Modern Principles of
ATHLETIC TRAINING

DANIEL D. ARNHEIM, D.P.E., A.T.,C.

Fellow, American College of Sports Medicine
Professor of Physical Education
Coordinator, Graduate Physical Education Program
California State University, Long Beach

Illustrated by
HELENE ARNHEIM, M.A.

SEVENTH EDITION

*With 1172 illustrations and
14 color photographs*

TIMES MIRROR/MOSBY COLLEGE PUBLISHING

ST. LOUIS   TORONTO   BOSTON   LOS ALTOS   1989

Publisher   Nancy K. Roberson
Senior Developmental Editor   Michelle A. Turenne
Project Manager   Suzanne Seeley
Production and Editing   Top Graphics
Designer   Rey Umali

Cover Art   Peter Fiore

Credits for all materials used by permission appear after index.

This text was revised based on the most up-to-date research and
suggestions made by individuals knowledgeable in the field of
athletic training. The author and publisher disclaim any
responsibility for any adverse effects or consequences from the
misapplication or injudicious use of information contained within
this text. It is also accepted as judicious that the athletic trainer
performing his or her duties is, at all times, working under the
guidance of a licensed physician.

SEVENTH EDITION

Library of Congress Cataloging in Publication Data

Arnheim, Daniel D.
   Modern principles of athletic training.

   Includes bibliographical references and index.
   1. Physical education and training.   2. Sports
medicine.   I. Title.
GV711.5.A76   1989   617'.1027   88-29499
ISBN 0-8016-0337-4

C/VH/VH   9 8 7 6 5 4

To Helene, my partner in life

PREFACE

PURPOSE OF TEXT

The seventh edition of *Modern Principles of Athletic Training*, as with all past editions, continues to provide the reader with the most current information possible in athletic training and sports medicine. Since the first edition appeared over 27 years ago, this text has been considered the leader in the field of athletic training throughout the world. The seventh edition continues this tradition.

The essential philosophy of the seventh edition of *Modern Principles of Athletic Training* remains the same as in the past editions, starting in 1962. This book is primarily designed to lead the student from *general* to *specific* concepts. As the reader progresses from beginning to end, he or she will gradually begin to understand the complex subject of athletic training/sports medicine. With understanding, an increased grasp of medical and scientific vocabulary also results. As in every past edition, a major premise is that prevention of adverse health conditions is always of the utmost importance.

WHO IS IT WRITTEN FOR?

Modern Principles of Athletic Training is designed primarily as an introductory text to the field of athletic training. It is designed for both athletic trainers and coaches as well as for courses concerned with the scientific and clinical foundations of athletic training and sports medicine. Practicing athletic trainers, physical therapists, and other health and safety specialists involved with sports will also find this text valuable.

The extent of the knowledge explosion in the field of sports medicine in general and athletic training in particular is truly mind-boggling. The athletic trainer is broadly becoming a specialist in numerous aspects of an athlete's health and safety. More specifically, he or she is becoming a specialist in orthopedic therapy.

The seventh edition is the result of the compilation of personal research and observation, detailed reviews and feedback from instructors using the sixth edition, and student comments.

NEW CONTENT FEATURES

1. New Chapter 10 on General Assessment Procedures provides a comprehensive chapter on fundamental assessment procedures and techniques, as the athletic trainer is increasingly becoming a specialist in the area of evaluation.
2. New Chapter 11 on Environmental Considerations conveys the function of athletic training in helping the athlete adapt to environmental extremes of hyperthermia, hypothermia, altitude, air pollution, and circadian dysrhythmia. Also included are discussions on preventing, recognizing, and managing adverse environmental conditions.
3. Because coaches and athletic trainers are becoming increasingly responsible for the athletic training of older athletes and wheelchair athletes, new information has been added to Chapter 3, Physical Conditioning and Training, which addresses the health and safety factors and unique problems of these two populations.

4. Because of the current concern about doping in sports, Chapter 15, Drug Use and Abuse in Sports, addresses recognition and the problems inherent in a drug testing program.

5. Coverage of sexually transmitted diseases has been expanded in Chapter 25, Other Health Conditions Related to Sports, with additional coverage of acquired immune deficiency syndrome (AIDS), since coaches and athletic trainers are increasingly viewed as counselors.

6. All taping techniques have been relocated in Chapter 12, Taping and Bandaging, for a more centralized presentation. This reorganization reinforces taping and bandaging as only one of the many skills and techniques that the coach and athletic trainer must have.

ORGANIZATIONAL CHANGES

To better help students understand the flow of ideas, the seventh edition has been changed from four to five parts.

Part One has been retitled *Introduction* and reduced from three to two chapters. Chapter 1, General Considerations, has been updated on such issues as professional organizations, concerns for sports health and safety, and risk factors inherent in sports activities. Chapter 2, The Athletic Training Program, discusses both the athletic trainer and the athletic training program. These two topics have been brought together to provide better continuity of ideas. Chapter 2 looks at the major roles of personnel and the services they provide in sports health and safety. The role of the athletic trainer is discussed in detail.

Part Two has been retitled *Injury Prevention*. The purpose of this organizational change was to bring together major areas of sports injury prevention. Chapter 3, Physical Conditioning and Training, provides an in-depth look at the many exercise variables that assist in injury prevention. A suggested flexibility exercise series has been added. Chapter 4, Nutritional Considerations, looks at all aspects of an athlete's diet and discusses such issues as fadism, the pregame meal, alternative eating patterns, and eating disorders. A number of tables have also been added to guide the athlete nutritionally. Chapter 5, Protective Sports Devices, has been given a major updating and revision to include both commercial and customized protective equipment as well as other sports devices. Psychogenic Considerations, from the sixth edition, is now Chapter 6 and retitled Psychological Stresses. Performance psychology has been removed and more focus has now been placed on the psychological aspects of injury prevention and other health factors.

To provide a more logical division of organizational structure, Part Three of the sixth edition, *Foundations of Injury Causations, Prevention, and Management*, has been divided into two parts. Part Three, *Basic Foundations of Sports Trauma*, consists of two chapters. Chapter 7, Mechanism, Characteristics, and Classification of Sports Injuries, represents a major revision of the sixth edition's Chapters 9 and 10. It discusses injuries from a cellular point of view, as well as mechanical forces that produce injuries and the body's susceptibility to sports trauma. Acute and chronic injuries are classified according to current medical terminology. Chapter 8, Tissue Response to Injury, has been reorganized and updated. The pain discussion has been expanded to include sclerotomic and dermatomic pain responses.

Part Four, *Management Skills,* consists of seven chapters. Chapter 9, Emergency Procedures, has an expanded discussion of shock. Chapter 10, General Assessment Procedures, is new, introducing the important topic of evaluation. Chapter 11, Environmental Considerations, also a new chapter, addresses the numerous environmental factors that impinge on the athlete. Chapter 12, Taping and Bandaging, has been extensively revised. It now includes the taping techniques formerly found in the chapters on musculoskeletal injuries. Chapter 13, Therapeutic Modalities, has received major updating. It not only cites examples, but now also provides a fundamental inroduction to this important area. Chapter 14, Exercise Rehabilitation, has been revised to include more of the important exercise elements commonly carried out in athletic training/sports medicine, such as proprioception, body mechanics, cardiovascular conditioning, and joint arthrokinematics. Both proprioceptive neuromuscular facilitation (PNF) and psychological aspects of sports rehabilitation have been expanded. Chapter 15, Drug Use and Abuse in Sports, formerly titled Pharmacology in Sports, discusses over-the-counter drugs in more detail, expands the discussion of prescription drugs and drug abuse, and has an added section on drug testing.

Part Five, *Specific Sports Conditions,* consists of Chapters 16 through 25, all of which have received major updating. Throughout Part Five the terms etiology, symptoms and signs, prevention, and management have been consistently applied for ease of reading and better understanding. Discussions have been expanded on musculoskeletal problems, injury prevention, and pathomechanics producing overuse stress syndromes. Chapter 22 is retitled The Head and the Thoracic and Cervical Spine for a better description of the order of contents. Chapter 25, Other Health Conditions Related to Sports, has been revised to include sexually transmitted diseases, including AIDS, as well as menstrual irregularities, the female reproductive system and physical activity, and sudden unexpected deaths in young athletes.

PEDAGOGICAL AIDS

Numerous pedagogical devices are included in this edition:
1. *Chapter Objectives* Goals begin each chapter to reinforce important key concepts to be learned.
2. *Margin information* Key concepts, selected definitions, helpful training tips, and illustrations are placed in the margin throughout the text for added emphasis and ease of reading and studying.
3. *Anatomy* Where applicable, extensive discussion of anatomy is presented and illustrated throughout the text.
4. *Boxed material within chapters* Important information has been boxed to make key information easier to find and to enhance the text's flexibility and appearance.
5. *Color throughout text* Color is used throughout the text to accentuate and clarify illustrations as well as textual material.
6. *New photos and line drawings* Many new photos and color line drawings have been added.

7. *Color illustrations* Fourteen full-color illustrations are included in Chapter 16 to depict common skin conditions.
8. *Management plans* In selected chapters, sample management plans are presented as examples of treatment procedures.
9. *Chapter summaries* Each chapter's salient points are summarized to reinforce key content.
10. *Review questions and class activities* New to this edition, at the end of each chapter, are review questions and class activities for enhancing the learning process.
11. *References* References have been extensively updated to provide the most complete and current information available.
12. *Annotated bibliography* For students and instructors who want to expand on the information presented in each chapter, an annotated bibliography has been provided.
13. *A detailed glossary* An extensive list of key terms and their definitions is presented to reinforce information in one convenient location.
14. *Appendix* The appendix contains suggested athletic training equipment, suggested supplies, a checklist for the athletic trainer's kit, and a conversion table for metric units of measure.

ANCILLARIES
Instructor's Manual

Developed for the seventh edition, the Instructor's Manual includes:
- Brief chapter overviews
- Learning objectives
- Key terminology
- Discussion questions
- Class activities
- Worksheets
- Worksheet answer keys
- Test Bank
- Appendixes of additional resources
- Transparency masters
- Perforated format, ready for immediate use

In total, approximately 2000 examination questions are included. Reviewed by instructors of the course for accuracy and currentness, each chapter contains true-false, multiple choice, and completion test questions. The worksheets in each chapter also include a separate Test Bank of matching, short answer, listing, essay, and personal or injury assessment questions that can be used as self-testing tools for students or as additional sources for examination questions.

The Instructor's Manual was prepared by Marcia Anderson, M.S., A.T.,C., Director of the Athletic Training program at Bridgewater State College, Bridgewater, Massachusetts.

Transparencies

Twenty-four acetate transparencies of important illustrations, tables, and charts are available to maximize the instructor's teaching and the student's learning process.

ACKNOWLEDGMENTS

As in every edition, there have been countless people involved with the final product. I would like to sincerely thank the following people:

My wife Helene, who, as always, has been an equal partner. She has put in countless hours of work reading manuscripts, making suggestions, drawing, and typing. Without her, the seventh edition would have been impossible.

A special expression of thanks goes out to student athletic trainer Mary Aja and to all the students she organized for photo sessions. They are Kam Barley, Doris Paloma, Guy Mohr, Susan Webb, Erik Linde, Lisa Fort, Kirk Mori, Marlan Wiley, Kerri Zaleski, Matt Grueisen, Kathy Walsh, and Michelle Paul.

Special thanks is also extended to Times Mirror/Mosby College Publishing for allowing a great deal of creative license. My sincere appreciation goes to my developmental editor, Michelle Turenne. When I was sure I was sinking from overwork, she managed to keep me afloat. Appreciation is also extended to my project manager, Suzanne Seeley, who is always so patient and helpful.

The publisher's reviewers for this edition greatly helped me to move in the right direction. Many thanks are extended to:

Bill Bean
University of Utah
Salt Lake City, Utah

Cheryl L. Birkhead
Eastern Illinois University
Charleston, Illinois

David A. Boyland
State University of New York
College at Cortland
Cortland, New York

Deloss Brubaker
U.S. Sports Academy
Daphne, Alabama

Julie Cain
University of Texas at Austin
Austin, Texas
Formerly of Central Michigan University
Mount Pleasant, Michigan

Jerry R. Elledge
Texas A&M University
College Station, Texas

Daniel J. Gales
Lock Haven University
Lock Haven, Pennslyvania

Dennis P. McManus
Plymouth State College
Plymouth, New Hampshire

Tamra Patton
San Jose State University
San Jose, California

Sincere gratitude is extended to William E. Prentice, Ph.D., University of North Carolina, Chapel Hill, who carefully read and criticized Chapter 13, Therapeutic Modalities.

Daniel D. Arnheim

CONTENTS IN BRIEF

Part Five

SPECIFIC SPORTS CONDITIONS

APPENDIXES

CONTENTS

Part Four
MANAGEMENT SKILLS

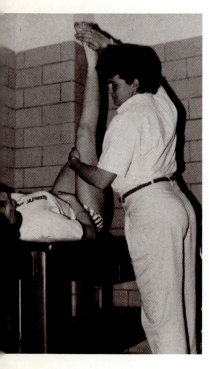

Part Five
SPECIFIC SPORTS CONDITIONS

16   SKIN DISORDERS, 456

APPENDIXES

COLOR PHOTOGRAPHS

Modern Principles of
ATHLETIC TRAINING

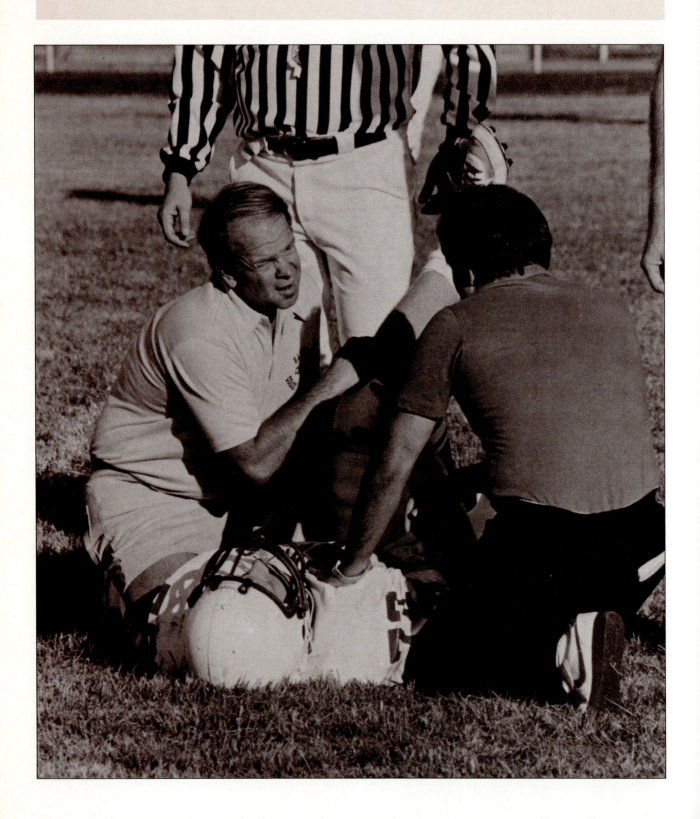

INTRODUCTION

Part One explores the origins of athletic training, the current status of sports injuries, and the present challenges for preventing and caring for these injuries. The major attributes of the athletic trainer and the athletic training program are discussed in detail.

CHAPTER 1

General Considerations

When you finish this chapter, you should be able to

Describe the historical foundations of athletic training

Identify the differences between professional organizations dedicated to athletic training and sports medicine

Contrast and evaluate the value of different ways and/or systems for collecting injury data

Compare the types and incidence of injuries in collision, contact, and noncontact sports

Explain how injury risks can be determined in sports

A thletic training is that aspect of sports that is basically concerned with all aspects of the athlete's health and safety. Although millions of individuals participate in organized and recreational sports, there is a relatively low incidence of fatalities or catastrophic injuries among them. A major problem, however, lies with the millions of sports participants who incur injuries or illnesses that could have been prevented and who later, as a consequence, develop more serious chronic conditions. Athletes in organized sports have every right to expect that their health and safety be kept as the highest of priorities.

HISTORICAL PERSPECTIVES

Athletic training and sports medicine have a varied and, in some ways, very complex history from prewritten times up to the present. This history consists of a compilation of the histories of exercise, medicine, physical therapy, physical education, and sport.[39]

Early History

The drive to compete in many early societies was very important. Sports developed over a period of time as a means of competing in a relatively peaceful and nonharmful way.

Early civilizations show little evidence of highly organized sports. It was not until the rise of Greek civilization that strongly organized sports began to evolve. Establishment of the Panhellenic Games, which were originally religious festivals, the most famous of which were the Olympic Games, in time produced coaches,

The history of athletic training draws from the histories of exercise, medicine, physical therapy, physical education, and sports.

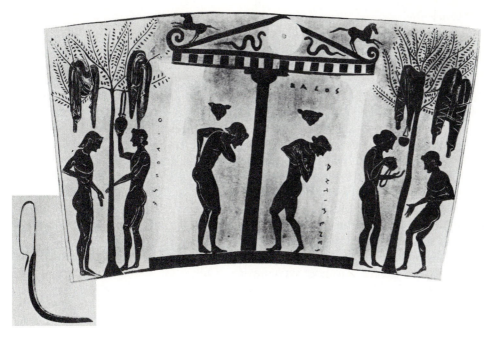

Figure 1-1

Ancient shower. The athlete removes sand, dust, and oil with a strigil (small instrument at left) before showering. The strigil and oil bottle were part of the athlete's equipment.

trainers,* and physicians to assist the athlete in reaching optimum performance.[17] Many of the roles that emerged during this early period are the same in modern sports.

With the appearance of the professional athlete in Athenian society, the *gymnastes* came into existence. These men trained their pupils in the skills and techniques of the sports of their day and a rudimentary knowledge of anatomy, physiology, and dietetics to keep the athletes in good condition. Later, the medical *gymnastai* appeared on the scene. Their concern was conditioning the athlete and maintaining him at a high peak of physical efficiency.[11,12] Possessing some knowledge of diet, rest, and exercise and the effect that each has on physical development and performance, they made use of hot baths, massage, anodynes, and other measures (Figure 1-1). The *paidotribai* (literally "youth or boy rubbers," who ranged in age from 7 to 20 years) and the *aleiptes* (anointers, who used various oils, powders, and massage in their ministrations) were also professional trainers, and the techniques of massage, the prescription of diet, and the general fitness of the athlete were their particular concerns.[11,17]

Perhaps the greatest of all the Greek trainers, Herodicus of Megara, was considered a physician as well as an athletic trainer. He performed his duties almost 300 years before Galen, and his chief claim to fame is that he was the teacher of Hippocrates, who was to become the "father of modern medicine."[12] As far as can be determined, Herodicus was the first physician to recommend exercise as a method of treatment for disease. Asclepiades, in the time of Christ, used exercise and massage as a method of treatment.

*Here the word trainers is used to denote people who helped the athlete reach top physical condition.

When the Olympic Games came into existence, women were not only forbidden to participate but were also forbidden to watch, on pain of death. In later years, the Heraea Games were instituted and were held secretly every 4 years between the Olympiads, with participation restricted to women. As time went on, attitudes became much more liberal, and eventually women were permitted limited participation in many of the games, principally wrestling, running, and chariot racing.[17] Scattered references in ancient history shed scant light on women's sports. With the rise of Sparta, women were encouraged to participate in strenuous physical activities such as running, throwing the javelin, and wrestling. The aim of Spartan society was to develop the strongest, healthiest females possible to serve as mothers of the future Spartan soldiers who would be developed to represent the epitome of physical perfection. It may well be that women's training started at this time. The Roman conquest of Greece put an end to the many games, and, as with the men, active participation by women in sports declined until it was more-or-less nonexistent.

Professional trainers were very much a part of the scene in ancient Rome. Early in his career, Galen, who later served as court physician to Marcus Aurelius, was physician to the gladiatorial school at Pergamum. He and others of his time wrote at considerable length about the salutary effects of proper diet, rest, abstinence from strong drink and sexual indulgence, and exercise as prerequisites for physical conditioning. For certain particularly demanding events, such as boxing, wrestling, and the pankration (a combination of both), the eating of meat was stressed, and a psychological approach was used in selecting athletes for certain events.

For many centuries after the fall of the Roman Empire there was a complete lack of interest in sports activities. It was not until the beginning of the Renaissance that these activities slowly gained popularity. Athletic training as we know it came into existence during the late nineteenth century with the firm establishment of intercollegiate and interscholastic athletes in the United States. The first athletic trainers of this era were hangers-on who "rubbed down" the athlete. Since they possessed no technical knowledge, their athletic training techniques usually consisted of a rub, the application of some type of counterirritant, and occasionally the prescription of various home remedies and poultices. Many of those earlier athletic trainers were persons of questionable background and experience. As a result, it has taken many years for the athletic trainer to attain the status of a bona fide member of the athletic staff.

Modern Athletic Training and Sports Medicine

Currently, that aspect of sports known as athletic training is one of the fastest-growing fields in sports medicine.

A Confusion of Terms

The terms *training* and *athletic training, trainer* and *athletic trainer* are confused more often outside than inside the United States. Historically, training implies the act of coaching or teaching. In comparison, athletic training has traditionally become known as the field that is concerned with the athlete's health and safety. A trainer refers to someone who trains dogs or horses or functions in coaching or teaching areas. The athletic trainer is one who is a specialist in athletic training. A title that is gaining increasing favor for this speciality is *sports therapist*.

The Field of Sports Medicine

Sports medicine is a term that has many connotations, depending on who or what group is using it. One of the major organizations using this expression is the American College of Sports Medicine (ACSM). It broadly designates sports medicine as multi-disciplinary, including the physiological, biomechanical, psychological, and pathological phenomena associated with exercise and sports.[1] The clinical application of the work of these disciplines is performed to improve and maintain an individual's functional capacities for physical labor, exercise, and sports. It also includes the prevention and treatment of diseases and injuries related to exercise and sports.[22]

The Field of Athletic Training

Athletic training has evolved into a major influence in athletes' lives. Growth of the athletic trainer's role from ancient times to the present has aptly been described thus: "The days of 'the rubber,' the know-it-all, the jack-of-all-trades and the master of all is over."[36] This change occurred rapidly after World War I and the appearance of the athletic trainer in intercollegiate athletics. During this period the major influence in developing the athletic trainer as a specialist in preventing and managing athletic injuries resulted from the work of Dr. S.E. Bilik, a physician who wrote the first major text (1917) on athletic training and care of athletic injuries.[3] Since that time more and more colleges and universities have been offering courses in athletic training, and today there are very few students majoring in physical education or physical therapy who are not offered some formal experience in athletic training and sports medicine (Figure 1-2).

Figure 1-2

The field of athletic training is a major link between the sports program and the medical community.

Athletic training must be considered as a specialization under the broad field of sports medicine.

The field of athletic training, as a specialization, provides a major link between the sports program and the medical community for the implementation of injury prevention, emergency care, and rehabilitation procedures.[20] It has evolved as a major paramedical profession since 1950, when the National Athletic Trainers' Association (NATA) was formed.[32] The primary purpose for its formation was to establish professional standards for the athletic trainer.

Growth of Professional Organizations

Many professional organizations that are dedicated to achieving health and safety in sports have developed in the twentieth century.

The twentieth century brought with it the development of a number of professional organizations dedicated to athletic training and sports medicine. Professional organizations have many goals: (1) to upgrade the field by devising and maintaining a set of professional standards, including a code of ethics; (2) to bring together professionally competent individuals to exchange ideas, to stimulate research, and promote critical thinking; and (3) to give individuals an opportunity to work as a group with a singleness of purpose, thereby making it possible for them to achieve objectives that, separately, they could not accomplish. Addresses for these organizations are in the box below.

Federation of Sports Medicine Among the first major organizations was the Federation of Sports Medicine, created in 1928 at the Olympic Winter Games in St. Moritz, Switzerland. This organization is multi-disciplinary, including many disciplines that are concerned with the physically active individual. To some degree the American College of Sports Medicine has patterned itself after this organization.

American College of Sports Medicine As discussed previously, the American College of Sports Medicine is interested in the study of all aspects of sports. Established in 1954, its membership is composed of medical doctors, doctors of philosophy, physical educators, athletic trainers, coaches, exercise physiologists, biomechanists, and others interested in sports. It holds national and regional conferences and meetings devoted to exploring the many aspects of sports medicine, and it publishes a quarterly magazine, *Medicine and Science in Sports.*

ADDRESSES OF PROFESSIONAL ORGANIZATIONS

American Academy of Pediatrics, Sports Committee, 1801 Hinman Ave., Evanston, IL 60204.

American Board of Physical Therapy Specialists, American Physical Therapy Association, 1111 North Fairfax St., Alexandria, VA 22314.

American College of Sports Medicine, 1440 Monroe St., Madison, WI 53706.

American Orthopaedic Society for Sports Medicine, Suite 202, 70 West Hubbard, Chicago, IL 60610.

National Athletic Trainers' Association, Inc., 112 South Pitt St., Greenville, NC 27834.

National Collegiate Athletic Association, Competitive Safeguards and Medical Aspects of Sports Committee, P.O. Box 1906, Mission, KS 66201.

The National Federation of State High School Athletic Associations, 11724 Plaza Circle, P.O. Box 20626, Kansas City, MO 64195.

This journal includes articles in French, Italian, German, and English and provides complete translations in English of all articles. It reports the recent developments in the field of sports medicine on a worldwide basis.

Orthopaedic Society for Sports Medicine The Orthopaedic Society for Sports Medicine was created in 1971 and is concerned with research and education. Its official bimonthly publication is the *American Journal of Sports Medicine*.

American Academy of Pediatrics, Sports Committee The American Academy of Pediatrics, Sports Committee, was organized in 1979. Its prime goal is to educate all physicians, especially pediatricians, about the special needs of children who participate in sports. Between 1979 and 1983, this committee developed guidelines that were incorporated in a report, *Sports Medicine: Health Care for Young Athletes,* edited by Nathan J. Smith, M.D.

National Athletic Trainers' Association Before the formation of the National Athletic Trainers' Association in 1950, athletic trainers occupied a somewhat insecure place in the athletic program. Since that time, as a result of the raising of professional standards and the establishment of a code of ethics, there has indeed been considerable professional advancement. The association accepts as members only those who are properly qualified and who are prepared to subscribe to a code of ethics and to uphold the standards of the Association. It publishes a quarterly journal, *Athletic Training: the Journal of the National Athletic Trainers' Association,* and holds an annual convention at which the members have an opportunity to keep abreast of new developments and to exchange ideas through clinical programs. The organization is constantly working to improve both the quality and the status of athletic training.

American Physical Therapy Association, Sports Physical Therapy Section In 1981, the section Sports Physical Therapy, of the American Physical Therapy Association, became official. Standards for clinical competence were established. Its official journal is the *Journal of Orthpaedic and Sports Physical Therapy.*[26]

Other Health-Related Organizations

Many other health-related professions have, over the years, become interested in the health and safety aspects of sports; thus dentists, podiatrists and chiropractors also provide varied services to the athlete. Besides national organizations that are interested in athletic health and safety, there are state and local associations, which are extensions of the larger bodies. National, state, and local sports organizations have all provided extensive support to the reduction of illness and injury risk to the athlete.

Other journals that provide an excellent service to the field of athletic training and sports medicine are *The International Journal of Sports Medicine,* which is published in English by Thieme-Stratton, Inc., New York, and *The Journal of Sports Medicine and Physical Fitness,* by Edizioni Minerva Medica SPA, ADIS Press Ltd., Auckland 10, New Zealand. *The Physician and Sportsmedicine,* published by McGraw-Hill, Inc., is a major publication directed to the health and safety aspects of sports.

SURVEILLANCE OF SPORTS INJURIES

By their very nature sports activities invite injury. The "all-out" exertion required, the numerous situations requiring body contact, and play that involves the striking and throwing of missiles establish hazards that are either directly or indirectly responsible for the many different injuries suffered by athletes.

A report on sports injuries and deaths in secondary schools and colleges in the United States, based on the survey mandated by section 826 of Public Law 93-380, was released by the National Center for Education Statistics, a division of the Department of Health, Education and Welfare (HEW). The report indicates that well over 4.2 million men and women participate annually in varsity sports in secondary schools, colleges, and universities throughout the United States.[5] More than 1.25 million girls and 3.5 million boys engage in interscholastic sports; over 30 million children aged 6 to 12 are involved in out-of-school programs.[28] These figures are more than double those of the early 1960s; half of the sports participants are female.

Because of the vast number of people involved with organized and recreational sports and the number of injuries sustained from these activities, accurate data acquisition is essential. Although methods are much improved over the past, many weaknesses exist in systematic data collection and analysis of sports injuries.[4]

The state of the art of sports injury surveillance is at this time unsatisfactory.[7] Currently most local, state, and federal systems are concerned with the accident or injury only after it has happened, and they focus on injuries requiring medical assistance or that cause time loss or restricted activity.

> The epidemiological approach toward injury data collection provides the most information.

The ideal system takes an epidemiological approach that studies the relationship of various factors that influence the frequency and distribution of sports injuries. Some of the factors that should be collected and studied are listed in the boxes on p. 9.

Using Injury Data

Valid, reliable sports injury data can materially help decrease injuries. If properly interpreted, the data can be used to modify rules, assist coaches and players in understanding risks, and help manufacturers evaluate their product against the overall market.[27] The public, especially parents, needs to understand the risks inherent in a particular sport, and insurance companies that insure athletes need to know risks to set reasonable costs.[27]

National Data Gathering Systems

A number of data collection systems tabulate the incidence of sports injuries. The most often mentioned systems are the National Safety Council, Annual Survey of Football Injury Research, National Football Head and Neck Injury Registry, National Electronic Injury Surveillance System (NEISS), and National High School Injury Registry (NHSIR).

National Safety Council

The National Safety Council* is a nongovernmental, nonprofit public service organization. It draws sports injuries data from a variety of sources, including educational institutions.

*National Safety Council, 444 North Michican Ave., Chicago, IL 60611.

EXTRINSIC FACTORS RELATED TO SPORTS INJURIES

Exposure to an injury situation
    Potential hazards and unique risks of the sport
    Position played
    Playing time
    Competitive level
Amount of practice and training
Environment
    Type and condition of playing surface
    Weather conditions
    Time of day
    Time of season
    Crowd control
    Laxity of officials
Equipment
    Protective equipment
    Footwear

INTRINSIC FACTORS RELATED TO SPORTS INJURIES

Age
Gender
Neuromuscular, structural, and performance aspects
    Somatotype   Physical maturation
    Strength   Postural alignment
    Endurance   Previous injuries
    Muscular tightness Timing
    Joint stability   Rhythm
    Balance   Reaction time
    Agility   Steadiness
    Speed   Accuracy
    Coordination
Mental and psychological aspects
    Innate intelligence
    Innate creativity
    Innate motivation
    Innate discipline
    Innate skill level
    Past experience in sports
    Need to take risks of injury

Annual Survey of Football Injury Research

In 1931 the American Football Coaches Association (AFCA) began the first Annual Survey of Football Fatalities. In 1980 this title was changed to Annual Survey of Football Injury Research. Every year, with the exception of 1942, data have been collected about public school, college, professional, and sandlot football. Information is gathered through personal contact interviews and questionnaires.[29] The sponsoring organizations of this survey are as follows:

American Football Coaches Association
Durham, North Carolina

National Collegiate Athletic Association
Shawnee Mission, Kansas

National Federation of State High School Associations
Kansas City, Missouri

This survey classifies football fatalities as being *direct* or *indirect*. Direct fatalities are those resulting directly from participation in football. Indirect fatalities are produced by systemic failure caused by the exertion of playing football or by a complication that arose from a nonfatal football injury.

In 1977 the AFCA and the National Collegiate Athletic Association (NCAA) instituted national surveillance of catastrophic football injuries. Catastrophic, in this instance, refers to cervical neck injury, leading to paralysis and permanent central nervous system damage (quadriplegia).

National Football Head and Neck Injury Registry

The National Football Head and Neck Injury Registry was established by Dr. J.S. Torg, Professor of Orthopaedic Surgery and Director of Sports Medicine Center at the University of Pennsylvania in Philadelphia. The registry collects data on an annual basis and compiles it epidemiologically. The registry indicates that craniocerebral death at all levels of participation is relatively constant for the period 1975 through 1984, averaging 7.8 deaths per year. In contrast, the annual incidence of permanent cervical quadriplegias at all levels of participation shows a significant decrease since 1977, the first year following major rule changes.[41]

National Electronic Injury Surveillance System (NEISS)

In 1972 the federal government established the Consumer Product Safety Act (CPSA), which created and granted broad authority to the Consumer Product Safety Commission to enforce the safety standards of more than 10,000 products that may be risky to the consumer.[4] To perform this mission, the National Electronic Injury Surveillance System (NEISS)* was established. Data on injuries related to consumer products are monitored 24 hours a day from a selected sample of 5000 hospital emergency rooms nationwide. Sports injuries represent 25% of all injuries reported by NEISS.[4] It should be noted that a product may be related to an injury but not be the direct cause of that injury.

Once a product is considered hazardous, the commission can seize the product or create standards to decrease the risk.[7] Also, manufacturers and distributors of

*National Electronic Injury Surveillance System, U.S. Consumer Products Safety Commission, Directorate for Epidemiology, National Injury Information Clearinghouse, Washington, D.C.

sports recreational equipment must report to the commission about any product that is potentially hazardous or defective.[7] The commission can also research the reasons that a sports or recreational product is hazardous.[4]

National High School Injury Registry

Sponsored by the National Athletic Trainers' Association (NATA), the National High School Injury Registry (NHSIR) is a nationwide reporting system that sampled 6544 high school football players in 1986. The rate and severity of football injuries was monitored by 105 NATA-certified athletic trainers.[34] Of the minor injuries, 74.9% required less than 7 days to heal; 16.15% injuries were considered moderate, with the football player missing 8 to 21 days of participation; 8.6% of the injuries were major, with the athlete missing more than 21 days of participation.[34]

The types of injuries sustained were 28.8% general, 28.1% ligamentous sprains, 21.3% muscular strains, 6.6% fractures, and 5.7% neurotrauma. General illness such as influenza and infection composed 5.1%, musculoskeletal inflammatory problems, 2.9%, and thermotraumas, 1.4%.[34]

The Incidence of Injuries

An **accident** is defined as an unplanned event capable of resulting in loss of time, property damage, injury, disablement, or even death.[8] On the other hand, an **injury** may be defined as damage to the body that restricts activity and/or causes disability to such an extent that the athlete is confined to his or her bed.[8] In general, the incidence of sports injuries can be studied epidemiologically from many points of view—in terms of age of occurrence, gender, body regions that sustain injuries, and/or the occurrence in different sports. When examined, sports are usually classified according to the risk, or chances, of their occurring under similar circumstances. Sports classified as the *collision types* have a higher risk potential for fatalities, catastrophic neck injuries, and severe musculoskeletal injuries when compared to sports that are categorized as *contact* or *noncontact*.

When considering athletes in all sports, recreational and organized, who participate in sports in 1 year's time, there is a 50% chance of their sustaining some injury. Of the 50 million estimated sports injuries per year, 50% require only minor care and no restriction of activity.[8] Ninety percent of injuries are muscle contusions, minor joint sprains, and muscle strains; however, 10% of the injuries lead to microtrauma complications and eventually to a severe, chronic condition in later life.

For sports injuries that must be medically treated, sprains or strains, fractures, dislocations, and contusions are the most common.[9] In terms of the body regions most often injured, the knee has the highest incidence, with the ankle second, and the upper limb third. For both males and females the most commonly injured body part is the knee, followed by the ankle; however, males have a much higher incidence of shoulder or upper-arm injuries than females.[9]

Collision Sports

In collision sports, athletes use their bodies to deter or punish opponents. American football, ice hockey, and rugby are the most common collision sports in the United States.

accident
An act that occurs by chance or without intention.

injury
An act that damages or hurts.

Risk of injury is determined by the type of sport—collision, contact, or noncontact.

American Football

Of all the organized sports, American football has the highest incidence of serious injuries.

American tackle football is the nation's—if not the world's—most injurious sport (Figure 1-3). It is also one of the most popular, with approximately 3 million high school and 75,000 college participants annually. Of this number, more than 300,000 high school participants, 35,000 college players, and half of all National Football League players will be injured in one season.[40,42]

The National High School Injury Registry (NHSIR) has indicated that most injuries occur during practice and that offensive linemen sustain 20% of all reported injuries, whereas defensive linemen accounted for 19%. Most injuries result from direct impact (43.9%).[34]

A major problem in American football is that of knee injuries. It has been estimated that there are at least 125,000 knee injuries annually, with approximately 35,000 needing surgery each year.

Football fatalities   There has been a significant drop in fatalities in organized football since 1976 when the NCAA and the National Federation of State High School Associations (NFSHSA) made a rule to prevent the use of the head as a primary and initial contact area in blocking and tackling.[29]

Direct fatalities   Most direct fatalities in football occur from injury to the head, followed by neck injuries (20%) and internal injuries (9%). Most direct fatalities occur during regularly scheduled games, with the largest number during October. Since 1976, tackling has claimed the majority of lives. There were seven direct football fatalities in 1985 at the college, high school, and youth league levels.[30] Six of these fatalities were from head injuries, and one was from a ruptured spleen.[30]

The National Operating Committee on Standards for Athletic Equipment (NOCSAE) played a role in the decline of football fatalities. NOCSAE developed

Figure 1-3

In collision sports, athletes use their bodies to deter or punish opponents

helmet safety standards that were adopted and implemented in 1978 by the NCAA and in 1980 for all high school players.

Although football helmets have been substantially improved since the beginning of American football, concussions continue to be a frequent injury, especially in high school. No helmet is capable of completely protecting the brain against shock. Cervical neck injuries are the result of improper techniques in blocking and tackling rather than the fault of the helmet per se, since the helmet cannot adequately protect the back of the neck (see Chapter 5, *Protective Sports Devices*).

Indirect fatalities   Each year a number of football deaths are attributed to indirect causes. Among these fatalities, heart failure and heat stroke, which is highly preventable, have the highest incidence.

Catastrophic neck injuries   Besides fatalities, there is major concern about catastrophic neck injuries sustained in football. A catastrophic neck injury is a permanent spinal injury that leaves the athlete a quadriplegic. As with fatalities, catastrophic neck injuries are decreasing to some extent, with this decrease attributable to the enforcement of stricter rules in the use of the head in blocking and tackling. Most of these injuries occur to backfield players during game situations when on defense and when tackling. From 1977 to 1985, there were 88 permanent cervical cord injuries, 74 in high school and 14 in college football.[30] In 1985, there were seven catastrophic neck injuries in American Football.[30]

Even though the number of catastrophic injuries from all sports is relatively low, the emotional and economic cost to the athlete, family, and society is staggering (see Chapter 2, *The Athletic Training Program*).

Ice Hockey

Ice hockey is an extremely fast, physically demanding and aggressive sport (Figure 1-4). Over 2 million athletes compete in ice hockey throughout the world. Because of the nature of this sport, fatalities, although uncommon, have occurred. The most common cause of death has been being hit by a stick or a hockey puck.[33]

A 5-year study of a major collegiate hockey team indicated that injuries about the shoulder (34.5%), upper extremities (28.8%), and lower extremities (33.8%) were fairly equally divided into thirds. The highest percentage of injuries was sustained in game situations, with the second half of the game the most dangerous time for both practice and actual game playing. The most common injuries were incisions or lacerations (28.9%) and contusions (19.4%). It is imperative that players wear both head and face protection.

Fifty percent to 70% of eye and face injuries result from improper stick use, and 15% to 25% result from fighting or other aggressive action that is unrelated to actual play.[43]

Various surveys have indicated that forwards are injured more often than defense men. Goaltenders are especially vulnerable to clavicular and neck injuries, particularly when contact with the goal itself ensues. The elbows and the insides of the knees are other vulnerable areas. Improvements in equipment design should provide better goalie protection. Figures indicate that the hockey stick is responsible for over one third of all hockey injuries, almost twice the number caused by the hockey puck. Stricter rule enforcement and perhaps an increase in the penalties for stick violations and for fighting, plus continued improvements in protective equipment, will decrease the number of injuries.[15]

Figure 1-4

The most common cause of death in ice hockey is being hit by a stick or hockey puck.

Figure 1-5

A potential injury situation in rugby, a game of precision, skill, and forceful body contact.

Rugby Football

As a collision sport, rugby football is one of the safest. Since it is played with no protective equipment or padding and with short-cleated shoes, the incidence, severity, or the types of injuries cannot be compared to American football. The highest incidence of injuries occurs to the shoulder, followed by injuries to the head, the neck, and the knee (Figure 1-5). The most-reported injuries are sprains and strains in the lower extremities.[13] Generally, bruises, contusions, and minor lacerations most commonly occur on the hands and the face, with injuries to the knee and ankle next in frequency. Injuries to the knee's meniscus are more common than ligamentous injuries, with occasional injuries occurring to the neck, particularly during a scrum.[2]

Contact Sports

Contact sports include basketball, baseball, field hockey, touch and flag football, judo, lacrosse, rodeo, soccer, softball, water polo, and wrestling. Basketball, baseball and softball, soccer football, and lacrosse are discussed as representative of contact sports.

Basketball

Basketball has the second highest rate of injury in competitive sports.[9] Originally conceived as a noncontact sport, it has evolved into a body-contact activity. Most of the injuries in basketball involve the knee, followed by ankle sprains, contusions to the hip or thigh and leg, and various injuries to the hand, wrists, and elbows.[9] Ankle and knee injuries occur in underbasket play or as the result of change-of-direction actions. The body build of basketball players is typically such that a high center of gravity induces relative instability, resulting in heavy falls to the floor. This is particularly obvious in rough underbasket play when a player

Figure 1-6

In contact sports some physical contact may be made which can produce injuries.

must leap off the floor to play the ball (Figure 1-6). In this situation even a relatively slight body contact with an opponent or a teammate anywhere below the hips could cause an upset. The acromioclavicular joint is very susceptible to injury in basketball players. Lacerations and abrasions occur more frequently in this sport than in football. Basketball has the highest incidence of injury (approximately double that of volleyball and field hockey, the next ranked) among women.

Baseball and Softball

In the 46 million individuals who participate in baseball and softball annually, approximately 900,000 injuries occur.[16] Most are caused by the ball, which is not only hard but travels at an extremely high rate of speed—some professional pitchers throw over 100 miles per hour. Little League pitchers have been timed at 55 to 70 miles per hour, and a batted ball can reach a velocity of 88 to 95 miles per hour.

Injuries to the hand, wrist, and forearm predominate, with mallet finger the most common. Wrist injuries, usually incurred in sliding, include sprains and occasional fractures; spike wounds and lacerations are not uncommon, usually resulting from collisions encountered in sliding or in playing the ball.

Over the years, Little League has kept an injury register and has done a great deal of research to reduce injuries to a minimum. The result has been the elimination of steel spikes and the institution of the on-deck circle, screening the dugouts, mandating the use of face and head protectors for the batters, and installing breakaway bases, all of which have resulted in a decrease in injuries.[16] The injury frequency is less than 2%, and the injuries are ones considered sufficient for medical attention and are mostly minor in nature. So-called Little League elbow, the result of excessive forceful throwing, such as in pitching, during one's early formative years has received considerable attention and study by the medical profession. Opinion is still divided as to whether such throwing has a detrimental residual effect that will limit activity in later years.

Fatalities do occur in baseball, usually to children who have been hit by a bat or baseball. The blows were to the head (of an athlete not wearing a protective head gear) or directly to the chest.[33]

Soccer Football

Undoubtedly soccer football is played by more individuals than any other sport in the world (Figure 1-7). It is the most popular sport in 135 countries. In the United States the sport is enjoying and unprecedented increase in participants and a marked increase in the number of spectators. Although soccer is played with a minimum of protective equipment, serious injuries are rare; however, deaths do occur. The main causes of death are collision with another player or the ground,

Figure 1-7

Although frequent forceful body contact often occurs in soccer, serious injuries are relatively rare; foot and leg injuries are common.

being hit in the head with a ball, and hitting a goalpost.[38] Death results from injuries to the brain or internal organs (e.g., the spleen), cardiovascular problems, or various rare medical conditions.

In Europe soccer injuries compose 50% to 60% of all sports injuries and from 3.5% to 10% of all the injuries treated in hospitals.[38] Injuries to the lower extremities seem to be most common. Sprains to the ankle joint are most frequent, followed by ruptured ligaments, injuries to the menisci, and fractures. Contusions of the forefoot and the metatarsals often occur. Although injuries to the upper extremities are least common, when they do occur, they are usually shoulder sprains with or without an accompanying rotator cuff tear. Fracture of the greater tuberosity of the humerus and separation of the acromioclavicular or the sternoclavicular joints are occasionally reported—usually the result of a fall. Many of the injuries reported, particularly those that affect the foot, the ankle, the knee, or the groin, are the result of overuse (from recurrent microtrauma).

Lacrosse and Field Hockey

Lacrosse, an original American sport, was invented by North American Indians. It is one of the fastest running sports played. It is played by both genders in more than 170 colleges and universities and in over 750 high schools and preparatory schools. Additionally there are many amateur and club lacrosse leagues.[21] Injuries in lacrosse, oddly enough, are neither as frequent nor as severe as one would expect, considering that it is a hard contact game involving the use of a stick (Figure 1-8). The use of protective helmets, face masks, gloves, and arm protectors for the players, with the goalie having the additional protection of a chest protector, has lessened the chance of serious injury. Additionally, the use of plastic sticks with molded plastic heads further contributes to the safety of the game.[21] Sprains and strains, especially of the lower extremities, apparently are the most common injuries. Abrasions, lacerations, and contusions, usually the result of stick contact or collision, are not infrequent. Joint injuries usually affect the ankles or the knees, and pulled hamstring muscles occasionally occur. Field hockey injury patterns apparently are similar to those found in lacrosse.

Figure 1-8

In spite of protective equipment, stick injuries are quite common in lacrosse.

Figure 1-9

Wrestling has a potential for numerous contact-related injuries.

Figure 1-10

The major injuries in waterpolo are to the shoulder and fingers.

Wrestling

In high schools throughout the country, wrestling is one of the most popular sports, averaging 300,000 to 400,000 participants yearly.[37] Wrestling has a considerable number of contact-related injuries, the most common affecting the knee, shoulder, and head and neck region, with injuries specifically to the menisci and the medial collateral ligament the most common (Figure 1-9).

One study found that 75.2 injuries were reported for 100 participants per season.[37] There are more injuries during practice than during competition, but the latter presents a higher risk situation, as does the takedown maneuver. Not infrequently, elbow hyperextension injuries, lateral meniscus injuries, and costochondral or sternoclavicular separations occur as a result of the sport of wrestling. In the past, severe illness and even death have occurred as a result of following improper procedures to make weight goals, but fortunately a more enlightened approach in recent years seems to be reducing such incidents.

Water Polo Injuries

Water polo is basically a team contact sport, combining both swimming and throwing. It uses a modified freestyle stroke, with the head out of the water and an "eggbeater" kick. The major injuries that are incurred are to the knee, from overuse of the shoulder, and from direct trauma to fingers and the face (Figure 1-10).[10]

Noncontact Sports

A great number of sports are classified as noncontact, including archery, badminton, bowling, crew rowing, cross-country running, curling, fencing, golf, gymnastics, riflery, skiing, squash, swimming, diving, tennis, track and field, and volleyball. Five noncontact sports are discussed that are representative of the vast array of physical stresses they can present: track and field, gymnastics, skiing, tennis, and swimming.

Track and Field

Track and field is extremely popular with men and women (Figure 1-11). Taking into consideration the high number of participants, it has very few fatalities and a relatively low injury rate. Fatalities in the past have usually indicated the presence of some organic impairment that directly or indirectly contributed to the fatality. In most cases death occurred as a consequence of a freak accident such as the athlete's being struck with an implement or projectile.

The recent proliferation of long-distance road races held in warm weather in which runners of both genders, ranging in age from 8 to 80 years, has led to a significant amount of heat injury. Long-distance events involving jogging, marathon running, and triathlons during recent years have increased the problems of overuse injuries.[44] In the sport of track and field muscle pulls, knee and ankle injuries, puncture wounds from shoe spikes, and abrasions are the most common injuries. Musculotendinous strains constitute approximately one third of the runner injuries, with approximately half of these strains affecting sprinters; stress fractures are more common in middle- and long-distance runners.[25] Most injuries occur in the running events, mainly occurring during sprinting.[44] The pole vault is the highest risk field event.[44]

Structural abnormalities, types of running shoe, running surface, and running intensity have been attributed to causing running injuries.[35]

Figure 1-11

The thigh is the most common area of injury in track and field participants.

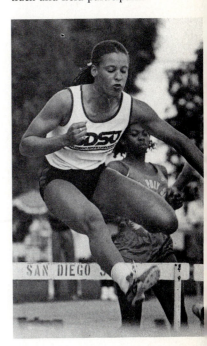

Figure 1-12

Gymnasts can sustain serious injuries to their shoulders, elbows, wrists, knees, and ankles.

Gymnastics

Gymnasts suffer from shoulder, elbow, and wrist injuries (Figure 1-12). A knee or ankle can also be injured, particularly in the tumbling phase of the floor exercise or in the execution of a dismount. Lacerations of the palm are still occasionally suffered, but the incidence is nowhere as great as it was before hand grips came into general use. Coaches or spotters not infrequently incur "spotter's elbow," medial epicondylitis, as the result of subjecting the elbow to unusually severe force in assisting a performer.

The most prevalent injuries requiring medical attention are ankle sprains. Severe knee injuries, as well as elbow dislocations, have also been reported.

Skiing

Alpine skiing is a unique sport because of the multiple conditions to which the skier is exposed. Three factors stand out when considering the injury rate of skiing: the skier, the ski equipment, and the environment. In recent years the injury rate in skiing has declined but not significantly.[19] The greatest decline has been to the lower leg, primarily ankle sprains. Twisting injuries leading to tibial fractures declined by 79%; however, boot top fractures declined only by 37%. The more serious knee injuries remain approximately the same. Knee injuries, at 20% of all injuries reported, represent the largest group of injuries. Injuries to the head and spine have declined. The usual causes of reported fatalities are head injuries, cardiac disease, or internal hemorrhage, which is usually caused by laceration of the spleen, the liver, or both.

Injuries of the upper extremities apparently are on the increase as a result of the forward lean prevalent in today's style of skiing, which is augmented by the

Figure 1-13

The high stiff boot and forward lean of today's alpine skier are producing a greater number of upper-extremity injuries.

forward flexion of high, stiff boots (Figure 1-13).[14] Women have proportionately more lower-extremity equipment–related injuries than men but do not show proportionately more of other types of injuries. Fifty percent of the injuries would be preventable if a safe, releasable ski binding were developed. Injury rates are higher in the under-25 age group, as would be expected, and tend to decrease as the skier's level of skill improves. Inexperienced skiers are especially prone to lower-extremity equipment–related injuries.

Cross-country skiing, it is estimated, has well over 4 million participants in the United States each year. Because cross-country skiing is performed mostly at state and federal parks or on unattended trails, accurate injury data are difficult to obtain. With the development of touring centers, constructed tracks, and trails, more consistent data are becoming available.[6]

Most cross-country injuries occur while the skier is going down hill. Upper-extremity injuries are the most common. The greatest number of lower-limb injuries result from the rotational forces involved in controlling and maneuvering the skis. Low-cut boots with pin bindings are the major cause of injuries.[23]

Tennis and Other Racquet Sports

Tennis, racquetball, squash, and other racquet sports present unique injury problems to the participants. Major sports-related injuries reported to the U.S. Consumer Product Safety Commission involved injury impact with a secondary object. Although racquet sports are low in terms of fatalities, they can be hazardous.

Tennis players suffer from many injuries (Figure 1-14). One of the most com-

Figure 1-14

Tennis players commonly sustain serious overuse injuries to their elbows, shoulders, or wrists.

Figure 1-15

The butterfly stroke can be a major cause of the rotator cuff impingement syndrome.

mon is overuse microtrauma to the elbow joint. "Tennis elbow," lateral humeral epicondylitis, has been estimated to occur in 31% of all men and women players. This injury is four times as frequent as the next most prevalent injury, ankle sprains (8%). On occasion the tennis player may injure a knee or shoulder and sustain bruises from falling on sliding of the court surface. As with most sports, many traumas could be prevented through a proper regimen of conditioning exercise and proper warm-up and cool down. Poor technique is believed to contribute to many tennis injury conditions.

Swimming

Swimmers engage in some of the hardest training of all the sports. Most participate in split training sessions daily during the competitive school year. They may swim 12,000 to 18,000 m daily. This type of hard training can lead to repetitive overuse microtrauma-type injuries (Figure 1-15). Commonly, injuries occur to the knee, shoulder, elbow, back, foot, and ankle.

INJURY RISK

As previously indicated, although millions of individuals participate in organized and recreational sports, there is a relatively low incidence of fatalities or catastrophic injuries. Ninety-eight percent of individuals with injuries requiring hospital emergency room medical attention are treated and released.[33] Deaths have been attributed to chest or trunk impact with thrown objects, other players, or nonyielding objects (for example, goalposts). Deaths have occurred when players were struck in the head by sports implements (bats, golf clubs, hockey sticks) or by missiles (baseballs, soccer balls, golf balls, hockey pucks). Deaths have also resulted when an individual received a direct blow to the head from another player or the ground. On record are a number of sports deaths in which a playing structure, such as a goalpost or backstop, fell on a participant.

The highest incidence of indirect sports death stems from heatstroke. Other less common indirect causes include cardiovascular and respiratory problems or congenital conditions not previously known.

Catastrophic injuries leading to cervical injury and quadriplegia are seen mainly in American football. Although the incidence is low for the number of players involved, it could be lowered even further if more precautions were taken.

In most popular organized and recreational sports activities, the legs and arms have the highest risk factor, with the head and face next. Muscle strains, joint sprains, contusions, and abrasions are the most frequent injuries sustained by the active sports participant.

It is the major goal of this text to provide the reader with the fundamentals necessary for preventing and managing illnesses and injuries common to the athlete. When considering the risks inherent in a particular sport, both extrinsic and intrinsic factors must be studied.[24] Thus information is gleaned from epidemiological data and the individual measurements of the athlete. The term extrinsic factors relates to the type of activity that is performed, the amount of exposure to injury, factors in the environment, and the equipment (see box on p. 9). On the other hand, the term intrinsic factors refers directly to the athlete and includes his or her age, gender, neuromuscular aspects, structural aspects, performance aspects, and mental and psychological aspects (see box on p. 9).

Sports injury risk is studied from intrinsic factors of the athlete and extrinsic factors such as exposure time, skill level, environment, and equipment.

The gathering of information that is intrinsic to the athlete is known as *profiling*.[31] In the past, profiles were made of an athlete to determine his or her potential for performance in a particular sport. More recently profiles are obtained as a means to prevent sports injuries. The profile is determined by taking the known performance demands of a particular sport and the risk factors that may be inherent to a particular sport and applying this data to the characteristics of an individual athlete.[18] Profiling often becomes a part of the athlete's physical examination.

With a thorough understanding of the risks inherent in a sport, every effort is made to reduce them through a program of prevention that includes extensive physical conditioning, good nutrition, and careful attention to the selection and fitting of all gear and equipment. Besides the physical aspects, the psychological and emotional aspects of competition must be addressed.

Although injury prevention is of primary concern, when injuries do occur, they must be cared for in the most expeditious manner possible. The athletic training team, including the coach, athletic trainer, and team physician, must work closely together to ensure all injuries are properly managed.

SUMMARY

Athletic training has a varied historical background. Its history consists of a compilation of historical influences, including exercise, medicine, physical therapy, and physical education. Early Greek and Roman history clearly reveals the coalition of specific roles that emerged for the care of the athlete. Athletic training in the United States resulted from the needs of football players. From this early beginning numerous organizations and professional groups have developed that are dedicated to the athlete's health and safety.

From a need to know the financial and personal impact sports injuries have on individuals and institutions, a number of data gathering systems have been developed. Those systems having the most value are epidemiological in nature. Injuries studied epidemiologically are in the sports categories of collision, contact, and noncontact. Fatalities and catastrophic neck injuries are relatively few but should be decreased further.

From studies of injuries, risks are determined and addressed. Injury risks are extrinsic and intrinsic. Extrinsic risks relate to exposure time, practice and training, environment, and equipment. Intrinsic risks relate to all aspects of the individual athlete, including physical and mental factors.

REVIEW QUESTIONS AND CLASS ACTIVITIES

1. How do modern athletic training and sports medicine compare with early Greek and Roman approaches for the care of the athlete?
2. What professional organizations are important to the field of athletic training?
3. Why is the epidemiological approach in the collection of injury data the most beneficial in terms of understanding the risks of particular sports?
4. Why are sports termed collision, contact, and noncontact?
5. What are the most common sports injuries, and to what part of the body do they most often occur?
6. Most fatal injuries occur to what part of the body?
7. Describe the catastrophic neck injury. Why is it so devastating to the athlete, the athlete's family, and society?
8. There are always risks when engaging in sports. How should they be determined? When determined, how may the information be used for prevention?

REFERENCES

1. American College of Sports Medicine, 1987 annual meeting, Las Vegas, Nev, May 27-30, 1987.
2. Baake, T: Rugby medicine: no more magic sponge, Phys Sportsmed 7:138, 1979.
3. Bilik, SE: The trainer's bible, New York, 1956, TJ Reed & Co.; originally published 1917.
4. Brown, VR: Government's role in data-gathering. In Vinger, PF, and Hoerner, EF, editors: Sports injuries, Boston, 1982, John Wright, PSG, Inc.
5. Calvert, R, Jr: Athletic injuries and deaths in secondary schools and colleges, 1975-76, Washington, DC, National Center for Education and Statistics.
6. Clancy, WG: Cross-country ski injuries. In Johnson, RJ, editor: Symposium on skiing injuries, Clinics in sports medicine, vol 1, no 2, Philadelphia, 1982, WB Saunders Co.
7. Damron, CF: Injury surveillance systems for sports. In Vinger PF, and Hoerner, EF, editors: Sports injuries, Boston, 1982, John Wright, PSG, Inc.
8. Dean, CH, and Hoerner, EF: Injury rates in team sports and individual recreation. In Vinger, PF, and Hoerner, EF, editors: Sports injuries, Boston, 1982, John Wright, PSG, Inc.
9. DeHaven, JE, and Lintner, DM: Athletic injuries: comparison by age, sport, and gender, Am J Sports Med 14(3)218, 1986.
10. Dominguez, RH: Water polo injuries. In Ciullo, JV, editor: Swimming, Clinics in sports medicine, vol 5, no 1, Philadelphia, 1986, WB Saunders Co.
11. Durant, W: The life of Greece, New York, 1939, Simon & Schuster, Inc.
12. Durant, W: Caesar and Christ, New York, 1944, Simon & Schuster, Inc.
13. Ekstrand, J, and Gillquist, J: Soccer injuries and their mechanisms: a prospective study, Med Sci Sports Exerc 15:267, 1983.
14. Ettlinger, CF, and Johnson, RJ: The state of the art in preventing equipment-related alpine ski injuries. In Johnson, RJ, editor: Symposium on skiing injuries, Clinics in sports medicine, vol 1, no 2, Philadelphia, 1982, WB Saunders Co.
15. Feriencik, K: Trends in ice hockey injuries: 1965-1977, Phys Sportsmed 7:81, 1979.
16. Hale, CJ: Protective equipment for baseball, Phys Sportsmed 7:59, 1979.
17. Harris, HA: Greek athletes and athletics, London, 1964, Hutchinson & Co.
18. Hershman, E: The profile for prevention of musculoskeletal injury. In Nicholas, JA, and Hershman, EB, editors: Symposium on profiling, Clinics in sports medicine, vol 3, no 1, Philadelphia, 1984, WB Saunders Co.
19. Johnson, RJ, and Ettlinger, CF: Alpine ski injuries: changes through the years. In Johnson, RJ, editor: Symposium on skiing injuries: Clinics in sports medicine, vol 1, no 2, Philadelphia, 1982, WB Saunders Co.
20. Kegerreis, S: Sports medicine: a functional definition, J Phys Ed Rec Dance 52(5):22, 1981.
21. Kulund, DN, et al.: Lacrosse injuries, Phys Sportsmed 7:82, 1979.
22. Lamb, DR: "Sports medicine"—what is it? ACSM President's report, Sports Med Bull 16:2, 1981.
23. Lyons, JW: Cross-country ski injuries, Phys Sportsmed 8:1, 1980.
24. Lysens, R, et al.: The predictability of sports injuries: a preliminary report, International Congress on Sports and Health, 22-23 Sept, 1983, Int J Sports Med 5:153, Nov 1984.
25. Lysholm, J, and Wiklander, J: Injuries in runners, Am J Sports Med 15(2):168, 1987.
26. Malone, T: Sports physical therapy specialization, J Orthop Sports Phys Ther 7:273, 1986.
27. Milner, EM: Proposals for improvement. In Vinger, PF, and Hoerner, EF, editors: Sports injuries, Boston, 1982, John Wright, PSG, Inc.
28. Mueller, FO, and Blyth, CS: Epidemiology of sports injuries in children. In Betts, JM, and Eichelberger, M, editors: Symposium on pediatric and adolescent sports medicine, Clinics in sports medicine, vol 1, no 3, Philadelphia, 1982, WB Saunders Co.

29. Mueller, FO, and Blyth, CS: Fatalities and catastrophic injuries in football, Phys Sportsmed 10:135, 1982.

30. Mueller, FO, and Blyth, CS: An update on football deaths and catastrophic injuries, Phys Sportsmed 14(10):139, 1986.

31. Nicholas, JA: The value of sports profiling. In Nicholas, JA, and Hershman, EB, editors: Symposium on profiling, Clinics in sports medicine, vol 3, no 1, Philadelphia, 1984, WB Saunders Co.

32. O'Shea, ME: A history of the National Athletic Trainers' Association, Greenville, NC, 1980, National Athletic Trainers' Association.

33. Overview of sports-related injuries in persons 5-14 years of age, Washington DC, Dec 1981, US Consumer Product Safety Commission.

34. Powell, J: 636,000 injuries annually in high school football, Ath Train 22:19, 1987.

35. Powell, KE, et al.: An epidemiological perspective on the causes of running injuries, Phys Sportsmed 14(6):100, 1986.

36. Rawlinson, R: Modern athletic training, North Palm Beach, Fla, 1980, The Athletic Institute.

37. Requa, RK, and Garrick, JG: Injuries in interscholastic wrestling, Phys Sportsmed 9:44, 1981.

38. Smodlaka, VN: Death on the soccer field and prevention, Phys Sportsmed 9:100, 1981.

39. Snook, GA: The history of sports medicine, part 1, Am J Sports Med 12:252, July/Aug 1984.

40. Thompson, N, et al.: High school football injuries: evaluation, Am J Sports Med 15:117, 1987.

41. Torg, JS, et al.: The national football head and neck injury registry: 14-year report on cervical quadriplegia (1971-1984). In Torg, JS, editor: Head and neck injuries, Clinics in sports medicine, vol 6, no 1, 1987, Philadelphia, WB Saunders Co.

42. Underwood, J: Football's unfolding tragedy, Reader's Digest 115:92, 1979.

43. Vinger, PF: Too great a risk spurred hockey mask development, Phys Sportsmed 5:70, 1977.

44. Watson, MD, et al.: Incidence of injuries in high school track and field and its relation to performance ability, Am J Sports Med 15(3):251, 1987.

ANNOTATED BIBLIOGRAPHY

Bilik, SE: The trainer's bible, ed 9, New York, 1956, TJ Reed & Co.
A classic book, first published in 1917, by a major pioneer in athletic training and sports medicine.

Nicholas, JA, and Hershman, EB, editors: Symposium on profiling, Clinics in sports medicine, vol 3, no 1, Philadelphia, 1984, WB Saunders Co.
A monograph that looks at all aspects of sports profiling. Profiling studies the demands of the sport and relates them to factors within the athlete. Profiling can be related to performance and/or injury prevention.

O'Shea, ME: A history of the National Athletic Trainers' Association, Greenville, NC, 1980, National Athletic Trainers' Association.
An interesting text about the history of the NATA that any student interested in athletic training as a career should read.

2

The Athletic Training Program

When you finish this chapter, you should be able to

Differentiate between the roles of the coach, the athletic trainer, and the team physician

Describe the professional qualifications of the athletic trainer, including his or her job description, successful personal qualities, licensure, and job opportunities

Explain the functions of support personnel in athletic training

List the major legal concerns of the coach and the athletic trainer in terms of sports injuries and how negligence can be avoided

Describe a functional athletic training facility

Identify the major administrative tasks, including facility upkeep and program operations, of the athletic training program

T his chapter introduces the field of athletic training to the reader. The growth of the athletic training profession has generally followed the growth of American football. Currently, athletic training is one of the fastest growing professions within sports medicine (see Chapter 1). In general, athletic training's major thrust is to ensure that the athlete's health and safety are maintained at the highest levels possible.

PERSONNEL

The primary athletic training team consists of the coach, the athletic trainer, and the team physician.

Athletic training must be considered a team effort.[19] The athletic training team involves a number of persons in performing its basic functions. Those people having the closest relationship to the athlete are the coach, the athletic trainer, and the team physician.[8]

The Coach

The coach is directly responsible for preventing injuries by seeing that the athlete has undergone a preventive injury conditioning program. He or she must ensure that sports equipment, especially protective equipment, is of the highest quality and is properly fitted. The coach must also make sure that protective equipment is properly maintained.[17] A coach must be keenly aware of what produces injuries in his or her particular sport and what measures must be taken to avoid them (Figure 2-1). A coach should be able, when called on to do so, to apply proper first aid. This is especially true in cases of serious head and spinal injuries.

Figure 2-1

The coach is directly responsible for preventing injuries in his or her sport.

It is essential that a coach have a thorough understanding of the skill techniques and environmental factors that may adversely affect the athlete. Poor biomechanics in skill areas such as throwing and running can lead to overuse injuries of the arms and legs, whereas overexposure to heat and humidity may cause death. Just because a coach is experienced in coaching does not mean that he or she knows proper skill techniques. It is essential that coaches engage in a continual process of education to further their knowledge in their particular sport. When a sports program or specific sport is without an athletic trainer, the coach very often takes over this role.

Coaches work closely with athletic trainers; therefore both must develop an awareness and an insight into each other's problems so that they can function as effectively as possible. The athletic trainer must develop patience and must earn the respect of the coaches so that his or her judgment in all training matters is fully accepted. In turn, the athletic trainer must avoid questioning the abilities of the coaches in their particular fields and must restrict opinions to athletic training matters. To avoid frustration and hard feelings, the coach must coach, and the athletic trainer must conduct athletic training matters. In terms of the health and well-being of the athlete, the physician and the athletic trainer have the "last word." This position must be backed at all times by the athletic director.

The Athletic Trainer

Athletic training, more specifically the athletic trainer, is a major link between the athletic program and the medical community for the implementation of injury preventive measures, emergency care, and injury management.[8] Ideally, every organized sports program should have a professional athletic trainer on its staff. This is especially true at the secondary school level. High school athletes deserve to have proper care of their injuries.[16]

Qualifications

Over the years, the athletic trainer has evolved into a highly educated and well-trained professional. The professional athletic trainer, having taken specific courses in athletic training, is expected to be a college graduate with extensive background in biological and health science. He or she should be certified by the National Athletic Trainers' Association (NATA) and should hold a cardiopulmonary resuscitation (CPR) certification.

NATA certification   Currently, there are two ways to become NATA certified: (1) by graduating from a college that has a NATA-approved curriculum and passing the national examination, or (2) by serving an internship and passing the national examination. As indicated by the Professional Education Committee of the NATA, an approved curriculum must include classes about the following:

Human anatomy
Human physiology
Exercise physiology
Kinesiology/biomechanics
Nutrition
Psychology
Personal and community health
Prevention and care of athletic injuries and illnesses
Evaluation of athletic injuries and illnesses
First aid and emergency care
Therapeutic modalities
Therapeutic exercises
Administration of athletic training programs
Instructional methods

As stated previously, certification by the NATA may be attained by an individual who attended a school that does not offer an approved curriculum; however, the candidate for certification must have spent a minimum of 1500 hours (during a minimum of 2 years and not more than 5 years) under the direction of an NATA-certified athletic trainer. Thirteen hundred of the hours must be attained in a traditional athletic training setting at the interscholastic, intercollegiate, or professional sports level. The additional 200 hours may be attained in acceptable, related areas.*

Individuals in an internship program must have at least one course in the following, as requested by the Board of Certification:

Personal health
Human anatomy
Kinesiology/biomechanics
Human physiology
Physiology of exercise
Basic athletic training
Advanced athletic training

For both curriculum and internship students, at least 25% of the clinical hours that are credited toward fulfilling the NATA certification requirements must have

---

*All requirements are subject to change. Students may contact the NATA Board of Certification, 1001 E. Fourth St., P.O. Drawer 1865, Greenville, NC 27835-1865, for updated information.

been spent during actual on-location practice and/or game coverage with one or more of the following high-risk sports: football, soccer, hockey, wrestling, basketball, gymnastics, lacrosse, volleyball, or rugby.

Major Functions

Athletic trainers are highly educated and well-trained professionals. Their major functions are injury prevention, recognition, and evaluation, and the management, treatment, disposition, rehabilitation, organization and administration, education, and counseling of the athlete.[15]

Injury prevention   The prevention of injury is a major goal of athletic training.[24] Athletic trainers must know how to create and carry out postseason, off-season, preseason, and in-season conditioning programs to assist the athlete in gaining and maintaining maximum physical conditioning. They must be skilled in constructing and applying all types of protective devices that support body parts, including adhesive taping, orthotic devices, and braces. Athletic trainers must determine whether athletic equipment is unsafe and ensure its proper maintenance. The athletic trainer monitors safe or unsafe environmental conditions such as temperature and humidity. The athletic trainer must also identify and protect preexisting physical conditions that might predispose the athlete to injury.

> The prevention of injury is a major goal of athletic training.

Injury recognition and evaluation   A primary aspect of athletic training is the recognition and evaluation of injuries.[24] The athletic trainer must have a thorough knowledge of human anatomy, physiology, kinesiology, and biomechanics to properly assess the seriousness of an injury. Knowledge and application of history-taking and injury inspection are essential. Through injury site palpation and estimation of range of motion, muscle strength, and joint flexibility and through neurological, sensory, and motor tests the athletic trainer determines the extent of injury.

Injury management or treatment and disposition   The athletic trainer is skilled in administering proper emergency care and making prompt, appropriate, medical referral.[24] When an injury occurs, the athletic trainer can skillfully apply emergency protective devices such as spine boards, cervical collars, bandages, and dressings and can oversee the transporting of the injured athlete without further tissue damage. With direction from the physician the athletic trainer performs a treatment regimen, using a variety of therapeutic methods, supportive procedures, or other techniques to aid recovery (Figure 2-2).

Figure 2-2

In treating the athlete, the athletic trainer carries out the directions of the physician.

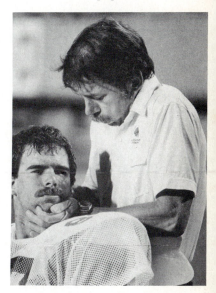

Injury rehabilitation   Once injured, the athlete is primarily concerned with full restoration.[24] The athletic trainer should be skilled in the use of a wide variety of means to encourage this restoration, including exercise and other therapeutic methods. The athletic trainer must be able to establish goals and a criteria for recovery and also be able to assess when, by objective measurement, the goals have been achieved.

Program organization and administration   To carry out an effective athletic training program there must be detailed organization and administration of all aspects of record keeping and facility upkeep.[24] Although the athletic training budget is often one of the largest in the entire athletic program, it is limited because of the demands placed on it; therefore it must be carefully managed. The purchase of supplies and equipment therefore becomes a constant concern of the athletic trainer. The athletic trainer initiates and carries out a health care service

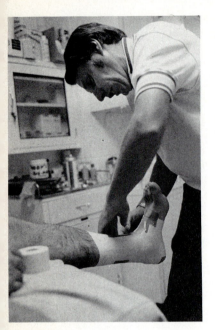

Figure 2-3

The athletic trainer must decide the degree to which each athlete will be served.

system for each injured athlete (Figure 2-3). A final but not least important factor is that policies and procedures must be established and carried out for daily operation of the athletic training program and support personnel.

Education and counseling   Athletic trainers are also educators and counselors.[24] They instruct athletes about all aspects of their condition, including the nature of the condition and procedures to be followed for fastest recovery.[13] They provide information about athletic training topics to coaches, faculty, and the community. They provide ongoing instruction to assistant athletic trainers and paraprofessionals working in the athletic training program. The athletic trainer may counsel athletes about emotional problems, including sexuality, drug abuse, and personal or social problems. For serious psychosocial difficulties the athletic trainer makes proper professional referrals.

Overview of the athletic trainer's duties   Duties of the athletic trainer should be detailed; an example of these duties follows[14]:

1. Work cooperatively with the coaches in setting up and carrying out a program of conditioning for athletes.
2. Administer first aid to injured athletes.
3. Obtain ambulances.
4. Apply protective or injury-preventive devices, such as taping, bandaging, or bracing.
5. Advise about equipment purchases.
6. Supervise fitting of protective equipment.
7. Work cooperatively with and under the direction of the physician about the following:
   a. Reconditioning procedures
   b. Operation of therapeutic devices and equipment
   c. Fitting of braces, guards, and other devices
   d. Referrals to the physician, health services, or hospital
   e. Assisting with physical examinations and physical fitness screening
8. Direct daily training room operations, including the following:
   a. Exercise rehabilitation and therapy programs
   b. Record keeping
   c. Requisitioning and storage of supplies
   d. Inventory and budget allocation
9. Provide training coverage of athletic events, both home and away.
10. Supervise and instruct assistant and student athletic trainers.
11. Counsel and advise athletes and coaches about matters pertaining to health.
12. Act as a clinical supervisor for students working toward NATA certification.
13. Conduct athletic training clinics and workshops periodically.

Personal Qualities

There is probably no field of endeavor that can provide more work excitement, variety of tasks, and personal satisfaction than athletic training. A person contemplating going into this field must love sports and enjoy the world of competition in which there is a level of intensity seldom matched in any other area.

An athletic trainer's personal qualities, not the facilities and equipment, deter-

mine his or her success. Personal qualities are the many characteristics that identify individuals in regard to their actions and reactions as members of society.
Personality is a complex of the many characteristics that together give an image
of the individual to those with whom he or she associates. The personal qualities
of athletic trainers are the most important, since they in turn work with many
complicated and diverse personalities. Although no attempt has been made to
establish a rank order, the qualities discussed in the following paragraphs are
essential if one desires to be a good athletic trainer.

Stamina and ability to adapt   Athletic training is not a field for a person
who likes an 8-to-5 job. Long, arduous hours of often strenuous work will sap
the reserve strength of anyone not in the best of physical and emotional health.
Athletic training requires abundant energy, vitality, and physical and emotional
stability. Every day brings new challenges and problems that must be solved. The
athletic trainer must be able to adapt to new situations with ease. A problem that
can happen in any ''helping profession'' and does on occasion occur among athletic trainers is burnout. This is a problem that can be avoided if addressed early.

A problem with burnout   The expression ''burnout'' is commonly used to describe the feelings of exhaustion and disinterest toward one's work. Clinically, it
is most often associated with the helping professions; however, it is seen in athletes and other types of individuals engaged in physically or emotionally demanding endeavors. Most persons who have been associated with sports have known
athletes, coaches, or athletic trainers who just ''drop out.'' They have become
dissatisfied and disinterested in what they have dedicated a major part of their
lives to. Signs of burnout include excessive anger, blaming others, guilt, being
tired and exhausted all day, sleep problems, high absenteeism, family problems,
and self-preoccupation. Drugs or alcohol may be consumed in an attempt to cope.

The very nature of athletic training is one of caring about and serving the
athlete. When the emotional demands of work overcome the professional's resources to cope, burnout may occur. Too many athletes to care for, the expectations of coaches to return an injured athlete to action, difficulties in caring for the
chronic conditions, and personality conflicts involving athletes, coaches, physicians, or administrators can leave the athletic trainer physically and emotionally
drained at the end of the day. Sources of emotional drain include little reward for
one's efforts, role conflicts, lack of autonomy, or a feeling of powerlessness to
deal with the problems at hand.[28] Commonly, the professional athletic trainer is
in a constant state of high emotional arousal and anxiety during the working day.

Individuals entering the field of athletic training must realize it is very demanding. Even though the field is often difficult, they must learn that they cannot be
''all things to all people.'' They must learn to say no when their health is at stake,
and they must make leisure time for themselves beyond their work.[5]

Empathy   Empathy refers to the capacity to enter into the the feeling or spirit
of another person. Athletic training is a field that requires the ability to sense
when an athlete is in distress, together with a desire to alleviate that stress.

Sense of humor   Many athletes rate having a sense of humor as the most
important attribute that an athletic trainer can have. Humor and wit help to release tension and provide an atmosphere that is relaxed. The athletic trainer who
is too serious or too clinical will have problems in adapting to the often ''light-
hearted'' setting of the sports world.

Athletic trainer's personal
qualities
   Stamina and ability to
      adapt
   Empathy
   Sense of humor
   Ability to communicate
   Intellectual curiosity
   Ethics

As a member of a helping
profession, the athletic
trainer is subject to
''burnout.''

Communication   Athletic training requires a constant flow of both oral and written communication. As an educator, psychologist, sports therapist, and administrator, the athletic trainer must be a good communicator.

Intellectual curiosity   The athletic trainer must always be a student. The field of athletic training is so diverse and ever changing that it requires constant study. The athletic trainer must have an active intellectual curiosity. Through reading professional journals and books, communicating with the team physician, and attending professional meetings the athletic trainer stays abreast of the field.

Ethics   The athletic trainer must act at all times with the highest standards of conduct and integrity. To ensure this behavior, NATA has developed a Code of Professional Practice.* Members who act in a manner that is unethical or unbecoming to the profession can ultimately lose their certification.

State Licensure

Many states throughout the United States require their athletic trainers to have a state license, certification, or registration.† Such measures help to delineate more specifically the practice of athletic training and avoids overlapping services with other health-related professions. These measures more clearly define the qualifications necessary to practice athletic training and should also specifically indicate the athletic trainer's relationship with the physician and other health professionals.

Professional Memberships

As a professional, the athletic trainer must be a member of and be active in professional organizations.

It is essential that an athletic trainer becomes a member and be active in professional organizations. Such organizations are continuously upgrading and refining the profession. They provide an ongoing source of information about changes occurring in the profession and include the National Athletic Trainers' Association, Inc., various state athletic training organizations, and The American College of Sports Medicine. Some athletic trainers are also physical therapists. Over the years there has become a close relationship between the NATA and the American Physical Therapy Association. Increasingly, physical therapists are becoming interested in working with physically active individuals.

Employment Opportunities

Athletic trainers work in a number of different settings
Secondary schools
School districts
Colleges and universities
Professional sports
Sports medicine clinics

Athletic trainers work in a number of different settings—in high schools, school districts, colleges, or universities, for professional teams, or in sports medicine clinics.

Secondary schools   It would be ideal to have certified athletic trainers serve every secondary school in the United States. Many of the physical problems that occur later from improperly managed sports injuries could be avoided initially if proper care from an athletic trainer had been provided. Many times a coach does all of his or her own athletic training, although in some cases, a coach is assigned additional athletic training responsibilities and is assisted by a student athletic

---

*National Athletic Trainers' Association, Inc., Code of Professional Practice, 1987, 1101 E. Fourth St., Greenville, NC 27858.
†National Athletic Trainers' Association, Inc., State Licensure, 1101 E. 4th St., Greenville, NC 27858.

trainer. If a secondary school hires an athletic trainer, it is commonly in a faculty-trainer capacity. This individual is usually employed as a teacher in one of the school's classroom disciplines and performs athletic training duties on a part-time or extracurricular basis. In this instance, compensation usually is on the basis of released time from teaching and/or a stipend as a coach.

Another means of obtaining high school or community college athletic training coverage is using a certified graduate student from a nearby college or university. The graduate student receives a graduate assistantship with a stipend paid by the secondary school or community college. In this situation both the graduate student and the school benefit.[16]

School districts   Some school districts have found it effective to employ a centrally placed certified athletic trainer. In this case the athletic trainer, who may be full- or part-time, is a nonteacher who serves a number of schools. The advantage is savings; the disadvantage is that one individual cannot provide the level of service usually required by a typical school.

Colleges or universities   At the college or university level the athletic training position varies considerably from institution to institution. In smaller institutions, the athletic trainer may be a half-time teacher in physical education and half-time athletic trainer (Figure 2-4). In some cases, if the athletic trainer is a physical therapist, rather than a teacher, he or she may spend part of the time in the school health center and part of the time in athletic training. Increasingly at the college level, athletic training services are being offered to members of the general student body who participate in intramural and club sports. In most colleges and universities the athletic trainer is full-time, does not teach, works in the department of athletics, and is paid by the state or from student union or alumni funds.

Figure 2-4

Both men and women athletic trainers have work opportunities at the college or university level.

Professional teams   The athletic trainer for professional sports teams usually performs specific team training duties for 6 months out of the year; the other 6 months are spent in off-season conditioning and individual rehabilitation. The athletic trainer working with a professional team is involved with only one sport and is paid according to contract, much like a player. Playoffs and championships could add substantially to the yearly income.

Sports medicine clinics   Because of the vast number of organized and recreational sports enthusiasts, sports medicine clinics are increasing in number throughout the country. Services provided by these clinics vary considerably. Some specialize in sports therapeutics; others include exercise physiology testing and biomechanics testing and analysis. Some of these programs are managed by a physician, others by a registered or licensed physical therapist. Commonly therapy is performed by physical therapists or physical therapy aides. In some cases, depending on state and local regulations, certified athletic trainers are employed in sports medicine clinics. Perhaps more athletic trainers will be hired in these clinics as they acquire state licensure.

Legal Concerns of the Coach and Athletic Trainer

In recent years negligence suits against teachers, coaches, athletic trainers, school officials, and physicians because of sports injuries have increased both in frequency and in the amount of damages awarded. An increasing awareness of the many risk factors present in physical activities has had a major effect on the coach and the athletic trainer in particular. A great deal of care must be taken in following coaching and athletic training procedures that conform to the legal guidelines governing liability.

Liability

Liability is the state of being legally responsible for the harm one causes another person.[25] It assumes that the coach or athletic trainer would act according to the standards of a reasonably prudent person. These standards require that the coach or the athletic trainer would function as any reasonable person of ordinary prudence (with comparable education, skills, and training) would act in a comparable situation.[25] In most cases in which someone has been charged with negligence, the actions of a hypothetical, reasonably prudent person have been compared with the actions of the defendant to ascertain whether the course of action followed by the defendant was in conformity with the judgment exercised by such a reasonably prudent person. The key phrase has been "reasonable care." Individuals who have many years of experience, who are well-educated in their field, and who are certified or licensed must act in accordance with this background.

Negligence is the failure to use ordinary or reasonable care—care that persons of ordinary prudence would exercise to avoid injury to themselves or to others under similar circumstances. This standard assumes that the individual is neither an exceptionally skillful individual nor an extraordinary cautious one but is a person of *reasonable* and *ordinary* prudence. Put another way, it is expected that the individual will bring a common-sense approach to the situation at hand and will exercise due care in its handling. An example of negligence is when an athletic trainer, through improper or careless handling of a therapeutic agent, seriously burns an athlete. Another illustration, occurring all too often in sports, is one in which a coach or an athletic trainer moves a possibly seriously injured athlete from the field of play to permit competition or practice to continue and does so either in an improper manner or before consulting those qualified to know the proper course of action. Should a serious or disabling injury result, the coach or the athletic trainer is liable.

Assumption of Risk

The courts generally acknowledge that hazards are present in sports through the concept of "assumption of risk." In other words, the individual, either by expressed or implied agreement, assumes the danger and hence relieves the other individual of legal responsibility to protect him or her; by so doing he or she agrees to take his or her own chances. This concept, however, is subject to many and varied interpretations in the courts, especially when a minor is involved, since he or she is not considered able to render a mature judgment about the risks inherent in the situation. Although athletes participating in a sports program are considered to assume a normal risk, this in no way exempts those in charge from exercising reasonable care and prudence in the conduct of such activities or from foreseeing and taking precautionary measures against accident-provoking circumstances.

Torts

Torts are legal wrongs committed against the person or property of another.[25] Such wrongs may emanate from an act of *omission*, wherein the individual fails to perform a legal duty, or from an act of *commission*, wherein he or she commits

---

Liability is the state of being legally responsible for the harm one causes another person.

an act that is not legally his or hers to perform. In either instance, if injury results, the person can be held liable. In the case of omission a coach or athletic trainer may fail to refer a seriously injured athlete for the proper medical attention. In the case of commission, the coach or athletic trainer may perform a medical treatment not within his or her legal province and from which serious medical complications develop.

Negligence

The tort concept of negligence is held by the courts when it is shown that an individual (1) does something that a reasonably prudent person would not do or (2) fails to do something that a reasonably prudent person would do under circumstances similar to those shown by the evidence.

It is expected that a person possessing more training in a given field or area will possess a correspondingly higher level of competence than, for example, a student. An individual will, therefore, be judged in terms of his or her performance in any situation in which legal liability may be assessed. It must be recognized that liability, per se, in all of its various aspects, is not assessed at the same level nationally but varies in interpretation from state to state and from area to area. It is therefore good to know and to acquire the level of competence expected in your particular area. In essence, negligence is conduct that results in the creation of an "unreasonable risk of harm to others."[29]

Medical Diagnoses

Medical diagnoses may be made *only* by a licensed physician, and any final decisions regarding such diagnoses are the physician's alone. There is a fine line indeed between the recognition of an injury and its diagnosis. Debating this difference serves no useful purpose other than to confound the distinction further. In situations in which time is of the essence, as is often the case in sports injuries, the ability to evaluate quickly, accurately, and decisively is vitally important. In such situations the coach or the athletic trainer must remain within the limits of his or her ability and training and must act in full accord with professional ethics.

In summary, the coach and athletic trainer, to be reasonable and prudent, must at all times consider the athletes' health and welfare.[2,3] The coach must follow these guidelines:

1. Warn the athlete of the potential dangers inherent in the sport.
2. Supervise constantly and attentively.
3. Properly prepare and condition the athlete.
4. Properly instruct the athlete in the skills of the sport.
5. Ensure that proper and safe equipment and facilities are used by the athlete at all times.

The athletic trainer should do as follows:

1. Develop and carefully follow an emergency plan.
2. Keep accurate records of all accidents and subsequent action(s).[20]
3. Make it a point to become familiar with the health status and medical history of the athletes under your care so you will be aware of those particular problems an athlete may have that could present a need for additional care or caution on your part.
4. Establish and maintain qualified and adequate supervision of the training room, its environs, facilities, and equipment at all times.

Medical diagnoses may be made only by a licensed physician.

5. If allowed by law, exercise extreme caution in the distribution of nonprescription medications, and do not dispense prescription drugs.
6. Use only those therapeutic methods that you are qualified to use and that the law states you can use.
7. Do not use or permit the presence of faulty or hazardous equipment.
8. Work cooperatively with the coach and the team physician in the selection and use of sports protective equipment, and insist that the best be obtained and properly fitted.
9. Do not permit injured players to participate unless cleared by the team physician. Players suffering a head injury should not be permitted to reenter the game. In some states a player who has suffered a concussion may not continue in the sport for the balance of the season.
10. Do not under any circumstances give a local anesthetic to enable an injured player to continue participation. It is dangerous as well as unethical.
11. Develop an understanding with the coaches that an injured athlete will not be allowed to reenter competition until, in the opinion of the team physician or the athletic trainer, he or she is mentally and physically able. Do not permit yourself to be pressured to clear an athlete until he or she is fully cleared by the physician.
12. Follow the expressed orders of the team physician at all times.
13. Use common sense in making decisions about the athlete's health and safety.

In the case of an injury the coach or athletic trainer must use reasonable care to prevent further injury until medical care is obtained.[11] NOTE: See Chapters 5 and 13 for additional comments.

The Team Physician

The team physician must have a full understanding of sports injuries. It is ideal that the team physician has a background in sports medicine. Currently physicians with varied specializations act as team physicians. They may be family physicians, pediatricians (specialist for children), internal medicine specialists, or orthopedic surgeons (specialists in the musculoskeletal system). These physicians may be medical doctors or doctors of osteopathy. Their primary duties entail the following:

1. Seeing that a complete medical history of each athlete is compiled and is readily available
2. Determining through a physical examination the athlete's health status
3. Diagnosing and treating injuries and other illnesses
4. Directing and advising the athletic trainer about health matters
5. Acting, when necessary, as an instructor to the athletic trainer, assistant athletic trainer, and student athletic trainers about special therapeutic methods, therapeutic problems, and related procedures
6. If possible, attending all games, athletic contests, scrimmages, and practices
7. Deciding when, on medical grounds, athletes should be disqualified from participation and when they may be permitted to reenter competition
8. Serving as an advisor to the athletic trainer and the coach and, when necessary, as a counselor to the athlete

9. Working closely with the school administrator, school dentist, athletic trainer, coach, and health services personnel to promote and maintain consistently high standards for the care of the athlete

Team physicians must have absolute authority in determining the health status of an athlete who wishes to participate in the sports program. They are the final authority in the determination of whether or not athletes should be permitted to take part in a given sports activity and when, following injury, they should be allowed to reenter competition. The physician's judgment must be based not only on medical knowledge but also on knowledge of the psychophysiological demands of a particular sport.[18]

Team physicians must have *absolute authority* in determining the health status of an athlete who wishes to participate in the sports program.

When a physician is asked to serve as a team physician, arrangements must be made with the employing educational institution about specific required responsibilities. Policies must be established regarding emergency care, legal liability, facilities, personnel relationships, and duties. The physician must work cooperatively with the athletic trainer and the coach in planning a training program for the prevention of sports injuries and for rehabilitation and reconditioning following injury. If it is not possible for the team physician to attend all practice sessions and competitive events or games, it is sometimes possible to establish a plan of rotation involving a number of physicians. In this plan any one physician need be present at only one or two activities a year. The rotation plan has proved quite practical in situations in which the school district is unable to afford a full-time physician or has so limited a budget that it must ask for volunteer medical coverage. In some instances the attending physician is paid a per-game stipend.

Support Personnel

A number of support health services may be used by a sports program. They may include a nurse, school health services, team orthopedist, team dentist, team podiatrist, team nutritionist, equipment personnel, and referees.

Support personnel concerned with the athlete's health and safety
Nurse
School health services
Team orthopedist
Team dentist
Team podiatrist
Team nutritionist
Equipment personnel
Referees

The Nurse

As a rule, the nurse is not usually responsible for the recognition of sports injuries. Education and background, however, render the nurse quite capable in the recognition of skin disease, infections, and minor irritations. The nurse works under the direction of the physician and in liaison with the athletic trainer and the school health services.

School Health Services

Colleges and universities maintain school health services that range from a department operating with one or two nurses and a physician available on a part-time basis to an elaborate setup comprised of a full complement of nursing services with a staff of full-time medical specialists and complete laboratory and hospital facilities. At the high school level health services are usually organized so that one or two nurses conduct the program under the direction of the school physician, who may serve a number of schools in a given area or district. This organization poses a problem, since it is often difficult to have qualified medical help at hand when it is needed. Local policy determines the procedure of referral for medical care. If such policies are lacking, the athletic trainer should see to it that an effective method is established for handling all athletes requiring medical care or opinion. The ultimate source of health care is the physician. The effectiveness of athletic health care service can be evaluated only to the extent to which it meets the following criteria:

1. Availability at every scheduled practice or contest of a person qualified and delegated to render emergency care to an injured or ill participant
2. Planned access to a physician by phone or nearby presence for prompt medical evaluation of the health care problems that warrant this attention
3. Planned access to a medical facility—including plans for communication and transportation

Team Orthopedist

Often the team physician has a speciality in family medicine or is an internist. In such cases serious musculoskeletal injuries are referred to an orthopedic surgeon who specializes in these disorders. Many colleges and universities have a team orthopedist on their staff.

Team Dentist

The role of team dentist is somewhat analogous to that of team physician. He or she serves as a dental consultant for the team and should be available for first aid and emergency care. Good communication between the dentist and the coach or athletic trainer should ensure a good dental program. There are three areas of responsibility for the team dentist:

1. Organizing and performing the preseason dental examination
2. Being available to provide emergency care when needed
3. Conducting the fitting of mouth protectors

Team Podiatrist

Podiatry, the specialized field dealing with the study and care of the foot, has become an integral part of sports health care. Many podiatrists are trained in surgical procedures, foot biomechanics, and the fitting and construction of orthotic devices for the shoe. Like the team dentist, a podiatrist should be available on a consultancy basis.

Team Nutritionist

Increasingly, individuals in the field of nutrition are becoming interested in athletics. Some large athletic training programs engage a nutritionist as a consultant who plans eating programs that are geared to the needs of a particular sport. He or she also assists individual athletes who need special nutritional counseling.

Equipment Personnel

Sports equipment personnel are becoming specialists in the purchase and proper fitting of protective equipment. They work closely with the coach and the athletic trainer.

Referees

Referees must be highly knowledgeable regarding rules and regulations, especially those that relate to the health and welfare of the athlete. They work cooperatively with the coach and the athletic trainer. They must be capable of checking the playing facility for dangerous situations and equipment that may predispose the athlete to injury.[8] They must routinely check athletes to ensure that they are wearing adequate protective pads.

ADMINISTRATIVE TASKS

Athletic training is a health care unit that requires careful organization and administration. Besides being a clinical practitioner, the head athletic trainer must be an administrator who performs both managerial and supervisory duties.[8] This section considers the policies and procedures that are necessary to the athletic training program.

Facilities

Essential to any sports program is the maximum use of facilities and the most effective use of equipment and supplies.

The athletic training facility is specially designed to meet the many requirements of the sports athletic training program (Figure 2-5). To accommodate the various functions of an athletic training program, it must serve as a health center for athletes.[12]

Size and Construction

An athletic training area of less than 1000 square feet is impractical. An athletic training facility 1000 to 1200 square feet in size is satisfactory for most school situations. The 1200 square foot area (40 by 30 feet) permits the handling of a sizable number of athletes at one time besides allowing ample room for the rather bulky equipment needed. A facility of this size is well suited for pregame preparation. Careful planning will determine whether a larger area is needed or is desirable.

The facility should have windows in at least one wall; the windows should be placed high enough above the floor to provide ample natural light and draft-free ventilation and to ensure privacy. An athletic training facility that is not properly equipped with vents can become exceedingly unpleasant smelling. To supplement natural ventilation, either an exhaust fan or, preferably, an air-conditioning system should be installed.

The walls and ceiling should be of either drywall or plaster construction and should be painted in a light pastel shade with a washable paint.

The floor should be of smooth-finished concrete, with a nonslip texture. On occasion cleats are worn in the facility, and a wooden floor may in time splinter and warp. Vinyl tile, although somewhat expensive, has been used as a floor covering with considerable success. The floors should be graded to slope toward strategically placed drain outlets.

Location

The athletic training facility should be located immediately adjacent to the dressing quarters of the athletes and should have three entrances: an outside entrance from the sports field and two inside entrances, leading from the men's and women's locker rooms. This arrangement makes it unnecessary to bring injured athletes in through the building and possibly through several doors; it also permits access when the rest of the building is not in use. Entrance doorways should be at least 44 inches wide; a double door at each entrance is preferable to allow easy passage of a wheelchair or a stretcher. A ramp at the outside entrance is safer and far more functional than are stairs. If an outside entrance is present, provisions should be made to protect against drafts, particularly during cold or inclement weather.

The training facility is a multipurpose area used for first aid, therapy and exercise rehabilitation, injury prevention, medical procedures such as the physical examination, and athletic training administration.

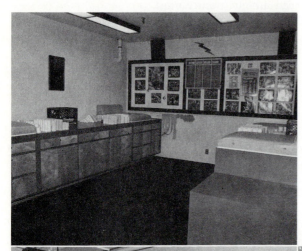

Figure 2-5

A modern athletic training room serves to carry out numerous functions.

Toilet facilities should be located adjacent to the athletic training room and should be readily accessible through a door in the training room.

The athletic training room should be located close to the shower rooms so that showers are readily available to dirt- or mud-covered athletes coming in for treatment.

Since the athletic training facility is the place where emergency treatment is given, its light, heat, and water sources should be independent from those for the rest of the building.

Illumination

The athletic training facility should be planned so that good natural illumination comes from high on one side. Work areas should be planned so that light comes from the left for right-handed athletic trainers and from the right for left-handed athletic trainers. Outdoor diffusers are preferable to shade for eliminating undue glare and controlling illumination.

Artificial lighting should be planned with the advice of a technical lighting engineer. The standard level of illumination recommended for athletic training facilities is 30 foot-candles at the height of 4 feet above the floor. Ceilings and walls, acting as reflective surfaces, aid in achieving an equable distribution and balance of light.

Light fixtures may be of several types. Since an even, nonglaring light is desired, a fixture that illuminates indirectly by casting direct light on the ceiling, from which it is reflected down and outward, is an excellent type. Fluorescent lights, when used with a diffuser, also provide a good source of light. Diffusers eliminate the flickering that is often an objectionable feature.

Special Service Sections

Apart from the storage and office space, a portion of the athletic training room should be divided into special sections, preferably by low walls or partitions. It should be noted, however, that space may not permit a separate area for each service section, and an overlapping of functions may be required.

Superficial thermal, mechanical, and cryotherapy therapy area   Superficial therapy consists of both heat and mechanical modalities. These modalities might include one or two infrared heat lamps, three or four tables for massage and passive mobilization, and two or three chairs or stools. This section should also facilitate cold therapy procedures such as ice massage.

Electrotherapy area   The electrotherapy area should constitute approximately 20% of the total special service area and is used for treatment by ultrasound, diathermy, or other electrotherapy methods. Equipment should include at least two treatment tables, several wooden chairs, one or two dispensing tables for holding supplies, shelves, and a storage cabinet for supplies and equipment. The area should contain a sufficient number of grounded outlets, preferably in the walls and several feet above the floor. It is advisable to place rubber mats or runners on each side of the treatment tables as a precautionary measure. This area must be under supervision at all times, and the storage cabinet should be kept locked when not in use.

Hydrotherapy area   The hydrotherapy area should constitute approximately 15% of the total special service area. The floor should slope toward a centrally located drain to prevent water from standing. Equipment should include two whirlpool baths, one permitting complete immersion of the body, a steam room or cabinet, several lavatories, and storage shelves. Since some of this equipment is electrically operated, considerable precaution must be observed. All electrical outlets should be placed 4 to 5 feet above the floor and should have spring-locked covers and water spray deflectors. All cords and wires must be kept clear of the floor to eliminate any possibility of electrical shock. To prevent water from entering the other areas, a slightly raised, rounded curb should be built at the entrance to the area. When an athletic training room is planned, ample outlets must be provided, for under no circumstances should two or more devices be operated from the same outlet. All outlets must be properly grounded.

Exercise rehabilitation area   Ideally an athletic training facility should accommodate injury reconditioning under the strict supervision of the athletic trainer. Selected pieces of resistance equipment should be made available. Depending on the existing space, shoulder wheels, knee exercisers, hand apparatus, and bicycle exercisers should be available to the injured athlete.

Taping, bandaging, and orthotics area   Each athletic training room should provide a place where taping, bandaging, and applying orthotic devices

Figure 2-6

An effective athletic training program must have appropriate facilities that are highly organized.

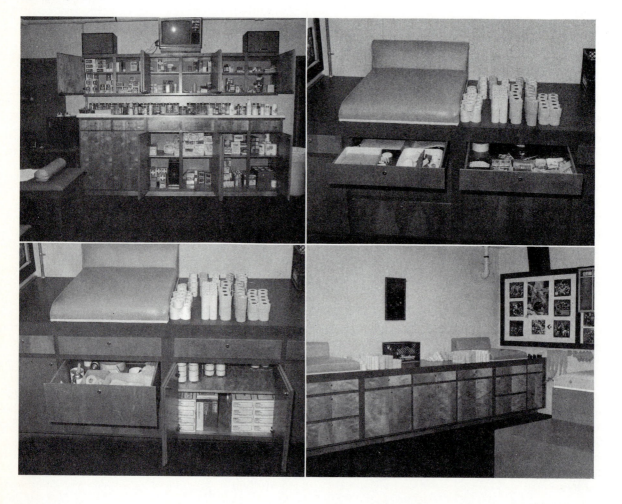

can be executed. This area should have three or four taping tables adjacent to a sink and a storage cabinet.

Physician's examination room   In colleges and universities the team physician has a special room. In this facility examinations and treatments may be given. This room contains an examining table, sink, locking storage cabinets, refrigerator, and small desk with a telephone. At all times, this facility must be kept locked to outsiders.

Storage Facilities

Many athletic training quarters lack ample storage space. Often storage facilities are located a considerable distance away, which is extremely inconvenient. In addition to the storage cabinets and shelves provided in each of the three special service areas, a small storage closet should be placed in the athletic trainer's office. All of these cabinets should be used for the storage of general supplies, as well as for the small specialized equipment used in the respective areas. A large walk-in closet, 80 to 100 square feet in area, is a necessity for the storage of bulky equipment, medical supplies, adhesive tape, bandages, and protective devices (Figure 2-6). A refrigerator for the storage of frozen water in styrofoam cups for ice massage and other necessities is also an important piece of equipment. Many athletic trainers prefer to place the refrigerator in their office, where it is readily accessible but still under close supervision. In small sports programs, a large refrigerator will probably be sufficient for all ice needs.

If at all possible, an ice-making machine should be installed in an auxilliary area to provide an ample and continuous supply of ice for treatment purposes.

Athletic Trainer's Office

A space 10 feet by 8 feet is ample for the athletic trainer's office. It should be located so that all areas of the training room can be well-supervised without the athletic trainer's having to leave the office. Glass partitions on two sides permit the athletic trainer, even while seated at the desk, to observe all activities. A desk, chair, tack board for clippings and other information, telephones, and a record file are the basic equipment. In some cases a computer is also housed in this office.

Because of the nature and character of the athletic training room and of the equipment and supplies within, this room should have an independent lock-and-key system so that it is accessible only to authorized personnel.

Hygiene and Sanitation

The practice of good hygiene and sanitation is of the utmost importance in an athletic training program. The prevention of infectious conditions is a direct responsibility of the athletic trainer, whose duty it is to see that all athletes are surrounded by as hygienic an environment as is possible and that each individual is practicing sound health habits.

Good hygiene and sanitation are essential for an athletic training program.

The athletic training facility   The use of the athletic training room as a place only for the prevention and care of sports injuries must be strictly observed. Too often the athletic training facility becomes a meeting or club room for the coaches and athletes. Unless definite rules are established and practiced, room cleanliness and sanitation become an impossible chore. Unsanitary practices or conditions must not be tolerated. The following are some important athletic training room policies:

1. *No cleated shoes are allowed.* Dirt and debris tend to cling to cleated shoes; therefore cleated shoes should be removed before entering the athletic training facility.
2. *Game equipment is kept outside.* Because game equipment such as balls and bats adds to the sanitation problem, it should be kept out of the athletic training room. Coaches and athletes must be continually reminded that the athletic training room is not a storage room for sports equipment.
3. *Shoes must be kept off treatment tables.* Because of the tendency of shoes to contaminate treatment tables, they must be removed before any care is given to the athlete.
4. *Athletes should shower before receiving treatment.* The athlete should make it a habit to shower before being treated if the treatment is not an emergency. This procedure helps keep tables and therapeutic modalities sanitary.
5. *Roughhousing and profanity should not be allowed.* Athletes must be continually reminded that the athletic training facility is placed for injury care and prevention. Horseplay and foul language lower the basic purpose of the athletic training room.

General cleanliness of the athletic training room cannot be stressed enough. Through the athletic trainer's example, the athlete may develop an appreciation for cleanliness and in turn develop wholesome personal health habits. Cleaning responsibilities in most schools are divided between the athletic training staff and the maintenance crew. Care of permanent building stuctures and trash disposal are usually the responsibilities of maintenance, whereas upkeep of specialized equipment falls within the province of the training staff.

Division of routine cleaning responsibilities may be organized as follows:
1. Maintenance crew
   a. Sweep floors daily.
   b. Clean and disinfect sinks and built-in tubs daily.
   c. Mop and disinfect hydrotherapy area twice a week.
   d. Refill paper towel and drinking cup dispensers as needed.
   e. Empty wastebaskets and dispose of trash daily.
2. Athletic training staff
   a. Clean and disinfect treatment table daily.
   b. Clean and disinfect hydrotherapy modalities daily.
   c. Clean and polish other therapeutic modalities weekly.

The gymnasium   Maintaining sanitation in sports is a continual battle in the athletic training environment. Practices such as passing a common towel to wipe off perspiration, using common water dispensers, or failing to change dirty clothing for clean are prevalent violations of sanitation in sports. The following is a suggested health practice check list, which may be used by the coach and the athletic trainer:
1. Facilities sanitation
   a. Are the gymnasium floors swept daily?
   b. Are drinking fountains, showers, sinks, and urinals and toilets cleaned and disinfected daily?
   c. Are lockers aired and sanitized frequently?
   d. Are mats cleaned routinely (wrestling mats and wall mats cleaned daily)?
2. Equipment and clothing issuance
   a. Are equipment and clothing fitted to the athlete to avoid skin irritations?

    b. Is swapping of equipment and clothes prevented?

    c. Is clothing laundered and changed frequently?

    d. Is wet clothing allowed to dry thoroughly before the athlete wears it again?

    e. Is individual attention given to proper shoe fit and upkeep?

    f. Is protective clothing provided during inclement weather or when the athlete is waiting on the sidelines?

    g. Are clean dry towels provided each day?

Emergency phone   The installation of an emergency phone adjacent to the major activities area is also desirable. It should be possible to use this phone to call outside for emergency aid and to contact the athletic training facilities when additional assistance is required.

The athlete   To promote good health among the athletes, the coach or the athletic trainer should encourage sound health habits. The following checklist may be a useful guide for coaches, athletic trainers, and athletes:

1. Are the athletes medically cleared to participate?
2. Is each athlete insured?
3. Does the athlete promptly report injuries, illnesses, and skin disorders to the coach or the athletic trainer?
4. Are good daily living habits of resting, sleeping, and proper nutrition practiced?
5. Do the athletes shower after practice?
6. Do they dry thoroughly and cool off before departing the gymnasium?
7. Do they avoid drinking from a common water dispenser?
8. Do they avoid use of a common towel?
9. Do they avoid exchanging gym clothes with teammates?
10. Do they practice good foot hygiene?
11. Do they avoid contact with teammates who have a contagious disease or infection?

Who Should Be Served?

A major factor in any athletic training program is the establishment of limits as to who is to be served by the athletic training staff. The individual athlete, the institution, and the community are considered.

The Athlete

The athletic trainer must decide the extent to which the athlete will be served. For example, will prevention and care activities be extended to athletes for the entire year, including summer and other vacations, or only during the competitive season? Also, the athletic trainer must decide what care will be rendered. Will it extend to all systemic illnesses or to just musculoskeletal problems?[8]

The Institution

A policy must be established as to who will be served by the athletic training program.[8] Often legal concerns and the school liability insurance dictate who is to be served other than the athlete. A policy should make it clear whether students other than athletes, athletes from other schools, faculty, and staff are to receive care. If so, how are they to be referred and medically directed? Also, it must be decided whether the athletic training program will act as a clinical setting for student athletic trainers.

The Community

A decision must be made as to which, if any, outside group or person in the community will be served by the athletic training staff. Again, legality and the institution's insurance program must be taken into consideration. If a policy is not delineated in this matter, outside persons may abuse the services of the athletic training facilities and staff.

Program Operations

Every athletic training program must develop policies and procedures that carefully delineate the daily routine of the program.

It is imperative that every athletic training program develop policies and procedures that carefully delineate the daily routine of the program. This is especially true for handling health problems and injuries.

The Preparticipation Health Examination

A major function of athletic training is the preparticipation health examination.

The primary purpose of the preseason health examination is to identify if an athlete is at risk when participating in a specific sport. Risk may consist of injury, reinjury, illness, or even death. Preseason health examinations must be given not only at the entry level but must be conducted during each season in which an athlete competes. Three types of examinations are commonly given—the locker room examination, an examination by a personal physician, and a station examination.

Name ______________________ Date __________

1. BP (sitting) ______/______
2. Vision: L 20/______ R 20/______ — CHECK IF NEGATIVE
3. Skin ______ ☐
   Mouth ______ ☐
   Eyes: Pupils L ______ R ______
4. Chest: PMI ______ ☐
   Pulses ______
   Rhythm ______
   Murmurs ______
   Lungs ______
5. Lymphatics: Cervical ______ ☐
   Axillary ______
   Abdomen: Organs ______ ☐
   ______
   Genitalia: ______ ☐
   Maturation Index ______
6. Orthopedic (conduct according to Figure 2-10): ☐
   Cervical spine/back ______
   Shoulders ______
   Arm/elbow/wrist/hold ______
   Knees ______
   ______
   Ankles ______
   ______
7. Other ☐

Figure 2-7

Preparticipation health examination physical evaluation.

Locker room examination "Locker room examination" refers to mass examination. Groups of athletes are examined by a team or volunteer physician in a cursory manner to satisfy the requirements of a particular sport. This method lacks a standardized history form and an examination that has a level of thoroughness (Figures 2-7 and 2-8). However, this is a screening examination that is highly specific and sports related. It should never be viewed as a complete physical examination.[23]

Personal physician Examination by a personal physician has the advantage of an in-depth history and an ideal physician-patient relationship. A disadvantage of this type of examination is that it may not be directed to detection of factors that predispose the athlete for a sports injury.[23]

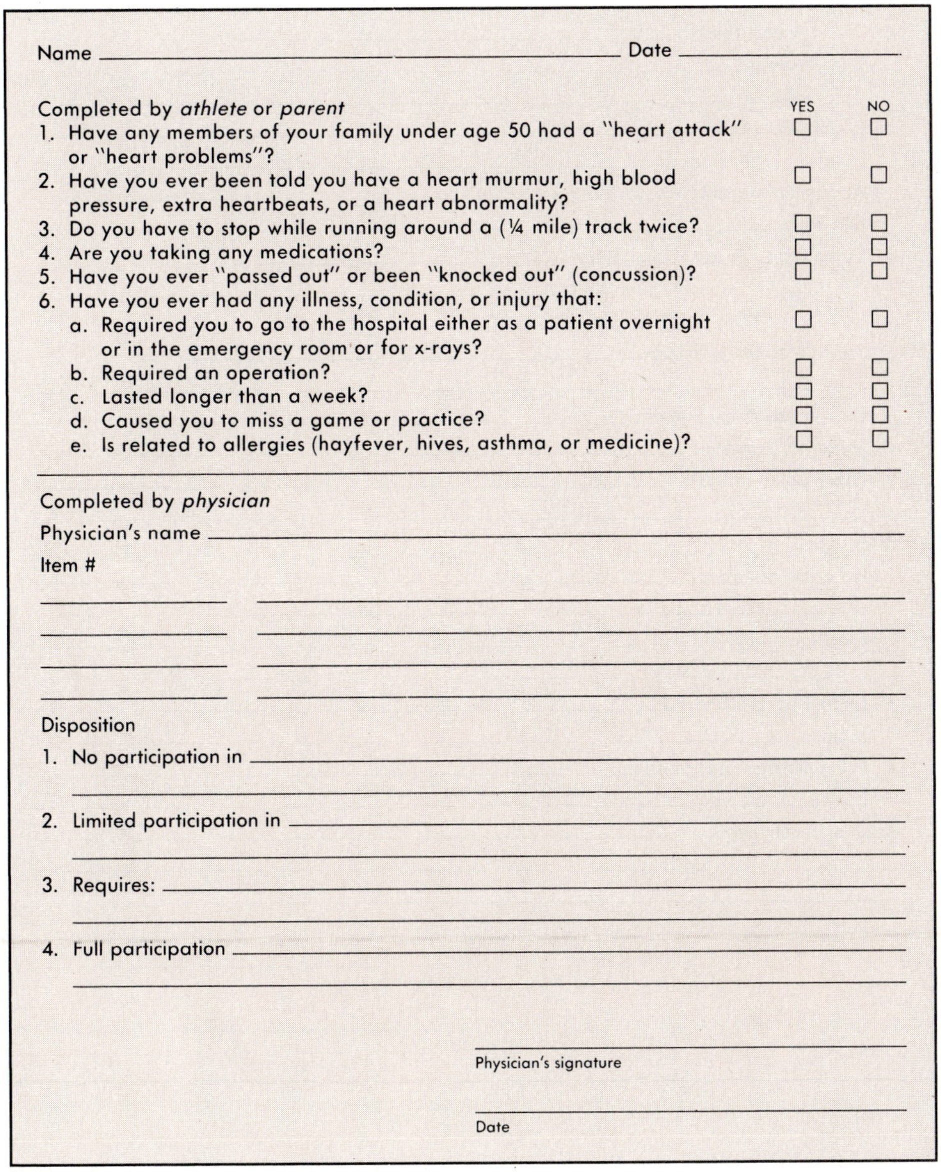

Figure 2-8

Preparticipation health examination history.

Name _____ Date _____

Completed by *athlete* or *parent*   YES   NO

1. Have any members of your family under age 50 had a "heart attack" or "heart problems"? ☐ ☐

2. Have you ever been told you have a heart murmur, high blood pressure, extra heartbeats, or a heart abnormality? ☐ ☐

3. Do you have to stop while running around a (¼ mile) track twice? ☐ ☐

4. Are you taking any medications? ☐ ☐

5. Have you ever "passed out" or been "knocked out" (concussion)? ☐ ☐

6. Have you ever had any illness, condition, or injury that:
    a. Required you to go to the hospital either as a patient overnight or in the emergency room or for x-rays? ☐ ☐
    b. Required an operation? ☐ ☐
    c. Lasted longer than a week? ☐ ☐
    d. Caused you to miss a game or practice? ☐ ☐
    e. Is related to allergies (hayfever, hives, asthma, or medicine)? ☐ ☐

Completed by *physician*

Physician's name _____

Item #

_____   _____
_____   _____
_____   _____
_____   _____

Disposition

1. No participation in _____

2. Limited participation in _____

3. Requires: _____

4. Full participation _____

_____
Physician's signature

_____
Date

Name _____ S.S. # _____

Height _____ Weight _____

CHECK IF
NEGATIVE

1. Blood pressure _____/_____   ☐

2. Vision

   Without glasses: R 20/_____   L 20/_____   ☐

   With glasses: R 20/_____   L 20/_____   ☐

3. Skin _____   ☐

   Mouth _____   ☐

   Pupil size: R _____   L _____   ☐

4. Chest: Pulses _____   ☐

           Heart rhythm _____   ☐

           Lungs _____   ☐

           Breast _____   ☐

5. Lymphatics: Cervical _____   ☐

                Axillary _____   ☐

   Abdominal organs _____   ☐

   Genitalia _____   ☐

6. Orthopedic: Postural alignment _____   ☐

                Cervical spine/back _____   ☐

                Leg _____   ☐

   Joint deformity/swelling _____   ☐

   Joint laxity _____   ☐

   Decreased range of motion _____   ☐

7. Urinalysis (Lab-Stix) _____   ☐

8. Other points noted _____

   _____

Disposition

1. No participation in _____

   _____

2. Clearance withheld until _____

   _____

3. Limited participation _____

   _____

4. Full, unlimited participation _____

   _____

Additional comments _____

_____

_____

_____

_____

Physician's signature

_____

Date

Figure 2-9

Preparticipation physical
examination—station report.

TABLE 2-1 Station Preparticipation Examination

Station	Points Noted	Personnel
1. Individual history; height, weight	Yes answers are probed in depth; height and weight relationships	Physician, nurse, or athletic trainer
2. Blood pressure, pulse	Upper limits: age 6 to 11—130/80; 12 and older—140/90; right arm is measured while athlete is seated	Student athletic trainer or manager
3. Snellen test	Upper limits of visual acuity—20/40	Student athletic trainer or manager
4. Skin, mouth, eyes	Suspicious looking skin infections and/or rashes, dental prosthesis or caries, unequal pupils	Physician, nurse, or athletic trainer
5. Chest	Heart abnormalities (e.g., murmurs, latent bronchospasm)	Physician
6. Lymphatics, abdomen, male genitalia	Adenopathy (cervical and axillary), abnormalities of genitalia, hernia	Physician or physician's assistant
7. Orthopedics	Postural asymmetry, decreased range of motion or strength, abnormal joint laxity	Physician, athletic trainer, physical therapist, or nurse practitioner
8. Urinalysis	After its collection in a paper cup, urine is tested for positive with a Lab-Stix	Student athletic trainer or manager
9. Review	History and physical examination reports are evaluated and the following decisions are made: (a) No sports participation (b) Limited participation (no participation in specific sports such as football or ice hockey) (c) Clearance withheld until certain conditions are met (e.g., additional tests are taken, rehabilitation is complete) (d) Full, unlimited participation is allowed	Physician

Station examination   The most thorough and sport-specific type of preparticipation examination is the "station examination" (Figure 2-9). This method can provide the athlete with a detailed examination in a short period of time. A team of nine people is needed to examine 30 or more athletes. The team should include two physicians, two medically trained nonphysicians (nurse, athletic trainer, physical therapist, or physician assistant), and five managers, student athletic trainers, or assistant coaches (Table 2-1).[23]

Orthopedic screening   Orthopedic screening is an essential part of the preparticipation health examination (Figure 2-10). Its purpose is to reveal past injuries that are inadequately rehabilitated or that have not been previously detected. The examination requires 90 seconds per individual athlete.[22]

Maturity assessment   Maturity assessment should be part of the preparticipation health examination as a means of protecting the young athlete.[4] Most commonly used methods are the circumpubertal (sexual maturity), skeletal, and dental assessments. Of the three, Tanner's five stages of assessment, indicating maturity of secondary sexual characteristics, is the most expedient for use in the station method of examination. The Tanner approach evaluates pubic hair and genitalia development in boys and pubic hair and breast development in girls. Other indicators that may be noted are facial and axillary hair. Stage one indicates that puberty is not evident, whereas stage five indicates full development. The crucial stage in terms of collision and high-intensity noncontact sports is stage three, in which there is the fastest bone growth. In this stage, the growth plates are two to five times weaker than the joint capsule and tendon attachments.[4] Young athletes in grades 7 to 12 must be matched by maturity, not age.[21]

Sport disqualification   As discussed previously, sports participation involves risks. Most disqualification conditions that are ascertained by a preparticipation health evaluation are noted in the medical history (Table 2-2).[22]

Figure 2-10

The orthopedic screening examination. Equipment that may be needed includes reflex hammer, tape measure, pin, and examining table.

ORTHOPEDIC SCREENING EXAMINATION	
Activity and Instruction	**To Determine**
Stand facing examiner	Acromioclavicular joints; general habitus
Look at ceiling, floor, over both shoulders; touch ears to shoulders	Cervical spine motion
Shrug shoulders (examiner resists)	Trapezius strength
Abduct shoulders 90° (examiner resists at 90°)	Deltoid strength
Full external rotation of arms	Shoulder motion
Flex and extend elbows	Elbow motion
Arms at sides, elbows 90° flexed; pronate and supinate wrists	Elbow and wrist motion
Spread fingers; make fist	Hand or finger motion and deformities
Tighten (contract) quadriceps; relax quadriceps	Symmetry and knee effusion; ankle effusion
"Duck walk" four steps (away from examiner with buttocks on heels)	Hip, knee, and ankle motion
Stand with back to examiner	Shoulder symmetry; scoliosis
Knees straight, touch toes	Scoliosis, hip motion, hamstring tightness
Raise up on toes, raise heels	Calf symmetry, leg strength

In general, the athlete who has lost one of two paired organs such as eyes or kidneys is cautioned against playing a collision or contact sport.[10] Such an athlete should be counseled into participating in a noncontact sport. The athlete with one testicle or one or both that are undescended must be apprised that there is a small risk, which is substantially minimized with the use of an athletic supporter and a protective device.[22]

TABLE 2-2 Disqualifying Conditions for Sports Participation

Conditions	Collision*	Contact†	Noncontact‡	Others§
General health				
Acute infections	X	X	X	X
Respiratory, genitourinary, infectious mononucleosis, hepatitis, active rheumatic fever, active tuberculosis				
Obvious physical immaturity in comparison with other competitors	X	X		
Hemorrhagic disease	X	X	X	
Hemophilia, purpura, and other serious bleeding tendencies				
Diabetes, inadequately controlled	X	X	X	X
Diabetes, controlled	‖	‖	‖	‖
Jaundice	X	X	X	X
Eyes				
Absence or loss of function of one eye	X	X		
Respiratory				
Tuberculosis (active or symptomatic)	X	X	X	X
Severe pulmonary insufficiency	X	X	X	X
Cardiovascular				
Mitral stenosis, aortic stenosis, aortic insufficiency, coarctation of aorta, cyanotic heart disease, recent carditis of any etiology	X	X	X	X
Hypertension on organic basis	X	X	X	X
Previous heart surgery for congenital or acquired heart disease	¶	¶	¶	¶
Liver, enlarged	X	X		
Skin				
Boils, impetigo, and herpes simplex gladiatorum	X	X		
Spleen, enlarged	X	X		
Hernia				
Inguinal or femoral hernia	X	X	X	

*Football, rugby, hockey, lacrosse, and so forth.
†Baseball, soccer, basketball, wrestling, and so forth.
‡Cross country, track, tennis, crew, swimming, and so forth.
§Bowling, golf, archery, field events, and so forth.
‖No exclusions.
¶Each individual should be judged on an individual basis in conjunction with his or her cardiologist and surgeon.   *Continued.*

TABLE 2-2 Disqualifying Conditions for Sports Participation—cont'd

Conditions	Collision	Contact	Noncontact	Others
Musculoskeletal				
Symptomatic abnormalities of inflammations	X	X	X	X
Functional inadequacy of the musculoskeletal system, congenital or acquired, incompatible with the contact or skill demands of the sport	X	X	X	
Neurological				
History of symptoms of previous serious head trauma or repeated concussions	X			
Controlled convulsive disorder	**	**	**	**
Convulsive disorder not moderately well controlled by medication	X			
Previous surgery on head	X	X		
Renal				
Absence of one kidney	X	X		
Renal disease	X	X	X	X
Genitalia				
Absence of one testicle	††	††	††	††
Undescended testicle	††	††	††	††

**Each patient should be judged on an individual basis. All things being equal, it is probably better to encourage a young boy or girl to participate in a noncontact sport rather than a contact sport. However, if a patient has a desire to play a contact sport and this is deemed a major ameliorating factor in his or her adjustment to school, associates, and the seizure disorder, serious consideration should be given to letting him or her participate if the seizures are moderately well controlled or the patient is under good medical management.

††The Committee approves the concept of contact sports participation for youths with only one testicle or with an undescended testicle(s), except in specific instances such as an inguinal canal undescended testicle(s), following appropriate medical evaluation to rule out unusual injury risk. However, the athlete, parents, and school authorities should be fully informed that participation in contact sports for youths with only one testicle carries a slight injury risk to the remaining healthy testicle. Fertility may be adversely affected following an injury. But the chances of an injury to a descended testicle are rare, and the injury risk can be further substantially minimized with an athletic supporter and protective device.

Insurance Requirements

It is essential that the athlete is fully insured.

Since 1971, there has been a significant increase in the number of lawsuits filed, caused, in part, by the steady increase in individuals who have become active in sports.[7] The costs of insurance have also significantly increased during this period. With more lawsuits and much higher medical costs there is a crisis in the insurance industry.[6] The major types of insurance about which individuals concerned with athletic training and sports medicine should have some understanding are general health insurance, catastrophic insurance, accident insurance, and liability insurance, as well as insurance for errors and omissions. There is a need to protect adequately all who are concerned with sports health and safety.

General health insurance Every athlete should have a general health insurance policy that covers illness, hospitalization, and emergency care. Some ''so-called'' comprehensive plans do not cover every health need. For example, they may cover physicians' care but not hospital charges. Many of these plans require large prepayments before the insurance takes effect. To cut pay-out costs, many insurance companies have begun to pay for preventive care (to reduce the need for hospitalization) and to limit where the individual can go for care.

Two ways to reduce costs have been the development of health maintenance organizations (HMOs) and preferred provider organizations (PPOs).[6] HMOs provide both preventive measures and limit where the individual can receive care. With the exception of an emergency, permission must be obtained before the individual can go to another provider.

PPOs provide discount health care but also limit where a person can go for treatment of an illness. The coach and/or athletic trainer must be apprised in advance where the ill athlete should be sent. Athletes sent to a facility not on the approved list may be required to pay for care, whereas if they are sent to a "preferred" facility, all costs are paid.[6] Added services such as physical therapy may be more easily attained and at no cost or much lower cost than with another insurance policy.

Accident insurance   Besides general health insurance, low-cost accident insurance is available to the student. It often covers accidents on school grounds while the student is in attendance. The purpose of this insurance is to protect against financial loss from medical and hospital bills, to encourage an injured student to receive prompt medical care, to encourage prompt reporting of injuries, and to relieve a school of financial responsibility.

The school's general insurance may be limited; thus accident insurance for a specific activity such as sports may be needed to provide additional protection.[6] This type of coverage is limited and does not require knowledge of fault, and the amount it pays is very limited. For very serious sport injuries requiring surgery and lengthy rehabilitation accident insurance is usually not adequate. This inadequacy can put families with limited budgets into a real financial bind. Of particular concern is insurance that does not adequately cover catastrophic injuries.

Catastrophic insurance   Although catastrophic injuries in sports participation are relatively uncommon, if they do occur, the consequences to the athlete, family, and institution, as well as society, can be staggering. In the past when available funds have been completely diminished, the family was forced to seek funding elsewhere, usually through a lawsuit. Organizations such as the NCAA and NAIA provide plans that deal with the problem of a lifetime that requires extensive medical and rehabilitative care because of a permanent disability.[6] Benefits begin when expenses have reached $25,000 and are then extended for a lifetime. At the secondary school level a program is offered to districts by the National Federation of State High School Associations (NFSHSA). This plan provides medical, rehabilitation, and transportation costs in excess of $10,000 not covered by other insurance benefits.[1]

Personal liability insurance   Most individual schools and school districts have general liability insurance to protect against damages that may arise from injuries occurring on school property. It covers claims of negligence on the part of individuals. Its major concern is whether supervision was reasonable and if unreasonable risk of harm was perceived by the sports participant.[27]

Because of the amount of litigation based on alleged negligence, premiums have become almost prohibitive for some schools. Typically, when a victim sues, the lawsuit has been a "shotgun approach," with the coach, athletic trainer, physician, school administrator, and school district all involved. If a protective piece of equipment is involved, the product manufacturer is also sued.

Because of the amount of litigation for alleged negligence, all professionals involved with the sports program must be fully protected by personal liability insurance.

To offset this shotgun mentality and to cover what is not covered by a general liability policy, *errors and omissions* liability insurance has evolved. It is designed to cover school employees, officers, and the district against suits claiming malpractice, wrongful actions, errors and omissions, and acts of negligence.[9] Even when working in a program having good liability coverage, each person within that program who works directly with students must have his or her own personal liability insurance.

As indicated, insurance that covers the athlete's health and safety can be very complex. It must be the concern of the coach and the athletic trainer that every athlete is adequately covered by a good, reliable insurance company. In some athletic programs the filing of claims becomes the responsibility of the athletic trainer. This task can be highly time-consuming, taking the athletic trainer away from his or her major role of directly working with the athlete. *Because of the intricacies and time involved with claim filing and follow-up communications with parents, doctors, and vendors, a staff person other than the athletic trainer should be assigned this responsibility.*

Budgetary Concerns

A major problem often facing athletic trainers is a budget of sufficient size.

One of the major problems faced by athletic trainers is to obtain a budget of sufficient size to permit them to perform a creditable job of athletic training. Most high schools fail to make any budgetary provisions for athletic training except for the purchase of tape, ankle wraps, and a training bag that contains a minimum amount of equipment. Many fail to provide a room and any of the special facilities that are needed to establish an effective athletic training program. Some school boards and administrators fail to recognize that the functions performed in the athletics training quarters are an essential component of the athletic program and that even if no specialist is used, the facilities are nonetheless necessary. Colleges and universities are not usually faced with this problem to the extent of high schools. By and large, athletic training is recognized as an important aspect of the athletic program.

Budgetary needs vary considerably within programs; some require only a few thousand dollars, whereas others spend hundreds of thousands of dollars. The amount spent on building and equipping a training facility, of course, is entirely a matter of local option. In purchasing equipment, immediate needs as well as availability of personnel to operate specialized equipment should be kept in mind.

Budget records should be kept on file so that they are available for use in projecting the following year's budgetary needs. They present a picture of the distribution of current funds and serve to substantiate future budgetary requests.

Expenditures for individual items vary in accordance with different training philosophies. Some athletic trainers may spend much of their budget on expendable supplies such as adhesive tape. An annual inventory must be conducted at the end of the year or before the ordering of supplies and equipment takes place. Accurate records must be kept to justify future requests.

Supplies   Supplies are expendable and usually are for injury prevention, first aid, and management. Examples of supplies are athletic training tape, germicides, and massage lubricants. (Appendix 2 provides some suggestions for individual programs.)

Equipment   The term equipment refers to those items that are not expendable. Equipment may be further divided into fixed and nonfixed. The term fixed does not necessarily mean that it cannot be moved but that it is not usually removed from the athletic training facility. Examples of fixed equipment are ice-makers, an isokinetic exercise device, and electrical therapeutic modalities. Non-fixed equipment refers to nonexpendable items that are less fixed, may be part of an athletic trainer's kit, or may be at the site where a sport is being held. Examples are blankets, scissors, and training kits. (See Appendix 1 for athletic training equipment, Appendix 2 for a list of suggested athletic supplies, and Appendix 3 for a checklist for the athletic trainer's kit.)

Personnel Coverage

A number of administrative functions are the responsibility of the athletic trainer. For example, athletic training coverage and record keeping, commonly called "paperwork," consume many hours per week.

Facility coverage   A major concern of any athletic department is that there is proper personnel coverage provided for the athletic training facility and specific sports. Depending on whether a school has a full-time athletic training staff, an athletic training facility may operate from 9 AM to 6 PM. Mornings are commonly reserved for treatments and exercise rehabilitation, early afternoons are for treatment, exercise rehabilitation, and preparation for practice or a contest, and late afternoons and early evenings are spent in injury management. High schools with limited available supervision may only be able to provide athletic training facility coverage in the afternoons and during vacation periods.

Sports coverage   Ideally, all sports should have a professional or at least a student athletic trainer in attendance at all practices and contests, both at home and away. The high-risk sports, ideally, should have professional athletic trainer and physician present at all practices and contests.

Record Keeping and Paper Work

Record keeping is a major responsibility of the athletic training program. Some athletic trainers object to keeping records and filling out forms, stating they have neither the time nor the inclination to be bookkeepers. Five major functions of athletic training require record keeping and paper work, including accident reports and injury disposition, daily treatment, health appraisal and injury risk or fitness profiles, athletic insurance coverage, and equipment and supply inventories.

Keeping adequate records is of major importance in the athletic training program.

Accident reports and injury disposition   An accident report serves as a record for future reference (Figures 2-11 and 2-12). If the emergency procedures followed are questioned at a later date, one's memory of the details may be somewhat hazy, but a report completed on the spot provides specific information. It should be noted that in a litigation situation questions may be asked of an athletic trainer about an injury that occurred 2 years in the past. All accident reports of this nature should be filed in the athletic trainer's office. It is well to make them out in triplicate so that one copy may be sent to the school health office, one to the physician, and one retained.

The treatment log   Each athletic facility should have a sign-in log available for the athlete who receives any service. Emphasis is placed on recording the treatments for the athlete who is receiving daily therapy for an injury. As with accident records and injury disposition, these records often have the status of legal documents and are used to establish certain facts in a civil litigation, an insurance action, or a criminal action following injury.

Personal information card   Always on file in athletic trainer's office is the athlete's personal information card (Figure 2-13). This card is completed by the

Figure 2-11

Athletic injury record form.

Name _____	Sport _____	Date: ___/___/___ Time: _____ Injury number: _____
Player I.D. _____	Age: _____ Location: _____	Intercollegiate-nonintercollegiate
Initial injury Recheck Reinjury	Preseason—Practice—Game	Incurred while participating in sport: yes_____ no _____
Description: How did it happen? _____		

Initial impression: _____

Site of injury	Body part		Structure	Treatment _____
1 Right	1 Head	25 MP joint	1 Skin	_____
2 Left	2 Face	26 PIP joint	2 Muscle	_____
3 Proximal	3 Eye	27 Abdomen	3 Fascia	_____
4 Distal	4 Nose	28 Hip	4 Bone	_____
5 Anterior	5 Ear	29 Thigh	5 Nerve	_____
6 Posterior	6 Mouth	30 Knee	6 Fat pad	_____
7 Medial	7 Neck	31 Patella	7 Tendon	_____
8 Lateral	8 Thorax	32 Lower leg	8 Ligament	_____
9 Other	9 Ribs	33 Ankle	9 Cartilage	_____
_____	10 Sternum	34 Achilles tendon	10 Capsule	_____
	11 Upper back	35 Foot	11 Compartment	_____
Site of evaluation	12 Low back	36 Toes	12 Dental	_____
1 SHS	13 Shoulder	37 Other	13 _____	_____
2 Athletic Trn Rm.	14 Rotator cuff	_____		Medication _____
3 Site-Competition	15 AC joint			_____
4 _____	16 Glenohumeral			_____
	17 Sternoclavicular	Nontraumatic	Nature of injury	_____
Procedures	18 Upper arm	1 Dermatological	1 Contusion	_____
1 Physical exam	19 Elbow	2 Allergy	2 Strain	_____
2 X-ray	20 Forearm	3 Influenza	3 Sprain	_____
3 Splint	21 Wrist	4 URI	4 Fracture	_____
4 Wrap	22 Hand	5 GU	5 Rupture	_____
5 Cast	23 Thumb	6 Systemic infect.	6 Tendonitis	_____
6 Aspiration	24 Finger	7 Local infect.	7 Bursitis	
7 Other		8 Other	8 Myositis	Prescription dispensed
_____		_____	9 Laceration	1 Antibiotics 5 Muscle relaxant
			10 Concussion	2 Antiinflammatory 6 Enzyme
Disposition	Referral	Disposition of injury	11 Avulsion	3 Decongestant 7 _____
1 SHS	1 Arthrogram	1 No part.	12 Abrasion	4 Analgesic
2 Trainer	2 Neurological	2 Part part.	13 _____	
3 Hospital	3 Int. Med.	3 Full part.		Injections
4 H.D.	4 Orthopedic		Degree	1 Steroids
5 Other	5 EENT		1° 2° 3°	2 Antibiotics
_____	6 Dentist			3 Steroids-xylo
	7 Other			4 _____
	_____	Previous injury _____		

```
┌─────────────────────────────────────────────────────────────────────┐
│                 CALIFORNIA STATE UNIVERSITY, LONG BEACH                │
│                      REPORT OF ATHLETIC INJURY                         │
│                                                                        │
│  Name _____ Date _____ Sport _____ Year  1  2  3  4  │
│  History of this injury:   Time _____ Location _____  │
│     How did it happen? (Student's own words): _____    │
│  _____  │
│  Previous injuries: _____   │
│  Initial impression: _____   │
│  _____  │
│  _____  │
│  Treatment: _____   │
│  Medication: _____   │
│  Disposition:   Referred (Circle) SHS, X-ray, Hospital, Other _____   │
│  Recheck—initial injury           (Initial) _____    │
│                                    Trainer              Team Physician │
└─────────────────────────────────────────────────────────────────────┘
```

Figure 2-12

Athletic injury report form.

```
┌─────────────────────────────────────────────────────────────────────┐
│                   ATHLETIC TRAINING INFORMATION CARD                   │
│                                                                        │
│  Name _____ Age ____ Sex ____ Student no. (S.S.#) _____  │
│  Sport _____                    │
│  School address _____ City _____ State _____   │
│        Zip _____ Phone _____                     │
│  Permanent address _____ City _____ State _____   │
│        Zip _____ Phone _____                     │
│  Parents' address _____ City _____ State _____   │
│        Zip _____ Phone _____                     │
│  Are you a junior college transfer?     Yes _____ No _____           │
│  Give the number of seasons completed at CSULB _____                  │
│  Do you or your parents have private health insurance?   Yes ____ No __│
│  Name of company _____ Policy number _____     │
│  In case of emergency notify _____ Phone _____ Relationship __  │
│  List major past injuries and dates _____     │
│  Medic Alert _____                           │
└─────────────────────────────────────────────────────────────────────┘
```

Figure 2-13

Sports participation card.

athlete at the time of the health examination and serves as a means of contacting the family, personal physician, and insurance company in case of emergency.

Supply and equipment inventory   As discussed previously, a major responsibility of the athletic trainer is to manage a budget, most of which is spent for equipment and supplies. Every year an inventory must be conducted and recorded on such items as new equipment needed, equipment that needs to be replaced or repaired, and the expendable supplies that need replenishing.

Annual reports   Most athletic departments require an annual report on the functions of the athletic training program. This report serves as a means for making program changes and improvements. It commonly includes the number of athletes served, a survey of the number and types of injuries, an analysis of the program, and recommendations for future improvements.

Computer use   Increasingly, computers are being used in athletic training (Figure 2-14). Athletic trainers who have access to a computer find that a great deal of information can be recorded for immediate and future use because of its almost limitless storing and retrieval capacities. There are hardware and software available for most of the functions that need storing. Besides record keeping and paper work, computer application can provide information about nutritional counseling and body composition, injury risk profiles based on other anthropometric measures, and the recording of isokinetic evaluation and exercise.[26]

> Computers are becoming an essential tool in the administration of the athletic training program.

Figure 2-14

Computers are becoming an essential tool in athletic training.

SUMMARY

Athletic training is a specialization within sports medicine, with its major concern the health and safety of athletes. The primary athletic training team consists of the coach, the athletic trainer, and the team physician. The coach must ensure that the environment and the equipment that is worn are the safest possible, that all injuries and illnesses are properly cared for, that skills are properly taught, and that conditioning is at the highest level.

The athletic trainer must be highly educated and a well-trained professional. The athletic trainer must be certified and, if possible, have a state license to practice. The successful athletic trainer is one who loves sports and the competitive environment. He or she must have an abundance of vitality and emotional stability and empathy for people who are in physical and/or emotional pain, as well as a sense of humor, the ability to communicate, and a desire to learn. All of the athletic trainer's actions must follow the highest standards of conduct.

At all times, the coach and the athletic trainer must act in a reasonable and prudent manner. A person who fails to act with reasonable care is considered negligent. The coach and the athletic trainer must, at all times, consider as paramount the health and well-being of the athlete. Legal liability or responsibility varies in its interpretation from state to state and from area to area.

The team physician can be in varied specializations. Team physicians, depending on the time they are committed to a specific sports program, can perform a variety of responsibilities. Some key responsibilities are performing the preparticipation health examination, diagnosing and treating illnesses and injuries, advising and teaching the athletic training staff, attending games, scrimmages, and practices, and counseling the athlete about health matters.

The athletic training program forms a health care unit requiring careful organization and administration. Of major concern is the maintenance of facilities, provision of proper supervision of special service sections, and performance of an effective preparticipation health examination. Insurance, budget, accident reporting, treatment logging, and annual reports are some of the record keeping responsibilities required of the athletic training program.

REVIEW QUESTIONS AND CLASS ACTIVITIES

1. Why is athletic training considered a team endeavor?
2. Contrast the coach's, athletic trainer's, and team physician's roles in athletic training.
3. What qualifications should the athletic trainer have in terms of education, certification, and personality?
4. What does a state licensure provide the athletic trainer?
5. Where can athletic trainers apply their professional preparation?
6. What are the major legal concerns of the coach and the athletic trainer in terms of liability, assumption of risk, torts, and negligence?
7. Contrast the act of recognizing an illness or injury with diagnosing it. Who can legally diagnose?
8. Describe the duties of the team physician.
9. What other health professionals could support the athletic training program?
10. What are the major administrative functions that a head athletic trainer must perform?
11. Design two athletic training facilities—one for a medium-size university and one for a large university.
12. Observe the activities in the athletic training facility. Pick both a slow time and a busy time to observe.
13. Why do hygiene and sanitation play an important role in athletic training? How should the athletic training facility be maintained?
14. Organize a preparticipation health examination for 90 football players.

15. Explain the importance of assessing a young person's level of physical maturity.
16. Debate what conditions constitute good grounds for medical disqualification from a sport.
17. Define the types of insurance necessary in sports.
18. Fully equip a new medium-size high school or college athletic training facility. Pick equipment from current catalogs.
19. Establish a reasonable budget for a small high school, a large high school, and a large college or university.
20. Identify the groups of individuals to be served in the athletic training facility.
21. Record keeping is a major function in athletic training. What records are necessary to keep? How can a computer help?

REFERENCES

1. Berg, R: 1984 catastrophic injury insurance: an end to costly litigation, Ath J 8:10, 1987.
2. Borkowski, RP: Coaches and the courts, First Aider 54(7):1, Summer 1985.
3. Borkowski, RP: Lawsuit less likely if safety comes first, First Aider, 55(2):11, Oct 1985.
4. Caine, DJ, and Broekhoff, J: Maturity assessment: a viable preventive measure against physical and psychological insult to the young athlete? Phys Sportsmed 15(3):67, 1987.
5. Capel, SA: Psychological and organizational factors related to burnout in athletic trainers, Ath Train 21:322, 1986.
6. Chambers, RL, et al.: Insurance types and coverages: knowledge to plan for the future (with a focus on motor skill activities and athletics), Phys Educator 44:233, 1986.
7. Clement, A: Patterns of litigation in physical education instruction. Paper presented at the American Association of Health, Physical Education, and Dance, National Convention and Exposition, Cincinnati, April, 1986.
8. Cutting VJ: Development of "A student handbook for prevention of athletic injuries," master's thesis, San Diego, 1985, San Diego State University.
9. Dodd, RB: Here is what liability responsibility means for athletics, Chicago Tribune, Feb 2, 1986.
10. Dorsen, PJ: Should athletes with one eye, kidney, or testicle play contact sports? Phys Sportsmed 14(7):130, 1986.

11. Drowatzky, JN: Legal duties and liability in athletic training, Ath Train 20:11, Spring 1985.
12. Forseth, EA: Consideration in planning small college athletic training facilities, Ath Train 21(1):22, 1986.
13. Furney, SR, and Patton, B: An examination of health counseling practices of athletic trainers, Ath Train 21:294, Winter 1985.
14. Gaunya, ST: The role of the trainer. In Vinger, PF, and Hoerner, EF, editors: Sports injuries, the unthwarted epidemic, Boston, 1982, John Wright, PSG, Inc.
15. Grace, P, and Ledderman, L: Role delineation study for the certification examination for entry-level athletic trainers, Ath Train 17:264, 1982.
16. Hossler, P: How to acquire an athletic trainer on the high school level, Ath Train 20:199, Fall 1985.
17. Lester, RA: The coach as codefendant: football in the 1980's. In Appenzeller, H, editor: Sports and law: contemporary issues, Charlottesville, Va, 1985, The Michie Co.
18. Loeffler, RD: On being a team physician, Sports Med Dig 9(2):1, 1987.
19. Lombardo, JA: Sports medicine: a team effort, Phys Sportsmed 13:72, April 1985.
20. Luschen, S, and Moore, W: Knowledge helps prevent sports-injury lawsuits, First Aider 56(6):4, 1987.
21. McKeag, DB: Preseason physical examination for the prevention of sports injuries, Sports Med 2:413, 1985.
22. Myers, C: Preparticipation health education. In Smith, NJ, editor: Sports

medicine: health care for young athletes, Evanston, Ill, 1983, Committee on Sports Medicine American Academy of Pediatrics.

23. Myers, GC, and Garrick, JG: The preseason examination of school and college athletes. In Strauss, RH, editor: Sports medicine, Philadelphia, 1984, WB Saunders Co.

24. National Athletic Trainers' Association: Code of ethics, Ath Train 19:66, Spring 1984.

25. Parcel, GS: Basic emergency care, ed 3, St. Louis, 1986, The CV Mosby Co.

26. Ray, R, and Shire, TL: An athletic training program in the computer age, Ath Train 21:212, 1986.

27. Reiner, NJ: Injury within our schools: can it affect you? J Natl Intraml-Rec Sports Assoc 6:56, 1982.

28. Vergamini, G: Professional burnout: implications for the athletic trainer, Ath Train 16:196, Fall 1981.

29. Yasser, R: Calculating risk, Sports Med Dig 9(2):5, 1987.

ANNOTATED BIBLIOGRAPHY

Appenzeller, H: Sports and law: contemporary issues, Charlottesville, Va, 1985, The Michie Co.
Exposes sports litigation from the perspectives of the athletic director, athlete, athletic trainer, coach, officials, and products liability expert. A chapter on the athletic trainer emphasizes the use of modalities and how this use relates to the practice of physical therapy in different states.

Bell, GW, editor: Professional preparation in athletic training, Champaign, Ill, 1982, Human Kinetics Publishing.
Represents a collection of papers presented at the National Athletic Trainers' Association's professional preparation conference in 1979 and 1980. Includes articles on athletic training in higher education, athletic injuries, preventing athletic injuries, and liability and management.

National Athletic Trainers' Association, Inc: Code of professional practice, 1001 E Fourth St, Greenville, NC 27858.
Contains a revision of the previous Code of Ethics of 1983. Includes ethical principles, membership standards, and certification standards.

Smith NJ, editor: Sports medicine: health care for young athlete, 1983 committee on sports medicine, Evanston, Ill, 1983. American Academy of Pediatrics.
Based on the concerns and needs of children who engage in sports. Covers the major health and safety aspects at this level.

INJURY PREVENTION

Part Two covers information fundamental to injury prevention. The four major areas of injury prevention are discussed in detail.

CHAPTER 3

Physical Conditioning and Training

When you finish this chapter, you should be able to

Identify the major conditioning seasons and the types of exercise that are performed in each season

Describe the value of specific conditioning exercises in injury prevention, including flexibility, strength development, and endurance

Contrast the ways that strength can be achieved through equipment and nonequipment approaches

Explain when an athlete has overexercised

Contrast the differences between genders in conditioning and training

Describe the major conditioning and training concerns in injury prevention for children, older persons, and disabled persons who compete

Lack of physical fitness is one of the primary causes of sports injury.

Physical conditioning for sports participation, besides preparing athletes for high-level performance, also prevents injuries. Coaches and athletic trainers alike now recognize that improper conditioning is one of the major causes of sports injuries. Muscular imbalance, improper timing caused by faulty neuromuscular coordination, inadequate ligamentous or tendinous strength, inadequate muscle or cardiovascular endurance, inadequate muscle bulk, problems of flexibility, and problems related to body composition are some of the primary causes of sports injuries directly attributable to insufficient or improper physical conditioning and training.

Training is usually defined as a systematic process of repetitive, progressive exercise or work, involving the learning process and acclimatization. The great sports medicine pioneer Dr. S.E. Bilik[4] correctly stated that the primary objective of intense sports conditioning and training must be as follows: "To put the body with extreme and exceptional care under the influence of all agents which promote its health and strength in order to enable it to meet extreme and exceptional demands upon it."

Through the use of systematic work increments, improved voluntary responses by the organs are attained; through constant repetition, the conscious movements become more automatic and more reflexive, requiring less concentration by the higher nerve centers and thus reducing the amount of energy expended through the elimination of movements unnecessary for performance of the desired task. Increasing the strenuousness of exercise in the ways suggested is an application of the *overload principle,* which holds that an activity must always be upgraded to a consistently higher level through maximum or near-maximum stimulation. In this way the metabolic level and the organic responses can be increased.

CONDITIONING OF SOFT AND BONY TISSUES

Properly graded conditioning can positively affect both the soft and bony tissues of the body (Figure 3-1). Connective tissue, comprising tendons, ligaments, and joint capsules, becomes increasingly more dense, and as a result, stronger. Stretched muscle fibers increase in their cross-sectioned width and in blood and nerve supply. Bones that are positively stressed will also increase their density and become stronger over a period of time. Conversely, soft tissue and bony tissue that are adversely stressed will become weakened over time. A good example of

Figure 3-1

Modern sports programs often require elaborate conditioning facilities and equipment to apply sound injury prevention methods.

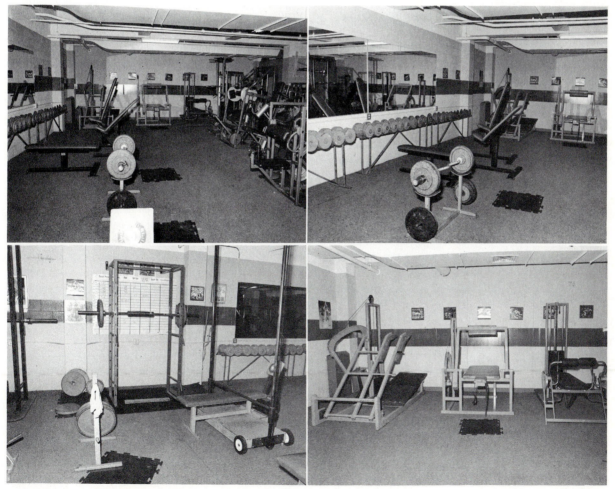

Continued.

Figure 3-1, cont'd

For legend see p. 65.

this process is described by Wolff's law, whereby changes in form and function of bones result in definite changes in their internal function.[2] A major basis for these changes apparently is the production of electrical potential that results from bony tensions and compression. In the case of bone, a negative potential is created on compression sites, and a positive potential at the tension site with less compression. This electrical activity in the bones apparently is involved with osteoblastic (bone formation) and osteoclastic (bone resorption) activity. This same principle may, in some way, be associated with tendon, ligament, and/or joint capsule collagen fiber formation and resorption. In the early stages of conditioning, tendinous, ligamentous, and capsular tissues, as well as bony tissue, absorb faster than they form collagen, placing them in a weakened condition. This resorption is followed by a gradual reversal of the process, and, over time, collagen formation is greater than its resorption. When a body part is immobilized following injury, collagen resorption takes precedence over formation (see Chapter 14, *Exercise Rehabilitation*).

It takes time and careful preparation to bring an athlete into competition at a level of fitness that will preclude early-season injury. The most dangerous period in any sport is the first 3 or 4 weeks of the season, principally because athletes frequently are lacking in flexibility, are often overweight, and many times are out of good physical condition when they report for initial practice. Another factor is lack of familiarity with most of the fundamentals of a sport, resulting in awkwardness and a consequent proneness to potential injury-provoking situations.

CONDITIONING SEASONS

No longer do serious athletes engage in just preseason conditioning and inseason competition. Sports conditioning is a year-round endeavor, often encompassing four training seasons: postseason, off-season, preseason, and in-season. This plan is especially appropriate for collision-type sports such as football. Gaunya[17] called this approach "the quadratic training cycle." For American tackle football, the postseason generally is from February to May; off-season, May to July; preseason, July to September; and in-season, September to January.

Postseason

Conditioning during the postseason is commonly dedicated to physical restoration. This period is particularly appropriate when the athlete has been injured during the in-season. This is a time when postsurgical rehabilitation takes place and detailed medical evaluations can be obtained.[17]

Sports conditioning often falls into four seasons: postseason, off-season, preseason, and in-season.

Off-Season

It is not essential that athletes continue an intensive conditioning program during the off-season, although it is usually a good idea for the athletic trainer and coach to encourage them to participate in another sport during this period. Such an activity should make certain physical demands embodying strength, endurance, and flexibility by means of running and general all-around physical performance. This activity will assist athletes in maintaining their level of fitness. In other words, the sport must be sufficiently demanding to require a good level of fitness to participate effectively. An excellent off-season sport for the football player would be wrestling or gymnastics. Track, especially cross-country, is a conditioner. Rope skipping as a conditioning activity lends itself to all sports and makes vigorous demands on the body.

If it is not feasible for athletes to participate in an off-season sport, a *detraining program* should be planned. Such a program permits gradual decrease in the usual work load and allows the athlete to exercise less frequently and less intensively. A weekly workout of moderate-to-strong intensity is usually all that is required, since physical fitness is retained for a considerable length of time after an active program of competition ends. The physically vigorous athlete tends to be quite active in the off-season too and, as a rule, will stay in reasonably good condition throughout the year.[17]

It must be kept in mind, however, that caloric intake must be decreased accordingly when the exercise load is decreased, since not as much energy is then burned. The overweight condition of many athletes when they report for preseason training is caused by their having continued a midseason appetite with an off-season activity load. Establishing regular training routines for the off-season enables the athletic trainer to keep a close check on athletes even if they are seen only at 2- or 3-week intervals. In this way extreme overweight or poor fitness can be forestalled.

Preseason

Athletic trainers should impress on their athletes the need for maintaining a reasonably high level of physical fitness during the off-season. If such advice is followed, the athlete will find preseason work relatively rewarding and any proneness to potential injury considerably diminished. No difficulty in reaching a state of athletic fitness suitable for competition within 6 to 8 weeks should then be experienced. During this preliminary period flexibility, endurance, and strength should be emphasized in a carefully graded developmental program. In such a program there must be wise and constant use of established physiological bases for improving physical condition and performance.

Many athletes, particularly in one-season sports, tend to reach their highest level of performance halfway through the season. As a result, they are truly efficient only half of the time. Conference and federation restrictions often hamper or prohibit effective preseason training, especially in football, and therefore compel the athlete to come into early-season competition before being physically fit for it. At the high school level 6 to 8 weeks of preseason conditioning afford the best insurance against susceptibility to injury and permit the athlete to enter competition in a good state of physical fitness, provided a carefully graded program is established and adhered to conscientiously. Recently, physicians have been adding their voices to the demands for a realistic approach to proper conditioning, and school administrators and the general public may see the need and effectiveness of permitting adequate and properly controlled preseason training.

In-Season

Intensive preseason conditioning programs, which bring the athlete to the competitive season, may not be maintained by the sport itself. Unless there is strenuous conditioning throughout the season, a problem of deconditioning may occur. Athletes who do not undergo maintenance conditioning may lose their entry level of physiological fitness.[17]

THE TEN CARDINAL CONDITIONING PRINCIPLES

The following 10 cardinal principles can be applied to sports conditioning to prevent injuries:

1. *Warming up*. See that proper and adequate warm-up procedures precede all activities.
2. *Gradualness*. Add small daily increments of work. REMEMBER: It takes 6 to 8 weeks to get into top-level condition.
3. *Timing*. Prevent overdoing. Relate all work to the athlete's general condition at the time. Practice periods should extend for 1 hour to 1 hour and 45 minutes, depending on the sport. REMEMBER: The tired athlete is prone to injury.
4. *Intensity*. Stress the intensity of the work rather than the quantity. Usually coaches and athletic trainers fail to work their athletes *hard* enough in terms of intensity. They make the mistake of prolonging the workout rather than increasing the tempo or the work load. As the degree of training increases, the intensity of training must also increase.
5. *Capacity level*. Expect from the athlete performance that is as close to his or her physiological limits as health and safety factors will allow. Only in working to capacity will the desired results be achieved.
6. *Strength*. Develop strength as a means of producing greater endurance and speed.
7. *Motivation*. Motivation is a prime factor in sports conditioning. Use circuit training and isometric exercises as means of further motivating the athlete.
8. *Specialization*. Exercise programs should include exercises for strength, relaxation, and flexibility. In addition, exercises geared to the demands made on the body in specific activities should be used to develop specialization.
9. *Relaxation*. Specific relaxation exercises, which aid in recovery from fatigue and tension, should be taught.
10. *Routine*. A daily routine of exercise, both in-season and off-season, should be established.

FOUNDATIONS OF CONDITIONING

Logan and Wallis[25] identified the SAID principle, which expressly relates to sports conditioning and training. SAID is an acronym for *s*pecific *a*daptation to *i*mposed *d*emands. The SAID principle indicates that conditioning and training are directed toward the specific demands of a given sport.

Gradually increasing the strenuousness of an exercise is an application of the overload principle.

The SAID principle indicates that conditioning and training should be directed toward the specific demands of a sport.

Fat and the Lean Body

The human body is generally composed of fat and a lean body mass. *Essential fat* is the survival fat that is stored around vital organs, in the bone marrow, and in the nervous system. It usually constitutes approximately 2% to 4% of the total body fat in adult males and 6% to 8% in adult females. Fat, other than essential fat, is primarily found subcutaneously. The normal total body fat is 13% to 15% for young adult males and 22% to 25% for young women.[5,10]

To prevent sports injuries, excess body fat should be avoided. Excess body fat is weight that is considered "dead" and not viable. This extra weight places an added stress on the body, especially the joints, and therefore results in an increased susceptibility to overuse problems.

Warming Up and Cooling Down

Both the processes of properly warming up and cooling down are believed by many authorities to have major implications in the prevention of sports injuries.[38]

Warming Up

Although warm-up is still a subject of study and results are somewhat conflicting, most evidence favors its use. The use of warm-up procedures has long been traditional in sports and is still advocated by most athletic trainers, coaches, and physicians as the means of preparing the body physiologically and psychologically for physical performance in the belief that it will not only improve performance but will lessen the possibilities of injury.[11] The term "warming up" in this discussion refers to the use of preliminary exercise procedures rather than the use of hot showers, massage, counterirritants, diathermy, or other forms of passive warm-up.

Warming up involves general body warming and warming specific body areas for the demands of the sport.

Warm-up is used as a preventive measure, although limited data exist to substantiate this. It is believed that a proper warm-up will prevent and/or reduce strains and the tearing of muscle fibers from their tendinous attachments. Most frequently the antagonist muscles are torn. Their inability to relax rapidly, plus the great contractile force of the agonist muscles added to the momentum of the moving part, subject the antagonists to a sudden severe strain that can result in a subsequent tearing of the fibers themselves, as well as their tendinous attachments. Proper warm-up can reduce or prevent muscle soreness.

Physiological purposes of warming up   The main purposes of warming up are to raise both the general body and the deep muscle temperatures and to stretch collagenous tissues to permit greater flexibility. This reduces the possibility of muscle tears and ligamentous sprains and helps to prevent muscle soreness. As cellular temperature increases, it is accompanied by a corresponding increase in the speed of the metabolic processes within the cells, since such processes are temperature dependent. For each degree of internal temperature rise there is a corresponding rise in the rate of metabolism of approximately 13%. At higher temperatures there is a faster and more complete dissociation of oxygen from the hemoglobin and myoglobins, and there is increased blood flow and reduced muscle viscosity, which improves the oxygen supply during work.[32,33] The transmission of nerve impulses speeds up as well. Overloading the muscle groups before engaging in power activities results in improved performance. It is thought that there is an increased level of excitation of the motor units that are called into play to handle the increased load and that these motor units are then carried over into the actual performance. The result is an increase in the athlete's physical working capacity.

It takes at least 15 to 30 minutes of gradual warm-up to bring the body to a state of readiness with its attendant rise in body temperature and to adequately mobilize the body physiology in terms of making a greater number of muscle capillaries available for extreme effort and of readying blood sugar and adrenaline. The time needed for satisfactory warm-up varies with the individual and tends to increase with age.

Warm-up differs in relation to the type of competition. It is advisable for athletes to warm-up in activities similar to the event in which they will compete. Accordingly, a sprinter would start by jogging a bit, practice a few starts, and use some stretching techniques and general body exercises. A baseball player might first use general body exercises, swing a bat through a number of practice swings, and do preliminary throwing, alternating these activities with stretching exercises. Both overload and the use of mimetic activities appear to be important for those events in which neuromuscular coordination is paramount. On cool days, warm-up should be increased in duration and should be performed in warm-up clothing.

The process of warming up   Warm-up generally falls into two categories: (1) the *general,* or *unrelated,* warm-up, which consists of activities that bring about a general warming of the body without having any relationship to the skills to be performed; and (2) *specific,* or *related,* warm-up, which is mimetic, that is, similar to or the same as skills to be performed in competition (running, throwing, swinging, etc.)

General warm-up   General warm-up procedures should consist of jogging or easy running and general exercises and stretching.[26] These procedures should mobilize the body for action and make it supple and free. They must be of sufficient duration and intensity to raise deep-tissue temperatures without developing marked fatigue. When athletes attain a state of sweating, they have raised their internal temperature to a desirable level. The nature of the warm-up varies to some degree in relation to the activity. Some procedures lend themselves well to athletic activities of all types and should be performed along with others that are specifically designed for the sport in which the athlete is to participate.

Specific event warm-up   After completing the general warm-up, the athletes should progress to those exercises that are specific for their events or activities. They should start at a moderate pace and then increase the tempo as they feel body temperature and cardiovascular increases taking place. The effects of warm-up may persist as long as 45 minutes. However, the closer the warm-up period is to the actual performance, the more beneficial it will be in terms of its effect on the performance. For the athlete to benefit optimally from warm-up, no more than 15 minutes should elapse between the completion of the warm-up and performing the activity itself.

Cooling Down

Cooling down, when applied to exercise, is the gradual diminishing of work intensity, which permits the return of both circulation and various other body functions to preexercise levels. From 30 seconds to 1 minute of jogging, followed by 3 to 5 minutes of walking, permits the body to effect the necessary readjustments.

Physiologically, an important reason for cooling down actively is that blood and muscle lactic acid levels decrease more rapidly during active recovery than during passive recovery. Gradually cooling down in this manner also keeps the muscle pumps, including the heart and the two legs, active and prevents blood from pooling in the extremities as would happen if the athlete suddenly stopped moving.

Proper cooling decreases blood and muscle lactic acid levels more rapidly.

Flexibility

Flexibility is defined as the range of movement of a specific joint or group of joints influenced by the associated bones and bony structures and the physiological characteristics of the muscles, tendons, ligaments, and the various other collagenous tissues surrounding the joint. Studies have indicated that an increase in the flexibility of inflexible joints tends to decrease the injuries to those joints. In most instances it is also contended that an increase in flexibility contributes to better athletic performance. Both of these considerations are important to the athletic trainer (Figure 3-2).

Good flexibility usually indicates that there are no adhesions or abnormalities present in or around the joints and that there are no serious muscular limitations. This allows the body to move freely and easily through the full range-of-joint flexion and extension without any unnecessary restrictions in the joints or the adjacent tissues. Examples of static flexibility exercises are shown on pp. 72-75.

Figure 3-2

Flexibility can be an important factor in decreasing sports injuries.

Hamstring stretch Starting position—sitting with legs straight, feet 8 inches apart. Keeping the knees straight, the athlete reaches forward and grasps either ankles or toes, depending on the extensibility of the hamstring muscles. **NOTE:** The stretch must first be felt in back of the knees and then in the low back.

Groin stretch Starting position—sitting with knees bent and the soles of the feet together and grasping both forefeet with both hands. Both elbows should rest on the lower legs. The athlete then leans the trunk forward while pressing downward on the bent legs at the same time.

Upper hamstring stretch Starting position—sitting with legs extended and grasping the right ankle with the left hand and underneath the knee with the right hand. The athlete then brings the leg as a unit toward the chest, stretching the hamstring muscles. **NOTE:** No pressure should be placed on the knee.

Achilles tendon (gastrocnemius) stretch Starting position—while facing a wall or other similar support, one leg is positioned back while leaning toward the wall. With the left foot flat, heel down, and knee straight, the stretch is to the gastrocnemius with the right knee bent. Stretch is focused on the Achilles tendon. The stretch can be varied by first stretching with the foot straight ahead, then adducted and, finally, abducted.

Hip flexor stretch Starting position—with the right foot flat, the knee is bent, and the left leg is extended straight backward. The trunk is then lowered as far as possible and positioned as far forward as possible. The stretch should be felt in the groin region.

Hamstring stretch

Groin stretch

Upper hamstring stretch

Achilles tendon stretch

Hip flexor stretch

Quadriceps stretch

Trunk and leg stretch

Lateral leg stretch

Sitting
low back
stretch

Rocking
low back
stretch

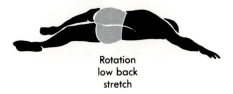

Rotation
low back
stretch

Quadriceps stretch Starting position—first the body is positioned on the left side, and the right foot is grasped with the right hand while the right knee is bent. To add to the stretch the hip is moved forward. The stretch is then repeated on the left side. **NOTE:** Avoid putting stress on the knee joint.

Trunk and leg stretch Starting position—with the arms extended overhead and legs straight, feet pointed, the athlete reaches overhead as far as possible and feet downward as much as possible. Stretching occurs to the posterior aspect of the arms, back, and legs.

Lateral trunk stretch Starting position—standing with feet shoulder-width apart with one hand on the hip and the other hand extended overhead. The trunk is then bent toward the hand on the hip, with the overhead arm stretching the lateral trunk.

Sitting low back stretch Starting position—sitting in a cross-leg position, the athlete leans forward, stretching the low back.

Rocking low back stretch Starting position—lying on the back, the knees are grasped with both hands, with the head curling forward far as possible toward the knees. In this position the athlete gently rocks back and forth.

Rotation low back stretch Starting position—lying on the back, the athlete places the left leg over the right, keeping the shoulders flat and the arms out to the side. A gentle stretch should be felt in the low back. This movement is repeated with the right leg placed over the left leg.

Spinal twist Starting position—sitting, legs fully extended; then the right leg is bent under the left leg. The heel of the left foot is then placed just in front of the bent right knee. Next, the trunk is twisted to the left, and the right elbow is positioned on the lateral aspect of the left knee. If possible, the foot or ankle of the right leg is grasped by the right hand. From this position the trunk and head are rotated toward the left while the right elbow pushes backward on the bent left knee. This sequence of movements is repeated on the opposite side.

Kneeling shoulder stretch Starting position—taking a four-point position, the arm or arms are extended as far in front of the head as possible. At the same time the trunk and face are lowered as much as possible to accentuate the stretch.

Double anterior shoulder stretch Starting position—both hands are grasped behind the back with elbows fully extended. In this position both arms are slowly raised as far as possible while maintaining a fully upright posture.

Single anterior shoulder stretch Starting position—standing fully upright, the left arm is placed behind the back, with the right arm raised to the side. In this position the right arm is pulled as far backward as possible, stretching the anterior shoulder.

Overhead shoulder stretch Starting position—both arms are raised above the head. The left elbow is bent and is grasped with the right hand. The left upper arm is then gently pulled toward the midline of the body. Repeat with the other side.

Overhead/behind back shoulder stretch Starting position—the left arm is raised overhead and the hand is positioned behind the head and as far down the back as possible. The right elbow is then placed behind the back, with the hand reaching upward as far as possible. Ideally, the fingers of both hands grasp. If grasping is not possible, connection can be made by holding onto a towel.

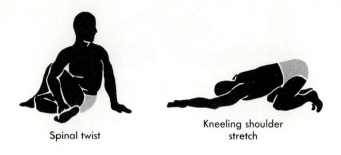

Spinal twist

Kneeling shoulder stretch

Double anterior shoulder stretch

Single anterior shoulder stretch

Overhead shoulder stretch

Overhead/behind back shoulder stretch

Neck rotation
stretch

Lateral neck
stretch

Front neck
stretch

Back neck
stretch

Neck rotation stretch Starting position—standing or sitting with good posture, slowly rotate head to the right until a gentle stretch is felt. Repeat on the left side.

Lateral neck stretch Starting position—standing or sitting with good posture, slowly bend the neck laterally and, if possible, touch the right ear to the tip of the right shoulder. Repeat on the opposite side.

Front neck stretch Starting position—standing or sitting with good posture, slowly extend the head back as far as possible, stretching the anterior neck muscles.

Back neck stretch Starting position—standing or sitting with good posture, slowly flex the head forward as far as possible, stretching the posterior neck muscles.

Most authorities in sports consider flexibility one of the most important objectives in conditioning athletes.[19] Good flexibility increases the athlete's ability to avoid some injuries. Since flexibility permits a greater range of movement within the joint, the ligaments and other connective tissues are not so easily strained or torn. It also permits greater freedom of movement in all directions. There apparently is a definite relationship between injury and joint flexibility. The "tight" or inflexible athlete performs with a considerable handicap in terms of movement, besides being much more injury prone. In some cases the very tight-jointed athletes are more susceptible to muscle strains and tears. Repetitive stretching of the collagenous or fascial ligamentous tissue over a long period of time permits the athlete to obtain an increased range of motion.

Conversely, **hyperflexibility**—flexibility beyond a joint's normal range—must be avoided, because loose-jointed players may be more prone to joint injuries such as subluxations and dislocations.[41] Extremes of flexibility are of little value and can result in joint weakness at certain angles. Flexibility, like strength, is specific to the joint and its surrounding tissues and varies in its natural degree among individuals.

The athlete with good flexibility can change the direction of a movement easily and is less likely to become injured if he or she should fall. The wise coach or athletic trainer will single out inflexible athletes and place them on a regimen of stretching exercises until they achieve a satisfactory degree of flexibility.

Conditioning should be performed gradually, with work added in small increments.

The "tight" or inflexible athlete performs with a considerable handicap in terms of movement.

hyperflexibility
Flexibility beyond a joint's normal range.

The athlete who gains improved flexibility and increased range of joint movement is able to use his or her body more effectively. In addition, when an injury situation is unavoidable, the joints involved very often can withstand a stress or torque considerably in excess of that which can be resisted by a less flexible person. Increased flexibility further aids in reducing impact shock such as that encountered in contact sports or in activities in which the body comes into forceful contact with a relatively unyielding surface (for example, the landing phase in gymnastics, jumping, or vaulting).

Increasing Flexibility

The development of flexibility is a slow process. The myotatic (stretch) reflex, which is invoked during a stretching maneuver, is a muscle-protective mechanism. The muscle itself actively resists stretch as the *result of a reflex inhibition* in the antagonist muscle (the inverse myotatic reflex), which tends to reduce activation. The amount and rate of response of a stretch reflex are proportional to the amount and rate of stretching; hence the use of a repetitive vigorous ballistic (rebound) stretching maneuver would cause the muscle to contract with proportional vigor—not a desirable response for either warm-ups or the attainment of flexibility.[37]

In general, three methods of stretching are used today to increase flexibility: *ballistic, static, and PNF stretching.* Ballistic (rebound) stretching should be avoided because it stimulates the myotatic reflex. The two methods that initiate the inverse myotatic reflex, which inhibits the stretching muscles and in turn facilitates further stretching, are the static and proprioceptive neuromuscular facilitation (PNF) stretching techniques (see Chapter 14, p. 402, for PNF stretching).

Principles of static stretching[45]

1. When to stretch
   a. After a general warm-up; before engaging in any vigorous conditioning activity or sports performance.
   b. After cooling down; following any vigorous activity.
2. How to stretch[1]
   a. Warm up musculoskeletal system through some repetitive activity, bringing skin to a light sweat (e.g., jogging, rope jumping).
   b. Begin with an *Easy Stretch*, holding for 20 to 30 seconds (this produces mild muscle tension and relaxation).
   c. When stretching, focus on muscle region that is pulling the body part into a stretch position (agonists).
   d. Following the Easy Stretch, proceed to the next phase—the Developmental Stretch; move to a moderate stretch position for 20 to 30 seconds.
   e. Avoid breath holding at all times. As the Developmental Stretch is performed, exhale the air from the lungs completely as the stretch is assumed; follow with breathing that is slow, relaxed, and rhythmic.
   f. Avoid severe, painful stretching. Overstretching an area will defeat the purpose of the activity.
   g. Each stretch may be executed from one to three times per day. The minimum number of stretch sessions per week is three. Ideally, athletes who have severe restriction of range of motion should stretch daily until a more normal range has been attained.

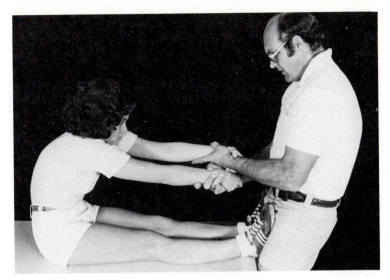

Figure 3-3

Releasing the muscles in the low back region can be accomplished by pulling back against an isometric resistance until fatigued, followed by 3 to 5 seconds of relaxation, and moving the trunk forward to a new position.

Muscle stretching through PNF   A number of PNF techniques are used for stretching—the slow reversal–hold, the contract-relax, and the hold-relax techniques. All three involve various combinations of alternating the contraction and relaxation of both agonist and antagonist muscles. All techniques consist of a 5- or 10-second pushing phase, followed by a 5- to 10-second relaxation phase (Figure 3-3).

For example, in using the slow-reversal–hold technique on the hamstring muscle, the following steps are executed: the athlete lies on his or her back with the knee extended and ankle flexed at 90 degrees. The athletic trainer or other operator flexes the athlete's leg at the hip joint until mild discomfort is felt in the hamstring region. At this time, the athlete pushes against the operator's resistance by contracting the hamstring muscle. After pushing 5 to 10 seconds, the athlete relaxes his or her hamstring, and the agonist quadricep muscle is contracted while the operator applies a passive stretch to further stretch the hamstrings. This process is repeated three times.

In the contract-relax technique, the hamstrings are actively (isotonically) contracted, moving the leg toward a flat surface on the push phase. The hold-relax method consists of a hamstring contraction against an immovable (isometric) resistance during the push phase. With both the contract-relax and the hold-relax techniques, there is a relaxation of hamstring and quadricep muscles, followed by a passive stretch of the hamstring muscles (see Chapter 14).

Muscle Strength

Muscles are complex types of tissue composed of contractible fibers that effect movement of an organ or body part. Here the focus is on skeletal muscles. *Strength* is defined as the capacity to exert force or as the ability to do work against resistance. The most noticeable change that takes place in the muscles as a result of regular and proper exercise is the increase in girth. However, this general rule—the girth of a muscle is proportional to the work done by it—does not

Size alone is not an index of muscle strength.

always hold true. For example, the weight training of men is usually associated with marked muscular hypertrophy, whereas women who engage in heavy weight training tend to develop sizable increases in strength but usually acquire very limited hypertrophy. The higher levels of testosterone found in the male are responsible for muscle hypertrophy in combination with an overload resistance program.[27] This principle of overload is one of the basic premises of strength training. Frequent repetitions, if not coincidental with increases in work load, are valueless for this purpose, although the total work load may be equal.

Muscular strength can show an increase of three times or more without a proportional increase in muscle bulk necessarily being indicated. However, exercise must be performed against near-maximum and gradually increasing resistance. Such resistance can be obtained either by lifting, pulling, or pushing against some resistive force that requires near-maximum effort for the individual; by moving the body at an ever-increasing rate of speed that is approaching the maximum level of performance; or by a combination of the two. It is important for the athletic trainer to know that a number of factors are involved in strength training. The speed, duration, number of repetitions, and vigor or force with which exercises are performed will determine the outcome of the program. The variable of individual difference is another factor that will affect the final result. Two athletes of the same gender following identical programs will not develop strength at the same rate, in the same manner, or to the same degree, because of varying inherent characteristics.

Types of Muscle Fibers

There are three basic types of muscle fibers:
Slow-twitch oxidative (SO)
Fast-twitch oxidative-glycolytic (FOG)
Fast-twitch glycolytic (FG)

Current opinion favors classifying muscle fibers into three basic types: the slow-twitch oxidative (SO) fiber, fast-twitch oxidative-glycolytic (FOG) fiber, and fast-twitch glycolytic (FG) fiber. Fast-twitch fibers are basically anaerobic; they do not depend on oxygen for their energy supply. In contrast, slow-twitch fibers are aerobic; they require oxygen for continued contraction. The preponderance of one fiber over another is related to inherited genetic factors that determine sports performance potential.[28] Fast-twitch fibers are responsible for speed or speed-power activities such as sprinting and weight lifting. Slow-twitch muscle fibers come into play in endurance activities such as long-distance running or cross-country skiing. The FOG fiber lies somewhere in the middle, but closer to the FG than to the SO category.

The way in which an individual trains determines the type of fiber developed. Slow, low-intensity work primarily uses slow-twitch fibers. Fast-twitch fibers are suited for power and speed; slow-twitch fibers contract slowly and are fatigue resistant.[28] Athletes in ball sports exhibit a wide variety of muscle fiber types and tend to be somewhere in the middle of the range.[28]

All work of low intensity may develop the slow-twitch fibers and fail to adequately develop strength and recruit fast-twitch fibers. The principle of specificity, which is discussed later in this chapter, must be adhered to.

General consensus favors the current theory that hypertrophy, the increase in muscle cross section, is caused by a development of the existing constituent fibers when strength exercises are used and by an increase in the total number of capillaries called into play when exercises of endurance are used. In other words, a gain in strength is accompanied by a significant increase in both the size of fibers and the number of capillaries in the muscle and by a resultant gain not only in power but also in speed and endurance.

Muscle Contraction and Exercise

Exercise for the development of strength is related to the type of muscle contraction.

Isometrics   Performance of an **isometric exercise** generates heat and energy by forcefully contracting the muscle in a *static* position, i.e., with no change in the length of the muscle or in the angle of the joint at which the contraction takes place. Attempting to lift or push an object that cannot be moved places the muscles in a state of isometric, or static, contraction. Isometric exercise is most effective when a maximum contraction is held for 6 seconds and the contraction is repeated from five to 10 times daily. Strength gained through an isometric program is specific to the joint angle at which the contraction takes place, so it is advisable to exercise throughout the full range-of-joint motion during each workout.

Isotonics   Shortening or lengthening the muscle, causing a skeletal part to move through a full range of motion, involves an isotonic contraction and hold. **Isotonic exercise** involves the moving of a resistive force, either a part of the body or some extraneous object and is referred to also as a *dynamic* contraction. An isotonic exercise does not involve the same fibers throughout a particular movement because the load remains constant regardless of the angle of contraction or the degree of fatigue engendered; consequently, the greatest strength gain appears in those fibers used in the initial part of the movement to overcome inertia. The least gain is at the midpoint of the contraction.

The major value of performing isotonic contraction in exercise is the increase or maintenance of joint range of motion. In addition, isotonic movements tend to promote muscular circulation and endurance. In performing an isotonic movement against resistance, the muscle should be first placed in stretch to ensure maximum innervation of muscle fibers. After full stretch, the body part is *concentrically* moved as far as possible and then *eccentrically* moved to the beginning position. A general rule for the most effective muscle training is to move the resistance as smoothly and quickly as possible and return it at a much slower rate. Slow, eccentric muscle contraction against resistance is known as **negative resistance**, enervating more muscle fibers than positive, or concentric contraction.

Recovery from muscular fatigue is more rapid in isotonic exercises than in isometric ones. Isotonic exercises in which the muscle works throughout its full range against an increasingly greater resistance are known as progressive resistance exercises (PRE) and were introduced by De Lorme and Watkins.[12] This type of exercise and its many variations have been shown to be superior to the isometric form for the development of strength and endurance. The De Lorme method uses a series of three sets of exercises with 10 repetitions each. The first set is performed against a resistance half of one's maximum, the second at three-quarters maximum, and the final set against full maximum. When one is able to successfully complete the full series, a weight increment (usually 5 pounds) is progressively added to the maximum. Numerous variations are used today, but none has been significantly different in its effectiveness. A training program using three sets each workout produces greater strength improvement than a program using one or two sets. Workouts three to four times weekly, with four to eight repetitions, produces the greatest strength. Another PRE method that is increasingly used for strength conditioning and rehabilitation is daily adjustable progressive resistive exercise (DAPRE), developed by Knight (see Chapter 14, p. 390).[23]

isometric exercise
Contracts the muscle statically without changing its length.

isotonic exercise
Shortens and lengthens the muscle through a complete range of motion.

negative resistance
Slow eccentric muscle contraction against resistance.

Fundamental principles of isotonic weight training   The following are suggested procedures for performing an isotonic free weight program:

1. Precede all weight training with a general warm-up.
2. Begin all isotonic contractions from a position of "on stretch"; immediately move into the concentric contraction.
3. Perform isotonic movements slowly and deliberately at approximately one-fifth maximum speed.
4. Apply the overload principle in all isotonic contractions. When you are able to complete the second or third series with some degree of ease, add more resistance.
5. Maintain good muscular balance by exercising both the agonist and antagonist muscles.
6. Confine heavy work to the off-season and the preseason period. A light-to-medium program can be maintained during the regular practice days of the competitive season, provided that it is confined to use of the weight schedule after the regular practice.
7. Work with weights every other day or no more than 4 days a week. This schedule allows ample time for reduction of soreness and stiffness.
8. Initiate the training program first in terms of general body development; then progress to exercises tailored to the specific sport or event, using the SAID principle and gearing to the type of muscle fiber involved in the activity.
9. Observe proper breathing procedures during lifting to assist in fixing the stabilizing muscles of the trunk, thereby giving a firm base from which to work. Inhale deeply as the lift is being executed, and exhale forcefully and smoothly at the end of the lift.
10. Evaluate your progress at certain intervals by testing maximum lifts.
11. Develop a recording system using cards or a notebook. Common isotonic resistive exercises with free weights are illustrated on pp. 81-84; Isometric exercises are shown on p. 85.

isokinetic exercise
Accommodating resistance exercise (ARE).

Isokinetics   Isokinetic exercise occurs through an *accommodating resistance exercise (ARE)*. It offers all the advantages of both isometric and isotonic exercises without their inherent weaknesses.[21] This method more nearly uses total involvement of the muscle fibers, since the resistance varies according to the angle of pull and the degree of fatigue developed throughout the exercise. The inertia of the resistance, a definite factor in the isotonic exercise, is not a factor in isokinetics, since the resistance automatically adjusts to the degree of force exerted against it, thus maintaining a constant and consistent force. Exercises can be performed throughout the entire range of the performer's speed, since most isokinetic exercise equipment has variable speed adjustments. A decided advantage of this type of exercise is that muscle soreness does not result. It is postulated that the muscle has a brief period of relaxation between repetitions, thus allowing the blood to circulate freely throughout the fibers and cleanse away the accumulated lactic acid and metabolites from the muscle cells. Isotonic exercises do not permit such relaxation, hence there is a buildup of fatigue products. Neither isokinetic nor isotonic resistance is superior to one another. The goal of training must be satisfied according to the SAID principle. Over the last few years, isokinetic resistance exercising has found a valuable place in rehabilitation, whereas free weights using isotonic principles have become increasingly popular in sports conditioning. (See

Text continued on p. 86.

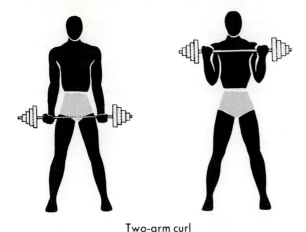

Two-arm curl

Half squat

Military press

Supine bench press

Two-arm curl Reverse or under grip and regular or upper grip. Starting position—feet in a side-stride stand, arms extended downward. Slowly flex elbows, bringing the barbell to a bent-arm position in front of chest. Return to starting position. **NOTE:** Keep elbows close to side of body. Alternate grasp on each series; three sets of 10 repetitions.

Half squat Heels are elevated approximately 1½ inches and a 20-inch bench is placed behind the buttocks to reduce the possibility of knee injury by serving as a "stop." Starting position—feet in a small side-stride stand, barbell resting on back of neck and shoulders. Slowly bend knees to half-squat position. Hold. Return to starting position; three sets of 10 repetitions.

Military press Starting position—feet in a side-stride stand, barbell raised to the bent-arm position in front of chest. Slowly extend arms overhead. Hold. Return to starting position; three sets of 10 repetitions.

Supine bench press Starting position—lying supine on a 20-inch bench, knees bent at right angles, feet flat on the floor, and barbell held at the chest. Slowly extend arms upward. Hold. Return to starting position; three sets of 10 repetitions.

Rowing exercise Starting position—feet in a small side-stride stand, arms extended downward with hands centered and in proximity of the bar, head resting on a folded towel placed on a table. Slowly pull the bar up to a position in front of the chest. Hold. Return to starting position; three sets of 10 repetitions. **NOTE:** This may also be done with the lifter assuming and maintaining an angle stand—that is, trunk flexed forward at the hips at approximately a right angle.

Side-arm raises Starting position—prone or supine position on a bench, arms downward, hands grasping 10-pound dumbbells. Slowly raise arms sideward to a horizontal position. Hold. Return to starting position. **CAUTION:** *Avoid locking the elbow joint in a complete extension, since this exerts severe strain on the joint.* Do three sets of 10 repetitions, alternating the prone and supine positions daily.

Leg curl Starting position—face-lying position with boot weight fixed to one foot. The leg is curled upward as far as possible and then slowly returned to its original position; three sets of 10 repetitions and then repeat with other leg.

Heel raise Starting position—feet in a small side-stride stand, balls of the feet on a 2-inch riser, barbell resting on the back of the neck and shoulders. Slowly rise on toes. Hold. Return to starting position. Variations may be performed by having the feet either toes out or toes in; three sets of 10 repetitions.

Rowing exercise

Side-arm raises

Leg curl

Heel raise

Press bar leg thrust

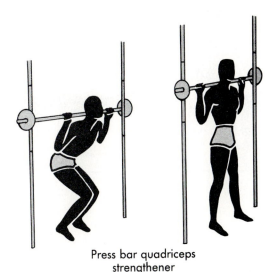

Press bar quadriceps
strengthener

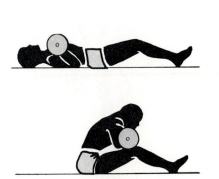

Abdominal curl

Press bar leg thrust Starting position—angle-lying position under the press bar, balls of the feet in contact with the bar or bar platform, legs in a half-flexed position. Slowly extend the knees, keeping the buttocks in contact with the floor. Hold. Return to starting position; three sets of 10 repetitions. **NOTE:** To provide for better contact, fasten to the bar an 8-inch by 12-inch board. This prevents the feet from slipping off the bar.

Press bar quadriceps strengthener Starting position—a half-crouched position under the bar. Shoulders and neck in contact with the bar. (A folded towel may be used as a pad.) Slowly extend knees to an erect position. Hold. Return to starting position; three sets of 10 repetitions. **CAUTION:** *Lift with the knee extensors, not the lower back muscles.*

Abdominal curl Starting position—hook-lying, feet anchored, and dumbbell weighing 15 to 25 pounds held on the upper chest. Curl the upper trunk upward and as far forward as possible. Return slowly to the starting position. Maintain a moderate tempo and steady rhythm and avoid bouncing up from the floor; three sets of 10 repetitions. Number can be increased as capacity for more work increases.

Supination-pronation Start with feet in small side-stride stand, elbow bent at a right angle to upper arm, and hand grasping a 20-pound dumbbell. Rotate the dumbbell alternately left and right, using the muscles of the forearm and wrist only; three sets of 10 repetitions.

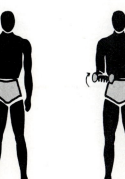

Supination-pronation

83

Wrist roll Begin with feet in a small side-stride stand. Slowly wind up a cord to which a 25-pound weight has been attached. Reverse the action, slowly unwinding the full length of the cord; three sets of five repetitions. **NOTE:** A wrist roller is easily constructed by securing one end of a 30-inch length of sash cord to the center of a 12-inch length of broomstick or dowel of a somewhat thicker diameter and the other end to a 25-pound weight.

Boot exercise Sit on plinth or table with lower legs hanging free over the edge and clear of the floor. A 20-pound boot is strapped to the foot. Do exercises involving knee flexion, extension, and inversion and eversion, flexion, and extension of the ankle. The weight should be increased in terms of ability to handle it. Each exercise should be done for three sets of 10 repetitions.

Crossed-arm swings Starting position—small side-stride stand, a 20-pound dumbbell in each hand, arms raised directly sideward to shoulder height. Slowly swing the arms forward in a horizontal plane, continuing until each arm has progressed across the other and is carried as far as possible. Arms are extended, but elbow joints should not be locked. Return slowly toward the starting position, carrying the arms horizontally as far backward as possible; three sets of 10 repetitions.

Wrist roll

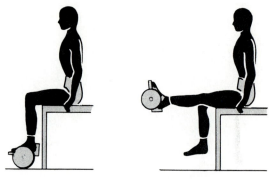

Boot exercise

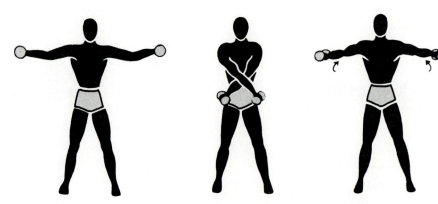

Crossed-arm swing

Stationary press
bar leg thrust

Stationary press
bar leg tensor

Wall press

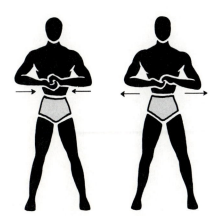

Shoulder-arm tensor

Stationary press bar leg thrust
Starting position—angle-lying position under the press bar, balls of the feet in contact with the bar or bar platform, legs in a half-flexed position. Press bar is locked into place. Exert maximum force against the immovable bar, sustaining full pressure for 6 to 10 seconds. Following a short period of relaxation (5 to 10 seconds) repeat the procedure two or three times. **NOTE:** Hips may be elevated by a 2-inch pad.

Stationary press bar leg tensor
Starting position—a half-crouched position under the bar, which is locked into place, shoulders and neck in contact with the bar. Exert maximum pressure against the bar by using the leg extensors and sustain full pressure for 6 to 10 seconds. Following a momentary relaxation, repeat the exercise two or three times.

Wall press   Starting position—stand in a small-side stride stand in either the corner of a room or a doorway, placing the hands against the walls or the sides of the opening at about shoulder height. The elbows should be bent to approximately the halfway point in the normal range. Exert maximum force against the opposing surface, holding the position for at least 6 to 10 seconds. Relax pressure momentarily. Repeat two or three times.

Shoulder-arm tensor   Starting position—feet in a small side-stride stand. Hook the fingers of the hands together, elbows bent so that hands are above waist height. Push the hands together forcefully, at the same time tensing the arm, shoulder, neck, and abdominal muscles. Hold for 6 to 10 seconds. Relax momentarily and then repeat the tensing action but reverse the hand action by pulling against the fingers with as much force as possible. Repeat two or three times.

TABLE 3-1 Comparison of Strength Exercises

	Isometric	Isotonic	Isokinetic	Variable Resistance (Nautilus)
Resistance	Accommodating at one angle	Constant	Accommodating through range of motion	Fixed ratio through range of motion
Velocity (speed)	Zero	Variable	Constant	Variable
Reciprocal contraction	None	None	Yes	None
Eccentric contraction	None	Yes	None	Yes
Safeness	Excellent	Poor	Excellent	Poor
Specificity to sport	Low	Medium	Very high	Medium
Motivation to exercise	Low	High	Medium	High

plyometric exercise
This type of exercise maximizes the myotatic or stretch reflex.

Chapter 14 for further discussion.) Also see Table 3-1 for a comparison of isometric, isotonic, and isokinetic exercise.

Plyometrics Plyometric exercise maximizes the myotatic or stretch reflex. By means of an eccentric (lengthening) contraction, the muscle is fully stretched ("on stretch") immediately preceding the concentric (shortening) contraction. The greater the stretch put on the muscle from its resting length immediately before the concentric contraction, the greater the load the muscle can lift or overcome. The rate of stretch is more critical than the magnitude of the stretch.

Plyometric training is sport specific—it uses hops, bounds, and depth jumps.[29] It should be noted that plyometrics can cause overuse tendon injuries in some athletes.

Means to Achieve Strength

Individuals can gain strength in numerous ways. This discussion briefly describes the more prevalent ways strength is developed; they are the nonequipment, equipment, and combined nonequipment and equipment approaches.

Nonequipment approaches Three nonequipment approaches are presently used in sports conditioning: calisthenics, or free exercise; partner or reciprocal, resistance; and self-resistance.

Calisthenics, or *free exercise,* is one of the more easily available means of developing strength. Isotonic movement exercises can be graded according to intensity by using gravity as an aid, ruling gravity out, moving against gravity, or using the body or body part as a resistance against gravity. Most calisthenics require the athlete to support the body or move the total body against the force of gravity. Push-ups are a good example of a vigorous antigravity free exercise. To be considered maximally effective, the isotonic calisthenic exercise, as in all types of exercise, must be performed in an exacting manner and in full range of motion. In most cases, 10 or more repetitions are performed for each exercise and are repeated in sets of two or three.

Some free exercises have a holding phase instead of using a full range of motion. Examples of them are back extensions and sit-ups. When the exercise produces maximum muscle tension, it is held between 6 and 10 seconds and then repeated one to three times.

Partner, or *reciprocal, resistance* exercise is an excellent approach to gaining strength and flexibility. It requires no equipment other than a partner who is approximately equal in size and strength. It is often highly motivating for both participants, and all types of exercise can be engaged using this method. When performing isokinetic resistance, the body part involved is taken into a stretched position by the partner. Resistance is accommodated through a complete range of motion. Three bouts of resistance usually are given for each exercise.

Equipment approaches   Numerous devices are designed to overload the musculature and develop strength. They range from individual pieces to entire conditioning systems and are generally categorized as isotonic/isometric and isokinetic.

Types of *isotonic/isometric equipment* are almost too numerous to mention. Some of the more standard stationary apparatus, chinning bars, parallel bars, and stall bars, have numerous possibilities for increasing strength. Another standard piece of equipment is the wall pulley weight, which progressively exercises the major joints and muscles.

Free weights are very popular and are used for developing strength through both isotonic and isometric contraction. Sports programs commonly have a variety of free weights, including dumbbells (Figure 3-4) and barbells (Figure 3-5). Dumbbells range from 2 to 2½ pounds to 50 to 75 pounds or more, and barbells range from 25 or 30 pounds to well over 200 pounds. Some people argue that free weights do not provide consistent muscle development through a full range of motion; however, they do help in the development of balance and coordination and exercise stabilizing and accessory muscles, which machine systems often do not adequately provide.

Figure 3-4

Dumbbells provide an excellent means for isotonic strength development.

Figure 3-5

Barbell free weights assist the athlete in developing isotonic strength, balance, and muscle coordination.

Figure 3-6

Many machine exercise systems provide a variety of exercise possibilities for the athlete.

Machine exercise systems, such as the *Universal Gym*, allow a variety of exercise possibilities such as sit-ups, parallel bar dips, bench presses, pull-downs, rowing exercises, knee extensions, knee curls, and biceps curls, as well as arm pressing (Figure 3-6). The Universal Gym uses graduated weights that are lifted by heavy cables as the athlete applies force against a bar.

Isokinetic machines provide an accommodating muscle resistance through a full range of motion. A maximum load is produced as the athlete dynamically performs work. The amount of resistance depends on the extent of force applied by the athlete. Machines designed for isokinetic resistance develop flexibility and coordination, as well as strength (Figure 3-7).

The *Nautilus machine* is one of the newest and most popular exercise systems. Nautilus training machines provide full range of movement and direct resistance to specific muscles or muscle groups. Both concentric and eccentric muscle contraction are maximally provided by special cams and counterweights. In this system, negative, or eccentric, work is accentuated. Although Nautilus is not an isokinetic system, it does provide some variable resistance through a full range of motion. Each machine provides body stabilization to afford isolation of a specific muscle or muscle group (Figure 3-8). This musculature isolation emphasizes negative, or eccentric, contraction. Because the amount of resistance varies during a full range of motion, resistance is indicated by the number of plates lifted, rather than the number of pounds.

Other examples of exercise systems, such as the *Mini-Gym,* provide opportunities for specific strength development related to sports activities. Using variable resistance devices, the athlete can concentrate on specific sports requirements (Figure 3-9).

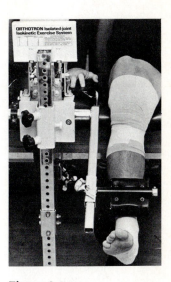

Figure 3-7

During isokinetic exercising the amount of resistance depends on the extent of force applied by the athlete.

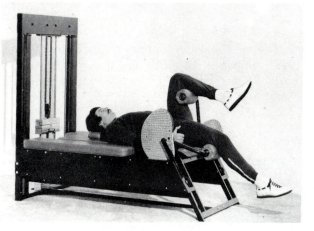

Figure 3-8

Nautilus training provides body stabilization and muscle group isolation.

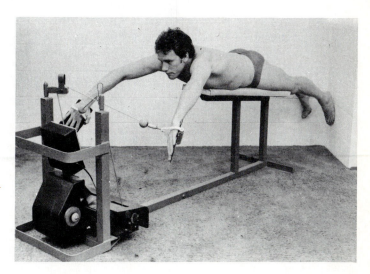

Figure 3-9

Exercise systems such as that provided by the Mini-Gym offer the athlete opportunities to concentrate on specific sports requirements.

Endurance and Stamina

The degree of ability to withstand fatigue is inherited, and the basis of the fatigue pattern is in each individuals's constitution.[8] Two factors modify an individual's capacity for improving endurance: (1) the ability to endure the pain and the discomforts of fatigue while endeavoring to improve the level of work tolerance; and (2) the body's ability to effect the necessary adjustments, which can enable an athlete to increase energy production to as much as 20 times the resting level when such a demand is made.

endurance

The ability of the body to undergo prolonged activity.

Endurance is the ability of the body to undergo prolonged activity. Endurance involves a number of elements, each of which is partially responsible for success or failure in sustaining physical performance (Figure 3-10). Endurance primarily depends on the various aspects of cardiac efficiency, which in turn influences the performance of the other portions of the human organism.

Training or conditioning builds a given economy, an efficiency in body adaptability, which is important as the body adjusts to the continued and prolonged stresses put on it while performing an activity that requires all-out or near-maximum performance over a considerable period of time.

Exercises for endurance improve muscle tonus. Endurance work improves circulation by calling into play more capillaries, thus providing the working muscles with more oxygen and fuel and facilitating removal of the metabolic by-products of the exercise.

Figure 3-10

Endurance is the ability of the body to perform prolonged activity.

As a muscle tires, it loses some of its ability to relax and thus increases the possibility of tearing. The character of a muscle is indicated not only by its ability to produce power over a period of time but also by its capacity to concurrently maintain its elasticity. As the muscle works, it restores its own oxygen and fuel supplies and disposes of metabolic products. As long as these two processes continue to operate at basically the same rate, the muscle can continue to work with efficiency. In fatigue the reaction time slows and is accompanied by stiffening or inability of the muscle to reach a condition of relaxation, which is a contributing factor to sports injuries.[22]

Training increases vital capacity (the maximum volume of air the lungs exchange in one respiratory cycle) and aids materially in establishing economy in the oxygen requirement. The conditioned athlete operates primarily on a "pay-as-you-go" basis as a result of his or her increased stroke volume and reduced heartbeat. An increase in the contractile power of the respiratory muscles, particularly the diaphragm, results in deeper respiration per breath. This enables the athlete to use a greater lung capacity and, consequently, to effect increased economy in the use of oxygen. The untrained individual attempts to compensate by increasing the rate of respiration and soon reaches a state of considerable respiratory indebtedness, which severely encumbers or even halts performance.

Endurance training not only significantly improves maximum oxygen consumption but also is a key factor in injury prevention. The fatigued athlete not only has a dminished reaction capacity, but because of muscular fatigue, is also less able to withstand extraneous forces, which means that such an athlete is more likely to sustain an injury under circumstances in which a better conditioned performer will not. Aerobic endurance training uses slow interval training.

Neuromuscular Coordination

Neuromuscular coordination is a complex interaction between muscles and nerves to perform a purposeful action. Major aspects of the coordination are the proprioceptors that are located in muscles, tendons, joints, and the labyrinth of the inner ear. Proprioceptors give the athlete knowledge of where the body is in space.

Athletes need to be able to recruit the appropriate muscles on demand. When recruitment of specific muscles is inappropriate, abnormal physical stresses can occur, leading to an acute or chronic injury.

Over-Exertional Muscle Problems

One ever-present problem in physical conditioning and training is that which stems from over exertion. Even though the gradual pattern of overloading the body is the best way for ultimate success, many athletes and even coaches believe that if there is no pain, there is no gain.

Exercise "overdosage" is reflected in muscle soreness, decreased joint flexibility, and general fatigue 24 hours after activity. Any one of the above, or even all, can be present. Four specific indicators of possible overexertion are acute muscle soreness, muscle stiffness, delayed muscle soreness, and muscle cramping.

Muscle soreness has long been a problem for the person engaging in physical conditioning. Two major types of muscle soreness are associated with severe exercise. The first, occurring immediately after exercise, is acute soreness, which is resolved when exercise has ceased. The second and more serious problem is de-

As a muscle tires, it loses some of its ability to relax.

stroke volume
The capacity of the heart to pump blood.

The two major types of muscle soreness associated with severe exercise are acute and delayed.

layed soreness, which is related mainly to early-season or unaccustomed work. Severe muscular discomfort occurs 24 to 48 hours after exercise.[16]

Acute-Onset Muscle Soreness

Acute-onset muscle soreness is related to an impedence of circulation, causing muscular ischemia. Lactic acid and potassium collect in the muscle and stimulate pain receptors.

Delayed-Onset Muscle Soreness

Compared to acute-onset soreness, delayed-onset muscle soreness (DOMS) increases in intensity for 2 to 3 days until it has completely disappeared within 7 days.[16]

The cause of DOMS apparently is sublethal and lethal damage to a small group of recruited muscle fibers.[6] The perception of soreness is caused by the activation of free nerve endings around selected muscle fibers.[6] The type of activity that causes the most soreness is eccentric exercise. Muscle fibers may take as long as 12 weeks to repair; therefore athletes need abundant recovery time.[15]

There are many ways to reduce the possibility of delayed muscle soreness. One is a gradual and complete warm-up before engaging in vigorous activity, followed by a careful cooling down. In the early part of training, careful attention should be paid to static stretching before and after activity. If there is extreme soreness, the application of ice packs or ice massage to the point of numbness (approximately 5 to 8 minutes) followed by a static stretch will often provide relief.

Muscle Stiffness

Muscle stiffness is contrasted to muscle soreness because it does not produce pain. It occurs when a group of muscles have been worked hard for a long period of time. The fluids that collect in the muscles during and after exercise are absorbed into the bloodstream at a very slow rate. As a result the muscle becomes swollen, shorter, and thicker and therefore resists stretching. Light exercise, massage, and passive mobilization assist in reducing stiffness.

Muscle Cramps

tonic
Muscle contraction marked by constant contraction that lasts for a period of time.

clonic
Involuntary muscle contraction marked by alternate contraction and relaxation in rapid succession.

Like muscle soreness and stiffness, muscle cramps can be a problem related to hard conditioning. The most common cramp is **tonic,** in which there is continuous muscle contraction. It is caused by the body's depletion of essential electrolytes or an interruption of synergism between opposing muscles. **Clonic,** or intermittent, contraction stemming from nerve irritation may rarely occur.

Gender Comparisons in Conditioning and Training

With proper conditioning and training, women and men can successfully compete in strenuous athletic activities at the highest levels of physical performance without physiological harm (Figure 3-11). As puberty, or the ability to reproduce, occurs (in girls from ages 9 to 16, and in boys from 13 to 15), anatomical and physiological differences arise. These differences can be an advantage or a disadvantage to the performances of the athletes.

Skeletal Differences

Comparatively, women have smaller bones and less articular surface area than men. Generally, women have shorter legs than men, giving them a lower center

Figure 3-11

As these two women soccer players indicate, with proper conditioning and athletic training both women and men can successfully compete in strenuous sports activities.

of gravity and more stability in balance activities. Men have longer bones that produce more force in striking, hitting, and kicking. Women have narrower shoulders, wider pelvises, and often, a greater varus angulation of the hip and valgus of the knees. This greater varus hip angulation and valgus of the knee have been blamed by many for the female susceptibility to overuse syndome in the hip and knee, especially in the unconditioned athlete.[18] Because of the anatomical gender differences, there are male and female variations in the basic skills of running, jumping, throwing, and arm-support activities.

Running

Because the female pelvis is frequently broader and shallower, causing the femur to articulate at a more acute angle than does that of the male, the obliquity of the femur tends to induce a lateral sway of the body in running. Frequently failure to lift the knees sufficiently and compensation by casting the lower leg and foot out to the side in the forward-carry phase causes the femur to be rotated inwardly. The casting accentuates the trunk sway, which becomes quite pronounced. During conditioning and coaching, good knee elevation, directly forward, coupled with straightforward foot placement, should be stressed.

Some women, as they run, tend to hug the upper arms and elbows tight against the body and swing the forearms out to the sides, meanwhile vigorously rotating the upper trunk and the shoulders in an attempt to offset the inward thigh rotation. In addition to the exaggerated trunk rotation, some girls and women keep the clenched fists tight against the chest, meanwhile alternately thrusting the elbows forward in a vigorous manner.

Jumping

In jumping sports events such as high jump and long jump, the female may, to some extent, have the same mechanical disadvantages as in running.

Women, with a lower center of gravity than men, are generally more stable and, as a result, are at a disadvantage in jumping activities. Disregarding any skeletal differences, the performance variation in jumping between male and female athletes may primarily be a result of the difference in strength.

Throwing and Support Activities

The shoulder width of the female is narrower than that of the male, and the breadth of the pelvis, augmented by the adipose pads over the hips, usually causes the arm to incline inward. Most women have a pronounced hyperextension of the elbow joint, often coupled with a decided outward angling of the forearm. These skeletal differences create difficulties in throwing, circling, or rotatory movements of the arm as a whole. This is true also in activities involving the support of the body by the arms, as encountered in gymnastics. In the latter the differences provide a distinct handicap, since both elbow and shoulder joints must function at somewhat unfavorable angles for weight bearing.

Body support activities can be difficult for women due to elbow hyperextension and forearm indication.

Muscular Strength

In proportion to weight and size, women's muscles are weaker than men's, possessing at maturity approximately half the strength of their male counterparts. Muscular strength is related to the size and anatomy of the body and is indicated in terms of its proportionate mass. Among males this mass constitutes approximately 43% and among women about 36% of the total. Differences in relative amounts of muscle tissue during puberty are the result of endocrine function, which causes the fundamental sex differences in terms of weight and development. Testosterone produces a marked increase in the weight of muscle tissue and an enlargement of the muscle fibers. Female hormones have a growth-inhibiting effect, but as with men, women's muscles develop in relation to the fundamental laws of exercise.

Chemical analysis of muscle fiber in athletes and nonathletes demonstrates that the differences between gender muscle fibers are in their size, not in the composition of the enzyme activity.[13] In endurance athletes, slow-twitch fiber is high for both women and men, constituting 63% and 60% respectively.[13] In sprint events, athletes in whom there is a predominance of fast-twitch fibers, the percentage is 76% for men and 73% for women.

Strength training   As is true for men, proper strength training is essential for women in preventing many injuries associated with sports participation.[18] As discussed earlier, muscle mass is hormonally regulated. "Within the male and female, the secretions of testosterone, androgen, and estrogen . . . vary considerably, which accounts for the marked differences in muscularity and general morphology among men and women."[18] A woman can increase muscle strength by as much as 44% without a significant gain in muscle mass.

Flexibility

Flexibility routines appropriate for men are also applicable to women. Women are more flexible than men. This does not mean women should not stretch before activity. It does, however, mean that anyone, male or female, who is hyperflexible in a certain joint should avoid overstretching that area.

In general women are more flexible than men.

Body Composition

Women have approximately 10% more adipose tissue than do men, although women long-distance runners will exhibit values well below that figure. The fat is stored at various depots around the body, as well as in a rather thick subcutaneous layer that serves as protection and insulation. Because of the subcutaneous layer, women are better able to withstand heat and cold than are men. The greater amount of adipose tissue may have some effect on the lower metabolic rate. Since fat is inert, it limits athletic performance, representing dead weight that must be carried by the athlete.

Women tend to accumulate fat on the thighs and around the hips, abdomen, and breasts, which would account generally for their greater relative weight in relation to size. The average female has approximately 7 pounds more of subcutaneous fat than her male counterpart, having a ratio of 22% to 25% fat to body weight as opposed to 14% for the male. Women athletes exhibit far less adiposity than nonathletes, having a range of from 10% to 15%. Among women distance runners, Wilmore[41] has found values as low as 6%. The type of athletic activity in which the sportswoman participates seems to affect her adiposity. For example, women runners are much leaner than women who compete in the weight events. Female athletes can and do approach the relative fat values attained by male athletes.[13]

Circulation

Both structural and physiological differences emphasize the fact that women should not be compared with men in terms of performance. They should be judged in terms relative only to the performance standards of their own gender. Gender has a definite influence on training, principally because of physiological differences in the capacity to perform exercises. In general, when performing moderate exercise, there is little significant difference between young men and women in respect to standards of performance, but the difference increases as the strenuousness of the activity increases. Women are subject to the same physiological laws as are men. However, they have a smaller heart and a faster pulse rate. They indicate a greater and more rapid increase in pulse rate at the beginning of exercise and a much slower recovery after exercise. The pulse rates of trained women athletes are approximately 10 beats per minute slower than those of nonathletes. Since the male possesses a larger heart, probably because of the fact that he has more muscle tissue, he has a larger circulation. Since heart rate is proportional to body size, a larger individual will have a slower heart rate; hence the male rate is some five to eight beats slower than that of the female, resulting in a greater cardiac output at a lower cardiac cost.

At rest the average number of red blood cells in the female is 4,500,000/mm as compared to 5,000,000/mm in the male. Postexercise values reflect an increase of approximately 1,000,000 for the male and a comparable rise for the female relative to the lower resting value. This rise is indicative of the compensatory adjustment to meet the demand for an increased oxygen supply. The female also has approximately 8% less hemoglobin.

At a given level of oxygen consumption women have a higher heart rate than do men. On the other hand, at a given heart rate men can transport more oxygen during submaximum and maximum work. In both sexes the maximum heart rate bears a linear relationship with an increased work load. Exhaustion, however, is reached at a lower rate of performance in women.

Blood pressure values, both diastolic and systolic, are from 5 to 10 mm Hg lower in the female. Pubertal systolic values, although reflecting some rise, are less pronounced than those of the male and will often indicate a slight decrease, which is maintained until age 18 or 19. After age 19 there is a slow but steady increase in both the male and female as age advances. After menopause most women show a systolic increase slightly higher than the comparable male.

Respiratory Function

Because of the smaller thoracic cavity, women respire more rapidly. They require less oxygen because of a lower metabolic rate and smaller body size. Trained athletes of both genders apparently use thier anaerobic processes to approximately the same level. Women breathe more shallowly, that is, with the upper part of the chest, whereas men tend to breathe more deeply and hence more diaphragmatically.

Vital capacity is the volume of air moved through the lungs from a maximum inspiration to a maximum expiration. It varies between the genders, since it bears a direct relationship to body size, area, and height. Although vital capacity does not predict performance by itself, it can be enhanced through training, and it determines performance capabilities. The vital capacity of the female is approximately 10% less than that of a male of the same size and age. The tendency to breathe with the upper part of the chest rather than from the diaphragm further limits the respiratory volume of the female. However, through training, diaphragmatic breathing can be developed.

The *oxygen pulse,* a measure used to determine how effectively the heart functions as a respiratory organ, is a relative measure involving blood volume, hemoglobin content, and body weight through which oxygen consumption is calculated in milliliters per heartbeat. There is a close relationship between the oxygen pulse rate of young women and young men who have similar heart rates while they are engaged in exercise of approximately 3600 ft-lb of work per minute. Both sexes reflect the same oxygen pulse rates at ages 12 to 15 years, but from 15 years up to ages 31 to 35 the male shows a rapid increase in values, as much as three times that of the female rate, which remains unchanged.

The *maximum aerobic power* of the female, the ability to use oxygen effectively, is also from 25% to 30% less than that of the male after age 12. Before that time both values are approximately the same. Both men and women peak out at age 18 years, after which there is a gradual decline. A comparison of the oxygen uptake values indicates similar levels per kilogram of body weight and it would seem that women, having a smaller body size, should have a higher value. It may well be that the smaller hemoglobin concentration restricts the full use of cardiac output for oxygen transport. Maximal oxygen uptake values (oxygen accepted by the tissues) are much higher for physically active females than for the more sedentary.

Metabolism

The metabolic rate of the female at all ages is from 6% to 10% lower than that of the male of comparable size when related to body surface area. When the basal metabolic rate is related to muscle mass, however, the gender difference disappears. This would indicate a significance to the resting heat disposition but not to muscular efficiency.

The calcium metabolic rate of the female is higher than that of the male, since ossification of her bones occurs at an earlier age. Thus the bones of the male are denser and more rugged because of the slower rate of ossification and the subsequent calcium retention.

Prepubertal and Pubertal Factors

During the prepubertal period, girls are the equal of, and often superior to, boys of the same age in activities requiring speed, strength, and endurance. The difference between men and women is not too apparent until after puberty. With the advent of puberty the gulf begins to widen, with the males continuing in a slower, gradual increase in strength, speed, and endurance.

Menarche   Menarche, the onset of the menses, normally occurs between the tenth and the seventeenth year, with the majority of girls usually entering it between 13 and 15 years.

There is some indication that strenuous training and competition may delay the onset of menarche. The greatest delay is related to the higher caliber competition. In itself, a delay in the first menses does not appear to pose any significant danger to the young female athlete. The late-maturing girl commonly has longer legs, narrower hips, and less adiposity and body weight for her height, all of which are more conducive to sports.

Menstruation   As interest and participation in girls' and women's sports grow, the various myths that have surrounded female participation and the effects of participation on menarche, menstruation, and childbirth are gradually being dispelled. Although the effects of sustained and strenuous training and competition on the menstrual cycle and the effects of menstruation on performance still cannot be fully explained with any degree of certainty, continued and increasing research is slowly clearing away the many unknowns of the past. Some of the research in the past has been contradictory and, on occasion, open to question. Current research appears to be answering some of the questions, although much needs still to be done.

The classic 28-day cycle consists of the follicular and luteal phases, each of which is approximately 14 days long. The menses vary from 3 to 7 days, with an average of 4 to 7 days (Figure 3-12).

The majority of women tend to show some variation in the length of their cycles, with these differences occurring principally because of differences in duration of the preovulatory phase rather than the premenstrual phase.

With the onset of menarche a cyclic hormone pattern commences, which establishes the menstrual cycle. These hormonal changes result from complex feedback mechanisms and specifically controlled interactions that occur between the hypothalamus, ovaries, and pituitary gland. Two gonadotropins induce the release of the egg from the mature follicle at midcycle (ovulation). They are FSH (follicle-stimulating hormone), which stimulates the maturation of an ovarian follicle, and LH (luteinizing hormone), which stimulates the development of the

During the prepubertal period, girls are the equal of, and often superior to, boys of the same age in activities requiring speed, strength, and endurance.

The onset of menarche may be delayed by strenuous training and competition.

Figure 3-12

Endocrine influences on the
menstrual cycle.

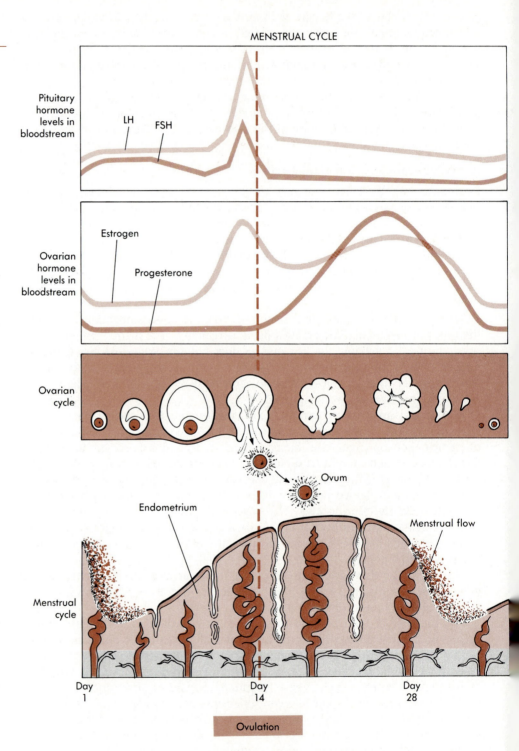

corpus luteum and the endocrine structure that secretes progesterone and estrogens. The control and eventual inhibition of the production of FSH when the follicle reaches maturity is brought about by the estrogenic steroids produced by the ovaries. Progesterone, a steroid hormone produced within the corpus luteum—a small body that develops within a ruptured ovarian follicle after ovulation—eventually inhibits production of LH. Estrogen is secreted principally by the luteal cells. Before onset of a new menstrual period, FSH levels are already rising, probably to initiate maturation of new follicles to reinstitute the next cycle.

For many years medical opinion held that little or no exercise should be taken during the menstrual period. Nevertheless, any athlete who is healthy gynecologically and whose menstrual cycles show no unusual or unfavorable changes either during or as the result of physical stress should be permitted to participate in sports activities at all times. Reproductive factors and menstrual irregularities are discussed in Chapter 25.

SPECIAL CONCERNS IN CONDITIONING AND TRAINING

Numerous areas of conditioning and training may present the athlete, athletic trainer, and coach with special concerns. Three of them are discussed briefly, including the child sports competitor, the older athlete, and the wheelchair athlete.

The Child Sports Competitor

Parents and professionals in the area of education, psychology, and medicine have long questioned whether vigorous physical training and competition are advisable for the immature child. Increasingly, children are engaging in intense programs of training that require many hours of daily commitment and may extend over many years. Swimmers may practice 2 hours, two times a day, covering 6000 to 10,000 meters each session in the water, and runners may cover as many as 70 miles each week.[43] Young gymnasts commonly practice as long as 6 hours a day, six times a week.[7]

The American Academy of Pediatrics has indicated that nearly universal participation of young children of both genders in competitive sports requires realistic guidelines. It is recognized that sports have an important effect on stamina and physiology and have lifelong values as recreational activities. The American Academy of Pediatrics also indicates that there is no physical reason to separate preadolescent girls and boys by gender in sports activities or recreational activities; however, separation of the genders should occur in collision-type sports when boys have acquired greater muscle mass in proportion to body weight, making participation with girls hazardous. All participants should be properly grouped by physical maturation, weight, size, and skill (Figure 3-13). Of major importance is for the child to always be given a proper physical examination before entering organized competitive sports. Also of importance is that coaches of children have some understanding of growth and development, injury causation, prevention of sports injuries, and the understanding and practice of correct coaching techniques. The American Academy of Pediatrics, however, does not consider the current preschool exercise movement beneficial to health of a child 3 years old or younger.[39,42]

Injury Epidemiology

There is a lack of in-depth accident statistics related to children and sports participation. Most of the current variance in data is based on personal medical opinion

Participation of young children of both genders in competitive sports requires realistic guidelines.

Figure 3-13

It is particularly important to match children in sports according to physical maturity, weight, size, and skill.

rather than on epidemiological study. From the information available, unsupervised play is far more dangerous than organized sports for the preadolescent participant (Figure 3-14).[27]

Physical Immaturity

Many professionals are concerned with the young athlete who has immature skeletal structures and engages in highly competitive sports. The degree of maturation is commonly measured by skeletal ossification. The skeleton does not completely mature until early adulthood. An example of this is the femur, which reaches full ossification at approximately 19 years of age. The main concern of opponents of vigorous competitive youth sports programs, especially the contact or collision variety, is injuries that could cause a premature cessation of growth in a particular bone. *Epiphyseal injuries* affecting growth plates, which are primarily cartilagenous in their immature state, can result from a number of activities. The following activities should be performed with great caution.[28]

Figure 3-14

Unsupervised play is generally more dangerous than organized sports activities.

- Falling, jumping, or landing with straight legs
- Excessive stress to the shoulder and elbow from repeated throwing motions
- Long-duration exercise involving weight bearing such as long-distance running
- Heavy weight lifting

Generally, according to the current data, youngsters adapt well to the same type of training routines used to train the mature athlete.[30,41]

Many physicians also are concerned with repeated microtraumas that occur to the young athlete over a period of time. Such small traumas can compound and produce chronic and, in some cases, degenerative conditions within the immature musculoskeletal system.

Extreme training intensity can increase a child's chance of sustaining an overuse injury.[7] Even though Wolff's law is at work when the growing child is experiencing intensive physical training, extreme care must be taken by coaches to avoid a considerable risk of injury.[7] "Proper supervision" are the key words in these circumstances.

The Child Athlete's Psyche

Another question that must be addressed is whether high-level sports competition is psychologically harmful to the emotionally immature. *Will a child who is placed under constant high-level competitive pressures, such as playing in all-star games, championships, or play-offs, develop emotional problems?* This is a difficult question. Some opinions indicate that no harm occurs, whereas others state undesirable behaviors may stem from this type of stress (Figure 3-15). Children have been known to display "burnout" from heavy training and high-pressure competition, which leads to a loss of interest in sports and exercise.

Many of the psychological problems associated with sports competition can be averted by educating parents and coaches that the joy of participation is the important thing, rather than winning at all cost. This is not to say that winning is not important, but it should be viewed as a reward for successful participation.

Another major factor is that children should not engage too early in specialization in any single physical activity that requires year-round conditioning. Normal physical and emotional growth and development are enhanced by a variety of activities. It is to be remembered: if it is not fun, it should not be done.

Figure 3-15

Constant high-level competitive psychological pressure can cause a child to become disinterested in sports and exercise.

Physical Training Intensity

How hard should children engage in physical training? Will such training adversely affect a child's heart, lungs, muscles, or bones? The answers to these questions can be either positive or negative, depending on many variables. Exercise is an essential element for normal growth and development. Children who are deprived of proper physical activity will fail to reach their growth potential. In fact, children who engage in physical training in preparation for sports competition will commonly have wider and stronger bones than less active children.[31]

Should a child between the ages of 9 and 12 years train with heavy resistance to increase strength? Heavy resistance, such as weight lifting, increases strength and the width and density of the skeletal structure. Although data are inconclusive, it is speculated that growing children should not engage in heavy resistance-type training programs. A safer approach is using a program of low weight and high repetition through a full range of motion or the use of isokinetic methods in which the resistance matches the force applied by the child. Of major importance is that children should avoid strength specialization. This avoidance is to prevent muscle and structural imbalances that may lead to eventual injury.

As with strength development, there is some contention as to the amount of stress that should be applied to a child's cardiovascular and respiratory system.

The human body at all ages, with an absence of pathological processes, has a great capacity to adapt to cardiorespiratory stress (Table 3-2). However, data are not available as to the effects of intense and long-term training on children. As with adults, children having low cardiorespiratory fitness respond most dramatically to such programs.

There must be a worldwide effort to control legally the participation of the young elite athlete. Above all, reasonable standards for training must be set, and dietary and hormonal manipulation must be condemned at every level of sports participation.

TABLE 3-2 Physiologic Characteristics of the Exercising Child, Which Have Relevance to Exercise Prescription[3]

Function	Compared with Adults	Implication for Exercise Prescription
Metabolic		
Maximal oxygen intake per kg body mass	Similar	Can perform endurance tasks reasonably well
Submaximal oxygen demand in running or walking	Higher	Greater fatigability in high-intensity tasks; greater heat production
Rate of anaerobic glycolysis	Lower	Lower capability in intense "anaerobic" tasks of 10 to 60 seconds' duration
On-transients of oxygen intake and postexertional recovery	Shorter	Well-suited to intermittent activities
Cardiovascular		
Cardiac output at given oxygen intake	Lower	Potential deficiency of peripheral blood supply during maximal exertion and in hot climates
Respiratory		
Submaximal ventilation, ventilatory equivalent, and respiratory frequency	Higher	Early fatigability in tasks that require large respiratory minute volume
Thermoregulatory		
Sweating rate	Lower	
Acclimatization to heat	Slower	Greater risk of heat-related illness on hot/humid days
Tolerance time in extreme heat	Shorter	
Body cooling in water	Faster	Potential hypothermia
Body core heating during dehydration	Greater	Fluid intake to be enforced repeatedly in prolonged activities
Perceptual		
Rating of perceived exertion	Lower	Child willing to continue exercise when physiologically strained

The Older Athlete

It is estimated that currently more than 22 million people in the U.S. population are over the age of 65 years, and by the year 1995, this figure will be over 50 million[36,44] There is some evidence, although still debated, that a lifelong habit of vigorous physical activity reduces the risk of cardiovascular disease. This, however, apparently does not hold true for the middle-aged person who begins exercising late in life.[20] Regular exercise has, in some cases, decreased the physiological decrement by as much as 50%.[36] The extremely fit person may have an increased level of high-density lipoprotein cholesterol (HDL-C) and decreased levels of low-density lipoprotein cholesterol (LDL-C), very low-density lipoprotein cholesterol (VLDL-C), total cholesterol, and triglycerides.[35] For the more sedentary person, aerobic endurance decreases in increments of approximately 5% per decade from age 25 to age 65, with some acceleration of that percentage thereafter.[35] Muscle strength generally remains at the young adult level until approximately 40 years of age and declines thereafter. By the time an individual reaches 65 years of age, 20% of his or her lean tissue has been lost. On the other hand, for persons who have engaged in a program of habitual physical activity throughout their lives, strength and endurance loss is minimum up to 65 years of age.[35]

Effects of Physical Activity on the Older Person

Elderly persons who engage in habitual physical activity will be able to have a longer period of independent living. During physical activity among the elderly, more opportunities for socialization and more positive mood states occur, and in some cases, many medical disorders associated with aging are lessened.[35] For example, problems such as obesity, hypertension, and bone demineralization (osteoporosis) can be delayed. However, once such an age-associated disorder is present, physical activity is not therapeutic to any extent.

The older person who engages in habitual physical activity will be able to enjoy a longer period of independent living.

Conditioning and Training Concerns

Increasingly, the athletic trainer and/or coach is becoming professionally involved with older persons who are concerned with optimizing their physical condition or with becoming involved in Master's Competition. At whatever level of activity, the participant must first have a complete physical examination, preferably including a cardiovascular stress test.[24]

History factors   Before monitoring the older athlete, the athletic trainer or coach must become familiar with his or her activity, as well as his or her medical history. A person who has had a life-long habit of exercising and/or sports participation should be much less at risk for sustaining medical trauma than one who has not been an athlete or physically active. Those people who sustain such risks have become sedentary over a long period of time or have never engaged in a pattern of habitual physical activity.

Of major concern are the prexisting health risks that the older person brings to physical conditioning and training. Some of them are as follows:

1. Obesity
2. Hypertension and other cardiovascular diseases (e.g., atherosclerosis)
3. Cardiorespiratory problems (e.g., asthma, chronic bronchitis, emphysema)
4. Chronic fatigue or depression
5. Arthritis or tendon degeneration
6. History of improperly rehabilitated musculoskeletal injuries
7. Diminished proprioception and balance when engaging in activity

---

GENERAL RULES FOR THE EXERCISING OLDER PERSON

1. Get a complete physical examination, including a cardiovascular stress test, before beginning exercise program.
2. When exercising
   a. Warm-up and cool down properly.
   b. Avoid extremes of hot and cold weather.
   c. Progress gradually, avoiding extreme fatigue.
   d. Stop activity if there is excessive breathlessness, chest pains, or abnormal heart response.
   e. Stop activity if there is an acute viral infection.
   f. Avoid sudden, unfamiliar movements such as rapid bending, twisting, and changes of direction.
   g. When possible, exercise with another person.
   h. Avoid severe isometric resistance actions.

Ideally a program of physical training for the older person should gradually progress to 30 minutes of activity, three to five times per week. The activity should cause a pleasant tiredness, but if full recovery in 24 hours does not occur, over exertion has occurred. The athletic trainer or coach *must* ensure that the participant performs the proper warm-up and cool down exercises and must eliminate training errors, as well as any poor techniques that may lead to eventual injury.

The Wheelchair Athlete

As sports for the disabled gain popularity, the involvement of the athletic trainer has also expanded. Through the efforts of organizations such as the National Wheelchair Athletic Association (NWAA), the National Wheelchair Basketball Association (NWBA), and the International Stoke Manderville Games Federation (ISMGF), wheelchair sports have made major strides in adaptive equipment, conditioning, and training (Figure 3-16).[14,40]

Based on regulations established by the NWAA, to be a wheelchair competitor, athletes must verify that they have a permanent neuromuscular-skeletal disability (e.g., a spinal cord disorder, poliomyelitis, or a below-limb amputation). All athletes must undergo special physical examinations to determine the following: (1) the level of the spinal lesion; (2) the muscle-group strengths in different areas of the body; (3) the muscle strength and control as it gives trunk balance; and (4) the level of amputation, if any.[2]

Functional Classification

In the last few years, there has been a lot of debate about what is the fairest wheelchair athlete classification system to use.[40] The most widely used system is the one developed by ISMGF,[34] which is as follows:

1a. Complete or incomplete quadriplegia, resulting from cervical lesions, involving both hands, with weakness of the triceps and with severe weak-

Figure 3-16

Adapted sports activities in track and field can accommodate persons with physical handicaps.

ness of the trunk and lower extremities, interfering with the sitting balance and the ability to walk.

1b. Complete or incomplete quadriplegia, resulting from cervical lesions involving both hands with normal or good triceps, with generalized weakness of trunk and lower extremities, interfering with the sitting balance and the ability to walk.

1c. Complete or incomplete quadriplegia, resulting from cervical lesions with normal or good triceps and normal or good finger flexors and extensors, with generalized weakness of trunk and lower extremities interfering with the sitting balance and the ability to walk.

2. Complete or incomplete paraplegia, T_1 to T_5 or comparable, with poor or nonexistent abdominal muscle strength and no useful sitting balance.

3. Complete or incomplete paraplegia T_5 to T_{10}, with upper-abdominal and spinal extensor muscle control, allowing poor sitting balance.

4. Complete or incomplete paraplegia, T_{10} or L_2 or comparable, with weak or nonexistent quadriceps strength and limited gluteal control.

5. Complete or incomplete paraplegia, lesion below I_2 or comparable, with good or fair quadriceps control.

Physiological Comparisons

The two factors that have influenced wheelchair sports in the last 10 years have been the development of lighter and more sport-specific wheelchairs and the improved fitness methods. The disabled athlete (e.g., the wheelchair racer) has a higher heart rate and higher blood pressure during activity when compared to the ablebodied runner.[14] This difference is caused by the contracting chest muscle that reduces the blood return from the lower extremities. In terms of wheelchair marathons, there is a significantly lower oxygen consumption (Vo_2) maximum value when compared to the ablebodied marathon runner.

TABLE 3-3 Wheelchair Sports Injuries and Their Prevention

Injury and Causes	Percent	Prevention Measures
Soft-tissue injuries, ligamentous injuries		
From falls, physical contact; overuse injuries to muscles and tendons; overexertion without proper warm-up	33	Perform routine stretching, warm-up and cool down; protect old injuries (splinting, taping); perform slow progression of conditioning exercises; rest and provide proper treatment of recurrent injuries
Blisters		
From friction (on hands from push rims and on back from wheelchair)	18	Allow skin to thicken; tape fingers, wear gloves, and pad seat post; wear a shirt
Abrasions/lacerations		
From finger contact with brake, armrest socket, or push rims; scraping inner arms on tires; trapping fingers between wheelchairs (basketball)	17	Remove all hazardous parts from wheelchair; wear arm guards on upper arms
Decubitus/pressure areas		
From friction and pressure on buttocks/sacrum from wheelchair design (knees elevated); sweat and moisture problems	7	Provide adequate cushioning under buttocks; perform routine skin checks and routine shifting of weight; provide proper nutrition, skin hygiene, absorbent clothing
Temperature regulation disorders		
From exposure to heat/cold; inadequate autonomic regulation; fluid loss/inadequate intake	3	Provide insulating clothing that assists heat convection; minimize exposure; replace fluids

Wheelchair Sports Injuries and Prevention

Over 5000 physically disabled individuals engage in organized athletic competition in the United States (Figure 3-17). The majority of their injuries during competition stem from track (28%), basketball (24%), and road racing (22%).[9] Table 3-3 lists the most common injuries, as well as possible ways to prevent them.

The athletic trainer working with an athlete with permanent spinal cord disability must fully understand the individual nature of the injury and its relationship to the sport. The athletic trainer must remember that spinal cord trauma causes varying sensory loss or sensation distortions below the level of injury. An incomplete lesion may cause a loss of vibratory sense and light or deep touch. There may be an inability to perspire in some areas of the body, thus creating some difficulty in cooling the body adequately during the summer heat. Problems of properly warming the body during the winter may also occur. Muscle spasticity contractures are an ever present problem. Because of a loss of sensation and circulation, pressure sores or decubitus ulcers are frequently encountered. They are deep ulcerations that form over bony protuberances (commonly the ischial tuberosities) from prolonged pressure such as can occur in a wheelchair. Routinely changing sitting positions in essential to these athletes.[2]

The spinal cord–disabled athlete may have varying sensory loss and sensation distortion below the level of the injury.

Figure 3-17

Tennis is a popular wheel chair activity.

SUMMARY

Proper physical conditioning for sports participation should prepare the athlete for a high-level performance, while helping to prevent injuries that are inherent to that sport. Through a gradual program of conditioning, both soft and bony tissue can become stronger through increased density.

Year-round conditioning is essential in most sports to assist in preventing injuries from a given sport. Postseason conditioning is concerned with injury rehabilitation, off-season conditioning with a degree of physical maintenance, and preseason with conditioning that meets the demands of a particular sport.

Physical conditioning must be concerned with the SAID principle—an acronym for *spe-cific adaptation to imposed demands*. It must work toward making the body as lean as possible commensurate with the athlete's sport.

A proper warm-up should precede conditioning, and a proper cool down should follow. It takes at least 15 to 30 minutes of gradual warm-up to bring the body to a state of readiness for vigorous sports training and participation. Warming up consists of general unrelated activity followed by a specific related activity.

Optimum flexibility is a necessary attribute for success in most sports. However, too much flexibility can allow joint trauma to occur, whereas too little flexibility can result in muscle tears or strains. Ballistic stretching exercises should be avoided. The safest means of increasing flexibility are static stretching and the PNF (proprioceptive neuromuscular facilitation) technique, consisting of slow-reversal–hold, contract-relax, and hold-relax methods.

Strength is that capacity to exert a force or the ability to perform work against a resistance. There are numerous means to achieving strength development, including isometric, isotonic, and isokinetic muscle contraction. Isometric exercise generates heat energy by forcefully contracting the muscle in a stable position that produces no change in the length of the muscle. Isotonic exercise involves shortening and lengthening a muscle through a complete range of motion. Isokinetic exercise involves shortening or lengthening the muscle, causing a skeletal part to be moved through an accommodating resistance exercise (ARE). Plyometric exercise maximizes the stretch reflex by first lengthening a muscle and then immediately shortening the muscle against a resistance. To avoid athletic injury, the athlete must have a high level of neuromuscular coordination, which involves a complex interaction between muscles and nerves to perform a purposeful and safe action.

Too much exercising can lead to the problems of over-exertional muscle soreness or injury. They include acute and chronic muscle soreness, muscle stiffness, and muscle cramps. Muscles that show signs of over exertion fail to function properly and are candidates for injury.

Women and men differ in their anatomical and physiological response to exercise. These differences may be of no consequence or may be an advantage or a disadvantage in terms of performance and/or injuries.

The child athlete/competitor who engages in intense physical activities is becoming more and more common. His or her physical immaturity must be taken into consideration when he or she undergoes conditioning and participates in a sport. Injuries to growth areas must be avoided.

Older athletes present unique problems when engaging in sports. There is general acceptance that habitual exercise can assist the older person to live longer. Care must be taken in determining the intensity and types of exercise in which they participate.

The number of disabled athletes who engage in wheelchair sports is also on the increase. The fairest classification system for competition may still have to be divised. Major injuries occur to the athletes' soft tissue as a result of falls, physical contact, and over exertion.

REVIEW QUESTIONS AND CLASS ACTIVITIES

1. Why is year-round conditioning so important for injury prevention?
2. In terms of injury prevention, list as many advantages as you can for conditioning.
3. How does the SAID principle relate to sports conditioning and injury prevention?
4. Relate lean body mass and body fat to the potential for sports injuries.
5. What is the value of proper warm-up and cool down to sports injury prevention?
6. Critically observe how a variety of sports use warm-up and cool down procedures.
7. Compare ways to increase flexibility and how they may decrease or increase the athlete's susceptibility to injury.
8. How may increasing strength decrease susceptibility to injury?
9. Compare different ways of increasing strength. How may each way be an advantage or a disadvantage to the athlete in terms of injury prevention?
10. Under what circumstances does over exertion occur? How can it be avoided?
11. Compare the genders' differences in sports performance and susceptibility to injuries.
12. Describe injury suseptibility caused by conditioning, training, and performance in the child, older athlete, and disabled athlete. How can these injuries be avoided?

REFERENCES

1. Anderson, B: Stretching, Fullerton, Cal, 1975, Anderson, Co.
2. Arnheim, DD, and Sinclair, WA: Physical education for special populations, Englewood Cliffs, N.J., 1985, Prentice-Hall, Inc.
3. Bar-or, O: Exercise in childhood. In Welsh, RP, and Shephard, RJ, editors: Current therapy in sports medicine, 1985-1986, Philadelphia, 1985, Brian C Decker, Publisher.
4. Bilik, SE: The trainer's bible, ed 9, New York, 1956, TJ Reed & Co, Publishers.
5. Body composition: a round table, Phys Sports 14(3):144, 1986.
6. Byrnes, WB, and Clarkson, PM: Delayed onset muscle soreness and training. In Katch, FI, and Freedson, PS: Clinics in sports medicine, vol 5, Philadelphia, 1986, WB Saunders Co.
7. Caine, DJ, and Lindner, KJ: Overuse injuries of growing bones: the young female gymnast at risk? Phys Sportsmed 12(12):51, 1985.
8. Costill, DJ: Recovery from training fatigue, Sports Med Dig, 8(8):6, 1986.
9. Curtis, JA, and Dillon, DA: Survey of wheelchair athletic injuries—common patterns and prevention. In Sherill, C, editor: Sports and disabled athletes. The 1984 Olympic scientific congress proceedings, vol 9, Champaign, Ill., 1986, Human Kinetics, Publisher.
10. Cutting, VJ: A student handbook for prevention of athletic injuries, master's thesis, San Diego, 1985, San Diego State University.
11. DeBruyn/Provost, P: The effects of various warming intensities and duration upon some physiological variables, Eur J Applied Physiol 43:93, 1980.
12. De Lorme, TL, and Watkins, AL: Progressive resistance exercise, New York, 1951, Appleton-Century-Crofts.
13. Drinkwater, BL: Physiological characteristics of female athletes. In Welsh, RP, and Shephard RP, editors: Current therapy in sports medicine, 1985-1986, Philadelphia, 1985, Brian C. Decker, Publisher.
14. Duda, H: Wheelers make strides, all disabled people win, Phys Sportsmed 13(10):156, 1985.
15. Evans, WJ: Exercise-induced skeletal muscle damage, Phys Sportsmed 15(1):89, 1987.
16. Francis, KT: Delayed muscle soreness: a review, J Orthop Sports Phys Ther 15:10, July/August 1983.
17. Gaunya, ST: The role of the trainer. In Vinger, PF, and Hoerner, EF, editors: Sports injuries, the unthwarted epidemic, Boston, 1981, John Wright, PSG Publishing Co, Inc.
18. Hunter, JY: Aspects of injuries to the lower extremity unique to the female athlete. In Nicholas, JA, and Hersh-

man, EP, editors: The lower extremity and spine in sports medicine, vol 1, St. Louis, 1986, The CV Mosby Co.

19. Hunter ST, et al.: Standards and norms of fitness and flexibility in high school athletes, Ath Train 20(3):210, 1985.

20. Jogging in middle age? Sports Med Dig 8(4):3, 1986.

21. Johnson, JH: A comparison of isokinetic and isotonic training for college women, Am Correct Ther J 34:176, Nov/Dec 1980.

22. Kirkendall, DT: Mobility: conditioning programs. In Gould, JA, and Davies, GJ, editors: Orthopaedic and sports physical therapy, vol 2, St. Louis, 1984, The CV Mosby Co.

23. Knight, KL: Guidelines for rehabilitation of sports injuries. In Harvey, JS, editor: Clinics in sports medicine, vol 4, no 3, Philadelphia, 1985, WB Saunders Co.

24. Kulund, DN: The injured athlete, Philadelphia, 1982, JB Lippincott Co.

25. Logan, GA, and Wallis, EL: Recent findings in learning and performance. Paper presented at the Southern Section Meeting, California Association for Health, Physical Education and Recreation, Pasadena, Cal, 1960.

26. Murphy, P: Warming up before stretching advised, Phys Sportsmed 14(3):45, 1986.

27. National Safety Council: Accident facts, Chicago, 1982.

28. Pate, RR: The principles of training. In Kulund, DN, editor: The injured athlete, Philadelphia, 1982, JB Lippincott Co.

29. Peterson, L, and Renström, P: Sports injuries, Chicago, 1986, Year Book Medical Publishers, Inc.

30. Pfeiffer, RD, and Francis RS: Effects of strength training on muscle development in prepubescent, pubescent, and postpubescent males, Phys Sportsmed 14(9):134, 1986.

31. Rutenfranz, J: Participation of children in elite sports, Pediatrician 13:7, 1986.

32. Semenick, D: Warmup and flexibility, Sports Med Guide 5(1):4, 1986.

33. Shellock, FG, and Prentice, WE: Warming-up and stretching for improved physical performance and prevention of sports-related injuries, Sports Med 2:267, 1985.

34. Shephard, RJ: Exercise for the disabled: the paraplegic. In Welsh, RP, and Shephard, RJ, editors: Current therapy in sports medicine 1985-1986, Philadelphia, 1985, Brian C Decker, Publisher.

35. Shephard, RJ: Physical training for the elderly. In Katch, FK, and Freedson PS, editors: Clinics in sports medicine, vol 5, Philadelphia, July 1986, WB Saunders Co.

36. Siegel, AJ: Exercise and aging. In Strauss, RH: Sports medicine, Philadelphia, 1984, W.B. Saunders Co.

37. Surberg, PR: Flexibility exercise reexamined, Ath Train 18:37, Spring 1983.

38. Töttössy, M: Warming up. In Kulund, DN, editor: The injured athlete, Philadelphia, 1981, JB Lippincott Co.

39. Ward, A: Born to jog: exercise programs for preschoolers, Phys Sportsmed 14(12):163, 1986.

40. Weiss, M, and Curtis, KA: Controversies in medical classification of wheelchair athletes. In Sherril, C, editor: Sports and disabled athletes, The 1984 Olympic scientific congress proceedings, vol 9, Champaign, Ill, 1986, Human Kinetics Publishers, Inc.

41. Wilmore, JH, and Seay, MG: Strength training for the young athlete, Sports Med Dig 9(1):4, 1987.

42. Wood, DA: Aerobic dance for children: resources and recommendations, Phys Sportsmed 14(3):225, 1986.

43. Zauner, CW, and Benson, NY: Physiological alterations in young swimmers during 3 years of intensive training, J Sport Med 21:179, June 1981.

44. Zeigler, RG, and Michael, RH: The Maryland Senior Olympic Games: challenging older athletes, Phys Sportsmed 13(8):159, 1985.

45. Zezoney, F: Stretching and flexibility in athletics, Sports Med Guide 4(3):8, 1985.

ANNOTATED BIBLIOGRAPHY

Anderson, B: Stretching, P.O. Box 2734, Fullerton, Cal 92633, 1975, Anderson Co.
An excellent text on the major subject of stretching. It presents an in-depth step-by-step program for increasing joint flexibility.

Garhammer, J: Strength training, New York, 1986, Harper & Row.
Provides an excellent presentation on the basics of strength training and conditioning.

Katch, FI, and Freedson, PS, editors: Clinics in sports medicine, vol 5, Philadelphia, 1986, WB Saunders Co.
A monograph that covers numerous current topics in the area of physical training. It provides both breadth and depth of information.

Keaghtch, JR: Weight training, Springfield, Ill, 1983, Charles C Thomas, Publisher.
Provides basic and advanced exercise programs using free weights, plus off-season and preseason conditioning programs.

Sharkey, BJ: Physiology of fitness, Champaign, Ill, 1984, Human Kinetics Publishers.
Written as a "how and why" of physical conditioning.

Sutton, JR, and Brach, RM, editors: Sports medicine for the mature athlete, Indianapolis, Ind, 1986, Benchmark Press, Inc.
Provides a collection of papers presented at the International Master's Sports Medicine Symposium held at the Toronto, Canada, 1985 Inaugural World Master's Games. Offers an in-depth look at the physiological performance and injury characteristics of the older athlete.

Nutritional Considerations

When you finish this chapter, you should be able to

Explain the importance of good nutrition in enhancing performance and preventing injuries

Discuss the importance of eating the correct amounts of the foods from the four food groups

Identify inappropriate eating practices

Explain the necessity of water in the athlete's diet

Describe the advantages or disadvantages of supplementing nutrients in the athlete's diet

Explain the advantages and disadvantages of carbohydrate and fat loading

Explain the advantages and disadvantages of a pre-event meal

Describe the vegetarian diet and the athlete who follows it

List the signs of bulimia and anorexia nervosa

Figure 4-1

The nutritional demands of most athletes are major, requiring an increase in the daily number of calories.

There is probably no field of endeavor in which food fallacies and myths are more prevalent than in physical fitness and sports participation (Figure 4-1).

In terms of injury prevention, many dietary practices are potentially dangerous, causing the athlete to be inadequately nourished and unable to recover properly from fatigue following activity. The chronically fatigued individual may be "an injury waiting to happen." Exercise makes metabolic demands on the body. Although competitive activities make more demands on the body than are made under normal circumstances, athletes are no different from other individuals in their need of proper nutrition. The repair of damaged tissues, recuperation of fatigued muscles, and regeneration of energy necessitate a balanced and adequate diet.

The athletic trainer and the coach must be able to provide scientific counsel on all aspects of nutrition.[30,31] He or she must understand the nutritional demands of a given sport. The value of dietary supplements, nutritional readiness for competition, and nutritional weight control must be clearly understood as well.

BASIC NUTRITIONAL GUIDELINES

Food contains nutrients that either supply energy, regulate the various body systems, or are concerned with the growth and repair of body tissues. How much,

Figure 4-2

Canada's Food Guide offers examples of appropriate food selection, which are important in an athlete's diet.

when, and what foods are consumed depend more on social, psychological, and satiety values than on nutritional considerations.[14] The foods commonly ingested are actually chemical substances that can be broken down into simpler substances by digestive enzymes. The body then uses the energy stored in these compounds.

Food is generally categorized into four groups: (1) milk and milk products; (2) meat, fish, nuts, beans, etc.; (3) breads and cereals; and (4) fruits and vegetables (Figure 4-2). Contained in these four food groups are essential nutrients, which must be provided by food because humans cannot synthesize them at a rate sufficient to meet the body's needs.[12] Table 4-1 presents essential nutrients as classified in 1985. Each is equally important in the athlete's diet.

The Athlete's Dietary Requirements

The athlete's energy for his or her bodily requirements comes from carbohydrates, protein, and fat. The distribution of daily **kilocalorie** ingestion is 55% or more carbohydrates, 10% to 12% proteins, and 25% to 30% fats, with only 10% of that saturated fats.[33]

kilocalorie
Amount of heat required to raise 1 kg of water 1° C.

TABLE 4-1 Essential Nutrients as Classified in 1985

Carbohydrate	Minerals	Vitamins
Glucose	Calcium*	*Fat soluble*
	Phosphorus	A$_1$ (retinol)*
Fat or lipid	Sodium†	D$_3$ (cholecalciferol)
Linoleic acid	Potassium	E (α-tocopherol)
	Sulfur	K
Protein	Chlorine	
Amino acids	Magnesium†	*Water soluble*
Leucine	Iron*	Thiamin‡
Isoleucine	Selenium	Riboflavin
Lysine	Zinc†	Niacin‡
Methionine	Manganese	Biotin
Phenylalanine	Copper	Folacin†
Threonine	Cobalt	B$_6$*
Tryptophan	Molybdenum	B$_{12}$
Valine	Iodine‡	Pantothenic acid
Histidine	Chromium	C
Nonessential nitrogen	Vanadium	
	Tin	**Water**
	Nickel	
	Silicon	

*Most likely to be a problem in the United States (based on Nationwide Food Consumption Survey, 1977-1978).
†Potential problems.
‡Previous problems; they have now been corrected.

Carbohydrates

Carbohydrates are organic compounds composed of carbon, hydrogen, and oxygen. The ratio of oxygen to hydrogen is 1:2, the same ratio found in water. Common carbohydrates are the starches and sugars found in foods such as breadstuffs, potatoes, and chocolate. During digestion the complex sugars found in foods are broken down into simple sugars that can be absorbed by the blood and tissues.

The sugars are carried to the liver where they are converted either into glycogen or glucose (blood sugar). Glycogen is stored in the liver and can be readily reconverted into glucose when the demands of exercise require it. Glucose is carried by the blood to the various cells of the body. Some of the glucose may be stored as glycogen in the muscle cells, but most is used immediately as energy at the cellular level. This is especially true of nerve cells, since they cannot use any other energy-yielding nutrient. Excess glucose that is not used as energy and has not been converted into glycogen is transformed into fat and is stored as a reserve energy source. Muscles use the carbohydrates first during the initial stages of exercise, and they use more for strenuous work than for moderate work. Endurance is directly related to the glycogen stores in the body. Carbohydrates are usually considered to be the primary body fuels, and fats assume the role of reserve stores.

Protein

Proteins are nitrogenous organic compounds that break down into amino acids that are transported by the blood to the tissues. Proteins are somewhat complex substances. Basically, they are composed of a great number of carbon atoms with which atoms of hydrogen, oxygen, and nitrogen are associated. Other elements such as iron, copper, sulfur, and phosphorus are also associated with proteins, but in small amounts.

Food proteins consist of amino acids in various and complex concentrations that form the "building blocks" of the body (see Table 4-1). Protein is a major factor in the body's growth and repair. However, some amino acids can feed into the cell's basic energy cycle. Use of amino acids is minimum during exercise, providing an insignificant energy contribution during it.[33]

Nutritional values of protein foods vary also, inasmuch as their values to the diet are determined by their amino acid pattern. Generally, animal proteins are considered more adequate than vegetable proteins, although each group has a wide range of biological values.

Amino acids are absorbed from the intestine and transported through the bloodstream to the various parts of the body. Amino acid molecules are deaminized by the liver cells, with a portion forming glucose and the remainder forming urea. Those molecules having the ability to form glucose are termed *glycogenic;* others, which bear a closer relationship to fatty acids, are classified as *ketogenic,* since they break down to acetic acid. Nitrogen is important as one of the key elements necessary for growth and repair. Amino acid that is not used undergoes a process of deamination during which the nitrogen is combined with carbon dioxide to form urea, which is excreted as urine within 4 hours after ingestion of this protein. This process necessitates an adequate daily intake of dietary protein to maintain a healthy growing state of the individual. In addition to their building and repairing properties, food proteins have considerable importance in maintaining the body's ability to resist infections and to effect good healing.

Lipids or Fats

Lipids, like carbohydrates, are composed of the elements carbon, hydrogen, and oxygen. The primary difference is in the ratio of oxygen to carbon and hydrogen. Simple carbohydrates may have a ratio of $1:2$ or $1:3$, but fats may range from $1:7$—that is, one oxygen to seven carbon and hydrogen atoms. Fats, or fatty compounds, are usually classified as saturated, monounsaturated, or polyunsaturated. In saturated fats each carbon atom in a molecular chain has two hydrogen atoms attached to it. Monounsaturated fats have one carbon atom in the chain that is free of hydrogen. In polyunsaturated fats two or more carbon atoms are free of hydrogen.

Fats provide more energy per gram than either carbohydrates or proteins, but body efficiency appears to be approximately 4.5% less with a fat diet than a carbohydrate diet. After digestion, fats are absorbed and deposited in muscle tissue and in other fat storehouses or depots around the body. These depots supply an energy reserve when needed, particularly if exercise demands are so protracted that they diminish the carbohydrate stores.

Fats are not as quickly digested as are other food elements. However, they must still be considered a basic source of muscular energy, since fats are used when the carbohydrate stores are depleted. More oxygen is needed by the athlete who is on a fat diet than would be required for a carbohydrate diet. This means that greater demands will be made on the respiratory system. For this reason it would not be feasible to place a distance runner, for instance, on a high-fat diet. Slow digestion, then, is characteristic of fat. In some instances the products of fat breakdown prove to be exceedingly irritating to the linings of the stomach and the digestive tract. This can cause a considerable amount of dietary distress and in some cases may cause diarrhea.

Americans, for the most part, consume too much fat. Most fats consumed are "hard," or saturated, fats. These fats have a higher melting point (solidification point) and are principally animal fats, dairy products, hydrogenated shortenings, chocolate, and coconut. Saturated fats tend to raise the cholesterol level of the blood. "Soft," or unsaturated, fats are classified as monounsaturated or polyunsaturated. Monounsaturated fats are generally free flowing and do not solidify even at low temperatures. Monounsaturated fats are found in fowl, olive, and peanut oils, and most nuts. These fats appear to be neutral in their effect on cholesterol. Polyunsaturated fats apparently lower the cholesterol level in the blood. Polyunsaturates are found in fish, various plant oils (corn, soybean, sunflower, safflower), and special margarines. Investigations have emphasized the prominence of fatty acid as one of the causes of atherosclerosis, a common form of arteriosclerosis (hardening of the arteries). Atherosclerosis is characterized by abnormal, cholesterol-containing deposits (plaques) on the inner layers of the blood vessels. It is one of the main causes of hypertension (high blood pressure). It must be stressed that the bulk of fat intake should consist of the polyunsaturated fats.[16]

Vitamins and Minerals

Vitamins and minerals are not sources of energy, nor do they contribute significantly to the substance of the body. They perform mainly as metabolic regulators and play a role in energy transformation. They usually act as coenzymes in enzyme systems.

coenzymes
Enzyme activators.

enzyme
An organic catalyst that can cause chemical changes in other substances without being changed itself.

As exercise levels are increased, there is not a concomitant need for the ingestion of more vitamins or minerals, with the possible exception of riboflavin.[33]

Vitamins   More misinformation has been disseminated about vitamins than about any other nutritional factor. Vitamins are essential for maintaining good health. A lack of vitamins in the diet leads to deficiency conditions, which express themselves in a variety of ways. The problem of vitamin deficiency is rarely caused by the lack of a single vitamin. It is, rather, the result of a multiple vitamin deficiency. A good, varied diet that includes a balance of the "basic four" food categories will supply all vitamin requirements.

Several vitamins can be made synthetically, and according to the available research, the body is unable to distinguish between the natural and the synthetic vitamins; either is used equally well. The body, however, cannot manufacture any of the vitamins except D, which is derived from sunshine. Thus it must obtain its requirements from the diet. Supplementary vitamins are of considerable value during postoperative or recuperative periods after illness or injury and are often prescribed by the physician to aid in the healing process.

TABLE 4-2 Summary of Fat-Soluble Vitamins

Vitamin	Physiological Functions	Results of Deficiency	Requirement	Food Sources
A				
Provitamin—β-carotene	Production of rhodopsin and other light-receptor pigments	Poor dark adaptation, night blindness, xerosis	Adult male—1000 μg retinal equivalent (RE) (5000 international units [IU]) Adult female—800 μg RE (4000 IU)	Liver, cream, butter, whole milk, egg yolk
Vitamin—retinol	Formation and maintenance of epithelial tissue Growth Reproduction Toxic in large amounts	Keratinization of epithelium Growth failure Reproductive failure	Pregnancy—1000 μg RE (6000 IU) Lactation—1200 μg RE (6000 IU) Children—400-800 μg RE (2000-4000 IU)	Green and yellow vegetables, yellow fruits Fortified margarine
D				
Provitamins—ergosterol (plants), 7-dehydrocholesterol (skin) Vitamins—D_2 (ergocalciferol) and D_3 (cholecalciferol)	1,25-dihydroxycholecalciferol, a major hormone regulator of bone mineral (calcium and phosphorus) metabolism Calcium and phosphorus absorption Toxic in large amounts	Faulty bone growth—rickets, osteomalacia	Adult—5-10 μg cholecalciferol (200-400 IU) Pregnancy and lactation—10-12.5 μg (400-5000 IU), depending on age Children—10 μg (400 IU)	Fortified milk Fortified margarine Fish oils Sunlight on skin
E				
Tocopherols	Antioxidation Hemopoiesis Related to action of selenium	Anemia in premature infants	Adults—8-10 mg α tocopherol equivalent (TE) Pregnancy and lactation—10-11 mg α TE Children—3-10 mg α TE	Vegetable oils
K				
K_1 (phylloquinone) K_2 (menaquinone) Analog—K_3 (menadione)	Activation of blood-clotting factors (e.g., prothrombin) by carboxylating glutamic acid residues Toxicity can be induced by water-soluble analogs	Hemorrhagic disease of the newborn Defective blood clotting Deficiency symptoms, which can be produced by coumarin anticoagulants and by antibiotic therapy	Adult—70-140 μg Children—15-100 μg Infants—12-20 μg	Cheese, egg yolk, liver Green leafy vegetables Synthesized by intestinal bacteria

TABLE 4-3 Summary of B-Complex Vitamins

Vitamin	Coenzymes: Physiological Function	Requirement	Food Source
Thiamin (B$_1$)	Carbohydrate metabolism, nervous system function	5 mg/1000 kcal	Pork, beef, liver, whole or enriched grains, legumes
Riboflavin (B$_2$)	General metabolism, cellular energy release, respiration	6 mg/1000 kcal	Milk, liver, enriched cereals
Niacin (nicotinic acid, nicotinamide)	General metabolism—cellular energy processes and respiration, carbohydrate metabolism, fat synthesis	14-20 mg niacin equivalent (NE)	Meat, peanuts, enriched grains (protein foods containing tryptophan)
Vitamin B$_6$ (pyridoxine, pyridoxal, pyridoxamine)	General metabolism—amino acid and protein metabolism, red blood cell (RBC) formation	2 mg	Wheat, corn, meat, liver
Pantothenic acid	General metabolism—energy and tissue metabolism	2-7 mg	Liver, eggs, milk
Biotin	General metabolism—synthesis of glycogen and fat; amino acid metabolism	35-200 μg	Egg yolk, liver
Folic acid (folacin)	General metabolism—regulates tissue processes, RBC formation	Infants—30-45 μg Children—100-400 μg Adults—400 μg	Liver, green leafy vegetables
Cobalamin (B$_{12}$)	General metabolism—maintenance of nerve tissue, RBC development		Liver, meat, milk, eggs, cheese

Vitamins are usually identified as either fat soluble or water soluble. Fat-soluble vitamins usually persist in the diet in a reasonably intact state; they are found in butter, fortified margarines, and liver and are not usually destroyed in cooking (Table 4-2). Vitamins A, D, E, and K are fat soluble. Little information is currently available concerning the biochemical role each of the fat-soluble vitamins plays, and there is some concern about their toxicity, since the amount of vitamin in excess of body needs is stored in the body. Vitamins A and K are present in a rather large variety of foods, whereas D and E are present in a limited number. Water-soluble vitamins grouped together as the B complex (Table 4-3) and vitamin C (Table 4-4) are often lost through cooking vitamin-containing foods in water and then disposing of the water in which they were cooked.

Minerals Inorganic salts are essential for good health and for life itself. Through metabolization these salts perform a number of vitally important services. As stated earlier, they aid in the formation of tissues, particularly the bones and teeth, and maintain the homeostatic or internal environment of the body through stabilizing a specific ion concentration. Table 4-5 summarizes the major minerals.

TABLE 4-4 Summary of Vitamin C (Ascorbic Acid)

Physiological Functions	Requirement	Food Sources

Antioxidation
Collagen biosynthesis
General metabolism
    Makes iron available for he-
      moglobin synthesis
    Influences conversion of
      folic acid to folinic acid
    Oxidation-reduction of the
      amino acids, phenylala-
      nine, and lyrosine
	60 mg	Fresh fruits, especially citrus
		Vegetables (e.g., tomatoes,
		    cabbage, potatoes, chili
		    peppers, broccoli)

Water

Water, one of the three prime necessities of life, comes from several sources to meet the body's physiological needs. Most of it is ingested in the daily diet either as fluid or as the fluid elements contained in the so-called solid foods. The remainder is a result of the oxidation of organic foodstuffs.

Water forms the bulk, approximately 75%, of all protoplasm, and it acts as a medium for the various enzymatic and chemical reactions. Water functions as a diluent of toxic wastes, thus preventing damage to the body and its organs from some of the toxic by-products of metabolism. This is especially true in the kidneys. Water aids in the transport of body fuels, elimination of waste materials, and regulation of body temperature by dissipating excess heat from the body through perspiration (Table 4-6).

Water balance must be maintained. Water loss usually approximates the water intake. If a salt deficit exists, the body will not retain water but will continue to eliminate it at a rate basically the same as that of the intake under normal situations. Dehydration must be prevented. Moderately severe or even severe exercise can be sustained quite comfortably over extended periods of time if the water intake is regulated to conform to the water loss. Small amounts given often are more effective in maintaining balance under severe heat and exercise conditions than are extremely large amounts given at greater intervals. Deprivation of water leads to more rapid dehydration, with subsequent impairment of performance. A daily intake of 2000 ml, more than 2 quarts, of water should be adequate in most instances but should be increased if sweating occurs. Some form of water should be available at all training sessions and games. It should be considered as much a part of the training/competitive regimen as any other phase. The withholding of water from athletes can neither be condoned morally nor can it be justified on physiological bascs. Encourage players to drink 500 ml of water before competition and 600 ml per hour when exercising (see Table 4-6).[22] When exercising in extremely hot weather, thirst is not a reliable guide to dehydration.[22] A little water sloshing in the stomach can do no harm.

Even during cold weather, dehydration can occur. When dehydration does occur, blood volume is lessened, making warming of the hands, toes, and face more difficult.[20]

TABLE 4-5 Summary of Major Minerals (required intake more than 100 mg/day)

Mineral	Metabolism	Physiological Functions	Requirement	Food Source
Calcium (Ca)	Absorption according to body need; requires Ca-binding protein and is regulated by vitamin D, parathyroid hormone, and calcitonin; absorption favored by protein, lactose, acidity	Constituent of bones and teeth Participates in blood clotting, nerve transmission, muscle action, cell membrane permeability, enzyme activation	Adults—800 mg Pregnancy and lactation—1200 mg Children—800-1200 mg	Milk, cheese Green, leafy vegetables Egg yolk Legumes, nuts
Phosphorus (P)	Absorption with Ca; aided by vitamin D and parathyroid hormone	Constituent of bones and teeth Participates in absorption of glucose and glycerol, transport of fatty acids, energy metabolism, buffer system	Adults—800 mg Pregnancy and lactation—1200 mg Infants—240-360 mg Children—800-1200 mg	Milk, cheese Meat, egg yolk Whole grains Legumes, nuts
Magnesium (Mg)	Absorption according to intake load; hindered by excess fat, phosphate, calcium, protein	Constituent of bones and teeth Coenzyme in general metabolism, smooth muscle action, neuromuscular irritability	Adults—300 mg Pregnancy and lactation—450 mg Infants—50-70 mg Children—150-400 mg	Milk, cheese Meat, seafood Whole grains Legumes, nuts
Sodium (Na)	Readily absorbed Excretion chiefly by kidney; controlled by aldosterone	Major factor in extracellular fluid, water balance, acid-base balance Cell membrane permeability, absorption of glucose Normal muscle irritability	Adults—1100-3300 mg Infants—115-350 mg Children—325-2700 mg	Salt (NaC1) Sodium compounds in baking and processing Milk, cheese Meat, eggs Carrots, beets, spinach, celery
Potassium (K)	Readily absorbed Secreted and reabsorbed in gastrointestinal circulation Excretion chiefly by kidney; regulated by aldosterone	Major cation in intracellular fluid, water balance, acid-base balance Normal muscle irritability Glycogen formation Protein synthesis	Adults—1875-5625 mg Infants—350-1275 mg Children—550-4575 mg	Fruits Vegetables Legumes, nuts Whole grains Meat
Chlorine (Cl)	Readily absorbed Excretion controlled by kidney	Major factor in extracellular fluid, water balance, acid-base balance, chloride-bicarbonate shift	Adults—1700-5100 mg Infants—275-1200 mg Children—500-4200 mg	Salt (NaCl)
Sulfur (S)	Absorbed in elemental form; split from amino acid sources (methionine and cystine) during digestion and absorbed into portal circulation	Essential constituent of protein structure Enzyme activity and energy metabolism Detoxification reactions	Diet adequate in protein contains adequate sulfur	Meat, egg Milk, cheese Legumes, nuts

TABLE 4-6 Typical Water Balance in Adults

Sources and Loss	Milliliters
Sources of water	
Liquid food	1100
Solid food	500-1000
Water of oxidation	300-400
TOTAL	1900-2500
Loss of water	
Urine	1000-1300
Perspiration and evaporation from skin	800-1000
Feces	100
TOTAL	1900-2400

EATING FOR SPORTS COMPETITION

There are numerous aspects of nutrition about which the athletic trainer typically must be able to advise the athlete. The major categories under this heading are supplementing the daily diet and eating practices.

Supplementing the Daily Diet

Traditionally, athletes engage in diet supplementation, intending to improve their performance. In many cases this supplementation fails to improve performance and, in some cases, is a hindrance. In this section seven topics will be discussed, including vitamins, minerals and electrolytes, iron supplementation, carbohydrates, fat loading, increasing protein content, and the liquid food supplements.

Vitamins and Minerals

Vitamin deficiency diseases are not as common in the United States today as they are in other parts of the world, since most Americans eat a reasonably well-balanced diet. However, a diet containing less than 35% to 45% of the Recommended Dietary Allowance (RDA) of B-complex vitamins can lead to decreased endurance capacity.[29] The depletion of vitamins A and C causes no such decrease in endurance.

Vitamin requirements do not increase during exercise, nor does exercise specifically reduce the amount of vitamin C or B-complex present.[5] As stated earlier, *vitamins per se are not an energy source.* Available evidence does not justify supplementing the diet of the athlete with vitamins to improve physical performance unless a preexisting vitamin deficiency exists.[28]

Taking vitamins in excessive quantities (megavitamin dosage) can, in certain circumstances, have deleterious effects and lead to vitamin toxicity from storage of vitamins A, D, and E. In extreme cases the toxicity can prove fatal. It would be more practical to attain desired vitamin levels through intelligent food selection and preparation rather than to rely on artificial supplements.[15]

No vitamins or minerals are safe if taken in megadoses. Because fat-soluble vitamins are stored in the body, if taken in an overdose, they can become toxic to the body. Even water-soluble vitamins, if taken in doses that saturate the body, can lead to physical problems. For example, B-complex vitamins can lead to limb

Vitamin requirements do not increase during exercise.

RECOGNIZING NUTRITION FRAUD

The "nutrition charlatan"
1. Advises the athlete to buy something he or she would not otherwise buy
2. Indicates that disease and poor athletic performance are the results of a poor diet
3. Indicates that most Americans are poorly nourished
4. Indicates that the soil has been depleted of nutrients and that the chemical fertilizers used cause malnutrition
5. Indicates that modern food processing and storage methods remove valuable nutrients from our food
6. Indicates that we are being poisoned by food additives, preservatives, and contaminants
7. Indicates that the athlete can eat poorly, as long as poor diet is offset by taking nutritional supplements
8. Recommends that every athlete take a daily vitamin and mineral supplement
9. Claims that "natural" vitamins are far superior to regularly available supplements

---

numbness, movement difficulties, and even paralysis. Niacin, in particular, if taken in large quantities, can cause extreme vasodilation, resulting in itching and bright red skin. Thiamin in megadoses can produce anaphylactic shock. Vitamin C, often thought completely safe in large doses, can lead to gastroenteritis, diarrhea, colitis, and kidney stones.[19]

Over ingestion of minerals can also cause physical problems for the athlete. Megadoses of sodium (salt tablets) and potassium can irritate the gastrointestinal tract and cause dehydration and muscle cramping. Too much chromium, a trace mineral, can cause damage to the liver and the kidneys. Selenium can produce fatigue and skin problems, whereas zinc, another trace mineral, can produce nausea, diarrhea, and dizziness, as well as interfere with the body's immune response.[3]

Athletes and coaches are easy prey for diet misinformation. Their desire to acquire the edge over the competitor often clouds common sense. The nutrition charlatan is "alive and well" in the sports world (see box above).[26]

Ingestion of the so-called sport or "electrolyte" beverages, of which there is a variety on the market, to replace water and electrolytes is of no special benefit; the need is more imagined than real, since the water and electrolyte losses can be met by increasing water intake and consuming food that has been slightly additionally salted. If a premixed electrolyte solution is used, it should be diluted with water in a 2:1 ratio for faster absorption into the bloodstream. Potassium needs can be met adequately through drinking an 8-ounce glass of orange juice, whereas a glass of tomato juice or similar fluid can supplement the diet for the most essential minerals.

The typical over-the-counter high-potency nutrient supplement uses a "shotgun" approach in its formula. In most cases the athlete consuming this product

TABLE 4-7 Typical Over-the-Counter High-Potency Nutrient Supplement ("Shotgun" Formula)

Nutrient	Adult RDA (%)	Adult RDA
Vitamin A	250	10,000 IU
Vitamin D	100	400 IU
Vitamin C	500	300 mg
Vitamin E	350	30 IU
Vitamin B_1	1500	15 mg
Vitamin B_2	800	10 mg
Vitamin B_6	500	10 mg
Vitamin B_{12}	160	5 μg
Folacin	100	400 μg
Biotin	100	200 μg
Niacin	900	100 mg
Calcium pantothenate	300	20 mg
Iron	150	15 mg
Calcium	12	100 mg
Iodine	50	0.05 mg
Magnesium	25	75 mg
Zinc	100	15 mg
Copper	33	1 mg
Manganese	20	1 mg

excretes excess amounts of water-soluble vitamins; however, and more importantly, he or she may develop toxic reactions from excess ingestion of fat-soluble vitamins and mineral elements (Table 4-7).[12]

Fluid and electrolyte replacement Electrolyte losses are primarily responsible for muscle cramping and intolerance to heat. Copious sweating results not only in a body water loss but in a mineral loss as well, particularly sodium, chloride, and, under extreme conditions, potassium (although generally potassium loss is negligible). These salts are electrically charged and are identified as ions or electrolytes. They are primarily concerned with the extracellular water (water outside of the cells), the significant reduction of which affects the body's control of the extracellular water. *Heavy sweating requires water replacement*, which is far more important than the replacement of electrolytes. Electrolytes can be adequately replaced after exercise by a balanced diet, which can, if need be, be salted slightly more than is usual. Free access to water (*ad libitum*) before, during, and after activity should be encouraged.

In most cases, plain water is a very effective and inexpensive means of fluid replacement for most types of exercise.[7] Commercial drinks, rather than adequately hydrating the athlete, may in fact hinder water absorption because of their high sugar content.[7] Drinks containing too much glucose, fructose, or sucrose are **hypertonic** and may draw water from blood plasma into the intestinal tract, dehydrating the athlete even more.[7,13]

For maximum absorption, sports drinks containing almost 5% sugar should be diluted with water to a 2.5% sugar solution. For most sports, electrolytes provided

Replacing fluid after heavy sweating is far more important than replacing electrolytes.

hypertonic
Having a higher osmotic pressure than a compared solution.

DIRECTIONS FOR FLUID INGESTION

When conditioning, training, and/or competing, the athlete should
1. Drink a pint (500 to 600 ml) of cold (40° to 50° F) water 15 to 30 minutes before exercise
2. Avoid highly sugared drinks ingested within an hour of exercise (this drink elevates blood glucose and insulin and may lead to hyperglycemia)
3. Ingest fluid that contains less than or equal to 2.5 g glucose per 100 ml water
4. Ingest fluid that contains a low concentration of ions (e.g., less than 0.2 g of sodium chloride and less than 0.2 g of potassium per quart [1000 ml] of fluid)

---

polymers
Natural or synthetic substances formed by the combination of two or more molecules of the same substance.

by commercial sports drinks are not needed unless the athlete is engaging in events such as ultramarathons.

A new group of sports drinks that uses glucose **polymers** has been introduced. These drinks have the advantage of not causing the hypertonic problems of other commercial solutions. These drinks are most appropriate for highly intense and prolonged events that severely deplete glycogen stores.[7,32]

During cold weather water is not as critical as in hot weather. Therefore, a stronger electrolyte solution that allows a slower, more steady release of fluid from the stomach should be used. As in hot weather, thirst is not an indicator of hydration (see box above).[32]

Calcium supplementation Calcium is by far the largest mineral amount present in the human body. Most dietary calcium comes from dairy products and some green leafy vegetables and grains. Calcium and phosphorous work closely together in bone and tooth formation, blood clotting, nerve transmission, muscle contraction and relaxation, cell membrane permeability, and enzyme activation.[33]

In general, calcium is expressly needed in children and in adolescents during their rapid growth period. In terms of sports participation, calcium supplementation apparently is not beneficial.[12]

Iron supplementation Iron deficiency, which is much more prevalent than usually thought, can affect muscular performance. Not infrequently, teenaged boys will exhibit an iron deficiency as the result of an inadequate diet and the demands of a rapid growth rate. Among female athletes, iron deficiency is not at all uncommon; borderline anemia may occur as a result of not getting enough dietary iron. The loss may be further compounded, particularly in the initial phases, by a strenuous training program wherein a temporary drop in plasma and hemoglobin results in so-called sports anemia, which is caused by the increased destruction of red blood cells. Should an iron deficiency be detected, iron supplementation should be introduced under medical supervision. The recommended daily dietary allowance for females from age 10 up through the reproductive years is 18 mg. Recent surveys have indicated that an average daily intake of only 11 to 12 mg, over a period of several years, results in an iron store depletion, with the hemoglobin levels falling below the anemia borderline of 12 g/100 ml of blood.[8] Adolescent female athletes apparently become more iron depleted than do nonathletes. This deficiency decreases their ability to work effectively, thus decreasing performance.[4]

Carbohydrate Increase and Loading

Carbohydrate intake should be significantly increased during the precontest period. Extra helpings of breads, cereals, potatoes, and sugar should be the rule. Bread and potatoes do not deserve their reputation as fattening foods. Potatoes should be eaten plain, that is, baked or boiled without the addition of milk, cream, or butter, which are the fattening agents. Bread, preferably, should be constituted from the less-refined flours or enriched by the restoration of the vitamins and minerals lost through refining. Since carbohydrates are most readily available and most easily absorbed in terms of metabolic demands, they are the first elements used for muscular work. Inasmuch as the final by-products of carbohydrate metabolism—carbon dioxide and water—are eliminated from the body through the lungs and the skin, no additional acid load is accumulated in the tissues.

The amount of glycogen stored in a muscle determines the endurance of that muscle. In activities that continue for half an hour or more and in which the aerobic energy demand is at a constant high level, the storing or loading of glycogen seems of value. It has been shown that endurance can be increased but not a track athlete's speed.[17,23] The amount of stored glycogen can easily be doubled through loading by increasing the carbohydrate ingestion.

To maximize the absorption of glycogen, the athlete should gradually taper the work intensity 1 week before the event. This work reduction should be followed by increased ingestion of carbohydrate foods 3 days before the competition.[23] Increasing pre-event ingestion of carbohydrates is of no particular use unless activity is sustained for 90 minutes or more, since events of short duration are not affected or modified by such "loading." Indeed, dehydration may develop. Marathon runners have shown no difference in carbohydrate stores during the first half of the race, but loading apparently has some advantage in the second half. Taking sweetened drinks during the latter part of the race seems to be of some help, but the explanation is open to question, since physiological evidence is moot. The apparent lift may be psychological; perhaps the fluid itself may have some bearing. It should be noted that carbohydrate ingestion has some risk. Depositing glycogen in the muscles this way also deposits three times as much water as glycogen, causing the athlete to feel heavy and stiff.[17]

Fat Loading

Recently some endurance athletes have tried fat loading in place of carbohydrate loading. Their intent was to have a better source of energy at their disposal. The deleterious effects of this procedure outweigh any benefits that may be derived.[6] Associated with fat loading is cardiac protein and potassium depletion, causing arrhythmias and increased levels of serum cholesterol as a result of the ingestion of butter, cheese, cream, and marbled beef.

Proteins

Massive doses of protein supplements are being taken in the belief that extra protein will stimulate muscle growth. Athletes need no more protein than the average individual; a well-balanced diet will supply adequate amounts not only of protein but also of all other nutritional needs. Protein supplementation is of no use as far as performance is concerned. Excessive protein supplementation not only leads to an increase in blood urea concentration but also may result in increased albumin excretion and nephritis. Muscle growth cannot be increased by eating high-protein foods. Only exercise can bring about an increase in muscle mass.

Intake of protein that exceeds the athlete's caloric requirement will only be stored as fat.[10] High intake of protein can lead to ketosis, dehydration, gouty arthritis, and loss of calcium in the body. The athlete who ingests a single amino acid supplement daily may actually interfere with the absorption of other essential amino acids.[2]

Liquid Food Supplements

A number of liquid food supplements have been produced and are being used by high school, college, university, and professional teams with some indications of success. These supplements supply from 225 to 400 calories per average serving, at a cost of approximately one fifth that of the pregame meal, which usually consists of steak. Athletes who have used these supplements, usually in approximately 925-calorie servings, report elimination of the usual pregame symptoms of "dry mouth," abdominal cramps, leg cramps, nervous defecation, and nausea.

Under ordinary conditions it usually takes approximately 4 hours for a full meal to pass through the stomach and the small intestine. Pregame emotional tension often delays the emptying of the stomach; therefore the undigested food mass remains in the stomach and upper bowel for a prolonged time, even up to or through the actual period of competition, and frequently results in nausea, vomiting, and cramps. This unabsorbed food mass is of no value to the athlete. According to team physicians who have experimented with the liquid food supplements, one of their major advantages is that they do clear both the stomach and the upper bowel before game time, thus making available the caloric energy that would otherwise still be in an unassimilated state. There is merit in the use of such food supplements for pregame meals.[1]

Dietary Practices

As in the area of supplementation, there are numerous fads and fallacies associated with eating habits of athletes. This section discusses pre-event nutrition, alternative eating patterns, weight management, and eating disorders among athletes.

Pre-Event Nutrition

Too often athletic trainers and coaches concern themselves principally with the meal immediately preceding competition and do not seem to realize that pre-event nutrition begins some time before that. Events that call for sudden bursts of all-out energy, rather than endurance or sustained effort, do not appear to be particularly affected or modified by pre-event nutrition. However, preparing for moderate or sustained effort that requires endurance includes consideration of nutrition approximately 48 hours preceding competition, since such events can be significantly affected by ingestion. The usual manifestation of precompetitive tension such as abdominal cramps, "dry mouth," acidosis, and other metabolic symptoms can be either reduced or eliminated to a considerable degree by careful attention to dietary considerations.

It is also wise to begin to gradually decrease the training program approximately 48 hours before competition. This is advocated because it enables the body

It takes approximately 4 hours for a full meal to pass through the stomach and small intestines.

Pre-event nutrition should begin at least 48 hours before the competition.

Resting and eating a high-carbohydrate diet 2 or 3 days before competition can store additional glycogen.

THE PREGAME MEAL

The athlete should
1. Eat 3 to 4 hours before competition
2. Avoid foods that are high in animal fat, protein, and sugar content
3. Avoid coffee and tea
4. Eat a meal that primarily contains complex carbohydrates
5. Drink water

---

to replenish certain essential stores and to reduce or eliminate various metabolites that might reduce performance. As has previously been shown, the glycogen stores of the body—specifically those in the liver, which normally consist of about 1500 calories—need to be built up to a full measure if an athlete is to compete well in an endurance event. In endurance events approximately 1500 calories are consumed during the first hour of effort, and continued exertion may result in an excessive depletion of the glycogen reserves of the body, with consequent hypoglycemia (notable reduction in blood sugar) and evident fatigue.

The use of liquid meals—which are nutritionally sound and contain the recommended daily dietary proportions of nutrients—as the meal immediately before performance is widely used and is recommended as a means of eliminating or reducing the pregame syndrome. Fluid is much easier to digest because it eliminates the liquefaction step in the stomach, an important factor under stress conditions, since nausea and vomiting are not infrequent accompaniments to preperformance tension. (See box above.)

Foods to avoid Foods of high cellulose content such as lettuce should be avoided, since they tend to increase the need for defecation. The elimination of highly spiced and of fatty or fried foods from the diet is also desirable because of the likelihood of gastrointestinal irritation.[17]

Protein content It is advisable to limit protein intake during the period just preceding competition, since proteins are a source of fixed acids, which can be eliminated from the body only through urinary excretion.

Sugar content Many athletic trainers and coaches advocate giving sugar, either in the form of lump sugar, dextrose tablets, glucose pills, or honey, as a means of improving athletic performance. Since sugar is a fuel food and therefore is active in muscle contractions, it has been reasoned that the feeding of supplementary sugar should have value as discussed earlier. All sugars notably retard gastric emptying; thus heavy sugar solutions tend to remain in the stomach for a considerable length of time, frequently causing gastric distress. Physiologically, when an individual is fed sugar, there is a tendency for the fluid required for its digestion to be drawn into the gastrointestinal tract, thus further dehydrating the organism.

Liquids Liquids should be low in fat content and readily absorbable. Above all, they should not cause laxation; therefore fruit juices should be restricted. Items such as prune juice, which has a high laxation factor, should be eliminated

All sugars retard gastric emptying; thus heavy sugar solutions tend to remain in the stomach for a long time, often causing gastric distress.

from the diet. Water intake should be normal. Cocoa, whether made from milk or water, is an excellent beverage to provide some variety and can be substituted for milk, juice, coffee, or tea as the occasion demands.

COFFEE AND TEA   At the high school level, drinking tea or coffee is not the usual practice among athletes, but it becomes more prevalent at the college and university level. For many years, tea, a caffeine-containing fluid, has traditionally been a part of the pregame meal. Caffeine induces a period of stimulation of the central nervous system that is followed by a period of depression. Because the athlete is usually excited and somewhat nervous during the precontest period, the addition of caffeine to the pregame meal may not be advisable. The same statements apply to the use of coffee. Tea and coffee are also diuretics; that is, they stimulate the flow of urine and thus may cause additional discomfort during the competitive period.

Time of the pre-event meal   The number and spacing of meals and the effect of food intake has been reported by several investigators. It is generally conceded that the pre-event meal should be consumed approximately 3 to 4 hours before competition. Eating a meal immediately before competition is not conducive to effective performance. The acute discomfort of attempting to perform physically on a full stomach provides a psychological impediment. Also, the increase in portal circulation required for digestion is achieved by withdrawing from the systemic circulation blood that would otherwise be readily available for the maintenance of physical work.

Alternative Eating Patterns

There is no scientific evidence that performance can generally be improved through control of the athlete's diet. Improvement in performance may be attributed to a balanced diet, if there have been previous dietary deficiencies. The main value of proper nutrition lies in preventing the deleterious effects of improper or inadequate nutrition.

Food fads are rampant among athletes. No food, vitamin, supplement, or hormone will substitute for sound nutrition and hard work. Dietary abuses are sometimes condoned by parents and coaches in the mistaken belief that they will help, whereas in reality many of them are deleterious.

The vegetarian athlete   Some athletes opt to eat a vegetarian diet. This decision can be based on religious, philosophical, or health reasons.[9] Types of vegetarian diets differ according to what animal products are ingested. For example, vegans eat only plant food, lacto-vegetarians ingest dairy products plus plant food, whereas the lacto-ovo vegetarian consumes eggs, dairy products, and plant food. Semi-vegetarians ingest animal meat but exclude red meat.[9]

The primary concern in the vegetarian diet is whether or not enough protein is being consumed because the essential amino acids are balanced better in animal products than in plant foods. The athlete, therefore, must carefully plan his or her diet to include all the essential amino acids (Table 4-8).

WEIGHT MANAGEMENT AND EATING DISORDERS

Gain or loss of weight in an athlete often poses a problem because the individual's ingrained eating habits are difficult to change. The athletic trainer's inability

TABLE 4-8 Complementary Plan Protein Sources

Food	Deficient Amino Acid	Complementary Protein
Grains	Isoleucine Lysine	Rice and legumes Corn and legumes Wheat and legumes Wheat, peanuts, and milk Wheat, sesame seeds, and soybeans Rice and sesame seeds Rice and brewer's yeast
Legumes	Tryptophan Methionine	Legumes and rice Beans and wheat Beans and corn Soybeans, rice, and wheat Soybeans, corn, and milk Soybeans, wheat, and sesame seeds Soybeans, peanuts, and sesame seeds
Nuts and seeds	Isoleucine Lysine	Peanuts, sesame seeds, and soybeans Sesame seeds and beans Sesame seeds, soybeans, and wheat Peanuts and sunflower seeds
Vegetables	Isoleucine Methionine	Lima beans Green peas and sesame seeds Brussel sprouts/Brazil nuts Cauliflower/mushrooms Broccoli Greens and millet/converted rice

to adequately supervise the athlete's meal program in terms of balance and quantity further complicates the problem. An intelligent and conscientious approach to weight control requires, on the part of both athletic trainer and athlete, some knowledge of what is involved. Such understanding allows athletes to better discipline themselves as to the quantity and kinds of foods they should eat.

The energy requirements of individuals are not at all constant but vary with age, sex, weight, current health status, and occupation. Body weight is determined in part by body build or somatotype. Because of these many variables, there is no shortcut or magic formula to weight control.

Overweight is simply the result of putting more energy into the body than is used. The principal cause is overeating coupled with inactivity. It is important that athletes develop good eating habits, restricting their use of fatty foods and modifying their carbohydrate intake. They must learn to eat less—overeating at the training table is a common fault—and to confine their intake to bulky, low-calorie foods (Table 4-9).

TABLE 4-9   Calorie Adjustment Required for Weight Loss

To lose 1 pound a week—500 fewer calories daily

Basis of estimation		
1 lb body fat	=	454 g
1 g pure fat	=	9 calories
1 g body fat	=	7.7 calories (some water in fat cells)
454 g × 9 calories/g	=	4086 calories/lb fat (pure fat)
454 g × 7.7 calories/g	=	3496 calories/lb body fat (or 3500 calories)
500 calories × 7 days	=	3500 calories = 1 lb body fat

Weight Management
Exercise and Weight Control

There has long been a misconception that exercise has little or no effect on caloric balance. Nothing could be further from the truth. Inactivity is probably the most important factor in weight gain. Eating habits do not readily change, but activity habits do. The measured costs, in energy expenditure, of various types of physical activities give an indication of the value of exercise as a means of weight control. This is exemplified by the added poundage that athletes usually acquire during the off-season. They continue their food intake at substantially the same rate but lower their activity level; therefore, the energy that is usually burned off through activity remains as adipose accretion.

Since the energy cost of exercise is proportional to body weight, overweight athletes require more energy and use more of their body reserves in performing a given activity than do persons who are not carrying excess poundage. If athletes permit themselves to become 20% or more overweight, the energy cost of their performance will increase the same amount, and they will be working at an inefficient level. A reduction in surplus weight, even when additional weight appears to be a desirable factor, generally results in a more efficiently functioning individual whose increase in usable energy will more than offset any apparent advantage dead weight would seem to give. If an increase in weight is desirable, it is better achieved through a gain in muscle bulk than through a gain in fat. Overnutrition can be a distinct hindrance to many types of performance, since the excess caloric intake causes excessive adipose tissue deposits, which tend to restrict body movement, thus adding to the work load and reducing the effective available surface for heat loss.

To lose weight one must increase physical activity and maintain a proper diet; only in this way can caloric expenditure be increased. Regular exercise tends to stabilize the weight, once the desired level is attained. In some sports, especially wrestling and weight lifting, it is sometimes necessary for the athlete to lose a few pounds so that he may make a specific weight class. Usually, most of the loss is achieved through dehydration and/or reducing the food intake (Figure 4-3).

Intense weight reduction during a short period of time may seriously impair performance. Ordinarily, weight reduction is effected within a period of 2 to 7 days. From 2 to 4½ pounds may be lost during this time. Avoiding fat foods and limiting the fluid intake, coupled with an exercise program to induce sweating, is the method customarily used. Dehydration impairs performance; in some individ-

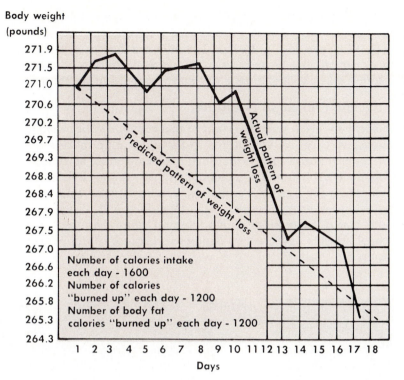

Body weight (pounds)

Number of calories intake each day - 1600
Number of calories "burned up" each day - 1200
Number of body fat calories "burned up" each day - 1200

Days

Figure 4-3

Changes in body weight of a very overweight person on a reducing diet. The progress chart of an actual patient shows how greatly body weight can fluctuate as a result of water retention even though daily calorie intake remains constant. This dieter accumulated water for 10 days while losing fat, then showed a rapid weight loss as water was eliminated.

uals dehydration of as little as 2% of the body weight causes a significant deterioration of work performance. If at all possible, weight reduction should be avoided. However, should athletic trainers be faced with an athlete's need for weight reduction, they should advocate a gradual loss over as long a period of time as is feasible under the circumstances to ensure the athlete's entering competition in a near-optimum state of fitness.

Crash Dieting

In an attempt to lose weight the athlete may go on a "crash" diet. Diets of this nature fail to recognize the basic problem in weight reduction—that of acquiring a change in eating habits. Athletes should be discouraged from attempting this type of program. The resulting lowered vitality makes the individual susceptible to colds and infections and produces weariness and weakness, which are reflected in a lowering of both the efficiency and the magnitude of physical performance. Besides crash dieting, the athlete may become desperate and become bulimic or may eventually develop anorexia nervosa.

Weight Maintenance or Gain

Weight gain can be accomplished through diet enrichment and exercise regulation. At times it may be advisable to advocate dietary supplementation between meals to increase caloric intake. Some reduction in the rigor of the daily training program, with an increase in the periods of rest and relaxation, helps in adding extra ounces. Such reductions in the training program should be consistent with maintaining the status quo of performance levels.

Many athletes must consume an extremely high number of kilocalories (kcals) per day just to maintain their current weight (some athletes expend well over 6000 kcals per day[24]). To help in this maintenance, nibbling food eight to ten times per day may be necessary. A liquid food supplement, containing 250 to 500 calories, taken several times a day may also assist in weight maintenance.[24]

Weight Control in Wrestling

Publicity in recent years has charged that certain coaches were requiring wrestlers to achieve excessive weight loss so that they could make a certain weight class for competition. If this is true, such practices cannot be condoned. They are not only undesirable from the standpoint of maintaining physical effectiveness but are also potentially harmful. A rapid decrease in weight, which is caused by extreme restrictions of caloric intake, is contraindicated immediately before or during periods that will require maximum physical effort. Also, weight reduction by high school athletes poses a serious problem because of the growth and maturation factors.

Figure 4-4

Great caution should be taken when wrestlers "make weight." Weight loss should not be extreme and should extend over a 5 to 6 week period.

Some coaches advocate "dryout" and *total fasting* in the beginning of a program of weight reduction. Usually they suggest elimination of carbohydrates and salt. Such an approach has serious implications to the athlete, since salt loss in the urine is greatly increased and this loss, coupled with the additional salt loss incurred through perspiration, greatly increases the possibility of a clinically identified sodium deficiency. When vigorous physical activity is performed, these features are not only magnified, but they may also lead to a renal shutdown. During such total fasts a decrease in heart size accompanies these hydrodynamic changes.

It is sometimes difficult to determine whether or not a person is overweight. Some athletes who appear overweight or who tip the scales above average standards are not overweight at all; they usually possess greater musculature and larger bones. In such situations a knowledge of somatotyping would be of value to the athletic trainer or coach.

Body fat that composes 5% to 7% of the total body weight is ideal. A fat content of 5% of total body weight is the ideal wrestling weight.

Weight loss during training should not exceed 2 to 5 pounds a week, and the conditioning program should be started at least 5 to 6 weeks before final decisions are made as to the final weight at which the athlete is to wrestle.[27] Once this weight is determined, he should not be permitted reduction to wrestle at a lower weight but should let his weight stabilize. Weight fluctuations impair physical performance (Figure 4-4).

A balanced diet, reduced somewhat in quantity, coupled with an adequate fluid and salt intake and with hard physical work is still the best way to reduce weight. The use of digitalis and other weight-loss drugs is strongly condemned.

Eating Disorders

There is an epidemic in our society, especially in sports. This problem is the inordinate concern with being overweight. Out of this obsession has emerged the eating disorders bulimia and anorexia nervosa. Both of these disorders are increasingly seen in athletes.[25]

Bulimia

The bulimic person is commonly female, ranging in age from adolescence to middle age. It is estimated that one out of every 200 American girls, ages 12 to 18 years (1% to 2% of the population), will develop patterns of bulimia and/or anorexia nervosa.[25] The bulimic individual typically gorges herself with thousands of calories after a period of starvation and then "purges" herself through induced vomiting and further fasting or through the use of laxatives or diuretics. This secretive binge-eating–purging cycle may go on for years.

Typically the bulimic athlete is Caucasian and belongs to a middle or upper-middle class family. She is perfectionistic, obedient, overcompliant, highly motivated, very successful academically, well-liked by her peers, and a good athlete.[24] She most commonly participates in gymnastics, track, and dance.[11] NOTE: Male wrestlers and gymnasts may also develop bulimia. (See box on p. 134.) The formal definition of bulimia is as follows: recurrent episodes of rapid, uncontrollable ingestion of large amounts of food in a short period of time, usually followed by purging, either by forced vomiting and/or abuse of laxatives or diuretics.

RECOGNIZING THE ATHLETE WITH AN EATING DISORDER

Signs to look for are athletes who display
1. Social isolation and withdrawal from friends and family
2. A lack of confidence in athletic abilities
3. Ritualistic eating behavior (e.g., organizing food on plate)
4. An obsession with counting calories
5. An obsession with constantly exercising, especially just before a meal
6. An obsession with weighing self
7. A constant overestimation of body size
8. Patterns of leaving the table directly after eating to go into the restroom
9. Problems related to eating disorders (e.g., malnutrition, menstrual irregularities, or chronic fatigue)

Bulimic girls are usually preoccupied with good diets and recipes and may prepare elaborate meals for others. Such binge-purge patterns can cause stomach rupture, disrupt heart rhythm, and cause liver damage. Stomach acids brought up by vomiting cause tooth decay and chronically inflame the mucous lining of the mouth and throat.

Anorexia Nervosa

It has been estimated that 30% to 50% of all individuals diagnosed as having anorexia nervosa also develop some symptoms of bulimia. Anorexia nervosa is characterized by a distorted body image and a major concern about weight gain. As with bulimia, anorexia nervosa affects mostly females. It usually begins in adolescence and can be mild without major consequences or can become life threatening. As many as 15% to 21% of those individuals diagnosed as anorexic will ultimately die from this disorder.

Despite being extremely thin, the athlete sees herself as too fat. These individuals deny hunger and are hyperactive, engaging in abnormal amounts of exercise such as aerobics or distance running.[18,21] In general, the anorexic individual is highly pliant (see box above).

The coach and athletic trainer must be sensitive to eating problems. Early intervention is essential. Any athlete with signs of bulimia or anorexia nervosa must be confronted in a kind, empathetic manner by the coach or athletic trainer. When detected, individuals with eating disorders must be referred for psychological or psychiatric treatment.

SUMMARY

The athlete requires proper nutrition to recover promptly from fatigue and to repair damaged tissue. Eating the correct amounts of nutrients in the basic food categories is extremely important to the athlete. Most athletic endeavors require that the athlete eat a diet consisting of 55% or more carbohydrates, 10% to 12% proteins, and 25% to 30% fats, of which only 10% are saturated fats.

Most proteins consist of amino acids in various combinations to form the ''building blocks'' of the body. Lipids or fats are composed of the same elements as carbohydrates, but they have a lower oxygen-to-carbon or oxygen-to-hydrogen ratio. To avoid arteriosclerosis, a greater abundance of polyunsaturated fats, compared to saturated fats, should be eaten by the athlete.

Vitamins and minerals are metabolic regulators that transform energy. Vitamins are classified as water soluble or fat soluble. A good, varied diet, including a balance of the ''basic four'' food categories, will supply all the essential vitamins. Minerals, like vitamins, are essential for good health and are provided by a good diet.

Water is one of the three prime necessities of life and comes from several sources to meet the body's needs. The athlete should drink at least 500 ml of water before competition and 600 ml per hour when exercising.

Athletes traditionally supplement their daily diets in many ways. In most cases, they have found that doing so does not improve their performance significantly. In some cases, supplementation can hinder performance and even predispose the athlete to eventual injury. However, iron supplementation may be of value for some teenaged boys and girls. Iron deficiency is not uncommon among female athletes.

The practice of increasing the amount of carbohydrates ingested helps the endurance athlete. Nevertheless, carbohydrate loading may help some athletes and hinder others. Fat loading should be avoided.

Pre-event nutrition varies according to the athlete. As a general rule, athletes should eat 3 to 4 hours before competition. Foods high in cellulose, meat proteins, fat, and sugar, as well as coffee and tea, should be avoided. Meals containing complex carbohydrates should be eaten along with water for hydration.

There is no scientific evidence to support the idea that performance can be generally improved through alternative eating patterns such as the vegetarian diet. The athlete who avoids eating animal flesh or all animal products must monitor his or her diet carefully to ensure all essential nutrients are eaten daily.

Extreme care must be taken when weight management is required for a specific sport. Severe weight loss can lead to serious illnesses or injuries. The best means to a healthy weight loss is eating from the basic four food categories daily in the correct percentages while reducing the amount of overall calories.

Eating disorders are a current problem among many participants in sports and dance. The obsession with weight loss can cause the eating disorders bulimia and anorexia nervosa to emerge. Bulimia's basic pattern is one of secretive binge eating and purging. Anorexia nervosa is a weight obsession characterized by a distorted body image. Anorexia sufferers see themselves as overweight when, in reality, they are markedly underweight.

REVIEW QUESTIONS AND CLASS ACTIVITIES

1. What is the value of good nutrition in terms of an athlete's performance and injury prevention?
2. Ask coaches of different sports about the type of diet they recommend for their athletes and their rationale for doing so.
3. Have a nutritionist talk to the class about food myths and fallacies.
4. Have each member of the class prepare a week's food diary; then compare it with other class members' diaries.
5. What are the daily dietary requirements of the basic four food groups? Should the requirements of the typical athlete's diet differ from them? If so, in what ways?
6. Have the class debate the value of vitamin and mineral supplements.
7. Describe the advantages and disadvantages of supplementing iron and calcium.
8. Is there some advantage to pre-event nutrition?
9. Are there advantages and/or disadvantages in the vegetarian diet for the athlete?

10. How should the athlete maintain proper weight? Discuss some of the abuses in this area.
11. Why do eating disorders occur among athletes?
12. Contrast the signs and symptoms of bulimia and anorexia nervosa. If a coach or athletic trainer is aware of an athlete who may have an eating disorder, what should he or she do?

REFERENCES

1. Adams, MM, et al.: Effect of a supplement on dietary intakes of female collegiate swimmers, Phys Sportsmed 10:122, July 1982.
2. Aronson, V: Protein and miscellaneous ergogenic aids, Phys Sportsmed 14(5):199, 1986.
3. Aronson, V: Vitamins and minerals as ergogenic aids, Phys Sportsmed 14(3):209, 1986.
4. Brown, RT, et al.: Iron status of adolescent female athletes, J Adolesc Health Care 6:349, Sept 1985.
5. Clark, N: Vitamin C: supplements, strength, psychology, Sports Med Dig 7(7):5, 1985.
6. Coleman, E: Fat loading? Sports Med Dig 8(1):7, 1986.
7. Coleman, E: Fluid replacement drinks, Sports Med Dig 8(7):6 1986.
8. Coleman, E: Iron deficiency in athletes, Sports Med Dig 8(3):5, 1986.
9. Coleman, E: The vegetarian athlete—general principles, Sports Med Dig 8(11):6, 1986.
10. Coleman, E: Protein requirements for athletes, Sports Med Dig 9(1):6, 1987.
11. Eating disorders in young athletes: a round table, Phys Sportsmed 13(11):89, 1985.
12. Guthrie, HA: Introductory nutrition, ed 6, St. Louis, 1986, The CV Mosby Co.
13. Hargreaves, M, et al.: Effect of fructose ingestion on muscle glycogen usage during exercise, Med Sci Sports Exerc 17:360, 1985.
14. Hecker, AL: Nutritional conditioning for athletic competiition. In Hecker, AL, editor: Clinics in sports medicine, Philadelphia, 1984, WB Saunders Co.
15. Katch, FI: Nutrition for the athlete. In Welsh, RP, and Shephard RJ, editors: Current therapy in sport medicine, 1985-1986, Philadelphia, 1985, Brian C Decker, Publisher.
16. Morgan, DW, et al.: HDL-C concentrations in weight-trained, endurance trained, and sedentary females, Phys Sportsmed 14(3):166, 1986.
17. Nelson, RA: Nutrition and physical performance, Phys Sportsmed 10:55, April, 1982.
18. Overdorf, VG: Conditioning for thinness: the dilemma of the eating disordered female athletes, JOHPERD 58:62, 1987.
19. Potera, C: Water-soluble vitamins not safe in megadoses, Phys Sportsmed 14(3):52, 1986.
20. Replacing body fluids is vital during winter, The First Aider, Gardner, Kan, Jan/Feb 1987, Cramer Products, Inc.
21. Rosen, LW, et al.: Pathogenic weight-control behavior in female athletes, Phys Sportsmed 14(1):79, 1986.
22. Shephard, RJ: Fluid and mineral needs. In Welsh, RP, and Shephard, RJ, editors: Current therapy in sports medicine, 1985-1986, Philadelphia, 1985, Brian C Decker, Publisher.
23. Sherman, WM: Carbohydrate, muscle glycogen, and improved performance, Phys Sportsmed 15(2):157, 1987.
24. Slavin, JL: Calorie supplements for athletes, Phys Sportsmed 15(2):157, 1986.
25. Slavin, JL: Eating disorders in athletes, JOHPERD 58(3):33, 1987.
26. Smith, NJ: Vitamins myths and food frauds, The First Aider, Gardner, Kan, 1986, Cramer Products, Inc.
27. Tipton, CM: Commentary: physicians should advise wrestlers about weight loss, Phys Sportsmed 15(1):160, 1987.
28. van der Beek, EJ: Vitamins and endurance training: food for running or faddish claims? Sports Med 2:175, 1985.
29. van der Beek, EJ: Vitamins and food fads of athletes. In Welsh, RP, and Shephard, RJ, editors: Current therapy in sports medicine, 1985-1986, Philadelphia, 1985, Brian C Decker, Publisher.

30. Vitti, GJ: Some nutrition guidelines, Sports Med Dig 8(9):4, 1986.
31. Wetch, PK, et al.: Nutritional education, body composition, and dietary intake of female college athletes, Phys Sportsmed 15(1):63, 1987.
32. Wiche, MK: Quenching the athlete's thirst, Phys Sportsmed 14(9):228, 1986.
33. Williams, SR: Essentials of nutrition and diet therapy, ed 4, St. Louis, 1986, The CV Mosby Co.

ANNOTATED BIBLIOGRAPHY

Guthrie, HA: Introductory nutrition, St. Louis, 1986, The CV Mosby Co.
As a foundation text, one of the most complete and easily understood. It covers all aspects of human nutrition.

Hecker, AL, editor: Symposium on nutritional aspects of exercise, Clinics in sports Medicine, vol 3, Philadelphia, 1984, WB Saunders Co.
Includes 15 chapters covering all aspects of nutrition and other ingesta that are intended to enhance sports competition.

Williams, MH: Nutritional aspects of human physical and athletic performance, ed 2, Springfield, Ill, 1985, Charles C Thomas, Publisher.
Includes up-to-date reviews about a wide range of sports nutrition topics, including nutrition for physical activity, weight control, and substance abuse.

Williams, SR: Essentials of nutrition and diet therapy, ed 4, St. Louis, 1986, The CV Mosby Co.
An excellent overview of the most pertinent aspects of nutrition. It meets the needs of the athletic trainer for a nutrition reference source.

Protective Sports Devices

When you finish this chapter, you should be able to

Identify the major legal ramifications related to manufacturing, buying, and issuing commercial protective equipment

Fit selected protective equipment properly (e.g., football helmets, shoulder pads, running shoes)

Differentiate between good and bad features of selected protective devices

Compare the advantages and disadvantages of customized versus commercial foot and ankle protective devices

Describe the controversies surrounding the use of certain protective devices—are they in fact weapons against opposing players, or do they really work?

Rate the protective value of various materials used in sports to make pads and orthotic devices

List the order of steps in making a customized foam pad with a thermomoldable shell

prophylactic
Refers to prevention, preservation, or protection.

Modifications and improvements in sports equipment are continually being made, especially for sports in which injury is common.[10] In this chapter, both commercial and **prophylactic** techniques are discussed.

COMMERCIAL EQUIPMENT

The proper selection and fit of sports equipment are essential in the prevention of many sports injuries. This is particularly true in direct contact and collision sports such as football, hockey, and lacrosse, but it can also be true in indirect contact sports such as basketball and soccer. Whenever protective sports equipment is selected and purchased, a major decision in the safeguarding of the athletes' health and welfare is being made.

Currently there is serious concern about the standards for protective sports equipment, particularly material durability standards—concerns that include who should set these standards, mass production of equipment, equipment testing methods, and requirements for wearing protective equipment. Some people are concerned that a piece of equipment that is protective to one athlete might in turn be used as a weapon against another athlete.

Standards are also needed for protective equipment maintenance, both to keep it in good repair and to determine when to throw it away. Too often old, worn-out, and ill-fitting equipment is passed down from the varsity players to the younger and often less-experienced players, compounding their risk of injury. Coaches must learn to be less concerned with the color, look, and style of a piece of equipment and more concerned with its ability to prevent injury.

A major step toward the improvement of sports equipment has been achieved through such groups as the American Society for Testing and Materials (ASTM).[1,17] Its Committee on Sports Equipment and Facilities, established in 1969, has been highly active in establishing "standardization of specifications, test methods, and recommended practices for sports equipment and facilities to minimize injury, and promotion of knowledge as it relates to protective equipment standards."[1,17] Engineering, chemistry, biomechanics, anatomy, physiology, physics, computer science, and other related disciplines are applied to solve problems inherent in safety standardization of sports equipment and facilities.

Legal Concerns

As with other aspects of sports participation, there is increasing litigation related to equipment. Manufacturers and purchasers of sports equipment must foresee all possible uses and misuses of the equipment and must warn the user of any potential risks inherent in the use or misuse of that equipment.[41]

To decrease the possibilities of sports injuries and litigation stemming from equipment, the practitioner should do the following:

1. Buy sports equipment from reputable manufacturers.
2. Buy the safest equipment that resources will permit.
3. Make sure that all equipment is assembled correctly. The person who assembles equipment must be competent to do so and must follow the manufacturer's instructions "to the letter."
4. Maintain all equipment properly, according to the manufacturer's guidelines.
5. Use equipment only for the purpose for which it was designed.
6. Warn athletes who use the equipment about all possible risks that using the equipment could entail.
7. Use great caution in the construction or customizing of any piece of equipment.
8. Use no defective equipment. All equipment must routinely be inspected for defects, and all defective equipment must be rendered unusable.

Commercial stock and custom protective devices differ considerably. Stock devices are premade and packaged and are for immediate use. Customized devices are constructed according to the individual characteristics of an athlete. Stock items may have problems with their sizing. In contrast, a custom device can be specifically sized and made to fit the protection and support needs of the individual. Both commercial and customizing devices are discussed in this chapter.

HEAD PROTECTION

Direct collision sports such as football and hockey require special protective equipment, especially for the head. Football provides more frequent opportunities for body contact than does hockey, but hockey players generally move faster and therefore create greater impact forces. Besides direct head contact, hockey has the added injury elements of swinging sticks and fast-moving pucks. Other sports using fast-moving projectiles are baseball, with its pitched ball and swinging bat, and track and field, with the javelin, discus, and heavy shot, which can also

produce serious head injuries. In recent years most helmet research has been conducted for football and ice hockey; however, some research has been performed
on baseball headgear.[13]

Football Helmets

A major influence on football helmet standardization in the United States has
been the research of Hodgson and Thomas[15] and the National Operating Committee on Standards for Athletic Equipment (NOCSAE) for football helmet certification. To be NOCSAE approved, a helmet must be able to tolerate forces applied to many different areas of it. Football helmets typically must withstand
repeated blows and high-mass–low-velocity impacts such as running into a goalpost or hitting the ground with the head.

> Football helmets must withstand repeated blows that are of high mass and low velocity.

Testing new football helmets to ensure their safety does not guarantee that they
will remain safe. A random selection of helmets from a high school football team
showed that 75% of those that were 3 years old failed the NOCSAE test.[16]

Schools must provide the athlete with quality equipment. This especially is true
of the football helmet. All helmets must have a NOCSAE certification. Even
though a helmet is certified does not mean that it is completely "failsafe." Athletes, as well as their parents, must be apprised of the dangers that are inherent
in any sport, particularly football.[4] To make this especially clear, the NOCSAE has
adopted the following recommended warning to be placed on all football helmets:

> Do not use this helmet to butt, ram or spear an opposing player. This is in viola-
> tion of football rules, and can result in severe head, brain, neck injury, paralysis or
> death to you and possible injury to your opponent. There is a risk these injuries may
> also occur as a result of accidental contact without intent to butt, ram or spear. No
> helmet can prevent all such injuries.[23]

Each player's helmet must have a visible exterior warning label ensuring that
players have been made aware of the risks involved in the game of American
football. The label must be attached to each helmet by both the manufacturer and
the reconditioner.[43]

Many types of helmets are in use today. They currently fall into two categories:
(1) padded, and (2) air and fluid (Figure 5-1). There are also helmets that are
combinations of the two types. In general, the helmet should adhere to the following fit standards[42]:

1. The helmet should fit snugly around all parts of the player's head (front,
   sides and crown), and there should be no gaps between the pads and the
   head or face.
2. It should cover the base of the skull. The pads placed at the back of the
   neck should be snug but not to the extent of discomfort.
3. It should not come down over the eyes. It should set (front edge) ¾ inch
   (1.91 cm) above the player's eyebrows.
4. The ear holes should match.
5. It should not shift when manual pressure is applied.
6. It should not recoil on impact.
7. The chin strap should be an equal distance from the center of the helmet.
   Straps must keep the helmet from moving up and down or side to side.
8. The cheek pads should fit snugly against the sides of the face.
9. The face mask should be attached securely to the helmet, allowing a complete field of vision.

Figure 5-1

Football helmets basically fall into two categories, air and fluid filled and padded.

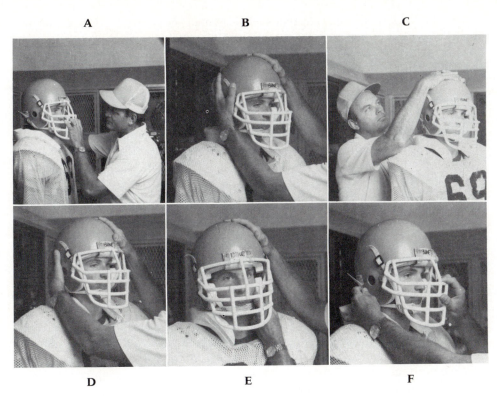

A   B   C

D   E   F

Figure 5-2

Fitting a football helmet. **A,** Pull down on face mask; helmet must not move. **B,** Turn helmet to position on the athlete's head. **C,** Push down on helmet; there must be no movement. **D,** Try to rock helmet back and forth; there must be no movement. **E,** Check for a snug jaw pad fit. **F,** Proper adjustment of the chin strap is necessary to ensure proper helmet fit.

Whichever football helmet is used, it must be routinely checked for proper fit, especially in the first few days that it is worn. A check for snugness should be made by inserting a tongue depressor between the head and the liner. Fit is proper when the tongue depressor is resisted firmly when moved back and forth. If air bladder helmets are used by a team that travels to a different altitude and air pressure, the helmet fit must be routinely rechecked.

Chin straps are also important in maintaining the proper head and helmet relationship. Two basic types of chin straps are in use today—a two-snap and a four-snap strap. Many coaches prefer the four-snap chin strap because it keeps the helmet from tilting forward and backward. The chin strap should always be locked so it cannot be released by a hard external force to the helmet (Figure 5-2).

Jaw pads are also essential to keep the helmet from rocking laterally. They should fit snugly against the player's cheek bones. Even if a helmets' ability to withstand the forces of the game is certified, it is of no avail if the helmet is not properly fitted or maintained.

Even high-quality helmets are of no use if not properly fitted or maintained.

Ice Hockey Helmets

As with football helmets, there has been a concerted effort to upgrade and standardize ice hockey helmets.[2] In contrast to football, blows to the head in ice hockey are usually singular rather than multiple. An ice hockey helmet must withstand both high-velocity impacts (e.g., being hit with a stick or a puck, which produces low mass and high velocity), as well as the high-mass–low velocity forces produced by running into the sideboard or falling on the ice. In each in-

Ice hockey helmets must withstand the high-velocity impact of a stick or puck and the low-velocity forces from falling or hitting a sideboard.

Figure 5-3

There is some question about how well baseball batting helmets protect against high-velocity impacts.

stance, the hockey helmet, like the football helmet, must be able to spread the impact over a large surface area through a firm exterior shell and, at the same time, be able to decelerate forces that act on the head through a proper energy-absorbing liner.[2]

Baseball Batting Helmets

Like ice hockey helmets, the baseball batting helmet must withstand high-velocity impacts. Unlike football and ice hockey, baseball has not produced a great deal of data on batting helmets.[13] It has been suggested, however, that baseball helmets do little to adequately dissipate the energy of the ball during impact (Figure 5-3). A possible answer is to add external padding or to improve the helmet's suspension.[13] Apparently the current use of helmets with an ear flap can afford some additional protection to the batter.

FACE PROTECTION

Devices that provide face protection fall into four categories: full face guards, mouth guards, ear guards, and eye protection devices.

Face Guards

Face guards are used in a variety of sports to protect against flying or carried objects during a collision with another player (Figure 5-4). Since the adoption of face guards and mouth guards for use in football, mouth injuries have been reduced more than 50% (Figure 5-5), but the incidence of neck injuries has increased significantly. The catcher in baseball, the goalie in hockey, and the la-

Figure 5-4

Sports such as fencing require complete face protection.

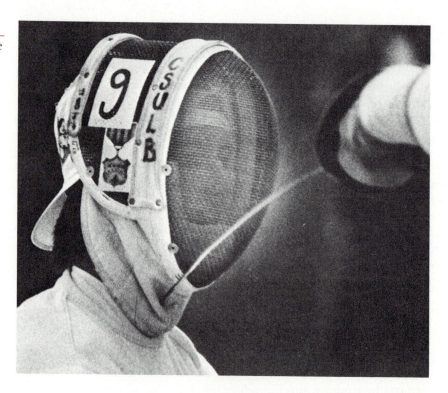

Figure 5-5

A variety of face guards are used in football.

Figure 5-6

Baseball catcher's mask.

crosse player should all be adequately protected against facial injuries, particularly lacerations and fractures (Figure 5-6).

A great variety of face masks and bars is available to the player, depending on the position played and the protection needed. In football no face protection should have less than two bars. Proper mounting of the face mask and bars is imperative for maximum safety. All mountings should be made in such a way that the bar attachments are flush with the helmet. A 3 inch (7.62 cm) space should exist between the top of the face guard and the lower edge of the helmet. No helmet should be drilled more than one time on each side. There should be a space of 1 to 1½ inches (3.81 cm) between the player's nose and the face guard. As with the helmet shell, pads, and chin strap, the face guard must be checked daily for defects.

In sports, the face may be protected by
    Face guards
    Mouth guards
    Ear guards
    Eye-protection devices

Mouth Guards

The majority of dental traumas can be prevented if the athlete wears a correctly fitted intraoral mouth guard, as compared to an extraoral type (Figure 5-7). In addition to protecting the teeth, the intraoral mouth guard absorbs the shock of chin blows and helps to prevent a possible cerebral concussion.[44] The mouth pro-

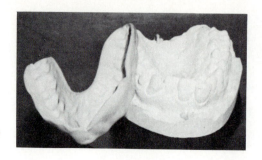

Figure 5-7

Customized mouth protector.

tector should give the athlete proper and tight fit, comfort, unrestricted breathing, and unimpeded speech during competition. A loose mouthpiece will soon be ejected onto the ground or left unused in the locker room. The athlete's air passages should not be obstructed in any way by the mouthpiece. It is best when the mouthpiece is retained on the upper jaw and projects backward only as far as the last molar, thus permitting speech. Maximum protection is afforded when the mouth guard is composed of a flexible, resilient material and is form fitted to the teeth and upper jaw.[7]

Three types of mouth guards are generally used in American football: ready-made, a commercial mouth guard formed after submersion in boiling water, and the custom-fabricated type, which is formed over a model made from an impression of the athlete's maxillary arch.[19] Many high schools and colleges now require that mouth guards be worn at all times during participation. For example, the National Collegiate Athletic Association (NCAA) mandates that all players wear a properly manufactured mouth guard. A time-out is charged a team if a player fails to wear the mouth guard.[19] To assist enforcement, official mouth guards are increasingly made in the most visible color possible—yellow.[44]

Ear Guards

With the exception of boxing and wrestling, most contact sports do not make a special practice of protecting the ears. Both boxing and wrestling can cause irritation of the ears to the point that permanent deformity can ensue. To avoid this problem special ear guards should be routinely worn. Recently a very effective ear protection has been developed for the water polo player (Figure 5-8).

Eye Protection Devices

The athlete who wears glasses must be protected during sports activities. Glasses broken during the heat of competitive battle can pose considerable danger. The eyes of the athlete can be protected by glass guards, case-hardened lenses, plastic lenses, or contact lenses.

Eye protection must be worn by all athletes who play sports that use fast-moving projectiles.

Spectacles

For the athlete who must wear corrective lenses, spectacles can be both a blessing and a nuisance. They may slip on sweat, get bent when hit, fog from perspiration, detract from peripheral vision, or be difficult to wear with protective headgear. Even with all these disadvantages, properly fitted and designed spectacles can provide adequate protection and withstand the rigors of the sport. If the athlete has glass lenses, they must be case-hardened to prevent them from splintering on impact. When a case-hardened lens breaks, it crumbles, eliminating the sharp

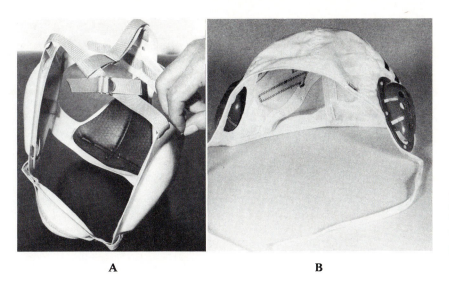

A   B

Figure 5-8

Ear protection. **A,** The wrestler's ear guard. **B,** Water polo player's ear protection.

edges that may penetrate the eye. The cost of this process is relatively low. The only disadvantages involved are that the weight of the glasses is heavier than average, and they may be scratched more easily than regular glasses.

Another possible sports advantage of glass-lensed spectacles is a process through which the lenses can become color tinted when exposed to ultraviolet rays from the sun and then return to a clear state when removed from the sun's rays. They are known as *photochromic lenses.*

Plastic lenses for spectacles are becoming increasingly popular with athletes. They are much lighter in weight than glass lenses; however, they are much more prone to scratching.

Contact Lenses

In many ways the athlete who is able to wear contact lenses without discomfort can avoid many of the inconveniences of spectacles. Their greatest advantage is probably the fact that they "become a part of the eye" and move with it.

Contact lenses come mainly in two types: the corneal type, which covers just the iris of the eye, and the scleral type, which covers the entire front of the eye, including the white, or scleral, portion. Peripheral vision, as well as astigmatism and corneal waviness, is improved through the use of contact lenses. Unlike regular glasses, contact lenses do not normally cloud during temperature changes. They also can be tinted to reduce glare. For example, yellow lenses can be used against ice glare and blue ones against glare from snow. One of the main difficulties with contact lenses is their high cost compared to regular glasses. Some other serious disadvantages of wearing contact lenses are the possibility of corneal irritation caused by dust getting under the lens and the possibility of a lens becoming dislodged during body contact. In addition, only certain individuals are able to wear contacts with comfort, and some individuals are unable to ever wear them because of certain eye idiosyncrasies. There is currently a trend toward athletes' preferring the soft, hydrophilic lenses to the hard type. Adjustment time for the soft lenses is shorter than for the hard, they can be more easily replaced, and they are more adaptable to the sports environment.

Figure 5-9

Athletes playing sports that involve small, fast projectiles should wear the closed type of eye guards.

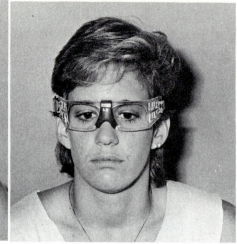

Figure 5-10

Standard football protective pads. This system uses open cell foam and air management to disperse a direct impact over the entire surface area of the pad, minimizing the blow to the athlete.

Eye and Glass Guards

It is essential that athletes take special precautions to protect their eyes, especially in those sports that use fast-moving projectiles and implements (Figure 5-9). Besides the more obvious sports of ice hockey, lacrosse, and baseball, the racquet sports also cause serious eye injury. Athletes not wearing spectacles should wear closed eye guards to protect the orbital cavity.[3] Athletes who normally wear spectacles with plastic or case-hardened lenses are to some degree already protected against eye injury from an implement or projectile; however, greater safety is afforded by the metal-rimmed frame that surrounds and fits over the athlete's glasses. The protection the guard affords is excellent, but it does hinder vision in some planes.

TRUNK AND THORAX PROTECTION

Trunk and thorax protection is essential in many contact and collision sports. Areas that are most exposed to impact forces must be properly covered with some material that offers protection against soft-tissue compression. Of particular concern are the exposed bony protuberances of the body that have insufficient soft tissue for protection such as shoulders, ribs, and spine, as well as external genitalia (Figures 5-10 and 5-11).

As discussed earlier, the problem that arises in the wearing of protective equipment is that, although it is armor against injury to the athlete wearing it, it can also serve as a weapon against all opponents. Standards must become more stringent in determining what equipment is absolutely necessary for body protection and at the same time is not itself a source of trauma.

Shoulder

Manufacturers of shoulder pads have made great strides toward protecting the football player against direct force to the shoulder muscle complex. There are two general types of pads: flat and cantilevered. The player who uses the shoulder a great deal in blocking and tackling requires the bulkier cantilevered type as compared to the quarterback or ball receiver who use the flat type. Over the years the

Figure 5-11

The ice hockey goalie's equipment represents the ultimate in body protection.

shoulder pad's front and rear panels have been extended along with the cantilever. The following are rules for fitting the football shoulder pad:

1. The tip of the inside shoulder pad should come in a direct line with the lateral aspect of the shoulder and the flap covering the deltoid muscle.
2. The neck opening must allow the athlete to extend the arm overhead without placing pressure on the neck but must not allow sliding back and forth.
3. Straps underneath the arm must hold the pads firmly but not so they constrict soft tissue.

Shoulder Restraint Braces

The shoulder braces (Figure 5-12) used in sports are essentially restraining devices for the chronically dislocated shoulder. Their purpose is to restrict the upper arm from being abducted more than 90 degrees and externally rotated, thus preventing it from being placed in a vulnerable position. Because of the ensuing limitation in range of motion of the arm, the athlete's capabilities are considerably reduced.

Breast Support

Until recently the primary concern for female breast protection had been against external forces that could cause bruising. With the vast increase in the number of physically active women, concern has been redirected to protecting the breasts against movement that stems from running and jumping. This is a particular problem for women with very heavy breasts. Many girls and women in the past may have avoided vigorous physical activity because of the discomfort felt from the uncontrolled movement of their breasts. Manufacturers are making a concerted effort to develop specialized brassieres for women who participate in all types of physical activity.

Figure 5-12

Shoulder restraint brace.

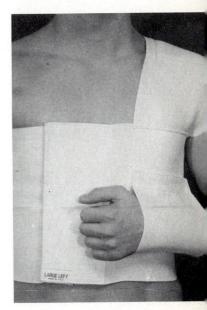

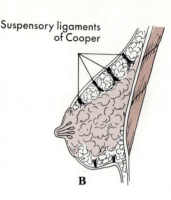

Figure 5-13

A, A sports bra must hold the breasts to the chest to avoid excessive motion. **B,** Cooper's ligament.

A brassiere should hold the breasts to the chest and prevent stretching of the Cooper's ligament, which causes premature sagging (Figure 5-13).[11]

Thorax

Manufacturers such as Bike Company and Casco provide similar equipment for thorax protection. Many of the thorax protectors and rib belts can be modified, replacing stock pads with customized thermomoldable plastic protective devices. A relatively recent item developed by a football player is the mesh body suit that has protective pads sewn into various areas (Figure 5-14). It is marketed as the Bennett 34 Body Gard. Recently many lightweight pads have been developed to protect the athlete against external forces. A jacket developed by Byron Donzis for the protection of a rib injury incorporates a pad composed of air-inflated, interconnected cylinders that protect against severe external forces.[6] This same principle has been used in the development of other protective pads (Figure 5-15).

Hips and Buttocks

Pads in the region of the hips and buttocks are often needed in collision and/or high-velocity sports such as hockey and football. Other athletes needing protection in this region are amateur boxers, snow skiers, equestrians, jockeys, and water skiers.[36] Two popular commercial pads are the girdle and belt types (Figure 5-16).

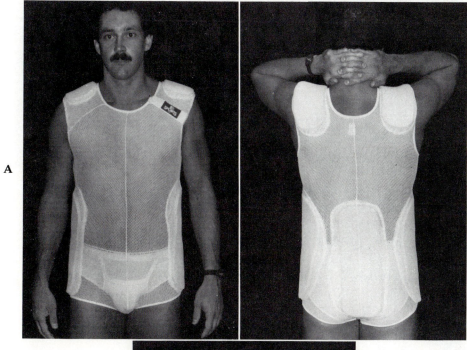

Figure 5-14

Bennett 34 Body Gard. **A,** front; **B,** Donzis flak jacket. **C,** side.

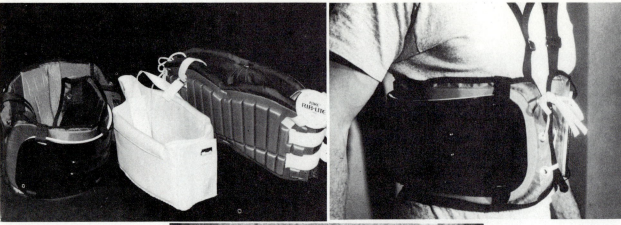

Figure 5-15

A, Donzis, Cosco, and Bike rib protectors. **B,** Donzis flak jacket. **C,** Cosco rib belt worn with insert molded to body.

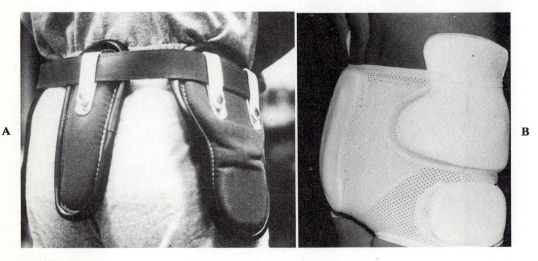

Figure 5-16

Girdle-style hip and coccygeal pad. **A,** Back. **B,** Side.

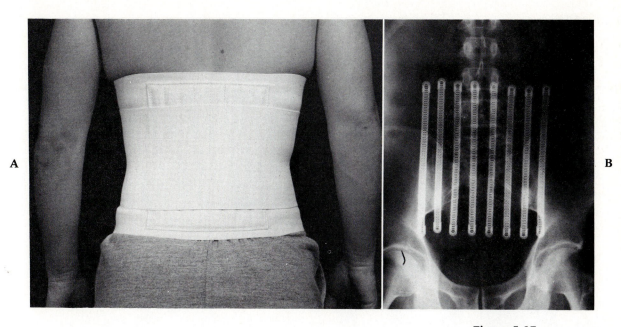

Figure 5-17

A, Lumbosacral corset. **B,** X-ray film showing corset stays.

Groin and Genitalia

Sports (e.g., hockey, lacrosse, and baseball) involving high-velocity projectiles require cup protection for male participants. It comes as a stock item that fits into place in a jockstrap, or athletic supporter.[36]

Abdominal and Low Back Supports

Because low back strain is a national problem, there are many gimmicks on the market that claim to give relief. Such devices may be classified as abdominal and low back supports. When freedom of activity is desired in sports, a rigid and nonyielding material may be handicapping. A material that permits movement and yet offers support is desirable. It may consist of an elastic fabric. In most cases of low back strain, supporting the abdominal viscera will alleviate considerable discomfort (Figure 5-17).

LIMB PROTECTION

Limbs, as with other areas of the body, can be exposed a great deal to sports injuries and can require protection or, where there is weakness, support. Compression and mild soft-tissue support can be provided by neoprene sleeves, and hard bony areas of the body can be protected by commercial pads (Figure 5-18). In contrast, the athlete with a history of injury that needs special protection and support may require a commercial brace.

Footwear

Footwear can mean the difference between success, failure, or injury in competition. It is essential that the coach, athletic trainer, and equipment personnel make every effort to fit their athletes with proper shoes and socks.

Figure 5-18

Types of Neoprene sleeves.

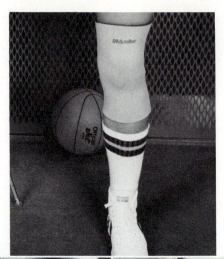

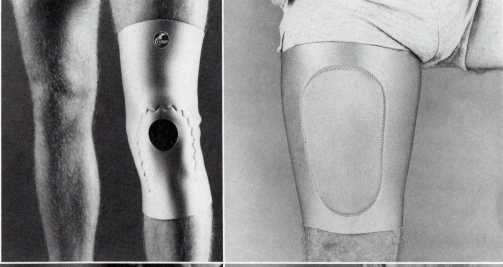

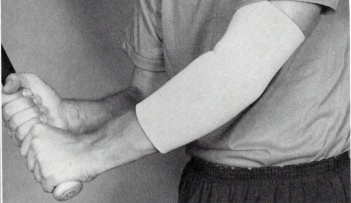

Figure 5-19

The tubular doubleknit sock can prevent friction in the shoe.

Socks

Poorly fitted socks can cause abnormal stresses on the foot. For example, socks that are too short crowd the toes, especially the fourth and fifth ones. Socks that are too long can also cause skin irritation because of wrinkles. All athletic socks should be clean, dry, and without holes to avoid irritations. Manufacturers are now providing a double-knit tubular sock without heels that decreases friction considerably within the shoe (Figure 5-19). The tubular sock without heels is especially good for the basketball player. The composition of the sock's material also should be noted. Cotton socks can be too bulky, whereas a combination of materials such as cotton and polyester is less bulky and dries faster.

Shoes

Even more damaging than improperly fitted socks are improperly fitted shoes. Chronic abnormal pressures to the foot can often cause permanent structural deformities, as well as potentially dangerous calluses and blisters. Besides these local problems, improperly fitted shoes result in mechanical disturbances that affect the body's total postural balance and may eventually lead to pathological conditions of the muscles and joints.

Shoe composition   The bare human foot is designed to function on uneven surfaces. Shoes were created to protect against harmful surfaces, but they should never interfere with natural functioning. Sports shoes, like all shoes, are constructed of different parts, each of which is designed to provide function, protection, and durability. Each sport places unique stresses and performance demands on the foot. In general, all sport shoes, like street shoes, are made of similar parts—a sole, uppers, heel counter, and toe box. The sole or bottom of a shoe is divided into an outer, middle, and inner section, each of which must be sturdy, flexible, and provide a degree of cushioning, depending on the specific sport requirements. A heel counter should support and cushion the heel, whereas the toe box protects and provides an area so that the toes do not become crowded. The uppers must give the foot support and freedom to withstand a high degree of stress (Figure 5-20).

Shoe fitting   Fitting sports footgear is always difficult, mainly because the individual's left foot varies in size and shape from the right foot. Therefore, measuring both feet is imperative. To fit the sports shoe properly, the athlete should approximate the conditions under which he or she will perform, such as wearing athletic socks, jumping up and down, or running. It is also desirable to fit the athlete's shoes at the end of the day to accommodate the gradual increase in size

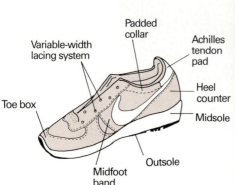

Toe box • Variable-width lacing system • Padded collar • Achilles tendon pad • Heel counter • Midsole • Outsole • Midfoot band

Figure 5-20

Properly fitted and constructed shoes can prevent foot injuries.

that occurs from the time of awakening. The athlete must carefully consider this shoe choice because he or she will be spending countless hours in those shoes (see box below for suggestions concerning shoe fitting).

During performance conditions the new shoe should feel snug but not too tight.[26] The sports shoe should be long enough that all toes can be fully extended without being cramped. Its width should permit full movement of the toes, including flexion, extension, and some spreading. A good point to remember is that the wide part of the shoe should match the wide part of the foot to allow the shoe to crease evenly when the athlete is on the balls of the feet. The shoe should bend (or "break") at its widest part; when the break of the shoe and the ball joint coincide, the fit is correct. However, if the break of the shoe is in back or in front of the normal bend of the foot (metatarsophalangeal joint), the shoe and the foot will be opposing one another, causing abnormal skin and structural stresses to occur. Two measurements must be considered when fitting shoes: (1) the distance from the heel to the metatarsophalangeal joint, and (2) the distance from the heel to the end of the longest toe. An individual's feet may be equal in length from the heels to the balls of the feet but different between heels and toes.

RUNNING SHOE DESIGN AND CONSTRUCTION

To avoid injury, the running shoe should[31]
1. Have a strong heel counter that fits well around the foot and locks the shoe around the foot
2. Always have good flexibility in the forefoot where toes bend
3. Preferably have a fairly high heel for the athlete with a tight Achilles tendon
4. Have a midsole that is moderately soft but does not flatten easily
5. Have a heel counter that is high enough to surround the foot but still allows room for an orthotic insert, if needed
6. Have a counter that is attached to the sole to avoid the possibility of its coming loose from attachment
7. Always be of quality construction

Figure 5-21

Variations in cleated shoes—the longer the cleat, the higher the incidence of injury.

Shoes, therefore, should be selected for the longer of the two measurements. Other factors to consider when buying the sports shoe are the stiffness of the sole and the width of the shank, or narrowest part of the sole. A shoe with a too rigid, nonyielding sole places a great deal of extra strain on the foot tendons. A shoe with too narrow a shank also places extra strain because it fails to adequately support the athlete's inner, longitudinal arches. Two other shoe features to consider are innersoles to reduce friction and built-in arch supports.

The cleated or specially soled sports shoe presents some additional problems in fitting. For example, American football uses the multi-short–cleated polyurethane sole and the five-in-front and two-in-back cleat arrangement with the soccer-type sole, both of which have cleats no longer than 0.5 inches (1.27 cm) (Figure 5-21). Special soled shoes are also worn when playing on a synthetic surface. If cleated shoes are used, no matter which sport, the cleats must be properly positioned under the two major weight-bearing joints and must not be felt through the soles of the shoes.

Commercial Foot Pads

Commercial foot pads are intended for use by the general public and are not usually designed to withstand the rigors of sports activities. Those commercial pads that are suited for sports are generally not durable enough for hard, extended use. If money is no object, the ready-made commercial pad has the advantage of saving time. Commercial pads are manufactured for almost every type of common structural foot condition, ranging from corns and bunions to fallen arches and pronated feet.[29] In general, excessive foot pronation often eventually leads to overuse injuries. Available to the athlete commercially are preorthotic and arch supports (Figure 5-22). Scholl 610.2, Spenco arch supports, Shea devices, and Foothotics "Ready to Dispense" orthotics are commonly used before more formal customized orthotic devices are made (see p. 161). They offer a compromise to the custom-made foot orthotics, providing some biomechanical control.[36] Indiscriminate use of these aids, however, may intensify the pathological condition or cause the athlete to delay seeing the team physician or team podiatrist for evaluation.

Figure 5-22

Ready-to-dispense orthotic device.

Figure 5-23

Heel cups and pads, including lifts of orthopedic felt.

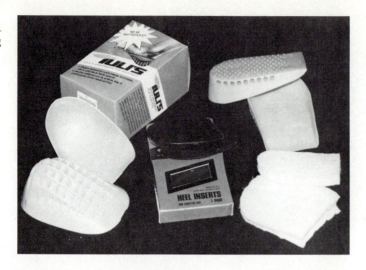

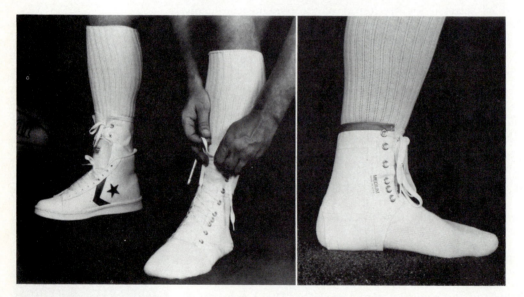

Figure 5-24

The spat-type commercial ankle support may give mild support to an uninjured ankle.

For the most part, foot devices are fabricated and customized from a variety of materials such as foam, felt, plaster, aluminum, and spring steel (see "Customizing Protective and Supportive Devices"). One item that historically began as a prefabricated device but now is commercial, is the heel cup, designed to reduce tissue shearing and shock (Figure 5-23).

Commercial Ankle Supports

Most commercial ankle supports are either a *elastic* or a *spat* type (Figure 5-24). The elastic type is a flexible, fibered sheath that slides over the foot and the ankle, purportedly giving mild support to a weak ankle. It has little use either as a strong support or as a protection to the postacute or chronically weakened ankle in

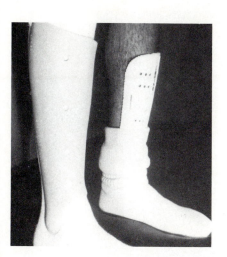

A
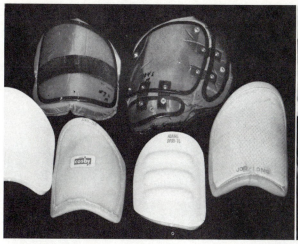
B
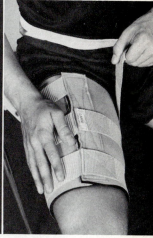

sports. The spat type is usually less resilient than the elastic type and has an open front that permits it to fit directly over the ankle and then tie snugly like a shoe. Some spats have vertical ribs to effect added inversion or eversion. Although providing some assistance, no commercial ankle support affords as much protection as does adhesive tape properly applied directly to the skin surface. Prophylatic ankle taping is superior to lace-on braces for the first 20 minutes of inversion activity. After 20 minutes, they are equal in their ability to support the ankle.[5] A fabricated orthoplast strip brace cut 3 or 4 inches (7.62 or 10.16 cm) wide is an effective semirigid support for sprained ankles.

Shin and Lower Leg

The shin is an area of the body that is commonly neglected in contact and collision type sports. Commerically marketed hard-shelled, molded shin guards are used in field hockey and soccer (Figure 5-25).

Thigh and Upper Leg

Thigh and upper leg protection is necessary in collision type sports such as hockey and football. Generally, pads slip into ready-made pockets in the sports suit or uniform (Figure 5-26). To avoid abnormal slipping within the pocket or to protect from injury, customized pads are constructed.

Knee Supports and Protective Devices

Knees are next in order to ankles and feet in terms of incidence of sports injury. As a result of the variety and rather high frequency of knee afflictions, many protective and supportive devices have been devised. The devices most frequently used in sports today are sleeves, pads, and braces.

Elastic knee pads or guards are extremely valuable in sports in which the athlete falls or receives a direct blow to the anterior aspect of the knee (Figure 5-27). An elastic sleeve containing a resilient pad may help to dissipate an anterior striking force but fails to protect the knee against lateral, medial, or twisting forces.

Figure 5-25 (Left)

Full shin guard.

Figure 5-26 (Right)

A, Protective pads.
B, Commercial supportive thigh braces.

Figure 5-27

Bike knee pad.

Figure 5-28

Medical collateral ligament brace.

Figure 5-29

A preventive knee brace designed to protect against a lateral force and to distribute load away from joint.

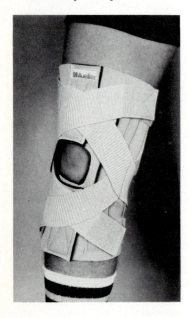

Knee Braces

There are a number of different knee braces on the market. Some consist of vertical rigid strips held in an elastic sleeve or an elastic sleeve containing rigid hinges to be placed on either side of the knee joint. These braces are extremely questionable as to their ability to act as a protection against initial or recurrent injury. Braces of the wrap-around type with rigid strips contained in less elastic material hold the knee more firmly in place (Figure 5-28).

The prophylactic knee brace   Currently, prophylactic knee bracing has become increasingly popular in high school, college, and professional football. The braces are usually used by players who are at greatest risk—offensive and defensive linemen, linebackers, and tight ends.[14] The braces vary, depending on the manufacturer, but commonly consist of a single-sided strut made of metal or heavy plastic, having a dual axis with a dual hinge. To date, anecdotal reports are divided, with some indicating a decrease in knee injuries and others reporting no difference or an increase in injuries.[20,38] More specifically, studies indicate that the effectiveness of prophylatic knee braces is highly controversial (Figure 5-29).[14,34] More studies need to be conducted concerning the relative strength of braces, whether they prestress the knee joint and produce injuries, whether in fact they actually can reduce injuries, and whether performance is adversely affected in any way.[20,39] Braces that are constructed based on surrogated limb testing apparently have a higher level of credibility in acting as a prophylactic knee device.[32]

The fitted knee brace   Following serious knee joint injury that produces chronic instability or necessitates surgery, a customized orthopedic knee brace may be prescribed for the athlete. The Lenox Hill and Pro Am braces are examples of braces that help stabilize the joint with rotary problems (see Figures 19-27 and 19-28).[21]

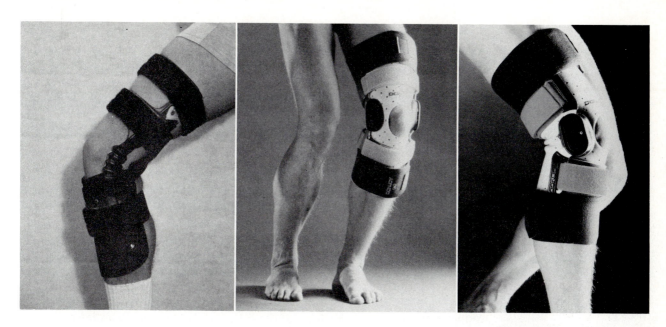

Figure 5-30

Postinjury knee braces.

Other popular knee devices are sleeves composed of elastic or neoprene material. Sleeves of this type provide mild soft-tissue support and, to some extent, retain body heat and help to reduce edema caused by tissue compression (Figure 5-30).

Hand, Wrist, and Elbow Protection

As with the lower limbs, the upper limbs require initial protection from injury, as well as prevention of further injury following a trauma. One of the finest physical instruments, the human hand, is perhaps one of the most neglected in terms of injury, especially in sports. Special attention must be paid to protecting the integrity of all aspects of the hand when encountering high-speed projectiles or receiving external forces that contuse or shear. Constant stress to the hand, as characterized by the force received by the hand of the baseball catcher, can lead to irreversible pathological damage in later life (Figure 5-31). The wrist and the el-

Figure 5-31

The hand is an often neglected area of the body in sports.

Figure 5-32

Commercial pads and braces.

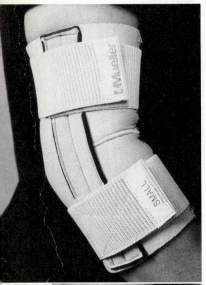

bow are also vulnerable to sports trauma and often need compression and/or support for protection (Figure 5-32).

CUSTOMIZING PROTECTIVE AND SUPPORTIVE DEVICES

A major requirement in athletic training and sports medicine is the construction of a variety of protective and supportive devices from many different materials. Three areas to be discussed are taping in sports, padding and bracing, and foot orthotics.

Prophylactic Taping in Sports

The use of adhesive substances in care of the external lesions goes back to ancient times. The Greek civilization is credited with formulating a healing paste composed of lead oxide, olive oil, and water, which was used for a wide variety of skin conditions. This composition was only recently changed by the addition of resin and yellow beeswax and, even more recently, rubber. Since its inception, adhesive tape has developed into a vital therapeutic adjunct.[30]

Two types of tape are generally used in sports medicine—linen and elastic. Linen, the most commonly used, is only slightly yielding, if at all. Elastic tape, in comparison, is made to stretch. Where linen tape rigidly holds a dressing, bandage, or body part in place, elastic tape compresses and moves as the body moves. One possible reason for more extensive use of linen tape is its lower cost. Also, waterproof, hypoallergenic, plastic-backed tape is available for wound dressing, and moleskin with a felt backing is available for support and cushioning.[40]

Adhesive Tape and Injury Prophylaxis

Adhesive tape as a prophylaxis has routinely been applied to ankles for many years; however, recently there has been controversy as to the real benefits, if any, ankle taping provides.

Tape as an Adjunct to Conditioning and Rehabilitation

Ankle taping to prevent injury should only be used as an adjunct to proper and extensive exercise. Tape should never be applied indiscriminantly, but only under highly controlled conditions.[18] The primary muscles of concern are the plantar muscles of the foot, the peroneal group, and the gastrocnemius-soleus complex. Special attention should be paid to stretching the heel cord. Heel cord tightness may be a major cause of lateral ankle sprain. When the heel cord is tight and the ankle is forced into dorsiflexion, the subtalar joint is placed into a supinated position, causing an increased stress on the ankle's lateral capsule.[28]

Athletes with normal or near-normal ankles should rely more on strengthening exercises than on artificial aids. When prophylaxis is needed in a high-risk sport, wraps may be preferable to rigid taping. Ankle taping should not become routine unless an honest effort at reconditioning has failed to adequately restore function to the ankle. An improperly applied wrap or taping can compound an injury and may even create postural imbalances that could adversely affect other parts of the body.[30] See boxes on p. 161 for arguments for and against routine ankle taping. **NOTE:** Proper tape application is discussed in Chapter 12, *Wound Dressing, Taping, and Bandaging,* and selected techniques are presented in chapters found in Part V.

ARGUMENTS FOR ROUTINE ANKLE TAPING

1. Wrapping or taping the ankles does not significantly hinder motor performance.[27]
2. Properly applied wraps and tapings, even though they loosen during activity, provide critical support at the limits of ankle movement.[36]
3. Because wraps and tapings do loosen in the initial period of activity, the midrange of ankle movement is allowed, thus moving adverse stress from the knee joint.[37]
4. High-risk sports such as football, basketball, and soccer should use ankle prophylaxis.[12]
5. Athletes having a history of recent ankle injury or chronically weak ankles should be given every possible protection against further insult.[24]
6. Statistics show that athletes who wear tape as an ankle prophylaxis have fewer injuries.[12]
7. Pressure of tape on the peroneus brevis muscle stimulates its action.[12]

ARGUMENTS AGAINST ROUTINE ANKLE TAPING

1. Tape is applied over movable skin.[9]
2. Moisture collects under tape, increasing its looseness.[9]
3. Constant taping for activity weakens supporting muscle tendons.[9]
4. Tape support is reduced 40% after 10 minutes of vigorous activity.[35]
5. Ankle wraps loosen 34% to 77% during exercise.[35]
6. Taping often replaces the practice of thoroughly exercising the ankle joint.[9]
7. The tradition of taping is based on folklore rather than on facts.[22]
8. Taping gives the athlete false security and soon becomes a psychological crutch.[9,22]
9. Because taping does not significantly reduce ankle torque, it does not decrease the athlete's potential for lower leg injury.[8]
10. There is indication that tape over a muscle facilitates its stabilization action through the stimulation of the skin receptors.[25]

Custom Pad and Orthotic Materials

There are many different materials available to the athletic trainer desiring to protect or support an injured area. In general, they can be divided into soft and hard materials (Figure 5-33).

Soft Materials

The major soft-material mediums found in training rooms are lamb's wool, cotton, gauze pads, adhesive felt or adhesive foam rubber felt, and an assortment of foam rubber in bulk.

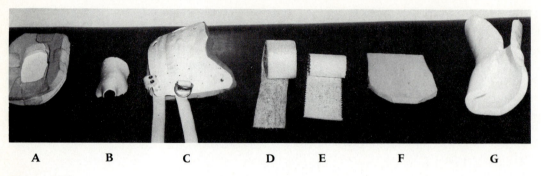

A   B   C   D   E   F   G

Figure 5-33

Types of sports orthoses.
A, Orthoplast with a foam
rubber doughnut;
B, Orthoplast splint;
C, Orthoplast rib protector
with a foam rubber pad;
D, fiberglass material for
splint construction; **E,** plaster
of paris material for cast
construction; **F,** foam rubber
pad; **G,** Aloplast foam
moldable material for
protective pad construction.

Lamb's wool is a material commonly used on and around the athlete's toes when circular protection is required. In contrast to cotton, lamb's wool does not pack but keeps its resiliency over a long period of time.

Gauze padding is less versatile than other pad materials. It is assembled in varying thicknesses and can be used as an absorbent or protective pad.

Cotton is probably the cheapest and most widely used material in sports. It has the ability to absorb, to hold emollients, and to offer a mild padding effect.

Adhesive felt (moleskin) or *sponge rubber* material contains an adhesive mass on one side, thus combining a cushioning effect with the ability to be held in a specific spot by the adhesive mass. It is a versatile material that is useful on all body parts.

Felt is a material composed of matted wool fibers pressed into varying thicknesses that range from ¼ to 1 inch (0.6 to 2.5 cm). Its benefit lies in its comfortable, semiresilient surface, which gives a firmer pressure than most sponge rubbers. Because felt will absorb perspiration, it clings to the skin, and it has less tendency to move than sponge rubber (Figure 5-34). Because of its absorbent qualities, it must be replaced daily. Currently, it is used as support and protection for some foot conditions.

Figure 5-34

Orthopedic felt, both 1/2- and
1/4-inch wide, with broad-
blade knife and large scissors
for contouring.

Foams are currently the major materials used for providing injury protection in sports. They come in many different thicknesses and densities (Figure 5-35). They are usually resilient, nonabsorbent, and able to protect the body against compressive forces. Some foams are open celled, whereas others are closed. The closed-cell type is preferable in sports because it rebounds and returns to its original shape quickly. Foams can be "easily worked," through cutting, shaping, and faceting.[36] Some foams are *thermomoldable* and, when heated, become highly pliant and easy to shape. When cooled, they retain the shape in which they were formed. A new class of foams are composed of viscoelastic polymers, of which Sorbothane is an example.[36] This foam has a very high energy-absorbing quality, but it also has a high density, making it heavy (Figure 5-36). Used in innersoles in sports shoes, it helps prevent blisters and also effectively absorbs vertical, front-to-back, and rotary shock caused by the foot. Foams generally range from ⅛ to ½ inch (0.3 to 1.25 cm) in thickness.

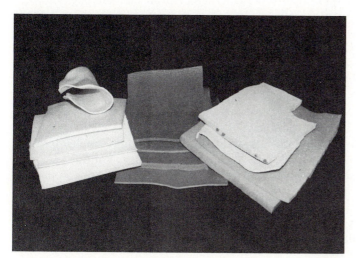

Figure 5-35

Foam assortment: thermomoldable *(left)*, closed celled *(center)*, and open celled *(right)*.

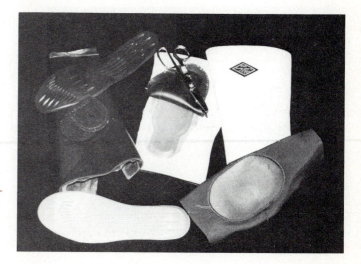

Figure 5-36

Sorbothane products, including sheet stock and insoles *(left)* and knee pads *(right)*.

Nonyielding Materials

A number of hard, nonyielding materials are used in athletic training for making protective shells and splints.

Thermomoldable plastics A number of plastic materials are becoming widely used in sports medicine for customized orthotics. They can brace, splint, and shield a body area. They can provide casting for a fracture, support for a foot defect, or a firm, nonyielding surface to protect a severe contusion.

Plastics used for these purposes differ in their chemical composition and reaction to heat. The three major categories are heatforming plastics, heatsetting plastics, and heatplastic foams.[33]

Heatforming plastics are of the low-temperature variety and are the most popular in athletic training. When heated to 140° to 180° F (60° to 82.2° C), depending on the material, the plastic can be accurately molded to a body part. Aquaplast (polyester sheets) and Orthoplast (synthetic rubber thermoplast) are popular types.

Heatsetting plastics require relatively higher temperatures for shaping. They are rigid and difficult to form, usually requiring a mold rather than being formed directly to the body part.[33] High-impact vinyl (polyvinyl chloride), Kydex (polyvinyl chloride acrylic), and Nyloplex (heatplastic acrylic) are examples of the more commonly used thermoforming plastics.

Heatplastic foams are plastics that have differences in density as a result of the addition of liquids, gas, or crystals. They are commonly used as shoe inserts and other body padding. Aloplast (polyethylene foam) and Plastazate (polyethylene foam) are two commonly used products.[33]

Usually the plastic is heated until soft and maleable. It is then molded into the desired shape and allowed to cool, thereby retaining its shape. Various pads and other materials can also be fastened in place. There may be limitations in the use of rigid thermomoldable plastics based on rules and regulations of various sport activities.

Casting materials Applying casts to injured body areas has long been a practice in sports medicine. The material or choice is fiberglass, using resin and a

Figure 5-37 (Left)

Casting material: fiberglass *(left)* and plaster *(right)*, including cast saw used to trim pictured skin guard.

Figure 5-38 (Right)

Glues and adhesive tapes.

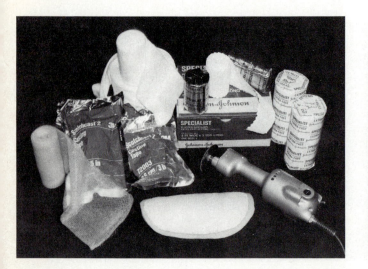

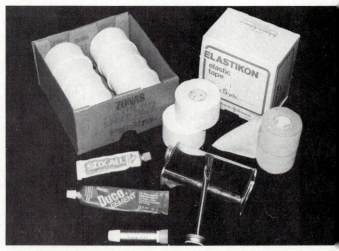

catalytic converter, plus water, to produce hardening. Besides casts, this material makes very effective shells for splints and protective pads. Once hardened, the fiberglass is trimmed to shape with a cast saw (Figure 5-37).

Tools Used for Customizing

Working with the various materials used to customize protective equipment requires the use of many different tools.[36] They include adhesives, adhesive tapes, heat sources, and shaping tools.

Adhesives   A number of adhesives are used in constructing custom protective equipment. Many cements and glues will join plastic to plastic or will join other combinations of material (Figure 5-38).

Adhesive tape   Adhesive tape is a major tool in holding various materials in place. Linen and elastic tape can hold pads to a rigid backing or to adhesive felt (moleskin) and can be used to protect against sharp edges.

Heat sources   To form thermomoldable plastics, a heat source must be available. Three sources are commonly found in training rooms: the commercial moist heat unit, a hot air gun or hair dryer, and/or an electric skillet or portable oven with a temperature control. The usual desired temperature is 160° F or higher (71° C).

Shaping tools   Commonly, the tools required to shape custom devices are heavy-duty scissors, sharp-bladed knives, and cast saws (Figure 5-39).

Holding materials in place   Once formed, customized protective equipment often must be secured in place. Fastening materials requires the availability of a great variety of different materials. For example, if something is to be held very secure, cotton herringbone–weave straps that are cut and riveted to the device may be desired. On the other hand, a Velcro fastener can be used when a device must be continually put on and removed. Leather can be cut and riveted in place to form hinge straps with buckles attached. Various types of laces can be laced through eyelets to hold something in place. Tools that allow for this type of construction include a portable drill, a hole punch, and an ice pick (Figure 5-40).

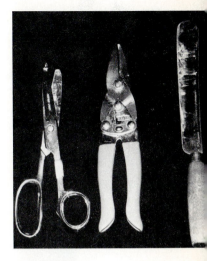

Figure 5-39

Scissors, tin snips, and broad-blade knife.

Figure 5-40

A, Fastening materials, including Velcro, Wet Wrap, leather, laces, rubber wraps, and hardware. **B,** Portable drill, hand-held hole punch, pop rivet gun, and ice pick for aligning and creating holes.

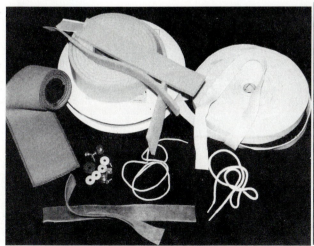

A

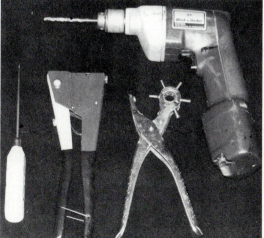

B

Figure 5-41

Constructing a hard-shell pad. **A,** Marking the area to be protected. **B,** Temporary foam insert to provide "bubble" relief. **C,** Heating plastic and wrapping it over temporary relief pad. **D,** Removing foam used to create "bubble." **E,** Trimmed shell.

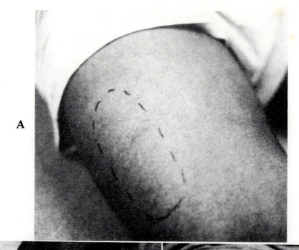

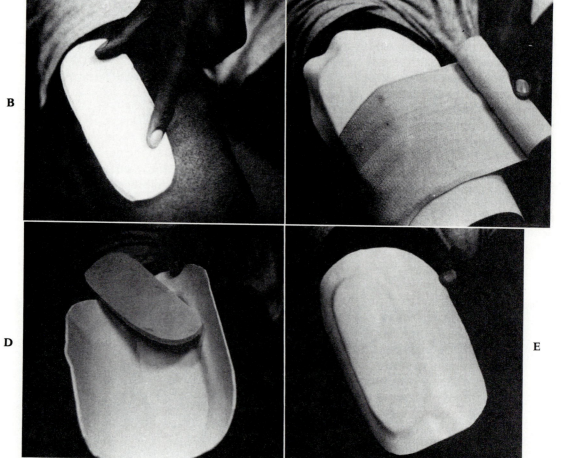

Customized Hard-Shell Pads

Commonly, an athlete who needs a hard-shell pad has acquired an injury, for example, a very painful contusion (bruise), that must be completely protected from further injury. To customize such a pad, the procedures should be followed that are presented in the box on p. 168, and in Figure 5-41.

Figure 5-41, cont'd

F, Doughnut-shaped foam lining. **G,** Doughnut combined with softer foam. **H,** Using an elastic wrap to secure pad.

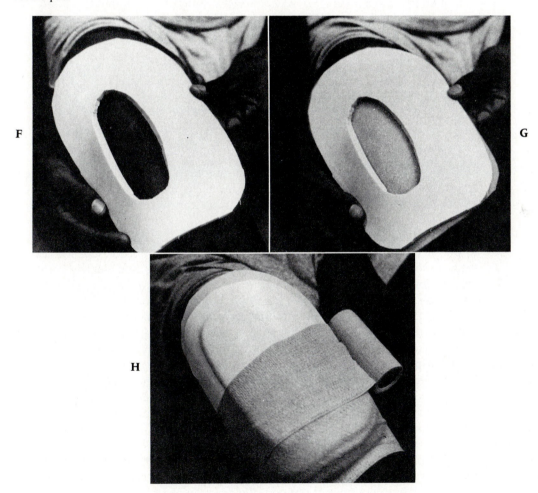

F
G
H

CONSTRUCTING A HARD-SHELL PAD

1. Select proper material and tools, which might include
   a. Thermomoldable plastic sheet.
   b. Scissors.
   c. Felt material.
2. Palpate and mark the margins of the tender area that needs protection.
3. Cut a felt piece to fit in the area of tenderness.
4. Heat plastic until malleable.
5. Place heated plastic over felt and wrap in place with an elastic wrap.
6. When cooled, remove elastic wrap and felt pad.
7. Trim shell to desired shape; a protective shell has now been made to provide a "bubble" relief.
8. If needed, add a softer inner layer of foam to distribute and lessen force further.
   a. Cut a doughnut-type hole in softer foam material the same size as the injury site.
   b. Cut foam the same shape as the hard shell.
   c. Use tape or an adhesive to affix the foam to the shell.

Custom Foot Orthotics

The athlete with serious biomechanical foot problems often requires a customized foot orthotic device. Measurement for this device is usually performed by an orthopedic surgeon or podiatrist. Foot orthotic devices prescribed by a professional are semisoft, semirigid, and rigid.

Semisoft orthotic device   This orthotic device is similar in its construction to the preorthotic device. The major advantage of this device is that it is easily made in the doctor's office, is inexpensive, and is almost immediately comfortable, having a relatively short "break-in" period. It can easily be modified with cork shims.

Construction of a semisoft orthotic device requires picking the correct size blank with the appropriate thickness and density. The foot is measured on the blank, followed by shaping and smoothing by a drum grinding wheel.[31]

Semirigid orthotic device   The semirigid orthotic device is constructed from maleable plastics such as polyethylene, polypropylene, and polyvinyl chloride. As the name implies, semirigid orthotic devices will "give" under great force.

Construction of this device requires casting the foot in a neutral position, then sending the cast to an outside laboratory for construction. The "break-in" period for this orthotic device is much longer than for the semisoft one.

Rigid orthotic device   The rigid orthotic device is the most expensive and most difficult one to construct. Providing the most rigid control, it is made from a cast of the foot in a neutral position. Rigid acrylic plastic is used by heating and pressing it over the mold. Of all three orthotic devices, the rigid one is the most difficult to fit, and its use has the highest degree of complications.[31]

SUMMARY

The proper selection and fitting of sports equipment are essentials in the prevention of many sports injuries. Because of the number of current litigations, sports equipment standards are of serious concern regarding the durability of the material and the fit and wear requirements of the equipment. Manufacturers must foresee all of the possible uses and misuses of their equipment and warn the user of any potential risks.

Head protection in many collision and contact sports is of concern to sports professionals. A major concern is that the football helmet be used for that which it was intended and not as a weapon. To avoid unwarranted litigation, a warning label must be placed on the outside of the helmet indicating that it is not "fail safe" and must be used as intended. Proper fit is also a major requirement.

Face protection is of major importance in sports that have fast-moving projectiles, use implements that are in close proximity to other athletes, and facilitate body collisions. Protecting teeth and eyes is of particular significance. The customized mouth guard, fitted to individual requirements, provides the best protection for the teeth and also protects against concussions. Eyes must be protected against projectiles and sports implements. The safest eye guard for the athlete not wearing contact lenses or spectacles is the closed type that completely protects the orbital cavity.

Many sports require protection of various parts of the athlete's body. American football players, ice hockey players, and baseball catchers are examples of players that require body protection. Commonly, the protection is for the shoulders, chest, thighs, ribs, hips, buttocks, groin, genitalia (male athletes), and breasts (female athletes).

Quality sportswear, properly fitted, is essential to prevent injuries. Socks must be clean, without holes, and made of appropriate materials. Shoes must be suited to the sport and must be fitted to the largest foot. The wide part of the foot must match the wide part of the shoe. If the shoe has cleats, they must be positioned at the metatarsophalangeal joints.

Currently, there are many stock pieces of specialized, protective equipment on the market. They may be designed to support ankles, knees, or other body parts. In addition to stock equipment, athletic trainers often construct customized equipment out of a variety of materials to pad injuries or support feet. Professionals such as orthopedists and podiatrists may devise orthopedic footwear and orthotic devices to improve the biomechanics of the athlete's foot.

REVIEW QUESTIONS AND CLASS ACTIVITIES

1. What are the legal responsibilities of the equipment manager, coach, and athletic trainer in terms of protective equipment?
2. Have the equipment manager of your sports program talk to your class about the purchase and fitting of equipment (e.g., football helmets and shoulder pads).
3. What are the differences between the helmet that protects against a fast-moving projectile and the one that protects against hard blows from an opponent?
4. What are the advantages of a custom-made mouth guard over the stock type?
5. What sports require ear guards?
6. Why are proper eye protection devices necessary in different sports? Identify the different types and their corresponding sports.
7. Which sports require trunk protection? Why? Which types of equipment are necessary?
8. Why is proper breast support so important to the woman with heavy breasts?
9. On what basis should different sports shoes by evaluated?
10. How should sports shoes be fitted?
11. When would you suggest a commercial foot pad to be used by an athlete?

12. Have a class debate about one of the following: the benefits of prophylactic taping versus the uselessness of prophylactic taping; commercial ankle supports versus no supports; and the current trend of using prophylactic knee braces versus not using braces.
13. What are the advantages and disadvantages of the *fitted* knee brace?
14. What is the relative value of commercial braces for the hand, wrist, and elbow?
15. You are given the responsibility to purchase materials that can be used for general padding or can be customized into special pads or other protective devices. What materials would you buy and why?
16. What steps would you take in making a hard-shell plastic pad?

REFERENCES

1. American Society for Testing and Materials, Committee F-8 on Sports Equipment and Facilities: Member information packet, Philadelphia, 1978.
2. Bishop, PJ, et al.: The ice hockey helmet: how effective is it? Phys Sportsmed 7:96, 1979.
3. Bishop, PJ: Performance eye protectors for squash and racquetball, Phys Sportsmed 10(3):62, 1982.
4. Bishop, PJ, et al.: An evaluation of football helmets under impact conditions, Am J Sports Med 12:233, May/June, 1984.
5. Bunch, RP, et al.: Ankle joint support: a comparison of reusable lace-on braces with taping and wrapping, Sports Med Guide, Prairie du Sac, Wis, Winter 1986, Meuller Sports Medicine, Inc.
6. Cain, TE, et al.: Use of the air inflated jacket in football, Am J Sports Med 9:240, 1981.
7. Castaldi, CR: Injuries to the teeth. In Vinger, PF, and Hoerner, EF, editors: Sports injuries: the unthwarted epidemic, Boston, 1981, John Wright PSG, Inc.
8. Fisher, RD: The measured effect of taping, joint range of motion, and their interaction upon the production of isometric ankle torques, Ath Train 17:218, 1982.
9. Freguson, AB, Jr: The case against ankle taping, J Sports Med 1:8, 1973.
10. Gardenswartz, A: Equipment for sports. In Appenzeller, O, and Atkinson, R, editors: Sports medicine, Baltimore, 1981, Urban & Schwarzenberg, Inc.
11. Gehlsen, G, and Albohm, M: Evaluation of sports bras, Phys Sportsmed 8:89, 1980.
12. Glick, JM: The prevention and treatment of ankle injuries, Am J Sports Med 4:4, 1976.
13. Goldsmith, W, and Kabo, JM: Performance of baseball headgear, Am Sports Med 14:262, 1986.
14. Hewson, GF, Jr, et al.: Prophylactic knee bracing in college football, Am J Sports Med 14:262, 1986.
15. Hodgson, VR, and Thomas, LM: Biomechanical study of football head impacts using a head model—condensed version, final report prepared for National Operating Committee on Standards for Athletic Equipment (NOCSAE), 1973.
16. Houston, JT: Helmet makers seek better product, tests. In More, M, editor: Football injury and equipment update, Phys Sportsmed 10:197, 1982.
17. Hulse, WF: Sports equipment standards. In Vinger, PF, and Hoerner, EF, editors: Sports injuries: the unthwarted epidemic, Boston, 1981, John Wright PSG, Inc.
18. Juvenal, JP: The effects of ankle taping on vertical jumping ability, Ath Train 7:5, 1972.
19. Keubker, WA, et al.: Do mouth-formed mouth guards meet the NCAA rules? Phys Sportsmed 14(6):69, 1986.
20. Knee braces to prevent injuries in football: a round table, Phys Sportsmed 14(4):108, 1986.
21. Knutzen, KM, et al.: A biomechanical analysis of two functional knee braces, Med Sci Sports Exerc 19(3):303, 1987.

22. Kozar, B: Effects of ankle taping upon dynamic balance, Ath Train 9:94, 1974.

23. Lester, RA: The coach as codefendant: football in the 1980's. In Appenzeller, H, editor: Sports and law: contemporary issues, Charlottesville, Va, 1985, The Michie Co.

24. Libera, D: Ankle taping, wrapping and injury prevention, Ath Train 7:73, 1972.

25. Loos, T, and Poelens, P: The effect of ankle tape on lower limb muscle activity, New York, 1984, Thieme-Stratton, Inc.

26. Martin, M: But does the shoe fit? In The First Aider, Gardner, Kan, Feb 1985, Cramer Products, Inc.

27. Mayhew, JL, and Riner, WF, Jr: Effects of ankle wrapping on motor performance, Ath Train 9:27, 1974.

28. McCluskey, GM: Prevention of ankle sprains, Am J Sports Med 4:151, 1976.

29. McKenzie, DC, et al.: Running shoes, orthotics, and injuries, Sports Med 2:334, 1985.

30. Meissner, L: Functional bandages. In Juprian, W, editor: Physical therapy for sports, Philadelphia, 1982, WB Saunders Co.

31. Micheli, LJ, et al.: Athletic footwear and modifications. In Nicholas, JA, and Hershman, EB, editors: The lower extremity and spine in sports medicine, vol 1, The CV Mosby Co, 1986, St. Louis.

32. Paulos, L, et al.: Biomechanics of lateral bracing, phase II. Review presented at the AAOS 51st annual meeting, San Francisco, Cal, Jan 22, 1987.

33. Peppard, A, and O'Donnell, M: A review of orthotic plastics, Ath Train 18:77, 1983.

34. Potera, C: Knee braces: questions raised about performance, Phys Sportsmed 13(9):153, 1985.

35. Rarick, L: The measurable support of the ankle joint by conventional methods of taping, J Bone Joint Surg 44A:1183, 1962.

36. Reese, RC, Jr, and Burruss, TP: Athletic training techniques and protective equipment. In Nicholas, JA, and Hershman, EB, editors: The lower extremity and spine, Sports Med, vol 1, St. Louis, 1986, The CV Mosby Co.

37. Reid, DC: Ankle injuries in sports, J Sports Med 1:3, 1973.

38. Rovere, GD, et al.: Prophylactic knee bracing in college football, Am J Sports Med 15:111, 1987.

39. Sforzo, GA, et al.: Knee brace wearing during exercise, Med Sci Sports Exerc 19(suppl):5, 1987.

40. Soos, TH: Taping the injured athlete. In Kulund, DN, editor: The injured athlete, Philadelphia, 1982, JB Lippincott Co.

41. Stotlar, DK: Athletic equipment: product liability gone awry, JOPERD 58:27, 1987.

42. Tobergate, E: Fitting the football helmet, Sports Med Guide, Prairie du Sac, Wis, Fall 1985, Meuller Sports Medicine, Inc.

43. Warning labels now required on outside of football helmets. The First Aider, Gardner, Kansas, 1986, Cramer Products, Inc.

44. Wilkinson, EE, and Powers, JM: Properties of custom-made mouth protector materials, Phys Sportsmed 14(6):77, 1986.

ANNOTATED BIBLIOGRAPHY

Ellison, AE, editor: Athletic training and sports medicine, Chicago, Ill, 1984, American Academy of Orthopaedic Surgeons.

Discusses all aspects of buying, fitting, and constructing protective equipment in Part 4, *Protective Equipment.*

Nicholas, JA, and Hershamm, EB, editors: The lower extremity and spine in sports medicine, vol 1, St. Louis, 1986, The CV Mosby Co.

Contains two excellent chapters on the subject of protective devices: Chapter 9, by RC Reese and TP Burruss, *Athletic Training Techniques* and *Protective Equipment;* and Chapter 20, by LJ Micheli, et al.: *Athletic Footwear and Modifications.*

Psychological Stresses

When you finish this chapter, you should be able to

Describe why and under what circumstances sports participation is a psychological stressor

Explain all the aspects of overtraining and staleness that stem from sports

Define the conflict adjustments that may occur as a result of becoming overstressed in sports

Identify physiological responses to stress

Describe how an athlete may respond psychologically to injuries or illnesses

Describe the roles of coaches, athletic trainers, and physicians when dealing with an overly stressed athlete

Mens sana in corpore sano, or "a sound mind in a sound body," is the concept of mind-body relationship that we have accepted since the time of the early Greeks. In recent years we have become increasingly concerned with the effect of psychological stress and its relationship to injury prevention and causation.

SPORTS AS A STRESSOR

Recently, the word **"stress"** has had a negative connotation. Rather, stress refers to a change. Stress is not all bad, nor is it all good. According to Pearsall,[11] stress is not something that an athlete can do to his or her body, but it is something that happens or that the brain tells the athlete is happening, which may be different from what has, in truth, been happening. When change occurs, the brain interprets that change and tells the body how to react to it. Selye[14] also considers stress as not necessarily implying a morbid change, but a change that could also be associated with intense pleasure. The concern here is the relationship between sports and abnormal stress (Figure 6-1).

Sports participation serves as both a physical and an emotional stressor. Stress can be a positive or negative influence. All living organisms are endowed with the ability to cope effectively with stressful situations. Pelletier[12] stated: "Without stress, there would be very little constructive activity or positive change." Negative stress can contribute to poor health, whereas positive stress produces growth

stress
The positive and negative forces that can disrupt the body's equilibrium.

Sports participation is both a physical and an emotional stressor.

172

and development. A healthy life must have a balance of stress; too little causes a "rusting out," and too much stress can cause "burnout."[15]

Athletes place their bodies in countless daily stress situations. Their bodies undergo numerous "fight-or-flight" reactions to avoid injury or other threatening situations. Inappropriate adjustment to fight-or-flight responses can eventually lead to emotional or physical illness.[6] An example of a normal reaction to stress is the "pregame response."

The Pregame Response

Pregame stress is a response with which everyone connected with sports is familiar. Before any event that is of significance to the performer, the symptoms manifest themselves in varying degrees. Continued exposure somewhat lessens but does not eradicate the effects: veteran athletes, public performers, politicians, and others will attest to still feeling one or more of these effects of tension.

Figure 6-1

Stress in sports, as in other endeavors, can be either "bad" or "good," depending on the brain's interpretation of it.

The pregame syndrome is one of nature's ways of preparing the individual for maximum effort and is the result of adrenomedullary activity. Epinephrine is released into the system with dramatic results. It is formed by the adrenal gland, located on the superior border of the kidney, and is released into the bloodstream in varying amounts. It is theorized that an epinephrine-like compound stimulates the adjacent dendrites and muscle cells when it is released as a result of the nerve impulse reaching the synapse or myoneural junctions. The adrenal hormones spread throughout the body and elicit a wide range of effects. These effects increase the physical performance of an individual in an emergency. This is accomplished through the following means:

1. Speedup of circulation and respiration, which increases the delivery of fuel to the muscles and the removal of metabolites and other wastes
2. Increase in glycogenolytic action, which increases the blood sugar content and supplies more fuel to the muscles
3. Increase in the metabolism of the cerebrum, which results in an increase in alertness and in the neuromuscular responses, thus improving physical performance.
4. Increase in the excitability of the neurons, which enhances motor activity and alertness

With the increase in blood pressure, heart rate, and endocrine stimulation, certain emotional symptoms appear such as a feeling of anxiety, breathlessness, "butterflies" in the stomach, and trembling. An athlete in a state of readiness for competition will exhibit these signs in varying degrees.

Also associated with these physiological responses is an extremely dry mouth (xerostomia). Stress causes a lack of normal salivary secretion. This problem can be relieved by chewing gum or sucking on a lemon. When the stress has been relieved, normal moisture returns. Another typical response to pre-event stress is that of diuresis and nervous defecation. Diuresis (increased flow of urine) and nervous defecation often accompany pregame tension and may be attributed to increased hormonal and nerve action. The increase in anxiety increases nerve irradiation and thus activates not only the adrenal glands but also the brain regions and visceral nerves that govern these functions, with the result that both bladder and bowel action are stimulated. Once the sports event has begun, the vast majority of the pregame nervous responses subside.

Figure 6-2

Signs of staleness can be deterred if there are maximum rewards for the athlete.

anxiety
A feeling of uncertainty or apprehension.

catecholamine
Active amines, epinephrine and norepinephrine, that affect the nervous and cardiovascular systems.

Overtraining and Staleness

Athletes who undergo prolonged stress because of overtraining can become stale. The term "stale" refers to a loss of vigor, initiative, and successful performance. This situation can be attributed to a wide variety of influences.

Causes of Staleness

The general cause of staleness in athletes is stress, usually occurring over a long period of time without adequate relief. Sometimes it is called athletic "burnout," much like psychological "burnout," which occurs in any field that has major responsibilities. (See Chapter 2, the section entitled *Athletic Trainer "Burnout"*.)

There are countless reasons why some athletes become stale. In fact, the athlete could be training too hard and long without proper rest. As discussed in Chapter 4, *Nutritional Considerations,* the athlete may not be eating enough carbohydrates to store glycogen for adequate fuel.

Although poor eating habits are an important cause of staleness, more often staleness is attributed to emotional problems stemming from daily worries, fears, and, most importantly, anxieties. **Anxiety** is one of the most common mental and emotional stress producers. It is reflected by a nondescript fear, a sense of apprehension, and restlessness. Typically the anxious athlete is unable to describe the problem. The athlete feels inadequate in a certain situation but is unable to say why. Heart palpitations, shortness of breath, sweaty palms, constriction in the throat, and headache may accompany anxiety. Children who are pushed too hard by parents may acquire a number of psychological problems. They may even fail purposely in their sport just to rid themselves of the painful stress of achieving. A coach who acts like a drill sergeant—one who continually gives negative reinforcements—will more than likely cause the athlete to develop symptoms of overstress.

Athletes are much more prone to signs of staleness if the rewards of their efforts are minimum. A losing season commonly causes many athletes to experience signs of staleness (Figure 6-2).[5]

Symptoms of Staleness

Staleness is evidenced by a wide variety of symptoms, among which are a deterioration in the usual standard of performance, chronic fatigue, apathy, loss of appetite, indigestion, weight loss, and inability to sleep or rest properly. Often athletes will exhibit higher blood pressure or an increased pulse rate, both at rest and during activity, as well as increased **catecholamine** excretions. All these signs indicate adrenal exhaustion. The athlete becomes irritable and restless, has to force himself or herself to practice, and exhibits signs of boredom and lassitude in respect to everything connected with the activity[4] (see the box on p. 175).

Abnormal Behavioral Response to Stress

An athlete who is under stress that is perceived as excessive may respond in a behavior that may be considered inappropriate. This type of behavior is categorized as "conflict adjustment."

RECOGNIZING SIGNS OF STALENESS IN ATHLETES

An athlete who is becoming stale will often display some or most of the following signs. He or she may

1. Show a decrease in performance level
2. Have difficulty falling asleep
3. Be awakened from sleep for no apparent reason
4. Experience a loss of appetite and a loss of weight; conversely, the athlete may overeat because of chronic worry
5. Have indigestion
6. Have difficulty concentrating
7. Have difficulty enjoying sex
8. Experience nausea for no apparent reason
9. Be prone to head colds and/or allergic reactions
10. Show behavioral signs of restlessness, irritability, anxiety, and/or depression
11. Have an elevated resting heart rate and elevated blood pressure
12. Display psychosomatic episodes of perceiving bodily pains such as sore muscles, especially before competing

Conflict Adjustment

The athlete who for one reason or another is under a great deal of mental and emotional stress may react as being in conflict. The adjustments of these conflicts may be inappropriate and reflect minor or even major behavioral problems.

Ambivalence   Ambivalence is typical of an individual in conflict. To want something and simultaneously reject it is characteristic of ambivalence. Some people achieve more satisfaction from one aspect and therefore encounter greater frustration in the other aspects of an activity. To express it differently, whatever they do to fulfill one motive opposes the other. Over a long period of time these people tend to develop an attitude of "Whatever I attempt to do is wrong or ends in failure." In such cases individuals tend to develop personality patterns that are revealed through various types of recognizable, overt behaviors. Thus the accident-prone athlete, the overly aggressive individual, and the complacent person all indicate outward manifestations of some hidden psychological problem. In some instances overt behavior is indicative of a specific failing or shortcoming that the individual seeks to mask by assuming a defensive posture.

Accident proneness   Accident-prone athletes have more than an average share of injuries. Injuries seem to seek them out, and normally insignificant or innocuous situations assume significance when they occur. They are easily involved in situations wherein they receive some injury, although others emerge unscathed. Ogilvie and Tutko[10] categorize the accident-prone athlete into three types: (1) the bona fide injured, (2) the psychologically injured, and (3) the malingerer. The *bona fide injured* athlete may have a series of rather severe injuries as the result of hostility directed toward the self, which is manifested in reckless and daredevil performances, thus inviting injury. The *psychologically injured* individual

Conflict adjustment examples in an athlete include
  Ambivalence
  Accident proneness
  Hostility/overaggressiveness
  Rationalization
  Sarcasm/criticism
  Foul language
  Defeatism
  Complacency
  Malingering

constantly complains of injury and pain, but no medically sound evidence is recognizable. The *malingerer* intentionally lies about an injury to get out of work.

Accident-prone individuals are most likely to suffer an accident toward the end of a long or sustained period of work. Accident proneness apparently is caused by a lack of ability to coordinate properly, as the result of either fatigue or emotional imbalance. Often the discouraged or apathetic athlete is accident prone. Athletic trainers and coaches have long observed that the competitor who is not emotionally stable stands an excellent chance of being injured.

Certain characteristics can be recognized in accident-prone athletes. Usually they are easily distracted and, as implied previously, generally exhibit emotional instability. In some instances they become extremely aggressive toward and intolerant of others, displaying an attitude of superiority. They actually enjoy some accidents because of the attention they attract. Some individuals of this type become almost permanent fixtures in the training room. Their high incidence of injury, plus the fact that they enjoy the ministrations and attention, make these individuals a real problem for the athletic trainer and the coach alike.

Hostility and overt aggressiveness Although aggressiveness is a desirable characteristic in sports, some athletes are hostile or overaggressive toward the opposition and team members and associates. Such feelings may indicate pregame tension or they may be the result of intensive training over a long period of time. Frequently, athletes who display aggressive tendencies falling into the latter category are "drawn fine" and need to ease their rigorous schedules for a while. Often feelings of hostility are released through competition, particularly in contact sports.

> Feelings of hostility are often released through competition, particularly in contact sports.

The coach or athletic trainer can handle the overly aggressive individual in several ways. He or she can attempt to channel the tendencies into more desirable avenues through careful counseling, or if the athlete seems amenable to reason, the trainer can get the athlete to recognize the problem and to attempt to solve it through changes in behavior. The latter method is not always effective, particularly when anger or hostility is evidenced during the discussion. A person in this frame of mind soon loses the ability to listen, reason, and think coherently and often becomes more symptomatic than usual. When neither the catharsis of competition, channeling, nor reasoning produces favorable results, the individual should be remanded to proper counseling channels for assistance. This type athlete is usually difficult to recondition.

Rationalization Many times the coach or athletic trainer will encounter athletes who use rationalization to a considerable degree. Such individuals advance seemingly plausible reasons for everything they do. Whenever errors, misunderstandings, or problems occur, although it is evident that the fault lies with them, they defend their position with the support of a somewhat credible explanation. The relationship to the athletic trainer and the training program takes the form of projection, usually involving feelings of persecution. Sometimes the position is taken that the athletic trainer is not interested in the athlete or in his or her rehabilitation and that this attitude is a result of some misunderstood action that has caused the athletic trainer to develop a feeling of personal animosity.

Individuals who show a pattern of this type are difficult to reach. They fail to follow training or reconditioning instructions, complaining that they cannot see the use of such procedures. They are convinced the procedures are giving them no positive results or are only aggravating the particular problem. Any attempt to point out specifics usually results in more rationalization. Not only do they fail to realize shortcomings, but they also refuse to accept them when they are made apparent. They cover their failures or confusion with specious reasoning that will, in their eyes, justify their actions.

The difficulties in working with this type of individual are nearly insurmountable. However, pressuring the athlete and consistently explaining the objectives often bring about positive results. Extreme cases should be referred to the school psychologist.

Sarcasm and criticism   Some athletes seek relief from emotional conflicts by turning to an excessive use of sarcasm or criticism. They incessantly find fault with equipment, training facilities, and gear. They are hypercritical of their wrappings and of other preventive or therapeutic actions. When queried, they take refuge in heavy sarcasm rather than attempting to critically evaluate their behavior and then take steps to eradicate their own faults. Answering such sarcasm with sarcasm tends to strengthen rather than attenuate the difficulty. Consequently, such individuals are best dealt with privately in efforts to help them recognize and overcome their shortcomings.

Foul language and profanity   The persons who persistently use foul or profane language often wish to distract attention from their failings or to compensate for feelings of insecurity. In some instances profanity may be a means of relieving inner tensions, but under no circumstances should the use of such language be tolerated. It has no place in sports. The usual, relaxed, after-practice atmosphere of the training room may reflect a feeling that the barriers are down and thus induce, in some individuals, a tendency to be careless with their language. Violators should promptly be admonished and told in no uncertain terms that such action is not and will not be tolerated.

Defeatism   Occasionally the coach or athletic trainer will encounter individuals who are defeatists. These individuals are quitters who give up easily, cannot see the use of continuing, and often use rationalization in an attempt to cover shortcomings. It is difficult to ascribe a specific reason for this attitude, since it often has rather deep psychological implications. These individuals are completely unreliable in competitive situations, since it is difficult to predict just when they will give up. Because they will not persist in treatment procedures, reconditioning is difficult.

The coach or athletic trainer may attempt to help these individuals develop more positive attitudes through counseling, but such attempts are not usually successful. It is better for them to secure the services of someone trained in the complexities of psychological diagnosis and treatment. As a rule, the defeatists or quitters do not last long in athletic competition. They either are dropped by the coach or give up athletics voluntarily because of preconceived ideas about their inability to succeed.

Complacency   Complacent athletes are so satisfied with their own abilities and merit that they do not endeavor to improve. These individuals present a trying problem both to the athletic trainer and to the coach because it is difficult to find adequate means of motivating such athletes. Methods that work for others are seldom effective with complacent athletes. Constant needling by the athletic trainer or coach may occasionally effect some motivation, but it is usually short

Pressuring the athlete and consistently explaining the objectives often have positive results.

Athletes using profanity should promptly be told that such behavior will not be tolerated.

lived. It is dispiriting when one recognizes that such individuals are performing well below optimum. It is difficult to get them to recognize their full potential, shake off the shackles of lethargy, and become efficiently functioning, contributing members of the team.

In the training room complacent athletes casually accept all ministrations but beyond this make little or no effort to assist with their own reconditioning. This complacency necessitates constant checking to ensure that they are following instructions and to provoke them into action. This is time consuming and also can prove vexing. The complacent athlete who makes no effort to respond is a detriment and should be dropped from the team.

Malingering   Certain athletes seek to escape practice and other responsibilities or to gain sympathy by feigning illness or injury. Frequently, such an individual is termed "con man" by athletic trainers and coaches, the term being self-evident. In many instances such an action may be difficult to detect. However, a history of repeated questionable incidents warrants thorough investigation. When a case of malingering is evident, the athletic trainer can usually handle it by direct means, that is, by letting the athlete know that the acting has been detected and that henceforth complaints had better be legitimate. Should the conduct continue, a conference between athletic trainer and coach is indicated. A persistent malingerer is of no value to the team and should be dropped.

Physiological Responses to Stress

Stress is a psychophysiological phenomenon. In other words, it is a combination of the mind and the body. As discussed earlier, sports, in every respect, are stressors. Physiologically, the body can experience three phases when stressed—alarm, resistance, and exhaustion. These reactions are commonly known as the General Adaptation Syndrome, or the GAS theory, as originally developed by Dr. Hans Selye.[12]

Alarm Stage

In the alarm phase, secretions from the adrenal gland sharply increase, creating the well-known "flight-or-fight" response. With adrenaline in the bloodstream, pupils dilate, hearing becomes more acute, muscles become more responsive, and blood pressure increases to facilitate the absorption of oxygen. In addition to these responses, respiration and heart rate increase to further prepare the body for action.

Resistance Stage

Following the alarm stage, the body gradually changes to the resistance stage. During this stage, the body prepares itself for coping by diminishing the adrenocortical secretions and directing stress to a particular body site. This stage is the body's way of resisting the stressor. Physiological response may remain high and could eventually lead to the final stage, exhaustion (Figure 6-3).

Exhaustion Stage

The exhaustion stage refers to an entire organ system, or a single organ, becoming dysfunctional and diseased as a result of chronic stress. It is generally accepted that chronic stress can adversely affect brain function, the autonomic nervous

Figure 6-3

The highly competitive athlete often has personality qualities that have to be carefully channeled to improve performances.

system, the endocrine system, and the immune system, eventually leading to a psychosomatic illness.[11]

Thus it is concluded that there are two kinds of stress—acute and chronic. During acute stress, the threat is immediate, and response is instantaneous. Physiologically, the body remains in the alarm stage. The primary reaction of the alarm stage is produced by the epinephrine and norepinephrine of the adrenal medulla. Chronic stress primarily involves the stages of resistance and exhaustion. During chronic stress, there is an increase of blood corticoids from the adrenal cortex.

STRESS RELATED TO INJURIES OR ILLNESS

An athlete who is taken out of a sport because of an injury or illness reacts in a personal way. The athlete who has trained diligently, has looked forward to a successful season, and is suddenly thwarted in that goal by an injury or illness can be emotionally devastated.

At the Time of Injury or Illness

At the time of serious injury or illness the athlete may normally fear the experience of pain or possible disability. There may be a sense of anxiety about suddenly becoming disabled and unable to continue sport participation. There also

TABLE 6-1 Emotional Emergency Care

Type of Emotional Reaction	Outward Signs	Trainer's Reactions	
		Yes	**No**
Normal	Weakness, trembling Nausea, vomiting Perspiration Diarrhea Fear, anxiety Heart pounding	Be calm and reassuring	Avoid pity
Overreaction	Excessive talking Argumentativeness Inappropriate joke telling Hyperactivity	Allow athlete to vent emotions	Avoid telling athlete he or she is acting abnormally
Underreaction	Depression; sitting or standing numbly Little talking if any Emotionless Confusion Failure to respond to questions	Be empathetic; encourage talking to express feelings	Avoid being abrupt; avoid pity

may be a sense of guilt about being unable to help the team or "letting down" the coach. Becoming suddenly dependent and somewhat helpless can cause anxiety in the usually independent and aggressive person.[7] The athlete may regress to childlike behavior, crying or displacing anger toward the coach or athletic trainer who is administering first aid. Also, in the very early period of injury, and sometimes later, the athlete may deny the injury altogether. Reaction of the athlete to a sudden injury may require immediate emotional support as shown in Table 6-1.

The Psychology of Loss

Psychological reactions to serious injury may include denial or disbelief, anger, bargaining, depression, or acceptance.

The athlete who has sustained an injury of such intensity that he or she is unable to perform for a long period will generally experience five reactions: denial or disbelief, anger, bargaining, depression, and acceptance of the situation (see box on p. 181). These reactions are typical for anyone who has experienced a sudden serious loss.

The coach and athletic trainer must realize that reactions to a sense of loss are normal and must allow the athlete to fully experience each reaction. A common error is to try to talk the person out of being angry or depressed. Athletic trainers must educate all of their injured charges to understand that rehabilitation and full recovery are a cooperative venture, with major responsibility resting on the athlete's shoulders.

Depression   The athlete who finds him or herself overstressed could experience mental depression. Along with the major signs of staleness, the athlete may

PSYCHOLOGICAL REACTIONS TO LOSS

Denial or Disbelief

On suddenly becoming disabled and unable to perform, the athlete will commonly deny the seriousness of the condition. When indications are that the injury is serious and will not heal before the end of the season, the athlete might respond by saying, "Not so, I'll be back in 2 weeks." This irrational thinking indicates denial of the true seriousness of the injury.

Anger

Anger commonly follows disbelief. As the athlete slowly becomes aware of the seriousness of the injury, a sense of anger develops. The athlete begins to ask, "Why me?" "What did I do wrong?" "Why am I being punished?" "It's not fair." Commonly, this anger becomes displaced toward other people. The athletic trainer may be blamed for not providing a good enough tape job, or another player may be blamed for causing the situation that set up the injury.

Bargaining

As anger becomes less intense, the athlete gradually becomes aware of the real nature of the injury and, with this awareness, begins to have doubts and fears about the situation, which leads to a need to bargain. Bargaining may be reflected in prayer, "God, if you will heal this injury in 3 weeks instead of 6, I'll go to church every Sunday." Or it may be reflected by pressure being put on the athletic trainer or physician to do his or her very best for a fast healing.

Depression

As the athlete becomes increasingly aware of the nature of the injury and that healing will take a specific length of time, depression can set in. Crying episodes may occur; there may be periods of insomnia, and the athlete may lose the desire for food.

Acceptance

Gradually, the athlete begins to feel less dejected and isolated and becomes resigned to the situation.

have feelings of worthlessness, self-reproach, and/or excessive and inappropriate guilt. This depression could be a temporary situational reaction.[1,16]

THE ROLE OF THE COACH, ATHLETIC TRAINER, AND PHYSICIAN

It is generally accepted that sports are stressors to the athlete. There is often a fine line between the athlete's reaching and maintaining peak performance and overtraining. Besides performance concerns, there are many peripheral stressors that can be imposed on the athlete such as unreasonable expectations by the athlete, the coaches, and/or the parents. Worries that stem from school, work, and family can also be major causes of emotional stress.

The Coach

The coach is often the first person to notice an athlete is overstressed. The athlete whose performance is declining and whose personality is changing may need a training program that is less demanding. A good talk with the athlete by the coach might reveal emotional and physical problems that need to be dealt with by a counselor/psychologist or a physician.

The Athletic Trainer

Injury prevention is *psychological,* as well as *physiological.* The athlete who enters a contest while angry, frustrated, or discouraged or while undergoing some other disturbing emotional state is more prone to injury than is the individual who is better adjusted emotionally. The angry player, for example, wants to vent ire in some way and therefore often loses perspective of desirable and approved conduct. In the grip of emotion, skill and coordination are sacrificed, with the result that an injury that otherwise would have been avoided can be sustained.

The athletic trainer must have some counseling skills.

Although athletic trainers are typically not educated as professional counselors or psychologists, nevertheless, they must be concerned with the feelings of the athletes they work with. No one can work closely with human beings without becoming involved with their emotions and, at times, their personal problems. The athletic trainer is usually a very caring person and, as such, is placed in numerous daily situations in which close interpersonal relationships are important. The athletic trainer must have appropriate counseling skills to confront an athlete's fears, frustrations, and daily crises and to refer individuals with serious emotional problems to the proper professionals.[13] To help reduce the athlete's muscle tension caused by stress, the athletic trainer is in a position to provide education in relaxation techniques.

Stress and Muscular Tension

Relaxation is usually defined as the elimination or diminution of tension. For our purposes, it is defined as the constructive use of tension, or *the ability of muscles to release contractual tension.* Muscle tension may be induced physiologically through exercise or psychogenically through anxiety, uncertainty, or other mental-emotional stressors. Emotional disturbances are reflected in muscle action, and situations that tend to increase such emotional tensions are thus indicated by increased muscular tensions. There are many causes of tensions; generally, normal fatigue, chronic fatigue, and over-activity are the principal ones. Before relaxation can occur, the causes for tension must be studied. In sports we are concerned with the release of tensions, either physical or psychogenic, within the muscles.

Emotional disturbances are reflected in muscle action. Situations that increase emotional tensions are thus indicated by increased muscular tensions.

As muscles tire, they lose some of their ability to release contractual tension (to relax). As a result, the elasticity of the muscle is considerably diminished. The endurances of a muscle is characterized by its ability to retain its elasticity. Hence, the degree of elasticity determines the degree of muscular efficiency. A muscle carefully conditioned for endurance will assume its maximum length after a long series of repeated actions. As a muscle fatigues, it steadily diminishes in irritability (its ability to respond to a stimulus) and elasticity because of the presence of increased metabolites. It loses its ability to readily give up eccentric (lengthening) contraction. The capability of a muscle to recuperate after a bout of exercise is considerably enhanced by the ability of the athlete to consciously relax.

Tension is a natural concomitant of any form of competitive endeavor. Properly channeled tension is an asset rather than a liability. Excessive tension, however, is detrimental not only to physical performance but also to the health of the athlete.

Relaxation Methods

Progressive muscle relaxation   To eliminate undesirable tensions athletes should be trained to use one of the various recognized techniques of relaxation, since reducing muscular tension decreases nervous tension and vice versa. A number of techniques for inducing relaxation have been advanced. Each has its proponents. Jacobson[8] has developed a technique that uses progressive relaxation. He recognized two types of relaxation: general and differential. General relaxation is obtained when all of the body's voluntary muscles are completely relaxed. Differential relaxation, in contrast, is the ability of agonist and antagonist muscles to reciprocally contract and relax with ease in the act of moving a body part. The Jacobson technique requires, as do other similar techniques, considerable practice before mastery is achieved. One hour, two or three times a week, is recommended. Practice can be performed on either a group or an individual basis. Once the basic principles are acquired, the athlete can use them when convenient and, in most instances, achieve a reasonable degree of success.[9]

Progressive muscle relaxation is probably the most extensively used technique for relaxation today.[8] It can be considered intense training in the awareness of tension and its release. Although over 200 sessions were prescribed in Jacobson's original method, a much smaller number can still be extremely effective. In the early stages of the method, the subject is instructed to actively tense major muscle groups for a few seconds and then release the muscle tension while consciously relaxing as much as possible. Progressive relaxation may be practiced in a reclining position or while seated in a chair. Each muscle group is tensed from 5 to 7 seconds, then relaxed for 20 to 30 seconds. In most cases, one repetition of the procedure is sufficient, however; if tension remains in the area, repeated contraction and relaxation is permitted. The sequence of tensing and releasing is systematically applied to the following body areas: the dominant hand and forearm; dominant upper arm; nondominant hand and forearm; nondominant upper arm; forehead; eyes and nose; cheeks and mouth; neck and throat; chest; back; respiratory muscles; abdomen; dominant upper leg, calf, and foot; and nondominant upper leg, calf, and foot. Throughout the session, a number of expressions for relaxing may be used: ''Let the tension dissolve. Let go of the tension. I am bringing my muscles to zero. Let the tension flow out of my body.''

After the athlete has become highly aware of the tension in the body, the contraction is gradually decreased until little remains. At this point, the athlete focuses on one area and mentally wills the tension to decrease to zero, or complete relaxation. Jacobson's session normally takes longer than the time allowed in a typical session or than the individual would want to spend. A short form can be developed that, although not as satisfactory, helps the individual become better aware of the body. *The essence of Jacobson's method is recognizing muscular tension and the conscious release of that tension.* The box on pp. 184-186 is a modified form of Jacobson's progressive relaxation method.

Quieting the anxious mind   Many times the athlete can reduce muscular tension at will but is unable to quell an active mind. A good example often occurs

JACOBSON'S PROGRESSIVE RELAXATION

Beginning Instructions
1. Get into a position that is relaxed and comfortable.
2. Breathe in and out easily and allow yourself to relax as much as possible.
3. Make yourself aware of your total body and the tensions that your muscles might have contained within them.

Arm Relaxation
1. Clench your right fist. Increase the grip more and more until you feel the tension created in your hand and forearm.
2. Slowly let go of the grip and allow the tension to flow out slowly until there is no tension left in your hand and forearm.
3. Feel how soft and relaxed the hand and forearm are and contrast this feeling with the left hand.
4. Repeat this procedure with the left hand, gripping hard and bringing the tension into the fist and forearm.
5. Now bend your right elbow and bring tension into the right biceps, tensing it as hard as you possibly can and observing the tightness of the muscle.
6. Relax and straighten the arm, allowing the tension to flow out.
7. Repeat the tension and relaxation technique with the left biceps.

The Head
1. Wrinkle your forehead as hard as you can and hold that tension for 5 seconds or longer.
2. Now relax and allow the forehead and face to completely smooth out.
3. Frown and feel the tension that comes in between the eyes and eyebrows.
4. Let go to a completely blank expression. Feel the tension flow out of your face.
5. Squint your eyes tighter and tighter, feeling the tension creep into the eyes.
6. Relax and gently allow your eyes to be closed without tension.
7. Clench your jaw, bite down hard, harder. Notice the tension in your jaw.
8. Relax. When you are relaxed, allow your lips to be slightly parted and your face completely without expression, without wrinkles or tension.
9. Stick your tongue up against the roof of your mouth as hard as possible, feeling the tension in the tongue and the mouth. Hold that tension.
10. Relax, allowing the face and the mouth to be completely relaxed. Allow the tongue to be suspended lightly in the mouth. Relax.
11. Bring your lips to form an O. Purse the lips hard together forming the letter O very hard so you feel the tension around the lips only.
12. Relax, allowing the tension to leave around the lips. Allow your lips to be slightly parted and tension completely gone from the face.

The Neck and Shoulders
1. By pressing your head back against the mat or chair, you feel the tension come into the neck region. Hold that tension. Be aware of it; sense it.
2. Now slowly allow the tension to leave, decreasing the amount of pressure applied until the tension has completely gone and there is as much relaxation as possible.
3. Bring your head forward so that your chin is pressing against your chest and tension is brought into the throat and back of your neck. Hold that tension.
4. Slowly return to the beginning position and feel the tension leave the neck and relax completely.

5. Shrug your shoulders upward, raising the tips of your shoulders as far as you can to the bottoms of the ears, hunching your head between your shoulders. Feel the tension creep into the tops of the shoulders. Hold that tension.
6. Now slowly let the tension leave by returning the shoulders to their original position. Allow the tension to completely leave the neck and shoulder region. Have a sense of bringing the muscles to zero, where they're completely at ease and without strain.

Respiration and the Trunk

1. As the body is completely relaxed and you have a sense of heaviness, allow your tension to move to your respiration. Fill the lungs completely and hold your breath upward to 5 seconds, feeling the tension come into the chest and upper back muscles.
2. Exhale slowly, allowing the air to go out slowly as you feel the tension being released slowly.
3. Now, while your breath is coming slowly and easily, sense the contrast of the breath holding to the breath that is coming freely and gently.
4. Tighten the abdominal muscles by pressing downward on the stomach. Note the tension that comes into the abdominal region, also in the respiratory center, as well as in the back region.
5. Relax the abdominal area and feel the tension leave the trunk region.
6. Slightly arch the back against the mat or back of the chair. This should be done without hyperextending or straining. Feel the tension that creeps into and along the spine. Hold that tension.
7. Now gradually allow the body to sink back into its original position and feel the tension leave the long muscles of the back.
8. Flatten the lower back by rolling the hips forward and feel the tension come into the lower back region. Hold that tension. Try to isolate that tension from all the other parts of your body.
9. Gradually return to the original position and feel the tension leave the body. Be aware of any of the tension that might have crept into your body regions that you have already relaxed. Allow your mind to scan your body; go back over the areas that you have released from tension and become aware of whether any tension has returned.

The Buttocks and Thighs

1. Press your buttocks muscles together, holding that area upward to 5 seconds. Try to isolate just the contraction of the buttocks region.
2. Now slowly allow the buttocks muscles to return to their normal state, relaxing completely.
3. Contract your thighs by straightening your knees. Hold that contraction, feeling the tension, isolating the tension just to that region, focusing just on the thigh region.
4. Slowly allow the tension to leave the region, bringing the entire body to a relaxed state, especially the thighs to a tensionless state.

Continued.

JACOBSON'S PROGRESSIVE RELAXATION—cont'd

The Buttocks and Thighs—cont'd

5. To bring the tension to the backs of the thighs, press your heels as hard as you can against the floor or mat, slightly bending the knees; bring the tension to the hamstring region and the back of the thighs. Hold this tension, study it, concentrate on it. Try to isolate the tension from other tensions that might have crept into the body.
6. Relax. Allow the tension to flow out. Return your legs to the original position, and let go of all the tensions of the body.

The Lower Legs and Feet

1. With the legs fully extended, point your foot downward as hard as possible, bringing tension into both calves. Hold that tension. Hold it as hard as you can without cramping.
2. Slowly allow the foot to return to a neutral position and allow relaxation to occur within the calf muscle. Bring it to zero if possible. No tension.
3. Curl the toes of the feet downward as hard as you can without pointing the foot downward, isolating the tension just in the bottoms of the feet and toes. Hold that tension. Isolate the tension, if possible, from the calves. Hold it; feel the tension on the bottoms of your feet.
4. Slowly relax and allow the tension to release from the foot as the toes straighten out.
5. Curl the toes backward toward the kneecaps and bring the foot back into dorsiflexion so you feel the tension in the tops of the toes, tops of the feet, and in the shin. Hold that tension. Be aware of it; study the tension.
6. After 5 seconds or longer, return to a neutral state where the foot is completely relaxed and the toes have returned to their normal position. Feel the tension leave your body.

---

at bedtime; the body may totally relax, but the mind continues to race with thoughts causing sleeplessness.

Meditation is a relaxation instrument used in virtually every culture dating back almost 3000 years. Many consider meditation to be an attitude rather than a technique or process. By increasing one's focus or attention, a greater conscious awareness is attained. It is not a pulling away from or a numbness against the realities of life. Practiced properly, meditation can reduce mental anxiety and muscular tension and create a climate for increased productivity. Meditation also affects the physiological functioning of the body in a positive way. In the sports setting, meditation is primarily important because of its potential for positively affecting various physiological aspects of the individual.

Benson[2] reported that meditation was not simply a relaxed state but also included the individual's capacity for focused attention. In studying transcendental meditation (TM), Benson observed a relaxation response that is hypometabolic, the counterpart of the fight-or-flight response, and that meditation affects the brain waves, as indicated on an encephalogram printout, producing calmness and relaxation. In TM it was found that after 3 to 5 minutes of meditation, the experienced meditator used 17% to 18% less oxygen and also produced less carbon dioxide. There was a slower respiratory rate and a significant fall in blood lactates, which are typically present in abnormal stress states. The heart rate and blood pressure decreased notably, and brain waves that are associated with a relaxed mental state increased. Further study identified four major components that are characteristic of almost every meditation system: (1) a mental device, (2) a passive attitude, (3) a decrease in muscle tone, and (4) a quiet environment.

Meditators focus on a constant mental stimulus such as a phrase repeated silently or audibly, a sound or a single word, or perhaps they gaze steadily at some object. In the passive attitude of meditation, a "don't work at it" approach is taken. As thoughts come into the consciousness, they are quietly turned away, and the individual returns to the focus of attention (see box below). For decreased muscle tone, a comfortable position is taken with the various major body areas relaxed and placed in as comfortable a position as possible. To effectively conduct a meditation session, a quiet environment is essential. Normally, the eyes are closed unless the meditator is focusing on some external object.[3]

THE MEDITATION TECHNIQUE

Quieting the Body

The athlete sits comfortably in a position that maintains a straight back, the head is erect, and the hands are placed lossely on each leg or on the arm of a chair with both feet firmly planted on the floor. To ensure a relaxed state, the meditator should mentally relax each body part, starting at the feet. If a great deal of tension is present, Jacobson's relaxation exercise might be appropriate, or several deep breaths are taken in and exhaled slowly and completely, allowing the body to settle more and more into a relaxed state after each emptying of the lungs.

The Meditative Technique

Once the athlete is in a quiet environment and fully physically relaxed, the meditative process can begin. With each exhalation the athlete emits self-talk of a short word. It is repeated over and over for 10 to 20 minutes. Such words as "peace" or "relaxed" are excellent relaxers; however, Benson[1] has suggested that the word "one" produces the same physiological responses as any other word. If extraneous thoughts come to mind, the meditator should passively disagree with the extraneous thought and return to the meditation.

After Meditating

After repeating the special word, the athlete comes back to physical reality slowly and very gently. As awareness increases, physical activity should also increase. Moving too quickly or standing up suddenly might produce light-headedness or dizziness.

The Physician

The team physician, as do the coach and the athletic trainer, plays an integral part with the athlete who is overly stressed. Many of the psychophysiological responses thought to be emotional are in fact caused by some undetected physical dysfunctions. Therefore, referral to the physician must be routine.

SUMMARY

Sports participation serves as both a physical and an emotional stressor. As with other endeavors, sports can be both a negative and positive stressor. A normal response to stress is the pregame response. In this response the body and mind speed up to meet the anticipated demands of competition.

An athlete who undergoes prolonged stress caused by overtraining can be stale. Another term for staleness is "burnout." The symptoms of staleness can stem from a variety of reasons other than emotions such as faulty diet or an unknown illness. A too-demanding coach or an athlete who is too intense can also cause overtraining.

The athlete who is overstressed may respond in a number of physiological and psychological ways such as having a higher-than-usual blood pressure, increased pulse rate, and increased catecholamine excretions. The athlete who continues at the reactive phase of stress eventually will become exhausted. Overstress can lead to adrenal exhaustion, causing a variety of psychoemotional problems. Conflict adjustment is one type of response to chronic stress.

The athlete may respond to chronic stress by experiencing muscle soreness caused by muscle tension. Emotional depression can also stem from stress, leading to feelings of worthlessness, self reproach, and/or excessive and inappropriate guilt.

Injuries and illness can cause chronic stress in the athlete. Often the athlete who is removed from sports participation for an extended period of time experiences the psychological reaction of loss. The five phases of loss psychology are denial or disbelief, anger, bargaining, depression, and acceptance.

The coach is the first in line to recognize an athlete who is overtraining or becoming stale. Staleness can result because the athlete has overtrained or because the coach teaches through negative reinforcement. The athletic trainer is also in a position to recognize subtle signs of an overstressed athlete. The physician may also become aware of an athlete who is "pushing too hard" or for other reasons is becoming "stressed out."

Two methods of reducing psychological stress can be taught to the athlete. If there is obvious muscle tension resulting from stress, Jacobson's Progressive Relaxation Method is appropriate. If, on the other hand, stress is causing more mental anxiety than muscle tension, meditation might be the preferred method.

REVIEW QUESTIONS AND CLASS ACTIVITIES

1. What is meant by good and bad stress?
2. How may a coach or an athlete cause the problem of overtraining and staleness?
3. What are the signs of conflict adjustment?
4. What does an athlete's reaction to pain have to do with psychological stress?
5. Depression can occur from chronic negative stress. What are depression's major signs?
6. Describe the GAS theory. Why may it be a factor in an athlete who is overstressed?
7. What is the psychology of loss? How may it relate to an athlete who becomes injured or ill?
8. Put yourself in place of a coach, an athletic trainer, and a physician. When viewed from each position, what indicators would reveal that the athlete is overstressed?
9. As an athletic trainer, how would you help an athlete to reduce muscle tension caused by overstress?

REFERENCES

1. Beck, AT: Depression: cause and treatment, Philadelphia, 1972, University of Pennsylvania Press.
2. Benson, HH: The relaxation response, New York, 1975, William Morrow & Co, Inc.
3. Benson HH: Beyond the relaxation response, New York, 1984, Times Books.
4. Costill, DL: Practical problems in sports physiology research, Res Q 59:378, 1985.
5. Costill, DL: Detection of overtraining, Sports Med Dig 8(5):4, 1986.
6. Dychtwald, K: Body-mind, New York, 1984, Jove Publishers.
7. Hafen, BQ: First aid for health emergencies, ed 4, St. Paul, Minn, 1988, West Publishing Co.
8. Jacobson, E: Progressive relaxation, ed 2, Chicago, 1938, University of Chicago Press.
9. Monat, A, and Lazarus, RS, editors: Stress and coping: an anthology, New York, 1977, Columbia University Press.
10. Ogilvie, BC, and Tutko, TA: Problem athletes and how to handle them, London, 1965, Pelham Books, Ltd.
11. Pearsall, P: Superimmunity, New York, 1987, McGraw-Hill Book Co.
12. Pelletier, KR: Mind as healer, mind as slayer, New York, 1977, Dell Publishing Co, Inc.
13. Salmi, HA: Exercise in the control of hypertension. In Welsh, RP, and Shepherd, RJ, editors: Current therapy in sports medicine 1985-1986, Philadelphia, 1985, Brian C Decker, Publisher.
14. Selye, H: Stress without distress, New York, 1974, JB Lippincott Co.
15. Truck, S: Teacher burnout and what to do about it, Navato, Cal, 1978, Academic Therapy Publications.
16. Willmer, P: Depression: a psychobiological synthesis, New York, 1985, John Wiley & Sons, Inc.

ANNOTATED BIBLIOGRAPHY

Monat, A, and Lazarus, RS, editors: Stress and coping: an anthology, New York, 1977, Columbia University Press.
A multiauthored book with detailed coverage about what stress is and how to cope with it.

Pearsall, P: Superimmunity, New York, 1987, McGraw-Hill Book Co.
An in-depth look at the relationship of emotions to health.

Pelletier, KR: Mind as healer, mind as slayer, New York, 1977, Dell Publishing Co, Inc.
Provides an in-depth discussion of the relationship of the mind to the cause and healing of disease.

Selye, H: Stress without distress, New York, 1974, JB Lippincott Co.
A practical guide to understanding the role of stress in life.

BASIC FOUNDATIONS OF SPORTS TRAUMA

Part Three imparts the diverse information necessary for understanding the body's susceptibility to sports injuries. It also covers classification of the injuries and tissue reaction to specific traumas.

CHAPTER 7

Mechanism, Characteristics, and Classification of Sports Injuries

When you finish this chapter, you should be able to

Identify the most common exposed skin injuries

Explain the normal structures comprising soft tissue and the specific mechanical forces that cause skin, internal soft-tissue, synovial joint, and bone injuries

Define the terms that describe the major injuries incurred during sports participation

Describe how epiphyseal injuries occur

Explain how pathomechanics can cause microtraumas and overuse injuries

Chapter 7 is concerned with the numerous general factors related to trauma in sports. Trauma, in this sense, refers to physical injuries stemming from an external or an internal force.[24] The purpose of this chapter is to provide a foundation for the understanding and management of specific sports injuries. It examines typical anatomical characteristics, mechanical forces, and other causative factors that produce sports injuries and arranges these injuries according to broad categories.

CONNECTIVE TISSUE CHARACTERISTICS

Connective tissue is the most prevalent tissue in the human body and plays an integral part in physical trauma and the healing process. Connective tissue connects, supports, transports, and defends. It attaches muscles to bones and bones to other bones. It supports the internal organs, as well as acts as a transport system through the blood. Several connective tissue cells defend against disease and provide a foundation for healing traumatic injuries. The intercellular substance may consist of one or more fibers, which are classified as reticular, elastic, or collagenous. The collagenous fiber, which is tough and strong, often occurs in bundles that are arranged to provide the greatest tensile strength. Collagen, in its hydrated form, is gelatin. Of all the protein compounds in the body, collagen is the most prevalent.

Reticular Connective Tissue

Reticular connective tissue is found in the spleen, lymph nodes, and bone marrow. It defends against microorganisms and harmful substances by filtrating blood and lymph through a reticular network. Reticular tissue also engages in phago-cytosis.

Loose Connective Tissue

Loose, ordinary connective tissue acts as a connection between different tissues and organs. It also provides a connection for superficial fascia.

Adipose Tissue (Fat)

Adipose tissue, or fat, is the type of connective tissue found under the skin and around organs. It provides protection, insulation, support, and a nutritional reserve.

Hemopoietic Connective Tissue

Hemopoietic connective tissue composes bone marrow and the lymphatic system. It forms red blood cells, leukocytes, and platelets. It also forms lymphocytes and monocytes, as well as some other connective tissue that is located in blood vessels. Blood is a form of connective tissue that is located in blood vessels and provides transportation and protection to the organism.

Dense Fibrous Connective Tissue

Dense fibrous connective tissue composes tendons, ligaments, aponeuroses, deep fascia, the dermis, capsules around organs (e.g., the kidney), and scar tissue. Its primary function is to provide a strong, flexible connection.

Tendinous Tissue

The tendon contains wavy parallel collagenous fibers that are organized in bundles surrounded by a gelatinous material that decreases friction.[6] Basically, a tendon attaches a muscle to a bone and concentrates a pulling force in a limited area. Tendons can produce and maintain a pull from 8700 to 18,000 pounds per square inch.[5] When a tendon is loaded by tension, the wavy collagenous fibers straighten in the direction of the load; when the tension is released, the collagen returns to its original shape.[6]

Ligamentous and Capsular Tissue

Ligaments and capsules, found in synovial joints, are similar in composition to tendons; however, they contain elastic fibers, and collagen fibers, that have a wavy configuration, which are irregular and have spiral arrangement. Attaching bone to bone, ligaments are strongest in their middle and weakest at their ends.[5] When an intact ligament is traumatically stretched, the injury often produces an avulsion-type fracture or tear at the ends, rather than in the middle. Avulsion fractures are more common when bone tissue is comparatively weaker than ligamentous tissue, as is evidenced in older individuals or postmenopausal women in whom significant osteoporosis has occurred or in children in whom the epiphyseal plates are relatively wide and soft.

Cartilage

Cartilage, as a connective tissue, provides firm and flexible support. It occurs throughout the body and consists of hyaline, fibrous, and elastic types. Cartilage is a semifirm type of connective tissue with a predominance of ground substance in the extracellular matrix. Within the ground substance are inset varying amounts of collagenous and elastic fibers.[3] Cartilage has a bluish-white or gray color and is semiopaque. It has no direct blood or nerve supply. Hyaline cartilage composes part of the nasal septum, the larynx, the trachea, the bronchi, and the articular ends of bones comprising the synovial joints. Fibrocartilage comprises the vertebral disks, symphysis pubis, and menisci of the knee joint. Elastic cartilage is found in the external ear and the eustachian tube.

Bone

Bone also contains an abundance of connective tissue. Rather than being soft and flexible, bone is hard and rigid because of calcification. Bone is comprised of 50% water and 50% solid material. The hard substance is composed mainly of cartilage impregnated with inorganic salts such as carbonate and phosphate of lime.

GENERAL INJURY MECHANISMS

Injuries related to sports participation can be caused primarily by the sport itself or can occur as a secondary event (Figure 7-1).[22]

Primary Injury

A primary injury is one that results directly from the stress imposed by a particular sport. The injury can be externally caused such as by body contact or use of a piece of equipment. The use of some implement such as a racquet or gymnastics equipment can produce instantaneous acute trauma or overuse microtrauma that becomes chronic from repeated stresses.[22]

Intrinsic injuries result from stresses created within the athlete. They can be acute or can become chronic over a long period of time.

Secondary Injury

Secondary problems can arise from an injury, especially if it has not been properly treated initially with ice, compression, elevation, and rest (ICE-R) or if the athlete has been allowed to return to competition too soon. An example of an early secondary problem after injury may be chronic swelling and weakness in a joint, whereas an example of later occurrence is arthritis that has developed in a joint many years after repeated sprains and improper care.

Nonconsequential causative factors refer to injuries or other problems that are not directly related to stress in a specific sport but adversely influence it. Periodic asthma attacks are an example of a nonconsequential causative factor that can adversely affect performance.[24]

SKIN TRAUMA

Generally, trauma that happens to the skin is visually exposed and is categorized as a skin wound. It is defined as a break in the continuity of the soft parts of body structures caused by a trauma to tissues.

Anatomical Characteristics

The skin, or integument, is the external covering of the body. It represents the body's largest organ system and essentially consists of two layers—the epidermis and the dermis (corium). Because of the soft, pliable nature of skin, it can be easily traumatized (see Chapter 16, *Skin Disorders,* for an in-depth discussion of anatomy).

Causative factors of sports injury.
  I. Consequential factors—primary
  A. Extrinsic (e.g., implemental, vehicular, environmental)
  B. Intrinsic (e.g., instantaneous, overuse)
 II. Nonconsequential factors (e.g., hereditary conditions, chronic conditions, asthma)

Continued.

Figure 7-1

A sports injury may result directly from the sport or may occur as a secondary event.

Figure 7-1, cont'd

For legend see p. 195.

TABLE 7-1 Soft-Tissue Trauma

Primary Tissue	Type	Mechanical Forces	Condition
Skin	Acute	Rubbing/friction	Blister
		Compression/contusion	Bruise
		Tearing	Laceration
		Tearing/ripping	Avulsion
		Penetrating	Puncture
Muscle/tendon	Acute	Compressional	Contusion
		Tension	Strain
	Chronic	Tension/shearing	Myositis/fasciitis
		Tension	Tendinitis/tenosynovitis
		Compression/tension	Bursitis
		Compression/tension	Ectopic calcification—myositis ossificans, calcific tendinitis

Injurious Mechanical Forces

Numerous mechanical forces can adversely affect the skin's integrity. These forces are friction or rubbing, scraping, compression or pressure, tearing, cutting, and penetrating.

Wound Classification

Wounds are classified according to the mechanical force that causes them (Table 7-1).

Blisters Continuous rubbing over the surface of the skin causes a collection of fluid below or within the epidermal layer called a blister.

Abrasions Abrasions are common conditions in which the skin is scraped against a rough surface. The epidermis and dermis are worn away, thus exposing numerous blood capillaries.

Skin bruise When a blow compresses or crushes the skin surface and produces bleeding under the skin, the condition is identified as a bruise, or contusion.

Laceration A laceration is a wound in which the flesh has been irregularly torn.

Skin avulsion Skin that is torn by the same mechanism as a laceration to the extent that tissue is completely ripped from its source is considered an avulsion injury.

Incision An incision wound is one in which the skin has been sharply cut.

Puncture wound Puncture wounds, as the name implies, are penetrations of the skin by a sharp object.

NOTE: Skin wounds (exposed injuries) are discussed in detail in Chapter 16, *Skin Disorders.*

SKELETAL MUSCLE TRAUMA

Skeletal muscles have an extremely high percentage of sports injuries.

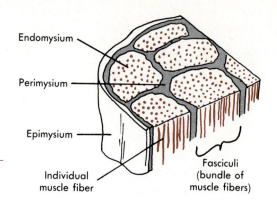

Figure 7-2

Connective tissue related to a skeletal muscle.

Anatomical Characteristics

Muscles are composed of contractile cells, or fibers, that produce movement. Muscle fibers have the ability to contract, plus the properties of irritability, conductivity, and elasticity. Three types of muscles are within the body—smooth, cardiac, and striated. Of major concern in sports medicine are conditions that affect striated, or skeletal, muscles. Within the fiber cell is a semifluid substance called sarcoplasm (cytoplasm). Myofibrils are surrounded by the endomysium, fiber bundles are surrounded by the perimysium, and the entire muscle is covered by the epimysium (Figure 7-2). The epimysium, perimysium, and endomysium may be combined with the fibrous tendon. The fibrous wrapping of a muscle may become a flat sheet of connective tissue (aponeurosis) that attaches to other muscles. Tendons and aponeuroses are extremely resilient to injuries. They will pull away from a bone, a bone will break, or a muscle will tear before tendons and aponeuroses are injured.

Skeletal muscles are generally well supplied with blood vessels that permeate throughout their structure. Arteries, veins, lymph vessels, and bundles of nerve fibers spread into the perimysium. A complex capillary network goes throughout the endomysium, coming into direct contact with the muscle fibers.

Injurious Mechanical Forces

Muscle tissue can be traumatized by three major mechanical forces: compression, tension, and shear (Figure 7-3).

Compression Force

Compression is a force that, with enough energy, crushes tissue. Soft tissue can withstand and absorb compression forces; however, when the force is excessive and can no longer be absorbed, a contusion, or bruise, occurs. Where constant submaximum compression exists over a period of time, the contacted tissue begins to develop an abnormal "wear."

Tension Force

Tension is the force that pulls and stretches tissue. Soft tissue that is suddenly stretched beyond its "yield point" will tear or rupture. When tissue containing a

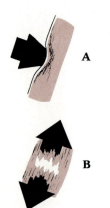

A

B

C

Figure 7-3

Mechanical forces can injure soft tissue. **A,** Compression. **B,** Tension. **C,** Shear.

preponderance of connective tissue such as fascia, tendons, ligaments, and muscle is placed in constant tension, collagen fibers weaken and are subject to injuries.

Shearing Force

A shearing force is one that moves across the parallel organization of collagen fibers. Like compression and tension, once shearing has exceeded the inherent strength of the tissue, injury occurs.

Muscle Injury Classification
Acute Muscle Injuries

The two categories of acute muscle injuries are contusions and strains.

Contusions   A bruise or contusion is received because of a sudden traumatic blow to the body. The intensity of a contusion can range from superficial to deep tissue compression and hemorrhage (Figure 7-4).

Interrupting the continuity of the circulatory system results in a flow of blood and lymph into the surrounding tissues. A hematoma (blood tumor) is formed by the localization of the extravasated blood into a clot, which becomes encapsulated by a connective tissue membrane. The speed of healing, as with all soft-tissue injuries, depends on the extent of tissue damage and internal bleeding.

Contusion or the crushing of soft tissue can penetrate to the skeletal structures, causing a bone bruise. The extent to which an athlete may be hampered by this condition depends on the location of the bruise and the force of the blow. Typical in cases of severe contusion are the following:

1. The athlete reports being struck a hard blow.
2. The blow causes pain and a transitory paralysis caused by pressure on and shock to the motor and sensory nerves.
3. Palpation often reveals a hard area, indurated because of internal hemorrhage.
4. Ecchymosis or tissue discoloration may take place.

Muscle contusions are usually rated by the extent the muscle is able to produce range of motion in a part. For example, a first-degree contusion will cause little movement restriction, a second-degree contusion will restrict some range of movement, and a third-degree injury usually severely restricts motion. It is noteworthy that a blow to a muscle can be so great that the related fascia is ruptured, allowing muscle tissue to protrude through it.

Strains   A strain is a stretch, tear, or rip in the muscle or adjacent tissue such as the fascia or muscle tendons (Figure 7-5). The cause of muscle strain is often obscure. Most often a strain is produced by an abnormal muscular contraction. The cause of this abnormality has been attributed to many factors. One popular theory suggests that a fault in the reciprocal coordination of the agonist and antagonist muscles takes place. The cause of this fault or incoordination is more or less a mystery. However, among the possible explanations advanced are that it may be related to (1) a mineral imbalance caused by profuse sweating, (2) fatigue metabolites collected in the muscle itself, or (3) a strength imbalance between agonist and antagonist muscles.

A strain may range from a minute separation of connective tissue and muscle fibers to a complete tendinous avulsion or muscle rupture (graded as *first, second,* or *third degree*). The resulting pathology is similar to that of the contusion or sprain, with capillary or blood vessel hemorrhage. The first-degree strain is ac-

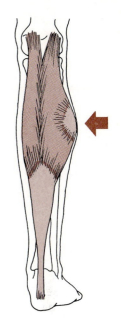

Figure 7-4

A contusion can range from a superficial to a deep-tissue compression *(arrow),* injuring cells and causing relative amounts of hemorrhage.

Figure 7-5

A strain can occur to any aspect of the musculo-tendinous unit. Depending on the amount of force, a strain can stretch or tear muscle fibers *(arrow)* or even avulse a tendon from a bone.

companied by local pain, which is increased by tension of the muscle, and a minor loss of strength. There is mild swelling, ecchymosis and local tenderness.[18] The second-degree strain is similar to the mild strain but has moderate signs and symptoms and impaired muscle function.[18] A third-degree strain has signs and symptoms that are severe, with a loss of muscle function and commonly a palpable defect in the muscle.[18] Healing takes place in a similar fashion, with the organization of a hematoma, absorption of the hematoma, and finally the formation of a cicatrix (scar) by fibroblastic repair. Detection of the injury is accomplished by understanding how the injury occurred and the administration of a muscle test to determine the specific locality. The muscles that have the highest incidence of strains in sports are the hamstring group, gastrocnemius, quadriceps group, hip flexors, hip adductor group, spinalis group of the back, deltoid, and rotator cuff group of the shoulder.

Tendon injuries   In tendons, collagen fibers will break if their physiological limits have been reached. A breaking point occurs after a 6% to 8% increase in length.[6] Because a tendon is usually double the strength of the muscle it serves, tears commonly occur at the muscle belly, musculotendinous junction, or bony attachment. Clinically, however, a constant abnormal tension on tendons increases elongation by the infiltration of fibroblasts, which will cause more collagenous tissue to be produced.[5] Repeated microtraumas can evolve into chronic muscle strain that resorbs collagen fibers and eventually weakens the tendon. Collagen resorption occurs in the early period of sports conditioning and during the immobilization of a part. During resorption collagenous tissues are weakened and susceptible to injury; therefore, a gradually paced conditioning program and early mobilization in the rehabilitation process are necessary.[7]

Muscle cramps and spasms   Leading to muscle and tendon injuries are muscle cramps and spasms. A cramp is usually a painful involuntary contraction of a skeletal muscle or muscle group. Cramps have been attributed to a lack of salt or other minerals or muscle fatigue. A reflex reaction caused by trauma of the musculoskeletal system is commonly called a spasm. The two types of cramps or spasms are the clonic type, with alternating involuntary muscular contraction and relaxation in quick succession, and the tonic type, with rigid muscle contraction that lasts over a period of time.

Chronic Muscle Injuries

As discussed previously, chronic injuries usually come with a slow progression over a long period of time. Often, repeated acute injuries can lead to a chronic condition. A constant irritation caused by poor performance techniques or a constant stress beyond physiological limits can eventually result in a chronic condition. These injuries are often attributed to overuse microtraumas.

Chronic muscle injuries are representative of a low-grade inflammatory process with a proliferation of fibroblasts and scarring. The acute injury that is improperly managed or that allows an athlete to return to activity before healing has completely occurred can cause chronic injury. The student should be especially knowledgeable about six chronic muscle conditions: myositis, tendinitis, tenosynovitis, bursitis, ectopic calcification, and muscle atrophy and contracture.

Myositis/fasciitis   In general, the term myositis means inflammation of muscle tissue. More specifically, it can be considered as a fibrocitis or connective tissue inflammation. Fascia that supports and separates muscle can also become chron-

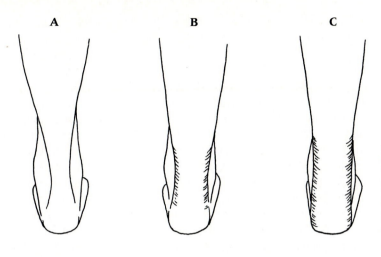

Figure 7-6

Tenosynovitis is an inflammation of the sheath covering a tendon. **A,** Normal. **B,** Strained. **C,** Chronic tenosynovitis.

ically inflamed following injury. A typical example of this condition is plantar fasciitis.

Tendinitis　Tendinitis has a gradual onset, diffuse tenderness because of repeated microtraumas, and degenerative changes. Obvious signs of tendinitis are swelling and pain that move with the tendon.

Tenosynovitis　Tenosynovitis is inflammation of the sheath covering a tendon. In its acute state there is rapid onset, articular crepitus, and diffuse swelling. In chronic tenosynovitis the tendons become locally thickened, with pain and articular crepitus present during movement (Figure 7-6).

Bursitis　The bursa is the fluid-filled sac found in places where friction might occur within body tissues. Bursae are predominantly located between bony prominences and muscles or tendons. Sudden irritation can cause acute bursitis and overuse of muscles or tendons, as well as constant external compression or trauma, can result in chronic bursitis. The signs and symptoms of bursitis include swelling, pain, and some loss of function. Repeated trauma may lead to calcific deposits and degeneration of the internal lining of the bursa.[11]

Ectopic calcification　Voluntary muscles can become chronically inflamed, resulting in myositis. An **ectopic** calcification known as *myositis ossificans* can occur in a muscle that directly overlies a bone. Two common sites for this condition are the quadriceps region of the thigh and the brachial muscle of the arm. In myositis ossificans osteoid material that resembles bone rapidly accumulates. If there is no repeated injury, the growth may subside completely in 9 to 12 months, or it may mature into a calcified area, at which time surgical removal can be accomplished with little fear of recurrence.[16] Occasionally, tendinitis leads to deposits of minerals, primarily lime, and is known as *calcific tendinitis*.

ectopic
Located in a place different from normal.

Atrophy and contracture　Two complications of muscle and tendon conditions are atrophy and contracture. Muscle atrophy is the wasting away of muscle tissue. Its main cause in athletes is immobilization of a body part, inactivity, or loss of nerve stimulation. A second complication to sport injuries is *muscle contracture,* an abnormal shortening of muscle tissue in which there is a great deal of resistance to passive stretch. Commonly associated with muscle injury, a contracture is associated with a joint that has developed unyielding and resisting scar tissue.

SYNOVIAL JOINTS

The joint of the human body is defined as the point where two bones join together. A joint must also transmit forces between participating bones.[13]

Anatomical Characteristics

The joint consists of cartilage and fibrous connective tissue. Joints are classified as immovable (synarthrotic), slightly movable (amphiarthrotic), and freely movable (diarthrotic). Diarthrotic joints are also called synovial articulations. Because of their ability to move freely and thus become more susceptible to trauma, joints are of major concern to the coach, the athletic trainer, and the physician. Anatomical characteristics of the synovial articulations consist of four features, which are as follows: (1) they have a capsule and/or ligaments; (2) the capsule is lined with a synovial membrane; (3) the opposing bone surfaces contain hyaline cartilage; and (4) there is a joint space (joint cavity) containing a small amount of fluid (synovial fluid) (Figure 7-7). In addition, there are nerves and blood supplied to the synovial articulation, and there are muscles that cross the joint or are intrinsic to it.

Joint Capsule

Bones of the diarthrotic joint are held together by a cuff of fibrous tissue known as the capsule, or capsular ligament. It consists of bundles of collagen and functions primarily to hold the bones together. It is extremely strong and can withstand cross-sectional forces of 500 kg/cm^2. Parts of the capsule become slack or taut, depending on the joint movements.

Ligaments

Ligaments are sheets or bundles of collagen fibers that form a connection between two bones. Ligaments fall into two categories: ones that are considered intrinsic and ones that are extrinsic to the joint. Intrinsic ligaments occur where the articular capsule has become thickened in some places. Extrinsic ligaments are separate from the capsular thickening.

A major factor in ligamentous injury is the viscoelastic tissue properties of ligaments and capsules. Viscoelastic refers to an extensibility when loaded that is time dependent.[14] Constant compression or tension will cause ligaments to deteriorate, whereas intermittent compression and tension increase strength and

Constant compression or tension will cause ligaments to deteriorate; intermittent compression and tension will increase strength and growth.

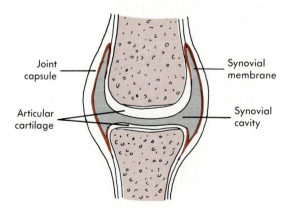

Joint capsule

Synovial membrane

Articular cartilage

Synovial cavity

Figure 7-7

Anatomy of the diarthrodial joint.

growth, especially at the bony attachment.[5] Chronic inflammation of ligamentous, capsular, and fascial tissue causes a shrinkage of collagen fibers; therefore, repeated microtraumas over time make capsules and ligaments highly susceptible to major acute injuries.

Ligaments act as protective backups for the joint. Primary protection occurs from the dynamic aspect of muscles and their tendons.[1] In a fast-loading situation, ligament failure ultimately will occur; however, the capsule and ligament do provide maximum protection during rapid movements. Nevertheless, capsular and ligamentous tissues are highly sensitive to the deprivation caused by normal stress through joint immobilization. On the other hand, they do respond positively to activities of daily living and to specific exercise.[1] Capsular and ligamentous tissue respond to Roux's law of functional adaptation: an organ will adapt itself structurally to an alteration, quantitative or qualitative, of function.[20]

Synovial Membrane and Synovial Fluid

Lining the synovial articular capsule is a synovial membrane that is comprised of connective tissue with flattened cells and villi (small projections) on its inner aspect. Fluid is secreted and absorbed by the synovial membrane. Synovial fluid has the consistency of egg whites and acts as a joint lubricant. It has the ability to vary its viscosity. During slow movement, the fluid becomes thick, whereas during fast movement, it thins. The presence of hyaluronic acid causes this variation in fluid thickness.

Articular Cartilage

As mentioned previously, the ends of the bones in a diarthrotic joint are covered by hyaline cartilage, which acts as a cushion for the bone ends. Its general appearance is smooth and pearly. Hyaline cartilage acts like a sponge in relation to synovial fluid. As movement occurs, it absorbs and squeezes out the fluid as pressures vary between the joint surfaces. Because of its great strength, the cartilage can be deformed without damage and can still return to its original shape. However, cartilagenous degeneration, producing microtrauma, may occur during the abnormal compressional forces that occur over a period of time.

Hyaline cartilage has no direct blood supply, receiving its nourishment from the synovial fluid—more specifically, from the synovial membrane located at its edges. Deeper aspects of the cartilage are fed by spaces (lacunae) in the adjacent bone.

Additional Synovial Joint Structures
Fat

In some joints such as the knee and elbow, there are pads of fat that lie between the synovial membrane and the capsule. They tend to fill in the spaces between the bones that form joints. As movement occurs, they move in and out of these spaccs.

Articular Disks

Some diarthrotic joints are provided with an additional fibrocartilagenous disk. These disks vary in shape and are connected to the capsule. They are found in joints where two planes of movement exist and may act as "spreaders" of the synovial fluid between the joint surfaces.

TABLE 7-2 General Relative Strength Grades in Selected Articulations

Articulation	Skeleton	Ligaments	Muscles
Ankle	Strong	Moderate	Weak
Knee	Weak	Moderate	Strong
Hip	Strong	Strong	Strong
Lumbosacral	Weak	Strong	Moderate
Lumbar vertebrae	Strong	Strong	Moderate
Thoracic vertebrae	Strong	Strong	Moderate
Cervical vertebrae	Weak	Moderate	Strong
Sternoclavicular	Weak	Weak	Weak
Acromioclavicular	Weak	Moderate	Weak
Glenohumeral	Weak	Moderate	Moderate
Elbow	Moderate	Strong	Strong
Wrist	Weak	Moderate	Moderate
Phalanges (toes and fingers)	Weak	Moderate	Moderate

Nerve Supply

The articular capsule, ligaments, outer aspects of the synovial membrane, and fat pads of the synovial joint are well supplied with nerves. The inner aspect of the synovial membrane, cartilage, and articular disks, if present, have nerves as well. Mechanoreceptors (encapsulated nerve endings) provide information about the relative position of the joint and are found in the fibrous capsule and ligaments. They are myelinated, whereas nonmyelinated fibers are pain receptors or blood vessel suppliers.

Types of Synovial Joints

Synovial joints are subdivided into six types—ball and socket, hinge, pivot, ellipsoidal, saddle, and gliding. *Ball and socket* joints allow all possible movement (e.g., shoulder and hip joints). *Hinge* joints allow only flexion and extension (e.g., elbow joint). *Pivot* joints permit rotation around an axis (e.g., cervical atlas and axis, proximal ends of radius and ulna. *Ellipsoidal* joints have an elliptical convex head in an elliptical concave socket (e.g., wrist joint). *Saddle-shaped* joints are reciprocally concavoconvex (e.g., carpometacarpal joint of the thumb). *Gliding* joints allow a small amount of gliding back and forth or sideways (e.g., joints between the carpal and tarsal bones and all of the joints between the articular processes of the vertebrae).

Functional Synovial Joint Characteristics

Synovial joints differ in their ability to withstand trauma, depending on their skeletal, ligamentous, and muscular organization. Table 7-2 provides a general guide to the relative strength of selected articulations in terms of sports participation.

Synovial Joint Stabilization

Muscle tension is important in limiting synovial joint movement. Limitation may be the result of contacting another body. When the joint capsule is overstretched, a reflex contraction of muscles in the area occurs to prevent overstretching. This reaction demonstrates Hilton's law, which states that the joint capsule, muscles moving that joint, and the skin overlying the insertion of the muscles have the same nerve supply. Ligaments, for the most part, are not extensible but can be extended as a result of the collagen fibers being arranged in bundles at right angles to one another. As the angles of the bundles are changed, ligaments can be extended without lengthening the collagen fiber.

In terms of stability, ligaments and capsular structures are highly important to joints. Characteristically, joints that are shallow and relatively poor fitting must depend on their capsular structures and/or muscles for major support. The knee is an example of an articulation that lacks bony congruence and depends mainly on muscles and ligaments for its support.

Besides moving limbs, muscles also provide joint stabilization to a greater or lesser extent and absorb the forces of load transmission. Muscles help stabilize joints in the following ways: (1) muscles that cross joints assist in maintaining proper articular alignment; and (2) some muscles attach directly to the articular capsule (shunt muscles) and, when stretched, also tighten the capsule. By becoming taut the shunt muscles prevent the articulations from separating and also assist in maintaining proper alignment.[5]

Articular Capsule and Ligaments

Capsular and ligamentous tissue maintains anatomical integrity and structural alignment of synovial joints. Both of these structures are similar in composition to tendons. However, they contain elastic fibers, and their collagenous fibers, although having many configurations, are irregular and have a spiral arrangement. Attaching bone to bone, ligaments are generally strongest in the middle and weakest at the ends.[5] In comparison to the fast, protective response of ligaments and capsular tissues, muscles respond much more slowly. For example, a muscle begins to develop protective tension within just a few hundredths of a second when overly stretched but will not fully respond until approximately one tenth of a second has elapsed.[6] The articular cartilage, which is classified as soft tissue, has three major mechanical functions: control of joint motion, joint stability, and force or load transmission.[12]

Motion control The shape of the articular surface determines what motion will occur. An enarthrodial joint or a ball and socket joint such as the hip is considered a universal joint, allowing movement in all planes. In contrast, a hinge joint such as the interphalangeal joint allows movement in only one plane.

Stability In general, bones that form a joint normally closely match with one another and produce varying degrees of stability, depending on their particular shape.

Load transmission The articular cartilage assists in transmitting a joint load smoothly and uniformly. The atmospheric pressure within the joint space must be kept constant at all times.

Injurious Mechanical Forces

Three major mechanical forces, when exceeding a synovial joint's normal protective response, can result in acute or chronic trauma. They include tension, including torsional forces, shear, and compression (Table 7-3).

A major factor in joint injuries is the viscoelastic tissue properties of ligaments

TABLE 7-3 Synovial Joint Trauma

Primary Tissue	Type	Mechanical Forces	Condition
Capsule	Acute	Tension/compression	Sprains Dislocation/subluxation Synovial swelling
	Chronic	Tension/compression/ shearing	Capsulitis Synovitis Bursitis
Articular cartilage (hyaline)	Chronic	Compression/shearing	Osteochondrosis Traumatic arthritis

and capsules. As mentioned previously, *viscoelastic* refers to the extensibility of collagen fibers that is time dependent. This extensibility is dependent on the rapidity of the movement. Constant compression or tension can cause ligaments and/or capsular tissue to deteriorate. In contrast, intermittent compression and tension will, over time, increase the overall strength, including that of the bony attachments of the connective tissue. Much like tension forces, torsional or twisting forces, when exceeding the relative strength of collagen fibers, can produce injury. Although occurring less often, a shearing action that cuts across the collagen fiber can traumatize capsular and ligamentous tissue. When articular cartilage fails to properly transmit the applied loads, tissue damage may occur. In other words, the bones and hyaline cartilage that form a joint become out of accordance with each other's compressional forces over a period of time and predispose the joint to degenerative changes.

Synovial Joint Injury Classification
Acute Joint Injuries

The major injuries that happen to synovial joints are sprains, subluxations, and dislocations.

Sprains   The sprain, one of the most common and disabling injuries seen in sports, is a traumatic joint twist that results in stretching or total tearing of the stabilizing connective tissues (Figure 7-8). When a joint is forced beyond its normal anatomical limits, microscopic and gross pathologies occur. Specifically, there is injury to ligaments, to the articular capsule and synovial membrane, and to the tendons crossing the joint. According to the extent of injury, sprains are graded in three degrees. A first-degree sprain is characterized by some pain, minimum loss of function, mild point tenderness, little or no swelling, and no abnormal motion when tested.[18] With a second-degree sprain, there is pain, moderate loss of function, swelling, and, in some cases, slight-to-moderate instability.[18] A third-degree, or severe, sprain is very painful, with major loss of function, marked instability, tenderness, and swelling.[18] A third-degree sprain may also represent a subluxation that has spontaneously been reduced.

Effusion of blood and synovial fluid into the joint cavity during a sprain produces joint swelling, local temperature increase, pain or point tenderness, and skin discoloration (ecchymosis). As with tendons, ligaments and/or capsules can experience forces that completely rupture or produce an avulsion fracture.

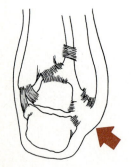

Figure 7-8

A sprain mainly involves ligamentous and capsular tissue *(arrow)*; however, tendons also can be secondarily involved. A joint that is forced beyond its anatomical limits can stretch and tear tissue and, on occasion, avulse ligaments from their bony attachments.

Ligaments and capsules heal slowly because of a relatively poor blood supply; however, their nerves are plentiful, often producing a great deal of pain when injured.

The joints that are most vulnerable to sprains in sports are the ankles, knees, and shoulders. Sprains occur least often to the wrists and elbows. Since it is often difficult to distinguish between joint sprains and tendon strains, the examiner should expect the worst possible condition and manage it accordingly. Repeated joint twisting can eventually result in chronic inflammation, degeneration, and arthritis.

Acute synovitis   The synovial membrane of a joint can be acutely injured by a contusion or a sprain. Irritation of the membrane causes an increase in fluid production, and swelling occurs. As the result, there is joint pain during motion, along with skin sensitivity from pressure at certain points. In a few days, with proper care, effusion and extravasated blood are absorbed, and swelling and pain diminish.

Subluxations and dislocations   Dislocations are second to fractures in terms of disabling the athlete. The highest incidence of dislocations involves the fingers and, next, the shoulder joint (Figure 7-9). Dislocations, which result primarily from forces causing the joint to go beyond its normal anatomical limits, are divided into two classes: *subluxations* and *luxations*. Subluxations are partial dislocations in which an incomplete separation between two articulating bones occurs. Luxations are complete dislocations, presenting a total disunion of bone apposition between the articulating surfaces.

Several important factors are important in recognizing and evaluating dislocations:

1. There is a loss of limb function. The athlete usually complains of having fallen or of having received a severe blow to a particular joint and then suddenly being unable to move that part.
2. Deformity is almost always apparent. Since the deformity can often be obscured by heavy musculature, it is important for the examiner to palpate the injured site to determine the loss of normal body contour. Comparison of the injured side with its normal counterpart often reveals distortions.
3. Swelling and point tenderness are immediately present.

At times, as with a fracture, x-ray examination is the only absolute diagnostic measure. First-time dislocations or joint separations may result in a rupture of the stabilizing ligamentous and tendinous tissues surrounding the joint and avulsion or pulling away from the bone. Trauma is often so violent that small chips of

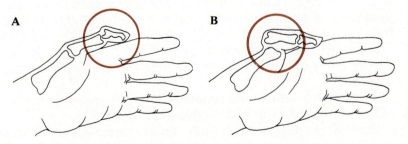

A   B

Figure 7-9

A joint that is forced beyond its anatomical limits can become partially dislocated (subluxated), **A,** or completely dislocated (luxated), **B.**

bone are torn away with the supporting structures, or the force may separate growth epiphyses or cause a complete fracture of the neck in long bones. These possibilities indicate the importance of administering complete and thorough medical attention to first-time dislocations. It has often been said, "Once a dislocation, always a dislocation." In most cases this statement is true, since once a joint has been either subluxated or completely luxated, the connective tissues that bind and hold it in its correct alignment are stretched to such an extent that the joint will be extremely vulnerable to subsequent dislocations. Chronic, recurring dislocations may take place without severe pain because of the somewhat slack condition of the stabilizing tissues.

A first-time dislocation should always be considered and treated as a possible fracture. Once it has been ascertained that the injury is a dislocation, a physician should be consulted for further evaluation. However, before the patient is taken to the physician, the injury should be properly splinted and supported to prevent any further damage.

> A first-time dislocation should always be considered a possible fracture.

Chronic Joint Injuries

As with other chronic physical injuries or problems occurring from sports participation, chronic synovial joint injuries stem from microtraumas and overuse. The two major categories in which they fall are osteochondrosis and traumatic arthritis (osteoarthritis and/or inflammation of surrounding soft tissues such as the bursal capsule and the synovium).[8] Another general expression for the chronic synovial conditions of the child or adolescent is articular epiphysial injury.

Osteochondrosis   Osteochondrosis is a category of conditions in which the causes are not well understood. A synonym for this condition, if it is located in a point such as the knee, is *osteochondritis dissecans* and, if located at a tubercle or tuberosity, *apophysitis.* Apophysial conditions are discussed in the section "Bone Trauma."

One suggested cause of osteochondrosis is aseptic necrosis in which circulation to the epiphysis has been disrupted. Another suggestion is that trauma causes particles of the articular cartilage to fracture, eventually resulting in fissures that penetrate to the subchondral bone. If trauma to a joint occurs, pieces of cartilage may be dislodged, which can cause joint locking, swelling, and pain. If the condition occurs in an apophysis, there may be an avulsion-type fracture and fragmentation of the epiphysis, along with pain, swelling, and disability.[16]

Traumatic arthritis   Traumatic arthritis is usually the result of microtraumas. With repeated trauma to the articular joint surfaces, the bone and synovium thicken, and there are pain, muscle spasm, and articular crepitus or grating on movement. Joint insult leading to arthritis can come from repeated sprains that leave a joint with weakened ligaments. There can be malalignment of the skeleton, which stresses joints, or it can arise from an irregular joint surface that stems from repeated articular chondral injuries. Loose bodies that have been dislodged from the articular surface can also irritate and produce arthritis. Athletes with joint injuries that are improperly immobilized or who are allowed to return to activity before proper healing has occurred may eventually be afflicted with arthritis.

> Athletes with improperly immobilized joint injuries or who are allowed to return to activity before proper healing has occurred may eventually be afflicted with arthritis.

Bursitis, capsulitis, and synovitis   The soft tissues that are an integral part of the synovial joint can develop chronic problems.

Bursitis   As discussed previously, bursae provide protection between tendons and bones, between tendons and ligaments, and between other structures where

there is friction. Bursae located in and around synovial joints can be acutely or, over a period of time, chronically inflamed. Bursitis in the knee, elbow, and shoulder is common among athletes.

Capsulitis and synovitis After repeated joint sprains or microtraumas, a chronic inflammatory condition, capsulitis, may occur. Usually associated with capsulitis is synovitis. Synovitis also occurs acutely, but with repeated joint injury or with joint injury that is improperly managed, a chronic condition can arise. Chronic synovitis involves active joint congestion with edema. As with the synovial lining of the bursa, the synovium of a joint can undergo degenerative tissue changes. The synovium becomes irregularly thickened, exudation is present, and a fibrous underlying tissue is present as well. Several movements may be restricted, and there may be joint noises such as grinding or creaking.

BONE TRAUMA

Bone provides shape and support for the body. As with soft tissue, it can be traumatized during sports participation.

Anatomical Characteristics

As discussed previously, bone is a specialized type of dense connective tissue, consisting of bone cells (osteocytes) that are fixed in a matrix, which consists of an intercellular material. The outer surface of a bone is composed of compact tissue, whereas the inner aspect is composed of a more porous tissue known as cancellous bone (Figure 7-10). Compact tissue is tunneled by a marrow cavity. Throughout the bone run countless branching canals, which contain blood vessels and lymphatic vessels. These canals form the Haversian system. On the outside of a bone is a tissue covering, the periosteum, which contains the blood supply to the bone.

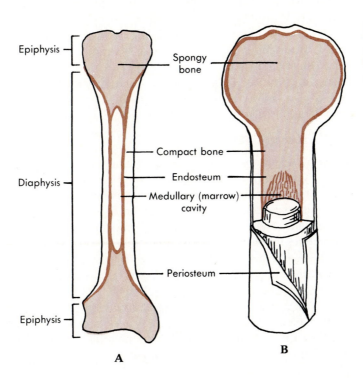

Figure 7-10

Anatomical characteristics of bone. **A,** Longitudinal section. **B,** Cutaway section.

Bone Functions

Bones perform five basic functions: body support, organ protection, movement (through joints and levers), a reservoir for calcium, and the formation of blood cells (hemopoiesis).

Types of Bone

Bones are classified according to their shapes. They include those bones that are flat, irregular, short, and long. Flat bones are in the skull, the ribs, and the scapulae; irregular bones are in the vertebral column and the skull. Short bones are primarily in the wrist and the ankle. Long bones are the most commonly injured ones in sports. They consist of the humerus, ulna, femur, tibia, fibula, and phalanges.

Flat, irregular, and short bones have the same inner cancellous bone over which is a layer of compact bone. A few irregular and flat bones (e.g., the vertebrae and the sternum) have some space in the cancellous bone that is filled with red marrow.

Gross Structures

The gross structures of bone that are visible to the naked eye include the diaphysis, epiphysis, articular cartilage, periosteum, medullary (marrow) cavity, and endosteum. The *diaphysis* is the main shaft of the long bone. It is hollow, cylindrical, and covered by compact bone. The *epiphysis* is located at the ends of long bones. It is bulbous in shape, providing space for the muscle attachments. The epiphysis is composed primarily of cancellous bone, giving it a spongelike appearance. As discussed previously, the ends of long bones are covered with a layer of *hyaline cartilage* that covers the joint surfaces of the epiphysis. This cartilage provides protection during movement and cushions jars and blows to the joint. A dense, white fibrous membrane, the *periosteum,* covers long bones except at joint surfaces. Many fibers, called Sharpey's fibers, from the periosteum penetrate the underlying bone. Interlacing with the periosteum are fibers from the muscle tendons. Throughout the periosteum on its inner layer exist countless blood vessels and osteoblasts (bone-forming cells). The blood vessels provide nutrition to the bone, and the osteoblasts provide bone growth and repair. The *medullar cavity,* which is a hollow tube in the long bone diaphysis, contains a yellow, fatty marrow in adults. Lining the medullar cavity is the *endosteum.*

Microscopic Structures

Calcium salts impregnate the intercellular substance of bone, making it very hard. Osteocytes are found in small, hollow spaces called *lacunae.* Running throughout the bone is the Haversian system, consisting of a central tube (Haversian canal) with alternate layers of intercellular matrix surrounding it in concentric cylinders. Haversian systems are the structural units of compact bone. Compact and cancellous bones differ in their structures. In bone that is compact, interspersed lamellae fill the spaces between adjacent Haversian systems. In cancellous bone, there are numerous open spaces located between thin processes called *trabeculae.* Trabeculae act like a scaffold, joining cancellous bone. They arrange themselves along the line of greatest stress, providing additional structural strength to the bone.

The blood circulation connects the periosteum with the Haversian canal through the Volkmann's canal. The medullary cavity and the bone marrow are supplied directly by one or more arteries.

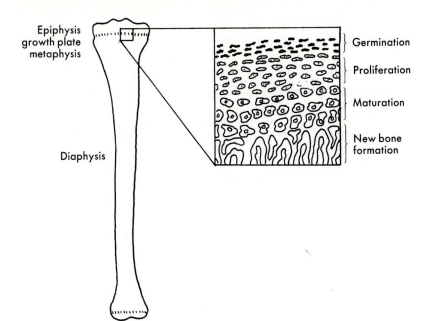

Epiphysis growth plate metaphysis

Germination

Proliferation

Maturation

New bone formation

Diaphysis

Figure 7-11

The epiphyseal growth plate is the cartilagenous disk located near the end of each long bone.

Bone Growth

In general, bone ossification occurs from the synthesis of bone's organic matrix by osteoblasts, followed immediately by the calcification of this matrix.

The epiphyseal growth plate is a cartilagenous disk located near the end of each long bone. Growth of the long bones depends on these plates. Ossification in long bones begins in the diaphysis and in both epiphyses. It proceeds from the diaphysis toward each epiphysis and from each epiphysis toward the diaphysis.[2] The growth plate has layers of cartilage cells in different stages of maturity with the more immature cells at one end and mature ones at the other end. As the cartilage cells mature, immature osteoblasts replace them later to produce solid bone (Figure 7-11). Epiphyseal growth plates are often less resistant to deforming forces than are ligaments of nearby joints or the outer shaft of the long bones; therefore, severe twisting or a blow to an arm or leg can result in disruption in growth.[17] Injury can prematurely close the growth plate, causing a loss of length in the bone. Growth plate dislocation can also cause deformity of the long bone.

Epiphyseal growth plate injuries have been classified by Salter-Harris[21] into five types as follows:

Type I   Complete separation of the epiphysis in relation to the metaphysis without fracture to the bone

Type II   Separation of the growth plate and a small portion of the metaphysis

Type III   Fracture of the epiphysis

Type IV   Fracture of a portion of the epiphysis and metaphysis

Type V   No displacement of the epiphysis, but the crushing force can cause a growth deformity

Bone diameter increases as the result of the combined action of osteoblasts and osteoclasts. Osteoblasts build new bone on the outside of the bone; at the same time osteoclasts increase the medullary cavity by breaking down bony tissue. Once a bone has reached its full size, there occurs a balance of bone formation and bone destruction, or osteogenesis and resorption, respectively. This process may be disrupted by factors in sports conditioning and/or participation. They may cause greater osteogenesis than resorption. Conversely, resorption may exceed osteogenesis in situations in which the athlete is out of shape but overtrains. On the other hand, females whose estrogen is decreased as the result of training may experience bone loss.[4] (See Chapter 25, *Other Health Conditions Related to Sports*.) In general, bone loss begins to exceed bone gain by ages 35 to 40. Gradually, bone is lost in the endosteal surfaces and then is gained on the outer surfaces. As the thickness of long bones decreases, they are less able to resist the forces of compression. This process also leads to increased bone porosity, known as osteoporosis.

As with other structures in the human body, bones are morphologically, biochemically, and biomechanically highly sensitive to both stress and stress deprivation. With this in mind, bone's functional adaptation follows Wolff's law[25]: *Every change in the form and function of a bone, or of its function alone, is followed by certain definite changes in its internal architecture and equally definite secondary alterations in its mathematical laws.*

Injurious Mechanical Forces

Because of its viscoelastic properties, bone will bend slightly. However, bone is generally brittle and is a poor shock absorber because of its mineral content. This brittleness increases under tension forces as opposed to compression forces.

Many factors of bone structure affect its strength. Anatomical strength or weakness can be affected by a bone's shape and its changes in shape or direction. A hollow cylinder is one of the strongest structures for resisting both bending and twisting as compared to a solid rod that has much less resistance to such forces.[9]

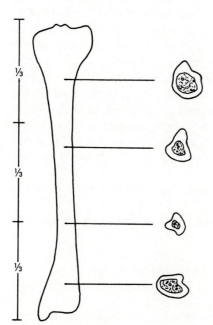

Figure 7-12

Anatomical strengths or weaknesses of a long bone can be affected by its shape, changes of direction, and hollowness.

This may be why bones such as the tibia are primarily cylinders. Most spiral fractures of the tibia occur at its middle and distal third, where the bone is most solid (Figure 7-12).

Anatomical Weak Points

Stress forces become concentrated where a long bone suddenly changes shape and direction. Long bones that change shape gradually are less prone to injury than those which change suddenly. The clavicle, for example, is prone to fracture because it changes from round to flat at the same time it changes direction.

Load Characteristics

Long bones can be stressed or loaded to fail by *tension, compression, bending, twisting* (torsion), and *shearing.* These forces, either singularly or in combination, can cause a variety of fractures. For example, spiral fractures are caused by twisting, whereas oblique fractures are caused by the combined forces of axial compression, bending, and torsion. Transverse fractures occur by bending (Figure 7-13).

Along with the type of stress, the amount of the load must be considered. The more complex the fracture, the more energy is required. Energy is used in deforming the bone and actually breaking the bony tissue, whereas some energy becomes dissipated in adjacent soft tissue.[9]

The rate of energy at which a force is applied to a long bone affects its failing point, sometimes called the *yield point.* At this point, the tissue tears or fractures.

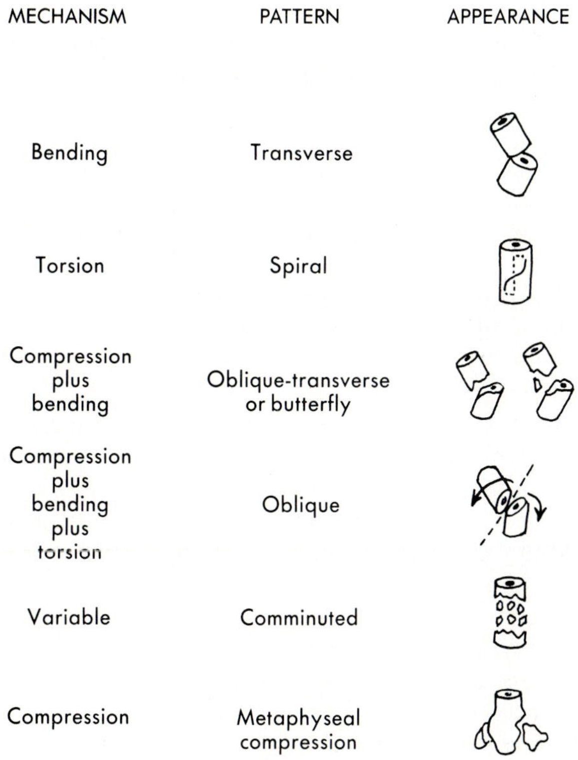

> Long bones can be stressed by tension, compression, bending, torsion, and shearing.

MECHANISM	PATTERN	APPEARANCE
Bending	Transverse	
Torsion	Spiral	
Compression plus bending	Oblique-transverse or butterfly	
Compression plus bending plus torsion	Oblique	
Variable	Comminuted	
Compression	Metaphyseal compression	

Figure 7-13

Mechanisms, patterns, and appearance of acute bone fractures.

Depending on the type of bony tissue, more energy is generally required to cause fracture in a shorter period of time than over a longer period of time.[22]

A bone's magnitude of stress and strain is most prevalent at its outer surface, gradually decreasing to zero at its center. When there is bending on the bone's shaft, tension occurs on one side and compression on the other side. Torsion, or rotary forces, apply tension to all parts of the bone.[15]

Bone Trauma Classification

Bone trauma can generally be classified as periostitis, acute fractures, stress fractures, and epiphyseal conditions.

Periostitis

An inflammation of the periosteum can result from various sports traumas, mainly contusion. It often appears as skin rigidity of the overlying muscles. It can occur as an acute episode or can become chronic.

Acute Bone Fractures

A bone fracture can be a partial or complete interruption in a bone's continuity and can occur without external exposure or can extend through the skin, creating an external wound (compound fracture). Fractures can result from direct trauma; in other words, the bone breaks directly at the site where a force is applied. When the fracture occurs some distance from where force is applied, it is called an indirect fracture. A sudden, violent muscle contraction or repetitive abnormal stress to a bone can also cause a fracture. Fractures must be considered one of the most serious hazards of sports and should be routinely suspected in musculoskeletal injuries. The following are more detailed descriptions of acute fractures.

Avulsion fracture   An avulsion fracture is the separation of a bone fragment from its cortex at an attachment of a ligament or tendon. This fracture usually occurs as a result of a sudden, powerful twist or stretch of a body part. An example of a ligamentous episode is the sudden eversion of the foot that causes the deltoid ligament to avulse bone away from the medial malleolus. An example of a tendinous avulsion is one that causes a patellar fracture, which occurs when an athlete falls forward while suddenly bending a knee. The stretch of the patellar tendon pulls a portion of the inferior patellar pole apart (Figure 7-14).

Blow-out fractures   Blow-out fractures occur to the wall of the eye orbit as the result of a blow to the eye.

Stress Fractures

Stress fractures have been variously called march, fatigue, and spontaneous fractures, although stress fracture is the most commonly used term. The exact cause of this fracture is not known, but there are a number of likely possibilities such as an overload caused by muscle contraction, an altered stress distribution in the bone accompanying muscle fatigue, a change in the ground reaction force such as going from a wood surface to a grass surface, and performing a rhythmically repetitive stress leading up to a vibratory summation point. The last possibility is favored by many authorities.[23] Rhythmic muscle action performed over a period of time at a subthreshold level causes the stress-bearing capacity of the bone to be exceeded, hence a stress fracture. A bone may become vulnerable to fracture during the first few weeks of intense physical activity or training. Weight-bearing

Figure 7-14

Mechanism of a tendinous avulsion fracture caused by the sartorius muscle's being abnormally stretched.

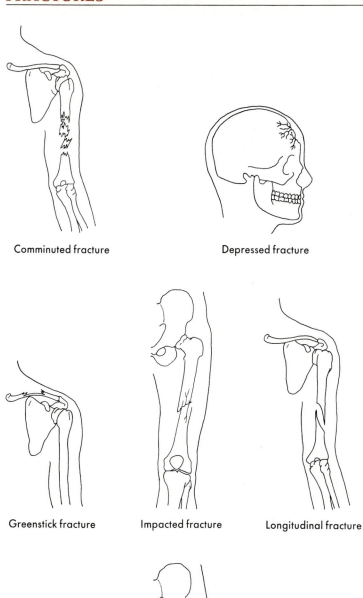

Comminuted fracture

Depressed fracture

Greenstick fracture

Impacted fracture

Longitudinal fracture

Oblique fracture

Comminuted fractures consist of three or more fragments at the fracture site. They could be caused by a hard blow or a fall in an awkward position. From the physician's point of view, these fractures impose a difficult healing situation because of the displacement of the bone fragments. Soft tissues are often interposed between the fragments, causing incomplete healing. Such cases may need surgical intervention.

Depressed fractures occur most often in flat bones such as those found in the skull. They are caused by falling and striking the head on a hard, immovable surface or by being hit with a hard object. Such injuries also result in gross pathology of soft areas.

Greenstick fractures are incomplete breaks in bones that have not completely ossified. They occur most frequently in the convex bone surface, with the concave surface remaining intact. The name is derived from the similarity of the fracture to the break in a green twig taken from a tree.

Impacted fractures can result from a fall from a height, which causes a long bone to receive, directly on its long axis, a force of such magnitude that the osseous tissue is compressed. This telescopes one part of the bone on the other. Impacted fractures require immediate splinting by the athletic trainer and traction by the physician to ensure a normal length of the injured limb.

Longitudinal fractures are those in which the bone splits along its length, often the result of jumping from a height and landing in such a way as to impact force or stress to the long axis.

Oblique fractures are similar to spiral fractures and occur when one end receives sudden torsion or twisting and the other end is fixed or stabilized.

Continued.

Serrated fractures in which the two bony fragments have a sawtooth, sharp-edged fracture line are usually caused by a direct blow. Because of the sharp and jagged edges, extensive internal damage, such as the severance of vital blood vessels and nerves, often occurs.

Spiral fractures have an S-shaped separation. They are fairly common in football and skiing, in which the foot is firmly planted and then the body is suddenly rotated in an opposing direction.

Transverse fractures occur in a straight line, more or less at right angles to the bone shaft. A direct outside blow usually causes this injury.

Contrecoup fractures occur on the side opposite to the part where trauma was initiated. Fracture of the skull is at times an example of the contrecoup. An athlete may be hit on one side of the head with such force that the brain and internal structures compress against the opposite side of the skull, causing a fracture.

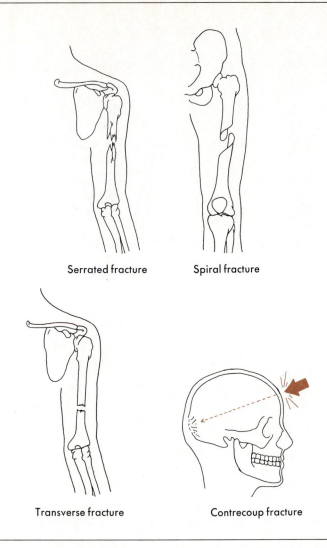

Serrated fracture   Spiral fracture

Transverse fracture   Contrecoup fracture

bones undergo bone resorption and become weaker before they become stronger. The sequence of events is suggested by Stanitski, McMaster, and Scranton[23] as resulting from increased muscular forces plus an increased rate of remodeling that leads to bone resorption and rarefaction, which progresses to produce increasingly more severe fractures. The four progressively severe fractures are focal microfractures, periosteal and/or endosteal response (stress fractures), linear fractures (stress fractures), and displaced fractures.

Typical responses for stress fractures in sports are as follows:
1. Coming back into competition too soon after an injury or illness
2. Going from one event to another without proper training in the second event
3. Starting initial training too quickly
4. Changing habits or the environment, (e.g., running surfaces, the bank of a track, or shoes)

In addition to these stresses, susceptibility to fracture can be increased by a variety of postural and foot conditions. Flatfeet, a short first metatarsal bone, or a hypermobile metatarsal region can predispose an athlete to stress fractures (see Chapter 18).

Early detection of the stress fracture may be difficult. Because of their frequency in a wide range of sports, stress fractures always must be suspected in

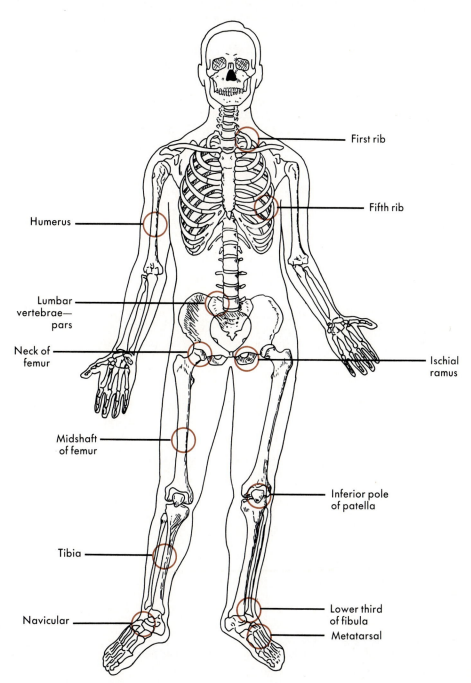

First rib

Fifth rib

Humerus

Lumbar vertebrae— pars

Neck of femur

Ischial ramus

Midshaft of femur

Inferior pole of patella

Tibia

Lower third of fibula

Navicular

Metatarsal

Figure 7-15

The most common stress fracture sites.

susceptible body areas that fail to respond to usual management. Until there is an obvious reaction in the bone, which may take several weeks, x-ray examination may fail to reveal any change. Although nonspecific, a bone scan can provide early indications in a given area.

The major signs of a stress fracture are swelling, focal tenderness, and pain. In the early stages of the fracture the athlete complains of pain when active but not at rest. Later, the pain is constant and becomes more intense at night. Percussion, by light tapping on the bone at a site other than the suspected fracture, will produce pain at the fracture site.

The most common sites of stress fracture are the tibia, fibula, metatarsal shaft, calcaneus, femur, pars interarticularis of the lumbar vertebrae, ribs, and humerus (Figure 7-15).

The management of stress fractures varies with the individual athlete, injury site, and extent of injury. Stress fractures that occur on the compression side of bone heal more rapidly and are managed more easily compared with those on the tension side. Stress fractures on the tension side can rapidly produce a complete fracture.

Epiphyseal Conditions

A musculoskeletal injury to a child or adolescent should always be considered a possible epiphyseal condition.

Three types of epiphyseal growth site injuries can be sustained by children and adolescents performing sports activities (Figure 7-16). They consist of injury to the epiphyseal growth plate, articular epiphyseal injuries, and apophyseal injuries. The most prevalent age range for these injuries is from 10 to 16 years.

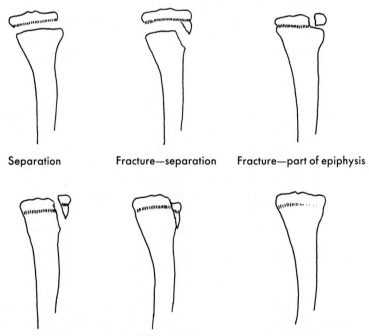

Separation   Fracture—separation   Fracture—part of epiphysis

Fracture—epiphysis and epiphyseal plate   Bony union—premature closing   Crushing of epiphyseal plate—may cause premature closure

Figure 7-16

Types of long bone epiphyseal injuries.

Apophyseal Injuries

The young, physically immature athlete is particularly prone to apophyseal injuries. The apophyses are "traction epiphyses" in contrast to the "pressure epiphyses" of the long bones. These apophyses serve as origins or insertions for muscles on growing bone that provide bone shape but not length. Common apophyseal avulsion conditions found in sports are Sever's disease and Osgood-Schlatter disease (Chapter 19).

NERVE TRAUMA

A number of abnormal nerve responses can be attributed to athletic participation or injury.

Anatomical Characteristics

The tissue that comprises the nervous system is throughout the body. It is composed of neurons, interstitial tissues, including neuroglia (supporting elements), neurilemma cells (the membranous sheath enveloping a nerve fiber), and satellite cells (flat epithelium-like cells forming the inner aspect of a double-layered capsule covering the neuron). Nerve tissue provides the body with its reception and response to stimuli.

Injurious Mechanical Forces

The two main forces that cause major nerve injuries are compression and tension. As with other tissues in the body, the injurious forces may be acute or chronic.

Nerve Injury Classification

Some of the more common nerve conditions are those that distort sensation or produce pain. Conditions that cause sensation distortion are as follows:

Hypoesthesia—a diminished sense of feeling

Hyperesthesia—an increased sense of feelings such as pain or touch

Paresthesia—a sensation of numbness, prickling, or tingling, which may occur from a direct blow or stretch to an area

Physical trauma, in general, produces pain as part of the inflammatory process (see Chapter 8, *Tissue Response to Injury*). Any number of traumas directly affecting nerves can also produce a variety of sensory responses, including pain. For example, a sudden nerve stretch or pinch can produce a sharp burning pain that radiates down a limb along with muscle weakness. *Neuritis,* a chronic nerve problem, can be caused by a variety of forces that usually have been repeated or continued for a long period of time. Symptoms of neuritis can range from minor nerve problems to paralysis.

Pain that is felt at a point of the body other than at its actual origin is commonly known as *referred pain.* Another manifestation of referred pain is a trigger point, which occurs in the muscular system but originates in some other distant body part.

BODY MECHANICS AND INJURY SUSCEPTIBILITY

If we carefully study the mechanical structure of the human body, it is amazing that humans can move so effectively in the upright posture. Not only must constant gravitational force be overcome, but the body also must be manipulated through space by a complex system of somewhat inefficient levers, fueled by a machinery that operates as an efficiency level of approximately 30%. The bony levers that move the body must overcome considerable resistance in the form of inertia and muscle viscosity and must work in most instances at an extremely unfavorable angle of pull. All these factors mitigate the effectiveness of lever action to the extent that most movement is achieved at an efficiency level of less than 25%.

In addition, more than half the total body weight is located in the upper part of the body, and this weight is supported by rather thin, articulated bones. Thus the center of gravity, which increases stability as it is lowered, is relatively high in the erect human body.

Despite these seeming inefficiencies, the body can compensate by making modifications or adjustments that depend on the task at hand. For example, the center of gravity may be lowered by widening the stance, the segmented body parts may function either as a single unit or as a series of finely coordinated units, or an increase in muscle power may be elicited in an effort to offset certain mechanical ineptitudes. Structural changes in bones, resulting from stresses placed on them, afford broader and more secure muscle anchorage and consequently aid in the development of more power.

Although the bones of the body are not primarily designed to withstand shock, the musculature serves as a shock absorber by absorbing impact and distributing it over a relatively large area, thereby lessening the concentration of the force on a small area of bone. Bones such as the shin and skull, however, which have little or no overlying musculature and thus are more susceptible to injury, should be afforded protection, especially in sports activities in which they are particularly vulnerable to blows.

In the upright posture human legs are long and straight, and the feet are adaptable for support and propulsion. The spine has three curves in the anteroposterior plane that help maintain balance. However, along with the invaluable advantages gained through an upright posture and an increased range of movement, there are some disadvantages. The mesenteries supporting the abdominal viscera would be more effective in a quadruped position. The constant gravitational pull plus the weight of the supported organs makes humans somewhat prone to have a protruded abdomen unless the abdominal muscles maintain sufficient tonicity to withstand these forces. The head, weighing close to 14 pounds, is balanced almost precariously on top of the seven small cervical vertebrae, which are sustained by the cervical neck ligaments and neck muscles. This cervical area is particularly vulnerable to injury, especially when excessive hyperflexion or hyperextension is encountered; hence strengthening of the neck muscles as a protective measure is vital in sports. Also, because of the length and great weight of the torso and head, the lumbosacral area of the spine is subjected to considerable strain and is particularly vulnerable to injury, especially in certain activities. For example, the twisting movements of golf and tennis and the excessive supportive demands sometimes made on the lumbosacral area in weight lifting or gymnastics often lead to low back strain or injury.

When determining the mechanical reasons for sports injuries to the musculoskeletal system, many factors stand out. Hereditary, congenital, or acquired defects may predispose an athlete to a specific type of injury. Anomalies in anatomical structure or in body build (somatotype) may make an athlete prone to certain injuries.

Postural Deviations

Postural deviations are often a major underlying cause of sports injuries.[10] Postural malalignment may be the result of unilateral muscle and soft-tissue asymmetries or bony asymmetries. As a result, the athlete engages in poor mechanics of movement (pathomechanics). Many sports activities are unilateral, thus leading to asymmetries in body development. The resulting imbalance is manifested by a postural deviation as the body seeks to reestablish itself in relation to its center of gravity. Often such deviations are a primary cause of injury. For example, a consistent pattern of knee injury may be related to asymmetries within the pelvis and the legs (short-leg syndrome). Unfortunately, not much in the form of remedial work is usually performed. As a result, an injury often becomes chronic—sometimes to the point that participation in a sport must be halted. When possible, the athletic trainer should seek to ameliorate or eliminate faulty postural conditions through therapy, working under the direction of an orthopedist or other qualified medical personnel. Remedial work of this type can complement the training program and, in most instances, may assist principally in maintaining sufficient bilateral development to minimize the more obvious undesirable effects of intensive unilateral development. Development of the antagonistic muscles to offset the power and force of the agonistic muscles will reinforce and establish stability and assist in the development and maintenance of good muscular balance. A number of postural conditions offer genuine hazards to athletes by making them exceedingly prone to specific injuries. Some of the more important are indicated in the following discussions of foot and leg anomalies, spinal anomalies, and various stress syndromes.

Genu Valgum (Knock-Knees)

Genu valgum (Figure 7-17, *A*) is an orthopedic disorder that presents a serious hazard to the knee joints. The weight-bearing line passes to the lateral side of the center of the knee joint as a result of the inward angling of the thigh and lower leg. This causes the body weight to be borne principally on the medial aspects of the articulating surfaces, thereby subjecting the medial collateral ligament to considerable strain and rendering the joint somewhat more unstable and prone to injury.

Genu Varum (Bowlegs)

Genu varum (Figure 7-17, *B*) is the opposite of genu valgum. The extra stress is placed on the fibular collateral ligament. In extreme cases of either of these conditions, athletes should be directed into a noncontact activity in which they are not subjected to the conditions of stress and force encountered in contact sports.

Spinal Anomalies

Kyphosis   An anteroposterior curvature of the spine wherein the convexity is directed posteriorly characterizes kyphosis, which is usually found in the cervicothoracic region (Figure 7-18). The condition is commonly called "round back." As a rule it is accompanied by a forward-thrust head, abducted scapulae, and a flat chest. Usually, activities that make great demands on the pectoral muscles are a primary cause in fostering this condition among athletes. Kyphotic athletes who have strong and well-developed but shortened pectoral muscles (such as are found frequently among basketball players, gymnasts, weightlifters, and—

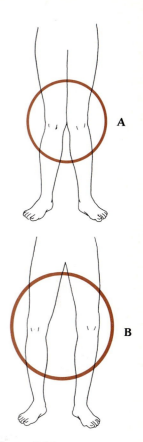

Figure 7-17

A, Genu valgum (knock-knees). **B,** Genu varum (bowlegs).

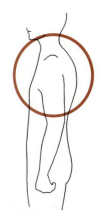

Figure 7-18

Kyphosis.

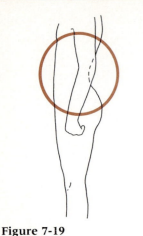

Figure 7-19

Lumbar lordosis.

Figure 7-20

Scoliosis.

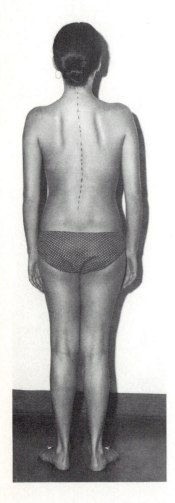

as a product of football stances—among football players) are quite susceptible to anterior dislocations of the arm, particularly when the arm is forced into an abducted and extended position accompanied by outward rotation.

Lumbar lordosis Lumbar lordosis is an abnormal anterior curvature of the lumbar spine, commonly called "hollow back" or "swayback" (Figure 7-19). A tightening of the lower back extensor muscles, contraction of the lumbar fascia, and corresponding stretching of the abdominal muscles are involved. Among football linemen this condition is further aggravated by the postural demands of the offensive stance. Gymnasts, particularly female gymnasts, are also subject to lumbar lordosis as the result of the strenuous muscular and ligamentous strains imposed on the lower back. In addition, the sport demands exceptional spinal flexibility, which also can be a factor. Spondylolysis (the breaking down of a vertebra or the occurrence of a stress fracture between the anterior and posterior portions of a vertebra) or spondylolisthesis (subluxation or slipping forward of the fifth lumbar vertebra and that portion of the spine above it over the base of the sacrum) can result as the spine's response to the excessive and strenuous physical demands being made on it. Lumbosacral strain, sacroiliac strain, and coccyalgia (pain in the coccygeal area) often may be traced to a lordotic condition as the predisposing cause. During active exercise there may be an overriding of the lumbosacral facets when an excessive lordosis is present; this can and often does result in trauma. The hamstring strain, sometimes suffered by trackmen, is often associated with a lordotic condition in which a lowering of the pubic arch produces a corresponding lift of the ischial tuberosity where the hamstrings originate. As a result, the latter are constantly in a state of stretch.

Scoliosis Scoliosis is defined as a lateral curvature of the spine and is a condition in which there is a rotary, lateral, curving deviation of the vertebrae from the median line of the body (Figure 7-20). Many of our sports are unilateral, and others have certain phases that tend to develop or aggravate this postural-orthopedic condition. Baseball pitching and high jumping using a one-foot takeoff are examples. Scoliotic athletes may be subject to severe epiphysitis or bursitis as a result of the excessive force demands made on the joint structures of the overdeveloped segment.

When a scoliotic condition is not directly attributable to a sport or a habit, it is usually caused by another structural condition, of which the most common probably is unequal leg length. When this condition exists, a lift built into the shoe will often correct the situation and permit the athlete to function normally.

Microtrauma and Overuse Syndrome

Injuries as a result of abnormal and repetitive stress and microtraumas fall into a class with certain identifiable syndromes. Such stress injuries frequently result in either limitation or curtailment of sports performance. Most of these injuries in athletes are directly related to the dynamics of running, throwing, or jumping. The injuries may result from constant and repetitive stresses placed on bones, joints, or soft tissues; from forcing a joint into an extreme range of motion; or from prolonged strenuous activity. Some of the injuries falling into this category may be relatively minor; still, they can prove to be quite disabling.[19] Among injuries classified as repetitive stress and microtrauma are Achilles tendinitis; splints; stress fractures, particularly of the fibula and second and fifth metatarsal bones; Osgood-Schlatter disease; runner's and jumper's knee; patellar chondromalacia;

apophyseal avulsion, especially in the lower extremities of growing athletes; and intertarsal neuroma.

Running Dynamics

Since many of the abnormal or continued stress syndromes bear a direct relationship to the act of running, the athletic trainer should have an understanding of what is involved in this gait. Running differs from walking in that the double period of support that occurs in walking is eliminated and a period of flight during which there is no contact with the ground is achieved. Basically there are three phases to the running gait: the push-off, the flight, and the landing. In running the foot strikes the ground almost directly under the center of gravity. This is not the case in walking. The resistive force, that is, the body weight and the backward pressure of the foot as it strikes the ground ahead of the body, is almost entirely eliminated in running. The supportive phase decreases, having an inverse relationship to the speed of the gait. In a sprint at a high rate of speed, the supportive phase is almost entirely propulsive. The legs alternate between a swinging phase, a brief supportive phase, and another swinging phase. Since the foot strikes the ground in advance of the body, there is a forward component of force in the thrust of the foot against the ground, which results in a backward counterpressure of the ground against the foot, slightly checking the forward momentum of the body. Most overuse injuries occur at this moment of impact. The counterpressure exists from the moment of foot-strike until the center of gravity has moved beyond the supporting foot. When the center of gravity has moved in front of the supporting foot, a propulsive force is engendered by the forceful thrust of the foot against the ground, resulting from the extension of the hip, knee, and ankle.

The mechanics of running are indeed similar to those of walking, differing, as previously stated, in the fact that the period of double support is eliminated and a period of flight supplants it. The force exerted consists of two components, horizontal and vertical, although the vertical component (unlike that in walking) is negligible because of the great increase in the horizontal component. Since the horizontal force is greatly increased, accompanied by a slight vertical increase, the angle between the leg and the ground during extension is smaller, and the pelvis is carried lower. Therefore, the weight is brought closer to the hip. The lowering of the pelvis requires greater flexion of the knee joint of the supporting leg, thus increasing the amount of extensor force developed by the driving leg. The increased knee flexion reduces the amount of time required to carry the leg forward to a position of extension.

Since speed is considerably increased in running and the body undergoes a period of flight, the force is greatly magnified when the swinging leg and foot strike the ground. In walking the heel of the swinging foot strikes the ground; but in running the leg reaches a full extension and has initiated the beginning of a backward movement. This causes the ball of the foot, rather than the heel, to make forceful contact with the supporting surface. In slow running, contact may be made with the heel first, the runner rolling along the lateral border to the ball of the foot as the leg reaches full backward extension. In sprinting, the weight is borne principally by the toes. At the moment of impact the foot may be in either dorsiflexion or plantar flexion, depending on whether the runner is moving slowly or rapidly. Placement of the foot may be a neutral position, or it may be toed out (pronation) or toed in (inversion). The latter two placements will exert considerable stress on the medial and lateral aspects of the foot, respectively. Pronation, the weakest position of the foot, is usually associated with a decided inward rotation of the thigh, which causes additional strain on the knee and hip joints, sometimes resulting in significant trauma. Continued overuse of the foot, particularly as encountered in distance running, leads to syndromes that are relatively common in activities in which repetitive pounding of the foot occurs in the foot-strike and the takeoff thrust phases of the gait (see Chapter 17 for a more detailed discussion of foot, ankle, and lower leg mechanics related to chronic injuries).

Throwing Dynamics

Throwing activities account for a considerable number of acute and chronic injuries to the elbow and shoulder joints.

Throwing activities account for a considerable number of acute and chronic injuries to the elbow and shoulder joints. Throwing is a unilateral action that subjects the arm to repetitive stresses of great intensity, particularly in sports activities such as pitching or javelin throwing. Should the thrower use incorrect techniques, the joints are affected by atypical stresses that result in trauma to the joint and its surrounding tissues. Throwing is a sequential pattern of movements in which each part of the body must perform a number of carefully timed and executed acts. For example, throwing a ball or javelin uses one particular pattern of movements; hurling the discus or hammer makes use of a similar complex, but with centrifugal force substituted for linear force and the type of terminal movements used in release being different. Putting the shot—a pushing rather than a throwing movement—has in its overall pattern a number of movements similar to those used in throwing a ball. Discus and hammer throwing seldom result in significant injury problems. However, hammer throwers, because of improper release of the hammer, on occasion may incur shoulder girdle injuries, particularly of the rotator cuff muscles and the middle and posterior deltoid.

In the act of throwing, momentum is transferred from the thrower's body to the object that is thrown. According to physical laws, the greater and heavier the mass, the greater the momentum needed to move it. Hence, as the size and weight of the object increase, more parts of the body are used to effect the summation of forces needed to accomplish the throw. The same is true in respect to the speed of the object: the greater the speed, the more body parts that must come into play to increase the body's momentum. Timing and sequence of action are of the utmost importance. They improve with correct practice.

In throwing, the arm acts as a sling or catapult, transferring and imparting momentum from the body to the ball. There are various types of throwing, with the overhand, sidearm, and underarm styles being the most common. The act of throwing is fairly complex and requires considerable coordination and timing if success is to be achieved.

Throwing or pitching involves three distinct phases: a preparatory or cocking phase, the delivery or acceleration phase, and the follow-through or terminal phase. Specific injuries appear peculiar to each phase. In throwing, the most powerful muscle groups are brought into play initially, progressing ultimately to the least powerful but the most coordinated (i.e., the legs, trunk, shoulder girdle, arm, forearm, and finally the hand). The body's center of gravity is transported in the direction of the throw as the leg opposite the throwing arm is first elevated and then moved forward and planted on the ground, thus stopping the forward movement of the leg and permitting the body weight to be transferred from the supporting leg to the moving leg. Initially the trunk rotates backward as the throwing arm and wrist are cocked, then rotates forward, continuing its rotation beyond the planted foot as the throwing arm moves forcibly from a position of extreme external rotation, abduction, and extension through flexion to forcible and complete extension in the terminal phase of the delivery, bringing into play the powerful internal rotators and adductors. These muscles exert a tremendous force on the distal and proximal humeral epiphysis and over a period of time create cumulative microtraumas that can result in shoulder problems or the so-called pitcher's or tennis elbow and eventually traumatic arthritis in the radiohumeral joint.

In throwing, the shoulder and the elbow seem particularly vulnerable to trauma. Uncoordinated or stress movements can subject either articulation to a considerable amount of abnormal force or torque. In pitching, with considerable speed being engendered, the forearm is the crucial element. The inward or outward rotation that is used to impart additional speed and action to the ball subjects the elbow and the shoulder to appreciable torque, which may become traumatizing if the action is improperly performed over a considerable period of time. The rotator cuff muscles, long head of the biceps brachii, pronator teres, anconeus, and deltoid are the muscles that are most affected in throwing.

Lesions of the pitching arm are quite common and are not restricted to the mature college or professional player. In the adolescent, bones are immature; the epiphyses are not closed and are somewhat susceptible to injury, particularly from pitching, wherein medial epicondyle epiphysis avulsion ("Little League elbow") and medial epicondylitis (pitcher's elbow) are not uncommon injuries.

The initial cocking phase may result in decreased internal and increased external humeral rotation, and tendinitis may occur in both the biceps and triceps muscles, as well as in the shoulder rotators.

The delivery or acceleration phase can cause tendinitis, involving the greater pectoral and latissimus dorsi muscles. "Little League shoulder," which results in osteochondrosis of the proximal humeral epiphysis or in a fracture of the proximal portion of the humeral shaft, can also result. This phase also subjects the elbow joint to considerable torque and stress, which may cause Little League elbow. Changes at the radiohumeral joint caused by compression forces may result in an aseptic necrosis of the radial head or osteochondritis dissecans of the capitulum of the humerus where it articulates with the radius. Bony spurs on both radius and ulna are not uncommon.

The final phase of the throw, the follow-through, has few problems other than the pronator teres syndrome, wherein pain is felt during the terminal pitching phase. This syndrome occurs most frequently among adults, since the forearm pronation is more pronounced in performing a "breaking" pitch (see Chapters 23 and 24).

Jumping Dynamics

In jumping activities the shock of takeoff and landing is transmitted to the lower limb or limbs. Improper takeoff or landing is responsible for a great many joint injuries. The force of the takeoff can cause a stress fracture to the foot or the ankle. The shock of an improper landing is frequently the cause of injury to the ankle, knee, or hip joint.

Severe torque results when the takeoff foot is either toed in or out. In either case the ligaments, particularly in the ankle or the knee joint, are subjected to an intense rotational shear force that usually results in torn ligaments, cartilages, or bone fracture. Improper landings from either the high jump or the long jump can cause lower limb injury, but the arms and neck are also vulnerable. The flop style of high jumping, wherein the bar is cleared by going over backward and the landing is on the back, can result in a cervical injury, especially to young and inexperienced jumpers.

Traumatic forces to the ankle joint frequently occur during jumping. Such twisting or shearing action can be damaging. Approximately 85% of all ankle injuries result from forced inversion, which causes tearing of the lateral ligaments. Eversion injuries usually result in the breaking off of the lateral malleolus, with some damage to the connective tissues on the medial aspect of the ankle.

Although the knee is the largest joint in the body, its shallowness renders it extremely vulnerable to injury. Medial, lateral, and twisting forces, such as encountered in most sports, subject the supportive ligamentous bands to severe strains. These injuries can occur after one violent traumatic incident, or they may result from the cumulative effects of repeated microtrauma. Such strain can result in the stretching or tearing of the supporting connective tissue, such as when the foot is firmly fixed and the body and leg go into or are in rotation. Hyperextension of the knee, wherein the knee is forced into a position beyond the normal 180-degree position, can result in severe joint trauma that may involve the synovial membrane or the deeper periosteal tissue. This commonly occurs in takeoff but can occur on landing, especially in gymnastics. Jumper's knee is an example of a condition resulting from repetitive microtrauma.

SUMMARY

Connective tissue is the most prevalent tissue in the human body and is the tissue that is most affected by traumatic sports injuries. The major component of connective tissue is collagenous fiber. Other fibers in connective tissue are reticular and elastic. Of major concern to sports medicine is dense fibrous connective tissue, comprising muscle tendons, joint capsular and ligamentous tissue, and cartilage.

Skin trauma can occur from a variety of forces (e.g., friction, scraping, compression, tearing, cutting, and puncturing) that produce, in order, blisters, skin bruises, lacerations, skin avulsions, incisions, and puncture wounds.

Skeletal muscle trauma from sports participation can involve any aspect of the muscle-tension unit. Forces that injure muscles are compression, tension, and shearing. Acute muscle injuries include contusions and strains. Avulsion fractures and muscle ruptures can occur from an acute episode. Chronic muscle conditions are myositis, fasciitis, tendinitis, tenosynovitis, and bursitis. Chronic muscle irritation can cause ectopic calcification, muscle disuse can cause atrophy, and immobilization can cause joint contracture.

Sports injuries to the synovial joints are common. Anatomically, synovial joints have relative strengths or weaknesses based on their ligamentous/capsular type and their muscle arrangements. Forces that can injure synovial joints are tension, compression, torsion, and shear. Sprains involve acute injury to ligaments and/or the joint capsule. A third-degree sprain may go so far as to cause ligament rupture or an avulsion fracture. Acute synovial joint injuries that go beyond the third degree may result in a dislocation. Two major chronic synovial joint conditions are osteochondrosis and traumatic arthritis. Other chronic conditions are bursitis, capsulitis, and synovitis.

Long bones can be anatomically susceptible to fractures because of their shape and as a result of changes in direction of the force applied to them. Mechanical forces that cause injury are compression, tension, bending, torsion, and shear. Bending and torsional forces are forms of tension. Acute fractures may include avulsion, blow-out, comminuted, depressed, greenstick, impacted, longitudinal, oblique, serrated, spiral, transverse, and contre-coup types. Stress fractures are commonly the result of overload to a given bone area. Stress fractures are apparently caused by an altered stress distribution or by the performance of a rhythmically repetitive action that leads to a vibratory summation and, thus, a fracture. Three major epiphyseal injuries in sports occur to the growth plate, the articular cartilage, and the apophysis.

Nerve trauma can be produced by overstretching or compression. As with other injuries, they can be acute or chronic. The sudden stretch of a nerve can cause a burning sensation. Abnormal pressure on a nerve can produce hypoesthesia, hyperesthesia, or paresthesia. A variety of traumas to nerves can produce acute pain or a chronic pain such as neuritis.

An athlete who has faulty body mechanics has a potential for injury. Postural deviations can increase the chances for pathomechanics. Improper use of the body in such activities as running, throwing, and jumping can predispose the athlete to an overuse injury.

REVIEW QUESTIONS AND CLASS ACTIVITIES

1. Describe the different types of connective tissue in the body. What role does connective tissue play in sports injuries?
2. Define primary and secondary injuries. Is there a relationship between them and acute and chronic injuries?
3. What mechanical forces injure skin?
4. List and define skin injuries.
5. Contrast contusions, strains, and sprains.
6. What mechanical forces traumatize the musculotendinous unit and the synovial joint? How are the forces similar to one another, and how are they different?
7. What forces gradually weaken tendons and ligaments?
8. Contrast two chronic synovial joint injuries.
9. List the structural characteristics that make a long bone susceptible to fracture.
10. What mechanical forces cause acute fracture of a bone?
11. How do stress fractures probably occur?
12. Describe the most common epiphyseal conditions that result from sports participation.
13. What are the relationships of postural deviations to sports injuries?
14. Discuss the concept of pathomechanics as it relates to microtraumas and overuse syndromes.

REFERENCES

1. Akeson, WH, et al.: The biology of ligaments. In Hunter, LY, and Funk, Jr, FJ, editors: Rehabilitation of the injured knee, St. Louis, 1984, The CV Mosby Co.
2. Anthony, CP, and Thibodeau, GA: Textbook of anatomy and physiology, ed 11, St. Louis, 1983, The CV Mosby Co.
3. Arnoczky, ST, and Torzilli, PA: The biology of cartilage. In Hunter, LY, and Funk, Jr, FJ, editors: Rehabilitation of the injured knee, St. Louis, 1984, The CV Mosby Co.
4. Bone loss in amenorrheic athletes, Sports med dig 9(8):6, 1987.
5. Cailliet, R: Soft tissue pain and disability, Philadelphia, 1977, FA Davis Co.
6. Ciulo, JV, and Zarins, B: Biomechanics of the musculotendinous unit: relation to athletic performance and injury. In Symposium on Olympic sports medicine, Clinics in sports medicine, vol 1, Philadelphia, 1982, WB Saunders Co.

7. Erikson, E, and Häggmark, T: Muscle and tension physiology. In Mack, RP, editor: Symposium on the foot and leg in running sports, American Academy of Orthopaedic Surgeons, St. Louis, 1982, The CV Mosby Co.

8. Geesink, RGT, et al.: Stress response of articular cartilage, Int J Sports Med 5:100, Nov 1984.

9. Gonza, ER: Biomechanics of long bone injuries. In Gonza, ER, and Harrington, IJ, editors: Biomechanics of musculoskeletal injury, Baltimore, 1982, The Williams & Wilkins Co.

10. Grace, TG: Muscle imbalance and extremity injury: a perplexing relationship, Sports Med 2:77, March/April 1985.

11. Hafen, BQ: First aid for health emergencies, St. Paul, Minn, 1981, West Publishing Co.

12. Harrington, IJ: Biomechanics of joint injuries. In Gonza, ER, and Harrington, IJ, editors: Biomechanics of musculoskeletal injury, Baltimore, 1982, The Williams & Wilkins Co.

13. Huson, A: Mechanics of joints, Int J Sports Med 5:83, Nov 1984.

14. Kotwick, JE: Biomechanics of the foot and ankle. In Torg, JS, editor: Symposium on ankle and foot problems in the athlete, Clinics in sports medicine, vol 1, Philadelphia, 1982, WB Saunders Co.

15. Markey, KL: Stress fractures. In Hunter-Griffin, LY, editor: Overuse injuries, Clinics in sports medicine, vol 6, Philadelphia, 1987, WB Saunders Co.

16. Maron, BR: Orthopedic aspects of sports medicine. In Appenzeller, O, and Atkinson, R, editors: Sports medicine, Baltimore, 1981, Urban & Schwarzenberg, Inc.

17. Micheli, LJ: Sports injuries in children and adolescents. In Straus, RH, editor: Sports medicine and physiology, Philadelphia, 1979, WB Saunders Co.

18. Rachun, A, editor: Standard nomenclature of athletic injuries, Monroe, Wis, 1976, American Medical Association.

19. Renström, P, and Johnson, RJ: Overuse injuries in sports: a review, Sports med 2:316, 1985.

20. Roux, W: Die Entwicklungsmechanic, Leipzig, 1905, W Englemann.

21. Salter, RB: Textbook of disorders and injuries of the musculoskeletal system, ed 2, Baltimore, 1983, Williams & Wilkins.

22. Sammarco, GJ, et al.: The biomechanics of torsional fractures: the effect of loading on ultimate properties, J Biomech 4:113, 1971.

23. Stanitski, CL, McMaster, JH, and Scranton, PE: On the nature of stress fractures, Am J Sports Med 6:391, 1978.

24. Williams, JGP: Color atlas of injury in sport, Chicago, 1980, Year Book Medical Publishers, Inc.

25. Wolff, J: Das Gesetz der Transformation der Knockan, Berlin, 1892, A Hirschwald.

ANNOTATED BIBLIOGRAPHY

Booher, JM, and Thibodeau, GA: Athletic injury assessment, St. Louis, 1985, The CV Mosby Co.
An excellent guide to the recognition, assessment, classification, and evaluation of athletic injuries.

Brown, LO, and Yavorsky, P: Locomotor biomechanics and pathomechanics: a review, J Orthop Sports Phys Ther 9:3, July 1987.
A review of current knowledge regarding clinical anatomy and arthrokinematics of the foot and ankle.

Grace, TG: Muscle imbalance and extremity injury: a perplexing relationship, Sports Med 2:77, March/April 1985.
Indicates that the relationship between muscle imbalance and extremity injury is perplexing and obscure. Much more research is needed in this area.

Standard nomenclature of athletic injuries, Monroe, Wis, 1976, American Medical Association.
An in-depth list of conditions in the fields of athletic training and sports medicine. Each condition is described in terms of its cause, symptoms, signs, complications, laboratory finding, x-ray findings, and pathology.

Subotnick, SI: The biomechanics of running: implications for the prevention of foot injuries, Sports Med 2:144, March/April 1985.

Indicates that it is essential to understand the biomechanics of running for overuse injuries to be effectively treated. Good foot balance and biomechanics should be provided when early signs of overuse injuries occur.

Williams, JGP: Color atlas of injury in sport, Chicago, 1980, Year Book Medical Publishers, Inc.

An excellent visual guide to the area of sports injuries. It covers the nature and incidence of sport injury, types of tissue damage, and regional injuries caused by a variety of sports activities.

Tissue Response to Injury

When you finish this chapter, you should be able to

Describe the major events in the healing of soft-tissue injuries, including acute and chronic conditions

Identify the general management concepts associated with soft-tissue injuries

List the major events in the healing of acute bone fractures

List the major characteristics of stress fracture healing

Explain why pain is commonly described as pain perception

Describe what is currently known about the cause of pain and how pain may be controlled

A student of the human body and sports medicine has to marvel at the process of healing. A common expression, "We know more about traveling into space than how the body repairs itself," tells it all. Although highly complicated and not fully understood, the basis of inflammation and the healing process should be studied as a foundation for initiating proper injury management. This chapter presents an overview of the major factors related to the inflammatory process. It is concerned with soft-tissue and skeletal response to injury and pain and factors that modify inflammation.

SOFT-TISSUE HEALING

Soft tissue is all tissues other than bone. The area that is discussed in this chapter is the tissue response to acute and chronic injuries.

Acute Injuries

Acute musculoskeletal injuries sustained in sports generally fall into three phases: the acute, reactive, or substrate inflammatory phase; the repair and regeneration phase; and the remodeling phase.

Phase I: Acute Phase

The acute phase of inflammation is the initial reaction of body tissue to an irritant or injury and is characteristic of the first 3 or 4 days after injury. The major outward signs are redness (rubor), heat (calor), swelling (tumor), pain (dolor), and, in some cases, loss of function (functio laesa). Dilation of blood vessels results in the swelling and redness caused by exudates. Pain may be produced by

Acute phase
  Redness
  Heat
  Swelling
  Pain
  Loss of function

specific chemical substances, by pressure on nerve endings, or by ischemia in the area of the injury.

An external or internal wound is associated with tissue death. In an acute phase, tissue death occurs from the actual trauma. Following trauma, cellular death may continue as a result of a lack of oxygen in the area. Continued death also occurs when the digestive enzymes of engulfing phagocytes spill over and kill normal cells. This fact points to the major importance of proper immediate care using ice, compression, elevation, rest, and immobilization of the injured part (see Chapter 11).

Acute inflammation is the fundamental reaction designed to protect, localize, and rid the body of some injurious agent in preparation for healing and repair. The main causative factors of inflammation are trauma, chemical agents, thermal extremes, and pathogenic organisms. The tissue irritants leading to the inflammatory process impose a number of vascular, cellular, and chemical responses.

Vascular events   At the time of trauma, before the usual signs of inflammation appear, a transitory **vasoconstriction,** with decreased blood flow, occurs and may last from a few seconds up to 10 minutes.[19] At the moment of vasoconstriction, coagulation begins to seal broken blood vessels, followed by the activation of chemical influences. Vasoconstriction is replaced by the dilation of venules, as well as arterioles and capillaries in the immediate area of the injury. **Vasodilation** brings with it a slowing of blood flow, increased blood viscosity, and stasis, which leads to swelling. With dilation also comes exudation of plasma and concentration of red blood cells (hemoconcentration). Much of the plasma **exudate** results from fluid seepage through the intact vessel lining that becomes more **permeable** and from higher pressure within the vessel. Permeability is relatively transient in mild injuries, lasting only a few minutes, with restoration to a preinjury state in 15 to 30 minutes.[1] In slightly more severe situations there may be a delay in response with a late onset of permeability. In such cases, permeability may not appear for many hours and then appears with some additional irritation and a display of rapid swelling lasting for an extended period of time.

A redistribution of leukocytes occurs within the intact vessels, caused in part by a slowing of circulation. These leukocytes move from the center of the blood flow to become concentrated, and then line up and adhere to the endothelial walls. This process is known as *margination* and *pavementing* and occurs mainly in venules. The leukocytes pass through the wall of the blood vessel by ameboid action, known as *diapedesis,* and are directed to the injury site by chemotaxis (a chemical attraction to the injury).

Cellular events   In phase I of acute inflammation, **mast cells** and **leukocytes** are in abundance. Mast cells are connective tissue cells that contain heparin (a blood anticoagulant) and histamine. Basophils, monocytes, and neutrophils are the major leukocytes. Basophil leukocytes are believed to bring anticoagulant substances to tissues that are inflamed and are present during both acute and chronic inflammatory healing phases. The neutrophils representing about 60% to 70% of the leukocytes arrive at injury site before the larger monocytes. They immigrate from the bloodstream. Neutrophils emigrate from the bloodstream through diapedesis and **phagocytosis** to ingest smaller debris than do monocytes. Phagocytosis is the process of ingesting material such as bacteria, dead cells, and other debris associated with disease, infection, or injury. The phagocyte commonly accomplishes this process by projecting cytoplasmic pseudopods, which

---

Cellular death continues after initial injury because of the following:
   Lack of oxygen caused by disruption of circulation
   Digestive enzymes of the engulfing phagocytes spill over to kill normal cells

Vascular events

vasoconstriction
Decrease in the diameter of a blood vessel.

vasodilation
Increase in the diameter of a blood vessel.

exudate
Fluid with a high protein content and containing cellular debris that comes from blood vessels and accumulates in the area of the injury.

permeable
Permitting the passage of a substance through a vessel wall.

Cellular events

mast cells
Connective tissue cells that contain heparin and histamine.

leukocytes
Consist of two types—granulocytes (e.g., basophils and neutrophils) and agranulocytes (e.g., monocytes and lymphocytes).

phagocytosis
Process of ingesting microorganisms, other cells, or foreign particles, commonly performed by monocytes (white blood cells).

Chemical mediators
  Histamine
  Serotonin
  Bradykinin
  Prostaglandins
  Leukotrienes

engulf the object and ingest the particle through enzymes. When the neutrophil disintegrates, it gives off enzymes called lysozomes, which digest engulfed material. These enzymes act as irritants and continue the inflammatory process. Neutrophils also have chemotactic properties, attracting other leukocytes to the injured area (Figure 8-1).[21] The monocyte, which is a nongranular leukocyte, occurs on the scene after the neutrophils, about 5 hours following injury. Monocytes transform themselves into large macrophages that have the ability to ingest large particles of bacteria and/or cellular debris.

Chemical mediators   Chemical mediators for the inflammatory process are stored and given off by various cells. Histamine, the first chemical to appear in inflammation is given off by blood platelets, basophil leukocytes, and mast cells. It is a major producer of arterial dilation, venule and capillary permeability. Serotonin is a powerful vasoconstrictor found in platelets and mast cells. With an increase in blood there is an increase in local metabolism. Permeability is produced by the contraction of the endothelial cells of the capillary wall, producing a gap between cells. Gaps allow plasma to leak plasma proteins, platelets, and leukocytes. Plasma proteases, with their ability to produce polypeptides, act as

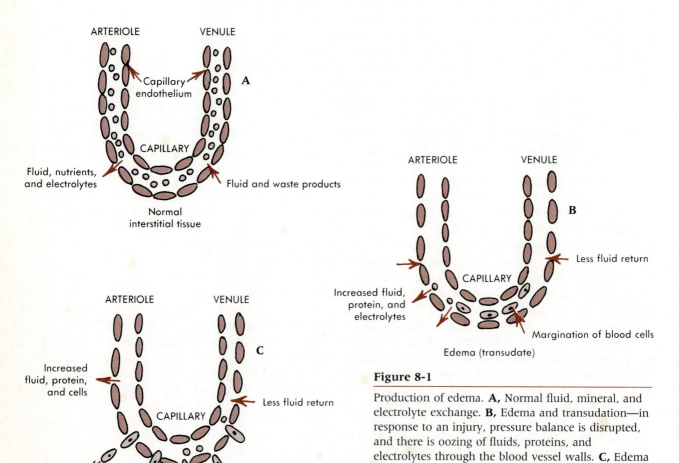

Figure 8-1

Production of edema. **A,** Normal fluid, mineral, and electrolyte exchange. **B,** Edema and transudation—in response to an injury, pressure balance is disrupted, and there is oozing of fluids, proteins, and electrolytes through the blood vessel walls. **C,** Edema and exudate—as inflammation continues, neutrophils and other blood cells emigrate into the surrounding tissue to form an exudate.

chemical mediators. A major plasma protease in inflammation is bradykinin. Bradykinin increases permeability and causes pain.

Heparin is also given off by mast cells and basophils, temporarily prevents blood coagulation. In addition, in the early stages of acute injury, prostaglandins and leukotrienes are produced. Both of these substances stem from arachidonic acid; however, prostaglandins are produced in almost all body tissues. They are stored in the cell membranes' phospholipids. Leukotrienes alter capillary permeability and, it is believed, play a significant role, along with prostaglandins, in all aspects of the inflammatory process. Prostaglandins apparently encourage, as well as inhibit, inflammation, depending on the conditions that are prevalent at the time.[7]

Complement system   The complement system includes enzymatic proteins in normal serum that can be activated by a variety of immune factors in chemicals. When activated, these components become involved with many aspects of the inflammatory process. Two important mechanisms they use are leukocyte chemotaxis and phagocytosis.

Complement system
  Leukocyte chemotaxis
  Phagocytosis

Bleeding and exudate   The extent of fluid in the injured area is highly dependent on the extent of damaged vessels and the permeability of the intact vessel. Blood coagulates in three stages. In the initial stage *thromboplastin* is formed, whereas in the second stage *prothrombin* is converted into *thrombin* under the influence of thromboplastin with calcium, and in the third stage thrombin changes from soluble *fibrinogen* into insoluble *fibrin*. The plasma exudate then coagulates into a network of fibrin and localizes the injured area.

Blood coagulation:
Thromboplastin +
Calcium = Prothrombin =
Thrombin = Fibrinogen =
Insoluble fibrin clot

Phase II: Repair and the Regenerative Phase

The term *repair* is synonymous with healing, whereas *regeneration* refers to the restoration of destroyed or lost tissue. Healing, which extends from the inflammatory phase (48 to 72 hours to approximately 6 weeks), occurs when the area has become clean through the removal of cellular debris, erthrocytes, and the fibrin clot.[7] Tissue repair is accomplished through three processes: (1) by resolution, in which there is little tissue damage and normal restoration; (2) by the formation of granulation tissue, occurring if resolution is delayed; and (3) by regeneration, the replacement of tissue by the same tissue.

Tissue repairs
  By resolution
  By granulation tissue
  By regeneration

The formation of scar tissue following trauma is a common occurrence; however, because scar tissue is less viable than normal tissue, the less scarring the better. When mature, scar tissue represents tissue that is firm, fibrous, inelastic, and devoid of capillary circulation. The type of scar tissue known as adhesion can complicate the recovery of joint or organ disabilities. Healing by scar tissue begins with an exudate, a fluid with a large content of protein and cellular debris that collects in the area of the injury site. From the exudate, a highly vascular mass develops known as granulation tissue. Infiltrating this mass is a proliferation of immature connective tissue (fibroblasts) and endothelial cells. Gradually the collagen protein substance, stemming from fibroblasts, forms a dense, fibrous scar. Collagenous fibers have the capacity to contract approximately 3 to 14 weeks after an injury and even as long as 6 months afterward in more severe cases.

Tissue repair depends on
  Elimination of debris
  Regeneration of
    endothelial cells
  Production of fibroblasts

During this stage, two types of healing occur. *Primary healing*, healing by first intention, takes place in an injury that has even and closely opposed edges, such as a cut or incision. With this type of injury, if the edges are held in very close approximation, a minimum of granulation tissue is produced. *Secondary healing*, healing by secondary intention, results when there are a gaping lesion and large tissue loss, leading to replacement by scar tissue. External wounds such as lacerations and internal musculoskeletal injuries commonly heal by secondary intention.

Regeneration   According to van der Meulen[19] "In man—unlike the salamander, which can regrow an amputated limb—the capacity for regeneration is limited to a few cells, which comprise the endothelial cells, the fibroblasts and the epithelial cells." The ability to regenerate following injury decreases with age. It is also associated with nutrition, general health of the individual, but most importantly, to the type of tissue that has been injured.

Repair and regeneration depend on three major factors: elimination of debris, the regeneration of endothelial cells, and the production of fibroblasts, which compose connective tissue throughout the body and form the basis of scar tissue. Typically in a traumatic event injured blood vessels become deprived of oxygen and die. Before repair and regeneration can occur, debris must be removed by phagocytosis. Stimulated by a lack of oxygen (hypoxia) and the action of macrophages, capillary buds begin to form in the walls of the intact vessels (Figure 8-2). From these buds grow immature vessels that form connections with other vessels. As these vessels become mature, more oxygenated blood is brought to the injured area. From the perivascular cells come the fibroblasts (immature fibrocytes) that migrate to the injury and form collagen substances, often within a few days of the injury.[19] The development of collagen is stimulated by lactic acid and vitamin C and depends on the proper amount of oxygen for its development.

Figure 8-2

Stimulated by hypoxia and action of macrophages, capillary buds begin to form in the walls of the intact vessels.

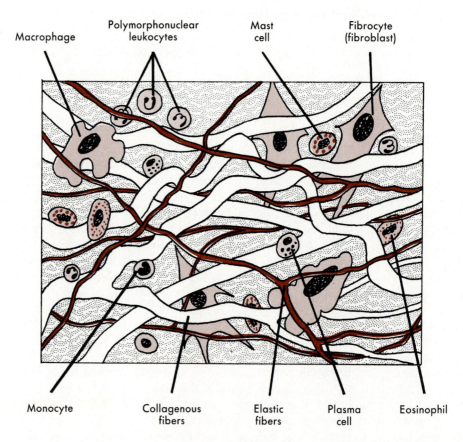

Macrophage   Polymorphonuclear   Mast   Fibrocyte
                    leukocytes   cell   (fibroblast)

Monocyte   Collagenous   Elastic   Plasma   Eosinophil
                  fibers   fibers   cell

Phase III: Remodeling Phase

Remodeling of the traumatized area overlaps that of repair and regeneration. Normally in acute injuries the first 3 to 6 weeks are characterized by increased production of scar tissue and the strength of its fibers. Strength of scar tissue continues to increase from 3 months to 1 year following injury. Ligamentous tissue takes as long as 1 year to become completely remodeled. To avoid a rigid, nonyielding scar, there must be a physiological balance between **synthesis** and **lysis.** The tensile strength of collagen apparently is specific to the mechanical forces imposed during the remodeling phase. Forces applied to the ligament during rehabilitative exercise will develop strength specifically in the direction that force is applied. If too early or excessive strain is placed on the injury, the healing process is extended. For proper healing of muscles and tendons, there must be careful consideration of when to mobilize the site. Early mobilization can assist in producing a more viable injury site; on the other hand, too long a period of immobilization can delay healing. The ideal of collagen remodeling is to have the healed area contain a preponderance of mature collagenous fibers that have a number of cross-linkages. As stated, collagen content and quality may be deficient for months following injury.[7]

> Remodeling depends on the amount and type of scar tissue present.
>
> **synthesis**
> The process of forming or building up.
>
> **lysis**
> A process of breaking down.

Chronic Inflammation

The chronic muscle and joint problem is an ever-present concern in sports. If an acute inflammation reaction fails to be resolved in 1 month, it is termed a subacute inflammation. If it lasts for months or even years, the condition is termed chronic. Chronic inflammation results from repeated acute microtraumas and overuse. Prominent features which are distinct from acute inflammation, are proliferation of connective tissue and tissue degeneration. The primary cells during chronic inflammation are lymphocytes, plasma cells, and macrophages (monocytes), whereas the most common cell type during acute inflammation is the neutrophil. It has been suggested that lymphocytes, although not normally phagocytic, may be used to stimulate fibroblasts to heal and to form scar tissue. The role of plasma cells is not clearly understood, however. Macrophages, present in both acute and chronic inflammation, are definitely phagocytic and actively engaged in repair and healing.

> Chronic inflammation can stem from repeated acute microtraumas and overuse.

Major chemicals found during chronic inflammation—although again, not fully understood—are the kinins (especially bradykinin), which also produce vasodilation, increased permeability, and pain. Prostaglandin, also seen in chronic conditions, does not produce pain but is a vasodilator and can be inhibited by aspirin.[3,16]

Modifying Soft-Tissue Healing

The healing process is unique in each athlete. In addition, different tissues vary in their ability to regenerate. For example, cartilage regenerates somewhat from the perichondrium, striated muscle is limited in its regeneration, and peripheral nerve fibers can regenerate if their damaged ends are opposed. Usually connective tissue will readily regenerate, but, as with all tissue, this possibility is dependent on the availability of nutrients.

Age and general nutrition can play a role in healing. The older athlete may be delayed in healing when compared to younger athletes. The injuries of an athlete with a poor nutritional status may heal more slowly than normal. Athletes with certain organic disorders may heal slowly. For example, blood conditions such as anemia and diabetes often inhibit the healing process.

Management Concepts

Many of the current treatment approaches are designed to enhance the healing process. They generally come under the headings of drugs to combat inflammation, thermal agents, physical modalities, mobilization, and exercise rehabilitation.

Drugs to treat inflammation   There is a current trend toward the use of antiprostaglandin medications or nonsteroidal anti-inflammatory drugs (NSAIDs). The intent of this practice is to decrease vasodilation and capillary permeability.[7] Questionable drugs are corticosteroids and dimethyl sulfoxide (DMSO) (see Chapter 15, *Drug Use and Abuse in Sports*).

Superficial thermal agents   Both cold and heat are used for different conditions. In general, heat aggravates acute inflammatory conditions, and cold depresses them. Conversely, in chronic conditions, heat may serve as a depressant (see Chapter 13, *Therapeutic Modalities*).

Physical modalities   A number of electrical procedures are increasing in popularity for the treatment of inflammation stemming from sports injuries. They come under the headings of penetrating heat devices such as microwave and ultrasound therapy and electrical stimulation, including transcutaneous electrical nerve stimulation (TENS) and electrical muscle stimulation (EMS) (see Chapter 12, *Therapeutic Modalities*).

Exercise rehabilitation   A major aim of soft-tissue rehabilitation through exercise is pain-free movement, full-strength power, and full extensibility of associated muscles.[14] The ligamentous tissue, if related to the injury, should become pain free, have full tensile strength, and full range of motion. The dynamic joint stabilizers should regain full strength and power.[14]

Immobilization of a part after injury or surgery is not always good for all injuries.[21] When a part is immobilized over an extended period of time, adverse biochemical changes occur in collagenous tissue. Early mobilization used in exercise rehabilitation that is highly controlled may enhance the healing process (see Chapter 14, *Exercise Rehabilitation*).[21]

FRACTURE HEALING

Those concerned with sports must fully realize the potential seriousness of a bone fracture. Coaches often become impatient for the athlete with a fracture to return to competition and sometimes become unjust in their criticism of the physician for being conservative. *Time* is required for proper bone union to take place.

The osteoblast is the cellular component of bone and forms its matrix; the osteocyte both forms and destroys bone, whereas osteoclasts destroy and resorb bone. The constant ongoing remodeling of bone is caused by osteocytes, whereas osteoclasts are related mainly to pathological responses (Figure 8-3). Osteoclasts come from the cambium layer of the periosteum, which is the fibrous covering of the bone, and are involved in bone healing. The inner cambium layer, in contrast to the highly vascular and dense external layer, is more cellular and less vascular. It serves as a foundation for blood vessels and provides a place for attaching muscles, tendons, and ligaments.

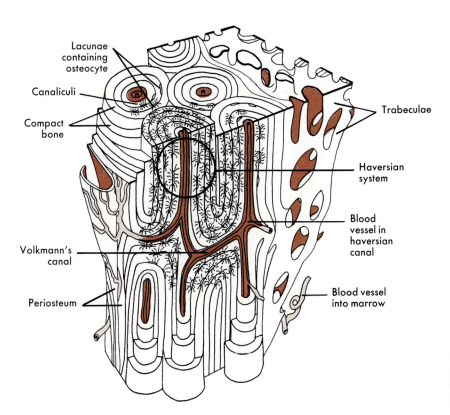

Figure 8-3

Bone is a complex organ in both growth and healing.

Skeletal fractures are discussed under the general headings of acute fractures and stress fractures of the bone.

Acute Fractures of the Bone

As with acute soft-tissue healing, healing of acute bone fractures involves a number of phases—acute, repair and regeneration, and remodeling. Trauma that produces a fracture often also causes extensive soft-tissue damage that must be healed.

Phase I: Acute Phase

Acute inflammation usually lasts approximately 4 days. When a bone fractures, there is trauma to the periosteum and surrounding soft tissue. With hemorrhaging, a hematoma accumulates in the medullary canal and surrounding soft tissue. The exposed ends of vascular channels become occluded with clotted blood accompanied by dying of the osteocytes, disrupting the intact blood supply. The dead bone and related soft tissue begin to elicit a typical inflammatory reaction, including vasodilation, plasma exudate, and inflammatory cells.

Phase II: Repair and Regeneration Phase

As with a soft-tissue injury, the hematoma begins its organization in granulation tissue and gradually builds a fibrous junction between the fractured ends. At this time the environment is acid, but it will slowly change to neutral or slightly alkaline. A major influx of capillary buds that carry endosteal cells from the bone's cambium layer occurs. These cells first produce a fibrous callus, then cartilage, and finally a woven bone. When there is an environment of high oxygen tension, fibrous tissue predominates, whereas when oxygen tension is low, cartilage develops. Bone will develop at the fracture site when oxygen tension and compression are in the proper amounts.

The soft callus, in general, is an unorganized network of woven bone formed at the ends of the broken bone that is later absorbed and replaced by bone. At the soft-callus stage, both internal and external calluses are produced that bring an influx of osteoblasts that begin to immobilize the fracture site. The internal and external calluses are formed by bone fragments that grow to bridge the fracture gap. The internal callus grows rapidly to create a rigid immobilization. Beginning in 3 to 4 weeks, and lasting 3 or 4 months, the hard callus forms. Hard callus is depicted by a gradual connecting of bone filament to the woven bone at the fractured ends. If there is less than satisfactory immobilization, a cartilagenous rather than bony union is produced. With adequate immobilization and compression, the bone ends become crossed with a new Haversian system that will eventually lead to the laying down of primary bone.

Phase III: Remodeling Phase

Remodeling occurs after the callus has been resorbed and trabecular bone is laid down along the lines of stress. Complete remodeling may take many years. The influence of bioelectrical stimulation (piezoelectric effect) is the basis for development of new trabecular bone to be laid down at the point of greatest stress. This influence is predicated on the fact that bone is electropositive on its convex side and electronegative on its concave side. The convex is considered the tension side, whereas the concave is the compression side. Significantly, osteoclasts are drawn to a positive electrical charge and osteoblasts to a negative electrical charge. Remodeling is considered complete when a fractured bone has been restored to its former shape or has developed a shape that can withstand imposed stresses.

Management of Acute Fractures

In the treatment of acute fractures the bones commonly must be immobilized completely until x-ray studies reveal that the hard callus has been formed. It is up to the physician to know the various types of fractures and the best form of immobilization for each specific fracture. During healing, fractures can keep an athlete out of participation in his or her particular sport for several weeks or months, depending on the nature, extent, and site of the fracture. During this period there are certain conditions that can seriously interfere with the healing process. Three such conditions are discussed below.

Conditions that interfere with fracture healing
Poor blood supply
Poor immobilization
Infection

1. If there is a *poor blood supply to the fractured area* and one of the parts of the broken bone is not properly supplied by the blood, that part will die and union or healing of the fracture will not take place. This condition is known as aseptic necrosis and often occurs in the head of the femur, the navicular bone in the wrist, the talus in the ankle, or isolated bone fragments. The condition is relatively rare among vital, healthy, young athletes except in the navicular bone of the wrist.

2. *Poor immobilization of the fracture site,* resulting from poor casting by the physician and permitting motion between the bone parts, may not only prevent

proper union but may also, in the event that union does transpire, cause deformity to develop.

3. *Infection* can materially interfere with the normal healing process, particularly in the case of a compound fracture, which offers an ideal situation for development of a severe streptococcal or staphylococcal infection. The increased use of modern antibiotics has considerably reduced the prevalence of these infections coincidental with or immediately following a fracture. The closed fracture is not immune to contamination, of course, since infections within the body or a poor blood supply can render it quite susceptible. If the fracture site should become and remain infected, the infection could interfere with the proper union of the bone. The interposition of soft parts between the severed ends of the bone—such as muscle, connective tissue, or other soft tissue immediately adjacent to the fracture—can prevent proper bone union, often necessitating surgical cleansing of the area of such tissues by a surgeon.

Healing of Stress Fractures

As discussed in Chapter 7, stress fractures may be created by cyclic forces that adversely load a bone at a susceptible site. Fractures may be the result of axial compression or tension created by the pull of muscles. As indicated, stress on ligamentous and bony tissue can be positive and can increase relative strength or can be negative and lead to tissue weakness.

As discussed previously, bone produces an electrical potential in response to the stress of tension and compression.[10] As a bone bends, tension is created on its convex side along with a positive electrical charge; conversely, on the concave or compressional side, a negative electrical charge is created.[10] Torsional forces produce tension circumferentially.[10] Constant tension caused by axial compression or stress by muscular activity can result in an increase in bone resorption and subsequently a microfracture.

As with the healing of acute fractures, healing of stress fractures involves restoring a balance of osteoclastic and osteoblastic activity. Achieving this balance requires recognition of the situation as early as possible. Stress fractures that go unhealed will eventually develop into complete cortical fractures that may, over a period of time, become displaced. A decrease in activity and elimination of other factors in training that cause stress will allow proper bone healing.

PAIN PERCEPTION

Pain is one of the major indicators of inflammation. Free nerve endings act as pain receptors and are commonly located in the superficial skin layers, bone periosteum, and joints.[20] In general, the most sensitive pain areas are the periosteum and the joint capsule. The subchondral bone, tendons, and ligaments are moderately pain sensitive. The synovium is insensitive to pain stimulation.[8]

Some pain receptors are stimulated by mechanical stresses such as tissue trauma and are considered as mechanosensitive pain receptors (non-nociceptors). Other pain receptors (nociceptors) are chemosensitive to such substances as bradykinin, serotonin, histamine, and prostaglandin. As pain continues over a period of time, the threshold of nerve receptors become progressively lower.[20] Tissue swelling and muscle spasm both stimulate mechanosensitive receptors. As a result of this pressure, blood flow decreases, causing ischemia together with a deficiency of oxygen (hypoxia). These events often produce a cycle of "pain-spasm-ischemia-hypoxia-pain."[6,20] The intention of many injury management procedures is to break through this cycle and, thereby, relieve pain.

As understanding of pain increases, there is a growing distinction between chronic and acute pain. Acute pain protects the body against something harmful. It is designed to immobilize the injured body part so it can heal. When it becomes chronic and fails to stop, pain ceases to serve a useful purpose.

Bonica[2] indicates that acute pain is a disagreeable sensation and an emotional experience caused by tissue damage or a noxious stimulus. For example, an acute pain experience happens when the big toe is stubbed, releasing substances in the tissue that send electrochemical impulses first to the spinal cord's dorsal horn, then relay them to the thalamus, which associates and synthesizes the stimuli, and finally relay the impulses to the cerebral cortex to be perceived as pain.

Projected (Referred) Pain

One major category of pain that professionals in the field of sports medicine/athletic training commonly encounter is projected, or referred, pain. Such pain occurs away from the actual site of irritation. This pain has been called an error in perception.[9] Each projected pain site must also be considered unique to each individual. Symptoms and signs vary according to the nerve fibers affected. Response may be motor, sensory, or both. The largest myelinated fibers (A-alpha) are the most sensitive to pressure (e.g., in a nerve root) and can produce paresthesia.[8] Three types of referred pain that may be common to athletes are myofascial, sclerotomic, and dermatomic pain.

Myofascial Pain

trigger points
Small hyperirritable areas within a muscle.

Acute and chronic musculoskeletal pain can be caused by myofascial trigger points. A **trigger point** is a specific sensitive area that has been referred to soft tissue. Such pain sites have variously been described as fibrositis, myositis, myalgia, myofascitiis, and muscular strain.[13] Trigger points are small hyperirritable areas within a muscle in which nerve impulses bombard the central nervous system and are expressed as a referred pain.[18]

There are two types of trigger points—active and latent. The active trigger point is hyperirritable and causes an obvious complaint. The latent trigger point, on the other hand, is dormant, producing no complaint except perhaps a loss of range of motion. The trigger point does not follow a usual area of distribution such as sclerotomes, dermatomes, or peripheral nerves. The trigger point pain area is called the *reference zone*, which could be close to the point or a considerable distance from the point.[12,13]

Sclerotomic and Dermatomic Pain

Deep pain, which can be either "slow" or "fast," may originate from sclerotomic, myotomic, and/or dermatomic nerve irritation or injury. A sclerotome is an area of bone or fascia that is supplied by a single nerve root. Myotomes are muscles supplied by a single nerve root. Dermatomes also are in an area of skin supplied by a single nerve root.

Sclerotomic pain is often called "slow pain" and is transported by the unmyelinated (C) fibers. Irritation of these fibers can cause deep, aching, and poorly localized pain. Sclerotomic pain impulses can be projected to regions in the brain such as the hypothalamus, limbic system, and reticular formation and cause depression, anxiety, fear, or anger. Autonomic changes may also occur, producing changes in vasomotor tone, blood pressure, and sweating.[8]

Irritation of a small, myelinated (A-delta) fiber can produce "fast," or dermatomic, pain. This pain, in contrast to sclerotomic pain, is sharp and well localized. Unlike sclerotomic pain, dermatomic pain projects mainly to the thalamus and is relayed directly to the cortex, skipping autonomic and affective responses.[8] (See Chapter 9 for further discussion of referred pain.)

Psychological Aspects of Pain

Pain, especially chronic pain, is a subjective, psychological phenomenon. When painful injuries are treated, the total athlete must be considered, not just the pain or condition. Even in the most well-adjusted person, pain will create emotional changes. Constant pain will often cause self-centeredness and an increased sense of dependency.

Athletes, like nonathletes, vary in their pain thresholds (Figure 8-4). Some can tolerate enormous pain, whereas others find mild pain almost unbearable. Pain apparently is worse at night because persons are alone and more aware of themselves, plus being devoid of external diversions.[15] Personality differences can also cause differences in pain toleration. For example, athletes who are anxious, dependent, and immature have less toleration for pain than those who are relaxed and emotionally in control.

A number of theories about how pain is produced and perceived by the brain have been advanced. Only in the last few decades has science demonstrated that pain is both a psychological and physiological phenomenon and is therefore

Figure 8-4

An athlete learns through conditioning to block the pain of minor injuries during rigorous activity.

unique to each individual. Sports activities demonstrate this fact clearly. Through conditioning, an athlete learns to endure the pain of rigorous activity and to block the sensations of a minor injury.

Managing Pain

Pain perception is a mixture of physiological and psychological factors that often produce major management problems. When a person suddenly stubs a toe or hits a finger with a hammer, he or she instantly rubs the area vigorously to diminish the pain. It is theorized that the act of rubbing releases the body's natural opiates, endorphins, which numb the injured area. In situations in which there is the cyclic condition of pain-spasm-ischemia-hypoxia-pain, reducing spasm and/or ischemia will often reduce pain. Anti-inflammatory drugs and drugs specifically designed to block pain impulses are beneficial in some cases. In recent years new theories of pain and its control have had great impact on sports medicine.

Figure 8-5

Scheme of the pain-modulating system in the dorsal horn of the spinal cord.

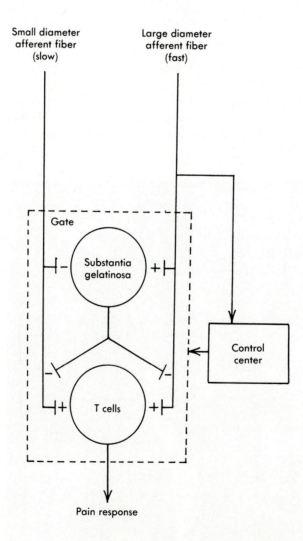

Theories of chronic pain control   Athletic training is concerned with basically healthy and physically active individuals; however, it still must address those musculoskeletal conditions that have become chronically painful. Currently there are a number of neurophysiological theories about controlling chronic pain through therapeutic means. Three of them are the "gate control" theory, control through a central biasing mechanism within the brain, and control through stimulating the endogenous, opiate-like endorphin substances produced by the pituitary gland. These theories must not be considered as discrete but as working in coordination with one another.

The gate theory   The gate theory, as developed by Melzack and Wall,[11] sets forth the idea that the spinal cord is organized in such a way that pain or other sensations may be experienced. An area located in the dorsal horn is thought able to cause inhibition of the pain impulses ascending to the brain cortex for perception. The area, or "gate," within the dorsal horn is composed of T cells and the *substantia gelatinosa*. T cells apparently are neurons that organize stimulus input and transmit the stimulus to the brain. The substantia gelatinosa functions as a gate-control system. It determines the stimulus input sent to the T cells from peripheral nerves. If the stimulus from a noxious material exceeds a certain threshold, pain is experienced (Figure 8-5). Apparently the smaller and slower nerve fibers carry pain impulses, whereas larger and faster nerve fibers carry other sensations. Impulses from the faster fibers arriving at the gate first inhibit pain impulses. In other words, stimulation of large, rapidly conducting fibers can selectively close the gate against the smaller pain fiber input. This concept explains why acupuncture, acupressure, cold, heat, and chemical skin irritation can provide some relief against pain. It also provides a rationale for the current success of transcutaneous electrical nerve stimulation (TENS).

Central biasing mechanism   Another consideration in pain control is a central biasing mechanism located in the brainstem. Within the brainstem is the raphe magnus nucleus in which neurons respond maximally to a noxious pain stimulus.[17] Apparently by stimulating the raphe magnus nucleus a gate-type mechanism is produced. This nucleus is rich in enkephalin hormone, a morphinelike substance, and the neurotransmitter serotonin.[4]

Endogenous opiates   In recent years specific opiate receptors have been found in the brain. Some of these opiates, such as etorphine, are 10,000 times as potent as morphine. Opiate receptors in the brain are located in the limbic system, spinoreticular tracts, thalamus, hypothalamus, and other pathways involved with pain reception. They are also found in the substantia gelatinosa and the vagus nerve.[5]

Besides opioid receptors, morphinelike substances have been identified in the brain and brainstem. A general term, *endorphins,* is given to two enkephalins and beta-endorphin, which are polypeptides. Beta-endorphin is found in areas of the brain and periphery, whereas enkephalins are found in the brainstem and pituitary gland. Beta-endorphin produces hypothermia and profound analgesia of the entire body.[5]

Releasing endorphin for the purpose of pain control has been attributed to low-frequency, 1 to 3 cycles per second, high-voltage electrical stimulation analgesia.[17] This also indicates why electroacupuncture relieves pain at trigger point sites.

SUMMARY

Response to sports injuries involves the soft and bony tissue and consists of acute and chronic inflammatory healing factors.

Acute soft-tissue healing consists of the acute, repair and regeneration, and remodeling phases. The acute phase lasts 3 to 4 days. During initial trauma transitory vasoconstriction occurs, followed by vasodilation and increased permeability. Through the process of chemotaxis, leukocytes, by means of diapedesis, are attracted to the injured area. Throughout the acute phase major cellular and chemical events are occurring. A complement system that consists of enzymatic proteins is also involved. An integral part of the acute phase is blood coagulation, which occurs in three stages. The second phase of soft-tissue healing, repair and regeneration, extends from the inflammatory phase of 48 to 72 hours to approximately 6 weeks. It consists of resolution, development of granulation tissue, and, finally, regeneration of lost tissue, depending on the extent of the injury. The two types of healing are generally known as primary, or first intention, and secondary, or second intention. Secondary healing develops more granulation tissue and, subsequently, has greater possibility of producing more scar tissue. Remodeling is the final phase of the healing process of soft tissue. Remodeling refers to a balance of tissue synthesis and lysis. To maximize this phase concern must be given to determining the extent of immobilization and mobilization of the injured part.

Inflammation that lasts for a long period of time is termed chronic, lasting for months or even years. It may occur as a result of acute microtrauma and overuse. The typical cells that are involved are lymphocytes, plasma cells, and monocytes. Scar tissue and degeneration are associated with chronic inflammation.

A number of factors such as nutrition and blood supply can modify the healing process. Anti-inflammatory drugs, thermal agents, physical modalities, and proper exercise procedures can positively alter the healing process.

Fractures can be acute or stress related. Healing of an acute fracture follows many of the phases of acute soft-tissue healing, with the exception of replacing osteocytes. Proper management, including immobilization when called for, is essential for bone healing and remodeling.

Pain is both a psychological and physiological phenomenon. Pain perception is subjective and may be described as "fast" and "slow." Acute pain is designed to protect the body, whereas chronic pain serves no useful purpose. Chronic pain is believed to be caused by a noxious stimulus that affects the high-threshold nociceptors in various tissue. Pain is managed by interrupting some aspect of the pain-spasm-ischemia-hypoxia-pain cycle. Interruption can be accomplished by certain drugs and therapeutic approaches such as TENS.

REVIEW QUESTIONS AND CLASS ACTIVITIES

1. Identify the outward signs of inflammation.
2. Describe the vascular, cellular, chemical, and complement system events that occur during acute soft-tissue healing.
3. How does soft tissue repair and regenerate itself after an acute injury?
4. What are the major implications of soft-tissue remodeling following injury?
5. Differentiate between acute and chronic inflammatory processes.
6. What are the reasons for using drugs, thermal agents, physical modalities, and exercise rehabilitation during the healing process?
7. Differentiate between acute soft-tissue healing and acute bone-fracture healing.
8. How does a stress fracture heal?
9. How does pain occur? Why is it generally described as pain perception?
10. What is projected, or referred, pain?
11. What are the major management concepts used in treating pain?

REFERENCES

1. Anderson, WAD, and Scotti, TM: Synopsis of pathology, ed 10, St. Louis, 1980, The CV Mosby Co.
2. Bonica, JJ: Pathophysiology in pain. In Current concepts of postoperative pain, New York, 1978, HP Publishing Co, Inc.
3. Bonta, IL, and Parnham, MJ: Prostaglandins and chronic inflammation, Biochem Pharmacol 27:1611, 1978.
4. Cailliet, R: Soft tissue pain and disability, Philadelphia, 1977, FA Davis Co.
5. Clark, WG: Goth's medical pharmacology, ed 12, St. Louis, 1988, The CV Mosby Co.
6. Guyton, AC: Textbook of medical physiology, ed 6, Philadelphia, 1981, WB Saunders Co.
7. Kellett, J: Acute soft tissue injuries—a review of the literature, Med Sci Sports Exerc 18:489, 1986.
8. Lynch, MK, and Kessler, RM: Pain. In Kessler, RM, and Hertling, D, editors: Management of common musculoskeletal disorders, Philadelphia, 1983, Harper & Row.
9. Magee, DJ: Orthopedic physical assessment, Philadelphia, 1987, WB Saunders Co.
10. Markey, KL: Stress fractures. In Hunter-Griffin, LY: Overuse injuries, Clinics in sports medicine, vol 6, Philadelphia, April 1987, WB Saunders Co.
11. Melzack, R, and Wall, PD: Pain mechanisms: a new theory, Science 150:971, 1965.
12. Nielsen, AJ: Spray and stretch for myofascial pain, Phys Ther 58:567, May 1978.
13. Nielsen, AJ: Case study: myofascial pain of the posterior shoulder relieved by spray and stretch, J Orthop Sports Phys Ther 3:21, Summer 1981.
14. Oakes, BW: Acute soft tissue injuries: nature and management, Aust Fam Phys 10(suppl):3, 1982.
15. Rusk, HA: Rehabilitation medicine, ed 4, St. Louis, 1977, The CV Mosby Co.
16. Schachter, M: Kallikreins (kininogenases)—a group of serine proteases with bioregulatory actions, Pharmacol Rev 31:1, 1979.
17. Stratton, SA: Role of endorphins in pain modulation, J Orthop Sports 3:200, 1982.
18. Travell, JG, and Rinzler, SH: The myofascial genesis of pain, Postgrad Med 11:425, 1952.
19. van der Meulen, JCH: Present state of knowledge on processes of healing in collagen structures, J Sports Med 3(suppl 1):4, 1982.
20. Wilkerson, GB: Inflammation in connective tissue: etiology and management, Ath Train 20:298, 1985.
21. Zarro, V: Mechanisms of inflammation and repair. In Michlovitz, SL, editor: Thermal agents in rehabilitation, Philadelphia, 1986, FA Davis Co.

ANNOTATED BIBLIOGRAPHY

Akeson, WH, et al.: The biology of ligaments; and Arnoczsky, ST, and Torzilli, PA: The biology of cartilage. In Hunter, LY, and Funk, Jr, FJ, editors: Rehabilitation of the injured knee, St. Louis, 1984, The CV Mosby Co.
An in-depth study in these two chapters of the healing of ligaments and cartilage at the cellular level.

Guck, TP: Stress management for chronic pain patients, J Orthop Sports Phys Ther 6:5, July/Aug 1984.
An overview of stress management procedures for pain patients.

Hunter-Griffin, LY, editor: Overuse injuries, Clinics in sports medicine, vol 6, Philadelphia, 1987, WB Saunders Co.
A monograph that provides a detailed presentation on the subject of overuse injuries stemming from sports participation. Major injuries are discussed in depth.

Kissane, JM, editor: Anderson's pathology, vols I and II, ed 9, St. Louis, 1989, The CV Mosby Co.
A two-volume in-depth presentation on the study of disease, involving changes in tissue structure and function. In Volume One, Chapter 2, *Inflammation and Healing,* and Chapter 4, *Injuries Caused by Physical Agents,* are particularly relevant to the study of athletic training.

Travell, JG, and Simons, DG: Myofascial pain and dysfunction: the trigger point manual, Baltimore, 1983, Williams & Wilkins.
A text about the pain and dysfunction occurring in myofascial tissues.

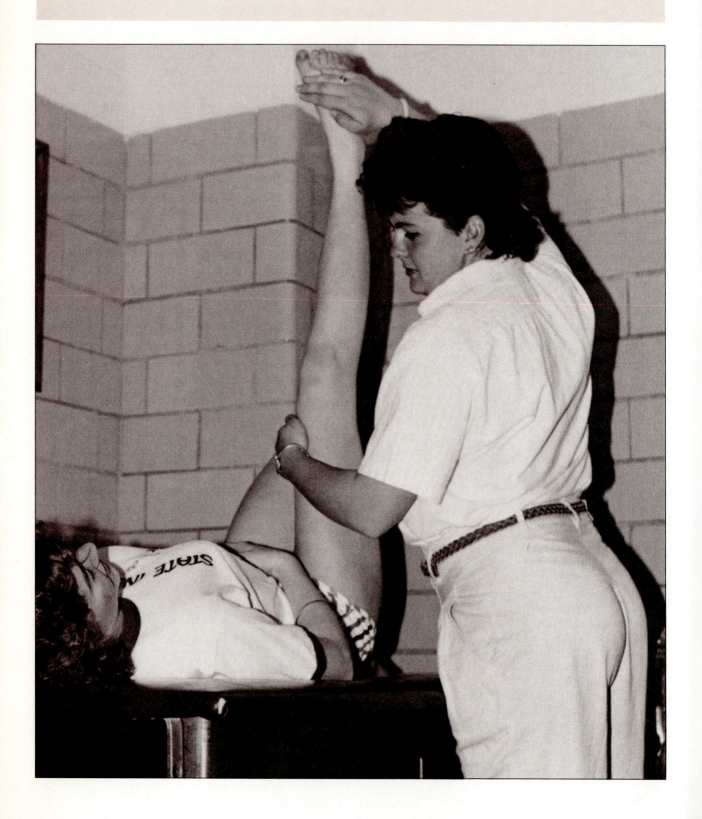

MANAGEMENT SKILLS

P art Four focuses on the skills necessary for managing a variety of situations that commonly occur in the fields of athletic training and sports medicine.

Emergency Procedures

When you finish this chapter, you should be able to

Establish an emergency system for a school sports program

Explain the importance of knowing cardiopulmonary resuscitation (CPR) and how to manage an obstructed airway

Describe the types of hemorrhage and their management

Assess the types of shock and their management

Describe the emergency management of musculoskeletal injuries

Time becomes critical in an emergency situation.

Most sports injuries do not result in life-or-death emergency situations, but when such situations do arise, prompt care is essential. Emergency is defined as ". . . an unforeseen combination of circumstances and the resulting state that calls for immediate action."[6] Time becomes the critical factor, and assistance to the injured individual must be based on knowledge of what to do and how to do it—how to perform effective aid immediately. There is no room for uncertainty, indecision, or error.

THE EMERGENCY PLAN

The prime concern of emergency aid is to maintain cardiovascular function, and indirectly, central nervous system function, since failure of any of these systems may lead to death. The key to emergency aid in the sports setting is the initial evaluation of the injured athlete. Time is of the essence, so this evaluation must be done rapidly and accurately so that proper aid can be rendered without delay. In some instances these first steps not only will be lifesaving but also may determine the degree and extent of permanent disability.

As discussed in Chapter 2, the athletic training team, consisting of the coach, the athletic trainer, and the team physician, must at all times act in a reasonable and prudent manner. This behavior is especially important during emergencies.

All sports programs mus have an emergency plan.

All sports programs must have an emergency plan that, when called on, can immediately be set in place. The following issues must be addressed when developing the emergency system:

1. Are location of phones and emergency telephone numbers well known? (Use 911 if available.)

2. Who is designated to make the telephone call? Who has the key to gates or padlocks, and who will open them?
3. What information should be given over the telephone?
   a. Type of emergency situation
   b. Type of suspected injury
   c. Present condition of the athlete
   d. Current assistance being given (e.g., cardiopulmonary resuscitation)
   e. Location of telephone being used
   f. Exact location of emergency (give names of streets and cross streets) and how to enter facility
4. Is there a separate emergency plan for each sport's fields, courts, and gymnasiums?
5. Have coaches, athletic trainers, athletic director, and other school personnel been apprised of the emergency plan? Do each of these individuals know his or her responsibilities when an emergency occurs?

Primary Injury Assessment

Primary injury assessment refers to the inspection and evaluation given as soon as possible after the occurrence of an injury. Specific examples are the recognition of vital signs, assessment of the unconscious athlete, and a primary musculoskeletal assessment. It must be remembered that all emergency situations require primary assessment procedures. Secondary assessment is discussed in Chapter 10, *General Assessment Procedures*.

Recognizing Vital Signs

The ability to recognize physiological signs of injury is essential to the proper handling of potentially critical injuries. When evaluating the seriously ill or injured athlete, the coach, athletic trainer, or physician must be aware of nine response areas: heart rate, breathing rate, blood pressure, temperature, skin color, pupils of the eye, movement, the presence of pain, and unconsciousness.

Pulse   The pulse is the direct extension of the functioning heart. In emergency situations it is usually determined at the carotid artery at the neck or the radial artery in the wrist (Figure 9-1). A normal pulse rate per minute for adults ranges between 60 and 80 beats and in children from 80 to 100 beats; however, it should be noted that trained athletes usually have slower pulses than the typical population.

Vital signs to observe
  Pulse
  Respiration
  Temperature
  Skin color
  Pupils
  State of consciousness
  Movement
  Abnormal nerve response

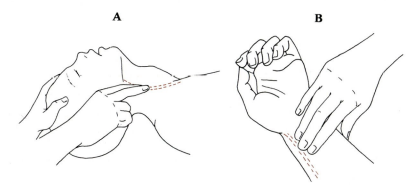

A   **B**

Figure 9-1

Pulse rate taken at the carotid artery, **A,** and radial artery, **B.**

An alteration of a pulse from the normal may indicate the presence of a pathological condition. For example, a *rapid but weak pulse* could mean shock, bleeding, diabetic coma, or heat exhaustion. A *rapid and strong pulse* may mean heatstroke or severe fright, and a *strong but slow pulse* could indicate a skull fracture or stroke, whereas *no pulse* means cardiac arrest or death.[2]

Respiration The normal breathing rate per minute is approximately 12 breaths in adults and 20 to 25 breaths in children. Breathing may be shallow (indicating shock), irregular, or gasping (indicating cardiac involvement). Frothy blood from the mouth indicates a chest injury, such as a fractured rib, that has affected a lung. Look, listen, and feel: *look* to ascertain whether the chest is rising or falling; *listen* for air passing in and out of the mouth or nose or both; and *feel* where the chest is moving.

Blood pressure Blood pressure, as measured by the sphygmomanometer, indicates the amount of force that is produced against the arterial walls. It is indicated at two pressure levels: systolic and diastolic. **Systolic blood pressure** occurs when the heart pumps blood, whereas **diastolic blood pressure** is the residual pressure present in the arteries when the heart is between beats. The normal systolic pressure for 15- to 20-year-old males ranges from 115 to 120 mm Hg. The diastolic pressure, on the other hand, usually ranges from 75 to 80 mm Hg. The normal blood pressure of females is usually 8 to 10 mm Hg lower than in males for both systolic and diastolic pressures. At the age of 15 to 20, a systolic pressure of 135 mm Hg and above may be excessive; also, 110 mm Hg and below may be considered too low. The outer ranges for diastolic pressure should not exceed 60 and 85 mm Hg, respectively. A lowered blood pressure could indicate hemorrhage, shock, heart attack, or internal organ injury.

Temperature Body temperature is maintained by water evaporation and heat radiation. It is normally 98.6° F (37° C). Temperature is measured with a thermometer, which is placed under the tongue, in the armpit, or, in case of unconsciousness, in the rectum. Changes in body temperature can be reflected in the skin. For example, a hot dry skin might indicate disease, infection, or overexposure to environmental heat. Cool, clammy skin could reflect trauma, shock, or heat exhaustion, whereas cool, dry skin is possibly the result of overexposure to cold.

A rise or fall of internal temperature may be caused by a variety of circumstances such as the onset of a communicable disease, cold exposure, pain, fear, or nervousness. Characteristically with the lowered temperature there may be chills with chattering teeth, blue lips, goose bumps, and pale skin.

Skin color For individuals who are lightly pigmented, the skin can be a good indicator of the state of health. In this instance, three colors are commonly identified in medical emergencies: red, white, and blue. A red skin color may indicate heatstroke, high blood pressure, or carbon monoxide poisoning. A pale, ashen, or white skin can mean insufficient circulation, shock, fright, hemorrhage, heat exhaustion, or insulin shock. Skin that is bluish in color (cyanotic), primarily noted in lips and fingernails, usually means that circulating blood is poorly oxygenated. This may indicate an airway obstruction or respiratory insufficiency.

Assessing a dark-skinned athlete is different from assessing a light-skinned athlete. These individuals normally have pink coloration of the nail beds and inside the lips, mouth, and tongue. When a dark-skinned person goes into shock, the skin around the mouth and nose will often have a grayish cast, whereas the tongue, inside of the mouth, the lips, and nail beds will have a bluish cast. Shock

---

systolic blood pressure
The pressure caused by the heart's pumping.

diastolic blood pressure
The residual pressure when the heart is between beats.

To convert Fahrenheit to centigrade (Celsius)
$$°C = (°F - 32) \div 1.8$$
To convert centigrade to Fahrenheit
$$°F = (1.8 \times °C) + 32$$

resulting from hemorrhage will cause the tongue and inside of the mouth to become a pale, grayish color instead of blue. Fever in these athletes can be noted by a red flush at the tips of the ears.[2]

Pupils   The pupils are extremely sensitive to situations affecting the nervous system. Although most persons have pupils of regular outline and equal size, some individuals normally have pupils that may be irregular and unequal. This disparity requires the coach or athletic trainer to know which of their athletes deviate from the norm.

A constricted pupil may indicate that the athlete is using a central nervous system–depressant drug. If one or both pupils are dilated, the athlete may have sustained a head injury, may be experiencing shock, heatstroke, or hemorrhage, or may have ingested a stimulant drug (Figure 9-2). The pupils' response to light should also be noted. If one or both pupils fail to accommodate to light, there may be brain injury or alcohol or drug poisoning. When examining an athlete's pupils, the examiner should note the presence of contact lenses or an artificial eye.

State of consciousness   When recognizing vital signs, the examiner must always note the athlete's state of consciousness. Normally the athlete is alert, aware of the environment, and responds quickly to vocal stimulation. Head injury, heatstroke, and diabetic coma can vary an individual's level of conscious awareness.

Movement   The inability to move a body part can indicate a serious central nervous system injury that has involved the motor system. An inability to move one side of the body could be caused by a head injury or cerebrovascular accident (stroke). Paralysis of the upper limb may indicate a spinal injury, inability to move the lower extremities could mean an injury below the neck, and pressure on the spinal cord could lead to limited use of the limbs.[2,7]

Abnormal nerve response   The injured athlete's pain or other reactions to adverse stimuli can provide valuable clues to the coach or athletic trainer. Numbness or tingling in a limb with or without movement can indicate nerve or cold damage. Blocking of a main artery can produce severe pain, loss of sensation, or lack of a pulse in a limb. A complete lack of pain or of awareness of serious but obvious injury may be caused by shock, hysteria, drug usage, or a spinal cord injury. Generalized or localized pain in the injured region probably means there is no injury to the spinal cord.[1]

The Unconscious Athlete

The state of unconsciousness provides one of the greatest dilemmas in sports. Whether it is advisable to move the athlete and allow the game to resume or to await the arrival of a physician is a question that too often is resolved hastily and without much forethought. Unconsciousness may be defined as a state of insensibility in which there is a lack of conscious awareness. This condition can be brought about by a blow to either the head or the solar plexus, or it may result from general shock. It is often difficult to determine the exact cause of unconsciousness (Table 9-1).

To recognize and evaluate the injury sustained by an unconscious athlete, use the following procedures:

1. Understand the sequence of the accident, either by having witnessed the event or by questioning other players and spectators.
2. After learning how the accident occurred, decide what part of the body was

Some athletes normally have irregular and unequal pupils.

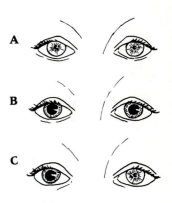

Figure 9-2

The pupils of the eyes are extremely sensitive to situations affecting the nervous system. **A,** Normal pupils. **B,** Dilated pupils. **C,** Irregular pupils.

TABLE 9-1 Evaluating the Unconscious Athlete

Functional Signs		Selected Conditions					
	Fainting	Concussion	Grand Mal Epilepsy	Brain Compression and Injury	Sunstroke	Diabetic Coma	Shock
Onset	Usually sudden	Usually sudden	Sudden	Usually gradual	Gradual or sudden	Gradual	Gradual
Mental	Complete unconsciousness	Confusion or unconsciousness	Unconsciousness	Unconsciousness gradually deepening	Delirium or unconsciousness	Drowsiness, later unconsciousness	Listlessness, later unconsciousness
Pulse	Feeble and fast	Feeble and irregular	Fast	Gradually slower	Fast and feeble	Fast and feeble	Fast and very feeble
Respiration	Quick and shallow	Shallow and irregular	Noisy, later deep and slow	Slow and noisy	Difficult	Deep and sighing	Rapid and shallow, with occasional deep sigh
Skin	Pale, cold, and clammy	Pale and cold	Livid, later pale	Hot and flushed	Very hot and dry	Livid, later pale	Pale, cold, and clammy
Pupils	Equal and dilated	Equal	Equal and dilated	Unequal	Equal	Equal	Equal and dilated
Paralysis	None	None	None	May be present in leg and/or arm	None	None	None
Convulsions	None	None	None	Present in some cases	Present in some cases	None	None
Breath	N/A	N/A	N/A	N/A	N/A	Acetone smell	N/A
Special features	Giddiness and sway before collapse	Signs of head injury, vomiting during recovery	Bites tongue, voids urine and feces, may injure self while falling	Signs of head injury, delayed onset of symptoms	Vomiting in some cases	In early stages, headache, restlessness, and nausea	May vomit; early stages: shivering, thirst, defective vision, and ear noises

most affected. Often no one is fully aware of just when or how the athlete was hurt. The position or attitude in which the athlete was found may therefore present an important key as to how the injury took place. It is a normal reaction for a person to pull away from an injuring force and to grasp at the painful area.

3. Do not move the unconscious athlete from the position found until a thorough examination has been made.

4. Make the examination as follows:

   a. First, check the ABCs of life support; if any of them are impaired, provide immediate first aid.

   b. Once life support is assured, start with the head and determine first whether there is bleeding or whether there is a straw-colored fluid coming from the nose, eyes, ears, or mouth. Look for bumps, lacerations, or deformities that may indicate a possible concussion or skull fracture.

   c. Check for shock.

   d. Moving down the body, check each part for deformities and, where possible, make a bilateral comparison. Palpate for abnormal movements and uneven surfaces.

   NOTE: Be extremely cautious testing the unconscious athlete because he or she may have a catastrophic neck injury.

Primary Musculoskeletal Assessment

A logical process must be used to evaluate accurately the extent of a musculoskeletal injury. One must be aware of the major signs that reveal the site, nature, and, above all, severity of the injury. Detection of these signs can be facilitated, as is true with all trauma, (1) *by understanding the mechanism or traumatic sequence* and (2) *methodically inspecting the injury.* Knowledge of the mechanism of an injury is extremely important in finding which area of the body is most affected. When the injury mechanism has been determined, the examiner proceeds to the next phase, physical inspection of the affected region. At this point information is gathered by what is seen, what is heard, and what is felt.

In an attempt to understand the mechanism of injury, a brief history of the complaint must be taken. The athlete is asked, if possible, about the events leading up to the injury and how it occurred. The athlete is further asked what was heard or felt when the injury took place. The athletic trainer makes a *visual observation* of the injured site and compares it to the uninjured body part. The initial visual examination can disclose obvious deformity, swelling, and skin discoloration.

Next, *auditory observation* of what was heard at the time of the injury is determined. Sounds occurring at the time of injury or during manual inspection yield pertinent information about the type and extent of pathology present. Such uncommon sounds as grating or harsh rubbing may indicate fracture. Joint sounds may be detected when either arthritis or internal derangement is present. Areas of the body that have abnormal amounts of fluid may produce sloshing sounds when gently palpated or moved. Such sounds as a snap, crack, or pop at the moment of injury often indicate bone breakage.

Finally, the region of the injury is gently palpated. Feeling, or *palpating,* a part with trained fingers can, in conjunction with visual and audible signs, indicate the nature of the injury. Palpation is started away from the injury and gradually moves towards it. As the examiner gently feels the injury and surrounding structures with the fingertips, several factors can be revealed: the extent of point tenderness, the extent of irritation (whether it is confined to soft tissue alone or extends to the bony tissue), and deformities that may not be detected by visual examination alone.

Decisions Made from the Primary Assessment

After a quick on-site injury inspection and evaluation, the athletic trainer makes the following decisions:

1. The seriousness of the injury
2. The type of first aid and immobilization necessary
3. Whether or not the injury warrants immediate referral to a physician for further assessment
4. The manner of transportation from the injury site to the sidelines, training room, or hospital.

All information about the initial history, signs, and symptoms of the injury must be documented, if possible, so that they may be described in detail to the physician.

OVERVIEW OF EMERGENCY CPR

It is essential that a careful evaluation of the injured person be made to determine whether or not cardiopulmonary resuscitation (CPR) should be conducted. The following is an overview of adult CPR and is not intended to be used by persons who are not certified in CPR. It should also be noted that, because of the serious nature of CPR, updates should routinely be studied through the American Red Cross and the American Heart Association.

First, establish unresponsiveness of the athlete by tapping or gently shaking his or her shoulder and shouting, "Are you okay?" Note that shaking should be avoided if there is a possible neck injury. If the athlete is unresponsive, call out for help, position the athlete for assistance, and then proceed with the ABCs of CPR.[6] The ABC mnemonic of CPR is easily remembered and indicates the sequential steps used for basic life support:

A Airway opened
B Breathing restored
C Circulation restored

Frequently, when A is restored, B and C will resume spontaneously, and it is then unnecessary to perform them. In some instances, the restoration of A and B obviates the necessity for step C. If the athlete is in a position other than supine, he or she must be carefully rolled over as a unit, avoiding any twisting of the body, since CPR can be administered only with the athlete lying flat on the back with knees straight or slightly flexed (see Figure 9-7). When performing CPR on an adult victim, the following sequence should be followed.

Airway Opened

1. **NOTE:** A face mask may have to be cut away before CPR can be rendered (Figure 9-3). Open the airway by using the head-tilt/chin-lift method. Lift chin with one hand while pushing down on victim's forehead with the other, avoiding the use of excessive force. The tongue is the most common cause of respiratory obstruction; the forward lift of the jaw raises the tongue away from the back of the throat, thus clearing the airway. **NOTE:** On victims with sus-

Decisions that can be made from the primary assessment
Seriousness of injury
Type of first aid required
Whether injury warrants physical referral
Type of transportation needed

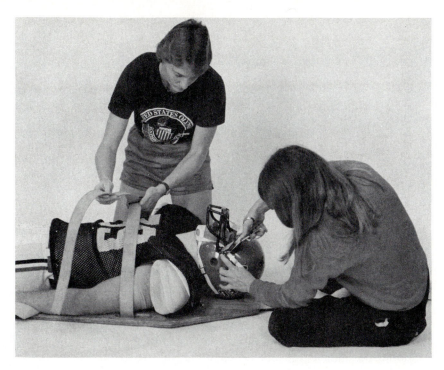

Figure 9-3

A face mask may have to be removed before CPR can be rendered.

pected head or neck injuries, perform a modified jaw maneuver. In this procedure displace the jaw forward only, keeping the head in a fixed, neutral position.

2. In an unconscious individual, since the tongue often acts as an impediment to respiration by blocking the airway, it is necessary to use the chin-lift maneuver. Lift the chin by placing the fingers of one hand under the lower jaw near the chin, lifting and bringing the chin forward, thus supporting the jaw and lifting the tongue. Avoid compressing the soft tissue under the jaw, since this could obstruct the airway. Avoid completely closing the mouth. The teeth should be slightly apart. *Look* to see if the chest rises and falls. *Listen* for air passing in or out of the nose or mouth. *Feel* on your cheek whether air is being expelled; this procedure should take 3 to 5 seconds.

3. If neither of the foregoing is sufficiently effective, additional forward displacement of the jaw can be affected by grasping each side of the lower jaw at the angles, thus displacing the lower mandible forward as the head is tilted backward. In executing this maneuver both elbows should rest on the same surface as that on which the victim is lying. Should the lips close, they can be opened by retracting the lower lip with a thumb. On individuals with suspected neck injuries this is the maneuver that should be used, since it can be performed effectively without extending the cervical spine.

4. If necessary, clear the mouth of any foreign objects such as vomitus, mouthpiece, dentures, or dislodged bridgework but do not waste a great deal of time.

5. If opening the athlete's airway does not cause spontaneous breathing, proceed to step B.

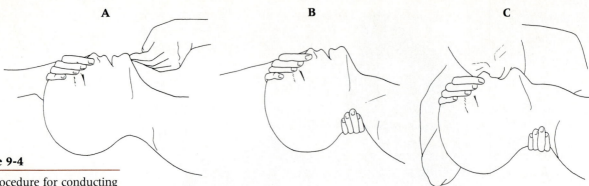

A   B   C

Figure 9-4

The procedure for conducting mouth-to-mouth resuscitation requires pinching the nose shut, **A,** moving the head back (if there is no neck injury), **B,** and after taking a deep breath, placing the mouth over the victim's mouth, **C,** thereby forming an airtight seal, and blowing until the chest rises.

Breathing Restored

1. With the hand that is on the athlete's forehead, pinch the nose shut, keeping the heel of the hand in place to hold the head back (if there is no neck injury) (Figure 9-4). Taking a deep breath, place your mouth over the athlete's mouth to provide an airtight seal and give two slow breaths at a rate of 1 to 1 ½ seconds per inflation. Observe the chest rise. Remove your mouth, and listen for the air to escape through passive exhalation.

2. Should the athlete still not be breathing, give two full, quick breaths, then check the carotid artery for the pulse. If the pulse is present, continue rescue breathing at the rate of one breath every 5 seconds. Recheck for continued pulse presence for 5 to 10 seconds after each series of 12 ventilations or after 1 minute when a single operator is functioning.

3. If no pulse is evident, then artificial circulation must be provided through cardiac compression coupled with the rescue breathing (step C). At the time no pulse is determined and before chest compressions are given, the Emergency Medical System (EMS) is activated.

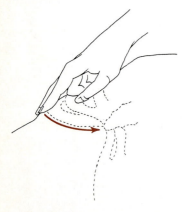

Figure 9-5

With the middle and index fingers of the hand closest to the waist, the lower margin of the victim's rib cage is located. The fingers are then run along the rib cage to the notch where the ribs meet the sternum. The middle finger is placed on the notch with the index finger next to it on the lower end of the sternum.

Circulation Restored

1. Maintain open airway. Position yourself close to the side of the athlete's chest. With the middle and index fingers of the hand closest to the waist, locate the lower margin of the athlete's rib cage on the side next to you (Figure 9-5).

2. Run the fingers up along the rib cage to the notch where the ribs meet the sternum.

3. Place the middle finger on the notch and the index finger next to it on the lower end of the sternum.

4. Next, the hand closest to the athlete's head is positioned on the lower half of the sternum next to the index finger of the first hand that located the notch; then the heel of that hand is placed on the long axis of the breastbone.

5. The first hand is then removed from the notch and placed on top of the hand on the sternum so that the heels of both hands are parallel and the fingers are directed straight away from the coach or athletic trainer (Figure 9-6).

6. Fingers can be extended or interlaced, but they must be kept *off* of the chest.

7. Elbows are kept in a locked position with arms straight and shoulders positioned over the hands, enabling the thrust to be straight down.

8. In a normal-size adult, enough force must be applied to depress the sternum 1½ to 2 inches (4 to 5 cm). After depression, there must be complete release of the sternum to allow the heart to refill. The time of release should equal the time of compression. For one or two operators compression must be given at the rate of 80 to 100 times per minute, maintaining a rate of 15 chest compressions to two quick breaths, thus alternating B and C.

9. When two rescuers are available, they are positioned at opposite sides of the athlete (Figure 9-7). The one providing the breathing does so by giving a breath after every five chest compressions, which are administered by the other rescuer at the rate of 80 to 100 compressions per minute. The carotid pulse must be checked frequently by the ventilator during chest compression to ascertain the effectiveness of the compression. In the beginning check after 10 sets of 15:2 have been completed, after which ventilation and compression should be interrupted during every few minutes of ventilation to determine whether spontaneous breathing and pulse have occurred. With the exception of inserting an airway and transporting, *never interrupt CPR for more than 5 seconds*. Adequate circulation must be maintained. Any interruption in compression permits the blood flow to drop to zero.

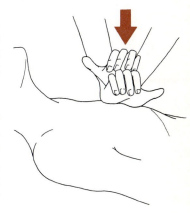

Figure 9-6

The heel of the headward hand is placed on the long axis of the lower half of the sternum next to the index finger of the first hand. The first hand is removed from the notch and placed on top of the hand on the sternum with fingers interlaced.

Number of Rescuers	Ratio of Compressions to Breaths	Rate of Compressions
1	15:2	80-100 times/min
2	5:1	80-100 times/min

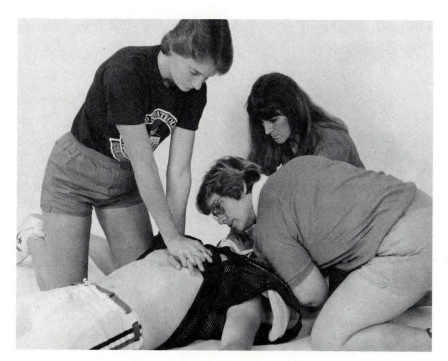

Figure 9-7

Cardiac compression, using two rescuers, interposes one breath for every five chest compressions. Third person in photo is an instructor and observer.

All coaches and athletic trainers must have current CPR certification.

Every coach and athletic trainer should be certified in CPR and should take a refresher examination at least once a year. It is wise to have all training assistants certified as well.

Obstructed Airway Management

Choking on foreign objects claims close to 3000 lives every year. Choking is a possibility in many sports activities; for example, an athlete may choke on a mouth guard, a broken bit of dental work, chewing gum, or even a "chaw" of tobacco. When such emergencies arise, early recognition and prompt, knowledgeable action are necessary to avert a tragedy. An unconscious person can choke also—the tongue may fall back in the throat, thus blocking the upper airway. Blood clots resulting from head, facial, or dental injuries may impede normal breathing, as may vomiting. When complete airway obstruction occurs, the individual is unable to speak, cough, or breathe. If the athlete is conscious, there is a tremendous effort made to breathe, the head is forced back, and the face initially is congested and then becomes cyanotic as oxygen deprivation is incurred. If partial airway obstruction is causing the choking, some air passage can be detected, but during a complete obstruction no air movement is discernible.

To relieve airway obstruction caused by foreign bodies, two maneuvers are recommended: (1) the Heimlich maneuver and (2) finger sweeps of the mouth and throat.

Heimlich Maneuver

As with CPR, the Heimlich maneuver (subdiaphragmatic abdominal thrusts) requires practice before proficiency is acquired. There are two methods of obstructed airway management, depending on whether the victim is in an erect position or has collapsed and is either unconscious or too heavy to lift. For the conscious victim the Heimlich maneuver is applied until he or she is relieved or becomes unconscious. In cases of unconsciousness, six to 10 abdominal thrusts are applied, followed by a finger sweep with an attempt at ventilation.

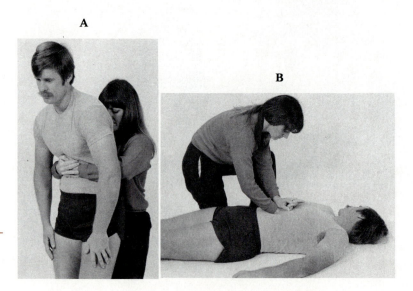

Figure 9-8

The Heimlich maneuver for an obstructed airway. **A,** Standing. **B,** Reclining.

Method A   Stand behind the athlete. Place both arms around the waist just above the belt line, and permit the athlete's head, arms, and upper trunk to hang forward (Figure 9-8, *A*). Grasp one fist with the other, placing the thumb side of the grasped fist immediately below the xiphoid process of the sternum, clear of the rib cage. Now sharply and forcefully thrust the fists into the abdomen, inward and upward, several times. This "hug" pushes up on the diaphragm, compressing the air in the lungs, creating forceful pressure against the blockage, and thus usually causing the obstruction to be promptly expelled. Repeat the maneuver six to 10 times in each series.

Method B   If the athlete is on the ground or on the floor, lay him or her on the back and straddle the thighs, keeping your weight fairly centered over your knees. Place the heel of your left hand against the back of your right hand and push sharply into the abdomen just above the belt line (note the position, Figure 9-8, *B*). Repeat this maneuver as many times as needed to expel the blockage. Care must be taken in either of these methods to avoid extreme force or applying force over the rib cage because fractures of the ribs and damage to the organs can result.

Finger Sweeping

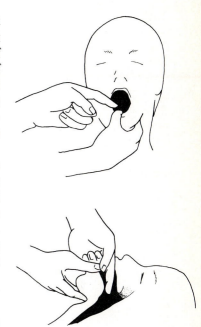

If a foreign object such as a mouth guard is lodged in the mouth or the throat and is visible, it may be possible to remove or release it with the fingers. Care must be taken that the probing does not drive the object deeper into the throat. It is usually impossible to open the mouth of a conscious victim who is in distress, so the Heimlich maneuver technique should be put to use immediately. In the unconscious athlete, turn the head either to the side or face up, open the mouth by grasping the tongue and the lower jaw, hold them firmly between the thumb and fingers, and lift—an action that pulls the tongue away from the back of the throat and from the impediment. If this is difficult to do, the crossed finger method can usually be used effectively. The index finger of the free hand (or if both hands are used, an assistant can probe) should be inserted into one side of the mouth along the cheek deeply into the throat; using a hooking maneuver, attempt to free the impediment, moving it into a position from which it can be removed (Figure 9-9). Attempt to ventilate after each sweep until the airway is open. Once the object is removed, if he or she is not already breathing, an attempt is made to ventilate the athlete.

Figure 9-9

Finger sweeping of the mouth is essential in attempting to remove a foreign object from a choking victim.

HEMORRHAGE

An abnormal external or internal discharge of blood is called a hemorrhage. The hemorrhage may be venous, capillary, or arterial and may be external or internal. Venous blood is characteristically dark red with a continuous flow, capillary bleeding exudes from tissue and is a reddish color, and arterial bleeding flows in spurts and is bright red.

External Bleeding

External bleeding stems from open skin wounds such as abrasions, incisions, lacerations, punctures, or avulsions (see Chapter 16 for further discussion). The control of external bleeding includes the use of direct pressure, elevation, and pressure points.

External bleeding can usually be managed by using direct pressure, elevation, or pressure points.

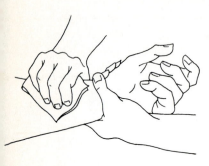

Figure 9-10

Direct pressure for the control of bleeding is applied with the hand over a sterile gauze pad.

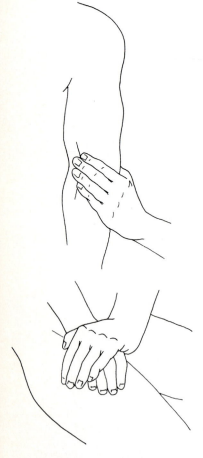

Figure 9-11

The two most common sites for direct pressure are the brachial artery and the femoral artery.

Direct Pressure

Pressure is directly applied with the hand over a sterile gauze pad. The pressure is applied firmly against the resistance of a bone (Figure 9-10).

Elevation

Elevation, in combination with direct pressure, provides an additional means for the reduction of external hemorrhage. Elevating a hemorrhaging part against gravity reduces blood pressure and, consequently, slows bleeding.[9]

Pressure Points

When direct pressure combined with elevation fails to slow hemorrhage, the use of pressure points may be the method of choice. Eleven points on each side of the body have been identified for controlling external bleeding; the two most commonly used are the brachial artery in the upper limb and the femoral artery in the lower limb. The brachial artery is compressed against the medial aspect of the humerus, and the femoral artery is compressed as it is detected within the femoral triangle (Figure 9-11).

Tourniquet

If more conservative means fail to control hemorrhage, a tourniquet may have to be applied. A tourniquet is seldom used in sports, and in most cases medical care can be administered in ample time. There are, of course, exceptions such as the ones that occur in snow when the injured person must be transported for a long distance, sometimes under trying conditions with limited help. Circumstances such as these may necessitate use of a tourniquet. The time of tourniquet application should always be indicated on a card that can be secured to the person of the injured athlete so that an accurate record can be kept of when to release and reset pressure. NOTE: *It must be remembered that if a tourniquet is left on for longer than 10 minutes, or if it is too narrow, a clot may result, along with nerve and blood vessel damage, which could lead to loss of a limb because of gangrene.* The most common error is applying the tourniquet too loosely and allowing the blood to seep out slowly. Although a loosely applied tourniquet will constrict the veins, it cannot occlude the deeper arteries; consequently, blood will still be lost. It is most important when using a tourniquet to take the pulse rate of the artery *below* the tourniquet to determine whether cessation of blood flow has occurred.

Internal Hemorrhage

Internal hemorrhage is invisible to the eye unless manifested through some body opening or identified through x-ray studies or other diagnostic techniques. Its danger lies in the difficulty of diagnosis. When internal hemorrhaging occurs, either subcutaneously such as in a bruise or contusion, intramuscularly, or in joints, the athlete may be moved without danger in most instances. However, the detection of bleeding within a body cavity such as the skull or thorax is of the utmost importance, since it could mean the difference between life and death. Because the symptoms are obscure, internal hemorrhage is difficult to diagnose properly. It has been said that, as a result of this difficulty athletes with internal injuries require hospitalization under complete and constant observation by a medical staff to determine the nature and extent of the injuries. All severe hemorrhaging will eventually result in shock and should therefore be treated on this premise. Even if there is no outward indication of shock, the athlete should be kept quiet and body heat should be maintained at a constant and suitable temperature (see section about shock for the preferred body position).

SHOCK

In any injury shock is a possibility, but when severe bleeding, fractures, or deep internal injuries are present, the development of shock is assured. Shock occurs when there is a diminished amount of fluid available to the circulatory system. As a result there are not enough oxygen-carrying blood cells available to the tissues, particularly those of the nervous system. This situation occurs when the vascular system loses its capacity to hold the fluid portion of the blood within its system because of dilation of the blood vessels within the body and disruption of the osmotic fluid balance (Figure 9-12). When this occurs, a quantity of plasma is lost from the blood vessels to the tissue spaces of the body, leaving the solid blood particles within the vessels and thus causing stagnation and slowing the blood flow. With this general collapse of the vascular system there is a widespread tissue death, which will eventually cause the death of the individual unless treatment is given.

Certain conditions such as extreme fatigue, extreme exposure to heat or cold, extreme dehydration of fluids and minerals, or illness predispose an athlete to shock.

In a situation in which there is a potential shock condition, there are other signs by which the athletic trainer or coach should assess the possibility of the athlete's lapsing into a state of shock as an aftermath of the injury. The most important clue to potential shock is the recognition of a severe injury. It may happen that none of the usual signs of shock is present.

The main types of shock are hypovolemic, respiratory, neurogenic, psychogenic, cardiogenic, septic, anaphylactic, and metabolic.[9]

Hypovolemic shock stems from trauma in which there is blood loss. Without enough blood in the circulatory system organs are not properly supplied with oxygen.

Signs of shock
  Blood pressure is low
  Systolic pressure is
    usually below 90 mm
    Hg
  Pulse is rapid and very
    weak
  Athlete may be drowsy
    and appear sluggish
  Respiration is shallow
    and extremely rapid

Figure 9-12

During shock, blood vessels dilate, causing the osmotic fluid balance to be disrupted and allowing plasma to become lost into tissue spaces.

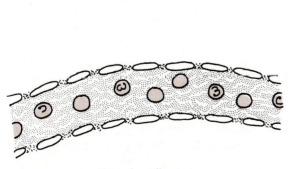

Normal capillary

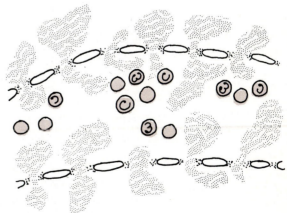

Dilated capillary

Respiratory shock occurs when the lungs are unable to supply enough oxygen to the circulating blood. Trauma that produces a pneumothorax or injury to the breathing control mechanism can produce respiratory shock.

Neurogenic shock is caused by the general dilation of blood vessels within the cardiovascular system. When it occurs, the typical 6 liters of blood can no longer fill the system. As a result the cardiovascular system can no longer supply oxygen to the body.

Psychogenic shock refers to what is commonly known as fainting (syncope). It is caused when there is temporary dilation of blood vessels, reducing the normal amount of blood in the brain.

Cardiogenic shock refers to the inadequacy of the heart to pump enough blood to the body.

Septic shock occurs from a severe, usually bacterial, infection. Toxins liberated from the bacteria cause small blood vessels in the body to dilate.

Anaphylactic shock is the result of a severe allergic reaction caused by foods, insect stings, drugs, or inhaling dusts, pollens, or other substances.

Metabolic shock happens when a severe illness such as diabetes goes untreated. Another cause is an extreme loss of bodily fluid (e.g., through urination, vomiting, or diarrhea).

Symptoms and Signs

The major characteristic of shock is marked paleness of the skin that may lead to cyanosis. As the condition progresses, the face takes on a pinched expression with staring of the eyes, which often lose their luster and become dilated. The pulse becomes weak and rapid, with the breathing rate increased and shallow. Blood pressure decreases, and in severe situations there is urinary retention and fecal incontinence. If conscious, the athlete may display a disinterest in his or her surroundings or may display irritability, restlessness, or excitement. There may also be extreme thirst.[9]

Management

Depending on the causative factor for the shock, the following emergency care should be given:

1. Maintain body heat, using warm but not hot blankets.
2. Elevate the feet and legs 8 to 12 inches for most situations.

However, shock management does vary according to the type of injury.[9] For example, for a neck injury, the athlete should be immobilized as found; for a head injury, his or her head and shoulders should be elevated; and for a leg fracture, his or her leg should be kept level and should be raised after splinting.

Shock can also be compounded or initially produced by the psychological reaction of the athlete to an injury situation. Fear or the sudden realization that a serious situation has occurred can result in shock. In the case of a psychological reaction to an injury the athlete should be instructed to lie down and avoid viewing the injury. This athlete should be handled with patience and gentleness, but firmness as well. Spectators should be kept away from the injured athlete. Reassurance is of vital concern to the injured individual. The person should be given immediate comfort through the loosening of clothing. Nothing should be given by mouth until a physician has determined that no surgical procedures are indicated.

MUSCULOSKELETAL INJURIES

Because musculoskeletal injuries are extremely common in sports, a knowledge of their immediate care is necessary. Three areas of first aid are highly important: (1) control of hemorrhage and management of early inflammation, muscle spasm, and pain; (2) splinting; and (3) handling and transportation.

Hemorrhage, Inflammation, Muscle Spasm, and Pain Management

Of major importance in musculoskeletal injuries is the initial control of hemorrhage, early inflammation, muscle spasm, and pain. The acronym for this process is ICE (ice, compression, and elevation). Added to this is the important factor of rest.

> ICE-R (ice, compression, elevation, and rest) are essential in the emergency care of musculoskeletal injuries.

Ice, Compression, Elevation, and Rest (ICE-R)

Ice (cold application)　Cold, primarily ice in various forms, is an effective first aid agent. It is not clear exactly how cold acts physiologically. It is known to reduce pain and spasm and to minimize enzyme activity, thus reducing tissue necrosis.[8] Cold application thus decreases the chances of swelling that occur for 4 to 6 hours following injury. There is some uncertainty about what extent vasoconstriction plays in the reduction of swelling. Cold makes blood more viscous, lessens capillary permeability, and decreases the blood flow to the injured area.[4] Cold applied to a recent injury will lower metabolism and the tissue demands for oxygen and reduce hypoxia. This benefit extends to uninjured tissue, preventing injury-related tissue death from spreading to adjacent normal cellular structures.[4] It should be noted however, that prolonged application of cold can cause tissue damage.[10]

For best results, ice packs (crushed ice and towel) should be applied directly to the skin. Frozen gel packs should not be used directly against the skin, because they reach much lower temperatures than ice packs. A good rule of thumb is to apply a cold pack to a recent injury for a 20-minute period and repeat every 1 to 1½ hours throughout the waking day. Depending on the severity and site of the injury, cold may be applied intermittently for 1 to 72 hours. For example, a mild strain will probably require one or two 20-minute periods of cold application, whereas a severe knee or ankle sprain might need 3 days of intermittent cold. If in doubt about the severity of an injury, it is best to extend the time ICE-R is applied.

Compression　In most cases immediate compression of an acute injury is considered an important adjunct to cold and elevation and in some cases may be superior to them.[11] Placing external pressure on an injury assists in decreasing hemorrhage and hematoma formation. Fluid seepage into interstitial spaces is retarded by compression, and absorption is facilitated.[11] However, application of compression to the anterior compartment syndrome would be contraindicated.

Many types of compression are available. An elastic wrap that has been soaked in water and frozen in a refrigerator can provide both compression and cold when applied to a recent injury. Pads can be cut from felt or foam rubber to fit difficult-to-compress body areas. A horseshoe-shaped pad, for example, placed around the malleolus in combination with an elastic wrap and tape, provides an excellent way to prevent or reduce ankle edema (Figure 9-13). Although cold is applied intermittently, compression should be maintained throughout the day. At night it

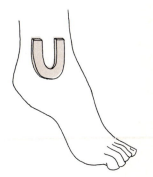

Figure 9-13

A horseshoe-shaped pad can be placed around the malleolus to reduce edema.

is best to remove the wrap completely and elevate the body part above the heart to avoid pooling of fluids when the body processes slow down.

Elevation   Along with cold and compression, elevation reduces internal bleeding. By elevating the affected part above the level of the heart, bleeding is reduced, and venous return is encouraged, further reducing swelling.

Rest   Rest is essential for musculoskeletal injuries. This can be achieved by not moving the part or can be guaranteed by the application of tape, wraps, splints, casts, and the assistance of a cane or crutches. Immobilization of an injury for the first 2 or 3 days after injury helps to ensure healing of the wound without complication. Too early movement will only increase hemorrhage and the extent of disability, prolonging recovery.

An ICE-R schedule

1. Evaluate the extent of injury.
2. Apply crushed ice in a moist towel pack to the injury.
3. Hold ice pack firmly against the injury site with an elastic wrap.
4. Elevate injured body part above the level of the heart.
5. After 20 minutes, remove ice pack.
6. Replace ice pack with a compress wrap and pad.
7. Elevate injured body part.
8. Reapply ice pack in 1 to 1 ½ hours, and, depending on degree of injury, continue this rotation until injury resolution has taken place and healing has begun.
9. When retiring, remove elastic wrap.
10. Elevate injured part above the heart.
11. When arising the next day, ICE-R is begun again and carried on throughout the day.
12. With second- or third-degree injury, continue this same process for 2 or 3 days.

Emergency Splinting

> A suspected fracture must be splinted before the athlete is moved.

Any suspected fracture should always be splinted before the athlete is moved. Transporting a person with a fracture without proper immobilization can result in increased tissue damage, hemorrhage, and shock. Conceivably a mishandled fracture could cause death. Therefore, a thorough knowledge of splinting techniques is important (Figure 9-14).

The application of splints should be a simple process through the use of emergency splints. In most instances the coach or athletic trainer does not have to improvise a splint, since such devices are readily available in most sports settings. The use of padded boards is recommended. They are easily available, can be considered disposable, and are easy to apply. Commercial basswood splints are excellent, as are disposable cardboard and clear plastic commercial splints. The clear plastic splint is inflated with air around the affected part and can be used for extremity splinting, but its use requires some special training (Figure 9-15). This splint provides support and moderate pressure to the body part and affords a clear view of the site for x-ray examination. The inflatable splint should *not* be used if it will alter a fracture deformity. For fractures of the femur the half-ring type of traction splint offers the best support and immobilization but takes considerable practice to master. A compound fracture must be carefully dressed to avoid additional contamination.

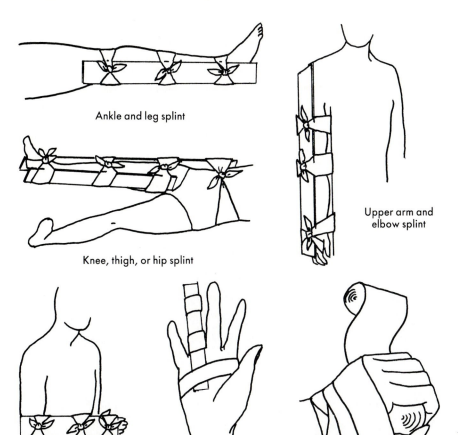

Ankle and leg splint

Knee, thigh, or hip splint

Upper arm and
elbow splint

Forearm splint

Hand and
finger splint

Gauze roll splint

Figure 9-14

Any suspected fracture
should routinely be splinted.

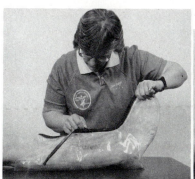

Figure 9-15

The air splint provides
excellent support, as well as a
clear site for x-ray
examination.

Whatever the material used, the principles of good splinting remain the same. Two major concepts of splinting are (1) to splint from one joint above the fracture to one joint below the fracture and (2) to splint where the athlete lies. If at all possible, do not move the athlete until he or she has been splinted.

Splinting of Lower-Limb Fractures

Fractures of the ankle or leg require immobilization of the foot and knee. Any fracture involving the knee, thigh, or hip needs splinting of all the lower-limb joints and one side of the trunk (Figure 9-16).

Figure 9-16

Application of a half-ring traction splint for a fracture of the femur.

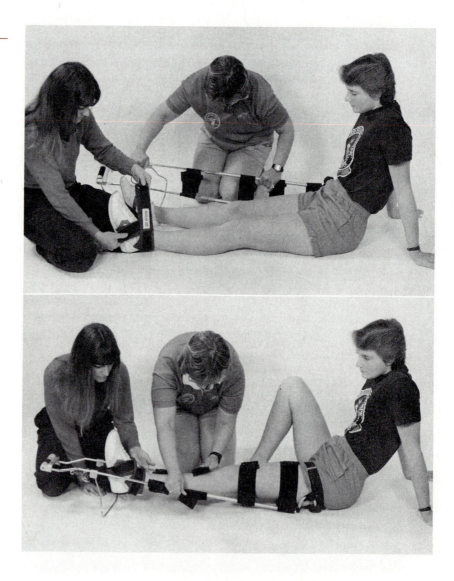

Splinting of Upper-Limb Fractures

Fractures around the shoulder complex are immobilized by a sling and swathe bandage, with the upper limb bound to the body securely. Upper-arm and elbow fractures must be splinted, with immobilization effected in a straight-arm position to lessen bone override. Lower-arm and wrist fractures should be splinted in a position of forearm flexion and should be supported by a sling. Hand and finger dislocations and fractures should be splinted with tongue depressors, gauze rolls, or aluminum splints.

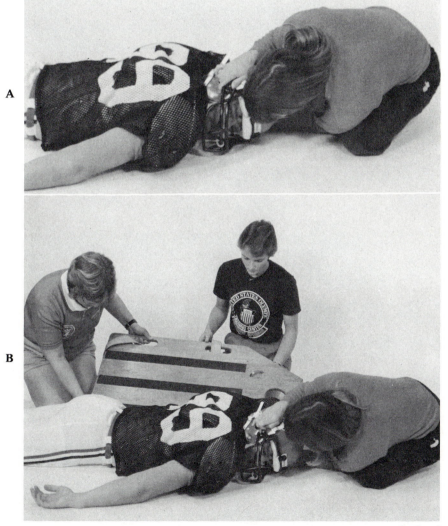

Figure 9-17

A, When moving an unconscious athlete, first establish whether the athlete is breathing and has a pulse. *An unconscious athlete must always be treated as having a serious neck injury.* If lying prone, the athlete must be turned over for CPR or to be secured to a spine board for possible cervical fracture. All of the athlete's extremities are placed in axial alignment with one athletic trainer stabilizing the athlete's neck and head. **B,** The spine board is placed as close to the athlete as possible.

Continued.

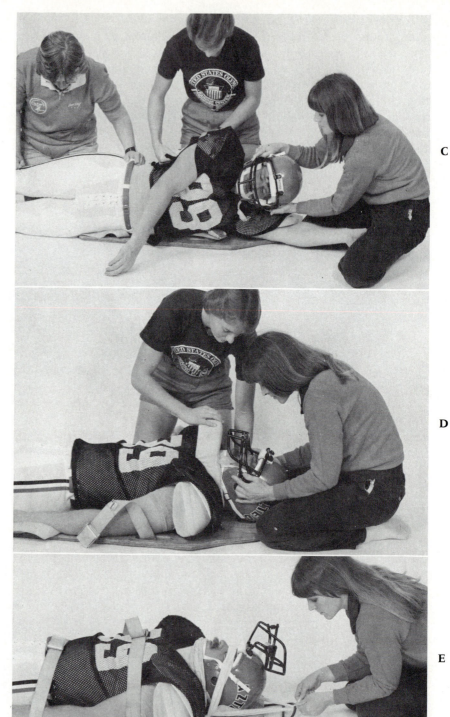

C

D

E

Figure 9-17, cont'd

C, Each assistant is responsible for one of the athlete's segments. When the athletic trainer (captain) gives the command "roll," the athlete is moved as a unit onto the spine board. **D,** At all times, the captain continues to stabilize the athlete's neck. **E,** The head and neck are stabilized onto the spine board by means of a chin strap secured to metal loops, and finally the trunk and lower limbs are secured to the spine board by straps.

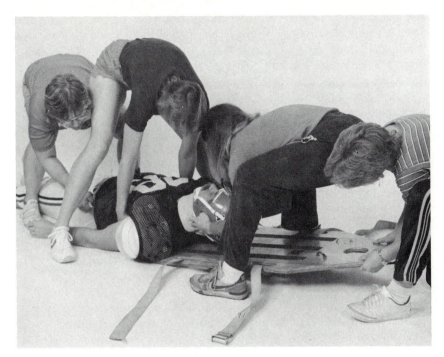

Figure 9-18

An alternate method of placing the athlete on a spine board is the straddle slide method.

Splinting of the Spine and Pelvis

Injuries involving a possible spine or pelvic fracture are best splinted and moved using a spine board (Figures 9-17 and 9-18). When such injuries are suspected, *the coach or athletic trainer should not, under any circumstances, move the injured athlete except under the express direction of a physician.*

HANDLING THE INJURED ATHLETE

Moving, lifting, and transporting the injured athlete must be executed so as to prevent further injury. Emergency aid authorities have suggested that improper handling causes more additional insult to injuries than any other emergency procedure.[2,3,5] There is no excuse for poor handling of the injured athlete.

Moving the Injured Athlete

It is very important that an unconscious athlete or one believed to have a spinal fracture be moved like a "log." The athlete who is unconscious and unable to describe the injury in terms of sensation and site *must be treated as having a severe cervical injury.*

    Suspected spinal injury   A suspected spinal injury requires extremely careful handling and is best left to properly trained ambulance attendants or certified paramedics who are more skilled and have the proper equipment for such transport. If such personnel are not available, moving should be done under the express direction of a physician or athletic trainer, and a spine board should be used (see Figure 9-17, *A-E*). One danger inherent in moving an athlete with a suspected spinal injury, in particular a cervical injury, is the tendency of the neck and head to turn because of the victim's inability to control his or her movements. Torque so induced creates considerable possibility of spinal cord or root damage when small fractures are present. The most important principle in transporting an individual on a spine board is *to keep the head and neck in alignment with the long axis of the body.* In such cases it should be best to have one individual whose sole responsibility is to ensure and maintain proper positioning of the head and neck until the head is secured to a backboard.

Suspected severe neck injury   Once an injury to the neck has been recognized as severe, a physician and an ambulance should be summoned immediately. Primary emergency care involves maintaining normal breathing, treating for shock, and keeping the athlete quiet and in the position found until medical assistance arrives. Ideally, transportation should not be attempted until the physician has examined the athlete and has given permission to move him or her. The athlete should be transported while lying on the back with the curve of the neck supported by a rolled-up towel or pad or encased in a stabilization collar. Neck stabilization must be maintained throughout transportation, first to the ambulance, then to the hospital, and throughout the hospital procedure. If stabilization is not continued, additional cord damage and paralysis may ensue.

These steps should be followed when moving an unconscious athlete:
1. Establish whether the athlete is breathing and has a pulse.
2. Plan to move the athlete on a spine board.
3. If the athlete is lying prone, he or she must be turned over for CPR or to be secured to the spine board. *An unconscious athlete or one with a possible cervical fracture is transported face up. An athlete with a spinal fracture in the lower trunk area is transported face down.*[2]
   a. Place all extremities in an axial alignment (see Figure 19-17, *A*).
   b. To roll the athlete over requires four or five persons, with the "captain" of the team protecting the athlete's head and neck. The neck must be stabilized and must not be moved from its original position, no matter how distorted it may appear.
   c. The spine board is placed close to the side of the athlete (see Figure 9-17, *B*).
   d. Each assistant is responsible for one of the athlete's body segments. One assistant is responsible for turning the trunk, another the hips, another the thighs, and the last the lower legs.
4. With the spine board close to the athlete's side, the captain gives the command to roll him or her onto the board as one unit (see Figure 9-17, *C*).
5. On the board, the athlete's head and neck continue to be stabilized by the captain (see Figure 9-17, *D*).
6. If the athlete is a football player, the helmet is *not* removed; however, the face guard is removed or lifted away from the face for possible CPR. NOTE: To remove the face guard, the plastic fasteners holding it to the helmet are cut.
7. The head and neck are next stabilized on the spine board by a chin strap secured to metal loops. Finally, the trunk and lower limbs are secured to the spine board by straps (see Figure 9-17, *E*).

An alternate method of moving the athlete onto a spine board, if he or she is face up, is the *straddle slide method.* Five persons are used—a captain stationed at the athlete's head and three or four assistants. One assistant is in charge of lifting the athlete's trunk, one the hips, and one the legs. On the command "lift" by the captain, the athlete is lifted while the fourth assistant slides a spine board under the athlete between the feet of the captain and assistants (Figure 9-18).

Transporting the Injured Athlete

As with moving, transporting the injured athlete must be executed so as to prevent further injury. There is no excuse for the use of poor transportation techniques in sports. Planning should take into consideration all the possible transportation methods and the necessary equipment to execute them. Capable persons, stretchers, and even an ambulance may be needed to transport the injured athlete. Four modes of assisting in travel are used: ambulatory aid, manual conveyance, stretcher carrying, and vehicular transfer.

Great caution must be taken when transporting the injured athlete.

Ambulatory aid   Ambulatory aid (Figure 9-19) is that support or assistance given to an injured athlete who is able to walk. Before the athlete is allowed to walk, he or she should be carefully scrutinized to make sure that the injuries are minor. Whenever serious injuries are suspected, walking should be prohibited. Complete support should be given on both sides of the athlete. The athlete's arms are draped over the assistants' shoulders, and their arms encircle his or her back.

Manual conveyance   Manual conveyance (Figure 9-20) may be used to move a mildly injured individual a greater distance than could be walked with ease. As with the use of ambulatory aid, any decision to carry the athlete must be made only after a complete examination to determine the existence of potentially serious conditions. The most convenient carry is performed by two assistants.

Figure 9-19

The ambulatory aid method of transporting a mildly injured athlete.

Figure 9-20

Manual conveyance method for transporting a mildly injured athlete.

Stretcher carrying Whenever a serious injury is suspected, the best and safest mode of transportation for a short distance is by stretcher. With each segment of the body supported, the athlete is gently lifted and placed on the stretcher, which is carried adequately by four assistants, two supporting the ends of the stretcher and two supporting either side (Figure 9-21). Any person with an injury serious enough to require the use of a stretcher must be carefully examined before being moved.

When transporting a person with a limb injury, be certain the injury is splinted properly before transport. Athletes with shoulder injuries are more comfortably moved in a semi-setting position, unless other injuries preclude such positioning. If injury to the upper extremity is such that flexion of the elbow is not possible, the individual should be transported on a stretcher with the limb properly splinted and carried at the side, with adequate padding placed between the arm and the body.

Figure 9-21

Whenever a serious injury is suspected, a stretcher is the safest method of transporting the athlete.

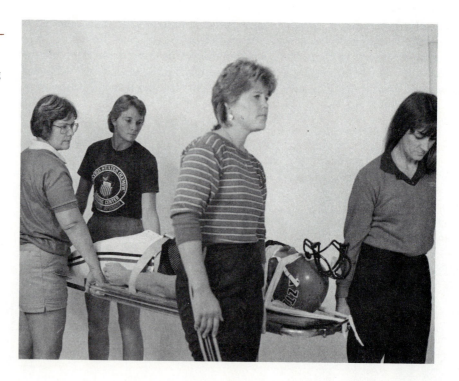

Emergency Emotional Care

Besides responding to the emergency physical requirements of an injury, the coach and the athletic trainer must respond appropriately to the emotions engendered by the situation.

The American Psychiatric Association has set forth major principles for the emergency care of emotional reactions to trauma.[3] They are as follows:

1. Accept everyone's right to personal feelings, since everyone comes from a unique background and has had different emotional experiences. Do not tell the injured person how he or she should feel. Show empathy, not pity.
2. Accept the injured person's limitations as real.
3. Athletic trainers must accept their own limitations as providers of first aid.

In general, the athletic trainer dealing with injured athletes' emotions should be empathetic and calm, making it obvious that their feelings are understood and accepted. See Table 6-1 for the emotional reaction after trauma and what an athletic trainer should and should not do.

SUMMARY

An emergency is defined as ". . . an unforeseen combination of circumstances and the resulting state that calls for immediate action."[6] The prime concern of emergency aid is to maintain cardiovascular function and, indirectly, central nervous system function. All sports programs should have an emergency system that is activated anytime an athlete is seriously injured.

Primary assessment may include determining if the ABCs of life support procedures are required and a thorough understanding of an athlete's vital signs. Other situations in which primary assessment procedures are performed are in cases of musculoskeletal injury or when an athlete is unconscious.

The mnemonic for cardiopulmonary resuscitation is ABC: A—airway opened; B—breathing restored; C—circulation restored. When using one rescuer, the ratio of compression to breaths is 15:2, with 80 to 100 compressions per minute. When using two rescuers, the ratio of compressions to breaths is 5:1, with 80 to 100 compressions per minute. To relieve an obstructed airway the Heimlich maneuver and/or the finger sweep of the throat should be performed.

Hemorrhage can occur externally and internally. External bleeding can be controlled by direct pressure, by elevation, and, as a last resort, by a tourniquet. Internal hemorrhage can occur subcutaneously, intramuscularly, or within a body cavity.

Shock can occur from a variety of situations. Shock can be hypovolemic, respiratory, neurogenic, psychogenic, cardiogenic, septic, anaphylactic, and metabolic. Symptoms may include skin paleness, dilated eyes, weak and rapid pulse, and rapid, shallow breathing. Management might include keeping the body warm and level but elevating the feet.

Ice, compression, elevation, and rest (ICE-R) should be used for the immediate care of a musculoskeletal injury. It should be applied for 10 to 20 minutes every 1 to 1½ hours throughout the waking day. A severe injury may require this procedure for 3 days.

Any suspected fracture should be splinted before the athlete is moved. The clear plastic air splint provides support, pressure, and a clear view for x-ray examination. Two major concepts of splinting are to splint from one joint above to one joint below the fracture. Do not move the athlete until the fracture has been splinted.

Great care must be taken in moving the seriously injured athlete. The unconscious athlete must be handled as though he or she has a cervical fracture. Moving an athlete with a suspected serious neck injury must be performed only by persons specifically trained to do so. A spine board should be used, avoiding any movement of the cervical region.

Athletes who are injured will respond emotionally to the situation. Their feelings must be understood and fully accepted by the coach and the athletic trainer.

REVIEW QUESTIONS AND CLASS ACTIVITIES

1. Why should every sports program in a school have an emergency system?
2. What decisions are made from a primary assessment?
3. What should be included in every emergency system?
4. How do you recognize vital life signs?
5. What are the ABCs of life support?
6. Identify the major steps in giving CPR and managing an obstructed airway. When may these procedures be used in a sports setting?
7. List the steps for examining a primary musculoskeletal condition.
8. Differentiate between the functional signs associated with selected conditions that result in loss of consciousness.
9. What are the types of hemorrhage that can occur in sports? How should each be managed?
10. There are numerous types of shock that can occur from a sports injury or illness; list them and their management.
11. What first aid procedures are used to decrease hemorrhage, inflammation, muscle spasm, and pain from a musculoskeletal injury?
12. Describe the basic concepts of emergency splinting.
13. How should an athlete with a suspected spinal injury be transported?
14. What assist techniques can be used when transporting an athlete with a suspected musculoskeletal injury?
15. Describe methods that should be used when dealing with an injured athlete's emotional response to the injury.

REFERENCES

1. Emergency care and transportation of the sick and injured, ed 2, Chicago, 1977, American Academy of Orthopaedic Surgeons.
2. Hafen, BQ: First aid for health emergencies, ed 4, St. Paul, Minn, 1988, West Publishing Co.
3. Henderson, J: Emergency medical guide, ed 4, New York, 1978, McGraw-Hill Book Co.
4. Knight, KL: ICE for immediate care of injuries, Phys Sportsmed 10:137, 1982.
5. Parcel, GS: Basic emergency care of the sick and injured, ed 3, St. Louis, 1985, The CV Mosby Co.
6. Standards and guidelines for cardiopulmonary resuscitation (CPR) and emergency cardiac care (ECC), JAMA 255:2841, 1986.
7. Stephenson, HE, Jr, (editor): Immediate care of the acutely ill and injured, ed 2, St. Louis, 1978, The CV Mosby Co.
8. Thorsson, O, et al: The effect of local cold application on intramuscular blood flow at rest and after running, Med Sci Sports Exerc 17:710, Dec 1985.
9. Thygerson, AL: First aid and emergency care workbook, National Safety Council, Boston, 1987, Jones and Bartlett Publishers, Inc.
10. Walton, M, et al.: Effects of ice packs on tissue temperatures at various depths before and after quadriceps hematoma: studies using sheep, J Orthop Sports Phys Ther 8:294, 1986.
11. Wilkerson, GB: External compression for controlling traumatic edema, Phys Sportsmed 13:96, 1985.

ANNOTATED BIBLIOGRAPHY

doCarmo, PB: Basic EMT skills and equipment, St. Louis, 1988, The CV Mosby Co.
Contains information about the skills required for basic emergency medical techniques.

Hafen, BQ: First aid for health emergencies, ed 4, St. Paul, Minn, 1988, West Publishing Co.
Presents in-depth coverage of emergency care. Of particular interest are chapters on shock, psychological first aid, bone, joint, and muscle injuries.

Judd, RL, and Ponsell, DD: Mosby's first responder: the critical first minutes, St. Louis, 1987, The CV Mosby Co.
A complete guide to emergency care.

Parcel, GS: Basic emergency care of the sick and injured, ed 3, St. Louis, 1985, The CV Mosby Co.
Presents wide coverage of emergency care. Of special interest are Chapter 2, *Legal Considerations Involved in Emergency Care by Nonmedical Personnel,* and Section III, *Trauma Emergencies.*

10

General Assessment Procedures

When you finish this chapter, you should be able to

Explain the importance of primary and secondary assessment in sports medicine and athletic training

List the major terms used in assessment

Describe the procedures and signs to watch for in a primary emergency assessment

Demonstrate a complete secondary musculoskeletal assessment

Describe additional tests that a physician might request to gain additional information for diagnosis

The assessment of sports injuries is a proficiency that all athletic trainers and sports physicians must have. As one of the most important members of the sports medicine team, the athletic trainer is charged with performing accurate and detailed assessment under a number of specific circumstances. As discussed in Chapter 9, the athletic trainer often performs primary or on-site injury assessment. In other words, the athletic trainer is often the first person to inspect and evaluate the athlete's injury, usually almost immediately after it has occurred. Under circumstances that do not require first aid or emergency care, assessment is often performed at a place other than where the injury occurred and has generally been called secondary or more detailed assessment.

INJURY RECOGNITION VERSUS DIAGNOSIS

Although athletic trainers and coaches recognize and evaluate sports injuries, by law they cannot make a diagnosis. A diagnosis denotes what disease, injury, or syndrome a person has or is believed to have. Making a diagnosis is usually reserved for individuals specifically licensed by a state to do so. Health professionals such as physicians can generally diagnose. Health professionals restricted to diagnosing one body area are dentists, who are limited to diagnosing mouth disorders, podiatrists, who are limited to diagnosing disorders of the human foot, and optometrists, who are limited to determining refractory problems of the eyes and prescribing lenses to increase the efficiency of vision. Chiropractors usually base their diagnoses on the relationship of the body's structure to its overall function. In some states, nurse practitioners may perform limited diagnoses.

Athletic trainers recognize and evaluate sports injuries, but by law they cannot make diagnoses.

FOUNDATIONAL REQUIREMENTS

The examiner of athletes with sports injuries must have a general knowledge of normal human anatomy and biomechanics and an understanding of the major hazards inherent in a particular sport. Without this information, accurate assessment becomes impossible.

The examiner of sports injuries must have a thorough knowledge of human anatomy and its function and of the hazards inherent in sports.

Normal Human Anatomy
Surface Anatomy

Understanding typical surface or topographical anatomy is essential when evaluating a possible injury. Key surface landmarks provide the examiner with indications of the normal or injured anatomical structures lying underneath the skin.[3]

Body planes and anatomical directions   Associated with surface anatomy is the understanding of body planes and anatomical directions. Body planes are used as points of reference from which positions of body parts are indicated. The three most commonly mentioned planes are the midsagittal, transverse, and frontal (or coronal) planes (Figure 10-1). Anatomical directions refer to the relative position of one part to another (Figure 10-2).

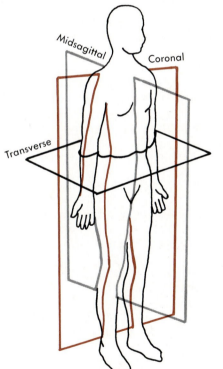

Figure 10-1

Knowledge of body planes helps provide points of reference.

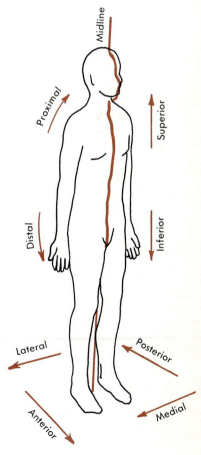

Figure 10-2

Anatomical directions refer to the relative position of one body part to another.

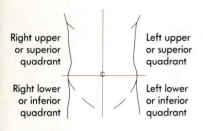

Figure 10-3

Knowledge about the four abdominopelvic quadrants helps in injury assessment.

biomechanics

Application of mechanical forces to living organisms.

Abdominopelvic quadrants   The abdominopelvic quadrants are the four corresponding regions of the abdomen that are divided for evaluative and diagnostic purposes (Figure 10-3).

Musculoskeletal System

Anyone examining the muscoloskeletal system for sports injuries must have an in-depth knowledge of both structural and functional anatomy. This knowledge encompasses the major joints and bony structures, as well as skeletal musculature. A knowledge of neural anatomy is also of major importance, particularly that which is involved in movement control and sensation, along with the neural factors that influence superficial and deep pain.

Standard musculoskeletal terminology for bodily positions and deviations   When assessing the musculoskeletal system, a standard terminology must be used to convey more precisely information to others who may become professionally involved with the athlete. These terms are found in Table 10-1.

Biomechanics   The understanding of biomechanics is the foundation for the assessment of musculoskeletal sports injuries. **Biomechanics** is the application of mechanical forces, which may stem from within or outside of the body, to living

TABLE 10-1 Standard Orthopedic Definitions for Positions and Deviations

Terms	Definition
Abduction	To draw away or deviate from the midline of the body
Adduction	To deviate toward or draw toward the midline of the body
Eversion	Turning outward
Extension	To straighten; when the part distal to a joint extends, it straightens
External rotation	Rotary motion in the transverse plane away from the midline
Flexion	To bend; when a joint is flexed, the part distal to the joint bends
Internal rotation	Rotary motion in the transverse plane toward the midline
Inversion	Turning inward
Kyphosis	An increased rounding of the normal thoracic curve of the spine
Lordosis	The anterior concavity in the curvature of the lumbar and cervical spines when viewed from the side
Pronation	Assuming the foot is in a prone position, a combination of eversion and abduction movements, resulting in a lowering of the medial margin of the foot; when applied to the hand, it means the palm is turned downward
Supination	To assume a supine position; applied to the foot, it refers to raising the medial margin of the foot; applied to the palm of the hand, it refers to turning the palm upward
Valgus	Deviation of a part or portion of the extremity distal to a joint toward the midline of the body
Varus	Deviation of a part or portion of an extremity distal to a joint away from the midline of the body

organisms. Of major concern is pathomechanics, which may precede an injury. **Pathomechanics** refers to mechanical forces that are applied to the body because of a structural body deviation, leading to faulty alignment. Pathomechanics often cause overuse syndromes.

Knowing sport hazards   The more the examiner of sports injuries knows about how a sport is performed and its potential for trauma, the better an injury assessment can be. To fully understand injuries that occur in a sport, a detailed knowledge of the correct kinesiological and biomechanical principles that should be applied is necessary. Violation of these principles can lead to repetitive and overuse syndromes. Understanding how an acute or chronic injury might occur helps the examiner "zero in" more directly on tissues that have been affected.

ASSESSING SPORTS INJURIES

Injury evaluation is an essential part of athletic training. Each examiner must develop his or her own systematic approach to injury evaluation. Three distinct evaluations are commonly conducted: (1) the primary, or on-site, injury inspection and evaluation; (2) the secondary, or off-site, injury evaluation; and (3) the evaluation for determining the progress of a specific treatment regimen.

The primary assessment involves first aid, the determination of serious injuries, and the proper disposition of the injured athlete. Secondary assessment concerns the detailed sequence of procedures that determine the nature, site, and severity of an injury. From the secondary assessment the examiner can decide whether referral to another health professional is necessary. Portions of the secondary assessment sequence may be used to determine the progress of a treatment regimen.

Descriptive Assessment Terms

When assessing sports injuries, selected terms are used to describe and characterize what is being learned about the condition. The student should become very familiar with these terms.

Etiology refers to the cause of an injury or disease. In sports medicine, the term *mechanism* is exchanged for etiology.

After understanding of an injury's etiology, symptoms and signs are ascertained. *Symptom* refers to a perceptible change in an athlete's body or its functions that indicates an injury or disease. Symptoms are subjective and are described by the athlete to the coach, athletic trainer, or physician. In comparison, a *sign* is objective, being definitive and obvious as an indicator for a specific condition. Signs are often determined when the athlete is examined.

After it is inspected, an injury may be assigned a *degree* or *grade*. First, second, or third degree corresponds to an injury that is mild, moderate, or severe, respectively. Sometimes grade is used in place of degree, depending on the examiner's preference. To add to this confusion, grades may be combined with degrees. For example, the first degree may be divided into two grades. Thus a first-degree/grade one injury would be very mild, whereas a first-degree/grade two injury would be more serious; however, it would be less serious than a second-degree, or moderate, injury. In most cases, a grade three condition corresponds with moderate injury, and a grade-four condition corresponds with severe injury. To avoid confusion, students must carefully read, in detail, the description of the injury and make their own logical designation.

pathomechanics
Mechanical forces that are applied to a living organism and adversely change the body's structure and function.

Diagnosis denotes the name of a specific condition. To establish the diagnosis of an athlete's injury or illness, all aspects of the condition must be studied. Once all the possible information has been gathered about the athlete's condition, a *prognosis* is made. This is a prediction of the course of the condition. In other words, the athlete is told what is to be expected as the injury heals. The amount of pain, swelling, and/or loss of function is discussed. Prognosis also refers to the length of time predicted for complete recovery. For the athlete, prognosis translates into "the length of time before I can compete."

Sequela refers to a condition following and resulting from a disease or injury. It refers to the development of an additional condition as a complication of an existing disease or injury. For example, pneumonia might result from a bout with the "flu," or osteoarthritis might follow a severe joint sprain.

The term *syndrome* is used throughout the text and refers to a group of symptoms and signs that, together, indicate a particular injury or disease.

Secondary Assessment

Secondary assessment
consists of
  History
  General observation
  Physical examination

Secondary assessment is more thoroughly performed once the athlete has been removed from the site of initial injury to a place of comfort and safety. This detailed assessment may be performed on the sidelines, in an emergency room, in the training room, or in a sports medicine clinic. Further inspection and evaluation may be performed when the injury is still in an acute phase or has become

---

MUSCULOSKELETAL ASSESSMENT SEQUENCE

1. History
   a. Past
   b. Present
2. Observation
   a. General
   b. Specific
3. Examination
   a. Palpation
      (1) Bony
      (2) Soft tissue
   b. Movement
      (1) Active
      (2) Passive
      (3) Resistive
   c. Neurological
      (1) Muscle testing
      (2) Reflex testing
      (3) Sensation testing
   d. Special tests
   e. Testing joint play
   f. Functional evaluation
   g. Postural evaluation

---

chronic and/or recurrent. Assessment falls under three broad headings: history, general observation, and physical examination. *There are numerous special tests that provide additional information about the extent of injuries.* The following discussion provides the student with a brief overview of some of the steps and techniques that can be used in a secondary assessment. (Chapters 17 through 24 provide the reader with specific injury assessment procedures.)

History

Obtaining as much information as possible about the injury is of major importance to the examiner. Understanding how the injury may have occurred and listening to the complaints of the athlete and how key questions are answered can provide important clues to the exact nature of the injury. The examiner becomes a detective in pursuit of as much accurate information as possible, which will lead to a determination of the true nature of the injury. From the history, the examiner develops strategies for further examination and possible immediate and follow-up management.

When obtaining a history, the examiner should do the following:
1. Be calm and reassuring.
2. Express questions that are simple, not leading.
3. Listen carefully to the athlete's complaints.

Questions might be stated under specific headings in an attempt to get as complete a historical picture as possible. In many cases, a history becomes very clearcut because the mechanism, trauma, and pathology are obvious, whereas in other situations, symptoms and signs may be obscured.

HISTORY OF MUSCULOSKELETAL INJURIES

Information to Obtain

Chief complaints and present problem(s).

If pain is present, its location, character, duration, variation, aggravation, distribution or radiation, intensity, and course.

Is the pain increased or decreased by specific activities or stresses?

What situation or trauma caused the problem?

Has the problem occurred before; if so, when and how was it treated? Was treatment successful?

The primary complaint   If conscious and coherent, the athlete is encouraged to describe the injury in detail. How did it occur? When did it occur? Has this happened before? If so, when? Was something heard or felt when it occurred? If the athlete is unable to describe accurately how the injury occurred, perhaps a teammate or someone who observed the event can do so.

The injury location   Ask the athlete to locate the area of complaint by pointing to it with one finger only. If the athlete can point to a specific pain site, it is probably a localized injury. On the other hand, if the exact pain site cannot be indicated, the injury may be generalized and nonspecific.

Determining whether the injury is acute or chronic   Ask the athlete how long he or she has had the symptoms and how frequently they appear.

Pain characteristics   What type of pain is it? Nerve pain is sharp, bright, and/or burning. Bone pain tends to be localized and piercing. Pain in the vascular system tends to be poorly localized, aching, and referred from another area. Muscle pain is often dull, aching, and referred to another area.[6] Determining pain origin makes the evaluation of musculoskeletal injuries difficult. The deeper the injury site the more difficult it is to match the pain with the site of trauma. This factor often causes treatment to be performed at the wrong site. Conversely, the closer the injury is to the body surface the better the elicited pain corresponds with the site of pain stimulation.[5]

Does the pain change at different times? Pain that subsides during activity usually indicates a chronic inflammation. Pain that increases in a joint throughout the day indicates a progressive increase in edema.

Does the athlete feel sensations other than pain? Pressure on nerve roots can produce pain and/or a sensation of "pins and needles" (paresthesia). What movement, if any, causes pain or other sensations?

Joint responses   If the injury is related to a joint, is there instability? Does the joint feel as though it will give way? Does the joint lock and unlock? Positive responses may indicate that the joint has a loose body that is catching or that is inhibiting the normal muscular support in the area.

OBSERVATION OF MUSCULOSKELETAL INJURIES

Concerns During Observation

Is there obvious soft-tissue and/or bone deformity?
Are limb positions symmetrical?
How do the limbs' size, shape, color, temperature, and muscle tone compare?
Are there trophic changes of the skin?
Are there skin sites in which there is heat, swelling, and/or redness?
Is the athlete willing to move a body part?
Does the athlete display facial expressions indicating pain?

General Observation

Along with gaining knowledge and understanding of the athlete's major complaint from a history, general observation is also performed, often at the same time the history is taken. What is observed is commonly modified by the athlete's major complaints. The following are suggested as specific points to observe:

1. How does the athlete move? Is there a limp? Are movements abnormally slow, jerky, asynchronous, or is movement not allowed in a body part?
2. Is the body held stiffly to protect against pain? Does the athlete's facial expression indicate pain or lack of sleep?
3. Are there any obvious body asymmetries? Is there an obvious deformity? Does soft tissue appear swollen or wasted as a result of atrophy? Are there

unnatural protrusions such as occur with a dislocation or a fracture? Is there a postural malalignment?

4. Are there abnormal sounds such as crepitus when the athlete moves?
5. Does a body area appear inflamed? Are there swelling, heat, and redness?

Physical Examination

In performing a more detailed examination of the musculoskeletal system, the examiner engages in palpation, movement assessment, neurological assessment, and special tests of specific body areas, such as testing joint play and posture when called for. At certain times functional tests are also given.

Palpation   Some examiners use palpation in the beginning of the examination procedure, whereas others only use it when they believe they have identified the specific injury site by other assessment means.[2,6] In some cases, palpation would be beneficial at both the beginning and the end of the examination. The two areas of palpation are bony and soft tissue. As with all examination procedures, palpation must be performed systematically, starting with very light pressure followed by gradually deeper pressure and usually beginning away from the site of complaint, gradually moving towards it.

Bony palpation   Both the injured and noninjured sites should be palpated and compared. The sense of touch might reveal an abnormal gap at a joint, swelling on a bone, joints that are misaligned, or abnormal protruberances associated with a joint or a bone.

Soft-tissue palpation   Through palpation, with the athlete as relaxed as possible, normal soft-tissue relationships can be ascertained. Tissue deviations such as swellings, lumps, gaps, and abnormal muscle tensions and temperature variations can be detected. The palpation of soft tissue can detect where ligaments or tendons have torn. Variations in the shape of structures, differences in tissue tightness and textures, differentiation of tissue that is pliable and soft from tissue that is more resilient, as well as pulsations, tremors, and other involuntary muscle twitching can be discerned. Excessive skin dryness and moisture can also be noted. Abnormal skin sensations such as diminished sensation (dysesthesia), numbness (anesthesia), or increased sensation (hyperesthesia) can be noted. Like bony palpation, soft-tissue palpation must be performed on both sides of the body for comparison.

Movement assessment   Movement assessment divides into three subcategories: active, passive, and resisted isometric movement. Each test is repeated several times to determine whether symptoms are decreased or exacerbated, whether there is a progressive increase in weakness, and whether circulation is impeded.[2,6] When tissues are stretched and contracted, both subjective and objective information is provided to the examiner.

> Movement examination includes
> Active movement
> Passive movement
> Resisted isometric movement

Active movement   According to Cyriax,[2] active movement (movement that is performed solely by the patient) indicates three factors: an ability and willingness to execute certain movements, muscular power, and range of active movement. Active movement may be normal, limited, or excessive.[2] Active movement limitations may be caused by pain, spasm, contracture, or compression. Active and passive joint range of motion can be measured using goniometry. Muscle grading can also be determined by manual testing (see section about neurological examination and Table 10-3).

JOINT RANGE OF MOTION   Goniometry, which measures joint range of motion, is an essential procedure during the early, intermediate, and late stages of injury. Full range of motion of an affected body part is a major criterion for the return of the athlete to participation.

Although a number of different types of goniometers are on the market, the most commonly used are ones that measure 0 to 180 degrees in each direction. The arms of the instrument are usually 12 to 16 inches (30 to 40 cm) long, with one arm stationary and the other fully movable.[8]

To ensure accuracy and reliability the tester must use specific body positions and anatomical landmarks. Figures 10-4 to 10-20 depict the proper position for the athlete and the placement of the goniometer (Table 10-2).

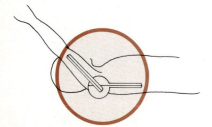

Figure 10-4

Shoulder flexion. The stationary arm is placed along the midaxillary line of the trunk in line with the greater trochanter of the femur. The moving arm is placed along the humerus and in line with the lateral condyle of the humerus.

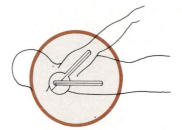

Figure 10-5

Shoulder extension using the same landmarks shown in Figure 10-4.

Figure 10-6

Shoulder abduction. The stationary arm is positioned parallel to floor at the side of the body posterior to the axillary line. The moving arm is placed on the posterior aspect of the arm parallel to the posterior midline of the body, pointing toward the olecranon process.

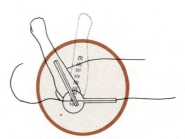

Figure 10-7

Lateral and medial shoulder rotation with the elbow flexed at 90 degrees. The stationary arm is placed parallel to the table. The center of goniometer is placed at the olecranon process, and the moving arm is placed along the dorsal midline of the forearm between the styloid process.

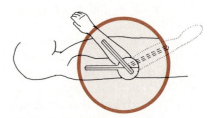

Figure 10-8

Elbow extension and flexion. The stationary arm is positioned along the lateral midline of the humerus toward the acromion process. The moving arm is positioned along the lateral midline of the radius, pointing to the styloid process.

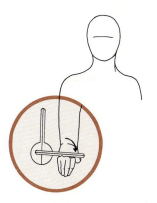

Figure 10-9

Forearm pronation. The stationary arm is placed on the back of the wrist parallel to the long axis of the humerus. The moving arm is placed along the back of the hand after movement has been performed.

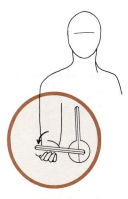

Figure 10-10

Forearm supination. The goniometer is placed on the volar (palm) side of the hand.

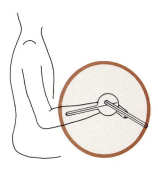

Figure 10-11

Wrist flexion and extension. The stationary arm is positioned along the lateral midline of the ulna pointing toward the medial epicondyle. The moving arm parallels the fifth metacarpal bone.

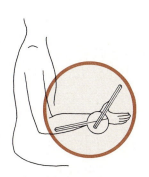

Figure 10-12

Radial flexion. The stationary arm is positioned along the midline of the back of the forearm between the ulna and radius, pointing toward the lateral epicondyle of the humerus. The moving arm is positioned along the third metacarpophalangeal joint of the third digit.

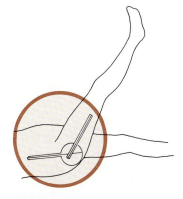

Figure 10-13

Hip flexion. The stationary arm is placed along a line from the crest of the ilium, femur, and greater trochanter. The moving arm is positioned in line with the femur, pointing toward the lateral condyle of the femur.

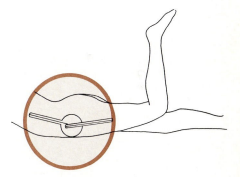

Figure 10-14

Hip extension. The goniometer is placed in the same position as in Figure 10-13, but the athlete takes a prone position.

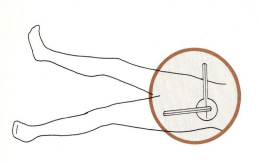

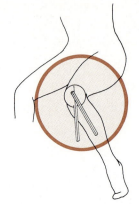

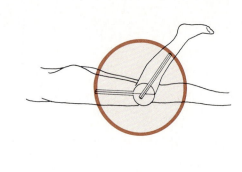

Figure 10-15

Hip abduction and adduction with the athlete in a supine position. The stationary arm is positioned between the anterior superior iliac spine. The moving arm parallels the anterior aspect of the femur, pointing toward the middle of the patella.

Figure 10-16

Medial and lateral rotation in a sitting position. The stationary arm is positioned along the middle of the tibia. The center of the goniometer is in the midpatellar region. The moving arm is in the same position as the stationary arm.

Figure 10-17

Knee flexion and extension in supine position. The stationary arm is positioned along the lateral femur, pointing toward the lateral condyle of the greater trochanter. The moving arm is placed parallel to the lateral midline of fibula toward the lateral malleolus.

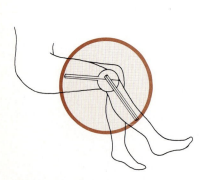

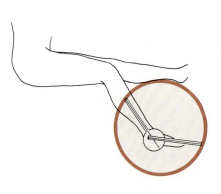

Figure 10-18

Knee extension and flexion while sitting on a table. The stationary arm is parallel to the lateral aspect of the femur. The center of the goniometer is at the lateral condyle of the femur. The moving arm is parallel to the fibula.

Figure 10-19

Ankle dorsiflexion and plantar flexion. The stationary arm is parallel to the lateral midline of the fibula in line with the lateral malleolus and head of the fibula. The moving arm is placed parallel to the lateral midline of the fifth metatarsal bone.

Figure 10-20

Foot abduction and adduction. The stationary arm is positioned on the plantar aspect of the foot from the center of the heel and between the second and third toes.

TABLE 10-2 Range of Joint Motion

Joint	Action	Degrees of Motion
Shoulder	Flexion	180
	Extension	45
	Adduction	40
	Abduction	180
	Medial rotation	90
	Lateral rotation	90
Elbow	Flexion	145
Forearm	Pronation	80
	Supination	85
Wrist	Flexion	80
	Extension	70
	Abduction	20
	Adduction	45
Hip	Flexion	125
	Extension	10
	Abduction	45
	Adduction	40
	Medial rotation	45
	Lateral rotation	45
Knee	Flexion	140
Ankle	Flexion	45
	Extension	20
Foot	Inversion	40
	Eversion	20

Passive movement   Passive movement refers to movement that is performed completely by the examiner. With the athlete relaxed, the body part is moved through as full a range of motion as possible. This type of assessment is basically designed to determine the condition of the inert tissue, or that tissue that surrounds a joint, excluding the musculature. As the part is moved, the examiner determines what is felt at the end of the movement, or "end feel." Magee[6] describes three typical end feels: bone to bone, soft-tissue approximation, and tissue stretch. With bone-to-bone end feel, there is a rigid unyielding feeling that is painless. In soft-tissue approximation, there is a feeling that further movement is being resisted by muscle bulk. In tissue-stretch end feel, the examiner feels a "springy" resistance.

Resisted isometric movements   The purpose of assessment through resisted isometric movement is to determine the status of a particular muscle or muscle group. It is performed following passive movement, while the part is held in a resting or midrange position. No joint movement is allowed to avoid tensing the inert joint tissues. The design of this procedure is to detect specific pain sites and/or muscular and tendinous weaknesses. The athlete is asked to contract the part as much as possible, while the examiner provides resistance accordingly. The following are some of the findings that this assessment can provide the examiner[2,6]:

Passive movement refers to movement that is performed completely by the examiner.

1. *Weak and painless*—a possible third-degree strain or muscle rupture
2. *Weak and painful*—a possible fracture at a joint site
3. *Strong and painful*—a possible tear of a muscle or tendon
4. *Strong and painfree*—no muscle lesion present

Neurological Examination

The neurological examination usually follows the movement examination. It consists of three major areas: muscle testing, reflex testing, and sensation testing.

Muscle testing   Whenever feasible and there is no danger of aggravating the injury, muscle strength should be tested and compared to the unaffected side of the body. Muscles should be graded according to Table 10-3.

TABLE 10-3 Manual Muscle Strength Grading

Grade	Percentage (%)	Value of Concentration	Muscle Strength
5	100	Normal	Complete range of motion (ROM) against gravity, with full resistance
4	75	Good	Complete ROM against gravity, with some resistance
3	50	Fair	Complete ROM against gravity, with no resistance
2	25	Poor	Complete ROM, with gravity omitted
1	10	Trace	Evidence of slight contractility, with no joint motion
0	0	Zero	No evidence of muscle contractility

Reflex testing   Reflex refers to an involuntary response following a stimulus. In terms of the neurological examination, there are two types of reflexes—superficial and deep. A superficial reflex is caused by sudden irritation of the skin or other areas. A deep reflex is caused by stimulation of structures underneath the skin such as tendons or bones. When a tendon is percussed, an involuntary muscle contraction stemming from the stimulation of a specific nerve or nerve root should occur. Table 10-4 shows how reflexes may be graded.

TABLE 10-4 Reflex Grading

	Grade	Definition
Absence of a reflex	0	Areflexia
Diminished reflex	1	Hyporeflexia
Average reflex	2	
Exaggerated reflex	3	Hyperreflexia
Clonus	4	Spasmodic alteration of muscle contraction and relaxation, indicating a nerve irritation

Sensation testing   A major component of musculoskeletal assessment is determining the distribution of peripheral nerves and dermatomes. Peripheral nerve distribution, although varying with individuals, is more predictable than dermatome distribution.[6] As the examination progresses, the examiner scrutinizes the variance, if any, in sensation from one side of the body to the other or on the

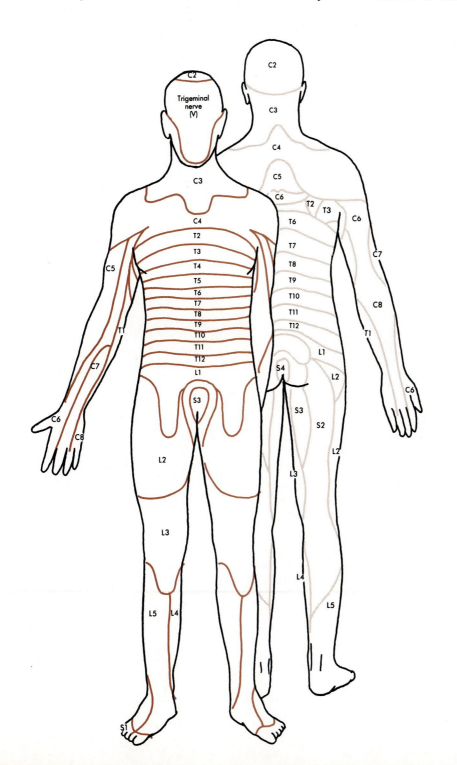

Figure 10-21

Numbness, referred pain, or other nerve involvements often follow the segmental distribution of spinal nerves on the skin's surface.

same side. Superficial sensation is commonly tested with a pin, and deep pain may be elicited by squeezing the muscle of the specific body part.[9] In testing for altered sensation, referred pain should be considered a possibility (Figures 10-21 and 10-22).

Determining projected referred pain   As discussed in Chapter 8, a complaint of deep, burning pain or an ache that is diffused or of a painful area with no signs of disorder or malfunctioning is most likely referred pain.[2] Cyriax[2] considers that the common sites for pain referral are, in order of importance, joint capsule, tendon, muscle, ligament, and bursa. Pressures from the dura mater and/or nerve sheath can also produce referred pain or other sensory responses. Palpation of what is thought the area at fault often is misleading. Detecting the selective tension of the tissue at fault is one of the best means for gathering correct data. Some musculoskeletal pain is caused by myofascial trigger points, which are not related to deeper, referred-type pain. Palpation is used to determine the presence or absence of tense tissue bands and tender trigger points.

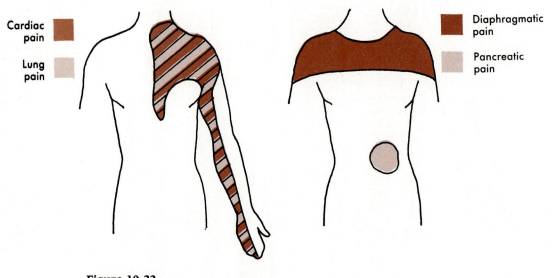

Figure 10-22

Some typical clinical presentations of referred somatic pain from organs with pathological conditions.

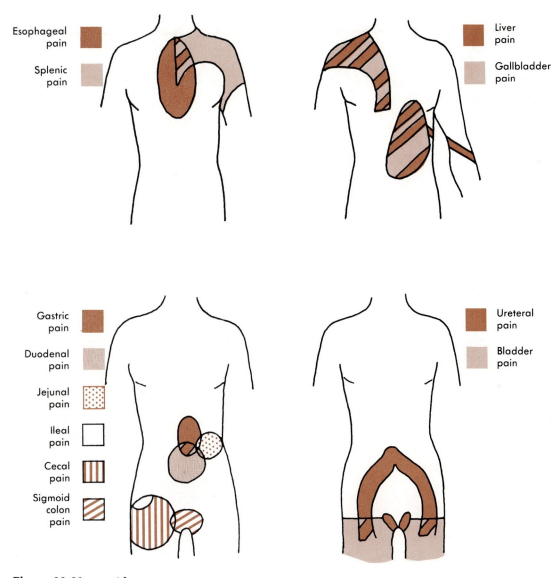

Figure 10-22, cont'd

Some typical clinical presentations of referred somatic pain from organs with pathological conditions.

Continued.

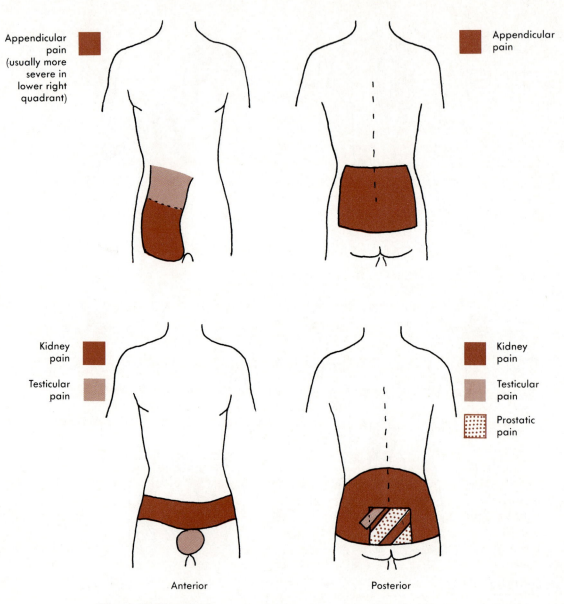

Figure 10-22, cont'd

Some typical clinical presentations of referred somatic pain
from organs with pathological conditions.

Special Tests

Special tests have been designed for almost every body region as means for detecting specific pathologies. They are often used to substantiate what has been learned from other testing. For example, special tests are commonly used to determine ligament stability, impingement signs, tightness of specific structures, blood circulation, muscle imbalance, and body alignment discrepancies (see Chapters 17 through 24).

Testing Joint Play

Joint play refers to that movement, found in diathroidial joints, that is not voluntary but accessory, being revealed by specific stresses applied by the examiner. A joint that has lost its joint play is dysfunctional, leading to pathology. Techniques of joint mobilization are designed to free these joints.[6] To be tested, the joint is positioned in the position of least strain, which is often called the loose-pack position.[4,6]

> Joint play is movement that is not voluntary but accessory.

Postural Examination

As discussed in Chapter 7, many cases of injuries in athletes can be attributed to body malalignments. Musculoskeletal assessment might be one area of a postural examination. It is designed to test for malalignments and asymmetries by viewing the body in comparison to a grid or plumb line (see Figure 21-17).

Functional Evaluation

The functional evaluation of an athlete may be performed early in the initial examination or be made to determine whether or not rehabilitation has been successful. It is an important factor that precedes the return to full sports participation. A functional evaluation proceeds gradually from very little stress to one that mimics the actual stress that would normally come from full sports participation. The major concern is whether the athlete has regained full strength, joint stability, and coordination and is pain free. A lack of any one of these three abilities may be a factor in excluding the athlete from his or her sport.

> Functional examination determines if there is full strength, joint stability, and coordination and if the part is pain free.

Gaining Additional Information

The physician, as does the athletic trainer, often performs a detailed musculoskeletal examination. Often, the physician and the athletic trainer will discuss and compare their individual findings. Because the physician is legally charged with the diagnosis and course of treatment, he or she may have to acquire and compare additional information, which may come from roentgenograms (x-rays), arthrography, arthroscopy, or myelography or through the new imaging techniques such as computed tomography, bone scanning, magnetic resonance imaging, and sonography. Other tests might include electromyography, determining nerve conduction velocity, synovial fluid analysis, and blood evaluation.

> Many new imaging techniques are now available as a means to diagnosing sports injuries:
> Computed tomography
> Bone scanning
> Magnetic resonance imaging
> Sonography

Roentgenograms (X-rays)

An x-ray examination is designed to rule out serious disease such as an infection or neoplasm. It assists the physician in determining fractures and dislocations or any bone abnormality that may be present. An experienced physician can detect some soft-tissue factors such as joint swelling and ectopic bone development in ligaments and tendons.[1]

Arthrography

Arthrography refers to the visual study of a joint through x-ray study after injection of an opaque dye, air, or a combination of air and opaque dye into the joint space. This procedure can show the disruption of soft tissue and loose bodies in the joint.

Arthroscopy

Arthroscopy uses a fiber optic arthroscope to view the inside of a joint.

The fiber optic arthroscope has been increasingly used by orthopedists. It is considered more accurate than the arthrogram but is more invasive, requiring anesthesia and a small incision for the introduction of the arthroscope (endoscope) into the joint space. While the arthroscope is in the joint, the surgeon can perform surgical procedures such as removing loose bodies and, in some cases, suturing torn tissues.[7]

Myelography

During myelography an opaque dye is introduced into the spinal canal (epidural space) through a lumbar puncture. While the patient is tilted, the dye is allowed to flow to different levels of the spinal cord. Using this contrast medium, physicians can detect conditions such as tumors, nerve root compression, and disk disease, as well as other diseases within the spinal cord.

Computed Tomography

Computed tomography (CT) penetrates the body with a thin fan-shaped x-ray beam, producing a cross-sectional view of tissues. Unlike x-ray studies, this viewing can be performed from many angles. As the machine scans, a computer compares the many views; these electrical signals are then processed by a computer into a visual image.

Bone Scanning

A bone scan involves the introduction of a radioactive tracer such as technetium-99 intravenously. By imaging the entire skeleton or part of a skeleton, bony lesions such as stress fractures can be detected.

Magnetic Resonance Imaging

Magnetic resonance imaging (MRI) surrounds the body with powerful electromagnets, creating a field as much as 600,000 times as strong as that of the Earth.[10] The magnetic current focuses on hydrogen atoms in water molecules and aligns them; when the current is shut off, the atoms continue to spin, emitting an energy that is detected by the computer. The hydrogen atoms in different tissue spin at different rates, thus producing different images. In many ways MRI provides images more clearly than CT scanning.

Sonography

Sonography is the use of sound waves to view the interior of the body. It uses a piezoelectric crystal that converts electrical pulses into vibrations that can penetrate the body. The sound waves reflect back to the crystal, which reconverts them into electric signals and forms a picture.

Electromyography

Various muscular conditions can be detected by using electromyography. Electromyography refers to a muscular contraction that follows an electrical stimulation. The procedure consists of inserting a very thin electrode needle into the muscle to be studied. Motor unit potentials can be observed on an oscilloscope screen or from a graphic recording called an electromyogram. Denervated muscles, as well as nerve root compression or other nerve compression sites, can be detected by electromyography.[1] Other muscle disease can be confirmed through this method.

Nerve Conduction Velocity

Determining the conduction velocity of a nerve may provide key information to the physician about a number of neuromuscular conditions. After a stimulus is applied to a peripheral nerve, the speed in which a muscle action occurs is measured. Delays in conduction might indicate nerve compression or other muscular and/or nerve disease.

Synovial Fluid Analysis

On occasion, the physician will opt to make an analysis of an athlete's synovial fluid. The purpose of this test is to detect whether an infection is present. The test also confirms the diagnosis of gout and differentiates noninflammatory joint disease such as degenerative arthritis from inflammatory conditions such as rheumatoid arthritis.[1]

Analysis of synovial fluid and of blood can be used to detect musculoskeletal infections.

Blood Testing

The physician may decide to run blood tests on the athlete when a systemic disease or acute joint infection is suspected. One test could check the sedimentation rate, which is the speed at which red blood cells settle. An abnormal rate is considered a nonspecific indicator of an inflammatory condition, as well as of disease. Blood testing might include a complete blood count in which an increase in leukocytes could indicate an acute joint infection.[1] Some tests are for more serious musculoskeletal diseases such as rheumatoid arthritis, systemic lupus erythematosus, scleroderma, or gouty arthritis.

SUMMARY

Injury assessment is a proficiency needed by all athletic trainers and sports physicians. In sports medicine, assessment is used in first aid and under secondary circumstances.

Athletic trainers recognize and evaluate, whereas physicians, according to the law, diagnose sports injuries. Diagnosis refers to naming a disease, injury, or syndrome.

To assess effectively, an examiner of athletes with sports injuries must have a foundation in a number of areas. This foundation consists of a thorough background in human anatomy, including surface anatomy, body planes, and anatomical directions. Of particular importance is an in-depth understanding of the musculoskeletal system, with special focus on adverse biomechanical forces, which become pathomechanical. Every examiner of sports trauma must have a clear knowledge of injuries that can be sustained in a particular sport.

After they are assessed, sports injuries must be described in a similar manner, using the following terms: etiology or mechanism, symptoms and signs, and the degree of trauma that is considered to have occurred. A diagnosis is made by a physician who then establishes a prognosis for the condition.

Assessment may be categorized into the primary emergency, or first aid, type and the secondary, more detailed, follow-up type. Secondary assessment consists of a more detailed procedure. It consists of three major areas: history, general observation, and the actual physical examination. The physical examination includes palpation, movement assessment, and the neurological examination. Special tests may also be warranted, depending on the body site. Joint play testing, a postural examination, and a functional evaluation are other possible assessments that may be used by an examiner.

Besides the assessment procedures mentioned, a physical examination may require additional information before an accurate diagnosis can be made. This information may include a variety of x-ray examinations, as well as examination through other imaging procedures such as bone scanning, magnetic resonance imaging, or sonography. When there is muscle injury, electromyography and/or determining nerve conduction velocity may be used. In cases of suspected infection, a synovial fluid analysis or blood tests may be required.

REVIEW QUESTIONS AND CLASS ACTIVITIES

1. Differentiate between injury recognition and diagnosis of it.
2. What basic knowledge must the examiner have before making an injury assessment?
3. Explain the key terminology necessary to communicate the results of an assessment.
4. What are the ABCs of life support?
5. How should an examiner take a history? What questions should be asked?
6. Describe palpation and when and how it should be performed?
7. What can be ascertained from active, passive, and resisted isometric movement?
8. Explain how muscle testing, reflex testing, and sensation testing are performed.
9. What part do special tests, testing joint play, and postural examination play in injury assessment?
10. When should a functional evaluation be given?
11. What insights can a physician gain by having special laboratory tests performed? Describe each test in detail.

REFERENCES

1. Birnbaum, JS: The musculoskeletal manual, New York, 1982, Academic Press, Inc.
2. Cyriax, J: Textbook of orthopaedic medicine, ed 8, London, 1982, Bailliere Tindale.
3. Ellison, AE, chairman, editorial board: Athletic training and sports medicine, Chicago, 1984, American Academy of Orthopaedic Surgeons.
4. Kaltenborn, FM: Mobilization of the extremity joints: examination and basic treatments, Oslo, 1980, Olaf Norlis Bokhandel.
5. Lynch, MK, and Kessler, RM: Pain. In Kessler, RM, and Hertling, D, editors: Management of common musculoskeletal disorders, Philadelphia, 1983, Harper & Row, Publishers.
6. Magee, DL: Orthopedic physical assessment, Philadelphia, 1987, WB Saunders Co.
7. Minkoff, J, and Putterman, E: The unheralded value of arthroscopy using local anesthetic for diagnostic specificity and intraoperative corroboration of therapeutic achievement. In Minkoff, J, and Sherman, OH, editors: Clinics in sports medicine, vol 6, no 3, Philadelphia, July 1987, WB Saunders Co.
8. Moore, ML: Clinical assessment of joint motion. In Basmajian, JF, editor: Therapeutic exercise, ed 3, Baltimore, 1978, The Williams & Wilkins Co.
9. Post, M: Physical examination of the musculoskeletal system, Chicago, 1987, Year Book Medical Publishers, Inc.
10. Sochurek, H: Medicine's new vision, Natl Geogr 171:2, Jan 1987.

ANNOTATED BIBLIOGRAPHY

Birnbaum, JS: The musculoskeletal manual, New York, 1982, Academic Press, Inc.
An outstanding text addressed directly to Written for medical professionals who require a direct and simple approach for recognizing and managing musculoskeletal problems. A great number of the conditions discussed relate to sports trauma.

Booher, JM, and Thibodeau, GA: Athletic injury assessment, St. Louis, 1985, The CV Mosby Co.
An outstanding text addressed directly to the practitioner in sports medicine/athletic training. All aspects of musculoskeletal and internal sports injuries are considered.

Cyriax, J, and Cyriax, P: Illustrated manual of orthopaedic medicine, London, 1983, Butterworth & Co. (Publishers), Ltd.
A beautifully color-illustrated text designed for diagnosing and providing Cyriax management to musculoskeletal conditions.

Hoppenfeld, S: Physical examination of the spine and extremities, New York, 1976, Appleton-Century-Crofts.
Presents an easy to follow, methodical, and in-depth procedure for examining musculoskeletal conditions.

Magee, DJ: Orthopedic physical assessment, Philadelphia, 1987, WB Saunders Co.
An extremely well-illustrated book, with excellent depth of coverage. Its strength lies in its coverage of injuries commonly found during athletic training.

Post, M: Physical examination of the musculoskeletal system, Chicago, 1987, Year Book Medical Publishers, Inc.
A text that has been contributed to by many experts in the field of orthopedic examination. Each major joint is covered in detail.

11

Environmental Considerations

When you finish this chapter, you should be able to

Describe the physiology of hyperthermia and the clinical signs of heat stress and how they can be prevented

Identify the causes of hypothermia and the major cold disorders and how they may be prevented

Describe the problems that high altitude might present to the athlete and how they can be managed

List the problems that are presented to the athlete by air pollution and how they can be avoided

Discuss what effect circadian dysrhythmia may have on athletes and the best procedures in handling any problems that may arise

E nvironmental stress can adversely affect an athlete's performance and, in some instances, can pose a serious health threat. Five environmental categories are of major concern to the coach, athletic trainer, and sports physician: hyperthermia, hypothermia, altitude, air pollution, and circadian dysrhythmia.

HYPERTHERMIA

A major concern in sports is the problem of hyperthermia. Among football players and distance runners in high school and college there has been a number of deaths caused by hyperthermia.

It is vitally important that the coaching staff and athletic trainer have knowledge about temperature and humidity factors to assist them in planning practice. They should be able to use the sling psychrometer, an instrument used to establish the wet-bulb, globe temperature index. The coach or athletic trainer must clearly understand when environmental heat and humidity are at a dangerous level and act accordingly. In addition, the clinical symptoms and signs of heat stress must be recognized and managed properly (Figure 11-1).

Heat is eliminated from the body through conduction, convection, evaporation, and radiation. Body temperature regulation results almost entirely through cutaneous cooling from the evaporation of sweat. During exercise there is some respiratory heat loss, but the amount is relatively small. The effectiveness of sweat evaporation is strongly influenced by relative humidity and wind velocity and

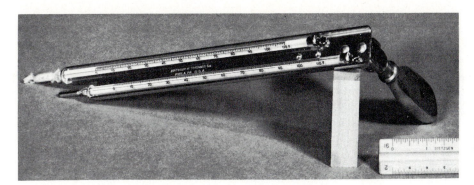

Figure 11-1

Sling psychrometer used to determine relative humidity.

under the most ideal conditions does not exceed 70% to 80%. When temperature exceeds 80° F (25.7° C), sweating is the only effective means that the body has of heat dissipation. However, when a high temperature is accompanied by high humidity, a condition with serious implications exists, since high humidity reduces the rate of evaporation *without* diminishing sweating. The stage is set for heat exhaustion and/or heatstroke unless certain precautionary measures have been observed. When a person's temperature reaches 106° F (41.1° C), the chances of survival are exceedingly slim.

An average runner may lose from 1.5 to 2.5 L/hr through active sweating; much greater amounts can be lost by football players in warm weather activity. Seldom is more than 50% of this fluid loss replaced, even though replacement fluids are taken **ad libitum,** since athletes usually find it uncomfortable to exercise vigorously with a full stomach, which could interfere with the respiratory muscles. The problem in fluid replacement is how rapidly the fluid can be eliminated from the stomach into the intestine, from which it can enter the bloodstream. Cold drinks (45° to 55° F [7.2° to 12.8° C]) tend to empty more rapidly from the stomach than do warmer drinks and offer no particular threat to a normal heart or in inducing cramps.

ad libitum
To the amount desired.

Sweating occurs whether or not the athlete drinks water, and if the sweat losses are not replaced by fluid intake over a period of several hours, dehydration results. Sweat is always hypotonic; that is, it contains a lower concentration of salt than does the blood, and its loss establishes a deficit of water in excess of the salt deficit. This is reflected in several physiological changes, which may manifest themselves in peripheral vascular collapse, renal decompensation, and uremia.[7]

Athletes must have unlimited access to water. Failure to permit *ad libitum* access will not only undermine their playing potentialities but also may be responsible for permitting a dangerous situation to develop that could conceivably have fatal consequences (Figure 11-2).

Women are apparently more physiologically efficient in body temperature regulation than men; although they possess as many heat-activated sweat glands as men, they sweat less and manifest a higher heart rate when working in heat. Although slight differences exist, the same precautionary measures apply to both genders.

Body build must be considered when determining individual susceptibility to heat stress. Overweight individuals may have as much as 18% greater heat pro-

Figure 11-2

Athletes must have unlimited access to water, especially in hot weather.

duction than an underweight individual, since metabolic heat is produced proportionately to surface area. It has been found that heat victims tend to be overweight. Death from heatstroke increases at a ratio of approximately 4 to 1 as body weight increases.

Prevention

The following should be considered when planning a training-competitive program that is likely to take place during hot weather:

1. Gradual acclimatization   This is probably the single most effective method of avoiding heat stress. Acclimatization should involve not only becoming accustomed to heat but also becoming acclimatized to exercise in hot temperatures.[9] A good preseason conditioning program, started well before the advent of the competitive season and carefully graded as to intensity, is recommended. During the first 5 or 6 days an 80% acclimatization can be achieved on the basis of a 2-hour practice period in the morning and a 2-hour practice period in the afternoon. Each should be broken down into 20 minutes of work alternated with 20 minutes of rest in the shade.

2. Identifying susceptible individuals   Athletes with a large muscle mass are particularly prone to heat illness.[11] Most deaths that occur among American football players are to interior lineman.[11] It must also be noted that fat produces more body heat than proteins or carbohydrates.[16] In addition, a considerable loss of fluid makes the athlete highly susceptible to heat illness (see "Weight Records").

The prevention of hyperthermia involves
   Gradual acclimatization
   Identification of susceptible individuals
   Lightweight uniforms
   Routine weight record keeping
   Unrestricted fluid replacement
   Well-balanced diet
   Routine temperature/humidity readings

3. Uniforms   Select uniforms on the basis of temperature and humidity. Initial practices should be conducted in short-sleeved tee shirts, shorts, and socks, moving gradually into short-sleeved net jerseys, lightweight pants, and socks as acclimatization proceeds. All early season practices and games should be conducted in light-weight uniforms with short-sleeved net jerseys and socks. Long sleeves and full stockings are indicated only when the temperature is low.

4. Weight records   Careful weight records of all players must be kept. Weights should be taken both before and after practice for at least the first 2 weeks of practice. If a sudden increase in temperature and/or humidity occurs during the season, a weight record should again be taken for a period of time. A loss of 3% to 5% of body weight will reduce blood volume and could lead to a health threat.[18]

5. Fluid replacement   Intake of water should be carefully observed. Athletes should have unlimited access to cold water at all times.

6. Diet   Generally, a well-balanced diet is essential. Fat intake should be somewhat minimized.

7. Temperature/humidity readings   Dry-bulb and wet-bulb readings should be taken on the field before practice. The purchase of a sling psychrometer for this purpose is recommended (see Figure 11-1). It is relatively inexpensive and uncomplicated to use. The relative humidity should be calculated. The following suggestions regarding temperature and humidity will serve as a guide:

Temperature (°F)	Humidity	Procedure
80°-90° (26.7° C-32.2° C)	Under 70%	Watch those athletes who tend toward obesity.
80°-90° (26.7° C-32.2° C)	Over 70%	Athletes should take a 10-minute rest every hour, and tee shirts should be changed when wet. All athletes should be under constant and careful supervision.
90°-100° (32.2° C-37.8° C)	Under 70%	
90°-100° (32.2° C-37.8° C)	Over 70%	Under these conditions it would be well to suspend practice. A shortened program conducted in shorts and tee shirts could be established.
Over 100° (37.8° C)		

Clinical Indications and Treatment

The box on p. 302 and Table 11-1 list the clinical symptoms of the various hyperthermal conditions and the indications for treatment. Although these tables call particular attention to some of the procedures for American football, the precautions, in general, have application to all sports. Football, because of the specialized equipment worn by the players, requires special consideration. To a degree, many uniforms are heat traps and serve to compound the environmental heat problem, which is not the case with the lighter uniforms.

TABLE 11-1 Heat Disorders: Treatment and Prevention

Disorders	Cause	Clinical Features and Diagnosis	Treatment	Prevention
Heat cramps	Hard work in heat; sweating heavily; salt intake inadequate	Muscle twitching and cramps, usually after midday; spasms; in arms, legs, abdomen; low serum sodium and chloride	Ingesting fluids and foods containing sodium chloride	Proper acclimatization; eating foods containing sodium chloride
Heat exhaustion	Prolonged sweating; inadequate replacement of body fluid losses; diarrhea; intestinal infection; predisposes to heatstroke	Excessive thirst, dry tongue and mouth; weight loss; fatigue; weakness; incoordination; mental dullness; small urine volume; elevated body temperature; high serum protein and sodium; reduced swelling	Bed rest in cool room, IV fluids if drinking is impaired; increase fluid intake to 6 to 8 L/day; sponge with cool water; keep record of body weight; keep fluid balance record; provide semiliquid food until salination is normal	Supply adequate water and other liquids. Provide adequate rest and opportunity for cooling
Heatstroke	Thermoregulatory failure of sudden onset	Abrupt onset, preceded by headache, vertigo, and fatigue, absence of sweating; hot, flushed dry skin; pulse rate increases rapidly and may reach 160 to 180; respiration increases; blood pressure seldom rises; temperature rises rapidly to 105 or 106° F (40 to 41° C); athlete feels as if he or she is burning up; diarrhea, vomiting; circulatory collapse may produce death; could lead to permanent brain damage	Heroic measures to reduce temperature must be taken immediately (e.g., full body immersion in cold water, air fan over body, massage limbs, etc.); temperature must be taken every 10 minutes and not allowed to fall below 101° F (38.5° C) to avoid converting hyperpyrexia to hypothermia; remove to hospital as soon as possible	Ensure proper acclimatization, proper hydration. Educate those supervising activities conducted in the heat. Adapt activities to environment. Screen participants with past history of heat illness

The recent popularity of distance running, especially road racing the marathon and the ultramarathon, has posed some problems in regard to potential heat stress injuries.[10]

HYPOTHERMIA

Cold weather is a frequent adjunct to many outdoor sports in which the sport itself does not require heavy protective clothing; consequently, the weather becomes a pertinent factor in injury susceptibility. In most instances, the activity itself enables the athlete to increase the metabolic rate sufficiently to be able to function physically in a normal manner and dissipate the resulting heat and perspiration through the usual physiological mechanisms. An athlete may fail to warm up sufficiently or may become chilled because of relative inactivity for vary-

Many sports played in cold weather do not require heavy protective clothing; thus weather becomes a factor in injury susceptibility.

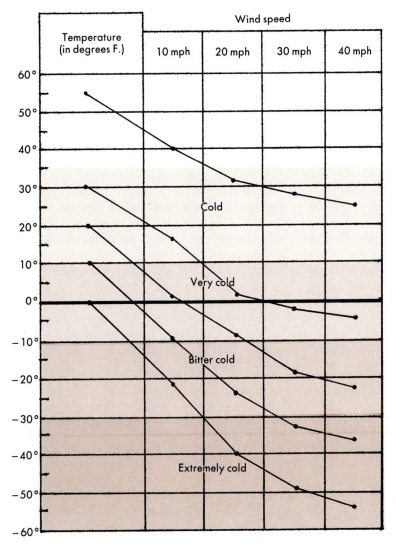

Figure 11-3

Low temperatures can pose serious problems for the athlete, but wind chill could be a critical factor.

ing periods of time demanded by the particular sport either during competition or training; consequently, the athlete is exceedingly prone to injury. Low temperatures alone can pose some problems, but, when such temperatures are further accentuated by wind, the chill factor becomes critical (Figure 11-3). For example, a runner proceeding at a pace of 10 mph directly into a wind of 5 mph creates a chill factor equivalent to a 15-mph headwind.

Sixty-five percent of heat that is produced by the body is lost through radiation. This loss occurs most often from the warm vascular areas of a head or neck that are uncovered.[2] Twenty percent of heat loss is through evaporation, of which two thirds is through the skin and one third is through the respiratory tract.[2]

During strenuous physical activity in cold weather as muscular fatigue builds up, the rate of exercise begins to drop and may reach a level wherein the body heat loss to the environment exceeds the metabolic heat protection, resulting in definite impairment of neuromuscular responses and exhaustion. A relatively small drop in body core temperature can induce shivering sufficient to materially affect one's neuromuscular coordination. Shivering ceases below a body temperature of 85° to 90° F (29.4° to 32.2° C). Death is imminent if the core temperature rises to 107° F (41.6° C) or drops to between 77° and 85° F (25° and 29° C).

Low temperatures accentuated by wind can pose major problems for athletes.

Preventing Hypothermia

Apparel for competitors must be geared to the weather. The function of such apparel is to provide a semitropical microclimate for the body and to prevent chilling. The clothing should not restrict movement, should be as lightweight as possible, and should consist of material that will permit the free passage of sweat and body heat that would otherwise accumulate on the skin or the clothing and provide a chilling factor when activity ceases. Preliminary to exercise, during activity breaks or rest periods, and at the termination of exercise, a warm-up suit should be worn to prevent chilling. Activity in cold, wet, and windy weather poses some problem, since such weather reduces the insulating values of the clothing worn; consequently the individual may be unable to achieve energy levels equal to the subsequent body heat losses. Runners who wish to continue outdoor work in cold weather should use lightweight insulative clothing and, if breathing cold air seems distressful, should use ski goggles and a ski face mask or should cover the mouth and nose with a free-hanging cloth.

Inadequate clothing, improper warm-up, and a high chill factor form a triad that can lead to musculoskeletal injury, chilblains, frostbite, or the minor respiratory disorders associated with lower tissue temperatures. For work or sports in temperatures below 32° F (0° C), it is advisable to add a layer of protective clothing for every 5 mph of wind.

Cold Disorders

As is true in a hot environment, there is need of fluid replacement in a cold environment. With reduced blood volume because of dehydration, there is less fluid available for warming the tissues.[12] Athletes performing in a cold environment should be weighed before and after practice, especially in the first 2 weeks of the season.[3] Severe overexposure to a cold climate occurs less often than hyperthermia does in a warm climate; however, it is still a major risk of winter sports, long distance running in cold weather, and swimming in cold water.[7]

General Body Cooling

A core temperature below 80° F (26.7° C) leads to unconsciousness. With a rectal temperature of 86.4° F (30.2° C), the athlete displays slurring of speech, clumsy movement, pupils that respond sluggishly, shallow respiration, and a heartbeat that may be irregular and slow.[1,7] The skin appears pale; the tissue of the lips, around the nose, and underneath the fingernails is a bluish hue (cyanosis). Muscle tonus increases, causing the neck and limbs to become stiff and rigid. Also occurring are metabolic pH changes, leading to acidosis, liver necrosis, uremia, renal failure, and seizures.[6]

Severe exposure to cold is a major medical emergency. The first concern is the maintenance of an airway. If the heart has stopped and the temperature is approximately 85° F (29° C) or less, it may be difficult to reestablish a heart rhythm. External rewarming should take place if the condition ranges from mild to moderate. Emergency rewarming at the site is to immerse the athlete's hands and forearms in water that is between 113° and 118° F (45° and 48° C). If the athlete is conscious, a hot drink may help in rewarming. Alcohol of any kind must be avoided because it vasodilates peripheral capillaries. In cases of severe cold exposure, rewarming too rapidly can cause the peripheral capillaries to become dilated, pulling blood and warmth from the core of the body. In a hospital setting, the athlete may be given warm enemas and warm intravenous solutions.

Common Cold Injuries

Local cooling of the body can result in tissue damage ranging from superficial to deep. Exposure to a damp, freezing cold can cause frostnip. In contrast, exposure to dry temperatures well below freezing more commonly produces a deep freezing type of frostbite.

Low freezing temperatures may cause ice crystals to form between or within the cells and may eventually destroy the cell. Local capillaries can be injured, blood clots may form, and blood may be shunted away from the injury site to ensure the survival of the nonaffected tissue.

Cold injuries in sports include
  Frostnip
  Frostbite

Frostnip

Frostnip involves ears, nose, cheeks, chin, fingers, and toes. It commonly occurs when there is a high wind, severe cold, or both. The skin initially appears very firm, with cold, painless areas that may peel or blister in 24 to 72 hours. Affected areas can be treated early by firm, sustained pressure of the hand (without rubbing), blowing hot breath on the spot, or, if the injury is to the fingertips, by placing them in the armpits.

Frostbite

Chilblains result from prolonged and constant exposure to cold for many hours. In time there is skin redness, swelling, tingling, and pain in the toes and fingers. This adverse response is caused by problems of peripheral circulation and can be avoided by preventing further cold exposure.

Superficial frostbite involves only the skin and subcutaneous tissue. The skin appears pale, hard, cold and waxy. Palpating the injured area will reveal a sense of hardness but with yielding of the underlying deeper tissue structures. When rewarming, the superficial frostbite will at first feel numb, then will sting and burn. Later the area may produce blisters and be painful for a number of weeks.

ENVIRONMENTAL CONDUCT OF SPORTS: PARTICULARLY FOOTBALL

I. General warning
  A. Most adverse reactions to environmental heat and humidity occur during the first few days of training.
  B. It is necessary to become thoroughly acclimatized to heat to successfully compete in hot and/or humid environments.
  C. Occurrence of a heat injury indicates poor supervision of the sports program.
II. Athletes who are most susceptible to heat injury
  A. Individuals unaccustomed to working in the heat.
  B. Overweight individuals, particularly large linemen.
  C. Eager athletes who constantly compete at capacity.
  D. Ill athletes who have an infection, fever, or gastrointestinal disturbance.
  E. Athletes who receive immunization injections and subsequently develop temperature elevations.
III. Prevention of heat injury
  A. Take complete medical history and provide physical examination.
    1. Include history of previous heat illnesses or fainting in the heat.
    2. Include inquiry about sweating and peripheral vascular defects.
  B. Evaluate general physical condition and type and duration of training activities for previous month.
    1. Extent of work in the heat.
    2. General training activities.
  C. Measure temperature and humidity on the practice or playing fields.
    1. Make measurements before and during training or competitive sessions.
    2. Adjust activity level to environmental conditions.
      a. Decrease activity if hot or humid.
      b. Eliminate unnecessary clothing when hot or humid.
  D. Acclimatize athletes to heat gradually.
    1. Acclimatization to heat requires work in the heat.
      a. Use recommended type and variety of warm weather workouts for preseason training.
      b. Provide graduated training program for first 7 to 10 days—and other abnormally hot or humid days.
    2. Provide adequate rest intervals and water replacement during the acclimatization period.
  E. Monitor body weight loss during activity in the heat.
    1. Body water should be replaced as it is lost.
      a. Allow additional water as desired by player.
      b. Provide salt on training tables (no salt tablets should be taken).
      c. Weigh each day before and after training or competition.
        (1) Treat athlete who loses excessive weight each day.
        (2) Treat well-conditioned athlete who continues to lose weight for several days.

    F. Monitor clothing and uniforms
        1. Provide lightweight clothing that is loose fitting at the neck, waist, and sleeves; use shorts and tee shirt at beginning of training.
        2. Avoid excessive padding and taping.
        3. Avoid use of long stockings, long sleeves, double jerseys, and other excess clothing.
        4. Avoid use of rubberized clothing or sweatsuits.
        5. Provide clean clothing daily—all items.
    G. Provide rest periods to dissipate accumulated body heat.
        1. Rest in cool, shaded area with some air movement.
        2. Avoid hot brick walls or hot benches.
        3. Loosen or remove jerseys or other garments.
        4. Take water during the rest period.

IV. Trouble signs: stop activity!

Headache	Diarrhea
Nausea	Cramps
Mental slowness	Seizures
Incoherence	Rigidity
Visual disturbance	Weak, rapid pulse
Fatigue	Pallor
Weakness	Flush
Unsteadiness	Faintness
Collapse	Chill
Unconsciousness	Cyanotic appearance
Vomiting	

Deep frostbite is a serious injury indicating tissues that are frozen. This is a medical emergency requiring immediate hospitalization. As with frostnip and superficial frostbite, the tissue is initially cold, hard, pale or white, and numb. Rapid rewarming is required, including hot drinks, heating pads, or hot water bottles that are 100° to 110° F (38° to 43° C). During rewarming, the tissue will become blotchy red, swollen, and extremely painful. Later the injury may become gangrenous, causing a loss of tissue.

ALTITUDE

Most athletic events are not conducted at high altitudes.

Most athletic events are not conducted at extreme altitudes. For example, Mexico City's elevation, which is 2350 meters high, is considered moderate, yet at this height there is a 7% to 8% decrease in maximum oxygen uptake.[15] This loss in maximum oxygen uptake represents a 4% to 8% deterioration in an athlete's performance in endurance events, depending on the duration of effort and lack of wind resistance. Often, the athlete's body compensates for this decrease in maximum oxygen uptake with corresponding tachycardia.[15] When the body is suddenly without its usual oxygen supply, hyperventilation can occur. Many of these responses are results of having fewer red blood cells than necessary to adequately capture the available oxygen in the air.[17]

Acclimatization

A major factor in altitude adaptation is the problem of oxygen deficiency. With a reduction in barometric pressure the partial pressure of oxygen in inspired air is also low. Under these circumstances the existing circulating red blood cells become less saturated, depriving tissue of needed oxygen.

An individual's acclimatization to high altitude depends on whether he or she is a native, resident, or visitor to the area. Natives of areas with high altitudes (e.g., the Andes and Nepal) have a larger chest capacity, more alveoli, more capillaries that transport blood to tissue, and a higher red blood cell level.[8] In contrast, the resident or individual who stays at a high altitude for months or years makes a partial acclimatization. His or her later adaptation includes the conservation of glucose, an increased number of mitochondria, which are the sources of energy in a cell, and increased formation of hemoglobin. In the visitor or person who is in an early stage of adaptation to high altitude, a number of responses represent a physiological struggle. The responses include increased breathing, increased heart action, increased hemoglobin in circulating blood, increased blood alkalinity, and increased myoglobin, as well as changes in the distribution of blood flow and cell enzyme activity.

There are many uncertainties about when to have an athlete go to an area of high altitude to compete. Some believe that 2 to 3 weeks before competition provides the best adjustment period, whereas others believe that, for psychological, as well as physiological, reasons, 3 days before competition is enough time.[15] This shorter time does allow time for the recovery of the acid/base balance in the blood but does not provide enough time for achieving a significant adjustment in blood volume and maximum cardiac output.[15]

Altitude Illness

Coaches and athletic trainers must be apprised that some of their athletes may become ill when suddenly subjected to high altitudes. These illnesses might include acute mountain sickness, pulmonary edema, and, when present in some athletes, an adverse reaction to the sickle cell trait.

Acute Mountain Sickness

One out of three individuals who go from a low to a moderate altitude of 7000 to 8000 feet will experience mild-to-moderate symptoms of acute mountain sickness. Symptoms include headache, nausea, vomiting, sleep disturbance, and dyspnea, which may last up to 3 days.[15] These symptoms have been attributed by some to a tissue disruption in the brain affecting the sodium and potassium balance. This imbalance can cause excess fluid retention within the cells and the subsequent occurrence of abnormal pressure.[15]

Pulmonary Edema

At an altitude of 9000 to 10,000 feet, high-altitude pulmonary edema may occur. Characteristically, lungs at this altitude will accumulate a small amount of fluid within the alveolar walls.[15] In most individuals this fluid is absorbed in a few days, but in some it continues to collect and to form pulmonary edema. Symptoms of high-altitude pulmonary edema are dyspnea, cough, headache, weakness, and, in some cases, unconsciousness.[15] The treatment of choice is to get the athlete to a lower altitude as soon as possible. When he or she is at a lower altitude, the condition rapidly resolves.

Sickle Cell Trait

Approximately 8% to 10% of American blacks (approximately 2 million persons) have the sickle cell trait. In most of them the trait is benign. The sickle cell trait relates to an abnormality of the structure of the red blood cell and its hemoglobin content.[4] When the abnormal hemoglobin molecules become deoxygenated as a result of exercise at a high altitude, the cells tend to clump together. This process causes the red blood cell to form into an abnormal "sickle" shape, which is easily destroyed. This condition can cause an enlarged spleen, which, in some cases, has been known to rupture at high altitudes.[15]

AIR POLLUTION

Air pollution is a major problem common in urban areas having large industries and heavy automobile traffic. There are two types of pollution: photochemical "haze" and smog. Photochemical haze consists of nitrogen dioxide and stagnant air that are acted on by sunlight to produce ozone.[17] Smog is produced by the combination of carbon monoxide and sulphur dioxide, which emanates from the combustion of a fossil fuel such as coal.

Air pollution is a major problem common in urban areas having large industries and heavy automobile traffic.

Ozone

Ozone is a form of oxygen in which three atoms of the element combine to form the molecule O_3. It is produced by a reaction of oxygen (O_2), nitrogen oxides, and hydrocarbon, plus sunlight.[14]

When individuals are engaged in physical tasks requiring minimum effort, an increase in ozone in the air does not usually reduce functional capacity in normal work output. However, when there is an increase in work output (e.g., during exercise), the work capacity is decreased. The athlete may experience shortness of breath, coughing, chest tightness, pain during deep breathing, nausea, eye irritation, fatigue, lung irritation, and a lowered resistance to lung infections. Over a period of time, individuals may become, to some degree, desensitized to ozone. Asthmatics are at greater risk when ozone levels increase.

Sulfur Dioxide

Sulfur dioxide (SO_2) is a colorless gas that is a component of burning coal or petroleum. As an air contaminant it causes an increased resistance to air movement in and out of the lungs, a decreased ability of the lungs to rid themselves of foreign matter, shortness of breath, coughing, fatigue, and increased susceptibility to lung diseases. Sulfur dioxide causes an adverse effect mostly on asthmatics and other sensitive individuals. Nose breathing lessens the effects of sulfur dioxide because the nasal mucosa acts as a sulfur dioxide scrubber.[5]

Carbon Monoxide

Carbon monoxide (CO) reduces the hemoglobins' ability to transport and release oxygen in the body.

Carbon monoxide (CO) is a colorless, odorless gas. In general, it reduces hemoglobin's ability to transport oxygen and restricts the release of oxygen to the tissue. Besides interfering in performance during exercise, carbon monoxide exposure interferes with various psychomotor, behavioral, or attention-related activities.[5]

Prevention

To avoid problems created by air pollution the athlete must stop or significantly decrease physical activity during periods of high pollution. If activity is conducted, it should be performed when commuter traffic has lessened and when ambient temperature has lowered. Ozone levels rise during dawn, peak at midday, and are much reduced after the late-afternoon rush hour. Running should be avoided on roads where there is concentration of auto emission and carbon monoxide.

CIRCADIAN DYSRHYTHMIA (JET LAG)

Jet power has made it possible to travel thousands of miles in just a few hours. Athletes and athletic teams are now quickly transported from one end of the country to the other and to foreign lands. For some, such travel induces a particular physiological stress, resulting in a syndrome that is identified as a *circadian dysrhythmia* and that reflects a desynchronization of the athlete's biological and biophysical time clock.

The term *circadian* (from the Latin *circa dies,* "about a day") implies a period of time of approximately 24 hours. The body maintains many cyclic mechanisms (circadian rhythms) that follow a pattern (e.g., the daily rise and fall of body temperature or the tidal ebb and flow of the cortical steroid secretion, which produces other effects on the metabolic system that are in themselves cyclical in nature). Body mechanisms adapt at varying rates to time changes. Some (e.g., protein metabolism) adjust immediately, whereas others take time, (e.g., the rise and fall of body temperature, which takes approximately 8 days). Others such as the adrenal hormones, which regulate metabolism, and other body functions may take as long as 3 weeks. Even intellectual proficiency or the ability to think clearly is cyclical. Younger individuals adjust more rapidly to time zone changes than do older people, although the differences are not great. The stress induced in jet travel occurs only when flying either east or west at high speed. There is 30% to

50% faster adaptation in individuals flying westward than in individuals flying eastward.[13] Travel north or south has no effect on the body unless several time zones are crossed in an east or west progression. The changes in time zones, illumination, and environment prove somewhat disruptive to the human physiological mechanisms, particularly when one flies through five or more time zones, as occurs in some international travel. Some people are much more susceptible to the syndrome than are others, but the symptoms can be sufficiently disruptive to interfere with one's ability to perform maximally in a competitive event. In some cases, an athlete will become ill for a short period of time with anorexia, severe headache, blurred vision, dizziness, insomnia, or extreme fatigue.

Adapting to Time-Zone Shifts

To assist in diminishing the effects of time-zone shifts, some of the following practices can be followed:

1. Depart well rested.
2. Choose daylight departures whenever possible.
3. Practice moderation in eating both before and during the flight and decrease protein intake.
4. Note that drugs such as trimethylxanthine (caffeine) and theophylline in tea help to shift the rhythm in a specific direction the moment they are given.
5. Change sleep patterns in preparation for travel across time zones.
6. For maximum performance, avoid hard training for 3 or 4 days after crossing time zones.[13]

SUMMARY

Environmental stress can adversely effect an athlete's performance, as well as pose a serious health problem. Hyperthermia is one of sport's major concerns. In times of high temperatures and humidity, the wet-bulb, globe temperature index should be routinely determined, using the sling psychrometer. Losing 3% or more of body weight because of fluid loss could pose a potential health problem.

Cold weather requires athletes to wear the correct apparel and to warm up properly before engaging in sports activities. The wind chill factor must always be considered when performing. As is true in a hot environment, the athlete must ingest adequate fluids when in cold conditions. Alcohol must be avoided at all times. Extreme cold exposure can cause conditions such as frost nip, chilblains, and frostbite.

An athlete going from a low altitude to one that is high in a very short time may encounter problems with performance and perhaps experience some health problems. Because it takes time for acclimatization to occur, there is a question as to when to bring the athlete to the higher altitude, especially if for an endurance event. Many coaches and athletic trainers believe that 3 days at the higher altitude will provide enough time for acclimatization to occur. Others believe a much longer time period is needed. If an athlete experiences a serious illness because of his or her presence at a particular altitude, he or she must be returned to a lower altitude as soon as possible.

Air pollution can produce a major decrement to performance and, in some cases, can cause illness. Increased ozone levels can cause respiratory distress, nausea, eye irritation, and fatigue. Sulfur dioxide, a colorless gas, can also cause physical reactions in some athletes and can be a serious problem for asthmatics. Carbon monoxide, a colorless and odorless gas, reduces hemoglobin's ability to use oxygen and, as a result, adversely affects performance.

Travel through different time zones can place a serious physiological stress on the athlete. This stress is called circadian dysrhythmia, or jet lag. This disruption of biological rhythm can adversely affect performance and may even produce health problems. The coach or athletic trainer must pay careful attention to helping the athlete acclimatize to time-zone shifting.

REVIEW QUESTIONS AND CLASS ACTIVITIES

1. How do temperature and humidity cause heat disorders?
2. What steps should be taken to avoid heat disorders?
3. Describe the symptoms and signs of the most common heat disorders.
4. How is heat lost from the body to produce hypothermia?
5. What should an athlete do to prevent heat loss?
6. Identify the physiological basis for the body's susceptibility to a cold disorder.
7. Describe the symptoms and signs of the major cold disorders affecting athletes.
8. What concerns should a coach or athletic trainer have when athletes are to perform an endurance sport at high altitudes?
9. What altitude illnesses might be expected among some athletes, and how should they be managed?
10. What adverse effects could high air concentrations of ozone, sulfur dioxide, and carbon monoxide have on the athlete? How should they be dealt with?
11. How can the adverse effects of circadian dysrhythmia be avoided or lessened?

REFERENCES

1. Appenzeller, O, and Atkinson, R: Temperature regulation and sports. In Appenzeller, O, and Atkinson, R, editors: Sports medicine, Baltimore, 1981, Urban & Schwarzenberg, Inc.
2. Bangs, CC: Cold injuries. In Strauss, RH, editor: Sports medicine, Philadelphia, 1984, WB Saunders Co.
3. Brotherhood, JR: Snow, cold and energy expenditure: a basis for fatigue and skiing accidents, Aust J Sci Med Sports 17:3, March 1985.
4. Eichner, ER: Sickle cell trait, exercise, and altitude, Phys Sportsmed 14(11): 144, 1986.
5. Folinsbee, LJ: Air pollution and exercise. In Welsh, RP, and Shephard, RJ, editors: Current therapy in sports medicine 1985-1986, Philadelphia, 1985, Brian C Decker, Publisher.
6. Frim, JJ: Hazards of cold air. In Welsh, RP, and Shephard, RJ, editors: Current therapy in sports medicine 1985-1986, Philadelphia, 1985, Brian C Decker, Publisher.
7. Gutmann, L: Temperature-related problems in athletic and recreational activities. In Joynt, RJ, editor: Semin Neurol 1(4):242, 1981.
8. Houston, CS: Man at altitude. In Strauss, RH, editor: Sports medicine, Philadelphia, 1984, WB Saunders Co.
9. Inbar, O: Exercise and heat. In Welsh RP, and Shephard, RJ, editors: Current therapy in sports medicine 1985-1986, Philadelphia, 1985, Brian C Decker, Publisher.
10. Moore, M: What are we learning from road races? Phys Sportsmed 10:151, 1982.
11. Murphy, RJ: Heat illness in the athlete, Ath Train 1, 1984.
12. Replacing body fluids is vital during winter, First Aider 56(4):1, 1987.
13. Rietveld, WJ: Time-zone shifts and international competition. In Welsh, RP, and Shephard, RJ, editors: Current therapy in sports medicine 1985-1986, Philadelphia, 1985, Brian C Decker, Publisher.
14. Schonfeld, SA, and Dixon, GF: The respiratory system. In Strauss, RH, editor: Sports medicine, Philadelphia, 1984, WB Saunders Co.
15. Shephard, RJ: Adjustment to high altitude. In Welsh, RP, and Shephard, RJ, editors: Current therapy in sports medicine 1985-1986, Philadelphia, 1985, Brian C Decker, Publisher.

16. Sinclair, RE: Be serious about siriasis: guidelines for avoiding heat injury during ''dog days,'' Postgrad Med 5:261, April 1985.

17. Stanitski, CL: Environmental problems of runners. In Drez, Jr, D: Symposium on running, Clinics in sports medicine, vol 4, no 4, Philadelphia, 1985, WB Saunders Co.

18. Stone, B: Dehydration and its effects upon endurance activity, Ath J 14:64, 1982.

ANNOTATED BIBLIOGRAPHY

Haymes, EM, and Wells, CL: Environment and human performance, Champaign, Ill, 1986, Human Kinetics Publishers, Inc.
Examines sports performance during a variety of environmental conditions. Two-hundred fifty references are reported.

Strauss, RH, editor: Sports medicine, Philadelphia, 1984, WB Saunders Co.
Provides four pertinent chapters on the subject of environmental disorders that could affect the athlete.

Wilkerson, JA, editor: Hypothermia, frostbite and other cold injuries, Seattle, Wash, 1986, The Mountaineers Books.
Provides a nontechnical approach to hypothermia and explains the importance of preparing for cold and how to recognize and manage cold injuries.

12

Taping and Bandaging

When you finish this chapter, you should be able to

Demonstrate basic skill in the use of taping in sports

Demonstrate the skillful application of tape for a variety of musculoskeletal problems

Demonstrate the application of the elastic wrap to major body parts

Demonstrate the application of triangular and cravat bandages

T aping and bandaging are major skills used for the care of injuries and the protection of the athlete. This chapter presents some of the more prevalent techniques used in sports medicine and athletic training.

TAPING

Historically, taping has emerged as an important part of athletic training. It is one area of proficiency that the athletic trainer has, and it must be equated with other proficiency areas such as customizing protective equipment and rehabilitation.

Tape Usage

Injury Care

When used for sports injuries, adhesive tape offers a number of possibilities:
- Retention of wound dressings
- Stabilization of compression-type bandages that are used to control external and internal hemorrhaging
- Support of recent injuries to prevent additional insult that might result from the activities of the athlete

Injury Protection

Protecting against acute injuries is another major use of tape support. This protection can be achieved by limiting the motion of a body part or by securing some special device (see Chapter 5).

Linen Adhesive Tape

Modern adhesive tape has great adaptability for use in sports because of its uniform adhesive mass, adhering qualities, and lightness, as well as the relative

When purchasing linen tape, consider
  Grade of backing
  Quality of adhesive mass
  Winding tension

strength of the backing materials. All of these qualities are of value in holding wound dressings in place and in supporting and protecting injured areas. This tape comes in a variety of sizes; 1-, 1½-, and 2-inch (2.5, 3.75, and 5 cm) widths are commonly used in sports medicine. The tape also comes in tubes or special packs. Some popular packs provide greater tape length on each spool. When linen tape is purchased, factors such as cost, grade of backing, quality of adhesive mass, and properties of unwinding should be considered.

Tape Grade

Linen-backed tape is most often graded according to the number of longitudinal and vertical fibers per inch of backing material. The heavier and more costly backing contains 85 or more longitudinal fibers and 65 vertical fibers per square inch. The lighter, less expensive grade has 65 or fewer longitudinal fibers and 45 vertical fibers.

Adhesive Mass

As a result of improvements in adhesive mass, certain essentials should be expected from tape. It should adhere readily when applied and should maintain this adherence despite profuse perspiration and activity. In addition to having adequate sticking properties, the mass must contain as few skin irritants as possible and must be able to be removed easily without leaving a mass residue or pulling away the superficial skin.

Winding Tension

The winding tension that a tape roll possesses is quite important to the operator. Sports place a unique demand on the unwinding quality of tape; if tape is to be applied for protection and support, there must be even and constant unwinding tension. In most cases a proper wind needs little additional tension to provide sufficient tightness.

Stretch Tape

Increasingly, tape with varying elasticity is being used in sports medicine, often in combination with linen tape. Because of its conforming qualities, stretch tape is used for the smaller, more angular body parts such as the feet, wrist, hands, and fingers. As with linen tape, stretch tape comes in a variety of widths.

Increasingly, tape with varying elasticity is being used in sports medicine.

Tape Storage

When storing tape, the following steps should be taken:
1. Store in a cool place such as in a low cupboard.
2. Stack so that the tape rests on its flat top or bottom to avoid distortion.

Store tape in a cool place, and stack it so that it rests on its flat top or bottom.

Using Adhesive Tape in Sports
Preparation for Taping

Special attention must be given when applying tape directly to the skin. Perspiration and dirt collected during sport activities will prevent tape from properly sticking to the skin. Whenever tape is used, the skin surface should be cleansed with soap and water to remove all dirt and oil. Hair should be removed by shaving to prevent additional irritation when the tape is removed. If additional adherence or protection from tape irritation is needed, a preparation containing rosin and a skin-toughening preparation should be applied. Commercial benzoin or skin tougheners offer astringent action and dry readily, leaving a tacky residue to which tape will adhere firmly.

Taping directly on skin provides maximum support. However, applying tape day after day can lead to skin irritation. To overcome this problem many athletic trainers sacrifice some support by using a protective covering to the skin. The most popular is a commercial, moderately elastic underwrap material that is extremely thin and fits snugly to the contours of the part to be taped. One commonly used underwrap material is polyester urethane foam, which is fine, porous, extremely lightweight, and resilient. Proper use of an underwrap requires the part to be shaved and sprayed with a tape adherent. When applied, underwrap material should be only one layer thick. It is also desirable to place a protective greased pad anterior and posterior to the ankle to prevent tape cuts and secondary infection.

Proper Taping Technique

Selection of the correct tape width for the body part to be taped depends on the area to be covered. The more acute the angles, the narrower the tape width must be to fit the many contours. For example, the hands and feet usually require ½-inch or 1-inch (1.25 or 2.5 cm) tape, the ankles require 1½-inch (3.75 cm) tape, and the larger skin areas such as thighs and back can accommodate 2- to 3-inch (5 to 7.5 cm) tape with ease. *NOTE: Supportive tape improperly applied can aggravate an existing injury or disrupt the mechanics of a body part, causing an initial injury to occur.*

Tearing Tape

Coaches and athletic trainers use various techniques in tearing tape (Figure 12-1). A method should be used that permits the operator to keep the tape roll in hand most of the time. The following is a suggested procedure:

1. Hold the tape roll in the preferred hand, with the index finger hooked through the center of the tape roll and the thumb pressing its outer edge.
2. With the other hand, grasp the loose end between the thumb and index finger.
3. With both hands in place, make a quick, scissorslike move to tear the tape.

Once the first thread is torn, tape tears easily.

When tearing is properly executed, the torn edges of the linen-backed tape are relatively straight, without curves, twists, or loose threads sticking out. Once the first thread is torn, the rest of the tape tears easily. Learning to tear tape effectively from many different positions is essential for speed and efficiency. Many tapes other than the linen-backed type cannot be torn manually and require a knife, scissors, or razor-blade cutter.

Rules for Tape Application

Included below are a few of the important rules to be observed in the use of adhesive tape. In practice the athletic trainer will identify others.

1. If the part to be taped is a joint, *place it in the position in which it is to be stabilized* or, if the part is musculature, *make the necessary allowance for contraction and expansion.*
2. *Overlap the tape at least half the width of the tape below.* Unless tape is overlapped sufficiently, the active athlete will separate it, thus exposing the underlying skin to irritation.

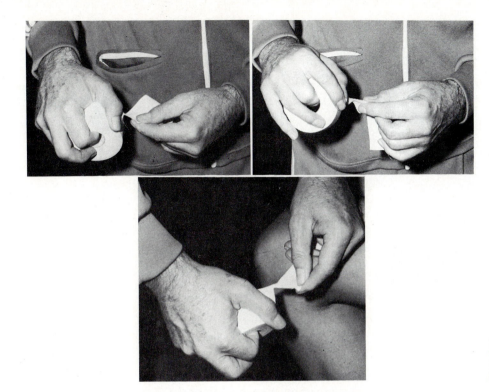

Figure 12-1

Methods of tearing linen-backed tape.

3. *Avoid continuous taping.* Tape continuously wrapped around a part may cause constriction. It is suggested that one turn be made at a time and that each encirclement be torn to overlap the starting end by approximately 1 inch. This rule is particularly true of the nonyielding linen-backed tape.

4. *Keep the tape roll in hand whenever possible.* By learning to keep the tape roll in the hand, seldom laying it down, and by learning to tear the tape, an operator can develop taping speed and accuracy.

5. *Smooth and mold the tape as it is laid on the skin.* To save additional time, tape strips should be smoothed and molded to the body part as they are put in place; this is done by stroking the top with the fingers, palms, and heels of both hands.

6. *Allow tape to fit the natural contour of the skin.* Each strip of tape must be laid in place with a particular purpose in mind. Linen-backed tape is not sufficiently elastic to bend around acute angles but must be allowed "to fall as it may," fitting naturally to the body contours. Failing to allow this fit creates wrinkles and gaps that can result in skin irritations.

7. *Start taping with an "anchor" piece and finish by applying a "lock" strip.* Taping should commence, if possible, by sticking the tape to an anchor piece that has encircled the part. This placement affords a good medium for the stabilization of succeeding tape strips, so that they will not be affected by the movement of the part.

8. *Where maximum support is desired, tape directly over skin surfaces.* In cases of sensitive skin, other mediums may be used as tape bases. With the use of artificial bases, some movement can be expected between the skin and the base.

Figure 12-2

To manually remove tape from the body, pull it in a direct line with the body.

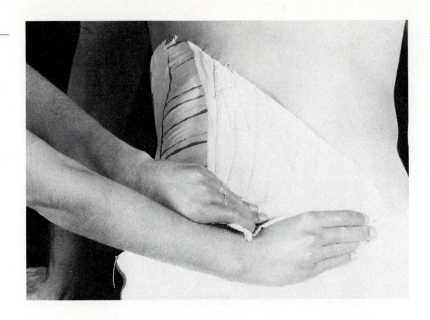

Removing Adhesive Tape

Tape usually can be removed from the skin by manual methods, by the use of tape scissors or tape cutters, or by chemical solvents.

Manual removal   When tape is pulled from the body, the operator must be careful not to tear or irritate the skin. Tape must not be wrenched in an outward direction from the skin but should be pulled in a direct line with the body (Figure 12-2).

Use of tape scissors or cutters   The characteristic tape scissors has a blunt nose that slips underneath the tape smoothly without gouging the skin. Precautions should be taken to avoid cutting the tape too near the site of the injury, lest the scissors aggravate the condition.

Use of chemical solvents   When an adhesive mass is left on the skin after taping, a chemical agent may have to be used. Commercial cleaning solvents often contain a highly flammable agent. Extreme care must be taken to store solvents in cool places and in tightly covered metal containers. Extensive inhalation of benzene fumes has a toxic effect. Adequate ventilation should be maintained when using solvents.

Common Taping Procedures
The Foot

The arch

ARCH TECHNIQUE NO. 1: With Pad Support

Arch taping with pad support uses the following procedures to strengthen weakened arches (Figure 12-3).

MATERIALS NEEDED: One roll of 1½-inch (3.8 cm) tape, tape adherent, and a ⅛- or ¼-inch (0.3 to 0.6 cm) adhesive foam rubber pad cut to fit the longitudinal arch.

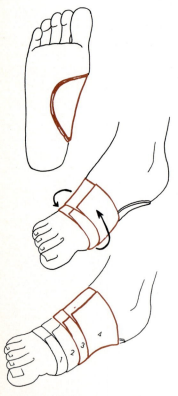

Figure 12-3

Arch taping technique no. 1, including an arch pad and circular tape strips.

POSITION OF THE ATHLETE: The athlete lies face downward on the table, with the foot that is to be taped extending approximately 6 inches (15 cm) over the edge of the table. To ensure proper position, allow the foot to hang in a relaxed position.

PROCEDURE:

1. Place a series of strips of tape directly around the arch or, if added support is required, around an arch pad and the arch. The first strip should be put on just above the metatarsal arch.
2. Each subsequent strip should overlap the preceding piece about half the width of the tape.

CAUTION: Avoid putting on so many strips of tape as to hamper the action of the ankle.

ARCH TECHNIQUE NO. 2: The X for the Longitudinal Arch

When using the figure-8 method for taping the longitudinal arch, the following steps are executed (Figure 12-4).

MATERIALS NEEDED: One roll of 1-inch tape and tape adherent.

POSITION OF THE ATHLETE: The athlete lies face downward on a table, with the affected foot extending approximately 6 inches (15 cm) over the edge of the table. To ensure proper position, allow the foot to hang in a relaxed natural position.

PROCEDURE

1. Lightly place an anchor strip around the ball of the foot, making certain not to constrict the action of the toes.
2. Start the next strip of tape from the medial edge of the anchor, moving it upward at an acute angle, crossing the center of the longitudinal arch, encircling the heel, and descending; then, crossing the arch again, end at the lateral aspect of the anchor.
3. Lock the first "cross" and each subsequent cross individually by using a single piece of tape placed around the ball of the foot.

NOTE: A variation of this method is to start and finish the X on each of the five metatarsal heads (Figure 12-5).

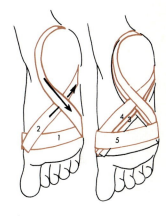

Figure 12-4

Arch taping technique no. 2 (**X** taping).

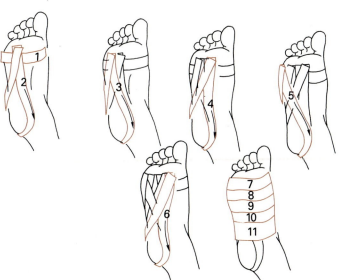

Figure 12-5

Alternate arch taping technique.

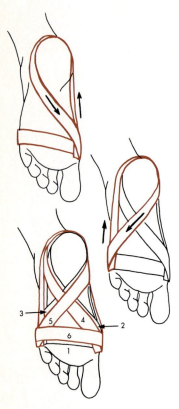

Figure 12-6

Arch taping technique no. 3 with double **X** and forefoot support.

ARCH TECHNIQUE NO. 3: The Double X and Forefoot Support

As its name implies, this taping both supports the longitudinal arch and stabilizes the forefoot into good alignment (Figure 12-6).

MATERIALS NEEDED: One roll of 1-inch (2.5 cm) tape and tape adherent.

POSITION OF THE ATHLETE: The athlete lies face down on a table, with the foot to be taped extending approximately 6 inches (15 cm) over the edge of the table.

PROCEDURE

1. Place an anchor strip around the ball of the foot.
2. Start the next strip on the side of the foot, beginning at the base of the great toe. Take the tape around the heel, crossing the arch, returning to the starting point.
3. The pattern of the third strip of tape is the same as the second strip except that it is started on the little toe side of the foot.
4. Lock each series of strips by placing tape around the ball joint. A completed procedure usually consists of a series of three strips.

LOWDYE TECHNIQUE

The LowDye technique is an excellent method for managing the fallen medial longitudinal arch, foot pronation, arch strains, and plantar fasciitis. Moleskin is cut in 3-inch (7.5 cm) strips to the shape of the sole of the foot. It should cover the head of the metatarsal bones and the calcaneus bone (Figure 12-7).[2]

MATERIALS NEEDED: One roll of 1-inch (2.5 cm), 1 roll of 2-inch (5 cm) tape and moleskin.

POSITION OF THE ATHLETE: The athlete sits with the foot in a neutral position with the first ray in plantar flexion.

PROCEDURE

1. Apply the moleskin to the sole of the foot, pulling it slightly downward before attaching it to the calcaneus.

Figure 12-7

LowDye taping technique for fallen medial longitudinal arch, foot pronation, arch strains, and plantar fasciitis.

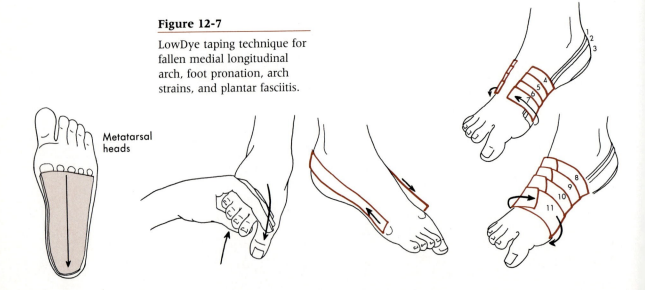

2. Grasp the forefoot with the thumb under the distal 2 to 5 metatarsal heads, pushing slightly upward, with the tips of the second and third fingers pushing downward on the first metatarsal head. While the foot is in this position, apply two or three 1-inch (2.5 cm) tape strips laterally, starting from the distal head of the fifth metatarsal bone and ending at the distal head of the first metatarsal bone. Keep these lateral strips below the outer malleolus.

3. Secure the moleskin and lateral tape strip by circling the forefoot with four or five 2-inch (5 cm) strips. Start at the lateral dorsum of the foot, circle under the plantar aspect, and finish at the medial dorsum of the foot.

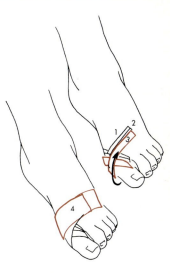

The toes

THE SPRAINED GREAT TOE

The following procedures are used for taping the great toe after a sprain (Figure 12-8).

MATERIALS NEEDED: One roll of 1-inch (2.5 cm) tape and tape adherent.

POSITION OF THE ATHLETE: The athlete assumes a sitting position.

PROCEDURE

1. The greatest support is given to the joint by a figure-8 taping. The series is started at an acute angle on the top of the foot, swinging down between the great and first toes, first encircling the great toe and then coming up, over, and across the starting point.
2. The above process is repeated, with each series started separately.
3. After the required number of figure-8 strips have been put in position, one lock piece should be placed around the ball of the foot.

Figure 12-8

Taping for a sprained great toe.

HAMMER, OR CLAWED, TOES

This technique is designed to reduce the pressure of the bent toes against the shoe (Figure 12-9).

MATERIALS NEEDED: One roll of ½-inch (1.25 cm) or 1-inch (2.5 cm) adhesive tape and tape adherent.

POSITION OF THE ATHLETE: The athlete sits on a table with the affected leg extended over the edge.

PROCEDURE

1. Tape one affected toe; then lace under the adjacent toe and over the next toe.
2. Tape can be attached to the next toe or can be continued and attached to the fifth toe.

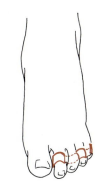

Figure 12-9

Taping for hammer, or clawed, toes.

FRACTURED TOES

MATERIALS NEEDED: One roll of ½- to 1-inch (1.25 to 2.5 cm) tape, ⅛-inch (0.82 cm) sponge rubber, and tape adherent.

POSITION OF THE ATHLETE: The athlete assumes a sitting position.

PROCEDURE

1. A ⅛-inch sponge rubber wedge is cut and placed between the affected toes.
2. Two to 3 circular tape pieces are placed around the toes (Figure 12-10). The concept of this technique is to splint the fractured toe with a nonfractured one.

Figure 12-10

Taping for fracture of a toe.

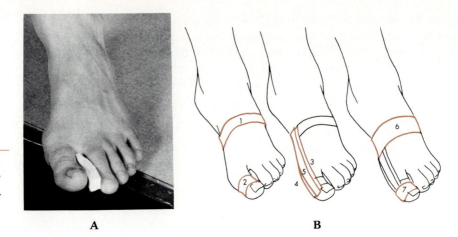

Figure 12-11

A, Wedging of the great toe can help reduce some of the abnormal stress of a bunion. **B,** Taping for the bunion.

A   B

BUNIONS

MATERIALS NEEDED: One roll of 1-inch (2.5 cm) tape, tape adherent, and ¼-inch (0.62 cm) sponge rubber or felt.

POSITION OF THE ATHLETE: The athlete assumes a sitting position.

PROCEDURE

1. The ¼-inch sponge rubber is cut to form a wedge between the great and second toes.
2. Anchor strips are placed to encircle the midfoot and distal aspect of the great toe (Figure 12-11).
3. Two or three stirrups are placed on the medial aspect of the great toe to hold the toe in proper alignment.

The Ankle Joint

ROUTINE NONINJURY

Ankle taping applied directly to the athlete's skin affords the greatest support; however, when applied and removed daily, skin irritation will occur. To avoid this problem an underwrap material should be applied (Figure 12-12). Before taping, follow these procedures:

1. Shave all the hair off the foot and ankle.
2. Apply a coating of a tape adherent to protect the skin and offer an adhering base.
   NOTE: It may be advisable to avoid the use of a tape adherent, especially in cases where the athlete has a history of developing tape blisters. In cases of skin sensitivity the ankle surface should be thoroughly cleansed of dirt and oil and an underwrap material applied; or one could tape directly to the skin.
3. If underwrap is not used, apply a gauze pad coated with friction-proofing material such as grease over the instep and to the back of the heel.
4. Do not apply tape if skin is cold or hot from a therapeutic treatment.

MATERIALS NEEDED: One roll of 1½-inch (3.8 cm) tape and tape adherent.

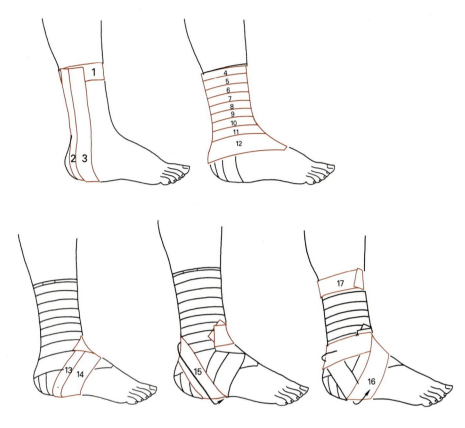

Figure 12-12

Routine noninjury ankle
taping.

POSITION OF THE ATHLETE: The athlete sits on a table with the leg extended and the
   foot held at a 90-degree angle.

PROCEDURE

1. A single anchor is placed around the ankle approximately 5 or 6 inches
   (12.7 to 15.2 cm) above the malleolus.
2. Two stirrups are applied in consecutive order, with care that each one overlaps half the width of the piece of tape it adjoins.
3. After the stirrups have been applied, 7 or 8 circular strips are put on, from
   the point of the anchor, moving downward until the malleolus is completely covered.
4. Next, two or three arch strips are applied.
5. The final support is given by a heel lock. Starting high on the instep, bring
   the tape along the ankle at a slight angle, hooking the heel, leading under
   the arch, then coming up on the opposite side, and finishing at the starting
   point. At this point the tape is torn to complete half of the heel lock. To
   complete the remaining half, execute the same procedure on the opposite
   side of the ankle.

OPEN BASKETWEAVE

This modification of the closed basketweave or Gibney technique is designed to
give freedom of movement in dorsiflexion and plantar flexion while providing
lateral and medial support and giving swelling room. Taping in this pattern (Fig-

ure 12-13) may be used immediately after an acute sprain in conjunction with a pressure bandage and cold applications, since it allows for swelling.

MATERIALS NEEDED: One roll of 1½-inch (3.8 cm) tape and tape adherent.

POSITION OF THE ATHLETE: The athlete sits on a table with the leg extended and the foot held at a 90-degree angle.

PROCEDURE

1. The procedures followed are the same as for the closed basketweave (Figure 12-14) with the exception of incomplete closures of the Gibney strips.

2. The gap between the Gibney ends should be locked by two pieces of tape running on either side of the instep.

   NOTE: Application of a 1½-inch (3.8 cm) elastic bandage placed over the open basketweave affords added control of swelling; however, it should be removed before retiring.

Of the many ankle taping techniques in vogue today, those using combinations of stirrups, basketweave pattern, and heel lock have been determined to offer the best support.

CLOSED BASKETWEAVE (GIBNEY)

The closed basketweave technique (Figure 12-14) offers strong tape support and is primarily used in athletic training for newly sprained or chronically weak ankles.

MATERIALS NEEDED: One roll of 1½-inch (3.8 cm) tape and tape adherent.

POSITION OF THE ATHLETE: The athlete sits on a table with the leg extended and the foot at a 90-degree angle.

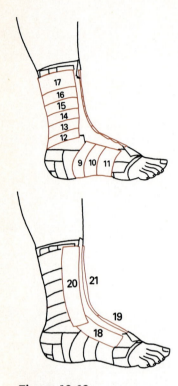

Figure 12-13

Open basketweave ankle taping.

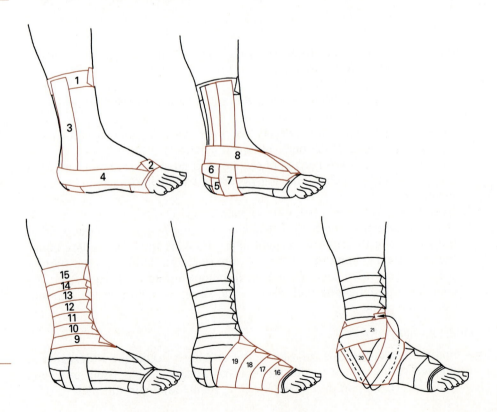

Figure 12-14

Closed basketweave ankle taping.

PROCEDURE

1. One anchor piece is placed around the ankle, approximately 5 or 6 inches (12.7 to 15.2 cm) above the malleolus, and a second anchor is placed around the arch and instep.

2. The first stirrup is then applied posteriorly to the malleolus and attached to the ankle stirrup.
   NOTE: When applying stirrups pull the foot into eversion for an inversion sprain and into a neutral position for an eversion sprain.

3. The first Gibney is started directly under the malleolus and is attached to the foot anchor.

4. In an alternating series, three stirrups and three Gibneys are placed on the ankle, with each piece of tape overlapping at least one half of the preceding strip.

5. After the basketweave series has been applied, the Gibney strips are continued up the ankle, thus giving circular support.

6. For arch support, two or three circular strips are applied.

7. After the conventional basket weave has been completed, a heel lock should be applied to ensure maximum stability.

CONTINUOUS STRETCH TAPE TECHNIQUE

This technique provides a fast alternative to other taping methods for the ankle (Figure 12-15).[1]

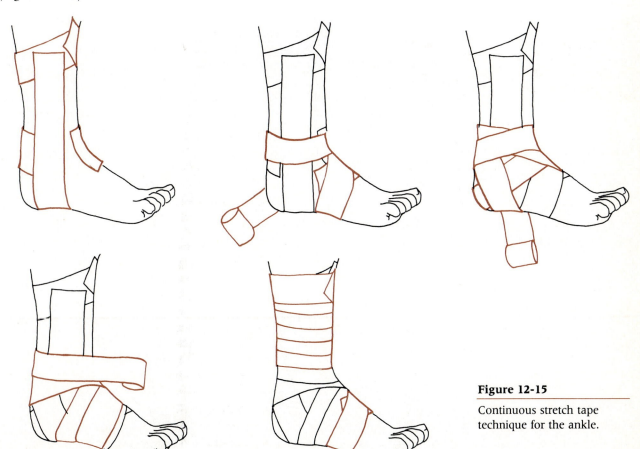

Figure 12-15

Continuous stretch tape technique for the ankle.

MATERIALS NEEDED: One roll of 1½-inch (3.75 cm) linen tape, one roll of 2-inch (5 cm) stretch tape, and tape adherent.

POSITION OF THE ATHLETE: The athlete sits on a table with the leg extended and the foot at a 90-degree angle.

PROCEDURE

1. One anchor strip is placed around the ankle approximately 5 to 6 inches (12.5 to 15 cm) above the malleolus.
2. Apply three stirrups, covering the malleoli.
3. The stretch tape is started in a medial-to-lateral direction around the mid-foot and continues in a figure-8 pattern to above the lateral malleolus.
4. The stretch tape is continued across the midfoot, then across the heel.
5. Two heel locks are applied, one in one direction and one in the reverse direction.
6. Next, repeat a figure-8 pattern followed by a spiral pattern, filling the space up to the anchor.
7. Use the lock technique at the top with a linen tape strip.

The Lower Leg

ACHILLES TENDON

Achilles tendon taping (Figure 12-16) is designed to prevent the Achilles tendon from overstretching.

MATERIALS NEEDED: One roll of 3-inch (7.5 cm) elastic tape, one roll of 1½-inch (3.8 cm) linen tape, and tape adherent.

POSITION OF THE ATHLETE: The athlete kneels or lies face down, with the affected foot hanging relaxed over the edge of the table.

PROCEDURE

1. Two anchors are applied with 1½-inch (3.8 cm) tape, one circling the leg loosely, approximately 7 to 9 inches (17.8 to 22.9 cm) above the malleoli, and the other encircling the ball of the foot.

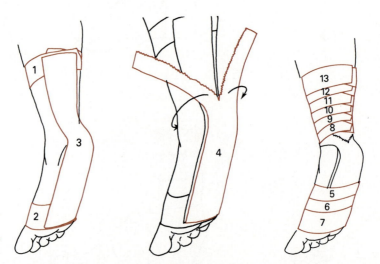

Figure 12-16

Achilles tendon taping.

2. Two strips of 3-inch (7.5 cm) elastic tape are cut approximately 8 to 10 inches (20 to 25 cm) long. The first strip is moderately stretched from the ball of the athlete's foot along its plantar aspect up to the Achilles tendon. The second elastic strip follows the course of the first except that it is cut and split down the middle lengthwise and the cut ends are wrapped around the lower leg to form a lock. **CAUTION:** Keep the wrapped ends above the level of the strain.

3. The series is completed by placing two or three lock strips of elastic tape loosely around the arch and five or six strips around the athlete's lower leg.

NOTE: Locking too tightly around the lower leg and foot will tend to restrict the normal action of the Achilles tendon and create more tissue irritation.

MEDIAL SHINSPLINTS

Proper taping can afford some relief of the symptoms of shinsplints (Figure 12-17).

MATERIALS NEEDED: One roll of 1½-inch (3.75 cm) linen or elastic tape and adherent.

POSITION OF THE ATHLETE: The athlete sits on a table with the knee bent and the foot flat on the table. The purpose of this position is to fully relax the muscles of the lower leg.

PROCEDURE

1. The operator first applies two anchor tape strips. The first anchor strip is applied to the anterolateral aspect of the ankle and lower leg and the second to the posterolateral aspect of the midcalf.

2. Starting at the lowest end of the first anchor, run a strip of tape to the back of the lower leg, spiraling it over the shin to attach on the lower end of the second anchor strip. Apply three strips of tape in this manner, with each progressively moving upward on the leg. As each strip comes across the strip, an effort should be made to pull the muscle toward the tibia.

3. After three pieces of tape have been applied, their ends are locked by one or two cross-strips.

4. After the procedure has been completed, an elastic wrap can be applied in a spiral fashion.

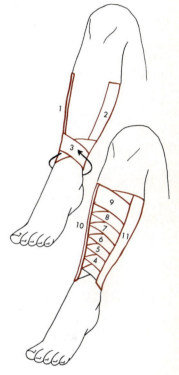

Figure 12-17

Taping for shinsplints.

The Knee

MEDIAL COLLATERAL LIGAMENT

As with ankle instabilities, the athlete with an unstable knee should never use tape and bracing as a replacement for proper exercise rehabilitation. If properly applied, taping can help protect the knee and become an aid in the rehabilitation process.[3]

MATERIALS NEEDED: One roll of 2-inch (5 cm) linen tape, one roll of 3-inch (7.5 cm) elastic tape, a 1-inch (2.5 cm) heel lift, and skin adherent.

POSITION OF THE ATHLETE: The athlete stands on a 3-foot (90 cm) table, with the injured knee held in a moderately relaxed position by a 1-inch (2.5 cm) heel lift. The hair is completely removed from an area 6 inches (15 cm) above to 6 inches (15 cm) below the patella.

PROCEDURE

1. A circular, 3-inch (7.5 cm) elastic anchor strip is placed lightly around the thigh and leg at the hairline.

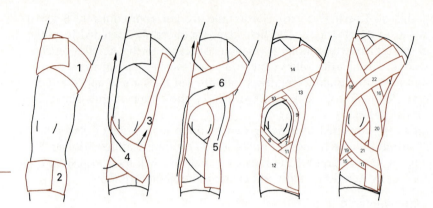

Figure 12-18

Taping for knee collateral
ligament injuries.

2. Twelve elastic tape strips are precut, each approximately 9 inches (22.5 cm)
   long. Stretched to their utmost, they are applied to the knee as indicated in
   Figure 12-18.
3. Finally, elastic tape is applied as locks for the basketweave. Two or three
   strips of 2-inch (5 cm) linen tape are cut to encircle the thigh and the leg.
   Some individuals find it advantageous to complete a knee taping by wrapping loosely with an elastic wrap, thus providing an added precaution
   against the tape's becoming loose from perspiration.

ROTARY INJURY KNEE INSTABILITY

The rotary taping method is designed to provide the knee with support when it
is unstable from injury to the medial collateral and anterior cruciate ligaments
(Figure 12-19).

MATERIALS NEEDED: One roll of 3-inch (7.5 cm) elastic tape, skin adherent, 4-inch
   (10 cm) gauze pad, and scissors.

POSITION OF THE ATHLETE: The athlete sits on a table with the affected knee flexed
   15 degrees.

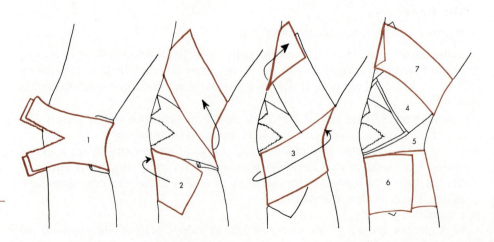

Figure 12-19

Taping for rotary injury knee
instability.

PROCEDURE

1. A 10-inch (25 cm) piece of elastic tape is cut with both the ends snipped. The gauze pad is placed in the center of the 10-inch (25 cm) piece of elastic tape.
2. The gauze with the elastic tape backing is placed in the popliteal fossa of the athlete's knee. Both ends of the tape are stretched to the fullest extent and are torn. The divided ends are placed firmly around the patella and are interlocked.
3. Starting at a midpoint on the gastrocnemius muscle, a 3-inch (7.5 cm) elastic tape strip is spiraled to the front of the leg, then behind, crossing the popliteal fossa, and around the thigh, finishing anteriorly.
4. Procedure 3 is repeated on the opposite side.
5. Three or four spiral strips may be applied for added strength.
6. Once in place, the spiral strips are locked by the application of two circular strips around the thigh and two around the calf.

NOTE: More rigidity can be achieved by tracing the spiral pattern with linen tape.

HYPEREXTENSION

Hyperextension taping (Figure 12-20) is designed to prevent the knee from hyperextending and also may be used for strained hamstring muscles or slackened cruciate ligaments.

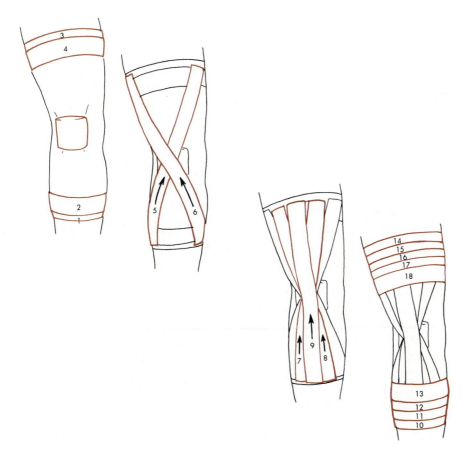

Figure 12-20

Hyperextension taping.

MATERIALS NEEDED: One roll of 2½-inch (5.5 cm) tape or 2-inch (5 cm) elastic tape, cotton or a 4-inch (10 cm) gauze pad, tape adherent, underwrap, and a 2-inch (5 cm) heel lift.

POSITION OF THE ATHLETE: The athlete's leg should be completely shaved above midthigh and below midcalf. The athlete stands on a 3-foot (90 cm) table with the injured knee flexed by a 2-inch (5 cm) heel lift.

PROCEDURE

1. Place two anchor strips at the hairlines, two around the thigh, and two around the leg. They should be applied loosely to allow for muscle expansion during exercise.
2. A gauze pad is placed at the popliteal space to protect the popliteal nerves and blood vessels from constriction by the tape.
3. Start the supporting tape strips by forming an X over the popliteal space.
4. Cross the tape again with two more strips and one up the middle of the leg.
5. Complete the technique by applying four or five locking strips around the thigh and calf.
6. Apply an additional series of strips if the athlete is heavily muscled.
7. Lock the supporting strips in place by applying two or three overlapping circles around the thigh and leg.

The Thigh

QUADRICEPS SUPPORT

The taping of the quadriceps muscle group (Figure 12-21) is designed to give support against the pull of gravity. In cases of moderate or severe contusions or strains, taping may afford protection or mild support and give confidence to the athlete. Various techniques fitted to the individual needs of the athletes can be used.

MATERIALS NEEDED: One roll of 2- or 1½-inch (5 or 3.75 cm) tape, skin toughener, and a 6-inch (15 cm) elastic bandage.

POSITION OF THE ATHLETE: The athlete stands on the massage table with leg extended.

PROCEDURE

1. Two anchor strips, each approximately 9 inches (22.5 cm) long, are placed respectively on the lateral and medial aspects of the thigh and are positioned half the distance between the anterior and posterior aspects.
2. Strips of tape are applied to the thigh, crossing one another to form an X. The crisscrosses are begun 2 or 3 inches (5 or 7.5 cm) above the kneecap and carried upward, overlapping one another. It is important that each tape strip be started from the anchor piece and carried upward and diagonally over the quadriceps, thus lifting against gravity. This procedure is continued until the quadriceps is completely covered.
3. After the diagonal series has been applied, a "lock strip" is placed longitudinally over the medial and lateral borders of the series.
4. To ensure more effective stability of the quadriceps taping, it is suggested that the entire thigh be encircled by either a 3-inch (7.5 cm) elastic tape or a 6-inch (15 cm) elastic bandage.

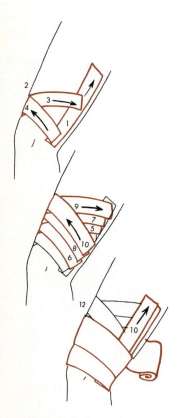

Figure 12-21

Quadriceps tape support.

HAMSTRING SUPPORT

It is extremely difficult to completely relieve the injured hamstring muscles by any wrapping or taping technique, but some stabilization can be afforded by each. The hamstring taping technique (Figure 12-22) is designed to stabilize the moderately to severely contused or torn hamstring muscles, enabling the athlete to continue to compete.

MATERIALS NEEDED: One roll of 2- or 1½-inch (5 or 3.75 cm) tape, skin toughener, and a roll of 3-inch (7.5 cm) elastic tape or a 6-inch (15 cm) elastic wrap.

POSITION OF THE ATHLETE: The athlete lies face downward or may stand on the table, with the affected limb flexed at approximately a 15-degree angle at the knee, so the hamstring muscle is relaxed and shortened.

PROCEDURE

1. This taping is applied in a way similar to the quadriceps technique. An anchor strip is placed on either side of the thigh, and then strips approximately 9 inches (22.5 cm) in length are crisscrossed diagonally upward on the posterior aspect of the thigh, forming an **X**.
2. After the hamstring area is covered with a series of crisscrosses, a longitudinal lock is applied on either side of the thigh.
3. Three-inch (7.5 cm) elastic tape or a 6-inch (15 cm) elastic wrap may be placed around the thigh to aid in holding the crisscross taping in place.

ILIAC SUPPORT

Iliac crest adhesive taping (Figure 12-23) is designed to support, protect, and immobilize the soft tissue surrounding the iliac crest.

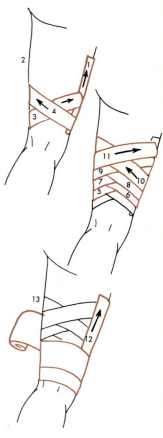

Figure 12-22

Hamstring taping.

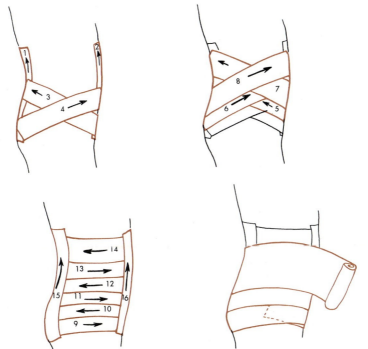

Figure 12-23

Iliac tape support.

MATERIALS NEEDED: One roll of 2-inch (5 cm) adhesive tape, 6-inch (15 cm) bandage, skin toughener, and tape adherent.

POSITION OF THE ATHLETE: The athlete stands on the floor, bending slightly laterally toward the injured side.

PROCEDURE

1. Two anchor strips, each approximately 9 inches (22.5 cm) long, are applied. One is placed longitudinally, just lateral to the sacrum and lumbar spine, and the other is placed lateral to the umbilicus.
2. Commencing 2 to 3 inches (5 to 7.5 cm) below the crest of the ilium, tape crisscrosses are placed from one anchor to the other, lifting the tissue against the pull of gravity. The crisscrosses are carried upward to a point just below the floating rib.
3. Lock strips are placed over approximately the same positions as the anchor strips.
4. If additional support is desired, horizontal strips should be laid on alternately in posteroanterior and anteroposterior directions.
5. Finally, a 6-inch (15 cm) elastic bandage is applied to additionally secure the tape in place and to prevent perspiration from loosening the taping.

The Shoulder

STERNOCLAVICULAR IMMOBILIZATION (Figure 12-24)

MATERIALS NEEDED: A felt pad of ¼-inch (0.63 cm) thickness, cut to a circumference of 4 inches (10 cm), 3-inch (7.5 cm) roll of elastic tape, two gauze pads, and tape adherent.

POSITION OF THE ATHLETE: Reduction of the most common sternoclavicular dislocation is performed by traction, with the athlete's arm abducted. Traction and abduction are maintained by an assistant while the immobilization taping is applied.

PROCEDURE

1. An anchor strip is applied around the chest at the level of the tenth rib while the chest is expanded.
2. A felt pad is laid over the sternoclavicular joint and gauze pads are applied over the athlete's nipples.

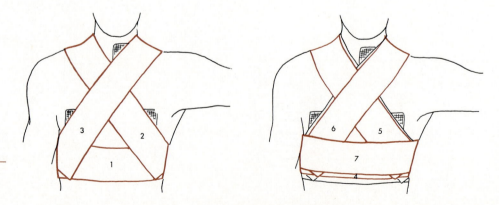

Figure 12-24

Sternoclavicular
immobilization.

3. Depending on the direction of displacement, tape pressure is applied over the felt pad. With the most common dislocation (that which is upward, forward, and anterior) taping is started from the back and is moved forward over the shoulder. The first pressure strip is taken from the anchor tape on the unaffected side and crosses over the injured site to finish on the front anchor strip.
4. A second strip is taken from the anchor strip on the affected side and crossed over the unaffected side to finish on the front anchor strip.
5. As many series of strips are applied as are needed to give complete immobilization. All series are locked in place by a tape strip placed over the ends.

ACROMIOCLAVICULAR SUPPORT

Protective acromioclavicular taping (Figure 12-25) is designed to stabilize the acromioclavicular articulation in proper alignment and still allow normal movement of the shoulder complex.

MATERIALS NEEDED: One ¼-inch (0.63 cm) thick felt pad, roll of 2-inch (5 cm) adhesive tape, tape adherent, 2-inch (5 cm) gauze pad, and 3-inch (7.5 cm) elastic bandage.

POSITION OF THE ATHLETE: The athlete sits in a chair with the affected arm resting in a position of abduction.

PROCEDURE
1. Three anchor strips are applied: the first in a three-quarter circle just below the deltoid muscle; the second, just below the nipple, encircling half the chest; and the third, over the trapezius muscle near the neck and then attaching to the second anchor in front and back.
2. The first and second strips of tape are applied from the front and back of the first anchor, crossing each other at the acromioclavicular articulation and attaching to the third anchor strip.
3. The third support strip is placed over the ends of the first and second pieces, following the line of the third anchor strip.
4. A fourth support strip is laid over the second anchor strip.
5. This basketweave pattern is continued until the entire shoulder complex is covered. It is followed by the application of a shoulder spica with an elastic bandage.

Figure 12-25

Protective acromioclavicular taping.

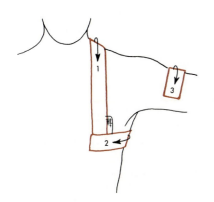

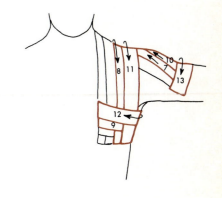

SHOULDER SUPPORT AND RESTRAINT

This taping is designed to support the soft tissues of the shoulder complex and to restrain the arm from abducting more than 90 degrees (Figure 12-26).

MATERIALS NEEDED: One roll of 2-inch (5 cm) tape, 2-inch (5 cm) gauze pad, cotton pad, tape adherent, and 3-inch (7.5 cm) elastic bandage.

POSITION OF THE ATHLETE: The athlete stands with the affected arm flexed at the elbow and the shoulder internally rotated.

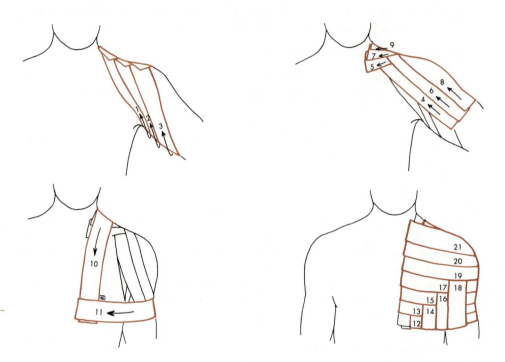

Figure 12-26

Taping for shoulder support and restraint.

PROCEDURE

1. The first phase is designed to support the capsule of the shoulder joint. After a cotton pad has been placed in the axilla, a series of three loops around the shoulder joint is applied. The first loop is started at the top of the athlete's scapula, is pulled forward across the acromion process, around the front of the shoulder, back underneath the axilla, over the back of the shoulder, crossing the acromion process again, and then is terminated at the clavicle. Each of the subsequent strips is begun down the shoulder half the width of the preceding strip.

2. Strips of tape are next run upward from a point just below the insertion of the deltoid muscle and crossed over the acromion process, completely covering the outer surface of the shoulder joint.

3. Before the final application of a basketweave shoulder taping, a gauze pad is placed over the nipple area. A strip of tape is laid over the shoulder near the neck and is carried to the nipple line in front and to the scapular line in back.

4. A second strip is taken from the end of the first strip, passes around the middle of the upper arm, and ends at the back end of the first strip.

5. The above alternation is continued with an overlapping of each preceding strip by at least half its width until the shoulder has been completely capped.
6. A shoulder spica is applied to keep the taping in place.

ELBOW RESTRICTION

The procedure for taping the elbow to prevent hyperextension follows (Figure 12-27).

MATERIALS NEEDED: One roll of 1½-inch (3.8 cm) tape, tape adherent, and 2-inch (5 cm) elastic bandage.

POSITION OF THE ATHLETE: The athlete stands with the affected elbow flexed at 90 degrees.

PROCEDURE

1. Apply two anchor strips loosely around the arm, approximately 2 inches (25 cm) to each side of the curve of the elbow (antecubital fossa).
2. Construct a checkrein by cutting a 10-inch (25 cm) and a 4-inch (10 cm) strip of tape and laying the 4-inch (10 cm) strip against the center of the 10-inch (25 cm) strip, blanking out that portion. Next place the checkrein so that it spans the two anchor strips, with the blanked-out side facing downward.
3. Place five additional 10-inch (25 cm) strips of tape over the basic checkrein.
4. Finish the procedure by securing the checkrein with three lock strips on each end. A figure-8 elastic wrap applied over the taping will prevent the tape from slipping because of perspiration.

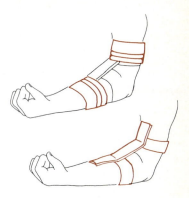

Figure 12-27

Elbow extension restriction taping.

The Wrist and Hand

WRIST TECHNIQUE NO. 1

This wrist taping (Figure 12-28) is designed for mild wrist strains or sprains.

MATERIALS NEEDED: One roll of 1-inch (2.5 cm) tape and tape adherent.

POSITION OF THE ATHLETE: The athlete stands with the affected hand flexed toward the injured side and the fingers moderately spread to increase the breadth of the wrist for the protection of nerves and blood vessels.

PROCEDURE

1. A strip of 1-inch (2.5 cm) tape, starting at the base of the wrist, is brought from the palmar side upward and around both sides of the wrist.
2. In the same pattern, with each strip overlapping the preceding one by at least half its width, three additional strips are laid in place.

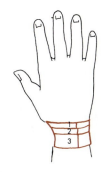

Figure 12-28

Wrist taping technique no. 1.

WRIST TECHNIQUE NO. 2

This wrist taping (Figure 12-29) is designed to stabilize and protect a badly injured wrist. The materials and positioning are the same as in technique 1.

MATERIALS NEEDED: One roll of 1-inch tape and tape adherent.

POSITION OF THE ATHLETE: The athlete stands with the affected hand flexed toward the injured side and the fingers moderately spread to increase the breadth of the wrist for the protection of nerves and blood vessels.

PROCEDURE

1. One anchor strip is applied around the wrist approximately 3 inches (7.5 cm) from the hand; another anchor strip encircles the spread hand.

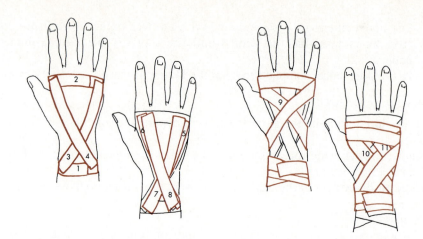

Figure 12-29

Wrist taping technique no. 2.

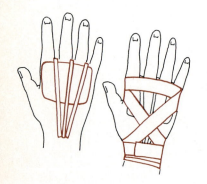

Figure 12-30

Bruised hand taping.

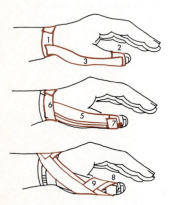

Figure 12-31

Sprained thumb taping.

2. With the wrist flexed toward the side of the injury, a strip of tape is taken from the anchor strip near the little finger and carried obliquely across the wrist joint to the wrist anchor strip. Another strip is taken from the anchor strip on the index finger side and carried across the wrist joint to the wrist anchor. This forms a crisscross over the wrist joint. A series of four or five crisscrosses may be applied, depending on the extent of splinting needed.
3. Over the crisscross taping, two or three series of figure-8 tapings are applied. Start by encircling the wrist once, carry a strip over the back of the hand obliquely, encircling the hand twice, and then carry another strip obliquely upward across the back of the hand to where the figure-8 started. This procedure should be repeated to ensure a strong, stabilizing taping.

BRUISED HAND

The following method is used to tape a bruised hand (Figure 12-30).

MATERIALS NEEDED: One roll of 1-inch (2.5 cm) adhesive tape, role of ½-inch (1.3 cm) tape, ¼-inch (0.63 cm) thick sponge rubber pad, and tape adherent.

POSITION OF THE ATHLETE: The fingers are spread moderately.

PROCEDURE

1. The protective pad is laid over the bruise and held in place by three strips of ½-inch (1.3 cm) tape laced through the webbing of the fingers.
2. A basic figure-8 made of 1-inch (2.5 cm) tape, is applied.

SPRAINED THUMB

Sprained thumb taping (Figure 12-31) is designed to give both protection for the muscle and joint and support to the thumb.

MATERIALS NEEDED: One role of 1-inch (2.5 cm) tape and tape adherent.

POSITION OF THE ATHLETE: The athlete should hold the injured thumb in a relaxed neutral position.

PROCEDURE

1. An anchor strip is placed loosely around the wrist and another around the distal end of the thumb.
2. From the anchor at the tip of the thumb to the anchor around the wrist,

four splint strips are applied in a series on the side of greater injury (dorsal or palmar side) and are held in place by one lock strip around the wrist and one encircling the tip of the thumb.

3. A series of three thumb spicas in now added. The first spica is started on the radial side at the base of the thumb and is carried under the thumb, completely encircling it, and then crossing the starting point. The strip should continue around the wrist and finish at the starting point. Each of the following spica strips should overlap the preceding strip by at least ⅔ inch (1.7 cm) and move downward on the thumb. The thumb spica with tape provides an excellent means of protection during recovery from an injury (Figure 12-32).

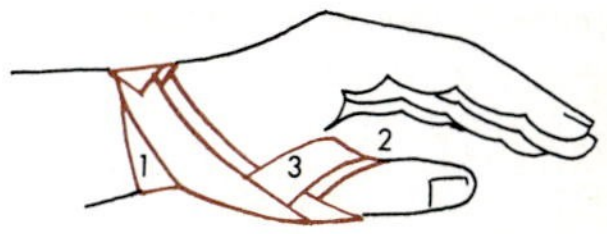

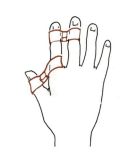

Figure 12-32

Thumb spica.

FINGER AND THUMB CHECKREINS

The finger or thumb that has been sprained may require the additional protection afforded by a restraining checkrein (Figure 12-33).

MATERIALS NEEDED: One role of 1-inch (2.5 cm) tape.

POSITION OF THE ATHLETE: The athlete spreads the injured fingers widely but within a range free of pain.

PROCEDURE

1. A strip of 1-inch (2.5 cm) tape, after encircling the middle phalanx of the injured finger, is brought over to the adjacent finger and encircles it also. The tape left between the two fingers, which are spread apart, is called the checkrein.

2. Additional strength is given by means of a lock strip that encircles the center of the checkrein.

Figure 12-33

Finger and thumb checkreins.

COMMON TYPES OF BANDAGES USED IN SPORTS MEDICINE

Two common bandages used in sports are the roller and the triangular.

Roller Bandages

Roller bandages are made of many materials; gauze, cotton cloth, and elastic wrapping are predominantly used in the training room. The width and length vary according to the body part to be bandaged. The sizes most frequently used are the 2-inch (5 cm) width by 6-yard (5½ m) length for hand, finger, toe, and head bandages; the 3-inch (7.5 cm) width by 10-yard (9 m) length for the extremities; and the 4-inch (10 cm) or 6-inch (15 cm) width by 10-yard length for thighs, groins, and trunk. For ease and convenience in the application of the roller bandage, the strips of material are first rolled into a cylinder. When a bandage is selected, it should be a single piece that is free from wrinkles, seams, or any other imperfections that may cause skin irritation.

Application

Application of the roller bandage must be executed in a specific manner to adequately achieve the purpose of the wrap. When a roller bandage is about to be placed on a body part, the roll should be held in the preferred hand with the loose end extending from the bottom of the roll. The back surface of the loose end is placed on the part and held in position by the other hand. The bandage cylinder is then unrolled and passed around the injured area. As the hand pulls the material from the roll, it also standardizes the bandage pressure and guides

To apply a roller bandage, hold it in the preferred hand with the loose end extending from the bottom of the roll.

the bandage in the proper direction. To anchor and stabilize the bandage, a number of turns, one on top of the other, are made. Circling a body part requires the operator to alternate the bandage roll from one hand to the other and back again.

To acquire maximum benefits from a roller bandage, it should be applied uniformly and firmly but not too tightly. Excessive or unequal pressure can hinder the normal blood flow within the part. The following points should be considered when using the roller bandage:

1. A body part should be wrapped in its position of maximum muscle contraction to ensure unhampered movement or circulation.
2. It is better to use a large number of turns with moderate tension than a limited number of turns applied too tightly.
3. Each turn of the bandage should be overlapped by at least one half of the overlying wrap to prevent the separation of the material while engaged in activity. Separation of the bandage turns tends to pinch and irritate the skin.
4. When limbs are wrapped, fingers and toes should be scrutinized often for signs of circulation impairment. Abnormally cold or cyanotic phalanges are signs of excessive bandage pressure.

The usual anchoring of roller bandages consists of several circular wraps directly overlying each other. Whenever possible, anchoring is commenced at the smallest circumference of a limb and is then moved upward. Wrists and ankles are the usual sites for anchoring bandages of the limbs. Bandages are applied to these areas in the following manner:

1. The loose end of the roller bandage is laid obliquely on the anterior aspects of the wrist or ankle and held in this position. The roll is then carried posteriorly under and completely around the limb and back to the starting point.
2. The triangular portion of the uncovered oblique end is folded over the second turn.
3. The folded triangle is covered by a third turn, thus finishing a secure anchor.

After a roller bandage has been applied, it is held in place by a *locking technique*. The method most often used to finish a wrap is that of firmly tying or pinning the bandage or placing adhesive tape over several overlying turns.

Once a bandage has been put on and has served its purpose, removal can be performed either by unwrapping or by carefully cutting with bandage scissors. Whatever method of bandage removal is used, extreme caution must be taken to avoid additional injury.

CLOTH ANKLE WRAP

Because tape is so expensive, the ankle wrap becomes an inexpensive and expedient means of mildly protecting ankles (Figure 12-34).

MATERIALS NEEDED: Each muslin wrap should be 1½ to 2 inches (3.8 to 5 cm) wide and from 72 to 96 inches (180 to 240 cm) long to ensure complete coverage and protection. The purpose of this wrap is to give mild support against lateral and medial motion of the ankle. It is applied over a sock.

POSITION OF THE ATHLETE: The athlete sits on a table, extending the leg and positioning the foot at a 90-degree angle. To avoid any distortion, it is important that the ankle be neither overflexed nor overextended.

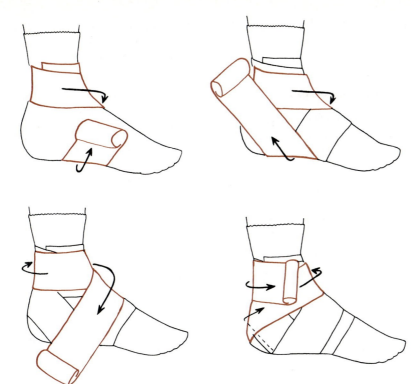

Figure 12-34

Ankle wrap.

PROCEDURE

1. Start the wrap above the instep around the ankle; circle the ankle and move it at an acute angle to the inside of the foot.
2. From the inside of the foot move the wrap under the arch, coming up on the outside and crossing at the beginning point, where it continues around the ankle, hooking the heel.
3. Then move the wrap up, inside, over the instep, and around the ankle, hooking the opposite side of the heel. This completes one series of the ankle wrap.
4. Complete a second series with the remaining material.

Elastic Wrap Techniques

ANKLE AND FOOT SPICA

The ankle and foot spica bandage (Figure 12-35) is primarily used in sports for the compression of new injuries, as well as for holding wound dressings in place.

MATERIALS NEEDED: Depending on the size of the ankle and foot, a 2- or 3-inch wrap is used.

POSITION OF THE ATHLETE: The athlete sits with ankle and foot extended over a table.

PROCEDURE

1. An anchor is placed around the foot near the metatarsal arch.
2. The elastic bandage is brought across the instep and around the heel and returned to the starting point.

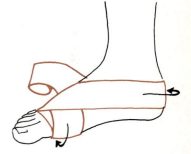

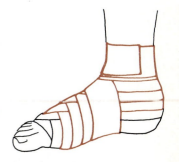

Figure 12-35

Ankle and foot spica.

3. The procedure is repeated several times, with each succeeding revolution progressing upward on the foot and the ankle.
4. Each spica is overlapped by approximately three fourths of the preceding bandage.

SPIRAL BANDAGE

The spiral bandage (Figure 12-36) is widely used in sports for covering a large area of a cylindrical part.

MATERIALS NEEDED: Depending on the size of the area, a 3- or 4-inch wrap is required.

POSITION OF THE ATHLETE: If the wrap is for the lower limb, the athlete bears weight on the opposite leg.

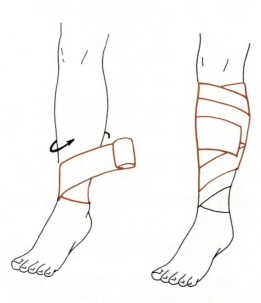

Figure 12-36

Spiral bandage.

PROCEDURE

1. The elastic spiral bandage is anchored at the smallest circumference of the limb and is wrapped, proceeding upward in a spiral against gravity.
2. To prevent the bandage from slipping down on a moving extremity, it is suggested that two pieces of tape be folded lengthwise and placed on the bandage at either side of the limb or that tape adherent be sprayed on the part.
3. After the bandage is anchored, it is carried upward in consecutive spiral turns, each overlapping the other by at least ½ inch.
4. The bandage is terminated by locking it with circular turns, which are then firmly secured by tape.

HIP SPICA FOR COMPRESSION

The hip spica (Figure 12-37) serves two purposes in sports. It holds analgesic packs in place and offers mild support to injured hip adductors or flexors.

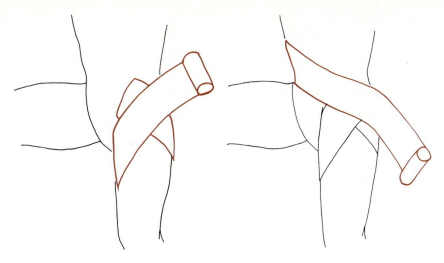

Figure 12-37

Hip spica.

MATERIALS NEEDED: In most cases a 6-inch wrap is used double its usual length.

POSITION OF THE ATHLETE: The athlete stands on a table, with his or her weight supported on the nonaffected leg.

PROCEDURE

1. Start the end of the roll at the upper part of the thigh and immediately encircle the upper thigh and groin, crossing the starting point.
2. When the starting end has been reached, the roll is taken completely around the waist to ensure against the wrap's slipping down; it should be brought around the wrist and firmly fixed above the crest of the ilium.
3. Continue by carrying the wrap around the thigh at groin level and up again around the waist; secure the end at the waist with adhesive tape.

NOTE: If movement restriction of the groin is needed, a hip spica wrap should be applied in reverse to Figure 12-38.

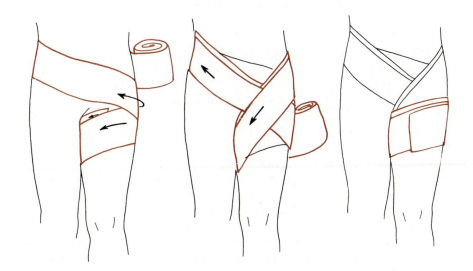

Figure 12-38

Elastic groin support.

GROIN SUPPORT

The following procedure is used to support the groin strain (Figure 12-38).

MATERIALS NEEDED: One roll of extra long 6-inch (15 cm) elastic bandage, a roll of 1½-inch (3.8 cm) adhesive tape, and nonsterile cotton.

POSITION OF THE ATHLETE: The athlete stands on a table with weight placed on the uninjured leg. The affected limb is relaxed and internally rotated. This procedure is different from that described earlier in which the wrap was used for pressure only.

PROCEDURE

1. A piece of nonsterile cotton is placed over the injured site.
2. The end of the elastic bandage is started at the upper part of the inner aspect of the thigh and is carried posteriorly around the thigh. Then it is brought across the lower abdomen and over the crest of the ilium on the opposite side of the body.
3. The wrap is continued around the back, repeating the same pattern and securing the wrap end with a 1½-inch (3.8 cm) adhesive tape.

SHOULDER SPICA

The shoulder spica (Figure 12-39) is used predominantly for the retention of wound dressings and for moderate muscular support.

MATERIALS NEEDED: One roll of extra length 4- to 6-inch elastic wrap, 1½-inch adhesive tape, and padding for axilla.

POSITION OF THE ATHLETE: Athlete stands with side toward the operator.

PROCEDURE

1. The axilla must be well padded to prevent skin irritation and constriction of blood vessels.
2. The bandage is anchored by one turn around the affected upper arm.
3. After anchoring the bandage around the arm on the injured side, the wrap is carried around the back under the unaffected arm and across the chest to the injured shoulder.
4. The affected arm is again encircled by the bandage, continuing around the back. Every figure-8 pattern moves progressively upward with an overlap of at least one half of the previous underlying wrap.

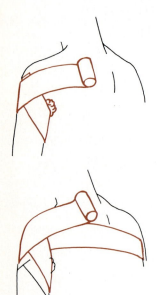

Figure 12-39

Elastic shoulder spica.

ELBOW FIGURE-8

The elbow figure-8 bandage (Figure 12-40) can be used to secure a dressing in the antecubital fossa or to restrain full extension in hyperextension injuries; when it is reversed, it can be used for conditions on the posterior aspect of the elbow.

MATERIALS NEEDED: One 3-inch elastic roll and 1½-inch adhesive tape.

POSITION OF THE ATHLETE: Athlete flexes elbow between 45 degrees and 90 degrees, depending on the restricted movement required.

PROCEDURE

1. Anchor the bandage by encircling the lower arm.
2. Bring the roll obliquely upward over the posterior aspect of the elbow.
3. Carry the roll obliquely upward, crossing the antecubital fossa; then pass once again completely around the upper arm and return to the beginning position by again crossing the antecubital fossa.
4. Continue the procedure as described, but for every new sequence move upward toward the elbow one half the width of the underlying wrap.

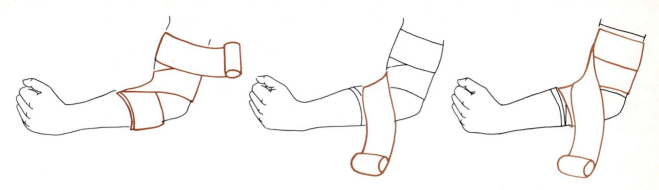

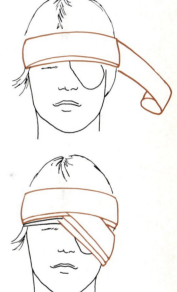

Figure 12-40

Elastic elbow figure-8.

EYE BANDAGE

For cases in which a bandage is needed to hold a dressing on an eye, the following procedure is suggested (Figure 12-41).

MATERIALS NEEDED: 2-inch gauze bandage roll, scissors, and ½- or 1-inch tape.

POSITION OF THE ATHLETE: Athlete sits in chair or on edge of table.

PROCEDURE

1. The bandage is started with a series of three circular turns around the head and then is brought obliquely down the back of the head.
2. From behind the head the bandage is carried forward underneath the earlobe and upward, crossing, respectively, the cheek bone, the injured eye, and the bridge of the nose; it is then returned to the original circular turns.
3. The head is encircled by the bandage, and the procedure is repeated with each wrap overlapping at least two thirds of the underlying material over the injured eye.
4. When at least three series have been applied over the injured eye, the bandage is locked after completion of a circular turn around the head.

JAW BANDAGE

Bandages properly applied can be used to hold dressings and to stabilize dislocated or fractured jaws (Figure 12-42).

Figure 12-41

Eye bandage.

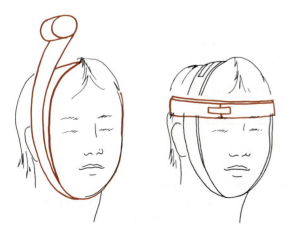

Figure 12-42

Jaw bandage.

MATERIALS NEEDED: 2- or 3-inch gauze bandage roll, scissors, and ½- or 2-inch tape.

POSITION OF THE ATHLETE: Athlete sits in chair or on edge of table.

PROCEDURE

1. The bandage is started by encircling the jaw and head in front of both ears several times.
2. The bandage is locked by a number of turns around the head.
3. Each of the two sets of turns is fastened with tape strips.

ARM OR LEG FIGURE-8

As with other figure-8 bandages, the arm or leg type (Figure 12-43) is used for keeping dressings in position, for holding splints in place, and for giving mild or moderate muscle support.

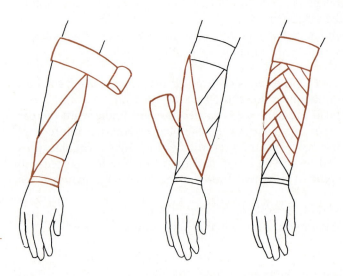

Figure 12-43

Arm or leg figure-8.

MATERIALS NEEDED: One 2- to 3-inch gauze roll, 1- or 1½-inch linen tape, and scissors.

POSITION OF THE ATHLETE: Athlete sits or stands with elbow slightly flexed.

PROCEDURE

1. An anchor is applied by circular turns around the wrist or ankle.
2. A spiral strip is carried diagonally upward to a point where one complete circular turn is executed.
3. The roll is then carried downward, crossing the spiral strip, to finish one figure-8.
4. The procedure is repeated until the injury site is thoroughly covered.

GAUZE CIRCULAR WRIST BANDAGE

Figure 12-44

Circular wrist bandage.

In training procedures the circular bandage (Figure 12-44) is used to cover a cylindrical area and to anchor other types of bandages.

MATERIALS NEEDED: One roll of 1- or 1½-inch gauze, 1-inch tape, and scissors.

POSITION OF THE ATHLETE: Athlete positions elbow at a 45-degree angle.

PROCEDURE

1. A turn is executed around the part at an oblique angle.
2. A small triangle of material is exposed by the oblique turn.
3. The triangle is bent over the first turn, with succeeding turns made over the turned down material locking it in palce.
4. After several turns have been made, the bandage is fastened at a point away from the injury.

GAUZE RECURRENT FINGER BANDAGE

This technique (Figure 12-45) is designed to hold a wound dressing on fingers.

MATERIALS NEEDED: One roll of ½-inch gauze, ½-inch tape, and scissors.

POSITION OF THE ATHLETE: Athlete positions elbow at a 45-degree angle.

PROCEDURE

1. The gauze roll starts at the base of the finger dorsally and is extended up the full length of the finger and back down on the volar aspect. This procedure can be performed several times, depending on the thickness required.
2. After the finger has been covered vertically, a spiral pattern is started at the base, initially moving up to the distal aspect of the finger and then proximally down, continuing several times.
3. The spiral pattern is completed at the finger's distal end and is secured by a piece of tape.

GAUZE HAND AND WRIST FIGURE-8

A figure-8 bandage (Figure 12-46) can be used for a mild wrist and hand support, as well as for holding dressings in place.

MATERIALS NEEDED: One roll of ½-inch gauze, ½-inch tape, and scissors.

POSITION OF THE ATHLETE: Athlete positions elbow at a 45-degree angle.

PROCEDURE

1. The anchor is executed with one or two turns around the palm of the hand.
2. The roll is then carried obliquely across the anterior or posterior portion of the hand, depending on the position of the wound, to the wrist, which it circles once; then it is returned to the primary anchor.
3. As many figures as needed are applied.

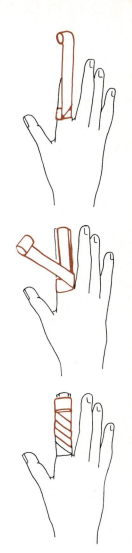

Figure 12-45

Recurrent finger bandage.

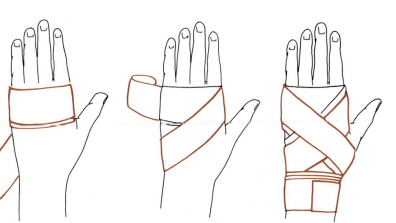

Figure 12-46

Hand and wrist figure-8.

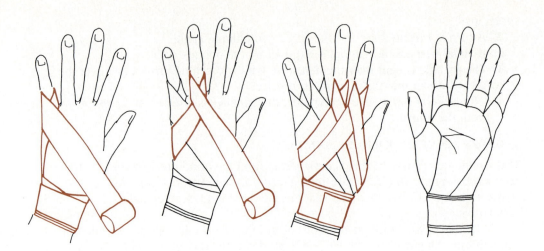

Figure 12-47

Demigauntlet bandage.

GAUZE DEMIGAUNTLET BANDAGE

The demigauntlet bandage (Figure 12-47) has considerable versatility in sports. It holds dressings on the back of the hand, and it also offers support and protection to knuckles. It may also be used in combination with linen and elastic tape to increase grip strength and to protect against calluses.

MATERIALS NEEDED: One roll of 1-inch gauze, ½-inch tape, and scissors.

POSITION OF THE ATHLETE: Athlete positions elbow at a 45-degree angle.

PROCEDURE

1. The bandage is anchored by circular turns at the wrist.
2. The roll is carried between the fourth and little fingers, encircling the little finger, and is brought once again across the back of the hand to the wrist.
3. The wrist is again encircled by the roll, which is carried to the next fingers consecutively until all digits and thumb have been wrapped.
4. Locking is executed at the wrist.

GAUZE FINGER BANDAGE

The finger bandage (Figure 12-48) can be used to hold dressings or tongue depressor splints in place.

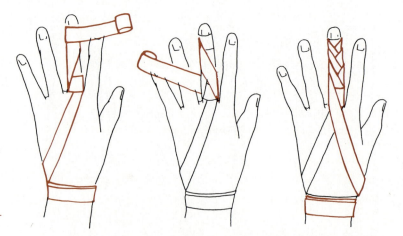

Figure 12-48

Finger bandage.

MATERIALS NEEDED: One roll of 1-inch gauze, ½-inch tape, and scissors.
POSITION OF THE ATHLETE: Athlete positions elbow at a 45-degree angle.
PROCEDURE

It is applied in a fashion similar to that used for the demigauntlet, with the exception that a spiral is carried downward to the tip of the finger and then back up to finish around the wrist.

Triangular and Cravat Bandages

Triangular and cravat bandages, usually made of cotton cloth, may be used where roller types are not applicable or available. Figure-8 and spica bandages are also used in sports medicine.

The triangular and cravat bandages are primarily used as first aid devices. They are valuable in emergency bandaging because of their ease and speed of application. In sports, the more diversified roller bandages are usually available and lend themselves more to the needs of the athlete. The principal use of the triangular bandage in athletic training is for arm slings. There are two basic kinds of slings, the cervical arm sling and the shoulder arm sling, and each has a specific purpose.

CERVICAL ARM SLING

The cervical arm sling (Figure 12-49) is designed to support the forearm, wrist, and hand. A triangular bandage is placed around the neck and under the bent arm that is to be supported.
MATERIALS NEEDED: One triangular bandage and one safety pin.
POSITION OF THE ATHLETE: The athlete stands with the affected arm bent at approx-
   imately a 70-degree angle.
PROCEDURE

1. The triangular bandage is positioned by the operator under the injured arm with the apex facing the elbow.
2. The end of the triangle nearest the body is carried over the shoulder of the injured arm; the other end is allowed to hang down loosely.
3. The loose end is pulled over the shoulder of the uninjured side.
4. The two ends of the bandage are tied in a square knot behind the neck. For the sake of comfort, the knot should be on either side of the neck, not directly in the middle.
5. The apex end of the triangle is brought around to the front of the elbow and fastened with a safety pin.

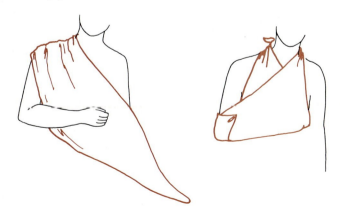

Figure 12-49

Cervical arm sling.

NOTE: In cases in which greater arm stabilization is required than that afforded by a sling, an additional bandage can be swathed about the upper arm and body (see Figure 12-51).

SHOULDER ARM SLING

The shoulder arm sling (Figure 12-50) is suggested for forearm support when there is an injury to the shoulder girdle or when the cervical arm sling is irritating to the athlete.

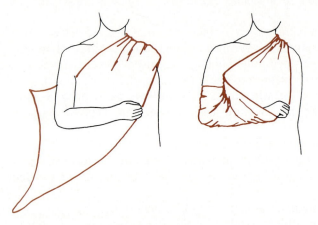

Figure 12-50

Shoulder arm sling.

MATERIALS NEEDED: One triangle bandage and one safety pin.

POSITION OF THE ATHLETE: The athlete stands with his injured arm bent at approximately a 70-degree angle.

PROCEDURE

1. The upper end of the shoulder sling is placed over the *uninjured* shoulder side.
2. The lower end of the triangle is brought over the forearm and drawn between the upper arm and the body, swinging around the athlete's back and then upward to meet the other end, where a square knot is tied.
3. The apex end of the triangle is brought around to the front of the elbow and fastened with a safety pin.

SLING AND SWATHE

The sling and swathe combination is designed to stabilize the arm securely in cases of shoulder dislocation or fracture (Figure 12-51).

Figure 12-51

Sling and swathe.

SUMMARY

Historically, taping has emerged as an important aspect of the field of athletic training. Sports tape is used in a variety of ways—as a means of holding wound dressing place, as support, and as protection against musculoskeletal injuries. For supporting and protecting musculoskeletal injuries, two types of tape are currently used—linen and stretch. Sports tape must be stored in a cool place and must be stacked on the flat side of each roll.

The skin of the athlete must be carefully prepared before tape is applied. The skin should first be carefully cleaned; then all hair should be removed. An adherent may next be applied, followed by an underwrap material, if need be, to help avoid skin irritation. When tape is applied, it must be done in a manner that provides the least amount of irritation and the maximum support. All tape applications require that great care is taken that the proper materials are used, that the proper position of the athlete is ensured, and that procedures are carefully followed.

The roller bandage is the most commonly used material in athletic training, with the elastic wrap second. Like taping, roller bandage application requires that directions be followed. Elastic wraps should be applied uniformly and firmly but not too tightly. Caution must be taken not to impede blood circulation.

Triangular and cravat bandages allow the trainer a number of bandage possibilities. Of major importance are the variations of slings that can be made.

REVIEW QUESTIONS AND CLASS ACTIVITIES

1. Demonstrate the correct way to dress a wound.
2. Observe the athletic trainer while he or she dresses wounds in the training room.
3. What aspects of backing, adhesive mass, and winding tension should be considered when purchasing athletic tape?
4. How should the skin be prepared when applying athletic tape?
5. Demonstrate proper use of the roller, triangular, and cravat bandages.

REFERENCES

1. The continuous technique of ankle support, Sports Med Guide 3(3):14, 1984.
2. Handling, KA: Taping procedure for an unstable knee, Ath Train 16:371, Sept/Oct 1984.
3. Kosmahl, EM, et al.: Painful plantar heel, plantar fasciitis, and calcaneal spur: etiology and treatment, J Orthop Sports Phys Ther 9(1):17, 1987.

ANNOTATED BIBLIOGRAPHY

Athletic training, National Athletic Training Association, PO Box 1865, Greenville, NC 27835-1865.
Each volume of this quarterly journal contains practical procedures for bandaging and taping, as well as for orthotic application.

Ellison, AD, editor and chairman: Athletic training and sports medicine, Chicago, 1984, American Academy of Orthopaedic Surgeons.
Part 3, "Taping and Bandaging," offers three chapters that provide taping and bandaging foundations, as well as important procedures common to athletic training and sports medicine.

First aider, Cramer Products, Inc, PO Box 1001, Gardner, Kansas 66030.
Published seven times throughout the school year, it contains useful taping and bandaging techniques that have been submitted by readers.

Sports med dig, PO Box 2160, Van Nuys, CA 91404-2160.
Many volumes of this monthly paper are dedicated to sports medicine discussions, bandaging and taping techniques, and major sports medicine problems.

Sports med guide, Mueller Sports Medicine, Inc, 1 Quench Dr, Prairie du Sac, WI 53578.
Published four times a year, this quarterly often presents, along with discussions on specific injuries, many innovative taping and bandaging techniques.

CHAPTER 13

Therapeutic Modalities

When you finish this chapter, you should be able to

Discuss the legal ramifications of treating the athlete with therapeutic modalities

Describe the theoretical uses of therapeutic heat, cold, and electrical stimulation

Apply a variety of thermotherapeutic and cryotherapeutic techniques

Differentiate therapeutic modalities that use the electromagnetic and acoustical energy spectrums

Discuss the reasons for using manual and mechanical therapeutic approaches

Describe, in detail, safe practices of all therapeutic modalities discussed in this chapter

Sports medicine, in general, and athletic training, specifically, increasingly are using a wide variety of therapeutic modalities. This chapter is designed as an introduction to those modalities that may be of special importance in sports medicine. The categories discussed include the legal concerns; thermal therapies, both superficial and penetrating; cryotherapy; electrical stimulations; and machine-assisted and manual therapies.

LEGAL CONCERNS

The use of therapeutic modalities in sports medicine must be performed with the greatest care possible. At no time can there be an indiscriminate use of any therapeutic modality. The athletic trainer must follow laws that specifically prohibit the use of certain therapeutic modalities. An athletic trainer who uses both superficial and penetrating modalities must have a thorough understanding of both their functions and the indications or contraindications for their use.

THERMOTHERAPY

The application of heat to treat disease and traumatic injuries has been used for centuries. Recently, however, its use in the immediate treatment phase of musculoskeletal injury has been replaced with cold application. Heat is an energy form that increases molecular activity by four methods of transfer, including conduction, convection, conversion, and radiation.[15] Thermotherapy modes are moist, dry, superficial, and deep.

The athletic trainer must carefully follow laws that prohibit him or her from use of certain therapeutic modalities.

Physical Principles

The transmission of heat energy is through **conduction, convection, radiation,** and **conversion.**

Conduction

Conduction occurs when heat is transferred from a warmer object to a cooler one. The ratio of this heat exchange is dependent on the temperature and the exposure time. Skin temperatures are basically influenced by the type of heat medium, the conductivity of the tissue, the quantity of blood flow in the area, and the speed at which heat is being dissipated.[15] To avoid tissue damage the temperature should never exceed 116.6° F (47° C). An exposure that includes close contact with a hot medium that has a temperature of 113° F (45° C) should not exceed 30 minutes. Examples of conductive therapeutic modalities are moist hot packs, paraffin baths, and electric heating pads.

Convection

Convection refers to the transference of heat through the movement of fluids or gases. Factors that influence convection heating are temperature, speed of movement, and the conductivity of the part.[15] The best example of thermotherapy through convection is the whirlpool bath.

Radiation

Radiation is the process whereby heat energy is transmitted through empty space. In other words, heat is transferred from one object through space to another object. Infrared heating and ultraviolet therapies are commonly used in sports medicine as radiation therapies.

Electromagnetic radiation   Every substance, if not at absolute zero, gives off electromagnetic radiation. This fact applies directly to many therapy modalities, including infrared devices, ultraviolet therapy, and shortwave and microwave diathermies. The common characteristics of radiant energy are (1) it can be transmitted without a medium for support, (2) all forms of radiant energy travel at 300 million meters per second in a vacuum, but the speed varies in different media, (3) energy waveforms travel in a straight line, and (4) the energy waveforms can be reflected, refracted, absorbed, or penetrated.

The electromagnetic radiation spectrum represents various regions classified according to wavelength and frequency. The formula for this is wavelength equals the velocity and frequency of the vibration or source. The longer the wavelength is, the lower the frequency will be, and, conversely, the shorter the wavelength, the higher the frequency. As mentioned previously, as a wave strikes an object it can be reflected, refracted, absorbed, or penetrated. In human tissue the energy must be absorbed before physiological changes occur. Generally radiation, with the longer wavelength, penetrates the deepest. The intensity of radiant energy varies inversely with the square of the distance from its source. Another factor that also holds true is that radiation is maximum when the angle of application is perpendicular to the surface.

Conversion

Conversion refers to the generation of heat from another energy form such as sound, electricity, and chemical agents. The mechanical energy produced by high-

conduction
Heating through direct contact with a hot medium.

convection
Heating indirectly through another medium such as air or liquid.

radiation
Transfer of heat through space from one object to another.

conversion
Heating through other forms of energy.

frequency sound waves will change to heat energy at tissue interfaces (ultrasound therapy).[15] The deep heat of diathermy can be produced by applying electrical currents of specific wavelengths to the skin. Chemical agents such as liniments and balms create a heat-type energy through counterirritation of sensory nerve endings.[15]

Physiological Effects of Heat

The body's response to heat depends on the type of heat energy applied, the intensity of the heat energy, the duration of application, and the unique tissue response to heat. For a physiological response to occur, heat must be absorbed into the tissue, causing an increase in molecular activity. Following the tissue's absorption of heat energy, heat is spread to adjacent tissue. To effect a therapeutic change that results in normal function of the absorbing tissue, the correct amount of heat must be applied. With too little, no change occurs; with too much, the tissue is damaged further.

There are still many unanswered questions about how heat produces therapeutic responses and what types of thermotherapy are most appropriate for a given condition. The desirable therapeutic effects of heat include (1) increasing the extensibility of collagen tissues, (2) decreasing joint stiffness, (3) reducing pain, (4) relieving muscle spasm, (5) reducing inflammation, edema, and exudates, and (6) increasing blood flow.[12]

> Heat has the capacity to increase the extensibility of collagen tissue.

Heat affects the extensibility of collagen tissue by increasing the viscous flow of collagen fibers and subsequently relaxing the tension. From a therapeutic point of view, heating contracted connective tissue permits an increase in extensibility through stretching. Muscle fibrosis, a contracted joint capsule, and scars can be effectively stretched while being heated or just after the heat is removed.[12] An increase in extensibility does not occur unless heat treatment is associated with stretching exercises.

Both heat and cold relieve pain, stimulating the free nerve endings and peripheral nerves by a ''gating'' mechanism or secretion of endorphins; after gating, cold numbs the area (see Chapter 8). Muscle spasm caused by **ischemia** can be relieved by heat, which increases blood flow to the area of injury. Heat is also believed to assist inflammation and swelling by a number of related factors such as raising temperature, increasing metabolism, reducing oxygen tension, lowering the pH level, increasing capillary permeability, and releasing histamine and bradykinin, which cause vasodilation. Histamine and bradykinin are released from some cells during acute and chronic inflammation. Heat is also produced by axon reflexes and vasomotor reflex change. Parasympathetic impulses stimulated by heat are believed to be one reason for vasodilation[12] (Table 13-1).

ischemia
Lack of blood supply to a body part.

Superficial Thermotherapy

Heat applied superficially to the skin directly increases the subcutaneous temperature and indirectly spreads to the deeper tissues. Muscle temperature increases through a reflexive effect on circulation and through conduction.[15] Comparatively, when heat is applied at the same temperature, moist heat causes a greater indirect increase in the deep-tissue temperature than does dry. Dry heat, in contrast to moist heat, can be tolerated at higher temperatures. Superficial heat application causes vasodilation that continues up to 1 hour after its removal.[4]

TABLE 13-1 Physiological Variables of Thermotherapy

Condition	Response to Therapy
Muscle spasm	Decreases
Pain perception	Decreases
Blood flow	Increases
Metabolic rate	Increases
Collagen elasticity	Decreases
Joint stiffness	Decreases
Capillary permeability	Increases
Edema	Increases

Special Considerations in the Use of Superficial Heat

In general, superficial heating of the skin is a safe therapeutic medium, assuming of course, that the heat is kept at a reasonable intensity and application is not for too long a period. The following are important contraindications and precautions to be taken when using superficial heat:

1. Never apply heat when there is a loss of sensation.
2. Never apply heat immediately after an injury.
3. Never apply heat when there is decreased arterial circulation.
4. Never apply heat directly to the eyes or the genitals.
5. Never heat the abdomen during pregnancy.

Moist Heat Therapies

Heated water is one of the most widely used therapeutic modalities in sports medicine. It is readily available for use in any sports medicine program. The greatest disadvantage of hydrotherapy is the difficulty in controlling the therapeutic effects, primarily as a result of the rapid dissipation of heat, which makes maintaining a constant tissue temperature difficult.

For the most part moist heat aids the healing process in some local conditions by causing higher superficial tissue temperatures; however, joint and muscle circulation increase little in temperature. Superficial tissue is a poor thermal conductor, and temperature rises quickly on the skin surface as compared to the underlying tissues.

Superfucial Tissue is

Superficial tissue is a poor thermal conductor.

Moist heat packs   Commercial moist heat packs, sometimes called Hydrocollator packs, heat by conduction.

Equipment   Moist heat packs contain silicate gel in a cotton pad, which is immersed in thermostatically controlled hot water at a temperature of 170° F (76.7° C). Each pad retains water and a constant heat level for 20 to 30 minutes. Six layers of toweling or commercial terry cloth are used between the packs and the skin (Figure 13-1).

Indications   The major value of the moist heat pack is that its use results in general relaxation and reduction of the pain-spasm-ischemia-hypoxia-pain cycle. There are limitations of the moist heat pack and all other superficial heating modalities: ". . . the deeper tissues, including the musculature, are usually not significantly heated because the heat transfer from the skin surface into deeper tis-

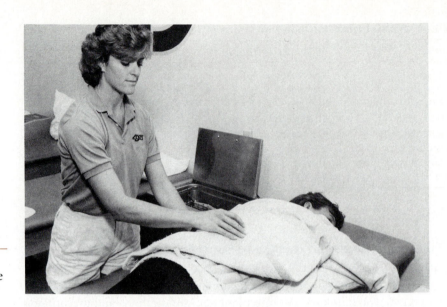

Figure 13-1

A protective layer of cloth must be applied between the skin and a moist heat pack.

sues is inhibited by the subcutaneous fat, which acts as a thermal insulator, and by the increased skin flow, which cools and carries away the heat externally applied."[12]

Application

1. Remove pack from water and allow to drain for a few seconds.
2. Cover pack with six layers of dry toweling or commercial cover.
3. Treat the area for 15 to 20 minutes.
4. As pack cools, remove layers of toweling to continue the heating.

Special considerations

1. Athlete should not be lying on packs.
2. Be sure athlete is comfortable at all times.

The whirlpool bath combines heated water and massaging action.

Whirlpool bath Whirlpool therapy is a combination of massage and water immersion. It has become one of the most popular thermotherapies used in sports medicine.

Equipment

1. There are generally three types of whirlpools: the "extremity" tank, which is used for treating legs and arms and is 15 inches wide, 28 to 32 inches long, and 18 to 25 inches deep; the "low boy" tank, which is approximately 24 inches wide, 52 to 62 inches long, and approximately 18 inches deep and used for full body immersion; and the "high boy" tank, which is designed for the hip or the leg and is 20 to 24 inches wide, 36 to 48 inches long, and 28 inches deep.[29]
2. The whirlpool is essentially a tank and a turbine motor, which regulates the movement of water and air. The amount of movement (agitation) is controlled by the amount of air that is emitted. The more air there is, the more water movement.[29]
3. The turbine motor can be moved up and down on a tubular column. It can also be rotated on the column and locked in place at a specific angle.

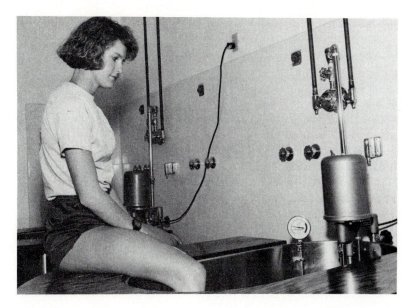

Figure 13-2

A whirlpool bath provides therapy through heat conduction and convection.

Indications

1. The whirlpool provides both conduction and convection. Conduction is achieved by the skin's contacting the higher water temperature. As the water swirls around the skin surface, convection occurs (Figure 13-2).
2. This medium assists the body part in reducing swelling, muscle spasm, and pain. Because of the buoyancy of the water, active movement of the part is also assisted.

TABLE 13-2 Whirlpool Temperatures

Descriptive Terms	Temperature
Very cold	>55° F (12.8° C)
Cold	55°-65° F (12.8°-18.3° C)
Tepid	80°-90° F (27°-33.5° C)
Neutral	92°-96° F (33.5°-35.5° C)
Warm	96°-98° F (35.5°-36.5° C)
Hot	98°-104° F (36.5°-40° C)

Application

1. Set water temperature according to Table 13-2. Some athletic trainers prefer to perform only cold water treatments, whereas others prefer to increase the temperature according to the healing phase of an acute injury. Chronic conditions normally require a higher water temperature.
2. Once the tank has been filled with water at the desired temperature, the athlete is comfortably positioned so that the part to be treated can be easily reached by the agitated water. In many cases it is best that the water jet is not placed directly on the part but to the side of the tank. This is particularly true

in the early stages of the acute injury. In cases in which the stream is concentrated directly toward the injury site, the site should be at least 8 to 10 inches from the jet.

3. The athletic trainer must use sound judgement in determining how long the whirlpool treatment should last.

4. The duration of treatment is of major concern for the athletic trainer. The maximum length of treatment time for acute injuries should not exceed 20 minutes. In the early stages of treating an acute injury, a graduated program should be implemented, increasing slowly on a daily basis—to 5 minutes, 10 minutes, 15 minutes, and finally to 20 minutes. A duration of 20 minutes is usually recommended for treatment of chronic injuries.

Special considerations

1. Great caution should be taken when an athlete undergoes full-body immersion because of the possibility of his or her experiencing lightheadedness.[2]

2. Whirlpool care is of major importance to avoid infection. The following procedures should be adhered to:
   a. Empty tank after use.
   b. Scrub inside of tank with a commercial disinfectant, rinse with clean water, and dry.
   c. Polish external surface of tank with a commercial stainless steel polish.

3. Safety is of major importance in the use of the whirlpool. All electrical outlets should have a ground fault circuit interrupter. At no time should the athlete turn the motor on or off. Ideally, the on/off switch should be a considerable distance from the machine.[29]

Paraffin bath   Paraffin is a popular method for applying heat to the distal extremities.

Paraffin bath therapy is particularly effective for injuries to the more angular body areas.

Equipment   The commercial paraffin bath is a thermostatically controlled unit, which maintains a temperature of 126° to 130° F (52° to 54° C). The paraffin mixture consists of a ratio of 2 pounds of paraffin wax to 1 gallon of mineral oil. Slats at the bottom of the container protect the athlete from burns and collect the settling dirt. Also required for treatment are plastic bags, paper towels, and towels.

Indications

1. The paraffin mixture provides 6 times the heat that is in water as a result of the lowering of paraffin's melting point by mineral oil.

2. This therapy is especially effective in treating chronic injuries occurring to the more angular areas of the body such as the hands, wrists, elbows, ankles, and feet.

Application

1. Therapy by means of the paraffin bath can be delivered in several ways. It can be applied as a pack or a soak or by painting the molten paraffin on an affected part. Packs, soaks, or a combination are the most commonly used methods in sports medicine.

2. Before therapy, the part to be treated is thoroughly cleaned and dried. Then the athlete dips the affected part into the paraffin bath and quickly pulls it out, allowing the accumulated wax to dry and form a solid covering. The process of dipping and withdrawing is repeated 6 to 12 times until the wax coating is ¼ to ½ inch (0.62 to 1.3 cm) thick.

3. If the pack technique is to be employed, the accumulated wax is allowed to solidify on the last withdrawal; then it is completely wrapped in a plastic material that in turn is wrapped with a towel. The packed body part is placed in

A   **B**

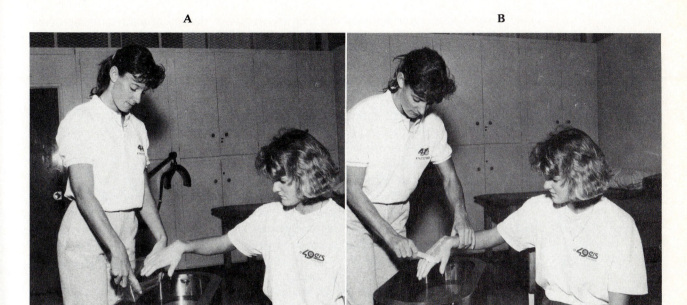

Figure 13-3

A paraffin bath is an excellent form of therapeutic heat for the distal extremities. **A,** After paraffin coating has been accomplished, the part is covered by a plastic material. **B,** When heat is no longer generated, the paraffin is scraped back into the container.

a position of rest for approximately 30 minutes or until heat is no longer generated. The covering is then removed and the paraffin is scraped back into the container.

4. If the soak technique is selected, the athlete is instructed to soak the wax-coated part in the hot wax container for 20 to 30 minutes without moving it, after which the part is removed from the container and the paraffin on it is allowed to solidify. The pack procedure can follow the soak or the paraffin coating can be scraped back into the container immediately after it hardens. Once the paraffin has been removed from the part, an oily residue remains that provides an excellent surface for massage (Figure 13-3).

Special considerations

1. Avoid paraffin bath therapy in areas where there is hemorrhaging or a decrease in normal circulation.
2. It is essential that the athlete clean the part thoroughly before therapy to avoid contaminating the mixture. In most cases, if this rule is closely adhered to, the mixture will only have to be replaced approximately every 6 months.[17]

Infrared radiation therapy Infrared radiations are invisible heat rays beyond the red end of the electromagnetic spectrum. Their wave length ranges from 7700 **Ångström units** to 1 millimeter.

Equipment When the decision is made to use infrared radiation, in most cases the infrared lamp is the modality of choice. More commonly known as a heat lamp, this device may be one of two types: luminous and nonluminous. Luminous infrared lamps are also classified as near-infrared, whereas nonluminous lamps are called far-infrared. The radiation generator commonly consists of a carbon or tungsten filament that heats rapidly.

Indications The value of infrared radiation as therapy is its ability to stimulate general circulation and provide some pain relief. Depending on the type of generator, skin penetration is approximately 2 mm. Although most of the heating is

Ångström units

Equal to 1 ten billionths of a meter (10^{-10} meters).

superficial, some temperature increase occurs to deeper structures through conduction. With this type of heating, only one body area can be treated; however, because it does not make direct body contact, no discomfort is felt.

Application

1. The lamp should be set 18 to 24 inches (17.72 to 23.62 cm) from the body part to be treated.
2. A moist towel should cover the skin to be heated.
3. Treatment duration ranges from 15 to 20 minutes.

Special considerations

1. Great care must be taken to avoid overheating and burning. Check skin often for the possibility of overheating.
2. Avoid this therapy if the athlete has circulatory or skin sensation problems.

Fluidotherapy   Fluidotherapy is becoming increasingly popular in sports medicine. It creates a therapeutic environment through dry heat and forced convection through a suspended airstream.

Equipment   Fluidotherapy units come in a variety of sizes, ranging from ones that treat distal extremities to ones that treat large body areas. The unit contains fine cellulose particles in which warm air is circulated. As the air is circulated, the cellulose particles become suspended, giving properties that are similar to liquid.[17] Fluidotherapy allows the athlete to tolerate much greater temperatures than would be possible using water or paraffin heat (Figure 13-4).

Indications   Fluidotherapy is successful, resulting in decreased pain, increased joint range of motion, and decreased spasm and swelling.

Application

1. Treatment temperature usually ranges from 100° to 113° F (37.8° to 45° C).
2. Particle agitation should be controlled for comfort.
3. Exercise can be performed while the athlete is in cabinet.
4. Athlete should be positioned for comfort.
5. Treatment duration is 15 to 20 minutes.

Contrast bath   Contrasting hot and cold water is a popular therapy in sports medicine. It is primarily used in the treatment of the extremities.

Equipment   The contrast bath technique requires the use of two containers, one to hold hot water at 105° to 110° F (40.6° to 43.3° C) and one to hold cold water at 50° to 65° F (10° to 18° C). A whirlpool can be used for the hot container, and a basin or bucket can be used for the cold.

Indications   The goal behind the use of the contrast bath is alternately to produce vasodilation from the hot water and vasoconstriction from the cold water. The hypothesis is that this procedure will increase local circulation in the treated limb and, to a lesser extent, on the contralateral limb.[29] This therapy may be advocated for treatment of swelling and chronic musculoskeletal injuries in which increased circulation is required.

Application

1. Limb is first placed in the warm water for 5 minutes and then is alternated to the cold water for 1 minute.
2. After the initial cycle, the athlete alternates 4 minutes warm water with 1 minute cold water (Figure 13-5).
3. Cycles are performed for 30 minutes.[24]

Special considerations

1. Care must be taken to keep water temperature constant.
2. Athlete should be kept as comfortable as possible throughout procedure.

Fluidotherapy consists of cellulose particles in which warm air is circulated.

Figure 13-4

Fluidotherapy units contain five cellulose particles in which warm air is circulated.

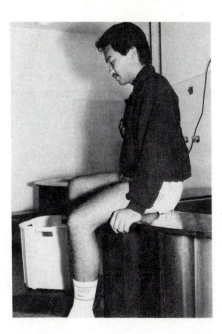

Figure 13-5

A contrast bath, which uses alternating cold water immersion and hot water immersion, is a popular therapy with many athletic trainers.

Alternative method   A second method of contrast that has become popular in sports medicine uses the concept of alternatively submerging the limb in an ice slush bath for 2 minutes and then in tepid water at 93° to 98° F (33.9° to 37.7° C) for 30 seconds. The baths are alternated for 15 minutes, beginning and ending with cold immersion.

Contrast bath procedure
Two minutes immersion in ice slush, followed by 30 seconds in tepid water (93° to 98° F [33.9° to 37.7° C]).

Penetrating Heat Therapies

Three types of penetrating heat are currently used for therapy. All heat by means of conversion. They consist of shortwave diathermy, microwave diathermy, and ultrasound therapy. Of the three, ultrasound therapy is most commonly used.

Major penetrating heat therapies
Shortwave diathermy
Microwave diathermy
Ultrasound therapy

Shortwave and Microwave Diathermies

Both shortwave and microwave diathermies heat the body's deeper tissue. Tissues with a higher water content (e.g., muscle) selectively absorb the heat delivered by shortwave and microwave diathermies.[8] The extent of muscle heating is dependent on the thickness of the subcutaneous fat layer. Both shortwave and microwave diathermies provide less heat penetration than ultrasound. In contrast to shortwave and microwave diathermies, ultrasonic vibration is not absorbed by fat and is therefore not influenced by its thickness.[8]

Shortwave diathermy   Shortwave diathermy heats deeper tissues by introducing a high-frequency electrical current. Shortwave diathermy is in essence a radio transmitter; the Federal Communications Commission (FCC) has assigned a wavelength of 7.5 m to 22 m and a frequency of 13.56 or 27.12 megacycles per second for therapeutic purposes.

There are two ways that shortwave diathermy can be used: through a condenser that uses electrostatic field heating or through electromagnetic or induction field heating.[10] In electrostatic field heating, the patient is a part of the circuit.[10] Heating is uneven because of different tissue resistance to energy flow, an application of Joule's law, which states that the greater the resistance or imped-

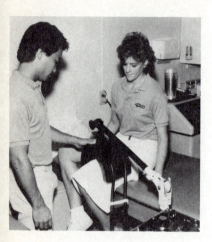

Figure 13-6

Short-wave diathermy, using the condensor applicator, can heat to a depth of 5 cm.

ance, the more heat will be developed. In electromagnetic field heating the patient is not part of the circuit but is heated by an electromagnetic field.

Equipment   In general, the shortwave diathermy unit consists of a power supply to a power amplifier and a frequency generator. It has an oscillator that produces high frequency (either 13.56 or 27.12 megacycles) and a power amplifier that converts alternating current (AC) to direct current (DC).[15] It also has a circuit that tunes in the patient automatically or manually as part of the circuitry (Figure 13-6).

The shortwave diathermy treatment applicators are either condensor or inductive types.[22] With the condensor, or field heating, the patient is a natural part of the circuit. The condensor applicator consists of electrodes that are formed by sheets of flexible or rigid metal covered by heavy insulation.

There are two types of inductive electrodes—the coil and the single drum unit. The inductive coil is comprised of a cable electrode, which ranges from 2 to 5 meters long, and is wound around the patient's part. Whereas the coil can heat generally, the single drum type is designed to treat a more specific area at a time.[10] Tissues with high water content such as blood and muscle are the most easily heated.

Indications   Shortwave diathermy is highly effective in cases of bursitis, capsulitis, osteoarthritis, deep muscle spasm, and strains. The depth of the inductive technique can be as much as 2 inches (5 cm). The condensor technique penetrates from 1 to 2 inches (2.5 to 5 cm). Tissue temperature can reach 107° F (41.7° C).

Application   If more superficial heating is desired, a condensor plate is used; when deeper therapy is desired, the induction coil should be used. A double-layered towel is placed between the applicator and the skin. When the patient is as comfortable as possible, he or she is tuned in with the oscillating circuit of the unit. In most cases the treatment times range from 20 to 30 minutes.

Special considerations
1. It is difficult to treat localized body areas.
2. Dosage is subjective.
3. There is less heating of skin and more chance for deep tissue burns.
4. Towels must be placed between the applicator and the skin. Towels absorb perspiration during treatment.
5. When there is loss of sensation, shortwave diathermy should not be used.
6. When metal such as implants is present, jewelry, a metal table, or intrauterine devices (IUDs) shortwave diathermy should not be administered.
7. Avoid use when the athlete is hemorrhaging, is pregnant, or has open wounds or contact lenses.
8. Diathermy cables or coils must not touch one another or any metal.
9. Avoid heating eyes, testicles, ovaries, bony prominences, and bone-growth areas.
10. A deep, aching sensation during treatment may indicate overheating.

Microwave diathermy   Clinical microwave diathermy generally has a wavelength of 12 cm to 33 cm and a FCC-assigned frequency of 915 to 2450 megacycles. Lower microwave frequencies (e.g., 915 megacycles per second) cause less conversion of energy into the subcutaneous tissue and, as a result, produce more uniform muscle heating.[8] Microwave diathermy heats deeper tissue by conversion. It is more easily absorbed in tissue with higher water content such as muscle and blood when compared to shortwave diathermy.[10]

TABLE 13-3 Sample Shortwave Diathermy and Microwave Diathermy Dosage

Dosage	Effect	Application
Lowest dose (I)	Just below the point of any sensation of heat (acute inflammatory process)	2 to 5 minutes daily for 2 weeks
Low dose (II)	Mild heat sensation, barely felt (subacute, resolving inflammatory process)	2 to 5 minutes daily for 2 weeks
Medium dose (III)	Moderate but pleasant heat sensation (subacute, re-solving inflammatory process)	2 to 30 minutes from 2 to 3 times weekly for 1 to 4 weeks
Heavy dose (IV)	Vigorous heating that causes a sensation that is well tolerated (chronic conditions); pain thresh-old should not be ex-ceeded	5 to 30 minutes for 2 to 3 times weekly for 1 to 4 weeks.

Equipment   In the microwave diathermy unit the alternating current (AC) is changed into direct currrent (DC). The unit consists of a magnetron oscillator, which is a tube that incorporates a complete oscillator circuit capable of generat-ing a radio frequency. A coaxial cable transports the energy from the magnetron oscillator to the applicator head. Within the delivery head is an antenna that radiates energy to the athlete. A commonly used spaced applicator is contained within a rectangular metallic reflector. It is suggested for use on flat or concave body surfaces.[10] The further away the reflector is from the skin, the greater body coverage will be with a proportional increase in wattage.

A coaxial cable consists of an insulated central conductor with tubular stranded conductors, which are separated by layers of insulation, laid over it concentrically.

Indications   Microwave diathermy is highly effective in treating conditions such as fibrositis, myositis, osteoarthritis, bursitis, calcific tendinitis, sprains, strains, and post-traumatic joint stiffness.[15] In an athlete with a subcutaneous fat thickness of 0.5 cm or less, microwave diathermy can penetrate tissue as much as 5 cm thick.[22]

Application   The athlete is made comfortable, and the microwave diathermy director is positioned at right angles to the part to be treated. The athlete's subjec-tive heat sensation is the major guide to dosage. As with shortwave diathermy, the microwave diathermy's therapeutic heat range is 104° to 113° F (40° to 45° C).[10] The length of treatment does not usually exceed 30 minutes. Lehmann,[13] Schliephakle,[25] and Kloth[10] have suggested a dosage scheme that can be used for both shortwave diathermy and microwave diathermy (Table 13-3). A towel must be placed over the skin to absorb any perspiration that accumulates.

Special considerations   The same considerations must be given to microwave diathermy as are given to shortwave diathermy. The applicator should never come in contact with the skin. At no time should heating exceed the athlete's pain threshold.[22]

Comparing microwave diathermy and shortwave diathermy   In gen-eral, shortwave and microwave diathermies penetrate the body to approximately the same depth; however, with parallel application of the shortwave diathermy, there apparently is deeper muscle heating and comparatively more skin heating with microwave diathermy.[15] Microwave diathermy heating is more localized than heating with shortwave diathermy.

Ultrasound Therapy

In recent years, ultrasound therapy has been the most commonly used deep therapeutic heat modality in sports medicine. For soft-tissue healing, ultrasound uses high-frequency sound waves beyond the audible range. Its energy is derived from the acoustical, rather than the electromagnetic, spectrum.[22] However, as with the shortwave and microwave diathermies, ultrasound therapy is a conversion type modality. Sound energy causes molecules in the tissues to vibrate, thus producing heat and mechanical energy.

> Ultrasound can be applied either to the skin or through a water medium.

The number of movements, or oscillations, in 1 second is referred to as the frequency of a sound wave. The number of oscillations occurring in 1 second is known as a hertz (Hz) unit. More commonly, 1 Hz equals 1 cycle per second, whereas 1 kHz equals 1000 cycles per second, and 1 mHz equals 1 million cycles per second.[30] The human ear cannot detect sound greater than 20,000 Hz; therefore, inaudible sound is considered ultrasound. When sound scatters and absorbs as it penetrates tissue, its energy is decreased (attenuation). Absorption of sound increases with an increase in frequency. Because it affords the best compromise between therapeutic heating and deep penetration, 1 mHz is the frequency most commonly used in ultrasound therapy.[30]

Tissue penetration depends on impedance or acoustical properties of the media that are proportional to tissue density.[15] Sound reflection occurs when adjacent tissues have different impedance. The greater the impedance, the greater is the reflection, and more heat is produced. The greatest heat is developed between bone and the adjacent soft-tissue interface.

Equipment   The main piece of equipment for delivering therapeutic ultrasound is a high-frequency generator, which provides an electrical current through a coaxial cable to a transducer contained within an applicator. In the applicator or transducer are crystals such as quartz that possess *piezoelectricity*. These crystals are in disks 2 to 3 mm thick and 1 to 3 cm in diameter.[30] The **piezoelectrical effect** causes expansion and contraction of the crystals, which produce oscillation voltage at the same frequency as the sound wave.[30]

> **piezoelectrical effect**
> Electrical current produced by applying pressure to certain crystals such as quartz.

The intensity of the ultrasound beam is determined by the amount of energy delivered to the sound head (applicator). It is expressed in the number of watts per square centimeter (watts/cm^2). As a therapeutic modality used in sports medicine, it ranges from 0.5 to 3.0 watts/cm^2.

Indications   In general, three types of effects occur from the application of ultrasound: thermal, mechanical, and chemical.[15]

> Ultrasound produces effects that are thermal, mechanical, and chemical.

Thermal effect   In terms of ultrasound properties, skin, fat, and muscle are similar. The greatest differences lie at the muscle-bone interface where temperature can increase to as high as 106.7° F (41.5° C). Joint capsules have been heated as high as 117.5° F (47.5° C) with ultrasound. Nerve tissue is twice as sensitive to ultrasound as muscle.[15]

Heat developed by ultrasound increases collagen tissue extensibility, alters blood flow, changes nerve conduction velocity, elevates pain threshold, raises enzymatic activity, and changes muscle contractibility.[17,30]

TABLE 13-4 Effects of Ultrasound Therapy

Type of Effect	Action in Area	Physiological Effect
Thermal	Volume heating	1.8° to 3.6° F (1° to 2° C)
	Structural heating	Temperature penetrates to depth of approximately 5 cm
Mechanical	Dispersion	"Micromassage" separates collagen
	Agitation	fibers as a result of effect on cement substance
Capillary changes	Alteration in capillary permeability	Hyperemia
		Absorption of exudate
Chemical	Accelerated metabolism	Increased ATP activity
		Increased cell membrane permeability

Mechanical effect   The mechanical effect results from mechanical vibration. At clinical intensities, dispersion and agitation of molecules, more commonly called "micromassage," occurs. This action acts on the cementum that holds collagen fibers together, causing a fiber separation.

Chemical effect   The clinical use of ultrasound accelerates enzyme activity, increases capillary permeability, and increases adenosine triphosphate (ATP) activity in skeletal muscle. ATP is an enzyme found in all cells, and, when it is split, energy is produced. Of particular interest is that the energy of muscle is stored in this compound.

Because of ultrasound's depth of treatment and its therapeutic effect on soft tissue, it especially increases the potential extensibility of connective tissue. Specifically, ultrasound can be the modality of choice for treating joint contractures, scar tissue, tendinitis, bursitis, skeletal muscle spasm, and pain.[17,30]

Conditions that develop an undesirable calcification are often treated with ultrasound. They often include calcific bursitis, calcific tendinitis, myositis ossificans, and exostosis. To date, it is not clear whether ultrasound, in fact, helps the resorption of calcium or only relieves the inflammation associated with the calcium deposit.[30] Skin conditions such as plantar warts have been successfully treated at dosages of 0.6 watts/cm^2 for 7 to 15 minutes, repeated for 2 to 15 sessions[17,30] (Table 13-4).

Application   As mentioned previously, there are a number of approaches in the use of ultrasound therapy. Currently, the moving ultrasound applicator and phonophoresis constitute one of the most commonly used methods in sports medicine.

Direct skin application   Because acoustic energy cannot travel through air and is reflected by the skin, there must be a coupling medium applied to the skin.[30] Coupling mediums can include a variety of materials, some of which are mineral oil or water-soluble creams or gels. The purpose of a coupler is to provide an airtight contact with the skin and a slick, friction-proof surface to glide over. When a water-soluble material is used, the skin should first be washed and dried to prevent air bubbles from hampering the flow of mechanical energy into the skin (Figure 13-7).

Stroking methods   Movement of the transducer can be in a circular pattern or

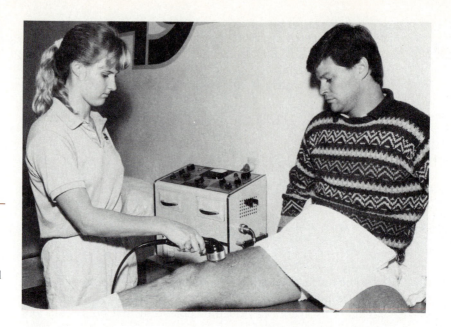

Figure 13-7

Ultrasound therapy, when applied directly to the skin, must be performed over a coupling medium because acoustic energy cannot travel through the air and skin reflection.

a stroking pattern. In the circular pattern the transducer is applied in small overlapping circles. In the stroking pattern the transducer is moved back and forth, overlapping the preceding stroke by half. Both techniques are performed slowly and deliberately. The field covered should not exceed 3 to 4 inches (7.5 to 10 cm). The pattern to use is determined mainly by the skin area to be treated. For example, the circular pattern is best for highly localized areas such as the shoulder, whereas in larger, more diffuse injury areas, the stroking pattern is best used. When a highly irregular surface area is to be given therapy, the underwater method should be used.

Underwater application   Underwater ultrasound is suggested for such irregular body parts as the wrist, hand, elbow, knee, ankle, and foot. The part is fully submerged in water; then the ultrasound head is submerged and positioned approximately 1 inch (2.5 cm) from the body part to be treated. The water medium provides an airtight coupling, allowing sound waves to travel at a constant velocity. To ensure uninterrupted therapy, air bubbles that form on the skin must be continually wiped away. The sound head is moved slowly in a circular or longitudinal pattern.

Dosage and treatment time   Dosage of ultrasound varies according to the depth of the tissue treated and the state of injury, such as subacute or chronic. Basically, 0.1 to 0.8 watts/cm^2 is regarded as low intensity, 0.8 to 1.5 watts/cm^2 is medium intensity, and 1.5 to 3 watts/cm^2 is high intensity. The duration of treatment time ranges from 3 to 8 minutes. Treatment ranges from daily to three times per week.

SPECIAL CONSIDERATIONS   Although ultrasound is a relatively safe modality, certain precautions must be taken, and in some situations ultrasound should never be used. Great care must be taken when treating anesthetized areas because the sensation of pain is one of the best indicators of overdosage. Great precautions must be used in areas that have reduced circulation. In general, ultrasound must not be applied to highly fluid areas of the body such as the eyes, ears, testes, brain, spinal cord, or heart. Reproductive organs and women who are pregnant also must be avoided. Acute injuries should not be treated with ultrasound. Epiphyseal areas in children should have only minimum ultrasound exposure.[30]

Ultrasound plus electrical stimulation   Some ultrasound units can combine ultrasound therapy with electrical stimulation. In this case, the transducer becomes the active electrode (Figure 13-8). These units are used on conditions requiring both increased circulation and decreased muscle spasm.[22]

PHONOPHORESIS   Phonophoresis is a method of driving molecules through the skin by ion transfer or by the mechanical vibration of the ultrasound.[24] Like iontophoresis, it is designed to move an entire molecule of medication into injured

Phonophoresis is a method of driving molecules through the skin through ultrasound.

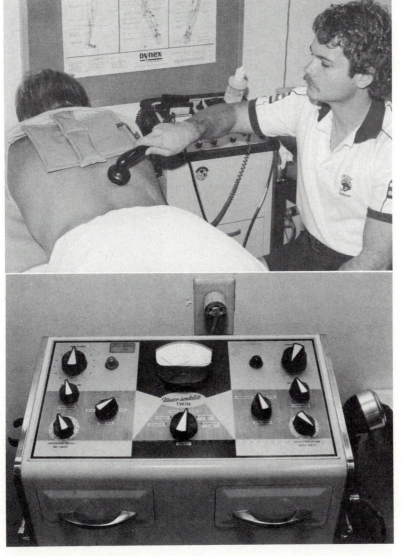

Figure 13-8

Some ultrasound units can combine ultrasound therapy and electrical stimulation. In this case the transducer becomes the active electrode.

tissues. Some sports medicine personnel prefer this to ionophoresis, indicating that it is less hazardous to the skin and that there is greater penetration.[23] As with ionophoresis, phonophoresis is predominately used to introduce a hydrocortisone and an anesthetic into the tissues. This method has been successful in treating painful trigger points, tendinitis, and bursitis.[23]

Many clinicians prefer to use a 10% hydrocortisone ointment.[15] Sometimes lidocaine is added to the cortisone to provide a local anesthetic effect. This medicine is massaged into the skin over an area of tendinitis, bursitis, or other chronic soft-tissue condition. The coupling gel is then spread over the medication, and the ultrasound is applied.

CRYOTHERAPY

The major therapeutic value of cold is its ability to produce anesthesia, allowing pain-free exercise.

Chapter 9, *Emergency Care*, states that application of cold for the first aid of trauma to the musculoskeletal system is a well-accepted practice in sports medicine. When applied intermittently for 20 minutes every 1½ waking hours, along with compression, elevation, and rest, it reduces many of the adverse conditions related to the inflammatory or reactive phase of an acute injury. Depending on the severity of the injury, ice, compression, elevation, and rest are performed from 1 to 72 hours.

Physical Principles

Cold as a therapeutic agent is within the broad heading of the electromagnetic spectrum and, more specifically, infrared radiation. When a cold object is applied to a warmer object, heat is abstracted. In terms of cryotherapy, the most common method for cold transfer to tissue is through conduction. The extent to which tissue is cooled depends on the cold medium that is being applied, the length of cold exposure, and the conductivity of the area being cooled.[18] In most cases the longer the cold exposure is, the deeper the cooling. At a temperature of 38.3° F (3.5° C), muscle temperatures can be reduced as deep as 4 cm. Cooling is dependent on the type of tissue. For example, tissue with a high water content, such as muscle, is an excellent cold conductor, whereas fat is very poor. Because of fat's low cold conductivity, it acts as the body's insulator.[18] Tissue that has previously been cooled takes longer to return to a normal temperature than that which has been heated.

The two most common means used to deliver cold as therapy to the body is through ice or cold packs or immersion in cool or cold water. The most effective type of packs contains wet ice, as compared to ice in a plastic container or commercial Crogen pack.[1] Wet ice is a more effective coolant because of the extent of internal energy that is needed to melt the ice.[18]

Physiological Effects of Cold

When cold is applied to skin for 15 minutes or less at a temperature of 50° F (10° C) or less, vasoconstriction of the arterioles and venules in the area occurs. This vasoconstriction is caused, in part, by the reflex action of the smooth muscles, which can result from stimulation of the sympathetic nervous system and adrenal medulla, causing a secretion of norepinephrine and epinephrine.[22] Also causing vasoconstriction is cooled blood circulating to the anterior hypothalamus. If cold is continuously applied for 15 to 30 minutes, an intermittent period of vasodilation occurs for 4 to 6 minutes. This period is known as the "hunting response,"

TABLE 13-5 Skin Response to Cold

Stage	Response	Estimated Time after Initiation
1	Cold sensation	0 to 3 minutes
2	Mild burning, aching	2 to 7 minutes
3	Relative cutaneous anesthesia	5 to 12 minutes

a reaction against tissue damage from too much cold exposure.[18] When the hunting response occurs, the tissue temperature does not return to preapplication levels. This response has primarily been observed in the appendages. Cold during this period also causes an increase in blood viscosity and a decrease in vasodilator metabolites.[22]

Cooling tissues can directly decrease a muscle spasm by slowing metabolism in the area, thus decreasing the waste products, which act as a muscle irritant and thus cause spasm, that may have accumulated in the area. A muscle spasm can also be decreased when cold is applied to decrease the muscle spindle's threshold and its myotactic reflex response and when cold increases the muscle's viscosity, slowing its ability to contract.[8]

Since the local application of cold can decrease an acute muscle spasm, the muscle becomes more amenable to stretch. A gentle stretch of a spastic muscle after an acute injury may be indicated; however, the stretching of long-standing contractures is contraindicated. Cold tends to cause collagen stiffness.[11]

Cold decreases free nerve-ending excitability, as well as the excitability of peripheral nerves. Analgesia is caused by raising the nerve's threshold.[8,26] Nerve fiber response to cold depends mainly on the presence of myelination and the diameter of the fiber. For example, most sensitive to cold are the small light-touch, cold, and gamma efferent myelinated fibers to the muscle spindles.[8] The next most sensitive to cold are the large myelinated fibers of the proprioceptors and alpha motor nerves.[8] The least sensitive to cold are the unmyelinated pain fibers and postganglionic sympathetic nerves.[8] Table 13-5 indicates the usual outward sequential response to cold application.

Cold, in general, is more penetrating than heat. Once a muscle has been cooled through the subcutaneous fat layer, cold's effects last longer than heat because fat acts as an insulator against rewarming.[11] The major problem is to penetrate the fat layer initially so that muscle cooling occurs. In individuals with less than ½ inch (1.25 cm) of subcutaneous fat, significant muscle cooling can occur after 10 minutes of cold application. In persons with more than ⅘ inch (2 cm) of subcutaneous fat, muscle temperatures barely drop after 10 minutes[11] (Table 13-6).

Another unique quality of cooling is its ability to decrease muscle fatigue and increase and maintain muscular contraction. This ability is attributed to decreasing the local metabolic rate and the tissue temperature.[11]

Special considerations Although adverse reactions to therapeutic cold application are uncommon, they do happen and are described as follows:
1. Cooling for an hour at 30.2° to 15.8° F (−1° to −9° C) produces redness and edema that lasts for 20 hours after exposure.[16] Frostbite has been known to occur in subfreezing temperatures of 26.6° to 24.8° F (−3° to −4° C).

The extent of cooling depends on the thickness of the subcutaneous fat layer.

TABLE 13-6 Physiological Variables of Cryotherapy

Variable	Effect
Muscle spasm	Decreases
Pain perception	Decreases
Blood flow	Decreases up to 10 minutes
Metabolic rate	Decreases
Collagen inelasticity	Increases
Joint stiffness	Increases
Capillary permeability	Increases
Edema	Controversial

2. Immersion at 41° F (5° C) increases limb fluid volume by 15%.
3. Exposure for 90 minutes at 57.2° to 60.8° F (14° to 16° C) can delay resolution of swelling up to 1 week.
4. Some individuals are allergic to cold, reacting with hives and joint pain and swelling.
5. **Raynaud's phenomenon** is a condition that causes vasospasm of digital arteries lasting for minutes to hours, which could lead to tissue death. The early signs of Raynaud's phenomenon are attacks of intermittent skin blanching or cyanosis of the fingers or toes, skin pallor followed by redness, and finally a return to normal color. Pain is uncommon, but numbness, tingling, or burning may occur during and shortly after an attack.
6. Paroxysmal cold hemoglobinuria is a rare disease that occurs minutes after cold exposure and may lead to renal dysfunction, secondary hypertension, and coma. Early symptoms are severe pain in the back and legs, headache, vomiting, diarrhea, and dark brown urine.
7. Although it is relatively uncommon, application of ice can cause nerve palsy. Nerve palsy occurs when cold is applied to a part that has motor nerves close to the skin surface, such as the peroneal nerve at the fibular head. Usually the condition resolves spontaneously with no significant problem. As a general rule, ice should not be applied longer than 20 to 30 minutes at any one time.

Raynaud's phenomenon
Condition in which cold exposure causes vasospasm of digital arteries.

Cryotherapeutic Methods

A number of methods of cold applications can be used therapeutically. The ones most commonly used in sports medicine are ice massage, cold or ice water immersion, ice packs, and vapocoolant sprays.

Ice Massage

Ice massage is a cryotherapeutic method that is performed on a small body area. It can be applied by the athletic trainer and the athlete alike.

Equipment   Water is frozen in a Styrofoam cup, which forms a cylinder of ice. When using this method, the Styrofoam is removed approximately an inch from the top of the cup. The remaining Styrofoam provides a handle to grasp while massaging. Another method is to fill a paper cup with water, with a tongue depressor added to act as a handle when the water is frozen. A towel should be present to absorb the water that is collected.

Indications   Ice massage is commonly used over a small muscle area such as the tendons, the belly of the muscle, the bursa, or over myofascial trigger points.

Application   Grasping the ice cylinder, the athletic trainer rubs the ice over the athlete's skin in overlapping circles, ranging in a 10 to 15 cm area for a period of 5 to 10 minutes. The athlete should experience the sensations of cold, burning, aching, and numbness. When analgesia has been reached, the athlete can engage in stretching and/or exercise (Figure 13-9).

Special considerations   In an athlete with normal circulation, tissue damage seldom occurs from cold application. The temperature of the tissue seldom goes below 59° F (15° C). The comfort of the athlete must be considered at all times.

Cold or Ice Water Immersion

Cold water immersion is a relatively simple means for treating a distal body part.

Equipment   Depending on the body part to be immersed, a variety of containers or basins can be used. In some cases, a small whirlpool can be used. Water and crushed ice are mixed together to reach a temperature of 50° F (10° C) to 60° F (15° C). Towels must be available for drying.

Indications   Where circumferential cooling of a body part is desired, cold or ice water immersion is preferred.

Application   The athlete immerses the body part into the water and proceeds through the four stages of cold response. This process may take 10 to 15 minutes. When the pain cycle has been interrupted, the part is removed from the water, and normal movement patterns are conducted. When pain returns, the part is reimmersed. This procedure may be repeated three times.

Special considerations   Because cold makes collagen tissue brittle, caution should be taken in allowing the athlete to return to full sports performance after receiving cold treatment. Over cooling can lead to frost bite. Any allergic response to cold should also be noted.

Ice Packs

The use of ice packs is another way to apply cryotherapy.

Equipment   There are a number of types of ice packs. As discussed previously, wet ice packs provide the best cooling properties. Flaked or crushed ice can be encased in a wet towel and placed on the part to be treated. Although not as efficient but less messy, a pack made by placing crushed or chipped ice in a self-sealing plastic bag may be used. If isopropyl alcohol is added at a 2:1 ratio, the packs can be put into a freezer and not completely frozen. When they are removed from the freezer, the packs easily fit the contour of the part. These packs are useful for approximately 15 or 20 minutes.[18] When the plastic packs are used, a wet towel should be placed between the skin and the pack. Besides toweling, an elastic wrap should be available and should be used to hold the pack firmly in place.

Indications   As with the other cryotherapeutic modalities, the four stages of cold are experienced, followed by normal movement patterns (Figure 13-10).

Special considerations   As with other modalities, excessive cold exposure must be avoided. With any indication of allergy to cold or of abnormal pain, the therapy should be aborted.

Cold therapy can begin 1 to 3 days after injury.

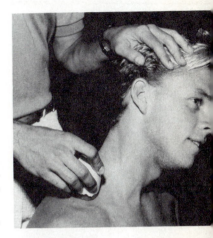

Figure 13-9

Ice massage can lead to an analgesia that can be followed by gentle muscle stretching.

Figure 13-10

Ice packs can be another way to apply cryotherapy.

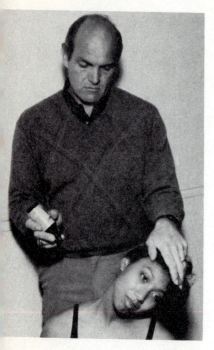

Figure 13-11

A vapocoolant spray such as Fluori-Methane can assist in reducing muscle spasm.

Vapocoolant Sprays

Increasingly, vapocoolant sprays are being used for treatment of musculoskeletal conditions attributed to sports activity.

Equipment   Currently the vapocoolant of choice is Fluori-Methane, a non-flammable, nontoxic substance. Under pressure in a bottle, it gives off a fine spray when inverted and an emitter is pressed.

Indications   The major value of a vapocoolant spray is its ability to reduce muscle spasm and increase range of motion. It is also a major treatment for myofascial pain and trigger points.

Application   When spraying vapocoolant spray to increase the athlete's range of motion in an area in which there is no trigger point, the following is performed:

1. The vapocoolant is held at a 30-degree angle, 12 to 18 inches (30 to 47 cm) from the skin.
2. The entire length of the muscle is sprayed from its proximal attachment to its distal attachment.
3. The skin is covered at a rate of approximately 10 cm per second and the spray is applied two or three times as a gradual stretch is applied.

When dealing with a possible trigger point, the first procedure is to determine its presence, then to alleviate it.

One method of determining an active trigger point is to reproduce the injured athlete's major pain complaint by pressing firmly on the site for 5 to 10 seconds. Another assessment technique is to elicit a "jump response" by placing the athlete's muscle under moderate tension, applying firm pressure, and briskly pulling a finger across the tight band of muscle. This procedure causes the tight band of muscle to contract and the athlete to wince or cry out.[19] The spray and stretch method[21] for treating trigger points and myofascial pain has become a major approach (Figure 13-11) and is performed as follows:

1. Position the athlete in a relaxed but well-supported position. The muscle that contains the trigger point is stretched (an exception to this is the sternocleidomastoid muscle).
2. Alert the athlete that the spray will feel cool.
3. Hold the Fluori-Methane bottle approximately 12 inches (30 cm) away from the skin to be sprayed.
4. Direct the spray at an acute angle in one direction toward the reference zone of pain.
5. Direct the spray to the full length of the muscle, including the reference zone of pain.
6. Begin firm stretching that is within the athlete's pain tolerance.
7. Continue spraying in parallel sweeps that are approximately ¼ inch (0.6 cm) apart at a speed of approximately 4 inches (10 cm) every second.
8. Cover the skin area one or two times.
9. Continue passive stretching while spraying (do not force the stretch; allow time for the muscle to "let go").
10. After the first session of spraying and stretching, warm the muscle with a hot pack or by vigorous massage.
11. A second session may be necessary after step 10.
12. When a stretch has been completed, have the athlete actively but gently move the part in a full range of motion.

13. Do not overload a muscle with strenuous exercise immediately after a stretch.
14. After an initial spraying and stretching session, instruct the athlete about stretch exercises that should be performed at home on a daily basis.

ELECTROTHERAPY

In recent years, the use of electrotherapy has significantly increased in sports medicine.

Physical Principles

In general, electricity is a form of energy that displays magnetic, chemical, mechanical, and thermal effects on tissue. It implies a flow of electrons between two points. Electrons are particles of matter that have a negative electrical charge and revolve around the core or nucleus of an atom. A proton located in the atom's nucleus represents a positive charge. The atom with more electrons than protons

Figure 13-12

The use of electrotherapy has significantly increased in sports medicine in recent years.

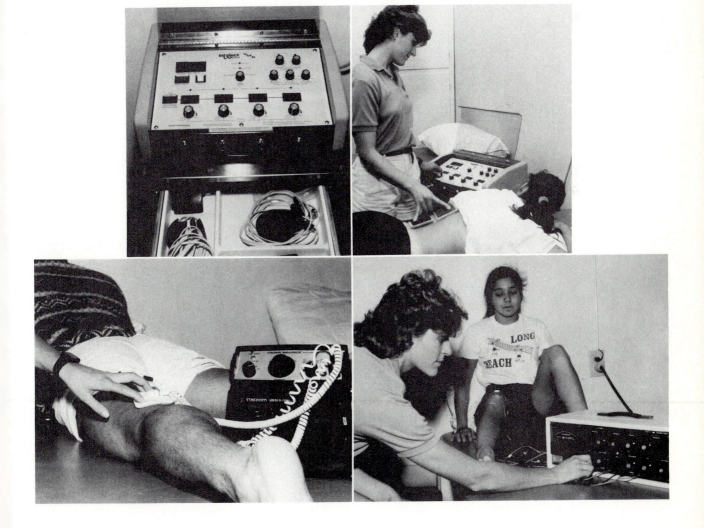

is negatively charged and, conversely, the atom with more protons is positively charged.

An *electrical current* refers to a string of loose electrons that pass along a conductor such as a nerve or wire. The intensity, or magnitude, of the current is measured in *amperes* (amp); 1 amp equals the rate of flow of 1 *coulomb* per second. A coulomb is a unit of electrical charge and is defined as the quantity of an electrical charge that can be transferred by 1 amp in 1 second.

Resistance to the passing of an electrical current along a conductor is measured in *ohms,* and the force that moves the current along is called *voltage* (V). One volt is the amount of electrical force required to send a current of 1 amp through a resistance of 1 ohm. In terms of electrotherapy, currents of 0 to 150 V are considered low-voltage currents, whereas those currents above 150 V are considered high voltage. The intensity of a current varies directly with the voltage and inversely with the resistance. Electrical power is measured in watts.

A frequency of an electrical current is expressed in cycles per second. In electrotherapy frequencies of less than 1000 cycles per second are low-frequency currents and 100,000 cycles per second are considered as high-frequency currents.

The human body has electrical conductivity because of positive and negative ions contained in tissue fluids. Tissue conductivity varies according to the amount of fluid it contains. For example, muscle tissue provides excellent conduction, whereas denser tissues such as tendons and fascia are poor conductors. An exception to this fact is that fat is a poor electrical conductor and acts as an insulator against electrical conduction (Figure 13-12).

Waveforms

Instruments used for electrotherapy produce varying waveforms, depending on the capabilities of the generator. Waveform refers to the shape, direction, amplitude, and duration of a particular electrical current (Figure 13-13).[20,22]

Direct current   Direct current (DC), or galvanic current, flows in one direction, with electrons moving from a negative to a positive pole. The first sensation the body experiences from direct-current is one of tingling, followed by a feeling of warmth.[15] Only if the direct current is interrupted will muscles contract.

Direct current can be of low or high frequency. The uninterrupted direct current is not usually used to produce muscular contraction; it is used to cause chemical reactions by breaking up nerve molecules into positively and negatively charged atoms and ions. The positively charged particles are pulled toward the negative pole and, conversely, the negatively charged particles are drawn toward the positive pole. Because of the reaction, direct current therapy increases blood flow and decreases swelling, spasm, and pain. Interrupted direct current and other currents that cause a muscle contraction can be used for reeducation after injury. Body parts that have been immobilized for a period of time tend to lose their memory for movement. Electrical muscle stimulation can assist in regaining that memory.

Alternating current   Alternating current (AC) refers to the flow of electrons that reverses direction once during each cycle. At a predetermined rate, two terminals in the generator change polarity from positive to negative and then back from negative and to positive.[15] Each cycle is composed of two half waves. There are three different AC waves: sine, square, and pulse (Figure 13-14).[15]

The current that flows without changing its waveform characteristics is known

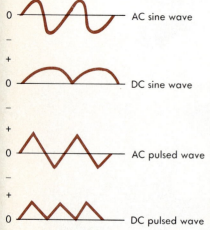

Figure 13-13

The term "wave forms" refers to the shape, direction, amplitude, and duration of a particular electrical current.

as a continuous current.[15] A current that is changed is a modulated current.[9] Current modulation occurs in three ways: as continuous, interrupted, or surged pulse. The surge causes a gradual rise to a peak of intensity and an immediate slow decline of intensity; in addition, a current can be modified, which is much like surge with the exception that peak intensity is maintained before a slow decrease occurs.[15] A pulse duration, or pulse width, of 120 to 300 msec in a bipolar waveform (positive then negative) produces the most comfortable muscle contraction.[15]

Low-Voltage Versus High-Voltage Currents

Voltage generators producing 150 volts (V) or less are categorized as producers of low-voltage current. Although they can cause muscle contractions, these generators are most effective in producing chemical and thermal reactions.[22]

High-voltage therapeutic units, which produce waveforms with amplitudes of more than 150 V, are highly effective in causing muscle contractions.[22] The high amplitude and short pulse widths allow nonirritating stimulation of both nerves and muscles.

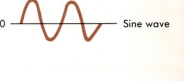

Figure 13-14

Three different AC waves— sine, square, and pulsed.

Pulsed Direct Current Muscle Stimulation

The use of pulsed direct current high-voltage stimulation is becoming increasingly popular in sports medicine. New devices are able to stimulate muscles and nerves directly.[15]

Pulse direct current high-voltage units stimulate muscles and nerves directly.

Indications   In general, electrical stimulation as therapy for athletes is used to decrease muscle atrophy, decrease swelling, reeducate movement, decrease pain, introduce anti-inflammatory and analgesic drugs through iontophoresis, and localized trigger points.[15]

Application   In electrotherapy, moist electrode pads are fixed directly to the skin. The smaller *active pad,* which brings the current to the body, can range from very small to 4 inches (10 cm) square; the larger *dispersal pad,* from which electrons leave the body, should be as large as possible. Because the current flows between the two pads, the distance between the pads depends on the type of muscle contraction desired. The closer the pads are, the shallower and more isolated the contraction; the farther apart the pads are, the deeper and more generalized the contraction. The physiological effects can occur anywhere between the two pads, but they usually occur at the active electrode, since current density is greater at this point.

Direct current is mainly used for its ability to reduce pain, reduce edema, stimulate denervated muscle, and perform iontophoresis. Interrupted, or pulsed, high-voltage direct current can stimulate muscle contraction as well as alternating current.[28] This pulsed high-voltage electrical stimulation is becoming the treatment of choice for acute pain, swelling, postoperative pain, and muscle reeducation.

In some cases a tetanizing current has relieved a muscle spasm. A frequency between 30 and 40 pulses/sec will produce tetanus. The tetanizing period should be relieved by a time of relaxation. A ratio of 1 to 3 is desirable, with 10 seconds of contraction followed by 30 seconds of relaxation. The treatment time should range from 15 to 30 minutes, two or three times a day.

Active exercising can be used while the muscles are being electrically stimulated. Electrical stimulation with exercise seems to increase muscle fiber innervation. Other therapies that can be effectively combined with electrical stimulation are ice pack treatments or cold water immersion. Care should be taken not to stimulate muscles immediately after an acute injury or to open wounds or incision sites.

Iontophoresis

Iontophoresis is the process whereby chemical ions are transported through the intact skin by an electrical current. Using a direct current low-voltage uninterrupted generator with positive and negative electrodes, the medication is transported into the body through the positive electrode.[7] The polarity of the electrode used in iontophoresis depends on the polarity of the ion introduced.[7] Medications of choice for treating musculoskeletal inflammatory conditions have commonly been pain relievers such as lidocaine (Xylocaine) and anti-inflammatory agents such as hydrocortisone or dexamethasone. Commonly, this treatment approach is for tendinitis, bursitis, myositis, and arthritis.

The anti-inflammatory medication and if desired, an analgesic are applied beneath the positive pole.

Transcutaneous Electrical Nerve Stimulation (TENS)

Transcutaneous electrical nerve stimulation (TENS) can stimulate the gating mechanism and facilitate the release of endogenous opiates.

In recent years, transcutaneous electrical nerve stimulation (TENS) has become popular for treating both acute and chronic pain. This approach stems from Melzack and Wall's gate-control theory of pain, as discussed in Chapter 8. It is theorized that through TENS there is inhibition of spinal cord neurons, direct peripheral blockage of nerve fibers, and activation of endogenous opiates such as endorphins. TENS units are designed to stimulate the afferent sensory nerve fibers, which respond best to a medium frequency of 2 to 150 pulses per second and with a pulse width of 40 to 500 m sec.[15] The TENS unit is commonly set just below the cite where a muscle contraction is produced.

The electrodes of TENS are placed at trigger points or dermatome sites adjacent to the injury or surgical incision. Because TENS does not cause muscle contraction, it can be used immediately after injury. TENS does not have to be worn continuously; ½ to 1 hour application will often relieve pain hours after it is removed. Another major value of TENS is that it allows pain-free exercise.

Special considerations   As with any modality, electrotherapy, in general, must be conducted with great caution. Protocols for a given stimulation unit and physical condition must be carefully adhered to. When using uninterrupted direct current, tissue damage can occur from excessive current. No stimulator should be placed over the carotid sinus, the abdomen of a pregnant woman, or where there is a pacemaker. When extremities are treated, the indifferent or dispersive electrodes should be placed on the same extremity and not the thorax to avoid having the current go through the heart.[20]

MANUAL AND MECHANICAL THERAPY

Massage and manipulation are types of manual therapy.

Mechanical or manual therapies include the direct use of the athletic trainer's hands (e.g., in massage and manipulation). A second category includes the machine-assisted therapies, such as traction and intermittent compression.[6]

Massage

Massage is defined as the systematic manipulation of the soft tissues of the body. The movements of gliding, compressing, stretching, percussing, and vibrating are regulated to produce specific responses in the athlete.[27]

Primarily, massage is separated into five basic categories: effleurage, pétrissage, friction, tapotement, and vibration. **Effleurage** is a technique in which the body or body part is stroked, with the heels and palms of the hands gliding over the body. **Pétrissage** is a technique in which soft tissue, held between the thumb and forefinger, is alternately rolled, lifted, and twisted to loosen tissue and stimulate fluid drainage. **Friction** movements are used successfully on joints and areas in which there is little soft tissue and on soft tissue that is indurated or in spasm. The fingers and thumbs move in circular patterns, stretching the underlying tissue, and thus increasing circulation to the part. **Tapotement** consists of cupping, hacking, and pincing movements. **Vibration** is the rapid shaking of tissue by hand or using a machine vibrator.

effleurage
Stroking.

pétrissage
Kneading.

friction
Heat producing.

tapotement
Percussion.

vibration
Rapid shaking.

Therapeutic Effects of Massage

Historically, wherever sports have been seriously undertaken, massage has been used in some form. Even today it is widely used throughout the world. Manipulation of soft tissue by massage is a useful adjunct to other modalities. Sports massage causes mechanical, physiological, and psychological responses, which are discussed below.

Mechanical responses   Mechanical responses to massage occur as a direct result of the graded pressures and movements of the hand on the body. Such actions encourage venous and lymphatic drainage and mildly stretch superficial and scar tissue. Connective tissue can be effectively stretched by friction massage, which helps to prevent rigidity in scar formation. When enforced inactivity is imposed on the athlete as the aftermath of an injury or when edema surrounds a joint, the stagnation of circulation may be prevented by using certain massage techniques.

Physiological responses   Massage can increase circulation and, as a result, increase metabolism to the musculature and aid in the removal of metabolites such as lactic acid.[27] It also helps overcome venostasis and edema by increasing circulation at and around the injury site, assisting in the normal venous blood return to the heart.

The *reflex effects* of massage are processes that, in response to nerve impulses initiated through rubbing the body, are transmitted to one organ by afferent nerve fibers and then respond back to another organ by efferent fibers. Reflex responses elicit a variety of organ reactions such as body relaxation, stimulation, and increased circulation.

Possible physiological responses of massage
Reflex effects
Relaxation
Stimulation
Increased circulation

Relaxation can be induced by slow, superficial stroking of the skin. It is a type of massage that is beneficial for tense, anxious athletes who may require gentle treatment.

Stimulation is attained by quick, brisk action that causes a contraction of superficial tissue. The benefits derived by the athlete are predominately psychological. He or she feels invigorated after intense manipulation of the tissue. In the early days of American sports, stimulation massage was given as a warm-up procedure, but it has gradually lost popularity because of the time involved and the recognition that it is relatively ineffectual physiologically.

Increased circulation is accomplished by mechanical and reflex stimuli. Together they cause the capillaries to dilate and be drained of fluid as a result of firm outside pressure, thus stimulating cell metabolism, eliminating toxins, and increasing lymphatic and venous circulation. In this way the healing process is aided.

Psychological responses   The tactile system is one of the most sensitive systems in the human organism. From earliest infancy humans respond psychologically to being touched. Because massage is the act of laying on of hands, it can be an important means for creating a bond of confidence between the athletic trainer and the athlete.

Sports Massage

Massage in sports is usually confined to a specific area and is seldom given to the full body. The time required for giving an adequate and complete body massage is excessive in athletics. It is not usually feasible to devote this much time to one athlete; 5 minutes is usually all that is required for massaging a given area.

Massage lubricants   To enable the hands to slide easily over the body, a friction-proofing medium must be used. Rubbing the dry body can cause gross skin irritation by tearing and breaking off the hair. Many mediums (e.g., fine powders, oil liniments, or almost any substance having a petroleum base) can be used to advantage as lubricants.

Positioning of the athlete   Proper positioning for massage is of great importance. The injured part must be made easily accessible; the athlete must be comfortable, and the part to be massaged must be relaxed.

Confidence   Lack of confidence in the person doing the massage is easily transmitted through inexperienced hands. Every effort should be made to think out the procedure to be used and to present a confident appearance to the athlete.

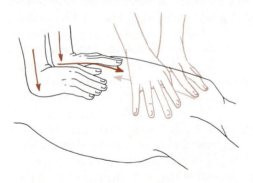

Figure 13-15

Effleurage.

Massage Procedures

Effleurage   Effleurage, or stroking (Figure 13-15), is divided into light and deep methods. Light stroking is designed primarily to be sedative. It is also used in the early stages of injury treatment. Deep stroking is a therapeutic compression of soft tissue, which encourages venous and lymphatic drainage. A different application of effleurage may be used for a specific body part.

Light and deep stroking of the back   A pillow or pad is placed under the athlete's pelvis to relax the low back region. When stroking the back, the heel of the hand is pushed upward on the back of the athlete to the heavy trapezius muscle, where the fingers encircle and lift the soft tissue (trapezial milking), and then trail down to where the stroke commenced. The stroke starts in the lower-lumbar area, as close as possible to the vertebral column. The hands stroke upward, covering the entire length of the spine and over the tops of the shoulders.

When the length of the spine has been covered, the fingers move out from the center approximately ½ inch (1.3 cm) and trail down the back to start the succeeding stroke. Progressively the hands move out to the periphery of the back until the whole area has been rubbed; then they proceed inward toward the center. To facilitate relaxation, as well as vascular drainage, the hands should maintain a definite rhythm and never lose contact with the athlete's back. Another excellent relaxation technique is to initiate a slow stroking directly over and down the full length of the spinal column.

Stroking of the lower limb   When effleurage is applied to a lower limb, the same principles as those used in back massage must be followed: begin the stroking at approximately the middle of the thigh, rubbing upward over the buttocks to the lower back, and then trail down to a point below the place where the stroke was initiated. Each stroke starts approximately ½ inch (1.3 cm) below the preceding one until the entire limb has been massaged. A pad should be placed under the knee and the ankle. Pressure should be applied lightly in these areas.

Stroking of the shoulder and arm   Effleurage to the arm is much like that to the lower limb. Stroking begins over the scapula and then moves over the upper chest region, progressing gradually down until stroking has been performed on the entire length of the arm.

Stroking variations   There are many variations in effleurage massage; some that are of particular value to sports injuries are pressure variations, the hand-over-hand method, and the cross body method.[27] *Pressure variations* range from very light to deep and vigorous stroking. Light stroking, as discussed previously, can induce relaxation or may be used when an area is especially sensitive to the touch; on the other hand, deep massage is designed to bring about definite physiological responses. Light and deep effleurage can be used alternately when both features are desired. The *hand-over-hand* stroking method is of special benefit to those surface areas that are particularly unyielding. It is performed by an alternate stroke in which one hand strokes, followed immediately by the overlaying of the other hand, somewhat like shingles on a roof (Figure 13-16). The *cross body* effleurage technique is an excellent massage for the low back region. The operator places a hand on each side of the athlete's spine. Both hands first stroke simultaneously away from the spine, then both hands at the same time stroke toward the spine (Figure 13-17).

Pétrissage   Kneading, or pétrissage (Figure 13-18), is a technique adaptable primarily to loose and heavy tissue areas such as the trapezius, the latissimus dorsi, or the triceps muscles. The procedure consists of picking up the muscle and skin tissue between the thumb and forefinger of each hand and rolling and twisting it in opposite directions. As one hand is rolling and twisting, the other begins to pick up the adjacent tissue. The kneading action wrings out the muscle, thus loosening adhesions and squeezing congestive materials into the general circulation. Picking up skin may cause an irritating pinch. Whenever possible, deep muscle tissue should be gathered and lifted.

Friction   The friction massage (Figure 13-19) is used often around joints and other areas where tissue is thin, as well as on tissues that are especially unyielding such as scars, adhesions, muscle spasms, and fascia. The action is initiated by bracing with the heels of the hands, then either holding the thumbs steady and moving the fingers in a circular motion or holding the fingers steady and moving the thumbs in a circular motion. Each method is adaptable to the type of area or articulation that is being massaged. The motion is started at a central point, and

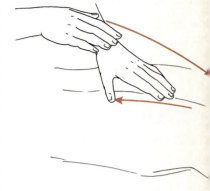

Figure 13-16

Hand-over-hand effleurage.

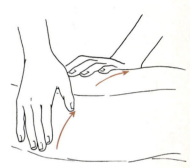

Figure 13-17

Cross-body effleurage.

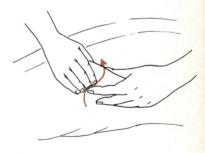

Figure 13-18

Pétrissage.

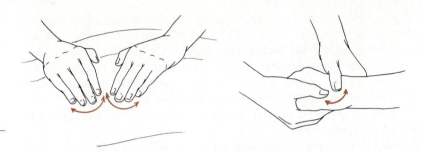

Figure 13-19

Friction massage.

then a circular movement is initiated, with the hands moving in opposite directions away from the center point. The purpose is to stretch the underlying tissue, develop friction in the area, and increase circulation around the joint.

Tapotement   The most popular methods of tapotement, or percussion, are the cupping, hacking, and pincerlike, or pincing movements.

Cupping   The cupping action produces an invigorating and stimulating sensation. It is a series of percussion movements, rapidly duplicated at a constant tempo. One's hands are cupped to such an extent that the beat emits a dull and hollow sound, quite opposite to the sound of the slap of the open hand. The hands move alternately, from the wrist, with the elbow flexed and the upper arm stabilized (Figure 13-20, *A*). The cupping action should be executed until the skin in the area develops a pinkish coloration.

Hacking   Hacking can be used in conjunction with cupping to bring about a varied stimulation of the sensory nerves (Figure 13-20, *B*). It is similar to cupping, except the hands are rotated externally and the ulnar, or little finger, border of the hand is the striking surface. Only the heavy muscle areas should be treated in this manner.

Pincing   Although pincing is not in the strictest sense percussive, it is placed under tapotement because of the vigor with which it is applied. Alternating hands lift small amounts of tissue between the first finger and thumb in quick, gentle pinching movements (Figure 13-20, *C*).

Vibration   Vibration is rapid movement that produces a quivering or trembling effect. It is mainly used in sports for its ability to relax and soothe. Although vibration can be done manually, the machine vibrator is usually the preferred modality.

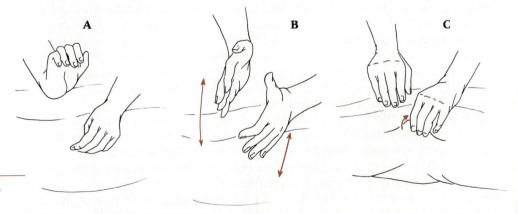

Figure 13-20

Tapotement. **A,** Cupping.
B, Hacking. **C,** Pincing.

Effective Massaging

Besides knowing the different kinds of massage, one should understand how to give the most effective massage. The following rules should be used whenever possible:

1. Make the athlete comfortable.
    a. Place the body in the proper position on the table.
    b. Place a pad under the areas of the body that are to be massaged.
    c. Keep the training room at a constant 72° F (22.2° C) temperature.
    d. Respect the athlete's privacy by draping him or her with a blanket or towel, exposing only the body parts to be massaged.
2. Develop a confident, gentle approach when massaging.
    a. Assume a position that is easy both on you and on the athlete.
    b. Avoid using too harsh a stroke, or further insult to the injury may result.
3. To ensure proper lymphatic and venous drainage, stroke toward the heart whenever possible.
4. Know when not to use massage.
    a. Never give a massage when there may be a local or general infection. To do so may encourage its spread or may aggravate the condition.
    b. Never apply massage directly over a recent injury; limit stroking to the periphery. Massaging over recent injuries may dislodge the clot organization and start bleeding.

Deep Transverse Massage

The transverse, or Cyriax, method of deep friction massage is increasingly being used in sports medicine. It is a specific technique for treating muscles, tendons, ligaments, and joint capsules. The major goal of transverse massage is to move transversely across a ligament or tendon to mobilize it as much as possible. This technique often precedes active exercise. According to Cyriax,[3] deep transverse friction massage restores mobility to a muscle in the same way that mobilization frees a joint.[5]

The position of the athletic trainer's hands is very important in gaining maximum strength and control. Four positions are suggested: index finger crossed over the middle finger, middle finger crossed over the index finger, two fingers side by side, and an opposed finger and thumb (Figure 13-21).

The massage must be directly over the site of lesion and pain. The fingers move with the skin and do not slide over it. Massage must be across the grain of the

> Transverse massage is a method of deep transverse friction massage.

Figure 13-21

Cyriax massage is a specific technique for muscle, tendons, ligaments, and joint capsules using a variety of hand positions. **A,** Index finger crossed over the middle finger. **B,** Middle finger crossed over the index finger. **C,** Two fingers side by side. **D,** Opposed finger and thumb.

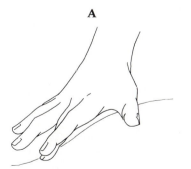
A

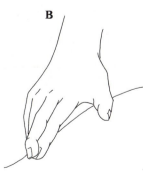
B

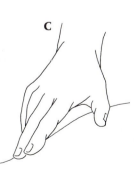
C

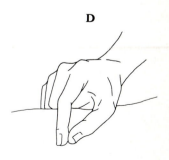
D

affected tissue. The thicker the structure, the more friction is given.[27] The technique is to sweep back and forth the full width of the tissue. Massage should not be given to acute injuries or over highly swollen tissues. A few minutes of this method will produce a numbness in the area, and exercise or mobilization can be instituted.

Manipulation Therapy

The use of manipulation in sports medicine is on the increase. Maitland[14] defines manipulation as passive movement of any kind. More specifically, it includes passive peripheral and vertebral joint movements that free the encumbered joints (Figure 13-22). Its primary purpose is to restore the accessory articular movements related to a normal range of physiological movement.[4] By improving joint motion through manipulation, there is implied positive change in muscles, ligaments, and neurogenic reflexes.[6] Contraindications for manipulative therapy are joint or bone disease, active inflammation, healing sprains or strains, disk injuries, and any possibility of fracture. At no time should an athletic trainer attempt manipulation without thorough education and practice under nonpathological conditions. An in-depth discussion of manipulative techniques is beyond the scope of this text.

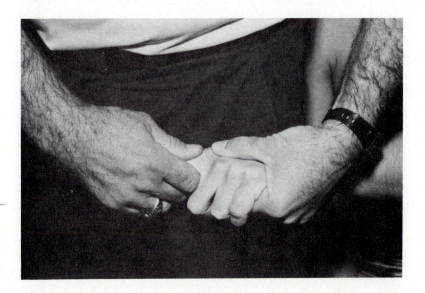

Figure 13-22

Joint manipulation is designed to passively move and to free encumbered peripheral and vertebral joints.

Machine or Manually Assisted Therapeutic Techniques

The two machine-assisted therapeutic modalities commonly used for musculoskeletal conditions are traction and intermittent compression.

Traction

Traction is the process of drawing or pulling. As therapy, it can be performed manually or by machine. Two body regions, the cervical and lumbar regions, are commonly provided traction. The primary reasons for drawing tension on tissue in this manner is to decrease pain, to reduce spasm, and to stretch fibrotic tissue (Figure 13-23). Traction in combination with moist heat can also increase local

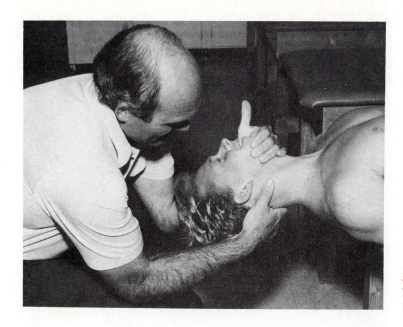

Figure 13-23

Traction can be performed mechanically or manually.

circulation. In many cases, traction is used to separate vertebral bodies to relieve compression on spinal nerves.[22]

Traction can be set to deliver either an intermittent or a sustained tension. Intermittent traction provides a gradual stretch, followed by a period of relaxation. It is more easily tolerated than continuous traction in the beginning of treatment. Traction interruption may occur as often as 16 times per minute. To enlarge the intervertebral foramen, continuous traction is the eventual goal. Cervical traction may range from 10 to 20 pounds, and lumbar traction may range from 65 to 200 pounds. The time of traction may range from 10 to 30 minutes.

Special considerations Traction should be avoided in the first 3 to 5 days of any acute sprain.[22] It should also be avoided when there is a possibility of bone or joint disease, tumors, osteoporosis, and, above all, fracture.

Intermittent Compressive Devices

In recent years, the use of devices designed to reduce edema has become increasingly popular in sports medicine. The two types of edema include that which is associated with the immediate acute injury and pitting edema, which occurs several hours later. Pitting edema is most effectively treated with intermittent compression. Controlled pressure applied to the swollen part encourages venous and lymphatic drainage.

Intermittent compression is performed by using a boot or sleeve that is put over the swollen part and, at preselected times, is intermittently filled with air (Figure 13-24). Some units are also combined with a refrigerant fluid to cool the part.

The amount of pressure varies with the body part to be treated. Pressure in the arms varies from 30 to 50 mm Hg and in the legs from 60 to 70 mm Hg, with the athlete establishing a comfort level. The time sequence is subjective, varying from 1 minute on and 2 minutes off, followed by 2 minutes on and 1 minute off

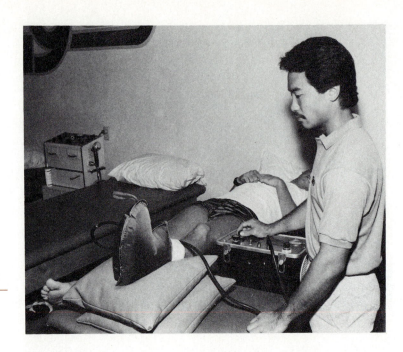

Figure 13-24

Intermittent compressive devices are designed to reduce edema after injury.

to 4 minutes on and 1 minute off. The length of treatment can vary from 10 minutes to 4 hours. The limb must always be maintained above the athlete's heart.

SUMMARY

To avoid legal problems, therapeutic modalities must be used with extreme care. Before any modality is used, there must be a thorough understanding of its function and when it should and should not be used.

Heat energy is transmitted through conduction, convection, radiation, and conversion. Conduction occurs when heat is transferred from a warmer object to a cooler one. Convection heating occurs by means of fluid or gas movement. Radiation is heat energy that is transmitted through empty space. Conversion, on the other hand, is heat that is generated when one energy is changed to another.

Thermotherapy increases blood flow, increases collagen viscosity, decreases joint stiffness, and reduces pain and muscle spasm. When the body's temperature is raised, tissue metabolism is increased, vascular permeability is increased, and chemicals such as histamine, bradykinin, and serotonin are released.

Superficial therapeutic heat should not be applied when there is a loss of sensation, immediately after an acute injury, when there is decreased arterial bleeding, over the eyes or genitals, and over the abdomen of a pregnant woman. Types of superficial heat are moist heat packs, whirlpool bath, paraffin bath, heat lamp, fluidotherapy, and contrast bath.

Penetrating heat therapies include shortwave diathermy, microwave diathermy, and ultrasound therapy. Both shortwave and microwave diathermies produce heat through the electromagnetic energy radiation spectrum, whereas ultrasound produces heat through acoustical energy. The contraindications for use of shortwave diathermy and microwave diathermy are basically the same as for superficial heating, with the additional restrictions of no implants, jewelry, or intrauterine devices. Care must be taken not to cross the cables. Ultrasound therapy heats through sound energy, which creates a mechanical vibration that is converted to heat energy within the body. Heating occurs in the denser tissue such as bone and connective tissue. More heat is built up at tissue interfaces. Ultrasound produces thermal, mechanical, and chemical changes within the body. It can be combined with electrical stimulation and used to drive molecules through the skin with the method known as phonophoresis.

Cold used for a therapeutic purpose as well as part of an emergency procedure is extremely popular in sports medicine. Cold, comparatively, penetrates deeper than superficial heat. Therapy is usually performed when the tissue has reached a relative anesthesia. Cryotherapy decreases muscle spasm, pain perception, and blood flow. It increases the inelasticity of collagen fibers, joint stiffness, and capillary permeability. Common cryotherapy procedures are cold water immersion, ice massage, ice packs, and the use of vapocoolant sprays.

In recent years, the use of electrotherapy has significantly increased in sports medicine. Direct current (DC), or galvanic current, flows in one direction. DC can produce a chemical effect that, in turn, increases circulation. DC that is interrupted will cause muscles to contract. Alternating current (AC) will also cause muscles to contract. A variety of electrical stimulators such as low-voltage or high-voltage currents are used in sports medicine. A small electrical generator called a transcutaneous electrical nerve stimulator (TENS) that can be either AC or DC is designed to inhibit pain through the gate mechanism and through stimulation of endogenous opiates.

A number of different manual and mechanical therapeutic approaches are used in sports medicine. They include systematic manipulation of the skin and consist of a number of different procedures, including effleurage, pétrissage, friction, vibration, and tapotement. A deep transverse massage technique is used on connective tissue. Manipulation therapy is currently used to restore accessory articular movements. Two machine-assisted therapeutic modalities popular in sports medicine are traction, especially of the cervical and lumbar regions, and intermittent compressive machines, which are used to reduce edema.

REVIEW QUESTIONS AND CLASS ACTIVITIES

1. Explain the legal factors that a coach or athletic trainer should consider before using a therapeutic modality.
2. Describe the physical principles related to thermotherapy.
3. What physiological changes occur when heat is applied to the body?
4. Contrast superficial and penetrating therapeutic heat.
5. Give an example of modalities that heat through conduction, convection, radiation, and conversion.
6. Demonstrate the use of a superficial and a penetrating therapeutic heat modality.
7. Contrast shortwave diathermy, microwave diathermy, and ultrasound therapy.
8. Compare the application of phonophoresis to iontophoresis.
9. Compare therapy delivered through heat to that through cold. When would you use each?
10. Describe the physical principles and the physiological effects thought to occur with cryotherapy.
11. Demonstrate the proper technique in using a variety of cryotherapeutic approaches.
12. Contrast the safety precautions that must be taken when using a thermotherapeutic modality and a cryotherapeutic modality.
13. Describe the different electrotherapeutic modalities available to the athletic trainer. What are the physical principles that underly these modalities?
14. How does the transcutaneous electrical nerve stimulation (TENS) concept apparently work?
15. How are muscles electrically stimulated to contract?
16. Describe the relative values of the following manual or mechanical therapies: massage, manipulation, traction, and intermittent compression.

REFERENCES

1. Belitsky, RB, et al.: Evaluation of the effectiveness of wet ice, dry ice, and Crogen packs in reducing skin temperature, Phys Ther 67(7):1080, July 1987.
2. Bell, AT, and Horton, PG: The use and abuse of hydrotherapy in athletics: a review, Ath Train 22:115, 1987.
3. Cyriax, J: Treatment of manipulation and deep massage, ed 6, New York 1959, Paul B Hoeber, Inc.
4. Dalzell, M: The physiotherapists armamentarium. In Welsh, RP, and Shephard, RJ, editors: Current therapy in sports medicine, 1985-1986, Philadelphia, 1985, Brian C Decker, Publisher.
5. deBruijn, R: Deep transverse friction: its analgesic effect, Int J Sports Med 5:35, Nov 1984.
6. Haldemann, S: Spinal manipulative therapy in sports medicine. In Spencer, CW, editor: Injuries to the spine, Clinics in sports medicine, vol 5, no 2, Philadelphia, 1986, WB Saunders Co.
7. Harris, PR: Iontophoresis: clinical research in musculoskeletal inflammatory conditions, J Orthop Sports Phys Ther 4:109, Fall 1982.
8. Hunter, LY: Physical therapy modalities. In Hunter, LY, and Funk, FJ, editors: Rehabilitation of the injured knee, St. Louis, 1984, The CV Mosby Co.
9. Jacobs, SR, et al.: Electrical stimulation of muscle. In Stillwell, GK, editor: Therapeutic electricity and ultraviolet radiation, ed 3, Baltimore, 1983, The Williams & Wilkins Co.
10. Kloth, L: Shortwave and microwave diathermy. In Michlovitz, SL, editor: Thermal agents in rehabilitation, Philadelphia, 1986, FA Davis Co.
11. Lehmann, JF, and DeLateur, BJ: Cryotherapy. In Lehmann, JF, editor: Therapeutic heat and cold, ed 3, Baltimore, 1982, The Williams & Wilkins Co.
12. Lehmann, JF, and DeLateur, BJ: Therapeutic heat. In Lehmann, JF, editor: Therapeutic heat and cold, ed 3, Baltimore, 1982, The Williams & Wilkins Co.
13. Lehmann, JF, et al.: Comparison of relative heating patterns produced in tissues by exposure to microwave energy at frequencies of 2450 to 900 megacycles, Arch Phys Med Rehabil 46:307, 1965.
14. Maitland, GD: Peripheral manipulation, ed 2, Boston, 1977, Butterworth & Co (Publishers), Ltd.
15. Marino, M: Principles of therapeutic modalities: implications for sports injuries. In Nicholas, J, and Hershman, EB, editors: The lower extremity and spine in sports medicine, vol 1, St. Louis, 1986, the CV Mosby Co.
16. McMaster, WC: Cryotherapy, Phys Sportsmed 10:112, Nov 1982.
17. Michlovitz, SL: Biophysical principles of heating and superficial heat agents. In Michlovitz, SL, editor: Thermal agents in rehabilitation, Philadelphia, 1986, FA Davis Co.
18. Michlovitz, SL: Cryotherapy: the use of cold as a therapeutic agent. In Michlovitz, SL, editor: Thermal agents in rehabilitation, Philadelphia, 1986, FA Davis Co.
19. Nielsen, AJ: Case study: myofascial pain of posterior shoulder relieved by spray and stretch, J Orthop Sports Phys Ther 3:21, Summer 1981.
20. Patterson, RP: Instrumentation for electrotherapy. In Stillwell, GK, editor: Therapeutic electricity and ultraviolet radiation, ed 3, Baltimore, 1983, The Williams & Wilkins Co.
21. Peppard, A, and Riegter, HF: Trigger point therapy for myofascial pain, Phys Sportsmed 9:161, June 1981.
22. Prentice, WE: Therapeutic modalities in sport medicine, St. Louis, 1986, Times Mirror/Mosby College Publishing.
23. Quillin, WS: Ultrasonic phonophoresis, Phys Sportsmed 10:211, June 1982.
24. Rusk, HA: Rehabilitation medicine, ed 4, St. Louis, 1977, The CV Mosby Co.
25. Schliephakle, E: Carrying out treatment. In Throm, H, editor: Introduction to shortwave and microwave therapy, ed 3, Springfield, Ill, 1966, Charles C Thomas, Publisher.
26. Sherman, M: Which treatment to recommend? Hot or cold? Am Pharm NS20:46, Aug 1980.

27. Tappan, FM: Massage techniques, New York, 1964, Macmillan, Inc.
28. Thorsteinsson, G: Electrical stimulation for analgesia. In Stillwell, GK, editor: Therapeutic electricity and ultraviolet radiation, ed 7, Baltimore, 1983, The Williams & Wilkins Co.
29. Walsh, M: Hydrotherapy: the use of water as a therapeutic agent. In Michlovitz, SL, editor: Thermal agents in rehabilitation, Philadelphia, 1986, FA Davis Co.
30. Ziskin, MC, and Michlovitz, SL: Therapeutic ultrasound. In Michlovitz, SL, editor: Thermal agents in rehabilitation, Philadelphia, 1986, FA Davis Co.

ANNOTATED BIBLIOGRAPHY

Cyriax, J, and Cyriax, P: Illustrated manual of orthopaedic medicine, Boston, 1983, Butterworth & Co (Publishers) Inc.
An excellent text covering the diagnosis and treatment of pain caused by orthopaedic problems. It provides excellent coverage of one system of joint manipulation and massage.

Knight, KL: Cryotherapy: theory, technique, and physiology, Chattanooga, Tenn, 1985, Chattanooga Corp.
Presents excellent coverage, both theoretical and practical, of one of the most widely used therapeutic approaches in sports medicine and athletic training—cryotherapy. It is clearly written and easily applied.

Maitland, GD: Peripheral manipulation, ed 2, Boston, 1977, Butterworth & Co (Publishers), Ltd.
Provides the reader with a theory and application of peripheral joint manipulation.

Maitland, GD: Vertebral manipulation, ed 4, Boston, 1977, Butterworth & Co (Publishers), Ltd.
Provides the reader with theoretical and practical applications of vertebral joint manipulation.

Michlovitz, SL, editor: Thermal agents in rehabilitation, Philadelphia, 1986, FA Davis Co.
An excellent text about understanding of the foundations and use of thermal agents in sports medicine and athletic training. It provides detailed discussions of inflammation, pain, superficial heat and cold, and the therapeutic use of ultrasound, shortwave, and microwave diathermies.

Prentice, WE: Therapeutic modalities in sports medicine, St. Louis, 1986, Times Mirror/Mosby College Publishing.
A complete guide to therapeutic modalities (not including exercise rehabilitation) in sports medicine and athletic training.

Stillwell, GK, editor: Therapeutic electricity and ultraviolet radiation, ed 3, Baltimore, 1983, The Williams & Wilkins Co.
Details therapeutic electricity and ultraviolet therapy and provides an excellent foundation in the use of these modalities.

Travell, JG, and Simons, DG: Myofascial pain and dysfunction, Baltimore, 1983, The Williams & Wilkins Co.
A valuable text about myofascial trigger points. It provides a clear understanding of trigger-point evaluation in the upper body and the treatment of choice as well as muscle stretch following the application of a vapocoolant.

Exercise Rehabilitation

When you finish this chapter, you should be able to

Describe the consequences of sudden inactivity and injury immobilization

Explain the importance of early injury mobility

Describe how exercise may be coordinated with other therapeutic modalities

Compare therapeutic and conditioning exercises

Describe the numerous elements that may compose an exercise rehabilitation program

Describe the uses of hydrotherapeutic and proprioceptive neuromuscular facilitation exercises in sports medicine

Fit crutches and/or a cane to an athlete

E xercise rehabilitation is one of the most important therapeutic tools available to the athletic trainer, therapist, or coach.[1] Exercise, properly used and combined with other therapeutic modalities, can help the athlete return safely to competition. Rehabilitation refers to the restoration of the athlete to a preinjury level of physical and psychological competitive fitness. Too often athletes, after injury, return to their sport before they have fully recovered, thereby risking a more serious injury.

An injured athlete should be monitored throughout the entire convalescent and reconditioning periods by both the athletic trainer and the physician. At no time should the immediate or future health of the athlete be endangered as a result of hasty decisions; at the same time, the dedicated athlete should be given every possible opportunity to compete, provided that such competition does not pose undue risk. The final decision in this matter must rest with the physician in charge.

It has been said that a good substitute is always more valuable than an injured star. There must be full cooperation between coach, athletic trainer, and physician in helping to restore the athlete to the proper level of competitive fitness. Rehabilitation through exercise is considered one factor in the total therapy regimen.

Exercise rehabilitation after a sports injury is the combined responsibility of all individuals connected with a specific sport. To devise a program that is most conducive to the good of the athlete, basic objectives that consider his or her needs must be developed. In addition to maintaining a good psychological climate, the

The physician makes the final decision about when an athlete can return to competition.

objectives are to (1) prevent deconditioning of the total body and (2) rehabilitate the injured part without hampering the healing process.

Preventing deconditioning involves keeping the body physically fit while the injury heals. In establishing a conditioning program, emphasis should be placed on maintaining strength, flexibility, endurance, and coordination of the total body. Whenever possible, athletes should engage in activities that will aid them in their sport but will not endanger recovery from the injury. Contralateral exercises should be introduced when they can be performed without pain or stress to the injured body part. If possible, all uninvolved body parts and joints should be exercised daily to maintain a reasonable degree of general strength and endurance.

Restoring the injured part is so important that a rehabilitation program must be started as soon as possible. An injured part, particularly a joint or the musculature, must be prevented from developing disuse degeneration. Disuse will result in atrophy, muscle contractures, inflexibility, and delays in healing because of circulatory impairment. This is not to imply that sports injuries should be "run off or worked through." Rather, a proper balance between resting and exercising should be maintained. Besides the physical aspect of rehabilitation, the mental and emotional aspects must also always be considered.

SUDDEN PHYSICAL INACTIVITY AND INJURY IMMOBILIZATION

The human body is a dynamic moving entity that requires physical activity to maintain proper physical function. When an injury occurs, two problems immediately arise that must be addressed. First is the generalized loss of physical fitness that occurs when activity is stopped, and second is the specific inactivity of the injured part, resulting from protective splinting of the soft tissue and, in some cases, immobilization by some external means.

Effects of General Inactivity

A person with a high level of physical fitness will experience a rapid generalized loss of this fitness when exercise is suddenly stopped. With this sudden lack of activity, rapid generalized loss of muscle strength, endurance, and coordination occurs. Whenever possible, the athlete, without aggravating the injury, must continue to exercise the entire body.

A sudden loss of physical activity leads to a generalized loss of physical fitness.

Effects of Immobilization

When an injured body is immobilized for a period of time, a number of disuse problems adversely effect muscle, joints, ligaments, bone, and the cardiovascular system.

Muscle and Immobilization

When a body part is immobilized for as short a period as 24 hours, definite adverse muscular changes occur.[4]

Atrophy and fiber type conversion Disuse of a body part quickly leads to a loss of muscle mass. The greatest atrophy occurs in the type I (slow-twitch) fibers. Over time, the slow-twitch fibers develop fast-twitch characteristics.[13] Slow-twitch fibers also diminish in number without type II (fast-twitch) fibers lessening in number.[19] A muscle that is immobilized in a lengthened or neutral

Immobilization of a part causes atrophy of slow-twitch muscle fibers.

position tends to atrophy less. In some cases, muscle lengthening may produce enlargement.[13] In contrast, immobilizing a muscle in a shortened position encourages atrophy and greater loss of contractile function.[4,13] In addition to maintaining an immobilized muscle in a lengthened position, atrophy can also be prevented through isometric contraction and electrical stimulation of the muscles.[13]

As the unused muscle decreases in size because of atrophy, protein is also lost. Protein synthesis decreases as much as 35%.[13] When activity is resumed, normal protein synthesis is reestablished.

Motor neuron discharge Immobilization decreases motor neuron discharge between 5% and 15%. Once immobilization has been removed, the original motor neuron discharge returns within about 1 week.[13]

Joints and Immobilization

Joint immobilization decreases normal lubrication.

Immobilization of joints causes loss of normal compression, which, in turn, leads to a decrease in lubrication that subsequently causes degeneration. This degeneration occurs because the articular cartilage is deprived of its normal nutrition.[13] The use of continuously active motion, electrical muscle stimulation, and/or hinged casts has, in some cases, retarded loss of articular cartilage.[4]

Ligament and Bone and Immobilization

When a joint is immobilized, it loses its primary purpose, which is stabilization. Both ligaments and bones respond to normal stress by maintaining their strength or becoming stronger. However, when stress is eliminated or decreased, ligament and bone become weaker.[13] Once immobilization has been removed, high-frequency, low-duration endurance exercise positively increases the mechanical properties of ligaments.[13] Endurance activities tend to increase both the production and the hypertrophy of the collagen fibers. Full remodeling of ligaments after immobilization may take as long as 12 months or more.[13]

Cardiovascular System and Immobilization

As with other structures, the cardiovascular system is adversely affected by immobilization. The resting heart rate increases approximately one-half beat per minute each day of immobilization. The stroke volume, maximum oxygen uptake, distal volume, and vital capacity decrease concurrently with the increase in heart rate.[13]

EARLY HEALING

Continuous passive movement is used to avoid articular cartilage degeneration.

When the injury is removed from immobilization, healing is in its early stages. Over time, a gradual increase in connective tissue density and tensile strength of muscle must occur.[4] In other words, stress is gradually increased through the application of exercise. The extent of exercising must depend on the amount of healing that has occurred and the absence of swelling, muscle spasm, and pain. Performance of therapeutic exercise must be pain free. In this early period there must be careful coordination of exercise with the application of physical modalities that deliver heat, cold, or electrical stimulation to muscles.[10] When edema and muscle spasm are decreased, muscle function is enhanced. Both heat and cold can increase the muscle's possibilities for stretch. A number of studies indicate that high-voltage direct current stimulation that is uninterrupted, in combination with cold, can relieve acute pain and edema and thus allow a greater range of motion.[17] Although their effectiveness is questionable when compared to active muscle contraction, electrostimulation units are becoming increasingly popular, especially when used after surgery to prevent extensive atrophy.[15] Massage and gentle mobilization may also be used to reduce spasm, increase circulation, and reduce pain. With swelling and pain there is a reflexive inhibition of muscle contraction.[4] In some cases of joint injury, mobilization is performed as soon as possible to avoid articular cartilage degeneration; for example, the continuous passive movement machine may be used after knee surgery.

THERAPEUTIC EXERCISE VERSUS CONDITIONING EXERCISE

Exercise is an essential factor in sports conditioning, injury prevention, and injury rehabilitation. Chapter 3, *Physical Conditioning and Training*, describes in some detail exercise used for physical conditioning and training. Whereas this chapter overlaps somewhat, it is specifically concerned with restoring normal body function after injury. In contrast to conditioning, therapeutic exercise, as one adjunct in the rehabilitation of sports injuries, can be defined as "the perception of bodily movement to correct an impairment, to improve musculoskeletal function, or to maintain a state of well-being."[12]

MAJOR ELEMENTS OF EXERCISE REHABILITATION

Before an injured athlete can be reinstated into full sports competition, a number of his or her physical conditioning factors must be returned to the preinjury state. They include the maintenance of general body conditioning and, when there is a musculoskeletal injury, the restoration of muscle strength, endurance, flexibility, proprioception (balance), agility, speed, coordination (skill patterns), cardiovascular endurance, and full reconditioning.

Elements of exercise rehabilitation include
General body conditioning
Muscle strength and endurance
Flexibility exercises
Proprioception
Body mechanics
Cardiovascular conditioning
Rehabilitation of joint arthrokinematics
Completion of healing and restoration of function
Psychological aspects

General Body Conditioning

It is essential that an injured athlete maintain the conditioning level of the unaffected parts of the body. There are two reasons for this premise: (1) when the injured body part is restored, the rest of the body must be ready to compete; and (2) there is some indication that conditioning of the body in general, in addition to that for the injured part, through some neural irradiation assists in the rehabilitation of the injured part.

Muscular Strength and Endurance

Muscular strength is one of the most essential factors in restoring the function of a body part to preinjury status. Isometric, isokinetic, and isotonic exercises can benefit rehabilitation. Whatever type of strength exercise is used, the pain it may produce should be carefully monitored. A major goal of performing strength exercise is that it be pain free.

Isometric Exercise

Isometric exercises are commonly performed in the early phase of rehabilitation when a joint is immobilized for a period of time. Isometrics increase static strength and assist in decreasing the amount of atrophy. Isometrics also can lessen swelling by causing a pumping action to remove fluid accumulation and by preventing the neural dissociation of proprioceptors.

Disadvantages for the use of isometrics in rehabilitation are the same as for conditioning. Primarily, strength develops specifically for the angle of the joint that is exercised. No functional force or eccentric work is developed. Other major difficulties are motivation and measuring the force that is being applied.

Isotonic Exercise

Isotonic exercise consists of concentric and eccentric muscle loading. During rehabilitation, it can progress from active to resistive-type exercises. The greatest tension and force are produced by eccentric contractions. When a particular joint is immobilized, joints that are distal and proximal to it can be exercised, using both concentric and eccentric movements. In cases where a concentric movement cannot be initiated, an eccentric exercise may be instituted; for example, following knee surgery and after the athlete can execute quadriceps sets, straight leg raises are performed. If the leg cannot be raised, it may be passively lifted by the athletic trainer or by a sling that is controlled by the athlete and then eccentrically lowered.

The advantage of isotonic resistive rehabilitative exercise is that it is relatively inexpensive, it provides a means for progressive exercise increases, and it is performed through a full range of motion. Both muscle strength and muscle endurance can be developed, and normal movement patterns can be developed by the variance of workloads and the increase in repetitions, sets, and weight increments. Through this variance of conditions the athlete is motivated throughout the rehabilitative process.

A current isotonic technique popular in sports medicine is Daily Adjustable Progressive Resistance Exercise (DAPRE). Developed by Knight,[10] its primary purpose is to determine the optimum time needed to increase resistance or the optimum amount of resistance that should be added. Four sets of exercises are initiated by a muscle group. During sets one and two, 10 and six repetitions are performed against one half and three fourths of the predetermined working weight, respectively. During the third set the athlete initiates as many repetitions as possible while using the full working weight. The number of repetitions executed on the third set establishes the adjusted weight for the fourth set. During the fourth set the number of repetitions performed is used to determine the adjusted working weight for the next day (Tables 14-1 and 14-2). The ideal working

TABLE 14-1 The DAPRE Technique

Set	Portion of Working Weight Used	Number of Repetitions
1	½	10
2	¾	6
3	Full	Maximum*
4	Adjusted	Maximum†

*The number of repetitions performed during the third set is used to determine the adjusted working weight for the fourth set according to the guidelines in Table 14-2.
†The number of repetitions performed during the fourth set is used to determine the adjusted working weight for the next day according to the guidelines in Table 14-2.

TABLE 14-2 Guidelines for Adjusting the DAPRE Technique

Number of Repetitions Performed during Set	Adjustment to Working Weight for	
	Fourth Set*	Next Day†
0-2	Decrease 5-10 lb	Repeat the set
3-4	Decrease 0-5 lb	Stay the same
5-7	Stay the same	Increase 5-10 lb
8-12	Increase 5-10 lb	Increase 5-15 lb
13-to . . .	Increase 10-15 lb	Increase 10-20 lb

*The number of repetitions performed during the third set is used to determine the adjusted working weight for the fourth set according to the guidelines in Table 14-1.
†The number of repetitions performed during the fourth set is used to determine the adjusted working weight for the next day according to the guidelines in Table 14-1.

weight is that which can be performed in six repetitions. If more repetitions can be performed, the resistance is too light; conversely, if six repetitions cannot be performed, there is too much resistance.[10]

As a means to early rehabilitation, isotonic resistance may have some disadvantages. For example, the muscle becomes loaded at the weakest point in the range of motion, and, if performed too soon or too vigorously, a reactive traumatic synovitis may occur. This type of exercise can produce muscle ischemia and can cause soreness, especially with eccentric resistive movement. If machines are used, in contrast to free weights, exercise is limited to only one muscle group. Another disadvantage of machines and free weights is that they do not allow exercises to be performed in a diagonal or functional plane. It is also difficult to exercise at functional velocities without producing additional injuries.

Isokinetic Exercise

Increasingly, isokinetic exercise is used in the rehabilitative process. Using fixed speed and variable resistance, the athlete is completely accommodated throughout the range of motion. Maximum loading occurs throughout the entire range of motion (Figure 14-1). Isokinetics is highly efficient and is a very safe means for achieving resistance rehabilitative exercises and accommodating to pain and fatigue.

Isokinetic exercise is performed at high speeds, which have a tendency to decrease the joint's compressive forces. Comparatively, fast-speed exercises produce fewer negative effects on joints than do slow-speed exercises. Short-arc submaximal isokinetics spreads out synovial fluid that helps to nourish the articular cartilage and, therefore, prevent deterioration.[3] It also develops neurophysiological "patterning" for functional speed and movements demanded by specific sports.

One major disadvantage is the cost of isokinetic equipment, which is very expensive and requires highly trained personnel to perform testing and rehabilitation. Another disadvantage is the inconvenience of continually changing equipment attachments to accommodate the exercise requirements of specific joints. If more than one joint needs exercise, a great deal of time may be involved.[3]

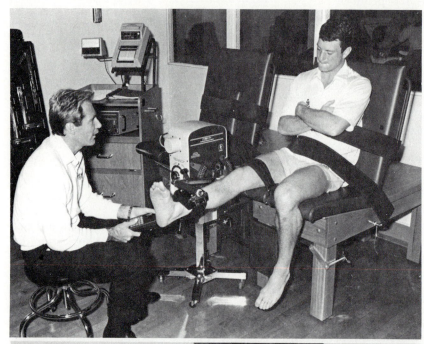

A

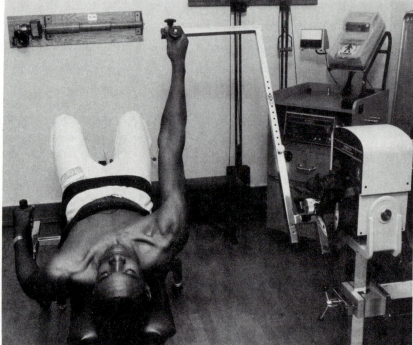

B

Figure 14-1

Isokinetics. **A,** A valuable
and reliable means to joint
testing. **B,** A highly safe
means for gaining strength in
the rehabilitation setting.

Flexibility Exercises

A decrease in the extensibility of soft tissue after athletic injury is very common. This decrease may be attributed to pain, muscle spasm, or neural inhibition related to an acute injury.[10] Immobilization of a part after surgery or injury can result in the development of adhesions or contractures, which limit range of motion (ROM). Flexibility after immobilization can be increased by passive stretching (PROM), active static stretching (AROM), and proprioceptive neuromuscular facilitation (PNF), using hold-relax or contract-relax techniques. Often heat, cold, or electrical muscle stimulation is used in combination with flexibility exercises.

To prevent degeneration of the articular cartilage or to maintain range of motion after injury and/or surgery, continuous passive movement (CPM) may be prescribed. The purpose of continuous passive movement is to provide nourishment to the articular cartilage through movement, thereby preventing further damage caused by inactivity. Continuous passive movement may be applied through commercially available machines or a stationary bicycle. Stationary cycle pedaling is performed by the noninjured leg, with the injured leg moving passively.

Proprioception

When there is an immobilized acute joint injury or a chronic joint condition with swelling, there are generally problems with proprioception. Exercise programs incorporating proprioceptive neuromuscular facilitation patterning, isokinetic exercise, the use of balance devices (e.g., tilt or wobble boards), and cryokinetics can help reestablish normal proprioception.

Body Mechanics

Body mechanics must always be a concern when considering a program of physical rehabilitation. Sports afflictions often produce postural asymmetrical behavior. An arm in a sling or leg in a cast is an example of a situation that disturbs the symmetry of the body and places abnormal stress on the musculoskeletal system. The athletic trainer should insist that the athlete maintain proper postural balance while recovering from an injury.

Cardiovascular Conditioning

As stated previously, when an athlete suddenly becomes inactive because of an injury, there is a significant decline in cardiovascular fitness. To prevent this decline the athlete must engage in activities that maintain or improve this system. Depending on the nature of the injury, there are a number of possible activities open to the athlete. Pool activities provide an excellent means for injury rehabilitation. Cycling also can positively stress the cardiovascular system (Figure 14-2). When there is a lower-limb injury, one-legged cycling and interval training can be performed on the bicycle. Other activities such as using the Nordic Trak (cross country skiing) and running may be used.[3]

Rehabilitation of Joint Arthrokinematics

When there is a joint injury, there is often a disruption of normal joint motion. As discussed in Chapter 13, manual therapy techniques can help restore a joint's physiological and accessory (component or joint play) movements. These techniques are often combined with active exercise.

Figure 14-2

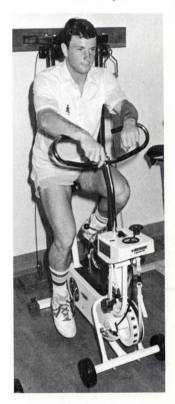

Cycling for the injured athlete may be one way to maintain the cardiovascular system.

Completion of Healing and Functional Restoration

In Chapter 8, *Tissue Response to Injury*, it was mentioned that soft-tissue healing during the remodeling phase takes much longer than previously thought. Rehabilitation, besides eliminating swelling and pain, must fully accomplish restoration of the range of motion, strength, and size, shape, and configuration of collagen tissue. Over time, with the assistance of a graduated program of specific exercises and functional activities, collagen fibers will return to their full and biomechanical function.[3]

The goal near the end of the rehabilitative process is to gradually enable the athlete to perform functional skills that replicate skills within the specific sport. The ideal is to return the athlete to full function without impairment or potential for reinjury.

The final stages of rehabilitation are concerned with reestablishing coordination and speed of movement. Before returning to a sport ready to resume full activity, an athlete must be able to perform at the same level of proficiency and have the same potential for delaying fatigue as before he or she became hurt. An athlete who is not at full capacity or who favors an injured part will most likely become reinjured or develop associated problems.

Psychological Aspects of Sports Rehabilitation

As discussed in Chapter 6, *Psychological Stress*, numerous psychological variables are inherent in any athlete with a sports injury. Typically, the athlete who is suddenly prevented from participation for an extended period of time will experience psychological reactions to loss (denial or disbelief, anger, bargaining, depression, and acceptance). A sport, to the serious athlete, is a direct extension of who he or she is as a person. When this sport is taken away, the athlete may feel that his or her sense of self-worth has also been taken away.[5] If a program of rehabilitation is to be successful, the athlete's emotional state and preconceived ideas about the injury and how it can be healed must be addressed. Three factors are of major importance in improving the athlete's emotional state during rehabilitation: (1) establishing rapport; (2) establishing a sense of cooperation; and (3) viewing exercise rehabilitation as an educational process.

The psychology of sports rehabilitation must include establishing
Rapport
A sense of cooperation
Exercise rehabilitation as an educational process
Competitive confidence

Rapport

The term rapport means a relationship of mutual trust and understanding. The athlete must thoroughly trust the athletic trainer or therapist to achieve maximum rehabilitation, and he or she must believe that at all times his or her best interests are being considered.

Cooperation

A highly motivated athlete begrudges every moment spent out of action and can become somewhat difficult to handle if the rehabilitative process moves slowly. Often the athlete blames the physician and/or the athletic trainer for not doing all they can. To avoid this situation, very early in the rehabilitative process the athlete must be taught that getting well or healing is a cooperative undertaking. It must be established that the athlete, physician, and athletic trainer are a team, all working towards the same ends—the return of the athlete to full function as soon as physiologically possible. To ensure this atmosphere the athlete must feel free to vent frustrations, to ask questions, and to expect clear answers about any aspect of the rehabilitative process. The athlete must feel a major responsibility to come into the training room on time and not skip appointments. He or she must be motivated to perform all exercises correctly and to perform all home assignments on a regular basis.

Many injured athletes lack patience. Nevertheless, patience and desire are necessary adjuncts in securing a reasonable rate of recovery.

Sports Rehabilitation as an Educational Process

To ensure maximum positive responses from the athlete in all aspects of rehabilitation, continual education must occur. All education is provided in layman's language or is commensurate with the athlete's background and education. The following is a list of educational matters to address carefully:

1. Describe the nature of the injury clearly, using anatomy charts or other visual aids. The athlete must fully understand the nature of his or her injury and its prognosis based on similar cases. A false hope for a fast ''comeback'' should not be engendered, when in reality a full recovery may be doubtful.
2. Explain how the healing process occurs and estimate the time needed for such healing.
3. Describe in detail the consequences of not following proper procedures.
4. Describe an overall rehabilitative plan, including progressive steps or phases within the plan.
5. Explain each physical modality and/or exercise and how it works and/or its specific purpose.
6. Make the athlete aware that his or her recovery depends as much on his or her attitude toward the rehabilitative process as on what therapy is being given. A positive attitude leads to a conscientious and persistent effort to speed recovery.

Regaining Competitive Confidence

Psychological rehabilitation is often as important as the restoration of the physical body. This is a commonly neglected factor in the total rehabilitative process. Very often an athlete returns to participation physically ready but psychologically ill-prepared. Although few athletes will admit it, when returning to participation, they often feel very anxious about getting hurt again (Figure 14-3). This very feeling may, in some ways, be a self-fulfilling prophecy. In other words, anxiety can lead to muscle tension, which, in turn, can lead to disruption of normal coordination, thus producing conditions that are favorable for reinjury or for sustaining an injury to another body part.[18] The following are suggestions for helping an athlete regain competitive confidence:

1. Allow the athlete to regain full performance by progressing in small increments. Return might include, first, performing all the necessary skills away from the team. This action may be followed by engaging in a highly controlled, small-group practice and then attempting participation in full-team noncontact practice. The athlete should be encouraged to express freely any anxiety that may be felt and to engage in full contact only when anxiety is at a minimum.
2. One technique that an athletic trainer might teach the athlete is systematic desensitization. The athlete first learns to consciously relax as much as possible through the Jacobson Progressive Relaxation Method.[7] When relaxation can be achieved at will, the athlete, with the help of the athletic trainer, develops a fear hierarchy related to returning to the sport and going ''all

SAMPLE EXERCISE REHABILITATION PLAN

Injury Situation

A high school football halfback received a second-degree sprain of the medial collateral ligament of the right knee joint. The athlete was given immediate care, consisting of cold packs, compression, and elevation. After examination, the physician immobilized the knee to 30 degrees of flexion with a soft brace for 2 weeks. After 1 week of immobilization, the athlete was released to the athletic trainer for exercise rehabilitation.

Injury Evaluation

Before starting exercise the athletic trainer evaluated the following:

1. *Range of motion*—goniometry indicated that it took 15 degrees to fully lock the knee and a total of 30 degrees for flexion.

2. *Strength grade*—the quadriceps muscle was graded as fair, having only approximately 10% of the strength of the unaffected quadriceps muscle. The hamstring muscles on the right side also demonstrated a fair grade, having only 15% of the strength of the left side. On the other hand, the gastrocnemius muscle was graded as good, having a 5% difference between the affected and unaffected leg.

3. *Circumference measurement*—circumference measurements were taken at three sites: 3, 6, and 9 inches (7.5, 15, and 22.5 cm) above the patella. Adding all measurements and comparing them to the unaffected side yielded a 1¼ inch (3.1 cm) discrepancy.

4. *Functional capacity*—observation of the athlete indicated a decided limp with a toe walk and an inability to keep the heel flat on the floor. Even with the toe-style walking, there was an inability to bear a great deal of weight.

Management Plan

1 **Management Phase**

Muscle tensing was performed from the time of immobilization. The athlete performed straight leg raises in the prone, supine, and side-lying positions and standing toe raises.

FREQUENCY: 10 to 15 times each waking hour.

2 **Management Phase**

Isometric exercise was added to the Phase 1 program for hamstring and quadriceps muscles (two or three contractions held for 6 seconds). Also, sandbag weights were added to the straight leg raises, starting with 5 lb and progressing to 15 lb (10 repetitions and three sets).

FREQUENCY: 2 or 3 times each day.

3	Management Phase	The brace was removed. The athlete performed leg swings while seated on the end of a table (10 to 20 repetitions) 3 times each day. This phase continued until 50% range of motion (ROM) and strength was achieved. The athlete walked in waist-high water daily.
4	Management Phase	Daily proprioceptive neuromuscular facilitation (PNF) knee patterns were initiated. The athlete began a walk/jog/run routine. Isotonic weight training was also started to restore muscle bulk. The criteria for moving to Phase 5 included 90% ROM, strength, and speed. FREQUENCY: 3 times each day.
5	Management Phase	The athlete practiced with the team but could not scrimmage until the criteria for recovery were satisfied. Flat footwear was worn instead of spiked shoes.

Criteria for Recovery

The ultimate goal of this reconditioning program was to return the athlete to sports participation at the same position as before injury. The criteria for recovery included the following.

1. Range of motion must be equal to that of the unaffected leg and must be pain free.
2. Strength of all major muscles associated with knee function must be equal to or exceed that of the unaffected leg. In rehabilitating an injured knee the lean muscle mass may be increased, but adipose tissue may be decreased, thus causing the circumferential measurement to be less than that of the unaffected leg.
3. Thigh circumference of the affected leg must not be less than 90% of that of the unaffected leg.
4. The functional capabilities of the athlete must permit walking and running without a limp, running at full speed, and 10 consecutive figure-8 patterns around goalposts.

out."[21] Each progressive step is imagined when the athlete is fully relaxed. As the progressive steps are imagined and fear is experienced at a specific step, the thought processes are halted. When coming to a point of anxiety, the athlete is taught to relax even more until the anxiety has passed.[14] The athlete then goes on to the next, more anxiety-producing event, with the relaxation process being repeated until no anxiety is again felt. When the athlete is able to complete the entire list of events without anxiety and has also completed the proper physical rehabilitation, he or she should be ready for competition (Table 14-3).

TABLE 14-3 Sample List of Steps for Systematic Desensitization of a Basketball Player After a Serious Ankle Sprain*

Imagine the Following

1. Coming into the locker room to dress for a game
2. Dressing for the game
3. Having ankles taped by the athletic trainer
4. Walking into the gym and beginning the warmup
5. Sitting on the bench watching the team play
6. Being called into the game
7. Running and positioning for an outside shot—the shot is good—you feel good
8. Going for a lay-up and coming down on the foot of the once-sprained ankle—you feel strong and well protected

*If the athlete feels anxious at any step, the process is stopped until further relaxation is achieved.

Figure 14-3

Tissue healing and the causation of pain are not clearly understood. However, what is known must be studied as a foundation for proper injury management.

DEVELOPING AN EXERCISE REHABILITATION PLAN

No exercise rehabilitation program can be properly undertaken without a carefully designed plan. The plan must consider as many variables as possible, including the injury situation and the actual management plan.

All exercise rehabilitation must be conducted as part of a carefully designed plan.

Injury Situation

Persons responsible for performing an exercise rehabilitation program must have as complete an understanding of the injury as possible. In other words, conditional to any exercise program is the knowledge of how the injury was sustained, the major anatomical structures affected, the degree or grade of trauma, and the stage or phase of the injury's healing (acute, subacute, or chronic).

The Management Plan

Very often the management plan follows the phases of the healing process and the functional capacity that is present in a part. Great care should be taken to coordinate exercise with other therapeutic modalities such as heat, cold, and electrical muscle stimulation. Swelling and muscle spasm limit movement and should always be considered when an exercise program is undertaken. Another major consideration in exercise therapy is to recognize exercise overdosage and to respond appropriately.

Exercise Overdosage

Engaging in exercise that is too intense or too prolonged can be detrimental to the progress of rehabilitation. The most obvious indicator of overdosage is an increase in swelling, spasm, and/or pain or discomfort lasting more than 3 hours. Another indicator of overdosage is a decrease in range of movement. When any sign of overdosage occurs, exercise must be diminished.

Exercise Intensity

In most injury situations, early exercise rehabilitation involves submaximum exercise performed in short bouts that are repeated many times daily. Exercise intensity is commensurate with healing. As recovery increases, the intensity of exercise also increases, with the exercise performed less often during the day and, ultimately, less often during the week. Finally, the athlete returns to a conditioning mode of exercise, which often includes high intensity three to four times per week.

Exercise Phases

Rehabilitative exercise in sports medicine can generally be subdivided into phases, depending on the nature of the injury. A unique phase that comes before elective surgery is the presurgical phase. After the presurgical exercise phase, five additional phases may possibly be identified: the postsurgical, or acute injury, exercise phase (phase 1), early exercise phase (phase 2), intermediate exercise phase (phase 3), advanced exercise phase (phase 4), and the initial sports reentry phase (phase 5). Not all injured athletes experience all phases in achieving full rehabilitation. Depending on the type of injury and the individual response to healing, phases may sometimes overlap. **NOTE:** If a phase or step approach to exercise therapy is selected, it must include all carefully considered goals and a criteria for advancing from one phase, or step, to another.

Presurgical Exercise Phase

If surgery can be postponed, exercise may be used as a means to improve its
outcome. By maintaining and, in some cases, increasing muscle tone and improving kinesthetic awareness, the athlete is prepared to continue the exercise rehabilitative program after surgery.

Postsurgical, or Acute Injury, Exercise Phase (Phase 1)

Exercise is often encouraged after surgery to the musculoskeletal system. Allman
states that "the optimal time for commencement of therapeutic exercise is approximately 24 hours after surgery or injury. An earlier beginning is often met by an unre-
ceptive and confused patient. Any beginning later than 24 hours must be considered
a loss of valuable time."[1] Exercise is used to avoid muscle atrophy and to ensure return to sports participation as quickly and safely as possible. Postsurgical exercise often repeats what was done presurgically. Commonly, the part surgically repaired is
immobilized by a cast, dressing, or sling. When immobilized, muscle tensing or isometrics may be used to maintain muscle strength. Unless contraindicated, joints that
are immediately adjacent (distal and proximal) to the immobilized part should be
gently exercised to maintain their strength and mobility.

When a part is immobilized after an acute injury, phase 1 allows for resolution
in the healing process to occur. In many cases, muscle setting and nonflexion
lifting activities such as straight leg raises may be performed while the injured
part is immobilized. Muscle setting is usually performed 10 to 15 times every
waking hour with each contraction held for approximately 6 seconds. Joints adjacent to the injury also may be exercised.

Early Exercise Phase (Phase 2)

The early exercise phase is a direct extension of the postsurgical, or acute injury,
phase. The primary goals of this phase are to restore full muscle contraction without pain and to maintain strength in muscles surrounding the immobilized part.
Muscle tensing is continued. Depending on the nature of the condition, isometric
exercise against resistance may be added. Joints that are close to the injury are
maintained in good condition by strengthening and mobility exercises.

Intermediate Exercise Phase (Phase 3)

When pain-free full muscle contraction has been achieved, the goals are to develop up to 50% range of motion of the unaffected part and 50% strength. A
third goal is to also restore near-normal neuromuscular coordination.

Advanced Exercise Phase (Phase 4)

The goals of phase 4 are to restore at least 90% of the athlete's range of motion
and strength. Also, the athlete is to undergo reconditioning for returning to his or
her sport. The primary goal in this phase is to fully restore power, flexibility,
endurance, speed, and agility of the injured part, as well as the entire body.

Initial Sports Reentry Phase (Phase 5)

Phase 5 of the exercise rehabilitation program involves returning to sports participation. In this phase, the underlying factors are gradualness and avoiding having
the athlete "overdo." In some cases, this phase is a period in which muscle bulk
is restored; in other instances, the athlete carefully tests the results of the exercise

rehabilitation process. It is essential that the athlete not return to competition before full range of movement, strength, and coordination have been attained.

Criteria for Full Recovery

All exercise rehabilitation plans must determine what is meant by complete recovery from an injury. Often it means that the athlete is fully reconditioned and has achieved full range of movement, strength, part size, proprioception, coordination, speed, and cardiovascular fitness, as well as overall fitness. Besides physical well-being, the athlete must also have regained full confidence to return to his or her sport.

ADDITIONAL APPROACHES TO EXERCISE REHABILITATION
Hydrotherapeutic Exercise

A sports medicine program that has access to a swimming pool is fortunate; however, a whirlpool bath can provide some of the same benefits. Water submersion offers an excellent environment for beginning a program of exercise therapy, or it can complement all phases of rehabilitation.

Because of buoyancy and hydrostatic pressure, submersion in a pool presents a versatile exercise environment that can be easily varied according to individual needs. With the proper technique, the athlete can reduce muscle spasm, relax tense muscles, increase the range of joint motion, reestablish correct movement patterns, and, above all, increase strength, power, and muscular endurance.[2]

Using the water's buoyancy and pressure, hydrotherapeutic exercise can be described as assistive, supportive, and resistive. As an *assistive* medium, the water's upthrust can increase range of motion, strength, and control. Starting below the water level, the athlete first allows the part to be carried passively upward, keeping within pain-free limits. As the athlete gains strength, movement is actively engaged in, and the buoyancy of the water becomes assistive. Progression of the movement can be initiated by increasing speed and making the water above the body part become a resistive medium (Figure 14-4).

A second use of water buoyancy is *support*. The limb normally will float just below the water's surface. In this position the limb is parallel to the surface of the water. As with the assistive technique, increasing the speed will make the move-

Exercise in water provides an excellent means for rehabilitation.

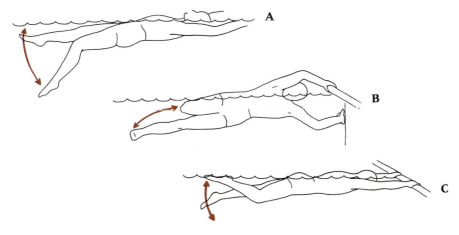

Figure 14-4

Use of the water's buoyance and pressure for progressive exercise. **A,** Body part floats upward passively. **B,** Using the water for buoyance. **C,** Using the water for resistance.

ment more difficult. Progression also can be accomplished by making the part less streamlined. In exercising the arm, the athlete can increase the difficulty by moving across the water with the flat of the hand or by using a hand paddle or webbed glove. Flippers can increase resistance to the leg.

A third use of water buoyance is *resistance.* The injured body part is moved downward against the upward thrust of the water. Maximum resistance is attained by keeping the limb at a right angle to the water's surface. As with the supportive technique, the resistive technique can be made progressively more difficult by using different devices. Extra resistance is added by pushing or dragging flotation devices down into the water.

Besides specific exercising, the athlete can practice sports skills, using the water's buoyancy and resistance to an advantage. For example, locomotor or throwing skills can be practiced to regain normal movement patterns. The swimming pool can also provide an excellent medium for retaining or restoring functional capacities as well as restoring cardiovascular endurance. Wearing a flotation device around the waist, the athlete performs a variety of upper- and lower-limb movement patterns. While in 3 feet of water, movements of straight-ahead running, backward running, side stepping, figure-8s, and carioca can be performed while bearing full weight.[8]

Proprioceptive Neuromuscular Facilitation

Proprioceptive neuromuscular facilitation (PNF) is a method for promoting or hastening the response of the neuromuscular mechanism through stimulation of the proprioceptors.

Proprioceptive neuromuscular facilitation (PNF) was developed by Herman Kabat, M.D., in association with Margaret Knott and Dorothy Voss, two physical therapists, for the rehabilitation of various neuromuscular problems.[9] The basis of PNF is that muscle function does not occur in a straight line but is diagonal and spiral. PNF is defined as "methods of promoting or hastening the response of the neuromuscular mechanism through stimulation of the proprioceptors."[11]

PNF uses four major neurophysiological principles: muscle and joint activity, irradiation, Sherrington's law of successive induction, and Sherrington's law of reciprocal innervation. The major muscle and joint reflexes used are the muscle spindle, which is activated by stretch; Golgi's organ, which is activated by pressure and concerned with muscle tonus; deep pressure in receptors in joints; and the righting reflex. Irradiation or reinforcement refers to a strong voluntary muscle action against a resistance that will bring out a response in other muscle areas. Sherrington's law of successive induction indicates that flexion augments extension and extension augments flexion. Sherrington's law of reciprocal innervation refers to the voluntary or reflex contraction of a muscle that is associated with a simultaneous relaxation of its antagonist muscle because of an inhibitory response of the muscle spindle.[20]

Techniques of PNF

PNF procedures are generally used in rehabilitation for the purposes of facilitating strength and the increase of range of motion. Stretching is increased by rhythmic initiation and the techniques of contract-relax and the hold-relax. In contrast, strength can be facilitated by repeated contraction and the slow-reversal, the slow-reversal–hold-relax, and the rhythmic stabilization techniques.

Stretching techniques   To produce muscle relaxation through an inhibitory response for purposes of increasing range of motion, the following PNF techniques may be used.

Rhythmic initiation   Rhythmic initiation consists of a progressive series of first passive movement, then active assistive movement, followed by an active movement through an agonist pattern.[16] The purpose of this approach is for athletes who have very limited movement to progressively regain some range of motion.

Contract-relax   The affected body part is passively moved until resistance is felt. The athlete is then told to contract the antagonistic muscle isotonically. The rotation is resisted as much as possible by the athletic trainer for 10 seconds or until fatigue is felt by the athletic trainer. The athlete is instructed to ''relax'' or ''let go'' up to 5 seconds. The athletic trainer then moves the limb to a new stretch position. The exercise is repeated two or three times.

Hold-relax   The hold-relax technique is similar to contract-relax except that a maximum isometric contraction is used. The athlete moves the body part to the point of resistance and is told to ''hold.'' The tight muscles are isometrically resisted by the athletic trainer for 10 seconds. The athlete is then told to ''let go'' for up to 5 seconds, and the body part is either moved to a new range actively by the athlete or passively by the athletic trainer. This exercise is repeated two or three times.

Slow-reversal-hold-relax   The athlete actively moves the part to the limits of motion. This movement is followed by isometric contraction of the antagonist muscles, which is held for approximately 30 seconds or until fatigue is felt. The antagonists are then relaxed while the agonists are contracted, moving the part to a new limited range.[16]

Strengthening techniques   To assist the athlete in developing muscle strength, muscle endurance, and coordination, the following techniques are used.

Repeated contraction   Repeated contraction of a muscle or a muscle group is used when there is general weakness or weakness at one specific point. The athlete moves isotonically against the maximum resistance of the athletic trainer until fatigue is experienced. At the time fatigue is felt, stretch is applied to the muscle at that point in the range to facilitate greater strength production.[16] All resistance must be carefully accommodated to the strength of the athlete. Because the athlete is resisting as much as possible, this technique may be contraindicated for some injuries.

Slow reversal   The athlete moves through a complete range of motion against maximum resistance. Resistance is applied to facilitate antagonist and agonist muscle groups and to ensure smooth and rhythmical movement. It is important that reversals of the movement pattern be instituted before the previous pattern has been fully completed. The major benefits of this PNF technique is that it promotes normal reciprocal coordination of agonist and antagonist muscles.

Slow-reversal-hold   In this technique the athlete moves a body part isotonically using agonist muscles, followed immediately by an isometric contraction. The athlete is instructed to ''hold'' at the end of each isotonic movement. The primary purpose of this technique is to develop specific strength at a point in the range of movement.[16]

Rhythmic stabilization   Rhythmic stabilization uses an isometric contraction of the agonists, followed by an isometric contraction of the antagonist muscles.[11] With repeated co-contraction of these muscles, strength is maximum at this point.[16]

Spiral-diagonal patterns   Spiral-diagonal patterns are used as a means of gaining relaxation or stimulating strength development through the maximum stimulation of proprioceptors. The major components of movement taking place at a joint and focal point are flexion, extension, and rotation. Movement toward and across the midline of the body takes place with adduction, and movement across and away from the midline is associated with abduction. Outward or external rotation takes place with supination and inversion, whereas inward or internal rotation is associated with pronation and eversion.[11] Figures 14-5 through 14-24 are examples of PNF patterns that may be used for rehabilitating some sports injuries.

Principles for Developing PNF Patterns

Six basic principles are used in PNF[20]:
1. *Manual pressure*—hands are placed in the direction of the desired movement.
2. *Verbal and visual stimulation*—clear, concise instructions are given, and the movement can be seen by the athlete.
3. *Pressure and traction*—bringing the joint together causes pressure and increased stability, whereas traction pulls the joint apart and facilitates movement.
4. *Direct resistance*—isotonic and isometric. In isotonic resistance maximum resistance is given through the entire range of movement. With isometric resistance maximum tension is built until fatigue is felt and is followed by a gradual release.
5. *Functional patterns*—functional movements are used, using spiral and diagonal patterns, along with flexion, extension, adduction, abduction, and internal and external rotation.
6. *Proper timing*—muscles are encouraged to contract in proper sequence: distal to proximal and proximal to distal. In PNF stronger muscle components are used to facilitate weaker ones.

See Tables 14-4 and 14-7 and Figures 14-5 through 14-24.

TABLE 14-4 Lower-Extremity Patterns*

Body Region	Extension	Flexion
Hip	Bilateral extension	Bilateral flexion
	Right adduction; external rotation	Right adduction; external rotation
	Left abduction; internal rotation	Left abduction; internal rotation
Ankles	Bilateral plantar flexion	Bilateral dorsiflexion
	Right inversion	Right eversion
	Left eversion	Left inversion
Toes	Flexion	Extension

*Rotation is to the left.

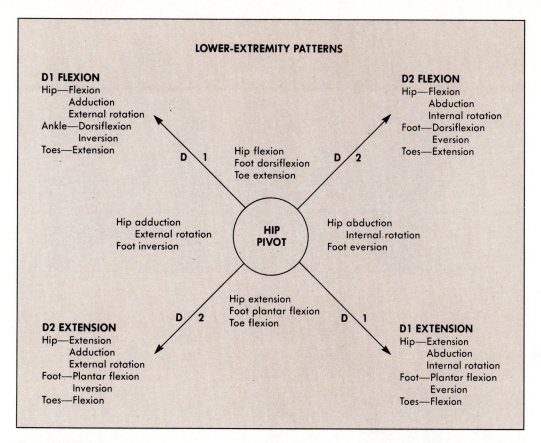

Figure 14-5

Diagrammatic representation of the
lower-extremity patterns.

TABLE 14-5 Lower-Extremity Patterns

Body Region	D1 Flexion	D1 Extension	D2 Flexion	D2 Extension
Hip	Flexion Adduction External rotation	Extension Abduction Internal rotation	Flexion Abduction Internal rotation	Extension Adduction External rotation
Knee	Flexion	Extension	Flexion	Extension
Ankle and foot	Dorsi-flexion Inversion	Plantar flexion Eversion	Dorsi-flexion Eversion	Plantar flexion Inversion
Toe	Extension	Flexion	Extension	Flexion

Figure 14-6

Ankle pattern. **A,** Start—ankle in dorsiflexion and foot in eversion. **B,** Finish.

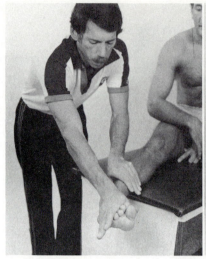
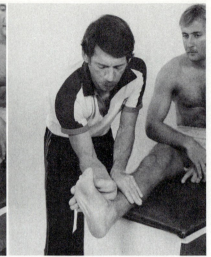

A B

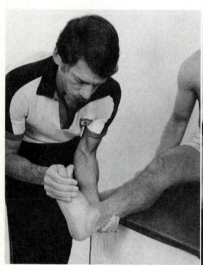
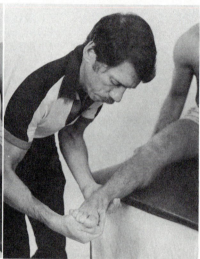

A B

Figure 14-7

Ankle pattern. **A,** Start—ankle in plantar flexion and foot in inversion. **B,** Finish.

Figure 14-8

Ankle pattern. **A,** Start—ankle in plantar flexion and foot in inversion. **B,** Finish.

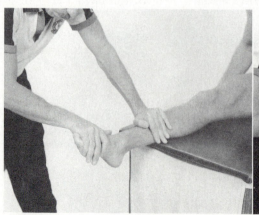
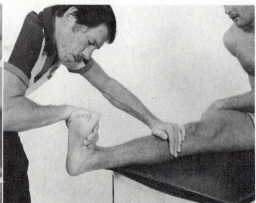

A B

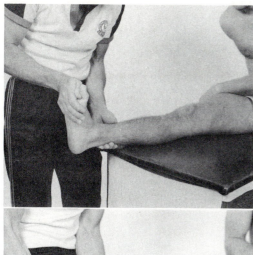

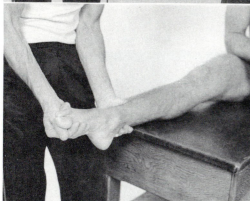

Figure 14-9

Ankle pattern. **A,** Start—ankle in dorsiflexion and foot in eversion. **B,** Finish.

Figure 14-10

Knee pattern. **A,** Start—knee extension with tibial external rotation, ankle dorsiflexion, and foot inversion with toes in tibial extension. **B,** Finish.

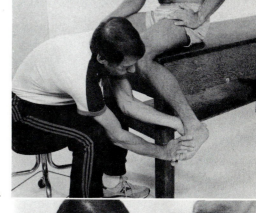

Figure 14-11

Knee pattern. **A,** Start—knee flexion with tibial internal rotation, ankle plantar flexion, and foot eversion with toes in fibular flexion. **B,** Finish.

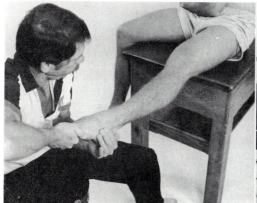

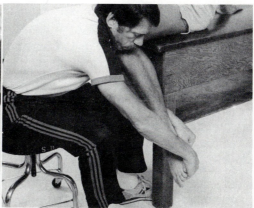

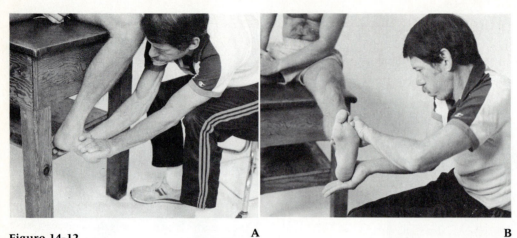

A   B

Figure 14-12

Knee pattern. **A,** Start—knee extension with tibial internal rotation, ankle dorsiflexion, and foot eversion with toes in fibular extension. **B,** Finish.

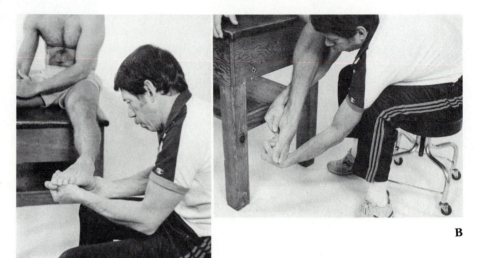

B

Figure 14-13

Knee pattern. **A,** Start—knee flexion with tibial external rotation, ankle plantar flexion, and foot inversion with toes in tibial flexion. **B,** Finish.

A

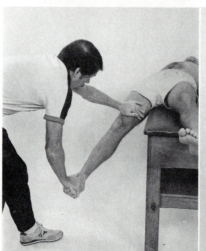

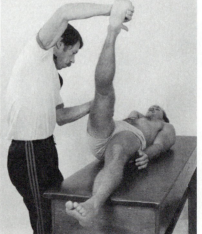

Figure 14-14

Hip pattern. **A,** Start—hip flexion, adduction, and external rotation. The knee is extended, ankle dorsiflexed, foot inverted, and toes extended tibially. **B,** Finish.

A   B

Figure 14-15

Hip pattern. **A,** Start—hip moving in extension, abduction, and internal rotation. The knee is extended, ankle plantar flexed, foot everted, and toes flexed toward the fibula. **B,** Finish.

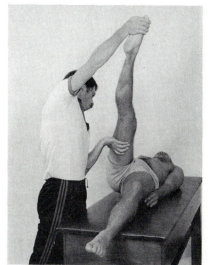

A

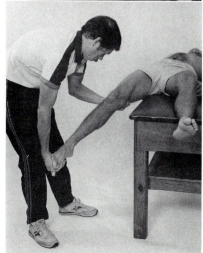

B

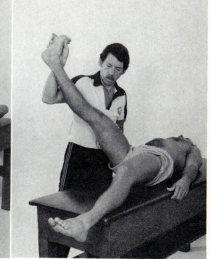

A

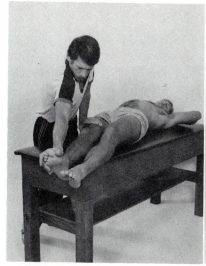

B

Figure 14-16

Hip pattern. **A,** Start—hip flexed, abducted, and internally rotated. The ankle is dorsiflexed, foot everted, and toes in fibular extension. **B,** Finish.

Figure 14-17

Hip pattern. **A,** Start—hip in extension, adducted, externally rotated with knee extended. The ankle is plantar flexed, foot everted, and toes flexed tibially. **B,** Finish.

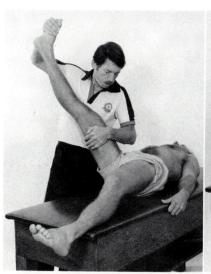

A

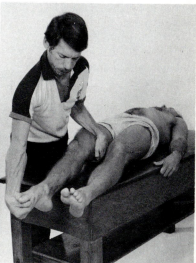

B

Figure 14-18

Bilateral hip pattern for abdominal and low back rehabilitation. **A,** Start— bilateral asymmetrical hip flexion with knee flexion for trunk flexors to left. *Athlete's right leg:* hip flexion, adduction, external rotation, and knee flexion. Ankle is dorsiflexed, foot inverted, and toes in tibial extension. *Athlete's left leg:* hip flexion, abduction, internal rotation, and knee flexion. Ankle is dorsiflexed, foot everted, and toes in fibular extension. **B,** Finish.

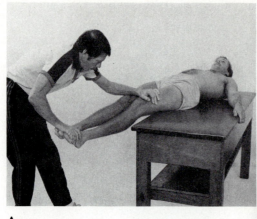
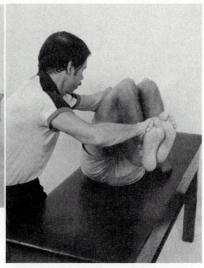

Figure 14-19

Bilateral hip pattern for abdominal and low back rehabilitation. **A,** Start— bilateral asymmetrical hip extension with knee extended for back extensors to the right. *Athlete's right leg* moves into hip extension, abduction, internal rotation, and knee extension. Ankle is plantar flexed, foot everted, and toes in fibular flexion. *Athlete's left leg* moves in hip extension, adduction, external rotation, and knee extension. Ankle is plantar flexed, foot inverted, and toes in tibial flexion. **B,** Finish.

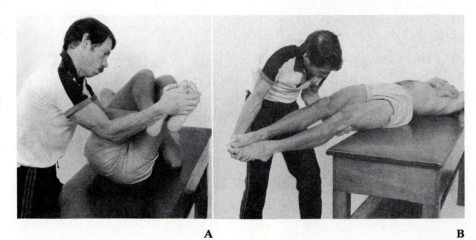

TABLE 14-6 Upper-Trunk Patterns*

Body Region	Extension (Lifting)	Flexion (Chopping)
Right upper extremity	Flexion Abduction External rotation	Extension Abduction Internal rotation
Left upper extremity (left hand grasps right forearm)	Flexion Adduction External rotation	Extension Adduction Internal rotation
Trunk	Rotates and extends to right	Rotates and flexes to right

*Rotation is to the right.

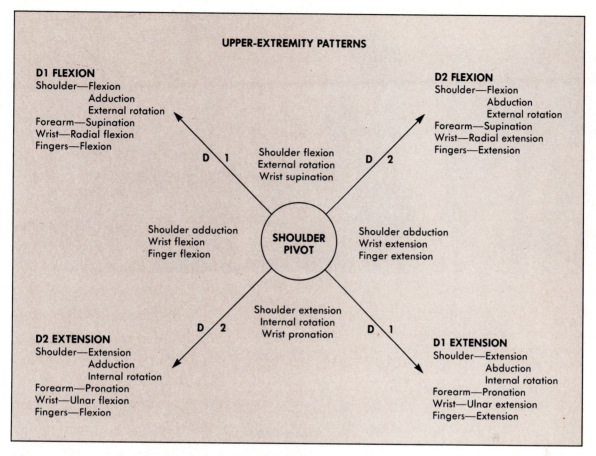

Figure 14-20

Diagrammatic representation of the upper-extremity patterns.

TABLE 14-7 Upper-Extremity Patterns

Body Region	D1 Flexion	D1 Extension	D2 Flexion	D2 Extension
Shoulder	Flexion Adduction External rotation	Extension Abduction Internal rotation	Flexion Abduction External rotation	Extension Adduction Internal rotation
Scapula	Elevation Protraction Upward rotation	Depression Retraction Downward rotation	Elevation Retraction Upward rotation	Depression Protraction Downward rotation
Forearm	Supination	Pronation	Supination	Pronation
Wrist	Radial flexion	Ulnar extension	Radial flexion	Ulnar flexion
Finger and thumb	Flexion	Extension	Extension	Flexion
	Adduction	Abduction	Abduction	Adduction

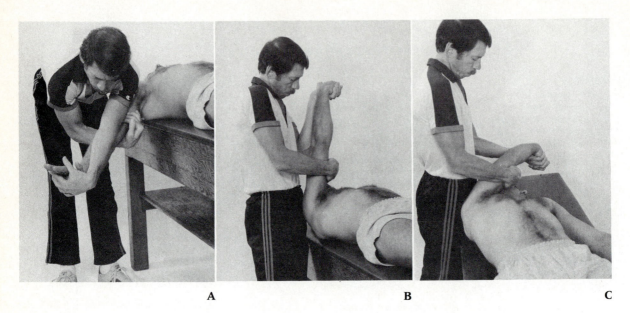

A   **B**   **C**

Figure 14-21

Shoulder pattern. **A,** Start—shoulder flexion, adduction,
external rotation. Forearm is supinated with wrist and
fingers in radial flexion. **B,** Continue motion. **C,** Finish.

Figure 14-22

Shoulder pattern. **A,** Start—shoulder extension, abduction,
internal rotation. Forearm moves into pronation, wrist and
fingers in ulnar extension. **B,** Continue motion. **C,** Finish.

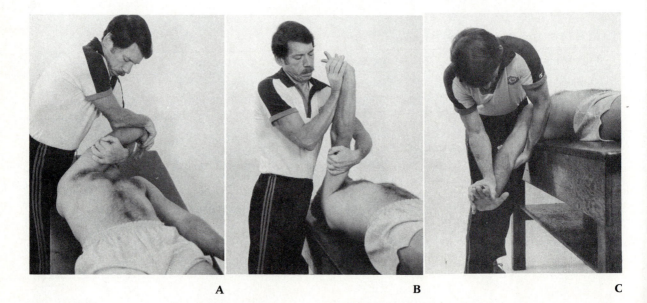

A   **B**   **C**

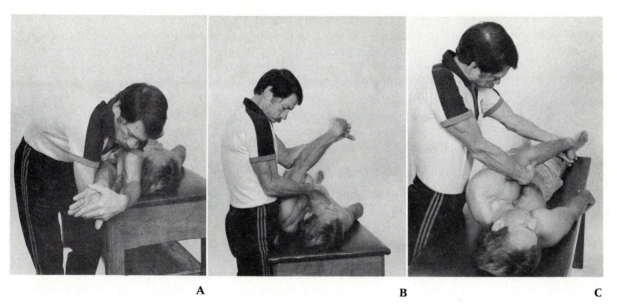

A   B   C

Figure 14-23

Shoulder pattern. **A,** Start—shoulder extension, adduction, and internal rotation. Forearm is pronated with wrist and fingers in ulnar flexion. **B,** Continue motion. **C,** Finish.

Figure 14-24

Shoulder pattern. **A,** Start—shoulder extension, adduction, and external rotation. Forearm is supinated with wrist and fingers in radial flexion. **B,** Continue motion. **C,** Finish.

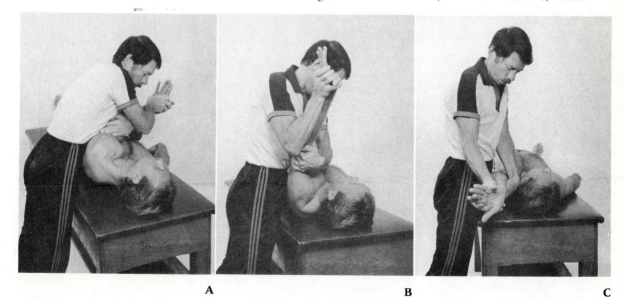

A   B   C

FITTING AND USING THE CRUTCH OR CANE

Properly fitting a crutch or cane is essential to avoid placing abnormal stresses on the body.

When an athlete has a lower-limb injury, weight bearing may be contraindicated. Situations of this type call for the use of a crutch or cane. Very often, the athlete is assigned one of these aids without proper fitting or instruction in their use. An improper fit and usage can place abnormal stresses on various body parts.[6] Constant pressure of the body weight on the crutch's axillary pads can cause crutch palsy. This pressure on the axillary radial nerves and blood vessels can lead to temporary or even permanent numbness in the hands. Faulty mechanics in the use of crutches or canes could produce chronic low back and/or hip strain.

Fitting the Athlete

The adjustable, wooden crutch is well-suited to the athlete. For a correct fit the athlete should wear low-heeled shoes and stand with good posture and the feet close together. The crutch length is determined first by placing the tip 6 inches (15 cm) from the outer margin of the shoe and 2 inches (5 cm) in front of the shoe. The underarm crutch brace is positioned 1 inch (2.5 cm) below the anterior fold of the axilla. Next, the hand brace is adjusted so that it is even with the athlete's hand and the elbow is flexed at approximately a 30-degree angle (Figure 14-25).

Fitting a cane to the athlete is relatively easy. Measurement is taken from the superior aspect of the greater trochanter of the femur to the floor while the athlete is wearing street shoes.

Walking with the Crutch or Cane

Many elements of crutch walking correspond with walking. The technique commonly used in sports injuries is the tripod method. In this method, the athlete swings through the crutches without making any surface contact with the injured

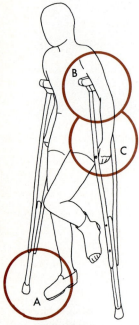

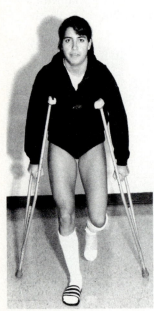

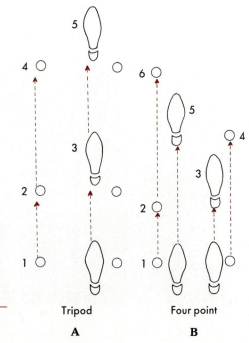

Figure 14-25

The crutch must be properly fitted to the athlete. *A,* The crutch tips are placed 6 inches [15 cm] from the outer margin of the shoe and 2 inches [5 cm] in front of the shoe. *B,* The underarm crutch brace is positioned 1 inch [2.5 cm] below the anterior fold of the axilla. *C,* The hand brace is placed even with the athlete's hand, with the elbow flexed approximately 30 degrees.

Figure 14-26

Crutch gait. **A,** Tripod method. **B,** Four-point gait.

Tripod

A

Four point

B

limb or by partially bearing weight with the injured limb. The following sequence is performed:

1. The athlete stands on one foot with the affected foot completely elevated or partially bearing weight.
2. Placing the crutch tips 12 to 15 inches (30 to 37.5 cm) ahead of the feet, the athlete leans forward, straightens the elbows, pulls the upper crosspiece firmly against the side of the chest, and swings or steps between the stationary crutches (Figure 14-26).
3. After moving through, the athlete recovers the crutches and again places the tips forward.

An alternate method is the four-point crutch gait. In this method, the athlete stands on both feet. One crutch is moved foward and the opposite foot is stepped foward. The crutch on the same side as the foot that moved foward moves just ahead of the foot. The opposite foot steps forward, followed by the crutch on the same side, and so on.

Once the athlete is able to move effectively on a level surface, negotiating stairs should be taught. As with level crutch walking, a tripod is maintained on stairs. In going upstairs, the unaffected support leg moves up one step while the body weight is supported by the hands. The full weight of the body is transferred to the support leg, followed by moving the crutch tips and affected leg to the step. In going downstairs, the crutch tips and the affected leg move down one step followed by the support leg. If a handrail is available, both crutches are held by the outside hand, and a similar pattern is followed as with the crutch on each side.

SUMMARY

Exercise rehabilitation is a major aspect of the injured athlete's total rehabilitation program. Two major goals of exercise rehabilitation are to prevent deconditioning and to restore the injured part to a preinjury state. Besides the physical aspect, the mental and emotional aspects of rehabilitation must always be considered.

Sudden general inactivity causes generalized loss of strength, endurance, and coordination. When a body part is injured, depending on the tissue affected, there is muscle atrophy, mainly in the slow-twitch fibers. A decrease in motor neuron discharge also occurs. Immobilized joints lose their ability to lubricate the articular cartilage and, as a result, are prone to degeneration. Bones become weaker when stress is eliminated. Part immobilization can also lead to a decrease in the heart's stroke volume, maximum oxygen uptake, and distal volume, along with an increase in heart rate.

Early mobility and other therapeutic modalities should be coordinated to maintain and increase tissue strength and to reduce swelling, muscle spasm, and pain. Early mobility assists articular cartilage degeneration.

Exercise rehabilitation has as its main goal the restoration of the injured body part to its preinjury status. It can incorporate many elements, depending on the nature of the injury. They may include general conditioning, muscle strength and endurance, flexibility, proprioception, body mechanics, joint arthrokinematics, and restoration of cardiovascular conditioning. Exercise rehabilitation continues until soft-tissue healing is completed and there is full functional restoration. Besides restoration of the physical aspect, a major concern is the psychological aspect, which permeates the entire rehabilitative process.

Any time rehabilitation is contemplated, a careful plan must be instituted. Every plan must be based on a clear understanding of the injury situation and the assessment that has been performed. Part of the rehabilitative plan includes the exercise instruction to be given, proper exercise positioning, and careful attention to exercise overdosage. The plan must include phases or steps that advance through the rehabilitative process until full recovery is acquired.

There are a number of different approaches to exercise rehabilitation, depending on the nature of the injury, the philosophy of the athletic trainer, and the available resources. Two approaches that are used extensively in sports medicine are hydrotherapeutic exercise and proprioceptive neuromuscular facilitation (PNF). Also included in the exercise rehabilitative process is teaching the proper use of crutches and canes.

REVIEW QUESTIONS AND CLASS ACTIVITIES

1. What occurs physiologically when an athlete is suddenly forced to stop physical activity?
2. Discuss the physiological effects of immobilization on muscles, ligaments, joints, and the cardiovascular system.
3. Physiologically, what is the advantage of early mobility after a sports injury?
4. How may exercise be coordinated with the therapy modalities of heat, cold, and electrical muscle stimulation?
5. Name the similarities and dissimilarities of therapeutic versus conditioning exercise.
6. Why must an athlete condition the body generally while an injury heals?
7. Critically compare the use of isometric, isotonic, and isokinetic exercises in rehabilitation.
8. How is flexibility restored after an injury?
9. How are proprioception and arthrokinematics adversely affected after a joint injury?
10. Why should there be a concern for restoring body mechanics following a sports injury?
11. Describe how to determine if an athlete is fully functionally restored after an injury.
12. Why is psychological rehabilitation as important as physical rehabilitation?
13. What is the importance of developing an exercise rehabilitation plan? Include the criteria for moving to various phases.
14. How may water be used in the exercise rehabilitative process?
15. Proprioceptive neuromuscular facilitation (PNF) includes stretching, strengthening, and movement-patterning techniques. How can these techniques apply to sports injuries?
16. Crutch and/or cane walking is often necessary during the rehabilitative process. How should crutches and canes be fitted and used?

REFERENCES

1. Allman, FL: Exercise in sports medicine. In Basmajian, JV, editor: Therapeutic exercise, ed 3, Baltimore, 1978, Williams & Wilkins.
2. Atkinson, GP, and Harrison, RA: Implications of health and safety in the work place in relation to hydrotherapy departments, Physiotherapy 76:146, Sept 1981.
3. Davies, GJ: Compendium of isokinetics in clinical usage, ed 2, LaCrosse, Wis, 1984, S & S Publishers.
4. Dickinson, A, and Bennett, KM: Therapeutic exercise. In Havey, JS, editor: Symposium on rehabilitation of the in-

jured athlete, Clinics in sports medicine, vol 4, no 3, Philadelphia, 1985, WB Saunders Co.
5. Faris, GJ: Psychologic aspects of athletic rehabilitation. In Harvey, JS, editor: Symposium on rehabilitation of the injured athlete, Clinics in sports medicine, vol 4, no 3, Philadelphia, 1985, WB Saunders Co.
6. Flood, DK: Proper fitting and use of crutches, Phys Sportsmed 11:75, March 1983.
7. Jacobson, E: Progressive relaxation, ed 2, Chicago, 1938, University of Chicago Press.
8. Loudon, JK: Pool therapy, Ath Train 22(4):326, 1987.

9. Kabat, H: Proprioceptive facilitation. In Licht, S, editor: Therapeutic exercise, Baltimore, 1965, Williams & Wilkins.

10. Knight, KJ: Guidelines for rehabilitation of sports injuries. In Harvey, JS, editor: Rehabilitation of the injured athlete, Clinics in sports medicine, vol 4, no 3, Philadelphia, 1985, WB Saunders Co.

11. Knott, M, and Voss, EE: Proprioceptive neuromuscular facilitation: patterns and techniques, ed 2, Philadelphia, 1968, Harper & Row, Publishers.

12. Kottke, FJ: Therapeutic exercise. In Kottke, FJ, et al.: Handbook of physical medicine and rehabilitation, ed 3, Philadelphia, 1982, WB Saunders Co.

13. Marino, M: Current concepts on rehabilitation in sports medicine: research and clinical interrelationships. In Nicholas, JA, and Hershman, EB, editors: The lower extremity and spine in sports medicine, vol 1, St. Louis, 1986, The CV Mosby Co.

14. McKay, M, et al.: Thoughts and feelings, Richmond, Cal, 1981, New Harbinger Publications.

15. Mohr, T, et al.: Comparison of isometric exercise and high volt galvanic stimulation on quadriceps femoris muscle strength, Phys Ther 65:606, May 1985.

16. Prentice, WE, and Kooima, EF: The use of proprioceptive neuromuscular facilitation techniques in rehabilitation of sport-related injury, Ath Train 21(1):26, 1986.

17. Ralston, DJ: High voltage galvanic stimulation, Ath Train 20(4):291, 1985.

18. Rotella, RJ: Psychological care of the injured athlete. In Kulund, D: The injured athlete, Philadelphia, 1982, JB Lippincott Co.

19. Smith, MJ: Muscle fiber types: their relationship to athletic training and rehabilitation. In Garron, GW, editor: Gymnastics, Clinics in sports medicine, vol 4, no 1, Philadelphia, 1985, WB Saunders Co.

20. Surburg, PR: Neuromuscular facilitation techniques in sportsmedicine, Phys Sportsmed 9:114, Sept 1981.

21. Wolpe, J: The practice of behavior therapy, ed 2, New York, 1973, Pergamon Press, Inc.

ANNOTATED BIBLIOGRAPHY

Davies, GJ: Compendium of isokinetics in clinical usage, ed 2, LaCrosse, Wis, 1984, S & S Publishers.
A complete monograph on the subject of isokinetic testing and exercise rehabilitation. It compares the advantages and disadvantages of isometric, isotonic, and isokinetic exercises.

Harvey, JS, editor: Symposium on rehabilitation of the injured athlete, Clinics in sports medicine, vol 4, no 3, Philadelphia, 1985, WB Saunders Co.
A monograph that provides the reader with the foundations necessary to establish a rehabilitation program, including exercise and the use of physical agents.

Kisner, C, and Colby, A: Therapeutic exercise: foundations and techniques, Philadelphia, 1986, FA Davis Co.
Provides a clear, concise presentation of the field of therapeutic exercise. It is well-suited to sports medicine and covers exercise for increasing range of motion and for treating soft tissues and bony and postsurgical problems extremely well.

Norkin, CC, and White, DJ: Measurement of joint motion: a guide to goniometry, Philadelphia, 1985, FA Davis Co.
A text designed to educate clinicians, educators, and students who desire to learn accurate goniometry. It is easy to read and well-illustrated.

Torg, JS, et al.: Rehabilitation of athletic injuries, Chicago, 1987, Year Book Medical Publishers, Inc.
Provides a systematic approach to sports injury diagnosis and rehabilitation.

15

Drug Use and Abuse in Sports

When you finish this chapter, you should be able to

Describe the major foundations of pharmacology and the safety precautions that must be taken from a legal standpoint in the sports medicine and athletic training fields

Delineate the differences between prescription and nonprescription drugs

Identify the most common drug categories used in sports medicine and athletic training, their active ingredients, and their reactions on the body

Identify substance categories that are designed to aid performance and those that are banned

Describe the physiological reactions to stimulants, narcotic analgesic drugs, beta blockers, diuretics, anabolic steroids, and growth hormone, as well as blood doping

Identify when athletes are abusing recreational drugs, provide education to the athletes, and, when necessary, provide proper counseling referral

Describe procedures for drug testing and express a philosophy about this matter

pharmacology
The study of drugs and their origin, nature, properties, and effects on living organisms.

Pharmacology is that branch of science that deals with the actions of drugs on biological systems, especially those drugs that are used in medicine for diagnostic and therapeutic purposes. Medications of all types, both prescription and nonprescription, are commonly used by athletes.

Relatively short sports seasons make any physical incapacity a crucial factor. The anxiety created in this situation can cause athletes, athletic trainers, coaches, and even physicians to overreact in ways that may be harmful; for example, they may advocate taking too much of a drug or taking it more often than indicated with the thought that "if a little bit is good, then more is better." In addition, the athlete may, unbeknown to the team physician or athletic trainer, be taking drugs prescribed by another physician, which could be a very dangerous practice (Figure 15-1).

This chapter is concerned with two areas of pharmacology: pharmaceuticals used for health problems that occur in sports and substance abuse, a major problem.

WHAT IS A DRUG?

The use of substances for the express purpose of treating some infirmity or disease dates back to early history. The ancient Egyptians were highly skilled in making and using medications, treating a wide range of external and internal conditions.

Figure 15-1

An athlete, without the knowledge of a team physician or athletic trainer, may be taking drugs prescribed by another physician that could lead to serious consequences.

Many of our common drugs such as aspirin and penicillin are derived from natural sources. Historically, medications were composed of roots, herbs, leaves, or other natural materials when they were identified or believed to have medicinal properties. Today many medications that originally came from nature are produced synthetically.

A **drug** is any chemical agent that affects living matter. Used in the treatment of disease, drugs may either be applied directly to a specific tissue or organ or be administered internally to affect the body systemically. When a drug enters the bloodstream by absorption through the gastrointestinal tract or through direct injection, it can affect specific tissues and organs far from the site of introduction.

drug
Any chemical substance that affects living matter.

DRUG VEHICLES

Although athletic trainers or coaches cannot dispense a prescription drug, they should have a basic comprehension of why, how, and by what means a drug is being delivered to the athlete's body. This section provides the reader with an elementary understanding of the vehicles in which a drug may be housed, how it may be administered, and the response it may have, both positive and negative.

A drug **vehicle** is a therapeutically inactive substance that transports a drug. A drug is housed in a vehicle that may be either a solid or a liquid. Some of the more common drug vehicles are listed below.

vehicle
The substance in which a drug is transported.

Liquid Preparations

1. *Aqueous solution*—sterile water containing a drug substance
2. *Elixir*—alcohol, sugar, and flavoring with a drug dissolved in solution, designed for internal consumption

3. *Liniment*—alcohol or oil containing a dissolved drug, designed for external massage
4. *Spirit*—a drug dissolved in water and alcohol or in alcohol alone
5. *Suspension*—undissolved powder in a fluid medium; must be mixed well by shaking before use
6. *Syrup*—a mixture of sugar and water containing a drug

Solid Preparations

1. *Ampule*—a closed glass receptacle containing a drug
2. *Capsule*—a gelatin receptacle containing a drug
3. *Ointment (emollient)*—a semisolid preparation of lanolin, petroleum jelly, or lard that suspends a drug
4. *Paste*—an inert powder combined with water
5. *Pill* or *tablet*—a drug powder compressed into a small oval, circle, square, or other form
6. *Plaster*—a drug in wax or resin, usually spread on a muslin cloth
7. *Poultice*—an externally applied, soft and moist paste containing a drug
8. *Powder*—a finely ground drug
9. *Suppository*—a medicated gelatin molded into a cone for placement in a body orifice, for example, the anal canal

DRUG ADMINISTRATION

Drugs can be administered internally or externally.

The administration of medications in athletes, as in any individuals, can be either internal or external and is based on the type of local or general response desired.

Internal Administration

Drugs and medications can be taken internally through inhalation, or they may be administered intradermally, intramuscularly, intranasally, intraspinally, intravenously, orally, rectally, or sublingually.

Inhalation is a means of bringing medication or substances to the respiratory tract. This method is most often used in sports to relieve the athlete of the discomfort of upper respiratory involvements such as colds and coughs. The vehicle for inhalation is normally water vapor, oxygen, or highly aromatic medications.

Intradermal (into the skin) or *subcutaneous* (under the cutaneous tissues) administration is usually accomplished through a hypodermic needle injection. Such introduction of medication is initiated when a rapid response is needed, but it does not produce as rapid a response as that following intramuscular or intravenous injection. Tests for allergic sensitivity are commonly given intradermally rather than subcutaneously.

Intramuscular injection means that the medication is given directly into the muscle tissue. The site for such an injection is usually the gluteal area or the deltoid muscle of the upper arm.

Intranasal application is varied according to the condition that is to be treated. The introduction of decongestants by using a menthol salve, a dropper, or an atomizer may relieve the discomfort of head colds and allergies.

Intraspinal injection may be indicated for any of the following purposes: (1) introduction of drugs to combat specific organisms that have entered the spinal cord; (2) injection of a substance such as procaine to anesthetize the lower limbs; or (3) withdrawal of spinal fluid to be studied.

Intravenous injection (into a vein) is given when an immediate reaction to the medication is desired. The drug enters the venous circulation and is spread instantly throughout the body.

Oral administration of medicines is the most common method of all. Forms such as tablets, capsules, powders, and liquids are easily administered orally.

Rectal administration of drugs is limited. In the past some medications have been introduced through the rectum to be absorbed by its mucous lining. Such methods have proved undesirable because of difficulties in regulating dosage. Drugs are primarily introduced into the rectum as an enema or to medicate disease conditions of the area.

Sublingual and *buccal* introductions of medicines usually consist of placing easily dissolved agents such as *troches* (or *lozenges*), tablets, or pills under the tongue or in the cheek. They dissolve slowly and are absorbed by the mucous lining. This method permits slow drug administration into the bloodstream.

External Administration

Medications administered externally may include **inunctions,** ointments, pastes, plasters, poultices, and solutions.

Inunctions are oily or medicated substances that are rubbed into the skin and result in a local or systemic reaction. Oil-base liniments or petroleum analgesic balms used as massage lubrications are examples of inunctions.

Ointments consisting of oil, lard, petroleum jelly, or lanolin combined with drugs are applied for long-lasting topical medication.

Pastes are ointments with a nonfat base, which are spread on cloth and usually produce a cooling effect on the skin.

Plasters are thicker than ointments and are spread either on cloth or paper or directly on the skin. They usually contain an irritant, are applied as a counterirritant, and are used for relieving pain, increasing circulation, and decreasing inflammation.

Solutions can be administered externally and are extremely varied, consisting principally of bacteriostatics. Antiseptics, disinfectants, vasoconstrictors, and liquid **rubefacients** are examples.

SAFETY IN USING DRUGS

As stated earlier, drugs of any kind can be harmful. It is therefore essential that the athletic trainer or coach becomes highly aware of the many ramifications inherent in drug safety.

Legal Concerns

The dispensing of drugs to the athlete by a member of the coaching staff or an athletic trainer, in a legal sense, is both clear and concise. At no time can anyone other than a person licensed by law legally prescribe drugs for an athlete. An athletic trainer, unless specifically allowed by state licensure, is not permitted to dispense a prescription drug. To fail to heed this fact can be a violation of the Federal Food, Drug, and Cosmetic Act and state statutes. A violation of these laws could mean legal problems for the physician, athletic trainer, school, school district, or even the league. The situation is not so cut and dried for nonprescription drugs. For example, most secondary schools do not allow the athletic trainer or coach to dispense nonprescription (over-the-counter [OTC]) drugs that are to be

inunctions
Oily or medicated substances (e.g., liniments) that are rubbed into the skin to produce a local or systemic effect.

rubefacients
Agents that redden the skin by increasing local circulation through dilation of blood vessels.

Unless allowed by state licensure, an athletic trainer may not dispense a prescription drug to an athlete.

taken internally by the athlete, including aspirin and over-the-counter cold remedies. The application of nonprescription wound medications is allowed by some secondary schools under the category of first aid. On the other hand, some high school athletic trainers in America are not allowed to apply even a wound medication in the name of first aid but can only clean the wound with soap and water; the athlete must then be sent to the school nurse for medication. The dispensing of vitamins and even dextrose may be specifically disallowed by some school districts. At the college or professional level, minors are not usually involved, and the dispensing of nonprescription medications may be less restrictive. It is assumed that athletes who are of legal age have the right to use whatever nonprescription drugs they choose; however, this right does not preclude the fact that the athletic trainer or coach must be reasonable and prudent about the types of nonprescription drugs offered to the athlete.

Generally, dispensing nonprescription medicinals by a member of the athletic staff to any athlete depends on the philosophy of the school district and must be under the direction of the team physician. As in all other areas of sports medicine and athletic training, one is obligated to act reasonably and prudently.

Pharmaceutical Drugs: Are They Safe Enough?

As stated many times before, no drug can be considered completely safe and harmless. If a drug is truly potent enough to effect some physiological action, then it is also strong enough, under some conditions, to be dangerous. All persons react individually to any drug. A given amount of a specific medication may result in no adverse reaction in one athlete, whereas another athlete may experience a pronounced adverse response. Both the athlete and the athletic trainer should be fully aware of any untoward effect a drug *may* have. It is essential that the athlete be instructed clearly about *when* specifically to take medications, with meals or not, and what not to combine with the drug, such as other drugs or specific foods.

Ingestion of some drugs can nullify the effects of another drug.

Some drugs can nullify the effect of another drug or can cause a serious antagonistic reaction. For example, calcium, which is found in a variety of foods, and even in some medications can nullify the effects of the powerful antibiotic tetracycline (Figure 15-2).

Drug Responses

Individuals react differently to the same medication, and different conditions may alter the effect of a drug on the athlete. Drugs themselves can be changed through age or improper preservation, as well as through the manner in which they are administered. Response variations also result from differences in each individual's size or age.

The following is a list of general body responses sometimes produced by drugs and medications:

1. *Addiction*—body response to certain types of drugs that produces both a physiological need and a psychological craving for the substance
2. *Antagonistic action*—result observed when medications, used together, have adverse effects or counteract one another
3. *Cumulative effect*—exaggerated drug effects, which occur when the body is unable to metabolize a drug as rapidly as it is administered; the accumulated, unmetabolized drug may cause unfavorable reactions
4. *Depressive action*—effect from drugs that slow down cell function

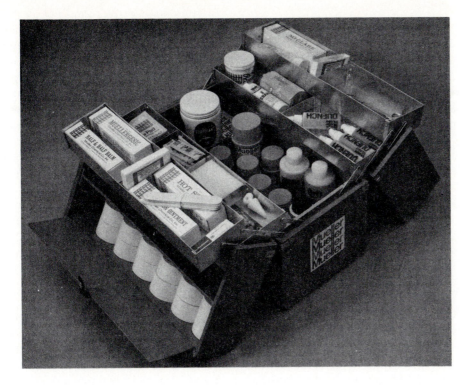

Figure 15-2

It must be remembered that all persons react individually to any drug.

5. *Habituation*—individual's development of a psychological need for a specific medication
6. *Hypersensitivity*—allergic response to a specific drug; such allergies may be demonstrated by a mild skin irritation, itching, a rash, or a severe anaphylactic reaction, which could be fatal
7. *Idiosyncrasy*—unusual reaction to a drug; a distinctive response
8. *Irritation*—process, as well as effect, caused by substances that result in a cellular change; mild irritation may stimulate cell activity, whereas moderate or severe irritation by a drug may decrease cell activity
9. *Paradoxical reaction*—a drug-induced effect that is the exact opposite of that which is therapeutically intended
10. *Potentiating*—a pharmaceutical that increases the effect of another; for example, codeine and aspirin—codeine is potentiated by aspirin, and therefore, less of it is required to relieve pain[38]
11. *Specific effect*—action usually produced by a drug in a select tissue or organ system
12. *Side effect*—the result of a medication that is given for a particular condition but affects other body areas or has effects other than those sought.
13. *Stimulation*—effect caused by drugs that speed up cell activity
14. *Synergistic effect*—result that occurs when drugs, given together, produce a greater reaction than when given alone
15. *Tolerance*—condition existing when a certain drug dosage is no longer able to give a therapeutic action and must therefore be increased

Alcohol and some foods, when mixed with drugs, produce adverse affects.

Alcohol should not be ingested with a wide variety of drugs, both prescription and nonprescription. A fatty diet may decrease a drug's effectiveness by interfering with its absorption.

Excessively acid foods such as fruits, carbonated drinks, or vegetable juice may cause adverse drug reactions.[38] The athletic trainer and coach must thoroughly know the athletes they work with. The possibility of an adverse drug reaction is everpresent and requires continual education and vigilance.

Nonprescription Medicinals

In most cases, the athletic trainer will be concerned only with nonprescription medications. A nonprescription drug is also called an over-the-counter drug; it is one that can be bought without a prescription.

There is a major difference between prescription and nonprescription drugs. A prescription drug is designed to relieve symptoms or cure a disease or injury. The OTC drug is not curative but is generally designed to relieve pain or inflammation. As with prescription drugs, great caution must be taken with OTC drugs.

Buying Medicinals

The pharmacist can provide the athletic trainer with information about the following
Lower-cost generic drugs
Drug effects
Shelf age
Dangers of drugs

One of the athletic department's best friends is the local pharmacist. The pharmacist can assist in the selection and purchase of nonprescription medicines, can save money by suggesting the lower priced generic drugs, and can act as a general advisor on what drugs are most effective, the age of a medicine, and even the inherent dangers in a specific drug.

All pharmaceuticals must be properly labeled, indicating clearly the content, date of purchase, expiration date, and any dangers or contraindications for use. However, most pharmacists do not place the expiration date on drugs; therefore, it is up to the athletic trainer or coach to find out this date and place it on the label. Those individuals buying medicinals should always learn the best ways to store them, including the correct temperature and moisture and the amount of light that may be tolerated. It is generally accepted that the more complex drugs are unstable.

PHARMACEUTICAL CLASSIFICATIONS

Certain types of pharmaceuticals used in sports are briefly defined in the following list. Some of them, as well as other selected drugs, are discussed in greater detail later in the chapter.

1. *Analgesics* or *anodynes*—pain-relieving drugs
2. *Anesthetics*—agents that produce local or general numbness to touch, pain, or stimulation
3. *Antacids*—substances that neutralize acidity; commonly used in the digestive tract
4. *Anticoagulants*—agents that prevent coagulation of blood
5. *Antidotes*—substances that prevent or counteract the action of a poison
6. *Antipruritics*—agents that relieve itching
7. *Antiseptics*—agents that kill bacteria or inhibit their growth and can be applied to living tissue
8. *Antispasmodics*—agents that relieve muscle spasm
9. *Antitussives*—agents that inhibit or prevent coughing
10. *Astringents*—agents that cause contraction or puckering action

11. *Bacteriostatics* and *fungistatics*—agents that retard or inhibit the growth of bacteria or fungi
12. *Carminatives*—agents that relieve flatulence (caused by gases) in the intestinal tract
13. *Cathartics*—agents used to evacuate substances from the bowels; active purgatives
14. *Caustics*—burning agents, capable of destroying living tissue
15. *Counterirritants*—agents applied locally to produce an inflammatory reaction for the relief of a deeper inflammation
16. *Depressants*—agents that diminish body functions or nerve activity
17. *Disinfectants*—agents that kill or inhibit the growth of microorganisms; should be applied only to nonliving materials
18. *Diuretics*—agents that increase the secretion of urine
19. *Emetics*—agents that cause vomiting
20. *Hemostatics*—substances that either slow down or stop bleeding or hemorrhage
21. *Irritants*—agents that cause irritation
22. *Narcotics*—drugs that produce analgesic and hypnotic effects
23. *Sedatives*—agents that quiet body activity
24. *Skeletal muscle relaxants*—drugs that depress neural activity within skeletal muscles
25. *Stimulants*—agents that temporarily increase functional activity
26. *Vasoconstrictors* and *vasodilators*—drugs that, respectively, constrict or dilate blood vessels

SELECTED THERAPEUTIC DRUGS IN SPORTS

In sports the use of drugs and medicinals is widespread, as in society in general, but it also is unique to the special needs of the athlete. This section is designed to discuss the most common medicinal practices in athletic training to date and specific drugs that are in use. The discussion includes both prescription and nonprescription drugs, with emphasis on what should most concern the coach or athletic trainer, and what the medications or materials are designed to accomplish.

Drugs to Combat Infection

Combating infection, especially skin infection, is of major importance in sports. Serious infection can cause countless hours of lost time and has even been the indirect cause of death.

Local Antiseptics and Disinfectants

Antiseptics are substances that can be placed on living tissue for the express purpose of either killing bacteria or inhibiting their growth. Disinfectants, on the other hand, are substances that combat microorganisms but should only be applied to nonliving objects. Other general names given to antiseptics and disinfectants are *germicides,* which are designed to destroy bacteria; *fungicides,* which kill fungi; *sporicides,* which destroy spores; and *sanitizers,* which minimize contamination by microorganisms.

Antiseptics act on disease-producing organisms by changing the protein structure of the organism, increasing its permeability, and inhibiting its metabolic processes.

Figure 15-3

Athletic trainers and coaches must understand the health belief systems in terms of the taking of medication of the athletes with whom they work.

Classification of local antiseptics
   Alcohols—ethyl alcohol and isopropyl alcohol
   Acids—acetic acid and boric acid
   Surface-active agents—quaternary ammonium compounds
   Phenols—hexachlorophene
   Halogenated compounds—iodine and iodophors
   Oxidizing agents—peroxides
   Metal compounds—mercury, silver, and zinc

In sports many agents are used to combat infection. Some of the most commonly used antiseptics and disinfectants in sports are the following: phenols, dyes, mercury compounds, silver compounds, halogens, oxidizing agents, alcohols, formaldehyde, boric acid, and soap.

Alcohol is one of the most widely used skin disinfectants. Ethyl alcohol (70% by weight) and isopropyl alcohol (70%) are equally effective. They are inexpensive and nonirritating, killing bacteria immediately, with the exception of spores. However, they have no long-lasting germicidal action. Besides being directly combined with other agents to form tinctures, alcohol acts independently on the skin as an antiseptic and astringent. In a 70% solution it can be used for disinfecting instruments. Because of alcohol's rapid rate of evaporation, it produces a mild anesthetic action and, when used as a massage agent, gives a refreshingly cool sensation. Combined with 20% benzoin, it is used in athletics as a topical skin dressing as a protective skin coating and astringent.

Acids are widely used both as antiseptics and astringents in a variety of skin preparations. Benzoic, salicylic, and undecylenic acids are all used in athlete's foot treatments. Whitefield's ointment contains both salicylic and benzoic acids, and Desenex powder, spray, and ointment contain undecylenic acid.

Among quaternary ammonium compounds, the most widely known and previously used is benzalkonium chloride (commonly known as Zephiran). Zephiran combined with an antirust compound is used in the disinfection of surgical instruments.

Phenol was one of the earliest antiseptics and disinfectants used by the medical profession. From its inception to the present it has been used to control disease organisms, both as an antiseptic and as a disinfectant. It is available in liquids of varying concentrations and emollients. Substances that are derived from phenol and that cause less irritation are now used more extensively. Some of these derivatives are resorcinol, thymol, and the common household disinfectant Lysol.

Halogens are chemical substances (chlorine, iodine, fluoride, and bromine) that are used for their antiseptic and disinfectant qualities. Iodophors or halogenated compounds, a combination of iodine and a carrier, create a much less irritating preparation than tincture of iodine. A popular iodophor is povidone-iodine complex (Betadine), which is an excellent germicide commonly used as a surgical scrub by the surgeon. Betadine as an antiseptic and germicide in athletic training has proved extremely successful on skin lesions such as lacerations, abrasions, and floor burns.

Oxidizing agents, as represented by hydrogen peroxide (3%) or potassium permanganate, are commonly used in athletic training. Hydrogen peroxide is an antiseptic that, because of its oxidation, affects bacteria but readily decomposes in the presence of organic substances such as blood and pus. For this reason it has little effect as an antiseptic. Contact with organic material produces an effervescence, during which no great destruction of bacteria takes place. The chief value of hydrogen peroxide in the care of wounds is its ability to cleanse the infected cutaneous and mucous membranes. Application of hydrogen peroxide to wounds results in the formation of an active effervescent gas that dislodges particles of wound material and debris and, by removing degenerated tissue, eliminates the wound as a likely environment for bacterial breeding. Hydrogen peroxide also possesses a styptic action as a result of encouraging fibrin development in open wounds. Because it is nontoxic, hydrogen peroxide may be used for cleansing mucous membranes. A diluted solution (50% water and 50% hydrogen peroxide) can be used for treating inflammatory conditions of the mouth and throat.

Metal compounds are widely used as antiseptics. For example, mercury and its derivatives are considered bacteriostatic because they inhibit certain enzymatic actions of the bacteria. Some popular mercury preparations are yellow mercuric oxide for infection of the conjunctiva, thimerosal (Merthiolate), nitromersol (Metaphen), and merbromin (Mercurochrome).

Some agents containing silver have both antiseptic and astringent effects. As with mercury, silver penetrates tissue protein and disrupts the function of the microorganism by inhibiting enzymatic action. Zinc is also used in both antiseptic and astringent skin preparations. Zinc sulfate ointment is used for conjunctivitis; zinc oxide is widely used in ointments and is a main ingredient of calamine lotion (Table 15-1).

Antifungal Agents

Many medicinal agents on the market are designed to treat fungi, which are commonly found in and around athletic facilities. The three most common fungi are *Epidermophyton, Trichophyton,* and *Candida albicans*.

In recent years there has been successful development and use of antifungal antibiotics such as nystatin (Mycostatin), amphotericin B (Fungi-zone), and griseofulvin. Both nystatin and amphotericin B seem to be effective against deep-seated fungous infections such as those caused by the *Monilia* strain, *Candida al-*

TABLE 15-1 Over-the-Counter First Aid Preparations for Skin Wounds

Category	Active Ingredients	Product Name and Manufacturer	How Delivered
Antiseptic	Ethyl alcohol (60% to 90%)	Alcare (Vestal)	Foam (62%)
	Isopropyl alcohol (50% to 9.3%)	Ethyl Rubbing Alcohol (Whiteworth)	Liquid (70%)
		Isopropyl Alcohol (Bowman)	Liquid (70%)
		(Eli Lilly Co.)	Liquid (91%)
		Zephiran (Winthrop-Breon Laboratories)	Tincture (1.7%), tincture spray (1.7%)
	Benzethonium chloride (0.5%) and benzocaine (13.6%)	Aerocaine (Aeroceuticals)	Spray
	Benzethonium chloride (0.1%) and benzocaine (10%)	Americaine First Aid (American Critical Care)	Spray
	Benzalkonium chloride (0.13%) and lidocaine (2.5%)	Bactine Antiseptic/Anesthetic First Aid Spray (Miles Laboratories Inc.)	Spray, liquid, aerosol
Wound protectant	Bacitracin	Baciguent (The Upjohn Co.) (fights gram-positive bacteria)	Ointment: 500 units/g
	Chlortetroagline hydrochloride	Aureomycin (Lederle) (fights gram-positive bacteria)	Ointment: 3%
	Neomycin sulfate	Myciguent (The Upjohn Co.) (active against gram-positive and some gram-negative bacteria)	Ointment: 5 mg/g (0.5%)
	Neosporin: 500 units polymyxin and B sulfate and 3.5 mg neomycin base (as sulfate) and 400 units/g bactracin	Neosporin (Burroughs Wellcome Co.)	Ointment

bicans. Griseofulvin, which is administered orally, produces an effective fungistatic action against the specific fungous species of *Microsporum, Trichophyton,* and *Epidermophyton*—all of which are associated with common athlete's foot. Given over a long period of time griseofulvin becomes a functioning part of the cutaneous tissues, especially the skin, hair, and nails, producing a prolonged and continuous fungistatic action. Tolnaftate (Tinactin), as well as the athlete's foot treatment acids mentioned previously, are topical medications for a superficial fungous infection caused by *Trichophyton* and other fungi.

Mechanical antiseptics, usually soaps that provide a cleansing and detergent action, remove pathogens from the skin.

Antibiotics

Antibiotics are chemical agents that are produced by microorganisms. Their useful action is primarily a result of their interfering with the necessary metabolic processes of pathogenic microorganisms. In sports they are used by the physician as either topical dressings or systemic medications. The indiscriminate use of an-

Indiscriminate antibiotic use can produce hypersensitivity and can prevent the development of natural immunity or resistance to infections.

tibiotics can produce extreme hypersensitivity or idiosyncrasies and can prevent the development of natural immunity or resistance to subsequent infections. The use of any antibiotic must be carefully controlled by the physician, who selects the drug on the basis of the most desirable type of administration and the amount of toxicity to the patient.

The antibiotics mentioned here are just a few of the many available. New types continue to be developed, mainly because, over a period of time, microorganisms often become resistant to a particular antibiotic, especially if it is indiscriminately used. Some of the more common antibiotics are penicillin, streptomycin, bacitracin, tetracycline, erythromycin, and the sulfonamides.

Penicillin as a prescription medication is probably the most important of the antibiotics; it is useful in a variety of skin and systemic infections. In general, penicillin interferes with the metabolism of the bacteria.

Streptomycin is a potent antibiotic that inhibits protein synthesis of bacteria. It is especially beneficial in treating respiratory tract infections.

Bacitracin has proved to be extremely valuable in sports in the last few years. Like penicillin, it has a broad spectrum of effectiveness as an antibacterial agent. In addition, it seldom causes sensitivity reactions when used topically in a salve, an advantage over penicillin.

Tetracyclines consist of a wide group of antibiotics that have a broad antibacterial spectrum. Their application, which is usually oral, modifies the infection rather than eradicating it completely.

Erythromycin is an effective agent against staphylococcal bacteria and has the same general spectrum as penicillin. It is normally used when penicillin-resistant organisms are present.

Sulfonamides are a group of synthetic antibiotics. In general, sulfonamides make pathogens vulnerable to phagocytes by inhibiting certain enzymatic actions. The most commonly used ones are sulfadiazine, sulfamerazine, sulfamethazine, and sulfisoxazole.

Drugs to Inhibit or Deaden Pain

Controlling pain in an athlete can involve innumerable drugs and procedures, depending on the beliefs of the athletic trainer, coach, or physician. As discussed in Chapter 8, why pain is often positively affected by certain methods is not clearly understood; however, some of the possible reasons are as follows:

1. The excitatory effect of an individual impulse is depressed.
2. An individual impulse is inhibited.
3. The perceived impulse is decreased.
4. Anxiety created by the pain or impending pain is decreased.

Counterirritants and Local Anesthetics

The inhibition of pain sensations through the skin is a major approach in sports. Analgesics give relief by causing a mild topical anesthesia in peripheral sensory nerve endings. Many chemical reactions on the skin can inhibit pain sensations through rapid evaporation, which causes a cooling action, or by counterirritating the skin. Irritating and counterirritating substances used in sports act as rubefacients (skin reddeners) and skin stimulants. They are becoming less popular than in the past. Their application causes a local increase in blood circulation, redness, and a rise in skin temperature. Frequently mild pain can be reduced by a **counterirritant,** which produces a stimulus to the skin of such intensity that the ath-

counterirritant
An agent that produces a mild inflammation and acts as an analgesic when applied locally to the skin.

lete is no longer aware of the pain. Some examples of counterirritants include liniments, analgesic balms, and heat (hot water) and cold (ice packs).

Spray coolants, because of their rapid evaporation, act as topical anesthetics to the skin. Several commercial coolants are presently on the market. Chloromethane is one of the most popular spray coolants currently used in sports. Cooling results so quickly that superficial freezing takes place, inhibiting pain impulses for a short time. Athletic trainers disagree as to the effectiveness of spray coolants. Some athletic trainers use them extensively for strains, sprains, and contusions. In my opinion spray coolants are useful only when other analgesics are not available.

Alcohol evaporates rapidly when applied to the skin, causing a refreshingly cool effect that gives a temporary analgesia.

Camphor may be considered a counterirritant when applied to the skin. It has mild antiseptic and skin-irritating qualities. Acting as a rubefacient, it relieves superficial tissue areas of congestion and pressure on sensory pain receptors.

Cold applications constrict blood vessels and numb sensory nerve endings.

Cold applications also immediately act to constrict blood vessels and to numb sensory nerve endings. Applications of ice packs or submersion of a part in ice water may completely anesthetize an area. If extreme cold is used, caution must be taken that tissue damage does not result.

Menthol is an alcohol taken from mint oils and is principally used as a local analgesic, counterirritant, and antiseptic. Most often in sports it is used with a petroleum base for treating cold symptoms and in analgesic balms.

Methyl salicylate is synthetic wintergreen used externally in sports as an analgesic, counterirritant, and antiseptic. Together with menthol and capsicum oleoresin (red pepper), it is one of the main constituents of analgesic balms and liniments.

TABLE 15-2 Some Over-the-Counter Pain, Fever, and Anti-Inflammatory Drugs Taken Internally

Product Name and Manufacturer	Dosage
Acetaminophen	
Tylenol, Regular Strength (McNeil Consumer Products Co.)	Tablets, 325 mg
Extra-Strength Datril (Bristol-Myers Co.)	Tablets, 500 mg
Aspirin (acetylsalicylic acid)	
A.S.A. tablets (Eli Lilly and Co.)	Tablets, 325 mg
Bayer Aspirin (Glenbrook Laboratories)	Tablets, 325 mg
Empirin (Burroughs Wellcome Co.)	Tablets, 325 mg
Choline salicylate anthropan (The Purdue-Frederick Co.)	Liquid, 870 mg/tsp (5ml)
Magnesium salicylate	
Doan's Pills (Jeffrey Martin)	Tablets, 325 mg

Local anesthetics are usually injected by the physician in and around injury sites for minor surgical procedures or to alleviate the pain of movement. Procaine hydrochloride is used extensively as a local anesthetic in sports, since its anesthesia is more concentrated than that of cocaine and does not cause blood vessel constriction (Table 15-2).

Narcotic Analgesics

Most narcotics used in medicine are derived directly from opium or are synthetic opiates. They depress pain impulses and the individual's respiratory centers. The two most often used derivatives are codeine and morphine.

Codeine resembles morphine in its action but is less potent. Its primary action is as a respiratory depressant; because of this action, it is found in many cough medicines.

Propoxyphene hydrochloride (Darvon) is a mild analgesic narcotic that is slightly stronger than aspirin in its pain relief. It is not an anti-inflammatory drug. Propoxyphene hydrochloride is addictive, and when combined with alcohol, tranquilizers, or other sedatives or depressants, it can be fatal.

Morphine depresses pain sensations to a greater extent than any other drug. It is also the most dangerous drug because of its ability to depress respiration and because of its habit-forming qualities. Morphine is never used in the following situations: (1) before a diagnosis has been made by the physician; (2) when the subject is unconscious; (3) when there is a head injury; or (4) when there is a decreased rate of breathing. It is never repeated within 2 hours.

Meperidine (Demerol) is the most commonly prescribed narcotic. It is used as a substitute for morphine for the relief of mild or moderate pain caused by muscular spasticity.

Drugs for the Central Nervous System

Drugs affect the central nervous system by either increasing or decreasing its irritability. In this section those drugs which decrease the irritability of the system are discussed. They are classified in two groups as follows: analgesics and antipyretics, and hypnotics and antianxiety drugs.

Analgesics and Antipyretics (Internally Administered and Over-the-Counter)

Central nervous system analgesics are those drugs designed to suppress all but the most severe pain, without the patient's losing consciousness. Their main action is on the nerves carrying the pain impulses to the brain. In most cases these drugs also act as antipyretics, inhibiting toxins from affecting the temperature control centers. They consist mainly of acetylsalicylic acid (aspirin: 5 to 15 grains) and acetaminophen.

Acetaminophen (Tylenol) is an effective analgesic and antipyretic. It raises the athlete's pain threshold and decreases fever by acting on the heat-regulating center in the hypothalamus. The usual adult dosage is one or two 325 mg tablets taken every 4 to 6 hours, not to exceed 12 tablets each day. Because it does not irritate the gastrointestinal system, it is often a replacement for aspirin in noninflammatory conditions.

Acetylsalicylic acid (aspirin) is one of the most widely used analgesics and antipyretics. It is also one of the most abused drugs in use today. A number of medications that have salicylates as a primary substance are on the market and are very effective in reducing pain, fever, and inflammation.

Hypnotics and Antianxiety Drugs

A hypnotic or antianxiety drug may be prescribed for an athlete who is under extreme tension. Benzodiazepines are the largest family of prescribed hypnotic and antianxiety drugs. The most commonly prescribed hypnotic drug in the United States is flurazepam (Dalmane). The most commonly prescribed tranquilizers of the benzodiazepine family in the United States are diazepam (Valium), oxazepam (Serax), lorazepam (Ativan), and alprazolam (Xanax).

Caution should always be used in dispensing analgesics for headaches and other complaints, since they may disguise symptoms of more serious pathological conditions.

Astringents

Astringents cause contraction of cells, arrest capillary bleeding, and coagulate the albumins of local tissues. Astringents applied to mucous membranes will harden tissue cells and decrease inflammatory exudates. Applied directly to the skin, an astringent will check hemorrhage and other secretions. The most popular astringents in sports are alum, boric acid, zinc oxide, and tannic acid.

Alum is used in sports mostly in powder form and is extensively applied as a styptic in the care of mouth ulcerations and in the control of excessive foot perspiration.

Boric acid is used both as an astringent and as a mild antiseptic. As an astringent it is used in powder form; it can be dusted on capillary bleeding areas or be used on the feet to control foot odors and excessive perspiration. Toxic reaction to boric acid may occur because of its high level of absorbability.

Zinc oxide in an ointment effects a soothing and astringent action. Used in the mass (sticky portion) of the adhesive tape, it helps to prevent undue skin softening when tape is applied. As an emollient, zinc oxide ointment can be applied to denuded skin areas and can effect a mild healing action without softening the skin excessively. It also provides a good drying agent for abrasions.

Tannic acid, when administered externally, has both astringent and hemostatic qualities. It is found in many training room preparations designed to toughen skin. It is effective and not dangerous when applied to small areas of the body (e.g., to a friction burn).

Drugs to Treat Itching

Pruritis (itching) is the result of irritation to the peripheral sensory nerves. It is a symptom, rather than a condition in itself, and leads to scratching, which in turn may cause infection. Many situations in sports can create pruritis. Perspiration combined with irritating clothing is a common cause of itching. To relieve itching, solutions and ointments containing either a mild topical anesthetic such as benzocaine or a cool, soothing agent such as calamine or menthol may be applied to the skin.

Perspiration combined with irritating clothing is a common cause of itching.

Calamine is one of the oldest medications used today. It is composed of zinc oxide powder with a small amount of ferric oxide, which gives it a pinkish color. In a lotion form it is combined with glycerin, bentonite magma (a suspending agent for insoluble drugs), and a solution of calcium hydroxide (lime water).

TABLE 15-3 Over-the-Counter Itch and Pain Remedies Applied to the Skin

Active Ingredients	Product Name and Manufacturer	How Delivered
Benzocaine (example of anesthetic)	Americaine Anesthetic (American Critical Care)	Spray 20%, cream 5%, ointment 5%
Camphor (East Asian camphor)		Liquid
Diphenhydromine hydrochloride, calamine, camphor	Caladryl Cream (Parke-Davis)	Cream: 1% diphenhydromine hydrochloride and 8% calamine, 0.1% camphor

Placed on the skin, calamine lotion acts as a soothing, protective coating in cases of itching dermatitis.

Caladryl is calamine combined with 1% diphenhydramine hydrochloride. It produces a very soothing lotion (Table 15-3).

Drugs to Loosen Horny Skin Layer

Because sports participation can create painful accumulations of the outermost horny layer of the skin on the hands and feet, warts, corns, and heavy calluses may require a keratolytic agent to loosen and/or encourage peeling of the top layer of skin. Resorcinol and salicylic acid are the most common drugs used for this purpose. They are commonly found in corn removal medications.

Protective Skin Coatings

Coatings may be applied to skin areas where protection from contamination, friction, or drying of tissues is needed. Protective coatings in sports consist mainly of substances containing storax or flexible collodion, plus adhesive tape.

Storax is a balsam derived from the trunk of *Liquidamber orientalis* or *Liquidamber styraciflua*. It occurs as a semiliquid, grayish, sticky, and opaque mass, which is used most often in a compound benzoin tincture as an adherent. Its qualities give a protective coating against tape and friction irritants.

Flexible collodion is a mixture of ethyl oxides, pyroxylin, alcohol, camphor, and castor oil. When applied to the skin, this solution evaporates rapidly, leaving a flexible cohesive film. Its use in sports is primarily for covering exposed tissue and protecting lacerated cuts from further irritation.

Adhesive tape offers a highly adaptable means for the protection of athletic affections.

Spray plastic coatings have been developed to cover external wounds, replacing the conventional cloth dressing. The danger of such coatings is that infection may be contained within the wound if it has not been properly cleansed.

Sun Screens

A number of sun screens are currently on the market. Many of these products contain para-aminobenzoic acid (PABA), which, when applied to the skin, combines with the stratum corneum to provide sun protection. Depending on the strength of the product, sunburning is prevented, but tanning is allowed, or both burning and tanning are prevented. Additional ingredients commonly used are podimate, oxybenzone, cinoxate, and others.[17]

Drugs to Treat Colds and Allergies

Drugs on the market designed to affect colds and allergies are almost too numerous to count. In general, they fall into three basic categories, all of which deal with the symptoms of the condition and not the causation. They are drugs dealing with nasal congestion, histamine reactions, and cough.

Nasal Decongestants and Antihistamines

Drugs that affect the nasal mucous membranes are basically vasoconstrictors, which reduce engorged tissue during upper respiratory tract involvements.

Decongestants   Decongestants that contain mild vasoconstricting agents such as phenylephrine hydrochloride (Neo-Synephrine) or naphazoline hydrochloride (Privine) are on the market. These agents, applied topically, are relatively safe. Only when used to excess do they cause undesirable side effects.

Antihistamines   Antihistamines are often added to nasal decongestants. Histamine is a protein substance contained in animal tissues that, when released into the general circulation, causes the reactions of an allergy. Histamine causes dilation of arteries and capillaries, skin flushing, and a rise in temperature. An antihistamine is a substance that opposes histamine action. Examples are diphenhydramine hydrochloride (Benadryl) and tripelennamine hydrochloride (Pyribenzamine). Nasal vasoconstrictors or decongestants can be overused by the athlete. For example, overuse of these medications can result in a reversal of vasoconstriction, or vasodilation, causing a rebound (reactive) edema to occur. Overuse can also cause the athlete to have elevated blood pressure, dizziness, heart palpitation, and drowsiness.

Some antihistamines have been found also to relieve the symptoms of *motion sickness* by depressing the central nervous system, particularly the nerves affecting the labyrinth of the ear. One of the most popular compounds used for motion sickness is dimenhydrinate (Dramamine).

An effective decongestant is pseudoephedrine hydrochloride (Sudafed). As a nonprescription drug it comes in tablets of 30 mg; prescription tablets for adults are 60 mg. Two tablets are recommended, four times a day. Sudafed is effective within ½ to 1 hour, by decongesting nasal passages and bronchioli.

> Overuse of nasal decongestants and antihistamines can cause elevated blood pressure, dizziness, heart palpitation, and drowsiness.

Cough Medicines

Cough medicines or antitussives help inhibit or prevent coughing. Their action may increase the fluid content so that expectoration is made easier, or they may relieve irritated mucous membranes by soothing or healing inflamed mucosa. Antitussives are available in liquid, capsule, pill, troche, or spray form. *Ammonium chloride* is used in many cough medicines to alleviate symptoms of inflamed mucous membranes. *Terpin hydrate* and *creosote* are substances that help to diminish bronchial secretions. *Codeine* is also commonly used but must be prescribed by a physician. It is a depressant and affects the reflex cough center in the brain.

Drugs to Treat Gastrointestinal Disorders

Disorders of the gastrointestinal tract include an upset stomach or formation of gas because of food incompatibilities and acute or chronic hyperacidity, which leads to inflammation of the mucous membrane of the intestinal tract. There is an ever-increasing incidence of ulcers among high school and college athletes, most of which are probably caused by the stress of anticipating sports performances. Poor eating habits may lead to digestive tract problems such as diarrhea or constipation. Drugs that elicit responses within the gastrointestinal tract are basically alkalies, carminatives, cathartics and laxatives, emetics, and hydrochloric and citric acids.

Poor eating habits may lead to digestive tract problems such as diarrhea or constipation.

Alkalies

Alkalies taken into the stomach relieve hyperacidity. The most common alkalies are sodium bicarbonate, calcium carbonate, magnesium carbonate, calcium hydroxide (lime water), and bismuth. They may be used in liquid, powder, or tablet form.

Carminatives

Carminatives are drugs that give relief from flatulence (gas). Their action on the digestive canal is to inhibit gas formation and aid in its expulsion. Peppermint and spearmint water are the most commonly used carminatives. They may be combined with alkalies to decrease the acid secretion of the stomach.

Laxatives

The use of laxatives in sports should always be under the direction of a physician. Constipation may be symptomatic of a serious disease condition. Indiscreet use of laxatives may render the athlete unable to have normal bowel movements. There is little need for healthy, active individuals to rely on artificial means for stool evacuation.

Emetics

Emetics are drugs that cause reverse peristalsis, or vomiting. This is usually a first-aid measure to rid the stomach of poison. In sports it may be used to rid the stomach of disagreeable food. A glass of warm water containing a teaspoonful of powdered mustard or salt or a glass of soapy water can cause regurgitation. A full glass of warm water and bicarbonate of soda will take the acidity from the vomitus. Probably the least time-consuming method to induce vomiting is to have the athlete tickle the back of the throat at the gag reflex center.

Drugs to Control Bleeding

Various drugs and medicines cause selective actions on the circulatory system, including vasoconstrictors and anticoagulants.

Vasoconstrictors

In sports vasoconstrictors are most often administered externally to sites of profuse bleeding. The drug most commonly used for this purpose is epinephrine (adrenaline), which is applied directly to a hemorrhaging area. It acts immediately to constrict damaged blood vessels and has been found extremely valuable in cases of epistaxis (nosebleed) in which normal procedures were inadequate.

Anticoagulants

Drugs that inhibit blood clotting may be used by the physician in cases of recent injury or in cases of blood vessel occlusion by a thrombus. The most common anticoagulants used by physicians in sports are heparin and coumarin derivatives.

Heparin is a substance that is derived from the lungs of domestic animals. It prolongs the clotting time of blood but will not dissolve a clot once it has developed. Heparin is used primarily to control extension of a thrombus that is already present.

Coumarin derivatives act by suppressing the formation of prothrombin in the liver. Given orally, they are used to slow clotting time in certain vascular disorders.

Drugs to Reduce Inflammation

Sports physicians have a wide choice of drugs at their disposal for treatment of inflammation. There is also a great variety of over-the-counter drugs that claim to deal effectively with inflammation of the musculoskeletal system. The problem of proper drug selection is tenuous, even for a physician, because of new drugs continually coming to the forefront; the situation is compounded by highly advertised over-the-counter preparations. Any drug selection, especially drugs designed to treat the inflammatory process, must be effective, must be appropriate for the highly physical athlete, and must not create any untoward adverse reactions. With these points in mind, the more generally accepted anti-inflammatory drugs are discussed.

Salicylates (Aspirin)

Aspirin is an anti-inflammatory agent, as well as an analgesic and antipyretic (as discussed earlier).

As an anti-inflammatory agent, aspirin is effective in conditions such as tendinitis, bursitis, chondromalacia, and tenosynovitis. It is believed to inhibit the release of prostaglandins, a major factor in the inflammatory process.[4] Aspirin has been associated with a number of adverse reactions that are primarily centered in the gastrointestinal region. They include difficulty in food digestion (dyspepsia), nausea, vomiting, and gastric bleeding. To reduce these complaints, buffered or enteric-coated aspirin should be ingested. Buffered aspirin prevents irritation because of its antacid properties, and enteric-coated aspirin dissolves in the small intestines instead of the stomach.

Other adverse reactions to aspirin, especially in high doses, are ear ringing or buzzing (tinnitus) and dizziness. In some cases, the athlete will report heart palpitations and/or tachycardia.

Dimethyl Sulfoxide (DMSO)

Dimethyl sulfoxide (DMSO) is one of the most controversial medicinals in sports medicine. Its unique properties have been described as a "wonder drug" by some and as "dangerous" by others. It has been actively investigated for its use with rheumatoid arthritis, brain swelling, scleroderma, sprains, and strains. However, questions as to its effectiveness and safety remain.

DMSO originally was a solvent used in the manufacturing of rayon and Orlon fibers, antifreeze, hydraulic fluid, paint, and varnish remover.

In terms of its medical use, DMSO is absorbed rapidly into the skin and bloodstream within 5 minutes of application.[26] Once absorbed, it permeates almost all tissue. One characteristic of DMSO is a taste and breath smell of garlic or oysters. Because of fast skin penetration it has been used as a vehicle for other drugs, such

Dimethyl sulfoxide (DMSO) is one of the most controversial drugs in sports medicine.

as hydrocortisone or hexachlorophene, into the body.[39] Another quality is that DMSO takes up water dramatically. It also is known to inhibit cholinesterase, which is an enzyme that catalyzes the hydrolysis of acetylcholine to choline and an anion. DMSO also breaks down collagen fibers while keeping elastic fibers intact.

In sports medicine, DMSO has been and is being used to decrease joint swelling, dispel hematomas and ecchymoses (black and blue areas), and generally promote the healing process. DMSO exacerbates inflammation by producing a histamine response, which promotes vasodilation. Pain is also decreased by the blockage of the C nerve fibers.

Reported side effects after DMSO treatment are relatively few. Some side effects are an occasional minor rash at the treatment site, generalized dermatitis, headache, nausea, and dizziness.[1] One extremely important factor is that tendons or ligaments may be weakened after prolonged DMSO treatment, thus precluding sports participation during and immediately after DMSO therapy.[6,27]

Enzymes

The use of enzyme drugs has become a popular means of caring for the injured athlete. Enzymes are used by physicians for various reasons, such as for the absorption of proteolytic enzymes and for clot lysis.

Varidase (streptokinase-streptodornase) is an enzyme taken from specific strains of streptococci. This mixture of enzymes is used topically for dissolving blood clots (streptokinase) and pus (streptodornase). For an athlete it may be mixed with hydrocortisone and lidocaine (Xylocaine) in treating a swollen joint. In general, varidase is an anti-inflammatory agent designed for the relief of pain, swelling, tenderness, and redness (erythema).

Bromelain (Ananase), on the other hand, contains proteolytic enzymes produced by the pineapple plant. Taken orally it decreases edema and pain and assists in tissue repair. Other commonly used agents are salicylates, especially aspirin, indomethacin (Indocin), and corticosteroids (cortisone).

Nonsteroidal Anti-Inflammatory Drugs

Indomethacin (Indocin) is a nonsteroidal drug that has anti-inflammatory, antipyretic, and analgesic properties. It is a strong inhibitor of prostaglandin synthesis and is effective for such chronic problems as rheumatoid arthritis and osteoarthritis.

Indomethacin can produce many adverse reactions and should be used cautiously. It can cause severe gastrointestinal tract reactions, drowsiness, headache, dizziness, depression, tinnitus, and a variety of other systemic reactions.

Ibuprofen (Motrin) is a nonsteroidal anti-inflammatory agent. Besides affecting inflammation, it also acts as an antipyretic and analgesic. Tablets are available in 300 and 400 mg. It is comparable to aspirin and better tolerated by some persons. Like many other anti-inflammatory agents, ibuprofen can cause gastric irritation, dizziness, headache, nervousness, and skin itching (pruritus).

Phenylbutazone (Butazolidin) is an extremely potent nonsteroidal antiinflammatory drug. It also is antipyretic and analgesic. Phenylbutazone is particularly useful for chronic musculoskeletal conditions such as acute arthritis, bursitis, and capsulitis. It can produce serious adverse reactions if not carefully administered by the physician. Gastric ulceration, anemia, fluid and electrolyte disturbances, liver damage, skin hemorrhaging, pruritus, kidney dysfunction, hypertension, heart inflammation, and an allergic reaction are a few of these adverse reactions.

Oxyphenbutazone (Tandearil), like phenylbutazone, is an extremely powerful drug. It also is a nonsteroidal agent that is anti-inflammatory, antipyretic, and pain inhibiting. The adverse reactions are similar to phenylbutazone.

Corticosteroids

Corticosteroids, of which cortisone is the most common, are used primarily for chronic inflammation of musculoskeletal and joint regions. Cortisone is a synthetic glucocorticoid that is usually given orally or by injection. Increasingly more caution is taken in the use of corticosteroids than was practiced in the past. Prolonged use of corticosteroids can produce the following serious complications:

1. Fluid and electrolyte disturbances (e.g., water retention caused by excess sodium levels)
2. Musculoskeletal and joint impairments (e.g., bone thinning and muscle and tendon weakness)
3. Dermatological problems (e.g., delayed wound healing)
4. Neurological impairments (e.g., vertigo, headache, convulsions)
5. Endocrine dysfunctions (e.g., menstrual irregularities)
6. Ophthalmic conditions (e.g., glaucoma)
7. Metabolic impairments (e.g., negative nitrogen balance, muscle wasting)

Cortisone is primarily administered by injection. Other ways are ionophoresis and phonophoresis. (See Chapter 13, *Therapeutic Modalities*.) Studies have indicated that cortisone injected directly into tendons, ligaments, and joint spaces can lead to weakness and degeneration. After cortisone treatment an athlete must not participate in sports for up to 6 weeks. Such activity will predispose the treated part to rupturing. Trigger points, tennis elbow, and plantar fasciitis have benefitted from corticosteroid treatment.[33]

Trigger points, tennis elbow, and plantar fasciitis have benefitted from corticosteroid treatment.

Drugs for Muscle Dysfunctions

The two most common muscle problems in sports are the ordinary muscle cramp, stemming from physical activity, and spasms, which are associated with musculoskeletal injury. Muscle cramps that commonly occur in the legs probably stem from fatigue and mineral deprivation or, perhaps, a muscle anoxia associated with some minor circulatory impairment. These cramps are often easily remediated through rest and restoration of mineral stores. However, skeletal relaxant agents designed to alleviate spasms of the musculature are widely used in both acute and chronic musculoskeletal conditions. If muscle spasms are relieved, pain can be diminished, and normal function can often be resumed. In recent years skeletal relaxants have been given by physicians to athletes immediately after musculoskeletal injury.

Drugs that produce muscular relaxation are divided into "peripheral" relaxants and "central" relaxants. Peripheral relaxants act on the myoneural junction by blocking the depolarization of the motor end-plate by acetylcholine. Central relaxants inhibit specific neuromuscular reflexes. Common skeletal muscle depressants that act on the central nervous system are mephenesin, methocarbamol (Robaxin), and carisoprodol (Soma). Because centrally acting muscle relaxants also act as sedatives or tranquilizers on the higher brain centers, there is growing speculation among physicians that these drugs are less specific to muscle relaxation than was once believed.

Most of these relaxants are dispensed in tablet form and ingested orally. These drugs relieve muscle spasms that have occurred from the traumatic injuries of sprains, strains, fractures, or dislocations.

PERFORMANCE AIDS

There is increasing concern about the number of athletes engaging in substance abuse. Some do so in an attempt to improve performance, whereas others engage in it as a recreational pursuit. Because of the inequities that result in competition and the health problems that can result, the use of these substances cannot be condoned.

Banned Substances and Methods

In sports medicine and athletic training, the administration of a drug that is designed to improve the competitor's performance is known as **"doping."** The International Olympic Committee (IOC) divides doping into three classes. Class I includes the following categories: stimulants, narcotics, anabolic steroids, beta blockers, and diuretics. Class II refers to blood reinjection (blood doping), and class III discusses the drugs such as alcohol, local anesthetics, and corticosteroids that are subject to certain restrictions.[22]

The IOC defines doping as "the administration or use of substances in any form alien to the body or of physiological substances in abnormal amounts and with abnormal methods by healthy persons with the exclusive aim of attaining an artificial and unfair increase in performance in sports."[12]

doping
The administration of a drug that is designed to improve the competitor's performance.

Stimulants

The intention of the athlete when he or she ingests a stimulant may be to increase alertness, to reduce fatigue, or, in some instances, to increase competitiveness and even produce hostility.[22] In general, some athletes respond to stimulants with a loss of judgment that may lead to personal injury or injury to others.

Two major categories of stimulants are psychomotor stimulant drugs and adrenergenic (sympathomimetic) drugs. Psychomotor stimulants are of two general types—amphetamines (e.g., metamphetamines) and non-amphetamines (e.g., methylphenidate and cocaine). The major actions of psychomotor stimulants result from the rapid turnover of catecholomines, which have a marked effect on the nervous and cardiovascular systems, metabolic rates, temperature, and smooth muscles. On the other hand, sympathomimetic drugs act directly on adrenergic receptors, or those that release catecholomines (i.e., epinephrine and norepinephrine) from nerve endings, and thus act indirectly on catecholamines. Ephedrine is an example of this type, and can, in high doses, cause mental stimulation and increased blood flow. As a result, it may also cause elevated blood pressure and headache, increased and irregular heart beat, anxiety, and tremor.[22] Another category of banned stimulant substances, analeptic drugs, includes central nervous system stimulants. The most prevalent analeptic used in our society is caffeine. Analeptics promote two main actions—general arousal and increased rate and depth of respiration. They also raise levels of reflex excitability, which could lead to convulsions. The major sites of action are the reticular activation system and the medulla.

Amphetamines and cocaine are the psychomotor drugs most commonly used in sports. Cocaine is discussed in the section "Recreational Drug Abuse." The sympathomimetic drugs present an extremely difficult problem in sports medicine because they are commonly found in cold remedies, nasal and ophthalmic decongestants, and most asthma preparations.[30] The IOC has approved some substances to be used by asthmatics who develop exercise-induced bronchospasms. These substances are selective B_2 agonists and consist of bitolterol, orciprenoline, rimiterol, salbutamol (albuterol), and terbutaline (in its aerosol form). Before an athlete engages in Olympic competition, his or her team physician must notify the IOC Medical Subcommission in writing concerning their usage.[30]

Amphetamines   Amphetamines are synthetic alkaloids that are extremely powerful and dangerous drugs. They may be injected, inhaled, or taken as tablets. Amphetamines are among the most abused drugs used with the goal of enhancing sports performance. In ordinary doses, amphetamines can produce euphoria, with an increased sense of well-being and heightened mental activity—until fatigue sets in (from lack of sleep), accompanied by nervousness, insomnia, and anorexia. In high doses, amphetamines reduce mental activity and impair performance of complicated motor skills. The athlete's behavior may become irrational. The chronic user may be "hung up" or, in other words, get stuck in a repetitive behavioral sequence. The perseveration may last for hours, becoming increasingly more irrational. The long-term, or even short-term, use of amphetamines can lead

---

STIMULANTS BANNED BY THE IOC, 1986*

Amfepramone	Furfenorex
Amfetaminil	Meclofenoxate
Amiphenazole	Mefenorex
Amphetamines	Methamphetamine
Benzphetamine	Methoxyphenamine
Caffeine	Methylephedrine
Cathine	Methylphenidate
Chlorphentermine	Morazone
Clobenzorex	Nikethamide
Clorprenaline	Pemoline
Cocaine	Penetrazol
Cropropamide (component of "micoren")	Phendimetrazine
Crothetamide (component of "micoren")	Phenmetrazine
Dimetamfetamine	Phentermine
Ephedrine	Phenylpropanolamine
Etafedrine	Pipradol
Ethamivan	Prolintane
Etilamfetamine	Propylhexedrine
Fencamfamin	Pyrovalerone
Fenetylline	Strychnine
Fenproporex	Any related compounds

*Any banned substance is subject to change. For current lists, write to the US Olympic Committee, Colorado Springs, Colorado 80909.

to "amphetamine psychosis," depicted by auditory and visual hallucinations and paranoid delusions.

Physiologically, high doses of amphetamines can cause mydriasis (abnormal pupillary dilation), increased blood pressure, hyperreflexia (increased reflect action), and hyperthermia.

In terms of their sports performance, athletes believe that amphetamines promote quickness and endurance, delay fatigue, and increase confidence, thereby causing increased aggressiveness.[19] Studies indicate that there is no improvement in performance, but there is an increased risk of injury, exhaustion, and circulatory collapse.[2]

Caffeine   Caffeine is an alkaloid found in coffee, tea, cocoa, and cola. It is a central nervous system stimulant and diuretic and also stimulates gastric secretion. One cup of coffee can contain from 100 to 150 mg of the alkaloid. In moderation, caffeine causes a stimulation of the cerebral cortex and medullar centers, resulting in wakefulness and mental alertness. In larger amounts and in individuals who ingest caffeine daily, it raises blood pressure, decreases and then increases the heart rate, and increases plasma levels of epinephrine, norepinephrine, and renin. It affects coordination, sleep, mood, behavior, and thinking processes.[32] In terms of exercise and sports performance, caffeine is controversial. Like amphetamines, caffeine can affect some athletes by acting as an ergogenic aid during prolonged exercise. The IOC considers caffeine a stimulant if the concentration in the athlete's urine exceeds 12 μg/ml (see box on p. 440).

Narcotic Analgesic Drugs

Narcotic analgesic drugs are derived directly from opium or are synthetic opiates. Morphine and codeine (methylmorphine) are examples of substances made from the alkaloid of opium. Narcotic analgesics are used for the management of moderate-to-severe pain. They have been banned by the IOC because of the high risk of physical and psychological dependency, as well as many other problems stemming from their usage. It is believed that slight-to-moderate pain can be effectively dealt with through drugs other than narcotics.[22] See box below.

NARCOTIC ANALGESIC DRUGS BANNED BY THE IOC, 1986

Alphaprodine	Ethylmorphine
Anileridine	Levorphanol
Buprenorphine	Methadone
Codeine	Morphine
Dextromoramide	Nalbuphine
Dextropropoxyphen	Pentazocine
Diamorphine (heroin)	Pethidine
Dihydrocodeine	Phenazocine
Dipipanone	Trimeperidine
Ethoheptazine	Any related compounds

BETA BLOCKERS BANNED BY THE IOC, 1986	
Acebutolol	Nadolol
Alprenolol	Oxprenolol
Atenolol	Propranolol
Labetalol	Sotalol
Metoprolol	Any related compounds

Beta Blockers

The "beta" in beta blockers refers to the type of adrenergic drug that blocks sympathetic nerve endings (see box above). (Another type of adrenergic agent would be an alpha blocker.) In recent years, beta blockers have been used in sports in which physical activity is of little or no importance such as in marksmanship. In these sports a steady hand is necessary, and heart rate and signs of nervousness must be kept to a minimum.[2] Beta blockers are one class of adrenergic agents that inhibit the action of catecholamines released from sympathetic nerve endings. Beta blockers produce relaxation of blood vessels. This relaxation, in turn, slows heart rate and decreases contractility of the heart muscle, thus decreasing cardiac output. Therapeutically, beta blockers are used for a variety of cardiac diseases, as well as in the treatment of hypertension.

Diuretics

Diuretic drugs increase kidney excretion by decreasing the kidney's resorption of sodium (see box below). The excretion of potassium and bicarbonate may also be increased. Therapeutically, diuretics are used for a variety of cardiovascular and respiratory conditions (e.g., hypertension) in which elimination of fluids from tissues is necessary. Sports participants have misused diuretics mainly in two ways—to reduce body weight quickly or to decrease a drug's concentration in the urine (increasing its excretion to avoid the detection of drug misuse).[22] In both cases, there are ethical and health grounds for banning certain classes of diuretics from use during Olympic competition.

DIURETICS BANNED BY THE IOC, 1986	
Acetazolamide	Diclofenamide
Amiloride	Ethacrynic acid
Bendroflumethiazide	Furosemide
Benzthiazide	Hydrochlorothiazide
Bumetanide	Mersalyl
Canrenone	Spironolactone
Chlormerodrin	Triamterene
Chlorthalidone	Any related compounds

ANABOLIC STEROIDS BANNED BY THE IOC, 1986

Bolasterone	Nandrolone decanoate
Boldenone	Norethandrolone
Clostebol	Oxandrolone
Dehydrochlormethyltestosterone	Oxymesterone
Fluoxymesterone	Oxymetholone
Mesterolone	Stanozolol
Metandienone	Testosterone
Metenolone	Any related compounds
Methyltestosterone	

Anabolic Steroids and Growth Hormone (GH)

Two substance classes related to the increase of muscle build, strength, power, and growth are the anabolic steroids and growth hormone (GH). Both are abused during sports participation.

Anabolic steroids   Androgenic hormones are basically a product of the male testes (see box above). Of these hormones, testosterone is the principal one and possesses the ability to function androgenically (the ability to stimulate male characteristics) and anabolically (the ability through an improved protein assimilation to increase muscle mass and weight, general growth, bone maturation, and virility). When prescribed by a physician to ameliorate or improve certain physiological conditions, these drugs have value.[15] In 1984, the American College of Sports Medicine (ACSM) reported that anabolic androgenic steroids taken with an adequate diet could contribute to an increase in body weight, and with a heavy resistance program there can be a significant gain in strength.[21] However, in sports, they constitute a major threat to the health of the athlete (see box below). Anabolic steroids present an ethical dilemma for the sport world. It is estimated that over a million young male and female athletes are taking them, with most being purchased through the black market.[8]

DELETERIOUS EFFECTS OF ANABOLIC STEROIDS

Teens—premature closure of long bones, acne, hirsutism, voice deepening, enlarged mammary glands (gynecomastia) of the male

Males—male-pattern baldness, acne, voice deepening, mood swings, aggressive behavior, decreased high-density lipoprotein, increased cholesterol, reduction in size of testicle, reduced testosterone production, changes in libido

Females—female-pattern baldness, acne, voice deepening (irreversible), increased facial hair, enlarged clitoris (irreversible), increased libido, menstrual irregularities, increased aggression, decreased body fat, increased appetite, decreased breast size

Abuse—may lead to liver tumors and cancer, heart disease, and hypertension

hirsutism
Excessive hair growth and/or
the presence of hair in
unusual places.

If these drugs are given to the prepubertal boy, a decrease in his ultimate height, because of the cessation of long bone growth, is a most certain hazard. Acne, hirsutism, a deepening of the voice in the prepubescent boy, and in some instances development of abnormally large mammary glands are among other androgen effects. The ingestion of steroids by females can result in **hirsutism** and a deepening of the voice as a result of vocal cord alteration.[35] When the dosage is halted, the hirsutism may cease, but the change of the vocal cords is irreversible. As the duration and dosage increase, the possibility of producing androgen effects also increases. Since self-administered overdosage seems to be the pattern of those who use steroids, the preceding statement is most significant.[16] Abuse of these drugs may also lead to cancer of the liver and prostate glands, as well as heart disease.

Usage of anabolic steroids is a major problem in sports that involve strength. Powerlifting, the throwing events in track and field and American football are some of the sports in which the usage of anabolic steroids is a serious problem.[5,37] Since female athletes are developing the attitude of "win at all costs," their abuse of anabolic steroids is also becoming a major health problem.[9]

Growth hormone (GH)   Growth Hormone (GH) is a polypeptide hormone produced by the somatrophic cells of the anterior region of the pituitary gland. It is released into circulation in a pulsating manner. This release can vary with age and the developmental periods of a person's life. A lack of GH can result in dwarfism. In the past, GH was in limited supply because it was extracted from cadavers. Now, however, it can be made synthetically and is more available.[24,36]

Experiments indicate that GH can increase muscle mass, skin thickness, connective tissues in muscle, and organ weight and can produce lax muscles and ligaments during rapid growth phases. It also increases body length and weight and decreases body fat percentage.[36]

The use of GH by athletes throughout the world is on the increase because it is more difficult to detect in urine than anabolic steroids.[2] There is currently a lack of concrete information about the effects of GH on the athlete who does not have a growth problem. It is known that an overabundance of GH in the body can lead to premature closure of long-bone growth sites or, conversely, can cause acromegaly, a condition that produces elongation and enlargement of bones of the extremities and thickening of bones and soft tissues of the face. Also associated with acromegaly is diabetes mellitus, cardiovascular disease, goiter, menstrual disorders, decreased sexual desire, and impotence. It decreases the life span up to 20 years. As with anabolic steroids, GH presents a serious problem for the sports world.

Other Drugs Subject to IOC Restriction[22]

The IOC indicates that, although it does not expressly prohibit alcohol, breath or blood alcohol levels may be determined at the request of the committee. Local anesthetics that are injected (excluding cocaine) are permitted, but they must be used as intra-articular injections. Corticosteroids have been abused for their ability to produce euphoria and certain side effects. They are, therefore, banned except for topical use or for inhalation therapy and intra-articular injections during the Olympic Games.

Blood Reinjection (Blood Doping)

Endurance, acclimatization, and altitude make increased metabolic demands on the body, which responds by increasing blood volume and red blood cells to meet the increased aerobic demands.

Recently researchers have replicated these physiological responses by removing 900 ml of blood, storing it, and reinfusing it after 6 weeks.[38] The reason for waiting at least 6 weeks before reinfusion is it takes that long for the athlete's body to reestablish a normal hemoglobin and red blood cell concentration. Using this method, endurance performance has been significantly improved.[38] From the standpoint of scientific research such experimentation has merit and is of interest. However, not only is use of such methods in competition unethical, but use by nonmedical personnel could prove to be dangerous.

In addition, there are serious risks with transfusing blood and related blood products. The risks include allergic reactions, kidney damage (if the wrong type of blood is used), fever, jaundice, the possibility of transmitting infectious diseases (viral hepatitis or acquired immune deficiency disease), or a blood overload, resulting in circulatory and metabolic shock.[11]

> Not only is the use of blood reinjection in competition unethical, but use by nonmedical personnel could prove dangerous.

RECREATIONAL DRUG ABUSE

As is true with the general public, recreational drug use has become a part of the world of sports. Reasons for using these substances may include to experiment, temporarily to escape from problems, or just to be part of a group (peer pressure). For some, recreational drug use leads to abuse and dependence. There are two general aspects of dependence—psychological and physical. *Psychological dependence* is the drive to repeat the ingestion of a drug to produce pleasure or to avoid discomfort. *Physical dependence* is the state of drug adaptation that manifests as the development of *tolerance* and, when the drug is removed, causes a *withdrawal syndrome*. Tolerance of a drug is the need to increase the dosage to create the effect that was obtained previously by smaller amounts. The withdrawal syndrome is one of an unpleasant physiological reaction when the drug is abruptly stopped. Some drugs that are abused by the athlete overlap with those thought to enhance performance. Examples include amphetamines and cocaine. Tobacco (nicotine), alcohol, cocaine, and marijuana are the most abused recreational drugs. The athletic trainer and/or coach might also come in contact with abuse by athletes of barbiturates, nonbarbiturate sedatives, psychotomimetic drugs, or different inhalants.

Tobacco

There are a number of current problems related to tobacco and sports. They can be divided into two headings—cigarette smoking and the use of smokeless tobacco.

Cigarette Smoking

On the basis of various investigations into the relationship between smoking and performance, the following conclusions can be drawn:

1. There is individual sensitivity to tobacco that may seriously affect performance in instances of relatively high sensitivity. Since over one third of the men studied indicated tobacco sensitivity, it may be wise to prohibit smoking by athletes.

2. Tobacco smoke has been associated with as many as 4700 different chemicals, many of which are toxic.

3. As few as 10 inhalations of cigarette smoke cause an average maximum decrease in airway conductance of 50%. This occurs in nonsmokers who inhale smoke secondhand as well.

4. Smoking reduces the oxygen-carrying capacity of the blood. A smoker's blood carries from five to as much as 10 times more carbon monoxide than normal; thus the red blood cells are prevented from picking up sufficient oxygen to meet the demands of the body's tissues. The carbon monoxide also tends to make arterial walls more permeable to fatty substances, a factor in atherosclerosis.

5. Smoking aggravates and accelerates the heart muscle cells through overstimulation of the sympathetic nervous system.

6. Total lung capacity and maximum breathing capacity are significantly decreased in heavy smokers; this is important to the athlete, since both changes would impair the capacity to take in oxygen and make it readily available for body use.

7. Smoking decreases pulmonary diffusing capacity.

8. After smoking, an accelerated thrombolic tendency is evidenced.

9. Smoking is a carcinogenic factor in lung cancer and is a contributing factor to heart disease.

The addictive chemical of tobacco is nicotine, which is one of the most toxic drugs. When ingested, it causes blood pressure elevation, increased bowel activity, and an antidiuretic action. Moderate tolerance and physical dependence occur. It also has been noted that passive inhalation of cigarette smoke can reduce maximum aerobic power and endurance capacity.[20]

Use of Smokeless Tobacco

It is estimated that over 7 million individuals use smokeless tobacco, which comes in three forms—loose-leaf, moist or dry powder (snuff), and compressed. The tobacco is placed between the cheek and the gum.[14] Then it is sucked and chewed. Aesthetically, this is an unsavory habit during which an athlete is continually spitting into a container. Besides the unpleasant appearance, the use of smokeless tobacco proposes an extremely serious health risk. Aggressive oral and throat cancer and periodontal destruction (with tooth loss) have been associated with this habit. The major substance injested is nitrosonornicotine, which is the drug responsible for this habit's addictiveness. This chemical makes smokeless tobacco a more addictive habit than smoking.[7] Smokeless tobacco increases heart rate but does not affect reaction time, movement time, or total response time among athletes or nonathletes.[10]

Coaches, athletic trainers, and professional athletes themselves must avoid the use of smokeless tobacco to present a positive role model.[18]

Alcohol

Alcohol consumption, at any time or in any amount, does not improve mental or physical abilities and should be avoided by athletes.

Alcohol is the number one abused drug in the United States.[39] Alcohol is absorbed directly into the bloodstream through the small intestine. It accumulates in the blood because alcohol absorption is faster than its oxidation. It acts as a central nervous system depressant, producing sedation and tranquility. Characteristically, alcohol consumption, at any time or in any amount, does not improve mental or physical abilities and should be completely avoided by athletes. Alcohol consumption on a large scale can lead to a moderate degree of tolerance. Alcohol has no place in sports participation.

Cocaine

Cocaine, sometimes called "coke," "snow," "toot," "happy dust," and "white girl," is a powerful central nervous system stimulant, as well as a local anesthetic and vasoconstrictor. Besides being a banned performance enhancer, it is one of the most abused recreational drugs. It can be inhaled, smoked, or injected (intravenously, subcutaneously, or intramuscularly).[3]

In high doses cocaine causes a sense of excitement and euphoria. On occasions it also produces hallucinations. Found in the leaves of the coca bush, when applied locally to the skin, it acts as an anesthetic; however, when taken into the body through inhalation, snorting, or injection, it acts on the central nervous system.

Habitual use of cocaine will not lead to physical tolerance or dependence but will cause psychological dependence and addiction. When cocaine is used recreationally, the athlete feels alert, self-satisfied, and powerful. Heavy usage can produce paranoid delusions and violent behavior. Overuse can lead to over-stimulation of the sympathetic nervous system and can cause tachycardia, hypertension, extra heartbeats, coronary vasoconstriction, strokes, pulmonary edema, aortic rupture, and sudden death.[3]

Marijuana

Marijuana is another one of the most abused drugs in Western society. It is more commonly called "grass," "weed," "pot," "dope," or "hemp." The marijuana cigarette is called a "joint," a "j," a "number," a "reefer," or a "root."

Marijuana is *not* a harmless drug. The components of marijuana smoke are similar to those of tobacco smoke and the same cellular changes are observed in the user.

Continued use leads to respiratory diseases such as asthma and bronchitis and a decrease in vital capacity of 15% to as much as 40% (certainly detrimental to physical performance). Among other deleterious effects are lowered sperm counts and testosterone levels. Evidence of interference with the functioning of the immune system and cellular metabolism has also been found. The most consistent sign is the increase in pulse rate, which averages close to 20% higher during exercise and is a definite factor in limiting performance.[31] Some decrease in leg, hand, and finger strength has been found at higher dosages. As with tobacco, marijuana must be considered carcinogenic.

Psychological effects such as a diminution of self-awareness and judgment, a slowdown of thinking, and a shorter attention span appear early in the use of the drug. Postmortem examinations of habitual users reveal not only cerebral atrophy but alterations of anatomical structures, which suggest irreversible brain damage. Marijuana also contains unique substances (cannabinoids) that are stored, in very much the same manner as are fat cells, throughout the body and in the brain tissues for weeks and even months. These stored quantities result in a cumulative deleterious effect on the habitual user.

A drug such as marijuana has no place in sports. Claims for its use are unsubstantiated, and the harmful effects, both immediate and long-term, are too significant to permit indulgence at any time.

Other Drugs

Although seen less often, the coach or athletic trainer may encounter the athlete who is using drugs such as barbituates, nonbarbituate sedatives, psychotomimetics, lysergic acid, or various inhalants.

Barbiturates

Barbiturates, also known as "goofballs" and "fool pills," are less popular than in the past. They produce both physical and psychological dependency, and they decrease mental activity and produce sedation.

Psychotomimetics

Psychotomimetics are considered psychotogenic (hallucinogenic) drugs. The best example of this type of drug is phencyclidine, or PCP (angel dust). As one of the most dangerous street drugs, it can produce excitement, perceptual distortions, impaired pain and touch perception, difficulty in speaking, and disorientation. Persons who ingest this substance often display feats of abnormal aggression and strength.

IDENTIFYING THE SUBSTANCE ABUSER

The following are signs of drug abuse:
1. Sudden personality changes
2. Severe mood swings
3. Changing peer groups
4. Decreased interest in extracurricular and leisure activities
5. Worsening grades
6. Disregard for household chores and curfews
7. Feeling of depression most of the time
8. Personal hygiene habits break down
9. Increased sleep and decreased eating
10. Clothes and skin smell of alcohol or marijuana
11. Sudden weight loss
12. Lying, cheating, stealing, etc.
13. Arrests for drunk driving or possessing illegal substances
14. Truancies from school
15. Loses or changes jobs frequently
16. Becomes defensive at the mention of drugs or alcohol
17. Increased isolation (spends time in room)
18. Family relationship deteriorates
19. Drug parphenalia (needles, empty bottles, etc.) found
20. Others make observations about negative behavior
21. Shows signs of intoxication
22. Constantly misses appointments
23. Falls asleep in class or at work
24. Has financial problems
25. Misses assignments or deadlines
26. Diminished productivity

Lysergic Acid

Lysergic acid (LSD) is a hallucinogenic drug. It produces central nervous system excitation and autonomic hyperactivity. It sometimes causes euphoria and, conversely, depression. The chief dangers of hallucinations are that they can cause severely impaired judgment and can lead to dangerous consequences. An example is the person who, because of hallucination and impaired judgment, believes he or she has the ability to fly and therefore attempts to do so, plunging from a deadly height.

Inhalants

A great number of substances are in a gaseous form and are highly volatile. This category of drug abuse, the use of inhalants, attracts the youngster. Among this group of drugs are the volatile nitrates, mainly amyl nitrate and isobutyl nitrate ("poppers" and "snappers"). Inhaling these chemicals produces a fleeting lightheadedness, euphoria, and headache and can enhance sexual orgasm. Other inhalants are certain glues, plastic cements, gasoline, brake and lighter fluid, paint and lacquer thinners, varnish remover, cleaning fluid (spot remover), and nail polish remover. All of these substances, if habitually inhaled, can lead to various physiological reactions and even death (see box on p. 448).

DRUG TESTING AND FIGHTING THE WAR AGAINST DRUGS

Drug testing began with the 1968 Olympic games. Since that time, each Olympic Committee has spent considerable amounts of money to equip a drug testing laboratory. In January 1986, the member institutions of the National Collegiate Athletic Association (NCAA) voted overwhelmingly to expand the NCAA drug education program to include mandatory drug testing during and after NCAA championship events. The major goals of both the organizations are to protect the health of athletes and to help ensure that competition is fair and equitable.[23]

Drug Testing

During a drug test a urine specimen is analyzed for any substances on the list of banned drugs. A careful procedure is followed to ensure that no cheating on the part of the athlete is taking place and to ensure as much accuracy as possible. The anonymity of the athlete is maintained at all times.

For routine screening, the more economical thin-layer chromatography (TLC) or gas-liquid chromatography (GLC) is used. When either one shows positive, to obtain positive drug identification, gas-chromatography mass spectrometry is used. Gas-chromatography mass spectrometry is extremely sensitive and is able to confirm selective drugs with almost 100% certainty,[30] and it provides legally admissible data.[34]

Probably any testing program, to be successful and not inhibited by financial problems, should be random. It must be realized that no system or device is completely "fail proof." False positives can occur. Great care must be taken that an athlete's personal rights are not violated.

The question of who should perform the routine collection and testing of urine arises when considering drug testing. In many programs, the athletic trainer is given this responsibility. This, however, undermines what the athletic trainer stands for—an impartial, unbiased health professional or friend who, in many cases, is a confidante to the athlete. Whenever possible, an outside organization should perform the drug testing program.[25] If the athletic trainer must be involved with the program, he or she should be divorced as much as possible from the actual testing phase of the program.[13]

Any drug testing program must be carefully designed and documented before implementation. Designing the program should be the responsibility of the team physician and the institution's lawyer. The testing program must stay within state legal guidelines and at all times must be confidential and concerned with the well-being of the athlete.[28]

Fighting the War Against Drugs

Substance abuse is rampant in our society and is a problem that must be immediately addressed by all who are involved directly or indirectly with athletes. Whenever possible, sports programs should have full-service programs that provide substance abuse education, counseling, and drug detection.

Athletes, parents, coaches, athletic trainers, physicians, and administrators must be educated about the dangers of drug abuse and the fact that it has no place in sports participation and recreation.[29] An in-depth program of education should be provided for the athletes, both formally in a classroom setting and informally as situations arise.

Counseling should be provided for all athletes who are abusing chemicals. Individual counseling, group counseling, and support groups should be available.

Detection must be part of every substance abuse program and can result from education about what to look for when an athlete is engaging in chemical abuse. Drug testing should be performed periodically in a random manner.

Above all, a sports program must engender the philosophy that "winning at all costs" is wrong. It is essential for athletes to believe that if they do their very best and adhere to the rules of the sport, they will be doing exactly what is expected of them.

SUMMARY

A drug is a substance that is designed to treat some human condition. It is transported in an inactive substance called a vehicle. The drug is administered to the athlete through external or internal means.

The use of any drug can be dangerous. There are no safe drugs. An athletic trainer, unless specifically allowed by state licensure, is not permitted to dispense a prescription drug. Allowing the dispensing of a nonprescription, or over-the-counter (OTC), drugs also varies depending on state law and local rules or statutes. The reason for this great caution in the dispensing of drugs is the individual differences in drug reactions.

As is true in the general public, the use of medicinals is extensive among athletes. Drugs used therapeutically in sports have a wide spectrum of uses, namely for treating infection, toughening skin, dealing with itching, providing protective coating, and dealing with cold symptoms, allergies, and gastrointestinal disorders. Of major importance in sports is the management of inflammation and pain, as well as specific muscle dysfunctions.

A major problem in sports participation is the extensive use of performance aids, consisting of drugs and blood doping. The International Olympic Committee (IOC) lists banned drugs under the headings of stimulants, narcotic analgesics, diuretics, and anabolic steroids. Blood doping has also been placed in the banned category.

A third area of concern is that of recreational drug abuse. This abuse is worldwide. It leads to serious psychological and physical health problems. The most prevalent substances that are abused are nicotine, alcohol, cocaine, and marijuana.

A current pressing dilemma is the decision of whether or not to test the athlete for drugs. Controversy arises over this situation in the areas of personal philosophy, education, and counseling. Of major importance is the avoidance of intrusion on the athlete's civil rights.

REVIEW QUESTIONS AND CLASS ACTIVITIES

1. What is the branch of science known as pharmacology, and what is the difference between a prescription and a nonprescription drug?
2. What is a drug vehicle? Give some examples of drug vehicles.
3. How can drugs be administered to an individual?
4. List what can be harmful in the purchase, storage, and use of over-the-counter drugs.
5. What are the legal implications if an athletic trainer administers prescription and non-prescription drugs?
6. List the responses to a drug that an athlete may experience.
7. Why must an athlete be concerned with foods that are ingested along with a drug?
8. List examples of common drugs used by athletes to combat infection, to inhibit or deaden pain, as narcotic analgesics, to affect the central nervous system, as astringents, for relieving itching, for treating colds and allergies, for treating gastrointestinal disorders, for reducing inflammation, and for treating muscle dysfunctions.
9. Discuss the use of performance aids such as drugs and blood doping.
10. How do stimulants enhance an athlete's performance? Do they, in fact, enhance it?
11. What are the purposes of narcotic analgesic drugs in sports? How do they affect performance?
12. What type athlete would use beta blockers? Why are they used?
13. Describe why anabolic steroids, diuretics, or growth hormones (GH) are used by athletes. What are their physiological effects on the athlete?
14. What are the deleterious effects of hormonal manipulation in sports?
15. Describe blood doping in sports. Why is it used? What are its dangers?
16. Have a member of the IOC explain the banned drug policy to the class.
17. Contrast psychological and physical dependence, tolerance, and withdrawal syndromes.
18. List the dangers of smokeless tobacco. List the effects of nicotine on the body.
19. Why is cocaine use a danger to the athlete?
20. Select a recreational drug to research. What are the physiological responses to it, and what dangers does it pose to the athlete?
21. How can an athlete who is abusing drugs be identified? Describe behavioral identification, as well as drug testing.
22. Select two committees to debate the issue of drug testing in athletics. One committee should take a pro-drug testing position, and the other a con position.
23. Discuss what might be the best possible way to curb drug abuse among athletes.

REFERENCES

1. Albrechtsen, SJ, and Harvey, JS: Dimethyl sulfoxide: biomechanical effects on tendons, Am J Sports Med 10:177, March 1982.
2. Bell, JA, and Doege, TC: Athlete's use and abuse of drugs, Phys Sportsmed 15(3):99, 1987.
3. Cantwell, JD, and Rose, FD: Cocaine and cardiovascular events, Phys Sportsmed 14(11):77, 1986.
4. Caron, R: Aspirin and athletics, Ath Train 16:56, Spring 1981.
5. Cohen, JC, et al.: Altered serum lipoprotein profiles in male and female power lifters ingesting anabolic steroids, Phys Sportsmed 14(6):131, 1986.
6. DMSO: Still on the scene, Sports Med Dig 9(5):6, 1987.
7. Duda, M: Snuffing out the use of smokeless tobacco, Phys Sportsmed 13(10):171, 1985.

8. Duda, M: Female athletes: targets for drug abuse, Phys Sportsmed 14(6):142, 1986.

9. Duda, M: Do anabolic steroids pose an ethical dilemma for U.S. physicians? Phys Sportsmed 14(11):173, 1986.

10. Edwards, SW, et al.: The effects of smokeless tobacco on heart rates and neuromuscular reactivity, Phys Sportsmed 15(7):141, 1987.

11. Eichner, ER: Blood doping: results and consequences from the laboratory and the field, Phys Sportsmed 15(1):121, 1987.

12. Ekblom, BT: Blood doping and performance. In Welsh, RP, and Shepard, RJ, editors: Current therapy in sports medicine, 1985-1986, Philadelphia, 1985, Brian C Decker Inc.

13. Erlich, NEP: The athletic trainer's role in drug testing, Ath Train 21:225, 1986.

14. Glover, ED, et al.: Implications of smokeless tobacco use among athletes, Phys Sportsmed 14(12):95, 1986.

15. Haupt, HA, and Rovere, GD: Anabolic steroids: a review of the literature, Am J Sports Med 12:469, Nov/Dec 1984.

16. Hickson, RC, and Kurowski, TG: Anabolic steroids and training. In Katch, FI, editor: Training, vol 5, no 3, Clinics in sports medicine, Philadelphia, 1986, WB Saunders Co.

17. Houston, BL: Sunscreen lotions may increase heat risks, Phys Sportsmed 10:27, Sept 1982.

18. Jones, RB: Commentary; prohibit smokeless tobacco use in athletic competition, Phys Sportsmed 15(7):148, 1987.

19. Lombardo, JA: Stimulants and athletic performance (part 1): amphetamines and caffeine, Phys Sportsmed 14(11): 128, 1986.

20. McMurray, RG, et al.: The effects of passive inhalation of cigarette smoke on exercise performance. In Krakauer, LJ, editor: The yearbook of sports medicine, Chicago, 1986, Yearbook Medical Publishers, Inc.

21. Miller, C: Anabolic steroids, an Australian sports physician goes public, Phys Sportsmed 14(11):167, 1986.

22. Miller, GD: A memorandum: list of doping classes and methods of doping, Colorado Springs, Col, 1986, Secretary General, United States Olympic Committee.

23. Murray, TH: Drug testing and moral responsibility, Phys Sportsmed 14(11): 47, 1986.

24. Murray, TH: Human growth hormone in sports, Phys Sportsmed 14(5):29, 1986.

25. O'Keefe AM: The case against drug testing, Psychol Today 21:34, 1987.

26. Olerud, J: DMSO—a literature review, NATA Clinical Symposium, Granite Falls, Wash, 1984, Marvl Productions. (Cassette.)

27. Percy, EC: DMSO; hazards outweigh benefits to athletes, The First Aider 56(2):1, 1986.

28. Pickett, AD: Drug testing: what are the rules? Ath Train 21:331, 1986.

29. Pincus, WH, and Cole, SL: Athletes and drugs: what is the coach's role? The First Aider, 56(3):8, 1986.

30. Puffer, JC: The use of drugs in swimming. In Ciullo, JV, editor: Swimming, vol 5, no 1, Clinics in sports medicine, Philadelphia, 1986, WB Saunders Co.

31. Renaud, AM, and Cormeir, Y: Acute effects of marijuana smoking on maximal exercise performance, Med Sci Sports Exerc 18:685, 1986.

32. Richner, ER: The caffeine controversy: effects on endurance and cholesterol, Phys Sportsmed 14(12):124, 1986.

33. Robbins, JR: Effects of steroids on ligaments and tendons, NATA Clinical Symposium, Granite Falls, Wash, 1984, Marvl Productions. (Cassette.)

34. Rovere, GD, et al.: Drug testing in a university athletic program: protocol and implementation, Phys Sportsmed 14(4):69, 1986.

35. Strauss, RH, et al.: Anabolic steroids use and perceived effects in 10 weight-trained women athletes, JAMA 253:2871, 1985.

36. Taylor, WN: Hormonal manipulation, Jefferson, NC, 1985, McFarland and Co Inc. Publishers.

37. Use of anabolic steroids by weight-trained women athletes, Sports Med Dig 8(3):7, 1986.

38. Wells, J: Adverse drug interaction in sports medicine, Ath Train 15:236, Winter 1980.

39. Wells, J: An evaluation of the present indications of dimethyl sulfoxide (DMSO) in sports medicine, Ath Train 17:26, Spring 1982.

ANNOTATED BIBLIOGRAPHY

American Pharmaceutical Association: Handbook of nonprescription drugs, ed 7, Washington, DC, 1982, The National Professional Society of Pharmacists.
Includes a complete description and evaluation of the most common nonprescription drugs.

Clark, WG: Goth's medical pharmacology, ed 12, St. Louis, 1988, The CV Mosby Co.
Presents modern pharmacology in a readable and easily understood manner.

Griffith, HW: Complete guide to prescription and non-prescription drugs, Tucson, Ariz, 1987, HP Books, Inc.
Presents 4000 brand and 490 generic drug titles and in-depth coverage of the side effects, warnings, and important information for safe drug use.

Physician's desk reference (PDR) for non-prescription drugs, ed 8, Oradell, NJ, 1987, Medical Economics Co.
An extensive guide to nonprescription drugs sold over-the-counter. Active ingredients and side effects are discussed thoroughly.

Physician's desk reference (PDR) for prescription drugs, ed 41, Oradell, NJ, 1987, Medical Economics Co.
A detailed reference guide for physicians, providing generic and chemical names, product categories, product identification through color photography, and detailed product information.

Taylor, WN: Hormonal manipulation, Jefferson, NC, 1985, McFarland and Co, Inc, Publishers.
A complete treatise on the subject of sports drug abuse, anabolic steroids, and growth hormone (GH).

Zimmerman, DR: The essential guide to nonprescription drugs, Philadelphia, 1983, Harper & Row, Publishers.
A complete guide to over-the-counter drugs, with each drug rated as to its effectiveness and safety.

SPECIFIC SPORTS CONDITIONS

P *art Five discusses the prevention, etiology, symptoms and signs, and management of the most common sports conditions.*

16

Skin Disorders

When you finish this chapter, you should be able to

Explain the structure and function of the skin and identify the major lesions that result from skin abnormalities

Describe in detail how skin trauma occurs, how it may be prevented, and how it may be managed

Identify skin infections that are potentially contagious

Describe the correct hygiene practices to use to avoid fungal infections

Contrast allergic, thermal, and chemical reactions of the skin

Identify infestations and insect bites and contrast them with other skin infections

I t is essential that athletic trainers and coaches understand conditions adversely affecting the skin and mucous membranes, especially highly contagious conditions.

SKIN ANATOMY AND FUNCTION

The skin is the largest organ of the human body. The average adult skin varies in total weight from 6 to 7½ pounds and is from ⅟₃₂ to ⅛ inch thick. It is composed of three layers—epidermis, dermis, and subcutis (Figure 16-1; Table 16-1).

Epidermis

The epidermis has multiple layers. It forms the outer sheath of the body and is composed of the stratum corneum, the pigment melanin, and appendages (hair, nails, sebaceous and sweat glands). It consists of two types of cells, the keratinocytes and the melanocytes. As these cells migrate outward toward the surface of the skin, the keratinocytes form the stratum corneum, which offers the greatest skin protection. The epidermis acts as a barrier against invading microorganisms, foreign particles from dirt debris, chemicals, and ultraviolet rays and also helps contain the body's water and electrolytes. Melanin, produced by melanocytes, protects the body against ultraviolet radiation.

Dermis

The dermis is a skin layer of irregular form, situated underneath the epidermis and composed of connective tissue that contains blood vessels, nerve endings,

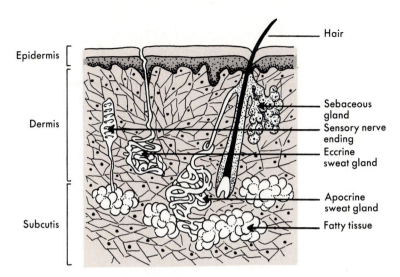

Epidermis [

Dermis

Subcutis

— Hair

— Sebaceous gland
— Sensory nerve ending
— Eccrine sweat gland

— Apocrine sweat gland
— Fatty tissue

Figure 16-1

The skin is the largest organ of the human body, weighing 6 to 7½ pounds in the adult.

TABLE 16-1 Outline of the Skin's Structure and Function

Layer	Subregion	Function
Epidermis	Stratum corneum	Prevents intrusion of microorganisms, debris, chemicals, ultraviolet radiation
		Prevents loss of water and electrolytes
		Performs heat regulation for conduction, radiation, convection
	Melanin (pigmentation)	Prevents intrusion of ultraviolet radiation
	Appendages	Contains eccrine and apocrine sweat glands, hair, nails and sebaceous glands
Dermis		Protects against physical trauma
		Contains sensory nerve endings
		Holds water and electrolytes
Subcutis		Stores fat, regulates heat

sweat glands, sebaceous glands, and hair follicles. The dermis forms a series of projections that reach into the epidermis, resulting in an interlocking arrangement and thereby preventing the epidermis from slipping off the dermis.

Hair and Sebaceous Glands

Hair grows from hair follicles contained in the skin. It extends into the dermis, where it is nourished by the blood capillaries. The sebaceous glands, which surround the hair, secrete an oily substance into the hair follicle. Persons who have overactive sebaceous glands may develop blackheads because of plugging of the hair follicle. Small muscles called *arrectores pilorum* connect to the hair at its root and, when contracted, serve to constrict the hair follicles and cause a "standing-on-end" effect or goose pimples. Such contractions increase the emission of oil and thereby help to protect the body from cold.

Sweat Glands

Sweat glands are necessary for cooling the surface of the body and the internal organs. There are two main types of glands: the eccrine glands, which are present at birth and are generally present throughout the skin, and the apocrine glands, which are much larger than the eccrine and mature during adolescence in conjunction with the axillary and pubic hair. Certain individuals with undersecreting sweat glands (dry skin) may be especially susceptible to various diseases. The fluid of the sweat gland contains antibacterial agents that are essential in controlling skin infections.

Nails

The nails are special horny cell structures that come from the skin (stratum germinativum) and protect the ends of the phalanges. They are embedded in skin at the base and along their sides and grow approximately ½ inch in 4 months.

Sensory Nerve Endings

Besides its many other functions, the dermis contains sensory nerve endings. These peripheral nerves provide the body with important protective information such as temperature changes and pain.

Subcutis

The subcutis region contains subcutaneous fat. This is the primary area for fat storage, producing internal temperature regulation and mobility of the skin over the internal body core.

SKIN LESIONS DEFINED

Skin that is healthy has a smooth, soft appearance. It is colored by a pigment known as melanin. An increased amount of blood in the skin capillaries may give a ruddy appearance, and an insufficient amount may give a pale effect.

The normal appearance of the skin can be altered by many factors, external and internal. Some changes may be signs of other involvements. The different intensities of paleness or redness of the skin, which is related to *redness of superficial capillaries,* may indicate a disease condition. *Excessive oiliness* or *dryness* of the skin may be hereditary. *Pigment variation* may result from an increase of sun exposure or from organic diseases; a yellowish discoloration, for example, is indicative of jaundice.

Skin abnormalities may be divided into primary and secondary lesions. Primary lesions include macules, papules, plaques, nodules, tumors, cysts, wheals, vesicles, bullae, and pustules (Figure 16-2; Table 16-2). Secondary lesions usually develop from primary lesions (Figure 16-3; Table 16-3).

MICROORGANISMS AND SKIN INFECTIONS

When an athlete is unable to defend adequately against the microorganisms that are ever present in the environment, skin infections can occur. They are associated with diseases, internal or external in nature, and are reflected in skin lesions. The microorganisms most common to skin infections among athletes are viruses, bacteria, and fungi.

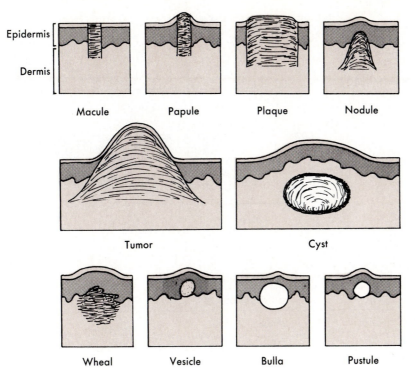

Figure 16-2

Typical primary skin lesions.

TABLE 16-2 Primary Skin Lesions

Type	Description	Example
Macule	A small, flat, circular discoloration smaller than 1 cm in diameter	Freckle or flat nevus
Papule	A solid elevation less than 1 cm in diameter	Wart
Plaque or patch	May be a macule or papule larger than 1 cm in diameter	Vitiligo patch (patches of depigmentation)
Nodule	A solid mass less than 1 cm, deeper into the dermis than a papule	Dermatofibroma (fibrosis tumor–like)
Tumor	Solid mass larger than 1 cm	Cavernous hemangioma (tumor filled with blood vessels)
Cyst	Encapsulated, fluid filled, in dermis or subcutis	Epidermoid cyst
Wheal	A papule or plaque caused by serum collection into the dermis, allergic reactions	Urticaria (hives)
Vesicle	Fluid-filled elevation less than 1 cm, just below epidermis	Smallpox, chickenpox
Bulla	Like a vesicle but larger	Second degree burn, friction blister
Pustule	Like vesicle or bullae but contains pus	Acne

Figure 16-3

Typical secondary skin
lesions.

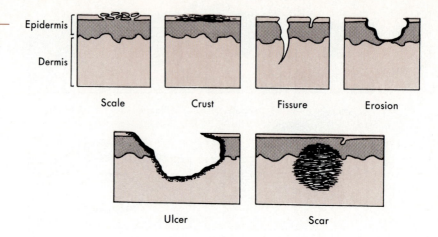

Scale   Crust   Fissure   Erosion

Ulcer   Scar

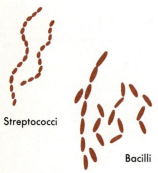

Streptococci

Bacilli

Staphylococci

Fungi

Figure 16-4

Common disease organisms.

TABLE 16-3 Secondary Skin Lesions

Type	Description	Example
Scales	Flakes of skin	Psoriasis
Crust	Dried fluid or exudates on skin	Impetigo
Fissures	Skin cracks	Chapping
Excoriation	Superficial scrape	Abrasion
Erosion	Loss of superficial epidermis	Scratches (superficial)
Ulcer	Destruction of entire epidermis	Pressure sore
Scar	Healing of dermis	Vaccination, laceration

Viruses

Viruses are minute infectious agents lacking independent metabolism but still having the capacity to reproduce. Reproduction can take place only within a living cell. The individual chemical particle (virion) includes nucleic acid and either deoxyribonucleic acid (DNA) or ribonucleic acid (RNA). The virus can attach to and enter a living cell and may multiply until it kills the cell and bursts out to reinfect other cells. Instead of killing the cell, the budlike growth may occur, with harm to the cell, or the virus may remain within a cell without ever causing an infection.

A number of skin infections are caused by a virus. Two of the most prevalent are the herpes virus and the verruca virus.[15] (See Chapter 25 for discussion of additional viral diseases.)

Bacteria

Bacteria are single-celled microorganisms that can only be seen with a microscope after being stained with specific dyes. They are of three major shapes: spherical (cocci), which occur in clumps; doublets, or chains, and rods (bacilli); and spirochetes, which are corkscrew-shaped. The three bacteria that are of major concern in sports are the staphylococcus, the streptococcus, and the bacillus (Figure 16-4).

Staphylococcus

Staphylococcus is a genus of gram-positive bacteria that commonly appear in clumps on the skin and in the upper-respiratory tract. It is the most prevalent cause of infections in which pus is present.

Streptococcus

Streptococcus is also a genus of gram-positive bacteria, but unlike staphylococci, it appears in long chains. Most species are harmless, but some are among the most dangerous bacteria affecting humans. They can be associated with serious systemic diseases such as scarlet fever and can be associated with staphylococci in skin diseases.

Bacillus

Bacillus is a genus of bacteria belonging to the family *Bacillaceae*. They are spore-forming and aerobic, and some are mobile. Most bacilli are not pathological; those that are can cause major systemic damage. *Bacillus* is presented here because of its relationship to the life-threatening disease tetanus, which is introduced through a skin wound. (See section "Punctures.")

Fungi

Fungi such as mushrooms, yeast, and molds are organisms with a true nucleus that contains chromosomes, but fungi lack chlorophyll and rigid cell walls. In most cases they are not pathogenic; however, some such as *Trichophyton* will attack skin, hair, and nails, *Candida,* a yeastlike fungus that is normally part of the flora of the skin, mouth, intestinal tract, and vaginal area can also lead to a variety of infections.

SKIN TRAUMA

Sports participation can place a great deal of mechanical force on the skin. Mechanical forces that can apply to the skin include friction, compression, shearing, stretching, scraping, tearing, avulsing, and puncturing, all of which can lead to painful and serious injuries.

Friction and Pressure Problems

Excessive rubbing back and forth over the skin, along with abnormal pressure, can cause hypertrophy of the stratum corneum, or horny layer, of the epidermis, especially on the soles of the feet and the palms of the hands. This condition is called keratoderma. Another expression for this process is callosity, or **keratosis.** This same mechanism can produce corns and blisters. Usually they occur in association with excessive perspiration (hyperhidrosis).

Keratosis of the Feet and Hands

Skin, typically the epidermal skin layer, increases in thickness when constant friction and pressure are externally applied. Excessive callus accumulation may occur over bony protuberances.

ETIOLOGY   Foot calluses may become excessive on an athlete who wears shoes that are too narrow or short. As with the foot, hand calluses can become painful when the subcutaneous fatty layer loses its elasticity, an important cushioning effect. The callus moves as a mass when pressure and a shearing force are applied.

Staphylococcus
Genus of gram-positive bacteria normally present on the skin and in the upper-respiratory tract and prevalent in localized infections.

Streptococcus
Genus of gram-positive bacteria found in the throat, respiratory tract, and intestinal tract.

keratosis
Excessive growth of the horny tissue layer.

This movement, coupled with a lack of blood supply, produces rips, tears, cracks, and ultimately, infection.[4]

PREVENTION Athletes whose shoes are properly fitted but who still develop heavy calluses commonly have foot mechanics problems that may require special orthotics. Special cushioning devices such as wedges, doughnuts, and arch supports may help to distribute the weight on the feet more evenly and thus reduce skin stress.[8] Excessive callus accumulation can be prevented by (1) wearing two pairs of socks, a thin cotton or nylon pair next to the skin and a heavy athletic pair over the cotton pair, or a single doubleknit sock, (2) wearing shoes that are the correct size and are in good condition, and (3) routinely applying materials such as petroleum jelly to reduce friction.

Hand calluses can also be controlled by proper toughening procedures and direct protection through the use of a special glove such as is used in batting or by the application of elastic tape or moleskin. The skin of the hands can be made more resistant to callosity by the routine application of astringents such as tannic acid or by salt water soaks. In sports such as gymnastics athletic trainers and athletes go to great lengths to protect the athletes' hands against tearing calluses. A protective device is a grip, which is a special type of hand covering that may include a wood dowel placed across the grip portion of the hand.

SYMPTOMS AND SIGNS The callus appears as a circumscribed thickening and hypertrophy of the horny layer of the skin. It may be ovular, elongated, brownish, and slightly elevated. Calluses may not be painful when pressure is applied.

MANAGEMENT Athletes who are prone to excess calluses should be encouraged to use an emery callus file after each shower. Massaging small amounts of lanolin into devitalized calluses once or twice a week after practice may help maintain some tissue elasticity. Once excessive formation has occurred, a keratolytic ointment, such as Whitefield's ointment, may be applied. Salicylic acid, 5% to 10%, in a flexible collodion, applied at night and peeled off in the morning, has also been beneficial. Before application of a keratolytic ointment, the athletic trainer might manually decrease the calluses' thickness by carefully paring with a sharp scalpel, sanding, or pumicing the surface. *Great care should be taken not to totally remove the callus and the protection it affords a pressure point.* A donut pad may be cut to size and placed on a pressure point to prevent pain.

Soft Corns and Hard Corns

Soft corns and hard corns are other examples of keratoses caused by abnormal skin pressure and friction.

ETIOLOGY A *hard corn (clavus durum)* is the most serious type of corn. It is caused by the pressure of improperly fitting shoes, the same mechanism that causes calluses. Hammer toes and hard corns are usually associated, with the hard corns that form on the tops of deformed toes (Figure 16-5, *A*). Symptoms are local pain and disability, with inflammation and thickening of soft tissue. Because of the chronic nature of this condition, it requires a physician's care.

A *soft corn (clavus molle)* is the result of the combination of wearing narrow shoes and having excessive foot perspiration. Because of the pressure of the shoe coupled with the exudation of moisture, the corn usually forms between the fourth and fifth toes (Figure 16-5, *B*). A circular area of thickened, white, macerated skin appears between the toes at the base of the proximal head of the phalanges. Both pain and inflammation are likely to be present.

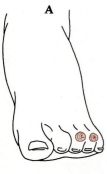

Figure 16-5

A, Hard corn (clavus durum); **B,** soft corn (clavus molle).

PREVENTION   The primary way to prevent a soft or hard corn is to wear properly fitted shoes. Soft corns can be avoided by wearing shoes that are wide enough. Conversely, hard corns can be avoided by wearing shoes that are long enough.

SYMPTOMS AND SIGNS   With a soft corn, the athlete complains of pain between the fourth and fifth toes. During inspection, the soft corn appears as a circular-shaped piece of thickened, white, macerated skin between the fourth and fifth toes at the base of the proximal head of the phalanges. In contrast, a hard corn is on the tops of hammer toes. The bony prominence of the toe is forced up, and it presses on the inner tops of the shoe, causing the corn to form. It appears hard and dry, with a callus that is sharply demarcated.

MANAGEMENT   The hard corn is difficult to manage. If pain and inflammation are major, referral to a podiatrist for surgical removal may be advisable. The athletic trainer may ameliorate the condition by having the athlete wear properly fitting shoes and socks and may alleviate further irritation of the corn by protecting it with a small felt pad or sponge pad, which can act as a buffer between the shoe and the toe.

In caring for a soft corn the best procedure is to have the athlete wear properly fitting shoes, keep the skin between the toes clean and dry, decrease pressure by keeping the toes separated with cotton or lamb's wool, and apply a keratolytic agent such as 40% salicylic acid in liquid or plasters.[8]

Blisters

A blister is a collection of fluid below or within the epidermal layer. Friction blisters are major problems among all types of athletes.

ETIOLOGY   Those athletes who use their hands extensively to use implements such as a bat, racket, club, or bar are prone to blisters. Feet are also prone to blistering when they are forced to slide back and forth within a shoe that is making sudden changes of position.

PREVENTION   Soft feet and hands, coupled with shearing skin stress, can produce severe blisters. A dusting of talcum powder or the application of petroleum jelly can protect the skin against abnormal friction. Wearing tubular socks or two pairs of socks, as for preventing calluses, is also desirable, particularly for athletes who have sensitive feet or feet that perspire excessively. Wearing the correct-size shoe is essential. The shoes must be broken in before they are worn for long periods of time. If, however, a friction area ("hot spot") does arise, the athlete has several options. The athlete can cover the irritated skin with a friction-proofing material such as petroleum jelly, place a "blanked-out" piece of tape tightly over the irritated area, or cover it with a piece of moleskin (Figure 16-6). Another method that has proved effective against blisters is the application of ice over skin areas that have developed abnormal friction.

SYMPTOMS AND SIGNS   The athlete normally will experience feeling a "hot spot," a sharp, burning sensation as the blister is formed, and the area of sensation should be examined immediately. The blister may be one which is very superficial, containing clear liquid. On the other hand, a blood blister may form in which deeper tissue is disrupted, causing blood vessels to rupture. Pain is caused by the pressure of the fluid.

MANAGEMENT   As stated previously, blister prevention is of paramount importance. Once developed, blisters can be a real problem for the athlete, as well as for the athletic trainer. The following are general rules for managing a blister:

Figure 16-6

A direct means of preventing a blister is to "blank out" a piece of tape and fit it tightly over an irritated skin area.

1. The intact blister
   a. Leave the blister intact for the first 24 hours. Often during that time, many of the symptoms will lessen.
   b. If the blister is large and in a place on the skin that will be continually irritated, clean it thoroughly with antiseptic soap.
   c. With a sterile scalpel, cut a small incision $\frac{1}{8}$ to $\frac{1}{4}$ inch long in the blister along the periphery of the raised tissue. The hole should be large enough that it will not become sealed.
   d. Disperse the fluid by applying a pressure pad, keeping the pad in place to prevent refilling.
   e. Once the fluid has been removed, clean the area again with an antiseptic such as povidone-iodine (Betadine) and cover it with an antibiotic ointment such as Neosporin.
   f. Place a donut pad around the dressed blister to avoid further irritation.
   g. Monitor the blistered area daily for the possibility of infection. If infection occurs, refer the athlete to a physician immediately.
   h. Replace the dressing if it becomes wet from fluid seepage. A wet environment encourages growth of the staphylcoccus bacteria and, therefore, infection.
   i. When the tenderness is completely gone (in approximately 5 to 6 days), denude the area; however, remove no skin if any tenderness persists.
2. The open (torn) blister
   a. Keep the open blister clean to avoid infection. In the beginning of management, carefully and thoroughly wash with soap and water. Once cleaned, rinse with liquid antiseptic. If the blister site is torn less than one half of its diameter, apply a liquid antiseptic and allow to dry; then apply an antibiotic ointment.
   b. Lay the flap of skin back over the treated tissue; then apply a sterile dressing and a donut pad.
   c. As when managing the intact blister, monitor the open blister daily for the possibility of infection.
3. The completely denuded blister
   a. If the blister is torn $\frac{1}{2}$ inch or more, completely remove the flap of skin, using sterile scissors.
   b. Completely clean the exposed tissue with soap and water. Apply a nonstinging antiseptic liquid such as benzalkonium.
   c. If the athlete has completed his or her activity, apply the "second-skin" dressing (New-Skin) by Spenco* to the raw area. When applied, this gel provides healing through the night.

Excessive Perspiration

Excessive perspiration can be a cause of serious skin irritation.

Excessive perspiration (hyperhidrosis) occurs in a small segment of the population. This problem can make the handling of sports objects difficult, causing both performance and safety problems. Emotional excitement often makes the situation worse. The chemical composition of hyperhidrotic perspiration from palms is syruplike in appearance and extremely high in sodium chloride. This problem also increases the possibility of skin irritations and often makes adherence of bandages

*Spenco Medical Corporation, Waco, Texas.

FOOT HYGIENE FOR EXCESSIVE PERSPIRATION AND ODOR

Before Practice

1. Apply an astringent such as 20% aluminum chloride in anhydrous ethyl alcohol (Drysol) to the skin and allow it to air dry.
2. Next, liberally apply a powder such as talcum, alum, or boric acid to the skin, socks, and sports footwear.

After Practice

1. After thoroughly washing and drying the feet, the same procedure is followed as before practice. An astringent is applied to the skin and an absorbent powder to street socks and shoes.
2. Footwear should be changed frequently.
3. Sports footwear should be liberally powdered after practice to absorb moisture during storage. Ideally a different pair of shoes should be worn daily.

difficult, especially where adhesive tape is necessary. This condition makes callus development, blisters, and intertrigo (chafing) much more likely to occur. Treatment of excessive perspiration should include using an astringent such as alcohol or an absorbent powder (see box above).

Chafing of the Skin

Chafing (intertrigo) of the skin is another condition that stems from friction or from rubbing the skin unduly.

ETIOLOGY Chafing occurs particularly in athletes who are obese or heavy limbed. It results from friction and maceration (softening) of the skin in a climate of heat and moisture.

SYMPTOMS AND SIGNS Repeated skin rubbing, as in the groin and axilla, can separate the keratin from the granular layer of the epidermis. This separation causes oozing wounds that develop into a crusting and cracking lesion.

PREVENTION To prevent intertrigo keep the skin dry, clean, and friction free. For groin conditions the athlete should wear loose, soft, cotton underwear. A male athlete should wear his supporter over a pair of loose cotton boxer shorts.

MANAGEMENT The chafed area should be cleansed once daily with mild soap and lukewarm water. Treatment of a chafed area includes wet packs, using a medicated solution such as Burrows 15 to 20 minutes, three times daily. This is followed by the application of a 1% hydrocortisone cream.

Ingrown Toenails

An ingrown toenail is a very common condition among athletes. The large toe is the most often affected. The nail grows into the lateral nailfold and enters the skin.[6]

ETIOLOGY In general, the ingrown nail results from the lateral pressure from poorly fitting shoes, improper toenail trimming, or trauma such as repeated pressure from sliding to the front of the shoe (Color Plate, Figure D).

Figure 16-7

Prevention of ingrown
toenails requires routine
trimming so that the margins
do not penetrate the skin on
the side of the nail.

Figure 16-8

Once an ingrown toenail
occurs, proper management is
necessary to avoid infection.
A, Applying a wisp of cotton
under the ingrown side;
B, cutting a V in the center of
the nail; **C,** shaving the top
of the nail thin.

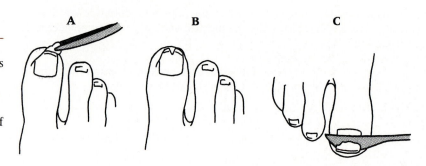

PREVENTION Because of the handicapping nature of this condition, prevention
of ingrown toenails is much preferred over management. Properly fitted shoes
and socks are essential. The toenails should be trimmed weekly by cutting straight
across, avoiding rounding so that the margins do not penetrate the tissue on the
side (Figure 16-7). The nail should be left sufficiently long so that it is clear of
the underlying skin yet still be cut short enough so as not to irritate the skin
through pushing against shoes or socks.

SYMPTOMS AND SIGNS The first indications of an ingrown toenail are pain and
swelling. If not treated early, the penetrated skin becomes severely inflamed and
purulent. The lateral nailfold is swollen and irritated.

MANAGEMENT There are a number of ways to manage the ingrown toenail. If
it is in the first stages of inflammation, a more conservative approach can be
taken.

1. Soak the toe in hot water (110° to 120° F) for approximately 20 minutes.
2. After soaking, the nail will be soft and pliable and may be pried out of the
   skin. Using sterile forceps or scissors, lift the nail from the soft tissue and
   insert a piece of cotton to keep the nail out of the skin (Figure 16-8). This
   also relieves the pain. Perform this procedure daily until the corner of the
   nail has grown past the irritated tissue.

If the condition becomes chronically irritated, a more aggressive approach is likely
to be taken.

1. After applying an antiseptic (e.g., 1% or 2% lidocaine), slip the nail-splitting
   scissor under the ingrown nail.
2. With the scissor inserted to the point of resistance, cut away and remove
   the wedge-shaped nail. Also remove the granulation tissue in the area.
   Keep a moist antiseptic compress in place until the inflammation has subsided.
3. Athletes with recurrent ingrown nails may require the use of phenol for
   permanent destruction of the lateral portion of the nail.

Wounds

Traumatic skin lesions, commonly termed wounds, are extremely prevalent in sports; abrasions, lacerations, and punctures are daily occurrences (Figure 16-9). To avoid infection, any wound, no matter how slight, must be cared for immediately (Table 16-4). In general all wounds must be cleansed with soap and water to rid them of microorganism contamination. Following cleansing, a dressing containing an antiseptic is applied. However, if the wound is to be examined by a physician, no medication should be added to the dressing. Most lacerations and puncture wounds should be treated by a physician. Uninfected abrasions are not

Signs of infection
Appear 2 to 7 days after injury
Red, swollen, hot, and tender wound
Swollen and painful lymph glands near the area of infection (groin, axilla, or neck)
Mild fever and headache

Figure 16-9

Wounds occurring in sports can present a serious problem of infection. **A1** and **A2,** Abrasion. **B,** Laceration. **C,** Puncture. **D,** Incision. **E1** and **E2,** Avulsion.

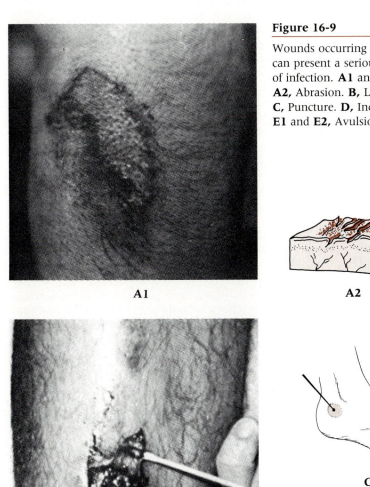

A1

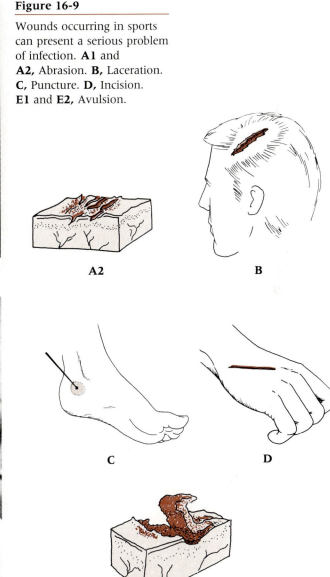

A2

B

C

D

E1

E2

TABLE 16-4 Care of External Wounds

Type of Wound	Action of Coach or Athletic Trainer	Initial Care	Follow-Up Care
Abrasion	Provide initial care. Wound seldom requires medical attention unless infected.	Cleanse abraded area with soap and water; debride with brush. Apply solution of hydrogen peroxide over abraded area; continue until foaming has subsided. Apply petroleum-based, medicated ointment to keep abraded surface moist—in sports, it is not desirable for abrasions to acquire a scab. Place a nonadhering sterile pad (Telpha pad) over the ointment.	Change dressing daily; look for signs of infection.
Laceration	Cleanse around wound; avoid wiping more contaminating agents into the area. Apply dry, sterile compress pad; refer to physician.	Complete cleansing and suturing are performed by physician; injections of tetanus toxoid are given if needed.	Change dressing daily; look for signs of infection.
Puncture	Cleanse around wound; avoid wiping more contaminating agents into the area. Apply dry, sterile compress pad; refer to physician.	Complete cleansing and injections of tetanus toxoid, if needed, are performed by physician.	Change dressing daily; look for signs of infection.
Incision	Clean around wound. Apply dry, sterile compress pad to control bleeding; refer to physician.	Cleanse wound. Suturing and injection of tetanus toxoid, if needed, are performed by physician.	Change dressing daily; look for signs of infection.
Avulsion	Clean around wound; save avulsed tissue. Apply dry, sterile compress pad to control bleeding; refer to physician.	Wound is cleansed thoroughly; avulsed skin is replaced and sutured by a physician; tetanus toxoid injection is administered if needed.	Change dressing daily; look for signs of infection.

usually referred to a physician. They are managed by debridement and thorough cleansing with soap and water, followed by the application of a moist dressing such as a medicated ointment. Using an ointment prevents accumulation of a crust and secondary infection. It is advisable that abrasions heal from the inside out to avoid the formation of scabs, which serve only to cover infected areas and are easily torn off by activity.

Skin Bruises

The consequence of a sudden compressive, blunt force to the skin is a bruise. The skin is not broken, but the soft tissue is traumatized. A first-degree bruise (ecchymosis) causes, in most cases, broken blood vessels and discoloration (black and blue). A great force affects the underlying structures, producing a bone or muscle contusion. ICE-R (*I*ce, *C*ompression, *E*levation, *R*est) is the treatment of choice to control the hemorrhage that may occur.

Abrasions

Abrasions are common conditions that occur when the skin is scraped against a rough surface. The top layer of skin is worn away, thus exposing numerous blood capillaries. This general exposure, with dirt and foreign materials scraping and penetrating the skin, increases the probability of infection unless the wound is properly debrided and cleansed.

Punctures

Puncture wounds can easily occur during physical activities and can be fatal. Direct penetration of tissues by a pointed object such as a track shoe spike can introduce the tentanus bacillus into the bloodstream, possibly making the athlete a victim of lockjaw. All puncture wounds and severe lacerations should be referred immediately to a physician.

Lacerations

Lacerations are also common in sports and occur when a sharp or pointed object tears the tissues, giving the wound the appearance of a jagged-edged cavity. As with abrasions, lacerations present an environment conducive to severe infection. The same mechanism that causes a laceration can also cause a skin avulsion, in which a piece of skin is completely ripped from its source.

Mouth lacerations   Lacerations of the mouth usually occur from a blow to the mouth that forces soft tissue against the teeth. Lacerations of the mouth occur most frequently to the lips and tongue. Deep cuts will need to be sutured by a physician, but most lacerations are minor and will not keep the athlete out of activity.

For inspecting this type of injury, the athlete should rinse the mouth with water, and then the athletic trainer should examine the teeth for possible fractures. After the extent of injury has been determined, a solution of hydrogen peroxide is used as an antiseptic and is followed by an astringent-antiseptic solution. Swelling and hemorrhaging can be controlled by having the athlete suck on ice.

Scalp lacerations   The care of scalp lacerations poses a special problem because of the general inaccessibility of these injuries. Bleeding is often extensive, which makes it difficult to pinpoint the site of the wound. Matted hair and dirt can also disguise the actual point of injury (see box on p. 470 for care).

Avulsion

Avulsion wounds occur when skin is torn from the body and are frequently associated with major bleeding. The avulsed tissue should be placed on moist gauze that is preferably saturated with saline solution. The tissue and gauze are put into a plastic bag that is then immersed in cold water and taken, along with the athlete, to the hospital for reattachment.

Incisions

Incisions are clearly cut wounds that often occur where a blow has been delivered over a sharp bone or over a bone that is poorly padded. They are not as serious as the other types of exposed wounds.

CARE OF SCALP LACERATIONS

MATERIALS NEEDED: Antiseptic soap, water, antiseptic, 4-inch (10 cm) gauze pads, sterile cotton, and hair clippers.

POSITION OF THE ATHLETE: The athlete lies on the table with the wound upward.

PROCEDURE

1. The entire area of bleeding is thoroughly cleansed with antiseptic soap and water. Washing the wound to remove dirt and debris is best done in lengthwise movements.
2. After the injury site is cleansed and dried, it is exposed and, if necessary, the hair is clipped away. Enough scalp should be exposed so that a bandage and tape may be applied.
3. Firm pressure or an astringent can be used to reduce bleeding if necessary.
4. Wounds that are more than ½ inch (1.25 cm) in length and ⅛ inch (0.3 cm) in depth should be referred to a physician for treatment. In less severe wounds the bleeding should be controlled and an antiseptic applied, followed by the application of a protective coating such as collodion and a sterile gauze pad. A tape adherent is then painted over the skin area to ensure that the tape sticks to the skin.

Wound Infection

All wounds are subject to infection from external contamination. The organism most often involved is the pyogenic *Staphylococcus.*

tetanus (lockjaw)
An acute, often fatal condition characterized by tonic muscular spasm, hyperreflexia, and lockjaw.

Tetanus   Tetanus (lockjaw) is an acute disease causing fever and convulsions. Tonic spasm of skeletal muscles is always a possibility for any nonimmunized athlete. The tetanus bacillus enters an open wound as a spore and, depending on individual susceptibility, acts on the motor end plate of the central nervous system. After initial childhood immunization by tetanus toxoid, boosters should be given every 10 years. An athlete not immunized should receive an injection of tetanus immune globulin (Hyper-Tet) immediately after injury.

WOUND DRESSINGS

bandage
A strip of cloth or other material used to cover a wound.

dressing
Covering, protective or supportive, that is applied to an injury or wound.

A **bandage,** when properly applied, can contribute decidedly to recovery from sports injuries. Bandages carelessly or improperly applied can cause discomfort, allow wound contamination, or even hamper repair and healing. In all cases bandages must be firmly applied—neither so tight that circulation is impaired nor so loose that the **dressing** is allowed to slip.

Skin lesions are extremely prevalent in sports; abrasions, lacerations, and puncture wounds are almost daily occurrences. It is of the utmost importance to the well being of the athlete that open wounds be cared for immediately. All wounds, even those that are relatively superficial, must be considered contaminated by microorganisms and therefore must be cleansed, medicated (when called for), and dressed. Wound dressing requires a sterile environment to prevent infections.

Individuals who perform wound management in sports often do not follow good principles of cleanliness. To alleviate this problem one must adhere to standard procedures in the prevention of wound contamination.

Training Room Practices in Wound Care

The following are suggested procedures to use in the athletic training room to cut down the possibility of wound infections. See Table 16-4 for more specific suggestions regarding the care of external wounds.

1. Make sure all instruments such as scissors, tweezers, and swabs are sterilized.
2. Clean hands thoroughly.
3. Clean in and around a skin lesion thoroughly.
4. Place a nonmedicated dressing over a lesion if the athlete is to be sent for medical attention.
5. Avoid touching any parts of a sterile dressing that may come in contact with a wound.
6. Place medication on a pad rather than directly on a lesion.
7. Secure the dressing with tape or a wrap; always avoid placing pressure directly over a lesion.

VIRAL INFECTIONS

As discussed previously, viruses are ultramicroscopic organisms that do not have enzyme systems but parasitize living cells. Entering a tissue cell, the virus exists as nucleic acid. Inside, the virus may stimulate the cell chemically to produce more virus until the host cell dies and/or the virus is ejected to infect additional cells.

Of the many viral infections that can directly infect the athlete, these very common ones will be discussed: the herpesviruses, wart-causing verrucas, and poxvirus (molluscum contagiosum).

Common viruses that attack the skin of athletes
Herpesvirus
Verruca
Poxvirus (molluscum contagiosum)

Herpes Simplex: Labialis and Gladiatorum

Herpes simplex is a strain of virus that is associated with skin and mucous membrane infection. Types 1 and 2 cause cutaneous lesions and are indistinguishable from one another (Color Plate, Figure A); however, type 1 is found, for the most part, extragenitally and type 2 genitally.[2] Both can, however, be found anywhere on the skin or mucous membrane.

ETIOLOGY   Herpes simplex is highly contagious and is usually transmitted directly through a lesion in the skin or mucous membrane. After the initial outbreak, it is thought to move down a sensory nerve's neurilemmal sheath to reside in a resting state in a local ganglion. Recurrent attacks can be triggered by sunlight, emotional disturbances, illness, fatigue, infection, or other situations that may stress the organism. However, sunlight does not adversely affect the reactivation rate if a sunscreen of SPF 15 is used.[9]

SYMPTOMS AND SIGNS   An early indication that a herpes infection is about to erupt is a tingling or hypersensitivity in the infected area 24 hours before the appearance of lesions. Local swelling occurs, followed by the appearance of vesicles. The athlete may feel generally ill with a headache and sore throat, lymph gland swelling, and pain in the area of lesions. The vesicles generally rupture in

1 to 3 days, spilling out a serous material that will form into a yellowish crust. The lesions will normally heal in 10 to 14 days.

Of the two areas of the body affected, herpes labialis (cold sore) is usually the least symptomatic. Herpes simplex gladiatorum is the more serious, with lesions commonly on the side of the face, neck, or shoulders.

MANAGEMENT Herpes simplex lesions are self-limiting. Therapy usually is directed toward reducing pain and promoting early healing.[2] Application of ice or liquid nitrogen during the early symptoms, before the appearance of lesions, effectively reduces later symptoms. Some treatment choices include drying the lesions with dyes, germicides, and hydrogen peroxide. Anti-inflammatory agents that contain topical hydrocortisone or other antibiotics may also be used.

Herpes simplex infection is so highly contagious that it may run rampant through an entire team in a very short time. Wrestlers having any signs of a herpes infection should be disqualified from body contact for at least 120 hours (5 days).[13]

COMPLICATIONS Herpes simplex, if not carefully managed, can lead to secondary infection. A major problem is keratoconjunctivitis, an inflammation of the cornea and conjunctiva that could lead to loss of vision and that must be considered a medical emergency.

Verruca Virus and Warts

Numerous forms of verruca exist, including the verruca plana (flat wart), verruca plantaris (plantar wart), and the condyloma acuminatum (venereal wart).

The verruca virus uses the skin's epidermal layer for reproduction and growth. The verruca wart enters the skin through a lesion that has been exposed to contaminated fields, floors, or clothing. Contamination can also occur from exposure to other warts.[10]

Verruca Plana

Verruca plana is associated with the common wart and is prevalent on the hands of children (Color Plate, Figure B).

SYMPTOMS AND SIGNS This wart appears as a small, round, elevated lesion with rough, dry surfaces. It may be painful if pressure is applied. These warts are subject to secondary bacterial infection, particularly if they are located on the hands or feet, where they may be constantly irritated.

MANAGEMENT Vulnerable warts need to be protected until they can be treated by a physician. Application of a topical salicylic acid preparation or liquid nitrogen or electrocautering are most common ways of managing this condition.

Verruca Plantaris

Plantar warts are usually found on the sole of the foot, on or adjacent to areas of abnormal weight bearing; however, they can spread to the hands and other body parts. They most commonly result from a fallen metatarsal arch or bruises to the ball of the foot, such as may be sustained during excessive jumping or running on the ball of the foot. Other names for this condition are papilloma and seed warts. Plantar warts are seen as areas with excessive epidermal thickening and cornification (Color Plate, Figure C). They produce general discomfort and point tenderness in the areas of excessive callus formation. Commonly the athlete complains that the condition feels as though he or she has stepped on broken glass.

SYMPTOMS AND SIGNS   A major characteristic of the plantar wart is its punctuation of hemorrhages, which looks like a cluster of small black seeds.

MANAGEMENT   There are many different approaches to the treatment of warts. In general, while the athlete is competing, a conservative approach is taken. Concern is to protect the wart against infection and to keep the growth of the warts under control. A common approach to controlling plantar warts is the careful paring away of accumulated callous tissue and application of a keratolytic such as 40% salicylic acid plaster. When the competitive season is over, the physician may decide to remove the wart by freezing it with liquid nitrogen or by electrodesiccation. Until its removal, a wart should be protected by a doughnut pad.

Poxvirus (Molluscum Contagiosum)

Molluscum contagiosum is a poxvirus infection. It is more contagious than warts, particularly during direct body contact activities such as wrestling.

SYMPTOMS AND SIGNS   Molluscum contagiosum appears as a small, pinkish, slightly raised, smooth-domed papule. When this condition is identified, it must be referred immediately to a physician.

MANAGEMENT   Treatment often consists of cleansing throughly and using a destructive procedure. Destructive procedures include the use of a powerful counterirritant such as cantharidin (Cantharone), surgical removal of the lesion, or cryosurgery, using nitrogen.

BACTERIAL INFECTIONS

Bacteria are single-celled, plantlike microorganisms that lack chlorophyll and may destroy blood cells. Bacterial infections are common complications of skin insults. Most of them are associated with strains of staphylococci and streptococci, particularly the *Staphylococcus aureus* strain, with the resultant production of purulent matter.

Athletes with bacterial infections associated with pus may pass the infection onto other athletes through direct contact.

Impetigo Contagiosa

Impetigo contagiosa is an extremely common skin disease, primarily observed in young adults, with the greatest number of cases occurring in late summer and early fall.

ETIOLOGY   Impetigo contagiosa is caused by streptococci, staphylococci, or a combination of these two bacteria. It is spread rapidly when athletes are in close contact with one another. Wrestling is a sport that is particularly at risk for spreading this disease.

SYMPTOMS AND SIGNS   Impetigo contagiosa is first characterized by mild itching and soreness, which are followed by the eruption of small vesicles that form into pustules and, later, yellow crustations (Color Plate, Figure E).

MANAGEMENT   Impetigo usually responds rapidly to proper treatment. This treatment consists of thorough cleansing of the crusted area, followed by the application of a topical antibacterial (see box on p. 474). Systemic antibiotics also are used.

Furuncles and Carbuncles

Two major skin problems affecting athletes are furuncles and carbuncles. Both, if traumatized, could lead to a serious systemic infection.

MANAGEMENT OF IMPETIGO

1. Wash vigorously four or five times daily, using a medicated cleansing agent and hot water to remove all the crustations.
2. After cleansing, dry the area by patting gently.
3. When completely dried, an antibiotic or prescribed medicated ointment may be applied.
4. Every precaution should be taken to make sure that the athlete used isolated gym clothing and towels to prevent the spread of the disease.

Furunculosis

Furuncles (boils) are common amoung athletes.

ETIOLOGY   Furuncles usually result from the irritation of hair follicles or sebaceous glands. The predominant infectious organisms are staphylococci, which produce a pustule.

SYMPTOMS AND SIGNS   The areas of the body most affected are the back of the neck, regions of the face, and the buttocks. The pustule becomes enlarged, reddened, and hard from internal pressure. As pressure increases, extreme pain and tenderness develop (Color Plate, Figure F). Most furuncles will mature and rupture spontaneously, emitting the contained pus. **NOTE**: Furuncles should *not* be squeezed, since squeezing forces the infection into adjacent tissue or extends it to other skin areas.

Furuncles on the face can be dangerous, particularly if they drain into veins that lead to venous sinuses of the brain. Such conditions should immediately be referred to a physician.

MANAGEMENT   Care of the furuncle involves protecting it from additional irritation, referring the athlete to a physician for antibiotic treatment, and keeping the athlete from contact with other team members while the boil is draining. The common practice of hot dressings or special drawing salves is not beneficial to the maturation of the boil.[8]

Carbuncles

ETIOLOGY   Carbuncles are similar to furuncles in their early stages, having also developed from the staphylococci.

SYMPTOMS AND SIGNS   The principal difference between it and a furuncle is that the carbuncle is larger and deeper and usually has several openings in the skin. It may produce fever and elevation of the white cell count. A carbuncle starts as a painful node that is covered by tight, reddish skin that later becomes very thin. The site of greatest occurrence is the back of the neck, where it appears early as a dark red, hard area and then in a few days emerges into a lesion that discharges yellowish-red pus from a number of places.

One must be aware of the dangers inherent in carbuncles—they may result in the athlete's developing an internal infection or may spread to adjacent tissue or to other athletes.

MANAGEMENT The most common treatment is surgical drainage combined with the administration of antibiotics. A warm compress is applied to promote circulation to the area.

Folliculitis

Folliculitis is an infection of the hair follicle. It is most prevalent in the hair follicles of the beard and the scalp (Figure 16-10). However, it can occur anywhere that hair exists on the body.

ETIOLOGY Folliculitis can be caused by comedones (blackheads) or, more commonly, by the ''ingrown'' hair, which grows inward and curls up to form an infected nodule. The infection occurs most often in areas in which hair is shaved or is rubbed with clothing such as the neck, face, buttocks, or thigh.

Many hair follicles may become involved through the extension of infection to contiguous sebaceous glands. Such spreading causes a general condition called

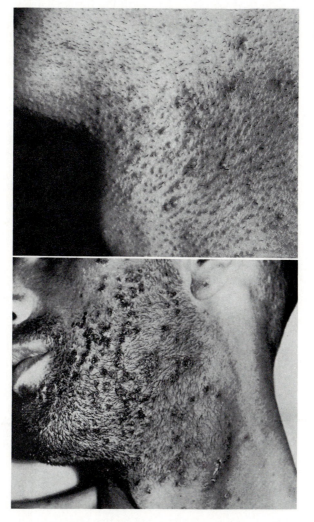

Figure 16-10

Folliculitis.

sycosis vulgaris or "barber's itch." It frequently occurs on the upper lip and forms a red, swollen area, exhibiting tenderness during palpation. Pus collects around the exposed hair, causing the hair to be easy to remove. Sycosis vulgaris should always be referred to a physician for treatment.

SYMPTOMS AND SIGNS   The condition starts with inflammation, followed by development of a papule or pustule at the mouth of the hair follicle. This is followed by development of a crust that may later slough off along with the hair. A deeper infection may cause scarring and permanent baldness (alopecia) in that area. The most common microorganism associated with this condition is staphylococcus.

MANAGEMENT   The management of acute folliculitis is similar to that of impetigo. Moist heat is applied intermittently to increase local circulation. Antibiotics may be applied locally, as well as systemically, depending on the scope of the condition.

Hidradenitis Suppurativa

Hidradenitis suppurativa is a chronic inflammatory condition of the apocrine glands or large sweat glands commonly found in the axilla, scrotum, labia majora, and nipples.

ETIOLOGY   The exact cause of this condition is unclear. Most believe it is caused by blockage of the apocrine gland ducts as a result of an inflammation. Some believe it is a keratinous plug of a hair follicle. The role of bacteria is not exactly known.

SYMPTOMS AND SIGNS   The condition begins as a small papule and grows to the size of a small tumor that is filled with purulent material. Deep dermal inflammation can occur, resulting in large abscesses that result in bands of scar tissue.[6] The contents of this lesion are highly infectious to the athlete and, when discharged, can infect other members of the team.

MANAGEMENT   Treatment of this problem includes avoiding the use of antiperspirants, deodorants, and shaving creams; using medicated soaps such as those containing chlorhexidine or povidone-iodine (Betadine); and applying a prescribed antibiotic lotion.

Comedones (Blackheads) and Pimples

Blackheads and pimples are common skin eruptions, which affect adolescents in particular. Both occur at the hair follicle where the oily secretion (sebum) accumulates. Sebum carries, besides its oily content, waste products that may aid in the initiation of a mild inflammatory condition if it should block a hair follicle. Blackheads and pimples occur primarily where the skin is oiliest—on the face, nose, chest, and upper back. The oilier an individual's skin, the more prone it is to blackheads. Frequent and thorough cleansing of the skin, using mild soap and hot water, will remove excess oil and consequently help to prevent blackheads.

Pimples may be caused by infected blackheads, skin infections, an inadequate diet, or internal imbalances. One should caution the athlete who has pimples or blackheads that squeezing will only cause additonal inflammation and infection.

Acne Vulgaris

Acne vulgaris is an inflammatory disease that involves the hair follicles and the sebaceous glands. It occurs near puberty and usually is less active after adolescence. Acne is characterized by blackheads, cysts, and pustules.

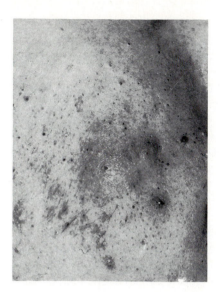

Figure 16-11

Acne vulgaris.

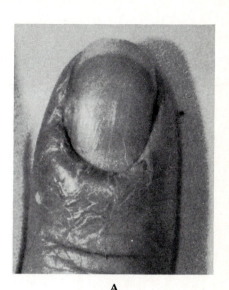

Figure 16-12

A, Paronychia is a common infection of the skin surrounding the nail. **B,** Cross section of finger.

A

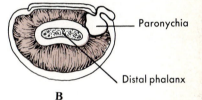

Paronychia

Distal phalanx

B

ETIOLOGY   Although most adolescents experience some form of acne, only a few develop an extremely disfiguring case (Figure 16-11). Its cause is not definitely known, but it has been suggested that sex hormone imbalance may be the major causal factor.

SYMPTOMS AND SIGNS   Acne begins as an improper functioning of the sebaceous glands with the formation of blackheads and inflammation, which in turn produces pustules on the face, neck, and back in varying depths. The superficial lesions usually dry spontaneously, whereas the deeper ones may become chronic and form disfiguring scars.

The athlete with a serious case of acne vulgaris has a scarring disease and because of it may have serious emotional problems. The individual may become nervous, shy, and even antisocial, with feelings of inferiority in interpersonal relations with peer groups. The athletic trainer's major responsibility in aiding athletes with acne is to help the athlete perform the wishes of the physician and to give constructive guidance and counsel.

MANAGEMENT   The care of acne is usually symptomatic, with the majority of cases following a similar pattern, including hormone therapy given by a physician and a routine of washing three times daily with a mild soap followed by the application of a drying agent. Other methods may be required such as the nightly application of keratolytic lotions (sulfur zinc or sulfur resorcinol), individual drainage of crusts or blackheads by the physician, and ultraviolet treatment.

Paronychia and Onychia

Fingernails and toenails are continually subject to injury and infection in sports. A common infection is paronychia, which is a purulent infection of the skin surrounding the nail (Figure 16-12).

ETIOLOGY   Paronychia and onychia develop from staphylococci, streptococci, and fungal organisms that accompany the contamination of open wounds or hangnails. It is common in football linemen, who regularly stick their fingers in dirt.

SYMPTOMS AND SIGNS   Acute paronychia has a rapid onset, with painful, bright red swelling of the proximal and lateral nail. An accumulation of purulent material occurs behind the cuticle.[6] The infection may spread and cause onychia, an inflammation of the nail bed.

MANAGEMENT   One should recognize paronychia early and have the athlete soak the affected finger or toe in a hot solution of Epsom salts or boric acid three times daily. A medicated ointment, preferably penicillin or 5% ammoniated mercury, should be applied between soakings. Every protection must be given the infected nail while the athlete is competing. Uncontrollable paronychia may require medical intervention, consisting of pus removal through a skin incision or the removal of a portion of the infected nail.

Conjunctivitis (Pinkeye)

ETIOLOGY   The conjunctiva of the eye is subject to inflammation from various causes. Colds, excessive light, dust, foreign bodies, and infections of the face may affect the conjunctiva.

SYMPTOMS AND SIGNS   Bacteria that enter the eye may cause itching, burning, watering, and sensitivity to light. The conjunctiva may become red and swollen, with an accumulation of pus. This condition can be highly infectious, spreading to the normal eye or to other individuals.

MANAGEMENT   An athlete exhibiting signs of conjunctivitis should be sent for medical care immediately. Conjunctivitis may be an indication of a more serious disease such as iritis or glaucoma.

Hordeolum (Sty)

A sty is an infection of the eyelash follicle or the sebaceous gland at the edge of the eyelid.

ETIOLOGY   The infection is usually caused by a staphylococcal organism, which has been spread by rubbing or by dust particles.

SYMPTOMS AND SIGNS   The condition starts as erythema of the eye, which localizes into a painful pustule within a few days.

MANAGEMENT   Treatment consists of the application of hot, moist compresses and an ointment of 1% yellow oxide or mercury. Recurrent sties require the attention of an ophthalmologist.

Ear Conditions

The earache is a common symptom for several different ear involvements. It often results from dermatitis of the external ear canal, from furuncles in the external canal, from eardrum inflammation, or from infections of the middle ear.

Infection of the external ear canal can arise from irritation caused by hardened wax (cerumen), foreign bodies, or insult caused by inserting hard objects into the ear. A general dermatitis may result or a localized infection may arise from a furuncle. The inflammation of the outer canal may infect the eardrum, causing sharp, intermittent pain. Another and more common cause of eardrum infection is an upper respiratory infection, which irritates and closes the eustachian tube, causing increased air pressure within the middle ear. The increased middle ear pressure combines with an inflammation and tends to create sharp stabbing pain, difficulty in hearing, and ringing in the ear. Ear infections require medical attention so that antibiotics and other medical procedures may be initiated.

Swimmer's Ear (External Otitis)

A common condition in athletes engaged in water sports is "swimmer's ear," or external otitis.

ETIOLOGY "Swimmer's ear" is a general term for ear infection caused by *Pseudomonas aeruginosa*, a type of gram-negative bacillus. Contrary to current thought among swimming coaches, swimmer's ear is not usually associated with a fungal infection. Water can become trapped in the ear canal as a result of obstructions created by cysts, bone growths, ear wax plugs, or swelling caused by allergies.[11]

Prevention of ear infection can best be attained by drying the ears thoroughly with a soft towel, using ear drops containing a mild acid (3% boric acid) and alcohol solution before and after each swim, and avoiding situations that can cause ear infections such as overexposure to cold wind or sticking foreign objects into the ear.

SYMPTOMS AND SIGNS The athlete may complain of itching, discharge, or even a partial hearing loss.

MANAGEMENT When the swimmer displays symptoms of external otitis, immediate referral to a physician must be made. Treatment may include acidification through drops into the ear to make an inhospitable environment for the gram-negative bacteria. Antibiotics may be used in athletes in whom inflammation is well established. Protection of the athlete with a mild ear infection can be successfully accomplished by plugging the ear with lamb's wool combined with lanolin.

FUNGAL INFECTIONS

Fungi cause several of the skin diseases found among athletes because sports produce an environment, at times, that is beneficial to their cultivation. Fungi grow best in unsanitary conditions combined with warmth, moisture, and darkness. Three categories of superficial fungal infections are discussed; dermatophytes, candidiasis (moniliasis), and tinea versicolor.

The fungus attacks mainly the keratin of the epidermis but may go as deep as the dermis through hair follicles. These organisms are given the common name of **ringworm (tinea)** and are classified according to the area of the body infected. Infection takes place within superficial keratinized tissue such as hair, skin, and nails. The extremely contagious spores of these fungi may be spread by direct contact, contaminated clothing, or dirty locker rooms and showers.

ringworm (tinea)
Common name given to many superficial fungal infections of the skin.

Dermatophytes (Ringworm Fungi)

Dermatophytes, also known as ringworm fungi, are the cause of most skin, nail, and hair fungal infections. They belong to three genera: *Microsporum*, *Trichophyton*, and *Epidermophyton*.

Tinea of the Scalp (Tinea Capitis)

SYMPTOMS AND SIGNS Tinea (ringworm) of the scalp (tinea capitis), beginning as a small papule on the scalp and spreading peripherally is most common among children. The lesions appear as small grayish scales, resulting in scattered bald patches. The primary sources of tinea capitis infection are contaminated animals, barber clippers, hairbrushes, or combs.

MANAGEMENT Griseofulvin is usually the treatment of choice. It is given in small doses over a period of time or in one large dose. A topical cream such as 1% clotrimazole may be used to help prevent the spread of the disease.

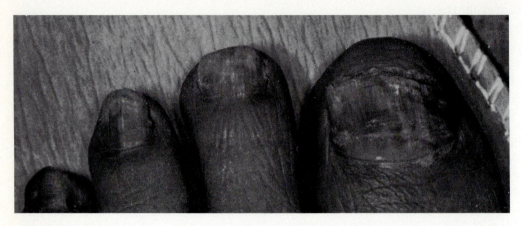

Figure 16-13

Tinea of the nail (tinea unguium).

Tinea of the Body (Tinea Corporis)

SYMPTOMS AND SIGNS   Tinea of the body (tinea corporis) mainly involves the upper extremities and the trunk. The lesions are characterized by ring-shaped, reddish, vesicular areas that may be scaly or crusted (Color Plate, Figure I). Excessive perspiration and friction increase susceptibility to the condition.

MANAGEMENT   Treatment usually consists of antifungal medication such as 2% miconazole cream or 1% clotrimazole cream or lotion.

Tinea of the Nail (Tinea Unguium)

SYMPTOMS AND SIGNS   Tinea of the nail (tinea unguium) is a fungous infection of the toenails and fingernails. It is often seen among athletes who are involved in water sports or who have chronic athlete's foot. Trauma predisposes the athlete to infection. It is often difficult for a physician to determine accurately what is the real cause of the disease. Many different organisms can adversely affect the nail plate. When infected, the nail becomes thickened, brittle, and separated from its bed (Figure 16-13).

MANAGEMENT   The treatment of tinea unguium can be very difficult. Oral therapy has not been found effective, and topical creams or lotions do not penetrate the nail. Surgical removal of the nail may have to be performed on the athlete with extremely infected nails.

Tinea of the Groin (Tinea Cruris)

Tinea of the groin (tinea cruris), more commonly called "jock rash" or "dhobie itch," appears as a bilateral and often symmetrical brownish or reddish lesion resembling the outline of a butterfly in the groin area.

SYMPTOMS AND SIGNS   The athlete complains of mild to moderate itching, resulting in scratching and the possibility of a secondary bacterial infection (Color Plate, Figure G).

MANAGEMENT   One must be able to identify lesions of tinea cruris and handle them accordingly. Conditions of this type must be treated until cured (Figure 16-14). Infection not responding to normal management must be referred to the team physician. Most ringworm infections will respond to many of the nonprescription medications that contain such ingredients as undecylenic acid, triacetin, or propionate-caprylate compound, which are available as aerosol sprays, liquids, powders, or ointments. Powder, because of its absorbent qualities, should be the only medication vehicle used in the groin area. Medications that are irritating or tend to mask the symptoms of a groin infection must be avoided.

Atypical or complicated groin infections must have medical attention. Many prescription medications that may be applied topically or orally and have dramatic effects on skin fungus are presently on the market.

Athlete's Foot (Tinea Pedis)

The foot is the most common area of the body that is infected by dermatophytes, usually by tinea pedis, or athlete's foot. *Tricophyton mentagrophytes* infect the space between the third and fourth digits and enter the plantar surface of the arch. The same organism attacks toenails. *Trichophyton rubrum* causes scaling and thickening of the soles. The athlete wearing shoes that are enclosed will sweat, encouraging fungal growth. However, contagion is based mainly on the athlete's individual susceptibility. There are other conditions that may also be thought to be athlete's foot, such as a dermatitis caused by allergy or an eczema-type skin infection (Color Plate, Figure H).

SYMPTOMS AND SIGNS Athlete's foot can reveal itself in many ways but appears most often as an extreme itching on the soles of the feet and between and on top of the toes. It appears as a rash, with small pimples or minute blisters that break and exude a yellowish serum (Figure 16-15). Scratching because of itchiness can cause the tissue to become inflamed and infected, manifesting a red, white, or gray scaling of the affected area.

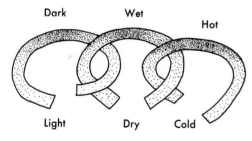

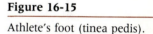

Figure 16-15

Athlete's foot (tinea pedis).

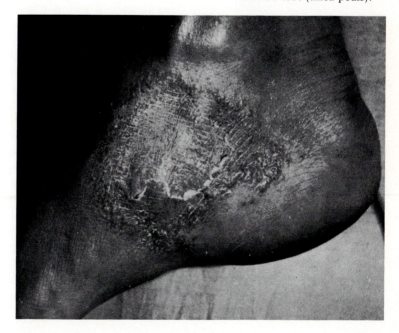

Figure 16-14

When managing a fungal infection, it is essential to break the chain of infection in one or more ways.

BASIC CARE OF ATHLETE'S FOOT

1. Keep the feet as dry as possible through frequent use of talcum powder.
2. Wear clean white socks to avoid reinfection, changing them daily.
3. Use a standard fungicide for specific medication. "Over-the-counter" medications such as Desenex and Tinactin are useful in the early stages of the infection. For stubborn cases see the team physician; a dermatologist may need to make a culture from foot scrapings to determine the best combatant to be used.

The best cure for the problem of athlete's foot is *prevention*. To keep the condition from spreading to other athletes, the following steps should be faithfully followed by individuals in the sports program:

1. All athletes should powder their feet daily.
2. One should dry the feet thoroughly, especially between and under the toes, after every shower.
3. One should keep sports shoes and street shoes dry by dusting them with powder daily.
4. All athletes should wear clean sports socks and street socks daily.
5. The shower and dressing rooms should be cleaned and disinfected daily.

MANAGEMENT   Griseofulvin is the most effective management for tinea pedis. Of major importance is good foot hygiene. Topical medications used for tinea corporis can be beneficial (see box above).[12]

Candidiasis (Moniliasis)

Candidiasis is a yeastlike fungus, which can produce skin, mucous, and internal infections.

ETIOLOGY   Candidiasis is caused by the yeastlike fungus *Candida albicans* and some other species. It will attack the skin, as well as other structures, if the environment is right. Weather that is hot and humid, along with tight clothing that rubs and poor hygiene, provides the ideal environment for fungal growth.

SYMPTOMS AND SIGNS   Among athletes, candidiasis can occur anywhere there is intertrigo, especially under the arms and in the groin area. In other words, it can occur anywhere skin touches skin when accompanied by heat and moisture. The coach or athletic trainer may mistake this condition for simple intertrigo. It appears with a bright red, moist, glistening base.[6] The border of this lesion, in contrast to that of intertrigo, is commonly rimmed with small red pustules. In cases in which it occurs where the skin is folded, a white, macerated border may surround the red area. Later, deep painful fissures may develop where the skin creases. Of major importance to the coach or athletic trainer is that *Candida albicans* can cause a systemic disease that may be life-threatening. Therefore, when suspected, immediate referral to a physician must be made.

MANAGEMENT   The first concern in treatment is to maintain a dry area. A cool, wet, medicated compress may be applied for 20 to 30 minutes several times per day to promote dryness. Depending on the site of the disease, an antibiotic salve or lotion containing miconazole may be applied. (**NOTE**: Genital candidiasis is discussed in Chapter 25, in the section "Sexually Transmitted Diseases.")

Tinea Versicolor

Tinea versicolor is a unique fungal infection and, therefore, is dealt with separately. It is a common fungal infection among young adults.

ETIOLOGY   Tinea versicolor is caused by a yeast called *Pityrosporum obiculare*. It is a normal part of the skin's flora, appearing commonly in areas in which sebaceous glands actively secrete body oils.

SYMPTOMS AND SIGNS   The fungus characteristically produces multiple, small, circular macules that are pink, brown, or white. In black persons, they appear hyperpigmented. They commonly occur on the abdomen, neck, and chest. The lesions do not tan when exposed to the sun and are usually asymptomatic.

MANAGEMENT   Treatment of tinea versicolor usually provides only temporary relief, and recurrences are common. The medication of choice is usually selenium sulfide (Selsum).

ALLERGIC, THERMAL, AND CHEMICAL SKIN REACTIONS

The skin can react adversely to a variety of nonpathogenic influences. Among the most common affecting athletes are allergies, temperature extremes, and chemical irritants.

Allergic Reactions

The skin displays allergic reactions in various ways (Color Plate, Figures K and L). An allergy is caused by an allergen, a protein toward which the body is hypersensitive. Causative factors may be food, drugs, clothing, dusts, pollens, plants, animals, heat, cold, or light, or the cause may be psychosomatic. The skin may reflect an allergy in several ways such as a reddening, elevated patches (urticaria or hives), or eczema. Reddening and swelling of the tissue may occur either locally or generally from an increased dilation of blood capillaries. Urticaria occurs as a red or white elevation (wheal) of the skin, characterized by a burning or an itching sensation. Eczema is a skin reaction in which small vesicles are produced, accompanied by itching and a crust formation.

> Skin reactions to allergy
>   Reddening
>   Elevated patches
>   Eczema

The athletic trainer should be able to recognize gross signs of allergic reactions and should then refer the athlete to the physician. Treatment usually includes avoidance of the sensitizing agents and use of an antipruritic agent (such as calamine location) and antihistamine drugs.

Allergic Contact Dermatitis

There are many substances in the sports environment to which the athlete may be allergic, causing a skin reaction.

ETIOLOGY   The most common plants that cause allergic contact dermatitis are poison ivy, poison oak, sumac, ragweed, and primrose. Over time the athlete may become allergic to topical medications such as antibiotics, antihistamines, anesthetics, or antiseptics. Chemicals commonly found in soaps, detergents, and deodorants can create a reaction. Also, the countless chemicals used in the manufacture of shoes and clothing and other materials have been known to produce allergic contact dermatitis.[1]

SYMPTOMS AND SIGNS   The period of onset from the time of initial exposure may range from 1 day to 1 week. Skin that is continually warm will develop signs earlier. The skin reacts with redness, swelling, and the formation of vesicles that ooze fluid and form a crust. A constant itch develops that is increased with heat and made worse with rubbing. Secondary infection is a common result of scratching (Color Plate, Figure J).

MANAGEMENT The most obvious treatment approach is to determine the irritant and avoid it. This may not always be simple and may require extensive testing. In the acute phase, tap water compresses or soaks soothe and dry the vesicles. In the nonacute stage topical corticosteroids may be beneficial.

Actinic Dermatitis (Sunburn)

Serious skin damage can occur from overexposure to the sun's rays. Actinic dermatitis (sunburn) is a precursor to this damage.[5]

ETIOLOGY Sunburn is a dermatitis caused by the ultraviolet radiation from the sun, and it varies in intensity from a mild erythema (pink color) to a severe, second-degree burn represented by itching, swelling, and blistering. Every protection should be given to athletes who have thin, white skin. Such persons are called *heliopaths;* their skin tends to absorb a greater amount of ultraviolet radiation than more pigmented individuals.

SYMPTOMS AND SIGNS If a large area of the skin is sunburned, the athlete may display all the symptoms of severe inflammation accompanied by shock. A sunburn can cause malfunctioning of the organs within the skin, which in turn may result in infection of structures such as hair follicles and sweat glands.

Sunburn appears 2 to 8 hours after exposure. Symptoms become most extreme in approximately 12 hours and dissipate in 72 to 96 hours.[3] After once receiving a severe sunburn, the skin is more susceptible to burning. The skin remains injured for months after a severe sunburn has been sustained. Prevention of sunburn should be accomplished by a gradual exposure to the rays of the sun, combined with use of a sunburn medication that will filter out most of the ultraviolet light. Individuals prone to burning should routinely wear a sunscreen such as para-aminobenzoic acid (PABA). Constant overexposure to the sun can lead to chronic skin thickening and damage.[3]

MANAGEMENT A sunburn is treated according to the degree or inflammation present. Mild burns can be aided by a soothing lotion that contains a mild anesthetic. Boric acid solution has also proved beneficial. Moderate and severe burns can be relieved by a tub bath in which a pound of cornstarch is used; a vinegar solution will also help. Severe sunburn may be treated by the physician with corticosteroids and other anti-inflammatory drugs.

It must be noted that ultraviolet radiation is not healthy—it can prematurely age the skin and can increase the chances of skin cancers. (Basal cell and squamous cell carcinomas are the most common cancers.[7])

Miliaria (Prickly Heat)

Prickly heat is common in sports and occurs most often during the heat of the year to those athletes who perspire profusely and who wear heavy clothing. Continued exposure to heat and moisture causes retention of perspiration by the sweat glands, resulting in itching and in burning vesicles and pustules. It occurs most often on the arms, trunk, and bending areas of the body. Care of prickly heat requires avoidance of overheating, frequent bathing with a nonirritating soap, wearing loose-fitting clothing, and the use of antipruritic lotions.

COMMON VIRAL INFECTIONS

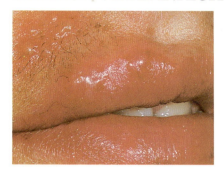

Figure A   Herpes simplex labialis.

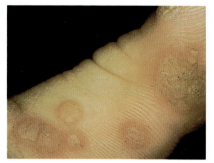

Figure B   Common warts.

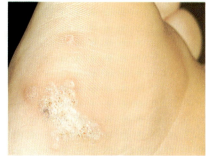

Figure C   Plantar warts on ball of foot.

COMMON BACTERIAL INFECTIONS

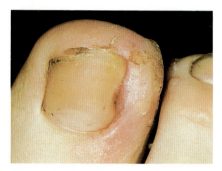

Figure D   Ingrown toenail.

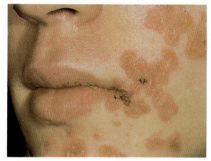

Figure E   Impetigo contagiosa.

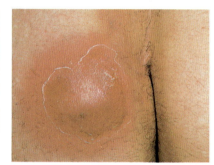

Figure F   Furuncle.

COMMON FUNGAL INFECTIONS

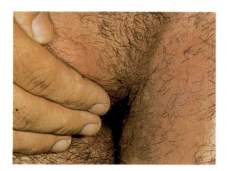

Figure G   Tinea of the groin (tinea cruris).

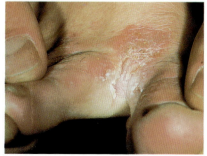

Figure H   Athlete's foot (tinea pedis).

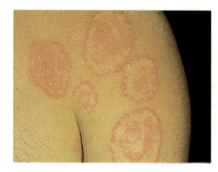

Figure I   Tinea of the body (tinea corporis).

COMMON SKIN REACTIONS

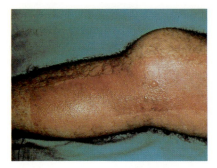

Figure J　Contact dermatitis.

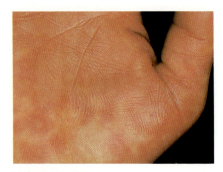

Figure K　Hives.

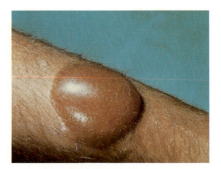

Figure L　Cold reaction.

COMMON SEXUALLY TRANSMITTED INFECTIONS

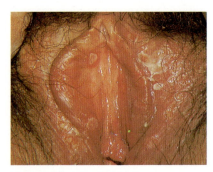

Figure M　Genital herpes simplex.

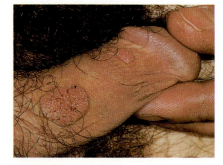

Figure N　Genital warts.

Chilblains

Chilblains is a common type of dermatitis caused by excessive exposure to cold. The tissue does not freeze but reacts with edema, reddening, possibly blistering, and a sensation of burning and itching. The parts of the body most often affected are the ears, face, hands, and feet. Treatment consists of exercise and a gradual warming of the part. Massage and application of heat are contraindicated in cases of chilblains. (See Chapter 11, *Environmental Considerations,* for more information about reactions to cold.)

INFESTATIONS AND BITES

Certain parasites cause dermatoses or skin irritations when they suck blood, inject venom, and even lay their eggs under the skin. Athletes who come in contact with these organisms may develop various symptoms such as itching, allergic skin reactions, and secondary infections from insult or scratching. The more common parasitic infestations in sports are caused by mites, crab lice, fleas, ticks, mosquitoes, and stinging insects such as bees, wasps, hornets, and yellow jackets.

Depending on the part of the country in which the athlete resides, parasites such as mites, crab lice, fleas, ticks, mosquitoes, and stinging insects can cause serious discomfort and infection.

Seven-Year Itch (Scabies)

ETIOLOGY   Seven-year itch (scabies) is a skin disease caused by the mite *Sarcoptes scabiei,* which produces extreme nocturnal itching. The parasitic itch mite is small, with the female causing the greatest irritation. The mite burrows a tunnel approximately ¼ to ½ inch (1.25 cm) long into the skin to deposit its eggs.

SYMPTOMS AND SIGNS   The mite's burrows appear as dark lines between the fingers, toes, body flexures, nipples, and genitalia. Excoriations, pustules, and papules caused by the resulting scratching frequently hide the true nature of the disease. The young mite matures in a few days and returns to the skin surface to repeat the cycle. The skin often develops a hypersensitivity to the mite, which produces extreme itching.

MANAGEMENT   Gamma benzene hexachloride (Lindane) has been identified as the most effective scabicide. It is available as a cream or a shampoo. Because of the athlete's itching and scratching, secondary infections are common and must also be treated (see box below for treatment).

TREATMENT OF SCABIES

1. The entire body should be thoroughly cleansed, with attention to skin lesions.
2. Bedding and clothing should be disinfected.
3. The coating of gamma benzene hexachloride (Lindane) should be applied on the lesions for 3 nights.
4. All individuals who have come in contact with the infected athlete should be examined by the physician.
5. Locker and game equipment must be disinfected.

Lice (Pediculosis)

ETIOLOGY   Pediculosis is an infestation by the louse, of which three types are parasitic to man. The *Pediculus capitis* (head louse) infests the head, where its eggs (nits) attach to the base of the hair shaft. The *Pthirus pubis* (crab louse) lives in the hair of the pubic region and lays it eggs at the hair base.

SYMPTOMS AND SIGNS   The *Pediculus corporis* (body louse) lives and lays its eggs in the seams of clothing. The louse is a carrier of many diseases; its bite causes an itching dermatitis, which, through subsequent scratching, provokes pustules and excoriations.

MANAGEMENT   Cure is quite rapid with the use of any of a number of parasiticides or lotions such as one composed of chlorophenothane 5.0 g, isopropyl alcohol 50 ml, and propylene glycol 50 ml, rubbed into the infected areas at night before retiring and again the following morning when arising. The area should not be washed for 7 to 10 days; then the lotion is reapplied. The lice cannot survive dryness. Good hygiene is of paramount importance in all infestations. All clothing, bedding, and toilet seats must be kept clean and sterile.

Fleas

ETIOLOGY   Fleas are small wingless insects that suck blood. Singly, their bites cause only minor discomfort to the recipient—unless the flea is a carrier of some contagious disease.

SYMPTOMS AND SIGNS   When there is a large number of biting fleas, a great deal of discomfort can occur. After attaching themselves to some moving object such as a dog or a human, most fleas bite in patterns of three. Fleas seem to concentrate their bites on the ankle and lower leg.

MANAGEMENT   Once the flea bite has been incurred, the main concern is to prevent itching with an antipruritic lotion such as calamine. Scratching the bite should be avoided to prevent a secondary infection. Areas in which fleas abound can be sprayed with selected insecticides containing malathion or some other effective insecticide.

Ticks

ETIOLOGY   Ticks are parasitic insects that have an affinity for the blood of many animals, including humans. They are carriers of a variety of microorganisms such as bacteria and viruses. Because ticks are commonly found on grass and bushes, they can easily become attached to the athlete who brushes against them.

SYMPTOMS AND SIGNS   Once attached, ticks burrow their head into the skin, becoming firmly fixed.

MANAGEMENT   To remove a tick, a heated device or alcohol is applied to its body, at which time it will withdraw its head. At no time should one attempt to pull the tick from the body; doing so may result in leaving the head of the tick embedded in the skin.

Mosquitoes

ETIOLOGY   Unless it is the carrier of a disease, the mosquito, as a blood sucker, produces a bite that causes only mild discomfort. Generally mosquitoes are attracted to lights, dark clothing, and warm, moist skin.

SYMPTOMS AND SIGNS   The mosquito bite produces a small reddish papule. Multiple bites may lead to a great deal of itching.

MANAGEMENT   Itching is most often relieved by the application of a topical medication such as calamine lotion. In climates where mosquitoes are prevalent, repellents should be used directly on the skin.

Stinging Insects

ETIOLOGY   Bees, wasps, hornets, and yellow jackets inflict a venomous sting that is temporarily painful for most individuals; however, some hypersensitive individuals may respond with an allergic reaction that may be fatal. Stings to the head, face, and neck are particularly dangerous to the athlete. Athletes having a history of allergic reactions from stings must be carefully scrutinized following a sting.

SYMPTOMS AND SIGNS   The allergic athlete may respond with an increase in heart rate, fast breathing, chest tightness, dizziness, sweating, and even loss of consciousness.[14]

MANAGEMENT   In uncomplicated sting cases, the stinging apparatus must be carefully removed with tweezers, followed by the application of a soothing medication. Detergent soap applied directly on the sting often produces an immediate lessening in symptoms. In severe reactions to a sting the athlete must be treated for severe shock and referred immediately to a physician. For sensitive athletes who perform outdoors, it should be suggested that they avoid using scented cosmetics, soap, colognes, or aftershave lotions and colorful, floral, or dark-colored clothing.

SUMMARY

The skin is the largest organ of the human body. In the average adult, skin varies in weight from 6 to 7½ lbs and is ¹⁄₃₂ to ⅛ inch thick. It is comprised of three layers, including the epidermis, the dermis, and the subcutis. The outermost layer, the epidermis, acts as protection against infections from a variety of sources. The dermis contains sweat glands, sebaceous glands, and hair follicles. The subcutis layer is the major area for fat storage and temperature regulation.

Primary skin lesions consist of the macule, papule, plaque, nodule, tumor, cyst, wheal, vesicle, bulla, and pustule. Secondary skin lesions are the scale, crust, fissure, erosion, ulcer, and scar. Causing skin lesions are microorganisms, trauma, allergies, temperature variations, chemicals, infestations, and insect bites.

Sports participation can place a great deal of mechanical force on the skin that can lead to many different problems. Abnormal friction causes keratosis and/or blisters and intertrigo. Hyperhidrosis adds to the problems of skin friction and infections. A tearing force can lacerate or avulse skin. Compression can bruise, scraping abrades, and a pointed object can puncture.

Providing immediate proper care is essential to avoid skin infections. Streptococcal and staphylococcal bacteria are associated with wound contamination, and the tetanus bacillus can cause lockjaw. All athletes should be immunized by the tetanus toxoid before they participate in sports.

Herpes simplex is a virus associated with herpes labialis and herpes gladiatorum. The verruca virus commonly is related to a variety of warts such as the plantar wart or the papilloma. The poxvirus causes molluscum contagiosum, a highly contagious wart spread by direct contact.

Impetigo contagiosa is a highly infectious disease among athletes and is associated with both the staphylococcal and streptococcal bacteria. Furuncles, carbuncles, and folliculitis are streptococcal-caused afflictions and can be spread by direct contact. Other bacterial skin conditions are hidradenitis suppurativa, acne vulgaris, paronychia, onychia, conjunctivitis, hordeolum, and external otitis (swimmer's ear).

The sports enviornment, which is often one of excessive moisture, warmth, and darkness, is conducive to fungal growth. An extremely common fungus, ringworm, is under the general heading of dermatophytes. The three genera of fungus for this condition are *Microsporum*, *Trichophyton*, and *Epidermophyton*. Under the right conditions, these fungi can attack a wide variety of body tissues. Candidiasis is a more serious form of infection caused by a yeastlike fungus, *Candida albicans*.

Athletes are also subject to many other causes of skin conditions—for example, allergies, extremes of heat or cold, and chemical irritations. One major problem that produces an insidious destruction of the skin is prolonged overexposure to sunlight.

Different parts of the country have problems with insect infestations and bites. Two of these problems are scabies (caused by mites) and pediculosis (from lice), and there are others that may be produced by fleas, ticks, mosquitoes, and stinging insects.

REVIEW QUESTIONS AND CLASS ACTIVITIES

1. Describe the skin's anatomy, functions, and lesions that are indicative of infection.
2. Contrast the microorganisms that are related to skin infections.
3. Relate the mechanical forces of friction, compression, shearing, stretching, scraping, tearing, avulsing, and puncturing to specific skin injuries.
4. List the steps to take in managing major skin traumas.
5. How should wounds be managed to avoid serious infections?
6. Characterize the different viruses that are associated with common skin infections that occur in sports.
7. What bacterial skin infections are commonly seen on athletes?
8. Tinea (ringworm) is a fungus that can be present on different parts of the body. Name the body parts.
9. How may skin infections related to microorganisms be avoided?
10. Why is candidiasis considered one of the most serious fungal infections in sports?
11. What allergic, thermal, and chemical skin reactions could an athlete sustain in the typical sports environment?
12. Different parts of the United States have their own problems with insects that infect the skin of humans. Identify the insects in your area that can cause problems to athletes. How may they be avoided?

REFERENCES

1. Barsky, HE: Allergic contact dermatitis: sensitizers, Dermatol Allerg 5:37, 1982.
2. Bergfeld, WF: Dermatologic problems in athletes. In Betts, JM, and Eichelberger, M, editors: Symposium on pediatric and adolescent sports medicine, Clinics in sports medicine, vol 1, no 3, Philadelphia, 1982, WB Saunders Co.
3. Bergfeld, WF: The skin. In Strauss, RH, editor: Sports medicine, Philadelphia, 1984, WB Saunders Co.
4. Bordelon, RL: Management of disorders of the forefoot and toenails associated with running. In Drez, D, editor: Symposium on running, vol 4, no 4, Clinics in sports medicine, Philadelphia, 1985, WB Saunders Co.
5. Davidson, T, and Wolfe, DP: Sunscreens, skin and your patient, Phys Sportsmed 14(8):65, 1986.
6. Habif, TP: Clinical dermatology, St. Louis, 1985, The CV Mosby Co.
7. Hanke, CW, et al.: Skin cancer in professional and amateur female golfers, Phys Sportsmed 13(8):51, 1985.
8. Liteplo, MG: Sports-related skin problems. In Vinger, PF, and Hoerner, EF,

editors: Sports injuries: the unthwarted epidemic, Boston, 1982, John Wright, PSG, Inc.

9. Mills, J, et al.: Recurrent herpes labialis in skiers: clinical observations and effect of sunscreen, Am J Sports Med 15:76, 1987.

10. Rees, RB: Warts: a clinician's view, Cutis 28:177, 1981.

11. Springer, GL, and Shapiro, ED: Fresh water swimming as a risk factor for otitis externa, a case-control study, Arch Environ Health 40:203, July/Aug 1985.

12. Stauffer, LW: How I manage athlete's foot, Phys Sportsmed 14(7):103, 1986.

13. Stauffer, LW: Skin disorders in athletes: identification and management, Phys Sportsmed 14(7):103, 1986.

14. Strauss, RH: Nontraumatic medical problems. In Strauss, RH, editor: Sports medicine in physiology, Philadelphia, 1979, WB Saunders Co.

15. Wallis, C: Viruses, p. 74, Time, Nov 3, 1986.

ANNOTATED BIBLIOGRAPHY

Habif, TP: Clinical dermatology, St. Louis, 1985, The CV Mosby Co.
An excellent, in-depth text about skin disease, diagnosis, and therapy that contains an extensive list of color photos and illustrations.

Smith, W: Dermatology and the athletic trainer, parts 1 and 2, NATA Clinical Symposium, Granite Falls, Wash, 1982, Marvl Productions. (Cassette.)
Two video cassettes covering skin diseases commonly seen in athletes.

Stewart, WD, et al.: Dermatology, ed 4, St. Louis, 1978, The CV Mosby Co.
An in-depth text about skin disease. Diseases common to athletes are extensively covered.

Williams, JGP: Color atlas of injury in sports, Chicago, 1980, Year Book Medical Publishers, Inc.
Presents extensive color illustrations of all aspects of sports injuries, including the area of dermatology.

The Foot, Ankle, and Lower Leg: Acute Injuries

When you finish this chapter, you should be able to

Identify the major anatomical components of the foot, ankle, and lower leg that are commonly injured in sports

Assess the foot, ankle, and lower leg after an acute injury

Report on the etiological factors, symptoms and signs, and management procedures for the major acute injuries in the foot, ankle, and lower leg

T he foot, ankle, and lower leg have one of the highest incidences of sports injuries. Because of this and the complicated nature of the anatomical structures of these body parts, injuries to this area represent a major challenge to the coach and athletic trainer.

THE FOOT
Basic Anatomy
Bones

The foot is designed basically for strength, flexibility, and coordinated movement. It also transmits throughout the body the stresses that create the locomotor activities of walking and running. It is comprised of 26 bones: 14 phalangeal, five metatarsal, and seven tarsal (Figure 17-1). The tarsal bones, which form the instep or ankle portion of the foot, consist of the talus, the calcaneus (os calcis), the navicular, cuboid, and the first, second, and third cuneiform bones.

Toes The toes are somewhat similar to the fingers in appearance but are much shorter and serve a different function. The toes are designed to give a wider base both for balance and for propelling the body forward. The first toe, or hallux, has two phalanges, and the other toes consist of three phalanges.

The two sesamoid bones are located beneath the first metatarsophalangeal joint. Their functions are to assist in reducing pressure in weight bearing, to alleviate undue friction during movement, and to act as sliding pulleys for tendons.

Metatarsus The metatarsis consists of five bones that lie between and articulate with the tarsals and the phalanges, thus forming the semimovable tarsometatarsal and metatarsophalangeal joints. Although there is little movement permitted, the ligamentous arrangement gives elasticity to the foot in weight bearing.

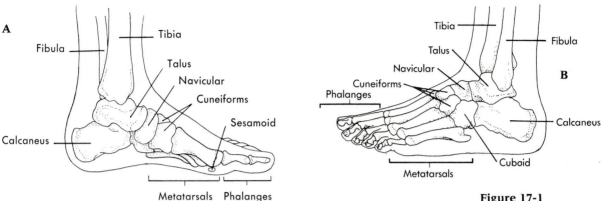

Figure 17-1

Bony structure of the foot. **A,** Medial aspect. **B,** Lateral aspect.

The metatarsophalangeal joints permit hinge action of the phalanges, which is similar to the action found between the hand and fingers. The first metatarsal is the largest and strongest and functions as the main body support during walking and running.

Tarsal bones   The tarsus, or ankle, consists of seven bones (tarsal bones), which are located between the bones of the lower leg and the metatarsus. These bones are important for support of the body and its locomotion. They consist of the calcaneus (os calis), talus (astragalus), cuboid (os cuboideum), navicular (scaphoid), and the first, second, and third cuneiform bones.

Calcaneus   The calcaneus is the largest tarsal bone. It supports the talus and shapes the heel; its main functions are to convey the body weight to the ground and act as a level attachment for the calf muscles.

The wider portion of the posterior extremity is called the tuberosity of the calcaneus. The medial and lateral tubercles are located on the inferior lateral and medial aspects, which provide the only parts that normally touch the ground.

Talus   The irregularly shaped talus is the most superior of the tarsal bones. It is situated on the calcaneus over a bony projection called the sustentaculum tali. The talus consists of a body, neck, and head. Uppermost is the trochlea, which articulates with the end of the tibia's medial and lateral malleoli. The trochlea is broader anteriorly than posteriorly, thus preventing forward slipping of the tibia during locomotion.

Because the talus fits principally into the space formed by the malleoli, little lateral movement is present unless the restrictive ligaments have been stretched. Because the uppermost articular surface of the talus is narrower posteriorly than anteriorly, dorsiflexion is limited. At a position of full dorsiflexion the anterior aspect of the medial collateral ligaments is taut,[13] whereas in plantar flexion internal rotation occurs because of the shape of the talus. The average range of motion is 10 degrees in dorsiflexion and 23 degrees in plantar flexion.

Navicular and cuboid bones   The navicular bone is positioned anterior to the talus on the medial aspect of the foot. Anteriorly the navicular bone articulates with the three cuneiform bones. The cuboid is positioned on the lateral aspect of the foot. It articulates posteriorly with the calcaneus and anteriorly with the fourth and fifth metatarsals.

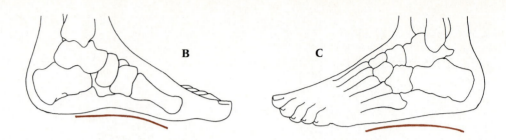

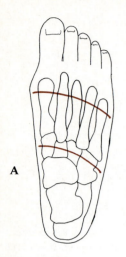

Figure 17-2

The arches of the foot.
A, Anterior metatarsal and transverse arches. **B,** Medial longitudinal arch. **C,** Lateral longitudinal arch.

Cuneiform bones   The three cuneiform bones are located between the navicular and the base of the three metatarsals on the medial aspect of the foot.

Arches of the Foot

The foot is structured, by means of ligamentous and bony arrangements, to form several arches. The arches assist the foot in supporting the body weight in an economical fashion, in absorbing the shock of weight bearing, and in providing a space on the plantar aspect of the foot for the blood vessels, nerves, and muscles. The arches' presence aids in giving the foot mobility and a small amount of prehensility. There are four arches: the medial longitudinal, the lateral longitudinal, the anterior metatarsal, and the transverse (Figure 17-2).

Medial longitudinal arch   The medial longitudinal arch originates along the medial border of the calcaneus and extends forward to the distal head of the first metatarsal. It is composed of the calcaneus, talus, navicular, first cuneiform, and first metatarsal. The main supporting ligament of the longitudinal arch is the plantar calcaneonavicular ligament, which acts as a sling by returning the arch to its normal position after it has been stretched. The tendon of the posterior tibialis muscle helps to reinforce the plantar calcaneonavicular ligament.

Lateral longitudinal arch   The outer longitudinal arch is on the lateral aspects of the foot and follows the same pattern as that of the inner longitudinal arch. It is formed by the calcaneus, cuboid, and fifth metatarsal bones. It is much lower and less flexible than the inner longitudinal arch.

Anterior metatarsal arch   The anterior metatarsal arch is shaped by the distal heads of the metatarsals. The arch has a semiovoid appearance, stretching from the first to the fifth metatarsal.

Transverse arch   The transverse arch extends across the transverse tarsal bones, primarily the cuboid and the internal cuneiform, and forms a half dome. It gives protection to soft tissue and increases the foot's mobility.

Plantar Aponeurosis

The plantar aponeurosis is a thick white band of fibrous tissue originating from the medial tuberosity of the calcaneus and ending at the proximal heads of the metatarsals. Along with ligaments, the plantar aponeurosis supports the foot against downward forces (Figure 17-3).

Joints

Joints of the foot are categorized into five regions: interphalangeal, metatarsophalangeal, intermetatarsal, tarsometatarsal, and intertarsal.

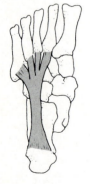

Figure 17-3

Plantar aponeurosis.

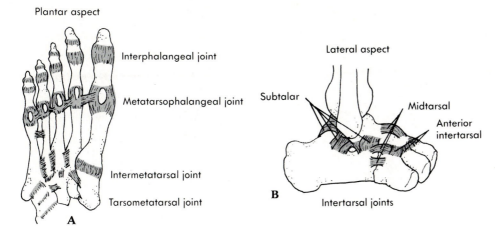

Figure 17-4

A, Ligaments of the interphalangeal, metatarsophalangeal, intermetatarsal, and tarsometatarsal joints. **B,** Ligaments of the intertarsal joints.

Interphalangeal joints   The interphalangeal joints are located at the distal extremities of the proximal and middle phalanges at the bases of the adjacent middle and terminal phalanges. These joints are designed only for flexion and extension. All interphalangeal joints have reinforcing collateral ligaments on their medial and lateral sides. Also located between the collateral ligaments on the plantar and dorsal surface are interphalangeal ligaments (Figure 17-4).

Metatarsophalangeal joints   The metatarsophalangeal joints are the condyloid type, which is permitted all forms of angular movement, with the exception of axial rotation; allowable movements include flexion, extension, adduction, and abduction. Each of these joints has collateral ligaments, as well as plantar and dorsal metatarsophalangeal ligaments.

Intermetatarsal joints   The intermetatarsal joints are sliding joints. They include two sets of articulations. One set consists of an articulation on each side of the base of the metatarsal bone, and the second articulations are on each side of the heads of the metatarsal bone. Each of these articulations permits only slight gliding movements. Shafts of the metatarsals are connected by interosseous ligaments. The bases are connected by plantar and dorsal ligaments, whereas the heads are attached by transverse metatarsal ligaments.

Tarsometatarsal joints   The tarsometatarsal joints are formed by the junction of the bases of the metatarsal bones with the tarsal bones. Their slight saddle-shape allows some gliding and thus a restricted amount of flexion, extension, adduction, and abduction. Metatarsal bones are attached to the tarsal bones by the dorsal and plantar tarsometatarsal ligaments. Interosseous ligaments connect the first cuneiform to the second metatarsal, the third cuneiform to the second metatarsal, and the fourth cuneiform to the third metatarsal.

Intertarsal joints   The intertarsal joints include the subtalar, midtarsal (transverse tarsal), and the anterior intertarsal (cuneonavicular) joints. In general, they are sliding joints. The subtalar joint is the articulation between the talus and the calcaneus. The midtarsal joint's articulation on the medial aspect is the talonavicular joint and on the lateral aspect is the calcaneocuboid joint. The anterior intertarsal or cuneonavicular joint is the articulation between the navicular and the cuneiform bones.

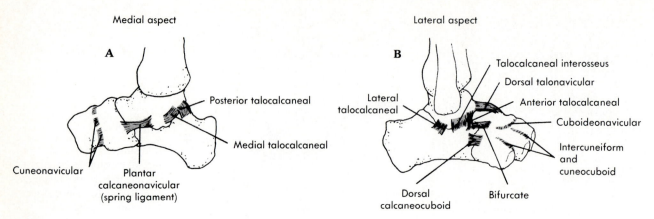

Figure 17-5

Ligaments of the subtalar
joint. **A,** Medial aspect.
B, Lateral aspect.

Movements of the intertarsal articulations are gliding, flexion, extension, abduction, adduction, inversion, and eversion. Gliding occurs primarily at the anterior intertarsal joint and provides shock absorption for the weight of the body. Slight flexion and extension occur at the midtarsal region. There are also slight abduction and adduction of the forefoot occurring at the talonavicular joint. Inversion and eversion occur at the subtalar and midtarsal joints. Inversion refers to the sole of the foot turning medially, and eversion refers to its turning laterally. Foot *pronation* refers to the combined movements of abduction and eversion. In contrast, foot *supination* is the combined movements of adduction and inversion.

Ligaments

The subtalar ligaments are the talocalcaneal interosseus and the anterior, posterior, lateral, and medial talocalcaneal (Figure 17-5). A major ligament is the plantar calcaneonavicular. It passes from the sustentaculum tali of the calcaneus to the navicular bone and supports the medial longitudinal arch. Because of its relatively large number of elastic fibers and its primary purpose of providing shock absorption, it is commonly called the spring ligament.

The primary ligaments of the midtarsal joint are the dorsal talonavicular, bifurcate, and dorsal calcaneocuboid. The midtarsal joint is given added strength in its plantar aspect by the long and plantar ligaments.

Ligaments of the anterior tarsal joints are divided into those of the cuneonavicular, cuboideonavicular, intercuneiform, and cuneocuboid joints. Each of these joints has both dorsal and plantar ligaments. The intercuneiform ligaments have three transverse bands, with one band connecting the first with the second and the second with the third cuneiform. A ligament also connects the third cuneiform with the cuboid bone.

Muscles and Movement

The movements of the foot are accomplished by numerous muscles (Figures 17-6 and 17-7; Table 17-1).

Dorsiflexion and plantar flexion   Dorsiflexion and plantar flexion of the foot take place at the ankle joint. The gastrocnemius, soleus, plantaris, peroneus longus, peroneus brevis, and tibialis posterior muscles (see Figure 17-38, *C* and *D*) are the plantar flexors. Dorsiflexion is accomplished by the tibialis anterior,

TABLE 17-1 Actions of the Intrinsic Foot Muscles

Location	Muscle	Action
Dorsal surface	Extensor digitorum brevis	Extension of first through fourth toes
First layer, plantar aspect	Abductor hallucis	Abduction and flexion of big toe
	Abductor digiti minimi pedis	Abduction and flexion of little toe
	Flexor digitorum brevis	Flexion of second through fifth toes
Second layer, plantar aspect	Quadratus plantae	Flexion of second through fifth toes
	Flexor digiti minimi brevis pedis	Flexion and abduction of little toe
	Lumbricalis pedis	Flexion of proximal phalanges and extension of distal phalanges of second through fifth toes; abduction of second toe; adduction of third, fourth, and fifth toes
Third layer, plantar aspect	Adductor hallucis	Adduction and flexion of big toe
	Flexor hallucis brevis	Flexion of big toe
Fourth layer, plantar aspect	Interosseus plantaris	Adduction of third, fourth, and fifth toes; flexion of these toes when acting with dorsal interossei
	Interosseus dorsalis pedis	When acting alone, first interosseus pulls second toe toward the big toe and pulls second, third, and fourth toes away from the big toe
		When acting with plantar interossei, flexion of second, third, and fourth toes

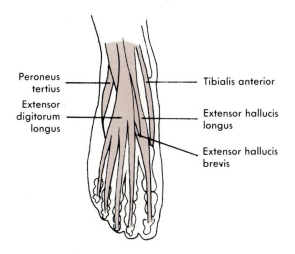

Figure 17-6

Muscles and tendons of the anterior aspect of the ankle and foot.

Peroneus tertius

Extensor digitorum longus

Tibialis anterior

Extensor hallucis longus

Extensor hallucis brevis

Figure 17-7

The movements of the foot are accomplished by a complex of many muscles.

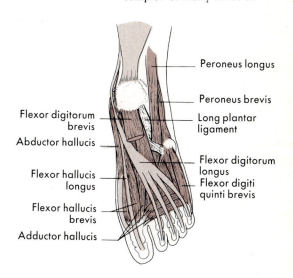

Flexor digitorum brevis

Abductor hallucis

Flexor hallucis longus

Flexor hallucis brevis

Adductor hallucis

Peroneus longus

Peroneus brevis

Long plantar ligament

Flexor digitorum longus

Flexor digiti quinti brevis

extensor digitorum longus, extensor hallucis longus and brevis, and peroneus tertius muscles (see Figure 17-6).

Inversion, adduction, and supination   The medial movements of the foot are produced by the same muscles as inversion, adduction (medial movement of the forefoot), and supination (a combination of inversion and adduction). Muscles that produce these movements pass behind and in front of the medial malleolus. Muscles passing behind are the tibialis posterior, flexor digitorum longus, and flexor hallucis longus (see Figure 17-38, *D*). Muscles passing in front of the medial malleolus are the tibialis anterior and the extensor hallucis longus (see Figure 17-38, *A*).

Eversion, abduction, and pronation   The lateral movements of the foot are caused by the same muscles that produce eversion, abduction (lateral movement of the forefoot), and pronation (a combination of eversion and abduction). Muscles passing behind the lateral malleolus are the peroneus longus and the peroneus brevis. Muscles passing in front of the lateral malleolus are the peroneus tertius and extensor digitorum longus (see Figure 17-38, *B*).

Movement of the phalanges   The movements of the phalanges are flexion, extension, abduction, and adduction. Flexion of the second, third, fourth, and fifth distal digits is executed by the flexor digitorum longus and the quadratus plantae. Flexion of the middle phalanges is performed by the flexor digitorum brevis, and flexion of the proximal phalanges is by the lumbricales and the interossei. The great toe is flexed by the flexor hallucis longus. The extension of all the middle phalanges is done by the abductor hallucis and abductor digiti quinti, the lumbricales, and the interossei. Extension of all distal phalanges is effected by the extensor digitorus longus, the extensor hallucis longus, and the extensor digitorum brevis. The adduction of the foot is performed by the interossei plantares and the adductor hallucis; abduction is by the interossei dorsales, the abductor hallucis, and the abductor digiti quinti.

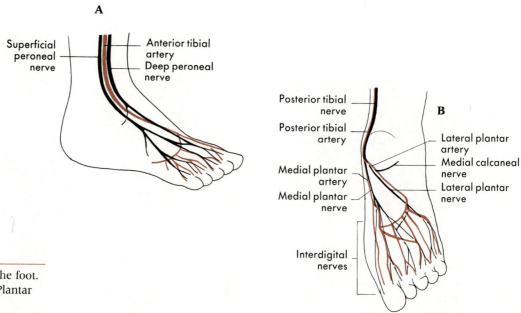

Figure 17-8

The major nerves of the foot. **A,** Dorsal aspect. **B,** Plantar aspect.

Blood and Nerve Supply

The major portion of the blood is supplied to the foot by the anterior and posterior tibial arteries. The dorsal venous arch and digital veins and the dorsal digital vein stem from the short and long saphenous veins.

The tibial nerve, largest division of the sciatic nerve, supplies the muscles of the back of the leg and the plantar aspect of the foot. The common peroneal nerve is a smaller division of the sciatic nerve and with its branches supplies the front of the leg and the foot (Figure 17-8).

FOOT ASSESSMENT

When assessing foot injuries, there must be a clear understanding that the foot is part of a "linkage" system that includes both the ankle and the lower leg. Acute injuries must be differentiated from those that had a relatively slow onset.

History

When making a decision about how to manage a foot injury, a quick assessment must be performed to determine the type of injury and its history. The following questions should be asked:

- How did the injury occur? Did it occur suddenly or come on slowly? Was the mechanism a sudden strain, twist, or blow to the foot?
- What type of pain? Is there muscle weakness? Are there noises such as crepitation during movement? Is there any alteration in sensation?
- Can you point to the exact site of pain?
- When is the pain or other symptoms more or less severe?
- On what type of surface have you been training?
- What type of footwear was being used during training? Is it appropriate for the type of training? Is discomfort increased when footwear is worn?
- Is this the first time this condition has occurred, or has it happened before? When, how often, under what circumstances?

General Observation

The athlete should be observed to determine the following:

- Whether he or she is favoring the foot, walking with a limp, or unable to bear weight
- Whether the injured part is deformed, swollen, or discolored
- Whether the foot changes color when weight bearing and non-weight bearing (changing rapidly from a darker to lighter pink when not weight bearing)
- Whether foot is well aligned and whether it maintains its shape on weight bearing

Physical Examination

The physical examination includes palpation, movement and neurological assessment, pulse measurement, and functional evaluation.

Palpation

Besides determining pain sites, swelling, deformities, palpation is used to determine and evaluate circulation.

Bony palpation If the site of the injury is uncertain, palpate the following bony sites for point tenderness:

Medial Aspect	Lateral Aspect
Medial calcaneus	Lateral calcaneus
Medial malleolus	Lateral malleolus
Sustentaculum tali	Sinus tarsi
Talar head	Peroneal tubercle
Navicular tubercle	Cuboid bone
First cuneiform	Styloid process (proximal head of the fifth metatarsal
First metatarsal	
First metatarsophalangeal joint	Fifth metatarsal
First phalanx	Fifth metatarsophalangeal joint
	Fifth phalanx

Dorsal Aspect	Plantar Aspect
Fourth, third, second metatarsals	Metatarsal heads
Fourth, third, second metatarsophalangeal joints	Medial calcaneal tubercle
Fourth, third, second phalanges	
Third and fourth cuneiform bones	

Soft-tissue palpation

Medial and Plantar Aspect	Lateral and Dorsal Aspect
Tibialis posterior tendon	Anterior talofibular ligament
Deltoid ligament	Calcaneofibular ligament
Calcaneonavicular ligament (spring ligament)	Posterior talofibular ligament
	Peroneal tendon
Medial longitudinal arch	Extensor tendons of toes
Plantar fascia	Tibialis anterior tendon
Bursal head of the first metatarsal bone	
Transverse arch	

Movement and Neurological Assessment

Both the extrinsic and the intrinsic foot muscles should be assessed for pain and range of motion during active, passive, and resistive isometric movement. Reflexes and cutaneous distribution should also be tested. Skin sensation should be noted for any alteration.

Tendon reflexes such as in the Achilles tendon (S_1 nerve root) should elicit a response when gently tapped. Sensation is tested by running the hands over the anterior, lateral, medial, and posterior surfaces of the foot and toes.[10]

Pulse

To ensure that there is proper blood circulation to the foot, the pulse is measured at the posterior tibial and dorsal pedis arteries (Figure 17-9).

Functional Evaluation

Passive, active, and resistive movement is performed in the numerous joints of the foot and adjacent ankle. Inspection is first performed while the athlete is on a table and then during weight bearing. Movement is performed in the following joints:

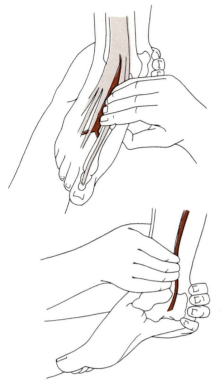

Figure 17-9

An ankle injury may impede blood flow, making routine measurement of the pulse extremely important.

1. Ankle
2. Talocalcaneal
3. Mid-dorsal with heel and ankle joints stabilized
4. Metatarsophalangeal
5. Interphalangeal

The foot is then inspected while the athlete stands and walks. The posture of the foot and whether it maintains the same shape in weight bearing as in non-weight bearing is noted. (See Chapter 18 for further discussion of foot posture.)

Foot Conditions

Most people will at some time develop foot problems. This development is attributed to the use of improper footwear, poor foot hygiene, or anatomical structural deviations that result from faulty postural alignments or abnormal stresses.

Many sports place exceptional demands on the feet—far beyond the normal daily requirements. The coach and the athletic trainer should be well aware of potential foot problems and should be capable of identifying, ameliorating, or preventing them whenever possible. Chapter 17 is mainly concerned with those acute conditions that affect the musculoskeletal system of the foot. Skin problems of the foot and proper shoe fit were discussed in Chapter 16.

Most people will at some time in their lives develop foot problems.

Acute Conditions of the Foot

Contusions   Two common contusions of the foot are the heel bruise and the instep bruise. Each can cause the athlete a great deal of discomfort and disability.

The athlete who is prone to heel bruises should routinely wear a padded heel cup.

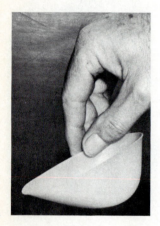

A

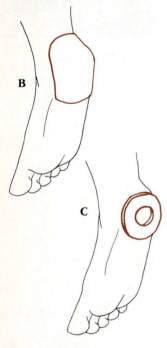

B

C

Figure 17-10

A and **B,** Heel protection achieved through the use of heel cup. **C,** Protective heel doughnut.

Heel bruise   Of the many contusions and bruises that an athlete may receive, there is none more disabling than the heel bruise. Sport activities that demand a sudden stop-and-go response or sudden change from a horizontal to a vertical movement (e.g., basketball, jumping, or the landing action in long jumping) are particularly likely to cause heel bruises. The heel has a thick, cornified skin layer and a heavy fat pad covering, but even this thick padding cannot protect against a sudden abnormal force directed to this area.

The major purpose of the tissue heel pad is to sustain hydraulic pressure through fat columns. Tissue compression is monitored by pressure nerve endings from the skin and plantar aponeurosis. Often the irritation is on the lateral aspect of the heel because of the heel strike in walking or running.[11]

SYMPTOMS AND SIGNS   When injury occurs, the athlete complains of severe pain in the heel and is unable to withstand the stress of weight bearing.

A bruise of the heel usually develops into chronic inflammation of the periosteum. Follow-up management of this condition should be started 2 to 3 days after insult, involving a variety of superficial and deep-heat therapies. If the athlete recognizes the problem in its acute stage, then he or she should adhere to the following procedures:

1. If possible, the athlete should not step on the heel for a period of at least 24 hours.
2. On the third and subsequent days the athlete can receive warm whirlpool and ultrasound or cold therapy.
3. If pain when walking has subsided by the third day, the athlete may resume moderate activity—with the protection of a heel cup, protective doughnut, or protective taping (Figure 17-10).

NOTE: Because of the nature of the site of this condition, it may recur throughout an entire season.

An athlete who is prone to or who needs protection from a heel bruise should routinely wear a heel cup with a foam rubber pad as a preventive aid. By surrounding the heel with a firm heelcup, traumatic forces are diffused.

The bruised instep   The bruised instep, like the bruised heel, can cause disability. It commonly occurs from the athlete's being stepped on or from being hit with a fast-moving hard projectile such as a baseball or hockey puck. Immediate application of cold compresses must be performed not only to control inflammation but, most importantly, to avoid swelling. Irritation of the synovial sheaths covering the extensor tendon can make wearing a shoe difficult. If the force is of great intensity, there is a good chance of fracture, requiring an x-ray. Once inflammation is reduced and the athlete returns to competition, a ⅛-inch (0.3 cm) pad protection should be worn directly on the skin over the bruise, as well as a rigid instep guard that is worn external to the shoe.

Foot strain   Insufficient conditioning of musculature, structural imbalance, or incorrect mechanics can cause the foot to become prone to strain. Common strains occur to the metatarsal arch, the longitudinal arch, and the plantar fascia.

Metatarsal arch strain   The athlete who has a fallen metatarsal arch or who has a pes cavus (high arch) is susceptible to strain. In both cases, malalignment of the forefoot subjects the flexor tendons to increased tension. Other conditions that produce the hypermobile and pronated foot may predispose the athlete to a metatarsal arch strain.

Longitudinal arch strain   Longitudinal arch strain is usually an early-season injury caused by subjecting the musculature of the foot to unaccustomed, severe exercise and forceful contact with hard playing surfaces. In this condition there is a flattening or depression of the longitudinal arch while the foot is in the mid-support phase, resulting in a strain to the arch. Such a strain may appear quite suddenly, or it may develop rather slowly throughout a considerable length of time.

SYMPTOMS AND SIGNS   As a rule, pain is experienced only when running is attempted and usually appears just below the medial malleolus and the posterior tibial tendon, accompanied by swelling and tenderness along the medial aspects of the foot. Prolonged strain will also involve the calcaneonavicular ligament and move progressively to the talonavicular joint and then to the articulation of the first cuneiform with the navicular. The flexor muscle of the great toe (flexor hallucis longus) often develops tenderness as a result of overuse in compensating for the stress on the arch ligaments.

MANAGEMENT   The management of a longitudinal arch strain involves immediate care of ICE-R followed by appropriate therapy, reduction of weight bearing, and exercise rehabilitation, following the procedures beginning on p. 504. Exercise and weight bearing must be performed pain free. Arch taping technique no. 1 or 2 might be used to allow earlier pain-free weight bearing (see Figures 12-3, 12-4, and 12-6).

Plantar fascia strain   Running the length of the sole of the foot is a broad band of dense connective tissue called the plantar aponeurosis. It is attached to the undersurface of the calcaneus at the back and fans out toward the front, with fibers and their various small branches attaching to the metatarsophalangeal articulations and merging into the capsular ligaments. Other fibers, arising from well within the aponeurosis, pass between the intrinsic muscles of the foot and the long flexor tendons of the sole and attach themselves to the deep fascia below the bones. The function of the plantar aponeurosis is to assist in maintaining the stability of the foot and in securing or bracing the longitudinal arch.

ETIOLOGICAL FACTORS   Strains to the fascia commonly occur during the early part of the season in sports that require running. The incidence is fairly high among tennis and basketball players and runners. The fascia is placed under strain either by extension of the toes or by depression of the longitudinal arch as the result of weight bearing. When the weight is principally on the heel, as in ordinary standing, the tension exerted on the fascia is negligible. However, when the weight is shifted to the ball of the foot (on the heads of the metatarsals), fascial tension is so increased that it equals approximately twice the body weight. In running, since the push-off phase involves both a forceful extension of the toes and a powerful thrust by the ball of the foot against a relatively unyielding surface, the degree of fascial tension is greatly increased.

Athletes who have a mild pes cavus are particularly prone to fascial strain. Modern street shoes, by nature of their design, take on the characteristics of splints and tend to restrict foot action to such an extent that the arch may become somewhat rigid because of shortening of the ligaments and other mild pathologies. The athlete, when changing from such footgear into a flexible gymnastic slipper or soft track shoe, often experiences trauma when subjecting the foot to stresses.

Trauma may also result from running improperly, either as the result of poor techniques or because of lordosis, a condition in which the increased forward tilt of the pelvis produces an unfavorable angle of foot-strike when there is considerable force exerted on the ball of the foot.

SYMPTOMS AND SIGNS   The athlete complains of having a sudden pain in the arch region that is relieved by becoming nonweight bearing. There are great difficulty in walking and an inability to run. During inspection there is **point tenderness** in the plantar aponeurosis, especially in the region of the epicondyle of the calcaneus. Swelling and later ecchymosis may be associated with this problem.

MANAGEMENT   Management is symptomatic. A heel doughnut may relieve some of the irritation, along with a heel lift, and a stiff shank will distribute the body weight more effectively. Also, performing a gradual stretch of the plantar muscle and the gastrocnemius-soleus complex will help relieve tension in that region. A gradual program of arch exercises should be performed. Plantar fasciitis is discussed in Chapter 18.

Foot sprain   Two sites where foot sprain may occur are the midfoot or forefoot and the phalanges.

Midfoot or forefoot sprain   Although not common, sprains of the midfoot or forefoot do occur. The most frequent mechanism is excessive dorsiflexion or plantar flexion of the toes or forefoot. Supportive ligaments are injured along with tendons. A common foot sprain among gymnasts and dancers occurs to the midtarsal ligament, caused by forced dorsiflexion and plantar flexion of the midfoot.

MANAGEMENT   Management usually consists of ICE-R and limitation in weight bearing. Tape support (see Chapter 12) helps relieve pain during weight bearing; also, placing the foot into a firm solid shoe with a rocker-bottom sole often prevents pain relief.

The sprained toe   Sprains of the phalangeal joint of the foot are caused most often by kicking some nonyielding object. Sprains result from a considerable force applied in such a manner as to extend the joint beyond its normal range of motion ("jamming" it) or to impart a twisting motion to the toe, thereby twisting and tearing the supporting tissues. Symptoms of an acute injury appear.

"Turf-toe" sprain of the first metatarsophalangeal joint   "Turf-toe" is the sprain of the metatarsophalangeal joint of the great toe. This injury results from the combination of the new artificial playing surfaces and flexible types of sport footwear.[3]

Fractures and dislocations   Because of the foot's susceptibility to trauma in sports, fractures or dislocations can occur. Any moderate to severe contusion or twisting force must be suspected as a fracture. X-ray examination should be routine in these situations.

Fractures and dislocations of the foot phalanges   Fractures of the phalanges (Figure 17-11) are usually the bone-crushing type such as may be incurred in kicking an object or stubbing a toe. Generally they are accompanied by swelling and discoloration. If the fracture is of the proximal phalanx of the great toe or of the distal phalanx and also involves the interphalangeal joint, it should be referred to an orthopedist.[2] If the break is in the bone shaft, adhesive tape is applied (see Chapter 12). However, if more than one toe is involved, a cast may be applied for a few days. As a rule 3 or 4 weeks of inactivity permits healing, although

point tenderness
Pain is produced when an injury site is palpated.

Fractures and dislocations of the foot phalanges can be caused by kicking an object or by stubbing a toe.

tenderness may persist for some time. A shoe with a wide toe box should be worn; in cases of great toe fracture, a stiff sole should be worn.

Dislocation of the phalanges is less common than fractures. If one occurs, it is a dorsal dislocation of the middle phalanx' proximal joint. The mechanism of injury is the same as for fractures. Reduction is usually performed easily without anesthesia by the physician.

Fractures of the metatarsals   Fractures of the metatarsals can be caused by direct force, such as being stepped on by another player, or by abnormal stress. They are characterized by swelling and pain. The most common acute fracture is to the base of the fifth metatarsal (Jones fracture) (Figure 17-12). It is normally caused by sharp inversion and plantar flexion of the foot. It has all the appearances of a severe sprain. Treatment is usually symptomatic, with ICE-R used to control swelling. Once swelling has subsided, a short leg walking cast is applied for 3 to 6 weeks. Ambulation is usually possible by the second week. A shoe with a large toe box should be worn. The injured toe should be taped to an adjacent toe in the same manner as for the fracture.

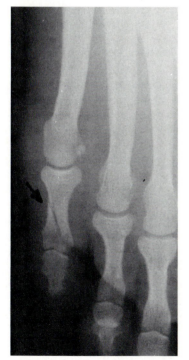

Figure 17-11

Fracture of the fifth phalanx.

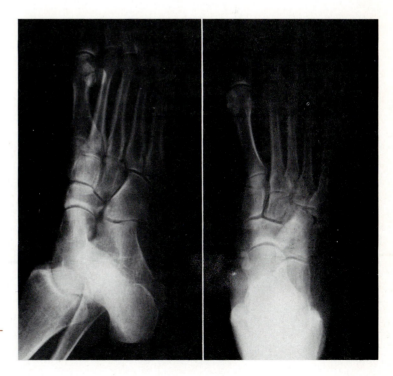

Figure 17-12

Fracture of the base of the fifth metatarsal.

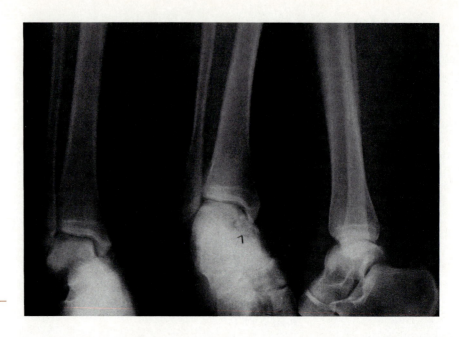

Figure 17-13

Fracture of the talar dome.

Fractures or dislocations of the talus Fracture or dislocation of the talus usually results from a severe ankle twist or being hit behind the leg while the foot is firmly planted on the ground (Figure 17-13). There are extreme pain and point tenderness at the distal end of the tibia. For accurate diagnosis an x-ray is essential. If the fracture is severe, there could be severance of the blood supply to the area—a condition that results in bone necrosis and may seriously jeopardize future sports participation by the athlete. The following procedures should be used:

1. The foot and ankle should be immobilized, and the athlete should be transported to a physician.
2. After the fracture has been reduced, the physician will usually cast the foot in a plaster boot for approximately 6 weeks and then allow only limited weight bearing on the injured leg for at least another 8 weeks.

Fracture of the os calis The os calis fracture is the most common fracture of the tarsus and is usually caused by a jump or fall from a height. There is usually extreme swelling and pain. There may be a serious threat that this condition will predispose the athlete to arthritis because of injury to the articulating surface. Reduction may be delayed for as much as 24 to 48 hours or until swelling has been reduced. In the interval the following steps should be initiated:

1. Cold and a pressure bandage should be applied intermittently for 24 to 48 hours.
2. The foot should be elevated immediately after the injury and maintained in this position for at least 24 hours or until definite medical treatment has been instituted.

Exercise Rehabilitation of the Foot

In most painful conditions of the foot, weight bearing is prohibited until pain has subsided significantly. During this period and until the athlete is ready to return

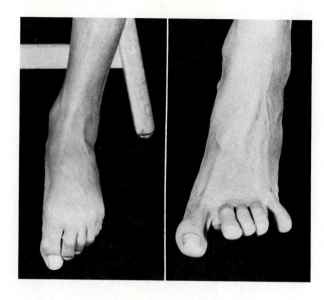

Figure 17-14

Gripping and spreading of the toes can be an excellent reconditioning exercise for the injured foot.

to full activity, a graduated program of exercise should be instituted. Exercises are divided into two stages. Each exercise should be performed three times a day with three to 10 repetitions of each exercise and should progress to two or three sets.

Stage 1

In Stage 1 primary exercises are used in the non-weight bearing or early phase of the condition. They include "writing the alphabet," picking up objects, ankle circumduction, and gripping and spreading.

1. *Writing the alphabet*—with the toes pointed, the athlete proceeds to write the complete alphabet in the air three times.
2. *Picking up objects*—the athlete picks up 10 small objects such as marbles with the toes and places them in a container.
3. *Ankle circumduction*—the ankle is circumducted in as extreme a range of motion as possible (10 circles in one direction and 10 circles in the other).
4. *Gripping and spreading*—of particular value to toes, gripping and spreading is conducted up to 10 repetitions (Figure 17-14).

Stage 2

Stage 2 exercises are added to Stage 1 when the athlete is just beginning to bear weight. They include the "towel gather" and "scoop" exercises.

1. *Towel gathering*—a towel is extended in front of the feet. The heels are firmly planted on the floor with the forefoot on the end of the towel. The athlete than attempts to pull the towel with the feet without lifting the heels from the floor. As execution becomes easier, a weight can be placed at the other end of the towel for added resistance. Each exercise should be performed 10 times (Figure 17-15). This exercise can also be used for exercising the foot in abduction and adduction.

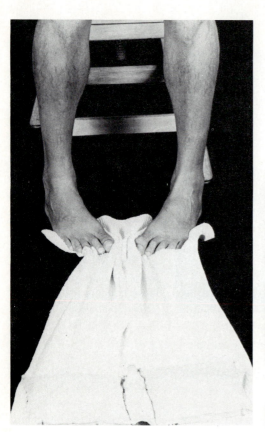

Figure 17-15

The towel gather exercise.

Figure 17-16

The towel scoop exercise.

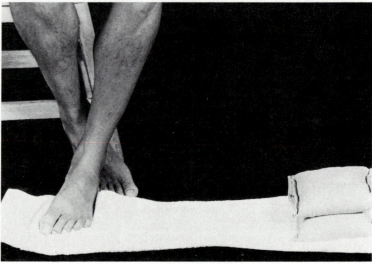

2. *Towel scoop*—a towel is folded in half and placed sideways on the floor. The athlete places the heel firmly on the floor, the forefoot on the end of the towel. To ensure the greatest stability of the exercising foot, it is backed up with the other foot. Without lifting the heel from the floor, the athlete scoops the towel forward with the forefoot. As with the towel gather exercise, a weight resistance can be added to the end of the towel. The exercise should be repeated up to 10 times (Figure 17-16).

THE ANKLE

Ankle injuries, especially to the ligamentous tissue, are the most frequent injuries in sports.[1] For the coach and the athletic trainer, understanding the complex nature of ankle injuries should be a major goal.

Basic Anatomy
Bones

The ankle joint, or talocrural articulation, is a hinge joint (ginglymus) that is formed by (1) the articular facet on the distal extremity of the tibia, which articulates with the superior articular surface (trochlea) of the talus, (2) the medial malleolus, which articulates with the medial surface of the trochlea of the talus, and (3) the lateral malleolus, which articulates with the lateral surface of the trochlea (Figure 17-17).

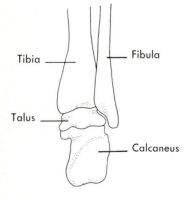

Tibia — Fibula

Talus —

— Calcaneus

Figure 17-17

The ankle is a hinge type joint formed by the tibia, fibula, and talus.

The talofibular articulation is formed by the lower end of the fibula with the talus. At its lower end the fibula develops a long projection, which extends along the lateral aspect of the talus and is called the *external malleolus*. It is located posterior to, and ½ inch lower than, the internal malleolus; like that of the internal malleolus, its border is roughened for ligamentous attachment.

The talus, the second largest tarsal and the main weight-bearing bone of the articulation, rests on the calcaneus and receives the articulating surfaces of the external and internal malleoli. Its almost square shape allows the ankle only two movements: dorsiflexion and plantar flexion. Because the talus is wider anteriorly than posteriorly, the most stable position of the ankle is with the foot in dorsiflexion. In this position the wider anterior aspect of the talus comes in contact with the narrower portion lying between the malleoli, gripping it tightly. By contrast, as the ankle moves into plantar flexion, the wider portion of the tibia is brought in contact with the narrower posterior aspect of the talus, a much less stable position than dorsiflexion.

> Because the talus is wider anteriorly than posteriorly, the most stable position of the ankle is with the foot in dorsiflexion.

Capsular and Ligamentous Support

The ligamentous support of the ankle (Figure 17-18) additionally fortifies its great bony strength. This support consists of the articular capsule, three lateral ligaments, and the medial or deltoid ligament. The three lateral ligaments include the anterior talofibular, the posterior talofibular, and the calcaneofibular (Table 17-2). A thin articular capsule encases the ankle joint and attaches to the borders of the bone involved. It is somewhat different from most other capsules in that it is

Figure 17-18

Major ligaments of the ankle. **A,** Lateral aspect. **B,** Medial aspect.

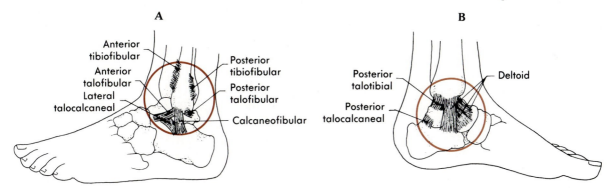

TABLE 17-2 Function of Key Ankle Ligaments

Ligament	Primary Function
Anterior talofibular	Restrains anterior displacement of talus
Calcaneofibular	Restrains inversion of calcaneus
Posterior talofibular	Restrains posterior displacement of talus
Deltoid	Prevents abduction and eversion of ankle and subtalar joint
	Prevents eversion, pronation, and anterior displacement of talus

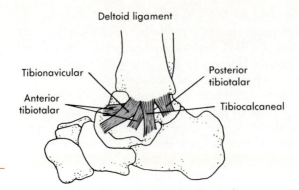

Figure 17-19

Medial ankle ligaments.

thick on the medial aspects of the joint but becomes a thin gauzelike membrane at the back.

The deltoid ligament is triangular shaped, attaching superiorly to the borders of the medial malleolus. It attaches inferiorly to the medial surface of the talus, to the sustentaculum tali of the calcaneus, and to the posterior margin of the navicular bone. The deltoid ligament is the primary resistance to foot eversion. It, along with the plantar calcaneonavicular (spring) ligament, also helps maintain the inner longitudinal arch. Although it should be considered as one ligament, the deltoid ligament includes superficial and deep fibers (Figure 17-19). Anteriorly are the anterior tibiotalar part and the tibionavicular part. Medially is the tibiocalcaneal part, and posteriorly is the posterior tibiotalar part.

Muscles and Movement

By far the weakest aspect of the ankle is its muscular arrangement, since the long muscle tendons that cross on all sides of the ankle afford maximum muscle leverage but minimum stabilization. The three lateral ligaments are the anterior talofibular, the calcaneofibular, and the posterior talofibular. The anterior talofibular ligament is attached superiorly to the anterior border of the lateral malleolus and inferiorly to the anterior margin of the lateral malleolar facet in the trochlea of the talus. The calcaneofibular ligament is the middle of the three lateral ligaments and attaches superiorly to the anterior border of the lateral malleolus and inferiorly to the middle of the lateral surface of the calcaneus. The most posterior of the lateral ligaments is the posterior talofibular ligament. From its attachment on the lateral malleolus, it moves horizontally to its medial attachment on the posterior aspect of the talus.

The movements of the ankle joint are dorsiflexion (flexion) and plantar flexion (extension). It can be generalized that muscles passing posterior to the lateral malleolus will produce ankle plantar flexion along with toe extension. It can also be generalized that anterior muscles serve to dorsiflex the foot and to produce toe flexion. The anterior muscles include the extensor hallucis longus, the extensor digitorum longus, the peroneus tertius, and the tibialis anterior. The posterior muscle group falls into three layers. At the superficial layer is the gastrocnemius, the middle layer includes the soleus and the plantaris, and the deep layer contains the tibialis posterior, the flexor digitorum longus, and the flexor hallucis longus.

Evaluating the Injured and Painful Ankle

The injured or painful ankle should be carefully evaluated to determine the possibility of fracture and whether medical referral is necessary.

History

The athlete's history may vary, depending on whether the problem is the result of sudden trauma or is of long standing.

The athlete with an acute sudden trauma to the ankle should be questioned about these factors:

1. What trauma or mechanism occurred?
2. What was heard when the injury occurred—a crack, snap, or pop?
3. What were the duration and the intensity of pain?
4. How disabling was the occurrence? Could the athlete walk right away, or was he or she unable to bear weight for a period of time?
5. Has a similar injury occurred before?
6. Was there immediate swelling, or did the swelling occur later (or at all)? Where did the swelling occur?

The athlete with a long-standing painful condition might be asked:

1. How much does it hurt?
2. Where does it hurt?
3. Under what circumstances does pain occur—when bearing weight, after activity, or when arising after a night's sleep?
4. What past ankle injuries have occurred?
5. What first aid and therapy, if any, were given for this occurrence?

General Inspection

The first inspection should be observation of the athlete's walk. Is the injured individual walking in the usual manner, on the toes, or is there an inability to bear any weight? When the athlete is seated, both ankles are compared for:

1. Position of the foot—a sprained ankle will usually be in a more inverted position
2. Range of ankle motion—normal range is approximately 20 degrees of dorsiflexion and 45 to 50 degrees of plantar flexion

Bony and Soft-Tissue Palpation

Palpation in the ankle region should start with key bony sites and ligaments and progress to the musculature, especially the major tendons in the area. The purpose of palpation in this region is to detect obvious structural defects, swellings, and localized tenderness (Figure 17-20). The following anatomical areas should be palpated:

1. Medial and lateral malleolus
2. Lower interosseus membrane
3. Tarsal navicular
4. Proximal head of the fifth metatarsal
5. Subtalar region
6. Deltoid ligament
7. Anterior talofibular ligament
8. Calcaneofibular ligament

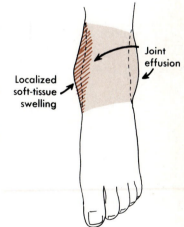

Figure 17-20

Local and diffused ankle swelling.

9. Posterior talofibular ligament
10. Anterior tibiofibular ligament
11. Achilles tendon
12. Peroneal tendons
13. Posterior tibialis tendon
14. Anterior tibialis tendon
15. Region of extensor tendons
16. Other areas when indicated

If the injury might have impeded blood flow to the ankle area, the pulse should be measured at the dorsal pedal artery and at the posterior tibial artery.

Tests for Joint Stability

A positive drawer sign of ankle stability is when the foot slides forward, sometimes making a clunking sound as it reaches its end point.

When there may be ankle joint instability as a result of repeated sprains, tests should be given. The most common sprain is the inversion type, which first involves the talofibular ligament. Because this ligament prevents the talus from sliding forward, the most appropriate test is the one that elicits the anterior drawer sign (Figure 17-21). The athlete sits on the edge of a treatment table with legs and feet relaxed. The athletic trainer or physician grasps the lower tibia in one hand and the calcaneus in the palm of the other hand. The tibia is then pushed backward as the calcaneus is pulled forward. A positive anterior drawer sign occurs when the foot slides forward, sometimes making a "clunking" sound as it reaches its end point.

Two other tests that may be used are those that test for torn anterior talofibular and calcaneofibular ligaments on the lateral side and the torn side. With the foot positioned at 90 degrees to the lower leg and stablized, the heel is inverted. If the talus rocks in the mortise, there is injury to both the anterior talofibular and calcaneofibular ligaments, and there is subsequent lateral ankle instability (Figure 17-22). The deltoid ligament can be tested in the same way, except that the heel is everted. As the heel is moved into eversion, a gap is felt between the medial malleolus and the calcaneus.

Figure 17-21

Anterior drawer test for ankle ligament stability.

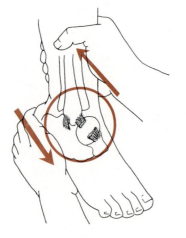

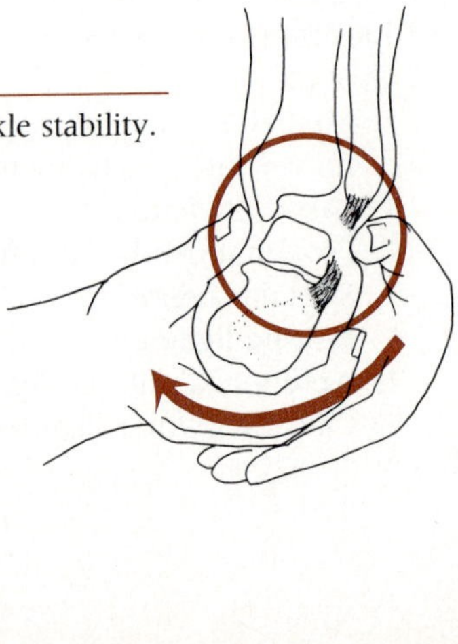

Figure 17-22

Testing lateral ankle stability.

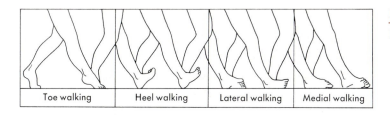

Figure 17-23

Evaluating ankle function.

Functional Evaluation

Muscle function is important in evaluating the ankle injury (Figure 17-23). *If the following movements aggravate a recent injury, they should be avoided.* While bearing weight on both feet, the athlete does the following:
1. Walks on toes (tests plantar flexion)
2. Walks on heels (tests dorsiflexion)
3. Walks on lateral border of feet (tests inversion)
4. Walks on medial border of feet (tests eversion)

Ankle Injury Prevention

Many ankle conditions, especially sprains, can be reduced by stretching the Achilles tendon, strengthening key muscles, proprioceptive training, wearing proper footwear, and, in some cases, proper taping.

Preventing ankle sprains is achieved by
  Stretching the Achilles tendon
  Strengthening key muscles
  Proprioceptive training
  Wearing proper footwear
  Taping when appropriate

Achilles Tendon Stretching

An ankle that can easily dorsiflex at least 15 degrees or more is essential for injury prevention. The athlete, especially one with tight Achilles tendons, should routinely stretch before and after practice (Figure 17-24).

Strength Training

Of major importance in ankle injury prevention is achieving both static and dynamic joint stability (Figure 17-25). A normal range of motion must be maintained, along with strength of the peroneal, plantar flexor, dorsal flexor, and extensor muscles.[14] The peroneals, mainly the peroneus longus muscle, must be exercised to afford eversion strength and to prevent the foot's being forced into inversion.

Proprioceptive Training

Athletes who have ankle injuries or who spend most of their time on even surfaces may develop a proprioceptive deficiency. Ankle ligamentous stability proprioception is also lost. The ankle and foot proprioceptive sense can be enhanced by locomotion over uneven surfaces or by spending time each day on a balance board (wobble board) (Figure 17-26).

Footwear

As discussed in Chapter 5, proper footwear can be an important factor in reducing injuries to both the foot and the ankle. Shoes should not be used in activities for which they were not intended—for example, running shoes designed for straight-ahead activity should not be used to play tennis, a sport demanding a great deal of lateral movement. Cleats on a shoe should not be centered in the middle of

A   B   C

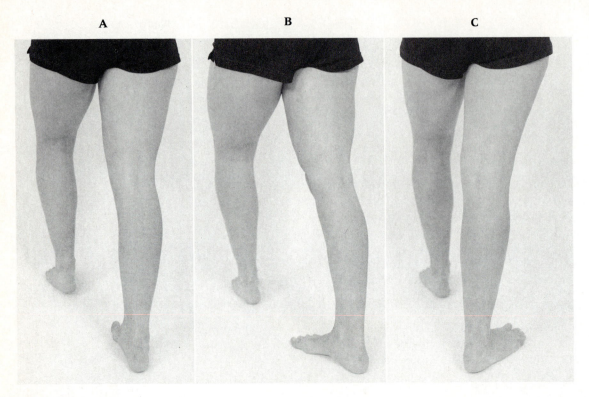

Figure 17-24

Stretching the Achilles tendon is essential in preventing ankle sprains. Stretching must be performed in all possible positions. **A,** Straight ahead. **B,** Adducted. **C,** Abducted.

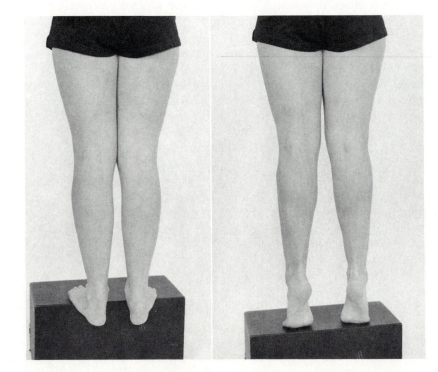

Figure 17-25

Strength training is essential for the prevention of ankle sprains.

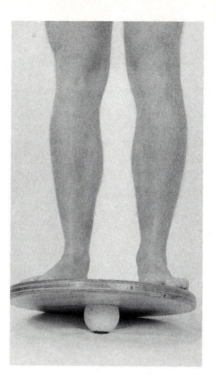

Figure 17-26

The wobble board is an excellent device for establishing ankle proprioception.

the sole but should be placed far enough on the border to avoid ankle sprains. High-top shoes, when worn by athletes with a history of ankle sprain, can offer greater support than low-top shoes.

Preventive Ankle Wrap and Taping

As discussed in Chapter 12, there is some doubt as to whether it is beneficial to routinely tape ankles that have no history of sprain. There is some indication that tape, properly applied, can provide some prophylactic protection. In the United States, millions of dollars are spent each year for the purchase of athletic tape. Poorly applied tape will do more harm than good. Tape that constricts soft tissue or disrupts normal biomechanical function can create serious injuries. Although taping is preferred, a much cheaper cloth muslin wrap may provide some protection (see Chapter 12). Lace-up supports and semirigid ankle braces are increasingly being used in place of tape. The Air Stirrup, which is a semirigid brace with inflatable air bags that conform to the ankle region, offers significant reduction to ankle inversion.[7]

Poorly applied ankle taping can do more harm than good to the athlete.

The Sprained Ankle

Because of their frequency and the disability that results, ankle sprains present a major problem for the coach, athletic trainer, and team physician. It has been said that a sprained ankle can be worse than a fracture. Fractures are usually conservatively cared for, with immobilization and activity restriction, whereas the athlete with a sprained ankle is often rushed through management and returned to activity before complete healing has occurred. Incompletely healed, the ankle becomes chronically inflamed and unstable, eventually causing a major problem for the athlete.

Mechanisms of Injury

Ankle sprains are generally caused by a sudden lateral or medial twist. The inversion sprain, in which the foot turns inward, is the most common type of ankle sprain because there is more bony stability on the lateral side, which tends to force the foot into inversion rather than eversion. If the force is great enough, inversion of the foot continues until the medial malleolus loses its stability and creates a fulcrum to further invert the ankle.[9] The peroneal or everting muscles resist the inverting force, and when they are no longer strong enough, the lateral ligaments become stretched or torn (Figure 17-27). Generally, most vertically loaded ankle sprains such as occur when an athlete comes down on another athlete's foot are more significant than horizontally loaded sprains because the vertically loaded sprain involves a greater amount of body weight applied directly to the ankle joint.

Usually a lateral ankle sprain involves either one or two torn ligaments. If it is a single ligament tear, it usually involves the anterior talofibular ligament, but if it is a double ligament tear with further inversion, the calcaneal fibular ligament also tears (see Figure 17-27). The tight heel cord forces the foot into inversion, making it more susceptible to a lateral sprain. In contrast, a foot that is pronated, hypermobile, or has a depressed medial longitudinal arch is more susceptible to medial arch and ankle injuries (Figure 17-28).

The eversion sprain occurs less frequently than the inversion sprain. The usual mechanism is the athlete's having suddenly stepped in a hole on the playing field, causing the foot to evert and abduct and the planted leg to rotate externally. With this mechanism the anterior tibiofibular ligament, interosseous ligament, and deltoid ligament may tear. With a tear of these ligaments, the talus is allowed to move laterally within the mortise, leading to ultimate degeneration within the joint. Also, there is abnormal space between the medial malleolus and the talus (Figure 17-29).

A sudden inversion force could be of such intensity as to produce a fracture of the lower leg. Unexpected wrenching of the lateral ligaments could cause a portion of bone to be avulsed from the malleolus (Figure 17-30). One extreme situation is when the lateral malleolus is avulsed by the calcaneofibular bone, and the talus rocks up against the medial malleolus to produce a second fracture. This sequence of events is known as the *bimalleolar fracture*.

MANAGEMENT   In managing a sprained ankle these first aid measures should be followed:

1. Determine the extent of the injury. The main purpose of the ankle sprain examination is to establish the injury severity and whether the ankle is stable or unstable. Swelling is *not* an indication of the severity of the injury. With the athlete in a seated position, a ligament laxity test may be given by the athletic trainer or the physician.
2. Use ICE-R (Figure 17-31).
   a. Apply an elastic pressure bandage around the perimeter of the malleolus at the site of the sprain to decrease internal bleeding.
   b. After the pressure bandage has been applied, decrease the temperature of the injured area by using ice packs. An elastic wrap that is thoroughly soaked in ice water and applied directly to the skin will cool faster when combined with an ice pack. Ice should be applied intermittently in 20 minute periods, 5 to 6 times a day. Do not expose the tissue to prolonged

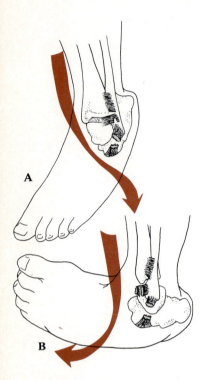

Figure 17-27

Mechanisms of an inversion ankle sprain.

The extent of ankle swelling is *not* an indicator of the severity of the injury.

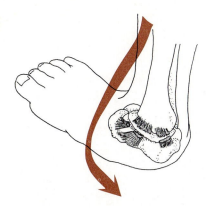

Figure 17-28

Mechanism of an eversion ankle sprain.

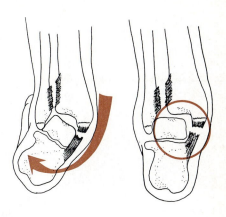

Figure 17-29

An eversion ankle sprain that creates an abnormal space between the medial malleolus and the talus.

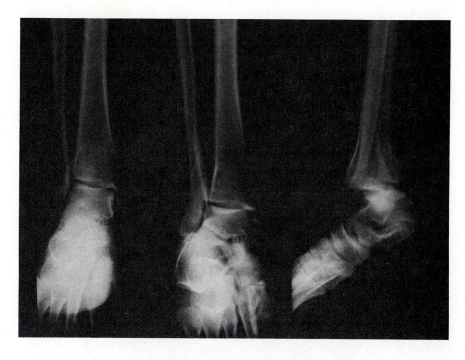

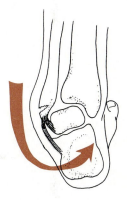

Figure 17-30

The same mechanism that produces an ankle sprain can also cause an avulsion fracture.

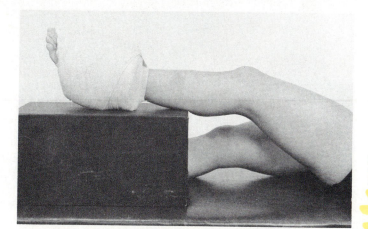

Figure 17-31

Application of ice, compression, elevation, and rest (ICE-R) is essential first aid for a sprained ankle.

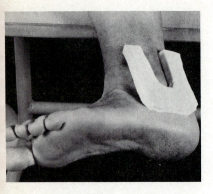

Figure 17-32

A horseshoe-shaped sponge rubber pad provides an excellent compress when held in place by an elastic wrap.

cooling. If a cold medium is not available, a horseshoe pad that is cut to fit around the malleolus and is held in place by an elastic wrap will help confine the internal hemorrhage (Figure 17-32).

    c. Promptly elevate the injured limb, if at all practical, so that fluid stasis of the internal hemorrhage does not take place.

    d. The open basketweave taping technique can also be used in conjunction with cold application (see Chapter 12).

NOTE: In most cases, if the ICE-R routine is carefully followed for 24 hours, articular and periarticular effusion can be limited.

3. If there is a possibility of fracture, splint the ankle and refer the athlete to the physician for x-ray examination and immobilization.

4. In most cases of moderate and severe ankle sprains, continue cold applications through the second or even the third day.

5. Begin heat therapy if hemorrhaging has stopped by the third day.

6. When a serious sprain has been ruled out, the physician may place the athlete in an Air Stirrup ankle brace, fit him or her with crutches, and instruct the athlete to continue with ICE three to four times per day (Figure 17-33).[16]

Lateral Ankle Sprains

Lateral ankle sprains are usually graded by the ligament or ligaments involved. A grade I or first degree sprain is concerned with the anterior talofibular ligament, a grade II with the calcaneofibular ligament, and a grade III with the posterior talofibular ligament. In each instance of injury, the foot is forcibly turned inward

Figure 17-33

The Air Stirrup ankle brace.

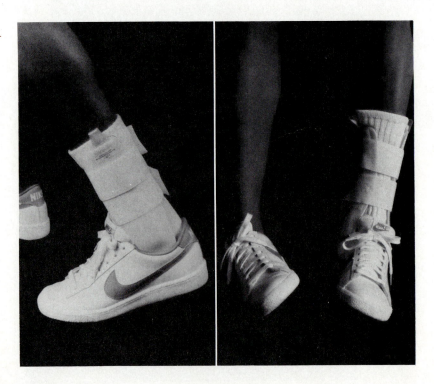

TABLE 17-3 Mechanisms of Ankle Sprain and Ligament Injury

Mechanisms	Area Injured
Plantar flexion or inversion	Anterior talofibular ligament Calcaneofibular ligament Posterior talofibular ligament Tibiofibular ligament (severe injury)
Inversion (uncommon)	Calcaneofibular ligament (along with anterior or posterior talofibular ligament)
Dorsiflexion	Tibiofibular ligament
Eversion	Deltoid ligament Tibiofibular ligament (severe injury) Interosseous membrane (as external rotation increases) Possible fibular fracture (proximal or distal)

on the leg such as when a basketball player jumps and comes down on the foot of another player. Inversion sprains can also occur when an individual is walking and running on an uneven surface or suddenly steps into a hole.[8,14]

First degree inversion ankle sprains   The first degree ankle sprain is the most common type of sprain. Most result from an inversion stress with the foot in *mild* plantar flexion, usually stretching the anterior talofibular ligament.

SYMPTOMS AND SIGNS   Mild pain and disability are present, with point tenderness and localized swelling over the area of the anterior talofibular ligament. The anterior drawer test is negative, with no ecchymosis and minimum loss of function.

MANAGEMENT   ICE-R is used for 20 minutes every few hours for 1 to 2 days. It may be advisable for the athlete to limit weight-bearing activities for a few days. An elastic wrap might provide comfortable pressure when weight bearing begins. When the athlete's ankle is pain free and not swollen, a routine of circumduction is begun. The athlete is instructed to circle the foot first 10 times in one direction then 10 times in the other several times per day. When the athlete returns to weight bearing, application of tape may provide an extra measure of protection.

A graduated exercise rehabilitation program is a major requirement in managing the first degree inversion sprain (see ''Exercise Rehabilitation of the Ankle and Lower Leg'' toward the end of this chapter).

Second degree inversion ankle sprains   Because it has a high incidence among sports participants and causes a great deal of disability with many days of lost time, the second degree ankle sprain is a major problem for the coach, athletic trainer, and physician.

SYMPTOMS AND SIGNS   The athlete usually complains that a tearing sensation was felt along with a pop or snap as the tissue gave way. Swelling is diffused with point tenderness at the sprain site. Some ecchymosis will occur 3 or 4 days after injury.

PATHOLOGICAL FINDINGS   The second degree ankle sprain may completely tear the anterior talofibular ligament and stretch and tear the calcaneofibular ligament. The anterior drawer test will elicit slight to moderate abnormal motion. This in-

MANAGEMENT PLAN FOR SECOND DEGREE ANKLE SPRAIN

Injury Situation

A male college senior-year lacrosse player stepped into a rut on the field, causing a major twist of the left ankle. At the time of injury the athlete felt a severe pain on the lateral aspect of the ankle before he fell to the ground.

Symptoms and Signs

After the injury the athlete complained of excruciating pain over the anterolateral aspect of the ankle. During palpation there was severe pain just under the lateral malleolus. A rapid, diffuse swelling occurred over the lateral ankle region, and an anterior drawer test showed some minor instability. X-ray examination indicated no fracture. The sprain was determined to be second degree.

Management Plan

1 Management Phase

GOALS: To control hemorrhage, swelling, pain, and spasm
ESTIMATED LENGTH OF TIME (ELT): 2-3 days

Therapy

IMMEDIATE CARE: Ice packs (20 min) intermittently 6-8 times daily
Athlete wears elastic wrap during waking hours and elevates leg
Foot is elevated on a pillow during sleep
Crutches are used to avoid weight bearing for at least 3-4 days or until athlete can walk without a limp
Open basketweave taping is applied for hemorrhage control (2-3 days)

Exercise Rehabilitation

Toe gripping and spreading if no pain is caused (10-15 times) every waking hour, starting on second day of injury
General body maintenance exercises are conducted three times a week as long as they do not aggravate the injury

2 Management Phase

GOALS: To decrease swelling and restore full muscle contraction without pain.
ELT: 4-7 days

Therapy

FOLLOW-UP CARE: All treatment is immediately followed by exercise
Ice pack (5-15 min) or ice massage (7 min) two or three times daily;
   or cold whirlpool (60° F, 10 min)
   or contrast baths (20 min);
   or massage above and below injury site (5 min)

Exercise Rehabilitation

Crutch walking is continued with a toe touch if athlete is unable to walk without a limp
Grip and spread toes (10-15 times) every waking hour
PNF ankle patterns three for four times daily
General body maintenance exercises are conducted three times a week as long as they do not aggravate the injury

3 Management Phase

GOALS: To restore 50% pain-free movement and restore strength

Therapy

All treatment is immediately followed by exercise
Ice pack (5-15 min) or ice massage (7 min) two or three times daily; or whirlpool (90° to 100 ° F) (10 to 15 min);
   or contrast baths (20 min);
   or massage above and below injury site (5 min);
   or ultrasound (0.5 watts/cm^2) (5 min)

	Exercise Rehabilitation	Avoid any exercise that produces pain or swelling Ankle circumduction (10-15 times each direction) two or three times daily Achilles tendon stretch from the floor (30 seconds) in each foot position (toe in, toe out, straight ahead) three or four times daily Toe raises (10 times—one to three sets) three or four times daily Eversion exercise using a towel or rubber tube or tire resistance three or four times daily Shifting body weight between injured and noninjured ankle (up to 20 times and as long as pain free) two or three times daily Progress to toe raises (10 to 15 times) two or three times daily PNF ankle patterns are continued two or three times daily Wobble board exercise (1-3 min) two or three times daily Progress to straight-ahead short step walking if it can be done without a limp General body maintenance exercises are conducted three times a week as long as they do not aggravate the injury
4	**Management Phase**	GOALS: To restore 90% range of motion (ROM), power, endurance, speed, and agility ELT: 1 week

	Therapy	All treatment is immediately followed by exercise
		Ice pack (5 min) or ice massage (7 min) once daily;
		   or whirlpool (100° to 120° F) (20 min);
		   or contrast baths (20 min);
		   or ultrasound (0.5 watts/cm^2) (5 min)

	Exercise Rehabilitation	Achilles tendon stretch using slant board (30 seconds each foot position) two or three times daily Toe raises using slant board and resistance (10 repetitions—one to three sets) two or three times daily Resistance ankle device to strengthen anterior, lateral, and medial muscles (starting with 2 lb and progressing to 10 lb) (one to three sets) two or three times daily Wobble board for ankle proprioception (begin at 1 min in each direction—progress to 5 min) three times daily Walk-jog routine as long as symptom free, can begin to alternately walk-jog-run-walk 25 yd straight ahead, jog 25 yd straight ahead; progress to walk 25 yd in lazy S or five figure-8s' progress to figure-8 running as fast as possible; when athlete is able to run 10 figure 8s or Z cuts as fast as possible and able to spring up in the air on the injured leg 10 times without pain, phase 5 can begin
5	**Management Phase**	The athlete is symptom free and has full ROM
	Exercise Rehabilitation	With the ankle protected by a tape or splint the athlete can return to practice Strengthening and ROM exercises should be continued daily
	Criteria for Returning to Competitive Lacrosse	1. The ankle is pain free during motion and no swelling is present. 2. Full ankle ROM and strength have been regained. 3. The athlete is able to run, jump, and make cutting movements as well as before injury.

jury degree can produce a persistently unstable ankle that recurrently becomes sprained and later develops traumatic arthritis.

MANAGEMENT ICE-R therapy should be used intermittently for 24 to 72 hours. X-ray examination should be routine for this degree of injury. The athlete should use crutches for 5 to 10 days to avoid bearing weight. A short leg walking cast or air cast (see Figure 17-33) may be applied for 2 or 3 days. Plantar and dorsiflexion exercises, if the athlete is pain free, may begin 48 hours after the injury occurs. Early exercise of this type helps to maintain range of motion and normal proprioception. Five to 10 minutes of ice pack application followed by 5 minutes of proprioceptive neuromuscular facilitation exercise improves strength, range of motion, and proprioception. After 1 or 2 weeks of non-weight bearing when swelling and pain have decreased, weight bearing can be resumed.

Taping in a closed basketweave technique may protect the ankle during the early stages of walking (see Figure 12-14). The athlete must be instructed to avoid walking or running on uneven or sloped surfaces for 2 to 3 weeks after weight bearing has begun.

Once hemorrhage has subsided, a therapy routine of superficial cold or heat should begin three times per day. Two or 3 weeks after the injury, circumduction exercises can be started. Gradually exercises can progress to resistive types.

COMPLICATIONS The second degree sprain, with its torn and stretched ligaments, tends to have a number of serious complications. Because of laxity there is a tendency to twist and sprain the ankle repeatedly. This recurrence over a period of time can lead to joint degeneration and traumatic arthritis. Once a second degree sprain has occurred, there must be a concerted effort to protect the ankle against future trauma.

Third degree inversion ankle sprains The third degree inversion ankle sprain is relatively uncommon in sports. When it does happen, it is quite disabling. Often the force causes the ankle to subluxate and then spontaneously reduce.

SYMPTOMS AND SIGNS The athlete complains of severe pain in the region of the lateral malleolus. Swelling is diffuse, with tenderness over the entire lateral area of the ankle. Where there is tearing of all three ligaments, results of the anterior and posterior drawer tests are positive.

PATHOLOGICAL FINDINGS This is a grade III injury that involves varying degrees of injury to the anterior talofibular, calcaneofibular, and posterior talofibular ligaments, as well as the joint capsule.

MANAGEMENT Normally ICE-R is used intermittently for 2 or 3 days. It is not uncommon for the physician to apply a short leg walking cast, when the swelling has subsided, for 4 to 6 weeks. In some cases a third degree ankle sprain is put into a cast for 3 weeks, followed by an air cast that can be removed for bouts of exercise.[4] Crutches are usually given to the athlete when the cast is removed. Circumduction exercises are begun immediately after the cast is removed, followed by a progressive program of strengthening. In some cases surgery is warranted to stabilize the athlete's ankle for future sports participation.

COMPLICATIONS The third degree ankle sprain creates significant joint laxity and instability. Because of this laxity the ankle joint becomes prone to severe degenerative forces.

Eversion Ankle Sprains

Eversion ankle sprains have a much lower incidence than inversion sprains; however, athletes who have pronated or hypermobile feet have a higher incidence of eversion sprains.

SYMPTOMS AND SIGNS   Depending on the degree of injury, the athlete complains of pain, sometimes severe, that occurs over the foot and lower leg. Usually the athlete is unable to bear weight on the foot. Both abduction and adduction causes pain, but pressing directly upward against the bottom of the foot does not cause pain.

COMPLICATIONS   An eversion sprain of second degree or more severity can produce significant joint instability. Because the deltoid ligament is involved with supporting the medial longitudinal arch, a sprain can cause weakness in this area. Repeated sprains could lead to pes planus (flatfoot).

> A second or third degree eversion sprain can adversely affect the medial longitudinal arch.

Injury to the Anterior or Posterior Tibiofibular Ligaments

The possibility in both the second and third degree inversion and eversion sprain of tearing either the anterior or posterior tibiofibular ligament is always present. The anterior tibiofibular ligament can be torn in an inversion sprain, whereas either or both ligaments can be torn in an eversion sprain. In both mechanisms, the tearing of one or both of these ligaments can widen the ankle mortise, leaving it unstable. With the widened mortise, an eversion or inversion motion will allow the talus to move laterally and medially more than 5 degrees. This condition is known as the *talar tilt*. One method for determining a posterior tibiofibular sprain is having the athlete bend the knee to relax the gastrocnemius muscle and passively dorsiflex the ankle. A positive test results in pain in the ankle sulcus.

> A talar tilt occurs when the ankle mortise is widened.

Ankle Fractures

There are a number of ways in which an ankle can be fractured or dislocated. A foot that is forcibly abducted on the leg can produce transverse and, on occasions, even comminuted fractures of the distal tibia and fibula. Also, forcible adduction of the foot on the leg can cause a transverse fracture of the distal tibia and fibula. In contrast, a foot that is planted, in combination with a leg that is forcibly rotated internally, can produce a fracture to the distal fibula and posterior tibia (Figure 17-34).[5]

Avulsion fractures, in which a chip of bone is pulled off by resistance of a ligament, are common in conjunction with second or third degree eversion or inversion sprains. In most cases of fracture, swelling and pain are extreme. There may be some or no deformity; however, if fracture is suspected, splinting is essential. ICE-R is used as soon as possible to control hemorrhage and swelling. Once swelling is reduced, casting can take place, allowing the athlete to bear weight. Immobilization will usually last for at least 6 to 8 weeks.

Acute Achilles Tendon Injuries
Achilles Tendon Strain

Achilles tendon strains are not uncommon in sports and occur most often as a result of a lack of coordination between the agonists and the antagonists following ankle sprains or sudden excessive dorsiflexion of the ankle.

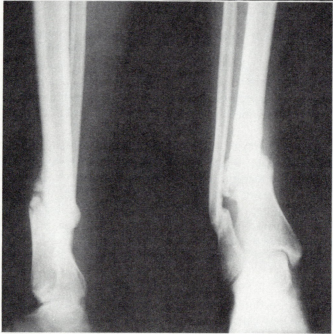

Figure 17-34

Ankle fractures or
dislocations can be major
sports injuries.

SYMPTOMS AND SIGNS   The resulting pathology may be mild to severe. The severe injury is usually thought of as a partial or complete avulsion or rupturing of the Achilles tendon. While receiving this injury, the athlete feels acute pain and extreme weakness on plantar foot flexion.

MANAGEMENT   The following are first aid measures to be applied:

1. As with other acute conditions, pressure is first applied with an elastic wrap together with cold application.
2. Unless the injury is minor, hemorrhage may be extensive, requiring ICE-R over an extended period of time.
3. After hemorrhaging has subsided, an elastic wrap can be lightly applied for continued pressure, and the athlete can be sent home. Management should begin the following day.

NOTE: The tendency for Achilles tendon trauma to readily develop into a chronic condition requires a conservative approach to therapy.

Management should be initiated in the following manner:

1. Follow-up therapy can usually begin on the third day and can continue on subsequent days, using hydromassage and analgesic packs until soreness has subsided.
2. Both heels, affected or unaffected, should be elevated by placing a sponge rubber pad in the heel of each street shoe. Elevation decreases the extension of the tendon and thereby relieves some of the irritation.
3. In a few days the athlete will be able to return to activity. The Achilles tendon should be restricted by a tape support and a sponge rubber heel lift placed in each athletic shoe (see Chapters 12 through 16). Heel lifts should be placed in both shoes or taped directly on the bottoms of both heels to avoid leg length asymmetry and subsequent adverse muscle and skeletal stresses.

It should be noted that correcting a rear foot valgus or varus may assist Achilles tendon problems.

Achilles Tendon Rupture

A rupture of the Achilles tendon (Figure 17-35) is a possibility in sports that require stop-and-go action. Although most common in athletes who are 30 years of age or older, rupture of the Achilles tendon can occur in athletes of any age. It usually occurs in an athlete with a history of chronic inflammation and gradual degeneration caused by microtears. The ultimate insult normally is the result of sudden pushing-off action of the forefoot with the knee being forced into complete extension.

SYMPTOMS AND SIGNS   When the rupture occurs, the athlete complains of a sudden snap or that something hit him or her in the lower leg. Severe pain, point tenderness, swelling, and discoloration are usually associated with the trauma. The major problem in the Achilles tendon rupture is accurate diagnosis. Often a partial rupture is thought to be a sprained ankle. Any acute injury to the Achilles tendon should be suspected as being a rupture. Signs indicative of a rupture are obvious indentation at the tendon site and/or a positive result to a Thompson test. The Thompson test (Figure 17-36) is performed by squeezing the calf muscle while the leg is extended and the foot is hanging over the edge of the table. A positive Thompson sign is one in which squeezing the calf muscle does not cause

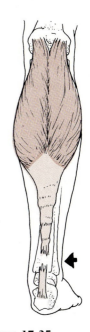

Figure 17-35

Achilles tendon rupture.

A ruptured Achilles tendon usually occurs when inflammation has been chronic.

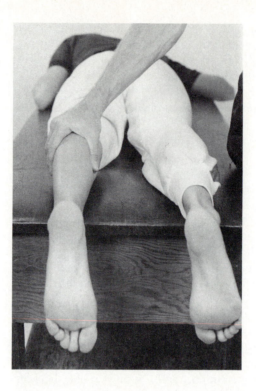

Figure 17-36

The Thompson test to determine an Achilles tendon rupture is performed by squeezing the calf muscle while the leg is extended. A positive result to the test is one in which the heel does not move.

the heel to move or pull upward or in which it moves less when compared to the uninjured leg. An Achilles tendon rupture usually occurs 2 to 6 cm proximal to its insertion onto the calcaneus.[6]

MANAGEMENT   Usual management of a complete Achilles tendon rupture is surgical repair. On occasion, however, the physician may decide on a conservative approach. When surgical correction is necessary, the ends of the tendon are surgically fixed with the foot in plantar flexion and the knee in flexion for approximately 4 weeks. Regaining full function from exercise rehabilitation will usually take more than 3 to 4 months.[13]

THE LOWER LEG
Functional Anatomy
Bony and Interosseal Structures

The portion of the lower extremity that lies between the knee and the ankle is defined as the leg and is comprised of the tibia, the fibula, and the soft tissues that surround them.

Tibia   The tibia, except for the femur, is the longest bone in the body and serves as the principal weight bearing bone of the leg. It is located on the medial or great toe side of the leg and is constructed with wide upper and lower ends to receive the condyles of the femur and the talus, respectively. The tibia is triangularly shaped in its upper two thirds but is rounded and more constricted in the lower third of its length. The most pronounced change occurs in the lower third of the shaft and produces an anatomical weakness that establishes this area as the site of most of the fractures occurring to the leg. The shaft of the tibia has three surfaces, the posterior, the medial, and the lateral. Primarily, the posterior and lateral surfaces are covered by muscle, whereas the medial surface is subcutaneous and, as a result, quite vulnerable to outside trauma.

Fibula   The fibula is long and slender and is located along the lateral aspect of the tibia, joining it in an arthrodial articulation at the upper end, just below the knee joint, and as a syndesmotic joint at the lower end. Both the upper and the lower tibiofibular joints are held in position by strong anterior and posterior ligaments. The main function of the fibula is to provide for the attachment of muscles. It serves to complete the groove for the enclosure of the talus in forming the ankle joint.

Interosseous membrane   The interosseous membrane is a strong sheet of fibrous tissue that extends between the fibula and the tibia. The fibers display an oblique downward-and-outward pattern. The oblique arrangement aids in diffusing the forces or stresses placed on the leg. It completely fills the tibiofibular space except for a small area at the superior aspect that is provided for the passage of the anterior tibial vessels.

Compartments

The soft tissue of the leg is contained within four compartments, which are bounded by heavy fascia (Figure 17-37). The *anterior compartment* holds the major structures for ankle dorsiflexion and foot and toe extension, which are the tibialis anterior, extensor hallucis longus, and extensor digitorum longus muscles, the

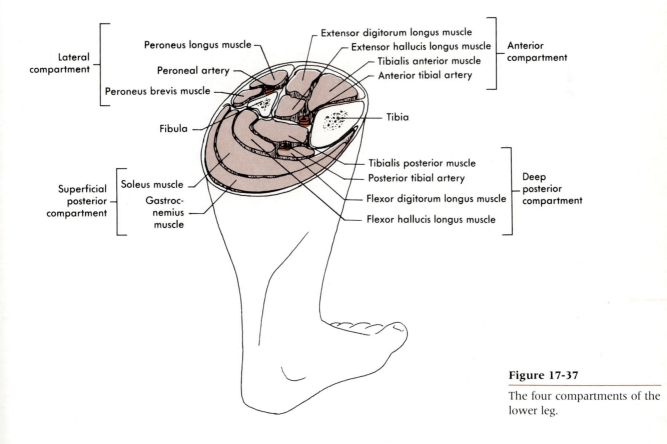

Figure 17-37

The four compartments of the lower leg.

anterior tibial nerve, and the tibial artery. A *lateral compartment* houses the perneus longus, brevis, and tertius muscles and the superficial branch of the peroneal nerve. The *superficial posterior compartment* is composed of the gastrocnemius muscle and the soleus muscle. These muscles plantar flex the ankle and control foot inversion and toe flexion. The *deep posterior compartment* houses the tibialis posterior, flexor digitorum longus, and flexor hallucis longus muscles and the posterior tibial artery. A major problem resulting from sports traumas can adversely affect these compartments, especially the anterior compartment. Such trauma can lead to swelling and neurological motor and sensory deficits (see further discussion later in this chapter).

Figure 17-38

Muscles of the lower leg. **A,** Anterior view; **B,** lateral view; **C,** posterior view superficial structures; and **D,** posterior view deep structures.

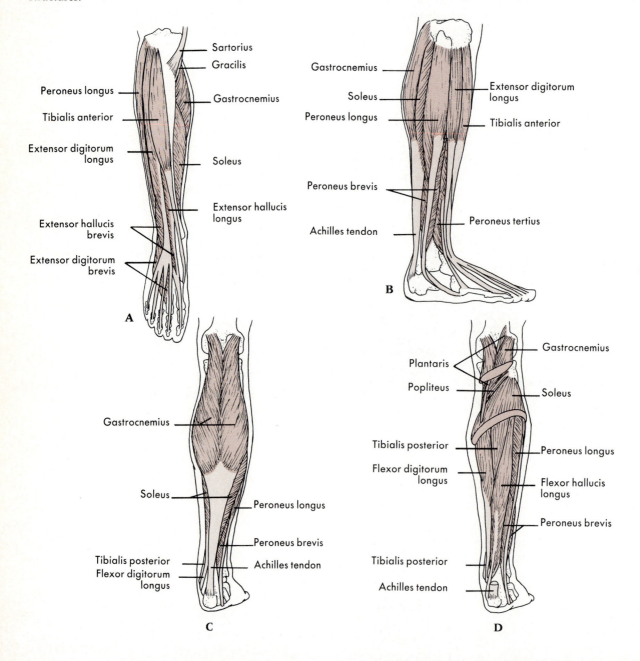

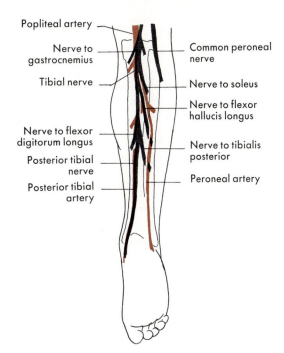

Popliteal artery

Nerve to gastrocnemius

Tibial nerve

Common peroneal nerve

Nerve to soleus

Nerve to flexor hallucis longus

Nerve to flexor digitorum longus

Posterior tibial nerve

Nerve to tibialis posterior

Peroneal artery

Posterior tibial artery

Figure 17-39

Blood and nerve supply of the lower leg.

Muscles

The lower leg is divided into posterior, anterior, and lateral muscular regions (Figure 17-38). The posterior region is divided into superficial and deep muscles. The superficial muscles include the gastrocnemius, plantaris, and soleus. The deep posterior group includes the tibialis posterior, flexor digitorum longus, and flexor hallucis longus. The anterior muscles consist of the anterior tibialis, extensor digitorum longus, peroneus tertius, and extensor hallucis longus. The lateral muscles are the peroneus brevis and longus.

Blood and Nerve Supply

The major nerves of the lower leg are the tibial and common peroneal stemming from the large sciatic nerve. The major arteries often accompany the nerves and are the posterior and anterior tibial arteries (Figure 17-39).

Assessment
Major Complaints

An athlete who complains of discomfort in the lower leg region should be asked the following:

1. How long has it been hurting?
2. Where is the pain or discomfort?
3. Has the feeling changed or is it numb?
4. Is there a feeling of warmth or coldness?
5. Is there any sense of muscle weakness or difficulty in walking?
6. How did the problem occur?

General Observation

The athlete is generally observed for the following:

1. Any postural deviations such as toeing in, which may indicate tibial torsion or genu valgum or varum; foot pronation should also be noted.
2. Any walking difficulty is noted, along with leg deformities or swellings.

Bony and Soft-Tissue Palpation

The tibia, fibula, and the musculature are palpated for pain sites and obvious defects and swellings.

Functional Evaluation

Passive, active, and resistive movement is given to the muscles of the lower leg.

Special Tests

When fracture is suspected, a percussive blow can be given to the tibia or fibula below or above the suspected site. Percussion can also be applied upward on the bottom of the heel. Such blows set up a vibratory force that resonates at the fracture, causing pain.

Acute Leg Injuries

The leg is prone to a number of acute conditions, of which contusions and strains are most common. Although less common, fractures can occur in relation to direct trauma such as being struck by a blow or through torsional forces with the foot fixed to the ground.

Leg Contusions

The shin bruise   The shin, lying just under the skin, is exceedingly vulnerable and sensitive to blows or bumps. Because of the absence of muscular or adipose padding here, blows are not dissipated as they are elsewhere, and the periosteum receives the full force of any impact delivered to the shin. The periosteum surrounds bone surfaces, with the exception of the cartilaginous areas, and is composed of two fibrous layers that adhere closely to the bone, acting as a bed for blood vessels and bone-forming osteoblasts. Severe blows to the tibia often lead to a chronic inflammatory state of the cutaneous and periosteal tissue. The shin is an extremely difficult area to heal, particularly the lower third, which has a considerably smaller blood supply than the upper portion. An inadequately cared for injury to the periosteum may develop into ostemyelitis, a serious condition that results in the destruction and deterioration of bony tissue.

Severe blows to an unprotected shin can lead to a chronic inflammation.

In sports such as football and soccer in which the shin is particularly vulnerable, adequate padding should be provided. All injuries in this area are potentially serious; therefore minor shin lacerations or bruises should never be permitted to go untended.

Muscle contusions   Contusions of the leg, particularly in the area of the gastrocnemius muscle, are common in sports. A bruise in this area can produce an extremely handicapping injury for the athlete. A bruising blow to the leg will cause pain, weakness, and partial loss of the use of the limb. Palpation may reveal a hard, rigid, and somewhat inflexible area because of internal hemorrhage and muscle spasm.

When this condition occurs, it is advisable to stretch the muscles in the region immediately to prevent spasm and then, for approximately 1 hour, to apply a compress bandage and cold packs to control internal hemorrhaging.

If cold therapy or other superficial therapy such as massage and whirlpool do not return the athlete to normal activity within 2 to 3 days, the use of ultrasound may be warranted. An elastic wrap or tape support will stabilize the part and permit the athlete to participate without aggravation of the injury.

Acute Compartment Syndrome

The acute compartment syndrome resulting from exercise is much less common than the chronic or recurrent type. It is usually caused by performing unaccustomed exercise such as running a long distance.[12]

SYMPTOMS AND SIGNS   As an acute condition, the compartment continues to show signs of neurovascular compression after the athlete quits exercising. The following signs are characteristic of anterior compartment syndrome, by far the most common form: (1) weakness of foot dorsiflexion or extension of the great toe, (2) decreased ability of the peroneal tendon to evert the foot, and (3) paresthesia of the web between the first and second toe or over the foot's entire dorsal region.[15]

If by chance there is an acute posterior compartment syndrome, there are (1) weakness in plantar flexion, (2) weakness of great toe and lateral toe flexion, and (3) paresthesia of the sole of the foot.

MANAGEMENT   An acute compartment syndrome requires immediate decompression through the surgical release of the fascia covering the area. The incision may be left open and the leg splinted for a week.

NOTE: At no time should a pressure wrap be applied when this condition is suspected.

Leg Spasms and Muscle Strains

Muscle spasms   Spasms are sudden, violent, involuntary contractions of one or several muscles and may be either clonic or tonic. A *clonic* spasm is identified by intermittent contraction and relaxation, whereas the *tonic* type is identified by its constant state of muscle contraction without an intervening period of relaxation. Both of these types occur in sports. How and why muscle spasms happen to athletes is often difficult to ascertain. Fatigue, excess loss of fluid through perspiration, and inadequate reciprocal muscle coordination are some of the factors that may predispose an individual to a contracture. The leg, particularly the gastrocnemius muscle, is prone to this condition. It is usually difficult to predict the occurrence of spasm, since only the aforementioned criteria can be used as a guide.

MANAGEMENT   When a muscle goes into spasm there is severe pain and considerable apprehension on the part of the athlete. Management in such cases includes putting the athlete at ease and relaxing the contracted site. Firmly grasping the contracted muscle, together with a mild gradual type stretching, relieves most acute spasms. Vigorously rubbing an extremity during spasm often increases its intensity. In cases of recurrent spasm, the athletic trainer should make certain that fatigue or abnormal electrolyte loss is not a factor, since the loss of salt or other minerals can result in abnormal motor nerve impulses to skeletal muscles.

Calf strain ("tennis leg")   Contrary to past beliefs, the plantaris muscle seldom ruptures; however, more commonly the medial head of the gastrocnemius becomes strained and tears near its musculotendinous attachment. Sports such as tennis that require quick starts and stops can cause this gastrocnemius strain.

Figure 17-40

"Tennis leg" calf strain.

Usually the athlete makes a quick stop with the foot planted flat footed and suddenly extends the knee, placing stress on the medial head of the gastrocnemius (Figure 17-40). In most cases calf strain can be prevented by a regular routine of gradually stretching the calf region and exercising the antagonist and agonist muscles. If the pain is sustained, immediate application of ICE-R is necessary, followed by a gentle, gradual stretch routine. Follow-up care should include a regimen of cold, heat, and mild exercise, together with walking in low-heeled shoes, accentuating a heel-toe gait.

Leg Fractures

Fractures received during sports participation occur most often to the fingers, hands, face, and legs. Of leg fractures, the fibular fracture has the highest incidence and occurs principally to the middle third of the leg. Fractures of the tibia occur predominantly to the lower third.

Fractures of the shaft of the tibia and fibula result from either direct or indirect trauma during active participation in sports (Figure 17-41). There is often a marked bony displacement with deformity as a result of a strong pull of antagonistic muscles, causing an overriding of the bone ends, particularly if the athlete attempts to move or to stand on the limb after the injury. Crepitus and a temporary loss of limb function are usually present.

The pathology consists of marked soft-tissue insult and extensive internal hemorrhaging. The leg appears hard and swollen, which may indicate the beginning

Figure 17-41

Fracture of the tibia.

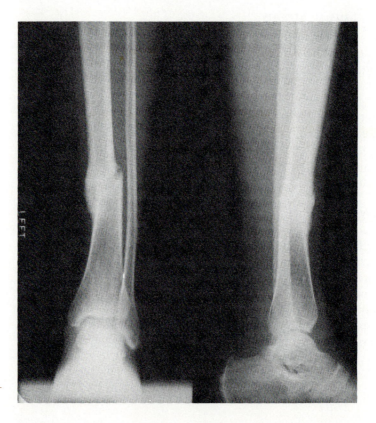

of Volkmann's contracture. Volkmann's contracture is the result of great internal tension caused by hemorrhage and swelling within closed fascial compartments, inhibiting the blood supply and resulting in necrosis of muscles and in contractures. In most cases, fracture reduction and cast immobilization are applied for 3 to 6 months, depending on the extent of the injury and any complications.

EXERCISE REHABILITATION OF THE ANKLE AND LOWER LEG

Many physicians think that a conservative approach should be taken in the treatment of sprained ankles by placing them in a cast and preventing any weight bearing for a period of at least 2 weeks. On the other hand, many sports physicians and athletic trainers maintain that the best method is the moderately active approach, in which the athlete returns to competition much sooner than with the conservative treatment and completes the therapy through activity. The best method for returning an athlete to action should be determined by the physician.

An athlete with a moderate or severe sprain should avoid weight bearing for at least 2 days and perhaps longer if there is pain and incapacitation. As the initial soreness decreases, the athlete should be encouraged to move the ankle as normally as possible—active dorsiflexion and plantar flexion should be emphasized, and inversion and eversion should be avoided. The athlete should use crutches to stand or walk. As the ankle heals, the athlete can be graduated from crutch walking to walking with a cane while the ankle is supported by tape. There must be complete healing before the athlete returns to vigorous activity. A good rule of thumb for determining when the athlete is able to return to a sport is to have the athlete stand, balancing full weight on the toes of the affected foot, and spring up and down. If this movement can be done without severe discomfort, it may be presumed that the athlete is able to resume a modified activity program with running. Maintaining tendon strength will aid the athlete when returning to the sport. The athlete's first concern should be to regain normal range of motion, after which a graded resistance exercise program can be started. All of the major muscles crossing the ankle joint must be considered in a reconditioning program. Of particular importance are the gastrocnemius and the muscles of foot inversion and eversion. Wearing cleated shoes should be avoided until there is full injury recovery. Too often athletes are permitted to return to their sport before adequate recovery has taken place, causing the ankle joint to become chronically inflamed. Besides a daily therapy program conducted by the coach or the athletic trainer, the athlete should be encouraged to engage in a home program—for example, ICE-R treatment followed by inner tube or other resistance exercises.

In most sports injuries that affect the leg, atrophy and contracture of the leg, thigh, or hip musculature occur. In addition to these conditions, a low-back imbalance may also occur and result in shortening of the injured limb. In dealing with leg injuries, one should strive to maintain strength and complete mobility of the knee, hip, and lower back. Rehabilitation depends on the site of the injury, its nature, and its extensiveness. Mobility should be attained and encouraged through passive stretching of the plantar and dorsal areas. When pain during movement has decreased, a progressive strengthening program should be established and a daily order of exercise maintained by the athlete.

It is suggested that rehabilitation exercises be performed two to three times daily, progressing from one to three sets of 10 repetitions. The athlete must con-

Too often athletes are permitted to return to their sport before adequate recovery has taken place, causing the ankle joint to become chronically inflamed.

sider all the major muscles associated with the foot, ankle, and lower leg. A program of three stages might include the following:

Stage 1—early rehabilitation (all exercises must be conducted pain free)

1. *Writing the alphabet*—with toes pointed, three times.
2. *Picking up objects* (e.g., marbles)—one at a time with the toes; place them in a container.
3. *Gripping and spreading toes*—10 repetitions.
4. *Ankle circumduction*—10 circles in one direction and 10 circles in the other.
5. *Flatfooted Achilles tendon stretching*—with foot flat on the floor, the Achilles tendon is stretched first with foot straight ahead, then adducted, and finally abducted. Each stretch is maintained for 20 to 30 seconds and repeated two to three times.
6. *Toe raises*—standing flat on floor, the athlete rises onto toes as far as possible, with toes pointed straight ahead, pointed in, and finally pointed out; 10 repetitions, two or three times.
7. *Walking on toes and heels*—the athlete walks 10 spaces forward on toes and 10 paces backward on heels. Repeated two or three times.

Stage 2—intermediate rehabilitation

1. *Towel gather*—10 repetitions, two or three times.
2. *Towel scoop*—10 repetitions, two or three times.

Figure 17-42

To maximize the strength of the Achilles tendon as much as possible, a toe raise must begin from a fully stretched position.

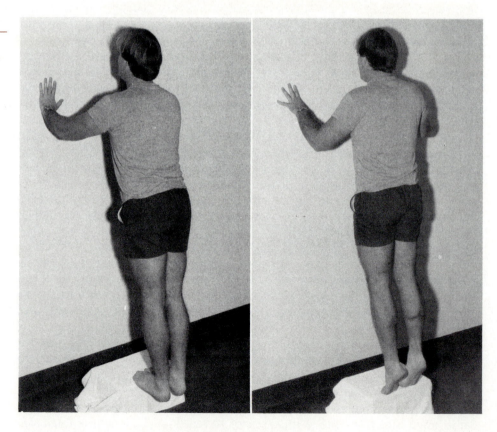

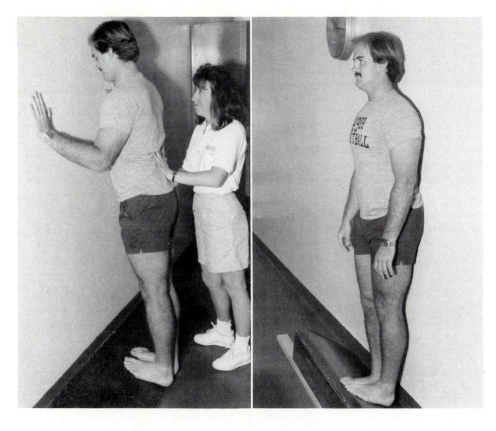

Figure 17-43

Incline boards can effectively stretch a constricted Achilles tendon.

3. *Achilles tendon stretching and toe raise*—the athlete stands with toes on a raised area such as a step with heels over the edge. The heels are raised as far as possible and then returned to stretch the Achilles tendon as much as possible. This movement is performed with toes pointed straight ahead, pointed in, and then pointed out; 10 repetitions, two or three times (Figures 17-42 and 17-43).

4. *Resistance with tubing*—exercise anterior, lateral, and medial leg muscles against a resistance such as surgical tubing or an inner tube strip. The tubing is attached around a stationary table or chair leg. The athlete places the tubing around the foot and pulls the forefoot into dorsiflexion and eversion, then reverses position and exercises the foot in plantar flexion inversion; 10 repetitions, three or four times (Figure 17-44).

5. *Manual resistance*—manual resistance can be applied by the athletic trainer or other person. The exercise is performed in a complete range of motion and in all four ankle movements. PNF patterns may be elected in place of straight patterns. Exercise is performed until fatigue or pain is felt. Manual resistance exercise should progress to the use of the elgin machine (Figure 17-45).

6. *Proprioceptive ankle training*—the athlete spends 3 to 5 minutes daily on a balance board (wobble board) to reestablish ankle proprioception (see Figure 17-21).

Figure 17-44

Thera band resistance material affords an excellent means to introduce an ankle or lower-leg strength exercise program. **A,** Plantar flexion. **B,** Dorsiflexion. **C,** Eversion.

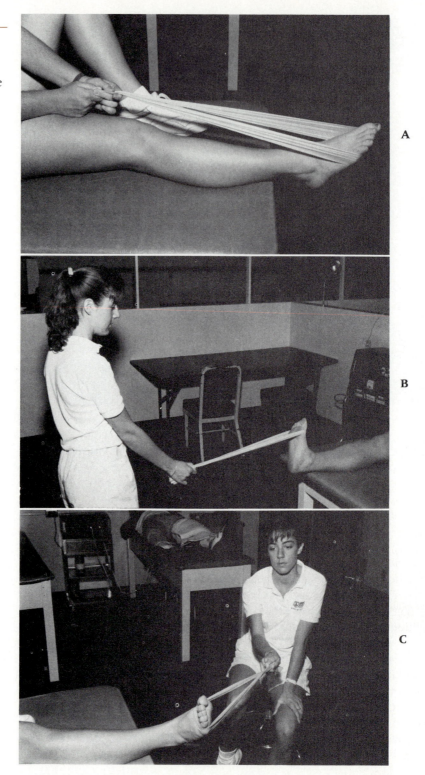

Stage 3—advanced rehabilitation

1. *Rope jumping*—5 to 10 minutes daily.
2. *Heel-toe and then on-toe running*—the athlete starts with heel-toe jogging until a mile distance can be performed easily. Jogging is then shifted to jogging 50 yards and on-toe running 50 yards, graduating to all on-toe running for 1 mile.
3. *Zigzag running*—the athlete runs a zigzag pattern, graduating from slow to full speed without favoring the leg.
4. *Backward running*—a final exercise for returning full ankle and lower leg function is running backward in an on-toe manner.

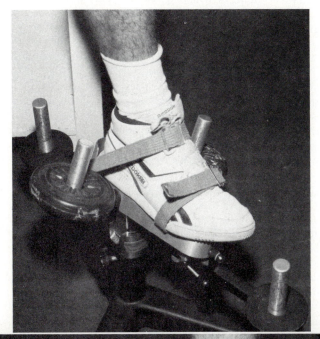

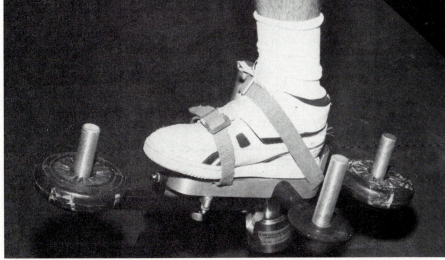

Figure 17-45

For a heavier resistance program the athlete may find using the Elgin machine beneficial.

SUMMARY

The human foot is a highly complicated anatomical structure, requiring a great deal of strength, flexibility, and coordinated movement. Complaints about foot injuries by athletes call for careful physical examination.

Common acute injuries are heel and instep bruises, arch strains, and sprains of the mid-foot, forefoot, and great toe. Fractures can occur to all areas of the foot.

Besides the use of other therapy modalities, the use of rehabilitative exercise is important for managing foot conditions.

The ankle has a high incidence of injury in sports activities. Although the ankle has a relatively strong bony arrangement in terms of its supportive soft tissue, it is very weak laterally. Despite its susceptibility to injuries, preventive procedures can be taken. Through stretching of the Achilles tendon, strength training, wearing proper footwear, and the application of appropriate taping or wrapping, many injuries can be prevented.

First, second, and third degree sprains must be managed by ICE-R during immediate care. Compression is achieved through application of sponge rubber and an elastic wrap. In the early stages, weight bearing should be eliminated or reduced through the use of crutches. A variety of therapeutic modalities, as well as exercise, are used in follow-up management.

The same mechanisms that strain an Achilles tendon can also cause rupture. The Thompson test is standard for determining a suspected Achilles tendon rupture. Repeated minor Achilles tendon tears can cause tissue degeneration and a subsequent rupture.

The lower leg is subject to contusion, muscle strains, and, less often, fractures. An acute compartment syndrome could lead to serious muscle weakness and paresthesia.

Exercise is an important approach for the rehabilitation of the ankle and the lower leg.

REVIEW QUESTIONS AND CLASS ACTIVITIES

1. Describe the anatomy of the foot, ankle, and lower leg.
2. Demonstrate assessment of the foot.
3. Why is the calcaneus prone to contusion, and how can contusion be prevented? How can it be managed?
4. Identify the type of acute strains occurring in the region of the foot. How can they be prevented? How can they be managed?
5. Where do sprains, dislocations, and fractures commonly occur in the foot? Discuss their symptoms and signs and how they can be cared for.
6. Describe exercise rehabilitation of the foot.
7. Demonstrate the steps that should be taken when assessing ankle injuries.
8. How can ankle injuries be prevented?
9. Describe how ankle sprains occur. Distinguish between first, second, and third degree types of ankle sprains.
10. Contrast the management of first, second, and third degree ankle sprains.
11. How can the anterior or posterior tibiofibular ligament be torn?
12. Describe acute sports injuries to the Achilles tendon. Indicate etiology and symptoms and signs.
13. Describe the anatomy of the lower leg.
14. How should the lower leg be assessed for possible injuries? What steps should be taken when assessing the lower leg for injuries?
15. Acute injuries to the lower leg are usually contusions and/or muscle strains. Discuss their etiology, symptoms and signs, and management.
16. Contrast an acute compartment syndrome with the chronic type described in Chapter 18.
17. How can a leg fracture occur?
18. Describe the steps that must be taken during exercise rehabilitation of the ankle and the lower leg.

REFERENCES

1. Balduini, FC, and Tetzlaff, J: Historical perspectives on injuries of the ligaments of the ankle. In Torg, JS, editor: Symposium on ankle and foot problems in the athlete, Clinics in sports medicine, vol 1, no 1, Philadelphia, 1982, WB Saunders Co.
2. Birnbaum, JS: The musculoskeletal manual, New York, 1982, Academic Press, Inc.
3. Black, HM, and Brand, RL: Injuries of the foot and ankle. In Scott, WN, et al., editors: Principles of sports medicine, Baltimore, 1984, The Williams & Wilkins Co.
4. Costello, BG: Ligament instability of the ankle. In Welsh, RP, and Shephard, RJ, editors: Current therapy in sports medicine 1985-1986, Philadelphia, 1985, Brian C Decker, Publisher.
5. Glick, JM, and Sampson, TG: Ankle and foot fractures in athletics. In Nicholas, JA, and Hershman, EB, editors: The lower extremity and spine in sports medicine, vol 1, St. Louis, 1986, The CV Mosby Co.
6. Hattrup, SJ, and Johnson, KA: A review of ruptures of the Achilles tendon, Foot Ankle 6:34, Aug 1985.
7. Kimura, IF, et al: Effect of the Air Stirrup in controlling ankle inversion stress. J Orthop Sports Phys Ther 9(5):190, 1987.
8. Knowles KG: Lateral collateral ligament injuries to the ankle, Postgraduate advances in sports medicine, I-X, Pennington, NJ, 1986, Forum Medicus, Inc.
9. Mack, RP: Ankle injuries in athletics. In Torg, JS, editor: Symposium on ankle and foot problems in the athlete, Clinics in sports medicine, vol 1, no 1, Philadelphia, 1982, WB Saunders Co.
10. Magee, DJ: Orthopedic physical assessment, Philadelphia, 1987, WB Saunders Co.
11. Miller, WE: The heel pad, Am J Sports Med 10:19, 1982.
12. Murbarak, S, and Hargens, A: Exertional compartment syndromes. In Mack, RP, editor: Symposium on the foot and leg in running sports, American Academy of Orthopaedic Surgeons, St. Louis, 1982, The CV Mosby Co.
13. O'Donoghue, DH: Treatment of injuries to athletes, ed 4, Philadelphia, 1984, WB Saunders Co.
14. Singer, KM, and Jones, DC: Ligament injuries of the ankle and foot. In Nicholas, JA, and Hershman, EB, editors: The lower extremity and spine in sports medicine, vol 1, St. Louis, 1986, The CV Mosby Co.
15. Wallensten, R, and Eriksson, E: Is medical lower leg pain (shinsplint) a chronic compartment syndrome? In Mack, RP, editor: Symposium on the foot and leg in running sports, American Academy of Orthopaedic Surgeons, St. Louis, 1982, The CV Mosby Co.
16. Weiker, GG: Sprains and pseudosprains of the athlete's ankle, Sports Med Dig 9(12):1, 1987.

ANNOTATED BIBLIOGRAPHY

Drez, Jr, D, editor: Symposium on running, Clinics in sports medicine, vol 4, no 4, Philadelphia, 1985, WB Saunders Co.
Covers the major factors concerned with injuries stemming primarily from long distance running. Subjects include the running shoe, biomechanics, mechanisms, and management of major injuries.

McMinn, RM, et al.: Color atlas of foot and ankle anatomy, Chicago, 1982, Year Book Medical Publishers, Inc.
Provides photographic illustrations of foot and ankle anatomy based on dissection.

Nicholas, JA, and Hershman, EB, editors: The lower extremity and spine, vol 1, St. Louis, 1986, The CV Mosby Co.
An in-depth medical text written for the physician and the sports therapist. The foot, ankle, and leg, including anatomy, biomechanics, and injuries are well-represented.

Torg, JS, editor: Ankle and foot problems in the athlete, Clinics in sports medicine, vol 1, no 1, Philadelphia, 1982, WB Saunders Co.
Presents 12 chapters on ankle and foot injuries, covering cause of injury, biomechanics, examination, prevention, and injury management.

18

The Foot, Ankle, and Lower Leg: Chronic and Overuse Injuries

When you finish this chapter, you should be able to

Explain the biomechanical and linkage relationships of chronic and overuse injuries of the foot, ankle, and lower leg

Discuss etiological factors, symptoms and signs, and management procedures for the major chronic and overuse sports injuries of the foot, ankle, and lower leg

Develop a management plan for major chronic and overuse sports injuries

C hronic and overuse stress injuries in the foot, ankle, or leg are becoming increasingly more of a problem in sports. Many reasons have been suggested for this situation; however, of major importance is the increase of running distance and other exercise intensity among both serious and recreational athletes (Figure 18-1).

FOOT BIOMECHANICAL IMPLICATIONS

A study of lower extremity chronic and overuse injuries related to sports participation must include some understanding of biomechanics of the foot, especially in the act of walking and running.

The human foot is designed to absorb shock for the entire body. Ankle dorsiflexion, knee and hip flexion, and eversion at the subtalar joint absorb the shock of making contact with surfaces that have no or varying resilience.[10]

Locomotion of any kind, but especially that which is imposed by sports activities, places great stress on the foot as it makes contact with a surface. If the foot is abnormally structured, pathological conditions may develop over time. A foot that functions normally will place no undue stress on itself or the other joints of the lower limb.[10] A foot with a structural malformation eventually may have overuse problems; foot malformations can lead to both soft-tissue and body deformities in the lower extremity.

The human foot provides shock absorption for the entire body.

Figure 18-1

With the increased popularity of distance running, chronic and overuse injuries are on the increase.

The Gait Cycle

The stance phase of gait includes contact (25%), midstance (40%), and propulsion (35%). In walking from heel-strike to heel-strike, 35% of the action consists of the swing phase, and 65% consists of the stance phase. During the initial surface contact or first 15% to 25% of the stance phase, the lower leg is internally rotated (Figure 18-2). When in contact with a surface, the foot is unable to rotate internally; it is the subtalar, or universal, joint that allows for this motion. During surface contact the subtalar joint normally pronates 6 to 8 degrees.[14] Pronation is the combined motion of calcaneal eversion, plantar flexion, and adduction of the talus. At the same time, the medial longitudinal arch flattens or lowers. Foot pronation is necessary for adaption to uneven surfaces. A flatfooted athlete may have as much as 10 to 12 degrees of navicular pronation. The more the subtalar joint pronates or everts, the more the tibia internally rotates. Tibial rotation is referred to the knee and hip joints, possibly leading to microtraumas and overuse problems.[14] Excessive internal rotation can be determined by the amount of patellar rotation. The patella rotates inwardly as much in the contact phase as it

The more the subtalar joint pronates or everts, the more the tibia internally rotates.

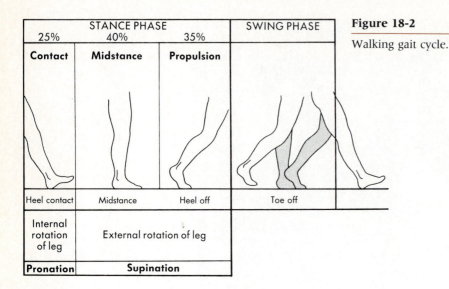

Figure 18-2

Walking gait cycle.

Figure 18-3

Foot bearing weight in walking as it moves from heel-strike to toe-off.

externally rotates during propulsion. More inward rotation than external rotation leads to excessive pronation in the subtalar joint.[17]

As the foot moves to the midstance, or fully loaded, position, it becomes increasingly more stable. As the full weight of the body is supported by the foot, the lower leg progressively moves from internal rotation to external rotation. As the leg externally rotates and the foot moves from a midstance position, the foot supinates. Supination begins with external rotation of the hip and raising of the medial longitudinal arch. The talus moves into dorsiflexion, and the calcaneus moves into inversion as the hindfoot moves into supination. The gastrocnemius, soleus, and posterior tibial are the major muscles for foot supination (Figure 18-3).[17] In this position the foot is normally rigid to provide a strong toe-off. Until toe-off the long peroneal muscle stabilizes the first metatarsal bone.

If an athlete has fallen arches or the stage of pronation is prolonged or the foot is inadequately stable during toe-off, injuries may occur. The converse of this is also true. A person with a cavus condition, indicated by an abnormally high arch and a rigid foot, has decreased subtalar, leg, and hip motion and subsequent shock absorption. The relative positions of the forefoot and the hindfoot generate abnormal forces to the foot, which are in turn transferred to the leg (Figure 18-4).

In running both feet are off the surface at the same time (Figure 18-5). Sprinters are on their toes during the support phase, whereas middle-distance runners may momentarily touch their heels during the support phase. Much like a walker, the jogger and the long-distance runner perform a heel-foot-toe action. Whatever the type of running, a **hypermobile foot** that allows too much pronation or fails at rigid stability in toe-off can eventually produce an injury. One indicator of how the running foot bears weight is to observe shoe wear (Figure 18-6).

hypermobile foot
Foot that allows too much pronation or fails at rigid stability in toe-off

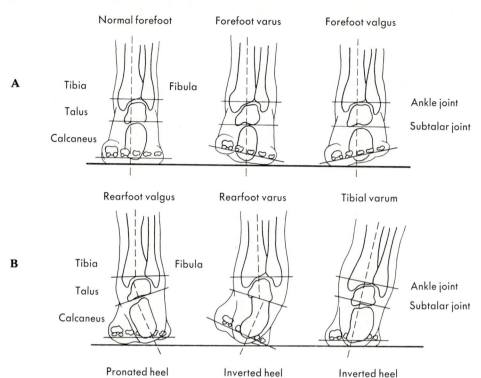

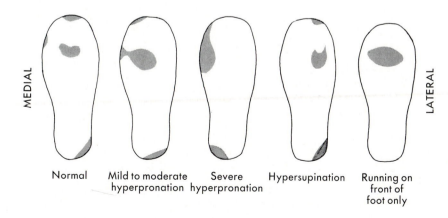

Figure 18-4

The relative positions of the forefoot and hindfoot generate abnormal forces to the foot, which are transferred to the leg. **A,** Anterior view. **B,** Posterior view.

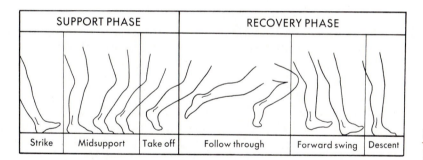

Figure 18-5

Running gait cycle.

Figure 18-6

Shoe wear can be an indicator of how the running foot is bearing weight.

Specific Joint Segments Related to Ambulation

Parks[17] emphasizes that all of the many foot segments are interdependent with one another. If one segment is weak, it adversely affects all other segments.

The Subtalar Joint

The subtalar joint must lock completely during the toe-off phase of locomotion and unlock in the contact phase, allowing pronation to occur. The position of the calcaneus during ambulation and stance is a good indicator of the habitual movement of the subtalar joint. At all times it should remain in a straight-line or vertical position.[17]

The Talonavicular Joint

The talonavicular joint moves independently from the hindfoot. In relation to the hindfoot it can dorsiflex and move in eversion and inversion. The talonavicular joint, like the subtalar joint, locks and unlocks. It has mobility during the first part of surface contact and should become highly stable before toe-off. Normally the talonavicular joint is positioned higher than the calcaneocuboid joint. If the subtalar joint is hypermobile, the talonavicular and calcaneocuboid joints become parallel and weakened, making them susceptible to surface forces. Another factor is that the surface stresses cause dorsiflexion of the forefoot on the hindfoot, thereby increasing hypermobility (Figure 18-7).

The Tarsometatarsal Joint

The tarsometatarsal joint comprises the cuboid; first, second, and third cuneiform; and bases of the metatarsal bones. These bones allow for great rotational forces when engaged in weight-bearing activities. They move as a unit, depending on the functioning of the talonavicular and subtalar joints. Also known as the Lisfranc joint, the tarsometatarsal joint is a locking device that provides foot stability. As the talonavicular joint becomes neutral or supinated, the tarsometatarsal joint becomes dorsally convex to resist the surface stress on the foot.[17] In pronation the tarsometatarsal joint loses its convexity, and the bones become more parallel to one another, thus causing the forefoot to become hypermobile.[17] The primary muscle support in this region is produced by the posterior tibial muscle pulling medially and the long and short peroneal muscles pulling laterally.

Figure 18-7

Stress sites in the hypermobile foot.

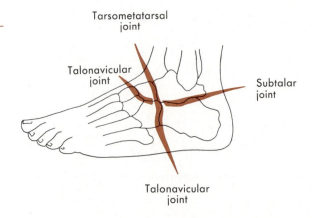

The Metatarsal Region

Together with subtalar, talonavicular, and tarsometatarsal interrelationships, foot stabilization depends on the functioning of the metatarsal joints.

The first metatarsal bone, along with the first cuneiform (first ray) bone, moves independently from the other metatarsal bones. As a main weight bearer, the first ray is concerned with body propulsion. An unstable first ray will cause forefoot pronation. Stabilization depends on the long peroneal muscle that attaches on the medial aspect of the first ray. The long peroneal muscle allows both plantar flexion of the first ray and foot abduction.[17] When there is habitual subtalar pronation, the long peroneal muscle loses its ability to effectively pull the first ray into plantar flexion and tends to adduct the foot. For mechanically effective toe-off to occur, the proximal head of the first ray must be lifted above the cuboid bone by the foot's moving into position of supination. Inadequate supination causes forefoot instability.

The fifth metatarsal bone, like the first metatarsal bone, moves independently. In plantar flexion it moves into adduction and inversion; conversely, in dorsiflexion it moves the foot into abduction and eversion. As with the other segments of the foot, stability of the fifth metatarsal bone depends on the relative position of the subtalar and talonavicular joints.[17]

THE FOOT, ANKLE, AND LOWER LEG AS A LINKAGE SYSTEM

As discussed in Chapter 7 and earlier in this chapter, there are a number of biomechanical factors that may be related to injuries of the lower-leg region. It is important when considering foot, ankle, and leg injuries that these segments are joined together to form a linkage system. With each movement of a body segment there is a direct effect on adjoining and distant body segments.[21] Each motion of the foot, ankle, and lower leg is closely linked with a proximal segment of the knee, hip, pelvis, and spine.[21]

A pathological problem occurring in one segment of the linkage system can produce problems in other segments within the system.[21] An example of this relationship is the gastrocnemius-soleus–Achilles tendon–plantar fascial system. If a muscle or muscles resist stretch, efficient eccentric contraction may be lacking. With this deficiency a sudden stretch occurring within this unit cannot be adequately accommodated and will result in a sudden opposing concentric contraction.[21] As a result, stress is produced on one or more of the muscles comprising the linkage. Injury most often happens to the weakest part of the linkage.[21] As described in Chapter 17, a sudden jerk of the linkage could lead to an acute Achilles tendon strain or rupture, to strain of the plantar fascia, or, if more insidious, to a chronic condition such as night cramps in the calf, Achilles tendinitis, plantar fasciitis (heel spur syndrome), or metatarsalgia (discussed later in this chapter).

FOOT CONDITIONS

Lower extremity stress injuries in sports often begin in the foot. In sports requiring extensive running, injuries can stem from biomechanical and weight transmission difficulties.

Foot Deformities and Structural Deviations
Foot Hypermobility versus Rigidity

The two major foot deformities commonly occurring in sports are those which are nonrigid and rigid.[10] A flexible deformed foot could eventually develop into one that is arthritic and rigid.

The degree the calcaneus is from being vertical and into the valgus, or everted, position indicates the amount of pronation. Calcaneal eversion of 5 to 10 degrees is considered mild-to-moderate flatfeet, and 10 degrees is severe.[10]

A calcaneus that is inverted 5 degrees is associated with a high-arched foot. In the flexible, high-arched foot, pronation will occur beyond the vertical position. However, a foot that is unable to go beyond verticle reflects a moderate-to-severe cavus deformity.[9,10]

Arch Conditions

Painful arches are usually the result of improperly fitting shoes, overweight, excessive activity on hard surfaces, overuse, faulty posture, or fatigue—any of which may cause a pathological condition in the supporting tissue of the arch. The symptoms in these cases are divided into three stages or degrees, each characterized by specific symptoms. The first-degree stage shows itself as a slight soreness in the arch. The second-degree stage is indicated by a chronic inflammatory condition that includes soreness, redness, swelling, and a slight visible drop in the arch. In the third degree a completely fallen arch is accompanied by extreme pain, immobility, and deformity.

Fallen anterior metatarsal arch   Activity on hard surfaces or prolonged stresses on the balls of the feet may cause weak or fallen anterior metatarsal arches (Figure 18-8). When the supporting ligaments and muscles lose their ability to retain the metatarsal heads in a domelike shape, falling of the arch results, thereby placing pressure on the nerves and blood vessels in the area. With this condition the athlete first notices irritation and redness on the ball of the foot. As the condition progresses, pain, callus formation, toe cramping, and often a severe burning sensation develop. Care of fallen anterior metatarsal arch conditions should include hydrotherapy, light friction massage, exercise, and metatarsal pads.

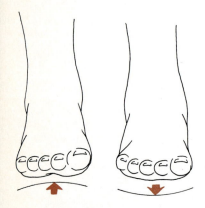

Figure 18-8

Normal metatarsal arch and fallen metatarsal arch.

CARE FOR ARCH CONDITIONS

1. Shoes should be fitted properly.
2. Hydrotherapy, especially a whirlpool, should be given three or four times daily at a temperature of 105° F (40.6° C) until the initial inflammation has subsided.
3. Deep therapy such as ultrasound can be used.
4. Arch orthotics may have to be used to ameliorate irritation of the weakened ligaments. If a pathological condition of the arch can be detected in the first-degree or second-degree stage, arch supports may be needed.
5. Weakened arches, if detected early, can be aided by an exercise program. If the arch is allowed to drop and the condition becomes chronic, exercising can offer little relief other than as a palliative aid.

Fallen medial longitudinal arch (flatfoot)   Various stresses weaken ligaments and muscles that support the arch, thus forcing the navicular bone downward (Figure 18-9). The athlete may complain of tiredness and tenderness in the arch and heel. Ankle sprains frequently result from weakened arches, and abnormal friction sites may develop within the shoe because of changes in weight distribution. This condition may be the result of several factors: shoes that cramp and deform the feet, weakened supportive tissues, overweight, postural anomalies that subject the arches to unaccustomed or unnatural strain, or overuse, which may be the result of repeatedly subjecting the arch to severe pounding through participation on an unyielding surface. Commonly, the fallen medial longitudinal arch is associated with foot pronation (see Figure 18-9).

Test for flexible and rigid flatfeet   The athlete is observed as full weight is borne on a foot and then is removed. A flexible flatfoot is one in which the medial longitudinal arch becomes flattened during weight bearing and produces an obvious arch after removal of that weight. Conversely, a rigid arch remains flat during both weight bearing and non-weight bearing.

Care includes the use of properly fitting shoes that give sufficient support to the arch or permit the normal anatomy of the foot to function, exercise, arch supports, and protective taping. In addition, when there is chronic pain, care should include daily hydrotherapy and friction massage until the inflammation has subsided.

Pes cavus   Pes cavus (Figure 18-10), commonly called clawfoot, hollow foot, or an abnormally high arch, is not as common as pes planus, or flatfeet. In the rigid type of pes cavus, shock absorption is poor and can lead to problems such as general foot pain, metatarsalgia, and clawed or hammer toes. Pes cavus also may be asymptomatic.

The accentuated high medial longitudinal arch may be congenital or indicate a neurological disorder. Commonly associated with this condition are clawed toes and abnormal shortening of the Achilles tendon. The Achilles tendon is directly linked with the plantar fascia (Figure 18-11). Also, because of the abnormal distribution of body weight, heavy calluses develop on the ball and the heel of the foot.

Figure 18-11

The Achilles tendon is directly linked with the plantar fascia. Achilles tendon stretching releases a tight medial longitudinal arch.

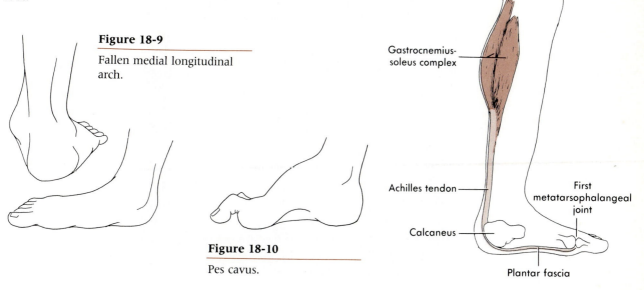

Figure 18-9

Fallen medial longitudinal arch.

Figure 18-10

Pes cavus.

Gastrocnemius-soleus complex

Achilles tendon

Calcaneus

First metatarsophalangeal joint

Plantar fascia

Conditions of the Forefoot, Ball of the Foot, and Toe

A number of deformities and structural deviations affect the forefoot and the ball of the foot. Among those conditions seen in sports are bunions, hallux valgus, bunionettes, sesamoiditis, metatarsalgia, interdigital neuroma, and Morton's syndrome.

Bunions (hallux valgus) and bunionettes (tailor's bunions)   A bunion is one of the most frequent painful deformities of the great toe (Figure 18-12).

ETIOLOGICAL FACTORS   The reasons a bunion develops are complex. Commonly it is associated with a congenital deformity of the first metatarsal head, combined with wearing shoes that are pointed, too narrow, too short, or have high heels. The bursa over the first metatarsophalangeal joint becomes inflamed and eventually thickens. The joint becomes enlarged and the great toe becomes malaligned, moving laterally toward the second toe, sometimes to such an extent that it eventually overlaps it. This type of bunion is also associated with a depressed or flattened transverse arch and a pronated foot.

The bunionette, or tailor's bunion, is much less common than hallux valgus and affects the fifth metatarsophalangeal joint. In this case, the little toe angulates toward the fourth toe.

In all bunions, both the flexor and extensor tendons are malpositioned, creating more angular stress on the joint.

NOTE: Sesamoid fractures and sesamoiditis could be secondary to hallux valgus.

SYMPTOMS AND SIGNS   In the beginning of bunion formation there is tenderness, swelling, and enlargement of the joint. Poor-fitting shoes increase the irri-

Figure 18-12

Mild bunion deformity of the left great toe.

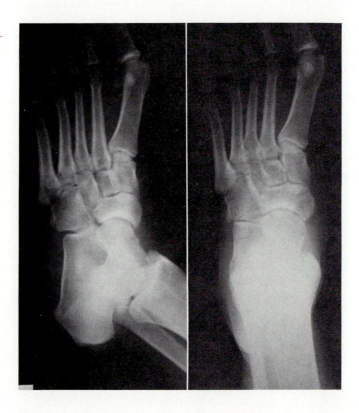

tation and pain. As the inflammation continues, angulation of the toe progresses, eventually leading to instability in the forefoot.

MANAGEMENT Each bunion has unique characteristics. Early recognition and care can often prevent increased irritation and deformity. Following are some management procedures:

1. Wear correctly fitting shoes with a wide toe box.
2. Place a felt or sponge rubber doughnut pad or lamb's wool over the medial side of the joint.
3. Wear a tape splint along with a resilient wedge placed between the great toe and the second toe (see Figure 12-11).
4. Apply thermal therapy or cryotherapy to reduce the inflammation.
5. Engage in daily foot exercises to strengthen both the extensor and flexor muscles.

If the condition progresses, a special orthotic device may help normalize foot mechanics. Surgery might be required in the later stages of this condition.

Sesamoiditis Pain and disability at the ball joint commonly reflect inflammation of the sesamoid bones. As the great toe passively undergoes dorsiflexion, the sesamoid bone becomes compressed upward, causing pain and discomfort.[3] This condition may be caused by roughening on the articular surface of the sesamoid bone or by abnormal pressure upward. Treatment usually includes placement of a doughnut pad around the sesamoid bone, wearing stiff-soled shoes, and, in some cases, a series of steroid injections.

Metatarsalgia Although **metatarsalgia** is a general term to describe pain in the ball of the foot, it is more commonly associated with pain under the second, and sometimes the third, metatarsal head. A heavy callus often forms in the area of pain. Figure 18-13 shows some of the more common pain sites in the foot.

metatarsalgia
A general term to describe pain in the ball of the foot

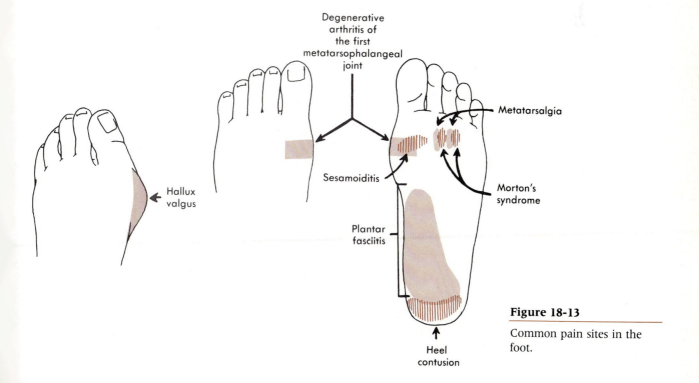

Figure 18-13

Common pain sites in the foot.

ETIOLOGICAL FACTORS One of the prevalent causes of metatarsalgia is restricted extensibility of the gastrocnemius-soleus system. Because of this restriction, the athlete shortens the midstance phase of the gait and emphasizes the toe-off phase, causing an excessive pressure under the forefoot.[7] This excess pressure over time causes a heavy callus to form in this region. As the forefoot bears weight, normal skin becomes pinched against the inelastic callus and produces pain.

Another cause of metatarsalgia is a fallen metatarsal arch. Normally the heads of the first and fifth metatarsal bones bear slightly more weight than the heads of second, third, and fourth metatarsal bones. The first metatarsal head bears two sixths of the body weight, the fifth bears slightly more than one sixth, and the second, third, and fourth bear one sixth. If the foot tends toward pronation or if the intermetatarsal ligaments are weak, allowing the foot to spread abnormally (splayed foot), occurrence of a fallen metatarsal arch is probable (Figure 18-14). As the transverse arch becomes flattened and the heads of the second, third, and fourth metatarsal bones become depressed, pain can result. A cavus deformity can also cause metatarsalgia.

MANAGEMENT Management of metatarsalgia usually consists of applying a pad to elevate the depressed metatarsal heads. **NOTE:** The pad is placed behind and not under the metatarsal heads (Figure 18-15). In severe cases a metatarsal bar may be applied (Figure 18-16). Abnormal callus buildup should be removed by paring or filing.

In an athlete in whom the etiology of metatarsalgia is primarily a gastrocnemius-soleus contracture, a regimen of static stretching should be performed several times per day. When his or her metatarsal arch is depressed as a result of weakness, a daily regimen of exercise should be practiced, concentrating on strengthening flexor and intrinsic muscles and stretching the Achilles tendon. A Thomas heel (Figure 18-17), which elevates the medial aspect of the heel from ⅛ to 3/16 inch (0.3 to 0.47 cm), also could prove beneficial.

METATARSAL PAD SUPPORT

The purpose of the metatarsal pad is to reestablish the normal relationships of the metatarsal bones. It can be purchased commercially or constructed out of felt or sponge rubber (Figure 18-18).

MATERIALS NEEDED: One roll of 1-inch tape (2.5 cm), a ⅛-inch (0.3 cm) adhesive felt oval cut to a 2-inch (5 cm) circumference, and tape adherent.

POSITION OF THE ATHLETE: The athlete sits on a table or chair with the plantar surface of the affected foot turned upward.

POSITION OF THE OPERATOR: The operator stands facing the plantar aspect of the athlete's foot.

PROCEDURE
1. The circular pad is placed just behind the metatarsal heads.
2. Approximately two or three circular strips of tape are placed loosely around the pad and foot.

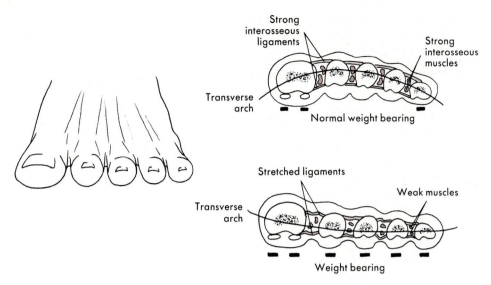

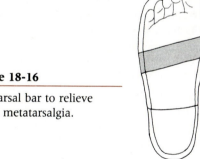

Figure 18-14

Normal weight bearing of the forefoot and abnormal spread (splayed foot).

Figure 18-15

Pad to elevate depressed metatarsal heads.

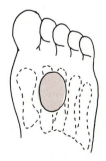

Figure 18-16

Metatarsal bar to relieve severe metatarsalgia.

Figure 18-17

The Thomas heel elevates the medial aspect of the calcaneus ⅛ to 3/16 inch (0.3 to 0.47 cm), which can help relieve pronation and metatarsalgia.

Figure 18-18

Metatarsal pad.

neuroma

A tumor that emanates from
a nerve.

Interdigital neuroma   Interdigital nerves travel between the metatarsal bones to innervate the toes. An interdigital **neuroma** emanates from and entraps the nerves. It usually involves the third plantar interdigital nerve, which innervates the third and fourth toes. Commonly, the interdigital neuroma causes swelling approximately ¾ inch (1.9 cm) long between the third and fourth distal metatarsal heads (Figure 18-19).

ETIOLOGICAL FACTORS   The interdigital nerves become entrapped between the metatarsal heads. This condition is more common among female athletes and is associated with the pronated foot and splayed toes.

SYMPTOMS AND SIGNS   The athlete complains of severe intermittent pain in the region of the nerve impingement. The pain radiates from the distal metatarsal heads to the tips of the toes and is often relieved when no weight is borne and the shoe is removed. During palpation between the distal metatarsal heads, radiating pain may be duplicated, and the tumor may be felt. Sometimes the skin between the metatarsal heads is numb.

MANAGEMENT   Conservative treatment of an interdigital neuroma includes the following:

1. Broad-toed shoe
2. Transverse arch support
3. Metatarsal bar
4. Foot orthotics
5. Injection of lidocaine and steroids

If conservative treatment is ineffective, surgical excision may provide complete relief.

Morton's syndrome   Another foot deformity causing major forefoot pain is Morton's syndrome. Metatarsalgia is produced by an abnormally short first metatarsal bone. Weight is borne mainly by the second metatarsal bone, and there is hypermobility between the first and second proximal metatarsal joints (Figure 18-20). The management is the same as that for foot pronation.

Toe Deformities

Hallux rigidus   Hallus rigidus is a painful condition caused by fusion or partial fusion of the first metatarsophalangeal joint. The great toe is unable to dorsiflex, causing the athlete to toe-off on the second, third, fourth, and fifth toes. Walking becomes awkward. Often, with complete fusion, pain disappears.

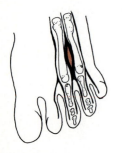

Figure 18-19

Interdigital neuroma.

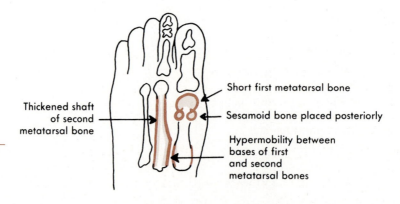

Thickened shaft
of second
metatarsal bone

Short first metatarsal bone

Sesamoid bone placed posteriorly

Hypermobility between
bases of first
and second
metatarsal bones

Figure 18-20

Morton's syndrome with an
abnormally short first
metatarsal bone.

Management usually includes placing a pad under the first metatarsal bone to prevent great toe dorsiflexion. A metatarsal bar on the shoe may help to avoid increasing the joint's irritation. Surgery may be the only means of recovering function.

Hammer or clawed toes   Hammer or clawed toes may be congenital, but more often the conditions are caused by wearing shoes that are too short over a long period of time, thus cramping the toes. Hammer toe usually involves the second or third toe, whereas clawed toes involve more than one toe. In both conditions the metatarsophalangeal and proximal interphalangeal joints become malaligned, along with overly contracted flexor tendons and overly stretched extensor tendons. Such deformities eventually result in the formation of hard corns or calluses on the exposed joints. Quite often surgery is the only cure. However, wearing proper shoes and using protective taping (see Figure 12-9) can help prevent irritation.

Figure 18-21

Overlapping toes.

Overlapping toes   Overlapping of the toes (Figure 18-21) may be congenital or may be brought about by improperly fitting footwear, particularly shoes that are too narrow. At times the condition indicates an outward projection of the great toe articulation or a drop in the longitudinal or metatarsal arch. As in the case of hammer toes, surgery is the only cure, but some therapeutic modalities such as a whirlpool bath can assist in alleviating inflammation. Taping may prevent some of the contractural tension within the sport shoe.

Chronic and Overuse Syndromes

Because of the hard use that feet receive in many sports, they are prone to chronic and overuse syndromes. This is especially true if weight-transmission or biomechanical problems exist. Because distance running is becoming increasingly popular, musculoskeletal problems of the feet are also becoming more prevalent.

Exostoses

Exostoses are benign bony outgrowths that protrude from the surface of a bone and are usually capped by cartilage. Sometimes called spurs, such outgrowths occur principally at the head of the first metatarsal bone on the dorsum of the foot (Figure 18-22). In certain instances, what may at first appear to be an exostosis actually may be a subluxation of the joints between the metatarsal and cuneiform bones. The causes of exostoses are highly variable, including hereditary influences, faulty patterns of walking and running, excessive weight, joint impingements, and continual use of ill-fitting footwear.

exostoses

Benign bony outgrowths that protrude from the surface of a bone and that are usually capped by cartilage.

Impingement exostoses   Impingement, one of the causes of exostoses, occurs when a joint is continually forced beyond the ranges of normal motion so that actual contact is effected by the bones comprising the joint. Continual contact creates inflammation and irritation, eventually activating formation of new bone, which builds up to such a degree that the bones contact each other. Extreme dorsiflexion, such as when the foot is at the end of the support period immediately before the forward-carry, may cause exostoses to form on the anterior articular lip of the tibia and the top of the talus as a consequence of the impingement.

SYMPTOMS AND SIGNS   Pain and tenderness are usually present, and performance is impaired, especially when the foot is in extreme dorsiflexion. This pain is usually apparent at the anterior aspect of the joint and may be severe enough to weaken the drive from the foot as it thrusts against the ground in the push-off, resulting in a loss of drive and speed.

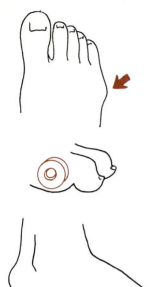

Figure 18-22

Exostoses (bony overgrowths). X-ray film of a
small plantar calcaneal exostotic spur.

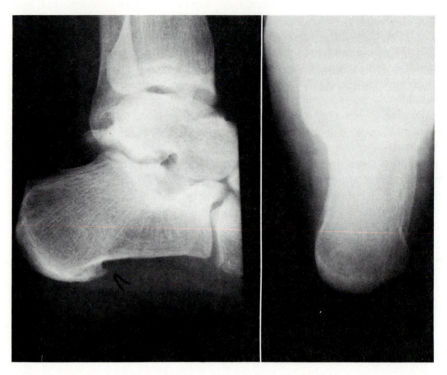

MANAGEMENT Some impingement spurring conditions are asymptomatic and
obviously require no treatment. For cases of impingement that are symptomatic,
surgery may be warranted to allow continued sports participation.[16]

Chronic irritation exostoses Poorly fitting shoes or a chronic irritation
may also predispose an area to exostoses, which usually appear either at the head
of the fifth metatarsal bone or as a calcaneal spur. If an exostosis becomes chronically irritated or disabling, surgery may be necessary. Sometimes protective
doughnuts and custom-made pads provide relief.

Postcalcaneal Bursitis (Retrocalcaneal Bursitis)

Figure 18-23

Postcalcaneal bursitis.

A common bursitis of the foot is postcalcaneal bursitis, which is located under the
skin just above the attachment of the Achilles tendon (Figure 18-23). It often
occurs because of pressure and rubbing by the upper edge of a sports shoe. Irritation produces an inflamed, swollen area. At the first sign of this condition a soft
resilient pad should be placed over the bursal site. If necessary, larger shoes with
a softer heel contour should be worn.

Apophysitis of the Calcaneus (Sever's Disease)

apophysitis
Inflammation of an
apophysis.

Calcaneal **apophysitis,** or Sever's disease, is one of the many osteochondroses
occurring to physically active athletes who are physically immature. This condi-

tion can be compared to Osgood-Schlatter disease. Instead of the tibial tubercle, Sever's disease is a traction-type injury at the epiphysis of an **apophysis** (bone protrusion) where the Achilles tendon attaches to the calcaneus. As with other such conditions, circulation to the epiphysis is disrupted, causing degeneration and sometimes fragmentation.

SYMPTOMS AND SIGNS   Pain occurs at the posterior heel below the attachment of the Achilles tendon insertion of the child or adolescent athlete. Pain occurs during vigorous activity and does not continue at rest.

MANAGEMENT   This condition is usually completely resolved when the apophysis closes. Until such time, relief can be provided by restricting dorsiflexion of the foot, which can be accomplished by elevating both heels with a ¼-inch (0.6 cm) lift. Commonly, rest for several weeks will relieve the symptoms so that activity can be resumed. However, when symptoms do not resolve, a walking cast may be needed for 6 to 8 weeks.

Plantar Fasciitis (Heel Spur Syndrome)

As a major support of the longitudinal arch, the plantar fascia biomechanically acts as a "bowstring."[13] Another chronic problem commonly associated with a resistance to stretch of the gastrocnemius-soleus–Achilles tendon–plantar fascial system is plantar fasciitis. This condition is the most frequent hind-foot problem among distance runners.[20]

A number of anatomical and biomechanical conditions have been studied as possible causes of plantar fasciitis. They include leg length inequality, greater pronation of the subtalar joint, inflexibility of the longitudinal arch, as well as tightness of the gastrocnemius-soleus unit.[22] Training shoes, stride length, and running surfaces have also been linked to this condition. To date, no one factor has been clearly delineated as a cause of plantar fasciitis.[22]

SYMPTOMS AND SIGNS   The athlete complains of anterior heel pain. During palpation the pain is usually localized on the plantar medial tuberosity of the calcaneus, radiating toward the sole of the foot. Often the pain intensifies when the athlete gets out of bed in the morning and first puts weight on the foot; however, the pain lessens after a few steps.[20] Pain also will be intensified when the toes and forefoot are forcibly dorsiflexed.

MANAGEMENT   Management of this condition follows the same procedures as for a chronic foot strain, including longitudinal arch support or LowDye arch support (see Figure 12-7). Of major importance is a vigorous regimen of Achilles tendon stretching, especially if the athlete's ankle cannot dosiflex 10 to 15 degrees from a neutral position. Stretching should be conducted at least three times a day in the positions of straight-ahead, toe-in, and toe-out. Techniques for stretching should follow the procedures discussed on pp. 511-513. The athlete should wear a shoe that is not too stiff and has a heel that is elevated ½ to ¾ inch (1.3 to 1.9 cm) above the level of the sole.[20] An oral anti-inflammatory medication or one injection of a corticosteroid may be used.

Cuboid Subluxation

Approximately 4% of athletes with plantar foot pain have cuboid syndrome. It is associated with a pronated foot, which causes a subluxation of the cuboid bone. The problem usually occurs in the early season after training on uneven surfaces or after a sudden twist of the foot. The pain is localized on the lateral side of the foot in the region of the cuboid bone. The primary reason for pain is the stress

apophysis

Bony outgrowth such as a tubercle or tuberosity.

placed on the long peroneal muscle when the foot is in pronation. In this position, the long-peroneal muscle allows the cuboid bone to move medially downward.

Management of the cuboid syndrome involves manipulating the bone into a correct position, rest, and application of an arch pad and tape support or an orthotic device. The physician will reduce the subluxation by dorsiflexing the ankle while plantar flexing the forefoot.

Stress Fractures of the Foot

More than 18% of all stress fractures in the body occur in the foot.

Metatarsal stress fracture   The most common stress fracture in the foot involves one or more metatarsal shafts. A fracture occurs most commonly to the second or third metatarsal bone (Figure 18-24). It occurs in the runner who has suddenly changed patterns of training such as increasing mileage, running hills, or running on a harder surface.

An athlete who has an atypical condition such as hallux valgus, flatfoot, or a short first metatarsal bone is more easily disposed toward incurring a stress fracture than is the individual whose foot is free of pathological or mechanical defects. A short first metatarsal bone is mechanically unable to make use of its strength and position to distribute the weight properly to the front part of the foot. Therefore excessive pressure and additional weight are transferred to the

Figure 18-24

Stress fractures of the third metatarsal bone.

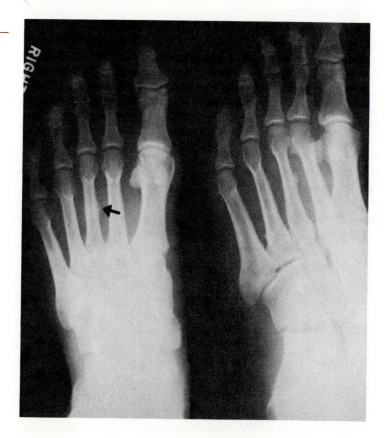

second metatarsal bone, resulting in traumatic changes and, on occasion, fracture. An x-ray examination may not detect this condition, requiring a bone scan to be performed.

Management of the painful metatarsal stress fracture usually consists of 3 or 4 days of crutch walking or wearing a short-leg walking cast for 1 to 2 weeks. Once the symptoms have significantly subsided, the athlete may resume weight bearing while walking. Shoes with firm soles should be worn. Tape support and therapy for swelling and tenderness should be given.

Running should not be resumed for 3 to 4 weeks, with intensity and/or mileage increased slowly. A more intense day should alternate with an easy day. The athlete must avoid toe running until bone tenderness is gone. Running should only be done on a soft, flat surface.

Calcaneal stress fracture   One of the bones of the foot known to develop stress fractures is the calcaneus. A calcaneal stress fracture is most prevalent among distance runners and is characterized by a sudden onset of constant pain in the plantar-calcaneal area. Pressure on the plantar-calcaneal tuberosity causes severe pain. The fracture fails to appear during x-ray examination for 4 to 6 weeks. Management is usually conservative for the first 2 or 3 weeks and includes rest, elastic wrap compression, elevation, and active range-of-motion exercises of the foot and ankle.[20] After 3 weeks and when pain subsides, activity within pain limits can be resumed gradually, with the athlete wearing a cushioned shoe.[20]

Hypertrophy of the second metatarsal bone   Milers and other distance runners who have engaged in strenuous athletic training and conditioning over a considerable span of time often suffer from hypertrophy of the second metatarsal bone. It is believed that the condition is caused by the strong thrust of the ball of the foot against the running surface during the pushing-off phase. As the foot begins its thrust, it is in a position of extreme dorsiflexion, usually with the center of gravity passing through or just forward of the ball of the foot. The extensor muscles of the foot and ankle bring maximum pressure to bear on the heads of the metatarsal bones. The resulting forces place great stress on this area; consequently, the second metatarsal bone, which receives a considerable share of the force, tends to enlarge or hypertrophy. This response illustrates the structure-function principle.

Chronic Ankle Tendon Conditions

Achilles tendinitis   Covering the Achilles tendon is a paratendon, which consists of fatty and areolar tissue that surrounds the tendon and fills the spaces around it. A jerk movement in the gastrocnemius-soleus system in which eccentric contraction is inefficient leads to microtears. Over time repeated injury leads to chronic-inflammation tissue degeneration. Sudden concentration of this system that was previously engaged in an eccentric contraction can lead to an Achilles tendon rupture.[22]

In chronic cases of Achilles tendinitis, mucoid nodules occur as a result of tissue degeneration. They must be surgically removed for healing to occur.

Other etiological factors are training errors such as hill running, increased mileage, intensive training sessions, and running on uneven surfaces.[7] Wearing a shoe that fails to stabilize the heel adequately, malalignment of the tibia vara, tight hamstrings, and cavus feet, as well as tightness of the gastrocnemius-soleus unit, can predispose an athlete to Achilles tendinitis.[7,13]

SYMPTOMS AND SIGNS   Achilles tendinitis is usually indicated by pain, swelling, crepitation, erythemia, weakness, restricted motion, and point tenderness.

MANAGEMENT   Management of Achilles tendinitis is initially conservative and includes using ice, gentle stretching, nonsteroidal anti-inflammatory medication, and rest. Runners must increase mileage and avoid hills and uneven surfaces. Foot alignment may be corrected by an orthotic device. A flexible shoe with a molded Achilles pad can be used to prevent irritation, and a 10 to 15 mm heel lift can be used to decrease tendon excursion.[7] In cases in which there is chronic degeneration, nodules may have to be surgically excised and defects repaired. Surgery is followed by placement in a short leg cast for 3 to 6 weeks, after which there is a gradual resumption of normal activities.

Achilles tendon bursitis   Achilles tendon bursitis usually occurs from over-stretching the Achilles tendon, resulting in constant inflammation of the Achilles bursa. This condition is chronic, developing gradually over a long period of time, and takes many days—sometimes weeks and even months—to heal properly. An excellent therapeutic approach is continued application of heat in as many forms as possible, especially through penetrating therapy such as ultrasound. All activity should be held to a minimum, and heel lifts should be placed in the shoes to relieve the Achilles tendon of as much tension as possible. After a workout, the tendon should be cooled with ice packs or ice massage. Static heel cord stretching is an excellent adjunct to heat therapy.

Peroneal tendon subluxation   The long and short peroneal tendons pass through a common groove located behind the lateral malleolus. The tendon is held in place by the peroneal retinaculum. A moderate-to-severe inversion sprain or forceful dorsiflexion of the ankle can tear the peroneal retinaculum, allowing the peroneal tendon to tear out of its groove. A common source of this injury is an athlete's suddenly stepping into a hole, forcing the foot into dorsiflexion and eversion.[8]

SYMPTOMS AND SIGNS   The athlete complains that in running or jumping the tendons snap out of the groove and then back in when stress is released. Eversion against manual resistance will often replicate the subluxation. The athlete experiences recurrent pain, snapping, and ankle instability.

MANAGEMENT   A conservative approach should be used first, including compression with a felt pad cut in a horseshoe-shaped pattern that surrounds the lateral malleolus. This compression can be reinforced with a rigid plastic or plaster splint until acute signs have subsided.[18] The time period for this conservative care is 5 to 6 weeks, followed by a gradual exercise rehabilitation program. If a conservative approach fails, surgery will be required.

Anterior tibial tendinitis   Anterior tibial tendinitis is a common condition of athletes or joggers who run downhill for an extended period of time. There is point tenderness over the anterior tibial tendon.

The athlete should be advised to rest or at least decrease the running time and distance and to avoid hills. In more serious cases ice packs, coupled with stretching before and after running, should help reduce the symptoms. A daily strengthening program also should be conducted. Oral anti-inflammatory medications may be required.

Posterior tibial tendinitis   Posterior tibial tendinitis is a common overuse condition among runners with hypermobility or pathologically pronated feet. As discussed previously, one of the major functions of the posterior tibial muscle is

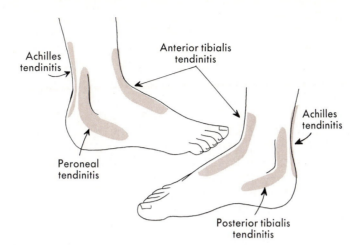

Figure 18-25

Common tendinitis of the foot and ankle region.

to pull the first metatarsal bone into plantar flexion. When there is major foot pronation of hypermobility, the posterior tibial tendon becomes overly stressed in its efforts to stabilize the first metatarsal bone.

Management consists of correcting the problem of pronation with a LowDye-type taping (see Figure 12-7) or an orthotic device. Measures such as rest or reducing the running distance should be taken to reduce the inflammation. Ice applications before and after activity, coupled with stretching, should reduce the symptoms. A daily strengthening routine should be engaged. Anti-inflammatory medication might be prescribed in more serious cases.

Peroneal tendinitis   Although not particularly common, peroneal tendinitis can be a problem in athletes with pes cavus. Because in pes cavus the foot tends to be placed in constant supination, which is resisted by the peroneal tendon, chronic inflammation can arise. Athletes who constantly bear weight on the outside of the foot also place chronic stress on the peroneal tendon.

As with all types of tendinitis in the lower extremities, the mechanics of walking and running should be observed. When faulty mechanics such as running on the outside of the foot occur, realignment with an orthotic device or taping should be used. In some cases a lateral heel wedge may help to reduce pain and discomfort. As with the other ankle tendons that are overused, the athlete with peroneal tendinitis should reduce activity, use ice routinely, and stretch and strengthen the tendon through eversion exercise (Figure 18-25).

REPETITIVE AND OVERUSE LEG PROBLEMS

A number of problems of the leg can be attributed to repetitive use and overuse. Three of these conditions are the medial tibial syndrome (shin-splints), exercise-induced compartment compression syndromes, and stress fractures.

Medial Tibial Syndrome

Medial tibial syndrome (shin-splints) is a general term applied to a variety of conditions that seasonally plague many athletes. It accounts for approximately 10% to 15% of all running injuries and up to 60% of all conditions that cause pain in athletes' legs.[2] It is characterized by pain and irritation in the shin region of the leg and is usually attributed to an inflammation localized primarily in the tendon of the posterior tibial muscle or long flexor muscles of the toes. How or why inflammation is produced in this area is often a mystery. It has been believed that chronic medial shin pain was a compartment syndrome; however, recent studies have discounted this view. Speculations advanced about the cause include faulty posture alignment, falling arches, muscle fatigue, overuse stress, body chemical imbalance, or a lack of proper reciprocal muscle coordination between the anterior and posterior aspects of the leg. All these factors, in various combinations or singly, may contribute to medial tibial syndrome.[6]

The pathological process of this condition is regarded as a myositis or periostitis that occurs either acutely, as in preseason preparation, or chronically, developing slowly throughout the entire competitive season. One should approach this situation through deductive thinking. First, all information about why a certain athlete may have acquired shin-splints must be gathered—examples include changing from a hard gymnasium floor activity to a soft field sport or exhibiting general fatigue after a strenuous season. Second, the athlete should be examined for possible structural body weaknesses. From this information an empirical analysis can be made as to the probable cause of shin-splints. However, persistent shin irritation and incapacitation must be referred to the physician for thorough examination. Conditions such as stress fractures, muscle herniations, or acute anterior tibial compartment syndromes (a severe swelling within the anterior fascia chamber) may resemble the symptoms of shin-splints. A number of authorities believe that shin-splints involve one of two syndromes: a tibial stress fracture or an overuse syndrome that can progress to an irreversible, exertional compartment syndrome.[4]

SYMPTOMS AND SIGNS   Four grades of pain can be attributed to medial tibial syndrome: grade I pain occurring after athletic activity; grade II pain occurring before and after activity but not affecting performance; grade III pain occurring before, during, and after athletic activity and affecting performance; and grade IV pain, so severe that performance is impossible.

MANAGEMENT   Management of medial tibial syndrome is as varied as its etiology. Constant heat in the form of whirlpools and ultrasound therapy give positive results and, together with supportive taping and gradual stretching, afford a good general approach to the problem. Phonophoresis and iontophoresis also have been effective.[19]

Ice massage to the shin region and taking two aspirins have been beneficial before a workout. Ice massage is applied for 10 minutes or until erythema occurs. Ice application should be followed by a gradual stretch to both the anterior and posterior aspects of the leg directly after the massage. Gradual stretching should be a routine procedure before and after physical activity for all athletes who have a history of shin-splints. Exercise must also accompany any therapy program, with special considerations of the calf muscle and the plantar and dorsiflexion movements of the foot. Use of taping is questionable but is used by some athletic trainers (see Figure 12-17).

Exercise-Induced Compartment Compression Syndromes

As discussed in Chapter 17, the leg is composed of four compartments. Each compartment is bound by fascial sheaths or by fascial sheaths and bone (see Figure 17-38). The anterior compartment contains the anterior tibial muscle, deep peroneal nerve, long extensor muscles of the toes, and both the anterior tibial artery and vein. The lateral compartment is composed of the superficial peroneal nerve and the long and short and peroneal muscles. Posteriorally, the leg has a deep and superficial compartment. The deep posterior compartment comprises the tibial muscle and flexor muscles of the toes, as well as the peroneal artery and vein, posterior tibial artery and vein, and tibial nerve. The superficial posterior compartment is composed of the soleus muscle and gastrocnemius and plantar tendons.

The exercise-induced compartment compression syndrome occurs most frequently among runners and athletes in sports such as soccer, which involve extensive running. The compartments most often affected are the anterior and deep posterior, with the anterior having by far the highest incidence. On occasion, the lateral compartment may be involved.

The compartment compression syndrome occurs when the tissue fluid pressure has increased because the confines of fascia and/or bone adversely compress muscles, blood vessels, and nerves. With the increase in fluid pressure, muscle ischemia that could lead to permanent disability occurs.[15]

> Exercise-induced compartment compression syndromes occur most commonly in runners and soccer players.

The exercise-induced compartment compression syndrome is classified as either acute or chronic or recurrent. The first type is an acute syndrome and is a medical emergency, requiring immediate decompression to prevent permanent damage. The acute exercise-induced compartment compression syndrome resembles a fracture or a severe contusion.

The second type is chronic or recurrent. Internal pressures rise slowly during exercise and subside after discontinuance of exercise. If exercise is not stopped in time, an acute emergency may occur. In chronic exercise-induced compartment compression syndrome, there is a constriction of blood vessels, producing ischemia and pain, but seldom neurological involvement.

Chronic Exertional Compartment Syndrome

The chronic exertional compartment syndrome is often confused by the coach or athletic trainer with shin-splints. It may also be confused with a stress fracture.

SYMPTOMS AND SIGNS The athlete commonly complains of an ache or sharp pain and pressure in the region of the anterior compartment when performing a particular activity.[23] The symptoms subside or go away completely when resting. When major symptoms are present, weakness in foot and toe extension and numbness in the dorsal region may occur.[15]

MANAGEMENT Often initial symptoms are aided by the application of ice and rest. However, recurrent conditions may require surgical release of the associated fascia. Once surgery is performed, the athlete is allowed to return home and begin a light program of exercise in 10 days.[1,5]

Stress Fracture of the Tibia or Fibula

Stress fractures to the tibia or fibula are a common overuse stress condition, especially among distance runners. Like many other overuse syndromes, athletes who have biomechanical foot problems are more prone to stress fractures of the lower leg. Athletes who have hypermobile pronated feet are more susceptible to fibular stress fracture, whereas those with rigid pes cavus are more prone to tibial stress fractures.[12] Runners frequently develop a stress fracture in the lower third of the leg; ballet dancers more commonly acquire one in the middle third.[8] Com-

> The athlete with hypermobile pronated feet is more susceptible to fibular stress fracture. The athlete with rigid pes cavus is more susceptible to tibial stress fractures.

MANAGEMENT PLAN FOR MEDIAL TIBIAL STRESS SYNDROME (SHIN-SPLINTS)

Injury Situation A female college field hockey player at the end of the competitive season began to feel severe discomfort in the medial aspect of the right shin.

Symptoms and Signs The athlete complained that her shin seemed to ache all the time but became more intense after practice or a game. During palpation there was severe point tenderness approximately 2 inches (5 cm) in length, beginning 4½ inches (11.25 cm) from the tip of the medial malleolus. The pain was the most severe along the medial posterior edge of the tibia. Further evaluation showed that the athlete had pronated feet. X-ray examination showed no indication of stress fracture; therefore, the injury was considered medial shin stress syndrome, or shin-splints, involving the long flexor muscle of the great toe and the posterior tibial muscle.

Management Plan

1

Management Phase	GOAL: To almost completely reduce pain and point tenderness ESTIMATED LENGTH OF TIME (ELT): 1 to 2 weeks
Therapy	IMMEDIATE CARE: Ice pack (5 to 15 min) or ice massage (7 min) followed by stretching three or four times daily LowDye taping or orthotic device is applied to the arch to correct pronation during weight bearing (see Chapter 12) (p 32_0)
Exercise Rehabilitation	Static stretch of Achilles tendon and anterior part of low leg; hold stretch 30 sec (two or three times); repeat set three or four times daily General body maintenance exercises are conducted if they do not aggravate injury, three times weekly

2

Management Phase	GOAL: Symptom free ELT: 1 week
Therapy	FOLLOW-UP CARE: Ice pack (5 to 15 min) or ice massage (7 min) and/or ultrasound (0.5 to 0.75 watts/cm^2) (5 to 10 min) two or three times daily Continue to wear arch taping or orthotic device when bearing weight.
Exercise Rehabilitation	Static stretch of lower leg followed by arch and plantar flexion exercises Towel gather (10 repetitions, one to three sets); progress from no resistance to 10 lb resistance, three times daily Towel scoop (10 repetitions, one to three sets); progress to 10 lb, three times daily Marble pickup, three times daily General body maintenance exercises are conducted if they do not aggravate injury, three times weekly

3	Management Phase	GOAL: To return to jogging ELT: 1 to 2 weeks
	Therapy	Cold application (5 to 15 min) to shin when stretching before jogging and after jogging, once daily
	Exercise Rehabilitation	Perform static stretch of lower leg before and after running, once daily Walk/jog on flat surface and avoid banked or crowned surfaces, once daily Athlete must cease activity immediately if any shin symptoms are felt
4	Management Phase	GOAL: To return to running ELT: 1 week
	Therapy	Cold applications (5 to 15 min) before prerun stretch and again after running, once daily
	Exercise Rehabilitation	Resume training: walk 1 mile in 15 min; then walk and jog to 8-min pace, once daily Resume running; try to run in toe-in manner
5	Management Phase	GOAL: Return to full-field hockey activity ELT: 1 to 2 weeks
	Therapy	Athlete practices cryokinetics before and after practice, once daily
	Exercise Rehabilitation	Athlete engages in full leg, strength, and endurance training along with reentry skill practice, once daily

Criteria for Returning to Competitive Field Hockey

1. Leg is symptom free after prolonged running.
2. The medial longitudinal arch has been strengthened along with correction of foot pronation through taping or an orthotic device.

monly, this type of stress fracture occurs to nonexperienced and nonconditioned runners.[11]

SYMPTOMS AND SIGNS The athlete complains of pain in the leg that is more intense during activity but relieved when resting. There is usually point tenderness, but it may be difficult to discern the difference between bone pain and soft-tissue pain. One technique for distinguishing bone pain from soft-tissue pain is bone percussion. The fibula or tibia is tapped firmly above the level of tenderness. Vibration travels along the bone to the fracture, which may respond with pain. Another percussive technique is to hit the heel upward from below; pain occurs at the fracture site.

Diagnosis of a stress fracture may be extremely difficult. X-ray examination may or may not detect a bone defect. A bone scan 1 to 3 hours after injection of radioactive material may reflect the stress fracture but does not clearly distinguish between a fracture or periostitis.

MANAGEMENT The following regimen may be used for a stress fracture of the leg:

1. Discontinue running or other stressful locomotor activities for at least 6 weeks.
2. When pain is severe, use crutch walking or wear a cast.
3. Weight bearing may be resumed as pain subsides.
4. Bicycling may be used before returning to running.
5. After at least 6 weeks and a pain-free period for at least 2 weeks, running can begin again.[3]
6. Biomechanical foot correction should be made.

RELATED PROBLEMS

Although lower-extremity stress injuries are usually concentrated in the foot, ankle, or leg, other body areas also can become involved. This is especially true for long-distance runners. Repetitive use and overuse of the lower extremity, particularly when there are biomechanical and subsequent weight-transmission discrepancies, can lead to problems in other regions of the body. Some of the more prevalent areas are the knee and hip.

The Knee

A common site for distance runners to have a stress problem is in the region of the knee. In some cases there may be chronic pain and swelling in the knee joint itself, possibly indicating a meniscal tear or degenerative articular cartilage changes. More commonly, the cause is patellar tendonitis, chondromalacia, iliotibial band tendinitis, or pes anserinus tendinitis (see Chapter 19).

The Thigh and Hip

As with the knee, the thigh and hip can sustain painful conditions that are attributed to overuse. Two conditions are on the rise in incidence because of the popularity of running. They are trochanteric bursitis and hamstring strain.

Running can place a strain on the middle gluteal muscles and the iliotibial band. When the athlete is in the stand phase, the middle gluteal muscle contracts to stabilize the pelvis. A leg-length discrepancy places additional stress on the hip that may cause the middle gluteal muscle to irritate the trochanteric bursa. The iliotibial band crossing the trochanter of the femur also can cause bursal irritation (see Chapter 20).[3]

The hamstring muscles can be adversely irritated by running. After contraction of the quadriceps muscles at heel-strike, the hamstring muscle contracts. If there is a significant difference in strength between the quadriceps muscle and the hamstring muscle or the athlete overstrides, forcing the hamstring to repeatedly contract from an extreme length, injury may occur (see Chapter 20).

Other injuries arising from the repetitive running motion are adductor groin strains or inflammation of the pubis symphysis (osteitis pubis). A foot-strike that is too wide from the center line or a pelvis that abducts excessively can lead to chronic adductor strain or osteitis pubis (see Chapter 20).

Running despite constant pain is foolish. Major problems such as stress or avulsion fractures may be present. Any continuous pain over a period of time should be referred for x-ray or bone scan examination.

A running foot-strike that is too wide can lead to chronic adductor strain or osteitis pubis.

SUMMARY

To more fully understand chronic and overuse stress injuries in the foot, ankle, and lower leg, foot biomechanics must be understood. There must also be an understanding of the foot, ankle, and lower leg as part of a linkage system.

Chronic and overuse foot conditions can lead to stress problems in the lower extremities. Common chronic problems occur to the arches of the foot, toes, and forefoot. The bunion, a common chronic condition, occurs when the great toe becomes deflected laterally. Metatarsalgia also is a chronic condition of the forefoot. Other problems include deformities such as hammer or clawed toes, bony outgrowths, heel bursitis, heel spurs, tendinitis, and stress fractures.

Chronic ankle conditions include Achilles tendinitis and Achilles tendon bursitis. Peroneal tendon subluxation and tendinitis of the anterior tibial, posterior tibial, and peroneal tendons are relatively common among athletes.

Overuse leg problems are common among athletes who engage in repetitive activities over a long period of time. Examples of these conditions are medial tibial syndrome (shinsplints), exercise-induced compartment compression syndromes, and various stress fractures of the lower leg. When there is body weight-transmission discrepancies, overuse problems can also occur to other regions of the body such as the knee, thigh, and hip.

REVIEW QUESTIONS AND CLASS ACTIVITIES

1. How does the foot function during the gait cycle?
2. The foot, ankle, and lower leg act as a linkage system. How can this fact explain an overuse injury?
3. What are the most common foot deformities? How do they occur?
4. Describe where and why exostoses occur in the foot region.
5. Compare postcalcaneal bursitis to apophysitis of the calcaneus in terms of symptoms and signs.
6. What are the possible causes of plantar fasciitis (heel spur syndrome)?
7. Discuss where and why stress fractures occur in the foot.
8. What major overuse tendon problems are associated with the ankle?
9. Describe chronic exertional problems that can occur to the lower leg.
10. How may chronic problems of the foot, ankle, or lower leg be transmitted to the knee, thigh, and hip?

REFERENCES

1. Balduini, FC: Compartment syndromes, Postgraduate advances in sports medicine, II-V, Berryville, Va, 1987, Forum Medicus, Inc.
2. Bates, P: Shinsplints: a literature review, Br J Sports Med 19:132, Sept 1985.
3. Birnbaum, JS: The musculoskeletal manual, New York, 1982, Academic Press, Inc.
4. Davey, JR: "Overuse" shinsplints, Sports Med Dig 7(10):1, 1985.
5. Detmer, DE, et al.: Chronic compartment syndrome: diagnosis, management, and outcomes, Am J Sports Med 13:162, May-June 1985.
6. Ekstrom, M: Lower-leg pain can stop athletes in their tracks, The First Aider 56(5):1, 1987.
7. Frey, CC, and Shereff, MJ: Tendon injuries about the ankle. In Yocum, LA, editor: Foot and ankle injuries, Clinics in sports medicine, vol 7, no 1, Philadelphia, 1988, WB Saunders Co.
8. Friedman, MJ: Injuries to the leg in athletes. In Nicholas, JA, and Hershman, EB, editors: The lower extremity and spine in sports medicine, vol 1, St. Louis, 1986, The CV Mosby Co.
9. Halback, J: Pronated foot disorders, Ath Train 16:53, Spring 1981.
10. Hoerner, EF: Foot and ankle injuries. In Vinger, PF, and Hoerner, EF: Sports injuries: the unthwarted epidemic, Boston, 1982, John Wright, PSG, Inc.
11. Jones, DC, and James, SL: Overuse injuries of the lower extremity: shin splints, iliotibial band friction syndrome, and exertional compartment syndromes. In Hunter-Griffin, LY, editor: Overuse injuries, Clinics in sports medicine, vol 6, no 2, Philadelphia, 1987, WB Saunders Co.
12. Kulund, DN: The injured athlete, Philadelphia, 1982, JB Lippincott Co.
13. Leach, RE, and Schepsis, AA: Achilles tendinitis, Postgraduate advances in sports medicine, I-VIII, Pennington, NJ, 1986, Forum Medicus, Inc.
14. Mann, RA: Biomechanics of running. In Mack, RP, editor: Symposium on the foot and leg in running, American Academy of Orthopaedic Surgeons, St. Louis, 1982, The CV Mosby Co.
15. Mubarak, S, and Hargens, A: Exertional compartment syndromes. In Mack, RP, editor: Symposium on the foot and leg in running sports, American Academy of Orthopaedic Surgeons, St. Louis, 1982, The CV Mosby Co.
16. O'Donoghue, DH: Treatment of injuries to athletes, ed 4, Philadelphia, 1984, WB Saunders Co.
17. Parks, RM: Biomechanics of the foot and lower extremity. In Appenzeller, O, and Atkinson, R, editors: Sports medicine, Baltimore, 1981, Urban & Schwarzenberg, Inc.
18. Singer, KM, and Jones, DC: Soft tissue conditions of the ankle and foot. In Nicholas, JA, and Hershman, EB, editors: The lower extremity and spine in sports medicine, vol 1, no 2, St. Louis, 1986, The CV Mosby Co.
19. Smith, W, et al.: Comparative study using four modalities in shinsplint trreatments, J Orthop Sports Phys Ther 8:77, 1986.
20. Waller, JF: Hindfoot and midfoot problems of the runner. In Mack, RP, editor: Symposium on the foot and leg in running sports, American Academy of Orthopaedic Surgeons, St. Louis, 1982, The CV Mosby Co.
21. Waller, JF, and Moddalo, A: The foot and ankle linkage system. In Nicholas, JA, and Hershman, EB, editors: The lower extremity and spine in sports medicine, vol 1, St. Louis, 1986, The CV Mosby Co.
22. Warren, BL, and Jones, CJ: Predicting plantar fasciitis in runners, Med Sci Sports Exerc 19:71, 1987.
23. Wiley, JP, et al.: A primary care perspective of chronic compartment syndrome of the leg, Phys Sportsmed 15(3):111, 1987.

ANNOTATED BIBLIOGRAPHY

Nicholas, JA, and Hershman, EB, editors: The lower extremity and spine in sports medicine, vols 1 and 2, St. Louis, 1986, The CV Mosby Co.

Present excellent articles about basic science, rehabilitation, regional injuries, the immature athlete, and sport specific injuries.

Nigg, BM: Biomechanics of running shoes, Champaign, Ill, 1986, Human Kinetics Publishers.

Describes the biomechanics of running, running shoe design and construction, and how to select a proper running shoe.

Yocum, LA, editor: Foot and ankle injuries, Clinics in sports medicine, vol 7, no 1, Philadelphia, 1988, WB Saunders Co.

This second of two editions (the first was dated March, 1982), provides a good overview of the major factors related to foot and ankle injuries and covers the current techniques in assessment and treatment of major injuries.

CHAPTER 19

The Knee and Related Structures

When you finish this chapter, you should be able to

Describe the normal structural and functional knee anatomy and relate it to major sports injuries

Assess the knee and related structures following injury

Establish a knee injury prevention program

Discuss etiological factors, symptoms and signs, and management procedures for the major knee joint conditions and related structures

Muscles and ligaments provide the main source of stability in the knee.

The knee is considered one of the most complex joints in the human body. Because so many sports place extreme stress on the knee, it is also one of the most traumatized joints. The knee, commonly considered a hinge joint (ginglymus), performs two principal actions, flexion and extension. Medial and lateral rotations of the tibia are possible but only to a limited degree. Since the knee is extremely weak in terms of its bony arrangement, compensation is provided through the support of ligaments and muscles (Figure 19-1). The knee is designed primarily to provide stability in weight bearing and mobility in locomotion; however, it is especially unstable laterally and medially (Figure 19-2).

ANATOMY
Structural Relationships

The distal end of the femur expands and forms the convex *lateral* and *medial condyles*, which are designed to articulate with the tibia and the patella. The articular surface of the medial condyle is longer from front to back than is the surface of the lateral condyle. Anteriorly, the two condyles from a hollowed area to receive the patella. The upper end of the tibia, designed to receive the condyles of the femur, consists of two *tuberosities,* which are divided posteriorly by a groove called the popliteal notch. Superiorly, the tuberosities have two shallow concavities that articulate with their respective femoral condyles. Separating these concavities, or articular facets, is a roughened area where the cruciate ligaments attach and from which a process commonly known as the tibial spine arises. The *patella* is the largest sesamoid bone in the body and lies within the tendon of the

Figure 19-1

The bony and ligamentous arrangement of the knee.

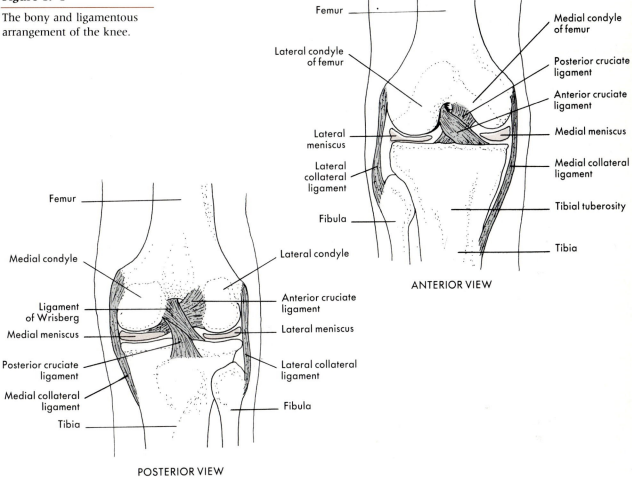

ANTERIOR VIEW

POSTERIOR VIEW

Figure 19-2

The knee is a highly complicated joint that is often traumatized during competitive sports.

quadriceps muscles. Its function is to give anterior protection to the knee joint and increased leverage to the knee on extension. All the articular surfaces of the femur, tibia, and patella are covered by *hyaline cartilage,* a smooth and pearly substance that serves mainly to reduce friction.

Articulations

The knee joint consists of several articulations: between the two femoral condyles and menisci, between the tibia and menisci, and between the patella and femur. The condyles of the femur move in a shallow depression formed by the tibia and additionally deepened by two semilunar cartilages (menisci).

Menisci

The *menisci* (Figure 19-3) are two oval-shaped (semilunar) fibrocartilages that deepen the articular facets of the tibia and cushion any stresses placed on the knee joint. The consistency of the menisci is much like that of the intervertebral disks. They are located medially and laterally on the tibial tuberosity. The menisci transmit one half of the contact force in the medial compartment and even a higher percentage of the contact load in the lateral compartment. The menisci help to stabilize the knee, especially the medial meniscus, when the knee is flexed at 90 degrees.

Medial meniscus   The medial meniscus is a C-shaped fibrocartilage, the circumference of which is attached firmly to the medial articular facet of the tibia and to the joint capsule by the coronary ligament. Posteriorly, it is also attached to fibers of the semimembranous muscle.

Lateral meniscus   The *lateral meniscus* forms an almost complete O and is attached to the lateral articular facet on the superior aspect of the tibia. The lateral meniscus also attaches loosely to the lateral articular capsule and to the popliteal tendon. The *Wrisberg ligament* is the part of the lateral meniscus that projects upward, close to the attachment of the posterior or cruciate ligament. The *transverse ligament* joins the anterior portions of the lateral and medial menisci.

Meniscal blood supply   Blood is supplied to each meniscus by the medial genicular artery. Although the menisci are, for the most part, **avascular,** the outer third does receive direct circulation. The inner two thirds of the menisci receive nourishment from being bathed by synovial fluid (see Figures 19-3 and 19-8).

Stabilizing Ligaments

The major ligaments of the knee, primarily the cruciate, capsular, and collateral, are secondary to the musculature in providing joint stability.

The cruciate ligaments   The *cruciate ligaments* account for a considerable amount of knee stability. They are two ligamentous bands that cross one another within the joint cavity of the knee. The *anterior cruciate ligament* attaches below and in front of the tibia; then, passing backward, it attaches laterally to the inner surface of the lateral condyle. The *posterior cruciate ligament,* the stronger of the two and primary stabilizer of the knee, crosses from the back of the tibia in an upward, forward, and medial direction and attaches to the anterior portion of the lateral surface of the medial condyle of the femur.

The anterior cruciate ligament   The anterior cruciate ligament comprises three twisted sections: the anteromedial, intermediate, and posterolateral sections.

Generally the meniscus has a poor blood supply.

avascular
Devoid of blood circulation.

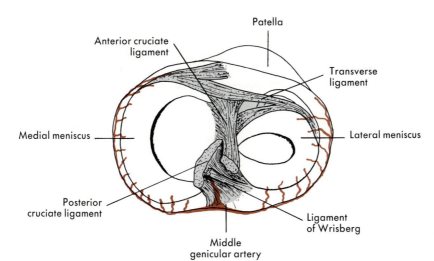

Anterior cruciate
ligament

Patella

Transverse
ligament

Medial meniscus

Lateral meniscus

Posterior
cruciate ligament

Ligament
of Wrisberg

Middle
genicular artery

Figure 19-3

Menisci of the knee.

In general, the anterior cruciate ligament prevents the femur from moving posteriorly during weight bearing. It also stabilizes the tibia against abnormal internal and external rotation.

When the knee is fully extended, the anteromedial section of the cruciate ligament is tight. In flexion the anteromedial fibers loosen and the posterolateral fibers tighten.[22] The anterior cruciate ligament works in conjunction with the thigh muscles, especially the hamstring muscle group, to stabilize the knee joint.[30]

The posterior cruciate ligament Some portion of the posterior cruciate ligament is taut throughout the full range of motion. It acts as a drag during the gliding phase of motion and resists internal rotation of the tibia. In general, the posterior cruciate ligament prevents hyperextension of the knee and femur, sliding forward during weight bearing.

Capsular and collateral ligaments Additional stabilization is provided the knee by the capsular and collateral ligaments. Besides stability, they also direct movement in a correct path. Although they move in synchrony, they are divided into the medial and lateral complexes.

Medial collateral ligament The superficial position of the medial (tibial) collateral ligament is separate from the deeper capsular ligament at the joint line. It attaches above on the medial epicondyle of the femur and below on the tibia, just beneath the attachment of the pes anserinus. The posterior aspect of the ligament blends into the deep posterior capsular ligament and semimembranous muscle. Fibers of the semimembranous muscle go through the capsule and attach to the posterior aspect of the medial meniscus, pulling it backward during knee flexion. Some of its fibers are taut through flexion and extension. Its major purpose is to prevent the knee from valgus and external rotating forces. The medial collateral ligament was thought to be the principal stabilizer of the knee in a valgus position when combined with rotation. It is now known that other structures such as the anterior cruciate ligament play an equal or greater part in this function.[18]

Deep medial capsular ligaments The deep medial capsular ligament is divided into three parts: the anterior, medial, and posterior capsular ligaments. The *ante-*

rior capsular ligament connects with the extension mechanism and the medial meniscus through the coronary ligament. It relaxes during knee extension and tightens during knee flexion. The primary purposes of the *medial capsular ligaments* are to attach the medial meniscus to the femur and to allow the tibia to move on the meniscus inferiorly. The *posterior capsular ligament* is sometimes called the posterior oblique ligament and attaches to the posterior medial aspect of the meniscus and intersperses with the semimembranous muscle.

Lateral collateral ligament and related structures   The lateral (fibular) collateral ligament is a round, fibrous cord shaped like a pencil. It is attached to the lateral epicondyle of the femur and to the head of the fibula. The lateral collateral ligament is taut during knee extension but relaxed during flexion.

Another stabilizing ligament of importance is the *arcuate ligament.* It is formed by a thickening of the lateral articular capsule. Its posterior aspect attaches to the fascia of the popliteal muscle and the posterior horn of the lateral meniscus.

Other structures that stabilize the knee laterally are the iliotibial band, popliteal muscle, and biceps muscle of the thigh. The iliotibial band, stemming from the tensor muscle of the fascia lata, attaches to the lateral epicondyle of the femur and lateral tibial tubercle (Gerdy's tubercle). It becomes tense during both extension and flexion. The popliteal muscle stabilizes the knee during flexion and, when contracting, protects the lateral meniscus by pulling it posteriorly.

The biceps muscle of the thigh also stabilizes the knee laterally by inserting into the fibular head, iliotibial band, and capsule.

Synovial Membrane and Bursae

The synovial membrane lines all of the articular surfaces and is internal to the cruciate ligaments. It is a highly vascularized, tubelike tissue, that extends upward along the anterior aspect of the femur and forms the suprapatellar bursa (Figure 19-4).

Bursae are protective synovia-filled sacs located in tissue sites that otherwise would become irritated because of friction (Figure 19-5). The knee has at least 11 bursae situated at points where friction is highly probable:

1. Suprapatellar
2. Popliteal
3. Medial gastrocnemius
4. Prepatellar
5. Superficial infrapatellar
6. Infrapatellar
7. Between the semimembranous and gastrocnemius muscles
8. Between the semimembranous muscle and tibial condyle
9. Between the lateral collateral ligament and biceps femoris muscle of the thigh
10. Between the medial collateral ligament and biceps femoris muscle of the thigh
11. Between the medial collateral ligament and pes anserinus

Patella

The patella is the largest sesamoid bone in the human body. It is located in the tendon of the quadriceps femoris muscle and is divided into three medial facets and a lateral facet that articulate with the femur (Figure 19-6). The lateral aspect

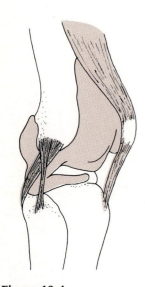

Figure 19-4

Synovial membrane of the knee.

Figure 19-5

Common bursae of the knee.

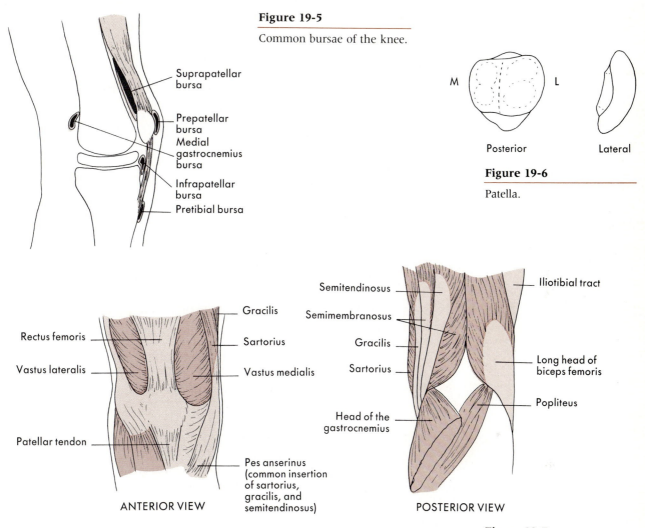

- Suprapatellar bursa
- Prepatellar bursa
- Medial gastrocnemius bursa
- Infrapatellar bursa
- Pretibial bursa

M — Posterior — L

Lateral

Figure 19-6

Patella.

POSTERIOR VIEW

- Semitendinosus
- Semimembranosus
- Gracilis
- Sartorius
- Head of the gastrocnemius
- Iliotibial tract
- Long head of biceps femoris
- Popliteus

ANTERIOR VIEW

- Rectus femoris
- Vastus lateralis
- Patellar tendon
- Gracilis
- Sartorius
- Vastus medialis
- Pes anserinus (common insertion of sartorius, gracilis, and semitendinosus)

Figure 19-7

Musculature of the knee.

of the patella is wider than the medial aspect. The patella articulates between the concavity provided by the femoral condyles. Tracking within this groove depends on the pull of the quadriceps muscle, infrapatellar ligament, depth of the femoral condyles, and shape of the patella.

Knee Musculature

For the knee to function properly, a number of muscles must work together in a highly complex fashion. The following is a list of knee actions and the muscles that initiate them (Figure 19-7):

1. Knee flexion is executed by the biceps muscle of the thigh, semitendinous, semimembranous, gracilis, sartorius, gastrocnemius, popliteal, and plantar muscles.
2. Knee extension is executed by the quadriceps muscle of the thigh, consisting of three vasti—the vastus medialis, vastus lateralis, and vastus intermedius—and by the rectus femoris.

Major actions of the knee
  Flexion
  Extension
  Gliding
  Rotation

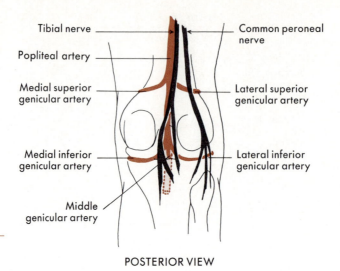

Tibial nerve ——————— Common peroneal nerve

Popliteal artery

Medial superior genicular artery ——————— Lateral superior genicular artery

Medial inferior genicular artery ——————— Lateral inferior genicular artery

Middle genicular artery

POSTERIOR VIEW

Figure 19-8

Blood and nerve supply to the knee.

3. Outward rotation of the tibia is controlled by the biceps muscle of the thigh; the anterior cruciate ligament and the quadriceps also control external rotation.
4. Inward rotation is accomplished by the popliteal, semitendinous, semimembranous, sartorius, and gracilis muscles. Rotation of the tibia is limited and can occur only when the knee is in a flexed position.

Blood and Nerve Supply

The main blood supply of the knee consists of the popliteal artery, which stems from the femoral artery. From the popliteal artery, five branches supply the knee: the medial and lateral superior genicular, middle genicular, and medial and lateral inferior genicular arteries. The primary nerves supplying the knee are the tibial and common peroneal nerves (Figure 19-8).

Functional Anatomy

The primary actions of the knee are flexion, extension, gliding, and rotation. Secondary movements consist of a slight internal (medial) and external (lateral) rotation of the tibia. The movements of flexion and extension take place above the menisci, whereas rotation is performed below the menisci. Rotation is caused mainly by the greater length of the medial condyle of the femur, which rolls forward more than does the lateral condyle.

The capsular ligaments are taut during full extension and to some extent relaxed during flexion. This is particularly true of the lateral collateral ligament; however, portions of the medial collateral ligament relax as flexion occurs. Relaxation of the more superficial collateral ligaments allows rotation to occur. In contrast, the deeper capsular ligament tightens to prevent excessive rotation of the tibia.

During extension there is external rotation of the tibia during the last 15 degrees of which the anterior cruciate ligament unwinds. In full extension the anterior cruciate ligament is taut, and it loosens during flexion. As the femur glides on the tibia, the posterior cruciate ligament becomes taut and prevents further gliding. In general, the anterior cruciate ligament stops excessive external rotation, stabilizes the knee in full extension, and prevents hyperextension. The posterior cruciate ligament prevents internal rotation, guides the knee in flexion, and acts as a drag during the initial glide phase of flexion.

In complete flexion, approximately 140 degrees, the range of the knee movement is limited by the extremely shortened position of the hamstring muscles, the extensibility of the quadriceps muscles, and the bulk of the hamstring muscles. In this position the femoral condyles rest on their corresponding menisci at a point that permits a small degree of inward rotation.[14]

The patella aids the knee during extension by lengthening the lever arm of the quadriceps muscle. It distributes the compressive stresses on the femur by increasing the contact area between the patellar tendon and the femur.[28] It also protects the patellar tendon against friction. During full extension the patella lies slightly lateral and proximal to the trochlea.[26] At 20 degrees of knee flexion there is tibial rotation, and the patella moves into the trochlea. At 30 degrees the patella is most prominent. At 30 degrees and more the patella moves deeper into the trochlea. At 90 degrees the patella again becomes positioned laterally.[26] When knee flexion is 135 degrees, the patella has moved laterally beyond the trochlea.

Knee Linkage System

As is true of other areas of the body, the knee is part of a linkage system. It is directly affected by the foot, ankle, and lower leg. The muscles that contribute to the capsular insertion have their origin, in part, in the region of the pelvis and hip joint.[7] Injuries to hamstring, rectus femoris, hip abductor, and hip extensor muscles limit hip movement and also place excessive stress on the knee joint.[7] Postural malalignment such as in athletes with lordosis, scoliosis, or leg length discrepancies must also be considered.[7]

ASSESSING THE KNEE JOINT

It is the responsibility of the team physician to diagnose the severity and exact nature of a knee injury. Although the physician is charged with the final evaluation, the coach or athletic trainer is usually the first person to observe the injury; therefore he or she is charged with initial evaluation and immediate care. The most important aspect of understanding what pathological process has taken place is to become familiar with the traumatic sequence and mechanisms of injury, either through having seen the injury occur or through learning its history (Figure 19-9). Often the team physician is not present when the injury occurs, and the athletic trainer must relate the pertinent information.[19]

Major Complaints

To determine the history and major complaints involved in a knee injury, the following questions should be asked

Current Injury

1. What were you doing when the knee was hurt?
2. What position was your body in?
3. Did the knee collapse?

Figure 19-9

It is extremely important to understand the sequence and mechanism of the knee injury before the pathological process can be understood.

4. Did you hear a noise or feel any sensation at the time of injury, such as a pop or crunch? (A pop could indicate an anterior cruciate tear, a crunch could be a sign of a torn meniscus, and a tearing sensation might indicate a capsular tear.)

5. Could you move the knee immediately after the injury? If not, was it locked in a bent or extended position? (Locking could mean a meniscal tear.) After being locked, how did it become unlocked?

6. Did swelling occur? If yes, was it immediate, or did it occur later? (Immediate swelling could indicate a cruciate or tibial fracture, whereas later swelling could indicate a capsular, synovial, or meniscal tear.)

7. Where was the pain? Was it local, all over, or did it move from one side of the knee to the other?

8. Have you hurt the knee before?

When first studying the injury, the athletic trainer or coach should observe whether the athlete is able to support body weight flatfootedly on the injured leg or whether it is necessary to stand and walk on the toes. Toe walking is an indication that the athlete is holding the knee in a splinted position to avoid pain or that the knee is being held in a flexed position by a wedge of dislocated meniscus. In first-time acute knee sprains, fluid and blood effusion is not usually apparent until after a 24-hour period. However, in an anterior cruciate ligament sprain or hemarthrosis it may occur during the first hour after injury. Swelling and ecchymosis will occur unless the effusion is arrested through the use of compression and cold packs.

Recurrent or Chronic Injury

1. What is your major complaint?
2. When did you first notice the condition?
3. Is there recurrent swelling?
4. Does the knee ever lock or catch? (If yes, it may be a torn meniscus or a loose body in the knee joint.)
5. Is there severe pain? Is it constant, or does it come and go?
6. Do you feel any grinding or grating sensations? (If yes, it could indicate chondromalacia or traumatic arthritis.)
7. Does your knee ever feel like it is going to give way or has it actually done so? (If yes and often, it may be a capsular, cruciate, or meniscal tear, a loose body, or a subluxating patella.)
8. What does it feel like to go up and down stairs? (Pain may indicate a patellar irritation or meniscal tear.)
9. What past treatment, if any, have you received for this condition?

Observation

If possible, the athlete with an injured knee should be observed in the following actions
Walking
Half-squatting
Going up and down stairs

A visual examination should be performed after the major complaints have been determined. The athlete should be observed in a number of situations: walking, half-squatting, and going up and down stairs. The leg also should be observed for alignment and symmetry or asymmetry.

Walking

1. Does the athlete walk with a limp, or is the walk free and easy? Is the athlete able to fully extend the knee during heel-strike?

2. Can the athlete fully bear weight on the affected leg?
3. Is the athlete able to perform a half-squat to extension?
4. Can the athlete go up and down stairs with ease? (If stairs are unavailable, stepping up on a box or stool will suffice.)

Leg Alignment

The athlete should be observed for leg alignment. Anteriorly, the athlete is evaluated for genu valgus, genu varum, and the position of the patella. Next, the athlete is observed from the side to ascertain conditions such as the hyperflexed or hyperextended knee.

Deviations in normal leg alignment may or may not be a factor in knee injury but should always be considered as a possible cause. As with any other body segment, leg alignment differs from person to person; however, obvious discrepancies could predispose the athlete to an acute or chronic injury.

Anteriorly, with the knees extended as much as possible, the following points should be noted:

1. Are the kneecaps level with each other?
2. Are the kneecaps facing forward?
3. Can the athlete touch the medial femoral condyles and medial malleoli?

Looking at the athlete's knees from the side:

1. Are the knees fully extended with only slight hyperextension?
2. Are both knees equally extended?

Leg alignment deviations that may predispose to injury Four major leg deviations could adversely affect the knee and patellofemoral joints: patellar malalignment, genu valgum (knock-knees), genu varum (bowlegs), and genu recurvatum (hyperextended knees).

Patellar malalignment Kneecaps that are rotated inward or outward from the center may be caused by a complex set of circumstances. For example, a combination of genu recurvatum, genu varum, and internal rotation, or anteversion, of the hip and internal rotation of the tibia could cause the kneecap to face inward. Interal rotation of the hip also may be associated with knock-knees, along with external rotation of the tibia, or tibial torsion. Athletes who toe-out when they walk may have an externally rotated hip, or retroversion. The normal angulation of the femoral neck after 8 years of age is 15 degrees; an increase of this angle is considered anteversion, and a decrease is considered retroversion. If an abnormal angulation seems to be a factor in a kneecap, malalignment or tibial torsion angles should be measured.

MEASURING FOR TIBIAL TORSION, FEMORAL ANTEVERSION AND RETROVERSION Tibial torsion is determined by having the athlete kneel on a stool with the foot relaxed. An imaginary line is drawn along the center of the thigh and lower leg, bisecting the middle of the heel and the bottom of the foot. Another line starts at the center of the middle toe and crosses the center of the heel. The angle formed by the two lines is measured (Figure 19-10); an angle measuring more or less than 15 degrees is a sign of tibial torsion.

Femoral anteversion or retroversion can be determined by the number of degrees the thigh rotates in each direction. As a rule, external rotation and internal rotation added together equal close to 100 degrees. If internal rotation exceeds 70 degrees, there may be anteversion of the hip.[5]

Hyperextension of the knee may result in internal rotation of the femur and

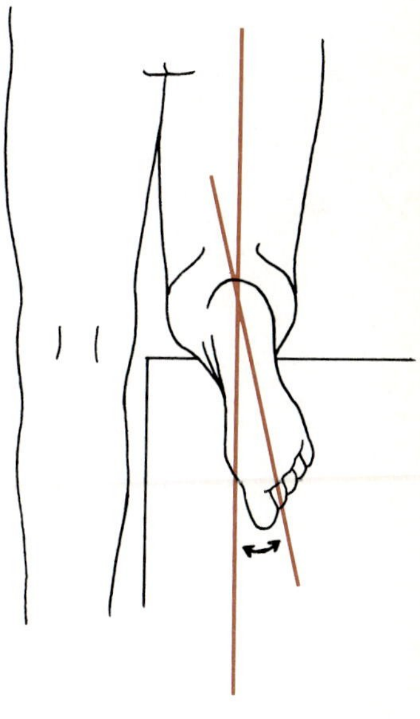

Figure 19-10

Measuring for tibial torsion.

external rotation of the tibia. The primary muscle that allows rotation in the lower leg is the posterior popliteal muscle, which normally rotates the lower leg inward on the femur. If there is posterior muscle weakness resulting in chronic knee hyperextension, the lower leg may be allowed to rotate outward on the femur. Internal rotation at the hip is caused by weak external rotator muscles or from foot pronation.

Genu valgum   The cause of genu valgum, or knock-knees, can be multiple. Normally, toddlers and very young children display knock-knees. When the legs have strengthened and the feet have become positioned more in line with the pelvis, the condition is usually corrected; however, obesity may prevent proper leg alignment from taking place. Commonly associated with knock-knees are pronated feet. Genu valgum places chronic tension on the ligamentous structures of the medial part of the knee, abnormal compression of the lateral aspect of the knee surface, and abnormal tightness of the iliotibial band. One or both legs may be affected, along with a weakening of the hip's external rotator muscles.

Genu varum   The two types of genu varum, or bowlegs, are structural and functional. The structural type, which is seldom seen in athletes, reflects a deviation of the femur and tibia. The more common functional, or postural, type usually is associated with knees that are hyperextended and femurs that are internally rotated. Quite often when genu recurvatum is corrected, so is genu varum.

Genu recurvatum   Genu recurvatum, or hyperextended knees, commonly occurs as a compensation for lordosis, or swayback. There is notable weakness and stretching of the hamstring muscles. Chronic hyperextension can produce undue anterior pressure on the knee joint and posterior ligaments and tendons.

Knee Symmetry or Asymmetry

The athletic trainer must establish whether both of the athlete's knees look the same:

1. Do the knees appear symmetrical?
2. Is one knee obviously swollen?
3. Is muscle atrophy apparent?

Leg-Length Discrepancy

Discrepancies in leg length can cause lateral tipping of the pelvis with some minor spinal curvature. In the nonactive person such discrepancies may not cause symptoms; however, in the physically active person a short leg could lead to problems of the entire lower limb, including the knee joint (p. 639).[23]

Bony Palpation

The bony structures of the knee are palpated for pain and deformities that might indicate a fracture or dislocation. The athlete sits on the edge of the training table or a bench. With the athlete's knee flexed to 90 degrees, the athletic trainer palpates the following bony structures:

Medial Aspect

1. Medial tibial plateau
2. Tibial tubercle
3. Medial femoral condyle
4. Adductor tubercle

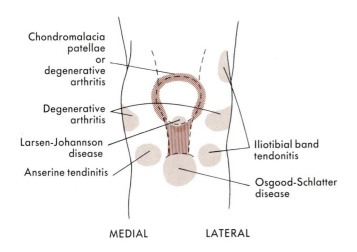

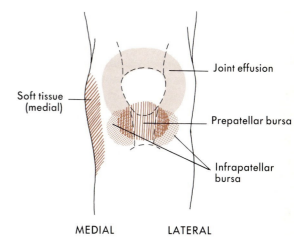

Figure 19-11 (Left)

Typical pain sites around the knee.

Figure 19-12 (Right)

Typical swelling sites around the knee.

Lateral Aspect

1. Lateral tibial plateau
2. Lateral tubercle
3. Lateral femoral condyle
4. Lateral epicondyle
5. Head of the fibula

Patella

1. Superior aspect
2. Around periphery with the knee relaxed
3. Around periphery with the knee in full extension

Capsular and Ligamentous Tissue Palpation

After palpation of the bony structures, the supportive structures should be palpated for pain and defects (Figure 19-11). The palpation sequence is the anterior capsule, lateral collateral ligament, and medial collateral ligament and capsular structures. Capsular tissue should be palpated at the joint line where most tears occur.

Soft-Tissue Palpation

Soft tissue around the knee should be palpated for symmetry of definition, defects of continuity indicating rupture or tears, and specific pain sites. Systematically the quadriceps muscle; patellar tendon; sartorius, gracilis, semitendinosus, and semimembranosus muscles; biceps tendon of the thigh; iliotibial band; popliteal fossa; popliteal muscle; and head of the gastrocnemius muscle should be felt for pain and defects.

Swelling Palpation

Of major importance to knee inspection and evaluation is palpating for joint effusion (Figure 19-12). Swelling caused by synovia or by blood in the joint, or **hemarthrosis,** must be determined. Blood in the knee joint feels heavy and moves like jelly, whereas synovial effusion feels light and, when pushed, runs easily back and forth.

hemarthrosis
Blood in a joint cavity.

Tests for Knee Ligament Stability

Both acute and chronic injury to the knee can produce ligamentous instability. It is advisable that the injured knee's stability be evaluated as soon after injury as possible. However, tests of this type should be performed only by well-trained professionals. The injured knee and uninjured knee are tested and contrasted to determine any differences in their stability.

Valgus and Varus Stress Tests

Valgus and varus stress tests are intended to reveal laxity of the medial and lateral stabilizing complexes, especially the collateral ligaments. The athlete lies supine with the leg extended. To test the medial side, the examiner holds the ankle firmly with one hand, while placing the other over the head of the fibula. The examiner then places a force inward in an attempt to open the side of the knee. This valgus stress is applied with the knee fully extended or at 0 degrees and at 15 degrees of flexion (Figure 19-13, *A*). The examiner reverses hand positions and tests the lateral side with a varus force on the fully extended knee and then with 30 degrees of flexion (Figure 19-13, *B*). **NOTE:** The hip must not be allowed to rotate during the test.

Cruciate Ligament Tests

A number of tests are currently being used to establish the integrity of the cruciate ligaments. They are the drawer test at 90 degrees of flexion, Lachman drawer test, and pivot-shift test.

Drawer test at 90 degrees of flexion   The athlete lies on the training table with the injured leg flexed, while the operator, facing the anterior aspect of the

Figure 19-13

Valgus and varus knee stress tests. **A,** Valgus. **B,** Varus.

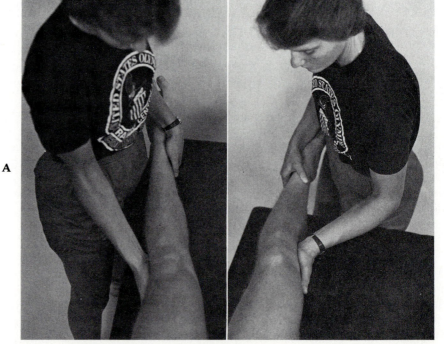

A   B

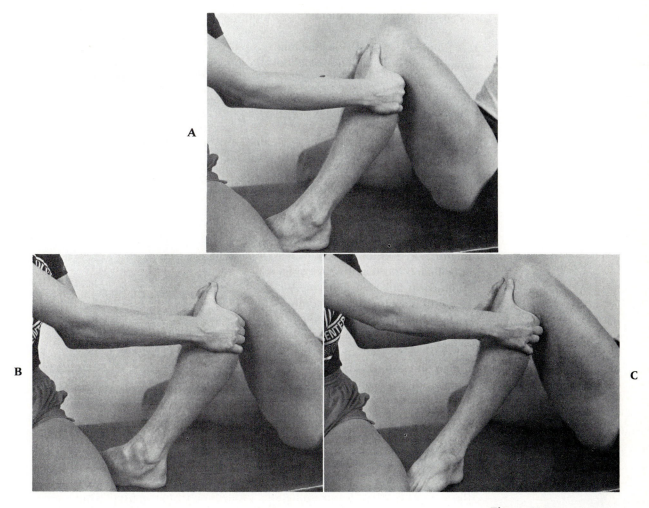

Figure 19-14

Drawer test for cruciate laxity. **A,** Knee at 90 degrees, with the foot pointing straight. **B,** Knee at 90 degrees, with the leg internally rotated. **C,** Knee at 90 degrees, with the leg externally rotated.

athlete's leg, encircles the upper portion of the leg, immediately below the knee joint, with both hands. The fingers of the tester are positioned in the popliteal space of the affected leg, with the thumbs on the medial and lateral joint lines (Figure 19-14, *A*). The index fingers of the tester are placed on the hamstring tendon to ensure that it is relaxed before the test is administered. The tibia's sliding forward from under the femur is considered a positive anterior drawer sign; conversely, the tibia's sliding backward is a positive posterior drawer sign.[15] If a positive anterior drawer sign occurs, the test should be repeated with the athlete's leg rotated internally 20 degrees and externally 15 degrees (Figure 19-14, *B* and *C*). Sliding forward of the tibia when the leg is externally rotated is an indication that the posteromedial aspect of the joint capsule, the anterior cruciate ligament, or possibly the medial collateral ligament could be torn. Movement when the leg is internally rotated indicates that the anterior cruciate ligament and posterolateral capsule may be torn.

The posterior cruciate ligament is tested in the same way as the anterior cruciate ligament but with the tibia moving posteriorly. A normal anterior shear is 5

Figure 19-15

A, Lachman drawer test for cruciate laxity. **B,** Alternate method.

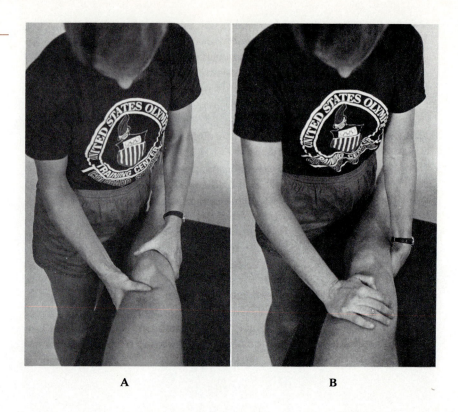

A

B

Figure 19-16

Pivot-shift test for antero-lateral rotary instability.

mm. Cailliet[8] indicates that shears of ½ inch, ½ to ¾ inch, and ¾ inch or more (1.3 cm, 1.3 to 1.9 cm, and 1.9 cm or more) correspond to one, two, and three degrees respectively.

Lachman drawer test   In recent years the Lachman drawer test has become preferred by many over the drawer test at 90 degrees of flexion (Figure 19-15). This is especially true for examinations immediately after injury.[20] One reason for using it immediately after an injury is that it does not force the knee into the painful 90-degree position, but tests it at a more comfortable 15 degrees. Another reason for its increased popularity is that it reduces the contraction of the hamstring muscles. The contraction causes a secondary knee stabilizing force that tends to mask the real extent of injury.[31] The Lachman drawer test is administered by positioning the knee in approximately 15 degrees of flexion, with the leg externally rotated. One hand of the examiner stabilizes the leg by grasping the distal end of the thigh, and the other hand graps the proximal aspect of the tibia, attempting to move it anteriorly.

Pivot-shift test   The pivot-shift test is designed to determine anterolateral rotary instability (Figure 19-16). It is most often used in chronic conditions and is a sensitive test when the anterior cruciate ligament has been torn. The athlete lies supine; one hand of the examiner is pressed against the head of the fibula, and the other hand grasps the athlete's ankle. To start, the lower leg is internally rotated and the knee is fully extended. The thigh is then flexed 30 degrees at the hip while the knee is also flexed, and a valgus force is applied by the examiner's upper hand. If there is anterior cruciate instability, a palpable shift will be felt, or a pop will be heard in the early stages of flexion.

Instrument assessment of cruciate ligament   As discussed previously, evaluating cruciate laxity can be very subjective. Increasingly, objective measures are being developed. One such device is the MED Metric's Knee Ligament Arthrometer. It is portable as well as accurate and reliable.[33]

Meniscal Tests

Determining a torn meniscus often can be difficult. The three most commonly used tests are the McMurray test, the Apley compression test, and the Apley distraction test.

The McMurray meniscal test   The McMurray test (Figure 19-17) is used to determine the presence of loose bodies within the knee. The athlete is positioned face up on the table, with the injured leg fully flexed. The examiner places one hand on the foot and one hand over the top of the knee, fingers touching the medial joint line. The ankle hand scribes a small circle and pulls the leg into extension. As this occurs, the hand on the knee feels for a "clicking" response. Medial meniscal tears can be detected when the lower leg is externally rotated, whereas internal rotation allows detection of lateral tears.

Figure 19-17

The McMurray meniscal test. **A** and **B,** Internal rotation of the lower leg into knee extension. **C** and **D,** External rotation of the lower leg into knee extension.

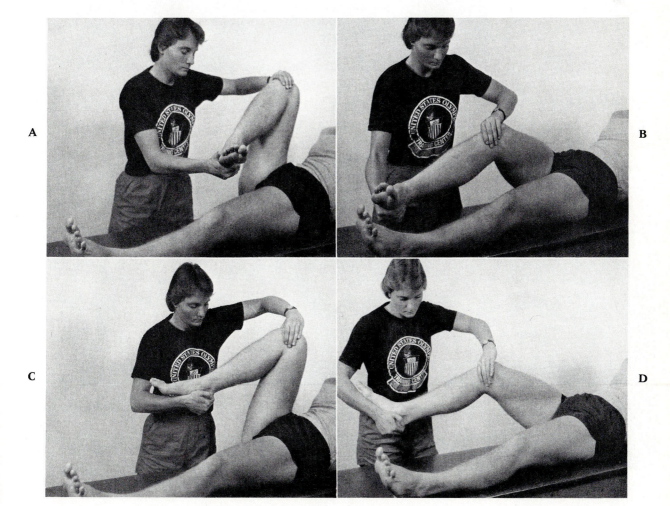

A

B

C

D

Figure 19-18

The Apley compression test.

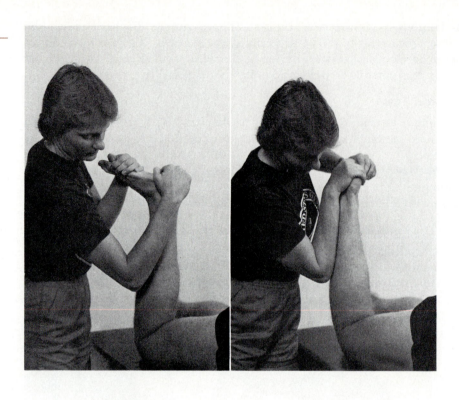

Figure 19-19

The Apley distraction test.

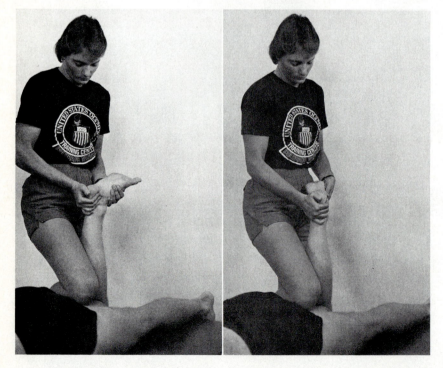

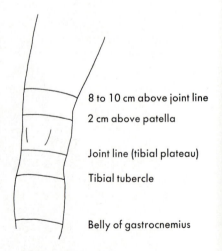

8 to 10 cm above joint line

2 cm above patella

Joint line (tibial plateau)

Tibial tubercle

Belly of gastrocnemius

Figure 19-20

The five sites for girth measurement.

The Apley compression test   The Apley compression test (Figure 19-18) is performed with the athlete lying face down and the affected leg flexed to 90 degrees. While stabilizing the thigh, a hard downward pressure is applied to the leg. The leg is then rotated back and forth. If pain results, a meniscal injury has occurred. A medial meniscal tear is noted by external rotation, and a lateral meniscal tear is noted by internal rotation of the lower leg.

The Apley distraction test   With the athlete in the same position as for the Apley compression test, the examiner applies traction to the leg while moving it back and forth (Figure 19-19). This maneuver distinguishes collateral ligamentous tears from capsular and meniscal tears. If the capsule or ligaments are affected, pain will occur; if the meniscus is torn, no pain will occur from the traction and rotation.[15]

Girth Measurement

A knee injury is almost always accompanied by an eventual decrease in the girth of the thigh musculature. The muscles most affected by disuse are the quadriceps group, which are "antigravity muscles" and assist humans in maintaining an erect, straight-leg position. They are in constant use in effecting movement. Atrophy results when a lower limb is favored and is not used to its potential. Measurement of the circumference of both thighs can often detect former leg injuries or determine the extent of exercise rehabilitation. Five sites have been suggested for girth measurement. These sites are the joint line, 8 to 10 cm above the tibial plateau, the level of the tibial tubercle, the belly of the gastrocnemius muscle measured in centimeters from the tibial tubercle, and 2 cm above the superior border of the patella recorded in centimeters above the tibial tubercle (Figure 19-20).

> Because the musculature of the knee atrophies so readily after an injury, girth measurements must be routinely taken.

Functional Examination

It is important that the athlete's knee also be tested for function. The athlete should be observed walking and, if possible, running, turning, performing figure-8s, backing up, and stopping. If the athlete can do a deep knee bend or duck walk without discomfort, it is doubtful that there is a meniscal tear. The resistive strength of the hamstring and quadriceps muscles should be compared to the strength of the knee known to be uninjured (Figure 19-21).

Figure 19-21

A, Testing quadriceps strength. **B,** Hamstring strength.

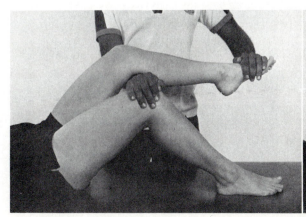
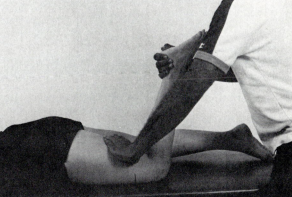

A   B

Patellar Examinations

Any knee evaluation should include inspection of the patella. Numerous evaluation procedures are associated with the patella and its surroundings. The following evaluation procedures can provide valuable information about possible reasons for knee discomfort and problems in functioning.[32]

Observation of the Patellar Position, Shape, and Alignment

The first aspect of examining the patella is one of observation. In terms of position, the patella may ride higher than usual, causing a tendency toward abnormal articulation. An indication of this condition is the patella that faces upward (patella alta) or downward (patella infra) rather than straight ahead when the athlete sits with the legs hanging over the end of a table with the knees flexed at a 45-degree angle. Observation can also tell the shape and size of the patella. Some patellas are smaller or larger than usual, and some display an abnormal shape, especially at the inferior pole. The symptomatic patella also should be observed for alignment with the nonsymptomatic patella. As discussed earlier, leg alignment problems such as hip anteversion, genu valgum, tibial torsion, and foot pronation can cause the patella to rotate inward, causing a tracking problem within the femoral groove.

The Q Angle

A Q angle greater than 20 degrees could predispose the athlete to patellar femoral pathology.

The Q angle is created when lines are drawn from the middle of the patella to the anterosuperior spine of the ilium and from the tubercle of the tibia through the center of the patella (Figure 19-22). It should be measured with the knee fully extended and with it flexed at 30 degrees. The normal angle is 10 degrees for males and 15 degrees for females. Q angles that exceed 20 degrees are considered excessive and could lead to a pathological condition in the patella.

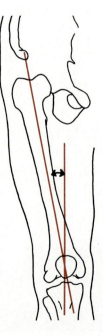

Figure 19-22

Measuring the Q angle of the knee.

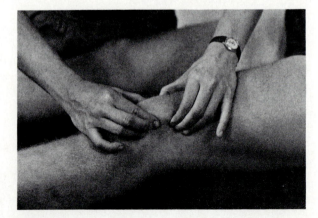

Figure 19-23

Palpating the periphery of the patella while the quadriceps muscle is fully relaxed.

Palpation of the Patella

With the quadriceps muscle fully relaxed, the patella is palpated around its periphery and under its sides for pain sites (Figure 19-23).

Patellar Compression, Patellar Grinding, and Apprehension Tests

With a rolled towel placed underneath the knee or with the knee held to create approximately 20 degrees of flexion, the patella is pressed downward into the femoral groove; it is then moved forward and backward (Figure 19-24). If the athlete feels pain or a grinding sound is heard during the patellar compression test, a pathological condition is probably present. With the knee still flexed, the patella is forced forward and is held in this position as the athlete extends the knee (Figure 19-25). A positive patellar grind test sign occurs pain and grinding are experienced by the athlete. Another test that indicates whether the patella can

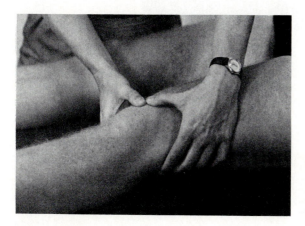

Figure 19-24

Patellar compression test. The patella is pressed downward in the femoral groove and moved forward and backward to elicit pain or crepitus.

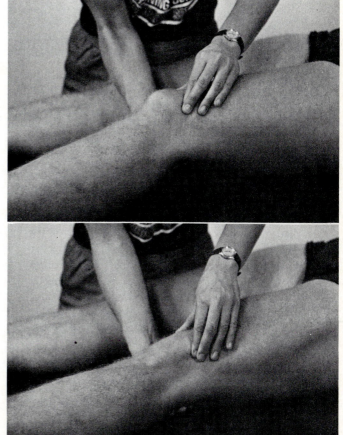

Figure 19-25

Patellar grind test. While the knee is flexed, the patella is forced forward, followed by the athlete's actively extending the knee. The test is positive if the athlete feels pain or grinding.

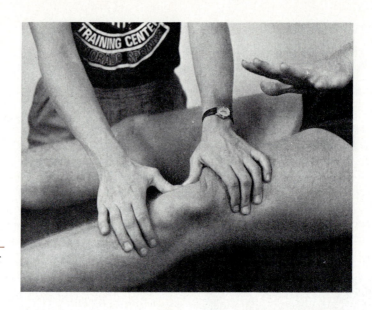

Figure 19-26

Patellar apprehension test for the easily subluxated or dislocated patella.

easily be subluxated or dislocated is known as the patellar apprehension test (Figure 19-26). With the knee and patella in a relaxed position, the examiner pushes the patella laterally. The athlete will express sudden apprehension at the point at which the patella begins to dislocate.[15]

PREVENTION OF KNEE INJURIES

Preventing knee injuries in sports is a complex problem. Of major importance are effective physical conditioning, rehabilitation and skill development, as well as shoe type. A questionable practice may be the routine use of protective bracing.

Physical Conditioning and Rehabilitation

To avoid knee injuries the athlete must be as highly conditioned as possible, meaning total body conditioning that includes strength, flexibility, cardiovascular and muscle endurance, agility, speed, and balance.[1] Specifically, the muscles surrounding the knee joint must be as strong as possible and flexible. The joints and soft tissue comprising the linkage system of which the knee is a part must also be considered sources of knee injury and, therefore, must be specifically conditioned for strength and flexibility. Depending on the requirements of a sport, a strength ratio should be acquired between the quadriceps and hamstring muscle groups. For example, in football players the hamstring muscles should have 60% to 70% of the strength of the quadriceps muscles. The gastrocnemius muscle should also be strengthened to help stabilize the knee. Although maximizing muscle strength may prevent some injuries, it fails to prevent rotary-type injuries.

Avoiding abnormal contraction of the muscles through flexibility exercises is a necessary protection for the knee. Gradual stretching of the knee musculature helps the muscle fibers become more extensible and elastic.[1] Of special concern in preventing knee injuries is extensibility of the hamstrings, erector spinae, groin, quadriceps, and gastrocnemius muscles.

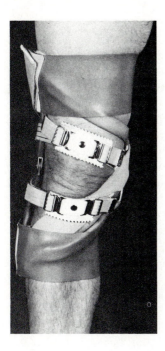

Figure 19-27

The Lenox Hill derotation knee brace.

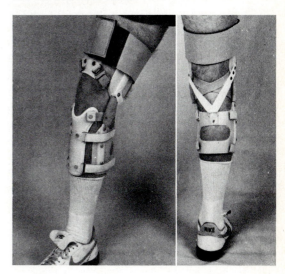

Figure 19-28

The Pro-Am knee brace.

Knees that have been injured must be properly rehabilitated. Repeated minor injuries to a knee make it susceptible to a major injury (see section entitled "Knee Joint Rehabilitation").

Shoe Type

During recent years, collision-type sports such as football have been using soccer-style shoes. The change from a few long conical cleats to a large number of cleats that are short (no longer than ½ inch [1.3 cm]) and broad has significantly reduced knee injuries in football. The higher number and shorter cleats are better because the foot does not become fixed to the surface and the shoe still allows for controlled running and cutting.

Protective Bracing

There is an increasing trend toward football players' wearing prophylactic knee braces to avoid injury. This practice is controversial (see Chapter 5). Knee braces are designed to provide protection against lateral and medial, but not rotary, forces. For athletes with a history of rotary instability, special orthopedic derotation knee braces are used (Figures 19-27 and 19-28).

KNEE JOINT INJURIES
Joint Contusions

ETIOLOGICAL FACTORS   A blow struck against the muscles crossing the knee joint can result in a handicapping condition. One of the muscles frequently involved is the vastus medialis of the quadriceps group, which is primarily involved in locking the knee in a position of full extension.

Because the knee joint and patella are poorly padded, they are prone to bruising.

SYMPTOMS AND SIGNS   Bruises of the vastus medialis produce all the appearances of a knee sprain, including severe pain, loss of movement, and signs of acute inflammation. Such bruising is often manifested by swelling and discoloration caused by the tearing of muscle tissue and blood vessels. If adequate first aid is given immediately, the knee will usually return to functional use 24 to 48 hours after the trauma.

Bruising of the capsular tissue that surrounds the knee joint is often associated with muscle contusions and deep bone bruises. A traumatic force delivered to capsular tissue may cause capillary bleeding, irritate the synovial membrane, and result in profuse fluid effusion into the joint cavity and surrounding spaces, thereby producing intra-articular swelling. Effusion often takes place slowly and almost imperceptibly. It is advisable to prevent the athlete from engaging in further activity for at least 24 hours after he or she receives a capsular bruise. Activity causes an increase in circulation and may cause extensive swelling and hematoma at the knee joint. Scar tissue develops wherever internal bleeding with clot organization is present. If this condition is repeated time after time, chronic synovitis or an arthritic sequela may develop.

MANAGEMENT   Care of a bruised knee depends on many factors. However, management principally depends on the location and severity of the contusion. The following procedures are suggested:

1. Apply compression bandages and cold until resolution has occurred.
2. Prescribe inactivity and rest for 24 hours.
3. If swelling occurs, continue cold application for 72 hours. If swelling and pain are intense, refer the athlete to the physician.
4. Once the acute stage has ended and the swelling has diminished to little or none, cold application with active range-of-motion exercises should be conducted within a pain-free range. If a gradual use of heat is elected, great caution should be taken to avoid swelling.
5. Allow the athlete to return to normal activity, with protective padding, when pain and the initial irritation have subsided.
6. If swelling is not resolved within a week, a chronic condition of either synovitis or bursitis may exist, indicating the need for rest and medical attention.

Figure 19-29

Baker's cyst in the popliteal fossa.

Bursitis

The knee has many bursae; the prepatellar, deep infrapatellar, and pretibial bursae are most often irritated.

Bursitis in the knee can be acute, chronic, or recurrent. Although any one of the numerous knee bursae can become inflamed, anteriorly the prepatellar, deep infrapatellar, and pretibial bursae have the highest incidence of irritation in sports (see Figure 19-5).

ETIOLOGICAL FACTORS   The prepatellar bursa often becomes inflamed from continued kneeling, and the deep infrapatellar becomes irritated from overuse of the patellar tendon.

SYMPTOMS AND SIGNS   Swelling in the knee posteriorly indicates an irritation of one of the bursae in this region. Swelling in the popliteal fossa could be a sign of *Baker's cyst* (Figure 19-29), which indicates distension of the gastrocnemius-semimembranous bursae.[15] Baker's cyst is commonly painless, causing no discomfort or disability. Some inflamed bursae may be painful and disabling because of the swelling and should be treated accordingly.

MANAGEMENT Management usually follows a pattern of eliminating the cause, prescribing rest, and reducing inflammation. Contrast baths may help reduce swelling. When the bursitis is chronic or recurrent and the synovium has thickened, use of aspiration and a steroid injection may be warranted.

Ligamentous Injuries

The major ligaments of the knee can be torn in isolation or in combination. Depending on the application of forces, injury can occur from a direct straight-line or single-plane force or from a rotary force.

Collateral Ligamentous and Capsular Injuries

Ligamentous and capsular sprains are the most frequently reported knee injuries that occur in sports.

Medial collateral ligamentous sprain

ETIOLOGICAL FACTORS Most knee sprains affect the medial collateral ligament as a result either of a direct blow from the lateral side, in a medial direction, or of a severe outward twist. Greater injury results from medial sprains than from lateral sprains because of their more direct relation to the articular capsule and the medial meniscus (Figure 19-30). Medial and lateral sprains occur in varying degrees, depending on knee position, previous injuries, the strength of muscles crossing the joint, the force and angle of the trauma, fixation of the foot, and conditions of the playing surface.

The position of the knee is important in establishing its vulnerability to traumatic sprains. Any position of the knee, from full extension to full flexion, can result in injury if there is sufficient force. Full extension tightens both lateral and medial ligaments. However, flexion affords a loss of stability to the lateral ligament but maintains stability in various portions of the broad medial ligament.[12] Medial collateral ligamentous sprains result most often from a violently adducted and internally rotated knee. The most prevalent mechanism of a lateral collateral ligamentous or capsular sprain is one in which the foot is everted and the knee is forced laterally into a varus position.

Speculation among medical authorities is that torn menisci seldom happen as the result of an initial trauma; most occur after the collateral ligaments have been stretched by repeated injury. Many mild-to-moderate sprains leave the knee unstable and thus vulnerable to additional internal derangements. The strength of the muscles crossing the knee joint is important in assisting the ligaments to support the articulation. These muscles should be conditioned to the highest possible degree for sports in which knee injuries are common. With the added support and protection of muscular strength, a state of readiness may be developed through proper athletic training.

The force and angle of the trauma usually determine the extent of injury that takes place. Even after witnessing the occurrence of a knee injury, it is difficult to predict the amount of tissue damage. The most revealing time for testing joint stability is immediately after injury before effusion masks the extent of derangement.

First-degree medial collateral ligamentous sprain A first-degree medial collateral ligamentous injury of the knee has the following characteristics (Figure 19-31):

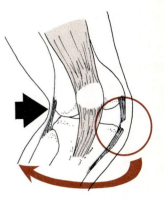

Figure 19-30

A valgus force with the tibia in external rotation injures the medial collateral and capsular ligaments, the medial meniscus, and sometimes the anterior cruciate ligaments.

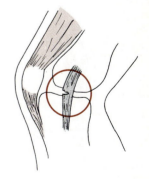

Figure 19-31

First-degree medial collateral ligamentous sprain.

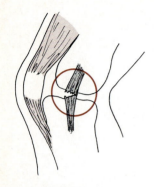

Figure 19-32

Second-degree medial collateral ligamentous sprain.

Figure 19-33

Knee immobilizer used after a ligamentous injury.

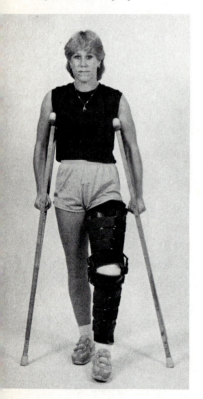

1. A few ligamentous fibers are torn and stretched.
2. The joint is stable during valgus stress tests.
3. There is little or no joint effusion.
4. There may be some joint stiffness and point tenderness just below the medial joint line.
5. Even with minor stiffness, there is almost full passive and active range of motion.

MANAGEMENT Immediate care consists of ICE-R for at least 24 hours. After immediate care, the following procedures should be undertaken:

1. Crutches are prescribed if the athlete is unable to walk without a limp.
2. Follow-up care may involve cryokinetics, including 5 minutes of ice pack treatment preceding exercise or a combination of cold and compression and/or ultrasound.
3. Proper exercise is essential, starting with Phase 1 of the knee joint rehabilitation procedures on p. 606.

Isometrics and straight-leg exercises are important until the knee can be moved without pain. The athlete then graduates to stationary bicycle riding or a high-speed isokinetic program. Proprioceptive neuromuscular function can also be an excellent means for rehabilitation.

The athlete is allowed to return to full participation when the knee has regained normal strength, power, flexibility, endurance, and coordination. Usually 1 to 3 weeks is necessary for recovery. When returning to activity, the athlete may require tape support for a short period.

Second-degree medial collateral ligamentous sprain Second-degree medial collateral ligamentous knee sprain indicates both miscroscopic and gross disruption of ligamentous fibers (Figure 19-32). The only structures involved are the medial collateral ligament and the medial capsular ligament. It is characterized by the following:

1. A complete tear of the deep capsular ligament and partial tear of the superficial layer of the medial collateral ligament or a partial tear of both areas.
2. No gross instability, but minimum or slight laxity during full extension. However, at 30 degrees of flexion and when the valgus stress test is performed, laxity may be as much as 5 to 15 degrees.
3. Slight or absent swelling unless the meniscus or anterior cruciate ligament has been torn. An acutely torn or pinched synovial membrane, subluxated or dislocated patella, or an osteochondral fracture can produce extensive swelling and hemarthrosis.
4. Moderate-to-severe joint tightness with an inability to fully, actively extend the knee. The athlete is unable to place the heel flat on the ground.
5. Definite loss of passive range of motion.
6. Pain in the medial joint line, with general weakness and instability.

MANAGEMENT

1. ICE-R for 48 to 72 hours.
2. Crutches are used with a three-point gait until the acute phase of injury is over and the athlete can walk without a limp.
3. Depending on the severity and possible complications, a full-leg cast or postoperative knee immobilizing splint may be applied by the physician (Figure 19-33).

4. Cryokinetics or other therapeutic modalities are used three or four times daily.

5. Isometric exercise along with exercise to all the adjacent joints is performed three or four times daily.

6. Depending on the extent of injury and swelling, the immobilizing splint is removed, and gentle range of movement may be performed. (See pp. 592-593 for a sample exercise rehabilitation program.)

7. Taping may be appropriate to provide some support and confidence to the athlete (see Figure 12-18).

Conservative care of the second-degree medial collateral ligamentous sprain has been successful. Studies show that there can be spontaneous ligamentous and capsular healing because other structures such as the anterior cruciate ligament also protect the knee against valgus and rotary movement.[35]

Third-degree medial collateral ligamentous sprain   Third-degree medial collateral ligamentous sprain means a complete tear of the supporting ligaments. The following are major symptoms and signs (Figure 19-34):

1. Complete loss of medial stability
2. Minimum-to-moderate swelling
3. Medial pain and point tenderness
4. Loss of range of motion because of effusion and hamstring spasm
5. The valgus stress test reveals some joint opening during full extension and significant opening at 30 degrees of flexion.

An anterior cruciate ligament tear or medial meniscal disruption may be present and should be tested for.

IMMEDIATE AND FOLLOW-UP CARE   ICE-R for 20 minutes every 2 hours during the waking day should be performed for at least 72 hours. In many cases, such an injury is surgically repaired as soon as possible after the acute inflammatory phase (3 or 4 days after injury). **NOTE:** In a third-degree medial collateral ligamentous sprain with significant valgus laxity while the knee is in full extension, there is a possibility that the posterior oblique ligament and posterior cruciate ligament are also involved.

Lateral collateral ligamentous sprain   Sprain of the lateral collateral ligament of the knee is much less prevalent than sprain of the medial collateral ligament.

ETIOLOGICAL FACTORS   The force to tear this ligament is varus, often with the tibia internally rotated (Figure 19-35). Because of the usually inaccessible medial

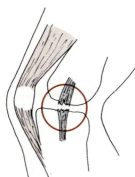

Figure 19-34

Third-degree medial collateral ligamentous sprain.

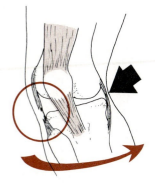

Figure 19-35

A varus force with the tibia internally rotated injures the lateral collateral ligament; in some cases both the cruciate ligaments and the attachments of the iliotibial band and biceps muscle of the thigh may be torn.

MANAGEMENT PLAN FOR MEDIAL COLLATERAL LIGAMENTOUS SPRAIN OF THE KNEE

Injury Situation

A female college soccer player injured her right knee in a game. The injury occurred in an attempt to recover the ball when she tripped on an opponent's foot, forcing her knee into a sudden valgus position. As the knee was forced inward, the athlete felt a sharp pain and a sense that the knee "gave way."

Symptoms and Signs

During inspection, the athlete complained of severe pain in the knee region. She was unable to bear full weight on the leg or to walk other than on the toe of the foot. Palpation by the athletic trainer revealed pain along the medial joint line. Varus and valgus stress tests were performed and found negative at full extension (0 degrees) but revealed some minor excursion at 30 degrees of flexion in the valgus test. All other knee tests proved negative. X-ray examination for fracture was negative. The injury was considered by the physician to be between a grade II and III medial collateral ligamentous sprain.

Management Plan

Because the knee was basically stable in all tests, surgery was ruled out, and a conservative therapy program was considered the best approach.

1

Management Phase

GOALS: To control hemorrhage, swelling, and pain
ESTIMATED LENGTH OF TIME (ELT): 3 days

Therapy

IMMEDIATE CARE: Apply ice pack (20 min) intermittently, six to eight times daily
Soft splint: an elastic wrap is worn
Leg is elevated whenever possible during day and night

Exercise Rehabilitation

Avoid weight bearing through crutch walking until athlete can walk without limp, 3 to 4 days
Isometric exercise (within pain-free limits; 10 to 15 times) to quadriceps and hamstring muscles (each contraction held 6 sec); may be done in conjunction with transcutaneous electrical nerve stimulation (TENS), every waking hour
Straight leg raises in all hip positions are added to isometrics 3 to 4 days after injury (each exercise is performed 10 to 15 times), every waking hour
General body maintenance exercises are conducted as long as they do not aggravate injury, three times a week

2

Management Phase

GOALS: To restore 50% range of motion (ROM), full muscle contraction
ELT: 4 to 7 days

Therapy

FOLLOW-UP CARE (all cold therapy is followed by exercise):
Ice pack (5 to 15 min) or ice massage (7 min) or cold whirlpool (60° F [15.5° C] for 10 min) three to four times daily

	Exercise Rehabilitation	Crutch walking is continued until athlete can walk without limp Isometrics and straight leg raises are continued, three to four times daily Active range-of-motion exercises are begun within pain-free limits using active movements and/or proprioceptive neuromuscular facilitation (PNF) hip and knee patterns, three to four times daily TENS is continued General body maintenance exercises are conducted as long as they do not aggravate injury, three times a week
3	**Management Phase**	GOALS: To restore 75% ROM, 50% full strength ELT: 10 to 14 days
	Therapy	Ice pack (5 to 15 min) or ice massage (10 min) followed by exercise
	Exercise Rehabilitation	Avoid any exercise that causes pain or swelling Isokinetic exercise starting at high speeds, once daily Isotonic exercise using progressive resistance exercise using daily adjustable progressive resistive exercise (DAPRE) concept (see p. 613) or PNF knee patterns or jogging in waist-high pool (20 min), once daily General body maintenance exercises are conducted as long as they do not aggravate injury, three times a week
4	**Management Phase**	GOALS: To restore 90% ROM, power, speed, and endurance and coordination ELT: 14 days
	Therapy	If symptom free, no therapy is required Continue program of DAPRE, three to four times a week Begin jogging on flat surfaces and progress from walk-run to running (3 miles) Begin figure-8 runs with obstacles 10 feet (3 m) apart, then decrease to 5 feet (1.5 m) apart at full speed
5	**Management Phase**	GOAL: To restore full muscle bulk and playing skill Work on maximum resistance, three to four times a week Begin practice while protected with tape and brace, once daily

Criteria for Returning to Competitive Soccer

1. The knee is symptom free.
2. The knee has full range of motion and strength equal to or exceeding the unaffected knee.
3. The athlete has full function and is able to jump and run a figure-8 at full speed.

Figure 19-36

Competitive skiing places extreme medial, lateral, and rotary stresses on the knee.

aspect, a direct blow is rare. In skiing, the lateral collateral ligament can be injured when the skier fails to hold a snowplow and the tips cross, throwing the body weight to the outside edge of the ski.[16] If the force or blow is severe enough, both cruciate ligaments, the attachments of the iliotibial band, and the biceps muscle may be torn. This same mechanism could also disrupt the lateral and even the medial meniscus (Figure 19-36). If the force is great enough, bony fragments can be avulsed from the femur or tibia. An avulsion can also occur through the combined pull of the lateral collateral ligament and biceps muscle on the head of the fibula.

SYMPTOMS AND SIGNS   The major symptoms and signs include the following:
1. Pain and point tenderness along the joint line.
2. Depending on the degree of injury, there is usually some joint instability with joint opening during the varus stress test at 30 degrees of knee flexion.
3. Swelling is usually minimum because of bleeding into joint spaces.
4. The greater the ligamentous injury, the less pain is felt during a varus stress test.

An injury can also occur to the peroneal nerve, causing temporary or permanent palsy. The common peroneal nerve originates from the sciatic nerve. It lies behind the head of the fibula and winds laterally around the neck of the fibula, where it branches into deep and superficial peroneal nerves (see Figure 19-8). Tears or entrapment of this nerve can produce varying weaknesses and paralysis of the lateral aspect of the lower leg. Injury of the peroneal nerve requires immediate medical attention.

MANAGEMENT   Management of the lateral collateral ligamentous injury should follow similar procedures as the medial collateral ligamentous injuries.

Cruciate Ligamentous Sprains

Anterior cruciate ligamentous sprain   The anterior cruciate ligament is most commonly the most seriously disrupted ligament in the knee.[20]

A lateral knee sprain can be caused by a varus force when the tibia is internally rotated.

ETIOLOGICAL FACTORS   The anterior cruciate ligament is most vulnerable to injury when the tibia is externally rotated and the knee is in a valgus position. The anterior cruciate ligament can sustain injury from a direct blow to the knee or from a single-plane force. The single-plane injury occurs when the lower leg is rotated while the foot is fixed. (Figure 19-37). In this situation, the anterior cruciate ligament becomes taut and vulnerable to sprain. An example occurs when an athlete who is running fast suddenly decelerates and makes a sharp "cutting" motion, causing an isolated tear of the anterior cruciate ligament. The same mechanism could be true of the skier when his or her ski catches in the snow and the body twists medially or laterally.

The two most common rotary injuries leading to knee instability are the anteromedial and anterolateral types. Anteromedial rotary motion can also tear the medial collateral ligament or both the medial and anterior cruciate ligaments. With anterolateral instability, the anterior cruciate ligament is also involved, along with a tear or laxity of the posterolateral capsule. Although the tear may be isolated, it could be associated with a meniscal or medial collateral ligamentous tear. Forced hyperflexion could also conceivably injure both the anterior and posterior cruciate ligaments.

Hyperextension from a force to the front of the knee with the foot planted can tear the anterior cruciate ligament (Figure 19-38) and, if severe enough, can also sprain the medial collateral ligament.

SYMPTOMS AND SIGNS   The anterior cruciate ligament sprain is extremely difficult to diagnose. The earlier the determination is made, the better because swelling will often mask the full extent of injury. In addition to swelling, this injury is associated with joint instability, and a positive drawer sign may be present.[13] The athlete often experiences a "pop," followed by immediate disability. The athlete complains that the knee feels like it is "coming apart." An athlete with this condition tends to stand pigeon-toed because doing so provides a sense of increased stability.

MANAGEMENT

Immediate care   Even with application of proper first aid and immediate ICE-R, swelling begins within 1 to 2 hours and becomes a notable hemarthrosis within 4 to 6 hours.[4] The athlete typically cannot walk without help.

If a clinical evaluation is inconclusive, an arthroscopic examination may be warranted to make a proper diagnosis.

Follow-up care   Anterior cruciate ligamentous injury could lead to serious knee instability; an intact anterior cruciate ligament is necessary for a knee to function in high-performance situations. Controversy exists among physicians about how best to treat an acute anterior cruciate ligamentous rupture and when surgery is warranted. It is well accepted that an unsatisfactorily treated anterior cruciate ligamentous rupture will eventually lead to major joint degeneration. Therefore a decision for or against surgery must be based on the athlete's age, the type of stress applied to the knee, and the amount of instability present, as well as the techniques available to the surgeon.[4] A simple surgical repair of the ligament may not establish the desired joint stability. Surgery may involve joint reconstruction, with transplantation of some external structure such as the pes anserinus, semitendinous muscle, tensor fascia lata, or patellar tendon to replace the lost anterior cruciate support. This type of surgery involves a significant hospital stay, 8 weeks or longer in casts and braces, and 6 months to 1 year of rehabilitation.[4]

Figure 19-37

A major mechanism causing an anterior cruciate tear occurs when a running athlete suddenly decelerates and makes a sharp "cutting" motion.

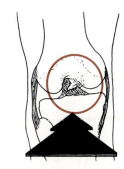

Figure 19-38

An anterior force with the foot planted can tear the anterior cruciate ligament.

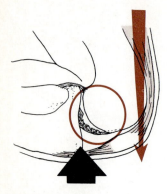

Figure 19-39

A fall or being hit on the anterior aspect of the bent knee can tear the posterior cruciate ligament.

The routine use of braces such as the Lenox-Hill derotation brace, along with rotary and hyperextension taping, can provide some protection during activity.[10,11]

Posterior cruciate ligamentous sprain   ==The posterior cruciate ligament has been called the most important ligament in the knee,== providing a central axis for rotation.[34] The posterior cruciate ligament is vulnerable to injury after the anterior cruciate ligament has been torn and the knee has been forced into hyperextension (see Figure 19-38).

ETIOLOGICAL FACTORS   The posterior cruciate ligament is most at risk when the knee is flexed to 90 degrees. Falling with full weight on the anterior aspect of the bent knee or receiving a hard blow to the front of the bent knee can tear the posterior cruciate ligament (Figure 19-39). In addition, it can be injured by a rotational force, which also affects the medial or lateral side of the knee.[34]

SYMPTOMS AND SIGNS   When the knee is examined at 30 degrees of flexion, a Lachman test will produce an increase in external rotation of the tibia. In contrast to the anterior cruciate ligamentous tear, the posterior cruciate ligamentous tear is usually not as tense and painful with hemarthrosis. In general, there is posterior pain, but the athlete may still display a functional arc of motion.[34]

MANAGEMENT   The usual first aid is administered. Surgery may be warranted when there is instability.

Meniscal Lesions

The medial meniscus has a much higher incidence of injury than the lateral meniscus. The higher number of medial meniscal lesions is basically a result of the coronary ligament attaching the meniscus peripherally to the tibia and also to the capsular ligament. The lateral meniscus does not attach to the capsular ligament and is more mobile during knee movement. Because of the attachment to the medial structures, the medial meniscus is prone to disruption from valgus and torsional forces.

ETIOLOGICAL FACTORS   A blow from the lateral side directed inward forces the knee into adduction, often tearing and stretching the medial collateral ligament; meanwhile, its fibers twist the medial meniscus outward. Repeated mild sprains reduce the strength of the knee to a state favorable for a cartilagenous tear through lessening its normal ligamentous stability. The most common mechanism is weight bearing combined with a rotary force while extending or flexing the knee. A cutting motion while running can distort the medial meniscus. Stretching of the anterior and posterior horns of the meniscus can produce a bowstring, or longitudinal-type, tear (Figure 19-40). Another way a longitudinal tear occurs is by forcefully extending the knee from a flexed position while the femur is internally rotated. During extension the medial meniscus is suddenly pulled back, causing the tear (see Figure 19-40). In contrast, the lateral meniscus can sustain an oblique tear by a forceful knee extension with the femur externally rotated.[8] A large number of medial meniscus lesions are the outcome of a sudden, strong internal rotation of the femur with a partially flexed knee while the foot is firmly planted. As a result of the force of this action, the cartilage is pulled out of its normal bed and pinched between the femoral condyles.

Meniscal lesions can be longitudinal, oblique, or transverse. Tears close to the periphery of a meniscus, because of its proximity to the coronary ligament and blood circulation, may heal over time if stress in the area is kept to a minimum.[3]

Figure 19-40

Common mechanisms of
injury to the meniscus.

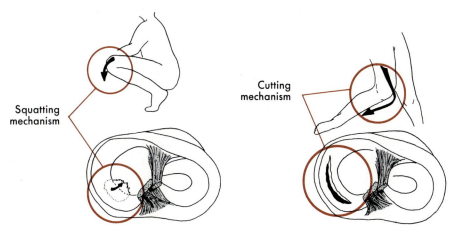

Squatting
mechanism

Cutting
mechanism

Tears that occur within the cartilage fail to heal because of lack of adequate blood
supply.

ACUTE SYMPTOMS AND SIGNS   An absolute diagnosis of cartilagenous injury is
difficult. For determining the possibility of such an injury, a complete history
should be obtained, which consists of information about past knee injury and an
understanding of how the present injury occurred. Diagnosis of meniscal injuries
should be made immediately after the injury has occurred and before muscle
spasm and swelling obscure the normal shape of the knee.

A meniscal tear may or may not result in the following:
1. Severe pain and loss of motion
2. A locked knee with inability to flex or extend fully
3. Pain in the area of the tear

MANAGEMENT OF THE ACUTE MENISCAL TEAR   If the knee is not locked but
shows indications of a tear, the physician might obtain an arthrogram, which is
an x-ray film of a joint that has been injected with radiopaque material. An arthrogram should rule out a fracture. An arthroscopic examination may also be
performed, whereby the physician can physically look inside the knee for deviations.

The knee that is locked by a displaced cartilage may require unlocking with
the athlete under anesthesia so that a detailed examination can be conducted. If
discomfort, disability, and locking of the knee continue, surgery may be required.
For the nonlocking acute meniscal lesion, immediate care should follow a second-
or third-degree sprain management pattern. The knee is managed by splinting,
crutch walking, muscle setting, and isometric exercise followed by gradual range-
of-motion and progressive resistance exercises.

CHRONIC SYMPTOMS AND SIGNS   Once a knee cartilage has been fractured, its
ruptured edges harden and may eventually atrophy. On occasion, portions of the
meniscus may become detached and wedge themselves between the articulating
surfaces of the tibia and femur, thus imposing a locking, "catching," or "giving
way" of the joint. Chronic meniscal lesions may also display recurrent swelling
and obvious muscle atrophy around the knee. The athlete may complain of an
inability to perform a full squat or to change direction quickly when running
without pain, a sense of the knee collapsing, or a "popping" sensation. Such

Simple surgical repair of the
torn anterior cruciate
ligament may not establish
proper stability.

symptoms and signs usually warrant surgical intervention. NOTE: *Symptomatic meniscal tears can eventually lead to serious articular degeneration with major impairment and disability.*

Knee Plica

The fetus has three synovial knee cavities whose internal walls, at 4 months, are gradually absorbed to form one chamber; however, in 20% of all individuals, the knee fails to fully absorb these cavities. In adult life these septa form synovial folds known as plicae.

ETIOLOGICAL FACTORS The most common synovial fold is the infrapatellar plica, which originates from the infrapatellar fat pad and extends superiorly in a fanlike manner. The second most common synovial fold is the suprapatellar plica, located in the suprapatellar pouch. The least common, but most subject to injury, is the mediopatellar plica, which is bandlike and begins on the medial wall of the knee joint and extends downward to insert into the synovial tissue that covers the infrapatellar fat pad.[25] Because most synovial plicae are pliable, most are asymptomatic; however, the mediopatellar plica may be thick, nonyielding, and fibrotic, causing a number of symptoms. The mediopatellar plica is associated with chondromalacia of the medial femoral condyle and patella.[6]

SYMPTOMS AND SIGNS The athlete may or may not have a history of knee injury. If symptoms are preceded by trauma, it is usually one of blunt force such as falling on the knee or of twisting with the foot planted. A major complaint is recurrent episodes of painful pseudolocking of the knee when sitting for a period of time. As the knee passes 15 to 20 degrees of flexion, a snap may be felt or heard. Such characteristics of locking and snapping could be misinterpreted as a torn meniscus. The athlete complains of pain while ascending or descending stairs or when squatting. Unlike meniscal injuries, there is little or no swelling and no ligamentous laxity.

Knee plicae that have become thick and hard are often mistaken for meniscal injuries.

MANAGEMENT A knee plica that becomes inflamed as a result of trauma is usually treated conservatively with rest, anti-inflammatory agents, and local heat. If the condition recurs, causing a chondromalacia of the femoral condyle or patella, the plica will require surgical excision.

Osteochondral Knee Fractures

Occasionally the same mechanisms that produce collateral ligamentous, cruciate ligamentous, or meniscal tears can shear off either a piece of bone attached to the anterior cartilage or cartilage alone. Twisting, sudden cutting, or being struck directly in the knee are typical causes of this condition. The athlete commonly hears a snap and feels the knee give way. Swelling is immediate and extensive because of hemarthrosis, and there is considerable pain. The diagnosis is usually confirmed by arthroscopic examination. Surgery is performed to replace the fragment as soon as possible to avoid joint degeneration and arthritis.

Osteochondritis Dissecans

Osteochondritis dissecans is a painful condition involving partial or complete separation of a piece of articular cartilage and subchondral bone. Both teenagers and adults can have this condition. The vast majority of fragments, over 85%, occur on the medial femoral condyle near the posterior cruciate ligament attachment.[9]

ETIOLOGICAL FACTORS The exact cause of osteochondritis dissecans is unknown. It usually has a very slow onset. A disruption of blood circulation has been suggested as a possible reason for this condition. Other possible factors are as follows:[8]

1. Repeated trauma to the medial condyle by the tibial tuberosity
2. Endocrine imbalance
3. Heredity

SYMPTOMS AND SIGNS The athlete with osteochondritis dissecans complains of a knee that aches, has recurrent swelling and, on occasion, may catch or lock. There may be atrophy of the quadriceps muscle and point tenderness.

MANAGEMENT For children usually rest and immobilization using a cylinder cast are prescribed. This management affords proper resolution of the injured cartilage and normal ossification of the underlying bone. As with many other osteochondroses, resolution may take as long as 1 year. For the teenager and adult, surgery such as multiple drilling in the area to stimulate healing, pinning loose fragments, or bone grafting may be warranted.

A knee that locks and unlocks during activity may indicate a fractured meniscus.

Loose Bodies within the Knee

Because of repeated trauma to the knee during sports activities, loose bodies ("joint mice") can develop within the joint cavity. Loose bodies can stem from osteochondritis dissecans, fragments from the menisci, pieces of torn synovial tissue, or a torn cruciate ligament. The loose body may move in the joint space and become lodged to cause locking, popping, and giving way. When the loose body becomes wedged between articulating surfaces, irritation can occur. If not surgically removed, the loose body can create conditions that lead to joint degeneration.

Injury to the Infrapatellar Fat Pad

The two most important fat pads of the knee are the infrapatellar fat pad and the suprapatellar fat pad. The infrapatellar fat pad lies between the synovial membrane on the anterior aspect of the joint and the patellar ligament, and the suprapatellar fat pad lies between the anterior surface and the suprapatellar bursa. Of the two pads, the infrapatellar is more often injured in sports, principally as a result of its large size and particular vulnerability during activity.

ETIOLOGICAL FACTORS The fat pad may become wedged between the knee articulations, irritated by chronic kneeling pressures, or traumatized by direct blows.

SYMPTOMS AND SIGNS Repeated injury to the fat pad produces capillary hemorrhaging and swelling of the fatty tissue; if the irritation continues, scarring and calcification may develop. The athlete may complain of pain below the patellar ligament, especially during knee extension, and the knee may display weakness, mild swelling, and stiffness during movement.

MANAGEMENT Care of acute fat pad injuries involves rest from irritating activities until inflammation has subsided, heel elevation of ½ to 1 inch (1.3 to 1.5 cm), and the therapeutic use of heat. Heel elevation prevents added irritation during full extension; applying hyperextension taping may also be necessary to prevent occurrence of full extension. Therapy should include heat applied throughout the day in the form of moist heat packs, whirlpool, or analgesic balm packs. Massage around the inflamed area may assist lymphatic drainage. However, avoid massaging directly over the joint itself. Quadriceps atrophy may be prevented by assigning a daily program of quadriceps "setting" or isometric exercises.

PATELLAR AND RELATED CONDITIONS

The position and function of the patella and surrounding structures expose it to a variety of traumas and diseases related to sports activities.

Patellar Fracture

Fractures of the patella can be caused by either direct or indirect trauma.

ETIOLOGICAL FACTORS   Most patellar fractures are the result of indirect violence in which a severe pull of the patellar tendon occurs against the femur when the knee is semiflexed. This position subjects the patella to maximum stress from the quadriceps tendon and the patellar ligament. Forcible muscle contraction may then fracture the patella at its lower half. Direct injury most often produces fragmentation with little displacement. Falls, jumping, or running may result in a fracture of the patella.

SYMPTOMS AND SIGNS   The fracture causes hemorrhage and joint effusion, resulting in generalized swelling. Indirect fracture causes capsular tearing, separation of bone fragments, and possible tearing of the quadriceps tendon. Direct fracture involves little bone separation.

MANAGEMENT   Diagnosis is accomplished through use of the history, palpation of separated fragments, and an x-ray confirmation. As soon as the examiner suspects a patellar fracture, a cold wrap should be applied, followed by an elastic compression wrap and splinting. The athletic trainer should then refer the athlete to the team physician. The athlete will normally be immobilized for 2 to 3 months.

Acute Patellar Subluxation or Dislocation

Knees that "give way" or "catch" have a number of possible pathological conditions
  Subluxating patella
  Meniscal tear
  Anterior cruciate
    ligamentous tear
  Hemarthrosis

When an athlete plants his or her foot, decelerates, and simultaneously cuts in an opposite direction from the weight-bearing foot, the thigh rotates internally while the lower leg rotates externally, causing a forced knee valgus. The quadriceps muscle attempts to pull in a straight line and as a result pulls the patella laterally—a force that may dislocate the patella. As a rule, displacement takes place outwardly, with the patella resting on the lateral condyle (Figure 19-41).

With this mechanism the patella is forced to slide laterally into a partial or full dislocation. Some athletes are more predisposed to this condition than others because of the following anatomical structures:

1. A wide pelvis with anteverted hips
2. Genu valgum, increasing the Q angle
3. Shallow femoral grooves
4. Flat lateral femoral condyles
5. High riding and flat patellas
6. Vastus medialis and ligamentous laxity with genu recurvatum and externally rotated tibias
7. Pronated feet
8. Externally pointing patellas

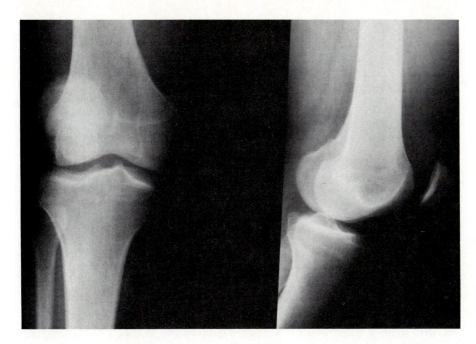

Figure 19-41

Fracture and dislocation of the patella.

The Subluxated Patella

An athlete who has a subluxated patella will complain that the knee catches or gives way. The knee may be swollen and painful. Pain is a result of swelling but also results because the medial capsular tissue has been stretched and torn. Because of the hemarthrosis, the knee is restricted in flexion and extension. There may also be a palpable tenderness over the adductor tubercle where the medial retinaculum (patellar femoral ligament) attaches.

The Dislocated Patella

An acute patellar dislocation is often associated with sudden twisting of the body while the foot or feet are planted.

SYMPTOMS AND SIGNS   The athlete experiences a complete loss of knee function, pain, and swelling, with the patella resting in an abnormal position. The physician immediately reduces the dislocation by applying mild pressure on the patella with the knee extended as much as possible. If a period of time has elapsed before reduction, a general anesthesia may have to be used. After aspiration of the joint hematoma, ice is applied, and the joint is splinted. A first-time patellar dislocation is always associated with a chondral or osteochondral fracture. X-ray evaluation is performed before and after reduction.

MANAGEMENT   To reduce a dislocation, the hip is flexed, and the patella is gently moved medially as the knee is slowly extended. After reduction the knee is immobilized in extension for 4 weeks or longer, and the athlete is instructed to use crutches when walking. During immobilization, isometric exercises are performed at the knee joint. After immobilization the athlete should wear a horseshoe-shaped felt pad that is held in place around the patella by an elastic wrap or that is sewn into an elastic sleeve that is worn while running or performing in sports (Figure 19-42). Commercial braces are also available.

Muscle rehabilitation should be concerned with all the musculature of the knee, thigh, and hip. Knee exercise should be confined to straight leg raises.

If surgery is performed, it is usually to release constrictive ligaments or to reconstruct the patellofemoral joint. It is important to strengthen and balance the strength of all musculature associated with the knee joint. Postural malalignments must be corrected as much as possible. Shoe orthotic devices may be used to reduce foot pronation, tibial torsion, and subsequently to reduce stress to the patellofemoral joint.

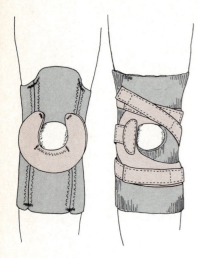

Figure 19-42

Special pads for the dislocated patella.

Patellofemoral Arthralgia

The patella, in relation to the femoral groove, can be subject to direct trauma or disease, leading to chronic pain and disability. Of major importance among athletes are those conditions that stem from abnormal patellar tracking within the femoral groove, of which the two most common are chrondomalacia and degenerative arthritis.[24]

Chondromalacia

Occurring most often among teenagers and young adults, chondromalacia is a gradual degenerative process (Figure 19-43). Cailliet[8] describes chondromalacia as undergoing three stages:

Stage 1	Swelling and softening of the articular cartilage
Stage 2	Fissuring of the softened articular cartilage
Stage 3	Deformation of the surface of the articular cartilage caused by fragmentation

ETIOLOGICAL FACTORS   The exact cause of chondromalacia is unknown. As indicated previously, abnormal patellar tracking could be a major etiological factor; however, individuals with normal tracking have acquired chondromalacia, and some individuals with abnormal tracking are free of it.[8] Abnormal patellofemoral tracking can be produced by the following:

1. Genu valgum
2. External tibial torsion
3. Foot pronation
4. Femoral anteversion
5. A quadriceps Q angle greater than 15 to 20 degrees
6. Patella alta
7. A shallow femoral groove
8. A shallow articular angle of the patella
9. An abnormal articular contour of the patella
10. Laxity of the quadriceps tendon

SYMPTOMS AND SIGNS   The athlete may experience pain in the anterior aspect of the knee while walking, running, ascending and descending stairs, or squatting. There may be recurrent swelling around the kneecap and a grating sensation when flexing and extending the knee.

The patella displays crepitation during the patellar grind test. During palpation there may be pain on the inferior border of the patella or when the patella is compressed within the femoral groove while the knee is passively flexed and extended. The athlete has one or more lower-limb alignment deviations.

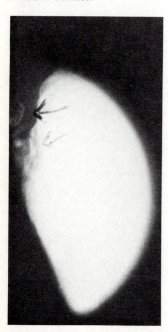

Figure 19-43

Chondromalacia with chipping away of the articular surface.

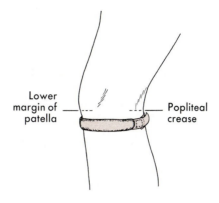

Lower margin of patella

Popliteal crease

Figure 19-44

The chondromalacia brace.

Degenerative Arthritis

Degenerative arthritis, in contrast to chondromalacia, occurs on the medial facet of the patella, which makes contact with the femur when the athlete performs a full squat.[8,25] Degeneration first occurs in the deeper portions of the articular cartilage, followed by blistering and fissuring that stems from the subchondral bone and appears on the surface of the patella.[8]

MANAGEMENT   In some cases, patellofemoral arthralgia is initially treated conservatively as follows:

1. Avoidance of irritating activities such as stair climbing and squatting
2. Isometric exercises that are pain free to strengthen the quadriceps and hamstring muscles
3. Oral anti-inflammatory agents, small doses of aspirin
4. Wearing of a chondromalacia brace (Figure 19-44)
5. Wearing of an orthotic device to correct pronation and reduce tibial torsion

If conservative measures fail to help, surgery may be the only alternative. Some of the following surgical measures may be indicated[8]:

1. Realignment procedures such as lateral release of the retinaculum, moving the insertion of the vastus medialis muscle forward
2. Shaving and smoothing the irregular surfaces of the patella and/or femoral condyle
3. In cases of degenerative arthritis removing the blister through drilling
4. Elevating the tibial tubercle
5. As a last resort completely removing the patella

Other Extensor Mechanism Problems

Many other extensor mechanism problems can occur in the physically active individual. They can occur in the immature adolescent's knee or as a result of jumping and running.

The Immature Extensor Mechanism

Two conditions common to the immature adolescent's knee are Osgood-Schlatter disease and Larsen-Johansson disease.

Osgood-Schlatter disease   Osgood-Schlatter disease is an apophysitis under the general classification of osteochondritis. To call this condition a disease is misleading because it is a number of conditions related to the epiphyseal growth center of the tibial tubercle. The tibial tubercle is an apophysis for the attachment of the patellar tendon.

Conditions that may be mistaken for one another
 Osgood-Schlatter disease
 Larsen-Johansson disease
 Jumper's or kicker's knee

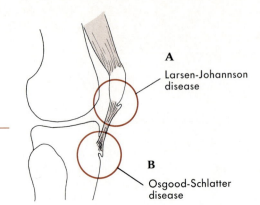

Figure 19-45

Two conditions of the immature extensor mechanism. **A,** Larsen-Johansson disease. **B,** Osgood-Schlatter disease.

ETIOLOGICAL FACTORS   The most commonly accepted cause of Osgood-Schlatter disease is repeated avulsion of the patellar tendon at the epiphysis of the tibial tubercle. Complete avulsion of the patellar tendon is a major complication of Osgood-Schlatter disease.

SYMPTOMS AND SIGNS   Repeated irritation causes swelling, hemorrhage, and gradual degeneration of the epiphysis as a result of impaired circulation. The athlete complains of severe pain when kneeling, jumping, and running. There is point tenderness over the anterior proximal tibial tubercle (Figure 19-45).

MANAGEMENT   Management is usually conservative and includes the following:

1. Stressful activities are decreased until the epiphyseal union occurs, within 6 months to 1 year.
2. Severe cases may require a cylindrical cast.
3. Ice is applied to the knee before and after activities.
4. Isometric strengthening of quadriceps and hamstring muscles is performed.
5. Surgery is performed only in the most severe cases.

Larsen-Johansson disease   Larsen-Johansson disease is similar to Osgood-Schlatter disease, but it occurs at the inferior pole of the patella (see Figure 19-45). As with Osgood-Schlatter disease, the cause is believed to be excessive repeated strain on the patellar tendon. Swelling, pain, and point tenderness characterize Larsen-Johansson disease. Later, degeneration can be noted during x-ray examination.

Jumper's and Kicker's Knee Problems

Jumping, as well as kicking or running, may place extreme tension on the knee extensor muscle complex. As a result of either one or more commonly repetitive injuries, tendinitis occurs in the patellar or quadriceps tendon. On rare occasions, a patellar tendon may completely fail and rupture.

Patellar or quadriceps tendinitis   Sudden or repetitive forceful extension of the knee may begin an inflammatory process that will eventually lead to tendon degeneration.

SYMPTOMS AND SIGNS   Patellar or quadriceps tendinitis can be described in three stages of pain:

Stage 1   Pain after sports activity
Stage 2   Pain during and after activity (the athlete is able to perform at the appropriate level)
Stage 3   Pain during activity and prolonged after activity (athletic performance is hampered) may progress to constant pain and complete rupture

MANAGEMENT Any pain in the extensor mechanism must preclude sudden explosive movement such as that characterized by heavy plyometric-type exercising. Many approaches to treating athletes with extensor mechanism disorders have been reported, including the use of ice, phonophoresis, iontophoresis, ultrasound, and various forms of superficial heat modalities such as whirlpool together with a program of exercise. There are three goals of rehabilitation: decreasing pain, restoring motion, and increasing strength, endurance, and function.[2] Increasingly, ultrasound is being used alternately with ice for pain relief.[2] Three minutes of ultrasound is followed with 2 minutes of cold.

Patellar tendon and quadriceps tendon ruptures A sudden powerful contraction of the quadriceps muscle with the weight of the body applied to the affected leg can cause a rupture.[29] The rupture may occur to the quadriceps tendon or to the patellar tendon. Usually rupture does not occur unless there has been an inflammatory condition over a period of time in the region of the knee extensor mechanism, causing tissue degeneration. Seldom does a rupture occur in the middle of the tendon, but usually it is torn from its attachment. The quadriceps tendon ruptures from the superior pole of the patella, whereas the patellar tendon ruptures from the inferior pole of the patella. Proper conservative care of jumper's knee is essential to avoid such a major injury. For athletes who use antiinflammatory drugs such as steroids, intense exercise involving the knee must be avoided.[25] Steroids injected directly into these tendons weaken collagen fibers and mask pain.[25]

Runner's and Cyclist's Knee

Runner's knee is a general expression for many repetitive and overuse conditions. Many runner's knee problems can be attributed to malalignment and structural asymmetries of the foot and lower leg, including leg-length discrepancy. Common are patellar tendinitis and patellofemoral problems that may lead to chondromalacia. Two conditions that are becoming increasingly prevalent among joggers, distance runners, and cyclists are **iliotibial band friction syndrome** and **pes anserinus tendinitis** or bursitis.

Iliotibial band friction syndrome Illiotibial band friction syndrome is an overuse condition commonly occurring in runners and cyclists having genu varum.[27] Irritation develops at the band's insertion and, where friction is created, over the lateral femoral condyle. Conducting Ober's test (p. 637) will cause pain at the point of irritation.

Pes anserinus tendinitis or bursitis The pes anserinus is where the sartorius, gracilis, and semitendinous muscles join to the tibia (see Figure 19-7). Associated with this condition is pes anserinus bursitis. In contrast to iliotibial band friction syndrome, inflammation results from excessive genu valgum and weakness of the vastus medialis muscle. This condition is commonly produced by running on a slope with one leg higher than the other.

iliotibial band friction syndrome
Runner's knee.

pes anserinus tendinitis
Cyclist's knee.

MANAGEMENT Management of runner's or cyclist's knee involves correction of foot and leg alignment problems. Therapy includes cold packs or ice massage before and after activity, proper warmup and stretching, and avoiding activities such as running on inclines that aggravate the problem. Other management procedures may include administering anti-inflammatory medications and using orthotic shoe devices to reduce leg conditions such as genu varum.[27]

The Collapsing Knee

Knee collapse can stem from a variety of reasons. The most common causes of frequent knee collapse include a weak quadriceps muscle; chronic instability of the medial collateral ligament, anterior cruciate ligament, or posterior capsule; a torn meniscus; loose bodies within the knee; and a subluxating patella. Chondromalacia and a torn meniscus have also caused the knee to give way.

KNEE JOINT REHABILITATION

The knee rehabilitation program has as its primary goal to restore the athlete's muscle strength, power, endurance, flexibility, and agility. In exercise rehabilitation of the knee, as with other programs of rehabilitation, each physician has his or her own approach. In general, however, knee rehabilitation falls into six major phases:

Preoperative phase
Phase 1   Postoperative or postinjury period
Phase 2   Early intermediate rehabilitation
Phase 3   Late intermediate rehabilitation
Phase 4   Advanced rehabilitation
Phase 5   Return to competition

Preoperative Phase

If there is to be elective knee surgery, it is essential that muscles surrounding the joint be as strong as possible. A well-conditioned knee will undergo surgery with fewer negative effects than one that is deconditioned. In addition to the knee joint, all adjacent joints should be conditioned as much as possible. Any exercise must not aggravate the condition by forcing the knee through a full range of motion (Table 19-1).

Phase 1

Rehabilitative exercise during the immediate postoperative or postinjury phase depends on the nature of surgery or type of injury sustained. Usually it is initiated 24 hours after an operation or an acute injury. This phase ideally should be a continuation of the presurgical phase to maintain normal function and to prevent muscle atrophy, but without knee flexion and extension.

Progression from one phase to another depends on the extent of soft-tissue healing, pain, joint mobilization, and residual joint instability.

Exercise rehabilitation of the postsurgical anterior instability may take as long as 1 year. The immediate postoperative period continues with the preoperative isometric exercises. Contractile muscle ability is emphasized during this period.[21] To augment the exercise, electrical stimulation or biofeedback training may be performed.[21] In knee rehabilitation after knee reconstruction, 4 to 6 weeks of

TABLE 19-1 Sample 3-Week Preoperative Phase for Uncomplicated Injury

Exercise	First Week	Second Week	Third Week
Quadriceps setting (6 sec maximum contraction, 2 sec rest for 5 min each waking hour)	+*	+	+
Straight leg raises against maximum resistance (hold 6 sec in up position followed by 2 sec rest) (in cases of anterior instability, the knee is bent between 20 and 30 degrees)			
Into hip extension	+	+	−†
Into hip abduction	+	+	−
Into hip adduction	+	+	−
Into hip flexion	+	+	−
Wall pulley (maximum resistance 10-15 repetitions three times a day)			
Into hip extension		+	+
Into hip flexion		+	+
Into hip abduction		+	+
Into hip adduction		+	+
Isokinetic knee flexion (of special importance to anterior instability repair)		+	+
PNF patterns for ankle, knee, and hip		+	+

*+, Performed.
†−, Optional.

immobilization may be needed while early healing takes place. This immobilization ensures that the sutures or attachments are maintained in a secure position. All joints adjacent to the knee are exercised maximally (Figure 19-46). During this phase only active motion is encouraged, along with crutch walking using a three-point gait. In anterior instability surgical cases, from 6 to 8 weeks of knee motion is progressively allowed through the use of a cast brace that allows 30 to 60 degrees of flexion. Each week 5 degrees of extension and 10 degrees of flexion are added until 90 degrees of flexion and −15 degrees of extension have been achieved. When leaving the hospital, the athlete is encouraged to engage in general conditioning activities to maintain the level of fitness.

Phase 2

Phase 2 is considered the early intermediate period of rehabilitation. It usually begins at the end of immobilization and when swelling is controlled, pain is minimum, and the athlete can flex the knee 90 degrees and extend it to −15 degrees. For the knee that has been surgically corrected for anterior instability, this phase may not commence for 10 to 12 weeks after surgery. Less complicated knee problems may begin this phase 3 to 4 weeks after injury. A major goal of Phase 2 is to restore biomechanical efficiency and achieve full mobilization and pain-free extension and flexion. Both the quadriceps and hamstring muscle groups must be strengthened; however, in anterior cruciate ligament repair, hamstring strength is emphasized over quadriceps strength. Using isotonic hamstring exercise does not produce an anterior drawer force on the tibia, as does isotonic quadriceps exercise (Table 19-2; Figure 19-47).

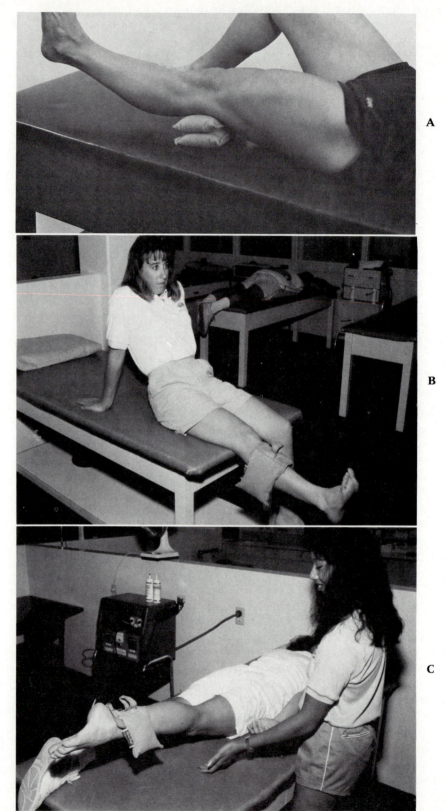

Figure 19-46

Knee exercises performed during the preoperative phase and Phase 1. **A,** Muscle setting. **B,** Sitting straight-leg raise with hip flexion. **C,** Straight-leg raise with hip extension.

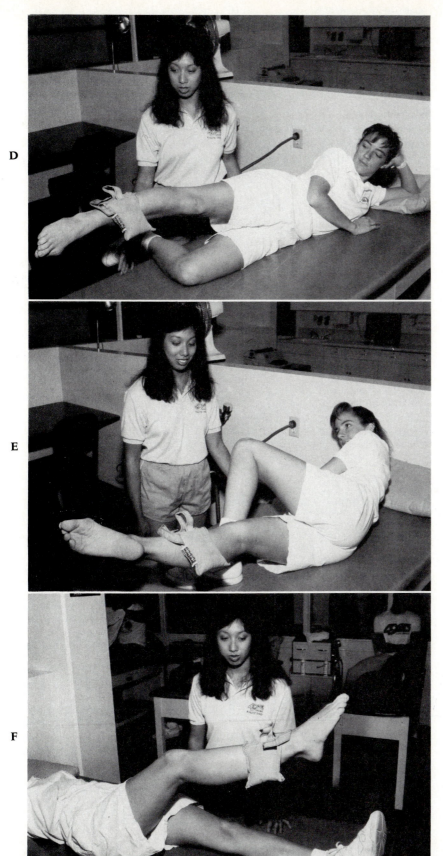

D

E

F

Figure 19-46, cont'd

D, Hip side raise (abduction)
E, Hip adduction. **F,** Back
lying with hip flexion.

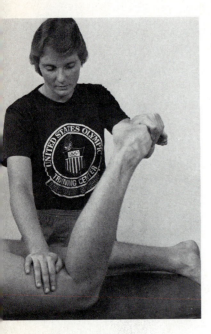

Figure 19-47

It is essential that hamstring muscle strength be increased in case of knee injury and surgery.

Phase 3

Phase 3 is considered the later intermediate stage of rehabilitation. The criteria for beginning Phase 3 are no swelling or inflammation and minimum to no pain with almost full range of motion. The athlete is able to walk without a limp. For the athlete who has undergone reconstruction of anterior instability, this phase may not be reached for 6 months or longer. This phase involves more intense exercising. Isokinetic or PNF exercises, isotonic or isometric resistance, and cycling exercises are the exercises of choice (Table 19-3).

TABLE 19-2 Phase 2 Knee Joint Rehabilitation

Exercise	Repetitions or Duration	Times per Day
Straight leg raises from all positions, maximum resistance (sandbags)	15-20	3
Straight leg pulling exercise in all positions, maximum resistance	15-20	3
Toe raises	15-20	3
PNF exercises (emphasize hamstring muscles for anterior cruciate ligament repair)	15-20	2-3
Stationary cycling; first both legs, then affected leg only	10-20 min	1-2
Modified isokinetic exercise (begin with low speed and progress gradually)	5-15	2-3

TABLE 19-3 Phase 3 Knee Joint Rehabilitation

Exercise	Repetitions or Duration	Times per Day
Isokinetic	Starting at 120 degrees/sec and progressing to 300 degrees/sec	1-2
PNF exercises		1
Stationary bicycling	3-5 miles as fast as possible (varied resistance)	1
Pes anserinus isometric exercise	6-sec contact	2-3
Isotonic exercise, maximum resistance		
Leg extension	15-20 repetitions	1
Leg flexion	15-20 repetitions	1
Leg press	15-20 repetitions	1
Balance activities		
On one leg	2-3 min	3
On 2-inch (5 cm) board (eyes open)	2-3 min	3
On wobble board (eyes closed)	2-3 min	3
Active static stretching of quadriceps and hamstring muscles	30 sec, each repeated 3 times	2-3
Jogging (jog-run for uncomplicated knee)	1-3 miles	1

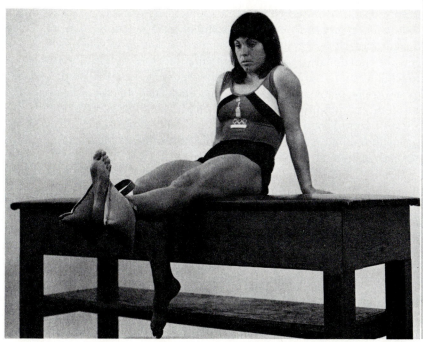

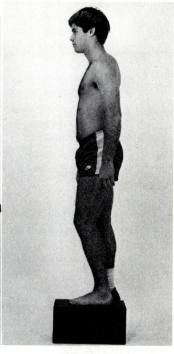

Figure 19-48

When an athlete is almost able to fully extend an injured knee against some resistance, he or she is ready for Phase 4 rehabilitation.

TABLE 19-4 Phase 4 Knee Joint Rehabilitation

Exercise	Repetitions or Duration	Times per Day or Week
Isokinetic	300 degrees/sec, 5 min	1 per day
Isotonic, maximum resistance		
Leg extension	15-20 repetitions,	3 times per week
Leg curls	three sets of 10	
Leg presses		
Half knee squats		
Toe raises		
Rope jumping	10-20 min	1 time per day
Stationary bicycling	10-20 min	1 time per day
Running	20 min	
Progress from slow running to fast and straight jog or straight run	2-3 miles	1 time per day
Progress to running circles in each direction, large figure-8s, weaving in and out of obstacles, and cutting maneuvers	1-2 miles	2 times

Phase 4

To enter Phase 4 of knee joint rehabilitation the athlete must have full range of motion, no symptoms, functional stability, and no more than a 10% deficit in strength, power, and endurance compared to the uninvolved leg. Phase 4 represents the functional stage of the rehabilitation program (Figure 19-48). As in ankle rehabilitation, the injured knee joint needs to regain dynamic control, requiring a variety of balance activities that stimulate the proprioceptors. Isokinetic resistance and proprioceptive neuromuscular facilitation (PNF) also help reestablish joint control and stability.[17] For the knee that has been treated surgically, especially with anterior instability reconstruction, this phase may not arrive until the tenth or twelfth month (Table 19-4).

Phase 5

Phase 5 is the athlete's reinstatement to competition. Exercise is no longer directed toward therapy but toward competitive conditioning. The knee now is symptom free and equal in every respect to the uninjured knee in terms of strength, power, and size (Figure 19-49).

DAPRE in Knee Exercise Rehabilitation

DAPRE

Daily adjustable progressive resistive exercise; a modification of the DeLorme method of exercise rehabilitation.

The **DAPRE** or daily adjustable progressive resistive exercise, as described in Chapter 14, is an excellent approach to knee rehabilitation following surgery (see pp. 390-391 and Tables 14-1 and 14-2). In this method daily strength increases are noted, and the athlete exercises at near optimum level. In the third and fourth sets as many full repetitions are performed as possible, with the number executed determining the weight to be added for the fourth set and for the first set in the next exercise session.

Criteria for Recovery and Returning to Sports

The criteria for recovery after a knee injury are sport specific. Every sport has certain requirements such as jumping, running, or cutting from one side to the other. These are feats that can be tested. As indicated previously, full range of motion, equal or almost equal circumference to the unaffected side, and full strength, power, endurance, and proprioception are also of major importance.

Maintenance

Once a serious knee injury has occurred, the knee tends to decondition quickly. It is important for the athlete to engage in a daily maintenance program. Immediately after practice the athlete should use either an isokinetic machine or exercise isotonically with weight resistance. Fifty percent of maximum resistance should keep the knee strong.

A collapse after a sudden change of direction may indicate ligamentous instability or a kneecap that has moved out of its articular groove. Catching and collapse can occur in a knee that has a disrupted meniscus, a patella that has an irregular articular surface, or a piece of articular cartilage that has broken loose in osteochondritis dissecans. If these conditions recur, bracing or surgery may be the treatment of choice.

Figure 19-49

In Phase 5 exercise rehabilitation the athlete has gained almost full strength power, and flexibility.

Patellofemoral Joint Rehabilitation

Patellofemoral joint exercise rehabilitation should be performed conservatively.

Injuries to the patellofemoral joint should be rehabilitated conservatively. All exercises should be pain free. Primarily, exercise rehabilitation consists of muscle setting and isometrics[8] (Table 19-5).[8]

TABLE 19-5 Patellofemoral Joint Rehabilitation

Exercise*	Repetitions or Duration	Times per Day
While lying on back with knee in full extension, contract quadriceps muscle isometrically, pulling patella toward abdomen; when pain free, progress to next exercise	Hold for 6 sec, rest 2 sec; repeat 2-3 times per session	1-2 times every waking hour
With 4-inch (10 cm) thick pad underneath popliteal fossa, extend knee fully	With 2-10 lb weight on ankle, hold extended position for 6 sec; repeat 2-3 times	1-2 times every waking hour
With 4-inch (10 cm) thick pad underneath popliteal fossa and knee fully extended, slowly, eccentrically lower knee to table	With 2-10 lb weight on ankle, repeat 2-3 times	1-2 times every waking hour
In front-lying position with pillow under abdomen, slowly curl knee to approximately 30-degree angle	With 2-10 lb weight on ankle, hold terminal position for 6 sec; repeat 2-3 times	1-2 times every waking hour
In front-lying position with pillow under abdomen, slowly lower leg eccentrically from 30-degree angle of flexion	With 2-10 lb weight on ankle, repeat leg exercise 2-3 times	1-2 times every waking hour

*All exercises must be within pain-free limitations.

SUMMARY

The knee is one of the most, if not the most, complex joints in the human body. As a hinge joint that also glides and has some rotation, it is also one of the most traumatized joints in sports. Three structures are most often injured: the medial and lateral collateral capsules and ligaments, the menisci, and the cruciate ligaments.

Prevention of knee injuries involves maximizing muscle strength and wearing appropriate shoes. Use of protective knee bracing may be questionable.

Acute knee conditions include superficial conditions such as contusions and bursitis. Ligamentous and capsular sprains occur frequently to the medial aspect of the knee and less often to the lateral aspect. The most common ligamentous injury occurs to the anterior cruciate ligament.

The immediate care of a knee sprain requires ice, compression, and elevation (ICE) for 20 minutes every 1½ hours during waking periods. ICE may be extended for several days, depending on the extent of the injury. Rest is also essential during this inflammatory phase.

A meniscus can be injured in a variety of ways, including a rotary force to the knee with the foot planted, a sudden valgus or varus force, or sudden flexion or extension of the knee. There may be severe pain and loss of motion, locking of the knee, and pain in the area of the tear.

Chronic knee joint problems can occur when the articular cartilage is disrupted. Sometimes pieces of cartilage or bone become loose bodies in the knee joint. These floating pieces can cause chronic knee inflammation, locking, catching, or giving way of the joint.

The patella and its surrounding area can develop a variety of injuries from sports activities. Some of these injuries are fracture, dislocation, and chronic articular degeneration such as chondromalacia. Other conditions in the region include Osgood-Schlatter disease and jumper's knee.

The goal of the knee rehabilitation program is to restore the athlete's muscular strength, power, endurance, flexibility, and agility. The program varies according to the sport and condition.

REVIEW QUESTIONS AND SUGGESTED ACTIVITIES

1. Describe the major structural and functional anatomical features of the knee.
2. Demonstrate the steps that should be taken when assessing the knee.
3. Explain how a knee injury can best be prevented. What injuries are most difficult to prevent?
4. Describe the symptoms, signs, and management of knee contusions and bursitis.
5. Distinguish collateral ligamentous sprains from cruciate sprains.
6. What is the difference between a meniscal lesion and a knee plica?
7. Explain how different fractures (e.g., patellar and epiphyseal fractures) may occur in this region of the knee.
8. Describe the relationship of loose bodies within the knee to osteochondritis dissecans.
9. How do the patella fracture and the patellar dislocation occur?
10. Compare the causes of patellofemoral arthralgia.
11. What types of injuries can occur to the extensor mechanism in a physically immature athlete?
12. Describe and compare the iliotibial band friction syndrome and pes anserinus tendinitis or bursitis.
13. What causes the knee to collapse?
14. Describe knee rehabilitation following conservative treatment of a second-degree medial collateral sprain and following surgical repair of a torn anterior cruciate ligament.

REFERENCES

1. Allman, Jr, FA: Conditioning for prevention of knee injuries. In Hunter, LY, and Funk, Jr, FJ, editors: Rehabilitation of the injured knee, St. Louis, 1984, The CV Mosby Co.

2. Antich, TJ, et al.: Physical therapy treatment of knee extensor mechanism disorders: comparison of four treatment modalities, J Orthop Sports Phys Ther 8:255, 1986.

3. Arnoczky, SP, and Warren, RF: Microvasculature of the human meniscus, Am J Sports Med 10:90, March/April 1982.

4. Berfeld, JA: Injury to the anterior cruciate ligament, Phys Sportsmed 10:47, Nov 1982

5. Birnbaum, JA: The musculoskeletal manual, New York, 1982, Academic Press, Inc.

6. Blackburn, Jr, TA, et al.: An introduction to the plica, J Orthop Sports Phys Ther 3:171, 1982.

7. Boland, Jr, AL: Soft tissue injuries of the knee. In Nicholas, JA, and Hershman, EB, editors: The lower extremity and spine in sports medicine, St. Louis, 1986, The CV Mosby Co.

8. Cailliet, R: Knee pain and disability, ed 2, Philadelphia, 1983, FA Davis Co.

9. Cameron, JC: Osteochondritis dissecans, osteochondral fractures, and osteoarthritis of the knee. In Welsh, RP, and Shephard, RJ, editors: Current therapy in sports medicine 1985-1986, Philadelphia, 1985, Brian C Decker, Publisher.

10. Colville, MR, et al.: The Lenox Hill brace: an evaluation of effectiveness in treating knee instability, Am J Sports Med 14:257, 1986.

11. Coughlin, L, et al.: Knee bracing and anterolateral rotary instability, Am J Sports Med 15:161, 1987.

12. Derscheid, FL, and Garrick, JG: Medial collateral ligament injuries in football, Am J Sports Med 9:365, 1981.

13. DiStefano, VJ: The enigmatic anterior cruciate ligament, Ath Train 16:244, 1981.

14. Frankel, VH, and Nordin, M: Biomechanics of the knee. In Hunter, LY, and Funk, Jr, FJ, editors: Rehabilitation of the injured knee, St. Louis, 1984, The CV Mosby Co.

15. Hoppenfeld, S: Physical examination of the spine and extremities, New York, 1976, Appleton-Century-Crofts.

16. Howe, J, and Johnson, RJ: Knee injuries in skiing, Symposium on skiing injuries, Clinics in sports medicine, vol 1, no 2, Philadelphia, 1982, WB Saunders Co.

17. Ihara, H, and Nakayama, A: Dynamic joint control training for knee ligament injuries, Am J Sports Med 14:309, 1986.

18. Inoue, M, et al.: Treatment of the medial collateral ligament injury: I: The importance of anterior cruciate ligament on the varus-valgus knee laxity, Am J Sports Med 15:15, 1987.

19. Jensen, JE, et al.: Systemic evaluation of acute knee injuries. In Larson, RL, and Singer, KM, editors: Clinics in sports medicine, vol 4, no 2, Philadelphia, 1985, WB Saunders Co.

20. Johnson, RJ: The anterior cruciate: a dilemma in sports medicine, Int J Sports Med 2:71, May 1982.

21. Jones, AL: Rehabilitation for anterior instability of the knee: preliminary report, J Orthop Sports Phys Ther 3:121, Winter 1982.

22. King, S, et al.: The anterior cruciate ligament: a review of recent concepts, J Orthop Sports Phys Ther 8:100, 1986.

23. Klein, KK: Developmental asymmetries of the weight bearing skeleton and its implications on knee stress and knee injury, Ath Train 17:207, 1982.

24. Kramer, PG: Patella malalignment syndrome: rationale to reduce excessive lateral pressure, J Orthop Sports Phys Ther 8:301, 1986.

25. Kulund, DN: The injured athlete, Philadelphia, 1982, JB Lippincott Co.

26. Nisonson, G, et al.: The knee. In Scott, WN, Nisonson, B, and Nicholas, JA, editors: Principles of sports medicine, Baltimore, 1984, Williams & Wilkins.

27. Olson, DW: Iliotibial band friction syndrome, Ath Train 21(1):32, 1986.

28. Peterson, L, and Frankel, VH: Biomechanics of the knee in athletics. In Nicholas, JA, and Hershman, JA, editors: The lower extremity and spine in sports medicine, vol 1, St. Louis, 1986, The CV Mosby Co.

29. Siwek, CW: Quadriceps and patellar tendon ruptures. In Welsh, RP, and Shephard, RJ, editors: Current therapy in sports medicine 1985-1986, Philadelphia, 1985, Brian C Decker, Publisher.

30. Solomonow, M, et al.: The synergistic action of the anterior cruciate ligament and thigh muscles in maintaining joint stability, Am J Sports Med 15(3):207, 1986.

31. Torsten, J, et al.: Clinical diagnosis of ruptures of the anterior cruciate ligament, Am J Sports Med 10:100, 1982.

32. Vitti, G: Patellofemoral joint lesions—pointers in evaluation, Sports Med Dig 8(12):6, 1986.

33. Weesner, CL, et al.: Clinical usage and application of instrumented cruciate ligament assessment, Ath Train 22:29, 1987.

34. Wickiewicz, TL, and Warren, RF: Posterior and postero-lateral instabilities of

the knee, Postgraduate advances in sports medicine, I-II, Pennington, NJ, 1985, Forum Medicus, Inc.

35. Woo, SL-Y, et al.: Treatment of the medial collateral ligament injury: II: Structure and function of canine knees in response to differing treatment regimens, Am J Sports Med 15:22, 1987.

ANNOTATED BIBLIOGRAPHY

Cailliet, R: Knee pain and disability, ed 2, Philadelphia, 1983, FA Davis Co.
Includes both structural and functional anatomy, as well as an in-depth discussion of acute and chronic knee conditions.

Hunter, LY, and Funk, Jr, FJ, editors: Rehabilitation of the injured knee, St. Louis, 1984, The CV Mosby Co.
Provides an in-depth look at the many complicated aspects of knee rehabilitation. This text presents both the theoretical and the practical aspects of rehabilitation.

Larson, RL, editor: Symposium on the knee, Clinics in sports medicine, vol 4, no 2, Philadelphia, 1985, WB Saunders Co.
An in-depth monograph about the knee. It presents 15 chapters covering all aspects of the athlete's knee.

Torg, JS, et al.: Rehabilitation of athletic injuries: an atlas of therapeutic exercises, Chicago, 1987, Year Book Medical Publishers, Inc.
Thorough coverage of exercise rehabilitation in sports medicine. Chapter 5, "The Knee," provides general coverage of the use of exercise for the most common problems seen in sports.

20

The Thigh, Hip, and Pelvis

When you finish this chapter, you should be able to

Describe the major anatomical features of the thigh, hip, and pelvis as they relate to sports injuries

Identify and evaluate the major sports injuries to the thigh, hip, and pelvis

Establish a management plan for a sports injury to the thigh, hip, or pelvis

A lthough the thigh, hip, and pelvis have relatively lower incidences of injury than the knee and lower limb, they still receive considerable trauma from a variety of sports activities. Of major concern are thigh strains and contusions and chronic and overuse stresses affecting the thigh and hip.

THE THIGH REGION
Anatomy

The thigh is generally considered that part of the leg between the hip and the knee. Several important anatomical units must be considered in terms of their relationship to sports injuries: the shaft of the femur, musculature, nerves and blood vessels, and the fascia that envelops the thigh.

The Femur

The femur (Figure 20-1) is the longest and strongest bone in the body and is designed to permit maximum mobility and support during locomotion. The cylindrical shaft is bowed forward and outward to accommodate the stresses placed on it during bending of the hip and knee and during weight bearing.

Thigh Musculature

The muscles of the thigh may be categorized according to their location: anterior, posterior, and medial.

Anterior thigh muscles The anterior thigh muscles consist of the sartorius and the quadriceps femoris group.

Sartorius The sartorius muscle (Figure 20-2) consists of a narrow band that is superficial throughout its whole length. It stems from the anterosuperior iliac spine and crosses obliquely downward and medially across the anterior aspect of the thigh where it attaches to the anteromedial aspect of the tibial head. It helps flex the thigh at the hip joint, abducts and outwardly rotates the thigh at the hip

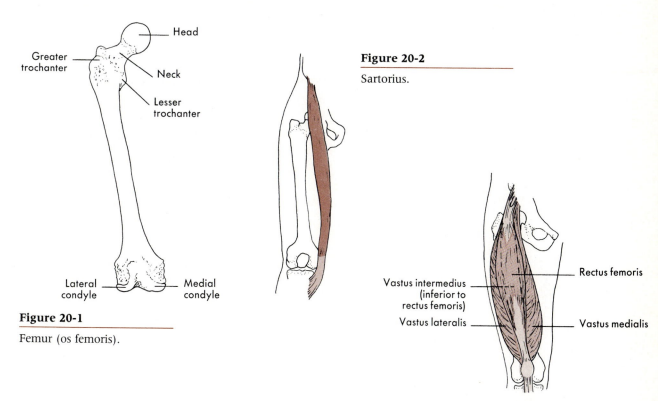

Figure 20-1

Femur (os femoris).

Figure 20-2

Sartorius.

Figure 20-3

Quadriceps femoris.

joint, and inwardly rotates the flexed knee. When the legs are stabilized, both muscles act to flex the pelvis on the thigh. When one leg's sartorius muscle contracts, the pelvis is rotated.

Quadriceps femoris   Normally the strongest of the thigh muscles, the quadriceps femoris muscle group (Figure 20-3) consists of four muscles: rectus femoris, vastus medialis, vastus lateralis, and vastus intermedius. These four muscles form a common tendon that attaches distally at the superior border of the patella and indirectly into the patellar ligament, which attaches to the tibial tuberosity.

Rectus femoris   The rectus femoris muscle is attached superiorly to the anterior inferior iliac spine and the ilium above the acetabulum and inferiorly to the patella and patellar ligament.

Vastus muscles   The vastus medialis and vastus lateralis muscles originate from the lateral and medial linea aspera of the femur, whereas the vastus intermedius muscle originates mainly from the anterior and lateral portion of the femur. Inferiorly, the three vastus muscles are attached to the rectus femoris muscle and to the lateral and proximal aspects of the patella. Of particular importance is the vastus medialis muscle, which serves as a major stabilizer for patellar tracking.

Function   The function of the quadriceps femoris muscle group is extension of the lower leg or the thigh on the lower leg. The rectus femoris muscle, with its pelvic attachment of the quadriceps muscles, is the only flexor of the thigh at the hip joint. The common peroneal nerve innervates the short head of the rectus femoris muscle, and the tibial portion of the sciatic nerve innervates the long head. This muscle group is innervated by the femoral nerve.

Posterior thigh muscles   The posterior thigh muscles include the popliteus and the hamstring muscles.

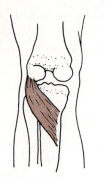

Figure 20-4

Popliteus.

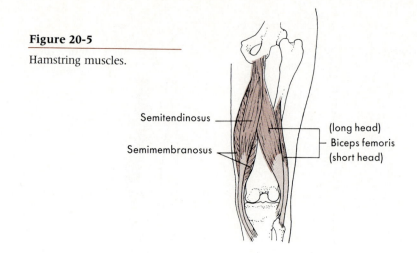

Figure 20-5

Hamstring muscles.

Popliteus muscle   The popliteus muscle stems from the lateral epicondyles of the femur (Figure 20-4). It passes downward to the posterior surface of the tibial shaft to the popliteal line. Its actions are flexion and inward rotation of the leg.

Hamstring muscles   Located posteriorly, the hamstring muscle group (Figure 20-5) consists of three muscles: the biceps femoris, semimembranosus, and semitendinosus muscles.

Biceps femoris   The biceps femoris muscle, as its name implies, has two heads. Its long head originates with the semitendinosus at the medial aspect of the ischial tuberosity. Its short head is attached to the linea aspera below the gluteus maximus attachment on the femur and medial to the attachment of the vastus lateralis. Both muscle heads attach with a common tendon to the head of the fibula.

Semitendinosus   The semitendinosus muscle originates at the medial aspect of the ischial tuberosity along with the biceps femoris muscle. Together with the semimembranosus muscle, the semitendinosus muscle attaches to the medial aspect of the proximal tibia. This attachment is just behind those of the sartorius and gracilis muscles, which all together form the pes anserinus tendon. The tibial branch of the sciatic nerve supplies this muscle.

Semimembranosus   The semimembranosus muscle originates from the lateral aspect of the upper half of the ischeal tuberosity. Moving downward, it attaches into the medial femoral condyle. It also attaches to the medial side of the tibia, the popliteus muscle fascia, and the posterior capsule of the knee joint. The tibial branch of the sciatic nerve supplies this muscle.

The hamstring muscles are biarticular, acting as extensors at the hip and flexors at the knee joint. Assisting the hamstrings in knee flexion are the sartorius, gracilis, popliteus, and gastrocnemius muscles. At the hip, hamstrings work in cooperation with the gluteus maximus to extend the hip. Lateral rotation of the leg at the knee is conducted by the biceps femoris muscle, whereas medial rotation is caused by both the semitendinosus and semimembranosus muscles.

Medial thigh muscles   The medial thigh muscles include the gracilis, pectineus, and three adductor muscles.

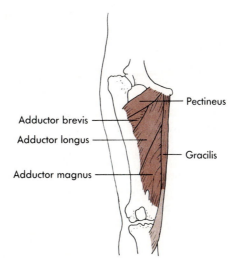

Figure 20-6

Hip adductors.

Gracilis, pectineus, adductor longus, brevis, and magnus   Five muscles comprise the medial bulk of the thigh. They are the sartorius, gracilis, adductor longus, brevis, and magnus muscles. All act as adductors and lateral rotators of the thigh at the hip joint (Figure 20-6).

Gracilis   The gracilis muscle is attached superiorly to the body of the inferior ramus of the pubis and inferiorly to the medial aspect of the proximal tibia. It is a relatively narrow-appearing muscle that adducts the thigh at the hip and flexes and medially rotates the leg at the knee joint. The anterior branch of the obturator nerve serves this muscle.

Pectineus   The pectineus muscle arises from the pectineal crest of the pubis and attaches distally on the pectineal line of the femur. As one of the adductors, it also flexes and outwardly rotates the thigh.

Adductor longus, brevis, and magnus   The adductor longus, brevis, and magnus muscles originate at the ramus of the pubis and attach inferiorly on the linea aspera of the femur. The muscles adduct the thigh at the hip and outwardly rotate the thigh. All of these muscles assist in the flexion of the thigh.

Soft-Tissue Thigh Injuries

Injuries to the thigh muscles are among the most common in sports. Contusions and strains occur most often, with the former having the higher incidence.[5]

Quadriceps Contusions

The quadriceps group is continually exposed to traumatic blows in a variety of vigorous sports. Contusions of the quadriceps display all the classic symptoms of most muscle bruises. They usually develop as the result of a severe impact to the relaxed thigh, compressing the muscle against the hard surface of the femur. At the instant of trauma, pain, a transitory loss of function, and immediate capillary effusion usually occur. The extent of the force and the degree of thigh relaxation determine the depth of the injury and the amount of structural and functional disruption that take place.[3]

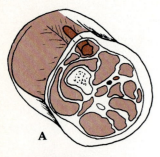

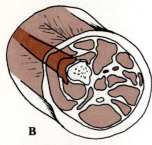

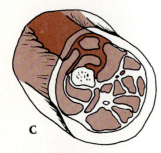

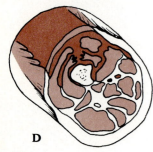

Figure 20-7

Quadriceps contusion.

SYMPTOMS AND SIGNS   Early detection and avoidance of profuse internal hemorrhage are vital, both in effecting a fast recovery by the athlete and in the prevention of widespread scarring. Detection of the charley horse is based on a history of injury, palpation, and a muscle function test. The athlete usually describes having been hit by a sharp blow to the thigh, which produced intense pain and weakness. Palpation may reveal a circumscribed swollen area that is painful to the touch. A function test is given to the quadriceps muscle. Injury to the quadriceps produces varying degrees of weakness and a decreased range of motion.

First-Degree Contusions

Grade I   The first-degree grade I quadriceps contusion represents a very superficial intramuscular bruise that produces mild hemorrhage, little pain, no swelling, and mild point tenderness at the site of the trauma. There is no restriction of the range of motion (Figure 20-7, *A*).

Grade II   The grade II contusion is deeper than grade I and produces mild pain, mild swelling, and point tenderness, with the athlete able to flex the knee no more than 90 degrees (Figure 20-7, *B*).

Second-Degree Contusions

The second-degree, or grade III, quadriceps contusion is of moderate intensity, causing pain, swelling, and a range of knee flexion that is less than 90 degrees, with an obvious limp present (Figure 20-7, *C*).

Third-Degree Contusions

The severe quadriceps, or grade IV, contusion represents a major disability. A blow may have been so intense as to split the fasciae latae, allowing the muscle to protrude (muscle herniation) (Figure 20-7, *D*). A characteristic deep intramuscular hematoma with an intermuscular spread is present. Pain is severe, and swelling may lead to hematoma. Movement of the knee is severely restricted, and the athlete has a decided limp.

MANAGEMENT   Compression by pressure bandage and the application of a cold medium can help control superficial hemorrhage, but it is doubtful whether pressure and cold will affect a deep contusion (Figure 20-8). This condition is managed in three stages:

Stage 1   Minimizing hemorrhaging through the ICE-R procedure, combined with performing isometric exercises for the quadriceps muscle. Crutches may be warranted in second- or third-degree contusions. Gentle passive stretching is performed while a cold pack is applied.

Stage 2   Using hydromassage, deep thermal therapy, or cryotherapy and stretching to regain normal range of movement.

Stage 3   Increasing to full function through a graduated program of resistive exercise and sports participation.

Generally the rehabilitation of a thigh contusion should be handled conservatively. Cold packs combined with gentle stretching may be a preferred treatment. If heat therapy is used, it should not be initiated until the acute phase of the injury has clearly passed. An elastic bandage should be worn to provide constant pressure and mild support to the quadriceps area. Manual massage and hydromassage are best delayed until resolution of the injury has begun. Exercise should

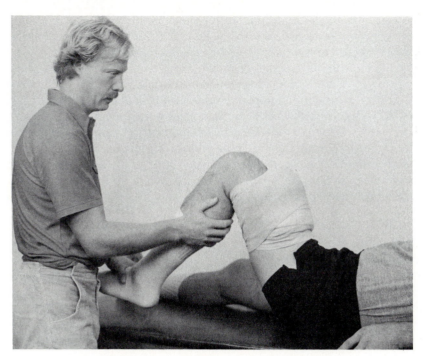

Figure 20-8

Immediate care of the thigh
contusion; applying cold pack
with a pressure bandage
along with a mild stretch
may provide some relief.

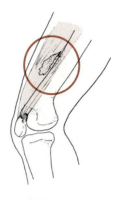

Figure 20-9

Myositis ossificans.

be graduated from mild stretching of the quadriceps area in the early stages of the
injury to swimming, if possible, and then to jogging and running. Exercise should
not be conducted if it produces pain.

Medical care of a thigh contusion may include surgical repair of a herniated
muscle or aspiration of a hematoma. Some physicians administer enzymes either
orally or through injection for the dissolution of the hematoma.

Once an athlete has sustained a second- or third-degree thigh contusion, great
care must be taken to avoid sustaining another one. The athlete should routinely
wear a protective pad held in place by an elastic wrap while engaged in sports
activity.

Myositis Ossificans

A severe blow or repeated blows to the thigh, usually to the quadriceps muscle,
can lead to ectopic bone production, or myositis ossificans. It commonly follows
bleeding into the quadriceps muscle and a hematoma. The contusion to the muscle causes disruption of the muscle fibers, capillaries, fibrous connective tissue,
and periosteum of the femur. Acute inflammation follows resolution of hemorrhage. The irritated tissue may then produce tissue formations resembling cartilage or bone. In 2 to 4 weeks, particles of bone may be noted during x-ray examination. If the injury is to a muscle belly, complete absorption or a decrease in
size of the formation may occur. This is less likely, however, if calcification is at
a muscle origin or insertion. In terms of bone attachment, some formations are
completely free of the femur, whereas one is stalklike and another is broadly
attached (Figure 20-9).

Myositis ossificans can
occur from
   A single severe blow
   Many blows to a muscle
     area
   Improper care of a
     contusion

Improper care of a thigh contusion can lead to myositis ossificans, the bony deposits or ossification in muscle. The following can initially cause the condition or, once present, aggravate it, causing it to become more pronounced:

1. Attempting to "run off" a quadriceps contusion
2. Too vigorous treatment of a contusion—for example, massage directly over the contusion, ultrasound therapy, or superficial heat to the thigh

MANAGEMENT Once myositis ossificans is apparent, treatment should be extremely conservative. If the condition is painful and restricts motion, the formation may be surgically removed after 1 year with much less likelihood of its return. Too early removal of the formation may cause it to return. Recurrent myositis ossificans may indicate a blood clotting problem such as hemophilia, which is a very rare condition.

Thigh Strains

In order of incidence of sports injury to the thigh, quadriceps contusions rank first, and hamstring strains rank second.

The two major areas for thigh strains are the quadriceps and hamstring groups. (Adductor muscle strain is discussed under hip and pelvic conditions.)

Quadriceps muscle strain Quadriceps tendon strain was discussed under jumper's problems in Chapter 19. However, on occasion, the rectus femoris muscle will become strained by a sudden stretch such as falling on a bent knee or sudden contraction such as occurs during jumping in volleyball or kicking in soccer. Usually it is associated with a muscle that is weakened or one that is overly constricted.

A tear in the region of the rectus femoris muscle may cause partial or complete disruption of muscle fibers. The incomplete tear may be located centrally within the muscle or more peripheral to the muscle.

SYMPTOMS AND SIGNS A peripheral quadriceps femoris muscle tear causes fewer symptoms than the deeper tear. In general, there is less point tenderness and less development of a hematoma.[17] A more centrally located partial muscle tear causes the athlete more pain and discomfort than the peripheral tear. With the deep tear there is a great deal of pain, point tenderness, spasm, and loss of function but with little discoloration from internal bleeding. In contrast, complete muscle tear of the rectus femoris muscle may leave the athlete with little disability and discomfort but with some deformity of the anterior thigh.

MANAGEMENT Immediate care involves using ICE and proper rest. The extent of the tear should be ascertained as soon as possible before swelling, if any, masks the degree of injury. Crutches may be warranted for the first, second, and third days. After the acute inflammatory phase has progressed to resolution and healing has begun, a regimen of isometric muscle contraction, within pain-free limits, can be initiated along with cryotherapy. Other therapy approaches such as cold whirlpool and ultrasound may also be used. Gentle stretching should not be started until the thigh is pain free. A neoprine or elastic sleeve (Figure 20-10) may be worn or taping (see Figure 12-21) may be used for soft-tissue support.

Hamstring strains Hamstring strains rank second in incidence of sports injuries to the thigh; of all the muscles of the thigh that are subject to strain, the hamstring has one of the highest incidences.

MECHANISM OF INJURY The exact cause of hamstring strain is not known. It is speculated that a quick change of the hamstring muscle from one of knee stabilization to that of extending the hip when running could be a major cause of

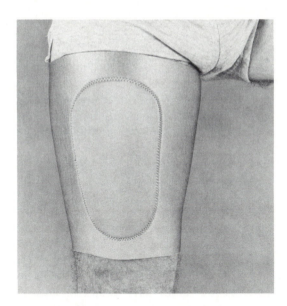

Figure 20-10

A neoprine sleeve may be worn for soft-tissue support.

Figure 20-11

There is a high incidence of hamstring strain in the sprint event of track and field.

strain (Figure 20-11). What leads to this muscle failure and deficiency in the complementary action of opposing muscles is not clearly understood. Some possible reasons are muscle fatigue, faulty posture, leg-length discrepancy, tight hamstrings, improper form, or imbalance of strength between hamstring muscle groups.[2] **NOTE**: Hamstring muscles function as decelerators of leg swing and commonly become injured when an athlete suddenly changes direction or starts to slow. In most athletes the hamstring muscle group should have a strength 60% to 70% of that of the quadriceps group.

It has been theorized that because the short head of the biceps femoris muscle may contract at the same time as the quadriceps muscle as a result of an idiosyncracy of nerve innervation, it is subject to the highest incidence of hamstring strain.

SYMPTOMS AND SIGNS   Hamstring strain can involve the muscle belly or bony attachment. The extent of injury can vary from the pulling apart of a few muscle fibers to a complete rupture or an avulsion fracture (Figure 20-12).

Capillary hemorrhage, pain, and immediate loss of function vary according to the degree of trauma. Discoloration may occur a day or two after injury.

First-degree hamstring strain usually is evidenced by muscle soreness during movement, accompanied by point tenderness. These strains are often difficult to detect when they first occur. Not until the athlete has cooled down after activity do irritation and stiffness become apparent. The soreness of the mild hamstring strain in most instances can be attributed to muscle spasm rather than to the tearing of tissue.

A second-degree strain of a hamstring muscle represents partial tearing of muscle fibers, identified by a sudden snap or tear of the muscle accompanied by severe pain and a loss of function during knee flexion.

Third-degree hamstring strains constitute the rupturing of tendinous and/or muscular tissue, involving major hemorrhage and disability.

MANAGEMENT Initially an ice pack, with crushed ice, and compression by an elastic wrap should be used. Activity should be reduced until soreness has been completely alleviated. Ballistic stretching and explosive sprinting must be avoided.[13]

In an athlete with a first-degree hamstring strain, as with the other degrees, before he or she is allowed to resume full sports participation, complete function of the injured part must be restored.

Second- and third-degree strains should be treated very conservatively. For second-degree strains, ICE-R should be used for 24 to 48 hours, and for third-degree strains, for 48 to 72 hours. After the early inflammatory phase of injury has stabilized, a treatment regimen of isometric exercise, cryotherapy, and ultrasound may be of benefit. In later stages of healing, gentle stretching within pain limits, jogging, stationary cycling, and isokinetic exercise at high speeds may be beneficial. Following elimination of soreness, the athlete may begin isotonic knee curls. Full recovery may take from 1 month to a full season.[9] Hamstring taping may be used as a muscle restraint (see Figure 12-22).

Strains are always a problem to the athlete, because they tend to recur as a result of the inelastic, fibrous scar tissue that sometimes forms during the healing process. The higher the incidence of strains at a particular muscle site, the greater the amount of scar tissue and the greater the likelihood of further injury will be. The fear of "another pulled muscle" becomes, to some individuals, almost a neurotic obsession, which is often more handicapping than the injury itself.

Muscle rehabilitation after injury should emphasize eccentric exercise (see Table 20-1).

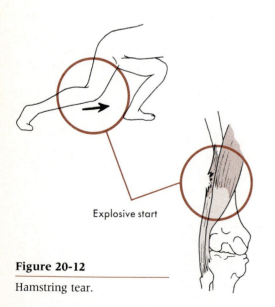

Explosive start

Figure 20-12

Hamstring tear.

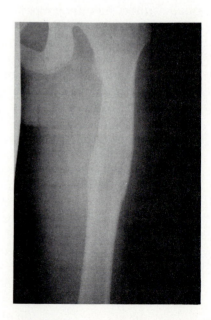

Figure 20-13

Old healed fracture of the femur.

Femoral Fractures
Acute Fractures

In sports, fractures of the femur occur most often in the shaft rather than at the bone ends and are almost always caused by a great force such as falling from a height or being hit directly by another participant. A fracture of the shaft most often takes place in the middle third of the bone because of the anatomical curve at this point, as well as the fact that the majority of direct blows are sustained in this area (Figure 20-13). Shock generally accompanies a fracture of the femur as a result of the extreme amount of pathology and pain associated with this injury. Bone displacement is usually present as a result of the great strength of the quadriceps muscle, which causes overriding of the bone fragments. Direct violence produces extensive soft-tissue injury, with lacerations of the vastus intermedius muscle, hemorrhaging, and muscle spasms.

A fractured femur is recognized by the classic signs of (1) deformity, with the thigh rotated outward; (2) a shortened thigh, caused by bone displacement; (3) loss of function; (4) pain and point tenderness; and (5) swelling of the soft tissues.

To prevent danger to the athlete's life and to ensure adequate reconditioning, immediate immobilization and referral to a physician must be made.

Femoral stress fractures   Although relatively uncommon, stress fractures of the femur are occurring more often than in the past. The possible reason is the popularity of jogging and the increased mileage covered by serious runners. Stress fractures should always be considered as a possibility when there is persistent pain.[4,11] The most common site is in the area of the femoral neck. For incomplete fractures rest and limited weight bearing constitute the usual treatment of choice. Complete stress fractures may have to be surgically pinned.

> Femoral stress fractures are becoming more prevalent because of the increased popularity of repetitive, sustained activities such as distance running.

THE HIP AND PELVIC REGION

Normal function of the hip and the pelvis is necessary for sports performance. Normal body movement is highly important for sports that predominantly use the lower extremities or the upper extremities. It must be remembered that the hip and the pelvis are part of the linkage system that transmits load from the foot to the spine and vice versa in all three planes of movement.[16]

Anatomy
Structural Relationships

The pelvis is a bony ring formed by the two innominate bones, the sacrum and the coccyx (Figure 20-14). Each innominate bone is composed of an ilium, ischium, and pubis. The functions of the pelvis are to support the spine and trunk and to transfer their weight to the lower limbs. In addition to providing skeletal support, the pelvis serves as a place of attachment for the trunk and thigh muscles and as protection for the pelvic viscera. The basin formed by the pelvis is separated into a false and a true pelvis. The false pelvis is composed of the wings of the ilium, and the true pelvis is composed of the coccyx, the ischium, and the pubis.

The *innominate bones* are composed of three bones that ossify and fuse early in life. They include the ilium, which is positioned superiorly and posteriorly; the pubis, which forms the anterior part; and the ischium, which is located inferiorly. Lodged between the innominate bones is the wedge-shaped *sacrum*, composed of

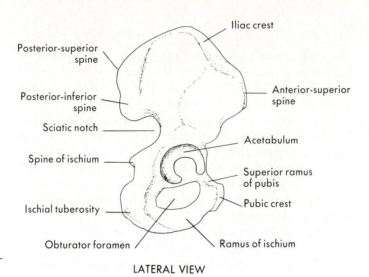

Posterior-superior spine
Posterior-inferior spine
Sciatic notch
Spine of ischium
Ischial tuberosity
Obturator foramen
Iliac crest
Anterior-superior spine
Acetabulum
Superior ramus of pubis
Pubic crest
Ramus of ischium

LATERAL VIEW

Figure 20-14

Pelvis.

five fused vertebrae. The sacrum is joined to other parts of the pelvis by strong ligaments, forming the sacroiliac joint. A small backward-forward movement is present at the sacroiliac junction. The *coccyx* is composed of four or five small, fused vertebral bodies that articulate with the sacrum.

The hip joint is formed by articulation of the femur with the innominate, or hip, bone. The spherical head of the femur fits into a deep socket, the acetabulum, which is padded at its center by a mass of fatty tissue. Surrounding its rim is a fibrocartilage known as the glenoid labrum. A loose sleeve of articular tissue is attached to the circumference of the acetabulum above and to the neck of the femur below. The capsule is lined by an extensive synovial membrane, and the iliofemoral, pubocapsular, and ischiocapsular ligaments give it strong reinforcement. Hyaline cartilage completely covers the head of the femur, with the exception of the fovea capitis, a small area in the center to which the ligamentum teres is attached. The ligamentum teres gives little support to the hip joint, having as its main function the transport of nutrient vessels to the head of the femur. Because of its bony, ligamentous, and muscular arrangements, this joint is considered by many to be the strongest articulation in the body.

Acetabulum   The acetabulum, a deep socket in the innominate bone, receives the articulating head of the femur. It forms an incomplete bony ring that is interrupted by a notch on the lower aspect of the socket. The ring is completed by the transverse ligament that crosses the notch. The socket faces forward, downward, and laterally.

Femoral head   The femoral head is a sphere fitting into the acetabulum in a medial, upward, and slightly forward direction.

Synovial membrane   The synovial membrane is a vascular tissue enclosing the hip joint in a tubular sleeve, with the upper portion surrounding the acetabulum. The lower portion is fastened to the circumference of the neck of the femur. Except for the ligamentum teres, which lies outside the synovial cavity, the membrane lines the acetabular socket.

Articular capsule   The articular capsule is a fibrous, sleevelike structure covering the synovial membrane, its upper end attaching to the glenoid labrum and

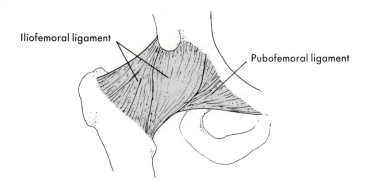

Iliofemoral ligament

Pubofemoral ligament

Figure 20-15

Ligaments of the hip.

its lower end to the neck of the femur. The fibers surrounding the femoral neck consist of circular fibers that serve as a tight collar. This area is called the *zona orbicularis* and acts in holding the femoral head in the acetabulum.

Ligaments   Many strong ligaments—the iliofemoral, the pubofemoral, and the ischiofemoral—reinforce the hip joint (Figure 20-15).

The *iliofemoral ligament* (Y ligament of Bigelow) is the strongest ligament of the body. It prevents hyperextension, controls external rotation and adduction of the thigh, and limits the pelvis during any backward rolling of the femoral head during weight bearing. It reinforces the anterior aspect of the capsule and is attached to the anterior iliac spine and the intertrochanteric line on the anterior aspect of the femur.

The *pubofemoral ligament* prevents excessive abduction of the thigh and is positioned anterior and inferior to the pelvis and femur.

The *ischiofemoral ligament* prevents excessive internal rotation and adduction of the thigh and is located posterior and superior to the articular capsule.

Bursae   The hip joint has many bursae. Clinically, the most important of them are the iliopsoas bursa and the deep trochanteric bursa. The iliopsoas bursa is located between the articular capsule and the iliopsoas muscle on the anterior aspect of the joint. The deep trochanteric bursa lies between the greater trochanter and the deep fibers of the gluteus maximus muscle.

Muscles of the Hip

The muscles comprising the hip can be divided into anterior and posterior groups. The anterior group includes the iliacus and psoas muscles. The posterior group's muscles include the tensor fasciae latae, gluteus maximus, gluteus medius, gluteus minimus, and the six deep outward rotators—the piriformis, superior gemellus, inferior gemellus, obturatorius internus, obturatorius externus, and quadratus femoris.

Anterior hip muscles   The iliacus and psoas muscles comprise the anterior hip muscles. The triangular-shaped iliacus is contained within the iliac fossa within the abdomen. Its tendon merges with the psoas major muscles, forming a common tendon that is called the iliopsoas. The iliopsoas attaches on the iliac fossa and part of the inner surface of the sacrum proximally, and it attaches distally on the lesser trochanter of the femur. The psoas muscle attaches proximally on the transverse processes and bodies of the lumbar vertebrae. Its distal attachment is on the lesser trochanter. The iliopsoas muscle flexes the thigh at the hip

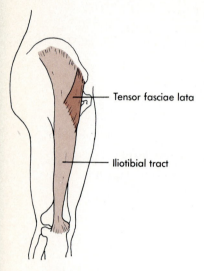

Figure 20-16

Tensor fasciae lata.

joint and tends to rotate the thigh outwardly and to adduct the thigh when free to move. When fixed, the iliopsoas assists in flexing the trunk and hip.

Posterior hip muscles The posterior muscles of the hip consist of the tensor fasciae latae, the three gluteal muscles, and the six deep outward rotators.

Tensor fasciae latae The tensor fasciae latae muscle is located on the upper anterior aspect of the lateral thigh (Figure 20-16). It is attached superiorly to the iliac crest just behind the anterior superior iliac spine and is inserted inferiorly into the iliotibial tract. Its primary action is flexion and medial rotation of the thigh. It is innervated by the superior gluteal nerve.

The gluteal region The gluteus maximus muscle forms the buttocks in the hip region. Lateral to and underneath the gluteus maximus are the gluteus medius and the gluteus minimus muscles (Figure 20-17, *A*). Underneath these larger muscles are much smaller muscles—the piriformis, the obturator internus, and the gemelli (Figure 20-17, *B* and *C*).

Gluteus maximus The gluteus maximus muscle is attached above to the posterior aspect of the iliac crest, the sacrum, and the coccyx, as well as to the fascia in the area. Inferiorly, this muscle attaches to the iliotibial tract and into the gluteal tuberosity of the femur between the linea aspera and greater trochanter. It acts as a lateral rotator of the thigh at the hip joint, as well as allows the body to rise from a sitting to a standing position and, through the attachment to the iliotibial tract, helps to extend the flexed knee. The inferior gluteal nerve supplies this muscle.

Gluteus medius The gluteus medius muscle is located lateral to the hip. It is attached superiorly to the lateral aspect of the ilium and inferiorly to the lateral aspect of the trochanter. The gluteus maximus muscle covers this muscle posteriorly, and it is covered anteriorly by the tensor fasciae latae. It acts primarily as a thigh abductor at the hip, with some flexion and medial rotation occurring from

Figure 20-17

Gluteal muscles.

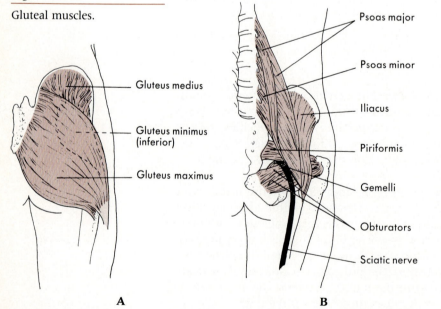

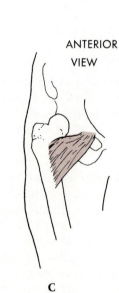

A B C

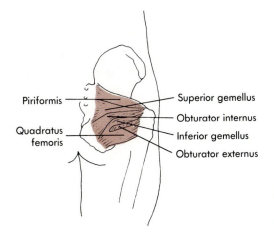

Figure 20-18

The six deep, outward rotators of the thigh.

its anterior aspect and some extension and lateral rotation occurring from its posterior aspect. It is innervated by the superior gluteal nerve.

Gluteus minimus The gluteus minimus muscle originates above the lateral aspect of the ilium and attaches inferiorly to the anterior aspect of the greater trochanter of the femur. Its main action is to cause medial rotation at the hip joint, whereas its secondary action is abduction of the thigh at the hip joint. It is innervated by the superior gluteus nerve.

Deep outward rotators The six deep outward rotator muscles are positioned behind the hip joint (Figure 20-18). They hold the head of the femur in the acetabulum.

Blood and Nerve Supply
Arteries

Opposite the fourth lumbar vertebra, the aorta divides to become the two common iliac arteries (Figure 20-19). They in turn pass downward to divide, opposite the sacroiliac joint, into the internal and external iliac arteries. Most of the branches of the internal iliac artery supply blood to the pelvic viscera. The external iliac artery, on the other hand, is the primary artery to the lower limb. It becomes the femoral artery as it passes behind the inguinal ligament, then moves in front of the thigh to the medial side, and passes in back of the thigh two thirds of the way down. It then becomes the popliteal artery, which goes behind the knee between the femoral condyles. For the most part, the femoral artery and its branches supply the muscles of the thigh.

Nerve Supply

The lumbar plexus is created by the intertwining of the fibers stemming from the first four lumbar nerves. The femoral nerve, a major nerve emerging from this plexus, later divides into many branches to supply the thigh and lower leg. Nerve fibers from the fourth and fifth lumbar nerves and the first, second, and third sacral nerves form the sacral plexus within the pelvic cavity, anterior to the piriformis muscle. Along with other nerves, the tibial and common peroneal nerves emerge from the sacral plexus and form the large sciatic nerve in the thigh (see Figure 20-19).

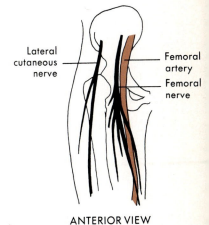

ANTERIOR VIEW

Figure 20-19

Blood and nerve supply to the hip region.

Assessing the Hip and External Pelvis

The hip and pelvis form the body's major power source for movement. The body's center of gravity is located just in front of the upper part of the sacrum. Injuries to the hip or pelvis cause the athlete major disability in either the lower limb or trunk or both.

Because of the close proximity of the hip and pelvis to the low back region, many evaluative procedures overlap.

Major Complaints

The athlete should be questioned about the site and type of pain, the extent of disability, and when the injury first occurred.

Observation

The athlete with an external pelvic pain must be observed for postural asymmetry.

The athlete should be observed for postural asymmetry while standing on one leg and during ambulation.

Postural asymmetry

1. From the front view, do the hips look even? A laterally tilted hip could mean a leg-length discrepancy and/or abnormal muscle contraction on one side of the hip or low back region.
2. From the side view, is the pelvis abnormally tilted anteriorly or posteriorly? This tilting may indicate lordosis or flat back, respectively.
3. In lower-limb alignment, is there indication of genu valgum, genu varum, foot pronation, or genu recurvatum? The patella should also be noted for relative position and alignment.
4. The posterior superior iliac spines, represented by the skin depressions above the buttocks, should be horizontal to one another. Uneven depressions could indicate that the pelvis is laterally tilted.

Standing on one leg   Standing on one leg may produce pain in the hip, abnormal movement of the symphysis pubis, or a fall of the pelvis on the opposite side as a result of abductor weakness.

Ambulation   The athlete should be observed during walking and sitting. Pain in the hip and pelvic region will normally be reflected in movement distortions.

Bony Palpation

The following bony sites should be palpated for pain and continuity:

Anteriorly	Posteriorly
1. Anterior superior iliac spine	1. Posterior superior iliac spines
2. Iliac crest	2. Ischial tuberosity
3. Greater trochanter	3. Sacroiliac joint
4. Pubic tubercles	

Soft-Tissue Palpation

The soft-tissue sites of major concern are those lying in the groin region, the femoral triangle, sciatic nerve, and major muscles.

Groin palpation   Groin pain could result from swollen lymph glands, indicating an infection, or from an adductor muscle strain. The adductors may have point tenderness at any point along their length. Resisted motion may make pain worse.

Muscle palpation   The following muscles should be palpated for pain, swelling, or fiber disruption:

Iliopsoas	Adductor longus and brevis
Sartorius	Adductor magnus
Rectus femoris at the hip joint	Gluteus medius
Gracilis	Gluteus maximus
Pectineus	Hamstring muscles at their origin

Functional Evaluation

The athlete is led through all possible hip movements, both passive and active, to evaluate range of motion and active and resistive strength (Figure 20-20). These movements are as follows:

Hip abduction
Hip adduction
Hip flexion
Hip extension
Hip internal and external rotation

Tests for hip flexion tightness   Contractures of the hip flexors are major causes of lordosis and susceptibility to groin pain and discomfort. Two tests can be used—the Kendall test and the Thomas test.

Kendall test   The athlete lies supine on a table with one knee flexed on the chest and the back completely flat (Figure 20-21). The other knee is flexed over the table's end. Normal extensibility of the hip flexors allows the thigh to touch the table, with the knee flexed approximately 70 degrees. Tight hip flexors are revealed by the inability of the thigh to lie flat on the table. If only the rectus femoris muscle is tight, the thigh will touch the table, but the knee will extend more than 70 degrees (Figure 20-22).

Thomas test   The Thomas test indicates whether hip contractures are present (Figure 20-23). The athlete lies supine on a table, arms across the chest, legs together and fully extended. The athletic trainer places one hand under the athlete's lumbar curve; one thigh is brought to the chest, flattening the spine. In this position the extended thigh should be flat on the table. If not, there is a hip contracture. When the athlete fully extends the leg again, the curve in the low back returns.

Femoral Anteversion and Retroversion

The athlete with a painful hip problem may also have a deformity in the relationship between the neck of the femur and the shaft of the femur. The normal angle of the femoral neck is 15 degrees anterior to the long axis of the shaft of the femur and femoral condyles. Athletes who walk in a toe-in manner may be reflecting a hip deformity in which the femoral neck is directed anteriorly (femoral anteversion). In contrast, athletes who walk in a pronounced toe-out manner may be displaying a condition in which the femoral neck is directed posteriorly (femoral retroversion) (Figure 20-24). Characteristic of femoral anteversion is internal hip rotation in excess of 35 degrees, and, in the case of femoral retroversion, an excess of the normal 45 degrees of external rotation.

Test for pathological conditions of the hip and sacroiliac joint   The Patrick test detects pathological conditions of the hip and sacroiliac joint (Figure 20-25). The athlete lies supine on the examining table. The foot on the side of

Figure 20-20

Manual muscle tests of the hip. **A,** Abduction.
B, Adduction. **C,** Flexion (iliopsoas muscle).
D, Extension. **E,** Internal rotation. **F,** External rotation.
G, Rectus femoris at the hip.

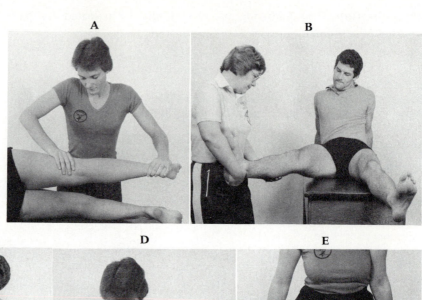

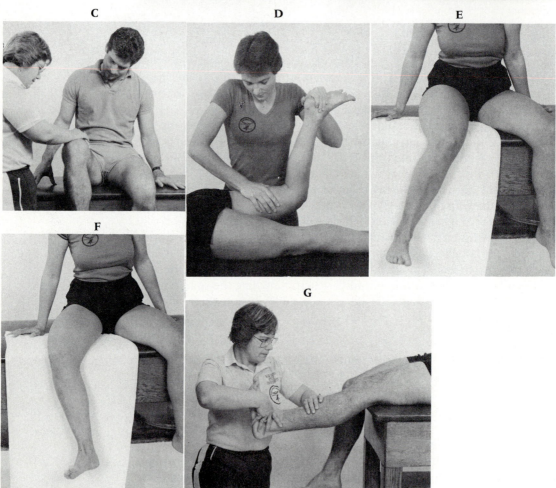

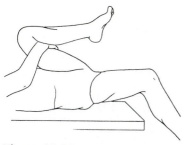

Figure 20-21

Kendall test for hip flexor tightness.

Figure 20-22

Demonstrating, **A,** extensible and, **B,** tight hip flexors.

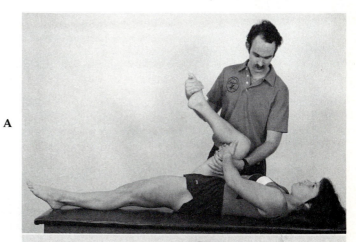

A

B

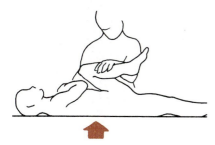

Figure 20-23

Thomas test for hip contractures.

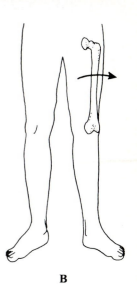

Figure 20-24

A, Anteversion of the femoral neck. When the knee is directed anteriorly, the femoral neck is directed *anteriorly* to some degree. **B,** Retroversion of the femoral neck. When the knee is directed anteriorly, the femoral neck is directed *posteriorly* to some degree.

A   B

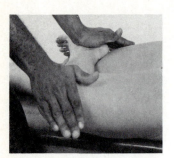

Figure 20-25

Test for a pathological condition of the hip and sacroiliac joint.

Figure 20-26

Testing for iliotibial band tightness.

Figure 20-27

A, Measuring for leg-length discrepancy. **B,** Anatomical discrepancy. **C,** Functional discrepancy.

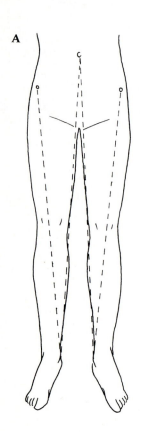

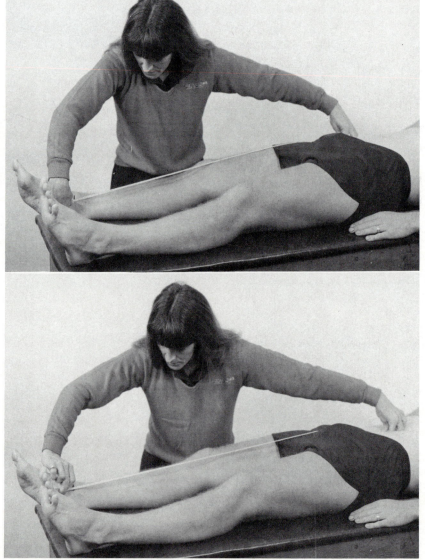

the painful sacroiliac is placed on the opposite extended knee. Pressure is then applied downward on the bent knee. Pain may be felt in the hip or sacroiliac joint.

Testing the Tensor Fasciae Latae and Iliotibial Band

Three tests that can be used to discern iliotibial band tightness and inflammation of the bursa overlying the lateral femoral epicondyle or direct irritation of the iliotibial band and periosteum are the Renne, Nobel, and Ober[14] (Figure 20-26).

Renne's test   While standing, the athlete supports full weight on the affected leg, with the knee bent at 30 to 40 degrees. A positive response of fasciae latae tightness occurs when pain is felt at the lateral femoral condyle.[14]

Nobel's test   The athlete's knee is flexed to 90 degrees, and pressure is applied to the lateral femoral epicondyle while the knee is gradually extended. A positive response occurs when severe pain is felt at the lateral femoral epicondyle with the knee at 30 degrees of flexion.[14]

Ober's test   The athlete lies on the unaffected side. With the knee flexed at 90 degrees, the affected thigh is abducted as far as possible. With the pelvis stabilized, the abducted thigh is then relaxed and allowed to drop into adduction. A contracted tensor fasciae latae or iliotibial band will keep the thigh in an abducted position, not allowing it to fall into adduction.[5,14]

Leg-Length Discrepancy

In individuals who are not physically active, leg-length discrepancies of over 1 inch may produce symptoms[17]; however, shortening as little as 3 mm (⅛ inch) may cause symptoms in highly active athletes. Such discrepancies can cause cumulative stresses to the lower limbs, hip, and pelvis or low back.

Leg-length discrepancy in an athlete can lead to stress-related physical injuries.

Measuring leg-length discrepancy   There are two types of leg-length discrepancy—true or anatomical shortening and apparent or functional shortening. X-ray examination is the most valid means of measurement. It is difficult to be completely accurate because of mobility of the soft tissue over bony landmarks (Figure 20-27, *A*).

Anatomical discrepancy   In an anatomical discrepancy, shortening may be equal throughout the lower limb or localized within the femur or lower leg. The athlete lies supine and fully extended on the table. Measurement is taken between the medial malleoli and the anterior superior iliac spine of each leg[6] (Figure 20-27, *B*).

Functional discrepancy   Functional leg shortening can occur as the result of lateral pelvic tilt (obliquely) or from a flexion or adduction deformity (Figure 20-27, *C*). Measurement is taken from the umbilicus to the medial malleoli of each ankle.

Groin Strain

The groin is that depression that lies between the thigh and the abdominal region. The musculature of this area includes the iliopsoas, the rectus femoris, and the adductor group (the gracilis, pectineus, adductor brevis, adductor longus, and adductor magnus). Any one of these muscles can be torn during sports activity and elicit what is commonly considered a groin strain (Figure 20-28). Any overextension of the groin musculature may result in a strain. Running, jumping, or twisting with external rotation can produce such injuries. Contrary to some opinions, the adductor group is more often torn than is the iliopsoas.

The groin strain presents one of the most difficult injuries to care for in sports.

MANAGEMENT PLAN FOR GROIN STRAIN

Injury Situation   A woman varsity basketball player had a history of tightness in her groin. During a game she suddenly rotated her trunk while also stretching to the right side. There was a sudden sharp pain and a sense of "giving way" in the left side of the groin that caused the athlete to immediately stop play and limp to the sidelines.

Symptoms and Signs   As the athlete described it to the athletic trainer, there was severe pain when rotating her trunk to the right and flexing her left hip. Inspection revealed the following:

1. There was major point tenderness in the groin, especially in the region of the adductor magnus muscle.
2. There was no pain during passive movement of the hip, but severe pain did occur during both active and resistive motion.
3. When the groin and hip were tested for injury, the hip joint, illiopsoas, and rectus femoris muscles were ruled out as having been injured; however, when the athlete adducted the hip from a stretch position, it caused her extreme discomfort.

Management Plan   Based on the athletic trainer's inspection, with findings confirmed by the physician, it was determined that the athlete had sustained a second-degree strain of the groin, particularly to the adductor magnus muscle.

1 **Management Phase**   GOALS: To control hemorrhage, pain, and spasms
ESTIMATED LENGTH OF TIME (ELT): 2 to 3 days

Therapy   IMMEDIATE CARE: ICE-R (20 min) intermittently, six to eight times daily
The athlete wears a 6-inch elastic hip spica

Exercise Rehabilitation   No exercise—as complete rest as possible

2 **Management Phase**   GOALS: To reduce pain, spasm, and restore full ability to contract without stretching the muscle.
ELT: 4 to 6 days

Therapy   FOLLOW-UP CARE: Ice massage (1 min) three to four times daily
Bipolar muscle stimulation above and below pain site (7 min)

Exercise Rehabilitation   PNF for hip rehabilitation three to four times daily (beginning approximately 6 days after injury)
OPTIONAL: "Jogging" in chest-level water (10 to 20 min) one or two times daily; must be done within pain-free limits
General body maintenance exercises are conducted three times a week as long as they do not aggravate the injury

3	**Management Phase**	GOALS: To reduce inflammation and return strength and flexibility
	Therapy	Muscle stimulation using the surge current at 7 or 8, depending on athlete's tolerance, together with ultrasound, set at 1 watt/cm^2 (7 min) once daily and cold therapy in the form of ice massage or ice packs (7 min) followed by exercise, two to three times daily
	Exercise Rehabilitation	PNF hip patterns two to three times daily following cold application, progressing to progressive-resistive exercise using pulley, isokinetic, or free weight (10 reps, three sets) once daily OPTIONAL: Flutter kick swimming once daily General body maintenance exercises are conducted three times a week as long as they do not aggravate the injury.
4	**Management Phase**	GOALS: To restore full power, endurance, speed, and extensibility
	Therapy	If symptom free, precede exercise with ice massage (7 min) or ice pack (5 to 15 min)
	Exercise Rehabilitation	Added to Phase 3 program, jogging on flat course slowly progressing to a 3-mile run once daily and then progressing to figure-8s, starting with obstacles 10 feet apart and gradually shortening distance to 5 feet, at full speed
5	**Management Phase**	GOAL: To return to sports competition
	Exercise Rehabilitation	Athlete gradually returns to precompetition exercise and a gradual return to competition while wearing a figure-8 elastic hip spica bandage for protection.

Criteria for Returning to Competitive Basketball

1. As measured by an isokinetic dynamometer, the athlete's injured hip should have strength equal to that of the uninjured hip.
2. Hip has full range of motion.
3. The athlete is able to run figure-8s around obstacles set 5 feet apart at full speed.

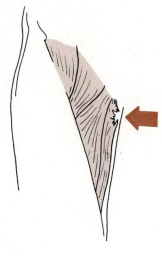

Figure 20-28

Many sports that require severe stretch of the hip region can cause a groin strain *(see arrow)*.

The strain can be felt as a sudden twinge or feeling of tearing during an active movement, or the athlete may not notice it until after termination of activity. As is characteristic of most tears, the groin strain also produces pain, weakness, and internal hemorrhage. If it is detected immediately after it occurs, the strain should be treated by intermittent ice, pressure, and rest for 48 to 72 hours.

Both passive, active, and resistive muscle tests should be given to ascertain the exact muscle or muscles that are involved.

Difficulty is frequently encountered when attempting to care for a groin strain. In these cases rest has been the best treatment. Daily whirlpool therapy or cryotherapy are palliative; ultrasound offers a more definite approach. Exercise should be delayed until the groin is pain free. Exercise rehabilitation should emphasize gradual stretching and restoration of the normal range of motion. Until normal flexibility and strength are developed, a protective spica bandage should be applied (see Figures 12-34 and 12-35). See Table 20-1 for suggestions about managing muscle-tendon injuries of the hip and pelvis.

Trochanteric Bursitis

Trochanteric bursitis is a relatively common condition of the greater trochanter of the femur. Although commonly called bursitis, it also could be an inflammation at the site the gluteus medius muscle inserts or the iliotibial band passes over the trochanter. It is most common among women runners who have an increased Q angle and/or a leg-length discrepancy. Management should include stopping running on inclined surfaces and correcting faulty running form and leg-length discrepancy. Cold packs or ice massage, together with gentle stretching, rest, and anti-inflammatory medication, may be helpful.

An increased Q angle and/or leg-length discrepancy can lead to trochanteric bursitis in women runners.

NOTE: The athletic trainer should, during an examination, be able to differentiate tenderness sites in the region of the hips and pelvis (Figure 20-29).

TABLE 20-1 Management of Muscle-Tendon Injuries of the Hip and Pelvis

Management	Phase I Acute, 1 to 72 hrs	Phase II Healing and Repair	Phase III Can Do Isometric Exercise Pain Free	Phase IV Range of Motion, 95% to Normal; Strength, 75% to Normal	Phase V 90% of Full Strength
			Stage of Healing		
Ice	X				
Compression	X				
Elevation	X				
Rest	X				
Nonsteroidal anti-inflammatory medication	X				
Contrast baths		X	X		
Whirlpool hydrotherapy		X	X		
Active range of motion		X	X		
Ultrasound		X	X		
Muscle stimulation		X	X		
Isometric exercise		X	X		
Isokinetic/isotonic exercise			X	X	
Stretching			X	X	
Aerobic exercise				X	
Proprioceptive activities				X	
Agility training				X	
Sport-specific activities				X	
Jogging				X	
Straight-ahead sprint				X	
Return to sport					X
Strength and flexibility maintenance					X

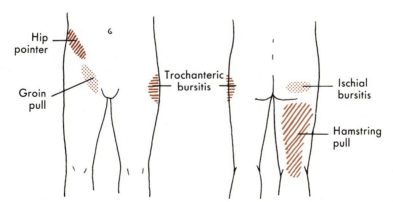

Figure 20-29

Tenderness sites in the region of the hip and pelvis.

Conditions of the Hip Joint

The hip joint, the strongest and best protected joint in the human body, is seldom seriously injured during sports activities.

Sprains of the Hip Joint

The hip joint is substantially supported by the ligamentous tissues and muscles that surround it, so any unusual movement that exceeds the normal range of motion may result in tearing of tissue. Such an injury may occur as the result of a violent twist, either produced through an impact force delivered by another participant or by forceful contact with another object, or sustained in a situation in which the foot is firmly planted and the trunk forced in an opposing direction. A hip sprain displays all the signs of a major acute injury but is best revealed through the athlete's inability to circumduct the thigh.

Dislocated Hip Joint

Dislocation of the hip joint rarely occurs in sports and then usually only as the end result of traumatic force directed along the long axis of the femur. Such dislocations are produced when the knee is bent. The most common displacement is one posterior to the acetabulum, with the femoral shaft adducted and flexed.

The luxation presents a picture of a flexed, adducted, and internally rotated thigh. Palpation will reveal that the head of the femur has moved to a position posterior to the acetabulum. A hip dislocation causes serious pathology by tearing capsular and ligamentous tissue. A fracture is often associated with this injury, accompanied by possible damage to the sciatic nerve.

MANAGEMENT   Medical attention must be secured immediatley after displacement, or muscle contractures may complicate the reduction. Immobilization usually consists of 2 weeks of bed rest and the use of a crutch for walking for a month or longer.

COMPLICATIONS   Complication of the posterior hip dislocation is likely, with the possibilities of a palsy of the sciatic nerve and/or later the development of osteoarthritis. Also, hip dislocation could lead to disruption of the blood supply to the head of the femur, which eventually leads to the degenerative condition known as avascular necrosis.

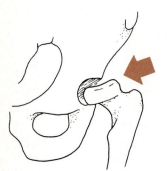

Figure 20-30

Legg-Perthes disease (coxa plana). Arrow indicates avascular necrosis of the femoral head.

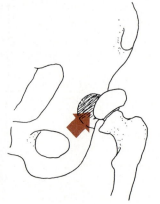

Figure 20-31

Slipped capital femoral epiphysis *(see arrow).*

Immature Hip Joint and Pelvic Problems

The coach or athletic trainer working with a child or adolescent should understand two major problems stemming from the immature hip joint. They are Legg-Perthe's avascular necrosis (coxa plana) and the slipped capital femoral epiphysis.[7]

Legg-Perthes Disease (Coxa Plana)

Legg-Perthes disease is avascular necrosis of the femoral head (Figure 20-30). It occurs in children ages 3 to 12 and in boys more often than in girls. The reason for this condition is not clearly understood. It is listed under the broad heading of osteochondroses. Because of a disruption of circulation at the head of the femur, articular cartilage becomes necrotic and flattens.

SYMPTOMS AND SIGNS   The young athlete commonly complains of pain in the groin that sometimes is referred to the abdomen or knee. Limping is also typical. The condition can have a rapid onset, but more often it comes on slowly over a number of months. Examination may show limited hip movement and pain.

MANAGEMENT   Care of this condition could mean complete bed rest to alleviate synovitis. A special brace to avoid direct weight bearing on the hip may have to be worn. If treated in time, the head of the femur will revascularize and reossify.

COMPLICATIONS   If the condition is not treated early enough, the head of the femur will become ill shaped, creating problems of osteoarthritis in later life.

> A young athlete complaining of pain in the groin, abdomen, or knee and walking with a limp may display signs of Legg-Perthes disease or a slipped capital femoral epiphysis.

Slipped Capital Femoral Epiphysis

The problem of a slipped capital femoral epiphysis (Figure 20-31) is found mostly in boys between the ages of 10 and 17 who are characteristically very tall and thin or are obese. Although idiopathic, it may be related to the effects of a growth hormone. One quarter of those seen are in both hips.

SYMPTOMS AND SIGNS   As with Legg-Perthes disease, the athlete has a pain in the groin that comes on suddenly as a result of trauma or over weeks or months as a result of prolonged stress. In the early stages of this condition signs may be minimum; however, in its most advanced stage there is hip and knee pain during passive and active motion, limitations of abduction, flexion, medial rotation, and a limp. X-ray examination may show femoral head slippage posteriorly and inferiorly.

MANAGEMENT   In minor slippage, rest and non-weight bearing may prevent further slipping. Major displacement usually requires corrective surgery.

COMPLICATIONS   If the slippage goes undetected or if surgery fails to properly restore normal hip mechanics, severe hip problems may occur in later life.

The Snapping Hip Phenomenon

The snapping hip phenomenon is common to dancers, gymnasts, and hurdlers, who use similar use of their hips.

ETIOLOGICAL FACTORS   The problem stems from habitual movements that predispose muscles around the hip to become imbalanced. This condition commonly occurs when the individual laterally rotates and flexes the hip joint as part of the exercise or dance routine. This condition is related to a structurally narrow pelvic width, greater range of motion of hip abduction, and less range of motion in lateral rotation. With hip stability becoming lessened, the hip joint capsule and ligaments and adductor muscles become less stable.

SYMPTOMS AND SIGNS   The athlete complains that snapping occurs, especially when balancing on one leg. Such a problem should not go unattended, especially if pain and inflammation are associated with the snapping.

MANAGEMENT   Management should focus on cryotherapy and ultrasound to stretch tight musculature and strengthen weak musculature in the hip region.

Pelvic Conditions

Athletes who perform activities involving violent jumping, running, and collisions can sustain serious acute and overuse injuries to the pelvic region (Figure 20-32). During running the pelvis rotates along a longitudinal axis proportionate to the amount of arm swing. It also tilts up and down as the leg engages in support and nonsupport.[1] This combination of motion causes shearing at the sacroiliac joint and symphysis pubis. There is also tilting of the pelvis, producing both a decrease and an increase in lumbar lordosis, depending on the slant of the running surface. Running downhill increased lumbar lordosis, and running uphill decreases it.[1]

Figure 20-32

Sports that include violent extension of the body can produce serious pelvic injuries.

Contusion (Hip Pointer)

Iliac crest contusion, commonly known as a hip pointer, occurs most often in contact sports (Figure 20-33).

ETIOLOGICAL FACTORS   The hip pointer results from a blow to an inadequately protected iliac crest. The hip pointer is considered one of the most handicapping injuries in sports and one that is difficult to manage. A direct force to the unprotected iliac crest causes severe pinching action to the soft tissue of that region.

SYMPTOMS AND SIGNS   Such an injury produces immediate pain, spasms, and transitory paralysis of the soft structures. As a result, the athlete is unable to rotate the trunk or to flex his thigh without pain.

MANAGEMENT   Cold and pressure should be applied immediately after injury and should be maintained intermittently for at least 48 hours. In severe cases bed rest for 1 to 2 days will speed recovery. It should be noted that the mechanisms of the hip pointer are the same as those for an iliac crest fracture or epiphyseal separation.

Referral to a physician must be made, and an x-ray examination must be performed. A variety of treatment procedures can be used for this injury. Ice massage and ultrasound have been found beneficial. Initially the injury may be injected with a steroid. Later, oral anti-inflammatory agents may be used. Recovery time usually ranges from 1 to 3 weeks. When the athlete resumes normal activity, a protective taping (see Figure 12-23) must be worn to prevent reinjury.

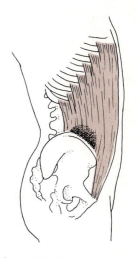

Figure 20-33

Hip pointer.

Osteitis Pubis

Since the popularity of distance running has increased, a condition known as osteitis pubis has become more prevalent.[15] It is also caused by the sports of soccer, football, and wrestling. As the result of repetitive stress on the pubic symphysis and adjacent bony structures by the pull of muscles in the area, a chronic inflammatory condition is created (Figure 20-34). The athlete has pain in the groin region and area of the symphysis pubis. There is point tenderness on the pubic tubercle and pain when such movements as running, sit-ups, and squats are performed.[1]

MANAGEMENT   Follow-up care usually consists of rest and an oral anti-inflammatory agent, with a gradual return to activity.

Fractures of the Pelvis

Acute fractures   The pelvis is an extremely strong structure, and fractures from sports activities are rare. Those fractures that occur are usually the result of direct trauma. A pelvic fracture should be suspected if an athlete has received a crushing type of trauma. Severe pain, loss of function, and shock are commonly associated with this injury. To further substantiate the possibility of a pelvic girdle fracture, one should gently examine the injury in the following manner:

1. Both hands are placed on the anterior superior spines of the ilium and are pressed downward and outward. If there is a fracture of the pelvic ring, pain will be elicited with little pressure.
2. Pressure is again gently applied by forcing the iliac spines inward and outward. In cases of pelvic ring fracture, pain will be produced during compression and spreading.

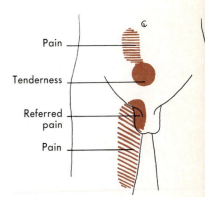

Pain —

Tenderness —

Referred pain —

Pain —

Figure 20-34

Osteitis pubis and other pain sites in the region of the pelvis and groin.

3. The possibility of acetabular and femoral head fractures also should be remembered. The distance between the anterior superior spine and the internal malleolus of both legs should be determined by a careful examination.

4. After measurement is taken, upward pressure should be applied to the femur against the acetabulum. A fracture at this point will produce pain during pressure.

If a pelvic fracture is suspected, the athlete should be immediately treated for shock and sent to a physician. The seriousness of a pelvic fracture depends mainly on the extent of shock and the possibility of internal organ injury.

Stress fractures   As with other stress fractures, repetitive cyclical forces created by ground resistance can produce stress fractures in the pelvis and the proximal femur.[18] They constitute approximately 16% of all stress fractures and are more common in women than in men.[8] The most common sites are the inferior pubic ramus, as well as the femoral neck and subtrochanteric area of the femur.[10]

Commonly, the athlete complains of groin pain, along with an aching sensation in the thigh that increases with activity and decreases with rest. Standing on one leg may be impossible. Deep palpation will cause severe point tenderness. Pelvic stress fracture has a tendency to occur during intensive interval training or competitive racing.

Rest is usually the treatment of choice for 2 to 5 months. Freestyle swimming can be performed for aerobic exercise. The breast stroke must be avoided.[12]

Avulsion fractures and apophysitis   The pelvis has a number of apophyses where major muscles make their attachments. An apophysis, or traction epiphysis, is a bony outgrowth and is contrasted to pressure epiphyses, which are the growth plates for long bones. The three most common sites for avulsion fractures and apophysitis in the pelvic region are the ischial tuberosity and the hamstring attachment, the anterior inferior iliac spine and the rectus femoris muscle attachment, and finally the anterior superior iliac spine where the sartorius muscle makes its attachment (Figure 20-35). Pain at these sites could mean an apophysitis. Severe pain and disability may be an indication of an avulsion fracture. X-ray examination should be routine for the possibility of avulsion or stress fracture in the area. Apophysitis demands rest, limited activity, and graduated exercise rehabilitation. Complete avulsion fractures require surgical repair.

Figure 20-35

Avulsion fractures to pelvic apophyses.

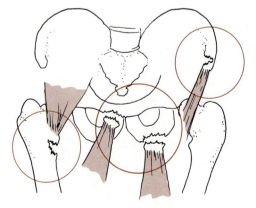

Thigh and Hip Rehabilitative Exercise

In general, exercise rehabilitation of the thigh is primarily concerned with the quadriceps and hamstring muscles. (Because of the relationship of thigh rehabilitation to the knee region, the reader is reminded to see Chapter 19). Normally the progression for strength is, first, muscle setting and isometric exercise until the muscle can be fully contracted, followed by active isotonic contraction, and then followed by isotonic progressive-resistant exercise or isokinetic exercise. PNF that uses both knee and hip patterns is also an excellent means of thigh rehabilitation. Flexibility exercises include gentle passive stretching, followed by gradual static stretching. PNF relaxation methods and/or more vigorous manual

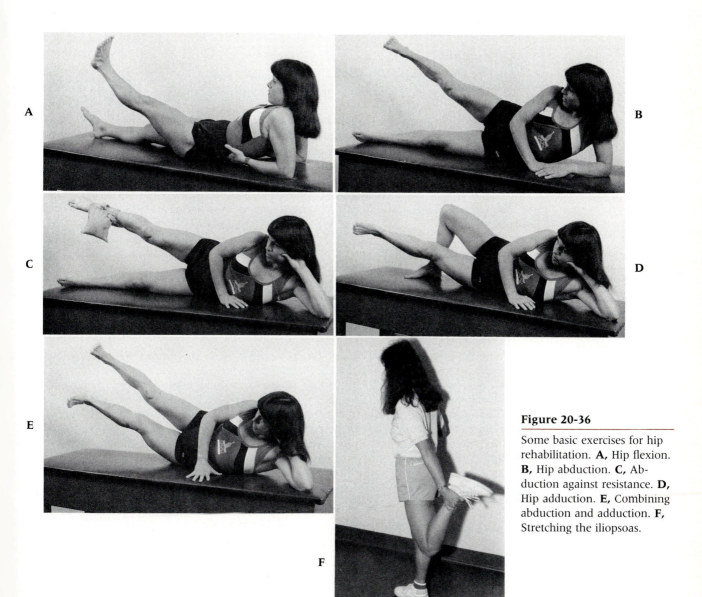

Figure 20-36

Some basic exercises for hip rehabilitation. **A,** Hip flexion. **B,** Hip abduction. **C,** Abduction against resistance. **D,** Hip adduction. **E,** Combining abduction and adduction. **F,** Stretching the iliopsoas.

stretching may also be used. As with strengthening, flexibility exercises are performed within pain-free limits.

When considering the reconditioning of the hip and groin region, one must consider its major movements: internal rotation, external rotation, adduction, abduction, extension, flexion, and the combined movement of internal and external circumduction. Because of the wide variety of possible movements, it is essential that exercise he conducted as soon as possible after injury, without aggravating the condition. When exercise is begun, it should be practiced within a pain-free range of movement. A program should be organized to start with free movement, leading up to resistive exercises. A general goal is to perform each exercise up to 10 to 15 repetitions, progressing from one set to three sets two or three times daily (Figure 20-36).

SUMMARY

The thigh is composed of the femoral shaft, musculature, nerves and blood vessels, and fascia that envelops the soft tissue. It is considered that part of the leg between the hip and the knee.

The quadriceps contusion and hamstring strain represent the most common sports injuries to the thigh, with the quadriceps contusion having the highest incidence. Of major importance in acute thigh contusion is early detection and the avoidance of internal bleeding. One major complication to repeated contusions is myositis ossificans.

Jumping or falling on a bent knee can strain the quadriceps muscle. A more common strain is that of the hamstring muscle; however, it is not clearly known why hamstring muscles become strained. Strain occurs most often to the short head of the biceps femoris muscle.

The femur can sustain both acute fractures and stress fractures. Acute fractures occur most often to the femoral shaft, usually from a direct blow. Femoral stress fractures are most common in the femoral neck.

The groin is the depression that lies between the thigh and the abdominal region. Groin strain can occur to any one of a number of muscles located in this region. Running, jumping, or twisting can produce a groin strain.

A common problem of women runners is trochanteric bursitis. An irritation occurs in the region of the greater trochanter of the femur.

The hip joint, the strongest and best protected joint in the human body, has a low incidence of acute sports injuries. More common are conditions stemming from an immature hip joint. They include Legg-Perthe disease (coxa plana) and the slipped capital femoral epiphysis.

The snapping hip phenomenon is one in which hip stability is lessened as a result of laxity of the hip joint, ligaments, and adductor muscles.

A common problem in the pelvic region is the hip pointer. This condition results from a blow to an inadequately protected iliac crest. The contusion causes pain, spasm, and malfunction of the muscles in the area. The pelvis can also sustain overuse conditions such as osteitis pubis, as well as both acute fractures and stress fractures.

REVIEW QUESTIONS AND SUGGESTED ACTIVITIES

1. Describe the major injuries to the thigh; include how contusions and strains are sustained and cared for.
2. How may hamstring strains be recognized and cared for?
3. How is a groin strain typically recognized and cared for?
4. What are the similarities and differences of coxa plana and a slipped capital femoral epiphysis?

REFERENCES

1. Boland, AL, and Hosea, TM: Hip and back pain in runners, Postgraduate advances in Sports Medicine, I-XII, Pennington, NJ, 1986, Forum Medicus, Inc.

2. Booher, J, and Moran, B: Evaluation and management of the acute hamstring injury, Sports Med Guide 4, April 1985.

3. Bull, CR: Soft tissue injury to the hip and thigh. In Welsh, RP, and Shephard, RJ, editors: Current therapy in sports medicine, 1985-1986, Philadelphia, 1985, Brian C Decker, Publisher.

4. Dimitris-Stilianos, K: Stress fractures of femoral neck in young athletes—report of 7 cases, J Bone Joint Surg 63B:33, 1981.

5. Fox, JM: Injuries to the thigh. In Nicholas, JA, and Hershman, EB, editors: The lower extremity and spine in sports medicine, vol 2, St. Louis, 1986, The CV Mosby Co.

6. Gogia, PP, and Braatz, JH: Validity and reliability of leg length measurements, J Orthop Sports Phys Ther 8:185, 1986.

7. Karlin, LI: Injuries to the hip and pelvis in the skeletally immature athlete. In Nicholas, JA, and Hershman, EB, editors: The lower extremity and spine in sports medicine, vol 2, St. Louis, 1986, The CV Mosby Co.

8. Kellam, JF: Fractures of the pelvis and femur. In Welsh, RP, and Shephard, RJ, editors: Current therapy in sports medicine, 1985-1986, Philadelphia, 1985, Brian C Decker, Publisher.

9. Klien, KK: Managing hamstring pulls in runners, The First Aider 56(6):15, 1987.

10. Lloyd-Smith, R, et al: A survey of overuse and traumatic hip and pelvic injuries in athletes, Phys Sportsmed 13(10):131, 1985.

11. Lomardo, SJ, and Benson, DW: Stress fractures of the femur in runners, Am J Sports Med 10:219, 1982.

12. Metzmaker, JN, and Pappas, AM: Avulsion fractures of the pelvis, Am J Sports Med 13:120, March/April 1985.

13. Miller, B: Evaluation and management of the acute hamstring injury, Sports Med Guide 15, April 1985.

14. Nobel, HB, Hajek, MR, and Porter, M: Diagnosis and treatment of iliotibial band tightness in runners, Phys Sportsmed 19:67, 1982.

15. Rold, JF, and Rold, BA: Pubic stress symphysitis in a female distance runner, Phys Sportsmed 14(6):61, 1986.

16. Sim, FH, and Scott, SG: Injuries of the pelvis and hip in athletics: anatomy and function. In Nicholas, JA, and Hershman, EB, editors: The lower extremity and spine in sports medicine, vol 2, St. Louis, 1986, The CV Mosby Co.

17. Sperryn, PN: Sport and medicine, Boston, 1983, Butterworth & Co, (Publishers), Ltd.

18. Sullivan, D, et al: Stress fractures in 51 runners, COOR 187:188, 1984.

ANNOTATED BIBLIOGRAPHY

Fox, JM: Injuries to the thigh. In Nicholas, JA, and Hershman, EB, editors: The lower extremity and spine in sports medicine, vol 2, St. Louis, 1986, The CV Mosby Co.
Presents a thorough discussion of thigh anatomy, physical examination, and sports injuries.

Sim, FH, and Scott, SG: Injuries of the pelvis and hip in athletics: anatomy and function. In Nicholas, JA, and Hershman, EB, editors: The lower extremity and spine in sports medicine, vol 2, St. Louis, 1986, The CV Mosby Co.
Provides a detailed discussion of hip and pelvic anatomy and sports injuries.

21

The Abdomen, Thorax, and Low Back

When you finish this chapter, you should be able to

Explain the anatomical ramifications of sports injuries of the abdomen, thorax, and low back

Identify major sports injuries of the abdomen

Recognize, evaluate, and manage sports injuries of the thorax

Recognize, evaluate, and manage low back conditions

T his chapter deals with major sports injuries to the trunk region—specifically, the abdomen, thorax, and low back. Although lower in incidence of injuries than the lower limbs, injury in the trunk region could be life threatening or could cause major long-term disability (Figure 21-1).

THE ABDOMEN
Anatomy

The abdominal cavity lies between the diaphragm and the pelvis and is bounded by the margin of the lower ribs, the abdominal muscles, and the vertebral column. Lying within this cavity are the abdominal viscera, which include the stomach and the lower intestinal tract, the urinary system, the liver, the kidneys, and the spleen.

The abdominal muscles are the rectus abdominis, the external oblique, the internal oblique, and the transverse abdominis (Figure 21-2). They are invested with both superficial and deep fasciae.

A heavy fascial sheath encloses the rectus abdominis muscle, holding it in its position but in no way restricting its motion. The inguinal ring, which serves as a passageway for the spermatic cord, is formed by the abdominal fascia.

Musculature

Rectus abdominis The rectus abdominis muscle, a trunk flexor, is attached to the rib cage above and to the pubis below. It is divided into three segments by transverse tendinous inscriptions; longitudinally it is divided by the linea alba. It functions in trunk flexion, rotation, and lateral flexion and in compression of the abdominal cavity.

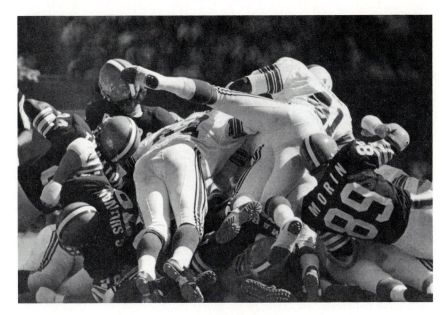

Figure 21-1

Collision sports can produce serious trunk injuries.

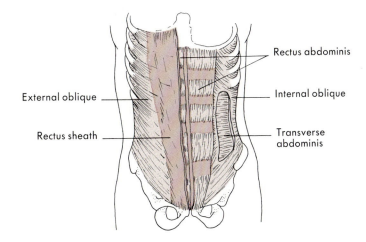

External oblique

Rectus sheath

Rectus abdominis

Internal oblique

Transverse abdominis

Figure 21-2

The abdominal musculature.

External oblique   The external oblique muscle is a broad, thin muscle that arises from slips attached to the borders of the lower eight ribs. It runs obliquely forward and downward and inserts on the anterior two thirds of the crest of the ilium, the pubic crest, and the fascia of the rectus abdominis and the linea alba at their lower front. Its principal functions are trunk flexion, rotation, lateral flexion, and compression.

Internal oblique   The internal oblique muscle forms the anterior and lateral aspects of the abdominal wall. Its fibers arise from the iliac crest, the upper half of the inguinal ligament, and the lumbar fascia. They run principally in an obliquely upward direction to the cartilages of the tenth, eleventh, and twelfth ribs on each side. The main functions of the internal oblique are trunk flexion, lateral flexion, and rotation.

Transverse abdominis   The transverse abdominis is the deepest of the abdominal muscles. Its fibers run transversely across the abdominal cavity, arising from the outer third of the inguinal ligament, the iliac crest, the lumbar fascia of the back, and the lower six ribs. It inserts into the linea alba and the front half of the iliac crest. The main functions of the transverse abdominis are to hold the abdominal contents in place and to aid in forced expiration. All the abdominal muscles work together in performing defecation, micturition, and forced expiration.

Abdominal Viscera

Solid internal organs are more at jeopardy from an injury than are hollow organs.

The abdominal viscera are composed of both hollow and solid organs. The hollow organs include vessels, tubes, and receptacles such as the stomach, intestines, gallbladder, and urinary bladder. The solid organs are the kidneys, spleen, liver, suprarenals, and pancreas (Figure 21-3). In internal injuries of the abdomen that occur in sports, the solid organs are most often affected. If a hollow organ is distended by its contents, it may have the same injury potential as a solid organ. Therefore it is desirable for athletes to have finished eating at least 3 hours before a sports contest so they can participate with stomach and bladder empty. Special anatomical considerations should be given to the kidney and spleen because of their relatively high incidence of injury in sports.

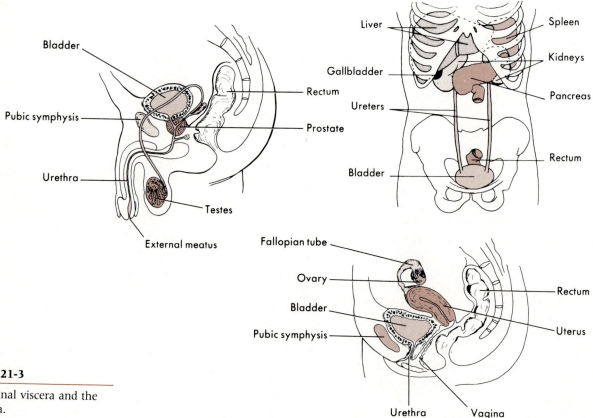

Figure 21-3

Abdominal viscera and the genitalia.

Kidneys   The kidneys are situated on each side of the spine, approximately in the center of the back. They are bean-shaped, approximately 4½ inches (11.25 cm) long, 2 inches (5 cm) wide, and 1 inch (2.5 cm) thick. The right kidney is usually slightly lower than the left because of the pressure of the liver. The uppermost surfaces of the kidneys are connected to the diaphragm by strong, ligamentous fibers. As breathing occurs, the kidneys move up and down as much as ½ inch (1.25 cm). The inferior aspect is positioned 1 to 2 inches (2.5 to 5 cm) above the iliac crest. Resting anterior to the left kidney are the stomach, spleen, pancreas, and small and large intestines. Organs that are situated anterior to the right kidney are the liver and the intestines. The peritoneum (the membrane that lines the abdominal cavity) does not invest the kidneys. Rather, the kidneys are surrounded by a fibrous capsule and by a layer of fat that in turn is encased in another fatty layer that connects it to the niche in which it lies.

Spleen   The spleen is the largest lymphatic organ in the body. It weighs approximately 6 ounces and is approximately 5 inches (12.5 cm) long. It lies under the diaphragm on the left side and behind the ninth, tenth, and eleventh ribs. It is surrounded by a fibrous capsule that is firmly invested by the peritoneum. The spleen's main functions are to serve as the following:

1. A reservoir of red blood cells
2. A regulator of the number of red blood cells in the general circulation
3. A destroyer of ineffective red cells
4. A producer of antibodies for immunological function
5. A producer of lymphocytes

Abdominal Injuries

Although abdominal injuries only comprise approximately 10% of sports injuries, they can require long recovery periods and can be life threatening.[13] The abdominal area is particularly vulnerable to injury in all contact sports. A blow can produce superficial or even deep internal injuries, depending on its location and intensity.[23] Strong abdominal muscles give good protection when they are tensed, but when relaxed, they are easily damaged. It is very important to protect the trunk region properly against the traumatic forces of collision sports. Good conditioning is essential, as is the use of proper protective equipment and the application of safety rules. Any athlete with a suspected internal injury must be referred immediately to a physician.[20]

Injuries to the Abdominal Wall

Contusions   Compressive forces that injure the abdominal wall are not common in sports. When they do happen, more often they occur in collision sports such as football or ice hockey; however, any sports implements or high-velocity projectiles can injure. Hockey goalies and baseball catchers would be very vulnerable to injury without their protective torso pads. Contusion may occur superficially to the abdominal skin or subcutaneous tissue or much deeper to the musculature. The extent and type of injury vary, depending on whether the force is blunt or penetrating.[20]

A contusion of the rectus abdominis muscle can be very disabling. A severe blow may cause a hematoma that develops under the fascial tissue surrounding this muscle. The pressure that results from hemorrhage causes pain and tightness in the region of the injury. A cold pack and a compression elastic wrap should be applied immediately after injury. Signs of possible internal injury must also be looked for in this type of injury.

Abdominal muscle strains   Sudden twisting of the trunk or reaching overhead can tear an abdominal muscle. Potentially these types of injuries can be very incapacitating, with severe pain and hematoma formation. Initially ice and an elastic wrap compress should be used. Treatment should be conservative, with exercise staying within pain-free limits.

Hernia   The term hernia refers to the protrusion of abdominal viscera through a portion of the abdominal wall. Hernias may be congenital or acquired. A congenital hernial sac is developed before birth and an acquired hernia after birth. Structurally a hernia has a mouth, a neck, and a body. The mouth, or hernial ring, is the opening from the abdominal cavity into the hernial protusion; the neck is the portion of the sac that joins the hernial ring and the body. The body is the sac that protrudes outside the abdominal cavity and contains portions of the abdominal organs.

The acquired hernia occurs when a natural weakness is further aggravated by either a strain or a direct blow. Athletes may develop this condition as the result of violent activity. An acquired hernia may be recognized by the following:

1. Previous history of a blow or strain to the groin area that has produced pain and prolonged discomfort
2. Superficial protrusion in the groin area that is increased by coughing
3. Reported feeling of weakness and pulling sensation in the groin area

The danger of a hernia in an athlete is the possibility that it may become irritated by falls or blows. Besides the aggravations caused by trauma, a condition may arise, commonly known as a strangulated hernia, in which the inguinal ring constricts the protruding sac and occludes normal blood circulation. If the strangulated hernia is not surgically repaired immediately, gangrene and death may ensue.

Hernias resulting from sports most often occur in the groin area; inguinal hernias (Figure 21-4), which occur in men (over 75%), and femoral hernias, most often occurring in women, are the most prevalent types. Externally the inguinal and femoral hernias appear similar because of the groin protrusion, but a considerable difference is indicated internally. The inguinal hernia results from an abnormal enlargement of the opening of the inguinal canal through which the vessels and nerves of the male reproductive system pass. In contrast to this, the femoral hernia arises in the canal that transports the vessels and nerves that go to the thigh and lower limb.

Under normal circumstances the inguinal and femoral canals are protected against abnormal opening by muscle control. When intra-abdominal tension is produced in these areas, muscles produce contraction around these canal openings. If the muscles fail to react or if they prove inadequate in their shutter action, abdominal contents may be pushed through the opening. Repeated protrusions serve to stretch and increase the size of the opening. Most physicians think that any athlete who has a hernia should be prohibited from engaging in hard physical activity until surgical repair has been made.

The treatment preferred by most physicians is surgery. Mechanical devices such as trusses, which prevent hernial protrusion, are for the most part unsuitable in sports because of the friction and irritation they produce. Exercise has been thought by many to be beneficial to a mild hernia, but such is not the case. Exercise will not affect the stretched inguinal or femoral canals positively.

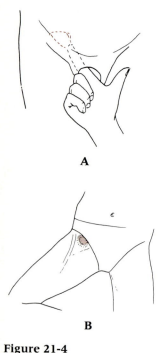

Figure 21-4

A, Inguinal hernia. **B,** Femoral hernia.

Intra-Abdominal Conditions

Stitch in the side   A "stitch in the side" is the name given an idiopathic condition that occurs in some athletes. It is best described as a cramplike pain that develops on either the left or right costal angle during hard physical activity. Sports that involve running apparently produce this condition.

The cause is obscure, although several hypotheses have been advanced. Among these causes are the following:

1. Constipation
2. Intestinal gas
3. Overeating
4. Diaphragmatic spasm as a result of poor conditioning
5. Lack of visceral support because of weak abdominal muscles
6. Distended spleen
7. Faulty breathing techniques leading to a lack of oxygen in the diaphragm
8. Ischemia of either the diaphragm or the intercostal muscles

Immediate care of a stitch in the side demands relaxation of the spasm, for which two methods have proved beneficial. First, the athlete is instructed to stretch the arm on the affected side as high as possible. If this is inadequate, flexing the trunk forward on the thighs may prove of some benefit.

Athletes with recurrent abdominal spasms may need special study. The identification of poor eating habits, poor elimination habits, or an inadequate athletic training program may explain the athlete's particular problem. It should be noted that a stitch in the side, although not considered serious, may require further evaluation by a physician if abdominal pains persist.

Blow to the solar plexus   A blow to the sympathetic celiac plexus (solar plexus) produces a transitory paralysis of the diaphragm ("wind knocked out").

SYMPTOMS AND SIGNS   Paralysis of the diaphragm stops respiration and leads to anoxia. When the athlete is unable to inhale, hysteria because of fear may result. It is necessary to allay such fears and instill confidence in the athlete. On occasion, the sudden lack of oxygen to the brain may cause an anoxic seizure. These symptoms are usually transitory.

MANAGEMENT   In dealing with an athlete who has had the wind knocked out of him or her, the athletic trainer should adhere to the following procedures:

1. Help the athlete overcome apprehension by talking in a confident manner.
2. Loosen the athlete's belt and the clothing around the abdomen; have the athlete bend the knees.
3. Encourage the athlete to relax by initiating short inspirations and long expirations.

Because of the fear of not being able to breathe, the athlete may hyperventilate, which means breathing at an abnormal rate. Hyperventilation results in the delivery of too much oxygen to the circulatory system and causes a variety of physical reactions such as dizziness, a lump in the throat, pounding heart, and fainting to occur.[11]

There should always be some concern that a blow hard enough to knock out the wind could also cause internal organ injury.

Ruptured spleen   Every year there are reports of athletes who suddenly die—hours, days, or even weeks after a severe blow received in a sports event. These deaths are often attributed to delayed hemorrhage of the spleen, the organ most often injured by blunt trauma.

An athlete with mononucleosis must not engage in any jarring activities.

Athletes who complain of external pain in the shoulders, trunk, or pelvis after a severe blow to the abdomen or back may be describing referred pain from an injury to an internal organ.

ETIOLOGICAL FACTORS Injuries to the spleen usually result from a fall or a direct blow to the left upper quadrant of the abdomen (see Figure 10-3).

Infectious mononucleosis predisposes the spleen to blunt trauma and may enlarge and weaken the spleen. Splenomegaly is present in 50% of the cases affected. An athlete with mononucleosis must not engage in any jarring activities. (See Chapter 25, p. 827.)

SYMPTOMS AND SIGNS The gross indications of a ruptured spleen must be recognized so that an immediate medical referral can be made. Indications include a history of a severe blow to the abdomen and possibly signs of shock, abdominal rigidity, nausea, and vomiting. There may be a reflex pain occurring approximately 30 minutes after injury, called Kehr's sign, which radiates to the left shoulder and one third of the way down the left arm (see Chapter 8).

COMPLICATIONS The great danger with a ruptured spleen lies in its ability to splint itself and then produce a delayed hemorrhage. Splinting of the spleen is formed by a loose hematoma formation and the constriction of the supporting and surrounding structures. Any slight strain may disrupt the splinting effect and allow the spleen to hemorrhage profusely into the abdominal cavity, causing the athlete to die of internal bleeding days or weeks after the injury. A ruptured spleen must be surgically removed.

Liver contusion Compared to other organ injuries from blunt trauma, injuries to the liver rank second.[13] In sports activities, however, liver injury is relatively infrequent. A hard blow to the right side of the rib cage can tear or seriously contuse the liver, especially if it has been enlarged as a result of some disease such as hepatitis. Such an injury can cause hemorrhage and shock, requiring immediate surgical intervention. Liver injury commonly produces a referred pain that is just below the right scapula, right shoulder, and substernal area and, on occasion, the anterior left side of the chest (see Chapter 8).

Hollow visceral organ injuries When compared to hollow organs, the solid organs are more often injured in sports; however, on rare occasions a severe blunt blow to the abdomen may cause rupture or laceration of the duodenum or other structures of the small intestine.

Injuries to the Genitourinary System

Kidney contusion The kidneys are seemingly well protected within the abdominal cavity. However, on occasion, contusions and even ruptures of these organs occur. The kidney may be susceptible to injury because of its normal distention by blood. A severe outside force, usually one applied to the back of the athlete, will cause abnormal extension of an engorged kidney, resulting in injury. The degree of renal injury depends on the extent of the distention and the angle and force of the blow. An athlete who has received a contusion of the kidney may display signs of shock, nausea, vomiting, rigidity of the back muscles, and hematuria (blood in the urine). As with other internal organs, kidney injury may cause referred pain to the outside of the body. Pain may be felt high in the costovertebral angle posteriorly and may radiate forward around the trunk into the lower abdominal region (see Chapter 8). Any athlete who reports having received a severe blow to the abdomen or back region should be instructed to urinate two or three times and to look for the appearance of blood in the urine. If there is any sign of hematuria, immediate referral to a physician must be made.

Medical care of the contused kidney usually consists of a 24-hour hospital observation, with a gradual increase of fluid intake. If the hemorrhage fails to stop, surgery may be indicated. Controllable contusions usually require 2 weeks of bed rest and close surveillance after activity is resumed. In questionable cases complete withdrawal from one active playing season may be required.

Injuries of the ureters, bladder, and urethra   On rare occasions a blunt force to the lower abdominal region may avulse a ureter or contuse or rupture the urinary bladder. Injury to the urinary bladder only arises if it is distended by urine.

After a severe blow to the pelvic region, the athlete may display the following recognizable signs:

1. Pain and discomfort in the lower abdomen, with the desire but inability to urinate
2. Abdominal rigidity
3. Nausea, vomiting, and signs of shock
4. Blood dripping from the urethra
5. Passing a great quantity of bloody urine, which indicates possible rupture of the kidney

With any contusion to the abdominal region, the possibility of internal damage must be considered, and after such trauma the athlete should be instructed to check periodically for blood in the urine. To lessen the possibility of rupture, the athlete must always empty the bladder before practice or game time. The bladder can also be irritated by intra-abdominal pressures during long-distance running. In this situation repeated impacts to the bladder's base are produced by the jarring of the abdominal contents, resulting in hemorrhage and blood in the urine. Bladder injury commonly causes referred pain to the lower trunk, including the upper thigh anteriorly and suprapubically (see Chapter 8).

Injury to the urethra is more common in men, because the male's urethra is longer and more exposed than the female's. Injury may produce severe perineal pain and swelling.[26]

Scrotal contusion   As the result of its considerable sensitivity and particular vulnerability, the scrotum may sustain a contusion that causes a very painful, nauseating, and disabling condition. As is characteristic of any contusion or bruise, there is hemorrhage, fluid effusion, and muscle spasm, the degree of which depends on the intensity of the impact to the tissue. Immediately following a scrotal contusion, the athlete must be put at ease, and testicular spasms must be reduced.

The following technique is used to relieve testicular spasm: the athlete is placed on his back and instructed to flex his thighs to his chest (Figure 21-5). This position will aid in reducing discomfort and relax the muscle spasm. After the pain has diminished, the athlete is helped from the playing area, and a cold pack is applied to the scrotum.

Spermatic cord torsion   Torsion of the spermatic cord results from the testicle's revolving in the scrotum after a direct blow to the area or as a result of coughing or vomiting. Cord torsion produces acute testicular pain, nausea, vomiting, and inflammation in the area. In this case, the athlete must receive immediate medical attention to prevent irreparable complications. Twisting of the spermatic cord may present the appearance of a cluster of swollen veins and may cause a dull pain combined with a heavy, dragging feeling in the scrotum. This condition may eventually lead to atrophy of the testicle. A physician should be consulted when this condition is suspected.

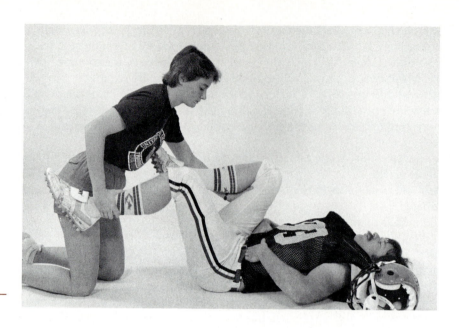

Figure 21-5

Reducing testicular spasm.

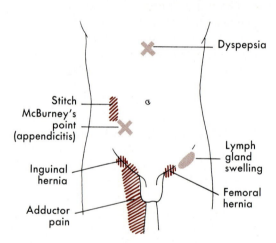

Figure 21-6

Common sites of abdominal pain.

Traumatic hydrocele of the tunica vaginalis   Traumatic hydrocele of the tunica vaginalis is an excess of fluid accumulation caused by a severe blow to the testicular region. After trauma the athlete complains of pain, swelling in the lower abdomen, and nausea. Cold packs should be applied to the scrotum, and referral to the physician should be made.

Gynecological injuries   In general the female reproductive organs have a low incidence of injury in sports; however, women water skiers do injure their vulvae when water is forced into the vagina and fallopian tubes, later causing infection. On occasion the external genital organs (vulva) of the female may become contused, resulting in hematoma.

Other Reasons for Abdominal Pain

A number of other abdominal pain sites can be disabling to the athlete. The athletic trainer should be able to discern the potentially more serious pain sites and refer the athlete accordingly. Indigestion or dyspepsia commonly causes pain just below the sternum. Appendicitis, typically when the appendix is in a normal position, creates pain at McBurney's point, which is one third the distance between the anterosuperior iliac spine and the umbilicus. Figure 21-6 shows some of the pain sites in the abdomen.

Pain at McBurney's point may indicate the athlete is having an appendicitis attack.

THE THORAX
Anatomy

The thorax is that portion of the body commonly known as the chest, which lies between the base of the neck and the diaphragm. It is contained within the thoracic vertebrae and the 12 pairs of ribs that give it conformation (Figure 21-7). Its main functions are to protect the vital respiratory and circulatory organs and to assist the lungs in inspiration and expiration during the breathing process. The ribs are flat bones that are attached to the thoracic vertebrae in the back and to the sternum in the front. The upper seven ribs are called sternal or true ribs, and each rib is joined to the sternum by a separate costal cartilage. The eighth, ninth, and tenth ribs (false ribs) have cartilages that join each other and the seventh rib before uniting with the sternum. The eleventh and twelfth ribs (floating ribs) remain unattached to the sternum but do have muscle attachments. The individual rib articulation produces a slight gliding action.

Thoracic Injuries

The chest is vulnerable to a variety of soft-tissue injuries, depending on the nature of the sport.

Breast Problems

It has been suggested that many women athletes can have breast problems in connection with their sports participation. Violent up and down and lateral movements of the breasts, such as are encountered in running and jumping, can bruise and strain the breast, especially in large-breasted women. Constant uncontrolled movement of the breast over a period of time can stretch the Cooper's ligament, which supports the breast at the chest wall, leading to premature ptosis of the breasts.[9]

Another condition occurring to the breasts is *runner's nipples,* in which the shirt rubs the nipples, causing an abrasion that can be prevented by placing a Band-Aid over each nipple before participation. *Bicyclist's nipples* can also occur as the result of a combination of cold and evaporation of sweat, causing the nipples to become painful. Wearing a Windbreaker can prevent this problem.[14]

Wearing a well-designed bra that has minimum elasticity and allows little vertical or horizontal breast movement is most desirable (see Figure 5-13). Breast injuries usually occur during physical contact with either an opponent or equipment. In sports such as fencing or field hockey, women athletes must be protected by wearing plastic cup-type brassieres.[9]

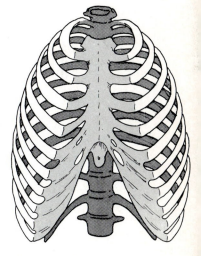

Figure 21-7

The thorax.

Rib Contusions

A blow to the rib cage can contuse intercostal muscles or, if severe enough, produce a fracture. Because the intercostal muscles are essential for the breathing mechanism, when they are bruised, both expiration and inspiration become very painful. Characteristically the pain is sharp during breathing, and there is point tenderness. X-ray examination should be routine in such an injury. ICE-R and anti-inflammatory agents are commonly used. As with most rib injuries, contusions to the thorax are self-limiting, responding best to rest and cessation of sports activities.

Rib Fractures

Rib fractures (Figure 21-8) are not uncommon in sports and have their highest incidence in collision sports, particularly in wrestling and football.

ETIOLOGICAL FACTORS Fractures can be caused by either direct or indirect traumas and can, infrequently, be the result of violent muscular contractions. A direct injury is the type caused by a kick or a well-placed block, with the fracture developing at the site of force application. An indirect fracture is produced as a result of general compression of the rib cage such as may occur in football or wrestling.

A rib fracture may be indicated by a severe, sharp pain during breathing.

The structural and functional disruption sustained in a rib fracture varies according to the type of injury that has been received. The direct fracture causes the most serious damage, since the external force fractures and displaces the ribs inwardly. Such a mechanism may completely displace the bone and cause an overriding of fragments. The jagged edges of the fragments may cut, tear, or perforate the tissue of the pleurae, causing hemothorax, or they may collapse one lung (pneumothorax). Contrary to the pattern with direct violence, the indirect type usually causes the rib to spring and fracture outward, producing an oblique or transverse fissure. Stress fracture of the first rib is becoming more prevalent. It can result from repeated arm movements such as are used in pitching. Stress fractures to other ribs have resulted from repeated coughing or laughing. Anytime an athlete complains of a dull ache in the thoracic region, he or she should be referred for x-ray examination.[10,17]

SYMPTOMS AND SIGNS The rib fracture is usually quite easily detected. The history informs the athletic trainer of the type and degree of force to which the rib cage has been subjected. After trauma, the athlete complains of having severe pain during inspiration and has point tenderness. A fracture of the rib will be readily evidenced by a severe sharp pain and possibly crepitus during palpation.

Figure 21-8

A rib fracture.

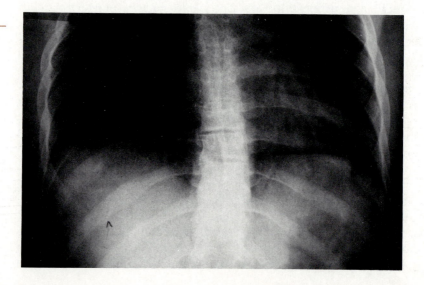

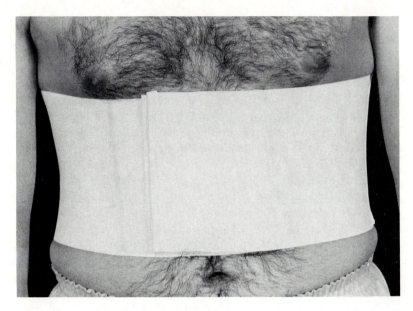

Figure 21-9

A commercial rib brace can provide moderate support to the thorax.

MANAGEMENT The athlete should be referred to the team physician for x-ray examination if there is any indication of fracture.

An uncomplicated rib fracture is often difficult to identify on x-ray film. Therefore the physician plans the treatment according to the symptoms presented. The rib fracture is usually managed with support and rest. Simple transverse or oblique fractures heal within 3 to 4 weeks. A rib brace can offer the athlete some rib cage stabilization and comfort (Figure 21-9).

Costochondral Separation and Dislocation

In sports activities the costochondral separation or dislocation has a higher incidence than fractures. This injury can occur from a direct blow to the anterolateral aspect of the thorax or indirectly from a sudden twist or a fall on a ball, compressing the rib cage. The costochondral injury displays many signs similar to the rib fracture, with the exception that pain is localized in the junction of the rib cartilage and rib (Figure 21-10).

SYMPTOMS AND SIGNS The athlete complains of sharp pain during sudden movement of the trunk, with difficulty in breathing deeply. There is point tenderness with swelling. In some cases there is a rib deformity and a complaint that the rib makes a crepitus noise as it moves in and out of place.

MANAGEMENT As with a rib fracture, the costochondral separation is managed by rest and immobilization by tape or a rib brace. Healing takes anywhere from 1 to 2 months, precluding any sports activities until the athlete is symptom free.

Muscle Conditions of the Thorax

The muscles of the thorax are the intercostals and the erector spinae, latissimus dorsi, trapezius, serratus anterior, serratus posterior, and pectoralis major—all of which are subject to contusions and strains in sports. The intercostals are especially assailable. Traumatic injuries occur most often from direct blows or sudden torsions of the athlete's trunk. Their care requires immediate pressure and appli-

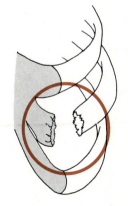

Figure 21-10

Costochondral separation.

cations of cold for approximately 1 hour; after hemorrhaging has been controlled, immobilization should be used.

Internal Complications

Internal thoracic complications resulting from sports trauma are rare. They pertain principally to injuries of the lung, pleurae, and/or intercostal arteries. Because of the seriousness of internal injuries, the athletic trainer should be able to recognize their basic signs. The most serious of the conditions are (1) pneumothorax, (2) hemothorax, (3) hemorrhaging into the lungs, (4) traumatic asphyxia, and (5) heart contusion.

Pneumothorax   Pneumothorax is a condition in which the pleural cavity becomes filled with air that has entered through an opening in the chest. As the negatively pressured pleural cavity fills with air, the lung on that side collapses. The loss of one lung may produce pain, difficulty in breathing, and anoxia.

Hemothorax   Hemothorax is the presence of blood within the pleural cavity. It results from the tearing or puncturing of the lung or pleural tissue, involving the blood vessels in the area. As with pneumothorax, pain, difficulty in breathing, and cyanosis develop.

A violent blow or compression of the chest without an accompanying rib fracture may cause a lung hemorrhage. This condition results in severe pain during breathing, dyspnea (difficult breathing), coughing up of frothy blood, and signs of shock. If these signs are observed, the athlete should be treated for shock and immediately referred to a physician.

Traumatic asphyxia   Traumatic asphyxia occurs as the result of a violent blow to or a compression of the rib cage, causing a cessation of breathing. Signs include purple discoloration of the upper trunk and head, with the conjunctivae of the eyes displaying a bright red color. A condition of this type demands immediate mouth-to-mouth resuscitation and medical attention.

Heart contusion   A heart contusion may occur when the heart is compressed between the sternum and the spine by a strong outside force, such as being hit by a pitched ball or bouncing a barbell off the chest in a bench press. This injury produces severe shock and heart pain. The heart goes into fibrillation, which is followed by death if medical attention is not administered immediately.

Sudden death syndrome   The most common cause of exercise-induced deaths is congenital cardiovascular abnormalities. The three most prevalent conditions are hypertrophic cardiomyopathy, anomalous origin of the left coronary artery, and Marfan's syndrome (see Chapter 25).[28]

THE LOW BACK
Anatomy of the Vertebral Column

The low back must be considered in the context of the entire spine. The lumbar, sacral, and coccygeal portions of the spine are discussed in this chapter, and the thoracic and cervical portions of the spine are discussed in Chapter 22.

Bony Structure

The spine or vertebral column is composed of 33 individual bones called vertebrae. Twenty-four are classified as movable, or true, and nine are classified as immovable, or false. The false vertebrae, which are fixed by fusion, form the sacrum and the coccyx. The design of the spine allows a high degree of flexibility forward and laterally and limited mobility backward. Rotation around a central axis in the areas of the neck and the lower back is also permitted.

The movable vertebrae are separated into three different divisions, according to location and function. The first division comprises the seven cervical vertebrae; the second, the 12 thoracic vertebrae; and the third, the five lumbar vertebrae. As the spinal segments progress downward from the cervical region, they grow increasingly larger to accommodate the upright posture of the body, as well as to contribute in weight bearing. Physiological curves also are present in the spinal column for adjusting to the upright stresses. These curves are, respectively, the cervical, thoracic, lumbar, and sacrococcygeal curves. The cervical and lumbar curves are convex anteriorly, whereas the thoracic and sacrococcygeal curves are convex posteriorly. The shape of the vertebrae is irregular, but the vertebrae possess certain characteristics that are common to all. Each vertebra consists of a neural arch through which the spinal cord passes and several projecting processes that serve as attachments for muscles and ligaments. Each neural arch has two laminae and two pedicles. The latter are bony processes that project backward from the body of the vertebrae and connect with the laminae. The laminae are flat bony processes occurring on either side of the neural arch and project backward and inward from the pedicles. With the exception of the first and second cervical vertebrae, each vertebra has a spinous and transverse process for muscular and ligamentous attachment, and all vertebrae have an articular process.

Intervertebral Articulations

Intervertebral articulations are between vertebral bodies and vertebral arches. Articulation between the bodies is of the symphysial type. There is an intervertebral disk composed of two components, the *annulus fibrosus* and the *nucleus pulposus.* The annulus fibrosus forms the periphery of the intervertebral disk and is composed of strong, fibrous tissue, with its fibers running in several different directions for strength. In the center is the semi-fluid nucleus pulposus compressed under pressure. The disks act as important shock absorbers for the spine. Besides motion at articulations between the bodies of the vertebrae, movement takes place at four articular processes that derive from the pedicles and laminae. The direction of movement of each vertebra is somewhat dependent on the direction in which the articular facets face.

Major Ligamentous Structures

The major ligaments that join the various vertebral parts are the anterior longitudinal, the posterior longitudinal, and the supraspinous (Figure 21-11). The anterior longitudinal ligament is a wide, strong band that extends the full length of the anterior surface of the vertebral bodies. The posterior longitudinal ligament is contained within the vertebral canal and extends the full length of the posterior aspect of the bodies of the vertebrae. Ligaments connect one lamina to another. The interspinous, supraspinous, and intertransverse ligaments stabilize the transverse and spinous processes, extending between adjacent vertebrae.

Movements of the Vertebral Column

The movements of the vertebral column are flexion and extension, right and left lateral flexion, and rotation to the left and right. The degree of movement differs in the various regions of the vertebral column. The cervical and lumbar regions

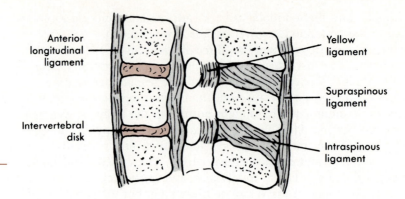

Figure 21-11

Major ligaments of the lumbar spine.

allow extension and flexion. Although the thoracic vertebrae have minimum movement, their combined movement between the first and twelfth thoracic vertebrae can account for 20 to 30 degrees of flexion and extension. Flexion and extension are most extensive at the fifth lumbar and the first sacral vertebrae and atlantooccipital joints.

Flexion of the trunk primarily involves lengthening of the deep and superficial back muscles and contraction of the rectus abdominus muscle. The psoas muscles also flex the lumbar spine. Trunk rotation is conducted by the oblique abdominal muscles—obliquus externus abdominis and obliquus internus abdominis. Lateral flexion is produced by the longitudinal muscles on the opposite side and the same side of the lumbar spine and by the intercostal muscles of the opposite side of the lumbar spine.

The Lumbar Vertebrae

The lumbar spine is usually composed of five vertebrae (Figure 21-12). They are the major support of the low back and are the strongest and most massive of the vertebrae. Movement occurs in all of the lumbar vertebrae; however, there is much less flexion than extension. Seventy-five percent of flexion occurs at the lumbosacral junction (L5-S1), whereas 15% to 70% occurs between L4 and L5; the rest of the lumbar vertebrae execute 5% to 10% of flexion.[5] The major muscle of extension is the erector spine or sacrospinalis, which is separated into the iliocostal, longissimus, and spinalis bands.

The Sacrum and Coccyx
The Sacrum

The sacrum is formed in the adult by the fusion of five vertebrae and, as part of the two hip bones, comprises the pelvis (Figure 21-13). The roots of the lumbar and sacral nerves, which form the lower portion of the cauda equina, pass through four foramina lateral to the five fused vertebrae.

The sacrum joins with the ilium to form the sacroiliac joint, which has a synovium and is lubricated by synovial fluid. During both sitting and standing the body's weight is transmitted through these joints. A complex of numerous ligaments serves to make these joints very stable.

The Coccyx

In the child the coccyx has four or five separate vertebrae, of which the lower three fuse in adulthood. The gluteus maximus muscle attaches to the coccyx posteriorly and to the levator ani muscles anteriorly.

Spinal Nerves and Peripheral Branches

Table 21-1 indicates the major spinal nerves and their peripheral branches in the lumbar region (Figure 21-14).

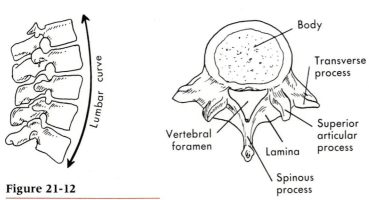

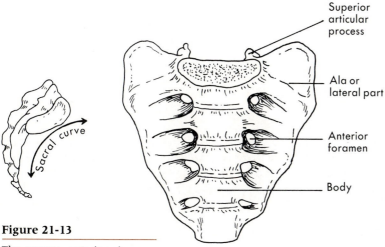

Figure 21-12

The lumbar vertebrae.

Figure 21-13

The sacrum, anterior view.

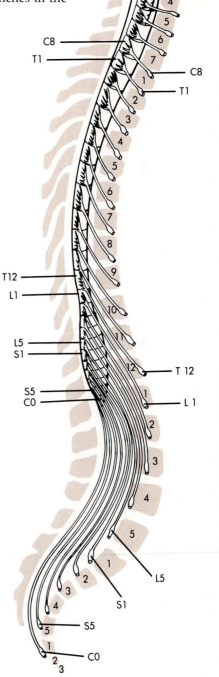

Figure 21-14

Spinal cord and the peripheral nerves.

TABLE 21-1 Spinal Nerves of the Lumbar, Sacral, and Coccygeal Regions

Spinal Nerves	Plexus Formed from Anterior Rami	Spinal Nerve Branches from Plexuses	Parts Supplied
Lumbar 1 2 3 4 5 Sacral 1 2 3 4 5 Coccygeal 1	Lumbosacral plexus	Iliohypogastric ⎫ Ilioinguinal ⎬ Sometimes fused Genitofemoral Lateral cutaneous of thigh Femoral Obturator Tibial (medial popliteal) Common peroneal (lateral popliteal) Nerves to hamstring muscles Gluteal nerves, superior and inferior Posterior cutaneous nerve Pudendal nerve	Sensory to anterior abdominal wall Sensory to anterior abdominal wall and external genitalia; motor to muscles of abdominal wall Sensory to skin of external genitalia and inguinal region Sensory to outer side of thigh Motor to quadriceps, sartorius, and iliacus muscles; sensory to front of thigh and medial side of lower leg (saphenous nerve) Motor to adductor muscles of thigh Motor to muscles of calf of leg; sensory to skin of calf of leg and sole of foot Motor to evertors and dorsiflexors of foot; sensory to lateral surface of leg and dorsal surface of foot Motor to muscles of back of thigh Motor to buttock muscles and tensor fasciae latae Sensory to skin of buttocks, posterior surface of thigh, and leg Motor to peroneal muscles; sensory to skin of perineum

Assessment of the Low Back

The athletic trainer should have a general knowledge of low back pain evaluation techniques. Differentiating superficial muscular conditions from deeper, more potentially disabling conditions is important in determining when or when not to refer the individual to a physician. Assessment techniques are also essential in determining the progress of rehabilitation (Figure 21-15).

Major Complaints

To determine the basis for the back pain, the following questions should be answered by the athlete:
1. Where does it hurt, and how long does the pain last?
2. What events precipitated the pain? Was there sudden, direct trauma such as being hit in the back, or was there a strain from a twist or lifting a heavy object? Did the pain come on slowly?
3. Does the pain radiate into the legs?
4. Is there a feeling of weakness, numbness, or tingling (paresthesia) in the legs or feet?

5. Which activities make the pain worse, and what things, if any, relieve the pain?
6. Has there been back pain before? What was done for it?

General Observation

The athlete should be observed with the entire body as exposed as possible. Observation should include kinetic activities such as walking and sitting, as well as static postural evaluation.

Kinetic observation   The athlete should be observed while walking, sitting, and rising from a chair. The following points should be noted:

1. Ease or lack of ease of movement
2. Whether the athlete favors one side of the body or body part more than the other
3. Movements that are painful or cannot be accomplished
4. Musculature that appears asymmetrically contracted
5. Observation of moving postural alignment from all positions, including feet, legs, pelvis, back, shoulders, and neck

Static Postural Observation

It is important next to observe the athlete's total static posture, with special attention paid to the low back, pelvis, and hips. When observing static posture, the athletic trainer must accept the fact that postural alignment varies considerably among individuals; therefore only obvious asymmetries should be considered. The athlete should be observed from all views—front, side, and back. The entire body is observed for vertical and horizontal alignment. To ensure accuracy of observation, a plumb line or posture screen may be of use (Figure 21-16). A trained observer with a good background in postural observation devices may not require any special devices. Figure 21-17 shows typical vertical alignment landmarks and more common postural deviations. Horizontal landmarks and deviations are indicated in Figure 21-18.

An important factor in low back pain is scoliosis, a lateral rotary curvature of the spine. The athlete with low back pain should be routinely evaluated for the possibility of scoliosis.[3] The following general postural signs should be looked for:

1. Head is tilted to one side.
2. Shoulder is lower on one side.
3. One shoulder is carried forward.
4. One scapula is lower and more prominent than the other.
5. Trunk is habitually bent to one side.
6. Space between the body and arm is greater on one side.
7. One hip is more prominent than the other.
8. Hips are tilted to one side (hip obliquity).
9. Ribs are more pronounced on one side.
10. One arm hangs longer than the other.
11. One arm hangs farther forward than the other.
12. One patella is lower than the other.
13. Marking spinous processes reveals a curvature (Figure 21-19).
14. Bending forward, the marked spine may straighten (functional) or remain twisted (structural). In this position, one side of the spine may be more prominent than the other (Figure 21-20). **NOTE:** The athlete should be observed for asymmetries while standing and sitting.

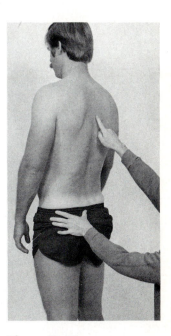

Figure 21-15

Observing spinal alignment.

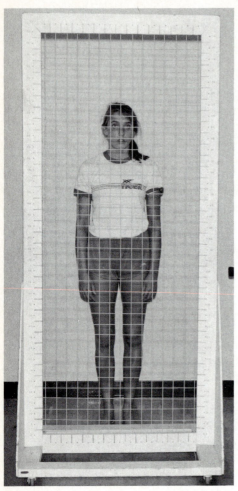

Figure 21-16

Using a grid can produce more accurate results during posture screening.

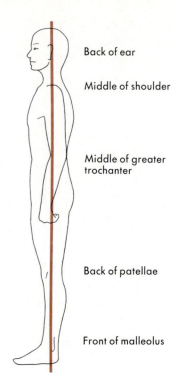

Figure 21-17

Typical vertical alignment landmarks.

- Back of ear
- Middle of shoulder
- Middle of greater trochanter
- Back of patellae
- Front of malleolus

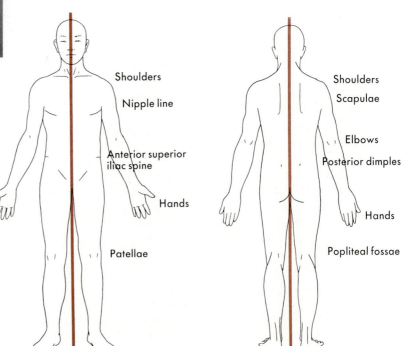

- Shoulders
- Nipple line
- Anterior superior iliac spine
- Hands
- Patellae

- Shoulders
- Scapulae
- Elbows
- Posterior dimples
- Hands
- Popliteal fossae

Figure 21-18

Typical horizontal alignment landmarks. (Colored line indicates vertical landmarks.)

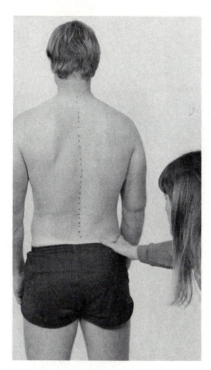

Figure 21-19

Marking spinous processes
can often reveal lateral rotary
curvatures.

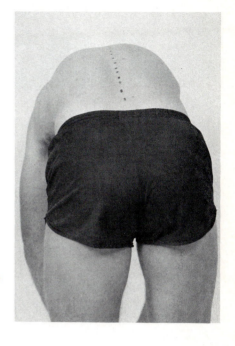

Figure 21-20

Bending forward may or may
not straighten the scoliotic
spine.

Postural changes resulting from chronic low back pain   Postural malalignment can produce low back pain, and chronic low back pain may result in
spasm and postural asymmetries. Loss of the normal lordotic curve can be caused
by a postural problem or muscle spasm. A lateral curvature of the low back region
may be a structural deformity of function resulting from muscle spasm.

Both static and dynamic
postural evaluations must be
performed in cases of low
back injuries.

More Detailed Inspection of the Low Back

Following general observation, a more detailed inspection should be given while
the athlete stands, lies supine, lies prone, and lies on the side.

Standing

1. The athlete is asked to point to the exact site of the pain.
2. The athlete's pelvis is palpated for unevenness (Figure 21-21, *A-C*).
3. Pain sites noted by the athlete are palpated for point tenderness.
4. Skeletal and musculature sites other than those noted by the athlete are
   also palpated to determine trigger points that may be referring pain.
5. The athlete is asked to actively flex forward, extend, flex laterally to the left
   and right, and rotate the trunk in each direction. Restricted motion, painful
   movements, and asymmetries are noted (Figure 21-22, *A-D*).
6. The sacroiliac joint can be tested for pain while the athlete is standing by
   firmly palpating its posterior aspects or by percussing it with the fist.

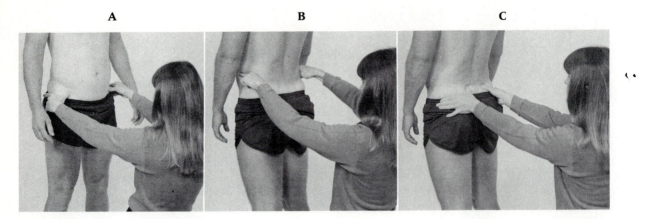

Figure 21-21

A, Testing hip level by comparing the level of the anterior superior iliac spine. **B,** Comparing hip level by palpating the crests of the ilium. **C,** Comparing hip level by palpating the posterior iliac spine.

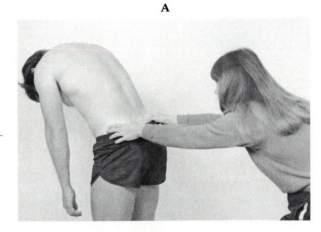

Figure 21-22

Looking for asymmetries and muscle spasms as the athlete goes into, **A,** forward flexion, **B,** back extension, **C,** lateral flexion, and **D,** trunk rotation.

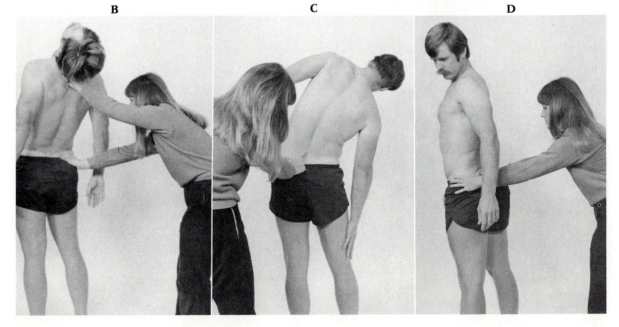

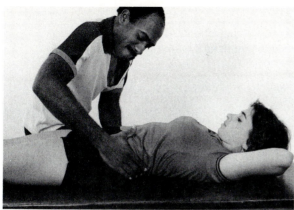

Figure 21-23

Testing the sacroiliac for a pathological condition by compressing the ilium.

Figure 21-24

Straight leg raising test to stretch the spinal cord or sciatic nerve.

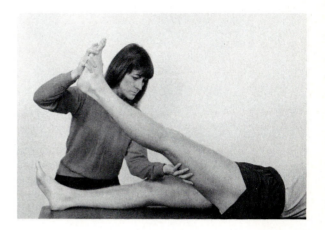

Supine

1. The athlete is measured for leg-length discrepancy (see Chapter 20, p. 637).
2. The sacroiliac joint is tested again by compressing inward on each side of the hip or downward and outward on each anterosuperior spine of the ilium (Figure 21-23).
3. The Patrick test (see p. 633) for hip problems can also determine pathological conditions of the sacroiliac.

Tests for nerve root irritation   Straight leg raising (Lesègue's sign) and its variations place a stretching movement on the dura mater.[7] It tests the fourth and fifth lumbar roots and the first, second, and third sacral nerve roots, which become the sciatic nerve, the largest nerve in the body.

Straight leg raising (affected side)   With the athlete lying flat on the table, the leg on the affected side is lifted by the heel as far as possible. If the test is positive, the athlete feels pain radiating down the leg as well as in the low back region (Figure 21-24). To confirm that pain stems from a nerve root involvement and not hamstring tightness, the leg is lowered to a point at which pain ceases. In this position the foot is then dorsiflexed and the neck flexed. If pain returns, it is a verification of a pathological condition of the nerve root.

Straight leg raising (unaffected side)   The examiner raises the athlete's unaffected leg. If pain occurs in the low back on the affected side as well as radiating along the sciatic nerve, this provides additional proof of nerve root inflammation.

The bowstring test   The bowstring test is another way to determine sciatic nerve irritation. The leg on the affected side is lifted until pain is felt. The knee is then flexed until the pain is relieved, at which time pressure is applied to the popliteal fossa. The test result is positive if pain is felt during palpation along the sciatic nerve (Figure 21-25).

A number of tests for low back injuries are designed to stretch the dura mater and subsequently test possible impingement on spinal nerves.

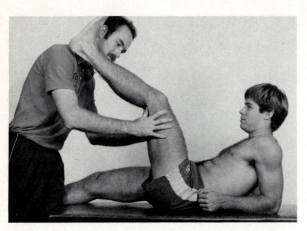

Figure 21-25

Bowstring test for nerve root involvement of the lumbar spine.

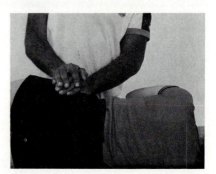

Figure 21-26

Sacroiliac compression test. The downward pressure of the hands on the pelvis will elicit pain in the S1 joint.

Side lying   The athlete lies on the pain-free side.

1. Sacroiliac compression test: the examiner places pressure downward on the lateral pelvis in line with the sacroiliac joint. If the athlete complains of pain in the sacroiliac joint, a pathological condition may be present (Figure 21-26).
2. When evaluating low back problems, the hip should also be evaluated (see Chapter 20).

Prone lying

1. Reverse straight leg raise: the athlete lies face down while the examiner lifts the affected leg.
2. If pain occurs in the low back, an L4 root compression may be present.

Functional Evaluation

Of major importance to the examination and evaluation of the low back is the testing of muscle strength in the lower extremities, of sensory loss, and of reflex inhibition.

Muscle strength   To help ascertain the nerve root involvement, the strength of major lower limb muscles should be determined (Table 21-2).

Sensation   When there is a nerve root involvement, sensation can be partially or completely disrupted. Table 21-3 indicates general disruption or loss of sensation as a result of the low back nerve root involvement (Figure 21-27).

TABLE 21-2 Muscle Weakness and Nerve Involvement

Muscles	Nerve Involvement			
Iliopsoas	T12	L1	L3	
Quadriceps	L2	L3	L4	Femoral nerve
Hip adductor group	L2	L3	L4	Obturator nerve
Extensor hallucis longus	L5	Deep peroneal nerve		
Anterior tibialis				
Gluteus medius				
Extensor digitorum longus and brevis				
Gastrocnemius, hamstring, gluteus maximus, peroneus longus and brevis	S1			

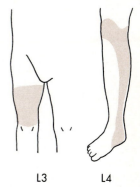

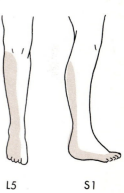

TABLE 21-3 Sensation

Region	Nerve Involvement		
Anterior thigh	L1	L2	L3
Knee	L4		
Inner lower leg and dorsum of foot	L5		
Heel, lateral malleolus, and plantar aspect of foot	S1		

Figure 21-27

Nerve root irritation in the low back region and alteration of lower limb sensation.

Reflexes Two reflexes are routinely measured—knee (patellar) and the Achilles tendon. A diminished or absent patellar reflex is an indication of an L4, L5, or S1 nerve root problem. In contrast, the Achilles tendon reflex can determine the presence or absence of an L3, L4, or L5 nerve root problem.

Along with the evaluation procedures mentioned in this chapter, further inspection would include a thorough testing of the pelvic and thigh regions (see Chapter 20).

Mechanisms of Low Back Pain in the Athlete

Back afflictions, particularly those of the lower back, are second only to foot problems in order of incidence to humans throughout their lives. In sports, back problems are relatively common and are most often the result of congenital, mechanical, or traumatic factors. Congenital back disorders are conditions that are present at birth. Many authorities think that the human back is still undergoing structural changes as a result of its upright position and therefore that humans are prone to slight spinal defects at birth, which later in life may cause improper body mechanics. The usual cause of back pain among athletes is overuse that produces strains and/or sprains of paravertebral muscles and ligaments.[24]

Congenital Anomalies

Anomalies of bony development are the underlying cause of many back problems in sports. Such conditions would have remained undiscovered had it not been for a blow or sudden twist that created an abnormal stress in the area of the anomaly.

The most common of these anomalies are excessive length of the transverse process of the fifth lumbar vertebra, incomplete closure of the neural arch *(spina bifida occulta)*, nonconformities of the spinous processes, atypical lumbosacral angles or articular facets, and incomplete closures of the vertebral laminae. All these anomalies may produce mechanical weaknesses that make the back prone to injury when it is subjected to excessive postural strains.

An example of a congenital defect that may develop into a more serious condition when aggravated by a blow or a sudden twist in sports is the condition of *spondylolisthesis.* Spondylolisthesis is a forward subluxation of the body of a vertebra, usually the fifth lumbar.

Mechanical Defects of the Spine

Mechanical back defects are caused mainly by faulty posture, obesity, or faulty body mechanics—all of which may affect the athlete's performance in sports. Traumatic forces produced in sports, either directly or indirectly, can result in contusions, sprains, and/or fractures. Sometimes even minor injuries can develop into chronic and recurrent conditions, which may have serious complications for the athlete. To aid fully in understanding a back complaint, a logical investigation should be made into the history and the site of any injury, the type of pain produced, and the extent of impairment of normal function.

Maintaining proper segmental alignment of the body during standing, sitting, lying, running, jumping, and throwing is of utmost importance for keeping the body in good condition. Habitual violations of the principles of good body mechanics occur in many sports and produce anatomical deficiencies that subject the body to constant abnormal muscular and ligamentous strain. In all cases of postural deformity the athletic trainer should determine the cause and attempt to rectify the condition through proper strength and mobilization exercises.

Back Trauma

That the athletic trainer possesses skill in recognizing and evaluating the extent of a sports injury to the back is of vital importance. Every football season there are stories of an athlete who has become paralyzed because of the mishandling of a fractured spine. Such conditions would not occur if field officials, coaches, and athletic trainers would use discretion, exercise good judgment, and be able to identify certain gross indications of serious spine involvement.

Preventing Initial Low Back Injuries in Sports

All conditioning programs in sports should include work for the prevention of back injuries. Prevention involves the following:

1. Correction, amelioration, or compensation of functional postural deviations
2. Maintenance or increase of trunk and general body flexibility
3. Increase of trunk and general body strength

Considerations in preventing low back injuries
Postural deviations must be corrected or compensated for
A balance of strength and flexibility in the trunk and pelvis must be maintained

One should be aware of any postural anomalies that the athletes possess; with this knowledge, one should establish individual corrective programs. Basic conditioning should include an emphasis on trunk flexibility. Every effort should be made to produce maximum range of motion in rotation and both lateral and forward flexion. Strength should be developed to the ultimate, with stress placed on developing the spinal extensors (erector spinae) and on developing abdominal strength to ensure proper postural alignment.

Conditions Causing Low Back Pain
Soft-Tissue Injuries

Soft-tissue injuries of the back most often occur to the lower back. Those that occur in sports are produced by acute twists, direct blows, or chronic strains resulting from faulty posture or from the use of poor body mechanics in the sport. Tearing or stretching of the supporting ligamentous tissue with secondary involvement of the musculature occurs. Repeated strains or sprains cause the stabilizing tissues to lose their supporting power, thus producing tissue laxity in the lower back area.

Back contusions   Back contusions rank second to strains and sprains in incidence. Because of its surface area the back is quite liable to bruises in sports; football produces the greatest number of these injuries. A history indicating a violent blow to the back could indicate an extremely serious condition. Contusion of the back must be distinguished from a vertebral fracture; in some instances this is possible only through an x-ray examination. The bruise causes local pain, muscle spasm, and point tenderness. A swollen area may be visible also. Cold and pressure should be applied immediately for approximately 24 hours or longer, followed by rest and a gradual introduction of various forms of superficial heat. If the bruise handicaps the movement of the athlete, deep therapy in the form of ultrasound or microwave diathermy may hasten recovery. Ice massage combined with gradual stretching benefits soft-tissue injuries in the region of the lower back. The time of incapacitation usually ranges from 2 days to 2 weeks.

Lower back strain and sprain   The mechanism of the typical lower back strain or sprain in sports activities usually occurs in two ways.[7] The first happens from a sudden, abrupt, violent extension contraction on an overloaded, unprepared, or underdeveloped spine, primarily in combination with trunk rotation. The second is the chronic strain commonly associated with faulty posture, usually excessive lumbar lordosis; however, conditions such as flat lower back or scoliosis can also predispose one to strain or sprain.[6]

Evaluation of the acute injury   Evaluation must be performed immediately after injury. The possibility of fracture must first be ruled out. Discomfort in the low back may be diffused or localized in one area. There is no radiating pain farther than the buttocks or thigh and no neurological involvement causing muscle weakness, sensation impairment, or reflex impairments.

Immediate and follow-up care   In the acute phase of this injury, it is essential that cold packs and/or ice massage be used intermittently throughout the day to decrease muscle spasm. Injuries of moderate-to-severe intensity may require complete bed rest to help break the pain–muscle spasm cycle. The physician may prescribe oral analgesic medication.

Cryotherapy, ultrasound, and an abdominal support (Figure 21-28) are often beneficial following the acute phase. A graduated program begins slowly in the subacute stage, following the suggested regimen on p. 681. Exercise must not cause pain.

The recurrent and chronic low back pain condition   Once an athlete has a moderate-to-severe episode of acute strain or sprain there is high probability that it will occur again. With each subsequent episode the stage is set for the common problem of "chronic low back pain." Recurrent or chronic low back pain can have many possible causes. Many episodes of strain or sprain can produce malalignment of the vertebral facets or eventually produce discogenic dis-

Figure 21-28

An abdominal brace must both support the abdomen and flatten the lumbar curve.

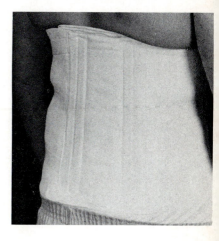

ease, causing nerve root compression and pain. Gradually this problem could lead to muscular weakness, impairments in sensation, and reflex responses. The older the athlete, the more prone he or she is to lower back injury. Incidence of this injury at the high school level is relatively low but becomes progressively greater at college and professional levels. In most cases, because of postural anomalies and numerous small injuries, a so-called acute back condition is the culmination of a progressive degeneration of long duration that is aggravated or accentuated by a blow or sudden twist. The injury is produced as the result of an existing anatomical vulnerability. The trunk and vertebral column press downward on the sacrum, whereas the lower limbs and pelvis force upward; thus an abnormal strain can be exerted when the athlete's trunk is twisted in one direction, while the hamstring muscles pull downward on the pelvis on the opposite side. Such stress, if applied to an inelastic, structurally deformed, or muscularly weak lower back, will produce pathology.

Sciatica   Sciatica is an inflammatory condition of the sciatic nerve that can accompany recurrent or chronic low back pain. It produces pain that follows the nerve pathway, posterior and medial to the thigh. The term *sciatica* has been incorrectly used as a general term to describe all lower back pain, without reference to exact causes. It is commonly associated with peripheral nerve root compression from intervertebral disk protrusion or structural irregularities within the intervertebral foramen. This nerve is particularly vulnerable to torsion or direct blows that tend to impose abnormal stretching and pressure on it as it emerges from the spine, thus effecting a traumatic condition. The sciatic nerve is also subject to trauma at the point at which it crosses over the ischial spine. Such a contusion can cause muscular spasm, placing direct pressure on the nerve.

Lumbar disk disease (intervertebral disk syndrome)   The lumbar disk is subject to constant abnormal stresses stemming from faulty body mechanics, trauma, or both, which, over a period of time, can cause degeneration, tears, and cracks in the annulus fibrosus. Various pressures within the intervertebral disks have been established.[21] When using intervertebral pressure in the standing position as a constant, it was found that pressure was *decreased* by 75% in the supine position and by 25% in the side lying position. Pressure was *increased* by 33% while sitting; by 33% while standing when slightly bent forward; by 45% while sitting when slightly bent forward; 52% while standing when bent far forward; and 63% while sitting when bent well forward.[21]

The area most often injured is the lumbar spine, particularly the disk lying between the fourth and fifth lumbar vertebrae. In sports, the mechanism of a disk injury is the same as for the lumbosacral sprain—a sudden twist that places abnormal strain on the lumbar region. Besides injuring soft tissues, such a strain may herniate an already degenerated disk by increasing the size of crack and allowing the nucleus pulposus to spill out (Figure 21-29). This protrusion of the nucleus pulposus may place pressure on the cord of spinal nerves, thus causing radiating pains similar to those of sciatica.

The movement that produces herniation or bulging of the nucleus pulposus may be excessive, and pain may be minimum or even absent. However, even without severe pain the athlete may complain of numbness along the nerve root and muscle weakness in the lower extremity.

Examination commonly reveals point tenderness and restricted movement. Straight leg and nerve root tests prove positive. Tendon reflexes are partially or

Individuals with lumbar disk disease should avoid performing forward-bending activities.

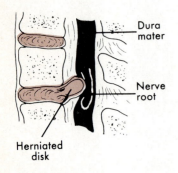

Dura mater

Nerve root

Herniated disk

Figure 21-29

Intervertebral disk syndrome.

completely blocked and dermatome sensation becomes decreased relative to the affected nerve root. Muscle weaknesses also become apparent. These symptoms and signs require immediate referral to an orthopedic surgeon or neurologist.[25]

Immediate and follow-up care   Treatment of disk disease usually includes the following[4,5]:

1. Strict bed rest for 1 to 2 weeks
2. Progressive ambulation
3. Anti-inflammatory agent and, on occasion, muscle relaxants
4. Analgesics and cryotherapy to break the pain–muscle spasm cycle (heat may be of value for its ability to relax muscles)
5. Tranquilizers to decrease the anxiety of the athlete forced to stay in bed

A condition that leads to a progressive bladder or bowel malfunction or severe paresis is considered a medical emergency. When symptom free, the athlete begins a daily program of exercise rehabilitation and postural education.

Spondylolysis   Spondylolysis refers to a degeneration of the vertebrae and, more commonly, a defect in the pars intermedia of the articular processes of the vertebrae (Figure 21-30). It is attributed to a congenital predisposition and/or repeated stress to this area. It is more common among boys.[15] Spondylolysis may produce no symptoms unless a disk herniation occurs or there is sudden trauma such as hyperextension. Sports movements that characteristically hyperextend the spine, such as the back arch in gymnastics, lifting weights, blocking in football, serving in tennis, spiking in volleyball, and the butterfly stroke in swimming, are most likely to cause this condition.[23] Commonly spondylolysis begins unilaterally and then extends to the other side of the vertebrae (Figure 21-31).

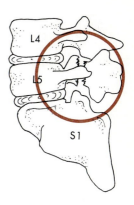

Figure 21-30

Spondylolysis.

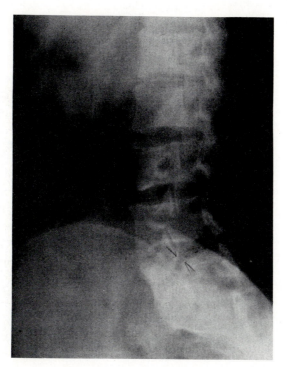

Figure 21-31

Spondylolysis of the fifth lumbar vertebrae.

MANAGEMENT PLAN FOR LUMBOSACRAL STRAIN

Injury Situation   A high school shot-putter came into the athletic training room complaining of a very sore back. He indicated that he woke up with the problem and was not sure how it occurred. Perhaps he had hurt it by doing dead lifts the day before or by throwing the shot incorrectly.

Symptoms and Signs   The athlete complained of a constant dull ache and an inability to flex, extend, or rotate the trunk without increasing the pain. Inspection of the injury indicated the following:

1. The athlete had a pronounced lumbar lordosis.
2. There was an obvious muscle contraction of the right erector spinae.
3. There was severe point tenderness in the right lumbar region.
4. The right pelvis was elevated.
5. Passive movement did not cause pain; however, active and resistive movements produced severe pain.
6. Range of movement in all directions was restricted.
7. All tests for nerve root, hip joint, and sacroiliac joint were negative.
8. Leg length was measured, and the athlete had a functional shortening but no apparent structural shortening.
9. Both the left and right hamstring muscle groups and iliopsoas muscles were abnormally tight.
10. X-ray examination showed no pathological conditions of the lumbar vertebrae.

Based on the examination, it was concluded that the athlete had sustained a first- to second-degree strain of the lumbar muscles, primarily in the right erector spinae region.

Management Plan

1	**Management Phase**	GOALS: To relieve muscle spasm and pain ESTIMATED LENGTH OF TIME (ELT): 2 or 3 days
	Therapy	IMMEDIATE CARE: Ice pack (20 min) followed by exercise and then by transcutaneous electrical nerve stimulation (TENS) (15 to 20 min), three to four times daily
	Exercise Rehabilitation	Following cold application, gentle passive stretch of low back region and hamstring and iliopsoas muscles—all within pain tolerance levels, three to four times daily
2	**Management Phase**	GOALS: To increase low back, hamstring, and iliopsoas range of motion (ROM) to at least begin postural correction ELT: fourth to seventh day of injury
	Therapy	FOLLOW-UP CARE: Ice massage followed by exercise two to three times daily If still painful, TENS therapy should be used

	Exercise Rehabilitation	Repeat Phase 1 exercise and begin proprioceptive neuromuscular facilitation (PNF) to hip and low back regions, two to three times daily; or static low back, hamstring, and iliopsoas stretching (two to three repetitions) and lower-abdominal strengthening two to three times daily Practice realigning pelvis General body maintenance exercises are conducted (as long as they do not aggravate the injury) three times a week
3	**Management Phase**	GOALS: 50% normal extensibility of the low back hamstring and iliopsoas muscles; appropriate abdominal strength ELT: eighth to twelfth day of injury
	Therapy	Ice massage or whirlpool once daily Ultrasound 1 to 1.5 watts/cm^2 once daily
	Exercise Rehabilitation	Repeat Phase 2 exercises once daily to continue reeducation of pelvic and lumbar alignment Add resistance training for abdominal strength General body maintenance exercises are conducted three times a week as long as they do not aggravate the injury
4	**Management Phase**	GOALS: To restore 90% of ROM, strength, and proper back alignment
	Exercise Rehabilitation	Return to weight training and shot-putting program three times a week Athlete is instructed about proper back alignment when shot-putting Athlete is to avoid dead lifting and to wear a lifting belt while weight training
5	**Management Phase**	GOALS: To return to full competition
	Exercise Rehabilitation	Return to normal training three times a week Gradual reentry into competition Using an abdominal support belt is advisable during practice and competition

Criteria for Returning to Competitive Shot-putting

The athlete's back must be as follows:
1. Pain and spasm free
2. Near normal in hamstring, low back, and iliopsoas extensibility
3. Making good progress toward correcting lumbar lordosis
4. Able to perform the shot-put with the spine and pelvis in good alignment

Management usually involves restricted activity and complete bed rest; bracing may also be required.

Rehabilitative exercise usually involves resolution of hyperlordosis.

Spondylolisthesis The condition spondylolisthesis is the forward slippage of a vertebra on the one below; it is commonly accompanied by spondylolysis and has the highest incidence with L5 on S1 (Figure 21-32). Although pars intermedia defects are more common among boys, the incidence of slippage is higher in girls.[15] The athlete with this condition will usually have a lumbar hyperlordosis postural impairment. A direct blow or sudden twist or chronic low back strain may cause the defective vertebra to displace itself forward on the sacrum. When this happens, the athlete complains of localized pain or a pain that radiates into both buttocks, stiffness in the lower back, and increased irritation after physical activity. The athlete with serious spondylolisthesis displays a short torso, heart-shaped buttocks, low rib cage, high iliac crest, and vertical sacrum; tight hamstring muscles and restricted hip extension may also be present. For the most part, these symptoms are the same for the majority of lower back problems; therefore, an x-ray film should be obtained to enable the physician to diagnose accurately. Discovery of a defective vertebra may be grounds for medical exclusion from collision and contact-type sports.

Conservative management of acute problems usually consists of bed rest and flexion of the lumbar spine.[5] Casting to reduce hyperlordosis may also be used. A slippage of 50% or more may cause a medical emergency, requiring surgical fusion of the spine.

Sacroiliac joint The sacroiliac is the junction formed by the ilium and the sacrum, and it is fortified by ligamentous tissue that allows little motion to take place. When the pelvis is abnormally rotated downward anteriorly, the majority of the weight of the upper trunk is carried back of the pelvis, producing stress at the sacroiliac joint. This abnormal postural alignment can cause pain and disability.

Lumbar vertebral fracture and dislocation Fractures of the vertebral column, in terms of bone injury, are not serious in themselves; but they pose dangers when related to spinal cord damage. Imprudent movement of a person with a fractured spine can cause irreparable damage to the spinal cord. All sports injuries involving the back should be considered fractures until proved differently by the physician. Lifting and moving the athlete should be executed in such a manner as to preclude twisting, and each body segment (neck, trunk, hips, and lower limbs) should be firmly supported. Vertebral fractures of the greatest concern in sports are compression fractures and fractures of the transverse and spinous processes.

The *compression fracture* may occur as a result of violent hyperflexion or jackknifing of the trunk. Falling from a height and landing on the feet or buttocks may also produce a compression fracture. The vertebrae that are most often compressed are those in the dorsolumbar curves. The vertebrae usually are crushed anteriorly by the traumatic force of the body above the site of injury. The crushed body may spread out fragments and protrude into the spinal canal, compressing and possibly even cutting the cord.

Recognition of the compression fracture is difficult without an x-ray examination. A basic evaluation may be made with a knowledge of the history and point tenderness over the affected vertebrae.

Spondylolysis can lead to the condition spondylolisthesis.

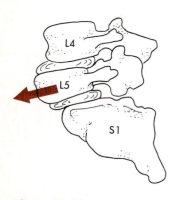

Figure 21-32

Spondylolisthesis.

Fractures of the transverse and spinous processes result most often from kicks or other direct blows to the back. Since these processes are surrounded by large muscles, fracture produces extensive soft-tissue injury. As fractures, these present little danger and will usually permit the athlete considerable activity within the range of pain tolerance. Most care and treatment will be oriented toward therapy of the soft-tissue pathology.

Coccyx Injuries

Coccygeal injuries in sports are prevalent and occur primarily from such direct blows as those that are received in forcibly sitting down, falling, or being kicked by an opponent. Most injuries to the coccyx are the result of contusions.

Athletes with persistent coccyalgia should be referred to a physician for x-ray and rectal examinations. Pain in the coccygeal region is often prolonged and at times chronic. Such conditions are identified by the term *coccygodynia* and occur as a result of an irritation to the coccygeal plexus.

Treatment consists of analgesics and a ring seat to relieve the pressure on the coccyx while sitting. Palliative measures such as sitz baths or whirlpool in warm water might alleviate some of the pain. It should be noted that pain with a fractured coccyx may last for many months. Once a coccygeal injury has healed, the athlete should be protected against reinjury by appropriately applied padding.

Rehabilitation of Low Back Pain

The following treatment procedures are used to a greater or lesser degree, depending on the type and extent of the pathological condition:
   1. Limitation of activity
   2. Anti-inflammatory and muscle relaxant medications
   3. Cold and/or heat application and ultrasound
   4. Passive exercise
   5. Active progressive exercise
   6. Relaxation training
   7. Transcutaneous electrical nerve stimulation (TENS) application
   8. Education for proper back usage

Limitation of Activity

Limiting physical activity is essential during acute episodes of low back pain. It can also be a positive influence in chronic pain. The least strain on the back is in the fully recumbant position. In the case of a chronic or a subacute lower back condition, a *firm mattress will afford better rest and relaxation of the lower back.* Placing a ¾ inch plywood board over the entire area of the bed underneath the athlete's mattress prevents the mattress from sagging in the wrong places and gives a firm, stable surface for the injured back. The athlete lies supine with hips flexed by elevating the legs with pillows. It is also interesting to note that sleeping on a water bed will often relieve the symptoms of a low back problem if the athlete lies on his or her back. However, in some cases, the firm mattress or water bed may create more pain and discomfort. The value of a water bed is that it supports the body curves equally, decreasing abnormal pressures to any one body area.

Medications

Analgesics and oral anti-inflammatory agents are commonly given to inhibit pain. If a highly active athlete becomes severely depressed over suddenly being severely physically restricted, an antidepressant may be given. On occasion muscle relaxants are also given.

Cold or Heat Application

Local ice application reduces the pain–muscle spasm cycle. Superficial heat can also provide relaxation and reduction of spasm. Ultrasound and mild muscle stimulation can be used to relieve spasm and discomfort.

Exercise and Low Back Disorders

Exercise is a common approach to managing athletes with low back disorders.[18] Many exercise approaches such as flexion and extension, passive and active exercises, postural programs, and exercise that may be predominantly isometric, isometric, isokinetic, or aerobic are available to the athletic trainer.[18] Selecting the correct program may be difficult because research data supporting a specific approach are very sparse.

Exactly how exercise relieves symptoms is not known. Pain is known to be relieved by a program of gradual stretching and strengthening.[18] Biomechanically, functional improvement occurs through a program of gradual progressive loading, along with stretching. Passive or active range of motion is necessary for stretching contracted muscles. Many exercises are designed to regain the normal lumbar curve.

The Williams flexion exercises, for many years, have been popular for reducing low back pain. However, in recent years they have waned in popularity, with extension exercise becoming increasingly popular. Flexion exercise is based on empirical knowledge acquired from clinical observation. Its basic premise is that much of lumbosacral pain is caused by overextension that can be relieved through lumbar flexion.[12] It is also theorized that lumbar flexion relieves pain produced by the impingement of the facet joints and the intervertebral foramen.[18] See Figure 21-A for low back exercises for strength and flexibility.

Like flexion exercises, the use of extension exercises has an empirical base acquired by observing patients with low back pain. Those individuals who seem to respond most have decreased lumbar lordosis.[7] Through extension exercises the normal lumbar lordosis is regained.[19] It is thought that regaining lumbosacral motion during extension improves the biomechanics of the spine and, as a result, relieves pain.[18] Extension exercise is thought to shift posteriorly displaced nucleus pulposa within the disk anteriorly.[18]

Passive Exercise

If the condition is muscular and discogenic disease has been ruled out, a mild passive stretch can help reduce muscle spasm. Passive stretching of the hamstrings and the iliopsoas muscle may allow a more coordinated lumbar pelvic rhythm to take place without pain and discomfort. Lumbar vertebral mobilization techniques may also be of some benefit if performed gently (see Chapter 13).

Figure 21-A

Low back exercises for strength and flexibility.

Relax.

Pelvic tilt.

Knee to chest.

Both knees to chest.

Erect pelvic tilt.

Leg raise.

Uncurling the trunk.

Heel cord stretch.

Hamstring stretch.

Hip flexion stretch.

Active Progressive Exercise

Active exercise is a major aspect of low back rehabilitation. Once the pain and spasm have subsided, active exercise should begin. The major goals of exercise are to establish normal flexibility and strength and to develop good postural habits in all aspects of daily activities.

Exercise should not be engaged in too vigorously before pain has diminished significantly. The first exercise phase should include pelvic tilt, alternate knees to chest, and double knee to chest. **NOTE:** All exercises within each phase should start with three repetitions and be increased each day by one, until 10 repetitions can be performed (if a position is held, it should be done for a count of six).

Stage 1—low back exercises

Pelvic tilt   The athlete lies supine in a "hook-lying" position, with feet flat on the mat or floor. The abdomen is contracted, and the back is flattened firmly against the surface.

After 10 repetitions of this exercise, the athlete, while keeping the lumbar spine as flat as possible, raises the pelvis 3 to 4 inches and holds this position for 6 seconds.

Alternate knee to chest   While the athlete is lying supine, one knee is brought slowly toward the chest. Both hands grasp the posterior thigh and gently pull it slowly to an end point for a count of six. The leg is returned slowly to its starting point, and the other leg is exercised in the same way.

Double knee to chest   While in a hook-lying position the athlete grasps under both bent knees and pulls them slowly and gently as far as possible toward the chest and holds the end point (Figure 21-33).

Stage 2—low back exercises
When the low back is relatively pain free, the athlete can move to Phase 2 exercises, which include overhead low back stretch, hip flexor stretch, hamstring stretch, single leg raise, abdominal curl-up, and lateral flexion stretch.

Hip flexor stretch   The hip flexor stretch releases tension associated with the lumbar curve. Placing one leg on the seat of a chair or bench with the support leg fully extended, the athlete settles the body weight downward, stretching the iliopsoas muscle on the side of the extended leg (Figure 21-34).

Single leg raise   The single leg raise stretches the low back and hamstrings and strengthens hip flexors and abdominal muscles. The athlete takes a supine position with one knee bent and the other straight. Keeping the back flat, the straight leg is raised as far as possible and returned slowly. The athlete completes up to 10 repetitions and then changes legs. This exercise can be made progressively more difficult by gradually extending the bent knee over a period of time until it is extended like the exercising leg.

Abdominal curl-up   The athlete assumes a hook-lying position, squeezes the buttocks together, contracts abdominal muscles, flexes the neck and places the chin on the chest, rolls shoulders forward, and slowly slides hands up the thighs to an end point. This exercise progresses from hands sliding up the thighs, to arms crossing the chest, and finally to hands laced behind the neck.

Lateral trunk flexion   The athlete stands with feet apart and slightly bends the knee on the side of the direction of the stretch. The trunk is then laterally flexed without backward extension or forward flexion. All movements are gently but progressively increased.[5]

Figure 21-33

Double knee to chest.

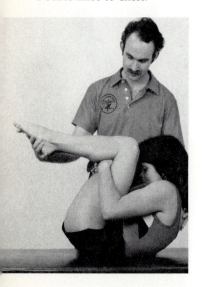

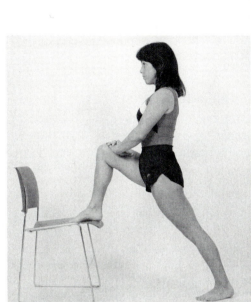

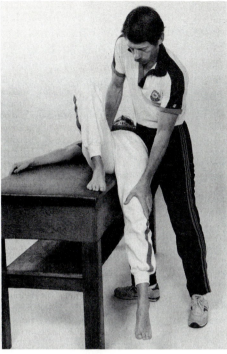

Figure 21-34

Hip flexor stretches.

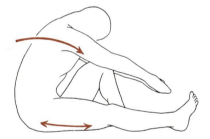

Figure 21-35

Hamstring stretching for low back strain.

Hamstring stretching for low back pain   Hamstring stretching for low back pain should not be conducted with both legs extended.[5] To protect the back against further irritation, one leg is stretched at a time. The leg not being stretched is placed in a hooked position to alleviate strain on the back. The stretch should be gradually increased, not ballistically stretched (Figure 21-35).

Wall back flattener   The wall back flattener exercise is designed to educate the athlete about the proper pelvic position, to stretch low back muscles, and to strengthen the lower abdominal muscles. The athlete stands approximately 8 to 12 inches from a wall facing outward, knees slightly bent, with the pelvis and low back pressed flat against the wall. The athlete then bends foward, rounding the back as much as possible, and then slowly returns to a fully upright position, attempting to touch each vertebrae to the wall.

Relaxation and Low Back Pain

An important aspect of treating athletes with low back pain is progressive relaxation. With constant pain comes anxiety and increased muscular tension that compounds the low back problem. By systematically contracting and completely "letting go" of the body's major muscles, the athlete learns to recognize abnormal tension and to consciously relax the muscles. The most popular method of progressive relaxation is the Jacobson[16] method, which can be found in modified form in a number of different texts.[1,2]

Transcutaneous Electrical Nerve Stimulation (TENS)

Application of a TENS device has been beneficial in a high percentage of cases of low back pain.[5] However, not every machine is equally effective in all cases of low back pain. There must be experimentation as to type of machine, wave form, and sites of application.[6]

Manual Therapeutic Procedures and Traction

Manual therapeutic procedures and traction have been used extensively over the years to treat low back pain.

Manual therapeutic procedures   The two manual therapeutic procedures currently being used for the management of low back pain are proprioceptive neuromuscular facilitation (PNF) and manipulation.

PNF   There is a high success rate in using PNF principles to increase range of motion and strength. Besides increasing flexibility and strength, muscles are reeducated to reestablish lost pelvic lumbar rhythm and proprioception. Rhythmic stabilization using isometric exercise can develop co-contraction of antagonistic muscle groups.[27]

Manipulation   Traditionally, spinal manipulation has been associated with competitive sports.[12] It is broadly defined as all procedures using the hands, including massage, myofascial stretching, and manipulation of spinal tissues. A major question is whether manipulation relieves low back pain. There is evidence that manipulation can relieve acute low back pain; however, there is, as yet, no evidence that manipulation produces any positive long-term effects.[12] In comparison to conservative treatments such as bedrest, analgesic medications, corsets, exercises, traction, ultrasound, massage, and back reeducation, manipulation is considered being as good a therapeutic approach.[7] **NOTE:** At no time should stretching be applied until there is absolute knowledge that no fracture is present and stretching will not aggravate a serious existing injury.

LOW BACK ROTATION STRETCH

Indications   Increasing the range of motion of the lower back often relieves the irritation of strain and chronic fibromyositis.

Positioning   The athlete lies in a supine position with hips turned laterally to the trunk, the upper leg flexed at a 90-degree angle. The operator stands at the middle of the table, facing the athlete, and places the hand that is on the side of the athlete's feet directly on the side of the knee, positioning the other hand on the athlete's shoulder.

Execution   In this position the operator stabilizes the athlete's shoulder and with a scissors action pushes the pelvis foward, thereby initiating a stretch (Figure 21-36).

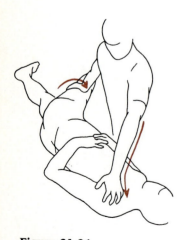

Figure 21-36

Low back rotation stretch.

Precautions   Do not stretch if there is a possibility of a fracture. Do not thrust, but stretch with an even and steady movement. *Do not stretch beyond normal pain limitations.*

LOW BACK SCISSORS STRETCH

Indications   This mild stretch is to be used with an effleurage massage of the back; it helps to relax and loosen contracted tissue.

Positioning   The athlete lies prone with arms at the side. The operator stands transversely at the middle of the table, on the side opposite the one to be stretched. With the hand nearest the athlete's feet, the operator grasps the antero-superior iliac spine and places the heel of the other hand on the lumbar area of the spine, directly over the transverse process (Figure 21-37).

Execution   The operator pulls upward on the anterosuperior spine and simultaneously pushes downward on the lower thoracic and lumbar area of the spine.

Precautions   Do not stretch if there is a possibility of fracture or if the athlete complains of tenderness at the anterosuperior spine of the ilium. In the latter instance, a pad should be placed on the site before it is grasped.

TRUNK ROTATION STRETCH

Indications   Limited ranges of motion during trunk rotation may be increased by use of the trunk rotation stretch.

Positioning   The athlete sits on a stool or chair with the hips placed against the back of the chair and the feet planted firmly on the floor (Figure 21-38). The operator stands to one side of the chair, facing the athlete. The operator then places his or her outside leg over the knees of the athlete, stabilizing the lower limbs. Reaching around the back of the athlete's upper trunk, the athlete grasps the shoulder nearest to the back of the chair and pulls it toward him or her. Simultaneously, the operator places a free hand on the athlete's near shoulder and pushes forward, thus effecting a forced torsion of the athlete's upper trunk.

Execution   The athlete exhales during trunk rotation, which should be executed with a slow and even pressure, beyond the point of restriction. It is desirable that the athlete have at least a 90-degree range of motion.

Precautions   Make certain that the athlete's hips are maintained in a stabilized position against the back of the chair. **NOTE:** Do not attempt to stretch when the athlete's lungs are expanded.

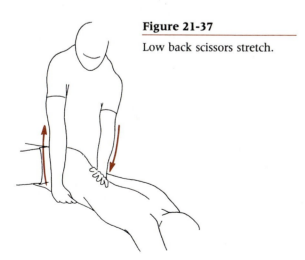

Figure 21-37

Low back scissors stretch.

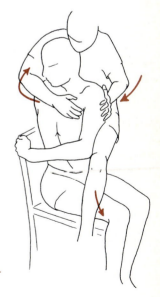

Figure 21-38

Trunk rotation stretch.

Traction   Traction is the treatment of choice when there is a small protrusion of the nucleus pulposus. Through traction, the lumbar vertebrae are distracted, a subatmospheric pressure is created, tending to pull the protrusion to its original position, and there is tightening of the longitudinal ligament, tending to push the protrusion toward its original position within the disk.[8] Sustained traction for at least 30 minutes with a force commensurate with body weight is preferred. A 35 kg/80 lb force would be the minimum for a small woman, and 80 kg/180 lb force would be the minimum for a large man.[8] Traction is usually applied daily (five times per week) for 2 weeks.

Educating for the Proper Care of the Back

Bed rest
1. Do not stay in one position too long.
2. The bed should be flat and firm.
3. Do not sleep on the abdomen.
4. Do not sleep on the back with legs fully extended.
5. If sleeping on the back, a pillow should be placed under the knees.
6. Ideally, sleep on the side.
7. Arms should never be extended overhead.

Sitting
1. Do not sit for long periods.
2. Avoid sitting forward on a chair with back arched.
3. Sit on a firm, straight-backed chair.
4. The low back should be slightly rounded or positioned firmly against the back of the chair.
5. The feet should be flat on the floor with knees above the level of the hips (if unable to adequately raise the hips, the feet should be placed on a stool).
6. Avoid sitting with legs straight and raised on a stool.

Driving
1. Move seat so that knees are higher than the hips (pedals must be reached without stretching).
2. Avoid leaning forward.
3. Wear seat and shoulder harnesses.

Standing
1. If standing in one spot for a long period of time:
   a. Shift position from one foot to another.
   b. Place one foot on a stool.
2. Stand tall, flatten low back, and relax knees.
3. Avoid arching back.

Lifting and carrying
1. To pick up an object:
   a. Bend at knees and not the waist.
   b. Do not twist to pick up an object—face it squarely.
   c. Tuck in buttocks and tighten abdomen.
2. To carry an object:
   a. Hold object close to body.
   b. Hold object at waist level.
   c. Do not carry object on one side of the body—if it must be carried unbalanced, change from one side to the other.

SUMMARY

The abdominal region can sustain a superficial or deep internal injury from a blow. Good conditioning that strengthens the abdominal muscles is essential to prevent contusions and strains.

Of the two common hernias, inguinal and femoral, the most prevalent is the inguinal hernia. These conditions can be congenital or acquired. The major danger in each occurs when the protruding sac becomes constricted and circulation is impeded.

Two additional abdominal problems are the "stitch in the side" and a blow to the solar plexus. The causes of the cramplike stitch in the side are obscure, although poor eating habits, poor elimination habits, or inadequate training habits are possibilities. A blow to the solar plexus produces transitory paralysis of the diaphragm, which stops breathing for a short while.

The two major internal organs that can be injured in sports are the spleen and the kidney. A direct blow to the abdomen or a jarring fall can rupture the spleen. Shock, abdominal rigidity, nausea, and vomiting are signs of spleen injury. Although well-protected, the kidney can be contused by a severe blow to the athlete's back. Signs of contusion are shock, nausea, vomiting, and rigidity of the back muscles.

The thoracic region can sustain a number of different sports injuries such as rib contusions, fractures, separations, and dislocations. Internal thoracic complications include pneumothorax, hemothorax, traumatic asphyxia, and even heart contusions.

The low back can sustain a number of different injuries from sports activities. Prevention of low back injuries includes correcting or compensating for postural deviations, maintaining or increasing trunk and general body flexibility, and increasing trunk and general body strength.

Many low back problems stem from congenital defects such as spina bifida occulta or spondylolisthesis. Faulty posture is commonly the cause of mechanical defects in the spine. Faulty mechanics of the low back can eventually lead to the serious condition lumbar disk disease. As with any musculoskeletal region, the low back can sustain traumatic sports injuries such as contusions, strains, and sprains.

REVIEW QUESTIONS AND SUGGESTED ACTIVITIES

1. Explain how the abdominal wall sustains sports injuries. How can they be prevented?
2. Distinguish an inguinal hernia or a femoral hernia from a groin strain.
3. Describe the signs of a "stitch in the side."
4. How do you manage an athlete who has had his or her wind knocked out?
5. Contrast the signs of a ruptured spleen with signs of a severely contused kidney.
6. What are the most common sports injuries to the genitourinary system?
7. Differentiate between rib contusions, rib fractures, and costochondral separations.
8. Compare the signs of pneumothorax, hemothorax, and traumatic asphyxia.
9. List the possible causes of sudden death syndrome among athletes.
10. Demonstrate assessment procedures of the low back.
11. How can low back strains or sprains be prevented?
12. How does a lumbar disk become ruptured?
13. Why does spondylolysis lead to spondylolisthesis?
14. Explain the rationale for rehabilitating the chronically painful low back.

REFERENCES

1. Arnheim, DD, and Sinclair, WA: Physical education for special populations, Englewood Cliffs, NJ, 1985, Prentice-Hall, Inc.
2. Auxter, D, and Pyfer, J: Principles and methods of adapted physical education, St. Louis, 1985, The CV Mosby Co.
3. Becker, T: Scoliosis in the adolescent athlete, Sports Med Guide 2(4):1, 1983.

4. Birnbaum, JS: The muscloskeletal manual, New York, 1982, Academic Press, Inc.

5. Cailliet, R: Low back pain, ed 3, Philadelphia, 1981, FA Davis Co.

6. Cantu, RC: Low back injuries. In Vinger, PE, and Hoerner, EF, editors: Sports injuries: the unthwarted epidemic, Boston, 1982, John Wright, PSG, Inc.

7. Cyriax, J: Textbook of orthopaedic medicine, vol 1, Diagnosis of soft tissue lesions, ed 8, London, 1982, Bailliere, Tindall.

8. Cyriax, J, and Cyrian, P: Illustrated manual of orthopaedic medicine, London, 1983, Butterworth & Co (Publishers), Ltd.

9. Gehlsen, G, and Albohm, M: Evaluation of sports bras, Phys Sportsmed 8:89, 1980.

10. Gurtler, H, Pavlov, H, and Torg, JS: Stress fracture of the ipsilateral first rib in a pitcher, Am J Sports Med 13:277, July/Aug 1985.

11. Hafen, GQ: First aid in health emergencies, ed 3, New York, 1984, West Publishing Co.

12. Haldeman, S: Spinal manipulative therapy in sports medicine. In Spencer III, CW: Injuries to the spine, Clinics in sports medicine, vol 5, no 2, Philadelphia, 1986, WB Saunders Co.

13. Haycock, CE: How I manage abdominal injuries, Phys Sportsmed 14(6):86, 1986.

14. Haycock, CE: How I manage breast problems in athletes, Phys Sportsmed 15(3):89, 1987.

15. Jackson, DW, and Ciullo, JV: Injuries of the spine in the skeletally immature athlete. In Nicholas, JA, and Hershman, EB, editors: The lower extremity and spine in sports medicine, vol 2, St. Louis, 1986, The CV Mosby Co.

16. Jacobson, E: Progressive relaxation, ed 2, Chicago, 1938, University of Chicago Press.

17. Lankenner, Jr, PA, and Micheli, LJ: Stress fracture of the first rib: a case re-

port, J Bone Joint Surg 67A:159, Jan 1985.

18. Lee, CK: The use of exercise and muscle testing in the rehabilitation of spinal disorders. In Spencer III, CW, editor: Injuries to the spine, Clinics in sports medicine, vol 5, no 2, Philadelphia, 1986, WB Saunders Co.

19. McKenzie, RA: Prophylaxis in current low back pain, NZ Med J 89:22, 1979.

20. Moncure, AC, and Wilkins, EW: Injuries involving the abdomen, viscera, and genitourinary system. In Vinger, PF, and Hoerner, EF, editors: Sports injuries: the unthwarted epidemic, Boston, 1982, John Wright, PSG, Inc.

21. Nachemson, A, and Elfstrom, G: Intravital dynamic pressure measurements in lumbar discs, Scand J Rehabil Med Suppl 1, 1969.

22. O'Donoghue, DH: Treatment of injuries in athletes, Philadelphia, 1984, WB Saunders Co.

23. O'Leary, P, and Borardo, R: The diagnosis and treatment of injuries of the spine in athletes. In Nicholas, JA, and Hershman, EB, editors: The lower extremity and spine in sports medicine, vol 2, St. Louis, 1986, The CV Mosby Co.

24. Rovere, GD: Low back pain in athletes, Phys Sportsmed 15(1):105, 1987.

25. Schafer, MF: Low back injuries in athletes, Sports Med Dig 8(7):1, 1986.

26. Schiller, WR: General surgery and sports medicine. In Appenzeller, O, and Atkinson, R, editors: Sports medicine, Baltimore, 1981, Urban & Schwarzenberg.

27. Teitz, CC: Rehabilitation of neck and low back injuries. In Harvey, JS, editor: Symposium on rehabilitation of the injured athlete, Clinics in sports medicine, vol 4, no 3, Philadelphia, 1985, WB Saunders Co.

28. Thompson, PD, and McGhee, JR: Cardiac evaluation of the competitive athlete. In Strauss, RH, editor: Sports medicine, Philadelphia, 1984, WB Saunders Co.

ANNOTATED BIBLIOGRAPHY

Cailliet, R: Low back pain syndrome, ed 3, Philadelphia, 1981, FA Davis Co.
Presents the subject of low back pain in a clear, concise, and interesting manner.

Spencer III, CW, editor: Injuries to the spine, Clinics in sports medicine, vol 5, no 2, Philadelphia, 1986, WB Saunders Co.
Includes coverage of spinal injuries stemming from sports participation. Acute and overuse injuries are discussed in-depth.

Stauffer, ES: The American Academy of Orthopaedic Surgeons instruction course lectures, vol XXXIV, St. Louis, 1985, The CV Mosby Co.
Contains excellent courses about the low back, scoliosis, cervical spine, shoulder, and upper extremity, as well as rehabilitation in sports medicine.

22

The Head and the Thoracic and Cervical Spine

When you finish this chapter, you should be able to

Describe the anatomy of the upper spine, head, and face and relate it to sports injuries

Recognize and evaluate major sports injuries of the upper spine, head, and face

Perform proper immediate and follow-up management of injuries to the upper spine, head, and face

Sports injuries to the upper spine, head, or face could have major consequences for the athlete. A serious facial injury could lead to disfigurement or loss of sight or might even be life threatening. Injury to the head could result in major cerebral involvement, whereas an upper spinal injury could result in paralysis.

THORACIC SPINE
Anatomy

The thoracic spine consists of 12 vertebrae. The first through the tenth thoracic vertebrae articulate with ribs through articular facets. Attached to all thoracic spinous processes is the trapezius muscle; the rhomboid muscle is attached to the upper spinous processes; and the latissimus dorsi muscle is attached to the lower spinous processes. Deeper muscles of the back also attach to spinous and transverse processes (Figure 22-1).

Evaluating the Thoracic Spine
Major Complaints

Pain in the upper back can be caused by a variety of conditions: pain could be referred from some visceral disorder, it could be of muscular origin, or it could be caused by a nerve root irritation. Having the athlete respond to the following questions should provide important information:

1. What kind of pain do you feel? Describe it.
2. What is the duration, location, and intensity of the pain? (For example, is it constant? intermittent?)

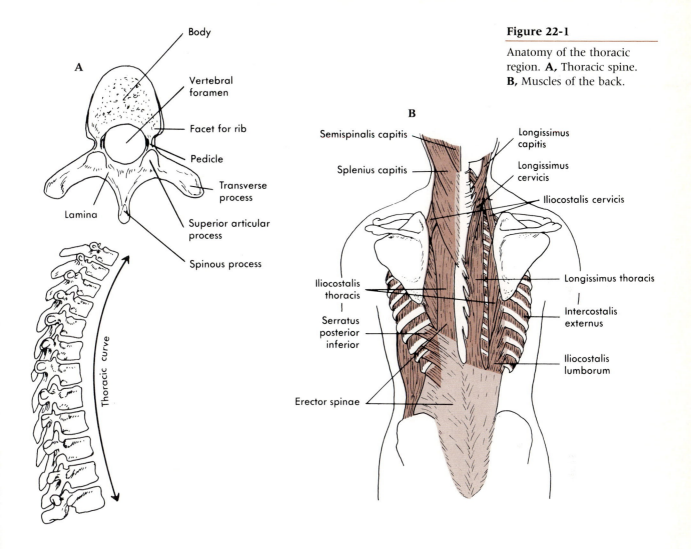

Figure 22-1

Anatomy of the thoracic region. **A,** Thoracic spine. **B,** Muscles of the back.

3. What makes the pain more or less intense?
4. Did the pain come on gradually or suddenly?
5. Do you feel numbness or tingling anywhere?
6. Have you been treated for this problem before? If so, was the result satisfactory?

General observation The athlete is examined posteriorly and laterally for the following:

1. Kyphosis (abnormal convexity of the curvature of the thoracic spine)
2. Flat back (decreased curvature of the thoracic spine)
3. Scoliosis (lateral rotary deviation of the spine)

A collapsed vertebra will often produce thoracic back protrusion, whereas a flat low back or kyphosis of the upper lumbar and lower thoracic spine may indicate Scheuermann's disease (adolescent osteochondrosis).[6] Viewed laterally, a decrease of the normal lumbar curve with extensive kyphosis of the thoracic spine could indicate ankylosing spondylitis.[6]

In evaluating the thoracic spine, all postural deviations must be noted.

Young athletes who complain of thoracic spine pain may in fact have
   Spondylolysis
   Spondylolisthesis
   Scoliosis
   Scheuermann's disease

Bony and Soft-Tissue Palpation

Starting at the twelfth thoracic vertebra, all thoracic and cervical vertebrae are palpated for pain and possible defects. Also palpated are the spinous and transverse processes, adjacent ribs in the thoracic region, and the intercostal and posterior back and shoulder muscles.

Active resistive and passive movement

Active movement   The athlete is first asked to flex, extend, laterally flex, and rotate the neck. Pain accompanying the movement in the upper back region could be referred from a lesion of the cervical disk. Additionally, pain in the scapular area could stem from an irritation of the long thoracic or suprascapular nerves, requiring evaluation of the shoulder complex (see Chapter 23). The athlete should also be asked to flex forward and laterally and to extend and rotate the trunk. Pain felt during movement may indicate nerve root irritation to the lower thoracic region.

After active movement, the same motions are resisted. Pain accompanying resisted movements can reveal muscle strains in the thoracic and abdominal regions.

Following active movement, the athlete is passively moved while seated in a chair with hips and legs stabilized. The athlete's trunk is passively rotated first one direction and then the other. Pain accompanying this passive movement may indicate a pathological condition of the joint.

Thoracic Spine Injuries

Back Conditions in the Young Athlete

Because young athletes are much less likely to sustain back strains and nerve root irritation, back pain could indicate a vertebral growth disturbance. Three such conditions that could have serious disabling consequences are spondylolithesis (see Chapter 21), scoliosis, and Scheuermann's disease.

Scoliosis   Scoliosis was discussed in Chapter 9 in relation to injury mechanism and in Chapter 21 in relation to low back pain. Any time a young athlete complains of back pain, scoliosis should be considered. Because a lateral-rotary condition of the spine can be progressively quite disabling if not promptly treated, referral to a physician must be made at once by the athletic trainer.

Scheuermann's disease (osteochondrosis of the spine)   Scheuermann's disease is a degeneration of vertebral epiphyseal endplates. This degeneration allows the disk's nucleus pulposus to prolapse into a vertebral body. Characteristically there is an accentuation of the kyphotic curve and backache in the young athlete. Adolescents engaging in sports such as gymnastics and swimming—the butterfly stroke particularly—are prone to this condition.[29]

ETIOLOGICAL FACTORS   Scheuermann's disease is idiopathic, but the occurrence of multiple minor injuries to the vertebral epiphyses seems to be an etiological factor. These injuries apparently disrupt circulation to the epiphyseal endplate, causing avascular necrosis.

SYMPTOMS AND SIGNS   In the initial stages, the young athlete will have kyphosis of the thoracic spine and lumbar lordosis without back pain. In later stages, there is point tenderness over the spinous processes, and the young athlete may complain of backache at the end of a very physically active day. Hamstring muscles are characteristically very tight.

MANAGEMENT   The major goal of management is to prevent progressive kyphosis. In the early stages of the disease, extension exercises and postural education are beneficial. Bracing, rest, and anti-inflammatory medication may also be helpful. The athlete may stay active but should avoid aggravating movements.

CERVICAL SPINE
Anatomy

Because of the vulnerability of the cervical spine to sports injuries, athletic trainers should be familiar with its anatomy and mechanism and with means of evaluating injuries (Figure 22-2). The cervical spine consists of seven vertebrae, with the

Figure 22-2

Many sports place a great deal of stress on the upper spine.

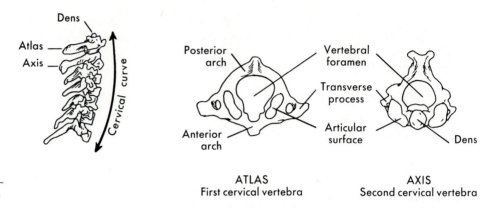

Figure 22-3

Cervical spine, atlas, and axis.

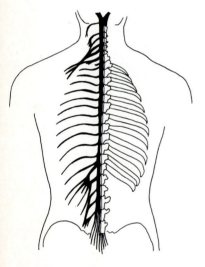

Figure 22-4

Relationship of cord and spinal nerves to the vertebral column.

first two differing from the other true vertebrae (Figure 22-3). These first two are called the atlas and the axis, respectively, and they function together to support the head on the spinal column and to permit cervical rotation. The *atlas,* named for its function of supporting the head, displays no body or spinous processes and is composed of lateral masses that are connected to the anterior and posterior arches. The upper surfaces articulate with the occipital condyles of the skull and allow flexion and extension but little lateral movement. The arches of the atlas form a bony ring sufficiently large to accommodate the odontoid process and the medulla of the spinal cord. The *axis,* or epistropheus, is the second cervical vertebra and is designed to allow the skull and atlas to rotate on it. Its primary difference from a typical vertebra is the presence of a toothlike projection from the vertebral body that fits into the ring of the atlas. This projection is called the odontoid process. The great mobility of the cervical spine is attributed to the flattened, oblique facing of its articular facets and to the horizontal positioning of the spinous processes.

The *spinal cord* is that portion of the central nervous system that is contained within the vertebral canal of the spinal column. It extends from the foramen magnum of the cranium to the filum terminale in the vicinity of the first or second lumbar vertebra. The lumbar roots and the sacral nerves form a horselike tail called the cauda equina.

Thirty-one pairs of *spinal nerves* extend from the sides of the spinal cord: eight cervical, 12 thoracic, five lumbar, five sacral, and one coccygeal (Figure 22-4). Each of these nerves has an anterior root (motor root) and a posterior one (sensory root). The two roots in each case join together and form a single spinal nerve, which passes downward and outward through the intervetebral foramen. As the spinal nerves are conducted through the intervertebral foramen, they pass near the articular processes of the vertebrae. Any abnormal movement of these processes, such as in a dislocation or a fracture, may expose the spinal nerves to injury. Injuries that occur below the third lumbar vertebra usually result in nerve root damage but do not cause spinal cord damage.

Cervical Spine Injuries

The very mobile neck carrying the relatively heavy head can incur a wide range of sports injuries.

Because the neck is so mobile, it is extremely vulnerable to a wide range of sports injuries. Although relatively uncommon, severe sports injury to the neck can produce catastrophic impairment of the spinal cord.

Assessment of Neck Injuries

Evaluation of the neck injury can be divided into on-site emergency evaluation and off-site (sidelines or athletic training room) evaluation.

Primary assessment   As discussed previously, serious injuries to the head or neck must be taken into consideration in the emergency plan that has been previously created. All personnel must know what to do immediately and must perform their responsibilities with great skill. All equipment such as spine boards must be available in their proper place and must be properly maintained. In football, bolt cutters and a sharp knife must be available to assist in removal of a face mask (see Figure 9-3 for procedures to be followed when there is a suspected cervical injury). Unconscious athletes should be treated as though they have a cervical fracture.

An athlete who has sustained a neck injury in which fracture has been ruled out should be carefully evaluated (Figure 22-5). Any one or more of the following signs should preclude the athlete from further sports participation:
1. Neck pain during passive, active, or resistive movement
2. Tingling or burning sensation in the neck, shoulder, or arm
3. Neck motion that causes paresthesia or hypoesthesia
4. Muscle weakness in the upper or lower limbs

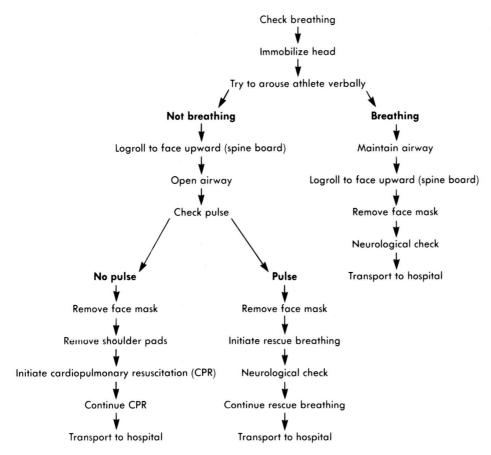

Figure 22-5

Procedures for assessing a suspected cervical injury

Secondary assessment and emergency management Even when an athlete comes into the athletic training room for an evaluation of neck discomfort, fracture should always be considered as a possibility until it is ruled out. If there is doubt about a fracture, immediate referral to a physician for x-ray examination should be made.

Major complaints The following factors should be considered:

1. How did the pain begin? (For example, a sudden twist, a hit to the head or neck)
2. Does the athlete have faulty posture?
3. Does the athlete complain of radiating pain or tingling or prickling sensations?
4. Is there numbness in the arm or hand?
5. Is there a crackling or creaking sensation during movement?
6. What precipitates pain? (For example, tension stress, sitting for long periods, sudden head movements)
7. What activities relieve the neck pain?
8. Does the athlete have a history of neck problems or injuries? If so, what actions were taken? (For example, x-ray films, physical therapy, traction, manipulation)

General observation The athlete is observed for the following:

1. Postural alignment
2. How the head is carried
3. Favoring the neck by holding it in a restricted position

Bony palpation The following areas are palpated:

1. Transverse processes
2. Spinous processes
3. Mastoid processes
4. Occiput

Soft tissue palpation Muscles in the region of the neck are palpated from their origin to their insertion. Trigger points and tonus asymmetries are also noted in the following:

1. Sternocleidomastoid muscle
2. Upper trapezius muscle
3. Throat areas (e.g., cartilages)

Functional evaluation Both active and passive movements, including flexion, extension, rotation, and lateral flexion, are observed for range of motion (Figure 22-6). Strength of the major neck muscles is next determined, followed by testing of the shoulders and arms (Table 22-1).

Sensation Nerve root irritation within the neck can alter skin sensations, depending on the peripheral nerves involved. As a result the athlete may complain of a "pins and needles" sensation corresponding to selected dermatome regions (Figure 22-7).

Mechanisms of Neck Injuries

The neck can be seriously injured by the following traumatic events (Figure 22-8):

**TABLE 22-1 Resistive Motion to Determine Muscle Weakness
Related to Neck Injury**

Resistive Motion	Major Muscles Involved	Nerves
Neck flexion	Sternocleidomastoidius	Cranial 11
		Cervical 2 and 3
Neck extension	Upper trapezius	Cranial 11
		Cervical 3 and 4
		Dorsal, primary divisions of the cervical nerves
	Splenius capitis	Cervical 4-8
Neck lateral flexion	Scalenus anticus, medius, and posticus	Anterior, primary divisions of the lower nerves
Neck lateral rotation	Sternocleidomastoidius	Cranial 11
		Cervical 2 and 3
Shoulder shrug (scapular elevation)	Upper trapezius	Cranial 11
	Levator scapulae	Cervical 3 and 4
	Anterior deltoideus	Cervical 5 and 6
Shoulder flexing	Coracobrachialis	Cervical 6 and 7
Shoulder extension	Deltoidius	Cervical 5 and 6
	Teres major	Cervical 5 and 6
	Latissimus dorsi	Cervical 6-8
Shoulder abduction	Middle deltoideus	Cervical 5 and 6
	Supraspinatus	Cervical 5
Shoulder lateral rotation	Subscapularis	Cervical 5 and 6
	Pectoralis major	Cervical 5-8
		Thoracic 1
	Latissimus dorsi	Cervical 6-8
	Teres major	Cervical 5 and 6
Elbow flexion	Biceps brachii	Cervical 5 and 6
	Brachialis	Cervical 5 and 6
	Brachioradialis	Cervical 5 and 6
Elbow extension	Triceps brachii	Cervical 7 and 8
Forearm supination	Biceps brachii	Cervical 5 and 6
	Supinator	Cervical 6
Forearm pronation	Pronator teres	Cervical 6 and 7
	Pronator quadratus	Cervical 8
		Thoracic 1
Wrist flexion	Flexor carpi radialis	Cervical 6 and 7
	Flexor carpi ulnaris	Cervical 8
		Thoracic 1
Wrist extension	Extensor carpi radialis	Cervical 6 and 7
	Extensor carpi radialis brevis	Cervical 6 and 7
	Extensor carpi ulnaris	Cervical 6-8
Finger flexion	Flexor digitorum superficialis	Cervical 7 and 8
		Thoracic 1
Finger extension	Extensor digitorum	Cervical 6-8
	Extensor indicis	Cervical 6-8
	Extendor digiti minimi	Cervical 6-8

Figure 22-6

In providing a functional evaluation of the neck, active movements are performed. **A,** Active flexion. **B,** Active extension. **C,** Active rotation. **D,** Active lateral flexion.

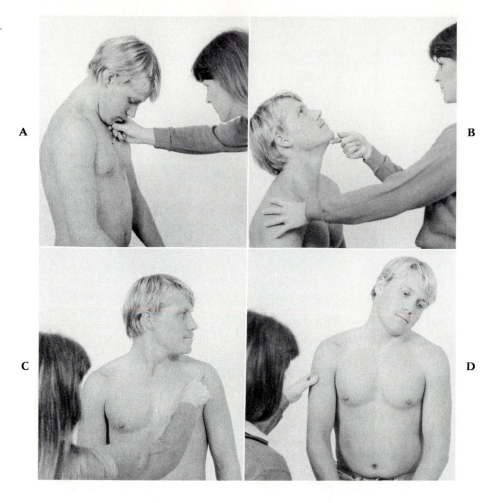

Figure 22-7

Alterations of skin sensation are reflected in dermatomes resulting from nerve root irritation.

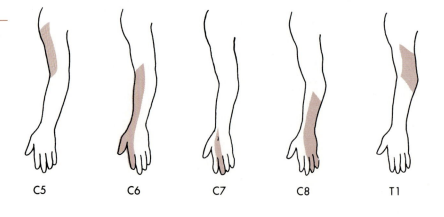

C5   C6   C7   C8   T1

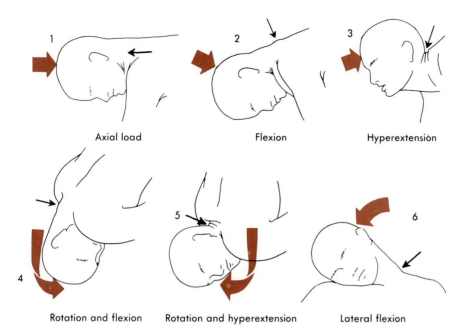

Axial load   Flexion   Hyperextension

Rotation and flexion   Rotation and hyperextension   Lateral flexion

Figure 22-8

Mechanisms of cervical injuries.

1. An axial load force to the top of the head
2. A flexion force
3. A hyperextension force
4. A flexion-rotation force
5. A hyperextension-rotation force
6. A lateral flexion force

The neck is also prone to subtle injuries stemming from stress, tension, and postural malalignments.

Sports and neck injuries A number of sports can place the cervical spine at risk. Among those activities in the highest risk category are diving, tackle football, and wrestling. Diving into shallow water causes many catastrophic neck injuries. The diver usually dives into water that is less than 5 feet deep, failing to keep the arms extended in front of the face; the head strikes the bottom, producing a cervical fracture at the C5 level.

Football helmets do not protect players against neck injury. In the illegal "spearing" situation, the athlete uses the helmet as a weapon by striking the opponent with its top. Most serious cervical injuries in football result from purposeful axial loading while spearing.[25] In other sports such as diving, wrestling, and bouncing on a trampoline the athlete's neck can be flexed at the time of contact, energy of the forward-moving body mass cannot be fully absorbed, and fracture or dislocation or both can occur. Many of the same forces can be applied in wrestling. In such trauma, paraplegia, quadriplegia, or death can result.

Prevention of Neck Injuries

Prevention of neck injuries depends on the flexibility of the neck, its muscle strength, the state of readiness of the athlete, a knowledge of proper technique, and the use of proper protective equipment. A normal range of neck movement

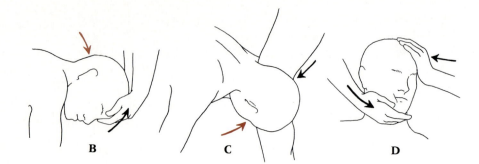

Figure 22-9

Manual resistance can provide an excellent means for helping to prevent neck injuries. **A,** Extension. **B,** Flexion. **C,** Lateral flexion. **D,** Rotation.

Long-necked football players or wrestlers are at risk and need to establish neck stability through strengthening exercises.

is necessary. Therefore neck flexibility exercises, coupled with neck-strengthening exercises, should be performed daily by the athlete.

During participation the athlete should constantly be in a ''state of readiness'' and, when making contact with an opponent, should ''bull'' the neck. This is accomplished by elevating both shoulders and isometrically contracting the muscles surrounding the neck.

Strength   Athletes with long, weak necks are especially at risk. Tackle football players and wrestlers must have highly stable necks. Specific strengthening exercises are essential for the development of this stability; a variety of different exercises that incorporate isotonic, isometric, or isokinetic contractions can be used. One of the best methods is manual resistance by the athlete or by a partner who selectively uses isometric and isokinetic resistance exercises.

Manual resistance should *not* be performed just before an individual engages in a collison-type sport such as football or ice hockey to avoid the danger of participating in these activities with fatigued neck muscles.

Manual neck resistance[21]

1. Extension, flexion, lateral flexion, and rotation are performed.
2. Each exercise is repeated four to six times in sets of three.
3. The resisting partner accommodates to the varied strength of the mover, through a full range of motion.
4. Weaker spots in the range of motion can be strengthened with isometric resistance that is held for 6 seconds (Figure 22-9).

Flexibility   In addition to strong muscles, the athlete's neck should have a full range of motion. Ideally the athlete should be able to place the chin on the chest and to extend the head back until the face is parallel with the ceiling. There should be at least 40 to 45 degrees of lateral flexion and enough rotation to allow the chin to reach a level even with the tip of the shoulder. Flexibility is increased through stretching exercises and strength exercises that are in full range of motion. Where flexibility is restricted, manual static stretching can be beneficial.

Protective neck devices   The protective neck roll and restrictive neck strap are used to reduce the severity of football neck injuries. The neck roll or collar can be custom-made, with stockinette placed over sponge rubber, a towel, or other resilient material, or can be of the commercial inflatable type. It should encircle the entire neck (Figure 22-10).

Restrictive neck straps are being used by some football teams. A 1½-inch (3.75 cm) wide semielastic strap is fixed to the back of the helmet and shoulder pad to restrict excessive flexion.

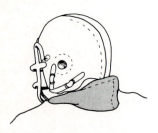

Figure 22-10

A collar for neck protection in football.

Neck Injuries

Contusions to the throat and neck   Blows to the neck do not occur frequently in sports, but occasionally an athlete may receive a kick or blow to the throat. One type of trauma is known as "clotheslining," in which the athlete strikes or is struck in the throat region. Such a force could conceivably injure the carotid artery, causing a clot to form that occludes the blood flow to the brain. This same clot could become dislodged and migrate to the brain.[19] In either case, serious brain damage may result. Immediately after throat trauma the athlete could experience severe pain and spasmodic coughing, speak with a hoarse voice, and complain of difficulty in swallowing.

A throat contusion could ultimately lead to brain damage.

Fracture of throat cartilages is rare, but it is possible and may be indicated by an inability to breathe and expectoration of frothy blood. Cyanosis may be present. Throat contusions are extremely uncomfortable and are often frightening to the athlete.

If the more severe signs appear, a physician should be called. In most situations cold may be applied intermittently to control superficial hemorrhage and swelling, and, after a 24-hour rest period, moist hot packs may be applied. For the most severe neck contusions, stabilization with a well-padded collar is beneficial.

Acute torticollis (wryneck)   Acute torticollis is a very common condition, more frequently called wryneck or stiffneck. The athlete usually complains of pain on one side of the neck when awakening. This problem typically follows exposure to a cold draft of air or holding the head in an unusual position over a period of time.

During inspection, there is palpable point tenderness and muscle spasm. Head movement is restricted to the side opposite the irritation. X-ray examination will rule out a more serious injury. Management usually involves wearing a cervical collar for several days to relieve muscle stress and daily therapy with superficial heat (Figure 22-11).

Figure 22-11

Wearing a soft cervical collar helps reduce pain and spasm in an athlete with an injured neck.

Acute strains of the neck and upper back   In a strain of the neck or upper back the athlete has usually turned the head suddenly or has forced flexion or extension. Muscles involved are typically the upper trapezius or sternocleidomastoid. Localized pain, point tenderness, and restricted motion are present. Care usually includes use of ICE-R immediately after the strain occurs and wearing a soft cervical collar. Follow-up management may include cryotherapy or superficial heat and analgesic medications as prescribed by the physician.

Cervical sprain (whiplash)   A cervical sprain can occur from the same mechanism as the strain but usually results from a more violent motion. More commonly the head snaps suddenly such as when the athlete is tackled or blocked while unprepared (Figure 22-12).

The sprain displays all the signs of the strained neck but to a much greater degree. Besides injury to the musculature, the sprained neck also produce tears in the major supporting tissue of the nuchal ligament and the interspinous and the supraspinous ligaments. Along with a sprain of the neck, an intervertebral disk may be ruptured.

SYMPTOMS AND SIGNS   Pain is not experienced initially but appears the day after the trauma. Pain stems from tissue tear and a protective muscle spasm that restricts motion.

MANAGEMENT   As soon as possible the athlete should have an x-ray examination to rule out the possibility of fracture, dislocation, or disk injury. Neurolog-

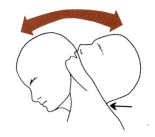

Figure 22-12

Whiplash.

MANAGEMENT PLAN FOR WHIPLASH SPRAIN OF THE NECK

Injury Situation

While at practice, a male ice hockey player was checked hard against the boards. Not being properly set for the force, his head was snapped vigorously backward into extension and forward into flexion. In this process the athlete experienced a sudden sharp pain and a tearing sensation at the base of the posterior neck region.

Symptoms and Signs

Initially the athlete complained to the athletic trainer that immediately after the injury there was a dull ache, stiffness, and weakness in the neck region. He also complained of headache, dizziness, and nausea approximately 1 hour after the injury.

Palpation revealed severe muscle spasm and point tenderness of the erector spinae muscles and the lateral aspect of the neck and upper shoulder. Gentle passive movement produced some pain. A soft neck collar was applied for immobilization. X-ray examination ruled out fracture, dislocation, or spinal cord injury. During further evaluation there was pain during both gentle active and resistive movement. The condition was considered to be a second-degree neck sprain with muscle involvement produced by a whiplash mechanism.

Management Plan

The nature of a neck sprain dictates that management should follow a conservative course. A soft cervical collar was to be worn 24 hours a day for the first 2 weeks or until the athlete was symptom free. Wearing this collar could be followed by wearing the brace just during the waking hours for 1 or 2 additional weeks.

1 **Management Phase**	GOALS: To control initial hemorrhage, swelling, spasm, and pain ESTIMATED LENGTH OF TIME (ELT): 2 to 3 days	
Therapy	IMMEDIATE CARE: Apply ice pack (20 min) intermittently six to eight times daily In some cases, transcutaneous electrical nerve stimulation (TENS) has been used successfully to reduce spasm and pain in the early stages of injury	
Exercise Rehabilitation	Wear soft cervical collar and avoid movement of the neck for 2 weeks Athlete is taught to hold head in good alignment in relation to shoulder and spine; this should be practiced every waking hour	
2 **Management Phase**	GOALS: To restore 50% active neck motion within pain free limits ELT: 7 days	
Therapy	FOLLOW-UP CARE: Ice pack (5 to 15 min) or ice massage (7 min) three or four times; precedes active motion	
Exercise Rehabilitation	Active stretching two or three times daily, including neck flexion with depressed shoulders, lateral neck flexion, and right and left head rotation; each position held 5 to 10 sec and repeated five times or within pain-free limits	

3	Management Phase	GOALS: To restore 90% neck range of motion and 50% strength ELT: 4 to 7 days
	Therapy	Ice pack (5 to 15 min) or ice massage (7 min) preceding exercise two to three times daily
	Exercise Rehabilitation	Gentle passive static stretching within pain-free limits (two to three times each direction) once daily; each stretch held for 20 to 30 seconds Manual isotonic resistive exercise to the neck performed once daily by the athlete or athletic trainer (five repetitions)
4	Management Phase	GOALS: To restore full range of motion and full strength ELT: 4 to 7 days
	Therapy	Ice pack (5 to 15 min) or ice massage (7 min) once daily preceding exercise
	Exercise Rehabilitation	Continue manual resistive exercise once daily; add resistance devices such as weighted helmet and/or Nautilus neck strengthener (three sets of 10 repetitions) using DAPRE concept, three times a week
5	Management Phase	GOALS: To return to ice hockey competition and full neck muscle bulk
	Exercise Rehabilitation	Work on maximum neck resistance 3 to 4 times daily Begin practice once daily with a neck roll protective brace during first few weeks of return

Criteria for Return to Competition Following Whiplash Neck Sprain

The neck of the athlete
1. Is completely symptom free
2. Has full range of motion
3. Has full strength and bulk

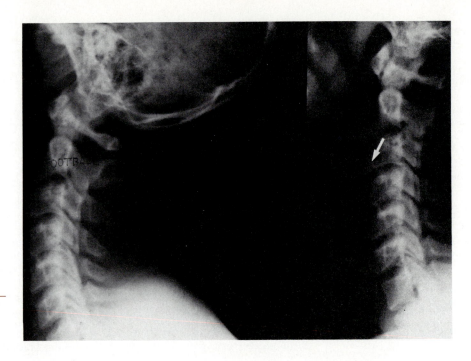

Figure 22-13

Fracture of the third cervical vertebra that resulted from playing football.

ical examination is performed by the physician to ascertain spinal cord or nerve root injury. A soft cervical collar is applied to reduce muscle spasm. ICE-R is used for 48 to 72 hours while the injury is in the acute stage of healing. In an athlete with a severe injury the physician may prescribe 2 to 3 days of bed rest, along with analgesics and anti-inflammation agents. Therapy might include cryotherapy or heat and massage. Mechanical traction may also be prescribed to relieve pain and muscle spasm.

Cervical fractures The cervical vertebrae can be fractured in a number of ways. A compression fracture is created by a sudden forced flexion of the neck, such as striking the head when diving into shallow water.[14] If the head is also rotated when making contact, a dislocation may occur along with the fracture. Fractures can also occur during a sudden forced hyperextension of the neck (Figure 22-13).

SYMPTOMS AND SIGNS The athlete may have one or more of the following signs of cervical fracture:

1. Cervical pain and pain in the chest and extremities
2. Numbness in trunk and/or limbs
3. Weakness or paralysis in limbs and/or trunk
4. A loss of bladder and/or bowel control
5. Neck point tenderness and restricted movement
6. Cervical muscle spasm

MANAGEMENT **NOTE:** An unconscious athlete should be treated as if a serious neck injury is present until this possibility is ruled out by the physician. Extreme caution must be used in moving the athlete. The athletic trainer must always be thinking of the possibility of the athlete's sustaining a catastrophic spinal injury from improper handling and transportation (see Chapter 9 for emergency care of spinal injuries).

Cervical dislocations Cervical dislocations are not common but occur much more frequently in sports than do fractures. They usually result from violent flexion and rotation of the head.[14] Most injuries of this type happen in pool diving accidents. The mechanism is analogous to the situation that occurs in football when blocks and tackles are poorly executed. The cervical vertebrae are more easily dislocated than are the vertebrae in other spinal regions, principally because of their nearness to the horizontally facing articular facets. The superior articular facet moves beyond its normal range of motion and either completely passes the inferior facet (luxation) or catches on its edge (subluxation). The latter is far more common and, as in the case of the complete luxation, most often affects the fourth, fifth, or sixth vertebra.

For the most part, a cervical dislocation produces many of the same signs as a fracture. Both can result in considerable pain, numbness, and muscle weakness or paralysis. The most easily discernible difference is the position of the neck in a dislocation: a unilateral dislocation causes the neck to be tilted toward the dislocated side with extreme muscle tightness on the elongated side and a relaxed muscle state on the tilted side.

A unilateral cervical dislocation can cause the neck to tilt toward the dislocated side, with tight muscles on the elongated side and relaxed muscles on the tilted side.

Cervical cord and peripheral nerve injuries Neck and back injuries should always be treated with caution, since they may cause paralysis. Because the spinal cord is well protected by a connective tissue sheath, fat, and fluid cushioning, vertebral dislocations and fractures seldom result in paralysis.

The spinal cord and nerve roots may be injured in five basic ways: laceration by bony fragments, hemorrhage (hematomyelia), contusion, shock, and stretching. These ways may be combined into a single trauma or may act as separate conditions.

Laceration Laceration of the cord is usually produced by the combined dislocation and fracture of a cervical vertebra. The jagged edges of the fragmented vertebral body cut and tear nerve roots or the spinal cord and cause varying degrees of paralysis below the point of injury.

Hemorrhage Hemorrhage develops from all vertebral fractures and from most dislocations, as well as from sprains and strains. It seldom causes harmful effects in the musculature, extradurally, or even within the arachnoid space, where it dissipates faster than it can accumulate. However, hemorrhage within the cord itself causes irreparable damage.

Contusion Contusion in the cord or nerve roots can arise from any force applied to the neck violently but without causing a cervical dislocation or fracture. Such an injury may result from sudden displacement of a vertebra that compresses the cord and then returns to its normal position. This compression causes edematous swelling within the cord, resulting in various degrees of temporary and/or permanent damage.

Spinal cord shock Occasionally a situation arises in which an athlete, after receiving a severe twist or snap of the neck, presents all the signs of a spinal cord injury. The athlete is unable to move certain parts of the body and complains of a numbness and a tingling sensation in his or her arms. After a short while all these signs leave; the athlete is then able to move his limbs quite freely and has no other symptoms other than a sore neck. This condition is considered a spinal cord shock and is caused by a mild contusion of the spinal cord. In such cases athletes should be cared for in the same manner used for any severe neck injury.

Cervical nerve stretch syndrome   Stretching (cervical nerve stretch syndrome), or cervical nerve pinch, is a condition that has received more recognition in recent years. Other terms for this condition are cervical radiculitis, "hot spots," "pinched nerve," or "burner." The mechanism of injury is one in which an athlete receives a violent lateral wrench of the neck from a head or shoulder block. The player complains of a burning sensation and pain extending from the neck down the arm to the base of the thumb, with some numbness and loss of function of the arm and hand that lasts 10 to 20 seconds. It is speculated that overriding of the articular facet has caused the electric-shock–like sensation. However, it also may be an indication of a slipped cervical disk or a congenital vertebral defect. Repeated nerve stretch may result in neuritis, muscular atrophy, and permanent damage. This condition requires immediate medical evaluation. After cervical nerve stretch, medical clearance is required before the athlete can return to sports activity. In some cases functional damage is such that an athlete must not participate in certain sports. Conditions for returning to the sport include above-average neck strength, wearing of protective neckwear, and not using the head and neck in a sports activity in such a way as to cause reinjury. A similar condition can be produced by a nerve compression.

Neck Rehabilitation

The neck should be pain free before exercise rehabilitation begins. The first consideration should be restoration of the neck's normal range of motion. If the athlete had a prior restricted range of motion, increasing it to a more normal range is desirable. A second goal is to strengthen the neck as much as possible.

Increasing Neck Mobility

All mobility exercises should be performed pain free. Stretching exercises include passive and active movement.

Passive and active stretching   The athlete sits in a straight-backed chair while the athletic trainer applies a gentle passive stretch. Extension, flexion, lateral flexion, and rotation in each direction is sustained for a count of six and repeated three times. Passive stretching should be conducted daily.

The athlete is also instructed to actively stretch the neck two to three times daily. Each exercise is performed for five to 10 repetitions, with each end point held for a count of six. All exercises are performed without force. Figure 22-14 shows forward flexion, extension, lateral flexion, and rotation.

Stretching can progress gradually to a more vigorous procedure such as the Billig procedure. In this exercise the athlete sits on a chair with one hand firmly grasping the seat of the chair and the other hand over the top of the head and placed on the ear on the side of the support hand. Keeping that hand in place, the athlete gently pulls the opposite side of the neck. Stretch should be held for 6 seconds (Figure 22-15). A rotary stretch in each direction can also be applied in the same manner by the athlete.

Manual neck-strengthening exercises   When the athlete has gained near-normal range of motion, a strength program should be instituted. All exercises should be conducted pain free. In the beginning each exercise is performed with the head in an upright position facing straight forward. Exercises are performed isometrically, with each resistance held for a count of six, starting with five repetitions and progressing to 10 repetitions (Figure 22-16).

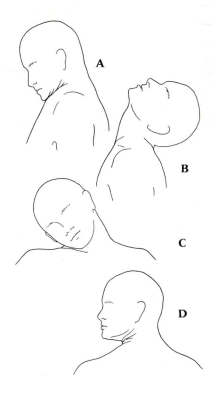

Figure 22-14

Active neck stretching is important in increasing neck mobility after injury. **A,** Forward flexion. **B,** Extension. **C,** Lateral flexion. **D,** Rotation.

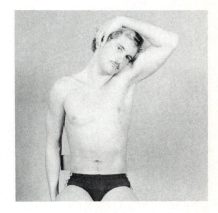

Figure 22-15

Stretching the lateral neck flexors by the Billig procedure.

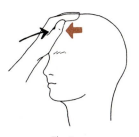

Flexion

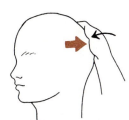

Extension

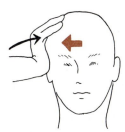

Lateral flexion

Rotation

Figure 22-16

Manual neck strengthening.

1. Flexion—press forehead against palm of hand.
2. Extension—lace fingers behind head and press head back against hands.
3. Lateral flexion—place palm on side of head and press head into palm.
4. Rotation—put one palm on side of forehead and the other at back of the head. Push with each hand, attempting to rotate head. Change hands and reverse direction.

Strengthening progresses to isotonic exercises through a full range of motion using manual resistance, special equipment such as a towel, or weighted devices (Figure 22-17). Each exercise is performed for 10 repetitions and two to three sets. **NOTE:** The athlete must be cautioned against overstressing the neck and must be encouraged to increase resistance gradually.

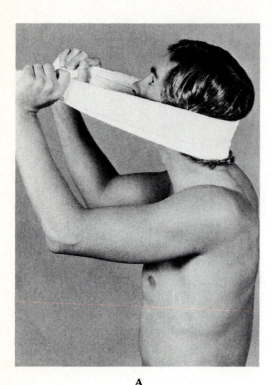

Figure 22-17

Neck strengthening through
the use of resistive devices.
A, Towel. **B,** Weight.
C, Nautilus.

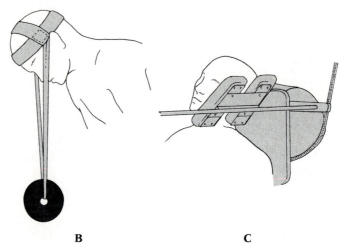

A   B   C

THE HEAD
Anatomy

The *brain*, or encephalon, is the part of the central nervous system that is contained within the bony cavity of the cranium and is divided into four sections: the cerebrum, the cerebellum, the pons, and the medulla oblongata.

Investing the spinal cord and the brain are the *meninges,* which are the three membranes that give protection to the brain and the spinal cord. Outermost is the dura mater, consisting of a dense, fibrous, and inelastic sheath that encloses the brain and cord. In some places it is attached directly to the vertebral canal, but for the most part a layer of fat that contains the vital arteries and veins separates this membrane from the bony wall and forms the epidural space. The arachnoid, an extremely delicate sheath, lines the dura mater and is attached directly to the spinal cord by many silklike tissue strands. The space between the arachnoid and the pia mater, the membrane that helps contain the spinal fluid, is called the subarachnoid space. The subarachnoid cavity projects upward and, running the full length of the spinal cord, connects with the ventricles of the brain. The pia mater is a thin, delicate, and highly vascularized membrane that adheres closely to the spinal cord and to the brain—the large extension of the cord that is housed within the skull (Figure 22-18).

Cerebrospinal fluid is contained between the arachnoid and the pia mater membrane and completely surrounds and suspends the brain. Its main function is to act as a cushion, helping to diminish the transmission of shocking forces.

Assessment of Cerebral Injuries

Cases of serious head injury almost always represent a life-threatening situation that requires that the athlete be admitted to a hospital within a crucial 30-minute period.

Primary Assessment

One must be adept at recognizing and interpreting the signs that an unconscious athlete presents. Priority first aid for any head injury must always deal with any life-threatening condition such as impaired airway or hemorrhage. When an athlete is unconscious, a neck injury is also assumed. Without moving the athlete, evaluation includes the following:

1. Looking for the possibility of airway obstruction. If breathing is obstructed, perform the following:
   a. Remove face mask by cutting it away from the helmet but leave helmet in place.
   b. Stabilize head and neck.
   c. Bring jaw forward to clear air passage (do not hyperextend neck).
   d. Take pulse: if absent cardiopulmonary resuscitation (CPR) is given; if present, oxygen may be given.
   e. **NOTE:** *Ammonia fumes should not be used for reviving an injured person.* The athlete who is dazed or unconscious, after smelling the pungent ammonia fumes, may jerk the head and exacerbate a spinal fracture.
2. A quick observation of the following physical signs of concussion and/or skull fracture:
   a. Face color may be red or pale.
   b. Skin may be cool or moist.
   c. Pulse, if present, may be strong and slow or rapid and weak.
   d. Breathing, if present, may be deep or shallow.
   e. Pupils may be dilated and/or unequal.
   f. Head may show swelling or deformity over area of injury.
3. The athlete is removed carefully from the playing site on a spine board as per Chapter 9 instructions.

If neck injuries are suspected in the unconscious athlete, the jaw is brought forward, but the neck is not hyperextended to clear the airway.

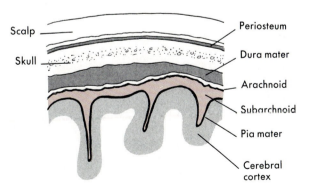

Scalp
Skull
Periosteum
Dura mater
Arachnoid
Subarchnoid
Pia mater
Cerebral cortex

Figure 22-18

The meninges covering the brain.

TABLE 22-2 Symptoms of Cerebral Concussion

Symptoms	First Degree		Second Degree	Third Degree
	Grade I	Grade II	Grade III	Grade IV
Disorientation	+	+	+ +	+ + +
Dizziness		+	+ +	+ + +
Amnesia		+	+ +	+ + +
Headache			+/+ +	+ + +
Loss of consciousness			+/+ +	+ + +
Problems in concentrating		+	+ +	+ + +
Tinnitus		+	+ +	+ + +
Balance problems		+	+ +	+ + +
Automatism			+/+ +	+ + +
Pupillary discrepancies			+/+ +	+ + +

+ Mild.
+ + Moderate.
+ + + Severe.

Secondary Assessment of the Athlete with a Cerebral Injury

Athletes with grade III or IV concussions having distinct clinical signs should automatically be sent to the hospital for medical care (for further discussion, see pp. 713-716). In grade I and II concussions it is often difficult for the athletic trainer to determine exactly how serious the problem is. Also, grade I and II conditions can slowly—or even quickly—deteriorate to a higher grade. This possibility makes certain evaluative procedures imperative even in so-called very minor cases (Table 22-2).

Questioning the athlete When the athlete regains consciousness, testing for mental orientation and memory should be done. Questions might include the following:

- What is your name?
- How old are you?
- Where are you?
- What game are you playing?
- What period is it?
- What is the score?
- What is your assignment on the 23 trap play?

After 5 or 10 minutes, repeat the questions that were previously asked.

Checking eye signs can yield crucial information about possible brain injury.

Testing eye signs Because of the direct connection between the eye and the brain, pupillary discrepancies provide important information. The athlete should be observed and tested for the following:

1. Dilated and/or irregular pupils. Checking pupil sizes may be particularly difficult at night and under artificial lights. To ensure accuracy, the athlete's pupil size should be compared with that of an official or another player present. It should be remembered, however, that some individuals normally have pupils that differ in size.
2. Blurred vision determined by difficulty or inability to read a game program or the score board.

3. Inability of the pupils to accommodate rapidly to light variance. Eye accommodation should be tested by covering one eye with a hand. The covered eye normally will dilate, whereas the uncovered pupil will remain the same. When the hand is removed, the previously covered pupil normally will accomodate readily to the light. A slow accommodating pupil may be an indicator of cerebral injury.

4. Inability of eyes to track smoothly. The athlete is asked to hold the head in a neutral position, eyes looking straight ahead. The athlete is then asked to follow the top of a pen or pencil, first up as far as possible, then down as far as possible. The eyes are observed for smooth movement and any signs of pain. Next, the tip of the pen or pencil is slowly moved from left to right to determine whether the eyes follow the tip smoothly across the midline of the face or whether they make involuntary movements. A constant involuntary back and forth, up and down, or rotary movement of the eyeball is call *nystagmus,* indicating possible cerebral involvement.

Testing balance   If the athlete can stand, the degree of unsteadiness must be noted. A cerebral concussion of grade II or more can produce balance difficulties (positive Romberg's sign). To test Romberg's sign the athlete is told to stand tall with the feet together, arms at sides, eyes closed. A positive sign is one in which the athlete begins to sway, cannot keep eyes closed, or obviously loses balance. Having the athlete attempt to stand on one foot is also a good indicator of balance.

Finger-to-nose test   The athlete stands tall with eyes closed and arms out to the side. The athlete is then asked to touch the index finger of one hand to the nose and then to touch the index finger of the other hand to the nose. Inability to perform this task with one or both fingers is an indication of physical disorientation and precludes reentry to the game.

Babinski test   A major test indicating injury to the brain from trauma is the Babinski. A pointed object is stroked across the plantar aspect of the sole of the foot, from the calcaneus along the lateral aspect of the sole of the forefoot. A positive Babinski sign is extension of the great toe and, on occasion, spreading of the other toes. A normal reaction is one in which the toes curl downward.

Monitoring the Grade I and II Head Concussion

An athlete with any degree of concussion should be sent immediately to the sports physician for treatment and observation. Brain injury may not be apparent until hours after the trauma occurs. The athlete may have to be observed closely throughout the night and be awakened approximately every 1 to 2 hours to check the level of consciousness and orientation.

Cerebral Injuries

Despite its considerable protection, the brain is subject to traumatic injury, and a great many of the head injuries incurred in sports have serious consequences. For this reason it is necessary to give special consideration to this part of the body. A constant supply of oxygen and blood to the brain is vital and critical to its survival. Although the incidence of serious head injuries from football had decreased in past years when compared to catastrophic neck injuries, their occurrence is of major concern. Every coach and athletic trainer must be able to recognize the signs of serious head injury to act appropriately.

TABLE 22-3 Cerebral Concussion Related to Consciousness and Amnesia

Grade	Symptoms
I	No amnesia and normal consciousness
II	Confusion and amnesia $\longrightarrow$ Normal consciousness with posttraumatic amnesia
III	Confusion and amnesia $\longrightarrow$ Normal consciousness wtih posttraumatic amnesia and retrograde amnesia
IV	**Coma** (paralytic) $\longrightarrow$ Confusion and amnesia
V	**Coma** $\longrightarrow$ Coma vigil
VI	$\longrightarrow$ Death

Most traumas of the head result from direct or indirect blows and may be classified as concussion injuries. It has been estimated that more than 250,000 concussions occur annually to football players.[4] Literally, "concussion" means an agitation or a shaking from being hit, and "cerebral concussion" refers to the agitation of the brain by either a direct or an indirect blow. Surgeons define concussion as a clinical syndrome characterized by immediate and transient impairment of neural functions such as alteration of consciousness, disturbance of vision, and equilibrium, caused by mechanical forces. The indirect concussion most often comes from either a violent fall, in which sitting down transmits a jarring effect through the vertebral column to the brain, or a blow to the chin. In most cases of cerebral concussion there is a short period of unconsciousness, having mild to severe results.

Most authorities agree that unconsciousness results from a brain anoxia that is caused by constriction of the blood vessels. Depending on the force of the blow and the tolerance of the athlete to withstand such a blow, varying degrees of cerebral hemorrhage, edema, and tissue laceration may occur that, in turn, will cause tissue changes. Because of the fluid suspension of the brain, a blow to the head can effect an injury to the brain either at the point of contact or on the opposite side. After the head is struck, the brain continues to move in the fluid and may be contused against the opposite side. This causes a *contrecoup type of injury*. An athlete who is knocked unconscious by a blow to the head may be presumed to have received some degree of concussion. Most often the blow simply stuns the athlete, who recovers quite rapidly.

In determining the extent of head injury one must be aware of basic gross signs by which concussions may be evaluated. There are many ways to grade cerebral injuries; the following represents one procedure. Concussions are described as mild, moderate, or severe and are graded from I through VI (Table 22-3).

Grade I Concussion

Grade I concussions are minimum in intensity and represent the most comon type in sports. In general the athlete becomes dazed and disoriented but does not become amnesic or have other signs associated with a more serious condition. There may also be a mild unsteadiness in gait. The athlete is completely lucid in 5 to 15 minutes.

Grade II Concussion

A grade II concussion is characterized by minor confusion that is caused by posttraumatic amnesia. Posttraumatic amnesia is reflected by the inability of the athlete to recall events that have occurred since the time of injury. There are also unsteadiness, ringing in the ears (tinnitus), and perhaps minor dizziness. A dull headache may also follow.[19] The athlete may also develop post-concussion syndrome, which is characterized by difficulty in concentrating, recurring headaches, and irritability. Athletes with post-concussion amnesia should not be permitted to return to play that day.[26] This amnesia may last for several weeks after the trauma, precluding sport participation until symptoms are completely gone.

Grade III Concussion

Grade III concussion includes all of the symptoms of grade II together with retrograde amnesia. Retrograde amnesia has occurred when the athlete is unable to recall recent events that occurred before the injury. There is also moderate tinnitus, mental confusion, balance disturbance, and headache. With a grade III concussion the athlete must not be allowed to return to activity until a thorough physical examination has been performed. An intracranial lesion that causes a gradual increase in intracranial pressure may be present.

Grade IV Concussion

A grade IV concussion involves that athlete who is "knocked out." This state is considered a paralytic coma, from which the athlete usually recovers in a few seconds or minutes.[26] While recovering, the athlete returns to consciousness through states of stupor and confusion, with or without delirium, to a semilucid state with automatism, and finally to full alertness. There almost always are posttraumatic amnesia and retrograde amnesia, along with post-concussion syndrome.

Conditions Indicating the Possibility of Increasing Intracranial Pressure

Headache
Nausea and vomiting
Unequal pupils
Disorientation
Progressive or sudden impairment in consciousness
Gradual increase in blood pressure
Decrease in pulse rate

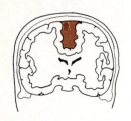

Figure 22-19

Intracranial hemorrhage.

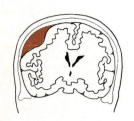

Figure 22-20

Epidural bleeding.

The three major types of intracranial hemorrhage are
  Epidural
  Subdural
  Intracerebral

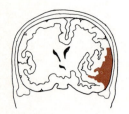

Figure 22-21

Subdural bleeding.

An emergency situation is present when there is a loss of consciousnes for more than several minutes and/or when there is a deteriorating neurological state. This situation demands immediate transportation to a hospital, with the athlete carried off the field on a spine board.

Grade V Concussion

A grade V concussion has occurred when the athlete is in a paralytic coma that is associated with secondary cardiorespiratory collapse.[26] The Glasgow Coma Scale may be used to determine an athlete's level of consciousness after cervical injury (Table 22-4).

Grade VI Death

The grade V concussion and coma may lead to a grade VI concussion and death.

Intracranial Hemorrhage

A blow to the head can cause intracranial bleeding. It may arise from rupture of a blood vessel's aneurysm or from tearing of a sinus separating the two brain hemispheres (Figure 22-19). Venous bleeding may be slow and insidious, whereas arterial hemorrhage may be evident in a few hours. In the beginning the athlete may be quite lucid, with few or none of the symptoms of serious head injury, and then gradaully display severe head pains, dizziness, nausea, inequality of pupil size, or sleepiness.[1] Later stages of cerebral hemorrhage are characterized by deteriorating consciousness, neck rigidity, depression of pulse and respiration, and convulsions. Of course, this becomes a life-and-death situation, necessitating urgent neurosurgical care.

Skull fracture Any time an athlete sustains a severe blow to the unprotected head, a skull fracture should be suspected. Skull fractures can be difficult to ascertain. Swelling of the scalp may mask a skull depression or deformity. Until the more obvious signs caused by intracranial bleeding are present, the skull fracture, even during x-ray examination, can be missed.

Epidural, subdural, and intracerebral hemorrhage There are three major types of intracranial hemorrhage: epidural, subdural, and intracerebral.

Epidural bleeding A blow to the head can cause a tear in one of the arteries in the dural membrane that covers the brain (Figure 22-20). It can result from a skull fracture or sudden shift of the brain. Because of arterial blood pressure, blood accumulation and the creation of a hematoma are extremely fast.[19] Often in only 10 to 20 minutes the athlete goes from appearing all right to having major signs of serious head injury. The pressure of the hematoma must be surgically relieved as soon as possible to avoid the possibility of death or permanent disability.

Subdural bleeding In subdural bleeding, veins are torn that bridge the dura mater to the brain.[18] A common mechanism of injury is one of contrecoup, in which the skull decelerates suddenly and the brain keeps moving, tearing blood vessels (Figure 22-21). Because of lower pressure, veins are the primary type of blood vessel injured. Hemorrhage is slow. Signs of brain injury may not appear for many hours after injury. Thus athletes who have sustained a hard blow to the head must be carefully observed for a 24-hour period for signs of pressure buildup within the skull.

TABLE 22-4 Glasgow Coma Scale

Type	Stimulus	Type of Response	Points
Eyes	Open	Spontaneously	4
		To verbal command	3
		To pain	2
		No response	1
	To verbal command	Obeys	6
	To painful stimulus*	Localized pain	5
		Flexion—withdrawal	4
		Flexion—abnormal (decorticate rigidity)	3
Best motor response		Extension (decerebrate rigidity)	2
		No response	1
Best verbal response†		Oriented and converses	5
		Disoriented and converses	4
		Inappropriate words	3
		Incomprehensible sounds	2
		No response	1
		TOTAL‡	3-15

*Apply knuckles to sternum; observe arms.
†Arouse patient with painful stimulus if necessary.
‡Lowest score is 3; highest score is 15.

Intracerebral bleeding   Intracerebral hemorrhage is bleeding within the brain itself. Most commonly it results from a compressive force to the brain[19] (Figure 22-22). Deterioration of neurological function occurs rapidly, requiring immediate hospitalization.

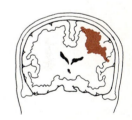

Figure 22-22

Intracerebral bleeding.

Returning to Competition After Cerebral Injury

There is always the question of whether an athlete who has been "knocked out" several times should continue in the sport. The team physician must be the final authority on whether an athlete continues to participate in a collision sport after head injury. Each athlete must be evaluated individually.[4] One serious concussion may warrant exclusion from the sport; on the other hand, a number of minor episodes may not. In making this decision, the physician must make sure that the athlete is as follows:

1. Normal neurologically
2. Normal in all vasomotor functions
3. Free of headaches
4. Free of seizure and has a normal electroencephalogram
5. Free of lightheadedness when suddenly changing body positions[19]

Secondary Conditions Associated with Cerebral Injury

In addition to the initial injury to the brain, many secondary conditions can also arise following head trauma. Some of the prevalent ones are cerebral hyperemia (primarily in children), cerebral edema, postinjury epilepsy and seizures, and migraine headaches.

Following a cerebral injury, an athlete must be free of symptoms and signs before returning to competition.

Cerebral hyperemia   A condition common to children with head injuries is cerebral hyperemia, resulting from cerebral blood vessel dilation and a rise in intracranial blood pressure.[1,3] As a result children develop headache, vomiting, and lethargy. Cerebral hyperemia can occur within a few minutes of injury and can subside in 12 hours.[1]

Cerebral edema   Cerebral edema is a localized swelling at the injury site. Within a 12-hour period the athlete may begin to develop edema, which causes headache and, on occasion, seizures.[1,19] Cerebral edema may last as long as 2 weeks and is not related to the intensity of trauma.

Seizures   Seizures can occur immediately after head trauma, indicating the possibility of brain injury. They have a higher incidence when the brain has been actually contused or there is intracranial bleeding. A small number of individuals who have sustained a severe cerebral injury will in time develop epilepsy.[1]

For athletes having a grand mal epileptic seizure, the following measures should be taken:

1. Maintain airway.
2. Make sure athlete is safe from injury.
3. Avoid sticking fingers into the athlete's mouth in an effort to withdraw the tongue.
4. Turn athlete's head to the side so that saliva and blood can drain out of the mouth.

The seizure will normally last only a couple of minutes. The athlete with epilepsy is discussed more fully in Chapter 25.

Migraine headaches   Migraine is a disorder characterized by recurrent attacks of severe headache with sudden onset, with or without visual or gastrointestinal problems. The athlete who has a history of repeated minor blows to the head such as those that may occur in soccer or who has sustained a major cerebral injury may, over a period of time, develop migraine headaches.[2,11] The exact cause is unknown, but it is believed by many to be a vascular disorder. Flashes of light, blindness in half the field of vision (hemianopia), and paresthesia are thought to be caused by vasoconstriction of intercerebral vessels. Headache is believed to be caused by dilation of scalp arteries. The athlete complains of a severe headache that is diffused throughout the head and often accompanied by nausea and vomiting. There is evidence of a familial predisposition for those athletes who experience migraine headaches following head injury.

THE FACE
Anatomy

The facial skin covers primarily subcutaneous bone with very little protective muscle, fascia, or fat. The supraorbital ridges house the frontal sinuses. In general the facial skeleton is composed of dense bony buttresses combined with thin sheets of bone.[30] The middle third of the face consists of the maxillary bone, which supports the nose and nasal passages.[30] The lower aspect of the face consists of the lower jaw or mandible. Besides supporting teeth, the mandible also supports the larynx, trachea, upper airway, and upper digestive tract[30] (Figure 22-23).

Facial Injuries

Serious injuries to the face have been reduced significantly from the past by requiring athletes to wear proper protection in high-risk sports (Figure 22-24). The most prevalent cause of facial injury is a direct blow that injures soft and bony tissue. Very common are skin abrasions, lacerations, and contusions; less common are fractures. Lacerations and abrasions are discussed in Chapter 16.

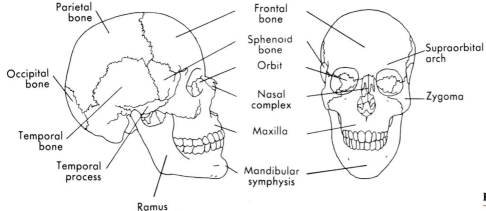

Figure 22-23

Bones of the face.

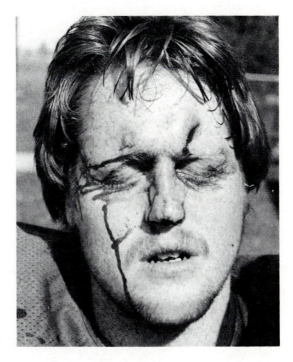

Figure 22-24

Skin wounds on the face must be carefully managed to avoid infection.

Figure 22-25

Mandibular fracture.

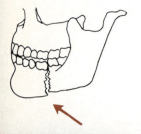

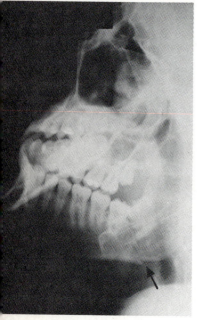

Injuries of the Mandible (Jaw)

Jaw fracture   Fractures of the lower jaw (Figure 22-25) occur most often in collision sports. They are second in incidence of all facial fractures. Because it has relatively little padding and sharp contours, the lower jaw is prone to injury from a direct blow. The most frequently fractured area is near the jaw's frontal angle.

SYMPTOMS AND SIGNS   The main indications of a fractured mandible are deformity, loss of normal occlusion of the teeth, pain when biting down, bleeding around teeth, and lower lip anesthesia.[12]

MANAGEMENT   Management usually includes cold packs to the side of the face, immobilization by a four-tailed bandage, and immediate referral to a physician.

Jaw dislocations   A dislocation of the jaw, or *mandibular luxation,* involves the temporomandibular joint, which is formed by the condyle of the mandible and the mandibular fossa of the temporal bone (Figure 22-26). This area has all the features of a hinge and gliding articulation. Because of its wide range of movement and the inequity of size between the mandibular condyle and the temporal fossa, the jaw is somewhat prone to dislocation. The mechanism of injury in dislocations is usually initiated by a side blow to the open mouth of the athlete, forcing the mandibular condyle forward out of the temporal fossa. This injury may occur as either a luxation (complete dislocation) or a subluxation (partial dislocation).

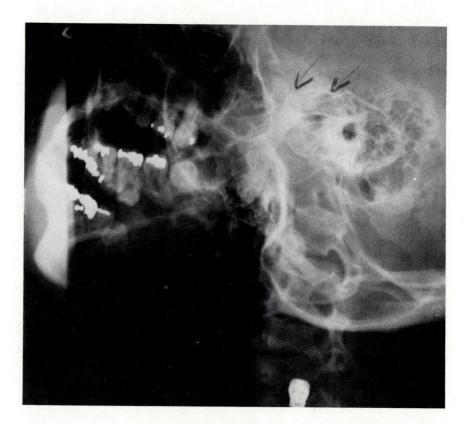

Figure 22-26

Dislocation of the jaw (right temporomandibular joint).

SYPMTOMS AND SIGNS   The major signs of the dislocated jaw are a locked-open position, with jaw movement being almost impossible, and/or an overriding mal-occlusion of the teeth.

MANAGEMENT   In cases of first-time jaw dislocation the initial treatment in-cludes immediately applying a cold compress to control hemorrhage, splinting the jaw through the use of a four-tailed bandage, and referring the athlete to a phy-sician for reduction. Without a physician it is not advisable to attempt the reduc-tion of a jaw dislocation unless it is of a chronically recurrent type.

Zygomatic (cheekbone) fracture   A fracture of the zygoma represents the third most common facial fracture.[30] Because of its nearness to the eye orbit, visual problems may also occur.

SYMPTOMS AND SIGNS   An obvious deformity occurs in the cheek region or a bony discrepancy can be felt during palpation. There is usually a nosebleed **(ep-istaxis),** and the athlete commonly complains of seeing double **(diplopia).**

Management   Care by the athletic trainer usually involves cold application for the control of edema and immediate referral to a physician.

Maxillary fracture   A severe blow to the upper jaw such as would be in-curred by being struck by a hockey puck or stick can fracture the maxilla. This ranks fourth in incidence of facial fracture.

SYMPTOMS AND SIGNS   After being struck a severe blow to the upper jaw, the athlete complains of pain while chewing, malocclusion, nosebleed, double vision and numbness in the lip and cheek region.

MANAGEMENT   Because bleeding is usually profuse, airway passages must be maintained. A brain injury may also be associated with this condition as with all injuries to the face and must be evaluated and managed accordingly. The athlete must be referred immediately for medical attention.

epistaxis
Nosebleed.

diplopia
Seeing double.

Dental Injuries

The tooth is a composite of mineral salts of which calcium and phosphorus are most abundant. That portion protruding from the gum, called the crown, is cov-ered by the hardest substance within the body, the enamel. The portion that ex-tends into the alveolar bone of the mouth is called the root and is covered by a thin, bony substance known as cementum. Underneath the enamel and cemen-tum lies the bulk of the tooth, a hard material known as dentin. Within the dentin is a central canal and chamber containing the pulp, a substance composed of nerves, lymphatics, and blood vessels that supply the entire tooth (Figure 22-27).

With the use of face guards and properly fitting mouth guards most dental injuries can be prevented (see Chapter 5). Any blow to the upper or lower jaw can potentially injure the teeth.[27] Injuries to the tooth below the gum line may repair themselves because of the abundant blood supply. However, fractures of the tooth below the gum line may not heal if there is an injury to the tooth pulp. Even though not obvious, a tooth could sustain a mild blow that disrupts its blood and nerve supply.[5]

The Fractured Tooth

Fracture of the crown of the tooth is an enamel fracture and can usually be re-paired by smoothing, capping, or even removal of the entire tooth. In contrast,

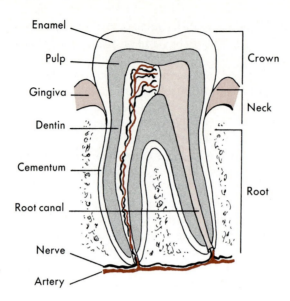

Figure 22-27

Normal tooth anatomy.

fractures that involve the dentin, exposing the pulp, may predispose the tooth to infection and tooth death.[13]

Teeth in which the enamel or dentin is chipped fail to rejuvenate because they lack a direct blood supply. They can be capped for the sake of appearance. A tooth that is fractured or loosened may be extremely painful because of the damaged or exposed nerve. In such cases a small amount of calcium hydroxide (Dycol) applied to the exposed nerve area will inhibit the pain until the athlete is seen by a dentist.

A fractured tooth is usually very sensitive to air and requires the athlete to keep the mouth closed. If there is no bleeding of the gums, the athlete can continue to play and see the dentist after the game.[5]

Partially or Completely Dislocated Tooth

A tooth that has been completely dislocated intact should be rinsed off with water and replaced in the socket.

A tooth that has been knocked crooked should be manually realigned to a normal position as soon as possible. One that has been totally knocked out should be cleaned with water and replaced in the tooth socket, if possible. If repositioning the dislocated tooth is difficult, the athlete should keep it under the tongue until the dentist can replace it.[5] If this is inconvenient, a dislodged tooth can also be kept in a glass of water. If a completely dislodged tooth is out of the mouth for more than 30 minutes, the chances of saving it are very tenuous; therefore the athlete should immediately be sent to the dentist for splinting.

Nasal Injuries
Nasal Fractures and Chondral Separation

A fracture of the nose is one of the most common fractures of the face.[8] It appears frequently as a separation of the frontal processes of the maxilla, a separation of the lateral cartilages, or a combination of the two (Figure 22-28).

SYMPTOMS AND SIGNS   The force of the blow to the nose may either come from the side or from a straight frontal force. A lateral force causes greater deformity than a "straight-on" blow. In nasal fractures hemorrhage is profuse because of laceration of the mucous lining. Swelling is immediate. Deformity is usually present if the nose has received a lateral blow. Gentle palpation may reveal abnormal mobility and emit a grating sound (crepitus).

MANAGEMENT   One should control the bleeding and then refer the athlete to a physician for x-ray examination and reduction of the fracture. Simple and uncomplicated fractures of the nose will not hinder or be unsafe for the athlete, and he or she will be able to return to competition within a few days. Adequate protection can be provided through splinting (Figure 22-29).

Figure 22-28

Nasal fracture.

Nasal Septal Injuries

A major nasal injury can occur to the septum. As with fracture, the mechanisms are caused by compression or lateral trauma.[22]

SYMPTOMS AND SIGNS   A careful evaluation of the nose must be made after the trauma. Injury commonly produces bleeding and, in some cases, a septal hematoma. The athlete complains of nasal pain.

MANAGEMENT   At the site where a hematoma may occur, compression is applied. When a hematoma is present, it must be drained immediately through a surgical incision through the nasal septal mucosa. After surgical drainage, a small wick is inserted for continued drainage, and the nose is firmly packed to prevent reformation of the hematoma. If a hematoma is neglected, an abscess will form, causing bone and cartilage loss and ultimately a difficult-too-correct deformity.[15]

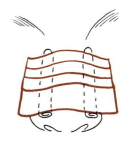

Figure 22-29

Splinting the fractured nose.

Nosebleed (Epistaxis)

Nosebleeds in sports are usually the result of direct blows that cause varying degrees of contusion to the septum.

SYMPTOMS AND SIGNS   Hemorrhages arise most often from the highly vascular anterior aspect of the nasal septum. In most situations the nosebleed presents only a minor problem and stops spontaneously after a short period of time. However, there are persistent types that require medical attention and, probably, cauterization.

NOSE SPLINTING

The following procedure is used for nose splinting.

MATERIALS NEEDED: Two pieces of gauze, each 2 inches (5 cm) long and rolled to the size of a pencil, three strips of 1½-inch (3.75 cm) tape, cut approximately 4 inches (10 cm) long; and clear tape adherent.

POSITION OF THE ATHLETE: The athlete lies supine on the training table.

PROCEDURE
  1. The rolled pieces of gauze are placed on either side of the athlete's nose.
  2. Gently but firmly, 4-inch (10 cm) lengths of tape are laid over the gauze rolls.

MANAGEMENT   The care of the athlete with an acute nosebleed is as follows:

1. The athlete lies on the same side as the bleeding septum, with his or her head comfortably elevated. (In this position the blood will be confined to one nostril.) Do not tip his or her head back.
2. A cold compress is placed over the nose.
3. The athlete applies finger pressure to the affected nostril for 5 minutes.

If the above method fails to stop the bleeding within 5 minutes, more extensive measures should be taken. With an applicator, paint the hemorrhage point with an astringent or a styptic such as tannic acid or epinephrine hydrochloride solution. The application of a gauze or cotton pledget will provide corking action and encourage blood clotting. If a pledget is used, the ends should protrude from the nostrils at least ½ inch to facilitate removal. After bleeding has ceased, the athlete may resume activity but should be reminded not to blow the nose under any circumstances for at least 2 hours after the initial insult.

Foreign Body in the Nose

During participation the athlete may have insects or debris lodge in one of his or her nostrils; if the object is large enough, the mucous lining of the nose will react by becoming inflamed and swollen. In most cases the foreign body will become dislodged if the nose is gently blown while the unaffected side in pinched shunt. Probing and blowing the nose violently will only cause additional irritation. The removal of difficult objects may be aided by placing a few drops of olive or mineral oil into the nostril to soothe and prevent swelling of the mucosa. If oil is unavailable, the application of a nasal vasoconstrictor will help to shrink the mucous membranes.

Ear Injuries

The ear (Figure 22-30) is responsible for the sense of hearing and equilibrium. It is composed of three parts: the external ear; the middle ear (tympanic membrane) lying just inside the skull; and the internal ear (labyrinth), which is formed, in part, by the temporal bone of the skull. The middle ear and internal ear are struc-

Figure 22-30

Ear anatomy. **A,** Normal external ear. **B,** Inner ear.

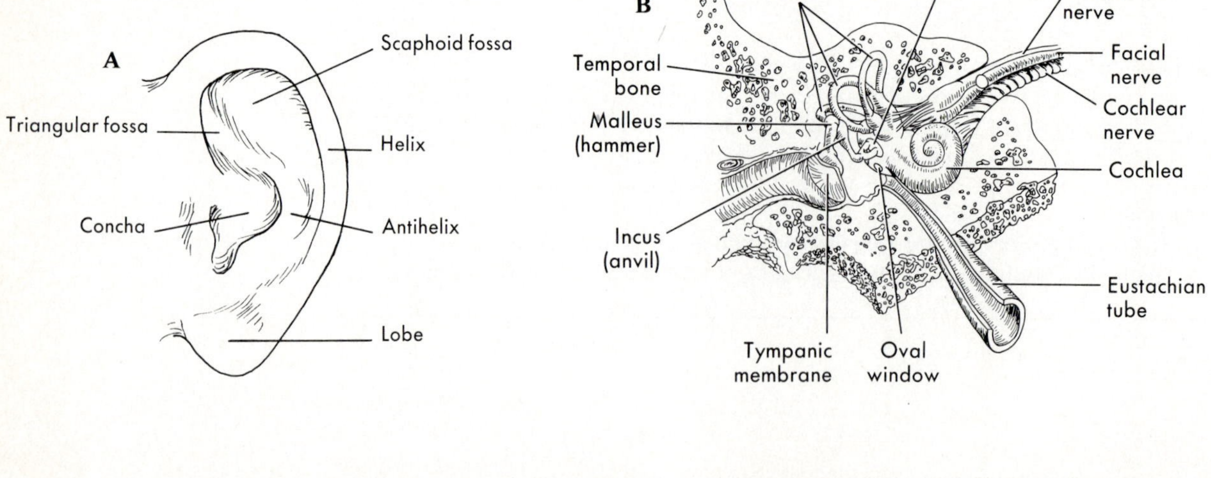

tured to transport auditory impulses to the brain. Aiding the organs of hearing and equalizing pressure between the middle and the internal ear is the eustachian tube, a canal that joins the nose and the middle ear.[17]

Sports injuries to the ear occur most often to the external portion. The external ear is separated into the auricle (pinna) and the external auditory canal (meatus). The auricle, which is shaped like a shell, collects and directs waves of sound into the auditory canal. It is composed of flexible yellow cartilage, muscles, and fat padding and is covered by a closely adhering, thin layer of skin. Most of the blood vessels and nerves of the auricle turn around its borders, with just a few penetrating the cartilage proper.

Figure 22-31

The cauliflower ear.

Hematoma Auris (Cauliflower Ear)

Contusions, wrenching, or extreme friction of the ear can lead to hematoma auris, commonly known as a "cauliflower ear"[15] (Figure 22-31).

ETIOLOGICAL FACTORS   This condition usually occurs from repeated injury to the ear and is seen most frequently in boxers and wrestlers. However, recently, it has been held to a minimum because of the protective measures that have been initiated.

SYMPTOMS AND SIGNS   Trauma may tear the overlying tissue away from the cartilaginous plate, resulting in hemorrhage and fluid accumulation. A hematoma usually forms before the limited circulation can absorb the fluid. If the hematoma goes unattended, a sequence of coagulation, organization, and fibrosis results in a keloid that appears elevated, rounded, white, nodular, and firm, resembling a cauliflower. Quite often it forms in the region of the helix fossa or concha; once developed, the keloid can be removed only through surgery. To prevent this disfiguring condition from arising, some friction-proofing agent such as petroleum jelly should be applied to the ears of athletes susceptible to this condition. They should also routinely wear ear guards in practice and in competition.

MANAGEMENT   If an ear becomes "hot" because of excessive rubbing or twisting, the immediate application of a cold pack to the affected spot will alleviate hemorrhage. Once swelling is present in the ear, special care should be taken to prevent the fluid from solidifying; a cold pack should be placed immediately over the ear and held tightly by an elastic bandage for at least 20 minutes. If the swelling is still present at the end of this time, aspiration by a physician is needed, usually followed by a rigid compress such as the silicone cast.

Foreign Body in the Ear

The ears offer an opening, as do the nose and eyes, in which objects can become caught. Usually these objects are pieces of debris or flying insects. They can be dislodged by having the athlete tilt the head to one side. If removal is difficult, syringing the ear with a solution of lukewarm water may remove the object. Care should be exercised to avoid striking the eardrum with the direct stream of water.

Pressure Injury (Otic Barotrauma)

Pressure injury to the ear, or otic barotrauma, occurs to athletes who are involved in such pursuits as diving, scuba diving, parachuting, and sports flying. Usually any change of ear pressure is equalized by swallowing, yawning, or chewing, which helps the eustachian tube to equalize the external air pressure with that on the eardrum.

With otic barotrauma the eustachian tube does not allow for air pressure equalization. Lack of pressure equalization may be attributed to nasal congestion from a cold, allergy, or other infection. Increased pressure can cause middle ear hemorrhaging and even a bursting of the tympanic membrane (eardrum). It is wise for an athlete with nasal congestion to avoid pressure changes. Referral should be made to an otolaryngologist.

Eye Injuries

Eye injuries account for approximately 1% of all sports injuries.[16] In the United States, baseball has the highest incidence of injuries (Table 22-5).

Eye Anatomy

The eye has many anatomical protective devices. It is firmly retained within an oval socket formed by the bones of the head. A cushion of soft fatty tissue surrounds it, and a thin skin flap (the eyelid), which functions by reflex action, covers the eye for protection. Foreign particles are prevented from entering the eye by the lashes and eyebrows, which act as a filtering system. A soft mucous lining that covers the inner conjunctiva transports and spreads tears, which are secreted by many accessory lacrimal glands. A larger lubricating organ is located above the eye and secrets heavy quantities of fluid through the lacrimal duct to help wash away foreign particles. The eye proper is well protected by the sclera, a tough white outer layer possessing a transparent center portion called the cornea (Figure 22-32).

Eye Protection

The eye can be injured in a number of different ways. Shattered eyeglass or goggle lenses can lacerate; ski pole tips can penetrate; and fingers, raquetballs, and larger projectiles can seriously compress and injure the eye. High-injury sports such as ice hockey, football, and lacrosse require full-face and helmet protection, whereas low-energy sports such as racquetball and tennis require eye guards that rest on

Figure 22-32

Eye anatomy.

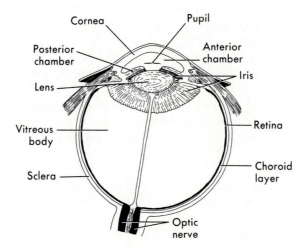

TABLE 22-5 Percentage of Sports Eye Injuries in the United States

Sport	Percent (%)
Baseball	27
Racquet sports	20
Basketball	20
Football and soccer	7
Ice hockey	4
Ball hockey	1

the face.[7,27] Protective devices must provide protection from front and lateral blows.[9,10]

Sport goggles can be made with highly impact-resistant polycarbonate lenses for refraction. The major problems with sports goggles are distortion of peripheral vision and the tendency for fogging under certain weather conditions (see Chapter 5).[24]

Primary Assessment

It is essential that any eye injury be evaluated immediately. To make an appropriate eye injury assessment the athletic trainer must have a properly equipped first aid kit.[23] The following is a list of items for use in the immediate care of eye injuries in sports:

1. Vision card for testing visual acuity
2. Pen light
3. Cotton tip applicators
4. Sterile ocular irrigating solution
5. Sterile eye patches
6. Plastic eye shields
7. Fluorescein strips
8. Plunger for removing contact lenses

The first concerns are to understand the mechanism of injury and if there is a related condition to the head, face, or neck. Evaluation steps are as follows[20]:

1. Inspect the external ocular structures for swelling and discoloration, penetrating objects, deformities, and movement of the lid.
2. Palpate the orbital rim for point tenderness or bony deformity.
3. Inspect the globe of the eye for lacerations, foreign bodies, hyphema, or deformities.
4. Inspect the conjunctiva and sclera for foreign bodies, hemorrhage, or deformities.
5. Determine pupillary response as performed for a possible cerebral injury, including pupil dilation and accommodation by covering the eye and then exposing it to light.
6. Determine visual acuity by asking the athlete to report what is seen when looking at some object with the unaffected eye covered. There may be blurring of vision, diplopia, or floating black specks or flashes of light, indicating serious eye involvement.[20]

SYMPTOMS INDICATING THE POSSIBILITY OF SERIOUS EYE INJURY

Blurred vision not clearing with blinking
Loss of all or part of the visual field
Pain that is sharp, stabbing, or throbbing
Double vision after injury

Initial Management of Eye Injuries

Extreme care must be taken with any eye injury
  Transport the athlete in a recumbent position
  Cover both eyes but put no pressure on the eye

Proper care of eye injuries is essential. The athletic trainer must use extreme caution in handling eye injuries. If there appears to be retinal detachment, perforation of the globe, foreign object embedded in the cornea, blood in the anterior chamber, decreased vision, loss of the visual field, poor pupillary adaptation, double vision, laceration, or impaired lid function, the athlete should be immediately referred to a hospital or an ophthalmologist.[20,27] Ideally, the athlete with a serious eye injury should be transported to the hospital by ambulance in a recumbent position (see box above). Both eyes must be covered during transport. At no time should pressure be applied to the eye. In case of surrounding soft-tissue injury, a cold compress can be applied for 30 to 60 minutes to control hemorrhage.[20]

Orbital Hematoma (Black Eye)

Although well protected, the eye may be bruised during sports activity. The severity of eye injuries varies from a mild bruise to an extremely serious condition affecting vision to the fracturing of the orbital cavity. Fortunately, most of the eye injuries sustained in sports are mild. A blow to the eye may initially injure the surrounding tissue and produce capillary bleeding into the tissue spaces. If the hemorrhage goes unchecked, the result may be a classic ''black eye.'' The signs of a more serious contusion may be displayed as a subconjunctival hemorrhage or as faulty vision.

Care of an eye contusion requires cold application for at least half an hour, plus a 24-hour rest period if the athlete has distorted vision. Under no circumstances should an athlete blow the nose following an acute eye injury. To do so might increase hemorrhaging.

Foreign Body in the Eye

Foreign bodies in the eye are a frequent occurrence in sports and are potentially dangerous. A foreign object produces considerable pain and disability. No attempt should be made to rub out the body or to remove it with the fingers. Have the athlete close the eye until the initial pain has subsided and then attempt to determine if the object is in the vicinity of the upper or lower lid. Foreign bodies in the lower lid are relatively easy to remove by depressing the tissue and then wiping it with a sterile cotton applicator. Foreign bodies in the area of the upper lid are usually much more difficult to localize. Two methods may be used; the first technique, which is quite simple, is performed as follows: gently pull the upper eyelid over the lower lid, as the subject looks downward. This causes tears

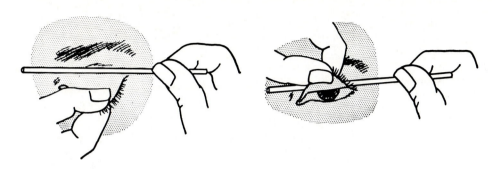

Figure 22-33

Removing foreign body from the eye.

to be produced, which may flush the object down on to the lower lid. If this method is unsuccessful, the second technique (see box below) should be used (Figure 22-33).

After the foreign particle is removed, the affected eye should be washed with a boric acid solution or with a commercial eyewash. Quite often after debridement there is a residual soreness, which may be alleviated by the application of petroleum jelly or some other mild ointment. If there is extreme difficulty in removing the foreign body or if it has become embedded in the eye itself, the eye should be closed and "patched" with a gauze pad, which is held in place by strips of tape. The athlete is referred to a physician as soon as possible.

Corneal Abrasions

An athlete who gets a foreign object in his or her eye will usually try to rub it away. In doing so, the cornea can become abraded. The athlete will complain of severe pain and watering of the eye, photophobia, and spasm of the orbicular muscle of the eyelid.[28] The eye should be patched, and the athlete should be sent to a physician. Corneal abrasion is diagnosed through application of a fluorescein strip to the abraded area, staining it a bright green.[27]

Hyphema

A blunt blow to the anterior aspect of the eye can produce a hyphema, which is a collection of blood within the anterior chamber. The blood settles inferiorly or

---

REMOVING A FOREIGN BODY FROM THE EYE

MATERIALS NEEDED: One applicator stick, sterile cotton-tipped applicator, eyecup, and eyewash (solution of boric acid).

POSITION OF THE ATHLETE: The athlete lies supine on a table.

PROCEDURE

1. Gently pull the eyelid down and lay an applicator stick crosswise at its base.
2. Have the athlete look down; then grasp the lashes and turn the lid back over the stick.
3. Holding the lid and the stick in place with one hand, use the sterile cotton swab to lift out the foreign body.

---

may fill the entire chamber. Vision is partially or completely blocked. The athletic trainer must be aware that a hyphema is a major eye injury that can lead to serious problems of the lens, choroid, or retina.[27]

Rupture of the Globe

A blow to the eye by an object smaller than the eye orbit produces extreme pressure that can rupture the globe. A golf ball or racquetball fits this category; however, larger objects such as a tennis ball or a fist will often fracture the bony orbit before the eye is overly compressed.[27] Even if it does not cause rupture, such a force can cause internal injury that may ultimately lead to blindness.

Blowout Fracture

A blow to the face that strikes the eye and orbital ridge can cause what is commonly called a blowout fracture of the orbit. Because of the sudden increase in internal pressure of the eye, the very thin bone located in the inferior aspect of the orbit can fracture. Hemorrhage occurs around the inferior margins of the eye. The athlete commonly complains of double vision and pain when moving the eye. With such symptoms and signs, immediate referral to a physician is necessary.

Retinal Detachment

A blow to the athlete's eye can partially or completely separate the retina from its underlying retinal pigment epithelium. Retinal detachment is more common among athletes who have myopia (nearsightedness). Detachment is painless; however, early signs include seeing specks floating before the eye, flashes of light, or blurred vision. As the detachment progresses, the athlete complains of a ''curtain'' falling over the field of vision. Any athlete with symptoms of detachment must be immediately referred to an ophthalmologist.

SUMMARY

The postural defect scoliosis, which is a lateral-rotary deviation of the spine, can be progressively disabling. Spondylolisthesis and Scheuermann's disease can also cause severe pain in the thoracic spine.

Because of its mobility, the cervical spine is vulnerable to a wide range of sports injuries. The catastrophic neck injury is one that produces varying degrees of quadriplegia. The unconscious athlete should be treated as if he or she has a serious neck injury. A major means for prevention of neck injury is maximizing the neck's strength and flexibility.

The neck and the upper back are subject to a number of acute noncatastrophic injuries, the most common of which are wryneck (or stiff neck), muscle strains, neck sprains (sometimes called whiplash), and throat contusion. The most serious neck injuries are cervical fracture and cervical dislocation.

Brain injuries, which can be life-threatening, often result from blows that can be classified as concussion injuries. Depending on the severity of the concussion, the athlete may display signs of disorientation, dizziness, amnesia, headache, loss of consciousness, problems in concentrating, tinnitus, balance problems, automatism, or pupillary discrepancies.

Brain concussion is categorized into six grades. In grade I the athlete becomes dazed and disoriented. In grade II the athlete displays minor confusion caused by a posttraumatic amnesia. There may also be minor dizziness, ringing in the ears, and a dull headache. Grade III concussion includes all of the symptoms of grade II, plus retrograde amnesia. Grade IV is of the ''knocked out'' athlete. There are posttraumatic amnesia and retrograde amnesia, along with post-concussion syndrome. The grade V concussion includes a paralytic coma, associated with a secondary cardiorespiratory collapse. A grade VI concussion is one in which coma leads to death.

The face is subject to many different types of traumatic sports injuries. The most common are facial wounds, with lacerations ranking at the top. Less common, but usually more serious, are injuries such as jaw fractures and dislocations, dental injuries, and nasal injuries. A potentially disfiguring ear injury is hematoma auris, or cauliflower ear. The eye is also at risk; therefore it is essential that the eye be protected against fast-moving projectiles.

REVIEW QUESTIONS AND SUGGESTED ACTIVITIES

1. What major sports conditions occur in the thoracic spine of young athletes?
2. Describe on-site emergency assessment of neck injuries.
3. Describe the causes of catastrophic neck injuries and how they may be prevented. Include practices, exercises, and protective devices in your answer.
4. Identify the major causes and immediate care of the following acute neck injuries—wryneck, whiplash, and throat contusion.
5. Describe the signs of the cervical neck stretch syndrome, which is commonly called the "burner."
6. Pair off with another student, with one acting as the coach or athletic trainer and the other as the injured athlete. The athlete simulates concussions of various grades. The coach or athletic trainer assesses the student, attempting to determine the grade of concussion.
7. List the on-site assessment steps that should be taken when cerebral injuries occur.
8. Demonstrate the following procedures in evaluating a cerebral injury—questioning the athlete, testing eye signs, testing balance, and the finger-to-nose test.
9. List the emergency procedures for treating a serious neck injury.
10. Contrast a grade II with a grade III concussion.
11. What immediate-care procedures should be performed for athletes with facial lacerations?
12. Describe the immediate care procedures that should be performed when a tooth is fractured and when it is dislocated.
13. Describe the procedures that should be performed for an athlete with a nose bleed.
14. How can cauliflower ear be prevented?
15. The eye can sustain an extremely serious injury during some sports activities. What are the major indicators of a possibly serious eye injury?

REFERENCES

1. Albright, L: Head and neck injuries. In Smith, NJ, editor: Sports medicine: health care for young athletes, Evanston, Ill, 1983, American Academy of Pediatrics.
2. Bennett, DR, et al.: Migraine precipitated by head trauma in athletes, Am J Sports Med 8:202, 1980.
3. Bruce, DA, et al.: Diffuse cerebral swelling following head injuries in children: the syndrome of "malignant brain edema." J Neurosurg 54:170, 1981.
4. Cantu, RC: Guidelines for return to contact sports after a cerebral concussion, Phys Sportsmed 14(10):75, 1986.
5. Castaldi, CR: Injuries to the teeth. In Vinger, PF, and Hoerner, EF, editors: Sports injuries: the unthwarted epidemic, Boston, 1982, John Wright, PSG, Inc.
6. Cyriax, J: Textbook of orthopaedic medicine, vol 1, Diagnosis of soft tissue lesions, ed 8, London, 1982, Bailliere Tindall.
7. Diamond, GR, et al.: Ophthalmologic injuries. In Betts, JM, and Dichelber-

ger, M, editors: Symposium on pediatric and adolescent sports medicine, Clinics in sports med, vol 1, no 3, Philadelphia, 1982, WB Saunders Co.

8. Douglas, LG: Facial injuries. In Welsh, PR, and Shephard, RJ, editors: Current therapy in sports medicine 1985-1986, Philadelphia, 1985, Brian C Decker, Publisher.

9. Esterbrook, M: Eye injuries in racket sports: a continuing problem, Phys Sportsmed 9:91, 1981.

10. Esterbrook, M: Eye protection for squash and racquetball players, Phys Sportsmed 9:79, 1981.

11. Garfinkle, D: Headache in athletes, Phys Sportsmed 11:67, 1983.

12. Halling, AH: The importance of clinical signs and symptoms in the evaluation of facial fractures, Ath Train 17:102, 1982.

13. Hildebrandt, JR: Dental and maxillofacial injuries. In Betts, JM, and Eichelberger, M, editors: Symposium on pediatric and adolescent sports medicine, Clinics in sports medicine, vol 1, no 3, Philadelphia, 1982, WB Saunders Co.

14. Jackson, DW, and Lohr, FT: Cervical spine injuries. In Spencer III, CW editor: Injuries to the spine, Clinics in sports medicine, vol 5, no 2, Philadelphia, 1986, WB Saunders Co.

15. McGrail, JS: Ear, nose, and throat injuries. In Welsh, PR, and Shephard, RJ, editors: Current therapy in sports medicine 1985-1986, Philadelphia, 1985, Brian C Decker, Publisher.

16. Pashby, RC, and Pashby, TJ: Ocular injuries in sport. In Welsh, PR, and Shephard, RJ, editors: Current therapy in sports medicine 1985-1986, Philadelphia, 1985, Brian C Decker, Publisher.

17. Podolsky, ML: Common ear problems due to trauma and temperature, Sports Med Dig 8(6):1, 1986.

18. Rimel, RW, et al.: Epidural hematoma in lacrosse, Phys Sportsmed 11:140, 1983.

19. Rockett, FY: Injuries involving the head and neck: clinical anatomic aspects. In Vinger, PF, and Hoerner, EF, editors: Sports injuries: the unthwarted epidemic, Boston, 1982, John Wright, PSG, Inc.

20. Sandusky, JC: Field evaluation of eye injuries, Ath Train 16:254, 1981.

21. Semenick, D: Preventing neck injuries: ten minute partner resistance neck and shoulder routing, Sports Med Guide 12, Fall 1985.

22. Sitler, M: Nasal septal injuries, Ath Train 21(1):10, 1986.

23. Smith, DJ: The trainer's role in the management of ocular injury, Ath Train 20:288, 1985.

24. Teig, DS, and Berman, AM: Vision options available to the athlete, Sports Med Dig, 8(2):1, 1986.

25. Torg, JS, and Vegso, JJ: Head and neck injuries in athletes (part I), Postgraduate advances in sports medicine, II-I, Berryville, Va, 1987, Forum Medicus, Inc.

26. Vegso, JJ, and Lehman, RC: Field evaluation and management of head and neck injuries. In Torg, JS, editor: Head and neck injuries, Clinics in sports medicine, vol 6, no 1, Philadelphia, 1987, WB Saunders Co.

27. Vinger, PF: Eye injuries. In Vinger, PF, and Hoerner, EF, editors: Sports injuries: the unthwarted epidemic, Boston, 1982, John Wright, PSG, Inc.

28. Vinger, PF: How I manage corneal abrasions and lacerations, Phys Sportsmed 14(5):170, 1986.

29. Wilson, FD, and Lindseth, RE: Adolescent "swimmer's back," Am J Sports Med 10:174, 1982.

30. Wilson, KS: Injuries to the face, ear-nose-throat and airway. In Vinger, PF, and Hoerner, EF, editors: Sports injuries: the unthwarted epidemic, Boston, 1982, John Wright, PSG, Inc.

ANNOTATED BIBLIOGRAPHY

Cailliet, R: Neck and arm pain, ed 2, Philadelphia, 1981, FA Davis Co.
 Discusses the complex subject of neck and arm pain in a clear, easy-to-understand manner.

Torg, JS, editor: Head and neck injuries, Clinics in sports medicine, vol 6, no 1, Philadelphia, 1987, WB Saunders Co.
 In-depth coverage of head and neck injuries stemming from sports activities. The mechanisms of these injuries are discussed, as well as their prevention, initial treatment, and rehabilitation.

The Shoulder Complex and Upper Arm

When you finish this chapter, you should be able to

Identify the major structural and functional anatomical features of the shoulder complex and relate them to sports injuries

Recognize and evaluate major sports injuries of the shoulder complex

Perform proper immediate and follow-up management

The shoulder complex, as the name implies, is an extremely complicated region of the body. Sports using the shoulder in repetitive activities such as throwing, blocking, tackling, or rolling over as in tumbling may produce a serious injury.

ANATOMY
Bony Structure

The bones that comprise the shoulder complex and shoulder joint are the clavicle, scapula, and humerus (Figure 23-1).

Clavicle

The clavicle is a slender bone approximately 6 inches (15 cm) long and shaped like a crank or the letter S. It supports the anterior portion of the shoulder, keeping it free from the thoracic cage. It extends from the sternum to the tip of the shoulder where it joins the acromion process of the scapula. The shape of the medial two thirds of the clavicle is primarily circular, whereas its lateral third assumes a flattened appearance. Also, the medial two thirds bend convexly forward, and the lateral third is concave. The point at which the clavicle changes shape and contour presents a structural weakness, and the largest number of fractures to the bone occur at this point. Lying superficially with no muscle or fat protection makes the clavicle subject to direct blows.

Scapula

The scapula is a flat, triangularly shaped bone that serves mainly as an articulating surface for the head of the humerus. It is located on the dorsal aspect of the thorax and has two prominent projections, the spine and the coracoid process. The spine divides the posterior aspect unequally. The superior dorsal aspect is a deep depression called the supraspinous fossa, and the area below, a more shallow depression, is called the infraspinous fossa. A hooklike projection called the coracoid process arises anteriorly from the scapula. It curves upward, forward, and outward in front of the glenoid fossa, which is the articulating cavity for the reception of the humeral head. The glenoid cavity is situated laterally on the scapula below the acromion.

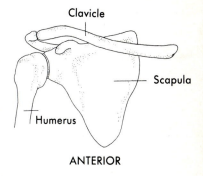

Humerus

The head of the humerus is spherical, with a shallow, constricted neck; it faces upward, inward, and backward, articulating with the scapula's shallow glenoid fossa. Circumscribing the humeral head is a slight groove called the anatomical neck, which is the attachment for the articular capsule of the glenohumeral joint. The greater and lesser tuberosities are located adjacent and immediately inferior to the head. The lesser tuberosity is positioned anteriorly and medially, with the greater tuberosity placed somewhat higher and laterally. Lying between the two tuberosities is a deep groove called the bicipital groove, which retains the long tendon of the biceps brachii muscle.

Figure 23-1

Bones of the shoulder complex.

Articulations

In all, there are four major articulations associated with the shoulder complex: the sternoclavicular joint, the acromioclavicular joint, the coracoclavicular joint, and the glenohumeral joint (Figure 23-2).

Sternoclavicular Joint

The clavicle articulates with the manubrium of the sternum to form the sternoclavicular joint, the only direct connection between the upper extremity and the trunk. The sternal articulating surface is larger than the sternum, causing the clavicle to rise much higher than the sternum. A fibrocartilaginous disk is interposed between the two articulating surfaces. It functions as a shock absorber against the medial forces and also helps to prevent any displacement upward. The articular disk is placed so that the clavicle moves on the disk, and the disk, in turn, moves separately on the sternum. The clavicle is permitted to move up and down, forward and backward, in combination, and in rotation.

The sternoclavicular joint is extremely weak because of its bony arrangement, but it is held securely by strong ligaments that tend to pull the sternal end of the clavicle downward and toward the sternum, in effect anchoring it. The main lig-

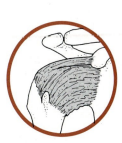

Sternoclavicular   Acromioclavicular   Coracoclavicular   Glenohumeral

Figure 23-2

Shoulder complex articulations.

aments are the anterior sternoclavicular, which prevents upward displacement of the clavicle; the posterior sternoclavicular, which also prevents upward displacement of the clavicle; the interclavicular, which prevents lateral displacement of the clavicle; and the costoclavicular, which prevents lateral and upward displacement of the clavicle.[17]

Some muscular support is given to the sternoclavicular joint by the subclavius, sternocleidomastoid, and sternohyoid muscles.

Acromioclavicular Joint

The acromioclavicular joint is a gliding articulation of the lateral end of the clavicle with the acromion process. This is a rather weak junction. A thin, fibrous sleeve surrounds the joint; additional reinforcement is given by the superior and inferior acromioclavicular ligaments and by the coracoclavicular ligaments.

Coracoclavicular Joint

The coracoclavicular joint is an amphiarthrodial, syndesmotic joint that permits only slight movement. It serves an important function in suspending the scapula and the clavicle and also in giving additional strength to the acromioclavicular joint. The coracoid process and the clavicle are joined by the coracoclavicular ligament, which is divided into the conoid part and the trapezoid part. The coracoclavicular ligament, because of the rotation of the clavicle on its long axis, develops some slack, which permits movement of the scapula at the acromioclavicular joint to take place.

Glenohumeral Joint

The glenohumeral joint (shoulder joint) is an enarthrodial, or ball-and-socket, joint in which the round head of the humerus articulates with the shallow glenoid cavity of the scapula. The cavity is deepened slightly by a fibrocartilagenous rim called the glenoid labrum. Surrounding the articulation is a loose, articular capsule. This capsule is strongly reinforced by the superior, middle, and inferior glenohumeral ligaments and by the tough coracohumeral ligament, which attaches to the coracoid process and to the greater tuberosity of the humerus. The long tendon of the biceps brachii muscle passes across the head of the humerus and then through the bicipital groove. In the anatomical position the long head of the biceps moves in close relationship with the humerus. The transverse ligament retains the long biceps tendon within the bicipital groove by passing over it from the lesser and the greater tuberosities converting the bicipital groove into a canal.

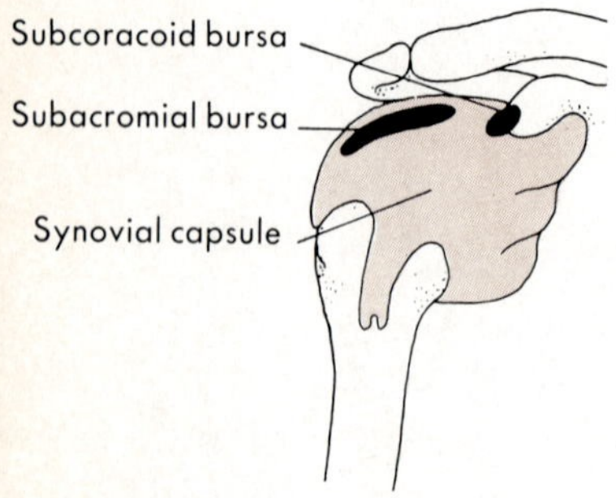

Bursa

Several bursae are located around the shoulder joint, the most important of which is the subacromial (subdeltoid) bursa (Figure 23-3), located between the acromial arch and the capsule and reinforced by the supraspinous tendon. It is easily subjected to traumatization by the deltoid muscle, which, as it contracts, may force the deeply seated bursa against the acromial shelf.

Musculature

The muscles that cross the shoulder joint assist in establishing stability to compensate for the weak bony and ligamentous arrangement. They may be separated

Subcoracoid bursa

Subacromial bursa

Synovial capsule

Figure 23-3

Synovial capsule and bursae of the shoulder.

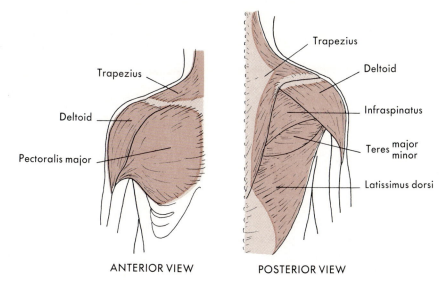

ANTERIOR VIEW   POSTERIOR VIEW

Figure 23-4

Shoulder musculature.

into two groups, one comprised of the more superficial muscles and the other composed of the deeper muscles (Figure 23-4). The superficial muscles arise from the thorax and shoulder complex and attach to the humeral shaft. They consist of the deltoid, greater pectoral, latissimus dorsi, and teres major. The deeper muscles originate from the scapula and attach to the humeral head. They consist of the supraspinatus, infraspinatus, subscapular, teres minor, and teres major muscles. These muscles constitute the short rotator muscles, commonly called the *rotator cuff*, whose tendons adhere to the articular capsule and serve as reinforcing structures.

Blood and Nerve Supply

The subclavian artery, which lies distal to the sternoclavicular joint, arches upward and outward, passes the anterior scalene muscle, and then moves downward laterally in back of the clavicle and in front of the first ribs. The subclavian artery continues on to become the axillary artery at the outer border of the first rib and, in the region of the teres major muscle in the upper arm, becomes the brachial artery (Figure 23-5).

The five anterior nerve rami, emanating from the fifth cervical vertebra through the first thoracic vertebra, subdivide and supply fibers to the skeleton and skin of the upper extremities. The subdivisions of the anterior rami create the complex nerve network called the *brachial plexus*. Stemming from this plexus are the much smaller nerves that serve the shoulders, arms, and hands. Trauma to the shoulder complex in athletes can place the brachial plexus in jeopardy of serious injury (see Figure 23-5).

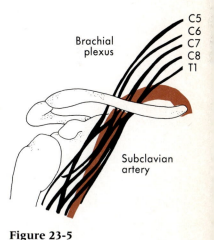

Figure 23-5

Brachial plexus and subclavian artery.

MOVEMENTS OF THE SHOULDER COMPLEX

The shoulder complex represents a multiaxial system that can produce both power and extreme range of motion[6] (Figure 23-6). Injuries to the shoulder joint usually result from its structural vulnerability, coupled with its extensive freedom of movement and a relatively poor correlation between the articular surfaces and the great strength of some of the surrounding musculature.[19]

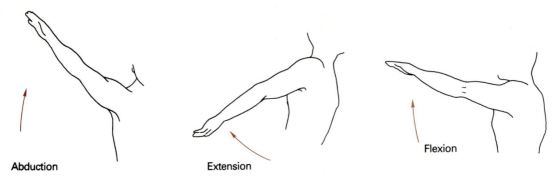

Abduction   Extension   Flexion

Figure 23-6

Movements of the shoulder.

To have a more comprehensive knowledge of the shoulder and its vulnerability to injury in sports, its complex movements must be understood. To assist in the understanding, consider the following analysis of the scapulohumeral rhythm, with the arm moving from the anatomical position through abduction to the vertical position.

Ratio: Arm to Scapular Movement

All the various components of the shoulder complex must move together rhythmically to perform a specific movement. The ratio of arm movement to scapular movement is considered to be approximately 2:1; in other words, 10 degrees of arm movement are comparable to five degrees of scapular movement. Although this ratio holds true for a complete zero to 180 degrees of scapulohumeral movement, it is variable between individuals. In some persons the scapula will rotate downward before it rotates upward, whereas in other individuals it will remain stabilized for the first 30 degrees. This preparatory period is called *scapular setting.*

Scapulohumeral Rhythm

Faulty scapulohumeral rhythm is one cause of chronic shoulder injuries.

Throughout the complete zero to 180 degrees of scapulohumeral movement, 120 degrees are attributed to the arm, and 60 degrees are accomplished within the shoulder complex. In the first 90 degrees of movement the arm moves approximately 50 degrees, and the shoulder complex moves 40 degrees, primarily within the sternoclavicular joint. As the arm moves upward, it rotates externally to allow the greater trochanter of the humerus to move out of the way of the acromion process; after 135 degrees of movement have taken place, or in the last stages of the vertical lift, approximately 20 degrees of motion take place within the acromioclavicular joint to complete the scapulohumeral rhythm. It also should be noted that the clavicle moves on its long axis posteriorly, in addition to elevating 40 degrees in the sternoclavicular joint and 20 degrees in the acromioclavicular joint. This posterior rotation slackens the coracoclavicular ligament, thus allowing the scapula to move in the acromioclavicular joint.

Muscles of the Scapulohumeral Rhythm

The muscles moving the arm in the scapulohumeral rhythm of arm abduction are (1) the prime moving mucles of arm abduction: the deltoid, supraspinous, and long head of the biceps when the arm is externally rotated; and (2) the guiding muscles (adductor group): the teres major, latissimus dorsi, greater pectoral, biceps brachii, and triceps. It is important that the head of the humerus be stabilized and maintained in relationship with the glenoid fossa. This requires a depression force to the head of the humerus by the infraspinous, teres minor, and subscapular muscles to counteract the upward force of the deltoid muscle. If the depressor muscles were not present, the head of the humerus would be jammed up against the acromion process and would traumatize the soft tissue lying principally between the subacromial bursa and the tendon of the supraspinous muscle. This depressor action is called a *force couple*.

The muscles moving the shoulder complex in scapulohumeral rhythm of arm abduction are (1) the prime moving muscles of upward rotation: the upper and lower trapezius and the serratus anterior (considered most important); and (2) the guiding muscles: the greater and lesser rhomboid, levator scapulae, lesser pectoral, and subscapular. The deltoid muscle tends to pull downward on the shoulder complex when the arm is at the side, and the upper trapezius stabilizes the shoulder complex in the first 30 degrees of arm abduction.

ASSESSMENT OF THE SHOULDER COMPLEX

The athlete who complains of pain in the shoulder region may be reflecting conditions other than in that area. Pain could be referred from a neck nerve root irritation or from an intrathoracic problem emanating from the heart, lungs, gallbladder, or other internal organs.

The shoulder complex is one of the most difficult regions of the body to evaluate. One reason for this difficulty is that the biomechanical demands placed on these structures during overhand accelerations and decelerations are, as yet, not clearly understood.[21]

Pain in the shoulder region may be referred from injury to an internal organ such as the spleen.

Major Complaints

It is essential that the evaluator understand the athlete's major complaints and possible mechanism of the injury. It is also necessary to know whether the condition was produced by a sudden trauma or was of slow onset. If the injury was of sudden onset, it must be determined whether the precipitating cause was from external and direct trauma or from some resistive force.[21] The following questions in regard to the athlete's complaints can help the evaluator determine the nature of the injury:

1. If the onset was gradual, what appeared to be the cause?
2. What is the duration and intensity of the pain? Where is the pain located?
3. Is there crepitus during movement, numbness, or distortion in temperature such as a cold or warm feeling?
4. Is there a feeling of weakness or a sense of fatigue?
5. What movement or body positions seem to aggravate or relieve the pain?
6. If therapy has been given before, what, if anything, offered pain relief, (e.g., cold, heat, massage, or analgesic medication)?

General Observations

The athlete should be generally observed while walking and standing. Observation during walking can reveal asymmetry of arm swing or leaning toward the painful shoulder.

The athlete is next observed from the front, side, and back while in a standing position. The evaluator looks for any postural asymmetries, bony or joint deformities, or muscle contractions and laxities.

Front View Observation

1. Are both shoulder tips even with one another, or is one depressed (indicating acromioclavicular sprain or dislocation)?
2. Is one shoulder pulled upward from a contracted muscle?
3. Is the lateral end of the clavicle prominent (indicating acromioclavicular sprain or dislocation)?
4. Is one lateral acromion process more prominent than the other (indicating a possible glenohumeral dislocation)?
5. Does the clavicular shaft appear deformed (indicating possible fracture)?
6. Is there loss of the normal lateral deltoid muscle contour (indicating glenohumeral dislocation)?
7. Is there an indentation in the upper biceps region (indicating rupture of bicipital tendon)?

Side View Observation

1. Is there thoracic kyphosis or shoulders slumped forward (indicating weakness of the erector muscles of the spine and tightness in the pectoral region)?
2. Is there forward or backward hang of the arm (indicating possible scoliosis)?

Back View Observation

1. Is there asymmetry such as a low shoulder, uneven scapulae, or winging of one scapular wing and not the other (indicating scoliosis)?
2. Is the scapula protracted because of constricted pectoral muscles?
3. Is there a distracted or winged scapula on one or both sides? (A winged scapula on both sides could indicate a general weakness of the serratus anterior muscles; if only one side is winged, the long thoracic nerve may be injured.)

Bony Palpation

With the evaluator standing behind the athlete, the shoulder is palpated anteriorly, laterally, and posteriorly. Both shoulders are palpated at the same time for pain sites and deformities.

Anterior Palpation

1. Sternoclavicular articulation
2. Clavicular shaft
3. Acromioclavicular articulation
4. Coracoid process
5. All aspects of the acromion process
6. Greater tuberosity of the humerus
7. Bicipital groove

Lateral Palpation

1. Underneath the acromion process
2. Greater tuberosity of the humerus

Posterior Palpation

1. Scapular spine
2. Vertebral border of the scapula
3. Lateral border of the scapula

Soft-Tissue Palpation

Palpation of the soft tissue of the shoulder detects pain sites, abnormal swelling or lumps, overly contracted muscle tissue, and trigger points. Trigger points are commonly found in the following muscles: levator scapulae, lesser rhomboid, supraspinous, infraspinous, scalene, deltoid, subscapular, teres major, trapezius, serratus anterior, and greater and lesser pectoral muscles.[22] As with bony palpation, the shoulder is palpated anteriorly, laterally, and posteriorly.

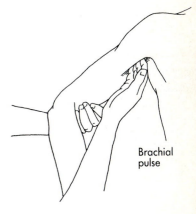

Brachial pulse

Anterior Palpation

1. Anterior deltoid muscle
2. Rotator cuff
3. Subdeltoid bursa
4. Greater pectoral muscle
5. Sternocleidomastoid muscle
6. Biceps muscle and tendon
7. Coracoacromial ligament
8. Glenohumeral ligament in supine position

Lateral Palpation

1. Glenohumeral capsule
2. Lateral deltoid muscle
3. Upper trapezius muscle

Posterior Palpation

1. Rhomboid muscles
2. Latissimus dorsi muscle
3. Serratus anterior muscle

Figure 23-7

Arterial pulses related to the shoulder.

Temperature

Skin temperature is subjectively assessed by comparing the back of the athlete's hands. A cold temperature can be an indication of blood vessel constriction, whereas an overly warm temperature may indicate an inflammatory condition.[21]

Circulatory and Neurological Assessment
Arterial Pulses

It is essential that athletes with shoulder complaints be evaluated for impaired circulation. In cases of shoulder complaints pulse rates are routinely obtained over the axillary, brachial, and radial arteries (Figure 23-7). The axillary artery is found in the axilla against the shaft of the humerus. The brachial artery is a continuation of the axillary artery and follows the medial border of the biceps brachii muscle toward the elbow. The radial pulse is found at the anterior medial aspect of the wrist. Taking the radial pulse provides an indication of the total circulation of the shoulder and arm.[21]

Injury to the shoulder complex can adversely affect skin sensation and the temperature of the arm and the leg.

Figure 23-8

Shoulder dermatomes.

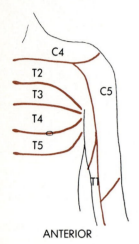

ANTERIOR

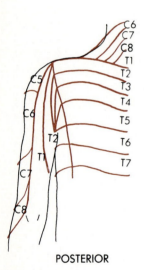

POSTERIOR

Figure 23-9

Scapulohumeral rhythm.

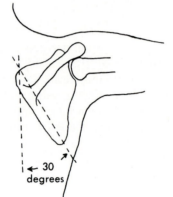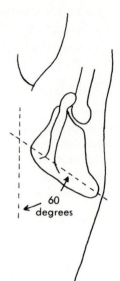

Sensation Testing

When there is injury to the shoulder complex, a routine test of cutaneous sensation should be performed. Dermatome levels are tested for pain and light pressure (Figure 23-8).

Functional Assessment
Range of Motion

The shoulder's range of motion is noted in all directions and compared to the nonsymptomatic limb. All motions should be performed both passively and then actively (Chapter 14).

Of major importance is noting whether the scapula and humerus are moving in a coordinated manner. This coordination is tested with the athlete abducting the arm through a full range of motion. The evaluator stands behind the athlete and notes when the arm first abducts 90 degrees without scapular motion. Since the humerus and scapula move together with a 2:1 ratio to full abduction, if the athlete's shoulder joint fails to follow this coordinated action, a fixation of the joint (frozen joint) may be present (Figure 23-9).

Muscle Strength

All major muscles associated with the shoulder complex should be tested for strength and pain (Table 23-1).

Special Assessment Procedures

A number of evaluation procedures can be used to determine the possibility of selected problems.

Serratus Anterior Muscle Weakness

The athlete performs a push-up movement against a wall. Winging of the scapula indicates weakness of the serratus anterior muscle. Winging of only one scapula could indicate an injury to the long thoracic nerve.

TABLE 23-1 Resistive Motion to Determine Muscle Weakness Related to Shoulder Injury

Resistive Motion	Major Muscles Involved	Nerves
Scapular	Serratus anterior	Cervical 6-8
Abduction	Trapezius (superior)	Accessory cranial
Elevation	Levator scapulae	Cervical 3 and 4
	Trapezius (inferior)	Accessory cranial
Depression	Trapezius (middle)	Accessory cranial
Adduction	Rhomboid	Cervical 5
Glenohumeral		
Flexion	Deltoid (anterior)	Cervical 5 and 6
Extension	Coracobrachial	Cervical 6 and 7
	Latissimus dorsi	Cervical 6-8
	Teres major	Cervical 5 and 6
	Deltoid (posterior)	Cervical 5 and 6
Abduction	Deltoid (middle)	Cervical 5 and 6
	Supraspinous	Cervical 5
Horizontal abduction	Deltoid (posterior)	Cervical 5 and 6
Horizontal adduction	Greater pectoral	Cervical 5-8
		Thoracic 1
Lateral rotation	Infraspinous	Cervical 5 and 6
	Teres minor	Cervical 5
Medial rotation	Teres major	Cervical 5 and 6

Evaluation of Acromioclavicular Joint Stability

The acromioclavicular joint is first palpated to ascertain separation of the acromion process and the distal head of the clavicle (Figure 23-10, *A*). Next, pressure is applied inward from the anterior and posterior aspects of the shoulder. An unstable acromioclavicular joint will show some excursion and pain (Figure 23-10, *B*). Finally, the evaluator grasps the athlete's wrist and pulls downward on the arm to detect whether the acromion process can be depressed (Figure 23-10, *C*).

Supraspinous Muscle Function

Drop arm test   The drop arm test is designed to determine tears of the rotator cuff, primarily of the supraspinous muscle. The athlete abducts the arm as far as possible and then slowly lowers it to 90 degrees. From this position the athlete with a torn supraspinous muscle will be unable to lower the arm further with control (Figure 23-11). If the athlete can hold the arm in a 90-degree position, a light tap on the wrist will cause the arm to fall.

Centinela supraspinous muscle test   Another test for supraspinous muscle strength and pain was developed at the Centinela Hospital Medical Center Biomechanics Laboratory in Inglewood, California (Figure 23-12).[27] The athlete brings both arms into 90 degrees of forward flexion and 30 degrees of horizontal abduction. In this position the arms are internally rotated as far as possible, thumbs pointing downward. A downward pressure is then applied by the evaluator. Weakness and pain can be detected, as well as comparative strength between the two arms.

The rotator cuff muscle that is most commonly injured is the supraspinous muscle.

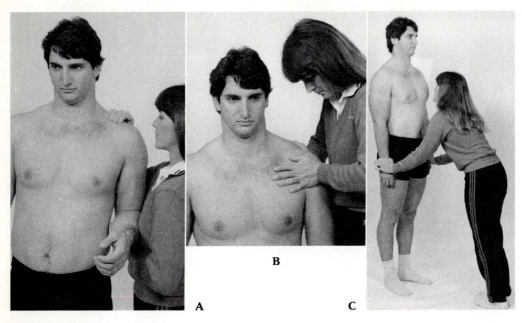

Figure 23-10

Evaluating the acromio-
clavicular joint. **A,** Palpating
the acromioclavicular joint.
B, Inward pressure on the
shoulder to test excursion.
C, Pulling down on the arm
to depress the acromion
process.

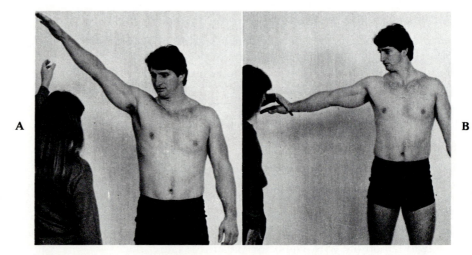

Figure 23-11

Drop arm test for supraspinous muscle stability. **A,** Lower
the arm to 90 degrees. **B,** The athletic trainer lightly taps
the wrist. The test is positive if the athlete is unable to hold
the 90-degree position.

Bicipital Tendinitis and Subluxation Test

The bicipital tendinitis and subluxation test indicates function of the long head of the biceps tendon. Keeping the elbow at 90 degrees, the athlete attempts to externally rotate the humerus against the resistance of the evaluator as the humerous is also being pulled downward. The test is positive if pain is felt in the region of the bicipital groove. If there is instability, the tendon will snap out of its groove (Figure 23-13).

Glenohumeral Instability

A number of procedures can be used to determine glenohumeral instability.

Pressure displacement   With the athlete's shoulder flexed and the arm supported in a completely relaxed position, an anteriorly unstable joint can be manually subluxated forward (Figure 23-14).

Figure 23-12

Centinela supraspinous muscle test.

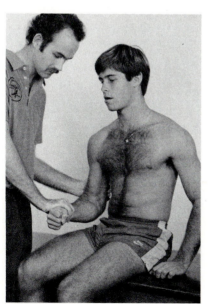

Figure 23-13

The bicipital tendinitis and subluxation test.

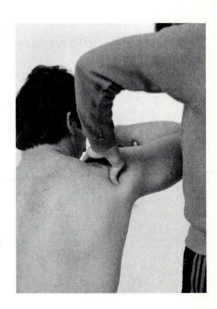

Figure 23-14

Pressure displacement test.

Apprehension test   With the arm abducted 90 degrees, the shoulder is slowly and gently externally rotated as far as the athlete will allow. The athlete with a history of anterior glenohumeral dislocation will show great apprehension that is reflected by a facial grimace before an end point can be reached. At no time should the evaluator force this movement[21,27] (Figure 23-15).

Posterior instability also can be determined through an apprehension maneuver. A posterior force is applied to the glenohumeral joint while the arm is internally rotated and moved into various degrees of flexion.[21]

Figure 23-15

Shoulder apprehension test.

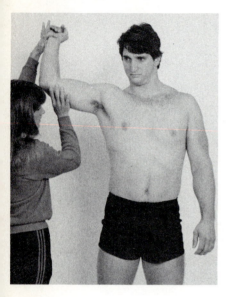

A   B

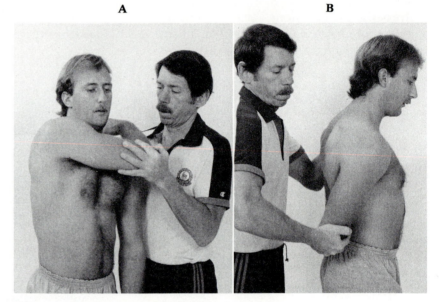

Figure 23-16

A, Horizontal adduction and, **B,** hyperextension for testing anterior and posterior capsular stability, and/or pain.

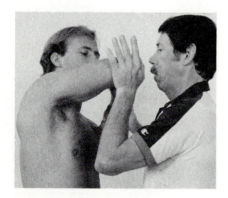

Figure 23-17

Impingement syndrome test.

Figure 23-18

Anterior scalene syndrome test.

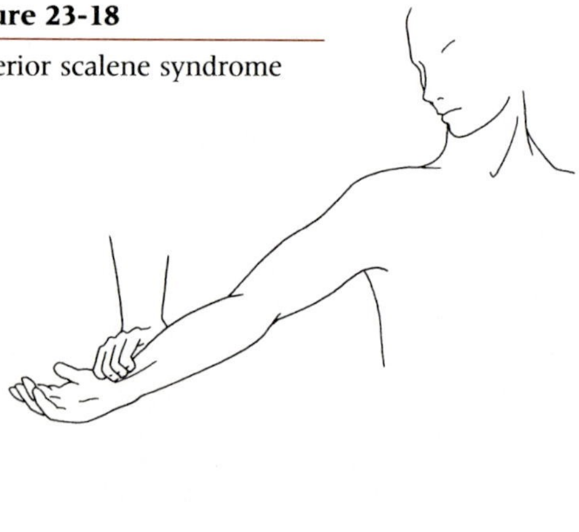

Anterior and Posterior Capsular Pain

The anterior and posterior capsule of the shoulder can be examined by pulling the arm into hyperextension and horizontal adduction (Figure 23-16).

Impingement Syndrome Tests

One reliable impingement syndrome test consists of forced flexion of the arm so that the head of the humerus is forced under the acromion process (Figure 23-17). A positive sign is indicated if the athlete feels pain and reacts with a grimace.

In another test the arm if flexed to 90 degrees and then vigorously rotated internally. This forces the greater tuberosity beneath the coracoacromial arch.

Special Tests for Neurovascular Syndromes of the Neck and Shoulders

Thoracic outlet compression syndrome tests

Anterior scalene syndrome test   The purpose of this test is to indicate whether the subclavian artery is being compressed as it enters into the outlet canal that lies between the heads of the anterior and middle scalene muscles. Compression can also occur between the cervical rib and the anterior scalene muscle. This maneuver is performed with the athlete seated on a stool, with both hands resting on the thighs. The athete's radial pulse is taken, first with the arm relaxed and then extended, while at the same time the athlete elevates the chin, turns the face toward the extended hand, and holds the breath (Figure 23-18). A positive test is one in which the pulse is depressed or stopped completely in the testing position.

Costoclavicular syndrome test   This test indicates whether the subclavian artery is being compressed between the first rib and the clavicle. The radial pulse is taken while the athlete stands in a stiff, military posture. The shoulders are in posterior abduction, the arms are extended, and the neck is hyperextended. A positive test is one in which the pulse is obliterated partially or totally (Figure 23-19).

Hyperabduction syndrome test   In an athlete with hyperabduction syndrome, the subclavian and axillary vessels and the brachial plexus are compressed as they move behind the pectoral muscle and beneath the coracoid process. To test for this syndrome, the athlete's radial pulse is taken while both hands are raised and the arms are fully extended overhead (Figure 23-20).

Mechanism of Injury

Chapter 7 discussed how the shoulder becomes injured in sports participation. Incorrectly performing the overhand throw, falling on the outstretched arm or shoulder tip, and forcing the shoulder into external or internal rotation while the arm is abducted are the most common mechanisms of shoulder injury.

PREVENTING SHOULDER INJURIES

Proper physical conditioning is of major importance in preventing many shoulder injuries. As with all preventive conditioning, the program should be directed toward general body development and development of specific body areas for a given sport.[15] If a sport places extreme, sustained demands on the arms and shoulders or if the shoulder is at risk for sudden traumatic injury, extensive conditioning must be used. Maximum strength of both intrinsic and extrinsic muscles must be gained, along with a full range of motion in all directions.

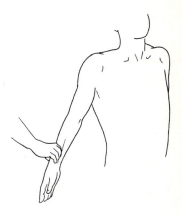

Figure 23-19

Costoclavicular syndrome test.

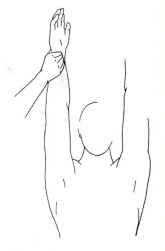

Figure 23-20

Hyperabduction syndrome test.

Proper warm-up must be performed gradually before explosive arm movements are attempted. This warm-up includes gaining a general increase in body temperature, followed by sport-specific stretching of selected muscles[7] (see Chapter 14).

All athletes in collision and contact sports should be instructed and drilled on how to fall properly. They must be taught not to try to catch themselves with an outstretched arm. Performing a shoulder roll is a safer way to absorb the shock of the fall. Specialized protective equipment such as shoulder pads must be properly fitted to avoid some shoulder injuries in tackle football.

To avoid overuse shoulder injuries, it is essential that athletes be correctly taught in the appropriate techniques of throwing, spiking, overhead smashing, overhand serving, proper crawl and butterfly swimming strokes, and tackling and blocking.

SHOULDER COMPLEX INJURIES
Contusions and Strains

Injuries to the soft tissue in the area of the shoulder complex are common in sports.

Contusions

Blows around the shoulder that produce injury are most prevalent in collision and contact sports. The muscles with the highest incidence are the upper trapezius and deltoid muscles. Characteristically, bruises in this area result in pain and restricted arm movement. The subcutaneous areas of the shoulder complex are subject to bruising in contact sports.

Contusion to the distal end of the clavicle   The most vulnerable part of the clavicle is the enlarged lateral end (acromial end), which forms a projection just before it joins the acromion process. Contusions of this type are often called *shoulder pointers,* and they may cause the athlete severe discomfort. Contusion to the lateral end of the clavicle causes a bone bruise and subsequent irritation to the periosteum. During initial inspection this injury may be mistaken for a first-degree acromioclavicular separation. Management requires proper immediate first aid and follow-up therapy. In most cases these conditions are self-limiting; when the athlete is able to move the shoulder freely, he or she can return to sports activities.

Injuries Resulting from the Throwing Motion

Overuse syndromes of the shoulder complex occur mainly in athletes who use repetitive throwing-type motions in activities such as baseball pitching, tennis serving and overhead smashing, and swimming the crawl or butterfly (Figure 23-21). Quarterbacking and volleyball spiking also can cause microtraumas, which can lead to an overuse syndrome. In addition, repetitive movements, plus the production of a large amount of force, may cause microtraumas to the soft tissue of the shoulder.[9] In general, these sport activities have three phases in common: cocking, acceleration, and the follow-through and deceleration phase.[16]

Cocking phase   The cocking phase can cause anterior shoulder pain as a result of strain of the greater pectoral muscle insertion and the origin of the anterior deltoid, long head of the biceps, or internal rotator muscles.

Acceleration phase   Friction injuries causing an impingement syndrome or bursitis in the region of the scapula and fatigue injuries can result in the following:

1. Tendinitis of the greater pectoral major muscle insertion
2. Tendinitis of the coracobrachial muscle and short head of the biceps where it joins the coracoid process
3. Synovitis of the sternoclavicular or acromioclavicular joint
4. "Little League shoulder," or osteochondrosis, of the proximal humeral epiphysis
5. Spontaneous throwing fractures of the proximal humerus stemming from a stress fracture

Follow-through and deceleration phase   In this phase an eccentric load from throwing may cause pain over the posterior rotator cuff and capsule ("posterior capsule syndrome").

Strains and Impingements

Strains around the shoulder complex are common in those sports that use the arms to overcome a resistance or propel an object. Strains to the musculature of the shoulder joint frequently affect the deltoid superficially and affect the tendons of the rotator cuff internally.

Rotator cuff strains   The principal rotator cuff tendon injured is that of the supraspinous muscle. The mechanism of shoulder strains occurs mainly as the result of a violent pull to the arm, an abnormal rotation, or a fall on the outstretched arm, tearing or even rupturing tendinous tissue. The throwing mechanism can produce a variety of abnormal stresses to the soft tissues of the shoulder (e.g., impingement, overstretching, torsion, subluxation, and entrapment of nerves and blood vessels). Besides throwing, swimming in freestyle and butterfly events also places great stress on the shoulder rotating mechanisms and can lead to an acute or chronic injury. A tear or complete rupture of one of the *rotator cuff tendons* (the subscapular, supraspinatus, infraspinatus, or teres minor) produces an extremely disabling condition in which pain, loss of function (particularly with the arm in abduction or external rotation), swelling, and point tenderness are symptoms. In a strain, passive movements seldom yield pain.

Rotator cuff impingement syndrome   The continual use of the arm or arms above the horizontal plane such as in swimming has been known to lead to an impingement syndrome.[4]

Impingement commonly happens to the supraspinous muscle at the anterior edge of the acromion and coracoacromial ligament.[7] It occurs most often in athletes less than 25 years old, in the weekend athlete 25 to 40 years old, and in workers 40 years or older.[2,26] (See p. 747 for impingement syndrome test.)

The major reason for impingement is the reduction of space for the supraspinous muscle to pass underneath the anterior acromion and coracoacromial ligament. This space reduction may be attributed to muscle hypertrophy and inflammation caused by microtraumas or contraction of the biceps tendon, forcing the humeral head forward.[2,7,14]

The rotator cuff impingement syndrome has been described in four stages.[10,11]

Stage I   A beginning injury to the supraspinous muscle and/or long head of the biceps tendon will produce the following symptoms and signs:

Figure 23-21

The tennis serve can be a major cause of overuse syndromes of the shoulder.

1. Aching after activity
2. Supraspinatus muscle symptoms
   a. Point tenderness over the greater tuberosity of the humerus
   b. Pain during abduction that becomes worse at 90 degrees
   c. Positive impingement sign
3. Biceps tendon symptoms
   a. Point tenderness over the biceps tendon
   b. Pain at the biceps tendon during straight-arm full flexion
   c. Positive sign during resisted supination–external rotation test
4. No palpable muscle defect
5. Inflammation with edema
6. Temporary thickening of the rotator cuff and the subacromial bursa
7. Possible atrophy and constriction of muscles in the region of the shoulder joint

Stage II   An impingement syndrome involving the supraspinatus muscle and at times also the long head of the biceps tendon and subacromial bursa will have the following symptoms and signs:

1. Aching during activity that becomes worse at night
2. Some restriction of arm movement
3. No obvious muscle defect
4. Some muscle fiber separation
5. Permanent thickening of the rotator cuff and the acromial bursa with scar tissue

Stage III   In this stage the athlete has the following symptoms and signs:

1. A long history of shoulder problems
2. Shoulder pain during activity with increased pain at night
3. A muscle defect of 1 cm or less
4. A possible partial muscle tear
5. Permanent thickening of the rotator cuff and the acromial bursa with scar tissue

Stage IV   Stage IV of the rotator cuff impingement syndrome includes the following:

1. A long history of shoulder problems
2. An obvious infraspinous and supraspinous wasting
3. Point tenderness over the greater tuberosity of the humerus, the anterior acromion, and the acromioclavicular joint
4. A great deal of pain when abducting the arm to 90 degrees
5. A muscle defect greater than 1 cm
6. Permanent thickening of the rotator cuff and the acromial bursa with scar tissue
7. Limited active and full passive range of motion
8. Weakness during abduction and external rotation
9. Possible degeneration of the clavicle
10. A positive impingement sign

Management of shoulder impingement injuries   Stages III and IV are usually treated by surgery. Stages I and II may be treated conservatively with cold or heat modalities or by a combination of electrostimulation and therapeutic exercise.[7]

Conservative treatment   For stage I and initially in stage II shoulder impingement injuries, a conservative approach to treatment is taken. If this approach is
unsatisfactory in a stage II condition, surgery may be warranted.

Early prevention and proper training   Proper training methods to prevent shoulder injuries must be undertaken for sports that involve throwing. Gradual warm-
up should emphasize slow stretching and maximizing the extensibility of all major
shoulder muscles. Strengthening shoulder muscles should be general at first and
then emphasize the external and internal rotator muscles for good glenohumeral
joint control.

Athletes displaying early symptoms of shoulder impingement must modify
their arm movements. A swimmer may have to decrease the distance he or she
swims or change to a different stroke. Those athletes who throw or who perform
throwinglike motions may have to decrease their force or develop a different technique.

Cold application   Athletes experiencing shoulder pain and inflammation might
benefit from cold application after workouts. This could be in the form of ice
massage or an ice chip pack.

Heat   Heat of any form should be avoided after workouts. However, heat may
be beneficial before workouts or at other times. Ultrasound is valuable in many
cases of impingement syndrome. Between 0.8 and 1.2 watts/cm^2, 5 minutes daily,
for 10 days is suggested.

Transcutaneous electrical nerve stimulation (TENS)   In many cases TENS is effective in relieving pain from shoulder impingement.

Anti-inflammatory medication   The physician may prescribe an oral anti-inflammatory drug for a short period of time.

Rest   A change of activity or complete rest may be warranted. Because a stage
I condition is reversible, it is essential to avoid the movement causing the irritation until the shoulder is symptom free.

Sprains
Sternoclavicular Sprain

A sternoclavicular sprain (Figure 23-22) is a relatively uncommon occurrence in
sports, but occasionally one may result from one of the various traumas affecting
the shoulder complex.

ETIOLOGICAL FACTORS   The mechanism of the injury can be initiated by an
indirect force transmitted through the humerus of the shoulder joint by direct
violence such as a blow that strikes the poorly padded clavicle or by twisting or
torsion of a posteriorly extended arm. Depending on the direction of force, the
medial end of the clavicle can be displaced upward and forward, either posteriorly
or anteriorly. Generally the clavicle is displaced upward and forward, slightly anteriorly.

SYMPTOMS AND SIGNS   Trauma resulting in a sprain to the sternoclavicular
joint can be described in three degrees. The *first-degree* sprain is characterized by
little pain and disability, with some point tenderness but no joint deformity. A
second-degree sprain displays subluxation of the sternoclavicular joint with visible
deformity, pain, swelling, point tenderness, and an inability to abduct the shoulder in full range or to bring the arm across the chest, indicating disruption of
stabilizing ligaments.

> Sprains can occur in the
> three major joints of the
> shoulder complex
> Sternoclavicular joint
> Acromioclavicular joint
> Glenohumeral joint

MANAGEMENT PLAN FOR ROTATOR CUFF TEAR

Injury Situation

During a match, a male wrestler had his left arm severely forced into external rotation while it was partially abducted. At the time of trauma, the athlete felt a sudden sharp pain and a "giving way" of the shoulder.

Symptoms and Signs

As the athlete left the mat, his injured arm was dangling limply. He complained to the athletic trainer that there was moderated to severe pain and weakness in the shoulder region. During inspection, there was point tenderness over the greater tuberosity of the humerus. Tests for supraspinous muscle injury were positive. Passive movement, however, did not produce pain, but active minimum resistance movement caused extreme pain. It was determined that the wrestler had sustained a second-degree rotator cuff tear.

Management Plan

The physician and athletic trainer decided on a nonsurgical, active exercise rehabilitation approach that included a short period of sling support and immobilization until the shoulder complex was pain free (approximately 1 week).

1

Management Phase	GOALS: To control hemorrhage and full static contraction of shoulder ESTIMATED LENGTH OF TIME (ELT): two or three days
Therapy	IMMEDIATE CARE: ICE-R (20 min or intermittently), six to eight times daily
Exercise Rehabilitation	Ball squeeze (10 to 15 repetitions), each waking hour Muscle setting while in sling; each contraction held 6 sec (10 to 15 repetitions), each waking hour General body maintenance exercises are conducted three times a week as long as they do not aggravate injury

2

Management Phase	GOALS: To be free of pain and swelling and be able to fully contract shoulder muscles ELT: 1 to 2 weeks
Therapy	FOLLOW-UP CARE: Ice pack applied (5 to 15 min) before exercise, three or four times daily

	Exercise Rehabilitation	While supine, athlete abducts and externally rotates arm and squeezes ball; each maximum squeeze is held for 6 sec (three or four times) as arm moves slowly into adduction and internal rotation within pain-free limits, each waking hour
		Codman's pendulum exercise (three sets of 10) within pain-free limits, each waking hour
		Finger wall or ladder climb (three or four times, 10 to 15 repetitions) within pain-free limits, each waking hour
		General body maintenance exercises are conducted three times a week as long as they do not aggravate injury
3	**Management Phase**	GOALS: 50% of normal pain-free range of motion (ROM), with 50% of normal strength and coordination
		ELT: 1 to 2 weeks
	Therapy	Ice pack (5 min) precedes pain-free exercise, two or three times daily
	Exercise Rehabilitation	Isolated movement against gravity with resistance as tolerated; each exercise progresses to three sets of 10, two or three times daily
		Isotonic and/or isokinetic exercise can be used; all shoulder movements are exercised
		Proprioceptive neuromuscular facilitation (PNF) and pool exercising also should be considered
		General body maintenance exercises are conducted as long as they do not aggravate injury, three times a week
4	**Management Phase**	GOALS: To restore at least 90% ROM, power, endurance, speed, and coordination
		ELT: 1 to 3 weeks
	Exercise Rehabilitation	Progressive resistance exercise using DeLorme specifications or daily adjustable progressive resistive exercise (DAPRE) concept, three times a week, using equipment such as free weights, Universal gym, and Nautilus equipment
5	**Management Phase**	GOALS: To restore usual shoulder muscle bulk for full sports participation
	Exercise Rehabilitation	Heavy overload program using Olympic weight equipment, three or four times a week

Criteria for Returning to Competitive Wrestling

1. The shoulder is symptom free in all movements.
2. The shoulder has full range of motion.
3. The shoulder has full strength and coordination.

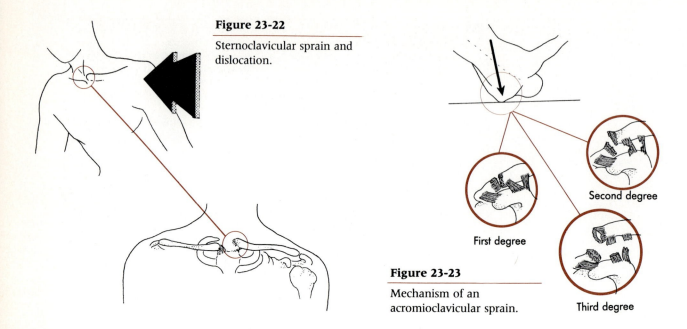

Figure 23-22

Sternoclavicular sprain and dislocation.

Figure 23-23

Mechanism of an acromioclavicular sprain.

First degree

Second degree

Third degree

The *third-degree* sprain, which is the most severe, presents a picture of complete dislocation with gross displacement of the clavicle at its sternal junction, swelling, and disability, indicating complete rupture of the sternoclavicular and costoclavicular ligaments. If the clavicle is displaced posteriorly, pressure may be placed on the blood vessels, esophagus, or trachea, causing a life-or-death situation.

MANAGEMENT   Care of this condition is based on returning the displaced clavicle to its original position, which is done by a physician, and immobilizing it at that point so that healing may take place. A deformity, primarily caused by formation of scar tissue at that point, is usually apparent after healing is completed. There is no loss of function. Immobilization (see Chapter 12 for immobilization technique) is usually maintained for 3 to 5 weeks, followed by graded reconditioning exercises. There is a high incidence of recurrence of sternoclavicular sprains.

Acromioclavicular Sprain

The acromioclavicular joint is extremely vulnerable to sprains among active sports participants, especially in collision sports. A program of prevention should entail proper fitting of protective equipment, conditioning to provide a balance of strength and flexibility to the entire shoulder complex, and teaching proper techniques of falling and the use of the arm in sports.

MECHANISM   The mechanism of an acromioclavicular sprain is most often induced by a direct blow to the tip of the shoulder, pushing the acromion process downward, or by an upward force exerted against the long axis of the humerus (Figure 23-23). The position of the arm during indirect injury is one of adduction and partial flexion. Depending on the extent of ligamentous involvement, the acromioclavicular sprain is graded as first, second, and third degree.

SYMPTOMS AND SIGNS   The *first-degree* acromioclavicular sprain reflects point tenderness and discomfort during movement at the junction between the acrom-

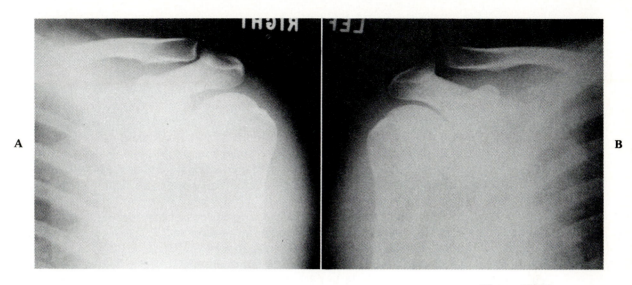

A   B

Figure 23-24

Comparison of, **A,** a normal shoulder with, **B,** a separated shoulder.

ion process and the outer end of the clavicle. There is no deformity, indicating only mild stretching of the acromioclavicular ligaments.

A *second-degree* sprain indicates rupture of the supporting superior and inferior acromioclavicular ligaments. There is definite displacement and prominence of the lateral end of the clavicle when compared to the unaffected side, especially when the acromioclavicular stress test is initiated (Figure 23-24). In this moderate sprain there is point tenderness during palpation of the injury site, and the athlete is unable to fully abduct through a full range of motion or to bring the arm completely across the chest. **NOTE:** The second-degree sprain may require surgery to restore stability.[1]

Although occurring infrequently, the *third-degree* injury is considered a dislocation, involving rupture of the acromioclavicular and coracoclavicular ligaments. The mechanics of a completely separated shoulder consist most often of a direct blow that forces the acromion process downward, backward, and inward while the clavicle is pushed down against the rib cage. In such an injury there is gross deformity and prominence of the outer clavicular head, severe pain, loss of movement, and instability of the shoulder complex.[1,25]

MANAGEMENT   Immediate care of the acromioclavicular sprain involves three basic procedures: (1) application of cold and pressure to control local hemorrhage, (2) stabilization of the joint by a sling and swathe bandage, and (3) referral to a physician for definitive diagnosis and treatment. Complete severance of the coracoclavicular ligament demands corrective surgery. Most second-degree sprains require 4 to 6 weeks for fibrous healing to take place, and an extended period is needed for the restoration of general shoulder strength and mobility. A regimen of superficial moist heat will aid in resolving soreness. Movement in the pain-free range will be restored after the use of ice packs.

Rehabilitation exercise is concerned with reconditioning the shoulder complex to the state it was before the injury. Full strength, flexibility, endurance, and function must be redeveloped. (See p. 768 for rehabilitation exercises.) Protective taping may help support the first-degree injury (see Figure 12-25).

Glenohumeral Joint Sprain

Sprains of the shoulder joint involve injury to the articular capsule. The pathological process of the sprain is comparable to that of an internal strain and often affects the rotator cuff muscles.

MECHANISM   The cause of this injury is the same as that which produces dislocations and strains. Anterior capsular sprains occur when the arm is forced into abduction (e.g., when making an arm tackle in football). Sprains can also occur from external rotation of the arm. A direct blow to the shoulder could also result in a sprain. The infraspinatus–teres minor muscle group is the most effective in controlling external rotation of the humerus and in reducing ligamentous injury.[3] The posterior capsule can be sprained by a forceful movement of the humerus posteriorly when the arm is flexed.

SYMPTOMS AND SIGNS   The athlete complains of pain during arm movement, especially when the sprain mechanism is reproduced. There may be decreased range of motion and pain during palpation.

MANAGEMENT   Care after acute trauma to the shoulder joint requires the use of a cold pack for 24 to 48 hours, elastic or adhesive compression, rest, and immobilization by a sling. After hemorrhage has subsided, a program of cryotherapy or ultrasound and massage may be added, and mild passive and active exercise is advocated for regaining full range of motion. Once the athlete can execute full shoulder range of movement without signs of pain, a resistance exercise program should be initiated. Any traumatic injury to the shoulder joint can lead to a subacute and chronic condition of either synovitis or bursitis, which in the absence of shoulder movement will allow muscle contractures, adhesions, and atrophy to develop, resulting in an ankylosed shoulder joint.

Subluxations and Dislocations

Shoulder dislocations account for up to 50% of all dislocations. The extreme range of all of its possible movements makes the shoulder joint highly susceptible

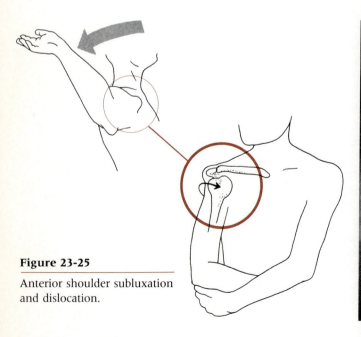

Figure 23-25

Anterior shoulder subluxation and dislocation.

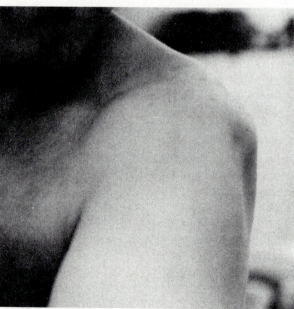

to dislocation. The most common kind of displacement is that occurring anteriorly (Figure 23-25). Of dislocations caused by direct trauma, 85% to 90% recur.[8]

Anterior Glenohumeral Dislocation

MECHANISM   A direct cause of anterior glenohumeral dislocation is a blow to the posterior or posterolateral aspect of the shoulder. A common indirect cause is the forced-abduction, external-rotation maneuver that forces the humeral head out of the glenoid socket (Figure 23-26).[5]

An arm tackle or an abnormal force to an arm that is executing a throw can produce a sequence of events resulting in a severe shoulder strain or dislocation. Less often a fall or inward rotation and abduction of an arm may result in serious shoulder joint injury.

In an anterior glenohumeral dislocation, the head of the humerus is forced out of its articular capsule in a forward direction past the glenoid labrum and then upward to rest under the coracoid process. The scope of the pathological process is quite extensive, with torn capsular and ligamentous tissue, possibly tendinous avulsion of the rotator cuff muscles, and profuse hemorrhage. A tear or detachment of the fibrocartilage labrum and elevation of the anterior scapula's periosteum occur. Healing is usually slow, and the detached labrum and capsule produce a permanent anterior defect called "Bankart lesion."[23] Another defect that occurs on the posterior lateral aspect of the humeral head is the Hill-Sacks lesion. It is caused by the compression of the cancellous bone of the head of the humerus against the anterior glenoid rim through the process of dislocation.[23] Additional complications may arise if the head of the humerus comes into contact with and injures the brachial nerves and vessels. The bicipital tendon also may be pulled from its canal as the result of a rupture of its transverse ligament.

SYMPTOMS AND SIGNS   The athlete with an anterior dislocation displays a flattened deltoid contour. Palpation of the axilla will reveal prominence of the humeral head. The athlete carries the affected arm in slight abduction and external rotation and is unable to touch the opposite shoulder with the hand of the affected arm. There is often severe pain and disability.

MANAGEMENT   Management of the shoulder dislocation requires immediate reduction by a physician, control of the hemorrhage by cold packs, immobilization, and the start of muscle reconditioning as soon as possible. The question often arises as to whether a first-time dislocation should be reduced or should receive medical attention. Physicians generally agree that a first-time dislocation may be associated with a fracture, and, therefore, its treatment is beyond the scope of a coach's or athletic trainer's duties. Recurrent dislocations do not present the same complications or attendant dangers as the acute type; however, risk is always involved. Reducing the anterior dislocation usually can be accomplished by applying traction to the abducted and flexed arm.[13]

After the dislocation has been reduced, immobolization and muscle rehabilitation are performed. Immobilization takes placc for approximately 3 weeks after reduction with the arm maintained in a relaxed position of adduction and internal rotation.[13] While immobilized, the athlete is instructed to perform isometric exercises for strengthening the internal and external rotator muscles. After immobilization, the strengthening program progresses from isometrics to resisting rubber tubing and then to dumbbells and other resistance devices. (See pp. 764-768

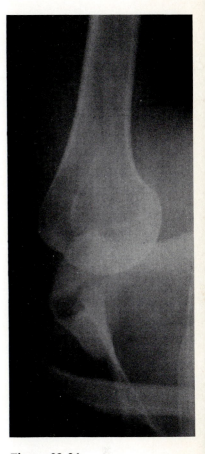

Figure 23-26

Subcoracoid dislocation of the humerus at the glenohumeral joint.

After exercise rehabilitation of an anterior shoulder dislocation, the athlete should have an internal and external rotation strength equal to at least 20% of body weight.

for rehabilitation of rotator cuff injuries.) A major criterion for the athlete's return to sports competition is that there must be internal and external rotation strength equal to 20% of the athlete's body weight.[13] Taping for shoulder restraint after dislocation has been performed throughout the years (see Figure 12-46).

Posterior Glenohumeral Dislocation

The posterior glenohumeral dislocation accounts for only 1% to 4.3% of all shoulder dislocations.[18]

MECHANISM   The mechanism of injury is usually a forced adduction and internal rotation of the shoulder or a fall on an extended and internally rotated arm.

SYMPTOMS AND SIGNS   Posterior glenohumeral dislocation produces severe pain and disability. The arm is often fixed in adduction and internal rotation. The deltoid muscle is flattened, the acromion and coracoid processes are prominent, and the head of the humerus also may be seen posteriorly.

MANAGEMENT   The athlete must be promptly referred to an orthopedic physician for x-ray examination and reduction. Reduction may have to be performed with the athlete under anesthesia. The procedure usually involves traction on the arm with the elbow bent, followed by adduction of the arm, with posterior pressure being applied to the humeral head anteriorly. While in traction the arm is slowly externally rotated and then internally rotated.[18]

The shoulder is immobilized in a position of external rotation and slight abduction for 3 to 6 weeks. After immobilization, an active program of range of motion and strengthening exercises are begun (p. 768).

The Unstable Shoulder: Recurrent Subluxation and Dislocation

Recurrent subluxation   Subluxation of the shoulder usually begins with one traumatic event that places an abnormal stress on the joint or by repeated less forceful movements that stress the joint capsule. Pitching, tennis serving, and crawl swimming may produce anterior capsular complaints, whereas swimming the backstroke or backhand stroking in tennis can cause problems with the posterior capsule. As the articular capsule becomes increasingly lax, more mobility of the glenohumeral head is allowed, eventually damaging the glenoid lip. With this damage and stretching of supportive ligamentous and tendinous structures, subluxation and dislocation can occur.[24]

When subluxation occurs, the athlete may complain that the shoulder felt like it came out of its socket, followed by sudden pain along the arm and numbness in the fingers.[20,24] The pain and numbness may last for several minutes, followed by extreme weakness of the entire arm. Tests for apprehension will be positive, and there is often point tenderness of the humeral head and positive signs of injury to the rotator cuff.[24]

In conservative management, the shoulder is immobilized with a sling and swathe for 5 to 6 weeks. After immobilization and a decrease in inflammation, an exercise program is instituted emphasizing the rotator cuff, rhomboid, latissimus dorsi, and serratus anterior muscles.[24] A gradual program of strength and flexibility development is performed over a 4- to 6-week period, followed by a slow return to sports activity over a period of 6 weeks.[24]

If a conservative approach is unsuccessful, surgery is usually performed. After surgery, a strength and development program is instituted.

Shoulder protection   Every protection should be given to the athlete who may be prone to recurrent dislocations. Restraint by means of adhesive taping and a harness appliance should be used during any sports activity. Repeated dislocations continue to stretch the supporting structures and damage the articulating hyaline cartilage, which may eventually result in an arthritic condition (see Chapter 12 for shoulder restraint).

Recurrent shoulder subluxation and dislocation reduction   With the permission of the team physician, the athletic trainer can assist the athlete in reducing a recurrent shoulder subluxation or dislocation. The safest method is by the *weight-on-the-wrist technique*. In this method the athlete lies between two tables, with the head resting on one table and the body on the other. The affected arm extends between the two tables with a 5- to 10-pound weight tied to the wrist. As the muscles of the shoulder relax, a spontaneous reduction occurs.

Shoulder Synovitis and Bursitis

The shoulder joint is subject to subacute chronic inflammatory conditions resulting from trauma or from overuse in an abnormal fashion. An injury of this type may develop from a direct blow, a fall on the outstretched hand, or the stress incurred in throwing an object. Inflammation can occur in the shoulder, extensively affecting the soft tissues surrounding it or specifically affecting various bursae (Figure 23-27). The bursa that is most often injured is the subacromial bursa, which lies underneath the deltoid muscle and the articular capsule and extends under the acromion process. The apparent pathological process in these conditions is fibrous buildup and fluid accumulation developing from a constant inflammatory state.

Figure 23-27

Sports such as pole vaulting place extreme stress on the arm and shoulder complex.

Recognition of these conditions follows the same course as in other shoulder afflictions.

SYMPTOMS AND SIGNS   The athlete is unable to move the shoulder, especially in abduction; rotation and muscle atrophy also may ensue because of disuse.

MANAGEMENT   Management of low-grade inflammatory conditions must be initiated somewhat empirically. In some instances both the superficial heat from moist pads or infrared rays and the deep heat of diathermy or ultrasound are beneficial. In other instances heat may be aggravating, so cold applications by cold pack may be more useful. Whatever the mode of treatment, the athlete must maintain a consistent program of exercise, with the emphasis placed on regaining a full range of motion, so that muscle contractures and adhesions do not immobilize the joint.

The *"frozen shoulder"* is a condition more characteristic of an older person, but occasionally it does occur in the athlete. It results from a chronically irritated shoulder joint that has had improper care. Constant, generalized inflammation causes degeneration of the soft tissues in the vicinity of the shoulder joint, resulting in an extreme limitation of movement. The main care of the frozen shoulder is a combination of deep heat therapy and mobilization exercise.

Fractures of the Shoulder Complex

Fractures in the shoulder complex can be caused directly by a blow on the bone or indirectly by a fall on either an outstretched arm or the point of the shoulder.

Clavicular Fractures

Clavicular fractures (Figure 23-28) are one of the most frequent fractures in sports. More than 80% occur in the middle third of the clavicle, which lacks ligamentous support.

More than 80% of all fractures to the clavicle occur in its middle third.

Figure 23-28

Clavicular fracture. **A,**
Associated brachial blood
vessels and nerves. **B,** X-ray
film of a comminuted
clavicular fracture.

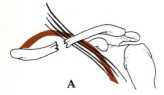

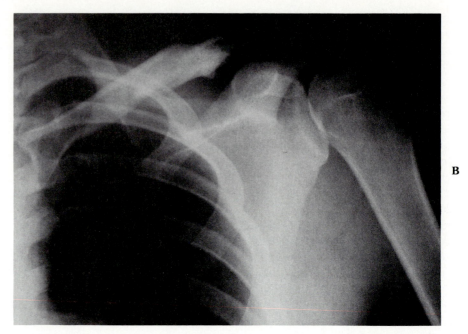

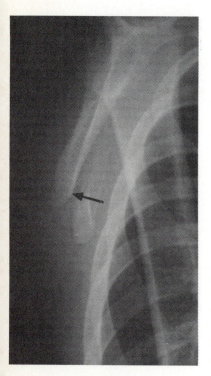

Figure 23-29

Fractures of the scapula are
infrequent in sports.

ETIOLOGICAL FACTORS   Clavicular fractures are caused by either a direct blow
or a transmitted force resulting from a fall on the outstretched arm. In junior and
senior high school athletes these fractures are usually the greenstick type.

SYMPTOMS AND SIGNS   The athlete with a fractured clavicle usually supports
the arm on the injured side and tilts his or her head toward that side, with the
chin turned to the opposite side. During inspection the injured clavicle appears a
little lower than the unaffected side. Palpation may also reveal swelling and mild
deformity.

MANAGEMENT   The clavicular fracture is cared for immediately by applying a
sling and swathe bandage and by treating the athlete for shock, if necessary. The
athlete is then referred to a physician, who in most instances will perform an x-
ray examination of the area and then apply a shoulder figure 8 wrapping that
will stabilize the shoulder in an upward and backward position.

Scapular Fractures

Fracture of the scapula is an infrequent injury in sports (Figure 23-29). Although
the scapula appears extremely vulnerable to trauma, it is well protected by a
heavy outer bony border and a cushion of muscle above and below. Those fractures that do occur happen as a result of force applied to the hand, elbow, or
shoulder joint. The fracture usually occurs when the humerus carries a force to
the scapula, as the serratus anterior muscle violently pulls the scapula forward at
the same time. Such a fracture may cause the athlete to have pain during shoulder movement, swelling, and point tenderness. When this injury is suspected, the
athlete should be given a supporting sling and sent directly to the sports physician.

Thoracic Outlet Compression Syndrome

A number of neurovascular problems that involve compression of the brachial plexus and subclavian artery can occur in the neck and shoulder.

ETIOLOGICAL FACTORS   Four possible causes have been identified:

1. Compression over a cervical rib
2. Spasm of the anterior scalene muscle
3. Compression of the brachial plexus, subclavian artery, and subclavian vein in the narrowed space between the first rib and clavicle (neurovascular bundle)
4. Compression of the smaller pectoral muscle over the subclavian and axillary vessels and brachial plexus as they pass beneath the coracoid process or between the clavicle and first rib

These problems may be attributed to a cervical rib anomaly—a supernumerary rib originating from a cervical vertebra and the thoracic rib.[12]

SYMPTOMS AND SIGNS   Abnormal pressure on the subclavian artery, subclavian vein, and brachial plexus produces a variety of symptoms[12]:

1. Paresthesia and pain
2. Sensation of cold
3. Impaired circulation that could lead to gangrene of the fingers
4. Muscle weakness
5. Muscle atrophy
6. Radial nerve palsy

Three tests can be given to determine vascular compression: the anterior scalene test, the costoclavicular test, and the hyperabduction test (p. 747).

MANAGEMENT   A conservative approach should be taken with early and mild cases of thoracic outlet syndromes. Conservative treatment is favorable in 50% to 80% of cases.[12]

The following measures may prove helpful:

1. Sling support and tension reduction
2. Anti-inflammatory medication
3. Exercises to strengthen the trapezius, serratus anterior, and erector muscles of the spine
4. Postural correction, especially in cases of drooped shoulders (Postural exercise should consist of those exercises that stretch and strengthen the muscles of the neck and shoulder girdle [Table 23-2].)

A number of neurovascular problems can occur within the thoracic outlet of the shoulder.

TABLE 23-2 Thoracic Outlet Syndrome Exercise

Stretch	Muscles Strengthened	Other Activities
Lateral neck	Serratus anterior	Codman's series
Neck rotation	Shoulder abduction	Deep breathing
Pectoralis muscle	Mid-trapezius	
Scalenus muscle	Shoulder shrug	
	Erector spinae	

UPPER-ARM CONDITIONS

The upper arm can sustain varied stress and trauma, depending on the nature of the sport. Crushing blows may be directed to the area by collision and contact sports; severe strain can be imposed by the throwing sports and sports such as gymnastics that afford muscle resistance.

Contusions

Contusions of the upper arm are frequent in contact sports. Although any muscle of the upper arm is subject to bruising, the area most often affected is the lateral aspect, primarily the brachial muscle and portions of the triceps and biceps muscles.

SYMPTOMS AND SIGNS   Bruises to the upper arm area can be particularly handicapping, especially if the radial nerve is contused through forceful contact with the humerus, producing transitory paralysis and consequent inability to use the extensor muscles of the forearm.

MANAGEMENT   Cold and pressure should be applied from 1 to 24 hours after injury, followed by cryotherapy or superficial heat therapy and massage. In most cases this condition responds rapidly to treatment, usually within a few days. If swelling and irritation last more than 2 or 3 weeks, *myositis ossificans* may have been stimulated, and massage must be stopped and protection afforded the athlete during sports participation.

Strains

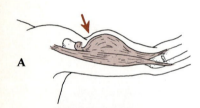

Acute and chronic strains are common in the arm. The muscles most commonly affected are the biceps, triceps, and pectoral muscles. Management of acute problems should follow usual procedures in immediate management. Two conditions that are unique to the arm area are bicipital tenosynovitis and biceps brachii rupture.

Bicipital Tenosynovitis

Tenosynovitis of the long head of the biceps muscle is common among athletes who execute a throwing movement as part of their event.

ETIOLOGICAL FACTORS   Bicipital tenosynovitis is more prevalent among pitchers, tennis players, and javelin throwers, for whom the repeated forced internal rotations of the upper arm may produce a chronic inflammatory condition in the vicinity of the synovial sheath of the long head of the biceps muscle. Complete rupture of the transverse ligament, which holds the biceps in its groove, may take place, or a constant inflammation may result in degenerative scarring or a subluxated tendon.

SYMPTOMS AND SIGNS   The athlete may complain of an ache in the anterior and medial areas of the shoulder; deep palpation reveals point tenderness in the region of the bicipital tendon.

MANAGEMENT   Such conditions are best cared for by a period of complete rest for 1 to 2 weeks, with daily applications of cryotherapy or ultrasound. After the initial aching has gone, a gradual program of reconditioning is begun.

Biceps Brachii Ruptures

Figure 23-30

A, Biceps brachii rupture.
B, Performing the iron cross on the rings can produce a biceps brachii rupture.

Ruptures of the biceps brachii (Figure 23-30) occur mainly in gymnasts who are engaged in power moves. The rupture commonly occurs near the origin of the muscle. The athlete usually hears a resounding snap and feels a sudden, intense pain at the point of injury. A protruding bulge may appear near the middle of the biceps. When asked to flex the elbow joint of the injured arm, the gymnast displays a definite weakness. Treatment should include immediately applying a cold pack to control hemorrhage, placing the arm in a sling, and referring the athlete to the physician. Surgical repair is usually indicated.

Fractures

Fractures of the humeral shaft (Figure 23-31) happen occasionally in sports, usually as the result of a direct blow or a fall on the arm. The type of fracture is usually comminuted or transverse, and a deformity is often produced because the bone fragments override each other as a result of strong muscular pull.

The pathological process is characteristic of most uncomplicated fractures, excpet that there may be a tendency for the radial nerve, which encircles the humeral shaft, to be severed by jagged bone edges, resulting in radial nerve paralysis and causing wrist drop and inability to perform forearm supination.

Recognition of this injury requires immediate application of a splint, treatment for shock, and referral to a physician. The athlete will be out of competition for approximately 3 to 4 months.

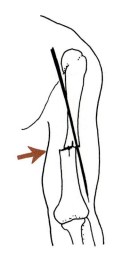

Figure 23-31

Humeral shaft fracture.

Fracture of the Upper Humerus

Fractures of the upper humerus (Figure 23-32) pose considerable danger to nerves and vessels of that area.

ETIOLOGICAL FACTORS Fractures of the humerus can result from a direct blow, a dislocation, or the impact received in falling onto the outstretched arm. Various parts of the end of the humerus may be involved, such as the anatomical neck, tuberosities, or surgical neck. This fracture may be mistaken for a shoulder dislocation. The greatest number of fractures take place at the surgical neck.

SYMPTOMS AND SIGNS It may be difficult to recognize a fracture of the upper humerus by visual inspection alone; therefore x-ray examination gives the only positive proof. Some of the more prevalent signs that may be present are pain, inability to move the arm, swelling, point tenderness, and discoloration of the superficial tissue. Because of the proximity of the axillary blood vessels and the brachial plexus, a fracture to the upper end of the humerus may result in severe hemorrhaging or paralysis.

MANAGEMENT A suspected fracture of this type warrants immediate support with a sling and swathe bandage and referral to a physician. Incapacitation may range from 2 to 6 months.

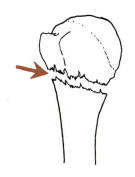

Figure 23-32

Fracture of the upper humerus.

Epiphyseal Fracture

Epiphyseal fracture of the head of the humerus (Figure 23-33) is much more common in the young athlete than is a bone fracture. An epiphyseal injury in the shoulder region occurs most frequently in individuals 10 years of age and younger. It is caused by a direct blow or by an indirect force traveling along the length of the axis of the humerus. This condition causes shortening of the arm, disability, swelling, point tenderness, and pain. There also may be a false joint. This type of injury should be suspected when the above signs appear in young athletes. Initial treatment should include splinting and immediate referral to a physician. Healing is initiated rapidly; immobilization is necessary for only approximately 3 weeks. The main danger of this injury lies in the possibility of damage to the epiphyseal growth centers of the humerus.

Figure 23-33

Epiphyseal fracture.

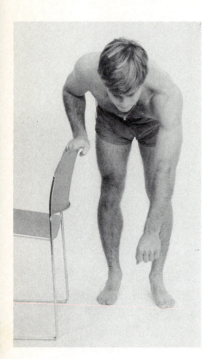

Figure 23-34

Codman's pendular exercise.

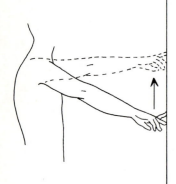

Figure 23-35

Finger wall climb.

REHABILITATION OF THE SHOULDER COMPLEX

The shoulder complex and especially the glenohumeral joint have a tendency to become highly restricted in motion after an injury and/or immobilization. In some cases, serious injury and immobilization lead to contractures and a tendency to develop fibrosis of the articular capsule. To prevent these problems, pain-free mobility is started as soon as possible without aggravating the injury.

Shoulder rehabilitation is highly complicated and depends on the nature of the injury and whether surgery has been performed. In general, rehabilitation progresses through early intermediate, and advanced exercise stages. Types of exercise can include isometrics, isotonics, isokinetics, stretching, or manual resistance using the principles of PNF. Often, all six are used in rehabilitation. Rotator cuff and impingement injuries, glenohumeral dislocations and subluxations, and acromioclavicular injuries are discussed to provide the student with an example of shoulder rehabilitation.

Rotator Cuff Injury Rehabilitation
Early Rehabilitation

At this stage, the rotator cuff is in a state of constriction after an injury or surgery. The primary goals are to establish pain-free active movement and minimum strength. TENS may be effective in reducing minor pain while exercising.

Ball squeeze   The athlete squeezes a tennis ball while performing pain-free shoulder movements in a sequence from abduction to flexion to external rotation and then moving to adduction, extension, and internal rotation (see Figure 24-56). This exercise is performed twice daily, 10 times in each direction.

Codman's pendular exercise   While bent over with the arm fully extended and the shoulder relaxed, the athlete moves the shoulder first in small circles in each direction and then in straight-line movements of flexion-extension and adduction-abduction. The distance of the swing is gradually increased. Exercises are performed twice daily with 10 movements in each direction (Figure 23-34).

Bar hang   The athlete grasps a horizontal bar overhead while supporting the body weight and standing on a chair. Gradually, the athlete allows the shoulder to take some of the body weight until it can take the entire weight without pain. The bar hang is performed one to three times for a count of five to 10 daily. NOTE: The bar hang, even in the last stages of rotator cuff rehabilitation, may cause impingement.

Finger wall climb   Standing an arm's distance away from a wall, the athlete finger-walks up until there is pain. The first walking occurs while the athlete stands facing the wall and then stands sideways to the wall. This is performed two or three times, twice daily (Figure 23-35).

Intermediate Rehabilitation

The athlete begins the intermediate phase of rehabilitation when the shoulder is pain free during muscle contraction. The goals of this stage are to increase range of motion and strength to almost preinjury status.

Codman's pendular exercise with resistance   Light dumbbell resistance is added to Codman's pendular exercise. As the weight is increased, the athlete stands upright, directing the dumbbell upward and outward and then upward and inward (Figure 23-36). The exercises are performed twice daily, 10 times in each direction.

Shoulder wheel   The shoulder wheel provides an excellent means of gaining both shoulder flexibility and strength. The athlete stands sideways to the wheel and performs 10 repetitions in each direction (Figure 23-37). The exercises are repeated two or three times and performed three or four times a week.

Dumbbell stretches   The athlete lies supine on a table or bench. Holding a 2- to 5-pound dumbbell in the hand with the elbow bent 90 degrees and the shoulder abducted 90 degrees, the athlete externally rotates as far as possible (Figure 23-38). Each stretch is maintained for 20 to 30 seconds and repeated two or three times.

The next exercise takes place with the athlete supine and the arm externally rotated and elevated 135 degrees in the frontal plane. The elbow is extended. While holding the dumbbell, the arm is extended as far as possible overhead.[15]

Figure 23-37

Reconditioning with the shoulder wheel.

Figure 23-36

Codman's pendular exercise with resistance.

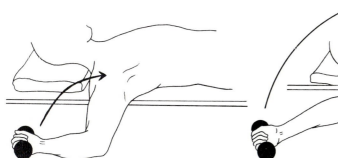

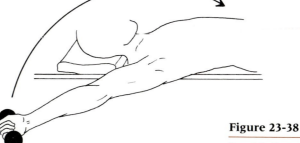

Figure 23-38

Dumbbell stretches.

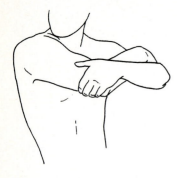

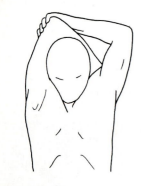

Self-stretching   To stretch the posterior capsule, the athlete moves the arm to 90 degrees of flexion and with the opposite hand pulls the elbow into horizontal adduction.[15] The exercise is performed twice daily, two or three times, holding each stretch for 20 to 30 seconds.

The inferior capsule is next stretched by placing the arm overhead as far as possible with the elbow flexed. The other hand grasps the opposite elbow to initiate the stretch[15] (Figure 23-39).

Dumbbell exercises   Strengthening the supraspinous muscle entails having the athlete sit with the arms abducted 90 degrees, horizontally flexed 30 degrees, and internally rotated. The athlete then lifts and lowers a dumbbell in each hand. The exercise is performed 10 times and repeated two or three times, three or four times a week.

To exercise the infraspinous and teres minor muscles, the athlete lies on the side, with the arm close to the body and the elbow bent 90 degrees. From a position of internal rotation, the athlete externally rotates the arm as far as possible (Figure 23-40). This exercise is repeated 10 times, twice for three sets, three or four times a week.

To exercise the subscapular muscle, the athlete lies supine, with the arm close to the side and the elbow flexed 90 degrees. From a position of full external rotation, the dumbbell is internally rotated as far as possible. The exercise is performed 10 times for two or three sets, three or four times a week.

Figure 23-39

Self-stretching.

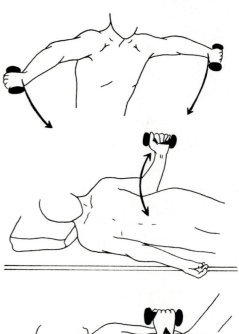

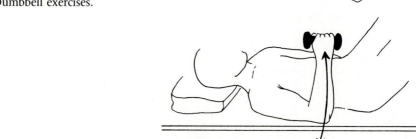

Figure 23-40

Dumbbell exercises.

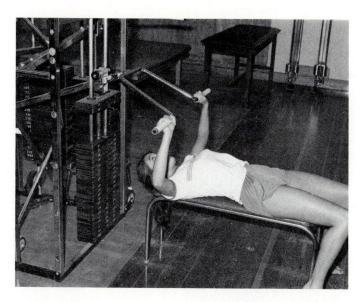

Figure 23-41

Bench presses.

Bench presses   The athlete progresses slowly from supporting a barbell or Universal weight in a bench-press position in a "locked-out" position (Figure 23-41). Gradually, the athlete begins to bend the elbows until a press can be performed from a full range of motion. Ten presses are performed for two or three sets, three times a week.

Upright rowing   A barbell is grasped in its center with both hands raised to a position underneath the athlete's chin (Figure 23-42). The exercise is performed 10 times for two or three sets, three times a week.

Isokinetic exercises   Isokinetic exercises also can be beneficial at this stage of rehabilitation. The athlete engages in shoulder flexion, abduction, adduction, internal and external rotation, elbow extension and flexion, and horizontal adduction and abduction (Figure 23-43).

Advanced Rehabilitation

Once the athlete has progressed to the advanced stage, there is full range of motion and near-normal strength. The purpose of advanced rehabilitation is to restore the athlete to competitive fitness. One program to develop extra strength along with flexibility might include the following:

1. Dumbbell alternate presses or barbell presses behind the neck
2. Dumbbell bench presses, incline dumbbell presses, flyers, or parallel bar dips
3. Bent-arm pullovers with a barbell
4. High pulls with a snatch grip
5. Straight-arm barbell pullovers with a weight of 30 pounds (grip progressively wider, with the weight remaining the same)

Exercise Rehabilitation after Rotatory Cuff Surgery

Exercise rehabilitation is begun the day after surgery.[10] The following is one rehabilitation approach for a pitcher recovering from rotator cuff surgery[10]:

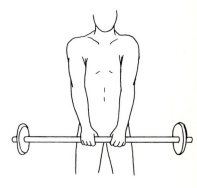

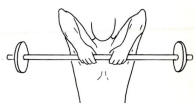

Figure 23-42

Upright rowing.

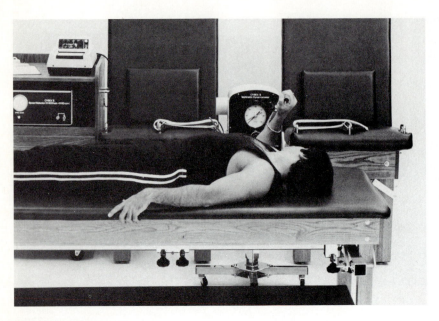

Figure 23-43

Shoulder exercises using the Cybex isokinetic system.

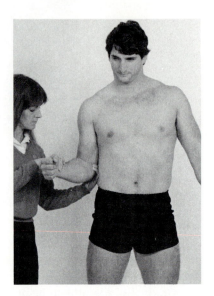

Figure 23-44

Strengthening the subscapular muscle for internal rotation.

1. Passive shoulder abduction and external rotation are performed in the first month.
2. Active asssistive exercise takes place during the second month.
3. Active range of motion, stretching, and more difficult exercises are performed from the third month on.
4. When full range of movement is acquired, usually by the end of the third month, throwing a ball for 30 feet is permitted.
5. During the fourth and fifth months, throwing distances are increased slowly.
6. In the sixth month, three-fourths speed throwing is allowed.
7. The seventh to twelfth months are spent in regaining general physical strength and endurance.
8. By the twelfth month, competitive pitching is allowed.

Glenohumeral Dislocation and Subluxation Rehabilitation

Exercise must be cautiously performed. For athletes who have not had surgery, exercise should be performed as follows:

1. In cases of anterior dislocation, avoid positions of abduction and external rotation and emphasize adduction, forward flexion, and internal rotation.
2. In cases of posterior dislocation, avoid positions of abduction and internal rotation.
3. Avoid wide barbell grips or dumbbell positions.
4. Exercises performed on a bench should be executed only in the top third of the movement.

5. Pressing exercises should be performed in the lower half of the range.
6. For the anterior glenohumeral dislocation, special emphasis should be paid to strengthening the subscapular and teres major muscles for internal rotation (Figure 23-44).
7. Exercise programming, in general, follows that for rotator cuff rehabilitation.

Acromioclavicular Injury Rehabilitation
Early Rehabilitation

Early rehabilitation begins after the acute stage of injury or after surgical intervention and stays within pain-free limits. Because of tightness and/or weakness, the trapezius, pectoral, deltoid, latissimus dorsi, and arm muscles receive major emphasis.

Shoulder range of motion   Shoulder range of motion is gently increased first through free movements that include flexion, abduction, and internal and external rotation. Each movement is repeated five to 10 times, twice daily. When these movements can be performed pain free, the athlete progresses to a towel-stretch sequence, including raising the arms overhead and stretching behind the back (Figure 23-45).

Light-resistance shrugs   The athlete exercises the upper trapezius muscle by performing shrugs against a light dumbbell resistance. **NOTE:** The weight should not be allowed to hang loosely, which strains the acromioclavicular joint. Light-resistance shrugs are performed five to 10 times, twice daily (Figure 23-46). This exercise should take the shoulder from an anterior position to elevation (shrugs) and then to a posterior position.

Upright rowing with light resistance   For strenghthening the anterior deltoid muscle, the athlete performs upright rowing against a light resistance. Each exercise is performed for five to 10 repetitions, twice daily.

Resistance exercises for arm biceps and triceps muscles   Elbow curls and extensions are performed with dumbbell resistance. The weight of the dumb-

Figure 23-45

Improving shoulder range of motion through towel exercising.

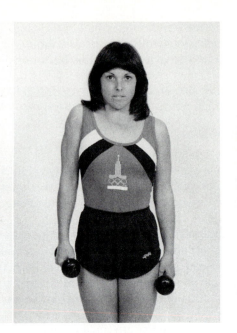

Figure 23-46

Dumbbell shoulder shrugs.

Figure 23-47

Shoulder shrugs with heavier resistance.

bell should not be so much as to pull the shoulder downward. Each exercise is repeated five to 10 times, twice daily.

Codman's pendular exercises   As in Figures 23-34 and 23-36, the athlete performs free exercise of Codman's pendular movement with limited weight. Movements are performed in a limited, pain-free range. This exercise is performed twice daily, and each movement is repeated five to 10 times.

Intermediate Rehabilitation

When the shoulder is pain free and has almost full range of motion, intermediate rehabilitation can begin. Exercise can now be performed with more resistance and vigor.

Shrugs with heavier resistance   Shoulder shrugs are performed against heavier resistance, such as that provided by the Universal apparatus (Figure 23-47). The emphasis is on the strength development of the upper trapezius muscle. This exercise is performed in two or three sets of 10 repetitions, three or four times a week.

Dumbbell exercises   A variety of exercises with progressively heavier dumbbells are performed as indicated in Figure 23-48. These exercises are performed in two or three sets of 10 repetitions, three or four times a week.

Overhead presses   Pressing a resistance overhead is valuable for strengthening the anterior deltoid muscle. Using a barbell or the Universal apparatus, the athlete presses as much weight as possible. This exercise is performed in two or three sets for 10 repetitions, three or four times a week (Figure 23-49).

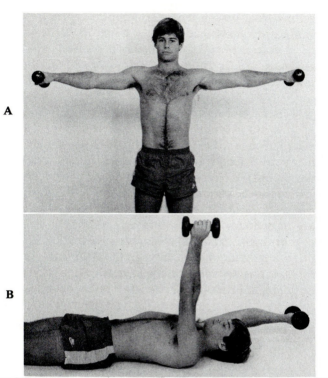

Figure 23-48

Variations in dumbbell exercise. **A,** Abduction. **B,** Flexion. **C,** Extension. **D,** Presses. **E,** Chest crosses.

Figure 23-49

Overhead press.

Figure 23-50

Push-ups.

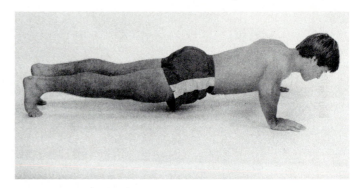

A   **B**   **C**

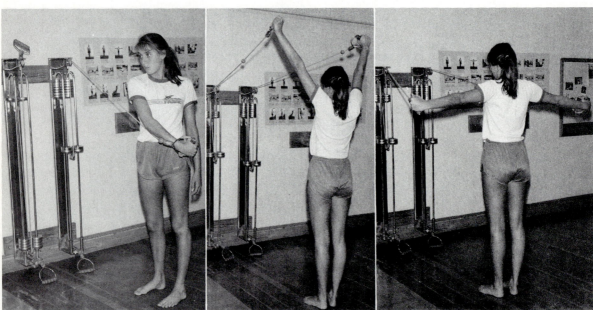

Figure 23-51

Variations in pulley exercises. **A,** Cross-chest pulley
exercise. **B,** High shoulder flexion. **C,** Horizontal abduction.

Push-ups   Push-ups are an excellent way to strengthen the shoulder complex, especially the anterior aspect of the shoulder and chest. Pushups are performed in two or three sets for 10 repetitions, three or four times a week (Figure 23-50).

Pulley exercises   Pulley exercises provide excellent intermediate rehabilitation for an acromioclavicular injury. Some of the possible exercises available are depicted in Figure 23-51. Each exercise should be conducted for two or three sets with 10 repetitions in each set, three or four times a week.

Dips and pull-ups   Parallel bar dips and horizontal bar pull-ups are also excellent intermediate exercises for shoulder rehabilitation. As with the other exercises, they should be performed in two or three sets of 10 repetitions, three or four times a week.

PNF for Shoulder Rehabilitation

PNF provides an excellent means of shoulder rehabilitation after an athletic injury. The principles of slow reversal described in Chapter 14 can help the injured shoulder develop strength and coordination.

SUMMARY

The shoulder complex is a highly complicated anatomical region that can sustain numerous sports injuries. Preventing shoulder complex injuries requires general body conditioning and specific conditioning for the demands of an individual sport. Proper warm-up and learning how to fall can also help prevent shoulder complex injuries.

Overuse injuries to the shoulder commonly stem from faulty form in pitching, tennis serving and overhead smashing, and swimming the crawl or butterfly stroke.

Contusions commonly occur to the soft tissue surrounding the shoulder complex, as well as to the clavicular region. Strains and impingements are common in sports that use the arms to overcome resistance or to propel objects. The rotator cuff muscles are common sites for strains and impingements. Sprains of the shoulder complex can occur at the sternoclavicular, acromioclavicular, and shoulder joints.

Shoulder joint dislocation is the second most common dislocation in sports. The most common dislocation is the anterior glenohumeral dislocation. The athlete displays a flattened deltoid contour and carries the arm in slight abduction and external rotation.

The shoulder joint is also subject to the chronic problem of bursitis. Bursitis can stem from overuse or a sudden strain. The most often injured is the subacromial bursa, which lies underneath the deltoid muscle and articular capsule and extends under the acromion process.

Fractures of the shoulder complex region can be caused directly by a blow to the bone or indirectly by a fall on either an outstretched arm or the point of a shoulder. The most prevalent fracture occurs to the clavicle.

Injuries to the upper arm include contusions, strains, and fractures. A relatively common chronic strain, called bicipital tenosynovitis, occurs to the tendon of the long head of the biceps. This tendon also can become ruptured. Fracture of the upper humeral shaft occurs only occasionally in sports, usually from a direct blow or a fall on the outstretched arm. A more common fracture site is the epiphysis of the humeral head of young athletes.

REVIEW QUESTIONS AND CLASS ACTIVITIES

1. How can shoulder injuries be prevented? Include conditioning and preventive equipment in your answer.
2. What are the usual causes of shoulder complex overuse injuries? How can some be related to improper throwing techniques?
3. Describe the shoulder point injury.
4. How can the supraspinatus muscle be injured? List the stages of injury.
5. Differentiate between the signs of a sternoclavicular sprain and an acromioclavicular sprain.
6. Describe the appearance of a glenohumeral sprain and differentiate it from a dislocation.
7. Why may a first-time shoulder joint dislocation be associated with a fracture?
8. Identify the reasons why glenohumeral subluxations and dislocations tend to recur. How are they commonly treated?
9. Why does the subacromial bursa develop chronic inflammation? Can this condition be prevented?
10. Discuss the symptoms and signs of a fractured clavicle.
11. How may an athlete acquire bicipital tenosynovitis? How does this condition lead to a ruptured biceps tendon?
12. Develop an exercise rehabilitation program for a rotator cuff injury; a glenohumeral dislocation; an acromioclavicular sprain.

REFERENCES

1. Bowers, KD: Treatment of acromioclavicular sprains in athletes, Phys Sportsmed 11:79, Jan 1983.
2. Brunet, ME, Haddad, RJ, and Porche, EB: Rotator cuff impingement syndromes in sports, Phys Sportsmed 10:86, Dec 1982.
3. Cain, TA, et al.: Anterior stability of the glenohumeral joint, Am J Sports Med 15:144, 1987.
4. Ciullo, JV: Swimmer's shoulder, Clinics in sports medicine, vol 5, no 1, Philadelphia, 1986, WB Saunders Co.
5. Grana, WA, et al.: How I manage acute anterior shoulder dislocations, Phys Sportsmed 15(4):88, 1987.
6. Hart, DL, and Carmichael, SW: Biomechanics of the shoulder, J Orthop Sports Phys Ther 6:229, Jan/Feb 1985.
7. Hawkins, RJ, and Hobeika, PE: Impingement syndrome in the athletic shoulder, Symposium on injuries to the shoulder in the athlete, Clinics in sports medicine, vol 2, no 2, Philadelphia, 1983, WB Saunders Co.
8. Henry, JH, and Genung, JA: Natural history of glenohumeral dislocation—revisited, Am J Sports Med 10(3):135, 1982.
9. Hill, JA: Overuse syndromes of the shoulder in athletes, Sports Med Dig 8(3):1, 1986.
10. Jobe FW: Serious rotator cuff injuries, Symposium on injuries to the shoulder in the athlete, Clinics in sports medicine, vol 2, no 2, Philadelphia, 1983, WB Saunders Co.
11. Jobe, FW, and Moynes, D: Delineation of diagnostic criteria and a rehabilitation program for the rotator cuff injuries, Am J Sports Med 10:336, 1982.
12. Lutz, Jr FR, and Gieck, JH: Thoracic outlet compression syndrome, Ath Train 21:302, 1986.
13. Matsen, FA, and Zuckerman, JD: Anterior glenohumeral instability, Symposium on injuries to the shoulder in the athlete, Clinics in sports medicine, vol 2, no 2, Philadelphia, 1983, WB Saunders Co.
14. McMaster, WC: Painful shoulder in swimmers: a diagnostic challenge, Phys Sportsmed 14(12):108, 1986.
15. Moynes, DR: Prevention of injury to the shoulder through exercises and therapy, Symposium on injuries to the shoulder in the athlete, Clinics in sports medicine, vol 2, no 2, Philadelphia, 1983, WB Saunders Co.

16. Richardson, AB: Overuse syndrome in baseball, tennis, gymnastics and swimming, Symposium on injuries to the shoulder in the athlete, Clinics in sports medicine, vol 2, no 2, Philadelphia, 1983, WB Saunders Co.

17. Salter, EG, et al.: Anatomical observations on the acromioclavicular joint and supporting ligaments, Am J Sports Med 15(3):199, 1987.

18. Samilson, RL, and Prieto, V: Posterior dislocation of the shoulder in athletes, Symposium on injuries to the shoulder in the athlete, Clinics in sports medicine, vol 2, no 2, Philadelphia, 1983, WB Saunders Co.

19. Schenkman, M, and Rugo de Cartaya, V: Kinesiology of the shoulder complex, J Orthop Sports Phys Ther 8:438, 1987.

20. Strauss, MD, et al: The shrugged-off shoulder: a comparison of paitents with recurrent shoulder subluxations and dislocations, Phys Sportsmed 11:85, March 1983.

21. Tank, R, and Halbach, J: Physical therapy evaluation of the shoulder complex in athletes, J Orthop Sports Phys Ther 3:108, Winter 1982.

22. Travell, JG, and Simons, DG: Myofascial pain and dysfunction, Baltimore, 1983, The Williams & Wilkins Co.

23. Tullos, HS, and Bennett, JB: The shoulder in sports. In Scott, WN, et al., editors: Principles of sports medicine, Baltimore, 1984, The Williams & Wilkins Co.

24. Warren, RF: Subluxation of the shoulder in athletes, Symposium on injuries to the shoulder in the athlete, Clinics in sports medicine, vol 2, no 2, Philadelphia, 1983, WB Saunders Co.

25. Wickiewicz, TL: Acromioclavicular and sternoclavicular injuries, Symposium on injuries to the shoulder in the athlete, Clinics in sports medicine, vol 2, no 2, Philadelphia, 1983, WB Saunders Co.

26. Wickiewicz, TL: The impingement syndrome, Postgraduate advances in sports medicine, I-V, Pennington, NJ, 1986, Forum Medicus, Inc.

27. Yocum, LA: Assessment of the shoulder, Symposium on injuries to the shoulder in the athlete, Clinics in sports medicine, vol 2, no 2, Philadelphia, 1983, WB Saunders Co.

ANNOTATED BIBLIOGRAPHY

American Academy of Orthopaedic Surgeons: Symposium on upper extremity injuries in athletes, St. Louis, 1986, The CV Mosby Co.
Covers basic anatomy, biomechanics, surgical and nonsurgical treatment, and detailed rehabilitation relating to upper-extremity injuries in sports.

Cailliet, R: Soft tissue pain and disability, Philadelphia, 1977, FA Davis Co.
Provides an excellent overview of the major conditions causing shoulder pain and their management in the chapter on shoulder pain.

Cailliet, R: Shoulder pain, ed 2, Philadelphia, 1981, FA Davis Co.
Covers the shoulder complex in detail, including its functional anatomy and major acute and chronic conditions.

Jobe, FW, editor: Symposium on injuries to the shoulder in the athlete, Clinics in sports medicine, vol 2, no 2, Philadelphia, 1983, WB Saunders Co.
A complete monograph on the athletic shoulder, including chapters about biomechanics, injury assessment, and epidemiology, and a discussion of the major shoulder injuries.

24

The Elbow, Forearm, Wrist, and Hand

When you finish this chapter, you should be able to

Describe the structural and functional anatomy of the elbow, forearm, wrist, and hand and relate it to sports injuries

Recognize and evaluate the major sports injuries to the elbow, forearm, wrist, and hand

Perform proper immediate and follow-up management of upper-limb injuries

The upper limb, including the elbow, forearm, wrist, and hand, is second to the lower limb in the number of sports injuries. Because of how it is used and its relative exposure, the upper limb is prone to acute and over use syndromes.

THE ELBOW JOINT
Anatomy
Structural Relationships

The elbow joint is composed of three bones: the humerus, the radius, and the ulna (Figure 24-1). The lower end of the humerus forms two articulating condyles. The lateral condyle is the capitulum, and the medial condyle is the trochlea. The rounded capitulum articulates with the concave head of the radius. The trochlea, which is spool shaped, fits into an articulating groove, the semilunar notch, which is provided by the ulna between the olecranon and coronoid processes. Above each condyle is a projection called the epicondyle. The structural design of the elbow joint permits flexion and extension through the articulation of the trochlea with the semilunar notch of the ulna. Forearm pronation and supination are made possible because the head of the radius rests against the capitulum freely without any bone limitations.

The capsule of the elbow, both anteriorly and posteriorly, is relatively thin and is covered by the brachial muscle in front and the triceps brachii behind. The capsule is reinforced by the ulnar and radial collateral ligaments. The ulnar collateral ligament is composed of a strong anterior band with weaker transverse and middle sheets. The radial collateral ligament does not attach to the radius,

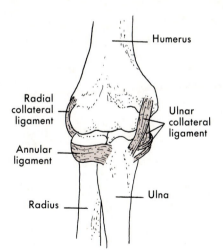

Figure 24-1

Bones and ligaments of the elbow.

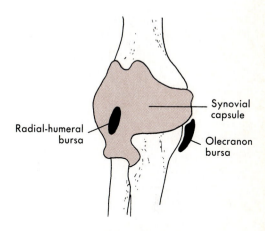

Figure 24-2

Synovium and bursa of the elbow.

which is free to rotate. The radius rotates in the radial notch of the ulna and is stabilized by a strong annular ligament. The annular ligament is attached to the anterior and posterior margins of the radial notch and encircles the head and neck of the radius.

Synovium and Bursa

A common synovial membrane invests the elbow and the superior radioulnar articulations, lubricating the deeper structures of the two joints; a sleevelike capsule surrounds the entire elbow joint. The most important bursae in the area of the elbow are the bicipital and olecranon bursae. The bicipital bursa lies in the anterior aspect of the bicipital tuberosity and cushions the tendon when the forearm is pronated. The olecranon bursa lies between the olecranon process and the skin, forming a liquid cushion (Figure 24-2).

Muscles

The muscles of the elbow consist of the biceps brachii and the brachial and brachioradial muscles, all of which in some way act in flexion. Extension is controlled by the triceps brachii muscle (Figure 24-3).

The biceps brachii and supinator muscles allow supination of the forearm, whereas the pronator teres and pronator quadratus act as pronators.

Blood and Nerve Supply

Superficial and close to the skin in front of the elbow lie the veins that return the blood of the forearm to the heart. Deep within the antecubital fossa lie the brachial and medial arteries that supply the area with oxygenated blood (Figure 24-4).

Nerves stemming from the fifth to eighth cervical vertebrae and first thoracic vertebra control the elbow muscles. In the cubital fossa these nerves become the musculocutaneous, radial, and median nerves (Table 24-1).

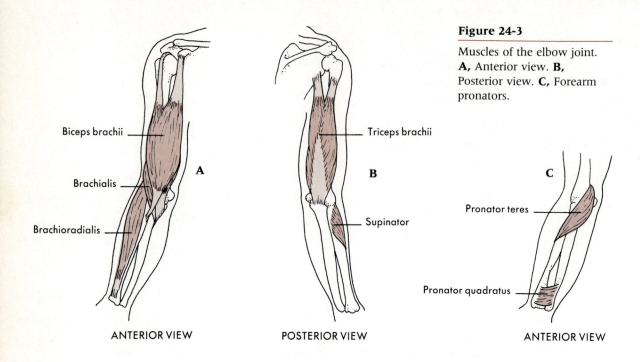

Figure 24-3

Muscles of the elbow joint.
A, Anterior view. **B,**
Posterior view. **C,** Forearm
pronators.

ANTERIOR VIEW   POSTERIOR VIEW   ANTERIOR VIEW

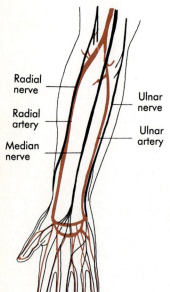

Figure 24-4

Arteries and nerves supplying
the elbow joint, wrist, and
hand.

TABLE 24-1 Resistive Motion to Determine Muscle Weakness Related to Elbow Injury

Resistive Motion	Major Muscles	Involved Nerves
Elbow flexion	Biceps brachii	Musculocutaneous (cervical 5 and 6)
	Brachial	Musculocutaneous (cervical 5 and 6)
	Brachioradial	Radial (cervical 5 and 6)
Elbow extension	Triceps brachii	Radial (cervical 7 and 8)
Forearm supination	Biceps brachii	Musculocutaneous (cervical 5 and 6)
	Supinator	Radial (cervical 6)
Forearm pronation	Pronator teres	Median (cervical 6 and 7)
	Pronator quadratus	Median (cervical 8, thoracic 1)

Assessment of the Elbow
Complaints

As with all sports injuries, the evaluator must first understand the possible mechanism of injury. The following questions will aid in evaluation of the elbow:

1. Is the pain or discomfort caused by a direct trauma such as falling on an outstretched arm or landing on the tip of a bent elbow?
2. Can the problem be attributed to sudden overextension of the elbow or to repeated overuse of a throwing-type motion?

The location and duration should be ascertained. As with shoulder pain, elbow pain or discomfort could be from internal organ dysfunction or referred from a nerve root irritation of nerve impingement.

1. Are there movements or positions of the arm that increase or decrease the pain?
2. Has a previous elbow injury been diagnosed or treated?
3. Is there a feeling of locking or crepitation during movement?

General Obervation

The athlete's elbow should be observed for obvious deformities and swelling. If permissible, the carrying angle, flexion, and extensibility of the elbow should be observed. If the carrying angle is abnormally increased, a cubitus valgus is present; if it is abnormally decreased, a cubitus varus is present (Figure 24-5). Too great or too little of an angle may be indication of a bony or epiphyseal fracture. The athlete is next observed for the extent of elbow flexion and extension. Both elbows are compared (Figure 24-6). A decrease in normal flexion, an inability to

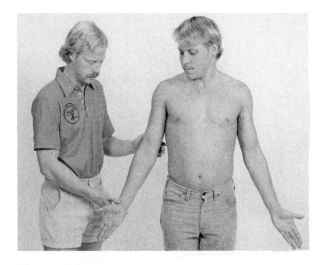

Figure 24-5

Testing for elbow carrying angle and the extent of cubitus valgus and cubitus varus.

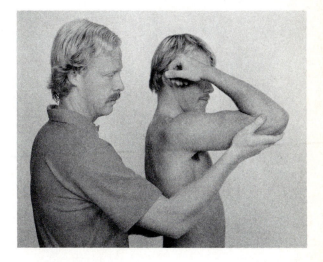

Figure 24-6

Testing for elbow flexion and extension.

extend fully, or extending beyond normal extension (cubitus recurvatus) could be precipitating reasons for joint problems (Figure 24-7). Next, the elbow is bent to a 45-degree angle and observed from the rear to determine whether or not the two epicondyles and olecranon process form an isosceles triangle (Figure 24-8).

Bony Palpation

Pain sites and deformities are determined through careful palpation of the epicondyles, olecranon process, distal aspect of the humerus, and proximal aspect of the ulna (Figure 24-9). The radial head also must be palpated, with the athlete's arm abducted and the elbow bent. The radial head is located approximately 1 inch (2.5 cm) distal to the lateral epicondyle. The athlete supinates and pronates the forearm while pressure is applied to the radial head. Pain during pressure may indicate a sprain of the annular ligament, a fracture, or a chronic articular condition of the radial head.

Figure 24-7

Determining whether the lateral and medial epicondyles, along with the olecranon process, form an isosceles triangle.

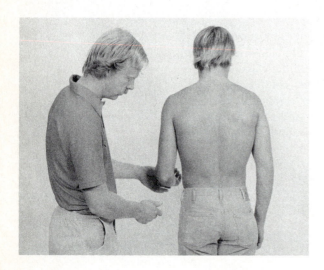

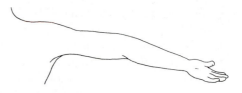

Figure 24-8

Testing for cubitus recurvatus (elbow hyperextension).

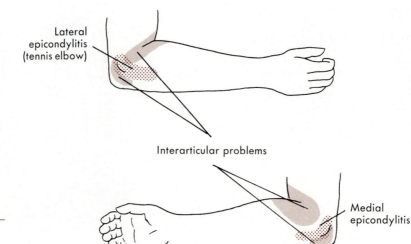

Lateral epicondylitis (tennis elbow)

Interarticular problems

Medial epicondylitis

Figure 24-9

Typical pain sites in the elbow region.

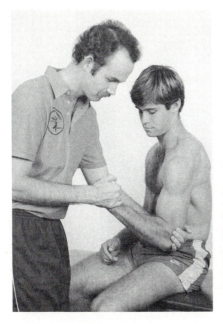

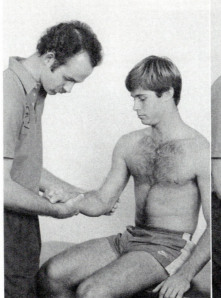

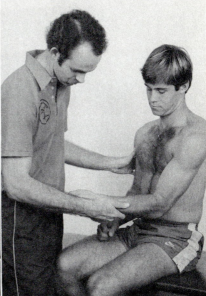

Figure 24-10   **Figure 24-11**

Soft-Tissue Palpation

Soft tissue includes the following:

1. Distal aspect of the wrist flexor muscles
2. Pronator teres muscle
3. Distal aspect of the wrist extensor muscles
4. Medial and lateral collateral ligaments
5. Brachioradial muscle
6. Biceps tendon
7. Antecubital fossa and its contents, including the brachial artery, pulses, and median nerve

Circulatory and Neurological Evaluation

With an elbow injury, a pulse routinely should be taken at the brachial artery, which is located in the antecubital fossa and the radial artery at the wrist.

Alteration of skin sensation also should be noted, which could indicate nerve root compression or irritation in the cervical or shoulder region or in the elbow itself. Additional nerve evaluation is made through testing active and resistive motion (see Table 24-1).

Functional Evaluation

The joint and the muscles are evaluated for pain sites and weakness through passive, active, and resistive motions, consisting of elbow flexion and extension (Figure 24-10) and forearm pronation and supination (Figure 24-11). Range of

Figure 24-10

Functional evaluation includes performing passive resistance flexion and extension to determine joint restrictions and pain sites.

Figure 24-11

Elbow evaluation includes performing passive, active, and resistive forearm pronation and supination.

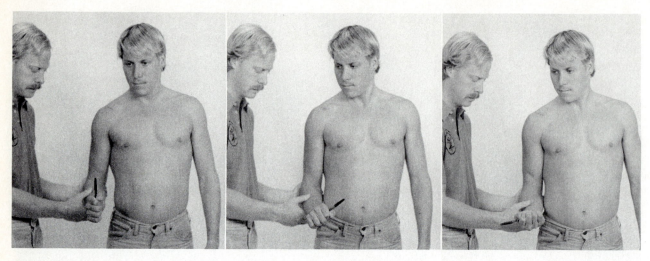

Figure 24-12

The range of motion of forearm pronation and supination is routinely observed in athletes with elbow conditions.

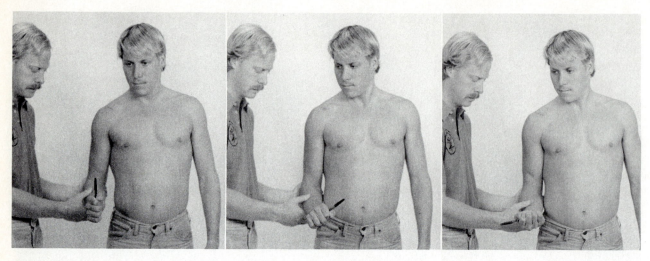

Pain site

Figure 24-13

Testing for capsular pain after hyperextension of the elbow. **A,** Wrist flexion. **B,** Wrist extension.

motion is particularly noted in passive and active pronation and supination (Figure 24-12).

Tests for Ligamentous and Capsular Injury

A test for capsular pain after hyperextension of the elbow is as follows:

1. Flex the elbow in a 45-degree position.
2. Flex the wrist as far as possible.
3. Extend the wrist as far as possible (Figure 24-13).

If joint pain is severe during this test, a moderate-to-severe sprain or fracture should be suspected.

The next test is for determining lateral and medial collateral ligamentous stability in the elbow. The following procedures should be conducted:

1. The evaluator grasps the athlete's wrist and extends the arm in an anatomical position.
2. The other hand of the evaluator is placed over either the lateral or medial epicondyle.
3. With the hand over the epicondyle acting as a fulcrum, the hand holding the athlete's wrist attempts to move the forearm.
4. In applying the stress, the evaluator notices whether there is an excursion or gapping of the lateral or medial collateral ligament (Figure 24-14).

SYMPTOMS AND SIGNS   The athlete complains of severe pain on the medial aspect of the elbow that becomes relieved by flexing the elbow. There is point tenderness on the medial epicondyle, distal aspect of the ulna, or lateral collateral ligament.

Tennis Elbow Test

Resistance is applied to the athlete's extended hand with the elbow flexed 45 degrees. A positive tennis elbow test will be moderate-to-severe pain at the lateral epicondyle (Figure 24-15).

Figure 24-14

Collateral ligament test of the elbow.

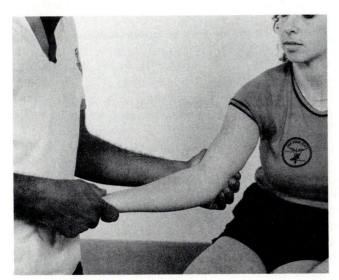

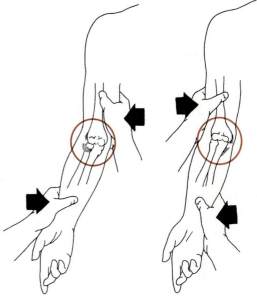

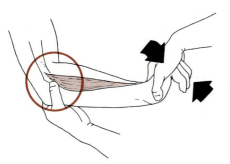

Figure 24-15

Tennis elbow test.

Mechanism of Elbow Injuries

As discussed in Chapter 7, elbow injuries can occur from a variety of mechanisms. The most common mechanisms of injury are overuse throwing and falling on the outstretched hand.

Injuries to the Elbow Region

The elbow is subject to injury in sports because of its broad range of motion, weak lateral bone arrangement, and relative exposure to soft-tissue damage in the vicinity of the joint.[23] Many sports place excessive stress on the elbow joint. Extreme locking of the elbow in gymnastics or using implements such as racquets, golf clubs, and javelins can cause injuries. The throwing mechanism in baseball pitching can injure the elbow during both the acceleration and follow-through phases.[16,24]

The two most common mechanisms of elbow injury
    Throwing
    Falling on the
        outstretched hand

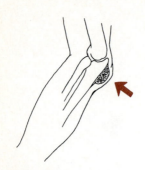

Figure 24-16

Olecranon bursitis.

Soft-Tissue Injuries Around the Elbow

Contusions   Because of its lack of padding and its general vulnerability, the elbow often becomes contused during contact sports. Bone bruises arise from a deep penetration or a succession of blows to the sharp projections of the elbow. A contusion of the elbow may swell rapidly after an irritation of the olecranon bursa or the synovial membrane and should be treated immediately with cold and pressure for at least 24 hours. If injury is severe, the athlete should be referred to a physician for x-ray examination to determine if a fracture exists.

Olecranon bursitis   The olecranon bursa (Figure 24-16), lying between the end of the olecranon process and the skin, is the most frequently injured bursa in the elbow. Its superficial location makes it prone to acute or chronic injury, particularly as the result of direct blows. The inflamed bursa produces pain, marked swelling, and point tenderness. Occasionally, swelling will appear almost spontaneously and without the usual pain and heat. If the condition is acute, a cold compress should be applied for at least 1 hour. Chronic olecranon bursitis requires a program of superficial therapy. In some cases, aspiration will hasten healing. Although seldom serious, olecranon bursitis can be annoying and should be well protected by padding while the athlete is engaged in competition.

Strains   The acute mechanisms of muscle strain associated with the elbow joint are usually excessive resistive motions such as a fall on the outstretched hand with the elbow in extension, forcing the joint into hyperextension. Repeated microtears that cause chronic injury are discussed under the section "Epicondylitis."

The biceps, brachial, and triceps muscles should be tested through active and resistive movement. The muscles of pronation and supination are also tested.

SYMPTOMS AND SIGNS   During active or resistive movement, the athlete complains of pain. There is usually point tenderness in the muscle, tendon, or lower part of the muscle belly.

MANAGEMENT   Immediate care includes ICE-R and sling support for the most severe cases. Follow-up management may include cryotherapy, ultrasound, and rehabilitative exercises. Conditions that cause moderate-to-severe loss of elbow function should routinely be referred for x-ray examination. It is important to rule out the possibility of an avulsion or epiphyseal fracture.

Elbow sprains   Sprains to the elbow are usually caused by hyperextension or valgus forces.

MANAGEMENT   Immediate care for elbow sprains consists of cold and a pressure bandage for at least 24 hours with sling support fixed at 45 degrees of flexion. After hemorrhage has been controlled, superficial heat treatments in the form of the whirlpool may be started and combined with massage above and below the injury. Like fractures and dislocations, strains also may result in abnormal bone proliferation if the area is massaged directly and too vigorously or is exercised too soon. The main concern should be to gently aid the elbow in regaining a full range of motion and then, when the time is right, to commence active exercises until full mobility and strength have returned. Taping can help and should restrain the elbow from further injury, or it may be used while the athlete is participating in sports (see Figure 12-27).

Epicondylitis   Epicondylitis is a chronic condition that may affect athletes who execute repeated forearm pronation and supination movements such as are performed in tennis, pitching, golf, javelin throwing, and fencing. The elbow is particularly predisposed to mechanical trauma in the activities of throwing and striking.

Epicondylitis is variously identified as "pitcher's elbow," "tennis elbow," "javelin thrower's arm," or "golfer's elbow." It is caused by the continuous forceful extension of the forearm accompanied by a severe twisting motion, such as when a pitcher throws a curve or screwball or when a tennis player applies English in returning a ball. The exact pathology is often difficult to determine. There are a number of possibilities that could elicit similar symptoms and signs (e.g., radio-humeral bursitis, periostitis of the common extensor tendon, or tendinitis of the common extensor or flexor tendon). Other causes having similar symptoms are myofasciitis, chrondromalacia of the elbow articulation, calcification in the region, or inflammation of other structures in the area.[19]

Pitcher's elbow   Baseball players who have begun pitching curve balls at too early an age appear especially vulnerable to pitcher's elbow. The constant, repetitive, and violent torsion and extension to which the elbow joint is subjected over a period of time, as in pitching a baseball game, results in the pronator teres muscle being torn from its origin on the lower aspect of the inner condyloid ridge of the humerus. Stress can also sprain and even rupture the medial collateral ligament. Inadequate warm-up before throwing is another cause of this condition.

Tennis elbow   In tennis players, improper techniques, poor conditioning, and a racket that is inappropriate for the level of play can cause severe stress in the elbow. Usually this syndrome is the result of continuous abuse, but on occasion it may result from a single incident.[17]

Javelin thrower's elbow   Javelin throwers, like baseball pitchers, can place a great deal of stress on the elbow. The medial collateral ligament can be sprained or ruptured; forceful extension of the elbow can fracture the olecranon process (Figure 24-17).

Common sports injuries that are forms of epicondylitis
  Pitcher's elbow
  Tennis elbow
  Javelin thrower's elbow
  Golfer's elbow

Figure 24-17

A, Repeated throwing actions can produce epicondylitis, a chronic elbow condition.
B, Javelin throwing places great strain on the elbow joint.

Golfer's elbow   The golfer's elbow (e.g., on a right-handed player) commonly involves microtears of the common flexor tendon of the medial condyle of the right elbow, much like tennis elbow, or it can occur in the lateral condyle of the leading left arm as the result of chronic strain of the extensor muscles.[10]

SYMPTOMS AND SIGNS OF EPICONDYLITIS   Regardless of the sport or exact location of the injury, the symptoms and signs of epicondylitis are similar. Pain around the lateral aspect of the epicondyle of the humerus is produced during pronation and supination. The pain may be centered at the epicondyle, or it may radiate down the arm. There is usually point tenderness and in some cases mild swelling. Passive movement of the arm in pronation and supination seldom elicits pain, although active movement does.

MANAGEMENT OF EPICONDYLITIS   Conservative management of moderate-to-severe epicondylitis usually includes use of a sling, rest, cryotherapy, and/or heat through the application of ultrasound. Analgesic and/or anti-inflammatory agents may be prescribed. A curvilinear brace applied just below the bend of the elbow is highly beneficial in reducing stress to the elbow. A conical brace provides counterforce, disseminating stress over a wide area and relieving the concentration of forces directly on the bony muscle attachments (Figure 24-18). For more severe cases elbow splinting and complete rest for 7 to 10 days may be warranted.[7] **NOTE:** In cases in which epicondylitis is related to tennis, there must be a concern for proper grip size and string tension.[1]

Elbow Osteochondritis Dissecans

> Elbow osteochondritis dissecans is similar to that in the knee but is less common.

Although osteochondritis dissecans is more common in knees, it also occurs in elbows. Its cause is unknown; however, impairment of the blood supply to the anterior surfaces leads to fragmentation and separation of a portion of the articular cartilage and bone, creating a loose body within the joint.

SYMPTOMS AND SIGNS   The adolescent athlete usually complains of sudden pain and locking of the elbow joint. Range of motion returns slowly over a few days. Swelling, pain, and crepitation may also occur.[2]

MANAGEMENT   If there are repeated episodes of locking, surgical removal of the loose bodies may be warranted. If they are not removed, traumatic arthritis can occur.

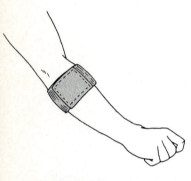

Figure 24-18

Counterforce brace for treatment of elbow epicondylitis.

Ulnar Nerve Injuries

> Athletes with a pronounced cubitus valgus are prone to injuring the ulnar nerve.

Because of the exposed position of the medial humeral condyle, the ulnar nerve is subject to a variety of problems. The athlete with a pronounced cubitus valgus may develop a friction problem. The ulnar nerve can also become recurrently dislocated because of a structural deformity. The ulnar nerve can become impinged by the arcuate ligament during flexion-type activities. Repeated direct pressure is another source of elbow joint irritation.

SYMPTOMS AND SIGNS   Rather than being painful, ulnar nerve injuries usually respond with a paresthesia to the fourth and fifth fingers.[10] The athlete complains of burning and tingling in the fourth and fifth fingers.

MANAGEMENT   The management of ulnar nerve injuries is conservative; aggravation of the nerve, such as placing direct pressure on it, is avoided. When stress on the nerve cannot be avoided, surgery may be performed to transpose it anteriorly to the elbow.[15]

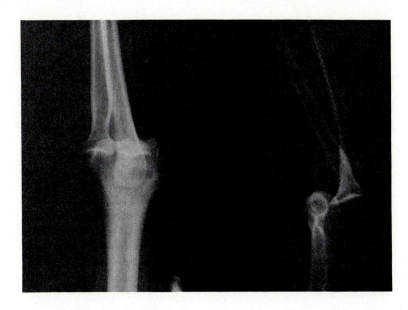

Figure 24-19

Elbow dislocation.

Dislocation of the Elbow

Dislocation of the elbow (Figure 24-19) has a high incidence in sports activity and is caused most often either by a fall on the outstretched hand with the elbow in a position of hyperextension or by a severe twist while it is in a flexed position. The bones of the ulna and radius may be displaced backward, forward, or laterally. By far the most common dislocation is one in which both the ulna and the radius are forced backward. The forward-displaced ulna or radius appears deformed. The olecranon process extends posteriorly, well beyond its normal alignment with the humerus. This dislocation may be distinguished from the supracondylar fracture by observing that the lateral and medial epicondyles are normally aligned with the shaft of the humerus.

SYMPTOMS AND SIGNS Elbow dislocations involve rupturing and tearing of most of the stabilizing ligamentous tissue, accompanied by profuse hemorrhage and swelling. There is severe pain and disability. The complications of such traumas include injury to the median and radial nerves, as well as to the major blood vessels and arteries, and—in almost every instance—myositis ossificans.

MANAGEMENT The primary responsibility is to apply cold and pressure immediately, then a sling, and to refer the athlete to a physician for reduction. Reducing an elbow dislocation should never be attempted by anyone other than a physician. It must be performed as soon as possible to prevent prolonged derangement of soft tissue. In most cases the physician will administer an anesthetic before reduction to relax muscles spasms. After reduction, the physician will often immobilize the elbow in a position of flexion and apply a sling suspension, which should be used for approximately 3 weeks. While the arm is maintained in flexion, the athlete should execute hand gripping and shoulder exercises. When initial healing has occurred, heat and gentle, passive exercise may be applied to help regain a full range of motion. Above all, massage and joint movements that are too strenuous should be avoided before complete healing has occurred because of

MANAGEMENT PLAN FOR POSTERIOR ELBOW DISLOCATION

Injury Situation

A female athlete fell from the uneven bars, landing on her outstretched left hand. The elbow was forced into hyperextension, dislocating the radial head posteriorly.

Symptoms and Signs

The athlete complained of extreme pain in the elbow region and numbness in the forearm and hand. From the side view the forearm appeared shortened. An obvious deformity was that the radial head stuck out beyond the posterior aspect of the elbow.

Management Plan

The athlete was referred immediately to a physician who performed an x-ray examination of the elbow to rule out fracture. After the x-ray examination, the elbow was reduced by the physician and placed in a cast and sling at 60 degrees for 6 weeks.

---

1 **Management Phase**

GOAL DURING IMMOBILIZATION PHASE: To maintain wrist and hand strength and shoulder range of motion while elbow is immobilized
ESTIMATED LENGTH OF TIME (ELT): 6 weeks

Exercise Rehabilitation

Ball squeeze (10 to 15 repetitions), each waking hour
Shoulder circles in all directions (10 to 15 repetitions), each waking hour. General body maintenance exercises are conducted three tmes a week as long as they do not aggravate injury

---

2 **Management Phase**

GOAL AFTER CAST IS REMOVED: To increase isometric strength and begin active range of motion
ELT: 2 to 3 weeks

Therapy

Ice packs (5 to 15 min) preceding exercise, three to four times daily

---

Exercise Rehabilitation

Continue exercises performed during immobilization phase, three to four times daily
Isometric exercise (two to three times), every waking hour
Pain-free active flexion and extension and forearm pronation and supination (10 to 15 repetitions), every waking hour; *avoid forcing movement*
Proprioceptive neuromuscular facilitation (PNF) also can be beneficial
General body maintenance exercises are conducted three times a week as long as they do not aggravate injury

---

3 **Management Phase**

GOALS: 50% full range of motion, 50% strength and coordination
ELT: 4 to 6 weeks

Therapy

Ice packs (5 to 15 min) preceding exercise, two to three times daily

	Exercise Rehabilitation	Isokinetic or isotonic exercise against dumbbell resistance, once daily, using daily adjustable progressive resistive exercise (DAPRE) concept PNF is also beneficial, emphasizing elbow flexion and extension and forearm supination and pronation General body maintenance exercises are conducted three times a week, as long as they do not aggravate injury
4	Management Phase	GOALS: To restore 90% of elbow range of motion and strength, including power, endurance, and coordination ELT: 4 to 6 weeks
	Therapy	Ice packs (5 to 15 min) preceding exercise
	Exercise Rehabilitation	Continue Phase 3 exercises and add isotonic machine resistance or free-weight barbell exercises; bar dips and chin-ups (10 repetitions), three to four times a week, can be added to routine
5	Management Phase	GOAL: To reenter competition ELT: 4 to 6 weeks
	Exercise Rehabilitation	Continue Phase 4 exercises three to four times a week Return to daily gymnastic practice within pain-free limits If elbow becomes symptomatic in any way such as pain, swelling, or decreased range of motion, athlete is to return to Phase 3 or 4 exercise program

Criteria for Returning to Competitive Gymnastics

The athlete must be able to do the following:

1. Extend and flex the elbow to at least 95% of the uninjured elbow
2. Pronate and supinate the forearm to at least 95% of the uninjured arm
3. Perform an elbow curl 10 times, for three sets, against a resistance equal to or greater than that which can be handled by the uninjured elbow (this could be measured by an isokinetic testing device)
4. Perform an elbow extension 10 times, for three sets, against a resistance equal to or greater than that which can be handled by the uninjured elbow (this also can be measured by an isokinetic testing device)
5. Pronate and supinate the forearm against a resistance equal to or greater than that which can be handled by the uninjured forearm
6. Perform 10 full bar dips
7. Perform 10 chin-ups
8. Perform a full routine on the uneven bars without causing discomfort

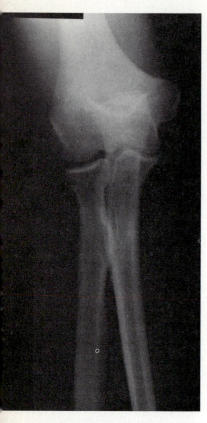

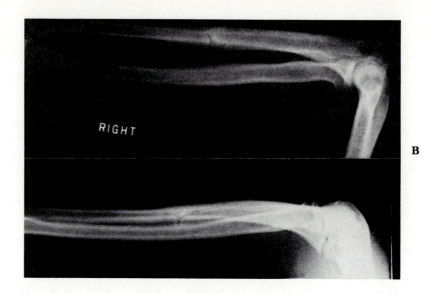

Figure 24-20

Fracture in region of the elbow. **A,** Impacted fracture of the head of the radius. **B,** Fracture of the head of the radius and the shaft of the ulna.

the high probability of encouraging myositis ossificans. Both range of movement and a strength program should be initiated by the athlete, but forced stretching must be avoided.

Fractures of the Elbow

An elbow fracture can occur in almost any sports event and is usually caused by a fall on the outstretched hand or the flexed elbow or by a direct blow to the elbow (Figure 24-20). Children and young athletes have a much higher rate of this injury than do adults. A fracture can take place in any one or more of the bones that compose the elbow. A fall on the outstretched hand quite often fractures the humerus above the condyles, the condyles proper, or the area between the condyles. The ulna and/or radius also may be the recipients of trauma, and direct force delivered to the olecranon process of the ulna or a force transmitted to the head of the radius may cause a fracture. An elbow fracture may or may not result in visible deformity. There usually will be hemorrhage, swelling, and muscle spasm in the injured area.

Volkmann's Contracture

Volkmann's contracture is a major complication of a serious elbow injury.

It is essential that athletes who sustain a serious elbow injury have their brachial or radial pulse monitored periodically to rule out the possibility of a Volkmann's contracture. It is most often associated with a humeral supracondylar fracture, which causes muscle spasm, swelling, or bone pressure on the brachial artery, inhibiting blood circulation to the forearm, wrist, and hand.

Such a contracture can become permanent. The first indication of this problem is pain in the forearm that becomes greater when the fingers are passively extended. This pain is followed by cessation of the bracial and radial pulses.

Rehabilitation of the Elbow

While the elbow is immobilized after an acute injury, the athlete should perform general body exercises, as well as exercises specific to the shoulder and wrist joint.

In some cases isometric exercise is appropriate while the elbow is immobilized. Maintaining the strength of these articulations will speed the recovery of the elbow. After the elbow has healed and free movement is permitted by the physician, the first consideration should be restoration of the normal range of movement (ROM). Lengthening the contracted tendons and supporting tissue around the elbow requires daily mild active exercises. **NOTE:** Passive stretching may be detrimental to the athlete regaining full ROM. Forced stretching must be avoided at all times. Proprioceptive neuromuscular facilitation and isokinetic exercises are valuable in the early and intermediate active stage of rehabilitation. When the full ROM has been regained (Figure 24-21), a graded, progressive, resistive exercise program should be initiated, including flexion, extension, pronation, and supination (Figure 24-22). Protective taping must be continued until full strength and flexibility has been restored. Long-standing chronic conditions of the elbow usually cause gradual debilitation of the surrounding soft tissue. Elbows with conditions of this type should be restored to the maximum state of conditioning without encouraging postinjury aggravation.

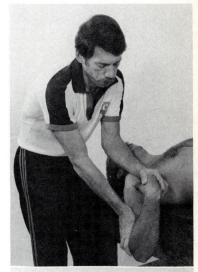

Figure 24-21

Restoring full range of movement is essential to elbow rehabilitation.

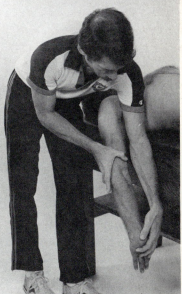

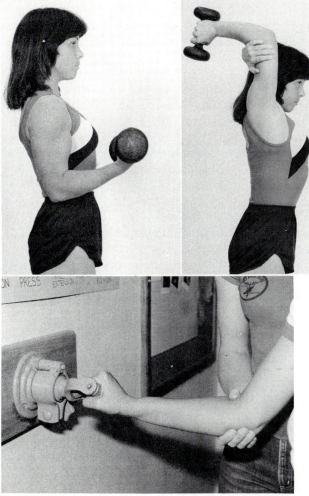

Figure 24-22

A very gradual program of progressive resistance exercise is important to elbow rehabilitation.

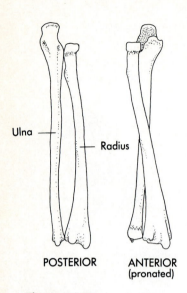

Ulna

Radius

POSTERIOR

ANTERIOR
(pronated)

Figure 24-23

Bones of the forearm.

THE FOREARM
Anatomy
Structural Relationships

The bones of the forearm are the ulna and the radius (Figure 24-23). The ulna, which may be thought of as a direct extension of the humerus, is long, straight, and larger at its upper end than at its lower end. The radius, considered an extension of the hand, is thicker at its lower end that at its upper end. The forearm has three articulations: the superior, middle, and distal radioulnar joints. The superior radioulnar articulation is a pivot joint, moving in a ring that is formed by the ulna and the annular ligament. The middle radioulnar joint, which is the junction between the shafts of the ulna and the radius, is held together by the oblique cord and the interosseous membrane. The oblique cord is a small band of ligamentous fibers that are attached to the lateral side of the ulna and pass downward and laterally to the radius. The interosseous membrane is a thin sheet of fibrous tissue that runs downward from the radius of the ulna and transmits forces directly through the hand from the radius to the ulna. The middle radioulnar joint provides a surface for muscle attachments; also, at the upper end, as at the lower end, there is an opening for blood vessels. The distal radioulnar joint is a pivot joint formed by the articulation of the head of the ulna with a small notch on the radius. It is held securely by the anterior and posterior radioulnar ligaments. The inferior ends of the radius and ulna are bound by an articular, triangular disk that allows radial movement of 180 degrees into supination and pronation.

Muscles

The forearm muscles consist of flexors and pronators that are positioned anteriorly and of extensors and supinators that lie posteriorly. The flexors of the wrist and fingers are separated into superficial muscles and deep muscles (Figure 24-24). The deep flexors arise from the ulna, the radius, and the interosseous tissue anteriorly, whereas the superficial flexors come from the internal humeral condyle. The extensors of the wrist and fingers originate on the posterior aspect and the external condyle of the humerus.

Blood and Nerve Supply

The major blood supply stems from the brachial artery, which divides into the radial and ulnar artery in the forearm.

Except for the flexor carpi ulnaris and half of the flexor digitorum profundus, most of the flexor muscles of the forearm are supplied by the median nerve. The majority of the extensor muscles are controlled by the radial nerve.

Evaluating Forearm Injuries

Sports injuries for the forearm are easily detectable because of the amount of exposure of both the ulna and the radius. Recognition of an injury is accomplished mainly through observation of the range of motion present and visible deviations and through the use of palpation. The forearm is first tested as to the amount of pronation and supination possible, 150 degrees being considered average. Next it is tested for wrist flexion and extension, with 150 degrees again considered normal. Injury may be reflected in the visible indications of deformity or paralysis. Palpation can reveal a false joint, bone fragments, or a lack of continuity between bones.

Injuries to the Forearm

Lying between the elbow joint and the wrist and hand, the forearm is indirectly influenced by injuries to these areas; however, direct injuries can also occur.

Contusions

The forearm is constantly exposed to bruising in contact sports such as football. The ulnar side receives the majority of blows in arm blocks and, consequently, the greater amount of bruising. Bruises to this area may be classified as acute or chronic. The acute contusion can result in a fracture, but this happens only rarely.

SYMPTOMS AND SIGNS   Most often a muscle or bone develops varying degrees of pain, swelling, and hematoma. The chronic contusion develops from repeated blows to the forearm with attendant multiple irritations. Heavy fibrosis may take the place of the hematoma, and a bony callus has been known to arise out of this condition.

MANAGEMENT   Care of the contused forearm requires proper attention in the acute stages through application of ICE-R for at least 1 hour, followed the next day by cryotherapy or superficial heat. Protection of the forearm is important for athletes who are prone to this condition. The best protection consists of a full-length sponge rubber pad for the forearm early in the season.

Strains

Forearm strain can occur in a variety of sports; most such injuries come from a severe static contraction. Repeated static contraction can lead to forearm splints.

Forearm splints   Forearm splints, like shin-splints, are difficult to manage. They occur most often in gymnasts, particularly to those who perform on the side horse.

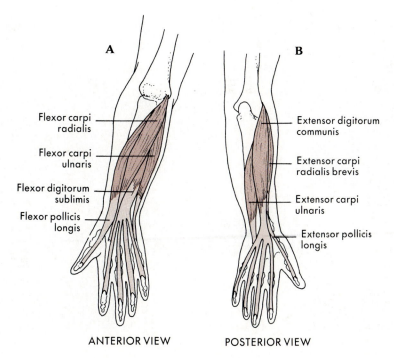

A

Flexor carpi radialis

Flexor carpi ulnaris

Flexor digitorum sublimis

Flexor pollicis longis

B

Extensor digitorum communis

Extensor carpi radialis brevis

Extensor carpi ulnaris

Extensor pollicis longis

ANTERIOR VIEW   POSTERIOR VIEW

Figure 24-24

Muscles of the forearm.
A, Anterior view.
B, Posterior view.

Forearm splints, like shin-splints, commonly occur either early or late in the sports season.

SYMPTOMS AND SIGNS   The main symptom is a dull ache between the extensor muscles, which cross the back of the forearm. There also may be weakness and extreme pain during muscle contraction. Palpation reveals an irritation of the interosseous membrane and surrounding tissue. The cause of this condition is uncertain; like shin-splints, forearm splints usually appear either early or late in the season, which indicates poor conditioning or fatigue, respectively. The pathological process is believed to result from the constant static muscle contractions of the forearm (e.g., those required to stabilize the side horse participant). Continued isometric contraction causes minute tears in the area of the interosseous membrane.

MANAGEMENT   Care of forearm splints is symptomatic. If the problem occurs in the early season, the athlete should concentrate on increasing the strength of the forearm through resistance exercises, but if it arises late in the season, emphasis should be placed on rest, cryotherapy, or heat and use of a supportive wrap during activity.

Fractures

Fractures of the forearm (Figure 24-25) are particularly common among active children and youths and occur as the result of a blow or a fall on the outstretched hand.[9] Fractures to the ulna or the radius singly are much rarer than simultaneous fractures to both. The break usually presents all the features of a long-bone fracture: pain, swelling, deformity, and a false joint. If there is a break in the upper third, the pronator teres muscle has a tendency to pull the forearm into an abduction deformity, whereas fractures of the lower portion of the arm are often in a neutral position. The older the athlete, the greater the danger is of extensive

Figure 24-25

A, A fracture of the radius and the ulna. **B,** A compound fracture of the ulna.

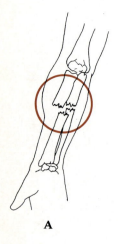

A

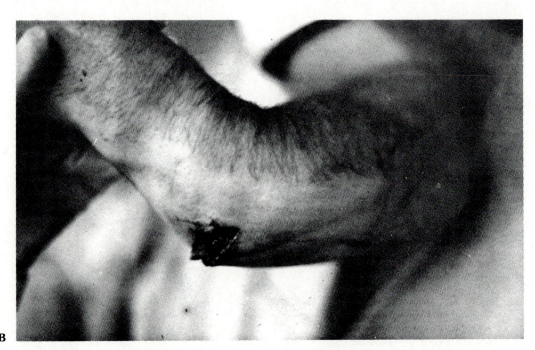

B

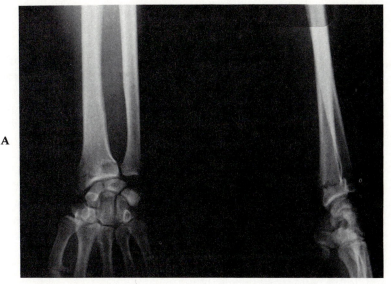

Figure 24-26

Colles' fracture. **A,** Fracture of the distal radial and ulnar styloid process. **B,** Common appearance of the forearm in Colles' fracture.

damage to soft tissue and the greater the possibility of paralysis from Volkmann's contractures.

To prevent complications from arising, a cold pack must be applied immediately to the fracture site, the arm splinted and put in a sling, and the athlete referred to a physician. The athlete will usually be incapacitated for approximately 8 weeks.

Colles' fracture   Colles' fractures (Figure 24-26) are among the most common types and involve the lower end of the radius and/or ulna. The mechanism of injury is usually a fall on the outstretched hand, forcing the radius and ulna backward and upward (hyperextension). Much less common is the reverse of Colles' fracture. The mechanism of this fracture is the result of a fall on the back of the hand.

SYMPTOMS AND SIGNS   In most cases there is forward displacement of the radius that causes a visible deformity to the wrist, which is commonly called a "silver fork" deformity. Sometimes no deformity is present, and the injury may be passed off as a bad sprain—to the detriment of the athlete. Bleeding is quite profuse in this area with the extravasated fluids causing extensive swelling in the wrist and, if unchecked, in the fingers and forearm. Ligamentous tissue is usually unharmed, but tendons may be torn and avulsed, and there may possibly be median nerve damage.

MANAGEMENT   The main responsibility is to apply a cold compress, splint the wrist, put the limb in a sling, and then refer the athlete to a physician for x-ray examination and immobilization. Severe sprains should always be treated as possible fractures. Lacking complications, the Colles' fracture will keep an athlete out of sports for 1 to 2 months. It should be noted that what appears to be a Colles' fracture in children and youths is often a lower epiphyseal separation. **NOTE:** Forearm exercise rehabilitation is discussed on pp. 811-812.

THE WRIST AND HAND
Anatomy
Structural Relationships

The wrist, or carpus, is formed by the union of the distal aspect of the radius and the articular disk of the ulna with three of the four proximal (of the eight diversely shaped) carpal bones. Appearing in order from the radial to the ulnar side in the first or proximal row are the navicular, lunate, triquetral, and pisiform bones; the distal row consists of the greater multangular (trapezium), lesser multangular (trapezoid), capitate, and hamate bones (Figure 24-27).

The concave surfaces of the lower ends of the radius and ulna articulate with the curve surfaces of the first row of carpal bones, with the exception of the pisiform, which articulates with the articular disk interposed between the head of the ulna and the triquetral bone. This radiocarpal joint is a condyloid joint and permits flexion, extension, abduction, and circumduction. Its major strength is drawn from the great number of tendons that cross it rather than from its bone structure or ligamentous arrangement. The articular capsule is a continuous cover formed by the merging of the radial and the ulnar collateral, volar radiocarpal, and dorsal radiocarpal ligaments.

The carpal bones   The carpal bones articulate with one another in arthrodial or gliding joints and combine their movements with those of the radiocarpal joint and the carpometacarpal articulations. They are stabilized by anterior, posterior, and connecting interosseous ligaments.

The metacarpal bones and phalanges   The metacarpal bones are five bones that join the carpal bones above and the phalanges below, forming metacarpophalangeal articulations of a condyloid type and permitting flexion, extension, abduction, adduction, and circumduction. As is true for the carpal bones, each joint has an articular capsule that is reinforced by collateral and accessory volar ligaments.

Figure 24-27

Bones of the wrist and hand.

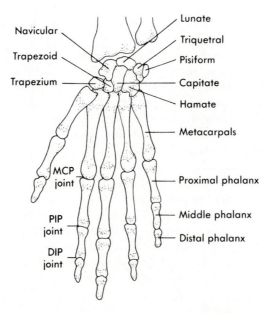

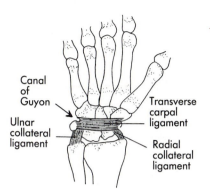

Figure 24-28

Ligaments of the wrist.

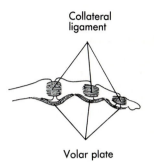

Figure 24-29

Ligaments of the phalanges.

The interphalangeal articulations are of the hinge type, permitting only flexion and extension. Their ligamentous and capsular support is basically the same as that of the metacarpophalangeal **(MCP)** joints.

The thumb varies slightly at its carpometacarpal joint and is classified as a saddle joint that allows rotation on its long axis in addition to the other metacarpophalangeal movements.

MCP
Metacarpophalangeal joint.

Ligaments

There are numerous wrist and hand ligaments; however, only those concerned with sports injuries are emphasized.

Ligaments of the wrist   The wrist is composed of many ligaments that bind the carpal bones to one another, to the ulna and radius, and to the proximal metacarpal bones. Of major interest in wrist injuries are the collateral ulnar ligament, extending from the tip of the styloid process of the ulna to the pisiform bone, and the triquetral bone and collateral radial ligament that extends from the styloid process to the radius to the navicular bone (scaphoid). Crossing the volar aspect of the carpal bones is the transverse capital ligament. This ligament serves as the roof of the carpal tunnel, in which the median nerve is often compressed (Figure 24-28).

Ligaments of the phalanges   The proximal interphalangeal **(PIP)** joints have the same design as the metacarpophalangeal joints. They comprise the collateral ligaments, palmar fibrocartilages, and a loose dorsal capsule or synovial membrane protected by an extensor expansion (Figure 24-29).

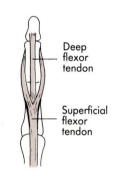

Figure 24-30

Tendons of the phalanges.

PIP
Proximal interphalangeal joint.

Musculature

The wrist and hand are a complex of extrinsic and intrinsic muscles. See Table 24-2 for the major muscles in the hand and wrist (Figure 24-30).

Blood and Nerve Supply

The arteries that supply the wrist and the hand are the radial and ulnar arteries. They create two arterial arches; the superficial palmar arch is the largest and most distal to the hand, and the second is the deep palmar arch.

The three major nerves of the hand are the ulnar, radial, and median nerves. The ulnar nerve comes to the hand by passing between the pisiform bone and the hook of the hamate bone. The radial nerve enters the wrist from the back of the

Circulation impairment must be noted as soon as possible in any wrist and hand injury.

TABLE 24-2 Resistive Motion to Determine Muscle Weakness Related to Wrist and Hand Injury

Resistive Motion	Major Muscles Involved	Nerves
Wrist flexion	Flexor carpi radialis	Median, cervical 6 and 7
	Flexor carpi ulnaris	Ulnar, cervical 8, thoracic 1
Wrist extension	Extensor carpi radialis longus	Radial, cervical 6 and 7
	Extensor carpi radialis brevis	Radial, cervical 6 and 7
	Extensor carpi ulnaris	Radial, cervical 6-8
Flexion of MCP joints of fingers	Lumbricalis manus	Median, ulnar, cervical 6-8
	Interossei dorsalis manus	Ulnar, cervical 8, thoracic 1
	Interossei palmares	Ulnar, cervical 8, thoracic 1
Flexion of PIP and DIP joints of fingers	Flexor digitorum superficialis	Median, cervical 7 and 8, thoracic 1
Extension of MCP joints of fingers	Extensor digitorum	Radial, cervical 6-8
	Extensor indicis	Radial, cervical 6-8
	Extensor digiti minimi	Radial, cervical 6-8
Finger abduction	Interossei dorsalis	Ulnar
	Abductor digiti	Cervical 8, thoracic 1
Finger adduction	Interossei palmares	Ulnar, cervical 8, thoracic 1
Thumb flexion	Flexor pollicis brevis	
	Lateral portion	Median, cervical 6 and 7
	Medial portion	Ulnar, cervical 8, thoracic 1
	Flexor pollicis longus	Cervical 8, thoracic 1
Thumb extension	Extensor pollicis brevis	Radial, cervical 6 and 7
	Extensor pollicis longus	Radial, cervical 6-8
Thumb abduction	Abductor pollicis longus	Radial, cervical 6 and 7
	Abductor pollicis brevis	Median, cervical 6 and 7
Thumb adduction	Adductor pollicis	Ulnar, cervical 8, thoracic 1
Thumb opposition	Opponens pollicis	Median, cervical 6 and 7
Fifth-finger opposition	Opponens digiti minimi	Ulnar, cervical 6 and 7

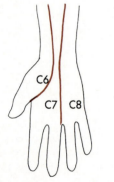

Figure 24-31

Sensory patterns of peripheral nerves in the hand.

forearm between the superficial and deep extensor muscles where it terminates in the back of the carpus. The median nerve enters the palm of the hand through the carpal tunnel (see Table 24-2).

The sensory pattern of peripheral nerves can be seen in Figure 24-31. The radial nerve may or may not follow this pattern.[4]

Assessment of the Wrist and Hand
Complaints

As with other conditions, the evaluator asks about the location and type of pain:

1. What increases or decreases the pain?
2. Has there been a history of trauma or overuse?
3. What therapy or medications, if any, have been given?

Observations

As the athlete is observed, arm and hand asymmetries are noted:

1. Are there any postural deviations?
2. Does the athlete hold the part in a stiff or protected manner?
3. Is the wrist or hand swollen?

Hand usage such as writing or unbuttoning a shirt is noted. The general attitude of the hand is observed (Figure 24-32). When the athlete is asked to open and close the hand, the evaluator notes whether this movement can be performed fully and rhythmically. Another general functional activity is to have the athlete touch the tip of the thumb to each fingertip several times. The last factor to be observed is the color of the fingernails. Nails that are very pale instead of pink may indicate a problem with blood circulation.

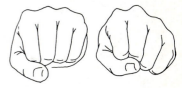

At rest

Normal fist   Clenched fist

Figure 24-32

General normal attitudes of the hand.

Bony Palpation

Wrist region   The bones of the wrist region are palpated for pain and defects. The following anatomical sites are palpated:

With the wrist in ulnar flexion
1. Radial styloid process
2. Navicular bone (scaphoid) through the anatomical snuffbox
3. Trapezium
4. First metacarpal bone

With the wrist straight
1. Distal head of the radius
2. Lunate bone
3. Capitate bone
4. Ulnar styloid
5. Triquetral bone
6. Pisiform bone
7. Hook of the hamate bone

Hand region
1. First metacarpal bone
2. MCP joint
3. Each phalanx, starting with the PIP joint, progressing to the distal interphalangeal **(DIP)** joint

DIP
Distal interphalangeal joint.

Soft-Tissue Palpation

Wrist region   Each tendon is palpated as it crosses the wrist region. Of major importance is the palpation of the six dorsal wrist tunnels, the carpal tunnel, and the canal of Guyon on the volar aspect. Pain at the site of the first tunnel may indicate stenosing tenosynovitis, or de Quervain's disease. Point tenderness is an indication for administering the de Quervain's test.

Hand region   The soft tissue of the hand is palpated as follows:
1. Thenar and hypothenar region
2. Palmar aponeurosis
3. Flexor muscles

Dorsal aspect
1. Extension tendons
2. Phalanges

Special Tests for the Hand and Wrist

Test for de Quervain's disease   The de Quervain's test is commonly called the Finklestein Test (Figure 24-33). The athlete makes a fist with the thumb

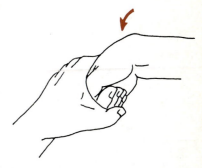

Figure 24-33

de Quervain's test.

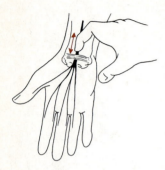

Figure 24-34

Tapping over the transverse carpal ligament to test for carpal tunnel syndrome (Tinel's sign).

tucked inside. The wrist is then deviated into ulnar flexion. Sharp pain is evidence of stenosing tenosynovitis. Pain over the carpal tunnel could mean a carpal tunnel syndrome affecting the median nerve. On occasion the flexor tendons also become trapped, making finger flexion difficult. Any symptoms of carpal tunnel syndrome are an indication for testing, using the tapping sign and wrist press test.

The tapping sign for carpal tunnel syndrome The tapping sign (Tinel's sign) for carpal tunnel syndrome is performed by tapping over the transverse carpal ligament. It is a positive test if pain or paresthesia is elicited (Figure 24-34).

Wrist press Another common test for carpal tunnel syndrome is the wrist press test (Phalen's test). The athlete is instructed to flex both wrists as far as possible and press them together. This position is held for approximately 1 minute. If this test is positive, pain will be produced in the region of the carpal tunnel (Figure 24-35).

Circulatory and Neurological Evaluation

The hands should be inspected to determine whether circulation is being impeded. The hands should be felt for their temperature. A cold hand or portion of a hand is a sign of decreased circulation. Pinching the fingernails can also help to indicate circulatory problems. Pinching will blanch the nail, and on release there should be rapid return of a pink color. Another objective test is the Allen test.

Testing the radial and ulnar arteries of the hand The Allen test is used to determine the function of the radial and ulnar arteries supplying the hand. The athlete is instructed to squeeze the hand tightly into a fist and then open it fully three or four times. While the athlete is holding the last fist, the evaluator places firm pressure over each artery. The athlete is then instructed to open the hand. The palm should now be blanched. One of the arteries is then released, and, if normal, the hand will instantly become red. The same process is repeated with the other artery (Figure 24-36).

The hand is next evaluated for sensation alterations, especially in cases of suspected tunnel impingements. Nerve involvements will be further evaluated when active and resistive movements are initiated.

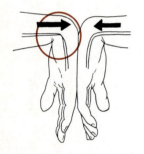

Figure 24-35

Wrist press for carpal tunnel syndrome (Phalen's test).

Figure 24-36

Testing the radial and ulnar arteries of the hand (Allen test).

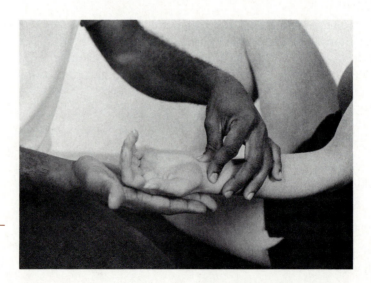

Functional Evaluation

Range of motion is noted in all movements of the wrist and fingers. Active and resistive movements are then compared to the uninjured wrist and hand. The following sequence should be conducted:

Wrist: Flexion, extension, radial and ulnar deviation

MCP joint: Flexion, extension

PIP and DIP joints: Flexion, extension

Finger: Abduction, adduction

MCP, PIP, and DIP joints of the thumb: Flexion and extension

Thumb: Abduction, adduction, opposition

Fifth finger: Opposition

Passive, active, and resistive movements are performed in the wrist and hand. Table 24-2 indicates resistive motions to use to determine the extent of strength of the major wrist and hand muscles.

Injuries to the Wrist

The wrist is the region between and including the distal ends of the radius and ulna and the bases of the metacarpals.[8] The wrist area includes the carpal bones and ligaments and the related fibrocartilaginous complex.

The main purposes of the wrist are to position the hand in space and to direct forces from the hand to the forearm and vice versa.[8] To accomplish these purposes there must be both stability and mobility. Injuries to the wrist usually occur from a fall on the outstretched hand or from repeated flexion, extension, or rotary movements. (Figure 24-37).

Strains and Sprains

It is often very difficult to dinstinguish between injury to the muscle tendons crossing the wrist joint or to the supporting structure of the carpal region. Therefore, emphasis is placed on the condition of wrist sprain, whereas strain will be considered in the discussion of the hand.

A sprain is by far the most common wrist injury and in most cases is the most poorly managed injury in sports. It can arise from any abnormal, forced movement of the wrist. Falling on the hyperextended wrist is the most common cause, but violent flexion or torsion will also tear supporting tissue. Since the main support of the wrist is derived from posterior and anterior ligaments that transport the major nutrient vessels to the carpal bones and stabilize the joint, repeated sprains may disrupt the blood supply and consequently the nutrition to the carpal bones.

SYMPTOMS AND SIGNS The sprained wrist may be differentiated from the carpal navicular fracture by recognition of the generalized swelling, tenderness, inability to flex the wrist, and absence of appreciable pain or irritation over the navicular bone. All athletes having severe sprains should be referred to a physician for x-ray examination to determine possible fractures.[12]

MANAGEMENT Mild and moderate sprains should be given cold therapy and compression for at least 24 to 48 hours, after which cryotherapy is performed or there is a gradual increase in heat therapy. It is desirable to have the athlete start hand-strengthening exercises almost immediately after the injury has occurred. Taping for support can benefit healing and help prevent further injury (see Chapter 12, Figures 12-28 and 12-29).

Nerve Compression in the Wrist Region

Because of the narrow spaces that some nerves must travel through the wrist to the hand, compression neuropathy or entrapment can occur. The two most common entrapments are of the median nerve, which travels through the carpal tunnel, and the ulnar nerve, which is compressed in the tunnel of Guyon between the pisiform bone and the hook of the hamate bone.

Figure 24-37

Wrist injuries commonly occur from falls on the outstretched hand or from repeated flexion, extension, lateral, or rotary movements.

Such compression causes a sharp or burning pain that is associated with an increase or decrease in skin sensitivity or paresthesia.[6] When chronic entrapment may cause irreversible nerve damage, unsuccessful conservative treatment can lead to surgical decompression. Conservative treatment of the athlete usually includes rest and anti-inflammatory medication. Varying degrees of muscle weakness can also follow.

de Quervain's disease   de Quervain's disease (also called Hoffman's disease) is a stenosing tenosynovitis in the thumb. The first tunnel of the wrist becomes contracted and narrowed as a result of inflammation of the synovial lining. The tendons that go through the first tunnel are the extensor pollicis brevis and abductor pollicis longus, which move through the same synovial sheath. Because the tendons move through a groove of the radiostyloid process, constant wrist movement can be a source of irritation.[28]

SYMPTOMS AND SIGNS   Athletes who use a great deal of wrist motion in their sport are prone to de Quervain's disease. Its symptom is aching, which may radiate into the hand or forearm.[6] Movements of the wrist tend to increase the pain, and there is a positive de Quervain's test. There is point tenderness and weakness during thumb extension and abduction, and there may be a painful snapping and catching of the tendons during movement.

MANAGEMENT   Management of de Quervain's disease involves immobilization, rest, cryotherapy, and anti-inflammatory medication. Ultrasound and ice massage are also beneficial.

Dislocations

Dislocations of the wrist are relatively infrequent in sports activity. Most occur from a forceful hyperextension of the hand. Of those dislocations that do happen, the bones that could be involved are the distal ends of the radius and ulna (Figure 24-38) and a carpal bone, the lunate being the most commonly affected.

Dislocation of the lunate bone   Dislocation of the lunate (Figure 24-39) is considered the most common dislocation of a carpal bone.

ETIOLOGICAL FACTORS   Dislocation occurs as a result of a fall on the outstretched hand, forcing open the space between the distal and proximal carpal bones. When the stretching force is released, the lunate bone is dislocated anteriorly (palmar side).

SYMPTOMS AND SIGNS   The primary signs of this condition are pain, swelling, and difficulty in executing wrist and finger flexion. There also may be numbness or even paralysis of the flexor muscles because of lunate pressure on the median nerve.

MANAGEMENT   This condition should be treated as acute, and the athlete sent to a physician for reduction of the dislocation. If it is not recognized early enough, bone deterioration may occur, requiring surgical removal. The usual time of disability and subsequent recovery totals 1 to 2 months.

Fractures

Fractures of the wrist commonly occur to the distal ends of the radius and ulna and to the carpal bones; the carpal navicular bone is most commonly affected, and the hamate bone is affected less often. Serious acute injuries to the wrist are usually caused by impact or by rotational forces. The most common mechanism is a fall on the outstretched hand.[27]

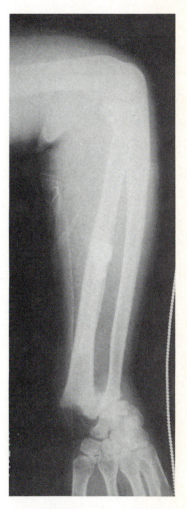

Figure 24-38

Dislocation of the distal radius and ulna.

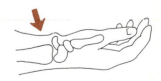

Figure 24-39

Dislocation of the lunate bone.

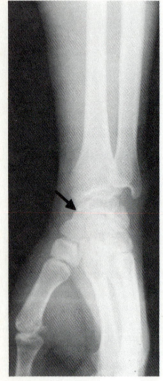

Figure 24-40

Carpal navicular fracture.

Navicular (scaphoid) fracture   The navicular bone is the most frequently fractured of the carpal bones.

ETIOLOGICAL FACTORS   The injury is usually caused by a force on the outstretched hand, which compresses the navicular bone between the radius and the second row of carpal bones[29] (Figure 24-40). This condition is often mistaken for a severe sprain, and as a result the required complete immobilization is not performed. Without proper splinting, the navicular fracture often fails to heal because of an inadequate supply of blood; thus degeneration and necrosis occur. This condition is often called "aseptic necrosis" of the navicular bone. It is necessary to try, in every way possible, to distinguish between a wrist sprain and a fracture of the navicular bone because a fracture necessitates immediate referral to a physician.

SYMPTOMS AND SIGNS   The signs of a recent navicular fracture include swelling in the area of the carpal bones, severe point tenderness of the navicular bone in the anatomical snuff-box (Figure 24-41), and navicular pain that is elicited by upward pressure exerted on the long axis of the thumb and by radial flexion.

MANAGEMENT   With these signs present, cold should be applied, the area splinted, and the athlete referred to a physician for x-ray study and casting. In most cases, cast immobilization lasts for approximately 8 weeks and is followed by strengthening exercises coupled with protective taping.

Hamate fracture   A fracture of the hamate bone can occur from a fall but more commonly occurs from being struck by an implement such as the handle of a tennis racket, a baseball bat, or a golf club. Wrist pain and weakness are experienced. Pull of the muscular attachments can cause nonunion; therefore casting is usually the treatment of choice.

Wrist Ganglion of the Tendon Sheath

The wrist ganglion (Figure 24-42) is often seen in sports. It is considered by many to be a herniation of the joint capsule or of the synovial sheath of a tendon; other authorities believe it to be a cystic structure. It usually appears slowly, after a wrist strain, and contains a clear, mucinous fluid. The ganglion most often appears on the back of the wrist but can appear at any tendinous point in the wrist

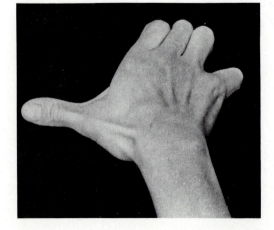

Figure 24-42

Wrist ganglion.

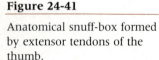

Figure 24-41

Anatomical snuff-box formed by extensor tendons of the thumb.

or hand. As it increases in size, it may be accompanied by mild pressure discomfort. An old method of treatment was first to break down the swelling through digital pressure and then apply a felt pressure pad for a period of time to encourage healing. A newer approach is the use of a combination of aspiration and chemical cauterization, with subsequent application of a pressure pad. Neither of these methods prevents the ganglion from recurring. Surgical removal is the best of the various methods of treatment.

Injuries to the Hand

Injuries to the hand occur frequently in sports, yet the injured hand is probably the most poorly managed of all body areas.

Contusions and Pressure Injuries of the Hand and Phalanges

The hand and phalanges, having an irregular bony structure combined with little protective fat and muscle padding, are prone to bruising in sports. This condition is easily identified from the history of trauma and the pain and swelling of soft tissues. Cold and compression should be applied immediately until hemorrhage has ceased, followed by gradual warming of the part in whirlpool or immersion baths. Although soreness is still present, protection should be given by a sponge rubber pad (see Figure 12-30).

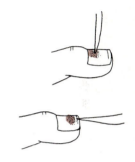

Figure 24-43

Releasing blood from beneath the fingernail, technique no. 1.

A particularly common contusion of the finger is bruising of the distal phalanx, which results in a *subungual hematoma* (contusion of the fingernail). This is an extremely painful condition because of the accumulation of blood underneath the fingernail. The athlete should place the finger in ice water until the hemorrhage ceases, and the pressure of blood should then be released (Figure 24-43 and the box below).

RELEASING BLOOD FROM BENEATH THE FINGERNAIL

The following are two common methods for releasing the pressure of the subungual hematoma.

MATERIALS NEEDED: Scalpel, small-gauge drill or paper clip, and antiseptic.

POSITION OF ATHLETE: The athlete sits with the injured hand, palm downward, on the table.

TECHNIQUE 1
1. The injured finger should first be coated with an antiseptic solution.
2. A sharp scalpel point, small-gauge drill, or paper clip is used to penetrate the injured nail through a rotary action. If the hematoma extends as far as the end of the nail, it may be best to release the blood by slipping the scalpel tip under the end of the nail.

TECHNIQUE 2
1. A paper clip is heated to a red-hot temperature.
2. The red-hot paper clip or small-gauge drill is laid on the surface of the nail with moderate pressure, resulting in melting a hole through the nail to the site of the bleeding.

Bowler's thumb A perineural fibrosis of the subcutaneous ulnar digital nerve of the thumb can occur from the pressure of a bowling ball thumbhole. With the development of fibrotic tissue around the ulnar nerve, the athlete senses pain, tingling during pressure to the irritated area, and numbness.

Early management includes decreasing the amount of bowling and padding of the thumbhole. If the condition continues, however, surgery may be warranted.

Handlebar palsy Handlebar palsy, or ulnar neuropathy, in bicyclists results from an abnormal amount of pressure on the hands. The bicyclist experiences numbness, weakness, and a loss of coordination of the ulnar side of the fourth and fifth fingers. It can occur in one or both hands.[4] To avoid this condition the bicyclist should wear gloves and have padded handlebars. It is also essential that the bicycle be of the proper size and handlebar height to avoid excessive body weight being forced forward onto the hands. Hand positions should be changed frequently during long trips. With prolonged symptoms the rider should avoid bicycling and be referred to a physician for treatment.

Tendon Conditions

Tendon injuries are common among athletes. As with many other hand injuries occurring in sports, they are characteristically neglected.[22]

Tenosynovitis The tendons of the wrist and hand can sustain irritation from repeated movement that results in tenosynovitis. An inflammation of the tendon sheath results in swelling, crepitation, and painful movement. Most commonly affected are the extensor tendons of the wrist: the extensor carpi ulnaris, extensor pollicis longus, extensor pollicis brevis, and abductor pollicis longus.

Trigger finger or thumb The trigger finger or thumb is another example of stenosing tenosynovitis. It most commonly occurs in a flexor tendon that runs through a common sheath with other tendons. Thickening of the sheath or tendon can occur, thus constricting the sliding tendon. A nodule in the synovium of the sheath adds to the difficulty of gliding.

SYMPTOMS AND SIGNS The athlete complains that when the finger or thumb is flexed, there is resistance to reextension, producing a snapping that is both palpable and audible. During palpation, tenderness is produced, and a lump can be felt at the base of the flexor tendon sheath.

MANAGEMENT Treatment initially is the same for de Quervain's disease; however, if it is unsuccessful, steroid injections may produce relief. If steroid injections do not provide relief, splinting the tendon sheath is the last option.

Mallet finger The mallet finger is common in sports, particularly in baseball and basketball. It is caused by a blow from a thrown ball that strikes the tip of the finger and avulses the extensor tendon from its insertion along with a piece of bone.

SYMPTOMS AND SIGNS The athlete is unable to extend the finger, carrying it at approximately a 30-degree angle. There is also point tenderness at the site of the injury, and the avulsed bone often can be palpated (Figure 24-44).

MANAGEMENT Pain, swelling, and discoloration from internal hemorrhage are present. The distal phalanx should immediately be splinted in a position of extension, cold should be applied to the area, and the athlete should be referred to a physician. Most physicians will splint the mallet finger into extension and the proximal phalanx into flexion for 4 to 6 weeks (Figure 24-45).

Two important forms of tenosynovitis
 deQuervain's disease
 Trigger finger or thumb

Figure 24-44
Mallet finger.

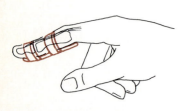
Figure 24-45
Splinting of the mallet finger.

Boutonnière deformity   The boutonnière, or buttonhole, deformity is caused by a rupture of the extensor tendon of the middle phalanx. Trauma occurs to the top of the middle finger, which forces the PIP joint into excessive flexion.

SYMPTOMS AND SIGNS   The athlete complains of severe pain and inability to extend the PIP joint. There is swelling, point tenderness, and an obvious deformity (Figure 24-46).

MANAGEMENT   Management of the boutonnière deformity includes cold application followed by splinting of the PIP joint in extension. **NOTE:** If this condition is inadequately splinted, the classic boutonnière deformity will develop. Splinting is continued for 5 to 8 weeks. While splinted, the athlete is encouraged to flex the distal phalanx[6] (Table 24-3).

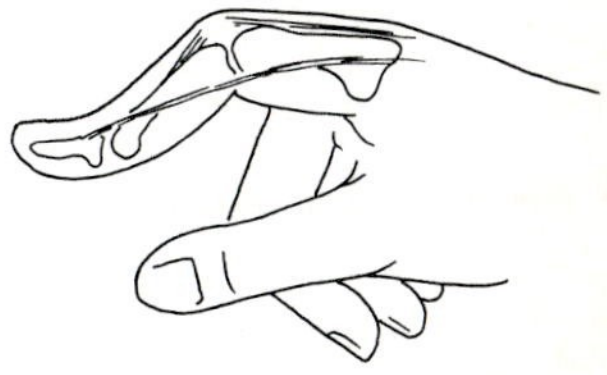

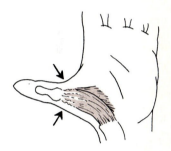

Figure 24-46

Boutonnière deformity.

Sprains, Dislocations, and Fractures

The phalanges, particularly the thumb (Figure 24-47), are prone to sprains caused by a blow delivered to the tip or by violent twisting.[27] The mechanism of injury is similar to that of fractures and dislocations.[14] The sprain, however, mainly affects the capsular, ligamentous, and tendinous tissues. Recognition is accomplished primarily through the history and the sprain symptoms: pain, marked swelling, and hematoma.[5]

Sprains of the metacarpophalangeal joint

Fingers   A sprain of the MCP joint often consists of disruption of the extensor tendon and an inability of the athlete to extend the joint fully. There may be obvious slipping of the extensor tendon[3] (see Table 24-3).

Gamekeeper's thumb   A sprain of the ulnar collateral ligament of the MCP joint of the thumb is common among athletes, especially skiers and tackle football players. The mechanism of injury is usually a forceful abduction of the proximal phalanx, which is occasionally combined with hyperextension.[11]

Figure 24-47

Sprained thumb.

TABLE 24-3   Conservative Treatment and Splinting of Finger Injuries

Injury	Constant Splinting	Begin Motion	Additional Splinting During Competition	Joint Position
Mallet finger	6-8 wk	6-8 wk	6-8 wk	Slight DIP hyperextension
Collateral ligament sprains	3 wk	2 wk	4-6 wk	30-degree flexion
PIP and DIP dislocations	3 wk	3 wk	3 wk	30-degree flexion
Phalangeal fractures	4-6 wk	4-6 wk	3 wk	N/A
PIP and DIP fractures	9-11 wk	3 wk	3 wk	30-degree flexion
Pseudoboutonnière volar plate injuries	5 wk	3 wk	3 wk	20- to 30-degree flexion
Boutonnière deformity	6-8 wk	6-8 wk	6-8 wk	PIP in extension; DIP and MCP not included
MCP fractures	3 wk	3 wk	4-6 wk	30-degree flexion
Flexor digitorum profundus repair	5 wk	3 wk	3 wk	Depends on repair

Since the stability of pinching can be severely deterred, proper immediate and follow-up care must be performed. If there is instability in the joints, the athlete should be immediately referred to an orthopedist. If the joint is stable, x-ray examination should routinely be performed to rule out fracture. Splinting of the thumb should be applied for protection over a 3-week period or until it is pain free. The splint, extending from the end of the thumb to above the wrist, is applied with the thumb in a neutral position.[20] After splinting, thumb spica taping should be worn during sports participation.

Sprains of the interphalangeal joints of the fingers   Interphalangeal finger sprains can include the PIP joint or the DIP joint. Injury can range from minor to complete tears of the collateral ligament, a volar plate tear, or a central extensor slip tear (see Table 24-3).

Collateral ligament sprain   A collateral ligament sprain of the interphalangeal joint is very common in sports such as basketball, volleyball, and football. A common mechanism is an axial force producing the ''jammed finger.''

SYMPTOMS AND SIGNS   There is severe point tenderness at the joint site, especially in the region of the collateral ligaments. There may be a lateral or medial instability when the joint is in 150 degrees of flexion. Collateral ligamentous injuries may be evaluated by the application of a valgus and varus joint stress test.

MANAGEMENT   Management includes ice packs for the acute stage, x-ray examinations, and splinting. Splinting of the PIP joint is usually at 30 to 40 degrees of flexion for 10 days. If the sprain is to the DIP joint, splinting a few days in full extension assists in the healing process. If the sprains are minor, taping the injured finger to a noninjured one will provide protective support. Later, a protective checkrein can be applied for either thumb or finger protection (see Figures 12-31 to 12-33).

Volar plate injury   The volar plate of the PIP joint is most commonly injured in sports from a severe hyperextension force. A distal tear may cause a ''swanneck deformity,'' whereas injury to the proximal part of the plate may cause a ''pseudoboutonnière deformity.[21] A major indication of a tear is that the PIP joint can be passively hyperextended in comparison to other PIP joints.

Management usually consists of splinting in 20 to 30 degrees of flexion for 5 weeks, followed by 3 weeks of active motion. A 30-degree extension block splint might be used after flexion splinting.[13]

Dislocations of the phalanges   Dislocations of the phalanges (Figure 24-48) have a high rate of occurrence in sports and are caused mainly by being hit on the tip of the finger by a ball (Figure 24-49). The force of injury is usually directed upward from the palmar side, displacing either the first or second joint dorsally. The resultant problem is primarily tearing of the supporting capsular tissue, accompanied by hemorrhaging. However, there may be a rupture of the flexor or extensor tendon and chip fractures in and around the dislocated joint. It is advisable to splint the dislocation as it is and refer all first-time dislocations to the team physician for reduction.[18]

To ensure the most complete healing of the dislocated PIP and DIP joints, splinting should be maintained for approximately 3 weeks in 30 degrees of flexion because inadequate immobilization could cause an unstable joint and/or excessive scar tissue and, possibly, a permanent deformity.

Special consideration must be given to dislocations of the thumb and any MCP finger joints (Figure 24-50). A properly functioning thumb is necessary for hand

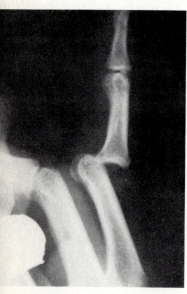

Figure 24-48

Being hit on the tip of a finger can produce enough force to dislocate it.

Figure 24-49

Volleyball produces a high percentage of finger injuries.

Figure 24-50

A thumb dislocation, if not properly managed, can seriously affect hand functioning.

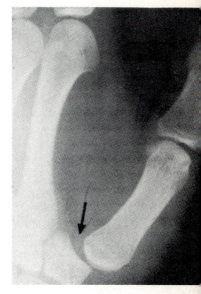

dexterity; consequently, any traumatic injury to the thumb should be considered serious. Thumb dislocations occur frequently at the second joint, resulting from a sharp blow to the distal end, with the trauma forcing the thumb into hyperextension and dislocating the second joint downward. Any dislocation of the MCP finger joints can lead to complications and require the immediate care of an orthopedist.[3]

Fractures of the metacarpal bones and phalanges The same mechanism that produces strains, sprains, and dislocations can cause fractures of the metacarpal bones and phalanges. Other mechanisms are of crushing injuries.

Fractures of the metacarpal bones Fractures of the metacarpal bones (Figure 24-51) are common in contact sports. They arise from striking an object with the fist or from having the hand stepped on. There are often pain, deformity, swelling, and abnormal mobility. In some cases no deformity occurs, and through palpation one is unable to distinguish between a severe contusion and a fracture. In this situation, digital pressure should be placed on the knuckles and the long axes of the metacarpal bones. Pressure will often reveal pain at the fracture site.[12] After the fracture is located, the hand should be splinted over a gauze roll splint, cold and pressure should be applied, and the athlete should be referred to a physician. Uncomplicated metacarpal fractures take approximately 1 month for complete healing.

A fracture of the first metacarpal's proximal end, which is often associated with a subluxation of the carpometacarpal of the thumb, is called a *Bennett fracture.*

Fractures of the phalanges Fractures of the phalanges are among the most common fractures in sports and can occur as the result of a variety of mechanisms: the fingers being stepped on, hit by a ball, or twisted. More concern should

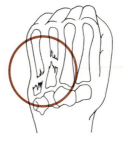

Figure 24-51

Fractures of the metacarpals.

be given to fractures of the middle and proximal phalanges because of possible involvement with the extensor or flexor tendons. Transverse, oblique, or spiral fractures should be referred to an orthopedist. Avulsion fractures are usually treated like a corresponding sprain[3] (Table 24-4). A deformity in an anterior direction usually occurs in proximal fractures. The finger must be splinted in flexion around a gauze roll or a curved splint to avoid full extension of the digit, which must be avoided at all times. Flexion splinting reduces the deformity by relaxing the flexor tendons. Fracture of the distal phalanx is less complicated than fracture of the middle or proximal phalanges, but it constitutes a painful injury that sometimes becomes complicated by a subungual hematoma (Figure 24-52). The major concerns are to control bleeding, to apply a splint properly, and then to refer the athlete to a physician.

TABLE 24-4 Avulsion Fractures

Avulsion Fracture	Corresponding Sprain
Corner of base of middle phalanx	Collateral ligament
Volar base of middle phalanx	Volar plate injury
Dorsal base of middle phalanx	Central extensor slip tear
Volar base of distal phalanx	Flexor profundus tear
Dorsal base of distal phalanx	Mallet finger

Figure 24-52

A fracture of the proximal phalanx is usually more serious than a fracture of the distal end.

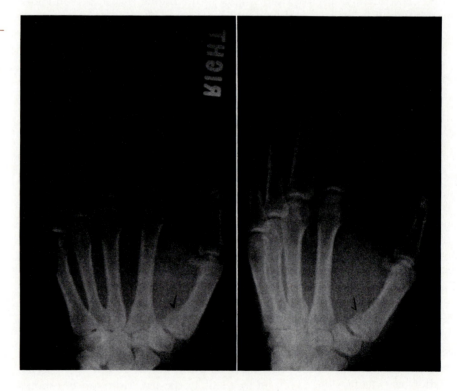

Rehabilitation of the Forearm, Wrist, and Hand

Reconditioning of the hand, wrist, and forearm must commence as early as possible. Immobilization of the forearm or wrist requires that the muscles be exercised almost immediately after an injury occurs if atrophy and contractures are to be prevented. The athlete is not ready for competition until full strength and mobility of the injured joint have been regained. Grip strength is an excellent way to determine the state of reconditioning of the hand, wrist, and forearm. The hand dynamometer may be used to ascertain strength increments during the process of rehabilitation. Full range of movement and strength must be considered for all the major articulations and muscles.

Once ligamentous or tendinous injuries have healed to the point that movement will not disrupt them, active mobilization is performed.[25,26] Exercise is graduated to increase grip and pinch strength. Some of the following exercises can be used with success. **NOTE:** All exercises should be performed in a pain-free range of motion. Such exercises should be performed in sets of 10, working toward an ultimate program of three sets of 10, two, or three times daily.

Suggested Forearm and Wrist Exercises

Proper forearm reconditioning is extremely important for injuries to the wrist and hand, as well as the forearm. An excellent beginning exercise is the towel twist, in which the athlete twists the towel in each direction as if wringing out water (Figure 24-53). A wrist roll exercise (Figure 24-54) against resistance is also an excellent forearm, wrist, and hand-strength developer. More specific strength development can be accomplished through the use of a resistance device such as a dumbbell. By stabilizing the bent elbow, the athlete can perform wrist flexion and extension and also forearm pronation and supination.

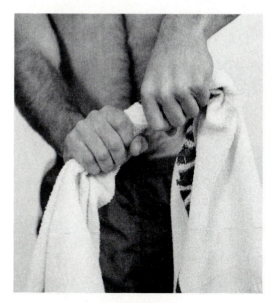

Figure 24-53

The towel twist exercise.

Figure 24-54

Wrist roll.

Wrist strength depends on forearm strength and freedom of movement in the wrist joint. Circumduction exercise helps to maintain joint integrity. Circling must be performed in each direction (Figure 24-55).

Suggested Hand and Wrist Exercises

Two exercises that are highly beneficial are gripping and spreading (Figure 24-56). Resistance exercises also can be used successfully for restoring grip strength.

Figure 24-55

Wrist circles and finger spread and grip.

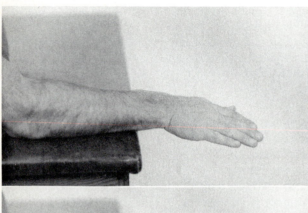
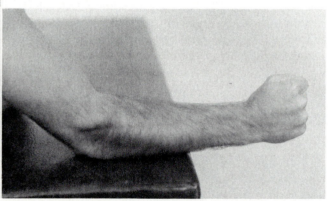
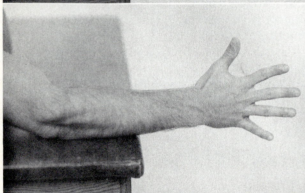

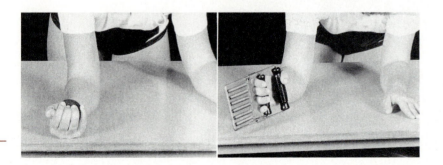

Figure 24-56

Restoring grip strength.

SUMMARY

The upper limb, including the elbow, forearm, wrist, and hand, is second to the lower limb in incidence of sports injuries.

The elbow is anatomically one of the more complex joints in the human body. The elbow joint allows the movements of flexion and extension and the radioulnar joint allows forearm pronation and supination. The major sports injuries of the elbow are contusions, strains, sprains, and dislocations. The chronic strain, which produces the pitcher's, tennis, javelin thrower's, and golfer's elbows, is more formally known as epicondylitis.

The forearm is composed of two bones, the ulna and the radius, as well as associated soft tissue. Sports injuries to the region commonly consist of contusions, chronic forearm splints, acute strains, and fractures.

Injuries to the wrist usually occur as the result of a fall or repeated movements of flexion, extension, and rotation. Common injuries are sprains, lunate carpal dislocation, navicular carpal fracture, and hamate fracture.

Injuries to the hand occur frequently in sports activities. Common injuries include those caused by contusions and chronic pressure, by tendons receiving sustained irritation, which leads to tenosynovitis, and by tendon avulsions. Sprains, dislocations, and fractures of the fingers are also common.

REVIEW QUESTIONS AND SUGGESTED ACTIVITIES

1. Describe how and why the elbow becomes chronically strained from throwing mechanisms.
2. Describe a dislocated elbow—its cause, appearance, and care.
3. How does the elbow sustain epicondylitis?
4. Compare elbow osteochondritis dissecans and knee osteochondritis dissecans. How does each occur?
5. What causes a Volkmann's contracture? How may it be detected early?
6. Discuss the many aspects of elbow exercise rehabilitation.
7. Compare forearm splints and shin-splints. How does each occur?
8. Describe the Colles' fracture of the forearm—its cause, appearance, and care.
9. What healing problems occur with navicular carpal fractures? Why?
10. How can a subungual hematoma be released?
11. What causes stenosing tenosynovitis in the hand?
12. Describe the circumstances that can produce a mallet finger and the boutonnière deformity in baseball players. What care should each condition receive?
13. A sprained thumb is common in sports activities. How does it occur, and what care should it receive?
14. Should a dislocated finger be reduced by a coach? Explain your answer.

REFERENCES

1. Allman, Jr, FL: Overuse injury to the elbow in the throwing sports. In Welsh, RP, and Shephard, RJ: Current therapy in sports medicine, 1985-1986, Philadelphia, 1985, Brian C Decker, Publisher.
2. Aronen, JG: Problems of the upper extremity in gymnastics. In Weiker, GG, editor: Symposium on gymnastics, Clinics in sports medicine, vol 4, no 1, Philadelphia, 1985, WB Saunders Co.
3. Birnbaum, JS: The musculoskeletal manual, New York 1982, Academic Press, Inc.
4. Burke, ER: Phys Sportsmed 9:53, April 1981.
5. Burnet, ME, and Haddad, Jr, RJ: Fractures and dislocations of the metacarpals and phalanges. In McCue III, FC, editor: Injuries to the elbow, forearm, and hand, Clinics in sports medicine, vol 5, no 4, Philadelphia, 1986, WB Saunders Co.

6. Cailliet R: Hand pain and impairment, ed 3, Philadelphia, 1982, FA Davis Co.

7. Cooney III, WP: Tennis elbow, Postgrad Med 15(76):45, 1984.

8. Culver, JE: Instabilities of the wrist. In McCue III, FC, editor: Injuries to the elbow, forearm, and hand, Clinics in sports medicine, vol 5, no 4, Philadelphia, 1986, WB Saunders Co.

9. Curtis, Jr, RJ, and Corley, Jr, FG: Fractures and dislocations of the forearm. In McCue III, FC, editor: Injuries to the elbow, forearm, and hand, clinics in sports medicine, vol 5, no 4, Philadelphia, 1986, WB Saunders Co.

10. Cyriax, J: Textbook of orthopaedic medicine, vol 1, Diagnosis of soft tissue lesions, ed 8, Eastborne, England, 1982, Pailliere Tindall.

11. Gerber, C, et al: Skier's thumb: surgical treatment of recent injuries to the ulnar collateral ligament of the thumb's metacarpophalangeal joint, Am J Sports Med 9:171, May/June 1981.

12. Gibeault, JD: Mismanaging hand injuries can lead to long-term disability, The First Aider 56(5):6, 1987.

13. Gieck, JH, and McCur III, FC: Splinting of finger injuries—a tip from the field, Ath Train 17:215, Fall 1982.

14. Isani, A, and Melone, Jr, CP: Ligamentous injuries of the hand in athletes. In McCue III, FC, editor: Injuries to the elbow, forearm, and hand, Clinics in sports medicine, vol 5, no 4, Philadelphia, 1986, WB Saunders Co.

15. Jobe, FW: Ulnar neuritis and medical collateral ligament instabilities in overarm throwers. In Welsh, RP, and Shephard, RJ, editors: Current therapy in sports medicine, 1985-1986, Philadelphia, 1985, Brian C Decker, Publisher.

16. Jobe, FW, and Nuber, G: Throwing injuries of the elbow. In McCue III, FC, editor: Injuries to the elbow, forearm, and hand, Clinics in sports medicine, vol 5, no 4, Philadelphia, 1986, WB Saunders Co.

17. Leach, RE, and Miller, JK: Lateral and medial epicondylitis of the elbow. In Hunter-Griffin, LY: Overuse injuries, Clinics in sports medicine, vol 6, no 2, Philadelphia, 1987, WB Saunders Co.

18. Leddy, JP: Athletic injuries to the hand and wrist, Postgraduate advances in sports medicine, I-IX, Pennington, NJ, 1986, Forum Medicus, Inc.

19. Lee, DG: "Tennis elbow": a manual therapist's perspective, J Orthop Sports Phys Ther 8:134, 1986.

20. Maroon, BR: Orthopedic aspects of sports medicine. In Appenzellar, O, and Atkinson, R, editors: Sports medicine, Baltimore, 1981, Urban & Schwarzenberg, Inc.

21. McCue III, FC: The elbow, wrist, and hand. In Kulund, DN: The injured athlete, Philadelphia, 1982, JB Lippincott Co.

22. McCue III, FC, and Wooten, SL: Closed tendon injuries of the hand in athletics. In McCue III, FC, editor: Injuries to the elbow, forearm, and hand, Clinics in sports medicine, vol 5, no 4, Philadelphia, 1986, WB Saunders Co.

23. Nirschl, RP: Soft-tissue injuries about the elbow. In McCue III, FC, editor: Injuries to the elbow, forearm, and hand, Clinics in sports medicine, vol 5, no 4, Philadelphia, 1986, WB Saunders Co.

24. Pappas, RM, Zawacki, RM, and Sullivan, TJ: Biomechanics of baseball pitching: a preliminary report, Am J Sports Med 13:216, July/Aug 1985.

25. Wilson, RL, and Carter, MS: Joint injuries in the hand: preservation of proximal interphalangeal joint function. In Hunter, JM, et al, editors: Rehabilitation of the hand, ed 2, St. Louis, 1984, The CV Mosby Co.

26. Wilson, RL, and Carter, MS: Management of hand fractures. In Hunter, JM, et al, editors: Rehabilitation of the hand, ed 2, St Louis, 1984, The CV Mosby Co.

27. Wright, CS: Fractures and dislocations in the hand and wrist. In Welsh, RP, and Shephard, RJ, editors: Current therapy in sports medicine, 1985-1986, Philadelphia, 1985, Brian C Decker, Publisher.

28. Wright, CS: Tendon injuries in the hand and wrist. In Welsh, RP, and Shephard, RJ, editors: Current therapy in sports medicine, 1985-1986, Philadelphia, 1985, Brian C Decker, Publisher.

29. Zemel, NP, and Stark, HH: Fractures and dislocations of the carpal bones. In McCue III, FC, editor: Injuries to the elbow, forearm, and hand, Clinics in sports medicine, vol 5, no 4, Philadelphia, 1986, WB Saunders Co.

ANNOTATED BIBLIOGRAPHY

Cailliet, R: Hand pain and impairment, ed 3, Philadelphia, 1982, FA Davis Co.
An excellent monograph about hand conditions that offers a thorough review of key anatomy and causes of injury and pain.

Hunter, JM, et al., editors: Rehabilitation of the hand, St. Louis, 1978, The CV Mosby Co.
Although written for the physician and therapist, includes parts that are of value to the coach or athletic trainer. The chapter about splinting is especially interesting.

McCue III, FC, editor: Injuries to the elbow, forearm, and hand, Clinics in sports medicine, vol 5, no 4, Philadelphia, 1986, WB Saunders Co.
Includes 13 chapters dedicated to elbow, forearm, and hand injuries caused by sports participation. Injury mechanisms, recognition, prevention, and management are stressed.

Petrone, FA, editor: American Academy of Orthopaedic Surgeons symposium on upper extremity injuries in athletes, St. Louis, 1986, The CV Mosby Co.
A compilation of papers about upper-extremity injuries that occur during sports participation.

Zarins, B, Andrews, JR, and Carson, WG, editors: Injuries to the throwing arm, The US Olympic Committee, Sports Medicine Council, Philadelphia, 1985, WB Saunders Co.
An outgrowth of two sports medicine conferences sponsored by the United States Olympic Committee and the United States Baseball Federation, this text contains chapters contributed by 30 experts in the field of sports medicine.

Other Health Conditions Related to Sports

When you finish this chapter, you should be able to

Identify symptoms and signs of common respiratory and gastrointestinal tract problems

Differentiate between diabetic coma and insulin shock and provide appropriate emergency care for both

Describe common contagious viral diseases

Describe appropriate action for caring for an athlete having an epileptic seizure

Identify signs of hypertension

Identify signs of the anemias and the sickle cell trait in athletes

Describe the symptoms and signs of major venereal diseases

Describe major menstrual irregularities and aspects concerning female reproduction in relation to sports participation

List reasons for sudden, unexplained death in young athletes

Besides the skin and musculoskeletal conditions already addressed, the athlete is subject to many other conditions. The athletic trainer, as a health and safety practitioner, should be able to recognize and give advice about a vast array of health problems. Chapter 25 presents the most prevalent and important of these health problems.

THE RESPIRATORY TRACT

Respiratory tract infections can be highly communicable among sports team members.

The respiratory tract is an organ system through which various communicable diseases can be transmitted. It is commonly the port of entry for acute infectious diseases that are spread from person to person or by direct contact. Some of the more prevalent conditions affecting athletes are the common cold, sinusitis, sore throat, asthma, hay fever, air pollution, and the "childhood" diseases, measles, chickenpox, and mumps.

The Common Cold (Coryza)

Upper respiratory tract infections, especially colds and associated conditions, are common in the sports program and can play havoc with entire teams.

ETIOLOGY   The common cold is attributed to filterable viruses which produces an infection of the upper respiratory tract within a susceptible individual.

SYMPTOMS AND SIGNS   The susceptible person is believed to be one who has, singly or in combination, any of the following characteristics:

1. Physical debilitation for overwork or lack of sleep
2. Chronic inflammation from a local infection
3. Inflammation of the nasal mucosa from an allergy
4. Inflammation of the nasal mucosa from breathing foreign substances such as dust
5. Sensitivity to stress

The onset of **coryza** is usually rapid, with symptoms varying in each individual. The typical effects are a general feeling of **malaise** with an accompanying headache, sneezing, and nasal discharge. Some individuals may register a fever of 100° to 102° F (38° to 39° C) and have chills. Various aches and pains may also accompany the symptoms. The nasal discharge starts as a watery secretion, gradually becoming thick and discolored from the inflammation. A cold may be centered in a specific area or may extend throughout the upper respiratory tract. Sinusitis and pharyngitis often result from the common cold. Many disorders begin with the same symptoms that a cold presents.

MANAGEMENT   Management of the cold is usually symptomatic, with emphasis placed on isolation, bed rest, and light eating. **Palliative** medications include aspirin for relieving general discomfort, medications for drying the secreting mucosa, and nasal drops or an inhaler containing ephedrine to relieve nasal congestion. If a cough is present, various syrups may be given to afford relief. Caution should be taken in disguising basic cold symptoms so that the athlete may return to activity sooner. Activity before complete recovery will only delay full recuperation and may possibly cause chronic associated conditions.

The prevention of colds is much more important than caring for them after they have become established. The methods of cold prevention that have proved most beneficial are (1) eating regular, well-balanced meals, (2) avoiding extreme fatigue, (3) avoiding undue temperature changes without adjustments of clothing to meet such changes, (4) maintaining cleanliness at all times, and (5) attempting to eliminate undue emotional stress.

Influenza

Influenza, the "flu," is one of the most persistent and debilitating diseases. It usually occurs in various forms as an annual epidemic, causing severe illness among the populace.

ETIOLOGY   Influenza is caused by myxoviruses classified as types A, B, and C. The virus enters the tissue's cell through its genetic material. Within the tissue, the virus multiplies and is released from the cell by a budding process, to be spread throughout the body.

SYMPTOMS AND SIGNS   The athlete with the flu will have the following symptoms: fever, cough, headache, malaise, and inflamed respiratory mucous membranes. Flu generally has an incubation period of 48 hours and comes on suddenly, accompanied by chills and a fever of 39° to 39.5° C (102° to 103° F), which develops over a 24-hour period. The athlete complains of a headache and general aches and pains—mainly in the back and legs. The headache increases in intensity, along with **photophobia** and aching at the back of the skull. There is often

coryza
Profuse nasal discharge.

malaise
Discomfort and uneasiness caused by an illness.

palliative
An agent that alleviates or eases but does not cure.

photophobia
Unusual intolerance to lights.

sore throat, burning in the chest, and in the beginning, a nonproductive cough, which later may develop into bronchitis. The skin is flushed, and the eyes are inflamed and watery. The acute stage of the disease usually lasts up to 5 days. Weakness, sweating, and fatigue may persist for many days. Flu prevention includes staying away from infected persons and maintaining good resistance through healthy living. Vaccines, including prevalent strains, may be given to individuals who are at risk such as pregnant women or people in frail health.

MANAGEMENT If the flu is uncomplicated, its management consists of bed rest. During the acute stage, the temperature often returns to normal. Symptomatic care such as aspirin, steam inhalation, cough medicines, and gargles may be given.

Sinusitis

There are numerous sinuses in the facial bony structure. These sinuses are hollow cavities lined with a mucous membrane, and each sinus is connected by a canal to the nasal passages. There are two basic groups of facial sinuses: (1) an anterior group composed of the maxillary, frontal, and ethmoidal sinuses and (2) a posterior group consisting of the sphenoidal and ethnoidal sinuses.

ETIOLOGY Inflammation of the sinuses may be acute, subacute, or chronic and can occur from any condition that hampers normal sinus ventilation and drainage. Sinusitis may occur after a cold, an allergy, measles, or other diseases that involve the upper respiratory tract. It is usually associated with streptococcal, pneumococcal, and staphylococcal organisms.

SYMPTOMS AND SIGNS Sinusitis can develop gradually or suddenly and is associated with headache, nasal and postnasal discharge, and a general feeling of malaise. There also may be accompanying fever and sore throat.

MANAGEMENT Because the infected sinuses lie close to the brain, sinusitis can be extremely dangerous. Cases of sinusitis should be managed by a physician who uses various methods to help evacuate and heal the inflamed sinuses. The most common treatment procedure consists of inhalation of steam and the use of vasoconstricting nose drops, combined with symptomatic therapy such as rest, a light diet, and aspirin.

The athlete should be instructed about the proper way to apply nose drops (Figure 25-1) and the safe way to blow the nose. The nose should be blown with the mouth open, and pressure should be applied to one nostril at a time to avoid additional sinus irritation or the spread of the infection.

Figure 25-1

Proper application of nose drops. **A,** Head tilted back. **B,** Head down.

A

B

Hay Fever (Pollinosis)

Hay fever, or pollinosis, is an acute seasonal allergic condition that results from airborne pollens.

ETIOLOGY Hay fever can occur during the spring as a reaction to tree pollens such as oak, elm, maple, alder, birch, and cottonwood. During the summer grass and weed pollens can be the culprits. In the fall, ragweed pollen is the prevalent cause. Airborne fungal spores also have been known to cause hay fever.

SYMPTOMS AND SIGNS In the early stages, the athlete's eyes, throat, mouth, and nose begin to itch, followed by watering of the eyes, sneezing, and a clear, watery, nasal discharge. The athlete may complain of a sinus-type headache, emotional irritability, difficulty in sleeping, red and swollen eyes and nasal mucous membranes, and a wheezing cough.[4]

MANAGEMENT Most athletes obtain relief from hay fever through oral antihistamines. To avoid the problem of sedation stemming from these drugs, the athlete may ingest a decongestant during the day and a long-reacting antihistamine before going to bed.

Sore Throat (Pharyngitis)

The sore throat, or pharyngitis, is usually of viral origin or is caused by streptococcal, pneumococcal, or straphylococcal organisms.[4]

ETIOLOGY A sore throat usually is associated with a common cold or sinusitis as the result of the postnasal drip. It may also be an indication of a more serious condition.

SYMPTOMS AND SIGNS Frequently pharyngitis starts as a dryness in the throat, progressing to soreness, with pain and swelling. It is sometimes accompanied by a headache, a fever of 101° to 102° F (38° to 39° C), chills, coughing, and a general feeling of fatigue. During examination, the throat may appear dark red and swollen, and mucous membranes may be coated.

MANAGEMENT In most cases bed rest is considered the best treatment, combined with the use of symptomatic medications such as aspirin and a hot saltwater gargle. Antibiotics and a silver nitrate throat swab may be used by a physician if other measures are inadequate.

Bronchitis and Asthma

Bronchitis and asthma are two major respiratory problems that bother some athletes. Sports performance can be inhibited by both of these health problems.

Bronchitis (Acute)

An inflammation of the "bronchial tubes" mucous membranes is call bronchitis. It occurs in both acute and chronic forms. If occurring in an athlete, bronchitis is more likely to be in the acute form.

ETIOLOGY Acute bronchitis usually occurs as an infectious winter disease that follows a common cold or other viral infection of the nasopharynx, throat, or tracheobronchial tree. Secondary to this inflammation is a bacterial infection that may follow overexposure to air pollution. Fatigue, malnutrition, and/or becoming chilled could be predisposing factors.

SYMPTOMS AND SIGNS The symptoms of an athlete with acute bronchitis usually start with an upper respiratory infection, nasal inflammation and profuse discharge, slight fever, sore throat, and back and muscle pains. A cough signals the beginning of bronchitis. In the beginning, the cough is dry, but in a few hours or days, a clear mucous secretion begins, becoming yellowish, indicating an infection. In most cases, the fever lasts 3 to 5 days, and the cough lasts 2 to 3 weeks or longer. The athlete may wheeze and rale when auscultation of the chest is performed. Pneumonia could complicate bronchitis.

To avoid bronchitis, it is advisable that an athlete not sleep in an area that is extremely cold or exercise in extremely cold air without wearing a face mask to warm inhaled air.

MANAGEMENT   Management of acute bronchitis involves rest until fever subsides, drinking 3 to 4 L of water per day, and ingesting an antipyretic analgesic, a cough suppressor, and an antibiotic (when severe lung infection is present) daily.

Asthma

ETIOLOGY   As one of the most common respiratory diseases, bronchial asthma can be produced from a number of stressors such as a viral respiratory tract infection, emotional upset, changes in barometric pressure or temperature, exercise, inhalation of a noxious odor, or exposure to a specific allergen.

SYMPTOMS AND SIGNS   Bronchial asthma is characterized by a spasm of the bronchial smooth muscles, edema, and inflammation of the mucous lining. In addition to asthma's narrowing of the airway, copious amounts of mucus are produced. Difficulty in breathing may cause the athlete to hyperventilate, resulting in dizziness. The attack may begin with coughing, wheezing, shortness of breath, and a sense of fatigue. See box on p. 821.

Exercise-Induced Bronchial Obstruction (Asthma)

ETIOLOGY   Exercise-induced bronchial obstruction is also known as exercise-induced asthma (EIA). It is a disease that occurs almost exclusively in asthmatic persons.[30]

SYMPTOMS AND SIGNS   An asthmatic attack can be stimulated by exercise in some individuals and can be provoked in others only on rare occasions during moderate exercise.[27,39] The exact cause of EIA is not clear. Metabolic acidosis, postexertional hypocapnia, stimulation of tracheal irritant receptors, adrenergic abnormalities such as a defective catecholamine metabolism, and psychological factors have been suggested as possible causes.[19,38] Loss of heat and water causes the greatest loss of airway reactivity. Eating certain foods such as shrimp, celery, and peanuts can cause EIA. Sinusitis can also trigger an attack in an individual with chronic asthma.[18]

MANAGEMENT   A number of studies have been performed to determine the most desirable exercise and training methods for EIA. Long continuous running causes the most severe bronchospasm.[28] Swimming is the least bronchospasm producing, which may be a result of the moist, warm air environment.[6] It is generally agreed that a regular exercise program can benefit asthmatics and non-asthmatics. Fewer symptoms occur with short intense work followed by rest compared to sustained exercise.[27] There should be gradual warm-up and cool down. The duration of exercise should build slowly to 30 to 40 minutes, four or five times a week. Exercise intensity and loading also should be graduated slowly. An example would be 10 to 30 seconds of work, followed by 30 to 90 seconds of rest. Aerosol asthmatic agents are taken before exercise.[2] Asthmatic athletes who receive medication for their condition should make sure that what they take is legal for competition.

MANAGEMENT OF THE ACUTE ASTHMATIC ATTACK

Athletes who have a history of asthma usually know how to care for themselves when attack occurs. However, the athletic trainer must be aware of what to look for and what to do if called on.

Early Symptoms and Signs

Anxious appearance
Sweating and paleness
Flared nostrils
Breathing with pursed lips
Fast breathing
Vomiting
Hunched over body posture
Physical fatigue unrelated to activity
Indentation in the notch below the Adam's apple
Rib spaces sink in as the athlete inhales
Coughing for no apparent reason
Excess throat clearing
Irregular, labored breathing or wheezing

Actions to Take

Attempt to relax and reassure the athlete.
If medication has been cleared by the team physician, have the athlete use it.
Encourage the athlete to drink water.
Have the athlete perform controlled breathing along with relaxation exercises.
If an environmental factor triggering the attack is known, remove it or the athlete
    from the area.
If these procedures do not help, immediate medical attention may be necessary.

THE GASTROINTESTINAL TRACT

Like any other individual, the athlete may develop various complaints of the digestive system. The athlete may display various disorders of the gastrointestinal tract as a result of poor eating habits or the stress engendered from competition. The responsibility of the athletic trainer in such cases is to be able to recognize the more severe conditions so that early referrals to a physician can be made. The following discussion of the digestive system disorders that are common in sports provides information on how to (1) give proper counsel to the athlete about the prevention of mouth and intestinal disorders, (2) recommend a proper diet, and (3) recognize deviations from the normal in these areas.

Mouth Disorders

Many different conditions involving the mouth appear during the course of a regular training program. Of them, the most commonly observed is dental caries (tooth decay), which is indicated by local decalcification of the tooth. Tooth decay is the result of an increase in mouth acids, usually from food fermentation. Any disorder within the oral environment that raises its acid content without adequate neutralization may result in tooth decay. Proper oral hygiene is necessary and should include the following: (1) eating wholesome foods and (2) brushing the teeth properly, immediately after meals.

The greatest single cause of tooth loss is gum disease, the symptoms of which usually display the following pattern: (1) gingivitis, (2) periodontitis, and (3) pyorrhea. Gingivitis is an inflammation of the gum tissue surrounding the teeth and can arise from irritation brought about by tartar (calculus) or bacterial infection. If not cared for properly, gingivitis can extend to the periodontal tissue and eventually to the alveolar bone that supports the teeth, resulting in eventual loss of the teeth.

Infections associated with dental caries and gum disease can completely debilitate an athlete. Therefore, an immediate referral to a dentist is important.

Indigestion (Dyspepsia)

Some athletes have certain food idiosyncrasies that cause them considerable distress after eating. Others develop reactions when eating before competition. The term given to digestive upset is indigestion (dyspepsia).

ETIOLOGY Indigestion can be caused by any number of conditions. The most common in sports are emotional stress, esophageal and stomach spasms, and/or inflammation of the mucous lining of the esophagus and stomach.

SYMPTOMS AND SIGNS These conditions cause an increased secretion of hydrochloric acid (sour stomach), nausea, and flatulence (gas).

MANAGEMENT Care of acute dyspepsia involves the elimination of irritating foods from the diet, development of regular eating habits, and avoidance of anxieties that may lead to gastric distress.

Constant irritation of the stomach may lead to chronic and more serious disorders such as gastritis, an inflammation of the stomach wall, or ulcerations of the gastrointestinal mucosa. Athletes who appear nervous and high-strung and suffer from dyspepsia should be examined by the sports physician.

Diarrhea

Diarrhea is abnormal stool looseness or passage of a fluid, unformed stool and is categorized as acute or chronic, according to the type present.

ETIOLOGY Diarrhea can be caused by problems in diet, inflammation of the intestinal lining, gastrointestinal infection, ingestion of certain drugs, and psychogenic factors.

SYMPTOMS AND SIGNS Diarrhea is characterized by abdominal cramps, nausea, and possibly vomiting, coupled with frequent elimination of stools, ranging from 3 to 20 a day. The infected person often has a loss of appetite and a light brown or gray, foul-smelling stool. Extreme weakness caused by fluid dehydration is usually present.

MANAGEMENT The cause of diarrhea is often difficult to establish. It is conceivable that any irritant may cause the loose stool. This can include an infestation of parasitic organisms or an emotional upset. Management of diarrhea requires a knowledge of its cause. Less severe cases can be cared for by (1) omitting foods that cause irritation, (2) drinking boiled milk, (3) eating bland food until symptoms have ceased, and (4) using pectins two or three times daily for the absorption of excess fluid.

Diarrhea could lead to fluid dehydration.

Constipation

Some athletes are subject to constipation, the failure of the bowels to evacuate feces.

ETIOLOGY   There are numerous causes of constipation, the most common of which are (1) lack of abdominal muscle tone, (2) insufficient moisture in the feces, causing it to be hard and dry, (3) lack of a sufficient proportion of roughage and bulk in the diet to stimulate peristalsis, (4) poor bowel habits, (5) nervousness and anxiety, and (6) overuse of laxatives and enemas.

MANAGEMENT   The best means of overcoming constipation is to regulate eating patterns to include foods that will encourage normal defecation. Cereals, fruits, vegetables, and fats stimulate bowel movement, whereas sugars and carbohydrates tend to inhibit it. Some persons become constipated as the result of psychological factors. In such cases it may be helpful to try to determine the causes of stress and, if need be, to refer the athlete to a physician or school psychologist for counseling. Above all, laxatives or enemas should be avoided unless their use has been prescribed by a physician.

Laxatives and enemas should be avoided to relieve constipation.

Hemorrhoids (Piles)

Hemorrhoids are varicosities of the hemorrhoidal venous plexus of the anus. There are both internal and external anal veins.

ETIOLOGY   Chronic constipation or straining at the stool may tend to stretch the anal veins, resulting in either a protrusion (prolapse) and bleeding of the internal or external veins or a thrombus in the external veins.

SYMPTOMS AND SIGNS   Most often hemorrhoids are painful nodular swellings near the sphincter of the anus. There may be slight bleeding and itching. The majority of hemorrhoids are self-limiting and spontaneously heal within 2 to 3 weeks.

MANAGEMENT   The management of hemorrhoids is mostly palliative and serves to eliminate discomfort until healing takes place. The following measures can be suggested:

1. Use of proper bowel habits
2. Ingestion of 1 tablespoon of mineral oil daily to assist in lubricating dry stool
3. Application of an astringent suppository (tannic acid)
4. Application of a local anesthetic to control pain and itching (dibucaine)

If palliative meaures are unsuccessful, surgery may be required.

Appendicitis

Appendicitis is discussed because of the importance of its early detection and the possibility of mistaking it for a common gastric complaint.

ETIOLOGY   Inflammation of the vermiform appendix can be chronic or acute; it is caused by a bacterial infection. In its early stages, the appendix becomes red and swollen; in later stages it may become gangrenous, rupturing into the bowels or peritoneal cavity and causing peritonitis.

SYMPTOMS AND SIGNS   The athlete may complain of a mild-to-severe cramp in the lower abdomen, associated with nausea, vomiting, and a low-grade fever ranging from 99° to 100° F (37° to 38° C). Later, the cramps may localize into a pain in the right side, and palpation may reveal tenderness at a point midway between the anterior superior spine of the ilium and the umbilicus (McBurney's point).

MANAGEMENT   If appendicitis is suspected, the athlete must be referred immediately to a physician for diagnostic tests. Surgery is the usual treatment.

Food Poisoning (Gastroenteritis)

Food poisoning, which may range from mild to severe, results from infectious organisms (bacteria of the salmonella group, certain staphylococci, streptococci, or dysentery bacilli) that enter the body in either food or drink.

ETIOLOGY   Contaminated foods result, especially during warm weather, when improper food refrigeration permits the organisms to multiply rapidly. Contamination can also occur if the food is handled by an infected food handler.

SYMPTOMS AND SIGNS   Infection results in nausea, vomiting, cramps, diarrhea, and anorexia. The symptoms of staphylococcal infections usually subside in 3 to 6 hours. Salmonella infection symptoms may last from 24 to 48 hours or more.

MANAGEMENT   Management requires rapid replacement of lost fluids and electrolytes, which in severe cases may need to be replaced intravenously. Bed rest is desirable in all but mild cases; as long as the nausea and vomiting continue, nothing should be given by mouth. If tolerated, light fluids or foods such as clear, strained broth, bouillon with a small amount of added salt, soft-cooked eggs, or bland cereals may be given.

DIABETES MELLITUS

Diabetes mellitus is a complex hereditary or developmental disease involving carbohydrate metabolism. Decreased effectiveness of or insufficient insulin is responsible for most cases. Until recently diabetics were usually discouraged or forbidden competitive sports participation. Today an ever-increasing number of diabetics are active sports participants, functioning effectively in almost all sports. Since the key to the control of diabetes is the control of blood sugar, the insulin-dependent athlete must constantly juggle food intake, insulin, and exercise to maintain the blood sugar in its proper range if he or she is to perform to maximum. Diet, exercise, and insulin are the major factors in the everyday life-style of the diabetic athlete, who must of necessity develop an ordered and specific living pattern to cope with the demands of daily existence and strenuous physical activity.[16]

Diabetic athletes engaging in vigorous physical activity should eat before exercising, and, if the exercise is protracted, should have hourly glucose supplementation. As a rule, the insulin dosage is not changed, but food intake is increased. The response of diabetics varies among individuals and depends on many variables. Although there are some hazards, with proper medical evaluation and planning by a consultant in metabolic diseases, diabetics can feel free to engage in most physical activities.[23]

Diabetic Coma and Insulin Shock

It is important that coaches and athletic trainers who work with athletes who have diabetes mellitus are aware of the major symptoms of diabetic coma and insulin shock and the proper actions to take when either one occurs.

Diabetic Coma

If not treated adequately through proper diet and/or intake of insulin, the diabetic athlete can develop acidosis.

ETIOLOGY   A loss of sodium, potassium, and ketone bodies through excessive urination produces a problem of ketoacidosis that can lead to coma.

SYMPTOMS AND SIGNS

Labored breathing or gasping for air

Fruity smelling breath caused by acetone

Nausea and vomiting

Thirst

Dry mucous lining of the mouth and flushed skin

Mental confusion or unconsciousness followed by coma

MANAGEMENT   Because of the life-threatening nature of diabetic coma, early detection of ketoacidosis is essential. The injection of insulin into the athlete will normally prevent coma.

Insulin Shock

ETIOLOGY   Unlike diabetic coma, insulin shock occurs when too much insulin is taken into the body and hypoglycemia results.

SYMPTOMS AND SIGNS   Insulin shock is characterized by the following:

Physical weakness

Moist and pale skin

Drooping

Normal or shallow respirations

MANAGEMENT   The diabetic athlete who engages in intense exercise and metabolizes large amounts of glycogen could inadvertently take too much insulin and thus have a severe reaction. To avoid this problem the athlete must adhere to a carefully planned diet that includes a snack before exercise. The snack should contain a combination of a complex carbohydrate and protein such as cheese and crackers. Activities that last for more than 30 to 40 minutes should be accompanied by snacks of simple carbohydrates. Some diabetics carry with them a lump of sugar or have candy or orange juice readily available in the event an insulin reaction seems imminent.

COMMON CONTAGIOUS VIRAL DISEASES

It is not within the purview of this text to describe in detail all the various infectious diseases to which athletes may be prone. However, on occasion an athlete may exhibit recognizable symptoms of such a disease; one should know the symptoms and be able to identify them (Table 25-1). A player or other athlete indicating such symptoms should be remanded to a physician without delay.

The virus is an extremely small organism that is visible only with an electron microscope. Viruses are a parasitic mode of **DNA** or **RNA** and reside in a cell. Along with the cell, viruses are provided with nutrition and their reproductive needs by the host systems.

DNA
Deoxyribonucleic acid.

RNA
Ribonucleic acid.

More than 300 viruses have been isolated, some of which are harmless to humans. But others are related to infectious diseases such as the common cold, most childhood diseases, and a majority of the upper respiratory tract diseases. Infectious mononucleosis, or "mono," is a common occurrence among athletes and is associated with Epstein-Barr virus. The newest of the venereal diseases to be identified, acquired immune deficiency syndrome (AIDS), is a viral disease as well (see pp. 833-834).

TABLE 25-1 Some Infectious Viral Diseases

Disease	Sites Involved	Mode of Transmission	Incubation Period	Chief Symptoms	Duration	Period of Contagion	Treatment	Prophylaxis
Measles (rubeola)	Skin, respiratory tract, and conjunctivae	Contact or droplet	7-14 days	Appearance—like common cold with fever, cough, conjunctivitis, photophobia, and spots in throat, followed by skin rash	4-7 days after symptoms appear	Just before coldlike symptoms through approximately 1 week after rash appears	Bed rest and use of smoked glasses; symptomatic	Vaccine available
German measles (rubella)	Skin, respiratory tract, and conjunctivae	Contact or droplet	14-21 days	Cold symptoms, skin rash, and swollen lymph nodes behind ear	1-2 days	2-4 days before rash through 5 days afterward	Symptomatic	Vaccine available; gamma globulin given in postexposure situations
Chicken pox (varicella)	Trunk; then face, neck, and limbs	Contact or droplet	14-21 days	Mild cold symptoms, followed by appearance of vesicles	1-2 weeks	1 day before onset through 6 days afterward	Symptomatic	Vaccine available, including zoster immune globulin (ZIG) or varicella-zoster immune globulin (VZIG)

Mumps (epidemic parotiditis)	Salivary glands	Prolonged contact or droplet	18-21 days	Headache, drowsiness, fever, abdominal pain, pain during chewing and swallowing, swelling of neck under jaw	10 days	1 week	Symptomatic	Temporary immunization by virus vaccine
Influenza (flu)	Respiratory tract	Droplet	1-2 days	Aching of low back, generalized aching, chills, headache, fever, and bronchitis	2-5 days	2-3 days	Symptomatic	Moderate temporary protection from polyvalent influenza virus
Cold (coryza)	Respiratory tract	Droplet	12 hours to 4 days	Mild fever, headache, chills, and nasal discharge	1-2 weeks	Not clearly identified	Symptomatic	Possible help from vitamins and/or cold vaccine; avoid exposure
Infectious mononucleosis	Trunk	Contact	4-7 weeks	Sore throat, fever, skin rash, general aching, and swelling of lymph glands	3-4 weeks	Low rate	Symptomatic	None; avoid extreme fatigue

CONVULSIVE DISORDERS (EPILEPSY)

Epilepsy is not a disease but is a symptom that can be manifested by a large number of underlying disorders. **Epilepsy** is defined as "a recurrent paroxysmal disorder of cerebral function characterized by a sudden, brief attack of altered consciousness, motor activity, sensory phenomena, or inappropriate behavior."[4]

ETIOLOGY   For some types of epilepsy there is a genetic predisposition and a low threshold to having seizures. In others, altered brain metabolism or a history of injury may be the cause. A seizure can range from extremely brief episodes (petit mal seizure) to major episodes (grand mal seizures), unconsciousness, and tonic-clonic muscle contractions.

SYMPTOMS AND SIGNS   Each person with epilepsy must be considered individually as to whether he or she should engage in competitive sports. It is generally agreed that if an individual has daily or even weekly major seizures, collision sports should be prohibited.[36] This prohibition is not because hitting the head will necessarily trigger a seizure, but that unconsciousness during participation could result in a serious injury. If the seizures are properly controlled by medication or only occur during sleep, little, if any, sports restriction should be imposed except for scuba diving, swimming alone, or participation at a great height.[9]

MANAGEMENT   Often the epileptic athlete will experience an **aura,** which is a sign of an impending seizure. In such instances the athlete can take measures to provide protection such as sitting or lying down. When a seizure occurs without warning, the following steps should be taken by the athletic trainer:

Be emotionally composed.

If possible, cushion the athlete's fall.

Keep the athlete away from injury-producing objects.

Loosen restricting clothing.

Prevent the athlete from biting the mouth by placing a soft cloth between the teeth.

Allow the athlete to awaken normally after the seizure.

HYPERTENSION

Hypertension, or high blood pressure, that goes uncontrolled for a long time can lead to disease of the cardiovascular system (Table 25-2).

Athletes who are believed to have mild to moderate hypertension should not participate in competitive sports until a thorough physical examination, including a maximum exercise stress test, has been given.[25] The hypertensive athlete should avoid isometric exercises and/or heavy isotonic resistance such as in weight lifting.[40]

TABLE 25-2   Age and Blood Pressure Limits

Age	Upper Blood Pressure Limits at Rest*
<10	130/75 mm Hg
10-15	140/85 mm Hg
15-20	145/90 mm Hg
>20	150/95 mm Hg

*If the upper limits of blood pressure are exceeded during three measurements, the athlete may have hypertension.

epilepsy
Recurrent paroxymal disorder characterized by sudden attacks of altered consciousness, motor activity, sensory phenomena, or inappropriate behavior.

For individuals who have major daily or weekly seizures, collision-type sports may be prohibited.

aura
Pre-epileptic phenomenon, involving visual sensation of fire or glow, along with other possible sensory hallucinations and dreamlike states.

Hypertension may be a factor excluding players from sports participation.

ANEMIA IN ATHLETES

Athletes who engage in aerobic exercise generally experience a mild lowering of their hemoglobin concentration.[11] It is not considered an adverse condition but one that is an adaptation to aerobic exercise. This occurrence may be noted in individuals immediately following exercise and is not true anemia. Another adaptation to exercise that is found in elite athletes is an increase in red cell mass.

Iron Deficiency Anemia

Iron deficiency is the most common form of true anemia among athletes.

ETIOLOGY　Three conditions occur during anemia: erythrocytes (red blood cells) are too small or too large, hemoglobin is decreased, and ferritin concentration is low. Ferritin is an iron-phosphorous-protein complex that normally contains 23% iron.

SYMPTOMS AND SIGNS　In the first stages of iron deficiency, the athlete's performance begins to decline. The athlete may complain of burning thighs and nausea from becoming anaerobic. Ice craving is also common.[11] Athletes with mild iron deficiency anemia may display some mild impairment in their maximum performance.[33] Determining serum ferritin is the most accurate test of iron status. Two factors must be checked by the physician: (1) the athlete's mean corpuscular volume (MCV), the average volume of individual cells in a cubic micron, and (2) the relative sizes of the erythrocytes.

MANAGEMENT　For men, iron deficiency is usually caused by blood loss in the gastrointestinal tract. For women, the most common causes are menstruation and not enough iron in the diet. If the athlete is a vegetarian, he or she might lack iron.[11] Aspirin or stress can irritate the gastrointestinal tract. The following are some ways to manage iron deficiency: (1) ensure proper diet, including more red meat or dark chicken; (2) avoid coffee or tea, which hampers iron absorption from grains; (3) ingest vitamin C sources, which enhance iron absorption; and (4) take an iron supplement, consisting of ferrous sulfate, 325 mg, three times per week.[11]

Footstrike Anemia

"Footstrike anemia," or **hemolysis,** is secondary to iron deficiency in athletes.

ETIOLOGY　The cause of footstrike anemia, as its name implies, is the impact of the foot as it strikes the floor surface. Impact forces serve to destroy normal erythrocytes within the vascular system.[11]

SYMPTOMS AND SIGNS　This hemolysis is characterized by mildly enlarged red cells, an increase in circulatory reticulocytes, and a decrease in the concentration of haptoglobin, which is a mucoprotein bound to hemoglobin and released into the plasma. Even with the athlete's wearing a well-designed and well-constructed running shoe, this condition can occur. Footstrike anemia varies according to the amount of running performed.[11]

MANAGEMENT　Footstrike anemia can be managed by decreasing the amount of running and by wearing proper running shoes. In addition, the athlete should be encouraged not to run on a nonyielding surface.

Sickle Cell Anemia

Sickle cell anemia is a chronic hereditary hemolytic anemia. Approximately 35% of the black population in the United States has this condition; 8% to 13% are

hemolysis
Destruction of red blood cells.

not anemic but carry this trait in their genes (sicklemia). The person with the sickle cell trait may participate in sports and never encounter problems until symptoms are brought on by some unusual circumstance.[37]

ETIOLOGY   In individuals with sickle cell anemia the red cells are sickle- or crescent-shaped. Within the red cells, an abnormal type of hemoglobin exists. It has been speculated that the sickling of the red blood cells results from an adaptation to malaria, which is prevalent in Africa. It is a recessive trait that is not sex-linked but is found in both parents.

The sickle cell has less potential for transporting oxygen and is fragile when compared to normal cells. A sickle cell's life span is 15 to 25 days, compared to the 120 days of a normal red cell; this short life of the sickle cell can produce severe anemia in individuals with acute sickle cell anemia. The cell's distorted shape inhibits its passage through the small blood vessels and can cause clustering of the cells and, consequently, clogging of the blood vessels, producing **thrombi,** which block circulation. For individuals having this condition, death can occur (in the severest cases of sickle cell anemia) from a stroke, heart disease, or an **embolus** in the lungs. Conversely, persons with sickle cell anemia may never experience any problems.

SYMPTOMS AND SIGNS   An athlete may never experience any complications from having the sickle cell trait. However, a sickle cell crisis can be brought on by exposure to high altitudes of by overheating of the skin, as is the case with a high fever.[20] Crisis symptoms include fever, severe fatigue, skin pallor, muscle weakness, and severe pain in the limbs and abdomen. Abdominal pain in the right upper quadrant may indicate a splenic syndrome in which there is an infarction. This is especially characteristic of a crisis triggered by a decrease in ambient oxygen while flying at high altitudes.[20] The athlete may also experience headache and convulsions.

MANAGEMENT   Treatment of a sickle cell crisis is usually symptomatic. The physician may elect to give anticoagulants and analgesics for pain.

SEXUALLY TRANSMITTED DISEASES

Sexually transmitted diseases are of major concern in sports because many athletes are in a period of life during which they are more sexually active than they will be at any other time during their life span. The venereal diseases with the highest incidence among the relatively young are nonspecific sexually transmitted infection (NSI), genital herpes, gonorrhea, genital candidiasis, condyloma acuminata (venereal warts), and acquired immune deficiency syndrome (AIDS).

Nonspecific Sexually Transmitted Infection

Nonspecific sexually transmitted infection (NSI), although not required to be reported to health officials, is considered by many the most common venereal disease in the United States. It is more common than gonorrhea.[4]

ETIOLOGY   The two organisms associated with NSI are ***Chlamydia trachomatis*** and *Ureaplasma urealyticum.* NSI is most commonly called chlamydia.

SYMPTOMS AND SIGNS   In the male, inflammation occurs along with a purulent discharge, 7 to 28 days after intercourse.[4] On occasion, painful urination and traces of blood in the urine occur. Most females with this infection are asymptomatic, but some may experience a vaginal discharge, painful urination, pelvic pain, and pain and inflammation in other sites.

thrombi
Plural of "thrombus"; a blood clot that blocks small blood vessels or a cavity of the heart.

embolus
A mass of undissolved matter.

Chlamydia trachomatis
A genus microorganism that can cause a wide variety of diseases in humans, one of which is venereal and causes nonspecific urethritis.

MANAGEMENT   A bacteriological examination is given to determine the exact organism(s) present. Once identified, the infection must be treated promptly to prevent complications. Organism identification and treatment must take place immediately in women who are pregnant. Chlamydial opthalmia neonatorum can cause conjunctivitis and pneumonia in the newborn from an infected mother.[4] Uncomplicated cases are usually treated with antibiotics. Approximately 20% of the sufferer's have one or more relapses.

Genital Herpes

Genital herpes is a venereal infection that is currently widespread among the populace.

ETIOLOGY   Type 2 herpes simplex virus is associated with genital herpes infection, which is now the most prevalent cause of genital ulcerations. After sexual contact signs of the disease appear in approximately 4 to 7 days.

SYMPTOMS AND SIGNS   The first signs in the male are itching and soreness, but women may be asymptomatic in the vagina and cervix. It is estimated that 50% to 60% of individuals who have had one attack of herpes genitalis will have no further episodes, or if they do, the lesions are few and insignificant. Like herpes labialis and gladiatorum, lesions develop that eventually become ulcerated with a red areola. Ulcerations crust and heal in approximately 10 days, leaving a scar (Color Plate, Figure M).

Of major importance to a pregnant woman with a history of genital herpes is whether there is an active infection when she is nearing delivery. Herpes simpex can be fatal to a newborn child. There is also some relationship (although this is unclear) between a higher incidence of cervical cancer and the incidence of herpes genitalis.[4]

MANAGEMENT   At this time there is no cure for genital herpes. Recently systemic medication, specifically antiviral medications such as acycloguanosine (Zovirax, Acyclovir) and vidarabine (Vira-A), are being used to lessen the early symptoms of the disease.[3]

Gonorrhea

Gonorrhea, commonly called "clap," is an acute venereal disease that can infect the urethra, cervix, and rectum.

ETIOLOGY   The organism of infection is the gonococcal bacteria *Neisseria gonorrhoeae*, which is usually spread through sexual intercourse.

SYMPTOMS AND SIGNS   In men the incubation period is 2 to 10 days. The onset of the disease is marked by a tingling sensation in the urethra, followed in 2 or 3 hours by greenish-yellow discharge of pus and painful urination. Sixty percent of infected women are asymptomatic. For those who have symptoms, onset is between 7 and 21 days. In these cases symptoms are very mild with some vaginal discharge. Gonorrheal infection of the throat and rectum are also possible.

Because of embarrassment some individuals fail to secure proper medical help for treatment of gonorrhea, and, although the initial symptoms will disappear, such an individual is not cured and can still spread the infection. Untreated gonorrhea becomes latent and will manifest itself in later years, usually causing sterility and/or arthritis. Treatment consists of large amounts of penicillin or other antibiotics. Recent experimental evidence suggests an increasing resistance of the gonococci to penicillin. Evidence of any of the symptoms should result in immediately remanding the individual to a physician for testing and treatment. *All sexual contact must be avoided* until it has been medically established that the disease is no longer active. Because of the latent residual effects that are the end result of several diseases in this group, including sterility and arthritis, immediate medical treatment is mandatory. Although outward signs may disappear, the disease is still insidiously present in the body. Additionally, such treatment will alleviate the discomfort that accompanies the initial stages of the disease.

MANAGEMENT Penicillin in high doses is usually the drug of choice. Other antibiotics may be used if the strain of bacteria is resistant to penicillin.

Trichomoniasis

Trichomoniasis affects 20% of all females and 5% to 10% of all males.

Trichomoniasis is an infection that affects 20% of all females during their reproductive years and 5% to 10% of males.

ETIOLOGY Trichomoniasis is caused by the flagellate protozoan *Trichomonas vaginalis.*

SYMPTOMS AND SIGNS The female with trichomoniasis typically has a vaginal discharge that is greenish-yellow and frothy. The disease causes irritation of the vulva, perineum, and thighs. The female may also experience painful urination. Males are usually asymptomatic, although some may experience a frothy, purulent urethral discharge.

MANAGEMENT Metronidazole, taken for 7 days, is usually the drug of choice in the treatment of trichomoniasis. Complete cure is required before the individual can again engage in sexual intercourse.

Genital Candidiasis

As discussed in Chapter 16, *Skin Disorders, Candida* (a genus of yeastlike fungi) is commonly part of the normal flora of the mouth, skin, intestinal tract, and vagina.

ETIOLOGY The *Candida* organism is one of the most common causes of vaginitis in women of reproductive age. The infection is usually transmitted sexually but also can stem from the intestine.

SYMPTOMS AND SIGNS As with other related conditions, the female complains of vulval irritation beginning with redness and severe pain, and a vaginal discharge (scanty). The male is usually asymptomatic but could develop some irritation and soreness of the glans penis, especially after intercourse. Rarely, a slight urethral discharge may occur.

MANAGEMENT Because of the highly infectious nature of this disease, all sexual contact should cease until completion of treatment. The drug nystatin (a fungicide) is usually inserted high into the vagina for 14 nights at bedtime. This treatment is immediately followed by application of nystatin cream to the labia, perineum, and perianal region.

Condyloma Acuminata (Venereal Warts)

Another sexually transmitted disease that should be recognized and referred to a physician is condyloma acuminata or venereal warts.

ETIOLOGY These warts are transmitted through sexual activity and commonly occur from poor hygiene. They appear on the glans penis, vulva, or anus.

SYMPTOMS AND SIGNS This form of wart virus produces nodules that have a cauliflower-like lesion or can be singular. In their early stage they are soft, moist, pink or red swellings that rapidly develop a stem with a flowerlike head. They may be mistaken for secondary syphilis or carcinoma (Color Plate, Figure N).

MANAGEMENT   Moist condylomas are often carefully treated by the physician with a solution containing 20% to 25% podophyllin. Dry warts may be treated with a freezing process such as liquid nitrogen.

Acquired Immune Deficiency Syndrome

Acquired immune deficiency syndrome (AIDS) is a fatal disease that attacks the body's immune system and prevents it from defending against otherwise non-threatening infections.

ETIOLOGY   AIDS is caused by the human immunodeficiency virus (HIV). This virus attacks the lymphocytes, which are the key to the human body's immune system. By suppressing the lymphocytes, the virus renders the body unable to ward off invading infections. The virus is a blood-borne disease that can be transmitted four ways: (1) sexual activity with an infected partner; (2) using infected hypodermic needles when injecting drugs; (3) receiving a blood or other blood-product transfusion from an AIDS victim; or (4) passage from the mother to her unborn child through the placenta. During sexual activity the virus can be passed through intercourse—either vaginal, anal, or oral.[1] AIDS cannot be spread through casual contact.

AIDS is the most serious venereal disease facing the world today. Reducing the risks of this disease involves practicing safe sex, which is having sexual intercourse while using a condom and eliminating multiple partners. Another solution is complete abstinence from sexual contact altogether.

SYMPTOMS AND SIGNS   As a viral disease, AIDS can result in varying degrees of sickness, although in some cases the virus produces no symptoms of illness. Some infected persons develop a less intense form of the disease known as AIDS-related complex (ARC), with the presence of certain clinical symptoms. ARC's symptoms might include loss of appetite, weight loss, fever, night sweating, diarrhea, and swollen lymphocytes. ARC may or may not progress into a complete case of AIDS.

The first symptom of AIDS is lymphadenopathy syndrome, characterized by persistently swollen lymph nodes. This symptom may be joined by fever, weight loss, night sweating, fatigue, diarrhea, a skin rash, and oral candidiasis, or thrush, which is a fungal infection. A dry cough, shortness of breath, and weight loss are all symptoms of pneumonia caused by *Pneumocystis carinii,* a leading indicator of AIDS. Other signs of AIDS are the development of purple blotches and bumps that form on the skin. They are indicators of Kaposi's sarcoma, a cancer of the capillary system. AIDS also can manifest cryptococcosis (a fungal infection that can cause meningitis), colitis, chronic herpes simplex (a virus that results in ul-cerating anal and oral herpes), cryptosporidiosis (an organismal infection causing prolonged diarrhea), and toxoplasmosis (a protozoan infection that invades the brain and lungs). Eventually, AIDS may cause dementia (a deterioration in cognition), memory loss, partial paralysis, loss of coordination and sight, and the development of tuberculosis.[41] AIDS is relatively new, so the maximum incubation period has not been established. The HIV virus is a lentivirus, or slow virus, which may take as long as 12 years to incubate. Most health officials set the average incubation period at 2 to 7 years.[41]

AIDS is a fatal disease that attacks the body's immune system.

MANAGEMENT At this time there is no cure or vaccine for AIDS. There are, however, drugs which are currently being developed and tested, that alleviate its symptoms or inhibit the multiplication of the virus. Twenty percent of all AIDS cases are among young, sexually active individuals (20 to 29 years old). There is major concern that this figure will rapidly increase. Education, counseling about safe sexual conduct, and early detection are of major importance in curbing the disease.

It is extremely important that coaches and athletic trainers are fully aware of the general symptoms and signs, as well as the management, of veneral diseases. An athlete who is concerned about having contracted a venereal disease will often ask a coach or athletic trainer, ''What does it look like when you have it?'' or ''What should one do if he or she thinks he or she has it?'' As with recreational drugs, all sports programs should provide opportunities for education and counseling, as well as immediate medical referral, for an athlete with the possibility of a venereal disease.

MENSTRUAL IRREGULARITIES AND THE FEMALE REPRODUCTIVE SYSTEM

Since women in the United States participate more in sports and are training harder than ever before in history, the question arises as to what impact these factors have on menstruation and reproduction.

Menstruation and Its Irregularities

amenorrhea
Absence or suppression of menstruation.

Menarche may be delayed in highly physically active women.[12] **Amenorrhea** (absence of menses) and oligomenorrhea (diminished flow) have been common in professional female ballet dancers, gymnasts, and long-distance runners.[7,8] Runners who decrease training, such as when they have an injury, often report a return of regular menses.[10] Weight gain, together with less intense exercise, also are reported to reverse amenorrhea and oligomenorrhea.[8] Because these irregularities may or may not be normal aspects of thinness and hard physical training, it is advisable that a physician be consulted.[32] To date, there is no indication that these conditions will adversely affect reproduction.[36] Almost any type of menstrual disorder can be caused by overly stressful and demanding sports activity—amenorrhea, dysmenorrhea, menorrhagia (excessive menstruation), oligomenorrhea, polymenorrhea (abnormal frequent menstruation), irregular periods, or any combination of these.[5]

In general, childbirth is not adversely affected by a history of hard physical exercise.

Dysmenorrhea

Girls who have moderate-to-severe dysmenorrhea require examination by a physician.

Dysmenorrhea (painful menstruation) apparently is prevalent among more active women; however, it is inconclusive whether specific sports participation can alleviate or produce dysmenorrhea. For girls with moderate to severe dysmenorrhea, gynecological consultation is warranted to rule out a pathological condition.[34]

Dysmenorrhea is caused by ischemia (a lack of normal blood flow to the pelvic organs) or by a possible hormonal imbalance. This syndrome, which is identified by cramps, nausea, lower abdominal pain, headache, and on occasion emotional lability is the most common menstrual disorder. Mild to vigorous exercises that help ameliorate dysmenorrhea are usually prescribed by physicians. Physicians generally advise a continuance of the usual sports participation during the menstrual period, provided the performance level of the individual does not drop be-low her customary level of ability. Among athletes, swimmers have the highest incidence of dysmenorrhea; it, along with menorrhagia, occurs most often, quite probably as the result of strenuous sports participation during the menses. Gen-erally, oligomenorrhea, amenorrhea, and irregular or scanty flow are more com-mon in sports that require strenuous exertion over a long period of time (e.g., long-distance running, rowing, cross-country skiing, basketball, tennis, or field hockey.)[22] Since great variation exists among female athletes in respect to the menstrual pattern, its effect on physical performance, and the effect of physical activity on the menstrual pattern, each individual must learn to make adjustments to her cycle that will permit her to function effectively and efficiently with a minimum of discomfort or restriction. Evidence to date indicates that top perfor-mances are possible in all phases of the cycle.

Bone Density and Amenorrhea

There is some indication that women who have not menstruated for a long period of time may be losing bone density.[17] When there is a significant decrease in circulating estrogen, a decrease in bone mass may occur.[22] Amenorrhea in ath-letes does respond to weight gain and reduction of work intensity.[26] Another factor in amenorrhea is that women athletes may prematurely lose bone mass, a loss that may increase risks of fractures.[24] There are also indications that women who have irregular menses have a higher incidence of musculoskeletal injury.[21] All women who stop menstruating should be examined by a physician.[35]

Contraceptives and Reproduction

Female athletes have been known to take extra oral contraceptive pills to delay menstruation during competition. This practice is not recommended because the pills should be taken no more than 21 days, followed by a 7-day break.[36] Side effects range from nausea, vomiting, fluid retention, and amenorrhea to the ex-treme effects of hypertension, double vision, and thrombophlebitis. Any use of oral contraceptives related to physical performance should be under the express direction and control of a physician. However, oral contraceptive use is okay for females with no medical problems and who have coitus at least twice a week. The new low-dose preparations, containing less than 50 mg of estrogen, add neg-ligible risks to the healthy woman.[34]

In general, athletes who wear intrauterine devices are free of problems. How-ever, intrauterine devices are not recommended for nulliparous (never borne a viable child) adolescents because of the associated risk of pelvic inflammatory disease.[36] On occasion the athlete may complain of a lower-abdominal cramp while being active. In such cases referral to a physician should be made (see Chapter 15).

For years it was widely stated that stressful physical exertion would strain or permanently damage the female reproductive organs. Experience and research, however, have indicated that this was but another myth. Clinical data compiled by a number of medical researchers add up to one conclusion: sports participation does not affect childbearing or childbirth in an adverse way but, on the contrary, serves this biological function in a positive way. Pregnancy may well be consid-ered a training period for the maternal organism inasmuch as the increases in blood volume and metabolism make rather intensive demands on the physiological systems. Strenuous to moderate physical activity continuing to the latter months of pregnancy should be viewed as preparatory.

During pregnancy women athletes exhibit high levels of muscle tonicity. It has been determined that women who suffer from a chronic disability after childbirth usually have a record of little or no physical exercise in the decade immediately preceding pregnancy. Generally, competition may be engaged in well into the third month of pregnancy unless bleeding or cramps are present and can fre-

---

AMERICAN COLLEGE OF OBSTETRICIANS AND GYNECOLOGISTS GUIDELINES FOR EXERCISE DURING PREGNANCY AND POSTPARTUM

1. Regular exercise (at least three times per week) is preferable to intermittent activity. Competitive activities should be discouraged.
2. Vigorous exercise should not be performed in hot, humid weather or during a period of febrile illness.
3. Ballistic movements (jerky, bouncy motions) should be avoided. Exercise should be done on a wooden floor or a tightly carpeted surface to reduce shock and provide a sure footing.
4. Deep flexion or extension of joints should be avoided because of connective tissue laxity. Activities that require jumping, jarring motions or rapid changes in direction should be avoided because of joint instability.
5. Vigorous exercise should be preceded by a 5-minute period of muscle warm-up. This can be accomplished by slow walking or stationary cycling with low resistance.
6. Vigorous exercise should be followed by a period of gradually declining activity that includes gentle stretching. Because connective tissue laxity increases the risk of joint injury, stretches should not be taken to the point of maximum resistance.
7. Heart rate should be measured at times of peak activity. Target heart rates and limits established in consultation with the physician should not be exceeded.
8. Care should be taken to gradually rise from the floor to avoid orthostatic hypotension. Some form of activity involving the legs should be continued for a brief period.
9. Liquids should be taken liberally before and after exercise to prevent dehydration. If necessary, activity should be interrupted to replenish fluids.
10. Women who have led sedentary life-styles should begin with physical activity of very low intensity and advance activity levels very gradually.
11. Activity should be stopped and the physician consulted if any unusual symptoms appear.

Pregnancy Only
1. Maternal heart rate should not exceed 140 beats per minute.
2. Strenuous activities should not exceed 15 minutes in duration.
3. No exercise should be performed in the supine position after the fourth month of gestation is completed.
4. Exercises that use the Valsalva maneuver should be avoided.
5. Caloric intake should be adequate to meet not only the extra energy needs of pregnancy but also of the exercise performed.
6. Maternal core temperature should not exceed 38° C.

quently be continued until the seventh month if no handicapping or physiological complications arise. Such activity may make pregnancy, childbirth, and postparturition less stressful. Many women athletes do not continue beyond the third month because of a drop in their performance that can result from a number of reasons, some related to their pregnancy, others perhaps psychological. It is during the first 3 months of pregnancy that the dangers of disturbing the pregnancy are greatest. After that period there is less danger to the mother and fetus, since the pregnancy is stabilized. There is no indication that mild-to-moderate exercise during pregnancy is harmful to fetal growth and development or causes reduced fetal mass, increased perinatal or neonatal mortality, or physical or mental retardation.[14,29] It has been found, however, that extreme exercise may lower birth weight.[15] See box on p. 836.

Many athletes compete during pregnancy with no ill effects. Most physicians, although advocating moderate activity during this period, believe that especially vigorous performance, particularly in activities in which there may be severe body contact or heavy jarring or falls, should be avoided.

SUDDEN UNEXPECTED DEATH IN YOUNG ATHLETES

It is considered catastrophic when a young athlete dies suddenly for no apparent reason. Most of these deaths occur in athletes 15 to 20 years old. It is essential that the coach and the athletic trainer recognize that, at any time, sudden unexpected death is always a possibility.

The causes of sudden unexpected death among athletes are highly variable. They can include infection, which could cause **septic shock, myocarditis,** or an existing respiratory infection that could lead to cardiac arrest.[31] Such abnormalities as cardiomyopathy (disease of the heart muscle), coronary artery irregularity (leading to heart ischemia), and **dysrhythmia** could also be causes of sudden death. Major blood vessels could have a congenital stenosis, or constriction.

Obstructive respiratory diseases such as asthma can result in sudden death because of drug toxicity or undertreatment.[13] Cold medications used during the early stages of a cold could be a factor in sudden death as well.

Even though there may be situations in which the athlete is not observed, it has been suggested that a major number of deaths could be avoided by recognizing the obvious signs, which are chest pains during exertion, shortness of breath, lightheadedness and fainting, and a tendency to fatigue easily.

septic shock
Shock caused by bacteria, especially gram-negative bacteria commonly seen in systemic infections.

myocarditis
Inflammation of the heart muscle.

dysrhythmia
Irregular heartbeats.

SUMMARY

Sports participation can lead to infections of the respiratory tract. Some of them are infections such as the common cold and influenza. Others may be related to air-obstructive conditions such as bronchitis or asthma. Hay fever (pollinosis) is also common among athletes as are varied inflammatory conditions such as sinusitis and pharyngitis.

Athletes are also subject to various gastrointestinal conditions that can adversely affect their performances. These conditions include mouth, gum, and tooth problems and digestive conditions such as dyspepsia, diarrhea, constipation, and hemorrhoids. Food poisoning can occur from various bacterial infections. Appendicitis is always a possibility and should be identified as early as possible.

Diabetes mellitus is a complex hereditary or developmental disease of carbohydrate metabolism. Athletes with this condition must carefully balance their diet, exercise, and insulin ingestion. Diabetics must be very cautious about the possibility of going into diabetic coma or insulin shock. Diabetic coma can occur if there is too little insulin in the system; conversely, insulin shock can occur from too much insulin in the body.

As is true in all young populations, athletes are susceptible to communicable viral diseases. Most of these viral diseases start with cold or flulike symptoms, which, in some cases, are followed by a skin rash. They may include chicken pox, measles, mumps, and infectious mononucleosis. Athletes who show symptoms of these conditions should be isolated from other athletes until the condition can be diagnosed by a physician.

Anemia in athletes usually is one of three types: iron deficiency anemia, footstrike anemia, and sickle cell anemia. Most often, iron deficiency anemia is a condition of a female. In an athlete with iron deficiency anemia, the erythrocytes are either too small or too large, hemoglobin is decreased, and the ferritin concentration is low. The athlete with footstrike anemia is usually heavyset and engages in an activity such as running in which the sustained impact forces destroy erythrocytes. The athlete with the sickle cell trait may have an adverse reaction at high altitudes where the sickle-shaped blood cell is unable to transport oxygen adequately.

Sexually transmitted disease has its highest incidence among younger sexually active persons. Since the highest number of athletes are in this highest risk age group, there should be great concern about the spread of these diseases. Many of these diseases such as genital herpes, condyloma acuminata, and acquired immune deficiency syndrome (AIDS) are caused by viral microorganisms. Some are caused by bacteria—for example, gonorrhea by *Neisseria gonorrhoeae* and nonspecific sexually transmitted infection by *Chlamydia trachomatis*. Others may be caused by a yeast infection (candidiasis) or a protozoa (tricomoniasis). To avoid these infections, "safe sex" is suggested, which involves the use of a condom, the elimination of multiple partners, or even complete abstinence from sexual intercourse altogether.

The highly active female may have menstrual irregularities, including dysmenorrhea, amenorrhea, oligomenorrhea, menorrhagia, and polymenorrhea. Contraception, reproduction, and pregnancy are issues that are continually addressed as they concern the female athlete.

The athlete who dies suddenly during physical activity is a major problem to be studied. Many cases have revealed the presence of existing heart and/or respiratory problems, whereas others remain a mystery.

REVIEW QUESTIONS AND CLASS ACTIVITIES

1. Contrast the symptoms and signs of respiratory tract conditions such as the common cold, flu, and hay fever.
2. Discuss and contrast bronchial obstructive diseases such as bronchitis and asthma. How do you care for an athlete with an acute asthmatic attack?
3. Describe the most common gastrointestinal complaints. How are they acquired and managed?
4. Contrast the symptoms and signs of an appendicitis attack and food poisoning.
5. What is diabetes mellitus? What value might exercise have for the person with diabetes mellitus? How are diabetic coma and insulin shock managed?
6. In a sports setting, what would be the indication that an athlete had a contagious disease?
7. What causes epilepsy? How should a grand mal seizure be managed?
8. Define hypertension. What dangers does it present to the athlete?
9. Describe the anemias that most often affect the athlete. How should each be managed?
10. Contrast the appearance and the management of the most common venereal diseases among athletes. How can they be prevented?
11. Discuss menstrual irregularities that occur in highly active athletes. Why do they occur? How should they be managed? How do they relate to reproduction?
12. Describe sudden unexpected death in young athletes.

REFERENCES

1. AIDS and children: American Red Cross/US Public Health Service, Washington, DC, Oct 15, 1986.
2. The asthmatic child and sports participation, Sports Med Dig 7(7):1 1985.
3. Bergfeld, WF: Dermatologic problems in athletes. In Symposium on pediatric and adolescent sports medicine, Clinics in sports medicine, Philadelphia, 1982, WB Saunders Co.
4. Berkow, R, editor: The Merck manual, ed 10, Rahway, NJ, 1983, Merck & Co, Inc.
5. Bonen, A, and Keizer, HA: Athletic menstrual cycle irregularity: endocrine response to exercise and training, Phys Sportsmed 12:78, Aug 1984.
6. Bungaord, A, et al.: Exercise induces asthma after swimming and bicycle exercise, Eur J Respir Dis 63:245, May 1982.
7. Caldwell, F: Menstrual irregularity in athletes: the unanswered question, Phys Sportsmed 10:79, April 1982.
8. Cohen, JL, et al.: Exercise, body weight and amenorrhea in professional ballet dance, Phys Sportsmed 10:79, April 1982.
9. Cowart, VS: Should epileptics exercise: Phys Sportsmed 14(9):183, 1986.
10. Dale, E, et al.: Menstrual dysfunction in distance runners, Obstet Gynecol 54:47, 1979.
11. Eichner, ER: The anemias of athletes, Phys Sportsmed 14(9):122, 1986.
12. Frisch, RE, et al.: Delayed menarche and amenorrhea in ballet dancer, N Engl J Med 303:17, 1980.
13. Galioto, FM: Identification and assessment of the child for sports participation: a cardiovascular approach. In Betts, JM, and Eichelberger, M, editors: Symposium in pediatric and adolescent sports medicine, vol 1, no 3, Clinics in sports medicine, Philadelphia, 1982, WB Saunders, Co.
14. Gauthier, MM: Guidelines for exercise during pregnancy: too little or too much? Phys Sportsmed 14(4): 162, 1986.
15. Gorski, J: Exercise during pregnancy: maternal and fetal responses: a brief review, Med Sci Sports Exerc 17:407, Aug 1985.
16. Holm, GAL, and Krotkiewski, MJ: Exercise in the treatment of diabetes mellitus. In Welsh, RP and Shephard, RJ, editors: Current therapy in sports medicine, 1985-1986, Philadelphia, 1985, Brian C Decker, Publisher.
17. Jacobsen, PC, et al.: Bone density in women: college athletes and older athletic women, J Orthop Res 2:328, 1985.
18. Katz, RM: Coping with exercise induced asthma in sports, Phys Sportsmed 15(7):101, 1987.
19. Kolski, GB: The athlete with asthma and allergies. In Betts, JM, and Eichelberger, M, editors: Symposium on pediatric and adolescent sports medicine, vol 1, no 1, Philadelphia, 1983, WB Saunders Co.
20. Lane, PA, and Githens, JH: Splenic syndrome at mountain altitudes in sickle cell: its occurrence in non-black persons, JAMA 253:2251, April 19, 1985.
21. Lloyd, T, et al.: Women athletes with menstrual irregularity have increased musculoskeletal injuries, Med Sci Sports Exerc 18:374, 1986.
22. Lutter, JM: Health concerns of women runners. In Driez, Jr, D, editor: Symposium on running, vol 4, no 4, Clinics in sports medicine, Philadelphia, 1985, WB Saunders Co.
23. Maehlum, S: Clinical application of exercise and training in diabetes mellitus, International Congress on Sports and Health, 22-23 Sept, 1983, Int J Sports Med 5:47, 1984.
24. Marcus, R, et al.: Menstrual function and bone mass in elite women distance runners: endocrine and metabolic feature, Ann Intern Med 102:158, Feb 1985.
25. Martin, RP: The heart in athletics. In Kulund, DN, editor: The injured athlete, Philadelphia, 1982, JB Lippincott Co.

26. Monahan, T: Treating athletic amenorrhea: a matter of instinct, Phys Sportsmed 15(7): 184, 1987.
27. Morton, AR: Physical activity and the asthmatic, Phys Sportsmed 9:51, March 1981.
28. Morton, AR: Continuous and intermittent running in the provocation of asthma, Ann Allergy 48:123, Feb 1982.
29. Mullinax, KM, and Dale, E: Some considerations of exercise during pregnancy. In Katch, FI, editor: Training, vol 5, no 3, Clinics in sports medicine, Philadelphia, 1986, WB Saunders Co.
30. Neijens, HJ, et al.: Exercise-induced bronchial obstruction. In Welsh RP, and Shephard, RJ editors: Current therapy in sports medicine, 1985-1986, Philadelphia, 1985, Brian C Decker, Publisher.
31. Newspiel, DR, and Kuller, LH: Sudden and unexpected natural death in childhood and adolescence, JAMA 254: 1321, Sept 13, 1985.
32. Sanborn, CF, et al.: Athletic amenorrhea: lack of association with body fat, Med Sci Sports Exerc 19(3):207, 1987.
33. Schoene, RB, et al.: Iron repletion decrease after maximal exercise and lactate concentration in female athletes with minimal iron deficiency anemia, J Lab Clin Med 102(8):306, 1983.
34. Shanghold, MM: Gynecologic concerns in women athletes. In Walsh, WM, editor: Symposium on the athletic woman, vol 3, no 4, Clinics in sports medicine, Philadelphia, 1984, WB Saunders Co.
35. Shanghold, MM: How I manage exercise-related menstrual disturbance, Phys Sportsmed 14(3):113, 1986.
36. Smith, NJ, editor: Sports participation for children and adolescents with chronic health problems. In Sports medicine health care for young athletes, Evanston, Ill, 1983, American Academy of Pediatrics.
37. Strong, WB: Sickle cell anemia and exercise. In Welsh, RP and Shephard, RJ, editors: Current therapy in sports medicine, 1985-1986, Philadelphia, 1985, Brian C Decker, Publisher.
38. Van Herwaarden, CLA: Exercise and training of individuals with chronic non-specific lung disease (CNSLD), Int J Sports Med Suppl 5:54, 1984.
39. Vay, RO: Exercise induced bronchiospasm, Sports Med Dig 7(7):1, 1985.
40. Walther, RJ, and Tifft, CP: High blood pressure in the competitive athlete: guidelines and recommendations, Phys Sportsmed 13(5):93, 1985.
41. Winkel, D: Conquering our fears, Press Telegram Newspaper, pp 1, 5, March 31, 1987.

ANNOTATED BIBLIOGRAPHY

Berg, KE: Diabetic's guide to health and fitness, Champaign, Ill, 1986. Life Enhancement Publications.
A practical approach to helping the person with diabetes lead a physically active life.

Krakauer, LJ, editor: Year book of sports medicine, Chicago, Ill, Year Book Medical Publishers, Inc.
A comprehensive book, published annually, that presents definitive abstracts of recent research and articles related to the broad field of sports medicine.

Kunz, JRM, and Finkel, AJ: Medical association family medical guide, New York, 1987, Random House, Inc.
A complete and up-to-date compendium of general health matters.

Shanghold, M, and Mirkin, G: The complete sports medicine book for women, New York, 1987, Simon and Schuster, Inc.
Explains what a woman should know about selecting a sport, choosing foods, and preventing and treating injuries and about menstruation, pregnancy, and menopause.

Tver, DF, and Hunt, HF: Encyclopedic dictionary of sports medicine, New York, 1987, Chapman and Hall.
Defines 635 terms, including ones from the fields of anatomy, physical fitness, sports illnesses, and injuries.

Suggested Equipment

Item	Quantities for Number of Participants per Year		
	Up to 200	200 to 400	400 to 600
Anatomy charts (set)	1	1	1
Ankle wrap roller	1	2	2
Athletic trainer's office equipment			
Bookshelf	1	1	1
Desk	1	1	1
Filing cabinet	1	1	1
Telephone	1	1	1
Athletic training kits	(available for each sport)		
Blankets	3	3	3
Braces			
Knee	*	*	*
Ankle	*	*	*
Back	*	*	*
Bulletin board	1	1	1
Callus file	6	12	18
Crutches	2 pairs	4 pairs	6 pairs
Diathermy (microwave or shortwave)	1	1	1
Drinking dispenser (per sport)	1	1	1
Electric clock	1	1	1
Electric muscle stimulator	1	1	1
Examining table (physician)	1	1	1
Eyecup	1	2	3
Flashlight (pencil type) (per kit)	1	2	3
Forceps (tweezers) (per kit)	3	3	3
Hair clippers	1	2	2
Hammer	1	1	1
Ice maker	1	1	1
Massage or treatment tables	2	4	6
Medicine dropper	3	6	9
Mirror (hand) (per kit)	3	5	7
Moist heat pack machine	1 small	1 small	1 large
Nail clippers (per kit)	1	2	2
Neck and back board	1	2	2
Oral screw (per kit)	(available for each first-aid kit)		
Oral thermometer (per kit)	1	2	3
Paraffin bath	optional	optional	1

*Should be on hand for each participant or funds available for purchase when need arises.

Item	Quantities for Number of Participants per Year		
	Up to 200	200 to 400	400 to 600
Pliers	1	2	3
Razor (safety, with blades)	1	2	3
Reconditioning equipment			
Barbells	*	*	*
Chinning bar	*	*	*
Dumbbells	*	*	*
Mats	*	*	*
Pulley weights	*	*	*
Shoe weights	*	*	*
Universal or Nautilus equipment	*	*	*
Isokinetic device (Cybex, Ortho-tron)	*	*	*
Refrigerator	1	1	1
Resuscitator	1	1	1
Safety pins	200	400	600
Scales and weight chart	1	2	3
Scalpel (per kit)	1	2	3
Scissors (per kit)			
All-purpose	2	3	4
Bandage	3	5	7
Surgical	2	2	2
Screwdriver	1	1	1
Shoehorn	3	5	7
Sink and washbasin	1	1	1
Splints (set of assorted pneumatic)	1	2	3
Sterilizer	optional	optional	1
Storage cupboards	†	†	†
Stretcher (folding)	1	1	1
Surgical lamp	1	1	1
Tape cutters	5	8	10
Taping tables	2	3	4
Ultrasound	1	1	1
Waste container	2	3	4
Wheelchair	(should be available)		
Whirlpool baths	1	2	3

†Dry, cool storage areas should be provided to house the bulk of the training supplies.

Suggested Supplies

Item	Quantities for Number of Participants per Year		
	Up to 200	200 to 400	400 to 600
Adhesive felt, ⅛-inch (0.3 cm)	2 rolls	4 rolls	6 rolls
Adhesive tape (linen backed)			
½-inch	3 tubes	5 tubes	7 tubes
1-inch	12 tubes	24 tubes	36 tubes
1½-inch	40 speed packs	77 speed packs	144 speed packs
2-inch	48 tubes	72 tubes	144 tubes
Analgesic balm	*	*	*
Ankle wrap (96 inch [240 cm] for men;	20	30	40
72 inch [180 cm] for women)	20	30	40
Antacid tablets	500	1000	1500
Antacid liquid (6-ounce)	2	3	4
Antiglare salve	5	10	15
Antiseptic powder (4-ounce)	1	2	3
Antiseptic soap (liquid, 6-ounce)	2	3	4
Bandages			
Band-Aids (sterile strips, box of 100)			
Assorted sizes	20 boxes	35 boxes	50 boxes
Butterfly (sterile strips)			
Medium	50	100	150
Small	50	100	150
Sterile pads (box of 100)			
2 by 2	5 boxes	10 boxes	15 boxes
3 by 3	5 boxes	10 boxes	15 boxes
Calamine lotion (4-ounce)	4	8	12
Collodion	1 pint	1 pint	2 pints
Combine (roll)	2 rolls	4 rolls	6 rolls
Cotton (sterile, 6-ounce)	2	3	4
Cotton-tipped applicators (box of 100)	6	12	18
Drinking cups (paper, box of 100)	6	8	10
Elastic bandages			
3-inch (7.5 cm)	12	24	48
4-inch (10 cm)	36	72	144
6-inch (15 cm)	12	24	48
Elastic knee caps			
Large	*	*	*
Medium	*	*	*
Small	*	*	*

*Should be on hand for each participant or funds available for purchase when need arises.

Item	Quantities for Number of Participants per Year		
	Up to 200	200 to 400	400 to 600
Elastic knee guards			
Large	*	*	*
Medium	*	*	*
Small	*	*	*
Elastic tape (3-inch [7.5 cm])	72 tubes	144 tubes	288 tubes
Elastic thigh caps			
Large	*	*	*
Medium	*	*	*
Small	*	*	*
Elastic thigh guards			
Large	*	*	*
Medium	*	*	*
Small	*	*	*
Eye wash (6-ounce)	2	3	4
Felt (36 by 44 inches [90 by 110 cm])			
¼-inch (0.6 cm)	1 sheet	2 sheets	3 sheets
½-inch (1.25 cm)	1 sheet	2 sheets	3 sheets
Flexible collodion	1 pint	2 pints	2 pints
Fluromethane (4-ounce)	2	4	6
Foot antifungus powder (4-ounce)	2	3	4
Foot antifungus salve (2-ounce)	6	12	18
Fungicides			
Ointments or solutions	1 pint	6 pints	9 pints
Powders (4-ounce can)	4 cans	8 cans	12 cans
Gauze (roll)			
1-inch (2.5 cm)	25 rolls	50 rolls	100 rolls
2-inch (5 cm)	25 rolls	50 rolls	100 rolls
3-inch (7.5 cm)	25 rolls	50 rolls	100 rolls
Germicides			
Alcohol (isopropyl)	5 pints	10 pints	15 pints
Boric acid (eyewash)	1 pint	2 pints	3 pints
Merthiolate (liquid)	1 pint	2 pints	3 pints
Nitrotan (liquid)	1 pint	2 pints	3 pints
Peroxide	1 pint	2 pints	3 pints
Grease (lubrication, 1-pound)	5	10	15
Gum rosin (adherent, 6-ounce)	1	1	1
Heat-treated plastic (¼-inch [0.6 cm]) (Orthoplast)	2 sheets	3 sheets	4 sheets
Heel cups (plastic)	5	10	15
Instant cold packs (dozen)	1	2	3
Internal agents			
Antacid tablets	200	300	500
Aspirin tablets	500	1000	1500
Dextrose tablets	2000	4000	6000
Liniment (6-ounce)	2	3	4
Massage lubricant	2 pints	4 pints	6 pints
Medicated ointments			
Athletic ointment	1 pound	2 pounds	3 pounds
Menthol ointment (4-ounce)	1	4	6
Zinc oxide	1 pound	2 pounds	2 pounds

Item	Quantities for Number of Participants per Year		
	Up to 200	200 to 400	400 to 600
Menthol spray (6-ounce)	2	3	4
Moleskin (12-inch [30 cm])	2 rolls	4 rolls	6 rolls
Neck and back board (emergency)	1	1	1
Nonadhering sterile pads, 3 by 3 (100)	2	4	6
Orthotic plastic material	*	*	*
Powder (corn starch)	1	1	1
Powdered rosin	*	*	*
Pretape material, 3-inch (7.5 cm)	1 case	2 cases	3 cases
Shoulder harness	*	*	*
Slings (triangular bandages)	5	10	15
Splints, air	1 set	1 set	1 set
Sponge rubber (vinyls), 36 by 44 inches (90 by 110 cm)			
⅛-inch (0.3 cm)	1 sheet	2 sheets	3 sheets
¼-inch (0.6 cm)	1 sheet	2 sheets	3 sheets
½-inch (1.25 cm)	1 sheet	2 sheets	3 sheets
Stockinette (3-inch [7.5 cm] roll)	1	3	6
Sun lotion, e.g., Paba (4-ounce)	4	8	12
Tape adherent (clear), spray cans (12-ounce)	6 cans	12 cans	12 cans
Tape remover	½ gallon	¾ gallon	1 gallon
Throat gargle, antiseptic (4-ounce), or lozenges	4	7	12
Tongue depressors	500	1000	1500
Waterproof tape (1-inch [2.5 cm])	6 rolls	12 rolls	36 rolls

Checklist for Athletic Trainer's Kit*

Item	Amount	Activity							
		Football-Rugby	Basketball-Volleyball-Soccer	Wrestling	Baseball	Track and Cross-Country	Water Polo and Swimming	Gymnastics	Tennis
Accident reports		X	X	X	X	X	X	X	X
Adhesive tape									
½-inch (1.25 cm)	1 roll	X	X	X	X	X		X	X
1 inch (2.5 cm)	2 rolls	X	X	X	X	X		X	X
1½-inch (3.75 cm)	3 rolls	X	X	X	X	X		X	X
2-inch (5 cm)	1 roll	X	X	X	X	X		X	X
Alcohol (isopropyl)	4 ounces	X	X	X	X	X	X	X	X
Ammonia ampules	10	X	X	X	X	X	X	X	X
Analgesic balm	½ pound	X	X	X	X	X	X	X	X
Ankle wraps	2	X	X		X	X			X
Antacid tablets or liquid	100	X	X	X	X	X	X	X	X
Antiglare salve	4 ounces	X			X				
Antiseptic powder	4 ounces	X	X	X	X	X	X	X	X
Antiseptic soap (liquid)	4 ounces	X	X	X	X	X	X	X	X
Aspirin tablets	100	X	X	X	X	X	X	X	X
Band-Aids (assorted sizes)	2 dozen	X	X	X	X	X	X	X	X
Butterfly bandages (sterile strip)									
Medium	6 dozen	X	X	X	X	X		X	
Small	6 dozen	X	X	X	X	X		X	
Contact case		X	X	X	X	X	X	X	X
Cotton (sterile)	1 ounce	X	X	X	X	X	X	X	X
Cotton-tipped applicators	2 dozen	X	X	X	X	X	X	X	X
Elastic bandages									
3-inch (7.5 cm)	2 rolls	X	X	X	X	X		X	X
4-inch (10 cm)	2 rolls	X	X	X	X	X		X	X
6 inch (15 cm)	2 rolls	X	X	X	X	X	X	X	X
Elastic tape roll (3-inch)	2 rolls	X	X	X	X	X		X	X

*Extra amounts of items such as tape and protective padding are carried in other bags.

		Activity							
Item	Amount	Football-Rugby	Basketball-Volleyball-Soccer	Wrestling	Baseball	Track and Cross-Country	Water Polo and Swimming	Gymnastics	Tennis
Eyewash	2 ounces	X	X	X	X	X	X	X	X
Felt									
¼-inch (0.6 cm)	6 by 6 sheet	X	X	X	X	X		X	X
½-inch (1.25 cm)	6 by 6 sheet	X							
Flexible collodion	2 ounces	X	X	X	X	X		X	
Foot antifungus powder	2 ounces	X	X	X	X	X	X	X	X
Forceps (tweezers)	1	X	X	X	X	X	X	X	X
Fungicide (salve)	2 ounces	X	X	X	X	X	X	X	X
Germicide (solution)	2 ounces	X	X	X	X	X	X	X	X
Grease (lubrication)		X	X	X	X	X			X
Gum rosin (adherent)	1 ounce	X	X		X	X			X
Heel cups	2			X		X		X	
Insurance information		X	X	X	X	X	X	X	X
Instant cold pack	2	X	X	X	X	X	X	X	X
Liniment	2 ounces	X	X	X	X	X	X	X	X
Medicated salve	2 ounces	X	X	X	X	X	X	X	X
Mirror (hand)	1	X	X	X	X	X	X	X	X
Moleskin	6 by 6 sheet	X	X	X	X	X		X	X
Nonadhering sterile pad (3 by 3)	12	X	X	X	X	X		X	X
Oral screw	1	X	X	X	X	X	X	X	X
Oral thermometer	1	X	X	X	X	X	X	X	X
Paper and pencil		X	X	X	X	X	X	X	X
Peroxide	2 ounces	X	X	X	X	X	X	X	X
Plastic cups		X	X	X	X	X	X	X	X
Salt tablets	50	X	X	X	X	X		X	X
Shoehorn	1	X	X	X	X	X			X
Sponge rubber									
⅛-inch (0.3 cm)	6 by 6 sheet	X	X	X	X	X		X	X
¼-inch (0.6 cm)	6 by 6 sheet	X	X	X	X	X		X	X
½-inch (1.25 cm)	6 by 6 sheet	X							
Sterile gauze pads (3 by 3)	6	X	X	X	X	X		X	X
Sun lotion	2 ounces	X	X	X	X	X	X	X	X
Surgical scissors	1	X	X	X	X	X	X	X	X
Tape adherent	6-ounce spray can	X	X	X	X	X		X	X
Tape remover	2 ounces	X	X	X	X	X	X	X	X
Tape scissors (pointed)	1	X	X	X	X	X	X	X	X
Tongue depressors	5	X	X	X	X	X	X	X	X
Triangular bandages	2	X	X	X	X	X	X	X	X
Waterproof tape (1-inch)	1 roll						X		

Unit of Measure

TEMPERATURE

To convert Fahrenheit temperature to Celsius (centigrade):

$$°C = (°F - 32) \div 1.8$$

To convert Celsius temperature to Fahrenheit:

$$°F = (1.8 \times °C) + 32$$

On the Fahrenheit scale, the freezing point of water is 32° F and the boiling point is 212° F. On the Celsius scale, the freezing point of water is 0° C, and the boiling point is 100° C.

DISTANCE

Equivalent Metric Unit	Equivalent English Unit
1 centimeter (cm)	0.3937 inch
2.54 centimeters	1 inch
1 meter (m)	3.28 feet; 1.09 yards
0.304 meters	1 foot
1 kilometer (km)	0.62 mile
1.61 kilometers	1 mile

POWER AND ENERGY

Power = Work divided by time; measured in horsepower (HP), watts, etc.

1 HP = 746 watts

Energy = Application of a force through a distance

1 kilocalorie (kcal) = Amount of energy required to heat 1 kilogram (kg) of water 1° Celsius

abduction Movement of a body part away from the midline of the body.

accident Occurring by chance or without intention.

acute injury An injury with sudden onset and short duration.

ad libitum Amount desired.

adduction Movement of a body part toward the midline of the body.

afferent nerves Nerves that transport messages toward the brain.

agonist muscles Muscles directly engaged in contraction as related to muscles that relax at the same time.

ambient Environmental (e.g., temperature or air that invests one's immediate environment).

ambulation Move or walk from place to place.

ameboid action Cellular action like that of an amoeba, using protoplasmic pseudopod.

analgesia Pain inhibition.

analgesic Agent that relieves pain without causing a complete loss of sensation.

anaphylaxis Increased susceptibility or sensitivity to a foreign protein or toxin as the result of previous exposure to it.

androgen Any substance that aids the development and controls the appearance of male characteristics.

anesthesia Partial or complete loss of sensation.

anomaly Deviation from the normal.

anorexia Lack or loss of appetite; aversion to food.

anorexia nervosa Eating disorder characterized by a distorted body image.

anoxia Lack of oxygen.

antagonist muscles Muscles that counteract the action of the agonist muscles.

anterior Before or in front of.

anteroposterior Refers to the position of front to back.

anteversion Tipping forward of a part as a whole, without bending.

antipyretic Agent that relieves or reduces fever.

apophysis Bony outgrowth to which muscles attach.

arrhythmical movement Irregular movement.

arthrogram Radiopaque material injected into a joint to facilitate the taking of an x-ray.

arthrokinematics Physiological and accessory movements of the joint.

arthroscopic examination Viewing the inside of a joint through an arthroscope, which uses a small camera lens.

asymmetry (body) Lack of symmetry of sides of the body.

atrophy Wasting away of tissue or of an organ; diminution of the size of a body part.

automatism Automatic behavior before consciousness or full awareness has been achieved after a brain concussion.

avascular necrosis Death of tissue caused by the lack of blood supply.

avulsion Forcible tearing away of a part or a structure.

axilla Arm pit.

Babinski reflex Dorsiflexion of the great toe when the sole of the foot is stimulated.

bacteria Morphologically, the simplest group of nongreen vegetable organisms, various species of which are involved in fermentation and putrefaction, the production of disease, and the fixing of atmospheric nitrogen; a schizomycete.

bacteriostatic Halting the growth of bacteria.

bandage Strip of cloth or other material used to cover a wound.

beta-endorphin Chemical substance produced in the brain.

biomechanics Branch of study that applies the laws of mechanics to living organisms and biological tissues.

bipedal Having two feet or moving on two feet.

BMR Basal metabolic rate.

bradykinin Peptide chemical that causes pain in an injured area.

buccal Pertaining to the cheek or mouth.

bulimia Binge-purge eating disorder.

bursitis Inflammation of a bursa, especially those bursae located between bony prominences and a muscle or tendon such as those of the shoulder and knee.

calcific tendinitis Deposition of calcium in a chronically inflamed tendon, especially the tendons of the shoulder.

calisthenic Exercise involving free movement without the aid of equipment.

calorie (large) Amount of heat required to raise 1 kg of water 1° C; used to express the fuel or energy value of food or the heat output of the organism; the amount of heat required to heat 1 lb of water to 4° F.

catastrophic injury Relates to a permanent injury of the spinal cord, leaving the athlete quadriplegic or paraplegic.

cerebrovascular accident Stroke.

chafing Superficial inflammation that develops when skin is subjected to friction.

chemotaxis Response to influence of chemical stimulation.

chiropractor One who practices a method for restoring normal condition by adjusting the segments of the spinal column.

chondromalacia Abnormal softening of cartilage.

chronic injury Injury with long onset and long duration.

cicatrix Scar or mark formed by fibrous connective tissue; left by a wound or sore.

circadian rhythm Biological time clock by which the body functions.

circumduct Act of moving a limb such as the arm or hip in a circular manner.

clonic muscle contraction Alternating involuntary muscle contraction and relaxation in quick succession.

collagen Main organic constituent of connective tissue.

collision sport Sport in which athletes use their bodies to deter or punish opponents.

colloid Liquid or gelatinous substance that retains particles of another substance in a state of suspension.

commission (legal liability) Person commits an act that is not legally his or hers to perform.

communicable disease Disease that may be transmitted directly or indirectly from one individual to another.

concentric muscle contraction Refers to muscle shortening.

conduction Heating through direct contact with a hot medium.

conjunctiva Mucous membrane that lines the eyes.

contact sport Sport in which athletes do make physical contact but not with the intent to produce bodily injury.

contrecoup brain injury After head is struck, brain continues to move within the skull, resulting in injury to the side opposite the force.

convection Heating indirectly through another medium such as air or liquid.

conversion Heating by other forms of energy (e.g., electricity).

convulsions Paroxysms of involuntary muscular contractions and relaxations.

core temperature Internal, or deep, body temperature monitored by cells in the hypothalamus, as opposed to shell, or peripheral, temperature, which is registered by that layer of insulation provided by the skin, subcutaneous tissues, and superficial portions of the muscle masses.

corticosteroid Steroid produced by the adrenal cortex.

counterirritant Agent that produces mild inflammation and acts, in turn, as an analgesic when applied locally to the skin (e.g., liniment).

crepitation Crackling sound heard during the movement of ends of a broken bone.

cryokinetics Cold application combined with exercise.

cryotherapy Cold therapy.

cubital fossa Triangular area on the anterior aspect of the forearm directly opposite the elbow joint (the bend of the elbow).

cyanosis Slightly bluish, grayish, slatelike, or dark purple discoloration of the skin caused by a reduced amount of blood hemoglobin.

DAPRE *D*aily *a*djustable *p*rogressive *r*esistive *e*xercise.

debride Removal of dirt and dead tissue from a wound.

deconditioning State in which the athlete's body loses its competitive fitness.

degeneration Deterioration of tissue.

dermatome Segmental skin area innervated by various spinal cord segments.

diapedesis Passage of blood cells through ameboid action through the intact capillary wall.

diarthrodial joint Ball and socket joint.

distal Farthest from a center, from the midline, or from the trunk.

dorsiflexion Bending toward the dorsum or rear; opposite of plantar flexion.

dorsum The back of a body part.

drug Any substance that, when taken into the living organism, may modify one or more of its functions.

eccentric muscle contraction Refers to muscle lengthening.

ecchymosis Black-and-blue skin discoloration caused by hemorrhage.

ectopic calcification Calcification occurring in an abnormal place.

edema Swelling as a result of the collection of fluid in connective tissue.

electrolyte Solution that is a conductor of electricity.

emetic Agent that induces vomiting.

endurance Body's ability to engage in prolonged physical activity.

enthesitis Group of conditions characterized by inflammation, fibrosis, and calcification around tendons, ligaments, and muscle insertions.

epidemiological approach Study of sports injuries, involving the relationship of as many factors as possible.

epiphysis Cartilaginous growth region of a bone.

epistaxis Nosebleed.

etiology Science dealing with causes of disease.

ethics Principles of morality.

eversion of the foot To turn the foot outward.

excoriation Removal of a piece or strip of skin.

exostosis Benign bony outgrowths, usually capped by cartilage, that protrude from the surface of a bone.

extraoral mouth guard Protective device that fits outside the mouth.

extravasation Escape of a fluid from its vessels into the surrounding tissues.

exudate Accumulation of fluid in an area.

facilitation To assist the progress of.

fascia Fibrous membrane that covers, supports, and separates muscles.

fasciitis Inflammation of fascia.

fibrinogen Blood plasma protein that is converted into a fibrin clot.

fibroblast Any cell component from which fibers are developed.

fibrocartilage Type of cartilage (e.g., intervertebral disks) in which the matrix contains thick bundles of collaginous fibers.

fibrosis Development of excessive fibrous connective tissue; fibroid degeneration.

foot pronation Combined foot movements of eversion and abduction.

foot supination Combined foot movements of inversion and abduction.

force couple Depressor action by the subscapularis, infraspinatus, and teres minor muscles to stabilize the head of the humerus and to counteract the upward force exerted by the deltoid muscle during abduction of the arm.

FSH *F*ollicle-*s*timulating *h*ormone.

GAS theory *G*eneral *a*daptation *s*yndrome.

genitourinary Pertaining to the reproductive and urinary organs.

genu recurvatum Hyperextension at the knee joint.

genu valgum Knock-knee.

genu varum Bow leg.

GH *G*rowth *h*ormone.

glycosuria Abnormally high proportion of sugar in the urine.

hemarthrosis Blood in a joint.

hematolytic Pertaining to the degeneration and disintegration of the blood.

hematoma Blood tumor.

hematuria Blood in the urine.

hemoglobin Coloring substance of the red blood cells.

hemoglobinuria Hemoglobin in the urine.

hemophilia Hereditary blood disease in which coagulation is greatly prolonged.

hemopoietic Forming blood cells.

hemorrhage Discharge of blood.

hemothorax Bloody fluid in the pleural cavity.

hertz (Hz) Number of sound waves per second.

homeostasis Maintenance of a steady state in the body's internal environment.

hyperemia Unusual amount of blood in a body part.

hyperextension Extreme stretching of a body part.

hyperhidrosis Excessive sweating; excessive foot perspiration.

hyperkeratosis Increased callus development.

hypermobility Extreme mobility of a joint.

hyperpnea Hyperventilation; increased minute volume of breathing; exaggerated deep breathing.

hypertension High blood pressure; abnormally high tension.

hyperthermia Extreme heat.

hypertrophy Enlargement of a part caused by an increase in the size of its cells.

hyperventilation Abnormally deep breathing that is prolonged, causing a depletion of carbon dioxide, a fall in blood pressure, and fainting.

hypoallergenic Low allergy producing.

hypoxia Lack of an adequate amount of oxygen.

ICE-R *I*ce, *c*ompression, *e*levation, and *r*est.

idiopathic Cause of a condition is unknown.

injury Act that damages or hurts.

innervation Nerve stimulation of a muscle.

interosseous membrane Connective tissue membrane between bones.

intertrigo Chafing of the skin.

inversion of the foot To turn the foot inward; inner border of the foot lifts.

ions Electrically charged atoms.

ipsilateral Situated on the same side.

ischemia Local anemia.

isokinetic muscle resistance Accommodating and variable resistance.

isometric muscle contraction Muscle contracts statically without a change in its length.

isotonic muscle contraction Muscle shortens and lengthens through a complete range of joint motion.

joint capsule Saclike structure that encloses the ends of bones in a diarthrodial joint.

keratolytic Loosening of the horny skin layer.

kinesthesia; kinesthesis Sensation or feeling of movement; the awareness one has of the spatial relationships of his or her body and its parts.

kyphosis Exaggeration of the normal curve of the thoracic spine.

labile Unsteady; not fixed and easily changed.

LH *L*uteinizing *h*ormone.

liability Legal responsibility to perform an act in a reasonable and prudent manner.

lordosis Abnormal lumbar vertebral convexity.

luxation Complete joint dislocation.

lysis To break down.

macerated skin Skin that has been softened through wetting.

margination Accumulation of leukocytes on blood vessel walls at the site of injury during early stages of inflammation.

menarche Onset of menstrual function.

microtrauma Microscopic lesion or injury.

muscle contracture Permanent contraction of a muscle as a result of spasm or paralysis.

myoglobin Respiratory protein in muscle tissue that is an oxygen carrier.

myositis Inflammation of muscle.

myositis ossificans Myositis marked by ossification of muscles.

necrosin Chemical substance that stems from inflamed tissue, causing changes in normal tissue.

negative resistance Slow eccentric muscle contraction against a resistance.

nerve entrapment Nerve compressed between bone or soft tissue.

neuritis Inflammation of a nerve.

neuroma Tumor consisting mostly of nerve cells and nerve fibers.

nociceptor Receptor of pain.

NOCSAE National Operating Committee on Standards for Athletic Equipment.

noncontact sport Sport in which athletes are not involved in any physical contact.

nystagmus Constant involuntary back and forth, up and down, or rotary movement of the eyeball.

omission (legal) Person fails to perform a legal duty.

orthopedic surgeon One who corrects deformities of the musculoskeletal system.

orthosis Used in sports as an appliance or apparatus to support, align, prevent, or correct deformities or to improve function of a movable body part.

orthotics Field of knowledge relating to orthoses and their use.

osteoarthritis Chronic disease involving joints in which there is destruction of articular cartilage and bony overgrowth.

osteochondral Refers to relationship of bone and cartilage.
osteochondritis Inflammation of bone and cartilage.
osteochondritis dissecans Fragment of cartiilage and underlying bone is detached from the articular surface.
osteochondrosis Disease state of a bone and its articular cartilage.

palpation Feeling an injury with the fingers.
paraplegia Paralysis of lower portion of the body and of both legs.
paresis Slight or incomplete paralysis.
paresthesia Abnormal or morbid sensation such as itching or prickling.
pathogenic Disease-producing.
pathology Science of the structural and functional manifestations of disease.
pediatrician Specialist in the treatment of children's diseases.
phagocytosis Destruction of injurious cells or particles by phagocytes (white blood cells).
phalanges Bones of the fingers and toes.
phalanx Any one of the bones of the fingers and toes.
pharmacology Science of drugs, their preparation, uses, and effects.
phonophoresis Introduction of ions of soluble salt into the body through ultrasound.
piezoelectric Production of an electric current as a result of pressure on certain crystals.
pneumothorax Collapse of a lung as a result of air in the pleural cavity.
podiatrist Practitioner who specializes in the study and care of the foot.
posterior Toward the rear or back.
primary assessment Initial first aid evaluation.
prognosis Prediction as to probable result of a disease or injury.
prophylaxis Guarding against injury or disease.
proprioceptor One of several receptors, each of which responds to stimuli elicited from within the body itself (e.g., the muscle spindles that invoke the myotatic or stretch reflex).
prostaglandin Acidic lipid widely distributed in the body; in musculoskeletal conditions it is concerned with vasodilation, a histaminelike effect; it is inhibited by aspirin.
prosthesis Replacement of an absent body part with an artificial part; the artificial part.
prothrombin Interacts with calcium to produce thrombin.
proximal Nearest to the point of reference.
psychogenic Of psychic origin; that which originates in the mind.
psychosomatic Showing effects of mind-body relationship; physical disorder caused or influenced by the mind (i.e., by the emotions).
purulent Consisting of or containing pus.

quadriplegia Paralysis affecting all four limbs.

radiation Emission and diffusion of rays of heat.
regeneration Repair, regrowth, or restoration of a part such as tissue.
residual That which remains; often used to describe a permanent condition reesulting from injury or disease (e.g., a limp or a paralysis).
resorption Act of removal by absorption.
retroversion Tilting or turning backward of a part.
revascularize Restoration of blood circulation to an injured area.
rotation Turning around an axis in an angular motion.

SAID principle *S*pecific *a*daptation to *i*mposed *d*emands.
scoliosis Lateral rotary curve of the spine.
secondary assessment Follow up; a more detailed examination.

seizure Sudden attack.

sequela Pathological condition that occurs as a consequence of another condition or event.

serotonin Hormone and neurotransmitter.

sign Objective evidence of an abnormal situation within the body.

stasis Blockage or stoppage of circulation.

stressor Anything that affects the body's physiological or psychological condition, upsetting the homeostatic balance.

subluxation Partial or incomplete dislocation of an articulation.

symptom Subjective evidence of an abnormal stiuation within the body.

syndrome Group of typical symptoms or conditions that characterize a deficiency or disease.

synergy To work in cooperation with.

synovitis Inflammation of the synovium.

synthesis To build up.

tendinitis Inflammation of a tendon.

tenosynovitis Inflammation of a tendon synovial sheath.

tetanus toxoid Tetanus toxin modified to produce active immunity against *Clostridium tetani.*

thermotherapy Heat therapy.

tonic muscle spasm Rigid muscle contraction that lasts over a period of time.

torsion Act or state of being twisted.

transitory paralysis Temporary paralysis.

trauma (plural—traumas or traumata) Wound or injury.

traumatic Pertaining to an injury or wound.

valgus Position of a body part that is bent outward.

varus Position of a body part that is bent inward.

vasoconstriction Decrease in the diameter of a blood vessel.

vasodilation Increase in the diameter of a blood vessel.

vasospasm Blood vessel spasm.

verruca Wart caused by a virus.

viscoelastic Any substance having both viscous and elastic properties.

viscosity Resistance to flow.

volar Referring to the palm or the sole.

CREDITS

Unit I Opener, Photo by Mark Dobson.

Chapter 1 *p. 5*, Bill Knight. Pro Photo, Inc.; *p. 13*, Bill Stover; *p. 17*, Courtesy California Lacrosse Assn.; *p. 21 (top)*, G. Robert Bishop; *p. 22*, Cramer Products, Inc., Gardner, Kans.

Chapter 2 *p. 27*, Cramer Products, Inc., Gardner, Kans.; *p. 46*, Adapted from American Academy of Pediatrics, Committee on Sports Medicine: Sports medicine: health care for young athletes, Nathan Smith (editor), p. 82, 1983, Evanston, Ill.; *p. 47*, Adapted from American Academy of Pediatrics, Committee on Sports Medicine: Sports medicine: health care for young athletes, Nathan Smith (editor), p. 84, 1983, Evanston, Ill.; *p. 49*, Adapted from Myers, G.C., and Garrick, J.G.: The preseason examination of school and college athletes. In Strauss, R.H. (editor): Sports medicine, Philadelphia, 1984, W.B. Saunders Co.; *p. 50*, Adapted from American Academy of Pediatrics, Committee on Sports Medicine: Sports medicine: health care for young athletes, Nathan Smith (editor), p. 80, 1983, Evanston, Ill.; *pp. 56, 57*, Courtesy D. Bailey, California State University—Long Beach.

Unit II Opener, Photo Researchers, Inc.; Christopher W. Morrow.

Chapter 3 *pp. 87, 88*, Courtesy Robert Freligh, California State University—Long Beach; *p. 98*, From Payne, W.A., and Hahn, D.B.: Understanding your health, ed. 2, St. Louis, 1989, Times Mirror/Mosby Publishing; *p. 102*, From Bar-or, O.: Exercise in childhood. In Welch, R.P., and Shepard, R.J. (editors): Current therapy in sports medicine, 1985-1986, Philadelphia, 1985, B.C. Decker, Inc.; *p. 105*, Photo by Curt Beamer, Courtesy Paralyzed Veterans of America: Sports 'n Spokes Magazine; *p. 106*, Adapted from Tables I and II, Curtis, K.A., and Dillon, D.A.: Survey of wheelchair athlete injuries—common patterns and prevention, pp. 211-216. In Sherill, C. (editor): Sports and Disabled Athletes, the 1984 Olympic Scientific Congress Proceedings, vol. 9, Human Kinetics Publishers, Inc., Champaign, Ill.; *p. 107*, Photo by Wendy Parks, Courtesy National Foundation of Wheelchair Tennis.

Chapter 4 *p. 113*, From "Canada's Food Guide," Health and Welfare Canada, 1983, and reproduced with the permission of the Minister of Supply and Services Canada; *pp. 114, 121, 123*, Adapted from Guthrie, H.A.: Introductory nutrition, ed. 7, St. Louis, 1989, Times Mirror/Mosby College Publishing; *pp. 117-120, 130*, Adapted from Williams, S.R.: Nutrition and diet therapy, ed. 6, St. Louis, 1989, Times Mirror/Mosby College Publishing; *p. 122*, Adapted from Smith, N.J.: Vitamin myths and food frauds, The First Aider 56(3):1, 1986, Gardner, Kans.; *p. 127*, Adapted from Bing, M.: The nutrition training table, Sports Medicine Digest 8(9):1, 1986; *p. 129*, Adapted from Lappe, F.M.: Diet for a small planet, ed. 5, New York, 1983, Ballantine Books; *p. 131*, Courtesy Pennwalt, Prescription Products Division, Pennwalt Corporation, Rochester, N.Y.; *p. 132*, Courtesy Cramer Products, Inc., Gardner, Kans.

Chapter 5 *pp. 140, 143 (top), 155*, Courtesy Robert Freligh, California State University—Long Beach; *p. 146 (bottom)*, Courtesy Donzis Protective Equipment, Houston, Tex.; *p. 147 (top)*, G. Robert Bishop; *pp. 147 (bottom), 152, 156-159, 160 (middle)*, Courtesy Mueller Sports Medicine, Inc.; *p. 148, A*, Photo by Douglas Child, Courtesy Creative Support Systems of California, Irvine, California; *pp. 149, 150, 155 (bottom), 156 (top), 157, 162 (bottom), 163-168*, From Nicholas, J.A., and Hershman, E.B.: The lower extremity and spine in sports medicine, vols. 1 and 2, St. Louis, 1986, The C.V. Mosby Co.; *pp. 158 (top), 159 (top left and right)*, Courtesy Don Joy Orthopedic, Carlsbad, Calif.

Chapter 6 *p. 179*, Courtesy Cramer Products, Inc., Gardner, Kans.; *p. 180*, Modified from Hafen, B.Q.: First aid for health emergencies, ed. 4, St. Paul, Minn., 1988, West Publishing Co. Source: U.S. Army.

Chapter 7 *p. 195 (bottom)*, Courtesy Cramer Products, Inc., Gardner, Kans.

Chapter 8 *p. 241*, Photo by Mark Dobson.

Unit IV Opener, Courtesy Bridgewater State College, Bridgewater, Mass.

Chapter 9 *p. 252*, Modified from International Medical Guide for Ships, World Health Organization, Geneva, Switzerland.

Chapter 10 *p. 278*, Adapted from Post, M.: Physical Examination of the Musculo-Skeletal System, Chicago, 1987, Yearbook Medical Publishers, Inc.; *p. 287*, Modified from Veterans Administration Standard Form A. Washington, D.C., U.S. Government Printing Office; *pp. 290-292*, From Boyd, C.E.: Referred visceral pain in athletics, Ath. Train. 15:20, 1980.

Chapter 11 *p. 300*, Courtesy Cramer Products, Inc., Gardner, Kans.; *p. 302*, Modified from Berkow, R.: The Merck manual of diagnosis and therapy, ed. 14, Rahway, N.J., 1982, Merck & Co., Inc.; *pp. 306-307*, Courtesy Burskirk, E.R., and Grasley, W.C.: Human performance laboratory, The Athletic Institute, The Pennsylvania State University.

Chapter 13 *p. 363*, Adapted from Marino, M.: Principles of therapeutic modalities: implications for sports injuries, p. 225. In Nicholas, J.A., and Hershman, E.B. (editors): The lower extremity and spine in sports medicine, St. Louis, 1986, The C.V. Mosby Co.

Chapter 14 *pp. 390, 391*, Adapted from Knight, K.J.: Guidelines for rehabilitation of sports injuries. In Harvey, J.S. (editor): Rehabilitation of the injured athlete, Clinics in Sports Medicine, vol. 4, no. 3, Philadelphia, 1985, W.B. Saunders Co.; *pp. 392 (left), 393*, Robert Freligh, California State University—Long Beach; *p. 398*, Courtesy Cramer Products, Inc., Gardner, Kans.; *pp. 404, 405, 410, 411*, From Prentice, N.E., and Kooima, E.F.: The use of proprioceptive neuromuscular facilitation techniques in rehabilitation of sport-related injury, Athletic Training 21(1):26, Spring 1986.

Chapter 15 *p. 423,* Courtesy Mueller Sports Medicine, Inc.; *p. 426,* Courtesy Cramer Products, Inc., Gardner, Kans.; *p. 448,* Adapted from Lombardo, J.A.: Drugs in sports. In Krakurer, L.J.: The yearbook of sports medicine, Chicago, 1986, Yearbook Medical Publishers Inc.

Unit V Opener, Photo by Mark Dobson.

Chapter 16 *p. 467 (top left),* From Booher, J., and Thibodeau, G.: Athletic injury assessment, St. Louis, 1989, Times Mirror/Mosby College Publishing; *p. 467 (bottom left),* Courtesy Dr. James Garrick; *pp. 475, 477 (left), 480, 481,* From Stewart, W.D., Danto, J.L., and Madden, S.: Dermatology: diagnosis and treatment of cutaneous disorders, ed. 4, St. Louis, 1978, The C.V. Mosby Co.; *Color plates (except L and J),* From Habif, T.P.: Clinical dermatology, St. Louis, 1985, The C.V. Mosby Co.; *Color plates (L and J),* From Bergfeld, W.F.: Dermatologic problems in athletics. In Betts, J.M., and Eichelberger, M. (editors): Symposium on pediatric and adolescent sports medicine, Clinics in Sports Medicine, vol. 1, no. 3, Philadelphia, 1982, W.B. Saunders Co.

Chapter 17 *p. 517,* Adapted from Singer, K.M., and Jones, D.C.: Ligament injuries of ankle and foot. In Nicholas, J.A., and Hershman, E.B. (editors): The lower extremity and spine in sports medicine, vol. 1, St. Louis, 1986, The C.V. Mosby Co.; *p. 522 (top),* Courtesy Cramer Products, Inc., Gardner, Kans.

Chapter 19 *p. 573,* Courtesy Cramer Products, Inc., Gardner, Kans.; *p. 582,* Courtesy Pro-Fit Orthotics, Linnfield, Mass.; *p. 594,* G. Robert Bishop; *p. 613,* From Knight, K.L., Am. J. Sports Med. 7:336, 1979.

Chapter 20 *p. 625,* Courtesy Mueller Sports Medicine, Inc.; *p. 641,* From Boland, A.L., and Hosea, J.M.: Hip and back pain in runners, Postgraduate Advances in Sports Medicine I-XII, Pennington, N.J., 1986, Forum Medicus, Inc.

Chapter 21 *p. 651,* G. Robert Bishop; *p. 666,* From Anthony, C.P., and Thibodeau, G.: Textbook of anatomy and physiology, ed. 12, St. Louis, 1987, Times Mirror/Mosby College Publishing.

Chapter 22 *p. 697,* Adapted from Vegso, J.: Field evaluation of head and neck injuries (unconscious athlete). In Torg, J.S. (editor): Athletic injuries to the head, neck and face, Philadelphia, 1982, Lea & Febiger; *p. 703,* Courtesy Mueller Sports Medicine, Inc.; *pp. 714, 715,* Adapted from Vegso, J.J., and Lehman, R.C.: Field evaluation and management of head and neck injuries. In Torg, J.S. (editor): Head and neck injuries, Clinics in Sports Medicine, vol. 6, no. 1, Philadelphia, 1987, W.B. Saunders Co.; *p. 727,* Adapted from Pashby, R.C., and Pashby, T.J.: Ocular injuries in sport. In Welsh, P.R., and Shepard, R.J. (editors): Current therapy in sports medicine 1985-1986, Philadelphia, 1985, B.C. Decker, Inc.; *p. 728,* Adapted from Vinger, P.F.: How I manage corneal abrasions and lacerations, Phys. Sportsmed. 14(5):170, 1986.

Chapter 24 *p. 807,* From Gieck, J.H., and McCue, F.C. III: Ath. Train. 17:215, Fall 1982; *p. 810,* From Birnbaum, J.S.: The musculoskeletal manual, New York, 1982, Academic Press, Inc.